# T&T Clark Handbook of the Old Testament

# T&T Clark Handbook of the Old Testament

## An Introduction to the Literature, Religion and History of the Old Testament

By
Jan Christian Gertz
Angelika Berlejung
Konrad Schmid
Markus Witte

t&t clark

**Published by T&T Clark International**
*A Continuum imprint*
The Tower Building, 11 York Road, London SE1 7NX
80 Maiden Lane, Suite 704, New York, NY 10038

www.continuumbooks.com



**British Library Cataloguing-in-Publication Data**
A catalogue record for this book is available from the British Library

ISBN: HB: 978-0-567-42529-4
PB: 978-0-567-25368-2

Typeset by Fakenham Prepress Solutions, Fakenham, Norfolk NR21 8NN
Printed and bound in India

# Table of Contents

# Preface

This book is an English translation of a German introduction into the literature, religion and history of the Old Testament/Hebrew Bible. It provides foundational information for deeper understanding of the Old Testament in academic settings, as well as for other intellectual interaction with the text. Although the bibliography is adjusted to the English-speaking community I have to admit that the English version still remains a work based on the German-speaking academic tradition. However, I hope that this book can provide a glimpse of recent European discussions about the literature, religion and history of the Old Testament. For the convenience of the reader, quotations from German or French texts have been translated into English.

The goal of this book is anything but modest, and given the present state of scholarship it issues a challenge: Old Testament studies are currently in a phase of profound reorientation in all their sub-disciplines. This makes the field quite exciting – and at the same time rather confusing if looked at from the outside. As a result few scholarly discussions influence the view of the Old Testament as held by the general public both within and outside the academic field. And consequently, confusion arises when more recent scholarly positions from Old Testament studies are presented to the larger public. Therefore it would hardly be appropriate if this *Handbook of the Old Testament* presented the consensus of the field independent of current challenges and trends in the scholarly discussion – for this would result in an even more pronounced distance between the academic discussion and the general public. Rather, in order to support an appropriate interaction with the Old Testament it is important to provide readers with the present state of affairs, even in places where no consensus exists.

The structure of the present volume corresponds to the task thus set before us. Introducing a subject means first of all defining a starting point and describing the methodology. As well as every historical and philological discipline, the point of departure for interaction with the literature, religion and history of the Old Testament is determined by the available sources – the texts of the Old Testament itself, the archaeological sources from the Levant as well as extra-biblical texts and iconographic sources from the Levant and the neighbouring cultures. Chapter 1 introduces these sources and their relationships to one another. Chapter 2 explains the academic use of those various sources. The subsequent survey of the political and religious history of ancient Israel in Chapter 3 clarifies the basis for a 'history of Israel'. Namely, how does the Old Testament depiction of history relate to the findings of modern historical studies? What are the differences between the time *in* the narrative and the time *of* the narrative? What differences should be noted when the terms 'Israel' and 'Canaan' appear? In which geographic and cultural location does the 'history of Israel' take place and how did this location influence the history of Israel? What do the most important terms of history and history of religions mean? The actual survey of the general and religious history of ancient Israel in 4 begins with the Late Bronze Age and continues into the Hellenistic Period. It thus deals with the period of the history of Israel addressed in the Old Testament narratives and the period in which the Old Testament texts have been written down.

The Chapters 5–30 are dedicated to the literature of the Old Testament and the history of its formation, including the apocrypha/deuterocanonical books. The sections and subsections are all structured identically: they begin with the most certain (scholarly) conclusions and move to the less certain. The beginning point is always the current text as it stands, introducing its content and structure ('Biblical Context'). Special attention is given to larger text complexes, including those reaching beyond single books. This step invites the reader to develop an individual reading of the Bible. For only a thorough knowledge of the text allows for productive and independent interaction with the various scholarly positions. The next step consists of communicating scholarship's most important textual observations, which throughout the history of interpretation have raised questions of textual development in the biblical books ('Textual Issues and Major Issues in the History of Critical Interpretation'). Textual peculiarities are never perceived and explained independently of previous scholarly discussions; instead our perception is affected by what others have perceived before us and how they have made sense of it. This is why references to the history of scholarship will also appear in this section. Here it has been especially important to focus on a few central perspectives and to explore exemplary problems. The following step assimilates these observations and constructs the (probable) historical development of the particular text ('Origins'). Like the section presenting the basic textual observations and history of scholarship, this section also concentrates only on the essentials, especially with regard to the secondary literature. Since nearly every sentence of the presentation suggests a whole library of further relevant literature, the reader can operate with the motto that the experts already know where to turn to and the rest does not need a full bibliography but is instead provided only with a few titles in order to find further literature easily. A brief presentation of the main theological themes of the particular text follows the history of textual development ('Theology'). Finally, each chapter concludes with remarks concerning the subsequent reception of the text both inside and outside the Bible ('Notes on the History of Reception'). These remarks can of course be merely exemplary and in these parts the origin of the authors is especially obvious, as one might expect.

As mentioned, the book contains discussions of the deuterocanonical books Judith, the Wisdom of Solomon (*Sapientia Salomonis*), Tobit, Jesus Sirach (*Ben Sira*), and Baruch together with the Letter of Jeremiah, 1–2 Maccabees, as well as the Prayer of Manesseh and the Additions to the books of Esther and Daniel. In order to continue the orientation on the general structure of the Hebrew Bible, the apocrypha, or deuterocanonical books, are presented in the concluding chapters on the literature of the Old Testament. Only the Additions to Esther and Daniel are included in the presentations of the respective book.

As indicated above, the presentation of the Old Testament literature contains notes on the theology of each individual literary work. By speaking about 'theology' the authors do not want to substantiate any present dogmatic position on biblical grounds. Rather, it is meant to reconstruct and examine critically the concepts of the respective biblical book. The methodology of the notes on theology is based on a particular conception of 'Old Testament Theology', which is developed in part VII. The chapters 31–34 include discussion of the history and problems of the discipline as well as the divergent views of what the subject matter of 'Old Testament Theology' might be.

I thank my co-authors for their stimulating collaboration and their willingness to provide competent assistance to the translation of their texts. I would also like to thank Jennifer Adams-Maßmann, Peter Altmann, Thomas Riplinger and Mark Biddle, who have prepared the translation, Steve McKenzie for bibliographical hints, and Laura Artes, Elisabeth Maikranz, Mike Rottmann and Friederike Schücking, who diligently and expertly assisted in the final stages of the editing process.

Jan Christian Gertz
Heidelberg, March 2011

# Technical Note

The individual sections and subsections in this book are generally preceded by several bibliographical references that offer the possibility for deeper study. The references named are typically understandable for a general audience. When the titles are also listed in the section 'Basic Literature for Old Testament Studies', only their shortened title is cited in the individual sections. However, if the titles do not appear in the later 'Basic Literature' bibliography, their full bibliographic information will appear in the individual section or subsection while they are cited in short form in the footnotes. Finally, if a title *only* appears in a footnote, then a full citation will be presented there, with later mentions of the title (in other footnotes) appearing in short form with a reference to the earlier full citation.

The bibliographic and all other abbreviations follow P. H. Alexander *et al.*, eds, *The SBL Handbook of Style: For Ancient Near Eastern, Biblical, and Early Christian Studies*. Peabody, Mass.: Hendrickson, 1999. In general, biblical proper names are cited according to the NRSV. Transliteration of Hebrew and Greek words follows the rules in the SBL Handbook of Style; other transliterations follow a simplified system based on the aforementioned.

References to the glossary are indicated by → and set in *italics*.

# Part I
## Sources and Methods

# 1

# Sources

(Angelika Berlejung – Translation by Thomas Riplinger)

## Chapter Outline



Bibliography 6.1 Extra-Biblical Sources: General and Methods.

## 1.1 Prolegomena

The Old Testament [OT] / Hebrew Bible is, through and through, both a theological book and a literary work of art. This collection of writings is not intended to present the creation of the world as an eyewitness report or the events of the history of Israel and Judah as a compendium of the history of Palestine. Instead, its purpose is to explain the People of Israel's past against the background of God's presence, and, in this way, to interpret the present experience of God's People in order to shape its future. In view of the Old Testament's literary nature and theological intention, it can be used, only with the greatest caution and careful critical study of the texts, as a reliable source not only for political historical inquiries such as the question: Did David's empire exist?, but also for religious-historical inquiries such as: Was cultic veneration of the dead found in Israel? Together, the books of the Hebrew Bible are a collection of literary works, influenced by particular opinions, convictions and tendencies, which they try to communicate to their readers. They represent at one and the same time a self-interpretation of Israelite history and a collection of theological texts with very different aims. They have in common, however, the confession of belief in Yhwh and the aim of convincing their readers of this faith by their testimony.[1] In doing so, the Old Testament sketches the history of God's people, embedded between the creation of the world at the beginning of times (Gen. 1) and the new creation at the end of time (Isa. 60.19). Within this overarching framework, it concentrates on tracing the history of God's people from the Exodus out of Egypt and the entry into the Promised Land, to the rebuilding of the Jerusalem temple after the → *exile* (Ezra 1–6.18) and down to the revolt of the Maccabees (1 Macc. 4.52–59; 2 Macc. 10.1–8). The period of time described here, recounted in the stories from the Exodus with the → *tabernacle* up to the rededication of the temple at the time of the Maccabees, is essentially identical to the succession of periods that Palestinian archaeology calls the Iron Age, the Babylonian-Persian and Hellenistic-Roman Periods (see the 'Chronology of Important Dates' in the Appendix).

The local setting of this history is the Levant. Back then, this region did not belong to the centre, but to the periphery of the ancient world. Beginning in the third millennium BCE, Palestine and Syria had become more and more marginal within the Mediterranean region, while, in the neighbouring regions, major cities, states and empires arose that would dominate world politics and the economy of the area for the following millennia: these were Egypt to the south, Anatolia to the north, Mesopotamia to the east, and Phoenicia with its coastal cities in the west. In the following centuries, Palestine repeatedly belonged to the sphere of influence of its expanding neighbours, and these in turn determined its political and economic destiny. However, many of the religious and social-political events in the Levant that were, in themselves, of great significance, were of little importance for the authors and redactors of the Old Testament, because they saw in them no relevance for the history of their belief in Yhwh. Accordingly, they omitted them or only mentioned them in passing.

For this reason, to identify what these writers saw as important for their writings and what they considered unimportant, to recognize what they emphasized, selected or passed over in silence, as well as to see how

1. See also M. Z. Brettler, *The Creation of History in Ancient Israel* (London: Routledge, 1995); J. Barr, *History and Ideology in the Old Testament: Biblical Studies at the End of a Millennium: The Hensley Henson Lectures for 1997 delivered to the University of Oxford* (Oxford: Oxford University Press, 2000); T. Ishida, *History and Historical Writing in Ancient Israel: Studies in Biblical Historiography* (Studies in the History and Culture of the Ancient Near East 16; Leiden: Brill, 1999).

they gave their own interpretation to processes and events against the background of the tendencies of their times, it is important to confront the biblical story with the other sources that have come down to us from the same world of experience and sometimes even describe the same events or processes from a different perspective. Only in this way can one discover what exactly the biblical authors sought to communicate to following generations. Only very rarely, this was merely historical information about some war taking place in some city somewhere in the Ancient Near East. Always, the intention was to give testimony to God's action and salvation of his people. However, the interpretative theological achievement of the biblical authors can only be appreciated against the background of an exegetical (re-)construction of the events as they actually happened (even when such reconstructions are always subject to the reservation of being only more or less probable hypotheses) and this (re-)construction requires that the historical event or process must be distinguished from theological interpretation. On the other hand, such historical (re-)construction of the events themselves with the methods of modern historiography is not always possible, because extra-biblical sources that could illuminate those events are often unavailable. In recent decades, however, there have been major advances in this respect. First of all, from Palestine itself, new extra-biblical written sources have been discovered, and, secondly, from the neighbouring regions and cultures, new materials have been found that allow new insights either verifying or correcting old ideas. In addition, the discipline known as 'Biblical Archaeology' or 'Archaeology of Palestine' has made major advances in the last decades and has expanded and refined its methods (for example, specialized disciplines like archaeobotany) so that much additional information can be gathered in order to put together a multifaceted picture of Palestine during biblical times. *Last but not least*, the growing fund of → *iconographic* sources from Palestine and its neighbouring cultures deserves mention. In recent years these iconographic sources have been made fruitful by the pioneering research of Othmar Keel and his students. The general rule, therefore, is that the more sources (archaeological evidence, biblical and extra-biblical texts, and images), methods and resulting interpretations we are ready to collect, apply and evaluate, the more we are able to describe the past culture and society of Palestine in a differentiated and well-ordered manner.

# 1.2 The Sources and Their Mutual Relationships

'The history does not lie in the sources but it needs sources to be written.'[2] It is the historian who raises an object to the status of a source, then treats and interprets it as such, and puts it in relation to other sources. For some time now, a debate has been going on among scholars about what written sources should be considered to be primary, secondary, tertiary and fourth level.[3]

### The Hierarchy of Sources

*Primary sources* are datable by archaeological methods. They are chronologically close to the event that they describe or to which they refer. The writers who produce these sources are usually the people who are themselves involved in the event or process or at least contemporary witnesses; thus letters, treaties and other written records belong to this category.

*Secondary sources* are more distant to the event, being copies or excerpts of the primary sources or commentaries upon them. The writers of these sources refer to information indirectly gained, for instance, from an archive; i.e., they refer to sources that they themselves could no longer personally verify.

*Tertiary sources* have an even greater temporal distance to their topic and rely heavily on secondary sources.

*Fourth-level sources* base themselves on secondary or tertiary sources without being able critically to assess their value or reliability.

This hierarchical classification of written sources is, in my opinion, an essential task, but it is not necessarily a guide to the evaluation of their historical reliability. A primary source in close proximity to the event does not automatically have a

2. Quotation according to C. Uehlinger, 'Bildquellen und "Geschichte Israels." Grundsätzliche Überlegungen und Fallbeispiele', in *Steine – Bilder – Texte: Historische Evidenz außerbiblischer und biblischer Quellen* (Arbeiten zur Bibel und ihrer Geschichte 5; ed. C. Hardmeier; Leipzig: Evangelische Verlagsanstalt, 2001), 25–77, esp. 31.

3. The impulse of E. A. Knauf, 'From History to Interpretation', in *The Fabric of History: Text, Artefact and Israel's Past* (JSOTSup 127; ed. D. V. Edelman; Sheffield: JSOT, 1991), 26–64 has often been discussed controversially. For the best survey of the contemporary debate, see the collection edited by C. Hardmeier, *Steine* (above, n. 2).

higher historical reliability in the sense of conveying information that is 'more factually accurate' than a secondary source with greater temporal distance to the event reported. For instance, royal → *annals*, although they are written close to the event described, may nevertheless be written with interpretative hindsight and make the account of the events fit into the ideological concepts of the court. Thus, the historical information given by a source always needs to be judged and evaluated in each single case by questioning, for instance, its contextual function and its pragmatic surroundings. Each source needs to be correlated with other sources and with already-gained empirical knowledge about the matter under discussion. The critical survey, evaluation and establishing of available resources as historical sources must be measured according to its degree of inter-subjective, testable plausibility and consensual objectivity (Jörn Rüsen),[4] a rule which applies both to the sources as such and to the historical (re-)constructions that depend on them.

Archaeological, → *iconographic*, and → *epigraphic* material is normally counted among the primary sources, since it derives from the same period. These primary sources may confirm each other, but may also present a different, complementary or even contrasting picture of the period in question and its historical and social interrelationships. In each case, the researcher is confronted with a problem of weighing the sources and, in the event of contradiction, of judging which source(es) should be taken as the more trustworthy. This problem is especially acute when historical (re)constructions that are based on such primary sources are confronted with (re-)constructions of the history of the southern Levant that have been made on the basis of the Old Testament – read as a historical source. According to the explanation given above, the Old Testament should not really be counted as a primary source for answering properly historical questions – but as it is often counted as such, the problem cannot be 'harmonized' (see below). In all such instances, in view of their immediate temporal proximity to the event in question, the archaeological sources should generally be preferred in answering such historical (!) questions. But, even here, one should be warned against exaggerated optimism, since the dating of archaeological remains is quite often difficult to pin down exactly; and, like the texts and the images, the archaeological evidence can be made to speak only through the interpretation of archaeologists and historians, who are not *always* in agreement. The local setting, stratification, function, material, comparative finds and dates often play an important role in shaping theories about, and (re-)constructions of the past. Likewise, the interpretation of iconographic material cannot always be certain.

4. J. Rüsen, *Rekonstruktion der Vergangenheit: Grundzüge einer Historik 2: Die Prinzipien der historischen Forschung* (Göttingen: Vandenhoeck & Ruprecht, 1986), 89–111.

> This is the case, for instance, when it comes to assigning the names of gods to the images of deities, when identifying captions do not accompany the images; in that case, the interpretations depend on the interpreter's research and previous knowledge as well as on the comparative material available for study. In addition, the function and the pragmatic context of the pictorial material likewise need to be assessed in order to evaluate its value as a historical source and its factual accuracy: e.g. the Assyrian reliefs do not depict real war scenes but reflect rather a politically correct idea of what should have happened.

On the basis of a single source group, the culture, history, society, and religion of a region within a particular period of time can only be (re-)constructed very incompletely; only the connection and correlation of different available sources with each other can help further to complete the picture (or pictures). Nevertheless, there will always remain unresolved problems, especially when historians make hypotheses to identify the reasons, processes, or interconnections that underlie such a (re-)construction.

> When the archaeological evidence unquestionably contradicts a biblical story (as in the case of Joshua 6, where the archaeological remains of ancient Jericho do not substantiate the biblical account of its conquest), it must be borne in mind that the Judean scribes who sketched the story of the ritual conquest of Jericho were theologians not annalists. They were not interested in writing a report of the events of the destruction of Jericho and the Israelite → *conquest* but in interpreting the ruins of Jericho as a sign of Yhwh's gift of the land to his people. A further example is the attitude toward images in 'Israel'. The iconographic evidence from 'Israel' demonstrates that it was a land rich in pictures and iconic motifs and that it not only had a long-standing, more or less continuous pictorial tradition, but also that it expressly cultivated that tradition. This evidence contradicts the biblical account that, from the beginnings of 'Israel', no images were made there because of the ban against images; the few exceptions mentioned in the Bible like the golden calf, were not seen as serious breaks in this otherwise consistent picture. Here too, the Old Testament theologians intended to make a programmatic theological statement rather than a descriptive historical one about their own past attitudes toward images. Thus, when archaeological, iconographic, or epigraphic evidence contradicts the biblical texts, we always have to keep in mind that the different sources have different intentions and express and communicate very different things. The aims and intentions of the statements of the two different complexes represented by the biblical and the extra-biblical sources are fundamentally different, and therefore they cannot and should not be harmonized.

Normally, biblical texts should not be counted as primary sources for historical inquiry because, as a rule, they were written down at considerable temporal distance to the events they relate to; this principle too, however, must be differentially applied from case to case. The time of the telling of the story, i.e. the time of the storytellers/scribes, must be distinguished from the time of the event or fact narrated. Furthermore, the biblical texts are often problematical because, today, we have them in a form created on the basis of different *Vorlagen* (pl. of *Vorlage*, i.e. the underlying biblical manuscript traditions) that have undergone a redactional process passing through different hands and that, quite often, cannot be dated precisely. Because of this feature and the underlying theological intentions of the text, the Old Testament should not be overestimated as a source for the (re-)construction of the political or religious history of Palestine, but it should also not be underestimated. A general rejection of the OT as a source for historical inquiry serves no purpose, because even secondary, tertiary and fourth-level sources have their value. Especially the younger Scriptures, in which the time of the storytelling is closer to the time narrated, often preserve valuable information about the social and political circumstances of the post-exilic period (→ *exile*). However, verifying the historical reliability of the biblical stories and of the Bible's historiography must always be done in terms of the individual facts and events: generalizing judgements about the trustworthiness or untrustworthiness of the OT account are of no use at all. The degree to which one can establish, through critical study and evaluation, the OT as a reliable historical source (and thus the veracity of the historical (re-)construction that is based on it) depends upon the ability to achieve inter-subjective, verifiable plausibility, and scholarly consensus. Without question, textual units that have only been hypothetically isolated and dated by historical criticism in order to identify a core of historical information will never evoke the same degree of plausibility and scholarly consensus that is evoked, for example, by a letter or some other object found in an archaeological context, or an artifact that can be localized and definitively dated.

In general, this discussion touches on the relationship between exegesis and biblical archaeology.[5] In the history of research, the roots of the latter derive from biblical studies. But, in the past decades, it has freed itself from previous aims

5. See J. K. Hoffmeier, *The Archaeology of the Bible* (Oxford: Lion, 2008); general: D. Stuart, *Old Testament Exegesis: A Handbook for Students and Pastors* (4th ed.; Louisville, Ky.: Westminster John Knox, 2009), § 4.7.5; J. R. Bartlett, 'What Has Archaeology to Do with the Bible – or Vice Versa?' in *Archaeology and Biblical Interpretation* (London/New York: Routledge, 1997), 1–19.

to support exegetic research and has taken its own place within the arena of Palestinian research. Biblical archaeology deals with Palestine, in particular, using the region's material remains over the whole course of its history as its principal sources. And it employs, in addition to strictly archaeological methods, also the methods of topography, climate research, → *anthropology*, botany, zoology, etc. For biblical archaeology as an independent scientific discipline, with its own methodology, the cooperation with biblical exegesis is indispensable, since both disciplines deal with the same subject, although each has its own premises, questions, sources, and methods. This interdisciplinarity, which aims at achieving a mutually complementary picture of the history and culture of Palestine, is largely restricted in practice to the temporal span from the second half of the second millennium to the Roman Period, i.e., the period covered by the story which the Old and New Testament narrate (narrated time). By looking simultaneously at the biblical sources, the archaeological finds, and the iconographic material of this period, one can gain a more nuanced picture, thanks to the different viewpoints, than when one leaves out any one of these sources. Still, biblical archaeology is not limited in scope to this relatively short 'biblically defined' period, and neither is its related discipline, biblical iconography. As part of the study of Palestine, both extend their research into other periods, for instance, to follow structures of *longue durée* (Ch. 3.2.2). Their task is no longer to verify or 'prove' Old and New Testament texts through archaeological evidence or to illustrate them with pictorial material. Nevertheless, the results of biblical archaeology (see Ch. 1.2.4 for iconography) can also be relevant for the interpretation of biblical texts. This relevance can refer, for instance, to issues concerning topographic features, *realia*, social structures, technology, means and routes of transportation, imported wares and motifs, trade, and much more: in short, biblical archaeology can give us a better picture of the everyday, real world surrounding the people who wrote the Old Testament and for whom the Old Testament was written.

## 1.2.1 The Biblical Sources

📖 Bibliography 1 Text Editions; 2.1 Concordances; 2.2 Concordances on CD-ROM; 2.3 Dictionaries; 3 Exegetical Methods (E. Tov, *Criticism*).

In contrast to the archaeological sources, the texts of the Old Testament as a source for political or religious history have the advantage that they recount the thoughts, argumentative strategies, theological conceptions, social criticism, critical or friendly attitudes to royal persons and power, and many other ideas of the people of the first millennium BCE. Nevertheless, one must take into consideration the fact that the Old Testament represents only a small selection of texts for any particular period. The only texts that were handed down as part of the tradition were those deemed relevant by the composers and redactors of the biblical books for their own belief in Yhwh and for promoting this belief: in practice, that meant that, for the most part, only those texts which were judged useful for supporting the orthodoxy of post-exilic Judaism were handed down. On top of that, in recent years, scholars have discovered that these surviving texts represent for the most part only the ideas and attitudes of the male upper-class of Jerusalem or indeed were drafted in those circles, so that the perspective of the northern kingdom of Israel and of the villages or small towns even of Judah (Micah for instance) is rarely expressed, and the viewpoints of women, children, or slaves are virtually never brought to expression.

## *1 The Text of the Old Testament, Contents and Literary Shape of the Scriptures*

The text of the Old Testament is attested in many ancient and medieval manuscripts in many different languages, i.e., the so-called textual witnesses, all of which show greater or lesser variations. No individual textual witness contains what could be termed 'the' biblical text, so work with the Bible always includes the study of all the textual sources with their variants and mutual correspondences. This requires text-critical methods (Ch. 2.1.1). Differences in the text even exist among the modern editions of the Masoretic Text (see below), the classical text of the Hebrew Bible, since they are based on different manuscripts. Even here, discrepancies can be found, for instance, with respect to the sequence of the biblical books, the chapter or verse distribution, variant letters or words, vocalizations or accents; thus, the Masoretic Text cannot simply be assumed to be 'the' biblical *Urtext*, i.e., the text assumed to be the one and only original version of the biblical text. Various hypotheses are offered to explain the fact that the different textual witnesses of the Hebrew Bible, even for one and the same biblical book, may offer identical, similar, slightly or even completely diverging texts or text lengths. The basic question has always been, whether unity or diversity originally prevailed. The idea of *one* single Urtext (since Paul de Lagarde [1827–1891]), from which all other textual witnesses depend genetically and were subsequently copied, is in fact a theoretical construct, and is rejected today by many exegetes (since Paul Kahle [1875–1964]). These more recent exegetes assume the existence of *several* original Urtexts with equal claims to authenticity. Diverse exegetes (e.g. Emanuel Tov, Hermann-Josef Stipp, Eugene Ulrich) now propose that the different Old Testament books have been re-edited time and again in the course of their history, even when their literary development appeared to have been completed and when they were accepted and circulated as definitive versions for use in worship and study, etc. These later revised editions, which now constitute the different witnesses of the Masoretic Text group, were meant to replace the allegedly 'final' versions of the biblical books already in circulation; yet they did not come to prevail everywhere. This led to the preservation of older versions, especially in remote communities like → *Qumran*, and, as in Alexandria, they even served as the *Vorlage* for translation. Merely by chance, then, the older versions have survived in the Septuagint (LXX; see below) and the Qumran finds, and they need to be taken account of within the framework of textual history. Especially for the books of Joshua, Samuel, Jeremiah, and Ezekiel, earlier versions, sometimes containing notable deviations from the versions handed down in the Masoretic Text group (and in the Vulgate, the Targumim, and the Peshitta, see below) – can be found in the LXX and in Qumran.

## *2 The Traditions and Translations*

'The' text of the Old Testament is an abstraction that has been patched together from many textual witnesses that may be quite dissimilar to each other. The most important witnesses include the following:

1 The *Masoretic Text* or *textus receptus* serves as the main text in critical editions. The name 'Masoretic Text' is misleading, since it suggests a uniformity that never existed in this way. The term stands for a *group* of related manuscripts. They correspond to the medieval representatives of the ancient text that had already been accepted as the sole authentic text as early as the first century CE by one main stream of Judaism, which had survived the events that occurred around 70 CE. It was, therefore, copied more often and more carefully than other versions, resulting in only slight variations in comparison to other traditions. Because of the carefulness of the copyists, from the beginning, few deviations have originated within this text group. Nevertheless, there never existed a single text that could be viewed as 'the' Masoretic Text, and, within the texts of this group, some variations did exist. Notwithstanding that fact, the ideal and intention of textual uniformity was increasingly implemented over the course of time, so that by the eighth or ninth century CE, at the latest, the Masoretic Text was practically fixed in a normative form.

The final form of the Masoretic Text, with vowel and accent markers, as well as the apparatus of the 'Masorah' (hence the name, see below), originated only in the Middle Ages, whereas the earlier versions of the text were written only in consonants with hardly any indications of vowels or accents. These purely consonantal texts are termed proto-Masoretic (attested in texts from the Judean desert, 3rd cent. BCE to 2nd cent. CE). Normally, the term 'Masoretic Text' is used only for the Masoretic tradition of Aaron Ben Asher and his family (early 10th cent. CE in Tiberias) and, therefore, for only one part of the representatives of the full tradition of the Masoretic text group. Thus the Masoretic Text (or, better, the Masoretic Text group) contains, on the one hand, the consonants that are attested in the proto-Masoretic texts from the time of the Second Temple on, and, on the other, the 'Masorah', including vowel and accent marks, para-textual elements (text divisions, scribal marks, such as *nun inversum* and *puncta extraordinaria*, *Kethib/Qere*,[6] etc.), together with the apparatus of the Masorah in the narrow sense, i.e. instructions for the handing down of the text. These additions were the creation of the so-called → *Masoretes* (i.e., those who transmit text). The standard scholarly edition of the Masoretic Text, the *Biblia Hebraica Stuttgartensia*, is based on the *Codex Petropolitanus* (formerly *Leningradensis*, hence the Siglum L) B19[A] from St. Petersburg, which was completed in 1008/9 CE and represents the oldest complete manuscript of the Tiberian text.

2 *The Samaritan Pentateuch* is the text of the Torah, i.e. only the first five books of the OT, that the Samaritans (see Ch. 3.2.1) have transmitted in a special form of the old Hebrew script. It came into existence around 100 BCE as a special version used by the Samaritan religious community. In → *Qumran*, texts have been found that are closely related to the Samaritan Pentateuch and are assumed to have been available to the Samaritans. These texts are called pre-Samaritan, because they share linguistic corrections and harmonizations with the Samaritan Pentateuch (in contrast to the Masoretic Text group), but they lack the typical characteristics of the Samaritan Pentateuch that reveal further changes in content and phonetics by comparison to the Masoretic Text group[7]. The most important readjustments of the contents in the Samaritan Pentateuch are changes concerning the central status of Shechem and Mount Gerizim and they are clearly based on the distinctive characteristics of the Samaritan religion.[8]

3 The texts from the *Judean Desert* (Qumran, Masada, Naḥal Ḥever, Wadi Murabba'at) are composed in Aramaic, Hebrew and Greek and include biblical, as well as extra-biblical texts. The biblical texts found at Qumran come from different periods, ranging between the 3rd cent. BCE and the 1st cent. CE, and derive from different places and scribal schools. Accordingly, they show a greater textual

6. A scribal mark that points to the fact that the written version of the text should be disregarded (*Kethib*, i.e., 'as it is written') and should be replaced by another word or words (*Qere*, i.e., 'that is to be read').
7. These texts are also named 'proto-Samaritan', but this classification is often mistakenly interpreted in the sense that these texts contained the beginnings of Samaritan features. Therefore 'pre-Samaritan' is preferable. See E. Tov, *Textual Criticism*, 81.
8. See I. Hjelm, *The Samaritans and Early Judaism* (JSOTSup 303; Copenhagen International Seminar 7; Sheffield: Sheffield Academic Press, 2000).

> diversity. The two main groups are the proto-Masoretic and the pre-Samaritan texts. Apart from these, there is another text group that attests to a special, probably typically Qumranic scribal practice (also applied to non-biblical texts) that uses its own orthography (e.g. often plene-writings), morphology (e.g. long forms of personal pronouns, pronominal suffixes), and other scribal usages (e.g. omission of the *litterae finales*, use of ancient Hebrew letters or cryptograms to mark special objects or the name of God). Noteworthy are also those texts that are close to the (re-)constructed Hebrew *Vorlage* of the Septuagint (e.g. 4QJer[bd]), as well as the large group of so-called independent texts, which, so far at least, cannot be attributed to any of the known textual groups and sometimes deviate significantly from all of them.

Among the various *translations* that were produced in antiquity and are based on different Hebrew *Vorlagen*, the most important are: the Septuagint (LXX), whose target language is Greek, together with its revisions, namely Theodotion, Aquila, Symmachus, and the fifth Column of the *Hexapla* of Origen (ca.185/6–253/4 CE) which are all based on the Masoretic Text group; then the Vulgate, whose target language is Latin and which is likewise based on the Masoretic Text group; and finally the Targumim, whose target language is Aramaic and which are also based on the Masoretic Text group. In general, each translation represents an interpretation made by the translator and depends therefore on his own philological competence, his stylistic preferences, and his theological or didactic intentions. Nevertheless, textual criticism is able with some precision to (re) construct from these translations the original Hebrew *Vorlagen* that each of the translators made use of. The criteria used for the (re)construction of such Hebrew *Vorlagen* on the basis of the translations are easily open to the accusation of subjectivity. The general rule is: a deviation of the translation from the text of the Masoretic Text group that cannot otherwise be explained either as the result of a theological or didactic interpretation or simply as a poor-quality translation, e.g. a mistaken reading, a change of letters, or a skipping of words in the translation, should be assumed to be based on a different Hebrew *Vorlage*. One can then attempt to translate back from the translation into Hebrew, in order to (re-)construct the assumed Hebrew *Vorlage*. Such (re-)constructions are plausible especially when they are supported by extra-Masoretic Hebrew readings. Often, however, we cannot determine whether a deviation from the text of the Masoretic Text group has been caused by a different Hebrew *Vorlage* or merely by the creative freedom of the translator.

The *Septuagint* (LXX), the translation of the Hebrew and Aramaic texts of the OT into Greek, which was the *lingua franca* in the Hellenistic Period, was a great boon to the community and school life of Hellenistic Judaism (→ *Hellenism*). At the same time, the Septuagint presented the Hebrew Bible to the Greek world for the first time. For Hellenistic Judaism, the New Testament authors, and the early Christian church, the Septuagint, not the Hebrew/Aramaic 'original' texts, constituted the decisive textual basis. Because of this version's importance, a broad spectrum of witnesses is available as a basis for (re-)constructing its original text, e.g. papyrus or letter fragments from the 2nd cent. BCE on, manuscripts written in uncials, or → *majuscules* from the 4th to 10th cent. CE[9]; manuscripts written in → *minuscules* or cursives from the 9th to 16th cent. CE). The name 'Septuagint' derives from the tradition that 72 (therefore, LXX = 70) elders from Jerusalem translated the Torah into Greek (Letter of Aristeas[10]) at the request of King Ptolemy II Philadelphus (283/2–246 BCE). Later, in the first centuries CE, this myth of origin was extended to all of the biblical books translated into Greek. The translation of the biblical books did, in fact, start with the Torah, probably in the first half of the 3rd cent. BCE in the Jewish → *diaspora community* of Alexandria, while the remaining books followed successively only during the course of the next two centuries (see prologue to Jesus Sirach from around 132 BCE, who knows of the Law, the Prophets, and some of the Writings in their Greek version). A dispute exists concerning whether, at the beginning of the LXX, only one translation existed for each single book of the Hebrew Bible (unity hypothesis; *Einheitshypothese*) or whether we should assume a later merging of different translation efforts (Targum hypothesis). This controversy seems to have been decided now in favour of the unity hypothesis. The Hebrew *Vorlage* of the LXX is, in part, quite different from other textual witnesses (e.g. the Masoretic Text group, the Targumim, the Peshitta [Syriac translation], and the Vulgate). The quality of the translation of each single book varies, and various early revisions tried to go back to the Hebrew original, e.g. Papyri Fouad 266 and Ryland 458 from the 2nd/1st cent. BCE; *Kaige*-Theodotion in the middle of the 1st cent. BCE; Aquila in 125 CE; Symmachus in the 2nd/3rd cent. CE. In the middle of the 3rd cent. CE, Origen took upon himself the task of organizing the various revisions and new translations of the LXX in his *Hexapla*, where he put side-by-side the Hebrew text, the Hebrew text in Greek transliteration, Aquila, Symmachus, LXX (the so-called Hexaplaric Recension) and *Kaige*-Theodotion (with translations of hitherto unknown *Vorlagen*).

The LXX includes besides the Greek translation of the 24 books of the Hebrew

9. Among them, the three most important manuscripts are: the Codex Vaticanus from the 4th cent. CE; the Codex Sinaiticus from the same period; and the Codex Alexandrinus from the 5th cent. CE.

10. D. De Crom, 'The Letter of Aristeas and the Authority of the Septuagint', *JSP* 17.2 (2008): 141–60. Full text of the Letter of Aristeas online: http://www.ccel.org/c/charles/otpseudepig/aristeas.htm (R. H. Charles).

→ *canon* (with abbreviations and additions) some other books that have been called → '*apocrypha*' (Greek: 'hidden things') by the Reformation churches since Andreas Bodenstein von Karlstadt (1486–1541) followed by Martin Luther (1483–1546), and → '*deuterocanonical literature*' by the Roman Catholic Church. The group of apocrypha/deuterocanonical books comprises works that were originally composed in the Greek language or works that have been translated into Greek from a Hebrew or Aramaic *Vorlage* (Jesus Sirach, Tobit). Additional books that are called *pseudepigrapha* (→ *pseudepigraphy*) by the Reformation churches and *apocrypha* by the Roman Catholic Church are also found in the LXX (see below, Part 3).

The *Vulgate* is a translation of the Hebrew Bible into Latin that was done between 390 and 405 CE by the church father, Jerome (ca. 342–420 CE). The Hebrew *Vorlage* of the Vulgate is nearly identical with the Masoretic text group, but the Vulgate also includes additional biblical texts not contained in the Hebrew Bible (see below, Part 3).

The *Targumim* (sing. 'targum') are translations of the OT into Aramaic. They came into existence during different periods when Aramaic was gaining primacy as a *lingua franca* in the Near East, especially from the Babylonian-Persian Period on. The oldest Targum fragments are known from Qumran. Also worthy of mention are the *Targum Onkelos* for the Pentateuch and the *Targum Jonathan* for the Prophets, both of which seem to have come into existence in Palestine before the end of the Bar Kokhba Revolt (132–135 CE). They were worked over, transmitted, and later vocalized in the communities and schools of the Babylonian Diaspora in the 4th cent. CE While the *Targum Onkelos* translates mainly the Hebrew text, the *Targum Jonathan* often offers a paraphrase with a tendency toward updating. The later Palestinian targumim – among them the targumim from the Cairo-Geniza (see excursus Ch. 27.2) from the 7th–11th cent. CE; the *Targum Neophyti* I, a manuscript from 1504, presumably going back to a lost 'original' dating between the 1st and 5th cent. CE – existed for the Pentateuch, the Prophets and for all Writings with the exception of Daniel and Ezra-Nehemiah. They show considerable variation and often represent the language type of Judeo-Palestinian Aramaic of the Byzantine Period.

## 3 Canonization

Together, the scriptures of the Old Testament along with those of the New Testament (in Roman Catholic tradition also including the deuterocanonical Scriptures) make up the 'canon' (*kanōn* 'measuring tape, norm'), i.e., the normative rule and guiding principle for Christian theology, proclamation and Christian praxis. In more general terms, 'canon' can be defined as any normative collection of holy texts or books for a religious community, which provide guiding principles and practical instructions for the institutions of that religious community (school, law, liturgy, theology) and to which the members of this religious community ascribe highest authority in comparison to other texts (Ch. 34).

Although the term 'canon' is Greek and its use as a term for the normative collection of Old and New Testament Scriptures derives from the church law of the 4th cent. CE, – modern Jews also sometimes use this term in English at least, but of course they restrict it to the Hebrew Bible – the basic idea of collecting normative texts and fixing their wording and sequence among themselves, in order to transmit them faithfully from one generation to the next, has much older roots (cf. the biblical commandment to preserve the text without addition or subtraction in Deut. 4.2; 13.1 [NRSV 12.32b]), and was long known in the Ancient Near East. In Mesopotamian schools, there existed 'canonical' lists from the very beginning of writing; these lists were ossified in form and sequence and belonged to the basic education of scribes.[11] Analogously, one can assume that the beginnings of the canonization of Old Testament Scripture originated in schools. The development of the Hebrew canon took place in several stages and over several centuries; the same applies to the Christian canon of the Bible. In order to write a full history of the canonization of the Hebrew Bible, it would be necessary to reconstruct a literary history for each of its single books and collections (Ch. 5–23). Still the precise historic beginnings of the canonization process remain largely in the dark. There are only two points of orientation that can be pinned down in terms of literature and date. For the first time in Sir. 44–50 (ca. 180 BCE), one encounters the idea of a fixed collection of biblical books. And it was only Flavius Josephus, about 93 CE (*Apion*. I, 8), who formulated explicitly the idea of a *completed* and unchangeable corpus of books, i.e. the Jewish canon, although he does not use this term. However, he assigns only 22 books to this corpus and, unfortunately, he does not name them.[12] That the first century CE was the time of the consolidation of the Hebrew Bible in respect to its contents can also be linked with the history of the text. After several centuries of textual diversity (see the findings in → *Qumran*), the biblical text of Judaism became consolidated in the first century CE in the shape of the proto-Masoretic text group (→ *Masoretes*). This was the result of various political as well as socio-religious factors, including the acceptance of the → *Septuagint* (LXX) by the Christian community (which led to its rejection by the Jewish community)

11. P. D. Gesche, *Schulunterricht in Babylonien im ersten Jahrtausend v. Chr.* (AOAT 275; Münster: Ugarit, 2001).

12. In contrast, the roughly contemporary *4 Ezra* 14 refers to 24 scriptures.

and the end of the Qumran community (70 CE). It was of doubtless importance that, after the destruction of the Second Temple, the priestly circles that transmitted the (proto-)Masoretic text group were the only organized group that could guarantee faithful textual transmission. Thus, their text tradition gained supremacy. Contrary to the tradition, there is no certain evidence that, during this period, any official meeting took place that could have decided on the canonical-authoritative status of the 24 books of the Hebrew canon in the version of the proto-Masoretic text group. The alleged rabbinical synod of Jabne/Jamnia, which supposedly met between 75 and 117 CE and made this decision, cannot be proven to have taken place.

The 24 books of the *Hebrew Bible* are divided into three parts: Torah (Law); Neviʾim (Prophets, i.e., Joshua to Malachi); and Ketuvim (Writings), which mirror the different stages of their acceptance into the canon, as well as their relationship among each other: the most important books come at the beginning. From the initial letters of each of the three parts T, N, and K, derives the word TaNaK also written Tanakh, which is used in the Jewish tradition to designate the Hebrew canon. In the Hebrew Bible the books of Samuel, 1 and 2 Kings, 1 and 2 Chronicles, Ezra and Nehemiah, as well as the 12 Minor Prophets are counted together as forming but one book each. That is why they add up to only 24 books in contrast to the 39 books counted in the Bibles of the Reformation tradition – additional books included in the Bibles of the Catholic and the Orthodox traditions yield an even higher number. The book of Daniel deserves special mention, because, despite its prophetic content, it is counted among the Ketuvim rather than the Neviʾim. This is usually explained by the late date of its completion, namely in the post-Maccabean Period, when presumably the canonization of the Neviʾim had already been completed and also or alternatively by the anti-apocalyptic tendency (→ *apocalyptic*) that reigned in Judaism at the time when the canon was completed (Ch. 21).

*English Bibles – Catholic, Orthodox and Protestant* – like the German versions, follow a different order than the Hebrew Bible, arranging the biblical books into three groups, which differ notably from the three sections of the Hebrew Bible: 1. historical books, 2. didactic books, and 3. prophetic books. This arrangement, which was already laid down in the LXX and was followed by the → *Vulgate*, corresponds to a three-step sequence of past, present and future (see table below). However, in this arrangement, the books Joshua to Kings, which the Hebrew Bible counts among the Neviʾim or prophetic books, are assigned to the historical books, so that, of the original Hebrew prophets, only Isaiah, Jeremiah, Ezekiel and the 12 'Minor Prophets' (taken as individual books) are assigned to the category of prophetic books, with Daniel being inserted into that group between Ezekiel and the Minor Prophets. Moreover, the LXX and the Vulgate contain additional books (and supplementary passages to some of the Hebrew books), which are not included in the Hebrew Bible. Depending on the nature of the contents, they insert these additions into appropriate places within the historical, didactic, or prophetic groups. Luther, in his German translation of the OT published in the complete Bible of 1534, placed these so-called 'apocrypha' (a term already used by Jerome to designate all the books of the Bible outside the Hebrew canon) in a separate section inserted between the Old and the New Testaments, so that they are also sometimes referred to as the 'inter-testamental books'. By contrast, the Catholic Church does not treat these books as 'apocrypha', but only as 'deuterocanonical' (second canon), a term in use since the 16th century. Thus Catholic versions of the Bible in English, e.g. the Douay-Rheims Bible (1582–1609), have continued to follow the practice of the Vulgate, leaving these books in their traditional places among the historical, didactic and prophetic books.

Until the 19th century, English Protestant versions of the Bible, including reprints of the King James Version (1611), generally followed the tradition begun by Luther and included the apocrypha in an inter-testamental section, sometimes with a warning about their non-authoritative character. However, in 1826, the British and Foreign Bible Society decided to refuse financial support to the publishing of Bibles containing the apocrypha, so that from then on until well into the 20th century they were generally omitted even in reprints of the King James Version. Only in 1964, did the American Bible Society officially lift its ban on their publication, and in 1966 the British and Foreign Bible Society followed suit. Meanwhile, already in 1957, the editors of the American Revised Standard Version (the OT portion appeared in 1951) had prepared a new English version of the apocrypha that was inserted into that version, usually as an appendix following the New Testament. More recent editions sometimes add as well the additional books of the LXX which are recognized as canonical by the Orthodox churches and insert all of these books together into an expanded inter-testamental section.

In addition to the Apocrypha (i.e., the additional scriptures of the LXX and Vulgate) described above, the Protestant tradition recognizes a number of other works related to the Bible as so-called 'pseudepigraphic works' (→ *pseudepigraphy*), whereas, in the Catholic tradition, these have traditionally been

| Hebrew Bible | LXX | Vulgate | NRSV |
|---|---|---|---|
| *Torah/Law* | *Historical Books* | *Pentateuchus* | |
| Genesis | Genesis | Genesis | Genesis |
| Exodus | Exodus | Exodus | Exodus |
| Leviticus | Leviticus | Leviticus | Leviticus |
| Numbers | Numbers | Numbers | Numbers |
| Deuteronomy | Deuteronomy | Deuteronomy | Deuteronomy |
| *Nevi'im/Prophets* | *see above* | *Libri Historici* | |
| *Former Prophets* | | | |
| Joshua | Joshua | Joshua | Joshua |
| Judges | Judges | Judges | Judges |
| (in Ketuvim) | Ruth | Ruth | Ruth |
| 1 + 2 Samuel | 1 + 2 Kings | 1 + 2 Kings | 1 + 2 Samuel |
| 1 + 2 Kings | 3 + 4 Kings | 3 + 4 Kings | 1 + 2 Kings |
| (in Ketuvim) | 1 + 2 Chronicles | 1 + 2 Chronicles (and Oratio Manassae) | 1 + 2 Chronicles |
| - | [1 Ezra (= 3 Ezra in Vulgate)] | 1 Ezra (= Ezra) | Ezra |
| (in Ketuvim) | 2 Ezra (= Ezra + Nehemiah) | 2 Ezra (= Nehemiah) [ | Nehemiah |
| - | - | 3 Ezra] | |
| - | - | [4 Ezra] | |
| (in Ketuvim) | Esther **+ Additions** | **Tobit** | Esther |
| - | **Judith** | **Judith** | |
| - | **Tobit** | Esther **+ Additions** | |
| | **1 + 2 Maccabees** | | |
| - | [3 + 4 Maccabees] | - | |
| *Latter Prophets* | *Didactic Books* | *Libri Didactici* | |
| Isaiah | | Job | Job |
| Jeremiah | Psalms | Psalms | Psalms |
| - | [Odes of Solomon and Oratio Manassae] | - | - |
| Ezekiel | Proverbs | Proverbs | Proverbs |
| Hosea | Ecclesiastes | Ecclesiastes | Ecclesiastes |
| Joel | Song of Songs | Song of Songs | Song of Solomon |
| | Job | | |
| - | **Wisdom of Solomon** | **Wisdom of Solomon** | |
| - | **Sirach** | **Sirach** | |
| Amos | [Psalms of Solomon] | | |
| Obadiah | | | |
| Jonah | | | |
| Micah | | | |
| Nahum | | | |
| Habakkuk | | | |
| Zephaniah | | | |
| Haggai | | | |
| Zechariah | | | |
| Malachi | | | |

| Hebrew Bible | LXX | Vulgate | NRSV |
|---|---|---|---|
| *Ketuvim/Writings* | *Prophetic Books* | *Libri Prophetici* | |
| Psalms | Hosea | Isaiah | Isaiah |
| Job | Amos | Jeremiah | Jeremiah |
| Proverbs | Micah | Lamentations | Lamentations |
| Ruth | Joel | **Baruch + Epistle of Jeremiah** | |
| Song of Songs | Obadiah | Ezekiel | Ezekiel |
| Ecclesiastes | Jonah | Daniel + **Additions (incl. Susannah, Bel and the Dragon)** | Daniel |
| Lamentations | Nahum | Hosea | Hosea |
| Esther | Habakkuk | Joel | Joel |
| Daniel | Zephaniah | Amos | Amos |
| Ezra + Nehemiah | Haggai | Obadiah | Obadiah |
| 1 + 2 Chronicles | Zechariah | Jonah | Jonah |
| | Malachi | Micah | Micah |
| | Isaiah | Nahum | Nahum |
| | Jeremiah | Habakkuk | Habakkuk |
| - | **Baruch** | Zephaniah | Zephaniah |
| | Lamentations | Haggai | Haggai |
| - | **Epistle of Jeremiah** | Zechariah | Zechariah |
| | Ezekiel | Malachi | Malachi |
| - | **Susannah = Dan 13** | **1 + 2 Maccabees** | |
| | Daniel + **Addittion 3.24–90 (Prayers of Azariah and of the Three Men in the Oven)** | | |
| - | **Bel and the Dragon = Dan. 14** | | |

called 'apocryphal' and they are equally considered to be outside the canon. To complicate matters, the mainstream Orthodox tradition does not use the term 'apocrypha' at all, preferring instead the Greek term 'anagignoskomena' (things that are read) to designate the additional scriptural texts of the LXX which it recognizes as canonical, and among these are a number of works that are regarded as 'apocryphal' in the Catholic tradition and in any case pseudepigraphic in both the Protestant and the Catholic traditions. Thus the term 'apocryphal books' is highly ambiguous and means different things according to the different confessional traditions. Correspondingly, the question of which texts should be counted as apocryphal or pseudepigraphic books of the Old Testament cannot always be clearly decided, especially since the boundaries separating them from other literary works like the New Testament apocrypha, the Qumranic literature, etc. are fluid.[13] The non-canonical, pseudepigraphic/apocryphal literature includes

13. A complete list can be found on www.uni-leipzig.de/~nt/asp/pseudep.htm. (in German).

works of very different genres: historical or legendary texts (*3 Ezra*, *3 Macc.*, *Aris. Ex.*), instructive works (*4 Macc.*, *Jub.*, *T. 12 Patr.*, *Mart. Isa.*, *L.A.E.*, *Jos. Asen.*), poetic writings (*Pss. Sol.*, *Odes Sol.*, *Pr. Man.*) and a large number of apocalypses (*Apoc. Ab.*, *As. Mos.*, *2 En.*, *1 En.*, *2 Bar.*, *3 Bar.*, *Sib. Or.*, 4 Ezra, *et al.*).

## Terminology

- Bible. The term 'Bible' derives from the Lebanese harbour town of Byblos, which was known in antiquity for the production and distribution of writing materials and books. 'Bible', therefore, means simply 'The Book'. For the Jewish religion, this is the collection of 22 or 24 (Flav. Jos., *Apion*. I, 8; *4 Ezra*. 14.42) books which constitutes the Hebrew Scriptures (i.e., Hebrew Bible, also called 'Scripture' or TNK/TaNaK; see above), while the Christian religion considers this collection to constitute only the first part of the Christian Bible, the second part consisting of the New Testament writings.
- Old Testament. The name 'Old Testament' was coined from the viewpoint of the NT and is applied to the first part of the Christian Bible (therefore, sometimes also called the 'First Testament'). The term is based upon Jer. 31.31–34, where a 'new → *covenant*' is proclaimed. The Hebrew word *běrît* 'covenant, treaty' corresponds to the Greek *diathēkē* and the Latin *testamentum*. In the last analysis, however, the term goes back to Paul's speech in 2 Cor. 3.14, where he uses the term 'old covenant' in connection with the reading of the Torah in the synagogue. The name 'Old Testament' gained ascendancy in Christianity already by the end of the 2nd cent. CE and was not meant pejoratively, i.e., 'old' was not understood in the sense of 'superseded' but rather in the sense of 'venerable and reliable', and it emphasizes the roots of the Christian Church within the Scriptures inherited from the Jews. Protestant Bible editions contain the books of the Hebrew Bible but not in the same order (Torah, Prophets, Writings), following instead a sequence that goes back to the LXX/Vulgate (past-present-future). The commitment of the Reformation to the original Hebrew text of the Bible (*veritas hebraica*) became a central issue in the 16th century, because the Scriptures alone were considered to be the normative criterion in questions of belief (*sola scriptura*). Thus, it was most important to identify as accurately as possible the original meaning of the texts in the original language. For this reason, only those scriptural texts were considered to be canonical, for which, according to the knowledge of the time, a Hebrew original existed. By contrast, Catholic Bible editions orient themselves mainly on the canon of the Septuagint and the Vulgate and thus contain, in addition, those books and passages that Protestants regard as 'apocryphal' and which Catholics treat as 'deuterocanonical'.
- The Greek Bible/Septuagint (LXX). The early Christian Church took over the Holy Scriptures of the Jews in the form and extent of this Greek translation of the OT. Until today, it is normative in the Eastern Orthodox churches. It contains the Scriptures of the Hebrew Bible and, in addition, the so-called apocryphal/deuterocanonical books, including some not contained in the Vulgate (see the preceding table). Almost all of these additional works were originally composed in Greek.

## 1.2.2 The Archaeological Sources from Palestine

Bibliography 6.3 Archaeology and Iconography. Further: Y. Meshorer, *A Treasury of Jewish Coins: From the Persian Period to Bar Kokhba*. Jerusalem: Yad Ben-Zvi, 2001.

As sources for the archaeology of Palestine, the material remains from the region are as numerous as they are diverse. Although the → *iconographic* and → *epigraphic* materials should be numbered among the archaeological remains, because of their special character and importance they will be treated here in separate chapters. In Palestine and in its neighbouring regions, there are many different types of evidence for ancient human activity in places that served as sites for settlement, cult, burial, or merely as temporary resting places.[14] Among them are:

(A) Artifacts in the sense of objects produced or shaped by human beings using the most diverse materials and techniques (including animal bones used both as tools and as materials). Among such artifacts are: mobile objects such as tools, jewellery, seals, furnishings, storage jars, figurines, etc.; immovable objects, i.e. fixed installations such as ovens, storage pits, storehouses, cisterns, reliefs carved in rock, etc.; complex architectural structures like buildings, walls, streets and roads, landscape improvements such as terraces, etc.; and objects designed for the expression and transmission of abstract ideas, i.e. objects bearing images or writing.
(B) Apart from such artifacts, there are also what may be called 'eco-facts', i.e., organic materials and elements of the natural environment that serve as signs of human activity.

In general, a distinction is made between the individual *find*, i.e. the individual object found, and the archaeological context in which it was found; this context, constituted by the sum total of what has been found at the site, is referred to as the *findings* (German: 'Befund'). These findings, however, represent only a momentary glimpse into a particular stage in the gradual process of decay of the objects, which have been accidentally preserved and now recovered. Thus, the objects found represent only a larger or smaller part of the sum total of the artifacts and eco-facts that had originally existed at the site.

14. Following C. Renfrew and P. Bahn, *Archaeology: Theories, Methods, and Practice* (4th ed.; London: Thames & Hudson, 2004, reprint 2006).

## 1.2.3 Extra-Biblical Text Sources from Palestine and the Neighbouring Cultures

Bibliography 6.2 Sources in Writing. Further: P. J. King and L. E. Stager, *Life in Biblical Israel,* Louisville: Westminster John Knox, 2001; F. M. Cross, *Leaves from an Epigrapher's Notebook: Collected Papers in Hebrew and West Semitic Palaeography and Epigraphy*. HSS 51. Winona Lake, Ind.: Eisenbrauns, 2003.

The extra-biblical written finds, discovered in Palestine itself, are written in different languages and scripts. There are texts in syllabic cuneiform, e.g. the Gilgamesh-Epic from Megiddo and the Letters from Taanach and Hazor, dating to the 2nd millennium BCE, the documents from Gezer, dating to the 1st mill. BCE,[15] and texts in the alphabetic cuneiform of Ugarit from Beth-Shemesh dating to the 14th/13th cent. BCE. Further, there are texts in Egyptian hieratic script, e.g. the → *ostraca* from Qubur al-Walaydah from the end of the 2nd mill. BCE, or in Egyptian hieroglyphs, e.g. from Beth-Shemesh and Beth-Shan of various dates. All of these were scripts that had been developed by the Mesopotamian, Ugaritic and Egyptian neighbours of Palestine. Soon after 2000 BCE, however, inhabitants of the Levant itself, perhaps Egyptians,[16] invented proto-forms of the alphabet as we know it, at first as a pure consonantal script that was more practical than any of the other scripts. From this 'old Canaanite' script[17] dating to the 12th/11th cent. BCE onward, a South Arabic and a Phoenician branch gradually developed. The latter became the point of departure for the Aramaic, Moabite, Ammonite, Edomite and ancient Hebrew alphabetic scripts (among others), which, because of their shared roots, strongly resemble each other. Also the ancient Greek script had its origin here. Texts in these scripts and the languages that use these scripts are well attested in Palestine and Syria.

15. For a survey, see W. Horowitz and T. Oshima, *Cuneiform in Canaan: Cuneiform Sources from the Land of Israel in Ancient Times* (Jerusalem: Israel Exploration Society, 2006).
16. See the proposal of G. J. Hamilton, *The Origins of the West Semitic Alphabet in Egyptian Scripts* (CBQMS 40; Washington: Catholic Biblical Association of America, 2006).
17. It is attested in the 16th–12th cent. BCE, among others, by difficult to decipher and interpret proto-Sinaic inscriptions from Serābit El-Ḫādim from the 16th/15th cent. BCE; by a votive inscription from Lachish ca. 13th cent. BCE; by an → *ostracon* from Beth-Shemesh ca. 12th cent. BCE.

## Languages and writing material

Seven ancient languages – Canaanite, Phoenician-Punic, Gileadite, Moabite, Ammonite, Edomite and Hebrew, together form the Canaanite language group, which along with Amorite, Ugaritic, and Aramaic, belongs to the family of Northwest Semitic languages. They share similarities, but also manifest differences. Even within any one of these languages, diachronic and synchronic orthographic, as well as linguistic differences can be observed. While diachronic variability can be placed within the framework of the history of a language and explained as such, synchronic variability should be interpreted as local variations. Thus, for example, one can understand the extra-biblical ancient Hebrew texts of the monarchic period as witnesses to two different regional idioms (dialects), the Israelite northern Hebrew (attested, e.g. in the → *ostraca* from Samaria) and the Judean southern Hebrew (attested, e.g. in the inscriptions from Jerusalem). With few exceptions (e.g. the genuine words of Hosea), the Scriptures of the OT are influenced by southern Hebrew (spoken until about 400 BCE) and middle Hebrew that developed from it (used from about 400 BCE until about 100 CE[18]). As the *lingua franca* of the Ancient Near East, from the 8th cent. BCE on, Aramaic increasingly replaced Akkadian, which had served in this function since the 2nd millennium. Initially used mainly as a language of diplomacy (see 2 Kgs 18.26; letter of Adon[19]), it became, from around 500 BCE, in the form of 'imperial Aramaic', the official language of the Achaemenid Empire, the common language of administration, commerce and literary texts in the Near East. Meanwhile, the Canaanite languages, among them Hebrew, became more and more marginalized so that it comes as no surprise that even in Palestine itself Aramaic was not only written but spoken (Neh. 8.8; 13.24), and that Aramaic texts are preserved in the Old Testament itself (Gen. 31.47; Jer. 10.11; Ezra 4.6–6.18; 7.12–26; Dan. 2.4b–7.28). With the overthrow of the Persian Empire (333/2 BCE), Aramaic was gradually replaced in the Near East by Greek, Persian, various East and West Aramaic dialects, and ultimately, in the 7th–10th cent. CE, by Arabic.

In principle, things could be written down on any material that was available. However, because organic materials like leather, parchment, wood, and papyrus only rarely (mainly in the desert!) can resist the grinding tooth of time, most of the extra-biblical texts from Palestine that have come down to us have been carved,scratched, chiselled, or hammered into stone, plaster, raw or fired clay, or metal, or written on these materials with ink. The types of texts transmitted (→ *'genre'*) are as diverse as the scripts, languages and writing materials, even when one considers only the extra-biblical written sources in Hebrew.[20] Since the monarchic period, there are

⇨

18. The terminology follows here K. Beyer, *ATTM*, 49.

19. B. Porten and A.Yardeni, *TADAE*, A 1.1.

20. For an overview of ancient Hebrew inscriptions, see G. I. Davies, *Ancient Hebrew Inscriptions: Corpus and Concordance* (Cambridge: Cambridge University Press, 1991); F. W. Dobbs-Allsopp, J. J. M. Roberts, C. L. Seow and R. E. Whitaker, *Hebrew Inscriptions: Texts from the Biblical Period of the Monarchy with Concordance* (New Haven, Conn.: Yale University Press, 2005).

ostraca (pieces of pottery on which texts were later written, including letters, lists and official documents), inscriptions on pieces of plaster, vessels of clay and other materials, building remains, stone slabs, ossuaries, sarcophaguses and tombs. Although inscribed weights, inventory lists, seals and stamps from Palestine that are inscribed with Hebrew signs offer no extensive connected texts (e.g. longer sentences or narratives), they do provide a glimpse into scribal practice and the local onomasticon (i.e., name giving) of a given period. From the Persian Period on, we also find coins as the bearers of writing. Special importance should be given to the extra-biblical Hebrew and Aramaic texts from the Judean Desert (papyrus, leather, parchment, copper scroll from → *Qumran*), which, apart from the biblical texts, contain writings of many different categories.

Extra-biblical text material cannot be sorted in a blanket manner into the categories of primary or secondary sources, but must be evaluated individually according to the nature of the material. Johannes Renz has argued that the simple use of temporal proximity as a formal criterion for primary sources and temporal remoteness for secondary sources is too general, and thus he has proposed a more differentiated model,[21] which, in addition to temporality, takes account of the diverse degrees of the subjectivity of the text and its function in context. The hierarchical classification of written sources which he proposes, begins with documents that stand in an immediate relationship to the historical event and in fact constitute a part of the event itself; these alone count for him as 'authentic primary sources'. To be distinguished from these are those texts which are likewise directly involved in the event, but represent a subjective point of view. After these, come documents which have been subsequently reworked after the fact, retrospective accounts of the event by persons who may or may not have participated in it, and texts which have arisen in the course of a complex, systematizing process of composition and reworking, such as annals, and ending with those textual witnesses that have passed through a long process of formation in the course of a literary tradition. However, the across-the-board distinction between objective and subjective documents is difficult to make in practice and very hard

21. J. Renz, 'Der Beitrag der althebräischen Epigraphik zur Exegese des Alten Testaments und zur Profan- und Religionsgeschichte Palästinas: Leistungen und Grenzen aufgezeigt am Beispiel der Inschriften des (ausgehenden) 7. Jahrhunderts vor Christus', in *Steine – Bilder – Texte* (ed. C. Hardmeier), 123–58, esp. 126–31 (above, n. 2).

to verify. Furthermore, in the concrete analysis of any particular source, the exact boundaries between these different categories are even more difficult to pin down, so that it seems more practical to stick to the traditional procedural distinction between primary and secondary sources based on the formal criteria of dating and temporal proximity without passing judgements about their reliability.

All Hebrew extra-biblical texts provide insights into the chronological development of the Hebrew script and language, as well as their geographically distinctive characteristics. Together with the additional text finds in other languages and scripts, they represent reliable sources for the (re-) construction of everyday culture (e.g. the Gezer calendar[22]), religious practices (e.g. votive inscription from Ekron, inscriptions from Kuntillet ʿAjrûd, funerary inscriptions from Khirbet el-Qôm, the Balaam Inscription from Tell Dēr-ʿAllā, amulet texts from Ketef Hinnom, the Greek inscription from Dan), for social, legal and economic conditions (e.g. ostraca from Samaria, Lachish, Arad, Idumean, and the ostracon from Məṣad Hăšavyāhū), and for political history (the Mesha Inscription, the Aramaic inscription from Tel Dan, the Siloam-Tunnel inscription,[23] the Nabonidus inscription from Jordan,[24] letters from the Judean desert), all of which need to be examined and taken into consideration.

Besides the texts that have been found in the Levant itself, there are extra-biblical written finds from surrounding Ancient Near Eastern and Egyptian regions that were composed in a diversity of languages (Akkadian, Sumerian, Hittite, Egyptian, Elamite, Phoenician, Ugaritic, Aramaic, etc.). These texts are studied by specialists of the related disciplines of Ancient Near Eastern Studies according to the canon of methods prevailing in their disciplines.[25] These sources are relevant for Palestinian and biblical studies because they resurrect the empires and cultures that dominated the ancient world in biblical times. Thus, their development and their characteristic features had, in one way or another, put their stamp on the Levant, which was always an area of transit and a 'threshold country' (see below Ch. 3.1) caught between its more

22. ANET, 320.

23. COS II, 145–6.

24. S. Dalley, 'The Selaʿ Sculpture: A Neo-Babylonian Rock Relief in Southern Jordan', *ADAJ* 41 (1997), 169–76.

25. German editions of the most important texts are comprised in *TUAT*. English translations are collected in *ANET* and *COS*.

powerful neighbours. Of special political-historical and religious-historical importance are the texts that directly or indirectly refer to events in Palestine, e.g. the annals of kings or pharaohs reporting campaigns in the region, the Tell el-ʿAmārna correspondence, the letters to the Assyrian kings from the western provinces, the black obelisk of Shalmaneser III), or those dealing with Israelite/Judean/Jewish → *diaspora* groups in their host countries, e.g. the texts from Dūr Katlimmu and āl-Yāḫudu[26]). The Aramaic papyri and ostraca from Egypt from the 7th cent. BCE to 4th cent. CE merit a special mention. They contain numerous texts sketching a vivid picture of events in Palestine (e.g. the letter of Adon[27]) or the socio-political, economic and religious life of the Jewish diaspora community of Elephantine.[28]

## 1.2.4 Iconographic Sources from Palestine and the Neighbouring Cultures.

Bibliography 6.3 Archaeology and Iconography; 9 History of Religion of Ancient Israel (O. Keel, *Geschichte Jerusalems*; idem and C. Uehlinger, *GGG*; B. A. Nakhai, *Archaeology*; Z. Zevit, *Religions*). Further: S. Schroer, *In Israel gab es Bilder: Nachrichten von darstellender Kunst im Alten Testament*. OBO 74. Fribourg: Academic Press/Göttingen: Vandenhoeck & Ruprecht, 1987; K. van der Toorn, ed., *The Image and the Book: Iconic Cults, Aniconism, and the Rise of Book Religion in Israel and the Ancient Near East*. CBET 21, Leuven: Peeters, 1997.

Religious ideas come to expression not only in texts, but also in all other forms of human communications, thus also in pictorial or iconic representations, whether these be painted, drawn, sketched, forged, cut out, engraved, scratched, chiselled, sculptured, or moulded, be they sophisticated or simple. Like all archaeological sources, such iconographic sources are accidental finds. For Palestinian studies, they are of extreme importance because, among other reasons, they are often attested in epochs without written sources and because

26. F. Joannès and A. Lemaire, 'Trois tablettes cunéiformes à onomastique ouest-sémitique', *Transeu* 17 (1999): 17–34 (contract from 498 BCE); K. Abraham, 'West Semitic and Judean Brides in Cuneiform Sources from the Sixth Century BCE', *AfO* 51 (2005/6): 198–219; idem, 'An Inheritance Division among Judeans in Babylonia from the Early Persian Period', in *New Seals and Inscriptions: Hebrew, Idumean, and Cuneiform* (ed. M. Lubetski; Sheffield: Phoenix, 2007), 206–21.
27. B. Porten and A. Yardeni, *TADAE*, A1.1.
28. Translated and edited in B. Porten and A. Yardeni, *TADAE*.

they are quite often made from materials less perishable than the writing materials – papyrus or leather – used in Palestine especially for larger texts. Contrary to the opinion that, because of the Old Testament's ban against images, there were no pictorial representations in ancient 'Israel', – a once common view still held in some circles – there is an abundance of iconographic source material in the region going back to the earliest periods and extending without a break (even in the monarchic period) up into the Islamic period, and this abundance of material is growing steadily thanks to ongoing excavations.

For quite some time now, the iconographic material from Palestine (the coastland and West and East Jordan) and its neighbouring regions (Egypt, Syria, Cyprus, Anatolia, Mesopotamia, Iran, etc.) has been collected and studied within the framework of individual scientific disciplines like Pre-historical Studies, Ancient Near Eastern Archaeology, Egyptology, etc.[29] and has been analysed more with respect to individual aspects and facets, than in terms of an overall view. This material provides valuable information about the life and ideas of a specific region, epoch and culture, as well as about prominent inter-cultural contacts (and sometimes even fashion trends) in a given period. Such inter-cultural contacts are reflected, for instance, in the inclusion of Egyptian hieroglyphics in Syrian and Palestinian seal-iconography. It is only since the works of Othmar Keel and his school that biblical iconography has come to be established as a distinctive discipline. It is dedicated predominantly to the study of pictorial material from or about Palestine (e.g. the Assyrian reliefs of Lachish). As already observed, biblical iconography is not at all limited in scope to the short span of time related in the Bible but extends deep into the other periods as well.[30]

In conclusion, it should also be noted that the most important materials on which pictures have been preserved in the ANE including Palestine and Egypt are: rock reliefs and murals, orthostate reliefs,[31] steles, wall paintings, graffiti, stamps or cylinder seals (rather less often in Palestine) and stamp or seal imprints, → *scarabs*, → *conoids*, full- or half-round statues or

29. The following works should be noted: E. Brunner-Traut, *Frühformen des Erkennens am Beispiel Ägyptens* (2nd ed.; Darmstadt: Wissenschaftliche Buchgesellschaft, 1992); J. Assmann, 'Die Macht der Bilder: Rahmenbedingungen ikonischen Handelns im Alten Ägypten', *Visible Religion* 7 (1990): 1–20; M. Bachmann, *Die strukturalistische Artefakt- und Kunstanalyse: Exposition der Grundlagen anhand der vorderorientalischen, ägyptischen und griechischen Kunst* (OBO 148; Fribourg: Academic Press/Göttingen: Vandenhoeck & Ruprecht, 1996).

30. This is apparent now in the broadly sketched work by O. Keel and S. Schroer, *IPIAO*.

31. An orthostate is a vertical basalt slab.

figurines of different materials (mostly metal, clay, stone, rarely wood) and sizes, decorations on furniture (ivory), tools, weapons, buildings such as temples and palaces, or grave paraphernalia, jewellery and decorations (rings, pendants, breastplates, etc.) and, from the Persian Period on, coins.

# 2

# Methods

(Angelika Berlejung – Translation by Thomas Riplinger)

## Chapter Outline



Bibliography 3 Exegetical Methods; 3.1.1 Discussion of Methods and Alternative Approaches – General; 3.1.2 Synchronic Methods: Canonical Approach, Structural Analysis, 'New Literary Criticism'. Further: R. N. Soulen and R. K. Soulen, *Handbook of Biblical Criticism*. Cambridge: James Clarke, 2002 (Reprint).

## 2.1 Exegetical Methods

The methodological approaches described in the following chapter have been developed to answer the principal exegetical question concerning the original meaning of the texts at the time of their origin. 'These approaches were not decreed by exegetes, but were [called forth] by the biblical subject matter itself, …'.[1] The purpose of exegesis (as one step of understanding the Old Testament) is to come as close as possible to the original historical sense of the text in its original historical setting, always in critical awareness of possible errors stemming from one's own preconceived notions. Exegesis, therefore, paves the way for the text itself. With the help provided by individual steps of the historical-critical method, the exegete attempts to disclose the meaning of the text reflected in both its historical development

1. O. H. Steck, *Old Testament Exegesis*, 20.

and its theological relevance, in order to penetrate its depth and to understand it. In this way, one can construct well-founded hypotheses about the historical development of the text from its earliest written or oral attestation until its present form. The starting point of this task is the observation that the majority of the biblical books were written neither by a single author, nor within a brief time period, nor even in one and the same place. The original compositions and their various redactions were composed, compiled and worked over during the course of many generations. This mainly productive phase of literary effort by the authors, the composers, the compilers and the redactors led to a generally stable form of the text. Then the mainly reproductive phase of the copyists, the transmitters and the translators took place. One must, however, take into account that copying a text could also include significant additions to that text, because the copyist was allowed to comment on or even to correct what he copied, and because interpretation of some sort is always a part of the translation process. Thus production and reproduction are closely related.

Recently, the diachronically oriented methods that interpret the biblical text as a historical object with different historical dimensions have been supplemented by synchronically oriented methods of biblical exegesis. The synchronically oriented approaches largely eschew historical questions and place the text in a time-neutral framework. They will be presented below, along with other methods of interpretation that are content-oriented or that aim at the application and actualization of the Bible.

## 2.1.1 Diachronic Methods: The Steps of the Historical-Critical Method

Bibliography 3 Exegetical Methods; 12 History of Exegesis and Reception of the Bible. Further: N. P. Lemche, *The Old Testament between Theology and History: A Critical Survey*. Louisville: Westminster John Knox, 2008, 44–69, 110–63.

The historical-critical method[2] places special value on separating the textual layers, clarifying questions of dating, and placing the text and its

2. For the history of the historical-critical method, see H.-J. Kraus, *Geschichte der historisch-kritischen Erforschung des Alten Testaments* (4th ed.; Neukirchen-Vluyn: Neukirchener, 1984 [1956]).

(re-)constructed stages and their compilations in their appropriate intellectual, cultural and social-historical contexts, and, if possible, relating them to particular historical events. By identifying the intentions of the author and the various redactors, this method can make important contributions to the reconstruction of the development of theological ideas as well. The historical-critical method comprises a set of separate steps that approach the Old Testament text as the literary product of an earlier time.

*Textual criticism*,[3] sometimes called 'lower criticism', is concerned with the (re-)construction of the assumed *Urtext* (or *Urtexts*, see below) underlying the current form of the biblical books and with the collection and analysis of the different text witnesses from the time of the books' 'completion' to the first printed editions of early modern times. This method includes the discussion of the relationship of the various textual witnesses to each other, as well as the weighing and investigation of practical conditions of their copying and textual transmission. Especially important is the documentation and evaluation of readings that deviate from the version that is taken to constitute the principal text, i.e. the so-called 'variants' or readings that represent quite different textual traditions. In critical editions of the Hebrew Bible, these are noted in the 'critical apparatus', where the Masoretic Text (→ *Masoretes*) serves as the principal text, to which the variants are compared. Textual criticism thus deals with the process and mechanisms of textual transmission: it is not concerned with the original process of the literary creation (= 'the writing') of the biblical books but rather with what happened to the texts afterwards, namely in the subsequent process of copying and transmitting them. In short, textual criticism tries to discover what the completed literary composition looked like at the point when the process of textual transmission began. It is not concerned with possible written stages the book may have gone through before it was completed in the form that has been handed down. This completed composition can be called the *Urtext* (a technical term borrowed from the German, meaning 'original/earliest text'); however, many exegetes now believe that often there were several such *Urtexts* (although strictly speaking an oxymoron) that existed simultaneously, e.g. in different geographical regions. Taking into account the relative trustworthiness of the various textual witnesses, the exegete attempts to determine which reading might have been the earliest, that is, the oldest variant from whence the others could have developed in the subsequent process of transmission. The method consists of distinguishing between unintentional mistakes (copying mistakes, such

3. See, E. Tov, *Text*; idem, *Textual Criticism of the Hebrew Bible* (2nd ed.; Minneapolis: Fortress, 2001).

as haplography, homoioarcton, homoioteleuton,[4] dittography,[5] letter transposition, false separation of words) and intentional deviations (smoothing out rough formulations, adding explanations, euphemisms, theological corrections). Traditional basic rules such as preference for the shorter or for the more difficult reading (*lectio brevior potior/lectio difficilior preferenda*) have been challenged as dubious simplifications.[6] In comparison to the earlier tendency to make value judgements about readings (worse/better), today one concentrates on establishing a relative chronological sequence, in order to describe the history of the text.

At the end of the composition process of a biblical book, a textual entity (or several alternative textual entities) emerged that was considered complete: this corresponded to what was above called the *Urtext(s)*, which then became the starting point for the ensuing process of copying and transmission. The history of the textual transmission process (and the recovery of the earliest completed text) is the object of textual criticism. The process leading up to this completed textual entity, namely, the history of the written and sometimes oral stages of the text on its way towards the final composition, is the object of a series of subsequent steps of the historical-critical method. However, the transition between the process of composition and redaction leading to the *Urtext(s)* and the process of transmission of this text(s) as witnessed in the various manuscript traditions is not a sharp one: the last redactor of the completed text was simultaneously an author and a copyist. As seen in this example, the transitions between the various methodological steps are fluid.

*Composition criticism*, as opposed to a possible pre-literary oral tradition, is the term we will use for what is called '*Literarkritik*' and '*Redaktionsgeschichte*' ('redaction history') in German. The use of the term 'literary criticism' to express what is involved here is problematical for a variety of reasons. Aside from the fact that 'literary criticism' in English is most often used outside of biblical exegesis in the general sense of literary studies, even within biblical studies the term has been used ambiguously: initially and sometimes even today, it was used more or less as a synonym for 'source criticism' particularly of the Pentateuch and some of the historical books, namely the attempt to identify a limited number of written documents, which a redactor pieced together to produce the final text. Occasionally, 'literary criticism' was used by exegetes as a general term for 'historical criticism' as a whole (as is sometimes the case for its counterpart,

4. Haplography is the inadvertent omission of a letter (or word) between two adjacent identical or similar letters (or words). *Homoioarcton* and *homoioteleuton* refer to the unintentional omission of a part of the text between repetitions of one or more identical or similar words in a particular context because the eye of the copyist or translator simply overlooked it. In *homoioarcton*, the repeated element is found at the beginning of the omitted part; in *homoioteleuton*, it is found at the end. Because it is often difficult to decide exactly what is involved, for the most part, one simply speaks of *parablepsis* as a general term for scribal mistakes due to inattention or oversight.
5. Dittography is the unintentional duplication of one or several letters or words.
6. See, e.g. E. Tov, *Text*, 255–6.

'source criticism'), i.e. for the general study of the historical setting of a particular biblical passage, including the persons, places and events mentioned in it. Increasingly, the term 'literary criticism' is used in 'its most basic meaning to refer to the process of analyzing and understanding parts of the Bible *as literature*,[7] examining technique, style, and other features in order to gain an appreciation for the intention and results of a given portion as a literary composition'.[8] To avoid confusion we shall not use the term 'literary criticism' as an equivalent to *Literarkritik* in the narrow sense described in the next paragraph, but we will speak instead of 'composition criticism'.

Like textual criticism described above, composition criticism is also based on the study of the textual witnesses, but it focuses on the development of the written text from its beginnings – the earliest layer – up to its final redaction as the 'completed' *Urtext*. In doing so, it divides the finished book into its various historical stages or editions and studies their character and presumed genesis. The identification of the growth of biblical texts and books can include various steps: consideration of the use of earlier *textual* sources ('source criticism', German: *Quellenkritik*), the use of certain oral or written genres or forms ('form criticism'), the use of various biblical and extra-biblical traditions ('tradition history'), and the gradual growth of texts through the introductions of larger or smaller additions by a redactor (editor) or redactors ('redaction history'). Composition criticism in this generic sense is based on the premise, founded on tensions observed in the text itself, that in the course of its genesis the text has gone through various hands in such a way that distinct stages and layers of development can be identified and individual component elements can be distinguished from one another.[9]

The composition-critical analysis and (re-)construction of the written tradition's history is subdivided into two phases, based on the need to distinguish between analytical methods identifying earlier stages and different layers, starting from the texts that have come down to us,[10] and the subsequent synthetical reconstruction of compilation, additions and editing processes of these components that produce the final form or *Urtext* of those books as presupposed by textual criticism described above (this phase is called 'redaction history', see next paragraph). In the first stage it is the task of historical-critical analysis to find traces of growth within the process of textual transmission that led to the

7. E.g. R. Alter, *Art*.
8. D. Stuart, *Old Testament Exegesis: A Handbook for Students and Pastors* (4th ed.; Louisville, Ky.: Westminster John Knox, 2009), 140.
9. Translator's note: With the approval of the author, this section has been substantially expanded and rewritten to make the matter more intelligible to the reader in the English-speaking world, where some of the distinctions made in the German discussions are not observed with such precision.
10. This earliest version established through composition criticism can be referred to as the 'basic document', and at times, confusingly, also as the *Urtext* of a particular book (e.g. *Ur-Deuteronomy*).

emergence of the final *Urtext* on the basis of reduplications, contradictions and textual inconsistencies. Based on those traces, individual elements that make up the various layers of the text are identified and delineated from each other. The result of this analysis is usually the division of the complete text or even of a complete book into a collection of smaller units, which manifest internal literary consistency and thus can be (re-)constructed as distinct original text elements that subsequently became part of the final composition. In an ensuing methodological step, the exact form, and the genre-specific homogeneity, and typical literary, conceptual and content-related characteristics of these units can then be investigated. Later additions can be identified as secondary, tertiary, etc. Because the decision about where tell-tale tensions are found in the text inevitably involves subjective judgements made by the individual exegete, these historical-critical analyses often turn out to be controversial and need to be proved in the course of the ensuing exegetical discussion.

Putting together the results of this critical analysis leads to the next phase called *redaction history* or *redaction criticism*,[11] which can often exercise a retrospective critical function regarding the foregoing analysis. Here the exegete assembles into larger units all of the isolated text fragments which appear to show the same hand and then attempts to construct a relative chronology of their subsequent growth, tracing the process of compilation by which the individual text elements or layers were gradually brought together to produce the final form of the book. In this way, the exegete (re-)constructs the successive stages and layers of literary growth of the component texts, i.e. of both the individual pericopes and the larger documents into which they later came to be incorporated, from the first written form of the individual fragments to the final composition of the book as a whole. In tracing this process, redaction criticism is particularly concerned with the theological or ideological profile of the compositions produced by the redactors, who deliberately worked over the already existing text elements either by compiling (→ *compilation*) them into larger units or by editorially correcting them to modify, interpret and update their meaning. In the course of this redactional process, the biblical texts were subjected to a tension between the need to preserve the original form of the text and the need to reshape and interpret it. The redactors were not merely re-productive adapters and compilers of their texts; they were also productive authors in their own right, who gave the texts new contextual meanings and theological interpretations. From the way the redactor received and reworked the textual material transmitted to him, it is possible to draw conclusions about the specific interests and intentions that guided his work and about the socio-political and historical developments to which he responded in his updating of the text. The overarching concept that determines the final shape of an individual text or a larger literary composition assembling related material, like the Book of Twelve (see Ch. 12), was in large measure the work of the (final) redactor.

11. N. P. Lemche, *Old Testament*, 64–9; O. H. Steck, *Exegesis*, 6.

*Form criticism* began as the study of the principles of the oral transmission and written pre-history of specific oral literary structures and types found in the biblical texts, treating in particular their more or less fixed and typical language structure ('genre style') and their underlying characteristic and often even institutionalized communicative situation (*'Sitz im Leben'*: literally, 'setting in life', though 'sociological setting' might be a more accurate rendering). Oral types or → *genres* (German: *Gattung*) represent typical forms of spoken expression that, independent of the individual text in which they have been transmitted in written form, manifest characteristic linguistic-literary structures and situational settings (*Sitz im Leben*). The method of form criticism was developed by Hermann Gunkel (1862–1932) at the end of the 19th/beginning of the 20th century in connection with his study of the Psalms and Genesis in opposition to the earlier methodological approach that searched primarily for written sources (i.e., the 'source criticism' employed in the identification of 'J', 'E', 'P', and 'D' in the Pentateuch). Its aim, among others, was to render individual biblical passages intelligible in terms of their genesis and linguistic-literary form in light of the language world and the sociological settings reflected in them. Historical criticism only gradually came to distinguish more clearly between the written phase of composition and redaction and the preceding oral phase, each with its respective genres. In recent decades, however, this methodological premise has come under criticism because scholars have increasingly raised questions about the transition from an oral to a written transmission phase and have raised doubts about the possibility of defining the genres on the basis of both form and content. Wolfgang Richter[12] has proposed separating the formal and the content-related aspects and treating the latter only after the former. He has also challenged the original assumption of form criticism that a particular formula remained unchanged in its original gestalt throughout the phase of oral transmission and only in the course of subsequent written history was then expanded upon and mingled with other structural elements. Klaus Berger[13] has proposed a 'new form history' that analyses 'the literary structures (*Forms*), their functions, and their histories as genres (*Gattungen*)', aiming to separate form history from questions of transmission history (see below).

In the meantime, form criticism has developed into a complex system of methods that, on the one hand, trace the linguistic development of the individual text units as determined by historical-critical analysis of the written text and, on the other hand, attempt to assign the individual text units to text types or classes and to identify the functions of such classes (= *genre analysis*): a) on the basis of structural relations as proposed by W. Richter; b) on the basis of

12. W. Richter, *Exegese als Literaturwissenschaft: Entwurf einer alttestamentlichen Literaturtheorie und Methodologie* (Göttingen: Vandenhoeck & Ruprecht, 1971).

13. K. Berger, *Einführung in die Formgeschichte* (Tübingen: Francke, 1987), 27.

communication-theory considerations as proposed by Christof Hardmeier;[14] and c) on the basis of their reception history as proposed by Klaus Berger[15]. Within genre analysis, questions are posed about the typical social-cultural background situations ('Sitz im Leben') of the genre as such. Such questions can only be answered on the basis of detailed knowledge of the interrelated social, economic, cultural and religious-historical context of Ancient 'Israel'. In actual practice, a genre can shift its 'Sitz im Leben' and develop from a primary genre to an imitated one. When this happens a text is indeed formulated by the author according to the fixed structural pattern proper to the genre (as it is known to him) but it is then used in an atypical manner, i.e. not in the normal function and 'Sitz im Leben' of the original genre. A classical example is the funeral dirge of Amos 5.1–3, which is set in the atypical context of a statement of prophetic judgement.

Following upon genre analysis, *genre history* investigates the diachronic development of a genre. To name the genres, terms are generally taken over from general literary studies because the Old Testament itself usually does not provide terms of its own, one of the rare exceptions being *māšāl* (proverb). It is important to note, however, that, although terms like novella, epos, etc., derive from general literary criticism, the specific structural pattern of the biblical genre is not always identical with the patterns found in other literatures.

*Transmission history* (German: Überlieferungsgeschichte): Martin Noth (1902–1968) originally introduced this term to describe the whole diachronic development of biblical texts from their very beginnings to their final gestalt. In recent decades, however, a stricter definition has become prevalent that limits transmission history to the pre-literary (oral) history of a text. Because oral transmission processes are difficult to pin down and enormously variable, it is extremely difficult to make plausible hypotheses about this process, and all such hypotheses depend on the results of preceding composition-critical and form-critical analyses which themselves are often controversial. Apart from that, the transition from oral transmission to stable literary texts often does not represent a clear-cut diachronic break, since oral and written versions can exist simultaneously and mutually influence each other. One must also consider the possibility that a written text may imitate typical characteristics of orality, e.g. characteristic formulae. As a result, transmission history has generally been abandoned in recent scholarship.

*Tradition criticism* is a step that can exist alongside of or next to such steps as composition or form criticism. In this methodological step, individual topics, ideas and motifs[16] that are contained in a biblical text but show evidence of

14. C. Hardmeier, *Texttheorie und Biblische Exegese: Zur rhetorischen Funktion der Trauermetaphorik in der Prophetie* (BEvT 79; München: Kaiser, 1978); idem, *Textwelten der Bibel entdecken: Grundlagen und Verfahren einer textpragmatischen Literaturwissenschaft der Bibel* (Textpragmatische Studien zur Literatur- und Kulturgeschichte der Hebräischen Bibel 1/1; Gütersloh: Gütersloher Verlagshaus 2003).

15. See footnote 13.

16. Motifs are the smallest dependent thematic building blocks in texts (e.g. 'wilted flower' as coined

independent transmission either in other biblical texts or the broader ancient Near Eastern context are isolated and investigated, e.g. through semantic field analysis[17] or comparison with extra-biblical texts and iconography. In semantic field analysis, one asks where a particular word came from, what development it underwent, under what conditions this development occurred, and with what aims it was used in the biblical text. Tradition criticism also studies inter-textual connections, like allusions or inner-biblical interpretations, in order to shed further light on the processes of biblical transmission and the transmitting agents, including their socio-cultural environment.

The various methodological steps or approaches within historical-critical analysis concerned with the linguistic gestalt and the diachronic connections related to content, composition and setting (*Sitz im Leben*) make differentiated exegesis possible for the biblical books in their received forms. Such an exegesis, gathering together the results of these various steps, can take the form either of a commentary, interpreting the text line-by-line or passage-by-passage, or of a monographic treatise in which the principal and secondary topics, the various concerns, and the intentions of the text are systematically presented and enlarged upon with hermeneutical reflections. Such comprehensive presentations normally also reflect the application of the synchronic methods, which will be described in the next section.

## 2.1.2 Synchronic Methods: Canonical Approach, Structural Analysis, Rhetorical Criticism, 'New Literary Criticism'.

Bibliography 3.1.2 Synchronic Methods.

One reaction to the failure of increasingly differentiated historical exegesis to produce consensus, i.e. in matters like the Pentateuchal debate (→ *Pentateuch*) or the hypothetical (re-)construction of text strata, has been the call in recent decades for a stronger and more 'objective' basis for exegesis. The name of

image for transient). Its investigation can be done within tradition history and is then sometimes called *motif criticism* or *history* (*Motivkritik* or *Motivgeschichte*).

17. One can search for relevant terms in the theological dictionaries to get a first overview of the tradition and its development. See *Theological Lexicon of the Old Testament* (ed. E. Jenni and C. Westermann); *Theological Dictionary of the Old Testament* (ed. G. J. Botterweck and H. Ringgren).

Brevard S. Childs[18] is synonymous with a form of exegesis in the context of the → *canon*, which deals with the interpretation of individual books and texts in their present 'canonical' form. This form is taken to be the definitive version, it is argued, because the decisions made by those shaping the individual biblical books and the canon as a whole should be taken seriously. This is known as the 'canonical approach'. It does not dismiss out of hand the diachronic questions, especially those of tradition and redaction history, since Childs insists that the final version is a reflection of the former tradition processes; but the canonical version (= final version) is decisive, because, in his view, the more recent interpretation given in the receiving community shows greater richness and variety than its earlier forms taken for themselves. In practice, this (problematical) assumption has led to growing disinterest in the historical dimensions of the text and to a tendency merely to re-phrase the existing text, reducing its multilayered historical meaning to a single mono-dimensional interpretation that takes into account only the narrow perspective and background of the current reader.

Much more developed synchronic exegetical approaches have emerged from linguistic structural analysis, e.g. by W. Richter, and narrative analysis, e.g. by Meir Sternberg.[19] In the structuralist approach, the given text is taken first as a formal linguistic phenomenon (formal aspect). Only after describing its formal characteristics does one attend to the internal contours of its meaning and then to interpreting its meaning as a whole (content aspect). In practice, it is difficult if not impossible to separate form and content in this way, especially treating the content aspects only after the formal aspects have been fully discussed. Moreover, this separation claims a high degree of objectivity in regard to the description of the formal aspects, although aesthetic criteria are operative; such claims are at best highly problematical.[20]

Narrative analysis is closely related to 'new literary criticism' and to narratology, a special discipline of the literary study of narrative structures. Narrative analysis is a collective term which includes a variety of synchronic,

18. B. S. Childs, *Introduction*; more recently idem, 'Critique of Recent Intertextual Canonical Interpretation', *ZAW* 115 (2003): 173–84; R. Rendtorff, G. T. Sheppard and D. Trobisch, *Canonical Criticism* (Biblical Interpretation Series 24; Leiden: Brill, 1997).

19. M. Sternberg, *Poetics*.

20. On the relationship of form and content, see the discussion in K. Berger, *Formgeschichte*, 72–84 (above, n. 13).

usually ahistorical approaches to the Bible.[21] It deals with the text in its current final form and seeks to plunge into the world of the text as it stands in order to follow the signals given by the text for constructing meaning. It analyses the text in terms of its linguistic form and its rhetorical formulation of sentences, episodes and scenes. This approach studies the intrinsic connection between form, content and intention, insisting that these cannot be isolated from one another. It asks about the overall conception of the text, the successive arrangement of its parts and the stages of the plot, as well as about the different points of view, e.g. those of the narrator or of the actors, that have found their way into the narrative. In addition, questions of biblical rhetoric (rhetorical criticism[22]), the reading process, and application in current contexts (see Ch. 2.1.3) can play a role.

Within a differentiated structural and narrative analysis, important observations can be made on the texts and the biblical books as a whole. This analysis can direct the exegete's attention to the text's structural signals, its overall coherence, and the literary devices it uses for linguistic expression. The problem with synchronically oriented exegesis is that it gives the impression that the final (or canonical) version provides an adequate and reliable basis for the understanding of the biblical text and that this basis stands above any and all hypothetical constructions. As noted above, a variety of textual traditions often existed side by side over longer periods of time, e.g. the different versions of the book of Jeremiah or Samuel. Moreover, the Hebrew texts were handed down in an unvocalized form for a long period of time. This phenomenon opens up the possibility not only of a variety of readings, which in some cases may even have been intended, but also of very different interpretations. This means that hypothetical conjectures are unavoidable and that decisions must be made about what is probable and what is improbable on the basis of solid arguments taking account of the history of the text. Consequently, diverse possibilities of interpretation exist. Based on responsible consideration and argumentation, even the ancient copyists and translators, e.g. those of the LXX and → *Vulgate*, were forced to discriminate between interpretations that are possible and those that are impossible. Today, we face the same challenge, and these decisions cannot be made without reference to the history of the text.[23]

21. See the research report by J. Vette, 'Narrative Poetics'.

22. See the outline of the method in D. F. Watson and A. J. Hauser, *Rhetorical Criticism of the Bible: A Comprehensive Bibliography with Notes on History & Method* (Leiden: Brill, 1994), 3–14.

23. On the synchronic and diachronic question, see D. Clines, 'Beyond Synchronic/Diachronic'.

## 2.1.3 Application-Oriented Methods: Feminism, Social History and Liberation Theology

Bibliography 3.1.3 Application-Oriented Methods

There are several new approaches to Old Testament texts that have gained increasing interest in the past few decades. They focus on the actualization and application of the biblical text and, therefore, are especially concerned with matters of content. In principle, these methods should not be seen as competitors or as alternatives to the historical-critical or to the synchronic methods described above. The points of view, for example, of feminist exegesis, e.g. by Athalya Brenner, Marie-Theres Wacker, Silvia Schroer,[24] of socio-historical exegesis, e.g. by Willy Schottroff,[25] of liberation-theological exegesis, e.g. by Milton Schwantes, J. Severino Croatto,[26] or of cultural anthropological exegesis, e.g. by B. Bernhard Lang[27], can easily exist within the framework of the methodological approaches of diachronic and synchronic exegesis. They can also be inserted as separate steps before or after historical-critical or synchronic text analysis. Thus it is neither necessary nor wise to create oppositions between these application-oriented approaches to the biblical text and those of the older, established historical or the more recent synchronic exegetical methods. Instead it is better to juxtapose them critically and creatively with one another and let them mutually enrich each other by disclosing further dimensions of meaning. As with any other method, interpreting the biblical text from the

24. L. Schottroff, S. Schroer and M.-T. Wacker, *Feminist Interpretation*; S. Schroer and S. Bietenhard, eds, *Feminist Interpretation of the Bible and the Hermeneutics of Liberation*, (Sheffield: Sheffield Academic Press, 2003).

25. W. Schottroff, *Gerechtigkeit lernen: Beiträge zur biblischen Sozialgeschichte* (TB 94; Gütersloh: Kaiser, 1999); see the articles collected in M. D. Carroll R., ed., *Rethinking Context, Rereading Texts: Contributions from the Social Sciences to Biblical Interpretation* (JSOTSup 299; Sheffield: Sheffield Academic Press, 2000).

26. M. Schwantes, 'Wege der biblischen Theologie in Latein Amerika', *EvT* 51 (1991): 8–19; see the articles collected in: L. E. Vaage, ed., *Subversive Scriptures: Revolutionary Christian Readings of the Bible in Latin America* (Valley Forge, Pa.: Trinity Press International, 1997); J. S. Croatto, *Exodus: A Hermeneutics of Freedom* (transl. S. Attanasio; Maryknoll, N.Y.: Orbis, 1981). Compare W. Kim, 'Liberation Theology and the Bible: A Methodological Consideration (A Response to J. Severino Croatto)', in *Reading the Hebrew Bible for a New Millennium: Form, Concept, and Theological Perspective* (ed. by idem *et al.*; Harrisburg, Pa.: Trinity Press International, 2000), 292–320.

27. B. Lang, 'Introduction: Anthropology as a New Model for Biblical Studies', in *Anthropological Approaches to the Old Testament* (IRT 8; Philadelphia: Fortress, 1985), 1–20.

viewpoints of feminism, social history, liberation theology, or cultural anthropology requires asking whether or not the results are inter-subjectively verifiable and supra-individually plausible. In the interpretation of each individual text, one must consider what presuppositions, premises, and models are involved, to what extent these have been reflected upon and openly acknowledged, and whether they in fact fit both the text and the topic at hand. On the level of argumentation, naturally, the aims and intentions of the exegete play a significant role in determining whether the appropriate methodology has been used, and, above all, how the available sources have been incorporated, analysed, and categorized. Thus, provided that the approaches have been carefully chosen and applied, application-oriented methods do not automatically imply a higher danger of selectivity and subjectivity in dealing with the texts than historical-critical methods: exegetic work is always(!) influenced by the presuppositions of the individual exegete.[28] For this reason, no exegete is ever free from the task of bringing to light personal presuppositions and submitting the results of one's exegetical work to the critical review of one's peers.

## 2.2 Methods of Biblical Archaeology/ Archaeology of Palestine

Bibliography 6.3 Archaeology and Iconography (C. Renfrew and P. Bahn, *Archaeology*). Further: J. Murphy-O'Connor, *The Holy Land: An Oxford Archaeological Guide from Earliest Times to 1700*. 5th rev. ed. Oxford: Oxford University Press, 2008; J. C. H. Laughlin, *Archaeology and the Bible*. London: Routledge, 2000, 17–32; I. Finkelstein and N. A. Silberman, *The Bible Unearthed: Archaeology's New Vision of Ancient Israel and the Origin of its Sacred Texts*. New York: Free Press, 2002.

Biblical archaeology, or the archaeology of Palestine,[29] is concerned with the material remains of Palestine as the principal evaluatable sources for all periods for which they are available. As in archaeology in general, the following methods

28. See already R. Bultmann, 'Ist voraussetzungslose Exegese möglich?', in *Rudolf Bultmann: Neues Testament und christliche Existenz: Theologische Aufsätze* (ed. A. Lindemann; Stuttgart: UTB, 2002), 258–66; D. J. A. Clines, *Interested Parties: The Ideology of Writers and Readers of the Hebrew Bible* (JSOTSup 205: Sheffield: Sheffield Academic Press, 1995), 24–5.
29. See the summary of this discussion in W. G. Dever, *What Did the Biblical Writers Know and When Did They Know It? What Archeology Can Tell Us About the Reality of Ancient Israel* (Grand Rapids, Mich.: Eerdmans, 2002), 60–2.

and techniques play a major role: aerial and satellite image analysis, cartographic ('Palestine Grid') and land surveying techniques, surface surveys and analysis, vertical stratigraphic excavations (with profile cuts), horizontal area and layer excavations to unveil building and settlement structures (settlement archaeology) and to unearth relicts of everyday objects, pottery, organic residues, architecture, tombs and tomb artifacts. Equally important are the examination of settlement patterns, including demographic examinations, of installations in and around the settlements, and the discoveries of landscape archaeology. The discoveries are collected, sorted, dated, documented, systemized and interpreted to answer historical questions of long, middle, or short term (Ch. 3.3.2). The interpretations of the finds and the results follow the methods and theoretical foundations of archaeology as a science of history and culture. Cooperation with other cultural disciplines like → *anthropology*, sociology, and ethnology, as well as with the natural sciences, e.g. botany, biology, climatology, geology, chemistry, physics, etc. also have their place, as do the dialogues with disciplines like Egyptology, Assyriology, Ancient Near Eastern Studies and Classical Archaeology (for their relationship to exegesis, see above Ch. 1.2). Most recently, the need to take account of Gender Studies has come to be recognized.

During the *surface analysis* in the course of an archaeological *survey* of a given area, all of the immediately visible remains of settlement and any still-existing monuments are systematically recorded. The potsherds that are found in the course of systematically walking over the surface of the area are collected, typologically sorted, documented and dated. These potsherds usually give an initial impression of what historical strata can be found under the surface. When this kind of examination encompasses a whole region and does not restrict itself to only one single location, it can yield an impression of how the investigated area developed in terms of settlement history, settlement pattern, settlement hierarchy and settlement density. Surveys can prepare the way for detailed excavations and can provide answers to questions regarding the surroundings of the excavation site such as the water supply system, the commercial routes, or the land use.[30] By contrast to the surface analysis, an *excavation* can only be made at *one* specific location with the aim of (re-)constructing the history of settlement or the buildings found at that site. Because in Palestine as elsewhere in the Near East people tended to settle at the same location over hundreds and thousands of years, erecting new buildings over the ruins of former mud brick constructions, in the course of time, settlement hills (Arabic *Tell*; plural *Tulul*) gradually were built up, typically taking the form of a low truncated cone with a flat top and sloping sides and

30. On natural science methods in archaeological field research (e.g. geophysical or chemical prospecting) and on the application of geographic information systems, see Ch. 2.2 Excursus.

standing out against their surroundings. Tells consist of overlaying horizontal beds (*strata*) containing the debris of earlier settlements, so that each individual overlying layer is younger than the underlying layers (**fig. 1**). During the excavation a relative chronology results from the examination of the layers of the strata (vertical trenching). Sites with only one or a few settlement layers are called by the Arabs 'Ḫirbe'. As they do not show a complex settlement diachrony, the excavation area in this case can often be larger. The expression 'Ḫirbe' can, however, also refer to the widely scattered stone remnants of former cities which especially in flat areas had been built during the periods of Hellenistic, Roman, or Byzantine culture and which follow their own patterns of construction.

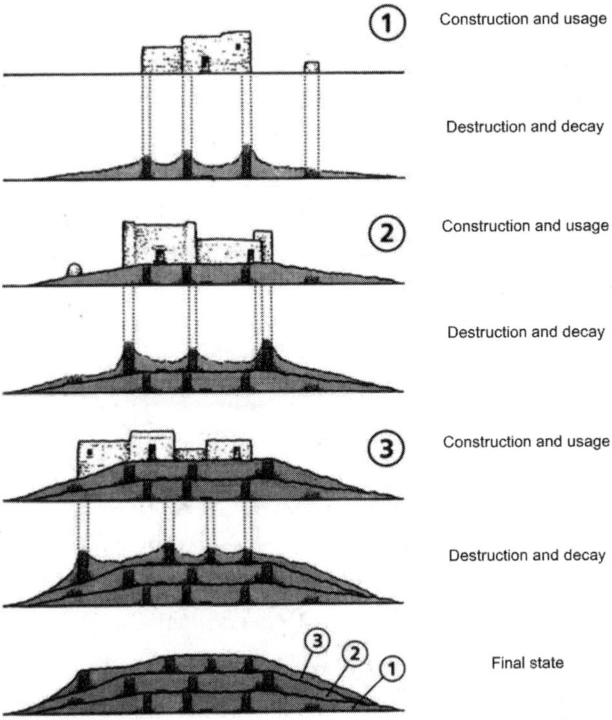


**Fig. 1:** Development of a Tell.

Modern archaeology does not aim at completely excavating a Tell or Ḫirbe, but only to collect enough significant material to give a plausible answer to basic archaeological, historical, or anthropological questions, for example determining the diachronic settlement history of the site on the basis of its stratigraphic levels, and to make it possible to check inter-subjectively any attempted (re)construction of the site's past by providing useful documentation of the material remains. Moreover, during the last decades investigation has shifted from concentrating on single settlements in isolation to studying as well the relationship of settlements to one another, analysing also their relationships to topographical features, and tracing human transformations of the natural landscape, e.g. the construction of terraces.

Back to the archaeological fieldwork and its documentation: For the examination of archaeological layers, the site under study is first measured and a plan is drawn up. The site is then divided into excavation areas; within these areas, individual excavation squares are laid out and plotted on the overall plan. Only then are the dig areas marked out on the site itself. In between the excavation squares (usually of 5 × 5 metres), gangways of about 1m in width are left standing. As the excavation progresses, the individual settlement layers (strata) become visible on the profiles showing on the vertical sides of these gangways, thus allowing each layer to be related to the corresponding layers of the rest of the site, in order to verify the stratigraphic sequence. Within each excavation square, layers are removed one by one. Floor levels are of special significance, since everything found above them necessarily dates to the time after their construction and thus allows a relative chronological dating of the material resting on them. All enclosed units (findings, *loci*) within a single layer, e.g. installations, walls, or rooms between walls, are assigned their own locus numbers, and all of the finds within the same locus are recorded as belonging together. Special small finds are photographed in their original setting, measured in three dimensions, and assigned a locus number. Specific observations, the progressive stages, and the results of the excavation must be documented continuously. Each horizontal level of the individual excavation squares (*plana*) should be mapped on as large a scale as possible, and the corresponding profiles, i.e. the vertical walls of the gangways, should be drawn on the same scale, since these drawings make it possible to re-examine the results of the excavation at a later date. Afterwards, one should also photograph both the *plana* and the profiles and describe them verbally as meticulously as possible. Small finds and pottery should be noted in the documentation with their locus numbers to assign them to their correct layers. In the post-excavation work, each stratum with its loci will be studied and correlated with those of other areas, so that gradually a comprehensive and coherent picture emerges for all the layers of the settlement. All layers need to be dated: for this purpose in pre-Persian times mostly pottery finds are used, concerning later times coins also are of help.[31]

31. For the identification of coins and the conversion of their dates see Y. Meshorer, *Samarian Coinage*

## Chronology and Dating

Because pottery forms, styles, and patterns have changed over the course of time, one can arrange the different layers excavated in a settlement by comparing their ceramics and arranging them according to a local chronology. Within the framework of a comparative stratigraphy, one can compare the single layer sequences of a settlement with those of other settlements and correlate them chronologically. Especially on the basis of pottery typology, one can compare the single layers of different settlements with relative exactness, thus constructing a regional, super-regional or countrywide *relative* chronology. Also other small finds can be classified using typological parallels and assigned to a chronology. Absolute chronology, however, remains a problem not only concerning dating based on pottery styles, but also by the use of dendrochronological analysis (determining the age of wood on the basis of its yearly growth rings), the thermoluminiscence method (determining the age of ceramics by testing for their energetic emissions), and the C-14 method (determining the age of substances containing carbon by measuring radioactive decay, according to the half-life of the radioactive carbon C-14-isotop). For the pre-Hellenistic periods, there are only a limited number of dates available that make it possible to link relative chronologies with specific events in an absolute chronology. Assyrian, Babylonian, or Egyptian campaign reports can be consulted, or events like the earthquake mentioned in Amos 1.1, that took place around 760 BCE, can be traced in some places by archaeological evidence. In each single case, however, the researcher must check whether the archaeologically visible destruction level can really be linked with the historical events known from textual sources. Absolute dates for Palestine can result from the collection and combination of different sources and methods, such as the already mentioned pottery dating, stratigraphy, dating by coins (only for the later levels), dating methods from natural sciences, datable or dated written sources from Palestine itself and from its neighbouring regions, and (for the earlier periods often decisive) the synchronisms between Palestine, Egypt and Mesopotamia. Dating of the last type depends, of course, on the Mesopotamian or Egyptian chronologies, which themselves have been the subject of discussion and modifications in recent decades.[32] A secure absolute chronology of Palestine covering Iron Age I or II is thus still lacking. Recently, there has been fierce debate between Israel Finkelstein and Amihai Mazar on this topic. Because Finkelstein has proposed to date the early Iron Age levels about 100 years later than previously assumed, his proposal is usually discussed

⇨

(Numismatic Studies and Researches 9; Jerusalem: The Israel Numismatic Society, 1999); idem, *A Treasury of Jewish Coins: From the Persian Period to Bar Kokhba* (Jerusalem: Yad Ben Zvi, 2001).

32. For a discussion about the high, middle and low chronologies in Egypt and Mesopotamia, see P. Åström, ed., *High, Middle or Low? Acts of an International Colloquium on Absolute Chronology Held at the University of Gothenburg, 20th-22nd August 1987* (3 vols; Göteborg: Åström, 1987/1989).

under the term 'low chronology.'[33] Finkelstein's proposal shakes the chronological foundations of the traditional 'history of Israel', and therefore polarizes both archaeologists and historians.

Meanwhile, additional chronologies have been proposed alongside these classical 'high' and 'low' chronologies. Deserving of special mention are the 'ultra-low chronology' of A. Gilboa and I. Sharon,[34] the modified 'high chronology' of Amihai Mazar[35] (Iron Age IIA from 1000/980 to 840/830 BCE), and the suggested compromise of Ze'ev Herzog and Lily Singer-Avitz[36] to separate within Iron Age IIA the chronology of the North from that of the South and to let this period comprise both the 10th century (= 'high chronology') and the 9th century (= 'low chronology'), and perhaps even the early 8th century as well. For the North, they distinguish three phases of Iron Age IIA: early Iron Age IIA (2nd half of 10th century), late Iron Age IIA in its main phase (early and mid-9th century), and final phase (last third of 9th century). In the South, by contrast, they see only two phases: the early Iron Age IIA (2nd half of 10th century) and the late Iron Age IIA (9th and perhaps early 8th century).

In any case, a consensus seems to be emerging that the campaign of Pharaoh Shishak I (926/920/917 BCE) did not mark the end of Iron Age IIA and that this period probably only ended with the campaign of Hazael (840/830/825) or even later, around 800 BCE. Because of the enlargement of Iron Age IIA, Iron Age IIB is reduced accordingly, so that it may have lasted only a few decades. These different chronological assignations can be illustrated by the example of Lachish.

Another question is the identification of an excavated settlement with a place whose name is known from biblical or extra-biblical ancient texts; this is one of the tasks of *historical topography*. To decide whether a particular location can be identified with an ancient place name, various types of evidence need to be taken into consideration. Modern Arabic place names may or may not reflect

33. I. Finkelstein, 'Bible Archaeology or the Archaeology of Palestine in the Iron Age', Levant 30 (1998): 167–74. For the state of the discussion see R. Kletter, 'Chronology and United Monarchy: A Methodological Review', *ZDPV* 120 (2004): 13–54.

34. A. Gilboa and I. Sharon, 'Early Iron Age Radiometric Dates from Tel Dor: Preliminary Implications for Phoenicia and Beyond', *Radiocarbon* 43 (2001): 1343–51.

35. A. Mazar, 'The Debate over the Chronology of the Iron Age in the Southern Levant: Its History, the Current Situation, and a Suggested Resolution', in *The Bible and Radiocarbon Dating: Archaeology, Text and Science* (ed. T. E. Levy and T. Higham; London: Equinox, 2005), 15–30.

36. Z. Herzog and L. Singer-Avitz, 'Sub-Dividing the Iron Age IIA in Northern Israel: A Suggested Solution to the Chronological Debate', *TA* 33 (2006): 163–95.

| | | Suggested Dating | | | | |
|---|---|---|---|---|---|---|
| **Strata** | **Character of Settlement** | **Mazar** | **Zimhoni** | **Finkelstein (1996)** | **NEAEHL** | **Herzog/Singer-Avitz (2006)** |
| I | large, fortified town, palace, 'solar shrine' | none | none | none | Babylonian/ Persian/ Hellenistic | None |
| II | small, fortified settlement, Lachish letters | Iron Age IIC | none | none | 701 to 587/6 | none |
| III | larger, fortified regional centre (destroyed by Sennacherib) | Iron Age IIB (840/30 to 732/701) | 785/748 to 701 | 785/748 to 701 | until 701 | 8th cent. |
| IV | fortified regional centre, palace A, 'cult chamber', solid wall, glacis, six-chamber gate, water installations and administrative building | Iron Age II A until 840/30 | until 785/748 | 825 to 785/748 | from 925 onwards | late Iron Age IIA, 9th cent. until possibly early 8th cent. |
| V | non-fortified settlement | Iron Age IIA from 1000/980 onwards | None | Iron Age IIA from 9th cent. on 'low chronology' | Iron Age IIA from 1000/925 'high chronology' | early Iron Age IIA from the mid of the 10th cent. |
| | | | **Settlement Gap** | | | |
| VI | non-fortified settlement, acropolis temple, administrative building | Iron Age IA 1200 to1140/30 | None | 1200 to 1150/30 | 1200 to 1150/30 | none |

the ancient name; obviously, all available literary (extra-biblical and biblical) as well as archaeological sources must be considered. Frequently, the results of such investigations are summarized in the production of a Bible atlas.[37] Such atlases, however, need to be revised and updated regularly according to the

37. See e.g. A. F. Rainey and R. S. Notley, eds, *Sacred Bridge*.

latest excavations and research results. Here, biblical archaeology can provide important background information for understanding those biblical texts, which require knowledge of the topographic features of Palestine.

In the end, we need to be reminded once more that the aim of biblical archaeology is to investigate the history of settlements and cultures, i.e. the history of long, medium and short duration, in Palestine (Ch. 3.2.2). Its task is not to verify or to refute the historicity of biblical texts, to confirm archaeological findings with the help of the Bible, or to harmonize archaeological data with the Bible. Obviously, however, when it comes to answering specific historical questions, all available sources, including the biblical texts (though not as primary sources for historical questions), need to be correlated, compared and critically examined in the course of historical (re-)construction.

## 2.3 Methods of Hebrew Epigraphy

Bibliography 6.1 General and Methods; 6.2 Sources in Writing. Further: W. M. Schniedewind, 'Problems in the Paleographic Dating of Inscriptions'. Pages 405–12 in *The Bible and Radiocarbon Dating: Archaeology, Text and Science*. Edited by T. E. Levy and T. Higham. London: Equinox, 2005.

*Hebrew epigraphy* deals with extra-biblical texts written in Hebrew, which for the most part have survived as inscriptions or tracings in stone, metal, ceramic, or other hard materials. Its first task is to clarify which texts are in Hebrew and which belong to some other language. The (Old) Hebrew writing tradition, as such, only developed during the 10th and 9th centuries BCE, thus, Hebrew epigraphy's object of investigation can only be found from this period on. A special problem is posed by the dating of texts that themselves bear no date. If they come from well-documented (and published!) excavations, one can usually date them with the aid of their archaeological context (stratigraphy and pottery dating). If this is not the case or if one needs to check the archaeological arguments against each other to support or correct the proposed dating, palaeographic analysis becomes important. Palaeography, therefore, is an integral part of the work with extra-biblical Hebrew texts (as it is for other languages as well). It focuses on the development of script(s), i.e. the sets of characters used for writing. It correlates letters of similar shape and meaning with considerations of the writing materials used and tries to establish a relative chronology for the development of the script. In a next step, for instance by comparison with datable sources, such as coins or dated inscriptions, typical shapes of individual letters can often be dated absolutely, which helps, in turn, to date undated texts having no documented archaeological context.

The earliest form of written Hebrew is the so-called Old Hebrew script that derives from the old Canaanite script (Ch. 1.2.3). Many biblical texts were also originally written in this consonant script. Only during the Second Temple Period was it replaced by the square script that derives from the Aramaic script, but even after the square script made its appearance (according to Talmudic Tradition [→ *Talmud*] introduced by Ezra), Old Hebrew script did not entirely fall out of use (see e.g. → *Qumran*). From this it follows that texts that are written in square script necessarily can only date to a relatively late stage, but the mere use of the Old Hebrew script does not necessarily guarantee an older date of the text. Orthography can also be of use for assigning a text to a certain period or region. This is because, in one and the same language, many words can be written in different ways without any difference in meaning, and such differences can be typical of a specific period or dialect. As with other languages, Hebrew orthography passed through several phases; a particularly important indicator is the increasing usage of consonantal letters as vowel-signs, so called *matres lectionis*.

Another important aspect of epigraphy can be the study of the attested textual → *genres*. Because texts do not exist independently of their writing materials, information about them can be gained from the objects on which and the instruments with which they were written. This information can provide external clues to the function and the *Sitz im Leben* of the text, e.g. inscriptions on cultic implements. In this way, it is possible to connect particular genres and formulae known from Old Hebrew inscriptions with a specific *Sitz im Leben*, to compare and to group them with their closer (North West Semitic) or their more remote (East/South Semitic) parallels, and often to identify local peculiarities or diachronic developments. Like all interpretations, such interpretations depend upon the interpreter, and they need to address the problem, that the original communication situation of a particular text, for instance the message that a letter was meant to answer, has generally been irretrievably lost.

It is important to date a text as precisely as possible: only then can one correlate its language, form, and contents with contemporary socio-political, economic, historical, or religious-historical developments. In the study of extra-biblical texts, beyond the philological study of the writing style, the orthography, the linguistics, the morphology, the semantics and the syntax of the text itself, it is important for both biblical scholars and biblical archaeologists to correlate the text with biblical, archaeological and → *iconographic* sources, to the extent that these are available. Because Hebrew epigraphy deals with extra-biblical Hebrew texts which are part of the world of the Old and New Testaments, it enters into a constructive dialogue with both biblical exegesis and biblical archaeology and iconography. The texts it studies can thus be used to (re)construct the cultural, religious, and historical background of the Old Testament world. Therefore Hebrew epigraphy makes an important contribution to the understanding of biblical texts and needs to be viewed as an additional and corrective tool both for biblical studies as such and for biblical archaeology and iconography.

## 2.4 Methods of Biblical Iconography/ Iconography of Palestine

Bibliography 6.1 General and Methods; 6.3 Archaeology and Iconography; 9 History of Religion of Ancient Israel. Further: A. Weissenrieder and F. Wendt, 'Images'.

Biblical *iconography* deals with Palestinian iconographic material from all relevant periods. Apart from archaeological methods for dating, it also uses, among others, the methods of art history, image semiotics,[38] and constructivist approaches. Images are 'artifacts, which were produced on specific objects, with specific instruments, according to specific technologies. They follow a system of conventions and rules that can be (re)-constructed empirically on the basis of surviving pictorial documents.'[39] They require interpretation, taking account of image semantics, image style, image function, and image pragmatics. As with the interpretation of texts and archaeological finds, it is the interpreter who makes the material speak. Image-bearing objects, techniques, choices of material, peculiarities in style, and motifs can all be arranged into meaningful groups, and their variations and innovations can be

38. T. Hölscher, 'Bilderwelt, Formensystem, Lebenskultur', *Studi italiani di filologia classica* 10 (1992): 460–83; A. Schelske, *Die kulturelle Bedeutung von Bildern: Soziologische und semiotische Überlegungen zur visuellen Kommunikation* (Wiesbaden: DUV, 1997); T. Hölscher, *The Language of Images in Roman Art* (Cambridge: Cambridge University Press, 2004).

39. C. Uehlinger, 'Bildquellen', 39 (above, Ch. 1 n. 2).

sorted either synchronically to trace regional developments or diachronically to show chronological developments.

As an independent field of research with its own methodology, biblical iconography involves cooperation with biblical archaeology and biblical exegesis, because these neighbouring areas all deal with one and the same general object, i.e. Palestine. As a scientific study of Palestine, biblical iconography, like biblical archaeology, is not limited to the short 'biblically determined' period from the second half of the second millennium until Roman times, but it also extends to periods beyond these limits in order to follow structures of *longue durée* (Ch. 3.2.2). No longer do scholars understand its task as merely verifying or illustrating Old or New Testament texts with iconographic material; it is now a discipline that stands on its own.

Biblical iconography, respectively the iconography of Palestine, collects and documents pictorial materials either found in or otherwise related to the region, to the extent that they can be dated on the basis of archaeological context and captions or on the basis of datable comparable objects (less often on the basis of the C14 method). It describes them in terms of their image-bearing objects, pictorial themes, pictorial organization, individual motifs etc., and analyses them in terms of picture composition, themes and decorations. It seeks to contextualize them, for example by grouping motifs into a typology, and by studying them in terms of the history of styles and motifs as well as in terms of general cultural and religious history.[40]

By considering the respective genres of the image-bearing objects (see below), one can investigate the iconographic evidence, the motifs, the underlying 'constellations' (complexes of ideas[41]), and their diachronic development in connection

40. For an initial survey of the material, ANEP is still to be recommended. See also O. Keel, *The Symbolism of the Biblical World: Ancient Near Eastern Iconography and the Book of Psalms* (transl. T. J. Hallet; Winona Lake, Ind.: Eisenbrauns, 1997).

41. For the term 'constellation' as used here, see O. Keel and C. Uehlinger, GGG, 6, pp. 13–14. The term was originally suggested by J. Assmann ('Die Zeugung des Sohnes: Bild, Spiel, Erzählung und das Problem des ägyptischen Mythos', in *Funktionen und Leistungen des Mythos: Drei altorientalische Beispiele* [OBO 48; ed. idem, W. Burkert and F. Stolz; Fribourg: Academic Press/ Göttingen: Vandenhoeck & Ruprecht, 1982], 13–61) to describe pre-mythological complexes of ideas or motifs – he uses the term 'Sinnkomplexe' – which only later were elaborated into full-blown mythical narratives. As examples Assmann cited the copulation of man and woman

and correlation with processes of society and history. In this connection, the scientific literature often speaks of iconology, a term which was coined and introduced by the art historian Erwin Panofsky[42] and accepted and used by Othmar Keel.[43] This gives rise to a three-step method, beginning with phenomenological description, followed by iconographic analysis, and ending in iconological interpretation. The latter interprets the picture as an indicator of its period, culture and society and presupposes a high degree of system conformity of the artifacts. Christoph Uehlinger[44] has in addition pointed out that aspects of 'conscious communication pragmatics' also play an important role with many artifacts. For this reason, the pragmatic context of the images, i.e. the living situation in which they appear and are used, needs to be considered for their interpretation. Apart from dealing with pictures and pictorial programmes in themselves,[45] biblical

as a sign of the fertilization of the earth or the struggle of a hero with a dragon as a symbol of a political or military struggle with an enemy. Such 'constellations of meaning' can serve as 'crystallization points' for a variety of mythical narratives in which they are subsequently elaborated. For the most part, they take the form of visual ideas – for this reason Assmann calls them 'icons' and 'referential images' – which can be isolated from the plot of the myths. Furthermore, he asserts that by comparison to the immense number of myths which make use of them, they are relatively few in number, since they rest on fundamental situations and relationships of human existence. The names of the protagonists and the details of the stories are secondary; what has priority and what remains constant is what Assmann calls the 'iconicity of the underlying constellation'. From this perspective, myths are nothing more than 'icons'/'constellations' elaborated into a story, and they can be reduced again, without losing their identity, to pure iconicity. This, in effect, is what happens in an iconographic image like a statue or a picture: the story is reduced again to the icon. Thus, according to Keel and Uehlinger one of the tasks of iconographic studies is to identify such underlying constellations within the pictorial images it studies, distinguishing what is primary and constant from secondary details that vary from piece to piece and can evolve diachronically and synchronically.

42. E. Panofsky, *Studies in Iconology: Humanistic Themes in the Art of the Renaissance* (Oxford: Oxford University Press, 1939; idem, 'Zum Problem der Beschreibung und Inhaltsdeutung von Werken der bildenden Kunst', in *Ikonographie und Ikonologie: Theorien – Entwicklung – Probleme: Bildende Kunst als Zeichensystem* 1 (ed. E. Kaemmerling; Köln: DuMont, $^{6}$1994), 185–206; idem, 'Ikonographie und Ikonologie', ibid., 207–25.

43. O. Keel, *Das Recht der Bilder, gesehen zu werden: Drei Fallstudien zur Methode der Interpretation altorientalischer Bilder* (OBO 122; Fribourg: Academic Press/Göttingen: Vandenhoeck & Ruprecht, 1992).

44. C. Uehlinger, 'Bildquellen' (above, Ch. 1 n. 2)

45. Image programmes can range over an enormous spectrum, from a simple symbol, like a star against a neutral ground, to highly complex scenes, in which diverse iconic elements (→

iconography is concerned with the correlation of images with the literary (→ *epigraphic*, as well as biblical) and other archaeological sources, to the extent that these are available. To the same degree that biblical iconography deals with images as part of the world of the Old and New Testament, it also enters into a constructive dialogue with text-oriented biblical studies. Images can be used in such a context to (re)construct the cultural and religious-historical background of the world of the Old Testament. In this way, biblical iconography can contribute substantially to the understanding of biblical texts and needs to be viewed as an additional and corrective tool to traditional text-oriented historical-critical biblical studies.

> In each individual case, the relationship between biblical and extra-biblical texts and images from Palestine or the Ancient Near East needs to be explained in a differentiated and argumentatively responsible way. Too rash or too general linkages hamper rather than help understanding of both the pictures and the texts. For this reason, it is necessary to look first at each medium in and of itself and only afterwards to correlate them in a subsequent synthetic step. This holds true especially for the cooperation of biblical iconography with biblical exegesis: only after the basic iconographical and exegetical work has been accomplished, the exploration of the relationship between the two should follow as a third step. If it emerges that Old Testament texts in fact have used motifs of contemporary iconography, it is often possible for biblical iconography to correlate the religious ideas expressed in the Old Testament with motifs of contemporary Ancient Near Eastern art, to compare them, and to interrogate and illuminate the texts against this canvas.[46] Images and texts, however, can also take up and use the same themes independently of each other; or the depictions and the texts may not share the same themes at all, but rather represent quite a different repertoire. Sometimes, interesting insights can be gained by pursuing such differences, e.g. how a certain object is treated in the Old Testament, e.g. sun/moon/stars as creations of Yhwh, whereas in art it is depicted differently, e.g. sun/moon/stars as

*anthropomorphic*, → *theriomorphic*, or symbolic images) are combined with decorative and space-filling elements.

46. This was still the aim of O. Keel, *Jahwe-Visionen und Siegelkunst: Eine neue Deutung der Majestätsschilderungen in Jes 6, Ez 1 und 10 und Sach 4* (SBS 84/85; Stuttgart: Katholisches Bibelwerk, 1977), 11–13. In the meantime, the focus of studies, especially by C. Uehlinger, has shifted more to the (re)construction of historical and religious-historical connections, see C. Uehlinger, ed., *Images as Media – Sources for the Cultural History of the Ancient Near East and the Eastern Mediterranean (1st Millennium BCE): Proceedings of an International Symposium held in Fribourg on November 25–29, 1997* (OBO 175, Fribourg: Academic Press/Göttingen: Vandenhoeck & Ruprecht, 2000).

deities, or is not depicted at all. The same holds conversely for image themes that are well attested iconographically, e.g. various female deities in pre-exilic 'Israel', whereas they are not mentioned or are repudiated in the Old Testament texts.

Depictions and texts each have their own specific means of expression and style. An important advantage of pictures is that they can show the viewer complex topics simultaneously: the relationship of several single elements to each other and to the whole is fixed in the picture and recognizable at one glance. However, the pictures of the Ancient Near East (and, therefore, Palestine as well) have certain typical features that must be taken into account to avoid misunderstandings. In the first place, the pictures are not, in general, to be understood as verisimilar depictions or copies of a reality, but rather as its interpretation. This means that depictions of cities and landscapes are idealized/stylized (e.g. Lachish reliefs; see below Ch. 4.2.1.3 **fig. 12**) and do not correspond to the actual architectonic features. Actions and events that happened after each other are often displayed immediately beside each other. Especially, depictions that were made by order of the respective king or Pharaoh had to represent historical events, the royal ideology, and the political or theological programmes in a visual way and needed to be 'politically correct'. Representations of humans or deities were also stylized. They were not conceived as portraits; instead, persons are shown as representatives of a certain role or function. Little or no attention was paid to individual features, either of human beings or of deities: thus, for example, the Israelite king Jehu of Israel on the Black Obelisk of the Assyrian king Shalmaneser III (858–824 BCE) is depicted in the same manner and attitude of humility as the subdued king Sua of Gilzanu (an area in modern Azerbaijan) on the same side of the stele (**fig. 2**).

Despite all these reservations, depictions of typical groups of deities or of humans (as well as situations of their encounters and interactions) can sometimes contain useful information about realia, e.g. what an altar looks like, or specific activities, e.g. prayer gestures, and in any case they provide valuable information about the system of religious symbols, as well as about culturally embedded social and religious ideas, structures, connections and practices.

**Fig. 2:** Jehu before the Assyrian king Shalmaneser III on the Black Obelisk.

# Part II
## History and Religion of Ancient Israel

# 3

# History and Religion of 'Israel'[1]: Basic Information

(Angelika Berlejung – Translation by Thomas Riplinger)

## Chapter Outline

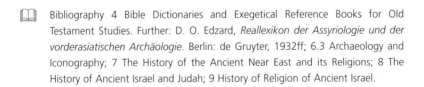

Bibliography 4 Bible Dictionaries and Exegetical Reference Books for Old Testament Studies. Further: D. O. Edzard, *Reallexikon der Assyriologie und der vorderasiatischen Archäologie*. Berlin: de Gruyter, 1932ff; 6.3 Archaeology and Iconography; 7 The History of the Ancient Near East and its Religions; 8 The History of Ancient Israel and Judah; 9 History of Religion of Ancient Israel.

1. The notion 'Israel' is used here only because it is already established and is commonly used in research and teaching. The history of the northern and southern kingdoms, and of the regions Samaria and Judah/Jehud/Judea, can only be treated adequately within the larger perspective of the history of Palestine and the southern Levant. From the eighth century BCE on, exilic and → *diaspora* groups were located in completely different geographical areas so that these must be treated in an even larger geographical perspective. Moreover, such regional and ethnic groups did not always understand themselves to be part of some collective entity called 'Israel', however this be understood.

# 3.1 The Premises: Israel versus Canaan, Yhwh versus Baal, and the Ancient Near East as the Background for Understanding the Biblical Scriptures

Bibliography 7 The History of the Ancient Near East and its Religions; Further: T. Staubli, *Das Image der Nomaden im Alten Israel und in der Ikonographie seiner sesshaften Nachbarn*. OBO 107. Fribourg: Academic Press/Göttingen: Vandenhoeck & Ruprecht, 1991.

Previously, it was assumed that Palestine was originally inhabited by an indigenous population and that, only later, new ethnic groups moved into the land and settled there, first the Canaanites, and then, from about 1200 BCE on, the Israelites; furthermore, it was assumed that these waves of immigration were responsible for decisive changes in Palestinian culture, history and religion. However, in the light of recent ethnological, archaeological and historical research, contemporary scholarship no longer starts from the premise that waves of immigrants from outside of Palestine either marked or caused significant breaks or major cultural changes in the land. In the new ethnological discussion,[2] the previously assumed sharp separation of ethnic groups ('peoples') has yielded to a much more complex understanding. Likewise, archaeological material, despite evident breaks and shifts in what has been handed down, shows numerous elements demonstrating overarching connection and constancy that point to continuity. Changes need not be caused by the arrival of new population groups; they can also be connected to internal shifts within the indigenous population structure and to other processes wholly within the society itself. Obviously, impulses from outside, be they trade contacts, foreign rule, or immigration, can also play a role, but that role needs to be assessed in each individual case.

While the Old Testament itself greatly emphasizes the fact that 'Israel' migrated into 'Canaan' and that the 'Israelites' and the 'Canaanites' were

2. See for example: S. Jones, *The Archaeology of Ethnicity: Constructing Identities in the Past and Present* (London: Routledge, 1997).

two distinct, mutually inimical and hostile people, today's scholars, when (re)constructing the history of Palestine, generally assume that it was not a large 'Israelite people' of Palestinian origin, who had resided in Egypt, but, at best, only a small group led by a man with the Egyptian name Moses, who (re?)migrated from Egypt to Palestine; and even this view is often challenged today. Moreover, scholars now generally believe that the most important social changes, which would eventually lead to the emergence of 'Israel', such as the transformation of indigenous[!] town inhabitants into village dwellers and even into nomads, were already in progress or had even already taken place before 'Israel' emerged. The thesis that pre-existing desert-dwelling Bedouin-like nomads forming the people of pre-state 'Israel' immigrated more or less as a compact group into the agrarian Canaanite territory with its largely urban structures can no longer be maintained. In the contemporary historical (re-)construction of society during this early period, that idea is increasingly yielding to a more supple notion of an essentially agrarian tribal society of village-dwelling farmers and sheep/goat breeders with notable regional diversity. The relationship between this rural population and the population of the cities, which also continued to exist in this period, was more a synthesis than an antithesis and the boundaries between the two were often fluid. The more recent theories about the → *conquest* interpret the development of 'Israel' as the result of a complex process involving the whole society within a multi-faceted cultural system located within the whole cultural landscape, so that 'Israel' in fact developed, for the most part, in and out of Canaan. In short, the Israelites were themselves largely Canaanites. Consequently, one can no longer assume that 'Israel' and 'Canaan' represent two distinct ethnic, social, or cultural systems or entities, e.g. desert nomads versus sedentary agriculturalists. Against this historical background, the opposition between 'Israel' and 'Canaan' as constructed by the Old Testament is increasingly seen not as a historical fact, but rather as an interpretative '*pattern*' (i.e. a paradigm for constructing an interpretation of the past rather than for giving an account of the past as it really happened) by which the Old Testament brings to expression a theological distance to its own previous background, language and ethnicity. This (re)interpretation was performed in an effort to provide the cultic communities of the exilic period (→ *exile*), at the earliest, with criteria for maintaining their separation from the outside world and for defining a self-identity within themselves.

This evaluation of the *'Israel' versus 'Canaan' pattern* is also important for the history of religion. In the past, different religious practices, e.g. rituals, festivals, cult images, or theological concepts, which had been attested, reinterpreted, or passed over in silence by the Old Testament, have often been assigned to categories like genuinely 'Israelite'-nomadic (often additionally qualified as → *monotheistic*, Yahwistic) or 'Canaanite'-agrarian (and by implication → *polytheistic*, magical, Baalistic). Against the background of what has been said above, such categorization is of little help and highly dubious, because it starts from the premise, that 'Israel' and 'Canaan' were two different entities. Thus preference should be given to scholarly proposals that reject such artificial and false contrasts between desert-dwelling nomads (= Israelites) and sedentary farmers (= Canaanites). Instead one must keep in mind that the pre-state situation in Palestine was one in which the cultural landscape included very different population groups living side by side, e.g. herdsmen, farmers and urban dwellers, craftsmen etc.

The origins and development of religious practices and ideas in Palestine have to be considered within a process of development involving the entire society with all its complexity, located within the framework of a shared cultural system, in which religious traditions of earlier periods subsequently not only came to be modified and transformed, but also were often simply received and maintained. Hence, one needs to attend not only to the changes, but also to the continuities. We must avoid assigning particular rituals, celebrations, or complexes of ideas to different ethnic groups or geographic entities, e.g. desert versus agricultural regions; instead, we need always to keep in mind the specific social groups that were the bearers of such religious practices and ideas. Similarly, the sharp opposition between Yhwh and Baal, which defines so much of the Old Testament, e.g. the Elijah stories, needs to be re-examined. For some years now, religious-historical studies have been making the point that the Yhwh of Israel and the Yhwh of Judah represent two different manifestations of an original weather god[3] that presumably had entered Palestine from the South, where this deity was originally at home. As a god of the Baal-Hadad-type,[4] which is well attested throughout the Ancient Near East, this deity could just as well be named Baal as Yhwh. Thus, Baal and Yhwh were not necessarily two entirely different deities, but, at least at certain times and in certain regions or circles, they were

3. H. Niehr, *Religionen*, 237. An immigration of Yhwh from the North rather than from the South has recently been suggested by H. Pfeiffer, *Jahwes Kommen von Süden: Jdc 5, Hab 3, Deut 33 und Ps 68 in ihrem literatur- und theologiegeschichtlichen Zusammenhang dargestellt* (FRLANT 211; Göttingen: Vandenhoeck & Ruprecht, 2005).

4. M. Weippert, 'Synkretismus und Monotheismus: Religionsinterne Konfliktbewältigung im alten Israel' (1990), in *Jahwe und die anderen Götter. Studien zur Religionsgeschichte des antiken Israel in ihrem syrisch-palästinischen Kontext* (FAT 18; Tübingen: Mohr Siebeck, 1997), 1–24, esp. 16–17.

> merely different names for one and the same god.[5] Only gradually, in a long and complex process of Syro-Palestinian religious history, did the specific belief in Yhwh crystallize out, first indeed only as belief in a highest god among others, and then, only later, as belief in the one and only God. This process extended over the course of the whole first millennium BCE, taking different tracks in the northern kingdom of Israel and the southern kingdom of Judah. Finally, in the time of the exile and the Second Temple, specific groups were responsible for introducing particularly decisive changes that led to an exclusivist Yahwism.

In the period under discussion here, Palestine was not only a transit land (land-bridge); it also showed typical characteristics of what is today called a 'threshold country', i.e. a developing country teetering on the verge of achieving 'modern' social, economic, cultural and political organization and independent statehood. Palestine's special geographic situation in a corridor connecting powerful neighbours to the north and south led, from early on, to economic, political and military incursions into this strategically important region by the neighbouring countries, which had consolidated themselves as states much earlier than Palestine (understood as comprising the northern kingdom of Israel and the southern kingdom of Judah together with the kingdoms of Moab, Ammon and Edom). During the most part of its history, the southern Levant was not an independent, autonomously administered political entity but was either split up into small regional units or was reduced to a colony, a vassal state, or a province of some foreign power. Thus, both the ruling powers and the boundaries of the Palestinian territories shifted, usually only slightly delayed, with the rise and fall of the currently prevailing foreign superpower or empire having ambitions for expansion in its direction, e.g. Egypt coming from the south, the Sea Peoples, among them the Philistines, coming from the Aegean, Aramaean groups coming from the north,[6] Assyrians, Babylonians, and later Persians coming from the east – succeeded in later times by the Greeks and subsequently the Romans, who took control of the region toward the end of biblical times. (**fig. 3**).

5. See M. Weippert, 'Synkretismus', 17 (above, n. 4).
6. The Hurrian and Hittite empires never really reached into Palestine. Their names are mentioned in the Old Testament only because they were used in an archaizing fashion.

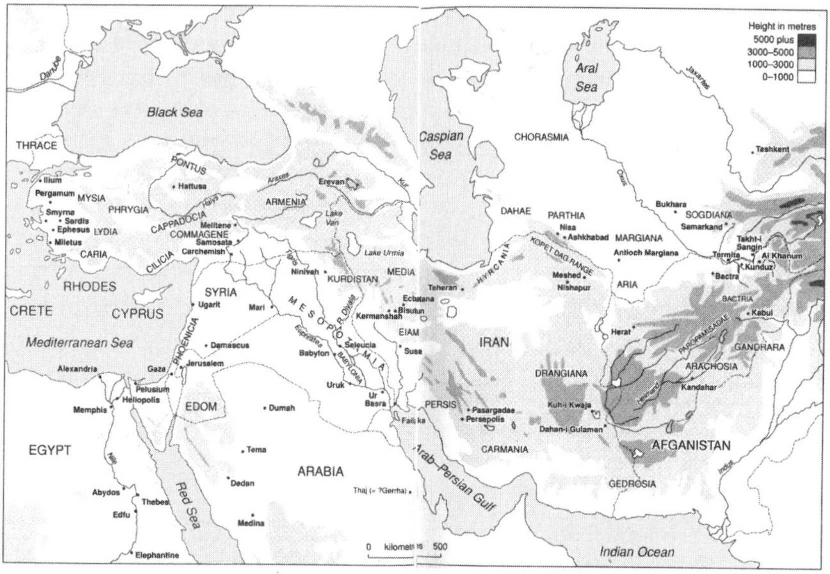


**Fig. 3:** Map of the Ancient Near East.

Not only foreign political supremacy and territorial ambitions influenced the cultural and religious development of Palestine, but also the trade contacts with its different neighbours, among them the Phoenician city states of the northern coastal regions, the inhabitants of Cyprus, and the northern and southern Arab tribes. Thus it becomes clear that both the secular history and the religious history of Palestine are immediately linked to the political events and developments within the region itself, and that they are also cross-linked with developments in the nearer, Syro-Phoenician-Arab environment as well as with the more remote Egyptian, Mesopotamian and Greek environments, and cannot therefore be adequately studied or described without knowledge of this larger context.

# 3.2 Terminology

## 3.2.1 The Terms Canaan, Israel/Israelite, Judah/Judean, Jehud, Judea, Jew, Samaritan and Palestine

📖 Bibliography 2.4 Atlases and Books on Applied Geography; 4 Bible Dictionaries and Exegetical Reference Books for Old Testament Studies.

Since the 18th cent. BCE, the term *Canaan*, whose etymology and meaning remains unclear, is attested as the name of a 'Canaanite' people known from a Mari letter. Canaan refers here to an area whose exact extent remains unknown.[7] In the 14th to 12th cent. BCE, the Egyptians called their southernmost Asiatic province by the Egyptian term '*kn*ʿ*n*'; this province was bordered in the west by the Mediterranean, in the east by the Jordan, in the south by the 'Brook of Egypt' (= Wādī l-ʿArīš or Wādī Gazze), extending to the southern tip of the Dead Sea, and in the north by a line somewhere north of Byblos. The capital of this province was Gaza. After the settlement of the Philistines in the southern coastal region in the 12th cent. BCE, the Egyptians lost control over this area, and the name of their province lost its importance. Among the Phoenicians and Carthaginians, the name Canaan appears only in texts of the Hellenistic and Roman periods. In these later texts, Canaan seems also to be the self-identification of Phoenicia (for example, Phoenician Laodicea in Canaan is identical with Greek Laodicea in Phoenicia, i.e. Beirut). Being a Canaanite was the self-identification of the Phoenicians. The same identification can be found in Mt. 15.22 and Mk 7.26. In the Old Testament, by contrast, the Canaanites appear only as the pre-settlers of the country, who, according to the factually inaccurate historical interpretation of the biblical authors and redactors, were driven out and defeated by the conquering 'Israelite' immigrant tribes (Deut. 1.7; Josh. 5.1; Judg. 1.27-36). Post-exilic (→ *exile*) biblical texts, however, use the term Canaan as a synonym for traders and merchants (Isa. 23.8; Zeph. 1.11; Job 40.30 [NRSV 41.6]; Prov. 31.24; Ezek. 17.4) implicitly equating Canaanites with the Phoenicians, who were the most famous, most successful, and thus most envied merchants of the region during this period, and the Phoenicians evidently used this equation themselves.

The meaning of the term '*Israel*' has undergone numerous changes during the course of history, and these can only be traced here quite briefly. In every case, it is important to observe the context in which one uses the term 'Israel' oneself or in which it is used by other authors in the literature. The earliest attestation for 'Israel' discovered to date is found on the so-called Israel stele of Pharaoh Merneptah (1213–1204 BCE): there it is said that the pharaoh, in the course of his eastern campaign, had devastated, inter alia, Canaan (i.e., the Egyptian province or Gaza), Ashkelon, Gezer, and Jenoʿam (6 km west of the southern tip of the lake Gennesaret). The text goes on: 'Israel is

7. M. Weippert, 'Kanaan', RlA 5:352–5.

devastated, it has no seed.'[8] Because 'Israel' is written here with the determinative for a people, one should interpret it as the designation of a population group rather than as one of a geographic area. Perhaps this battle is depicted on a relief in Karnak, the fourth scene of which represents a battle in an open countryside between the Egyptians and a people called 'Israel'.[9] Because the sequence of the places named in the inscription seems to follow the sequence of the campaign, it is usually assumed that the pharaoh went from Jeno'am southwards into the highlands, and there encountered his enemy 'Israel' in the Ephraimite mountains, where settlers from a tribe of that name are known to have lived in the villages and hamlets of the central or northern Palestinian highlands. How exactly this 'Israel' correlates with the 'Israel' of the later periods is a difficult question. In the first millennium BCE, the name 'Israel' was used for the northern kingdom that stretched (ideally), from south to north, from somewhere not far to the north of Jerusalem up to Dan in the far north; but according to archaeological finds the exact northern and eastern borders seem to have varied considerably during the first millennium.

The neighbouring southern kingdom, with its capital Jerusalem and a royal dynasty tracing itself back to David, was called *Judah*, thus appropriating the name of one of the southern tribes for its dynastically ruled state. The Old Testament assumes that at the time of David and Solomon both the northern and the southern regions were united in a single empire, to which it gives the term 'Israel'; if this was the case – it cannot be verified historically – this usage to refer to a united kingdom would have been of short duration. After the division, i.e. after the time of Solomon, the Old Testament again assumes the existence of two separate kingdoms with two different names: 'Israel' in the north and 'Judah' in the south. Following the end of the statehood of the northern kingdom as a result of the Assyrian conquest 722/721 BCE, there remained only the kingdom of Judah; nevertheless, the name 'Israel' survived and came, in fact, to be used also for the southern kingdom (Jer. 17.13). After 587/6 or 582 BCE, Judah likewise lost its independence, and its territory was included either into the Babylonian province of Samaria or made into a province of its own. We have to assume that the Persians took over, more or

8. *COS* II, 40–1.

9. F. J. Yurco, 'Merenptah's Canaanite Campaign', *Journal of the American Research Center in Egypt* 23 (1986): 189–215; idem, 'Merenptah's Canaanite Campaign and Israel's Origins', in *Exodus: The Egyptian Evidence* (ed. E. S. Frerichs and L. H. Lesko; Winona Lake, Ind.: Eisenbrauns, 1997), 27–55; idem, '3,200-Year-Old Picture of Israelites Found in Egypt', *BAR* 16.5 (1990): 20–38.

less unchanged, the situation as they found it when they conquered Babylon. The independent Persian province of Jehud is attested with certainty since the mid 5th century (Nehemiah), and is represented as embracing at least parts of the preceding state territory of Judah. Alongside this province of Jehud, there also existed a Persian province of Samaria, which presumably comprised roughly the state territory of the former northern kingdom of Israel. In Hellenistic times, under the name Judea, the former Persian province of Jehud became a part of the region subjected to the shifting influence of the Diadochi. For a short period, the Maccabees extended Judea to include not only ancient Judah but also the Samarian mountains, the coastal regions, and the area east of the Jordan. In 135 CE, the Romans renamed their province of Judea '*provincia syria palaestina*'. The term 'Jew' derives from Judah/Jehud/Judea and today expresses belonging to a people that understands itself as a religious rather than a political community.

The term *Samaritan* derives from the place-name 'Samaria' and was used for the inhabitants of both the city and the province of this name (2 Kgs 17.29). More recently, however, the term 'Samarian' has increasingly come into use to distinguish these geographically defined people from the members of the religious community of the Samaritans, which developed in the area around Mount Gerizim, where they had a temple of their own and where a small remnant still survives to this day. The precise origins of this religious community continue to be a matter of dispute, but the evidence clearly points to the post-exilic period (although exact dating is impossible), when a schism apparently developed between the Judean community associated with the Jerusalem temple and the northern Israelite community (the descendants of those who had not been deported by the Assyrians in the eighth century), who were associated with the temple in Shechem. The different scholarly opinions with regard to the dating of this schism base themselves on references from different texts dating between the Persian (Ezra 4.1-5), the early Hellenistic (Alexander the Great, Josephus, *Ant.* XI, 306–46), and the Hasmonean periods (128 [or 111] BCE, i.e. the destruction of the Gerizim temple by Johannes Hyrcanus[10]). Although palaeographic material[11] appears to support the later dating, it is now clear that already around 450 BCE, a temple existed on Mount Gerizim. Anti-Samaritan remarks in the Old Testament (2 Kgs 17.24-28)

10. Josephus, *Ant.* XIII, 254–7, with parallel text.

11. J. D. Purvis, *The Samaritan Pentateuch and the Origin of the Samaritan Sect* (HSM 2; Cambridge, Mass.: Harvard University Press, 1968), 18–28.

and in the rabbinic literature deny the Samaritans their common roots in the 'people of Israel' and the legitimacy of their Yhwh cult. Nevertheless, the Samaritans themselves believe in Yhwh as their one and only God, in Moses as their (only) prophet, and in the Torah (in the shape of the → *Samaritan Pentateuch*) as the unique law of God. For this distinct Jewish community, however, not Jerusalem but rather Mount Gerizim is seen as God's chosen place.

*Palestine* originally designated the settlement area of the Philistines (part of the Sea Peoples; Ch. 4.1.1) in the southern coastal plain, i.e. from south of Gaza down to the area of Jafo. Since Herodotus, *Hist.* I, 105; III, 91, the term 'Palestinian Syria' is attested, referring to the whole coastal strip between Egypt and Phoenicia. Thus the land was obviously still named after its inhabitants, the Philistines (= Palestinians). In 135 CE, the Roman province of Judea was renamed '*provincia syria palaestina*', and Jerusalem was renamed '*aelia capitolina*'. The area of the Roman province also included the agrarian region in the inner part of the country and was, therefore, considerably larger than the former settlement area of the Philistines (important settlements are Tell el-Fārʿa South, Gaza, Ashkelon, Ashdod, Gath, Ekron, Beth-Shemesh). From the 4th cent. CE on, the Roman provincial name became common in its abbreviated form, '*palaestina*'.

The terms '**Canaan**', '**Israel**', '**Judah**', '**Samaria**', and '**Palestine**' underwent various changes in the course of history, so that agreement about their specific usage is important. If these terms are used to designate political entities (kingdoms, provinces), one must recall that their borders could change within very short intervals.

- 'Canaan' designates the Egyptian province of the 14th to 12th cent. BCE. The name may occur as a self-designation of Phoenicians and is used in the Old Testament for the previous settlers of the Promised Land, from which the chosen people of God kept itself apart. The post-exilic texts usually see the Phoenicians as the prototype Canaanites.
- 'Israel' appears to have been originally a tribal complex inhabiting the central or northern Palestinian highlands, and in the 1st mill. BCE it became the name of the northern kingdom with its centre in Samaria. In the Old Testament, the term 'Israel' is used for the whole united monarchy under David and Solomon, which comprised both the northern kingdom of Israel and the southern kingdom of Judah; after the division, however, 'Israel' meant only the northern kingdom until its political end in 722/1 BCE Thereafter, 'Israel', however, could be used for the southern kingdom as well, thereby expressing a claim to

inheritance, and, independently from geographic borders, it came to be used to designate God's chosen people 'Israel' as a whole.

- 'Judah' was originally a tribal complex in the southern Palestinian highlands, and, in the 1st mill. BCE, it became the name of the southern kingdom with its centre in Jerusalem. After the political end of the southern kingdom, 'Judah' perhaps survived as the name of a Babylonian province, which later became the Persian province 'Jehud'. In Hellenistic-Roman times, the term 'Judea' came into use.
- 'Samaria' was the capital of the northern kingdom from the time of its king Omri, and later it became the name of the Assyrian, Babylonian and Persian provinces that were created out of the territory of the former northern kingdom. The inhabitants of the city and the province of Samaria are now called 'Samarians' to distinguish them from the so-called 'Samaritans', who are members of the religious community that developed in post-exilic times around the temple at Mount Gerizim.
- 'Palestine' originally designated the settlement area of the Philistines, later the coastal strip between Egypt and Phoenicia. In 135 CE, *'provincia syria palaestina'* became the new name of the Roman province of Judea.

Difficulties are raised concerning the terminology, especially in regard to the terms 'Israel' and 'Canaan'. In this book the usage is normally self-explanatory given the context; when it is ambiguous, the terms for God's People, 'Israel' and 'Israelites' and for their counterpart 'Canaan' and 'Canaanites' are put in quotation marks.

## 3.2.2 History, Stories, Historiography and Storytelling

Bibliography 8 The History of Ancient Israel and Judah. Further: E. A. Knauf, 'From History to Interpretation'. Pages 42–50 in *The Fabric of History: Text, Artifact and Israel's Past*. JSOTSup 127; ed. D. V. Edelman, Sheffield: JSOT, 1991; T. Krüger, 'Theoretische und methodische Probleme der Geschichte des alten Israel in der neueren Diskussion'. *VF* 53 (2008): 4–21 (research report).

In his seminal but not uncontroversial essay of 1991, Ernst Axel Knauf pointed out, with reference to Fernand Braudel, that history can and should be written on several levels. F. Braudel[12] distinguished: 1) long-term history (*histoire de la longue durée: temps géographique*), which is about the long-enduring structures of human life within its environment, in which changes, developments, and even cycles occur slowly and only gradually, extending over longer periods of time; 2) conjunctional history (*histoire conjoncturelle: temps social*), which traces the medium-term social, cultural, religious, and intellectual-historical

12. F. Braudel, *La Méditerranée et le monde méditerranéen à l'époque de Philippe II* (Paris: Colin, 1949).

developments and processes of shorter duration; and 3) history of events (*histoire événementielle: temps individuel*), which deals with single historic events, persons and places that are individually identifiable and datable. Textual sources, be they extra-biblical or biblical, as well as images in general, come only under consideration as sources for conjunctional and event-oriented history and must in every case be well-established through argumentation. By contrast, the *longue durée* history can only be (re-)constructed on the basis of geographical and archaeological findings, less often with the help of images showing the continuity of particular types of depiction. While Palestine can very well be the subject of a *longue durée* history, this is hardly possible for 'Israel' because of the lack of continuity of the reality intended by the term.

In the biblical texts, the distinction between *history* and *story*, i.e. historiography and storytelling, is not sharply drawn; by contrast, for contemporary scholars, thanks to presuppositions prevailing since the Enlightenment, it is impossible to ignore this distinction. However, both in the Ancient Near East and in the Old Testament, the telling of history also took place, albeit usually within the framework of storytelling, and thus it is in fact history within story. The bare facts (*bruta facta*) of any event are not at the core of the biblical (hi)storytelling; what counts is the significance of what is related within the framework of belief in Yhwh. Thus, it is the present situation of the author/redactor that is interpreted in the mode of (hi)storytelling. The Old Testament, therefore, was never a compendium of the history of Palestine nor was it intended to be. When historians nowadays propose to 'reconstruct' the history of Palestine according to modern historical science, the result, even when they make use of the best available resources, methods, and techniques, will always be a 'construct' reflecting the theories underlying their work. Every 'reconstruction' of history as it supposedly happened 'in fact', is thus in the last analysis a hypothetical construction created by the person who has written it.[13] Despite all these caveats, however, modern history writing is not fiction: historical events and processes can indeed be traced back to given structures or linked to explanations that evidence greater plausibility than alternatives. In fact, history writing as distinct from storytelling, already existed both

13. To remind ourselves of this fact, in the chapters on sources/methods and history/religious history, the terms 'reconstruction' and 'reconstruct' are put in quotation marks, or the prefix 're-' is marked by a hyphen. It would be better to renounce the term '(re-)construction' with a clear break between the two components, but common usage is too well established to insist on that. Thus, such a typographic signal is probably the easiest way to point to the problematic nature of the terms.

in the Ancient Near East as a whole and in Israel and Judah in particular, in the shape of → *annals* (Hebr. *dibrê hayyāmîm* = daily events) that were recorded in writing at the royal court. Excerpts from such annals also can be found in the Old Testament, but they are often difficult to delineate or even to identify as such, because they are embedded in larger literary units. The books Sam.–Kings (Chs 7.6.3.4 and 7.6.3.5), for example, were evidently not viewed by their authors/redactors as annals because, when it comes to information that would be of interest for historical or chronological questions, they explicitly distinguish themselves from the official annals (1 Kgs 14.19, 29). Their literary features and their theological intentions lie in another realm. These books, further deepened by different redactors in the course of their formation, are a commentary on history within the framework of the outline of a theological system that deliberately selected and arranged its material in specific ways in order to explain the reasons for the downfall of the kingdoms of Israel and Judah and to lay the foundations for the anticipated and hoped for new beginning. By contrast, 1 and 2 Chronicles are explicitly (secondarily?) characterized as annals (Ch. 23) by their titles '*dibrê hayyāmîm*'. At the same time, however, they are also a narrative interpretation of the Torah and the prophetic books, which were mined as sources, re-worked, and further narrated with the inclusion of additional traditions (*Sondergut*!). Also in this case, history and stories are linked, because 1 and 2 Chronicles also recount events in such a way as to interpret them in contemporary (i.e., Hellenistic) fashion. In this form, the history and the stories told in these books are accommodated into the views of the Chronicler and in their interpretation of the past they present a vision for a (better) future.

## 3.2.3 The Terms Monotheism, Polytheism, Monolatry, Henotheism and Poly-Yahwism

Bibliography 4 Bible Dictionaries and Exegetical Reference Books for Old Testament Studies.

The term → *monotheism* is a modern coinage first attested in 1660 in a work by Henry More. It describes the conviction that there is only one single God, who consequently is alone entitled to worship. A distinction is made today between exclusive and inclusive monotheism: while exclusive monotheism is marked by polemics against the (other) gods (= idols) and their worshippers, an inclusive monotheism remains more tolerant of polytheistic notions, because it sees behind the many different manifestations of gods a single, ultimate unity. By contrast, → *polytheism*, a term which first appears with Philo of Alexandria (ca. 25 BCE–25 CE), presupposes that there really exists a multitude of deities – often without an upper number limit – that can be the object of worship. Each of these gods is characterized by a distinct action-profile, and together they form a more or less structured pantheon. However, within polytheism, there can be a variety of forms that form a bridge to monotheism: e.g. → *monolatry* is the de facto adoration of only one god, despite the theoretical conviction that there are other deities as well. It is difficult to distinguish this concept from → *henotheism*, a term introduced by Friedrich Max Müller in 1860, to describe belief in one single god, who is credited with exercising at least temporary supremacy within the context of many other deities: the rest of the pantheon is under the command of this supreme deity, but a change at the top of the pantheon is not excluded. This phenomenon can also be called monarchic polytheism.

→ *Poly-yahwism* is a relatively new term, coined by Herbert Donner in 1973, that is linked with the theory (Manfred Weippert, Herbert Niehr) that in the northern kingdom and in Judah during the monarchic period, there existed a variety of local manifestations of Yhwh-deities. One of the starting points for this thesis was the observation that the inscriptions from Kuntillet ʿAjrûd, link the name of the god Yhwh with geographic names, speaking of the *Yhwh of Samaria*, the *Yhwh of Teman*. Two of the most important local forms of Yhwh are the Yhwh of Samaria, as the state god of the northern monarchy, and the Yhwh of Jerusalem, as the state god of Judah. It is possible that the → *Šĕma ʿ yiśrā ʾel* in Deut. 6.4 was originally meant as a protest against this kind of internal religious pluralism within Yhwh belief.[14]

The course of development of the Israelite-Judean religion, which at the end of the formation of the biblical tradition emerged as clearly monotheistic, has been (re-)constructed in different ways in the past. The earlier theory of an originally monotheistic Yahwism of the 'Israelite' people or at least the group around Moses, which (more or less successfully) managed to defend itself against 'Canaanite' polytheism, was based mainly on an uncritical re-narration of the biblical texts as they stand, with little regard for extra-biblical evidence. Increasingly, this view has given way to a much more nuanced religious history (mostly because of archaeological, → *iconographic*,

14. See, e.g. H. Donner, 'Hier sind deine Götter, Israel!' in *Wort und Geschichte: FS K. Elliger* (AOAT 18; ed. H. Gese and H. P. Rüger; Neukirchen-Vluyn: Neukirchener, 1973), 45–50.

and → *epigraphic* remains, but also because of texts such as Deut. 32.8-9, Pss 82, 89.6-8 (NRSV 89.5-7), and the results of historical-critical exegesis) which postulates a developmental model, assuming that the way from pre-exilic (→ *exile*) polytheism led via henotheism and monolatry to a multi-faceted monotheistic Yhwh, who in the process gradually absorbed the traces of earlier gods and goddesses.

## 3.3 The People and their Gods: Official Cult, Local Cult, Personal Piety/Domestic Cult, Everyday Cult and Festival Cult

K. van der Toorn, *Family Religion in Babylonia, Syria and Israel: Continuity and Change in the Forms of Religious Life*. SHANE 7. Leiden: Brill, 1996; R. Albertz and B. Becking, eds, *Yahwism after the Exile*. Studies in Theology and Religion 5. Assen: Royal van Gorcum, 2003; C. Meyers, *Households and Holiness: The Religious Culture of Israelite Women*: Minneapolis: Fortress, 2005.

Worship or cult, as the practical side of religion, is service to and for the gods (or sometimes deified ancestors), making use of all possible encoded forms of religious symbolic systems involving language, images, and actions.[15] In order to give structure to the different possible levels of cult practice, it has become customary for some time now, following works by Rainer Albertz and Bernhard Lang, to open up the classical sociologically oriented twofold differentiation between the centralized, supra-regional, urban and state-bound *official cult*, on the one hand, and the decentralized personal and *family cult or piety*, on the other, by introducing an intermediate level of the *local cult* that is linked to the place of settlement. The official cult sponsored by the king in the service of the city or territorial state took place at central sanctuaries with altar and temple building(s), and employed priests (sometimes also diviners and prophets) for the state gods, especially for the highest city or state god. By contrast, the rural, local

15. These are the three most important levels of representation in religious symbolic systems, see F. Stolz, 'Hierarchien der Darstellungsebenen religiöser Botschaft', in *Religionswissenschaft: Eine Einführung* (ed. H. Zinser; Berlin: Reimer, 1988), 55–72, here 55–7.

cult took place within families, kin groups, and tribal complexes and was celebrated by the leaders of these social units, generally at locally important open air sanctuaries, at cult places with an altar and sometimes with a cultic room or buildings, or at special niches at the city gate. Cult places of this type employed no official priests. The sanctuaries that were, inter alia, typical for Iron Age Palestine, are subsumed in Biblical studies for the most part under the biblical term 'high places' (Hebr. *bāmôt*). Personal piety found expression in the cult within the family's domestic space, and was dedicated to personal gods or ancestors. When, in this threefold model, a distinction is made between the levels of official, local and personal cult, we should always remember that the transition could be fluid; the temple cult that was sponsored from the official side could often, for instance, integrate a local sanctuary when there were good reasons for doing so. Pilgrimages and acts of dedication established bridges between the personal piety of individuals and the official cult. Cultic meals were usually part of the family cult that took place within the house, but on supra-regional holidays they could sometimes be celebrated also outside the house at jointly visited regional places of worship as a kind of cultic picnic.

Another distinction that is valid for all levels of cultic life is the differentiation between *everyday cult* and special *festival cult*. While the day-to-day rituals were characterized by regular routine, special rituals and liturgies were used on high holidays and during festival periods at the central temples as well as at the regional and local cult places, as befitting the event. Private cult as well could be shaped by regularly repeated festivals; in general, however, private cult was marked, for the most part, by important family and personal events, such as marriages, burials, or initiation rites, e.g. circumcision, that were staged as celebrations.[16]

In Palestine, from the earliest times, traces of family cult, but also of supra-familial, communal cults for the ancestors can be demonstrated both archaeologically and → *iconographically*. The findings are sometimes difficult to interpret, but, from the Neolithic period on, we can with certainty conclude that → *anthropomorphic* and → *theriomorphic*, as well as → *aniconic* objects were all used to represent deities or deified ancestors and were the centre of cultic practices. The earliest cult, as a

16. For the distinction between the recurring festivals and the single family celebrations see A. Berlejung, 'Heilige Zeiten: Ein Forschungsbericht', *Jahrbuch Biblische Theologie* 18 (2003): 3–61, esp. 4.

personal cult, took place within the family dwelling place; communal cult, by contrast, took place at a common open space or in the dwelling of the local chief. Buildings with exclusively cultic function for the community (= temples) can perhaps be traced back to the Neolithic, but definitely to the Chalcolithic (5,800 to 3,300 BCE). They are temples of the broad-room type (En-Gedi, Gīlat), which, in the cult room or *cella*, were furnished with a raised platform or dais for the deity, and with benches for depositing sacrifices and votive gifts. Together with accompanying buildings, installations, gates, and a so-called temenos wall, the temple as such could form part of a holy precinct (Greek: 'temenos'), for instance at En-Gedi. In the Early Bronze Period, double temples of the same type developed, for instance at Megiddo and Arad. Broad-room temples with a kind of open porch on the access side, bounded by the protruding sidewalls (= *antae*), can be found ever since Early Bronze Age III, e.g. Ḫirbet ez-Zeraqōn, Megiddo Temple 4040. Temples of the long-room type came from Mesopotamia and are attested in Palestine only from the Middle Bronze Age II on, for instance at Megiddo. Only from the Late Bronze Age on, did they become the most common temple type. Variants of this type are the long building with a closed front and the temple *in antis*. A special type is the *migdol* or fortification temple, which is the name for massive cultic buildings with towers and sometimes several levels, e.g. Megiddo Temple 2048. The tripartite long-room type is often encountered in the Late Bronze Age in Syria and Palestine. In this temple type, the long inner room is subdivided into a holy-of-holies/*cella*, a hall/*ante-cella*, and a covered vestibule or porch. This ground plan also corresponds to the Jerusalem temple as described in 1 Kgs 6–7; 2 Chr. 3–4; Ezek. 40–42) **(fig. 4)**.

With the end of the Late Bronze Age, the long-room type seems to have gradually passed out of use in Syria and Palestine. For Iron-Age urban temples in the Levant, a specific building type has now become known through excavation of the temple of Beth-Shan V (11th to 9th cent.) and temple 650 from Level I in Ekron (7th cent.) **(fig. 4c)**. The most important elements of this type are its longitudinal orientation, its side (and sometimes rear) adjoining rooms, and its two rows of pillars dividing the temple hall into three naves. These pillar temples derive from the pillar architecture of profane public buildings of the Iron Age.[17]

17. J. Kamlah, 'Der salomonische Tempel: Paradigma der Verknüpfung von biblischer Exegese und Archäologie für eine Rekonstruktion der Religionsgeschichte Israels', *VF* 53 (2008): 40–51.

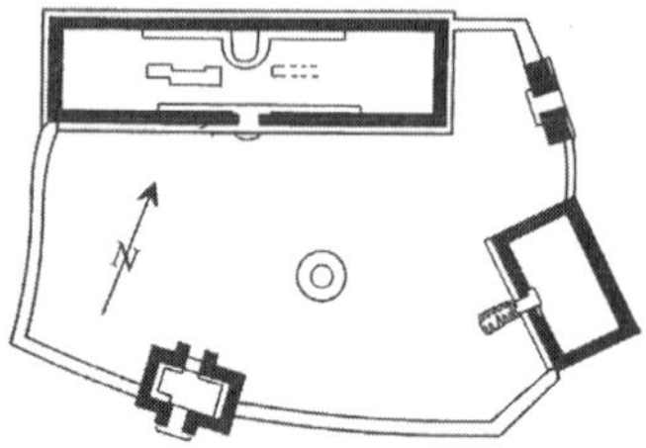

Fig. 4a Broad-room temple at En-Gedi

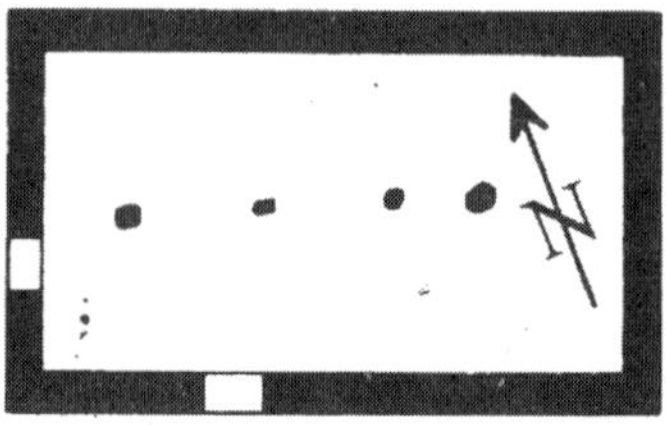

Fig. 4b Bent-axis temple at Naharīyā

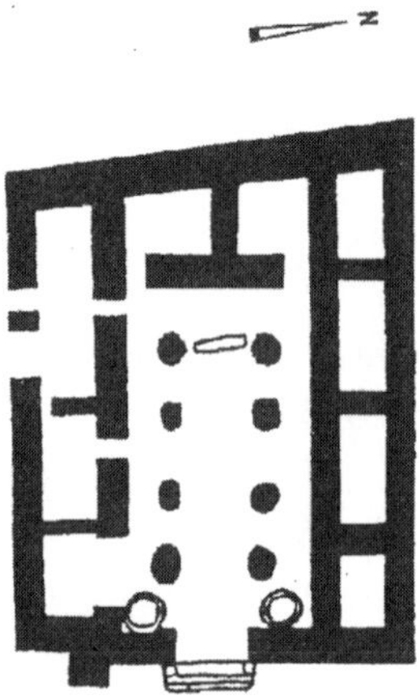

Fig. 4c Pillar temple at Ekron, 7th cent.

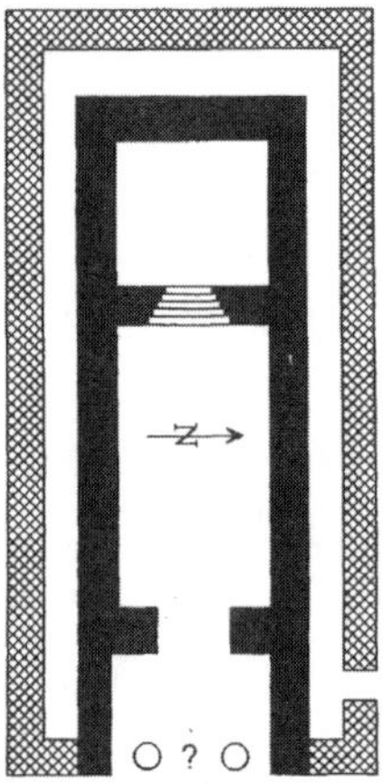

Fig. 4d Reconstruction of the Solomonic Temple

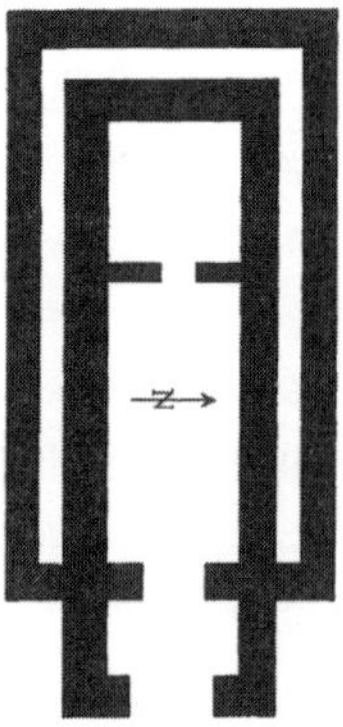

Fig. 4e Reconstruction of the Second Temple, according to Ezekiel

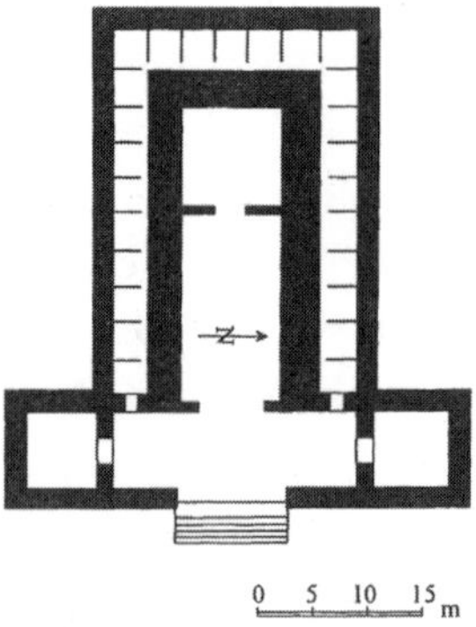


Fig. 4f Reconstruction of the Herodian Temple at Jerusalem

**Fig. 4:** Synopsis of types of temples and floor plan of the Jerusalem temple.

Archaeological, → *iconographic*, and the few → *epigraphic* sources reveal a picture of cultic life of the Iron-Age monarchies of 'Israel' and Judah that can well be understood as a sequel to the practices of previous epochs and can be compared with the cultic practices of contemporary neighbours. Thus, → *anthropomorphic* representations of diverse gods and goddesses attest to a certain diversity in the divine sphere. Evidence points, inter alia, to people placing their trust in local Yhwh manifestations and in 'Yhwh and his Asherah', who are epigraphically attested and who were presumably represented in images.[18] As representations of deities, → *theriomorphic* figures, e.g. bulls, and other iconic symbolic figures, e.g. the crescent moon, but also completely → *aniconic* objects, such as figureless stone stelae like the → *mazzeboth* and → *baetyls*, were in use alongside anthropomorphic images and were often the core, or at least a part, of cultic activities **(fig. 5)**. Altars were destined for sacrifices of different kinds as gifts to the deity. Temples as well as cultic sites were dispersed all over the country and were considered to be dwellings of the deities where a person could encounter them. Presumably, these sanctuaries were for the most part inhabited by the state and dynastic deity Yhwh, perhaps in his local manifestation and accompanied by Asherah as his consort. Depending on the cultic context, priestly actions were performed either by the heads of families (domestic cult), the chieftains of the clan or tribe (local cult), or by officials of the state (official cult), including the monarch himself. With the increasing complexity of the cult and its professionalization, the temple personnel differentiated into different groups of priests and other cult servants. In the state cult, they were subject to the king, who himself could occasionally act as the chief priest. Although, after the destruction of the main cities of Samaria and Jerusalem, the official cult for the most part ceased to exist, local and personal cult became further stabilized. After 587/6 BCE even in Judah, local cultic communities were able to consolidate themselves again,[19] especially in areas and at temples that had not been destroyed by the Babylonian conquerors, such as in the northern part of Judah and Benjamin. Mizpah and

18. See the suggestion of C. Uehlinger, 'Anthropomorphic Cult Statuary in Iron Age Palestine and the Search for Yahweh's Cult Images', in *The Image and the Book: Iconic Cults, Aniconism, and the Rise of Book Religion in Israel and the Ancient Near East* (CBET 21; ed. K. van der Toorn; Leuven: Peeters, 1997), 97–156, here 149–52.

19. H. M. Barstad, *The Myth of the Empty Land* (SO 28; Oslo: Scandinavian University Press, 1996), 19–20, 43–4, 47–55, and others.

**Fig. 5:** Survey of iconographically attested types of god's and goddesses.

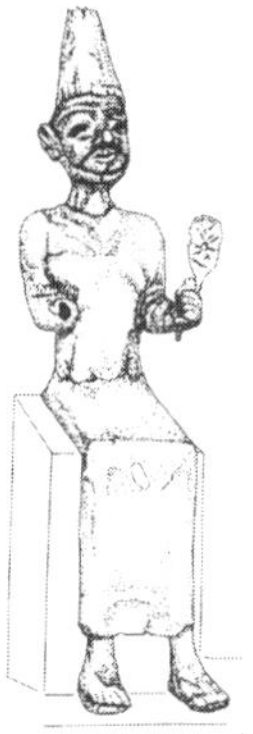

**Fig. 5a:** Enthroned god, Late Bronze Age, bronze figurine, sheathed with gold, from Megiddo, 25cm high.

**Fig. 5b:** Smiling god, Late Bronze Age, bronze figurine from Megiddo, 13cm high, the god Resheph with hand weapon and shield.

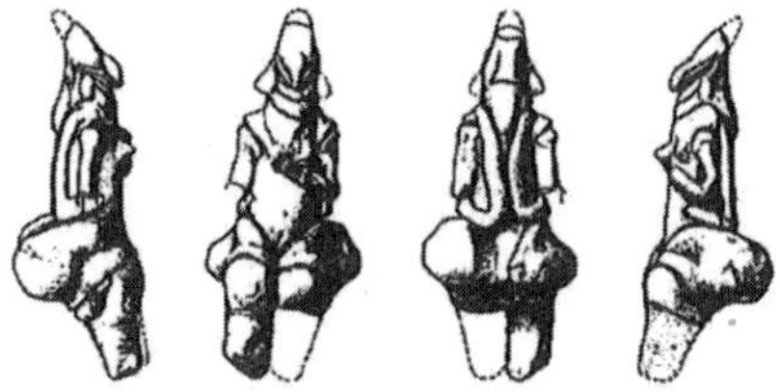

**Fig. 5c:** Mother goddess from Sha'ar ha-Golan, Neolithic.

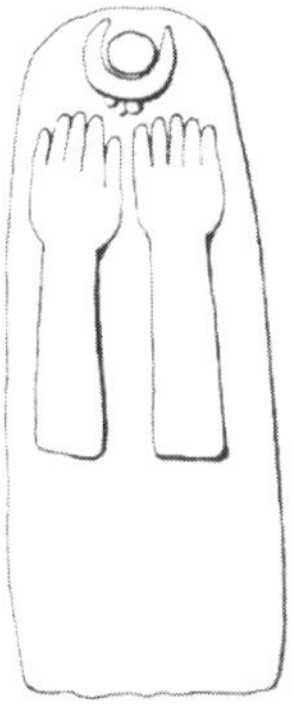

**Fig. 5d:** Stela with crescent moon and disc, stelae sanctuary of area c, Hazor, perhaps depiciting the moon god of Haron (North Syria), Middle Bronze Age.

**Fig. 5e:** Female deity 'Astarie plaque', Late Bronze/Early Iron Age, Tel Zeror.

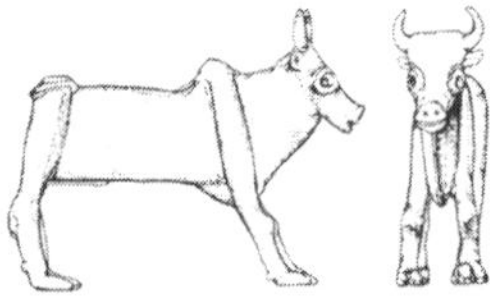

**Fig. 5f:** Bronze figurine, Iron Age I, open-air sanctuary East of Dothan, presumably depicting a weather god.

**Fig. 5g:** Smiting goddess, Dan, Iron Age IIB.

**Fig. 5h:** Terra-cotta figurine, goddess with child, Pella, Iron Age IIB.

**Fig. 5i:** Stelae and incense altars in the cultic niche of the temple at Arad, end of 8th cent. B.C.E.

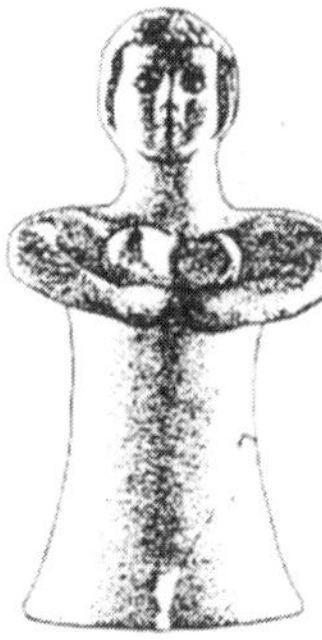

**Fig. 5j:** Female pillar figurine, Iron Age IIB/IIC.

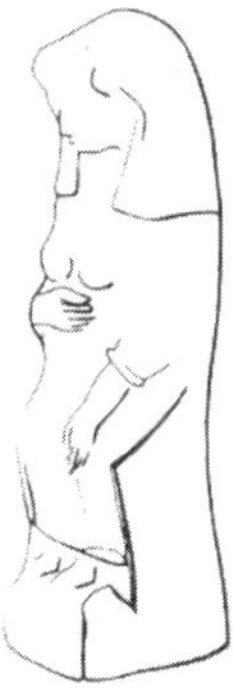

**Fig. 5k:** Seated pregnant lady; Iron Age III, Phoenicia.

**Fig. 5l:** Stelae of gods on throne of sphinxes, Ḫirbet et-Tayyiba, 47cm, 2nd cent. B.C.I.

Bethel seem to have been centres of supra-regional importance during the exilic period (→ *exile*), where the cultic traditions were maintained.[20] After only a short interruption, to a certain degree at least, even the temple cult in Jerusalem could be resumed at the altar within the ruins of the temple.[21] After the exile, partly with Persian help, a new official cult could take form around the Second Temple in Jerusalem. Because there was no longer a unifying figure, such as the king, to maintain the supra-regional official cult, this revived cult was based on the *one* central sanctuary in Jerusalem (Deut. 12), its priesthood, and the God Yhwh, who alone was to be worshipped there.[22] This cultic programme focused on Yhwh and on Jerusalem, reinterpreting elements of the pre-exilic cult, re-working and updating them, and adapting them to newly established theological standards. Nevertheless, this programme was not yet compulsory for all the cultic communities of Yhwh during the Second Temple period. For instance, the cultic life of the community around the Yhwh Temple on the Nile island of Elephantine took quite a different form. The existence of this temple itself contradicts the deuteronomic/deuteronomistic (→ *Deuteronomism*) demand for → *cult centralization*.[23] It was destroyed in 410 BCE by the Egyptians, and rebuilt with the knowledge of the Jerusalem priesthood and with Persian authorization. After the resumption of the official cult in Jerusalem in Persian times, various social, political and theological conflicts broke out during the Persian and Hellenistic Periods which, among other things, led, around 450 BCE, to

20. J. Blenkinsopp, 'The Judaean Priesthood during the Neo-Babylonian and Achaemenid Periods', *CBQ* 60 (1998): 25–43. For the topic of the cult in postwar times, see A. Berlejung, 'Notlösungen: Altorientalische Nachrichten über den Tempelkult in Nachkriegszeiten', in *Kein Land für sich allein: Studien zum Kulturkontakt in Kanaan, Israel/Palästina und Ebirnâri: FS M. Weippert* (OBO 186; ed. U. Hübner and E. A. Knauf; Fribourg: Academic Press/Göttingen: Vandenhoeck & Ruprecht, 2002), 196–230.

21. See S. Japhet, 'The Temple in the Restoration Period: Reality and Ideology', *USQR* 34 (1991): 195–251, esp. 224ff.

22. The deuteronomic/deuteronomistic demand for → *cult centralization* is often dated to the time of the Judean King Josiah (end of 7th cent.), based on 2 Kgs 22–23.

23. Except for its → *epigraphic* attestation, nothing is known about a Yhwh Temple in Idumea at Khirbet el-Qôm in the 4th cent. BCE; see A. Lemaire, 'Nouveau temple de Yaho (IV^e s. av. J.-C.)', in *'Basel und Bibel:' Collected Communications to the XVIIth Congress of the International Organization for the Study of the Old Testament Basel 2001* (BEATAJ 51; ed. M. Augustin and H. M. Niemann; Frankfurt a.M.: Lang, 2004), 265–73. Admittedly, however, the authenticity of the → *ostracon* R 59 is not beyond doubt.

the foundation of the cultic centre for the Samaritans on Mount Gerizim (Ch. 3.2.1), perhaps also to the building of a Yhwh Temple in Transjordan at 'Araq el-Emir by the Tobiade Hyrcanus at the beginning of the 2nd cent. BCE, and to the foundation of a Yhwh Temple in the Egyptian Leontopolis by Onias III/IV (around 169/between 163 and 145 BCE).[24] Another product of these conflicts was a kind of 'cultic reform' under the Seleucid Antiochus IV Epiphanes (175–164 BCE). The latter committed a sacrilege by building an altar for Zeus Olympius upon (or instead of) the altar of burnt offering in the Jerusalem temple, thereby provoking the Maccabean rebellion, led by the priestly family from Modein. From the Maccabees, the Hasmonean kingdom emerged in which, once again, the king functioned as a high priest. A further result of the conflicts in those times was probably the founding of the community of → *Qumran*, which (like the temples on Mount Gerizim and in Leontopolis) developed an anti-cult opposing the Jerusalem temple (see 1QS= 'Community Rule'). In Hellenistic and Roman times, especially in the Hellenized cities, temples for various deities were erected in the → *Hellenistic* building tradition at various places in Palestine, e.g. Samaria, Beth-Shan, Caesarea, and elsewhere.

## Excursus: (A.) Feast days, (B.) New Moon and Shabbat

A. The (re-)construction of the *liturgical year* in Israel and Judah is difficult. Extra-biblical sources that contain information about single feast days or the cultic calendar are only available from the 5th cent. BCE onward, e.g. Elephantine[25] (5th cent.), Wadī d-Dāliye (4th cent.), 1 *En* 72–82 (3rd cent.), Book of Jubilees (2nd cent.), texts from Qumran[26]. For earlier centuries, one has to rely on the biblical

24. According to Josephus, *Bell.* I, 31–33; VII, 420–432, it was Onias III. But according to Josephus, Ant. XII, 237.387–388; XIII, 62–73, the foundation goes back only to his son Onias IV. For this (and the rivalling Yhwh sanctuaries) see J. Frey, 'Temple and Rival Temple – The Cases of Elephantine, Mt. Gerizim, and Leontopolis', in *Gemeinde ohne Tempel/Community without Temple: Zur Substituierung und Transformation des Jerusalemer Tempels und seines Kults im Alten Testament, antiken Judentum und frühen Christentum* (WUNT 118; ed. B. Ego, A. Lange and P. Pilhofer; *Tübingen: Mohr Siebeck*, 1999), 171–203.
25. For the Passover-Mazzoth Papyrus, see B. Porten and A. Yardeni, *TADAE*, A4.1.
26. Concerning the calendar and timekeeping there, see J. VanderKam, *Calendars in the Dead Sea Scrolls: Measuring Time* (London: Routledge, 1998).

texts. From the Old Testament, several *feast calendars* are known, of which Exod. 23.14-17 and 34.18, 22-23 were previously considered to be the eldest. Meanwhile, their age and relation to one another has become disputed.[27] Apart from this dispute, one can question[28] whether Exod. 23.14-17 ever really functioned as a festival calendar as such for any historical cultic community; it is also quite possible that it represents simply a paradigmatic text, which prescribes only the basic parameters for the correct Israelite festival cult and that these were further developed in the texts of Exod. 34 and Deut. 16.1-17, which are evidently based on it. It remains unclear to what extent these biblical feast calendars can claim to be complete liturgical calendars. It likewise remains an open question, to what extent they reflect, select, or construct the pre-exilic cultic practice in Israel and Judah (and Palestine as a whole). The sources do not allow us to trace consistently local differentiations, i.e. in Judah, Israel, Jerusalem, or in the → *diaspora communities* of Babylonia and Egypt, or to trace diachronic developments. In any case, the Old Testament itself attests the existence of additional feast days, e.g. the feast celebrated around a dying god, (see Ezek. 8.14, i.e. the ritual wailing over Tammuz; Zech. 12.11, i.e. the mourning rites for Hadad-Rimmon) that evidently existed at least locally(?) and for some time(?), without ever being integrated into the aforementioned cultic calendars. According to the biblical feast calendars, Exod. 23.14-17; 34.18, 22-23 and Deut. 16.1-17, the yearly feast days in Israel and Judah (between which the Bible does not differentiate in this connection) consisted of (1.) the Feast of Unleavened Bread (Mazzoth), (2.) the Feast of Weeks (Shavuoth) and (3.) the harvest (autumn) feast or Feast of Tabernacles (Sukkoth), which are respectively listed in this order. This allows us to assume that the beginning of the cultic year was in spring. The rules for (4.) the Passover/Pesach feast originally stood separately from the calendars (Exod. 12) and only in Deut. 16 were they integrated therein. Groundbreaking work on the study of Israelite feast days was carried out by Julius Wellhausen (1844–1918),[29] who devoted a chapter to this topic in his *Prolegomena to the History of Israel* (transl.) in 1878. Since then, there has been more or less accord over the historical development of the three aforementioned feasts. Scholars assume that they were originally oriented toward events of the agricultural calendar were celebrated in the local communities and that, in later phases, they were repeatedly ⇨

27. E. Otto, *Das Deuteronomium: Politische Theologie und Rechtsreform in Juda und Assyrien* (BZAW 284; Berlin/NewYork: de Gruyter, 1999), 76–7, 325–7; S. Bar-On, 'The Festival Calendars in Exodus XXIII 14-19 and XXXIV 18-26', VT 48 (1998): 161–95.

28. So, e.g. D. Volgger, *Israel wird feiern: Untersuchung zu den Festtexten in Exodus bis Deuteronomium* (Arbeiten zu Text und Sprache im Alten Testament 73; St. Ottilien: EOS, 2002), 78 with n. 14.

29. J. Wellhausen, *Prolegomena to the History of Israel* (transl. and preface by W. R. Smith; Atlanta, Ga.: Scholars Press, 1994; transl. of *Prolegomena zur Geschichte Israels* [6th ed., Berlin/New York: de Gruyter, 1927; Student edition, 2001; 1st ed. 1878 under the title *Geschichte Israels*]), 65–90.

subjected to further interpretation.[30] Opinions sometimes differ about the chronological placement of certain developments, because the analysis and literary historical assessment of the complex biblical texts always has consequences for the (re-)construction of the cult history. Important historical turning points, which have influenced the development of festal practice and the interpretation of the feasts' contents, are usually pinpointed at the beginning of statehood in Israel and Judah, at the introduction of an official cult (under royal and priestly control) in the respective capitals, then at the end of the states of Israel and Judah and during the exile, when official cult was extinguished, and finally at the re-emergence of an official cult in the post-exilic period. The changes caused by these events cannot be discussed here in detail; instead, attention is called only to the overall tendency to historicize certain festivals within the OT by connecting them with events of 'Israel's' past. For example, → *Passover/Pesach* (in Exod. 12.21-23; 12.11-14), Mazzoth (in Exod. 23.15; 34.18; 12.17), and Passover/Pesach in connection with Mazzoth (in Deut. 16.1-8), as well as the → *Feast of Tabernacles* (only in Lev. 23.42-43) are presented as celebrations commemorating events of the Exodus and are connected with the idea of Yhwh's acts of salvation. The Feast of Weeks (in Deut. 16.12) is linked with the memory of slavery in Egypt, while in post-exilic times it becomes the commemoration of the → *covenant* on Sinai (Exod. 19.1; 2 Chr. 15.10-15; *Jub.* 1.1), of the covenant with Noah (*Jub.* 6.1-22), and of the covenant with Abraham (*Jub.* 14.10-20; 15.1). This historicization and theologization of the feasts originated in the intention of the biblical authors/redactors to shape their festal traditions according to their own theological programmes. Thus they connected the feasts with the central foundation myths that defined, according to the Old Testament, the identity of the ancient Israelites, thereby helping to define the identity of the post-exilic community.

1) The Mazzoth feast or Feast of Unleavened Bread (Exod. 23.15a; 34.18-20*) is a spring harvest festival and was celebrated at the beginning of the grain harvest. It did not originally have an exact date but depended on the actual beginning of the harvest within the first month (= March/April). It was supposed to last for seven days and was celebrated by eating unleavened bread at a festal meal.

2) The feast of Seven or Feast of Weeks (Shavuoth) (Exod. 34.22; Deut. 16.10, 16) or the harvest-feast (Exod. 23.16) was originally a one-day harvest thanksgiving connected with the first fruits of the barley harvest (Exod. 34.22). The rite of the offering of the firstlings (Deuteronomy 26), which was connected with this feast, was replaced in the text of Deut. 16.9-12 by non-specific voluntary gifts.

3) The feast of Ingathering, harvest or vintage (Exod. 23.16; 34.22) otherwise known as the Feast of Tabernacles (Sukkoth) (Deut. 16.13, 16; Lev. 23.34) was celebrated in autumn on the occasion of the vintage and olive harvests. The date of the feast varied and

30. For a general introduction, see E. Otto and T. Schramm, *Fest und Freude* (Kohlhammer-Taschenbücher 1003; Stuttgart: Kohlhammer, 1977), 9–76; J. C. VanderKam, 'Calendars, Ancient Israelite and Early Jewish', in *ABD* 1:814–20.

depended on the actual completion of the harvest before the wine and olive pressing. It is only more recent texts (Deut. 16.13-15) that broaden the one-day ritual into a festal series of seven days and fix (Lev. 23.34-36, 39-43; Num. 29.12-38) a precise date for it (15th to 21st day of the 7th month). As the most important custom connected with this feast, they introduce the binding of a festal bouquet (Lev. 23.40) and the dwelling for seven days in booths made of branches (Lev. 23.42). The Feast of Tabernacles was the greatest feast of the year; therefore, it was logical to connect it (at least on the literary level, whether this was historically correct remains unclear) with other events such as the consecration of the temple in 1 Kgs 8.2; the renewal of the covenant in Deut. 31.10; Neh. 8.14-15; and the consecration of the altar by the returnees in Ezra 3.4.

4) The Passover/Pesach *feast* was originally a feast celebrated in the family; in contrast to the other three yearly feasts, it was linked to animal husbandry and the non-sedentary life of herdsmen (not to be confused with a nomadic lifestyle) and to the warding off of demons (inter alia, because of the Hebrew root *psḥ* 'to push up/against/back'). According to Julius Wellhausen, its roots lay in the offering of firstborn animals; according to Leonhard Rost, however, they go back to the yearly change of grazing grounds, while Eckart Otto prefers to view the feast as linked with celebrations of the full moon after the spring equinox, supposedly to pacify divine anger.[31] The rite of Passover/Pesach (Exod. 12.21-23*) consists, in essence, of slaughtering a lamb and eating the roasted meat together at night and it is associated with a blood ritual, in which the head of the family smears the blood of the Passover/Pesach lamb on the doorframes and lintel of the house or tent. This blood-ritual is usually interpreted as an → *apotropaic* rite to protect the family from some danger, personified by the demonic 'destroyer', which could enter the house or tent. Passover/Pesach originally was independent of the Mazzoth feast. The linking of the two feasts in Deut. 16.1-8[32] had numerous consequences, among them, the detachment of Passover/Pesach from the family cult, the abandonment of the blood rite, the widening of the categories of sacrificial animals to include cattle as well as lambs/goats, the change from roasting to cooking the meat, the dating of the feast-cycle in the month Abib (later called Nisan). In Deuteronomy, the feast is historicized with reference to the exodus and with the call for lifelong commemoration, the Mazzoth bread is called 'food of distress', and abstinence from work is prescribed on the seventh day of the Mazzoth feast. All this is a product of the deuteronomic/deuteronomistic programme and was not left un-contradicted within the Old Testament.

⇨

31. J. Wellhausen, *Prolegomena*, 65–90 (above, n. 29); L. Rost, 'Weidewechsel und altisraelitischer Festkalender (1943)', in *Das kleine Credo und andere Studien zum Alten Testament* (Heidelberg: Quelle & Meyer, 1965), 101–12; E. Otto, 'Feste und Feiertage II. Altes Testament', *TRE* 11:96–106, esp. 98.

32. For the literary-critical debates about the text, see the summary on the state of research in C. Körting, *Der Schall des Schofar: Israels Feste im Herbst* (BZAW 285; Berlin/New York: de Gruyter, 1999), 40–50; S. Bar-On, 'The Festival Calendar of Deuteronomy', in *Deuteronomy* (ed. M. Weinfeld; Tel Aviv 1994), 133–8 [Hebr.].

In particular, the transformation of all four feasts, which were originally celebrated within the family or at the local sanctuary, into pilgrimage feasts that could be celebrated only at a central sanctuary, i.e. the Jerusalem temple (Deut. 16.1-17), belonged to the deuteronomic/deuteronomistic reform programme and did not come to prevail everywhere and for all times: it is opposed, for instance, by the festal programme of the → *Priestly Document*, which states that Passover/Pesach (Exod. 12.1-14*) is to be celebrated within the family and independently of a temple. Also in that tradition, the connection of Passover/Pesach with the Mazzoth feast and the changes in sacrificial material and its preparation are rejected and the Pesach blood rite is reintroduced. Further changes can be traced in later biblical texts, such as the festal calendar of Leviticus 23 or the sacrificial calendar of Numbers 28–29.[33] It is only in these texts that the exact dates of the four yearly feasts are fixed and correlated with each other. They add two additional feast days, the *New-year/New-moon day* on the 1st of the 7th month and the Day of Atonement on the 10th day of that month. The interpretation of the feast days also underwent changes: Leviticus 23 links them with the command to abstain from work and integrates them into the sacrificial cult by prescribing what offerings are to be made on them. Numbers 28–29 emphasizes the aspects of sin, → *atonement*, and admission of guilt[34] (see also Ezek. 45.18-25) and enlarges the sacrificial prescriptions. Finally, Ezra 6.19-22, Neh. 8.13-18 and Deuteronomy 31 shape the yearly festivals into foundational rites of the post-exilic cultic community. From the final version of the → *Pentateuch*, with its diverse versions of feast calendars and variant ritual instructions, from the Elephantine texts (Passover-Mazzoth Papyrus), and from the Book of Jubilees, it becomes clear that, even in the latest times, discussion was still going on about how, when, by whom, and where individual feast days should be celebrated. In later times, additional feasts were added to the original yearly feasts. These new feasts were conceived as commemorative festivals: Purim (14th/15th day of the 12th month Addar), whose origin probably goes back to Babylonia or Persia, is attested only from post-exilic times onwards (2 Macc. 15.36) and recalls, according to the legend in Esther 9, the salvation of the Jewish people who, with the help of Mordecai and Esther, escaped annihilation. Additional feasts find their roots in the Maccabean wars, e.g. the feast of the Re-consecration of the temple, which was celebrated on the 25th of the 9th month, Kislev, to commemorate the purification of the Jerusalem temple by Judas Maccabeus in 164 BCE (see 1 Macc. 4.36-61; 2 Macc. 1.18; 10.5-6 [→ *Hanukkah*])[35], the day of Nicanor, which was celebrated on the 13th day of

33. The feast and sacrificial calendars in Leviticus 23 and Numbers 28–29 have been discussed controversially. The latest consensus is expressed in C. Körting, *Schall*, 95–105 (Leviticus 23 as priestly composition); 211–22 (Numbers 28–29 as 'literary work of a priestly school' (transl.) and one of the latest texts of the Pentateuch; ibid., 213) (above, n. 32)).

34. For the connection of feasts and → *atonement* see E. Otto and T. Schramm, *Fest*, 69–70 (above, n. 30); C. Körting, *Schall*, 91–4, 263–6 (above, n. 32).

35. J. C. VanderKam, 'Hannukah: Its Timing and Significance According to 1 and 2 Maccabees', JSP 1 (1987): 23–40.

the 12th month, Addar, to commemorate the defeat of the Seleucid commander by Judas Maccabeus in 161 BCE (see 1 Macc. 7.26-50; 2 Macc. 15), and finally the feast commemorating the conquest of the Jerusalem citadel by Simon in 141 BCE, which was celebrated on the 23rd of the 2nd month, Ayyar (see 1 Macc. 13.49-52).

## B. New Moon and Shabbat

Apart from the yearly feasts, the New Moon and Shabbat are declared to be festal days (e.g. Amos 8.4-5; 2 Kgs 4.23; 1 Sam. 20.5-42; Ps. 81.4 [NRSV 81.3]; Ezek. 46.1-3; Num 28.11-15), implying that the moon cycle played a specific role in the cultic calendar with regard to feasts that were celebrated *monthly*. The *New Moon* at the beginning of each month was celebrated both in private celebrations (1 Sam. 20.5-42) and at the temple (Ps. 81.4 [NRSV 81.3]; Num. 28.11-15). This custom persisted well into post-exilic times (1 Chr. 23.31; 2 Chr. 2.3 [NRSV 2.4]; Neh. 10.34 [NRSV 10.33]). The *Shabbat*[36] was originally the day of the full moon, returning every month in the middle of the month and, thus, together with the new moon, giving structure to the month. The juxtaposition of New Moon and Shabbat is attested as being both pre-exilic (Hos. 2.13 [NRSV 2.11]; Isa. 1.13) and post-exilic (Ezek. 45.17; Neh. 10.34 [NRSV 10.33]) and reflects the custom of celebrating both the new and the full moon as feast days. At the earliest since the exilic period, the Shabbat was understood in the Old Testament as a *weekly* day of rest falling on the seventh day to commemorate Yhwh. Both versions of the → *Decalogue* (Exod. 20.8-11; Deut. 5.12-15) insist on its observance and, in this way, make it (together with the feast days) an identifying criterion for 'Israel'. As an institution of a day of rest with sacred character, the Shabbat structures everyday life in ever-recurring, short-term cycles of seven days. In deuteronomic theology, the Shabbat is understood to be a commemoration of slavery in Egypt (Deut. 5.12-15), whereas the Shabbat theology of the Priestly Document (Gen. 2.2-3; Exod. 20.11) explains it as connected with Yhwh's creation. The observance of Shabbat is commanded not only in the Decalogue, but also in the → *Covenant Code* (Exod. 23.12) and the cultic Decalogue (Exod. 34.21). In Hellenistic-Roman times, it represented the *single* distinguishing feature of Judaism to such an extent that it was preferable to die for observing the Shabbat than to break it (1 Macc. 2.32-38).

📖 A. Berlejung, 'Heilige Zeiten: Ein Forschungsbericht'. *Jahrbuch Biblische Theologie* 18 (2003): 3–61 (research report); J. A. Wagenaar, *Origin and Transformation of the Ancient Israelite Festival Calendar*. BZAR 6. Wiesbaden: Harrassowitz, 2005.

36. For the Shabbat, see G. F. Hasel, 'Sabbath', *ABD* 5:849–56; G. Robinson, *The Origin and Development of the Old Testament Sabbath* (Bangalore: United Theological College, 1998).

## 3.4 The People and their Dead/ Ancestors: Grave, Burial/Interment, Care for the Dead, Necromancy, Mortuary Cult/Ancestor Worship and Hopes of Resurrection

A. Berlejung, 'Tod und Leben nach den Vorstellungen der Israeliten: Ein ausgewählter Aspekt zu einer Metapher im Spannungsfeld von Leben und Tod'. Pages 465–502 in *Das biblische Weltbild und seine altorientalischen Kontexte*. FAT 32. Ed. by B. Ego and B. Janowski. Tübingen: Mohr Siebeck, 2001; J. Day, 'The Development of Belief in Life after Death in Ancient Israel'. Pages 259–82 in *After the Exile: Essays in Honour of Rex Mason*. Ed. by J. Barton and D. J. Reimer. Macon, Ga.: Mercer University Press, 1996; H. Hizmi and A. de Groot, eds, *Burial Caves and Sites in Judea and Samaria From the Bronze and Iron Ages*. Judea and Samaria Publications 4. Jerusalem: Israel Antiquities Authority, 2004.

Graves going back to the Middle Palaeolithic Age can be studied archaeologically in Palestine and allow glimpses into burial customs. The general custom was to inter the body; the burning of corpses is attested far less often. Already in the Natufian (12,500–9,400 BCE), the types of graves show remarkable variety, and, in the course of time, further differentiation took place, increasingly showing regional specification and adaptation of foreign, e.g. Egyptian, perhaps Philistine(?), Phoenician and Assyrian customs. The choice of burial type was evidently influenced by local features (caves in the rocky highlands, pits in the plains), as well as by local customs and/or perhaps contemporary trends. The graves of the Iron Age in Palestine continue the traditions of burial forms attested in the region during previous periods, especially those of the Late Bronze Age (pits, rock/cave, and chamber graves of various types, sarcophagi in the Egyptian tradition, e.g. from Beth-Shan, and bathtub coffins in the Assyrian tradition, e.g. from Megiddo, Shechem, are also attested. The burial or interment was part of a complex *rite de passage*, including (at least ideally) step-by-step preparations for the death of a relative, treatment of the corpse after death (washing, anointing, clothing, adorning, and laying it out), transfer to the grave, interment itself including the placement of grave goods (amulets, personal objects, food and drink, clothing), the sealing of the tomb, and the subsequent mourning rites. Thus, in a series of steps, the dead person was transferred from the world of the living into the world of the dead.

Those left behind accompanied him for a short and reversible part of the journey, but afterwards they were gradually re-integrated into everyday life by subsequent rites during a seven-day mourning period (1 Sam. 31.13). Burial and, eventually, a secondary burial (= burial of the remaining bones after corruption of the flesh, roughly a year later) and the ongoing care for the dead were tasks of the family, not of cultic personnel. Among the mourning rites attested in the Old Testament are the tearing of one's clothes, the wearing of a hairy mourning garment, fasting, putting ashes or dust on one's head, plucking or shearing one's hair, lamentation (guided by professional wailing women), and sometimes scarification of the skin.

Even after the burial, the deceased person remained part of his social unit. He could be visited and asked for advice (1 Samuel 28); could receive regular commemorative rituals (invocations of the name) and offerings with food and libations, or could share in special meals with the living. The Old Testament explicitly rejects such practices, which are well attested from Syria and Mesopotamia, but the biblical polemic against necromancy (= evocation[37] and consultation of the dead: Deut. 18.11; Lev. 19.31; 20.6, 27; Isa. 8.19; 65.4; 1 Samuel 28) and against offerings for the dead (Deut. 26.14), dating at the earliest from late exilic times (→ *exile*), attest to the fact that in 'Israel' and Judah it was acceptable and indeed customary, at least in the pre-exilic period,[38] to evoke the dead in necromantic rituals and to ask them for advice and support. Even late texts of the → *wisdom* literature emphasize that dead people do not know anything, and that it is thus not worth the trouble to consult them (Eccl. 9.4-6, 10; Job 14.21). On the basis of such texts, it appears that it was still thought necessary in this late period to argue against the convictions, widely prevalent in the Near East, that the dead, although not possessing any physical powers, retained exceptional insights that the living could make use of. After death, appropriate burial, and decomposition of the corpse, the dead were imagined to inhabit a subterranean, dusty and dark netherworld (Hebrew often *šĕ'ôl*). The surviving family members, independent of the social status of the deceased, had to maintain and support the dead person by repeatedly invoking their names and providing them with gifts of food and water (= care for the dead); however, only the highest personages received specific cultic veneration (= cult of the dead/ancestors). To what extent veneration of the type well known from Syria for deceased kings was accorded in 'Israel' to deified or divine ancestors, remains an open question. Cultic installations, such as are found in Iron Age graves, do not clearly prove such a practice; they might also have been

37. 'Evocation' means the calling up of a deceased from the netherworld.

38. With J. Tropper, 'Spirit of the Dead', in *DDD*$^2$:806–9.

intended only for the rituals performed at burial.[39] Repeatedly, in this connection, reference is made to the biblical *rephaim*: it is likely that the deified ancestral kings of the ruling dynasties of Ugarit (and Sidon, 6/5th century), who are also known as *rapi'uma*, are related to these biblical *rephaim* (see, e.g. Isa. 14.9). In Ugarit, but perhaps also in 7/6th-century Judah (Jer. 16.5), the *rephaim* were invited to participate in a banquet with the living at burials, perhaps, however, such banquets with the dead were held regularly, in order to maintain contact with them.

The belief in the resurrection of the individual is only attested from the Hellenistic period on: in the Ethiopic Book of Enoch and within the → *apocalyptic* texts, Dan. 12.2-3 and Isa. 26.19. Under → *Hellenistic* influence and the newly emerging belief in martyrdom, the text of 2 Maccabees 7 mentions both the resurrection of the body to eternal life and the immortality of the soul (2 Macc. 7.9, 14), together with the notion that deeds performed during one's lifetime will be recompensed after death. However, 2 Macc. 12.43-45 attests to the inconsistency of various ideas about resurrection; obviously there existed a broad spectrum of opinions. The dispute over resurrection also affected the factional conflicts between Sadducees and Pharisees: the former denied the resurrection (as Ecclesiastes 3 did); the latter endorsed it.

## 3.5 The Area: Geographical Characteristics of Palestine

Bibliography 2.4 Atlases and Books on Applied Geography (A. F. Rainey and R. S. Notley, eds., *Sacred Bridge*).

Palestine borders in the west on the Mediterranean. To the north, the mountain ridges of the Lebanon and Anti-Lebanon, with the impressive Mount Hermon, present a natural barrier. To the east (including Transjordan), the country gradually changes – due to a gradual decrease in precipitation from west to east – first into a steppe and then into a desert. The same shift occurs in the south – precipitation decreases from north to south – so that agriculture without artificial irrigation is only possible up to the area around Beersheba. Here in the south, the Wādī Gazze and further south again the Wādī l-ʿArīš form natural borders. The biblical formula 'from Dan to

39. Further, T. J. Lewis, *Cults of the Dead in Ancient Israel and Ugarit* (HSM 39; Atlanta, Ga.: Scholars, 1989), 179–81.

Beersheba' (Judg. 20.1; 1 Sam. 3.20 *et al.*), therefore, describes quite accurately the arable land of the southern Levant in its north-south extension. However, one should not imagine the borders with the adjacent regions as being sharply drawn; the transitions toward the steppe and desert regions of the Negev and the Sinai (which does not count as Palestine) in the south, to the Jordanian desert in the east, or to the coastal region of what is now Lebanon and Syria in the north were fluid.

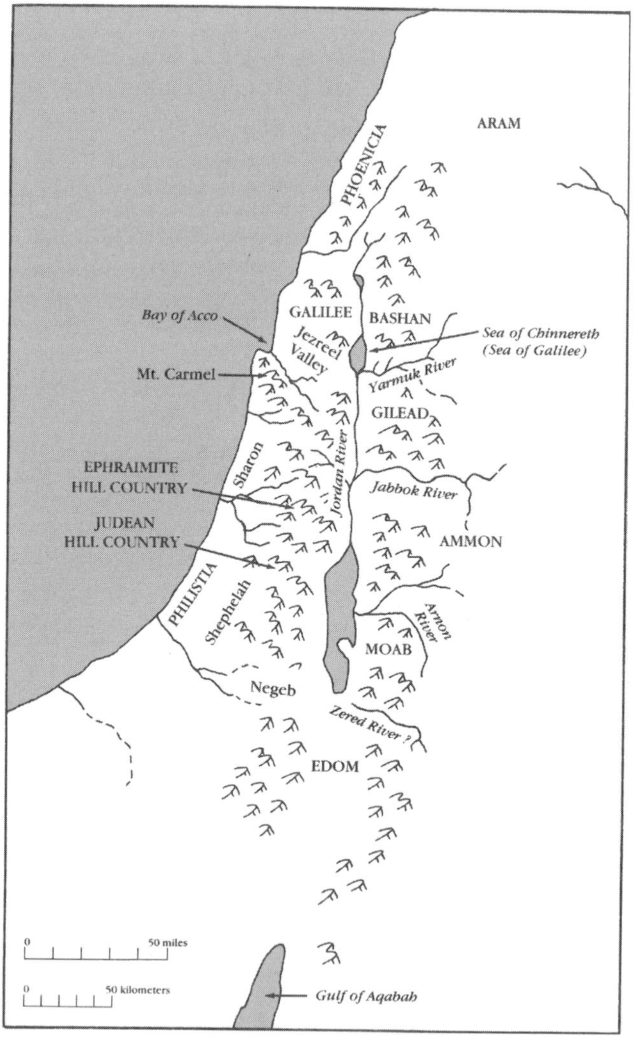


**Fig. 6:** Map of Palestine and its regions.

**Fig. 7:** The principal transit routes of Palestine.

Palestine comprises various regions (**fig. 6**) that differ notably with regard to their economic and infrastructural potential. River valleys and mountain ridges structure the landscape and the living space into small regional units. These geographic micro-zones influence the lifestyle and the cultural identity of their inhabitants. Depending on the amount of precipitation and other factors, the favourable conditions for settlement decrease from north to south and from west to east. The area west of the Jordan begins with a flat (Mt. Carmel being the exception) coastal region in the west, which during the Iron Age was in Phoenician hands in the north and in Philistine hands in the south. People there profited from the Mediterranean trade and the mostly fertile soils of the immediate vicinity. South of the Philistine coast lies the Negev coast, which was of special importance for the trade with Egypt. The relief of Palestine is structured from the coastal plain in the west towards the east as follows: the flat and narrow coastal strip of varying width (widening from north to south) is followed by the central/west Jordanian highlands/mountains (foothills of the Lebanon mountain range) that rise up to 1,000 m. The mountains are followed by a rift valley, which lies nearly everywhere below sea level (Lake Ḥūle, Lake Gennesaret, the Jordan trench, the Dead Sea, and the Wādī l-ʿAraba extending down to the Gulf of Eilat/Aqaba), and then by the mountain ridges of Transjordan with their high plains, reaching to over 1,000 m in height in the North, and up to 1,700 m in the South. Going from north to south, there is a conspicuous division of the central/west Jordanian mountains/highlands into a northern (Galilee) and a southern (Ephraimite and Judean highlands) district, which is caused by the intervening, agriculturally and strategically important Jezreel Valley. South of the Judean mountains/highlands, the hill region gradually gives way to the inhospitable rocky Negev. The area east of Jordan/Transjordan is dominated in the north by Mount Hermon and the foothills of the Anti-Lebanon and is structured by the deep canyons (in sequence from north to south) of the Jarmuk, Jabbok, Arnon and Sered. These canyons create separate regions (from north to south): Bashan, Gilead, Ammon, Moab, and Edom.

The geographic conditions also determine the lie of traffic and trade routes in Palestine. These follow natural features, such as the coastline, the mountain ridges and passes, and the desert fringe (**fig.** 7). As a transitional area between Syria, Anatolia, Mesopotamia, and Egypt, the north-south connection in Palestine was of greatest importance: in times of peace, it was used by traders; in times of war by armies. The most important north-south route was what the Romans used to call later the *via maris*. It started in Egypt, went along the coastline, passing through the Philistine cities (but not through Judah!) in a northerly direction, only to encounter a considerable barrier at the Carmel; this either had to be circumnavigated by passing through the inner part of the country or crossed over via dangerous and narrow passes. Beyond the Carmel, one could travel either via Hazor in a northerly direction towards Qatna or in a northeasterly direction to Damascus, or, if one chose to follow the coastal road again, one could proceed to the north via Acco, Tyre and Sidon on the Mediterranean shore. Another important traffic route was the so-called Kings' Highway that led through the territory east of the Jordan from the Red Sea via Dibon and Heshbon to Damascus. Also important was the mountain road through the territory west of the Jordan, which connected Beersheba, Hebron, Jerusalem, Shechem, and the Jezreel Valley. The ancient Incense Road, in contrast to the aforementioned routes, did not follow a north-south direction, but instead passed from east to west. It came from Arabia via Petra, following the southern fringes of Palestine towards Gaza.

## 3.6 Time: Calendar, Timekeeping and Chronology (again)

Bibliography 4 Bible Dictionaries and Exegetical Reference Books for Old Testament Studies. Further: R. De Vaux, *Ancient Israel: Its Life and Institutions*. Transl. by J. McHugh. Grand Rapids, Mich.: Eerdmans, 1997 (= *Les institutions de l'Ancien Testament I & II,* 1958/1960), 178–94.

The natural units of time and the calendar derived from them are determined by astronomical facts: one day corresponds to the apparent movement of the sun around the earth; one month corresponds to the revolution of the moon around the earth; one year corresponds to the orbiting of the earth around the sun. Some cultures prefer to base their calendar primarily on the lunar months, e.g. Mesopotamia, while others base themselves on the solar year, e.g. Egypt. One lunar year has 354 days, 8 hours, 48 minutes, and 36 seconds. The days missing by comparison to the solar year must then be offset by intercalating additional days or months, so that the calendar year corresponds to the seasonal rhythm determined by the sun. One solar year has 365 days, 5 hours, 48 minutes, and 46.43 seconds.

The (re-)construction of the ancient Israelite or Judean calendars is not easy, because the OT itself contains no calendar as such. Furthermore there are several systems in use for naming the months and for beginning the year (either in autumn or spring). Especially important, as an extra-biblical text, is the so-called Gezer Calendar from the 10th/9th cent.,[40] since it briefly sketches the agricultural year. From this text we know that at this time in Palestine the calendar year started in autumn. When exactly the Babylonian calendar, which begins the year at the equinox in spring, was adapted, remains disputed. Another problem is that one cannot exclude the possibility that the northern kingdom (Israel) and the southern kingdom (Judah) may, at least for some time, have followed different systems. The northern kingdom seems to have adapted the Mesopotamian custom as early as in the 8th cent. during the time of Assyrian hegemony;

40. For the text, see *ANET*, 320.

whereas Judah only adopted this practice much later under Babylonian influence. When exactly the beginning of the year in autumn was abandoned in Judah cannot be fixed precisely, but most likely it was during the reign of Eliakim/ Jehoiakim (609/8–598/7 BCE).[41]

During the post-exilic period (→ *exile*) the calendrical beginning of the year in spring was once again abandoned and (in the 1st cent. CE at the latest)[42] the older tradition of beginning the year in autumn was re-established. Regardless of when the new calendar year was supposed to begin, the course of the year was determined by the two equinoxes, dividing the year at the first and seventh month in two periods of six months each (Exod. 34.22 [autumn equinox], 2 Sam. 11.1 [spring equinox], Ezek. 45.18-20 [LXX!]). The 1st and the 7th months are thus of special importance in the OT festival calendars (Ch. 3.3 Excursus), since they contained the culminating points of the liturgical year. For both the pre-exilic and the post-exilic periods, it is best to assume that a moon calendar with intercalation was in use, although several (P) texts (Gen. 7.11; 8.14; 5.23) indicate that a solar calendar was also known. In the post-exilic and inter-testamental periods, several calendar systems (lunisolar and solar) existed alongside each other. The preference of the → *Qumran* community for the solar calendar meant that the dates of their feasts did not correspond to those in Jerusalem.

For the absolute dating of events, a calendar with cyclically recurring dates alone is of no use; it is necessary, in addition, to have some additional specification for an event that occurred only once and was not repeatable and which needs to be located within a recognized time-frame. For this purpose, dating according to the regnal years of kings is often used. In Egypt, this method of dating was introduced (after some pre-stages) from the 11th dynasty (2080–1937 BCE) onwards; in Babylonia, it was introduced from the Kassite period (about 1531 BCE) onwards; and, in the OT, it also came to be the prevailing practice. This method, however, is also prone to insecurity, when, for instance, co-regencies are concerned or the relationship between the year of the previous king's death and the year of accession of his successor to the throne cannot be determined. The OT knows not only the dating by the regnal years of Israelite or Judean kings (see for example Jer. 25.1, 3; 36.1) that is likewise attested in → *epigraphic* sources such as the → *ostraca* from Samaria[43] and Arad,[44] but

41. See R. De Vaux, *Ancient Israel*, 180–3, 188–93.

42. So E. Otto, 'Neujahrsfest', *Neues Bibel-Lexikon* 2:922–23; idem, 'Neujahr', *Neues Bibel-Lexikon* 2:922; compare also J. A. Wagenaar, *Origin and Transformation of the Ancient Israelite Festival Calendar* (BZAR 6; Wiesbaden: Harrassowitz, 2005), 22–4.

43. F. W. Dobbs-Allsopp *et al.*, *Hebrew Inscriptions*, 423–97.

44. *COS* III, 81–5.

it also uses dating by the ruling years of Babylonian kings (Nebuchadnezzar II, 2 Kgs 24.12; 25.8; Jer. 25.1 etc.; Evil-Merodach, 2 Kgs 25.27; Jer. 52.31) and Persian rulers (Hag. 1.1; Zech. 1.1). In this way it provides pointers to an inner-biblical synchronistic chronology: using synchronizations between Palestine, Egypt and Mesopotamia, it becomes possible to fit together the isolated dates mentioned in the sources into a relative chronological system comprising the whole Ancient Near East with many equations but also a considerable number of unknowns. The latter can be reduced by correlation with data from datable written sources, astronomical dates, pottery dating, and coins (if available), with stratigraphic results, and dating methods based on the natural sciences (see Ch. 2.2 Excursus). Nevertheless, it should be noted that, for the pre-Hellenistic period, there are practically no fixed benchmarks available that would allow one to fix beyond doubt the relative chronology with absolute dates. In general, for absolute dates in Palestine one must reckon with variations of from one to several years for dates in the 1st mill. BCE; with up to a few decades in the 2nd mill. BCE; and in the 3rd mill. BCE, upwards of 100 years. The further one goes back in time, the greater the possible variation. (For chronology, see Table Appendix I.)

# 4

# General and Religious History of 'Israel': A Historical Survey

(Angelika Berlejung – Translation by Thomas Riplinger

## Chapter Outline



## 4.1 The End of the Late Bronze Age (LB Age)

Bibliography 6.3 Archaeology and Iconography; 8 The History of Ancient Israel and Judah. Further: A. Killebrew, *Biblical Peoples and Ethnicity: An Archaeological Study of Egyptians, Canaanites, Philistines, and Early Israel, 1300–1100 BCE* Atlanta: SBL, 2005.

### 4.1.1 Society and Economy: The End of Egyptian Dominion over the Province of Canaan and the City-State Kingdoms

After an initial period of prosperity, the *Late Bronze Age* (1550–1200/1150 BCE), in which the urbanization of Palestine reached its highpoint, gradually slipped into an unstable period marked by the progressive decline not only of the city-state kingdoms under Egyptian dominion but also of the major empires themselves (Hittites, Egyptians, Mitanni), which had dominated the Near East in the second half of the 2nd millennium BCE (**fig. 8**).

During the time that the city-states of the coast and the lowlands of Palestine were under Egyptian control, the highlands in the LB Age were by and large a no-man's-land. Into this retreat area, various declassed population groups withdrew, which together were called Ḫapiru (identical with the *ʿApirū* mentioned in Egyptian and Akkadian texts since the end of the 3rd millennium and derived etymologically from ʿIbrī = Hebrews). There they formed small bands that lived from the surpluses of the city-states, which they time and again raided, so that they came to be regarded by the settled populace as a danger. In the Palestinian highlands on both sides of the Jordan, other groups of tent-dwelling pastoral groups organized in clans increasingly made their appearance, groups called Shasu in the Egyptian sources. These local nomadic groups often took over the abandoned villages (especially in the south) and practised there a → *subsistence economy* based on stockbreeding and agriculture. The majority of scholars today believe that these local nomadic clans in the course of the 13th and 12th centuries under Egyptian pressure increasingly merged with the Ḫapiru to form tribes. Pharaoh Merneptah (1213–1204 BCE) during his expedition against Palestine in 1208 BCE not only attacked the city-states of Ashkelon, Gezer etc. but also took on the non-urbanized population elements, namely the settlers of the tribe of 'Israel', who inhabited the villages and hamlets in the central and northern Palestinian highlands. Against them, he fought the battle described in his 'Israel Stela' (Ch. 3.2.1).[1] If the Pharaoh is to be taken at his word, that was the end of a very short history of 'Israel'. More than likely, however, like his predecessors, he simply returned to Egypt from this expedition with some prisoners of war (as from other Asian campaigns). This might explain the historical background of the presence in Egypt of a tribal group with the name 'Israel'. The Egyptian deportation practice normally affected only a part of the conquered population, so that this fate need not have affected all of the tribally organized farmers and herders of the central and northern Palestinian high country. Those who remained behind could thus become the fathers and mothers of the territorial states of Israel and Judah.

During the 13th century, new peoples made their appearance, among them the Aramaeans from the upper Ḫabūr-area and the Ṭur ʿAbdin or the 'Sea Peoples' from the Aegean, who involved the Egyptians and Hittites in warlike conflicts, which increasingly destabilized the region and marked the beginning of the Iron Age.

1. *COS* II, 40–1.

**Fig. 8:** Map of Syria and Palestine in the Late Bronze Age.

There is archaeological evidence for the destruction of many cities of the region around 1200 BCE (e.g. Hazor, Megiddo, Beth-Shan and Gezer). Responsibility can be assigned to various agents: (1) local princes battling out rivalries between the different Canaanite city-states; (2) Egyptian pharaohs of the 19th and 20th Dynasties carrying out expeditions against rebellious city kings in their former province; (3) indigenous Palestinian Ḫapiru or Shasu in their efforts to gain from the general chaos; (4) the 'Sea Peoples' on the way to the riches of Egypt. Most likely, shifting combinations of all four elements were at work. Archaeology makes it possible to verify the destruction of the cities in the 13th and 12th centuries, but it does not identify who was responsible. Whoever destroyed the cities of the Egyptian province of Canaan, the decline of this province had many causes and had already begun earlier.

## 4.1.2 Religion and Worship: The International Character of the Gods and the Dominance of Male Gods in the City Pantheons and City Temples

In the *Late Bronze Age*, as in the preceding Middle Bronze Age, temple complexes are found in cities and villages, as well as open worship areas

(Naharīyā LB I, Hazor), and places of private worship in dwellings. As usual, sacral architecture and → *iconography* reveals both the continuation of older traditions and the reception of new practices. In this period, the long-room temple with an inner sanctuary came to prevail (Hazor upper city since the MB Age IIC; Hazor lower city Area H) after the Syrian model. Nevertheless it was above all the Egyptian dominion that marked the province of Canaan and its worship. The Egyptian influence can, for instance, be recognized in the strong presence of Egyptian gods in the land.

In this connection, the temple of Hathor in Timna or her temple in Ṣerābiṭ el-Ḫādim (Sinai) deserve mention. Hathor, the goddess of beauty, of love and of foreign lands, is particularly well attested in southern Palestine, but she found her way far into the northern parts of the province of Canaan. In the LB Age, numerous Syro-Palestinian goddesses are represented in the style of Hathor, e.g. with cow horns, curly hair with a centre-parting, a horned crown with the sun-disk. As indicated by the ivories of Megiddo, the Egyptians also brought into Palestine Amun, Ptah, Maat, Re-Harachte and the grotesque God Bes, who, according to the seal-amulets of the Iron Age, evidently enjoyed considerable popularity. All in all, the Palestinian stamp seal-amulets reveal strong Egyptian influence and can well be regarded as the entrepôt for Egyptian religious influences in day-to-day living and in the private piety of individuals.

On the other hand, the Egyptians themselves participated in the worship of Palestinian deities. Thus one can observe that the intercultural contacts of the period led to a mutual exchange in the world of divinities: the originally Syro-Palestinian deities are egyptianized, and the originally Egyptian deities take on Syro-Palestinian characteristics. Often, the different deities are merged in function, symbolism and attributes (so for instance Baal with Seth), leading to an iconographic combination of elements originally having nothing to do with each other and to a theological transformation of the god's profile. Concerning the iconography of the native Palestinian divinities, one can observe how the motif of an enthroned or standing god, which had been rare in the MB Age, becomes the predominating motif in the LB Age bronze statuary, whereby the evidence shows that the image of the god of the smiting Baal/Hadad type takes priority among the bronze effigies found throughout the land (Megiddo, Lachish etc.). This impression is confirmed by the West Semitic personal names from Palestine, which are found in the Tell el-ʿAmārna-correspondence.[2] The warlike aspect of

2. These names manifest the dominance of Baal/Hadad/Addu as a theophoric element in names

the god (and of the ruler) is emphasized in this period as befits the war-torn political relationships of the period. Bronze images of goddesses, on the other hand, are found much less often. In contrast to earlier times, they are clothed in courtly dress. Their gesture marks them as authoritarian or warlike persons, corresponding by and large to the domination posture of the male deities. The naked goddesses of the earlier periods, whose gestures emphasize erotic aspects, are found from the LB Age on only in the form of metal pendants or cheap clay figurines or plaques. One can interpret this situation as an indication that the development begun in the Chalcolithic Period comes to a provisional peak in the LB Age. Whereas the official worship of the cities and city-states, as determined by the locally ruling men (indicated for instance by the attested personal names with → *theophoric elements*) is increasingly marked by their alliance with male deities, the goddesses continue to enjoy their former importance only in the local and private worship of this epoch.

## The Northwest Semitic Pantheon of the 2nd Millennium

In the pantheons of the city-states of Syria in the 3rd and 2nd millennia, various deities of very diverse origin (e.g. Sumerian, Hurrite, Semitic) were worshipped, as one sees especially from the literary texts from Ebla, Emar and Ugarit. The theological structure of the Ugarit pantheon of the 2nd millennium, as it is attested in the myths, is marked by the divine couple El (god of creatio+n and sustaining power) and Asherah (goddess of birthing and regenerating power, 'fruitfulness', also called Qudšu 'holiness') together with their children, the siblings Baal/Hadad (god of the weather, storms, rain, of seafaring, and, in general, of dynamic-aggressive power) and Anath (goddess with wild-warlike aspects, a huntress, foster-mother of kings and warriors – the earlier attribution of fertility aspects to her is now questioned (P. L. Day). Astarte (to be identified with the Mesopotamian Ishtar) was a fertility goddess with both warlike and erotic aspects. In addition, there were the two opponents of Baal, Mōt ('death', the one who threatens life, god of the underworld, summer heat, and ripe grain) and Yammu (the 'sea'), together with the Ugarit Hephaestus, Koṯar-wa-ḫasīs ('skilled and clever'). Lists of sacrifices and liturgical texts mention a wide variety of other divinities, the most important of which are the sun, Šapšu, which in Ugarit was feminine, and the moon Yari(ḫ) (known in the Mesopotamian area as Sin), who was masculine. The grain god Dagan is also attested as the father of Baal, having replaced El as the leading figure of the pantheon in the course of the 2nd millennium. The → *chthonic*

⇨

used by the upper classes of Palestine: see R. S. Hess, *Amarna Personal Names* (ASOR Dissertation Series 9; Winona Lake, Ind.: Eisenbrauns, 1993).

god Resheph counted as the cause of, but also as the protector against sickness. Likewise the divinized ancestors (Rapi'uma, see Ch. 3.4) could help against sickness.

There is disagreement about the extent to which the urban pantheon of the port city Ugarit in the middle of a rain-fed agricultural area can be generalized as a model for the religion of Palestine in the 2nd millennium. Place names there point to the sun-god Šamaš (Beth-Shemesh), the god of the evening light or the evening star Šalim (Jerusalem), the moon-god Yariḫ (Jericho), the chthonic god Horon (Beth-Horon), the grain-god Dagon (Beth-Dagon) and the weather-god Baal. As goddesses, Astarte (Ashtaroth) and Anath (Beth-Anath) are attested to. The latter appears to have played an especially important role in the Egyptian military posts Gaza and Beth-Shan towards the end of the 2nd millennium BCE. From Beth-Shan, two stelae of the LB Age with representations of Anath are known. Like the city-god of Beth-Shan, Mkl represented on another stela, Anath is portrayed here in Egyptian style. Iconographically, a large number of gods and goddesses are attested in Palestine for the 2nd millennium BCE, though unlike Mkl and Anath from Beth-Shan they are seldom identified by name through accompanying texts or otherwise brought together with divinities epigraphically (→ *epigraphy*) named.

# 4.2 From Iron Age[3] I to Iron Age IIC (ca. 1200/1150–587/6 BCE)

Bibliography 6.3 Archaeology and Iconography (I. Finkelstein, *Archaeology*; Z. Herzog, *Archaeology*; H. Weippert, *Palästina*, 344–681); 8 The History of Ancient Israel and Judah (G. Ahlström, *History*, 371–803; E. Pfoh, *Emergence*); 9 History of Religion of Ancient Israel (O. Keel/C. Uehlinger, *GGG*, 61–215); Further: R. D. Miller II, *Chieftains of the Highland Clans: A History of Israel in the 12th and 11th Centuries B.C.* Grand Rapids: Eerdmans, 2005.

## 4.2.1 Economy and Society: The Period of De-Urbanization and Settlement Growth, the Development of Tribes, Cities, Territorial States and Provinces

*1. Iron Age I (1200/1150–1000 BCE[4]).* Around 1200 BCE, the already weakened

3. Despite the nomenclature, iron is already found in the LB Age, and it gained large-scale economic importance only around the 10th cent. BCE.
4. On the end of the Iron Age I, see however Ch. 2.2.

Hittite Empire quickly came to an end due to famines, internal disturbances, and the incursions of the Sea Peoples. Not only the northern and middle Syrian territories were lost; even the capital Ḫattuša was destroyed. The Egyptian New Kingdom under the pharaohs of the 19th and 20th Dynasties managed once more to escape these dangers. Ramesses III (1187–1156 BCE) settled the Philistines (one of the Sea Peoples) in the southern coastal zone from Gaza to Jafo as a bulwark against other encroaching 'Sea People', thereby more or less willingly surrendering Egyptian influence in the economically important region. The Philistines quickly took control of the cities Gaza, Ashkelon, Ashdod, Ekron, Gath and Tell Qasīle and established themselves as the predominant upper class. They did not move further northwards but attempted to extend their influence into the interior. In the Iron Age, their cities dominated the southern coastal area and the Shephelah, where they resisted the general trend toward de-urbanization in the interior during Iron Age I. Ramesses III made various efforts to hold the Canaanite province: in Beth-Shan, he re-established a garrison; in Megiddo, the palace was restored. The end of the Egyptian province of Canaan is generally associated with the destruction of Lachish after Ramesses III, around 1150 BCE; however, the base of a statue shows that Ramesses VI (1145–1137 BCE) was present in Megiddo some years later. Thus, although the exact date of the end of Egyptian supremacy in Palestine remains controversial, it is generally recognized that the 12th cent. BCE (= Iron Age IA) was a time of Egyptian retreat in Palestine, generally marked – with local variations – by progressive de-urbanization, recession and impoverishment, so that the trend toward depression already evident in the LB Age continued to manifest itself. In this transition period, people shifted increasingly into a half- or non-sedentary way of life, indicated archaeologically by the evident reduction of the number of cities and settlements in the lowlands and the village character of the settlements which replaced the destroyed cities (when such successor settlements are present at all). By contrast, traces of settlement and (somewhat later) hamlets and villages are more often found in the highlands. The houses there are simple and functionally structured for pastoralists (direct entrance into the court, then into the building). Rare are the new foundations of fortified cities in Iron Age I, though they do occur. An example is the case of Kinneret linked with the settlement of the Aramaean tribe Geshur,[5] which established its local chiefdom

5. W. Dietrich and S. Münger, 'Zentrum und Peripherie – Die früheisenzeitliche Stadt Kinneret und ihr regionaler Kontext', in *Leben am See Gennesaret: Kulturgeschichtliche Entdeckungen in einer biblischen Region* (ed. G. Faßbeck, S. Fortner *et al.*; Mainz: Zabern, 2003), 43–6.

at the Sea of Galilee (**fig. 9**). Nevertheless, the former urban culture was not entirely lost; it persisted in the Philistine and Phoenician coastal cities and in places on the Beth-Shan Plain. The decline to village character did not take place there at all, and in Megiddo[6] it did not last long. When one considers the architecture and pottery of the successors of the destroyed settlements as well as of the new foundations of the 12th and 11th centuries, it becomes clear that in one and the same settlement, both continuity (e.g. still courtyard houses [Bethel, Ḫirbet el-Mšāš], carinated bowls) and change (new wall construction methods, pillared houses [Bethel], three- and four-room houses (**fig. 10**)[7] [Ḫirbet el-Mšāš], a new type of storage jar, the 'collared rim jar'[8]). Because these innovations appear to have originated in the villages of the central highlands, these findings are taken to mean that the settlers from these regions peacefully associated with the descendants of the former city-dwellers. Occasionally, it is argued that the new house types, construction techniques, and jar styles are typically 'Israelite',[9] however, on the basis of the discovery of the same 'specifica' in the region east of the Jordan and elsewhere, this opinion is now obsolete. All in all, it is problematical to attempt to bring together the findings of settlement history with ethnic and political categories. In place of ethnic models of explanation, more and more socio-economic interpretations are coming to the fore, explaining the changes as the result of the needs of rural societies with agrarian orientation. It is worthy of mention that, in this period, the older, LB Age urban culture mingles with the younger, Iron Age village traditions, and that a culturally specific differentiation between middle and northern Palestine, on the one hand, and southern Palestine, on the other, comes to the fore, which will be intensified in the later Iron Age.

6. H. M. Niemann, 'Kern-Israel im samarischen Bergland und seine zeitweilige Peripherie: Megiddo, die Jesreelebene und Galiläa im 11. bis 8. Jh. v.Chr: Archäologische Grundlegung, biblische Spiegelung und historische Konsequenzen', UF 35 (2003) [2004]: 421–85.

7. These houses consist of a broad-room (= dwelling area and stalls), with a court in front, which is divided by pillars into a covered area (working place) and an open area. When the broad-room is undivided, one speaks of a 'three-room house', the areas of the courtyard counting as two separate rooms; when the courtyard is divided into three separate spaces, one speaks of a 'four-room house'.

8. The neck of these ca. 1 m high storage jars shows a distinctive bulging collar around the rim, hence the name.

9. On this problem, see A. Mazar, 'From 1200 to 850 BCE: Remarks on Some Selected Archaeological Issues', in *Israel in Transition: From Late Bronze II to Iron IIa (c. 1250–850 BCE) 1. The Archaeology* (ed. L. L. Grabbe; New York: T&T Clark, 2008), 86–120, here 86–98.

**Fig. 9:** Map of the Early Iron age.

Having named the major events which will determine the course of the following period, namely the withdrawal of the Egyptians, the arrival of the Philistines in the south, and the penetration of the Aramaeans into the northern parts of Palestine, it is now time to sketch the events which took place in the region lying between these two spheres of influence:

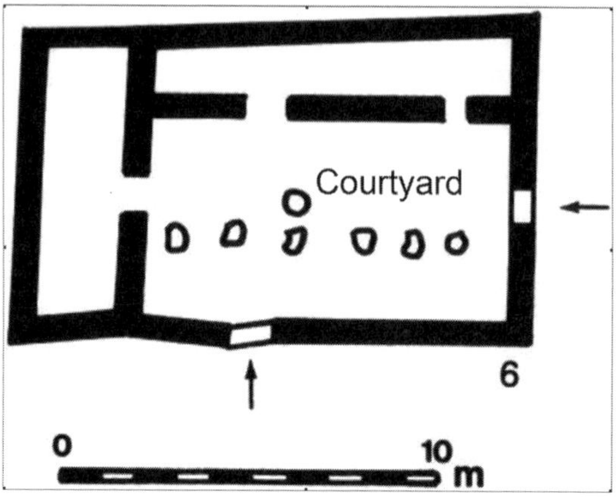


**Fig. 10:** Floor plan of a house with four rooms in Ḫirbet el-Mšāš.

## Excursus: Exodus and the 'Conquest'

**Exodus**: 'Israel', the Philistines, and the Aramaeans all entered the scene about the same time (Amos 9.7). Despite Deut. 26.5 'A wandering Aramaean was my ancestor', the Iron Age tribes of Palestine have nothing to do with the Aramaeans, but all the more to do with the inhabitants of the former Egyptian province of Canaan. Concerning the appearance of these tribes in the area west of the Jordan, there are a variety of hypotheses, which traditionally have been discussed under the term 'conquest'. Because in the Old Testament the 'conquest' by the people of 'Israel' (Ch. 3.2.1) is connected with the exodus, the discussion should begin with this point.

Subsequent to the older, uncritical acceptance of the account given by the OT, the first attempts to (re-)construct the historical events continued to presuppose that the people 'Israel' moved from Egypt, through the desert, into Palestine. Today there is general agreement that by no means the whole people 'Israel', but at best only a small portion had once been in Egypt and had fled from there. It is likewise agreed that the exodus cannot be separated from the person of Moses (Ch. 7.6.3 Excursus: Moses). This group, having fled from Egypt, appears to have become absorbed into the later tribes, to whom it communicated its faith in the experience of deliverance through Yhwh. It is possible, however, that the Egypt of the exodus did not in fact refer to Egypt in the geographical sense, but rather to Egypt in a political sense, so that a migration from southern Palestinian city-states could be interpreted as an exodus from Egypt. In this case, there would be no need to look for the presence of Asian Semites in Egypt proper, which would otherwise have constituted the logical presupposition for an exodus. Egyptian sources for the New Kingdom offer various indications pointing to the presence of Asians in Egypt as prisoners of war, economic refugees, slaves, migratory workers, mercenaries, or other victims of LB Age traffic in human beings. Extra-biblical sources for an exodus, however, do not exist.

**The 'Conquest':** 1. One model, reckoning with a warlike replacement of the urban culture of the province of Canaan by a village culture, is the model of conquest and immigration that corresponds to the account given in the book of Joshua. According to this model, the people 'Israel' had nothing to do with the 'Canaanites', whom they slaughtered at the command of God in various battles and whose land they occupied. This account not only contradicts the archaeological evidence of cultural continuity between the LB Age and Iron Age I, but also fails to fit intra-biblical traditions such as Judg. 1.16-36 with its 'negative list of possessions' ('negatives Besitzverzeichnis') – so Albrecht Alt (1883–1956) – listing the cities that could not be conquered. Concerning the ritualized wars with Jericho and Ai in Joshua 2; 6; and 8, which, in the light of archaeological findings, could never have taken place historically, compare Ch. 7.6.3.2.

2. Another model, reckoning this time with a peaceful transition from the urban culture of the province of Canaan to a village culture is the infiltration model (or territorial occupation model of Albrecht Alt).[10] In the course of their yearly wanderings between grazing areas (transhumance), herding local nomads from the desert areas peacefully entered the land and settled down on the margins of the agricultural areas (= 'Israelites'). Warlike conflicts between these 'Israelite' bands and the city-states arose only when the tribes had become strong enough and sought to expand their territories. This thesis fails, however, for several reasons. In the whole highland region, a settlement process is evident that in purely numerical terms cannot be explained by nomadic groups. Moreover, archaeological findings show that during Iron Age I new villages were founded in the lowlands as well, so that the new agrarian settlers evidently were not confined to marginal areas. Furthermore, the presuppositions of an opposition between 'nomads' and 'settlers' have been shown to be false, since in Palestine, from antiquity to the present, the transition from the one to the other style of life has often been fluid and cooperation between representatives of the two groups can often be observed.

3. The revolutionary occupation model (George E. Mendenhall; Norman K. Gottwald)[11] postulates that the lower classes of the LB Age city population took refuge in the highlands, where they established a new village society. This inner-Canaanite, revolutionary anti-urban movement was reinforced or perhaps even led by the exodus-group, which had come out of Egypt and succeeded in making its belief in the liberating God Yhwh plausible to their comrades-in-arms. This view is linked, however, by N. Gottwald among others, with social-romantic notions of the

⇨

10. A. Alt, 'Die Landnahme der Israeliten in Palästina, 1925', in *Kleine Schriften zur Geschichte des Volkes Israel I* (München: Beck, 1953), 89–125.

11. G. E. Mendenhall, *The Tenth Generation: The Origins of the Biblical Tradition* (Baltimore: Johns Hopkins University Press, 1973); N. K. Gottwald, *The Tribes of Yahweh. A Sociology of the Religion of Liberated Israel 1250-1050* BCE (Maryknoll, N.Y.: Orbis, 1979).

egalitarian structure of the early tribal constitutions for which there is no evidence whatsoever. Nevertheless, it has the advantage of explaining the archaeologically attested cultural continuity between the LB Age and Iron Age I, though it encounters the problem that the innovations of the Iron Age settlements can hardly be explained exclusively on the basis of a continuation of the urban culture of the LB Age.

4. By and large, the current discussion starts with the inner-Palestinian situation toward the end of the LB Age in order to explain what happened in Iron Age I. Since the biblical texts are not valuable historical sources for this period (Ch. 7.6.3.2), the archaeological findings showing both continuity and innovation between the two epochs, play a major role in this discussion. In particular, however, the identity of the people who founded the new village culture remains controversial. They could have been former city dwellers. who founded the new settlements (see Model 3; without the revolution hypothesis: Niels P. Lemche); they could also, however, have been a non-sedentary people (not necessarily from the desert), who, during a long period of economic symbiosis, gradually had taken over the culture of the city-states and, after the collapse of the latter, turned sedentary (Volkmar Fritz, Israel Finkelstein). A combination of these two positions is also conceivable and is the position taken here. In this view, the socio-political development of the LB Age/ Iron Age IA led to migration of the native population from the lowland cities into the highlands, where they settled together with Ḫapiru and Shasu (Ch. 4.1.1), who in the LB Age had occupied the otherwise unsettled territories. There, in Iron Age I, they formed the agricultural clans and tribes, from which the later tribal-states would develop. These tribes consisted of ethnically inhomogeneous groups that in large part consisted of former inhabitants of the city-states, i.e. 'Canaanites'. This anti-urban process did not take place everywhere and at the same time, and it extended well into the 10th century. The advantage of this model is that it accounts for the continuity of language (Hebrew is a Canaanite language) and culture (pottery, house architecture, → *iconography*), which exists between the early Iron Age tribes and the LB Age city-states, while explaining at the same time the transformations. The 'conquest' was thus an internal migration from the lowlands into the highlands, leading to the settlement of the latter. It consisted thus of a movement of people from the cities into a large number of villages.

📖 Bibliography 8 The History of Ancient Israel and Judah; Further: I. Finkelstein and N. Na'aman, 'Introduction: From Nomadism to Monarchy – the State of Research in 1992'. Pages 9–17 in *From Nomadism to Monarchy: Archaeological and Historical Aspects of Early Israel*. Jerusalem: Yad Izhak Ben-Zvi, 1994; N. Na'aman, 'The "Conquest of Canaan" in the Book of Joshua and in History'. Pages 218–81 in *ibid*.

With the archaeologically demonstrated growth of settlement of the highlands during Iron Age IB, the small settlements gradually grew into villages and the villages into regional centres. However diverse the origins of the new settlers may have been, they gradually formed into clans, tribes and tribal associations led by chieftains. Though many questions remain open, it is certain that the new population maintained the cultural heritage that had developed in Palestine. Concerning the social structure and the life of the tribes in the land, there is little source material to go on. It could well be that the book of Judges, when critically read, in fact preserves historical reminiscences of a time in which individual chieftains (Hebr.: *šōpĕṭîm,* falsely translated as 'judges') gained significant power (Gideon: Judg. 6–8) and created small tribal-states (Abimelech: Judges 9), which either made arrangements with their neighbors or attempted to cross swords with them (Judges 5). However, despite the redactional framing given in the book of Judges, there was no overarching superstructure embracing the whole of 'Israel'; each tribe was politically and militarily dependent upon the initiative of its leader (as one sees in the individual stories of the book of Judges). However, this does not exclude the possibility that, in the face of common danger, several tribes might unite in temporary alliances (Judges 5).

## The Organization of Agrarian Societies

Since earliest times, human social structure has been shaped by the family as a community of ancestry and descendence. Several families together constituted a clan. Regional political associations of clans with a chieftain or elder, often surrounded by a council of elders (clan chieftains) together constituted a tribe. The tribe is the political organization of non-urban society, whether this consists of settled or mobile farmers or stockbreeders. The name of a tribe may be derived from the name of the clan of the first chieftain who assumed leadership of the clan association, or the tribe may take its name from the geographic region in which the tribe's clans dwell (so Gilead, Ephraim). The social relations within a tribe are regulated by kinship structures. In this connection, genealogies play a major role, though they may not always represent real (i.e. biological) lineage, but instead may bring to expression the hierarchy of the clans or the tribes with respect to each other. Questions of justice are generally resolved on the basis of customary law, the rules of which have been handed down to all of the members of the group from their childhood (enculturation). The supreme judge in cases of conflict is the head of the family, of the clan or of the tribe, depending on the level on which the misdeed took place (Ch. 6.2 Excursus); there is no centrally organized judiciary.

2. In *Iron Age IIA (1000–926/900 BCE or 950/900–800/785/748 BCE[12])*, important changes took place. After the collapse of the Middle Assyrian Empire in the 11th century, Mesopotamia was organized anew. Under Ashur-dan II (934–912 BCE), the Neo-Assyrian Empire began to take form, though, for the time being, it did not threaten the west. The interior of Syria during this period was marked by the growing influence of the Aramaeans, who, after their first appearance on the scene (see above), gradually gained power and formed diverse tribal-kingdoms (= Aramaean states). Even in Palestine, an Aramaean tribal-kingdom formed around the Sea of Galilee: From the 10th cent. BCE on, a city some 6 ha large existed in Beth-Saida at the northern end of the Sea of Galilee; its palace structures, cultic installations, and city fortifications show the influence of Syrian culture. Probably, the city should be assigned to the Aramaean tribal-kingdom of Geshur, which fell victim to the expansion of Aram-Damascus into the lake district from the 9th cent. BCE on (1 Kgs 15.20). Much earlier (1st half of the 10th century), the Geshurite city Kinneret IV had been abandoned. Contrary to the biblical account which attributes the area to the tribe of Naphtali in the course of the 'conquest' (Josh. 19.35), this area was under Aramaean control in the 10th and 9th centuries, a situation which changed only temporarily in the course of the 8th century. (see below). The Syrian and northern Palestinian coastal region continued to be in Phoenician hands. Since ca. 1050 BCE, the Phoenicians, who can be seen as the heirs and transmitters of the LB Age urban culture (city-states with local dynasties and pantheons), had begun to acquire land in Palestine and Cyprus and later started the colonization of the Mediterranean coastal area by establishing trading posts (e.g. Malta and others) and founding cities. This led once again to the erection of an international economic system centred around the Mediterranean Sea. In the 10th cent. BCE, the kings of Tyre and Byblos were the principal exponents of the Phoenician long-distance trading monopoly. The southern coast of Palestine continued to be dominated by the Philistine cities. Phoenician economic expansion spread increasingly into the Syrian hinterland and into the middle and southern Palestinian coastal area. An important sign of the role of the Phoenicians in the ensuing development is not only the spread of Cypro-Phoenican pottery but also the reception of the Phoenician script by the cultures of the region and in the developing small states (Ch. 1.2.3).

In the archaeology of Palestine, Iron Age IIA generally is characterized as a time of re-urbanization (= renewal of urban culture), even though a clear

12. See the discussion of absolute dates in the chronology in Ch. 2.2.

north-south divide is evident. As in earlier epochs, the re-urbanization began in the centres that had preserved urban traditions during the transitional period. Given the nature of the case, these were the coastal region and the north. With respect to settlement development and population density, the Judean highlands were well behind northern Palestine and the southern coastal plains during Iron Age I and IIA. Whereas in the northern parts of Palestine the re-urbanization process had begun already in the 10th cent. BCE and the highland regions increasingly opened up to the coastal regions, this did not happen in the south until the 9th cent. BCE (see e.g. Lachish). In this differential development, the geographical proximity of northern Palestine to the Phoenician coastal cities undoubtedly played a major role. Effects of this economic impulse moving into northern Palestine from the west are the abandonment of the small settlements in the highlands, the increasing foundation of cities, and the development of villages into cities. Further indications are the revival of LB Age urban culture in Megiddo in the 10th century and the founding of the northern kingdom of Israel in the 1st half of the 9th century, followed, not long after, by the rise of Ammon and Moab (Edom a century later) in Transjordan. Only somewhat later did this influence reach southern Palestine, leading to the foundation of the state of Judah around the middle or end of the 9th cent. BCE. That the development from village culture and tribal chiefdoms (Iron Age IA), over settlement agglomerations and urban foundations, to tribal-kingdoms and kingdoms representing tribal-confederations (Iron Age IIA) and ultimately to full-fledged territorial states (as political organizational forms of urban societies; Iron Age IIB) could proceed so quickly in Palestine, is due to a variety of factors:

1. At this time, Palestine was not under the political dominion of any neighbouring major power.
2. In a development starting in the north and at the coast, it was possible to profit from the Phoenician economic upturn. This motivated the – till then only locally operating – tribal societies of the highlands first to increasing economic interaction with the valleys, then to the establishment of cities as commercial centres and migration thereto, and finally to supra-regional political amalgamation.
3. Re-urbanization, administration, and even kingship could build upon traditions of the LB Age in many places (e.g. Beth-Shan, Rehob, Megiddo, the coastal region), where they had never been extinguished. It is important to note, however, that although it was possible to build on the late LB Age city-state tradition, this tradition was significantly modified and further developed in Iron Age IIAB by the development of territorial states.

## The Formation of States in the Northern Kingdom of Israel and the Southern Kingdom of Judah:

Archaeologically, a process of settlement concentration and re-urbanization is manifest in Iron Age IIA. Nevertheless, it is not possible to establish clearly whether this process already corresponded, on the political level, to the development of territorial states with kings, capital cities, officials and supra-regional administration. An architecture characteristic of sovereignty, going beyond local dimensions and structures of administration (e.g. indicated by written documents), as signs of statehood has not yet been found for the 10th cent. BCE. Neither is there evidence of any building activity clearly pointing to a centrally planning and acting institution.[13] The archaeological findings in this connection reveal extremely modest conditions and indicate that in Iron Age IIA history began with the evolution of village culture and tribal chiefdoms into agglomerated settlements and revived cities with tribal-kingdoms or tribal-confederation kingdoms, whereas states in the proper sense (as political organizations of urban societies) only arose in the 9th cent. BCE and only then become recognizable in the material culture of Palestine. The cities of Iron Age IIA do not compare in size with those of the late Bronze Age. Jerusalem, for example, occupied only ca. 4 ha (suggesting a population of ca. 1,000), so that it is logically excluded that it should be seen as a central capital city, which, according to the biblical account, ruled over the early kingdom of Saul and over the united monarchy of the northern and southern kingdoms under David and Solomon in the 10th century, having its seat in Jerusalem – to say nothing of the large empire over which these kings are said to have ruled from Jerusalem. According to his own testimony, Pharaoh Shishak I marched in 926 (or 920/917[14]) BCE from Gaza via Gezer

13. The often-cited examples of Solomon's central building policy, Hazor X, Gezer VIII, and Megiddo VA/IVB belong in the 9th century: see I. Finkelstein, 'Omride Architecture', *ZDPV* 116 (2000): 114–38. The same holds for the '*large stone structure*', which Eilat Mazar excavated in Jerusalem, dating it to around 1000 BCE and identifying it with David's palace. See now I. Finkelstein, Z. Herzog *et al.*, 'Has King David's Palace in Jerusalem Been Found?' TA 34 (2007): 142–64. These walls belong to the remains of *several* buildings, which date from the 9th cent. BCE on into Hellenistic times.

The Negev fortifications of the 11th, 10th, and 9th centuries, which Helga Weippert among others interpreted as a kind of *limes* of the Davidic-Solomonic Empire (H. Weippert, *Palästina in vorhellenistischer Zeit.* [Handbuch der Archäologie, Vorderasien 2.1.; München: Beck, 1988], 484), have more recently been reinterpreted as refuges for the nomadic tribes of the region: see I. Finkelstein, 'The Iron Age "Fortresses" of the Negev – Sedentarization of Desert Nomads', *ErIsr* 18 (1985): 366–79.

14. See A. J. Shortland, 'Shishak, King of Egypt: The Challenge of Egyptian Calendrical Chronology', in *The Bible and Radiocarbon Dating: Archaeology, Text and Science* (ed. T. E. Levy and T. Higham; London: Equinox, 2005), 43–54.

to Megiddo with incursions into the interior (fragment of a stela from Megiddo[15]), without mentioning (contrary to 1 Kgs 14.25-28) Jerusalem, Rehoboam, David, Judah, Jeroboam I, 'Israel' or any rival kingdom. Megiddo, which in the 10th century (Stratum VIA) was a city-state in the tradition of the LB Age was officially taken into possession (victory stela) and made into the basis for further actions in the hinterland. The inscription of the Pharaoh gives no indication that either in the north or the south of Palestine there existed any political entity that might have opposed him as a serious opponent.

The agents of the processes of settlement agglomeration and re-urbanization of the 10th and 9th centuries BCE in Palestine were the diverse tribes of the respective regions, which under the leadership of the chieftain of the leading tribe and of his tribal seat had merged from the tribal chiefdoms of Iron Age I into a tribal-kingdom embracing a single tribe or occasionally into a kingdom encompassing a tribal-confederation composed of several tribes. The chieftain expanded his chieftain's compound into a palace within a city. The urban centre of the most important chieftain, which represented at the same time his power base and was organized as a city-state, served as the basis from which he could attack other tribal areas and their settlements when they did not attach themselves to him peacefully. Thus the urban seat of power of a tribal leader (who might call himself 'chieftain' or 'king') could develop into the centre of the territory ruled from this seat. The transition between a city-state with its hinterland and a territorial state with a capital is thus fluid. One can only really speak of a territorial state when – through the fusion of different cities with their hinterlands under the central organization and administration in the capital (= seat of the chieftain) – an organization had taken form on a level which included several cities; this took place only in Iron Age IIB.

In a way, these processes, which proceeded in structurally identical manner in the areas west and east of the Jordan, can still be recognized in the inscription of King Mesha of Moab from the middle of the 9th cent. BCE.[16] Starting from Dibon, his garrison city with a palace area for himself and a residential area for his warriors,

15. A further extra-biblical witness is the inscription on the Bubastis Portal at Karnak.

16. *COS* II, 137–8. S. Mittmann argues for a dating around 830 BCE, see S. Mittmann, 'Zwei "Rätsel" der Mēšaʿ-Inschrift: Mit einem Beitrag zur aramäischen Steleninschrift von Dan (*Tell el-Qāḍī*)', *ZDPV* 118 (2001): 33–65, esp. 53.

he went forth (like his father *Kmšyt*), to conquer and build up other cities in order to expand the area of his dominion. According to this inscription, he succeeded in putting to work in his building programme not only his own supporters and his prisoners of war, but also the local population. The cities (and their territories) to which he laid claim, were subjected to him on the basis of differing legal arrangements, which evidently could be changed.

In a certain sense, the chieftains with their tribal-states or tribal-confederation states centred on their residences revived the late LB Age traditions of the city-states with their Ḫapiru-mercenaries, when, relying on their 'powerbase' and the support of powerful troops with commanders fully committed to them, they attempted to expand the territory of their dominion. 1 Sam. 14.52; 22.6, with its presentation of Saul at Gibea and as chieftain over Benjamin, Ephraim and Gilead (2 Sam. 2.9), may well contain a reminiscence of similar conditions. Quite like Mesha, Saul appears to have emerged as the leader of a tribal-confederation and David too, practising the same tactics, became Saul's rival. On the whole, however, the OT is not a very reliable historical source for this period (Ch. 7.6). All the same, the description of the southern kingdom as the 'house of David' in the Aramaic inscription from Dan indicates that the southern kingdom (at least in the 2nd half of the 9th cent. BCE) was already – or still was – a kingdom only in the sense of a tribal-confederation, which (in analogy to the Aramaean tribal-kingdoms) had emerged through local concentration around the strong chieftain's personality of David and his dynastic successors and in dependence on their headquarter. The tribal-confederation state of Judah continued to look to David as its dynastic founder.[17]

## The Origin of Kingship in 'Israel'

The OT offers various reasons for the establishment of kingship in 'Israel'. The text of 1 Sam. 8.4-5, 20 suggests that kingship in 'Israel' was a foreign institution imported from its alien 'surroundings'. Only under external pressure could this institution be pushed through. In particular, in connection with 1 Sam. 13–15; 31, the threat to the interior tribes by the Philistines is repeatedly cited as the principal motive for the association of the tribes under the first (military) king Saul; however, this explanation

17. G. Lehmann and H. M. Niemann, 'Klanstruktur und charismatische Herrschaft: Juda und Jerusalem 1200–900 v.Chr.', *TQ* 186 (2006): 134–59.

owes more to the biblical construction of the tribes as forming a warrior community than to the real conditions. The introduction of monarchy into Palestine, be it in 'Israel', Judah, or Moab, represented a return to Late Bronze Age institutions typical of the area, although the kings of the Iron Age were concerned to extend the area of their dominion from that of a city-state with its hinterland to that of a territorial state (with fluid boundaries between the two). Kingship was thus by no means the result of coercion under external pressure or something alien to the segmentary, egalitarian or proto-democratic organization of the tribes of 'Israel'. This thesis of Albrecht Alt and Frank Crüsemann[18] (revitalized now with archaeological arguments by Avraham Faust[19]) can no longer be maintained on the basis of exegetical considerations, for the passages of the → *Deuteronomistic history* hostile to kingship have now been shown to rest on later insertions in the text.[20]

There is not even any historically confirmed information concerning the person of Solomon. In the scholarly discussion, one finds – alongside accounts based upon the Old Testament – various attempts at historical (re-) construction, all of which demonstrate only that the lack of extra-biblical sources cannot be compensated for by imagination. Thus Solomon has been described as a city-state king of Jerusalem in the LB Age tradition, who succeeded in integrating the Judaic tribal monarchy, although his attempts to extend his dominion towards the north (1 Kgs 4.7-19) were thwarted by Tyre among others.[21] According to another interpretation, he was a kind of vassal of King Hiram I of Tyre.[22] Still others see him as an entirely legendary founding

18. A. Alt, 'Das Königtum in den Reichen Israel und Juda, 1951', in *Kleine Schriften zur Geschichte des Volkes Israel II* (München: Beck, 1953), 116–34; F. Crüsemann, *Der Widerstand gegen das Königtum: Die antiköniglichen Texte des Alten Testaments und der Kampf um den frühen israelitischen Staat* (WMANT 49; Neukirchen: Neukirchener, 1978).

19. A. Faust, *Israel's Ethnogenesis: Settlement, Interaction, Expansion and Resistance* (London: Equinox, 2006), 92–107.

20. T. Veijola, *Das Königtum in der Beurteilung der deuteronomistischen Historiographie: Eine redaktionsgeschichtliche Untersuchung* (Helsinki: Suomalaisen Tiedeakatemian, 1977).

21. H. M. Niemann, 'Königtum in Israel', *RGG*$^4$ 4:1593–7; idem, 'Megiddo and Solomon: A Biblical Investigation in Relation to Archaeology', *TA* 27 (2000): 61–74; E. A. Knauf, 'King Solomon's Copper Supply', in *Phoenicia and the Bible: Proceedings of the Conference Held at the University of Leuven on the 15th and 16th of March 1990* (OLA 44; ed. E. Lipinski; Leuven: Peeters, 1991), 167–86.

22. H. Donner, *Geschichte*, 246.

figure projected into a former golden age.[23] All of this is no better confirmed historically than the stories of the OT (Ch. 7). Just as for the kingdom of David, so also for the kingdom of Solomon there are no archaeological or → *epigraphical* traces and even the OT does not hide the fact that for Solomon, as for Saul and David, the dates of their reigns were unknown, a sign that no → *annals* had been kept. The schematic claim to a ruling period of 40 years for both David and Solomon (1 Kgs 2.11; 11.42) replaces the ignorance of the real number by a rounded-off, ideal and programmatic number (40 years = a generation; a symbol of fullness).

3. *Iron Age IIB* (926/900–722/700 BCE or 800/785/748–722/700[24]) in Palestine is marked off chronologically on the one hand by the campaign of Pharaoh Shishak I (926 or 920/917 BCE) and on the other by the Assyrian conquest of Samaria (722/721 BCE) and the ensuing incorporation of the northern kingdom of Israel into the Assyrian province system. The Egyptian campaign in Palestine remained only an episode, though it cost Megiddo, the last surviving LB Age city-state in the Palestinian interior, its existence. The coastal area, during this period, continued to be controlled in the northern and middle portions by the southern Phoenician city-states Tyre and Sidon and in the southern portions by the Philistine cities. In Syria, in the 9th cent. BCE Aram-Damascus continued to grow and began to reach out into northern Palestine. In the 9th cent. BCE, the Aramaean tribal-kingdom of Geshur around the Sea of Galilee fell victim to this expansion. The presence of Aram-Damascus in the regions west and east of the Jordan was a political, economic and cultural factor in the 9th and 8th centuries BCE and essentially determined the fate of the whole region up till the fall of Damascus (732 BCE). For the Syro-Palestinian states, however, the greatest danger came from Mesopotamia with the strengthening of the Neo-Assyrian Empire, whose kings since Adad-Nirari II (912–891 BCE – he led campaigns against both the Babylonians and the Aramaeans) pursued imperial tendencies and under Ashurnasirpal II (884–858 BCE) also thrust mightily towards the west. Because, in the course of their western campaigns, the Assyrians until the reign of Shalmaneser III (858–824/823 BCE) were initially preoccupied with their

23. D. W. Jamieson-Drake, *Scribes and Schools in Monarchic Judah: A Socio-Archaeological Approach* (JSOTSup 109; Sheffield: Sheffield University Press, 1991); P. R. Davies, *In Search of 'Ancient Israel'* (JSOTSup 148; Sheffield: Sheffield University Press, 1992), 66–70; T. L. Thompson, *History*, 108–12.

24. On the debate about the beginning of Iron Age IIB, see Ch. 2.2.

western neighbours, the Aramaeans, a complex of mini-states was able to develop in the isolation of the Cis- and Transjordanian territories: these were associated with the names Israel (state god Yhwh), Judah (state god Yhwh), Moab (state god Chemosh) and Ammon (state god Milcom). Thus, from the middle of the 9th century on, one finds monumental architecture and a native administrative language in Moab (Mesha Inscription) and Ammon (citadel inscription from Amman) as signs of statehood.

In the region west of the Jordan, Iron Age IIB was archaeologically a time in which the north-south division of Palestine became increasingly apparent. Among other reasons, due to the geographical proximity to the Phoenicians and Aramaeans, the north had a greater share in the cultural, economic and political development of the whole region and clearly outstripped the south. Both the economic potential and the access to trade routes were unequally apportioned between northern and southern Palestine – we are talking from now on only about the West Jordanian region – which might explain why the development of the north and the south clearly drifted apart, e.g. in terms of both settlement density and urban structures. Although there is no extra-biblical evidence for statehood in 'Israel' or Judah in Iron Age IIA, the picture changes in Iron Age IIB. Noteworthy, however, is the distinction over against the LB Age, namely that (with the exception of the Philistine and Phoenician cities) it is not city-states but territorial states which come to prevail, even though it can be assumed that the Palestinian territorial states of the 9th century grew out of city-state residences from which dominion came to be extended to the surrounding territories and other cities. How efficient the administrative beginnings of the young states were, is difficult to say. Tendentially, one can reckon with a greater military, economic and political potential in the northern kingdom than in southern Judah, which perhaps never lost the character of a tribal-state kingdom, the Judah-Jerusalem of the Davidides, with only rudimentary administration and centralized planning. In what follows, the development of the north and the south will be treated separately.

*The North.* The developments in northern Palestine at the end of the 10th century and in the course of the 9th century present complex problems. According to the biblical account, Jeroboam I was able to unite the northern tribes and, as king, to found the state of 'Israel', which was concentrated around various residences (Shechem, Penuel, Tirzah) in the highlands (1 Kgs 12.25). According to the biblical account, the heads of the tribes assembled in Shechem played a central role in the foundation of this tribal-confederation kingdom, and Jeroboam remained in contact with them by shifting his residences around in their heartlands. According to 1 Kgs 12.20, Judah was reduced to a mini-state consisting of Jerusalem and the tribe of Judah, while the rest of the tribes followed Jeroboam I. Geographically, his dominion thus included the central highlands (Ephraim, Benjamin, Manasseh), the Jezreel Valley (Issachar) and Galilee (Zebulun, Naphtali, Asher) up to Dan in the north, with some possessions in Transjordan as well (Manasseh, Reuben, Gad). Although the historicity of Jeroboam I as king of the northern tribes is not questioned,[25] there is much controversy about what the northern kingdom actually looked like and what it included. On the basis of more recent archaeological research, it is often argued that Megiddo, the Jezreel Valley, the Beth-Shan Plains and Galilee (Kinneret, Hazor, Dan) were regions subjected to very chequered political history, in which the local elites at times pursued independence and often in their outward loyalties proved quite flexible (Aram or Israel). The Jezreel Valley and Galilee constituted an intermediate area between the Aramaeans and the 'Israelite' tribal groups as well as with respect to the economic power of the Phoenician coastland, so that these areas could or would not, without further ado, be integrated into the social and cultural structure of a tribal-confederation kingdom ruled from the central Palestinian highlands. Above, mention has already been made of the Aramaean tribal-kingdom of Geshur in the region. From the 9th cent. BCE on, Aram-Damascus was a permanent opponent of 'Israelite' claims, with both sides alternately claiming or actually holding Galilee and the Jezreel Valley. Against the background of the Aramaean expansion in the 10th and early 9th centuries BCE, there is not much room for the 'Israel' of Jeroboam I. Consequently, his kingdom shows itself to have been merely a tribal-confederation state of a central Palestinian society of highland peasants and herders with shifting residences, in short as a highland mini-state. This changed only with the military leader Omri, the founder of the first dynasty of the northern kingdom and the real 'founder' of that state, which is also called the 'Land of the House of Omri' by the Assyrians. Omri (882/878–871/870 BCE) founded a royal residence and military post in Samaria (1 Kgs 16.24), which till then had been a mere village[26] and which, from that time on, counted as the centre of his kingdom (for example for

25. The keeping of royal → *annals* appears to have begun with him; note the biblical information about exact periods of reign, which no longer use the rounded out number 40.

26. Whether Samaria should be described as a residence or as a capital, depends on how one defines the concepts, see H. M. Niemann, 'Royal Samaria – Capital or Residence? or: The Foundation of the City of Samaria by Sargon II', in *Ahab Agonistes: The Rise and Fall of the Omri Dynasty* (OTS 421; ed. L. L. Grabbe; London, T&T Clark 2005.

the Assyrians). Its existence has also been archaeologically verified.[27] Only under Omri's reign do the first clear signs of territorial statehood appear, manifested, for instance, in monumental stone architecture[28] for functional buildings with public character and in the construction of fortifications and city gates, perhaps even of a water supply system and storage buildings[29] in diverse supra-regionally significant administrative centres (Hazor X, Megiddo VA–IVB,[30] Jezreel, perhaps also Gezer VIII).

The choice of the cities to be built up reveals clear planning: Samaria as the royal acropolis in the highlands maintained continuity with the tribes of the heartland, Hazor served as a border fortress against the Aramaeans, and the cities of the lowlands occupied key positions connected with the traditions of LB Age urban culture and urban far-distance trade. Jezreel, likewise a foundation of Omri, was evidently intended to house the cavalry. The buildings and their dimensions presuppose a well-developed economic power and infrastructure for the Israel of Omri, with specialized crafts, competent architects, city planners, and a sufficient number of available construction workers.[31] Statelike structures are also evident in Omri's territorial claims in Transjordan, which were realized in fortifications there (the construction of Atarot and Jahaz as border fortresses, see the Mesha Inscription), in a developed language of administration, in mass production of ceramics, and also in the dynastic connections with Tyre (1 Kgs 16.31).

Only under Omri and his successors did the highland/mountain state 'Israel' expand beyond its heartland, transforming the tribal-confederation of the north

27. R. E. Tappy, *The Archaeology of Israelite Samaria I. Early Iron Age through the Ninth Century BCE* (HSS 44; Atlanta: Scholars, 1992); idem, *The Archaeology of Israelite Samaria II. The Eighth Century BCE.*, (HSS 50; Winona Lake, Ind.: Eisenbrauns, 2001).
28. On the characteristics of Omride architecture, see I. Finkelstein, *Omride Architecture*, passim: he calls attention especially to the podia, the extensive casemate walls, Proto-Ionic capitals, and bīt-ḫilāni-palaces, the last pointing to the Syrian influences in the new architecture.
29. The dating of the water supply system and the storage facilities is debated. I. Finkelstein, *Omride Architecture*, votes for later strata (Hazor VIII; Megiddo IVA) and their dating in the late 9th or early 8th centuries.
30. Toward the end of the 10th cent./early 9th cent., a modest village had again arisen in Megiddo, which in the 1st half of the 9th cent. was expanded into an unfortified settlement with new public buildings for the local administration (Stratum VA–IVB).
31. The population density of the northern kingdom in Iron Age II was significantly higher than that of Judah or the Transjordanian states; see M. Broshi and I. Finkelstein, 'The Population of Palestine in Iron Age II', BASOR 287 (1992): 47–60.

into the territorial state 'Israel'. The political course pursued by Omri and his successors clearly shows that the Samarian Kingdom was oriented toward the north (in the direction of Aram-Damascus and Phoenicia) and toward the east (Moab; see the Mesha Inscription). In both directions, the borders often presented a problem and were by no means fixed. Concretely, it was only for the rather short periods of 880–840/837 BCE (Omri to Jehoram/Joram) and 800–738/732 BCE (Joash to Pekah) that the Jezreel Valley, the Beth-Shan Plains and Galilee were under the influence of the kings of Samaria. Prior to Omri and from ca. 840/837–800 BCE, these economically important territories were dominated by the Aramaeans; after 738/732 BCE, they fell to the Assyrians. Omri's son Ahab (871/870–852/851 BCE) continued the expansive policy in Transjordan, at first with success (Mesha Inscription) and early on recognized the foreign political dangers in the north, to which he responded in a tactically clever manner: in 853 BCE, he joined up with Hadadezer of Damascus and the Phoenician cities to confront the Assyrian Shalmaneser III (858–824 BCE) at Qarqar[32] and, with his 2,000 chariots, contributed the largest contingent to the allied force. In the ensuing years, further incursions of the Assyrians could effectively be held off by the anti-Assyrian coalition. However, the succession in Aram-Damascus[33] (from Hadadezer to Hazael), military incursions of the Israelite king Jehoram/Joram into the territories claimed by the Aramaeans, and the conjoint murder of the kings Jehoram/Joram of Israel and Ahaziah of Judah (843/842 BCE), – ascribed to Hazael in the Dan Inscription,[34] but to the revolution of the usurpator Jehu in Israel according to the OT (2 Kgs 9.14-29; 2 Chr. 22.5-9) – soon put an end to this alliance. With the alliance broken, Jehu secured his kingdom by tribute payments to Shalmaneser III (841 BCE), who was moving west.[35] (**fig. 11**) but failed, despite all his efforts, to take Damascus. Because the Assyrian pressure on Aram-Damascus notably relaxed after 838 BCE, Hazael himself moved into northern Palestine around 837(?) BCE and destroyed Megiddo (Stratum IVB) among other places. Jezreel and Galilee were lost to the Aramaeans. After Hazael's conquest, Dan, Hazor and Beth-Saida were built up to become Aramaean centres. How far Hazael's conquests went is unclear. According to 2 Kgs 10.32-33; 12.18-19

32. *COS* II, 261–4.

33. Concerning Aram-Damascus, see E. Lipinski, *The Aramaeans: Their Ancient History, Culture, Religion* (OLA 100; Leuven: Peeters, 2000), 347–407.

34. *COS* II, 161–2.

35. *COS* II, 264–71.

(NRSV 12.17-18), he took Gilead and went as far as Gath,[36] imposing tribute on Joash of Judah (840–801 BCE).

**Fig. 11:** Kings from the ends of the world bringing tribute and prostrating before the Assyrian king – Black Obelisk (cf. Fig. 2).

Only when the Aramaeans themselves came under increasing pressure from the Assyrian Adad-Nirari III (809–781 BCE), did it become possible for the Samarian Kingdom once again to move out from its heartland in the mountains and to consolidate itself once again. This it did under Joash (800–785 BCE), who prudently paid tribute to Adad-nirari III in 796 BCE,[37] and also under his son Jeroboam II (785–745 BCE). Both kings succeeded in stimulating the development of a centralized state and an international economy and were able to recover portions of the northern territories, which had been lost to the

36. The rampart and fossa, siege constructions, and the burnt layer in Gath, which are dated to the end of the 9th cent. could correspond to this conquest; see C. S. Ehrlich, 'Die Suche nach Gat und die neuen Ausgrabungen auf Tell eṣ-Ṣāfī', in *Kein Land für sich allein: Studien zum Kulturkontakt in Kanaan, Israel/Palästina und Ebirnâri: FS M. Weippert* (OBO 186; ed. U. Hübner and E. A. Knauf; Fribourg: Academic Press/Göttingen: Vandenhoeck & Ruprecht, 2002), 56–69, esp. 62–6.

37. *COS* II, 276–7.

Aramaeans. Perhaps, the boundary between 'Israel' and Aram-Damascus for a time lay near Kinneret, for there, with Kinneret III around 800 BCE a fortress was built on the northern hill, though the foundation of a new city, Kinneret II took place only in the course of the 8th cent. BCE. This could be connected with the success of the Israelite king Joash (2 Kgs 13.25), who himself (or his son) might have founded a border fortress town there. Nevertheless, the military successes of Joash and Jeroboam II (2 Kgs 14.25; Amos 6.13-14) did not change the fact that although the southern and eastern coasts of the Sea of Galilee were in the hands of the northern kingdom, the northern and eastern coasts remained under Aramaean control until the fall of Aram-Damascus to the Assyrians in 732 BCE. The reigns of both kings marked a time of economic prosperity for the northern kingdom. In this period, Megiddo (Str. IVA) was built up to become a functional centre within the hierarchical structure of the state. Roughly 80 per cent of the constructions consisted of public administrative, economic, or military buildings, and the town was now, for the first time (!), secured by a city wall. All in all, the material culture of Galilee and the Jezreel Valley indicates evident material prosperity in the 8th century. From the first half of the 8th century, → *ostraca* have been found in Samaria[38] indicating the delivery of wine and oil to the royal court. Although the quantities were very modest, it is clear that the surrounding country had to supply them.

## Social Conflict and Prophetic Social Criticism

Despite the progressive development of the northern society to statehood, the agrarian tribal structures which had arisen in Iron Age I continued into Iron Age II. This led to the coexistence of an urban and statelike order on the one hand and a rural tribal order on the other, with differing attitudes towards the property of land. For the tribe, land tenure was a matter of inalienable family ownership; for the urban state administration and the growing class of large landholders, by contrast, it was interesting only as a capital investment. In the course of the development into a territorial state, local trade was transformed, with the barter and → *subsistence economy* being replaced by long-distance trade and a monetary economy (gold and silver coins appeared only in the Persian Period) seated in the cities. In addition to the need to maintain the king himself, a differentiated and expensive administrative organization became increasingly necessary, which also had to be supported by taxes. This put burdens on the rural population, which, under given circumstances, sank into debt bondage. The introduction of annuity capitalism had the result that

38. F. W. Dobbs-Allsopp *et al.*, *Hebrew Inscriptions*, 423–97.

the majority of peasants now tilled the soil as tenants of large landowners, who dwelt in the cities and lived off their annuities. This accelerated the development of a socially divided society, which was not arrested either by the socially critical prophecy of Amos (Amos 2.6-8; 3.9-15; 4.1-3; 5.7, 10-12) nor by legislative restrictions imposed on bank transactions (Exod. 22.25 [NRSV 22.26]; Lev. 25.36-37). In the 8th cent., in the northern kingdom and later in the southern kingdom, landed property came to be viewed more and more as capital, the proceeds of which were raked in by the owners living in the city. Increasingly, the tribal subsistence economy of the peasants was drawn into the whirlpool of a market economy. The 8th cent. was a time of economic upswing for the northern kingdom, but it also produced economic victims and upset social harmony, with the result that opposition arose. It is certainly no coincidence that the massive criticism of the royal court, of luxury, and of magnificent buildings becomes visible for the first time in the prophetic activity of Amos, who, according to Amos 1.1, himself belonged to the rural upper class.

R. Kessler, *The Social History of Ancient Israel: An Introduction*. Transl. by L. M. Maloney. Minneapolis: Fortress, 2008.

The weak period of the Neo-Assyrian Empire ended with Tiglath-Pileser III (745–726 BCE), who advanced against Babylonia and Syria. In 738 BCE Tiglath-Pileser III received tribute from Menahem of Israel (2 Kgs 15.18-20), from the Phoenician city-state kings, and from Rezin of Damascus among others.[39] During the following year, Tiglath-Pileser III was preoccupied with warfare in the north and east of his empire. It appears that the rulers in the west used this time to reorganize their resistance. In 734 BCE, the Assyrian king moved against the Philistines as far as Gaza (on the Egyptian border!) and took tribute from Ahas of Judah and from the kings of Ammon, Moab and Edom. In the following year, 733 or 732 BCE, Rezin of Damascus, Hiram II of Tyre, and Pekah of Israel revived the anti-Assyrian coalition. Judah refused to join the alliance, either because it was already (ever since 734) a loyal Assyrian vassal or because on this occasion it became such a vassal, asking Assyria for military help (2 Kgs 16; Isa. 7.1; Hos. 5). This provoked Israel and Damascus to force the king in Jerusalem to join them against Tiglath-Pileser III. Thus began the so-called Syro-Ephraimite War, from which the Assyrians gained the greatest benefit. In 732 BCE, Damascus fell and was turned into an Assyrian province. In the same year, Galilee, the Jezreel Valley, Megiddo,

39. *COS* II, 284–7.

Dor and Transjordan were lost to the Assyrians, who incorporated much of this territory into the Assyrian province of Megiddo[40] (Dor, Jezreel and Galilee) and transformed the eastern territories into the province Karnaim. The northern kingdom of Samaria was thus reduced to a small rump state, which was further weakened by deportations. The Assyrians replaced the unruly king Pekah of Israel with Hoshea. Hoshea, who was now a vassal of the Assyrians,[41] initially paid tribute, but used the opportunity of the death of Tiglath-Pileser III (727 BCE) for a rebellion (2 Kgs 15.29-30; 17.1-6), which the dead king's successor quickly put down. Shalmaneser V (726–722 BCE) besieged Samaria in 724/723 BCE and captured Hoshea (2 Kgs 17.4). In 722/721 BCE, Samaria was finally conquered, leading to further deportations of the citizens of Samaria and the surrounding highland areas. Because Shalmaneser V died in the winter of 722/721 BCE, it remained for his successor Sargon II to organize the new province. Perhaps he had to conquer Samaria once again in 720 BCE, for it is striking that he boasts of a conquest like that of Shalmaneser V.[42] Sargon II (722–705 BCE) transformed the rump state around Samaria into an Assyrian province (2 Kgs 17.5-6), built up the city into an Assyrian provincial capital of a province bearing the same name, installed an Assyrian governor, and settled Arabs in the place.[43] Megiddo as well was built up under the reign of Sargon II, who erected Assyrian administrative buildings there (ca. 719–716 BCE), since it was intended to serve as an important base for Assyrian expansion towards the Mediterranean and Egypt. Northern Palestine was thus integrated into the Assyrian provincial system. As Megiddo and the North Galilean Dan demonstrate, this was not necessarily disadvantageous. After the Assyrian destruction followed a period of intensive construction, so that Dan, for example, around 600 BCE achieved its greatest size since the Early Bronze Age. The Assyrian deportation policy did not change the northern kingdom as thoroughly

40. On this point, see A. M. Bagg, *Die Assyrer und das Westland. Studien zur historischen Geographie und Herrschaftspraxis in der Levante im 1. Jt. v.u.Z.* (Habilitationsschrift Berlin 2008; in print for OLA; Peeters: Leuven).

41. *COS* II, 287–8.

42. S. A. Fuchs, *Die Inschriften Sargons II. aus Khorsabad* (Göttingen: Cuvillier, 1994), 457–8; B. Becking, *The Fall of Samaria: An Historical and Archaeological Study* (SHANE 2; Leiden: Brill, 1992) reckons with two distinct conquests.

43. *COS* II, 293–9.

as 2 Kgs 17 suggests. The deportations affected in essence only the urban elite and the specialized artisans, so that, contrary to 2 Kgs 17.6, 24-41, the majority of the 'Israelites' remained in the land. The settlement of new population elements in Samaria introduced new peoples and cultural influences into the region, but in cultural and ethnic inhomogeneity there was nothing new. Northern Palestine (the coast, Galilee, the Jezreel Valley, the Beth-Shan Plains and the highlands) was never in the hands of a closed ethnic group during the Iron Age, for there – in quite different local and chronological dimensions – were to be found in addition to the descendants of the LB Age urban culture (see above), various highland tribes with highly complex pre-histories (see above), Aramaeans of diverse provenience, and Phoenicians. Into this melting-pot, the Assyrians brought new impulses with their appearance in the region – impulses which can be recognized in new architectonic traditions and new techniques in palace and urban construction, as well as in pottery.

*The South.* According to 1 Kgs 12.20 (NRSV 12.19), Judah was reduced to a mini-state consisting of Jerusalem and the tribe of Judah, whereas the rest of the tribes followed Jeroboam I. According to 1 Kgs 12.21 (NRSV 12.20), Rehoboam also ruled over Benjamin. The text of 2 Chr. 11.5-12 tells of extensive fortifications, which indicate a geographical extension of Rehoboam's dominion to include Jerusalem, the Judean mountains down to Hebron, and the Shephelah, but this is clearly a backwards projection of the situation prevailing under Hezekiah or Manasseh. Regarding the northern boundary, the biblical narratives reflect extended conflicts around the territory of the tribe of Benjamin (1 Kgs 14.30; 15.6, 16-22). Although there is little doubt about the historicity of Rehoboam as king of Jerusalem and Judah, there is considerable controversy about what this kingdom looked like and what it included. On the basis of more recent archaeological research, it is noted that the development towards real statehood reached Judah only with considerable delay, so that no material relics have been found from the 10th to the 9th cent. BCE pointing to a centrally organized, supra-regional territorial state. Monumental stone architecture, fortifications on the model of 2 Chr. 11, and written testimony are largely absent during this period. The latest discoveries of palace architecture in Jerusalem by Eilat Mazar are still controversial both as to their dating and as to their exact dimensions (see above fn. 13). The coastal hinterland of Judah was a highland area divided into small cell-like areas, in which a society of peasants and herders lived in isolated villages and hamlets. Both their living together and their survival were based on tribal organization and a → *subsistence economy*. From David on, the tribal kings/chieftains of Judah evidently had their seat in Jerusalem and were thus simultaneously city kings ruling over an urban centre (LB Age tradition) with a local upper class. The Judah of Rehoboam thus takes the form of a tribal-state for a society of highland peasants and herders centred in Jerusalem – in short a highland mini-state. The boundaries of the Judean territorial dominion constitute a difficult problem, for which different answers must be given for different periods, since they could shift quite quickly. Basically, Judah was confined on the west by the Philistine cities and on the north by the northern kingdom of Israel, but the exact course of the border was quite variable.

Recent archaeological investigations show that the Shephelah and the territory of the tribe of Benjamin were regions subjected to very chequered political history, in which the local tribal or village chieftains at times pursued independence or at other times exercised their loyalty to external powers in a very flexible manner (Israel or Judah, resp. Philistia or Judah).[44] The Shephelah constituted an intermediate area between the Philistines and the Judean tribes, which could not or would not be easily integrated into the social and cultural structure of a tribal-kingdom based on the Judean highland region.[45] Like its neighbour, Judah had a vital interest in the Shephelah and in the territory of the tribe of Benjamin, because both were very fertile areas. Moreover, the Shephelah, by reason of its location between the highlands and the coast, was predestined to be a location for intermediate trade from west to east, i.e. from the coast into the hinterland. In the material culture of the region, one finds both Philistine and Judean influence, confirming the role of the region as an intercultural intermediate area. However,

44. The (re-)constructions of the territorial boundaries are highly disparate in detail and very much debated. E. A. Knauf, 'Who Destroyed Beersheba II?' in *Kein Land für sich allein: Studien zum Kulturkontakt in Kanaan, Israel/Palästina und Ebirnâri: FS M. Weippert* (OBO 186; ed. U. Hübner and E. A. Knauf; Fribourg: Academic Press/Göttingen: Vandenhoeck & Ruprecht, 2002), 181–95, esp. 188 reckons with Judean dominion over Benjamin at the time of David and Solomon and again after Josiah. Only between ca. 850 and 701 BCE and again after Josiah was the Shephelah in Judean hands.

45. H. M. Niemann, 'Nachbarn und Gegner, Konkurrenten und Verwandte Judas: Die Philister zwischen Geographie und Ökonomie, Geschichte und Theologie', in *Kein Land für sich allein: Studien zum Kulturkontakt in Kanaan, Israel/Palästina und Ebirnâri: FS M. Weippert* (OBO 186; ed. U. Hübner and E. A. Knauf; Fribourg: Academic Press/Göttingen: Vandenhoeck & Ruprecht, 2002), 70–91.

> Judah could make good its claim on the Shephelah and Benjamin only when the political situation was such that the competitors were at a disadvantage. Judah had no chance when the northern kingdom of Israel was strong, when the Aramaean Hazael was on the march, when the Philistines were expanding toward the east, or when Assyria predominated. As a consequence, in Benjamin and the Shephelah, political control fluctuated in very short intervals, though the economic-technological predominance remained in the hands of the coastal inhabitants.

The Old Testament tells us that the relations between 'Israel' and Judah were at first full of conflict (1 Kgs 14.30; 15.6, 16). Only with the Omrides (i.e. ca. 880–843 BCE) did the situation change. Peaceful co-existence (1 Kgs 22.45 [NRSV 22.44]), foreign political cooperation (1 Kgs 22.4; 2 Kgs 3.7-9; 8.28-29), intermarriage between the royal houses (2 Kgs 8.18, 26) and the joint murder of the kings of Israel (Jehoram/Joram) and Judah (Ahaziah) by Jehu (2 Kgs 9.16-29) are all mentioned. With Athaliah (843–838 BCE), a female Omride even came to rule in Jerusalem for a short time (2 Kgs 11). Concerning the internal and foreign political situation of these times, very little is handed down with certainty. On the basis of 1 Kgs 22.2-38; 2 Kgs 9.16, 27; 14.8-14, 22-25 and with reference to the very modest archaeological evidence of urban development in Judah, a 'disguised vassal relationship of Judah with respect to Israel' has been postulated.[46] Likewise, the fact that the trading post Kuntillet ʿAjrûd (ca. 50 km South of Kadesh-Barnea) in the early 8th cent.[47] was evidently maintained by Phoenicians and inhabitants of the northern kingdom as indicated by personal names (whereas names of Judeans are absent), implies that Israel and its economic partner Phoenicia had more quickly recognized (and seized upon) the opportunities for far-distance trade than the southern kingdom, which at this time they may even have dominated politically.

In dependence upon the organizing measures of the Omrides (see above) and nudged by the coastal trade of the Philistines and Phoenicians, the first steps toward full statehood could make their appearance in Judah as well starting in the mid 9th cent. However, the inner-political situation of Jerusalem in the face of the Aramaean danger at its doorstep evidently remained quite unstable. According to the biblical account, Joash (838/837–799 BCE) succeeded Athaliah. He saw himself to be inferior to

46. H. Donner, *Geschichte*, 279.

47. I. Finkelstein and E. Piasetzky, 'The Date of Kuntillet ʿAjrud: The $^{14}$C Perspective', *TA* 35 (2008): 175–85.

the Aramaean king Hazael (2 Kgs 12.18-22 [NRSV 12.17-21) and was the victim of an assassination. Amaziah (799–771 BCE) succeeded him and in drastic miscalculation of the political and military situation became involved in warlike skirmishes with his northern colleague Joash of Israel (2 Kgs 14.8-14): he was defeated, and under the reign of the Israelite king Jeroboam II he was murdered in Lachish. The more-than-50-year reign of Uzziah (coregent since 785, king 771–734 BCE) and his son and coregent Jotham (757–742 BCE) marked a period of consolidation for Judah. Both rulers are only briefly mentioned in the OT (2 Kgs 15.1-7, 32-38), but their reigns coincide with the flourishing of the northern kingdom under Jeroboam II (as demonstrated by the material culture), with the rise of an economic upswing in Judah (e.g. oil and textile production in Beth-Shemesh), and with the first indications in the material culture of Judah of the foundation of centrally planned cities with statelike functions. Perhaps Judah was again dependent on the northern kingdom personified in Jeroboam II. The text of 2 Chr. 26.6-7 mentions a campaign of Uzziah against Gath, Jabneh (el) and Ashdod, which, however, cannot be verified archaeologically and which is historically rather improbable. Ashdod was for Judah the nearest Mediterranean port, but in the 8th cent., with a settlement area of some 30 ha, it was at the height of its power: only in 711 BCE was it captured and destroyed by Sargon II.

Whatever the case, after disparate beginnings from the middle of the 9th cent. BCE on, the socio-economic development to territorial statehood finally reached Judah in the 1st half of the 8th cent. – clearly later than in the north. The architecture of administrative and storage buildings and the water supply systems of the late 9th/early 8th centuries becomes visible in Lachish (Strata IV–III). This urban centre of the Shephelah was developed toward the turn of the 9th to 8th centuries into a garrison and residence city with imposing structures for defence and storage, and a raised palace area. In Beth-Shemesh, which already in the 10th and 9th centuries BCE was a locally significant settlement with cisterns, public buildings, and installations for the olive oil industry, an iron works is attested in the 9th cent. BCE which points to the increasing importance of iron technology. Despite its destruction in the 1st half of the 8th cent., the place regained prosperity in the further course of this century on the economic basis of its oil and textile production. The archaeological evidence shows that the cities of the south in the 9th and 8th centuries were significantly smaller than those of the northern kingdom and did not meet their urban standards.

This holds in particular for their absolute size, for the dimensions of the administrative buildings, and for the financial cost of the buildings, as well as for the frequency of luxury goods and written pieces. Judah remained essentially a city-state of Jerusalem with more or less hinterland depending on the political situation. Thus the Davidides lacked both the economic and the demographic means to erect architectonic monuments on the scale of Samaria or Jezreel. From an Aramaean or Assyrian perspective, Judah was too far away, too insignificant economically, and strategically only important if one planned to attack Egypt. For this reason, with the exception of Hazael in Gath, it by and large escaped Aramaean threats and even the first incursions of the Assyrians.[48] This situation changed with the reign of Ahaz of Judah (coregent since 742, king 734–723 BCE), who according to 2 Kgs 16 appealed to Tiglath-Pileser III for military support against the anti-Assyrian coalition of Israel and Aram-Damascus (see above). Perhaps Ahaz was already an Assyrian vassal at the time of his tribute payment in 734 BCE and was thus unwilling to take part in the revolt of the northern neighbours. It is also possible, however, that he became an Assyrian vassal only in the face of the Syro-Ephraimite threat in 733/2 BCE (Isa. 7.1) and called the Assyrians to his aid, professing his subjection to them in all due form in Damascus (2 Kgs 16.10). It is notable that with Ahaz the notion of 'Judah' as the name of the established state of the southern kingdom is for the first time attested outside the Bible.[49] Ahaz's son Hezekiah (723–695 BCE), under the impression of the Assyrian conquest of Samaria and the end of the northern kingdom 722/721 BCE, began systematically to protect his kingdom of Judah against the approaching threat. Chronologically, the construction of the Siloam Tunnel bringing the water of the Gihon spring directly into the fortified city (Siloam Pool) of Jerusalem (2 Kgs 20.20; 2 Chr. 32.30) belongs to these building measures and is → *epigraphically* attested by an inscription *in situ*.[50] During his reign, Jerusalem expanded for the first time from the city of David onto the western hill and was protected with surrounding fortifications. The growth of the city from 12 ha at the beginning of the 8th cent. to more than 50 ha towards the end of

48. The relative peace reigning in this period can be confirmed archaeologically, for example, in Mizpah, which was settled between the 10th and the 8th centuries without experiencing any notable destruction.

49. *COS* II, 289–90.

50. *COS* II, 145–6.

that century and into the 7th cent. is generally explained by the influx of refugees from the northern kingdom, who sought protection in Jerusalem. According to 2 Kgs 18.8, Hezekiah is said to have moved against Gaza, but as yet there is no confirmation of this action. In the late 8th cent., royal seals (*lmlk* = 'property of the king') begin to appear, which were used to mark the handles of large storage jars. Such jars have been found in the Judean fortress cities that Hezekiah of Judah had established. With their help, it is possible to define the territory ruled by Judah. The reign of Hezekiah was undoubtedly a time of flourishing and territorial expansion for Judah. The death of Sargon II (705 BCE) may well have tempted the Judean king to defy the Assyrians (2 Kgs 18.7) and to end the tribute payments. Sennacherib (705–681 BCE) sent a corresponding punitive expedition and left no doubt about the Assyrian interests in the west and their ability to enforce them. He himself led his third expedition, this time against Sidon, which led the kings of the Phoenician and Philistine coast (with few exceptions) as well as Ammon, Moab and Edom to secure their existence by paying tribute. Hezekiah of Judah, who apparently had entered into an agreement with anti-Assyrian parties in Ekron (he had captured king Padi) and the Egyptians, now came to the attention of the Assyrian king. After a clash between the Assyrian and the Egyptian armies at Elteke, Ekron was conquered and the king Padi, who had remained loyal to Assyria, was reinstalled by Sennacherib. The Judean cities and fortresses of the Shephelah, among them Lachish III (2 Kgs 18.13-14) (**fig. 12**),[51] and many other places were destroyed in 701 BCE. Deportations of portions of the Judean population followed. Then the Assyrian army turned against Jerusalem (2 Kgs 18.17; Isa. 36.2; 2 Chr. 32.9), but, for unknown reasons (plague of mice, pestilence in the camp, unrest in Assyria), it broke off the siege and returned to Assyria. In the biblical account (2 Kgs 19; Isa. 37), these events are treated as a miracle, which was attributed to the direct intervention of Yhwh (procured by the prophet Isaiah). According to both Assyrian and biblical accounts (2 Kgs 18.14-16), Hezekiah afterwards sent his tribute to the Assyrian king and thus freed his rump state around the city of Jerusalem once again from the prospect of a new

51. *COS* II, 302–4; C. Uehlinger, 'Clio in a World of Pictures – Another Look at the Lachish Reliefs from Sennacherib's Southwest Palace at Nineveh', in *'Like a Bird in a Cage': The Invasion of Sennacherib in 701 BCE* (JSOTSup 363; ed. L. L. Grabbe; Sheffield: Sheffield Academic Press, 2003), 221–305.

attack. Perhaps his goal was also to secure Assyrian protection against the Egyptians (2 Kgs 19.9 = Isa. 37.9[52]) who once again had demonstrated their Palestinian interests and at Elteke had not been thoroughly defeated. In the aftermath of these events, the Shephelah was permanently lost to Judah, being divided up among the Philistine vassal kings of Ashdod, Ekron and Gaza, who were loyal to Assyria. As in the north, the Assyrian conquest was not necessarily disadvantageous. Ekron profited in the 7th century. from the *pax assyriaca*: it became a major economic power (until its destruction by Nebuchadnezzar II at the end of the 7th century.), being a centre of oil trade (ca. 1000 t produced annually)[53] and textile industry under Assyrian oversight. Inscriptions from Ekron point to a Phoenician-Philistine community of interests in the coastal trade. In the 7th century, two Assyrian vassals appear to have cooperated in mutual interest: Judah supplied Ekron under Assyrian domination with raw materials and also perhaps with manpower. Thus, until the end of the Assyrian Empire, Judah remained a loyal vassal, with the result that the generations living under the reign of Manasseh (694–640 BCE) enjoyed a stable and prosperous period, though this is not adequately honoured in the Deuteronomistic interpretation of history.

*4. Iron Age IIC (722/700–587/586 BCE)*: In Palestine, Iron Age IIC is marked by the political end of the northern and southern kingdoms. In terms of foreign affairs, this period was a very chequered time, marked first by the high point of the Neo-Assyrian Empire, then by its downfall, and finally by the rise of the Neo-Babylonian Empire and various attempts to revive Egyptian predominance in the Levant. As noted above, after the death of Sargon II, his son Sennacherib (705–681 BCE) took control. Despite his frequent military expeditions, it was only under his son Esarhaddon (681–669 BCE) that the Neo-Assyrian Empire reached Egypt (the conquest of Memphis in 671) and thus its greatest extension. At first, Ashurbanipal (669–628/627 BCE) effectively put down revolts in Egypt (conquest of Memphis 667 and Thebes 664), but he had to relax his hold on the west in the course of the following decades

52. Tirhaka is an anachronism.

53. S. Gitin, 'Tel-Miqne-Ekron in the 7th century BCE: The Impact of Economic Innovation and Foreign Cultural Influences on a Neo-Assyrian Vassal City-State', in *Recent Excavations in Israel: A View to the West. Reports on Kabri, Nami, Miqne-Ekron, Dor, and Ashkelon* (ed. S. Gitin; Dubuque, Iowa: Kendall/Hunt, 1995), 61–79.

**Fig. 12:** Sennacherib's relief of the conquest of Lachish.

and to give up Egypt without a fight after the revolt of Psammetichus I. After 640 BCE, the first signs of the empire's decline make their appearance, making quick progress after Ashurbanipal's death and during the conflict over the royal succession between the two princes Ashur-etel-ilani and Sin-šar-iškun. The general Nabopolassar (626–605 BCE), the founder of the Chaldean Dynasty,[54] seized the Babylonian throne and joined with Cyaxares, King of the Medes, in an attack upon Assyria. In 614, the religious capital Assur and in 612 the political residence Nineveh were conquered (Nah. 2.2–3.19 [NRSV 2.1–3.19]). The remaining rump state of Ashur-uballit II centred in Haran came to an end in 609/608, although Pharaoh Neco II (610–595 BCE) evidently had come to the aid of the Assyrians. Egypt became the temporary heir of the western dominions, but was quickly succeeded by the Neo-Babylonian Empire, which really began only with Nebuchadnezzar II (605–562 BCE). The weak period of the Neo-Assyrian Empire (roughly after 640/630 BCE) and of its replacement by the Neo-Babylonian Empire was used by the Egyptians of the 26th Dynasty of Sais to renew their claims in the Syrian and Levantine land bridge, with the result that sooner or later a decision over the hegemony in the western territories had to be fought out between the Egyptian and the Babylonian heirs of the Neo-Assyrian Empire. Although Nabopolassar himself made no progress, his successor Nebuchadnezzar II, already as crown prince, early and efficiently took up the challenge, so that the beginning of his reign coincided with the decisive battle of Carchemish (605 BCE). The Egyptians were turned back and in the course of a series of Egyptian rearguard actions, Syro-Palestine fell to the Babylonians, who maintained their dominion more through frequent military incursions and razzias than through the establishment of systematic administrative or economic structures. The Neo-Babylonian Empire was short-lived. Already during the reign of Nabonidus (556–539 BCE) its last king, it hastened to its end, and around 539 BCE it was replaced by the Persian Empire under Cyrus II.

The former *northern kingdom*, after the Assyrian conquests, had been integrated into the Assyrian provincial system, which meant the end of its autonomy and the presence of Assyrian administrative officers, for whom residences had to be built in the provincial capitals. As a consequence, the Assyrians invested particularly in places like Megiddo and Samaria, from which the provincial administration was to be directed (see above),[55]

54. Only at this time does Ur become the city of the Chaldeans (Gen. 11.28, 31).

55. On the imprint of a royal seal of Sargon II, see O. Keel and C. Uehlinger, *GGG*, Ill. 278b.

while other settlements were abandoned after the Assyrian destruction (e.g. Kinneret). During the decline of the Neo-Assyrian Empire, Megiddo, as in earlier times, appears to have served as the base for Egyptian military operations toward the north (2 Kgs 23.29-30). The Babylonian conquests had little effect on the former Assyrian provincial centres in northern Palestine. In Megiddo the administrative area was abandoned on the eve of the Babylonian conquests, but the residential areas continued to be occupied at least in part. Relative continuity is also evident in Samaria, which was taken over as the centre of the Babylonian province bearing the same name. The region around Samaria and Galilee as well as the settlements immediately to the north of Jerusalem remained largely untouched by the Babylonian destructive measures.

*Judah,* after Hezekiah's futile revolt, remained an Assyrian vassal. His successor Manasseh (694–640 BCE) did nothing to change this arrangement and continued to pay tribute to Esarhaddon and Ashurbanipal, whose Egyptian campaigns he supported with military contingents.[56] Perhaps it was this strategically important support that secured the Judean kings' control over the Negev, where, in the 7th century, extensive re-urbanization and fortification measures have come to light. Here in the 7th century an upswing is evident, due, among other things to the booming trade with the Edomites and the Arabs.[57] The northern border of Judah in the direction of the neighbouring Assyrian province of Samaria ran only a few kilometres to the north of Jerusalem. The Shephelah remained lost to Judah from 701 BCE on and stood under Assyrian oversight, respectively under the control of Philistine vassals loyal to Assyria, a situation that did not change until the time of Josiah. That Judah continued to prosper during Iron Age IIC despite the loss of this agriculturally and economically important region and despite its enclosed situation is due to the political pragmatism of its kings and the economic opportunities of the *pax assyriaca.* Manasseh's (694–640 BCE) consistently friendly attitude towards Assyria secured for Judah the most flourishing period of its history, and the nearby Rāmat Rāḥēl V experienced an unparalleled boom in the 7th and early 6th centuries. For the first time (!) buildings with state functions were erected with ashlar masonry and proto-Ionic capitals were

56. *ANET*, 291.

57. However, one can also interpret the Edomite presence in the Negev and the Judean fortifications as a Judean attempt to protect themselves against incursions of the Edomites and/or Arabs.

used (Rāmat Rāḥēl). Many scholars ascribe this qualitative leap in the architecture in Judean territory to the influx of refugees from the northern kingdom, who brought their knowledge to bear in their place of refuge.[58] The technological transfer, as the expansion of the settlement area of Jerusalem in the 8th to 7th centuries, can also be related to the Assyrian, Philistine and Phoenician cooperation which is particularly evident in the cooperation with Ekron. According to 2 Kgs 21.23-24, Manasseh's son Amon (640–638 BCE) fell victim to a palace revolt supported by members of the upper class who pursued anti-Assyrian interests. With the enthronement of the underaged Josiah (638–609/8/7 BCE), this group was able to continue its policy for a whole decade, and the king apparently followed it when he came of age. The opportunities for anti-Assyrian cabal were more favourable than ever before. Around 640 BCE, at the latest with the death of Ashurbanipal,[59] the Assyrian weakness became perceptible in the western territories, and the pharaohs of the 26th Dynasty, who apparently had freed themselves from the Assyrians around 650 BCE immediately took advantage of the new situation. Egypt seized the opportunity to reclaim the area, where it believed itself to possess ancient rights. Thus an Egyptian renaissance occurred in Palestine, which, however, endured only until the Babylonian Empire under the Chaldean Dynasty grew strong enough to be willing and able to take over the succession of Assyria in the west. In the turmoil of the years from 640/630 BCE until 605 BCE the other mini-state kings of the Syro-Palestinian land bridge likewise tested out their chances, though these extended no further than Egypt allowed. Josiah and his successor came to feel this situation. The politics of Josiah's regent and of the king himself must be understood in this context. During this ruling period (638–609/608 BCE), Judah made territorial gains that would have been impossible in the times of Assyrian strength. The Shephelah again came under Judean control. Lachish (Stratum II), the principal guardian of the Judean highlands in the direction of the lowlands, was rebuilt and fortified. However, the new garrison town was notably smaller than its predecessor.

According to a Hebrew → *ostracon* from Məṣad Hăšavyāhū, a small fort ca. 2 km

58. Z. Herzog, *Archaeology*, 250.

59. D. S. Vanderhooft, *The Neo-Babylonian Empire and Babylon in the Latter Prophets* (HSM 59; Atlanta: Scholars, 1999), 69–81, argues for growing Egyptian influence from 640 BCE on.

South of Yavnē-Yām on the Mediterranean coast, which can be dated to the end of the 7th cent., Josiah (or his successor) succeeded in reaching out to the coast.[60] This could have been done with the help of Greek mercenaries, who, based on ceramic evidence, appear to have lived there. But this interpretation is not uncontested, for it is also conceivable to interpret the material evidence as indicating that the Judeans living there were under Egyptian command[61] and were serving in the fortress to protect a Greek trading post. The coastal fort demonstrates the meeting of Greek and Judean spheres of influence, whereby it either stood under direct or indirect (through the Judean vassal) Egyptian control.

The Negev as well remained in Judean hands in the time of Josiah. There is biblical evidence for attempts of the king (only after 612, the fall of Nineveh) to expand into the former territories of the northern kingdom (the tribe of Benjamin), which may have included a claim to take up its inheritance (Bethel: 2 Kgs 23.15). Against the background of the fact that Josiah met his death at Megiddo (!) at the hands of Pharaoh Neco II (2 Kgs 23.29-30), such plans for predominance in the north appear plausible. The lack of respect for Egyptian interests ultimately caused Josiah's dreams of expansion to fail. The exact circumstances of his death in 609/608 are unclear. Because 2 Kgs 23.29-30 makes no mention of a battle, it would appear that the pharaoh, who either intended to come to the aid of the Assyrian rump state in Haran or to protect the Egyptian hegemony in the region against the Babylonians (Josephus, *Ant.* X, 74–80), simply eliminated without a struggle a rebellious vassal in Egyptian eyes and a troublemaker who disrupted the politics of the major powers. Between 609 and 605 BCE, the Egyptians were still able to maintain their claims in Palestine and to dominate Judah. It was thus Pharaoh Neco II, who dethroned Josiah's dynastic successor Jehoahas (609/608) after only three months of rule, deported him to Egypt, and replaced him with Eliakim/Jehoiakim (609/608–598/597), who like his predecessors remained tributary to the pharaoh (2 Kgs 23.31-35).

The → *ostraca* of Arad VI[62] may well come from the reign of Eliakim/Jehoiakim. They are dated to around 600 BCE (in any case before 587) and refer to food rations for military personnel, among them the Kittim (i.e. Greek mercenaries in Judean service). In the same period, conflicts with the Edomites in the Negev occurred (Arad Ostraca Stratum VI No. 3, 21 and 24). There, numerous levels of destruction

60. *COS* III, 77–8; *AHI*, 76–7, No. 7.001.

61. On the state of the discussion, see D. S. Vanderhooft, *Empire*, 78–81 (above, n. 59).

62. *COS* III, 81–5; G. S. Davies, *Inscripitions*, 11–20.

dated around 600 BCE (e.g. in Kadesh-barnea) point to armed conflicts, though it remains an open question, whether they should be attributed to the Edomites, to the Egyptians under Neco II, or to the army of Nebuchadnezzar II.

Jehoiakim's Egyptian vassaldom ended only when it was replaced by Babylonian vassaldom. The Egyptian claims to Syro-Palestine were ended by the victory of the crown prince Nebuchadnezzar II in the battle of Carchemish in 605 BCE. With well-planned military expeditions, he conquered Syria, Palestine and the Phoenician coast. As king, he appeared in 604 BCE on the Palestinian coast and destroyed Ashkelon, followed by Ekron (603 or 601), Ashdod and Timna. The Aramaic letter of King Adon of Ekron[63] (an indication of the importance of Aramaic as the language of diplomacy in the region) demonstrates the orientation of the city's king toward Egypt, whose help he sought, as well as the unwillingness or inability of Egypt to give such help, and in general points to the desolate political situation prevailing in southern Palestine at the time. In 601 BCE, the expedition of the Babylonian king against Egypt failed,[64] with the result that the ruling classes in the hinterland state of Judah apparently became divided. One party (friendly to Egypt) saw the chance for a revolt against Babylonia (2 Kgs 24.1); the other called for restraint and warned against too much trust in Egypt (Jeremiah). Jehoiakim's refusal of tribute payments led to the expedition of Nebuchadnezzar II against Jerusalem, where Jehoiachin had meanwhile become king; he was forced to surrender the city. This first conquest of Jerusalem took place in 598/597 BCE (2 Kgs 24.1-16).[65] The Babylonians plundered the city and deported a portion of the ruling class to Babylon, where they were resettled. In this connection, it appears that the Negev fell to the Edomites. Among those deported, according to 2 Kgs 24.14, were the Davidide Jehoiachin with his family and the prophet Ezekiel (Ezek. 1.1-3). The Babylonians replaced Jehoiachin with Mattaniah/Zedekiah as king (2 Kgs 24.17, Ezek. 17.12-21), though in fact he was nothing more than a vice-regent. For the Deuteronomists (→ *Deuteronomism*), Zedekiah (598/597–587/586) was the last legitimate king of Judah. Although Zedekiah owed his reign to the Babylonians, he made the most fatal mistake a ruler could make in those times by failing to fulfil the duties of his vassalship. Behind this act of madness stood once again the intrigues of false counsellors

63. B. Porten and A. Yardeni, *TADAE*, A1.1.

64. *ANET*, 303–5.

65. *ANET*, 303–5.

and the deceptive reliance on Egyptian aid: although this time, the Egyptians came, they were unable to save him (Jer. 37.5-11). Jerusalem was besieged and conquered.[66] As a fugitive and rebellious vassal, Zedekiah was severely punished, blinded, and deported to Babylon (2 Kgs 25.7). The city and its temple were plundered, torn down, and burnt. A further deportation took place (2 Kgs 25.8-26). Jeremiah, whose warning prophecies of doom had appeared to the anti-Babylonian Zedekiah as nothing more than demoralizing, pro-Babylonian propaganda (Jer. 38.4, 24-25) appears to have been treated as a collaborator by the Babylonians and therefore set free (Jer. 40.4-6).

To the reign of Zedekiah belong the → *ostraca* from Lachish II,[67] which were addressed to the local commander Yā'ûš around 589–587 BCE. They attest to the tense situation of the garrisons in the Shephelah and to contacts with Egypt, which were designed to organize military aid (Ostracon No. 3, cf. the aid of Pharaoh Apries = Hofra according to Jer. 37.5–11; cf. Ezek. 17.15). Lachish II was destroyed (Jer. 34.7) along with diverse other places (Azekah; Rāmat Rāḥēl) in 587/586 BCE, though the exact date is unclear, because the route of the Babylonian army is not known. In the context of the events of 587/586, the southern Shephelah and the southern part of the Judean highlands came under Edomite control until Edom too was annexed by Nabonidus in 553/552 BCE.

According to 2 Kgs 25.22–26; Jer. 40.7–41.18, a Judean rump state or at least a provincial seat around Mizpah survived, where Gedaliah (not a Davidide but a member of the important Jerusalem family of Shaphan), who had been installed by the Babylonians, ruled. His exact status is unclear: he may have been a mere governor or perhaps he was in fact the last king of Judah, who was counselled by Jeremiah (Jer. 40.6). In any case, he surrounded himself with the pro-Babylonian (= anti-Egyptian) party in Mizpah, but then was murdered there by Judean fanatics led by the Davidide Ishmael in 582 BCE. This may have occurred with Ammonite support (Jer. 40.14) and Egyptian instigation, since it appears to be connected with the Babylonian conquest of Ammon and Moab (Josephus, *Ant. X*, 181), to a third deportation of Judeans (Jer. 52.30), and to a flight of refugees into Egypt (2 Kgs 25.26; Jer. 41–43).

66. The Babylonian military leaders mentioned in Jer. 39.3 have now been identified. Nabû-šarrūssu-ukīn rab ša rēši has recently been discovered by Michael Jursa on a receipt in the British Museum, London.

67. *COS* III, 78–81; G. S. Davies, *Inscriptions*, No. 1.002-1.006.

## 4.2.2 Religion and Cult: Local Pantheons, Open-Air Sanctuaries, State Gods and hardly any City Temples

*1. Iron Age I (1200/1150–1000 BCE[68]).* The cultic buildings of Iron Age I point to a time of cultural mixture, in which elements of diverse origin combined, and to a time of transition, in which, on the one hand, the LB Age traditions lived on, while, on the other hand, innovations also appear. All in all, only a few cultic buildings are known from Iron Age I, and all are located either in the cities of the coastal region (Tell el-Qasīle, Tell Abū Hawām) or in interior enclaves with surviving LB Age traditions (Beth-Shan V, the southern and perhaps also the northern temple). Here the tradition of the city temples evidently continued to be followed, although changes can also be observed, e.g. the ground plans are by no means derived from LB Age (see p. 78). For this reason, analogies from other areas of the Near East or the Aegean have often been invoked, but they have failed to convince. Perhaps one must think of a synthesis of elements from various sources. Architectonic traditions of the LB Age survived in Iron Age I at best only in the coastal regions (e.g. Gezer). Evidently the coastal regions and the interior went in different directions with respect to sacral architecture. In the village settlements of the highlands of the early Iron Age, no temples have yet been found, thus indicating that the population spared the costs of maintaining a permanent community ('official') temple cult, practising instead familial cult in the house (attested, for example, in Hazor) as well as local worship at open-air sanctuaries (= 'high places'). Stone settings with → *mazzeboth* ('bull site' East of Dothan; there also a bull in bronze) sufficed for the community's worship, which could take place in open sanctuaries, either within the villages (Arad) or outside of them. The pantheon was just as much affected by the decline of the Bronze Age city culture as the people themselves. The formerly well-differentiated city pantheons appear now in much reduced form, although, in the coastal region and isolated enclaves, Bronze Age traditions continued to be cultivated, and, especially on the southern coast, elements from the West (Cyprus, the Aegean) found increasing acceptance.[69] The withdrawal of the Egyptians had its effect. Egyptian divinities (Ptah, Hathor) tend to disappear. They retain

68. On the problem of the chronology, see Ch. 2.2.

69. The so-called Ashdoda, a goddess-figure in clay, who merges with her throne, is locally restricted to the Philistine cities and temporally restricted to but a short period during Iron Age I. She should be seen in connection with Mycenaean clay idols.

their position (Amun above all) especially in the cities with Egyptian and LB Age character, e.g. Beth-Shan, Megiddo, Lachish and Gaza, at least as long as the Egyptian presence continued there.

The metal statues of Iron Age I, which are found much less frequently than in the LB Age, represent almost exclusively the male divinities of the enthroned El or the standing Baal/Hadad types (Megiddo, Hazor *et al.*). Bronze bull statuettes (the 'bull-site' East of Dothan) are rare and should be interpreted as symbolic animals for male divinities of the Baal/Hadad type. Due to the economic recession and shortage of raw materials, most of the cultic objects found from this period are not made of valuable metal but rather of clay as a cheap substitute. In the → *iconography* of the clay figurines and plaques, one finds representations of bulls (Shilo) and only rarely → *anthropomorphic* deities (Beth-Shan Stratum S2). Very frequent, by contrast, are the anthropomorphic representations of naked or clothed goddesses, who are holding their breasts or a lotus plant and who may be with or without a child (e.g. Beth-Shemesh, Tell Abū Hawām, Beth-Shan). These findings indicate that the religious symbol system of the LB Age had survived, though, due to the lack of metals, one had to resort to clay for the production of cultic equipment. This is easily connected with the observation that in Iron Age I domestic and local worship took on increased importance.

The locally produced limestone seals show simple decoration with schematic representations of human beings, plants and animals. A new, typically local type takes the form of → *conoids*, which likewise bear representations of animals and the Syrian motif of the suckling mother animal (usually a cow, sometimes a caprid) with the head turned backwards. Perhaps, after the urban motifs of the LB Age, this points to the increased interest of the seal owners of Iron Age I in agricultural themes.[70] To the 21st Dynasty (1075–945 BCE), belong the so-called post-Ramessite mass-produced goods, i.e. seal amulets from Egypt (Tanis) with schematic gravure. Their iconographic themes are symbols of superiority, of triumph, and of (positively valued) aggressivity. Some of these motifs have been handed down into Iron Age I without consideration of their Egyptian origin or connections with the Egyptian royal iconography. They may also have been taken over in the local → *glyptic* (mostly of the southern coast). Then typical Egyptian elements (e.g. → *uraeus*) were omitted, the iconographic motif was generalized into a symbol of militant triumph, and thus (quasi 'de-egyptianized') integrated into the local symbol system.

Corresponding to the character of society in Iron Age I, which remained urban in only a few areas of retreat and elsewhere was typically agrarian, the heavenly pantheons of the cities remained attached to the Bronze Age traditions, whereas

70. So with O. Keel and C. Uehlinger, *GGG*, § 76.

a different situation should be postulated for the Palestinian village culture. The pantheons there, corresponding to the modest socio-economic differentiation of agrarian societies, were certainly much less complicated and the number of deities was much reduced. The divine head of the family, the clan, or the tribe was a male god with a female partner and perhaps children, whose number may have varied according to place and time. To them was dedicated the corresponding settlement's familial or local worship, so that one can reckon with a plurality of small local divine families and perhaps with the worship of family ancestors. → *Mazzeboth* served these deities (and also the ancestors) as signs of their presence, as did the rare metal and frequent clay statues, figurines and plaques. The pantheon of the Palestinian village culture during this transitional period, however, is archaeologically difficult to grasp. Because the roots of the later 'Israel' are thought to lie here, we find ourselves in a very regrettable situation, in which the consultation of the biblical texts likewise offers little help.

> The OT accounts of the idealized portrait of families in patriarchal times living together with their house deity and associated with diverse local, open-air sanctuaries (in Shechem: Gen. 12.6; 35.4; Mamre: Gen. 13.18; Bethel: Gen. 12.8; Beer-sheba: Gen. 21.33) reflect a later situation (Ch. 7.4). Albrecht Alt's famous hypothesis from the 'Gott der Väter' (= *God of the Fathers*; 1929)[71] has met devastating criticism (Ch. 7.4.2).[72] The same holds for Martin Noth's thesis of an 'Ancient Israelite → *amphictyony*'[73] existing in the period prior to statehood, namely a sacral tribal league (composed ultimately, in his view, of 12 tribes), i.e. an association of neighbouring peoples around a central sanctuary sacred to Yhwh (in his opinion, the → *ark of the covenant*), whose maintenance and support constituted its principal duty. Against this model, it was early on objected, that even the biblical account of the period before statehood knows nothing of a central sanctuary of the 12 tribes, that the ark is described not as a place of worship but as a cultic object, and that the number of 12 tribes represents a fiction inconsequently maintained even within the OT. Due to the lack of similarities in their constitutive elements, Noth's argument by analogy from the Greek and Old-Italic amphictyonies to the organization of the federation of (12) tribes prior to statehood rests on feet of clay.

71. A. Alt, 'Der Gott der Väter. Ein Beitrag zur Vorgeschichte der israelitischen Religion, 1929', in *Kleine Schriften zur Geschichte des Volkes Israel I* (München: Beck 1953), 1–78.
72. M. Köckert, *Vätergott und Väterverheißungen: Eine Auseinandersetzung mit Albrecht Alt und seinen Erben* (FRLANT 142; Göttingen: Vandenhoeck & Ruprecht, 1988); R. Smend, 'Albrecht Alt', in Astruc, 132–56.
73. M. Noth, *Das System der zwölf Stämme Israels* (BWANT IV, 1, Stuttgart: Kohlhammer, 1930). On this account and the most important counterarguments, see H. Donner, *Geschichte*, 72–6.

The society comprised of individual tribes of unknown number in the interior of Palestine was not a 'pan-Israelite' worship community; instead, each tribe, each clan, and each family relied, in cultic matters, on its own local or familial traditions, which it cultivated at local or domestic cultic places. In this connection, professional priests or priestesses would have been the exception, so that the performance of worship fell within the responsibilities of the head of the family, the clan, or the tribe. Perhaps, by analogy to wandering artisans and in connection with Judges 17, one might imagine wandering priests who offered their services for hire.

*2. Iron Age IIA (1000–926/900 or 950/900–800/785/748 BCE*[74]*)*: Although Iron Age IIA should be seen as a time of settlement agglomeration and revival of urban culture, the city temples, as known from the city-states of the LB Age, are absent for the most part (exceptions: Beth-Shan V and the coastal cities). These findings can be given different interpretations. When, in conformity with the biblical account, one places the beginning of statehood in the northern and southern kingdoms in the 10th cent. BCE, one can postulate that the state only maintained the 'national'[75] temples of the official state religion and neglected the other city sanctuaries as places of local worship.[76] Independent of the acceptance of the existence of full-blown states or of a Davidic-Solomonic Empire, one can note, however, that, in general, the newly arisen urban culture was sustained by different population elements than that of the old city-states of the LB Age. The population of the small towns now in the process of formation derived, for the most part, from the village culture of the highlands and continued to observe their customary religious practices of domestic and local cults in open-air sanctuaries and at home, seeing no need to establish city temples.[77] This means first that the religious traditions of the LB Age city-states did not continue unbroken into the cities of Iron Age II and

74. On the chronological discussions about Iron Age IIA, see Ch. 2.2.

75. To remind ourselves of the fact that the concept of 'nations' is a recent one in history, the terms 'nation' and 'national' are put in quotation marks. It would be better to renounce the term 'nation/-al' entirely, but its usage is too well established for that. Such indication is probably the easiest way to point out its problematics.

76. So H. Weippert, *Palästina*, 447–8.

77. The proposed 'sanctuary' in Lachish stratum V is a fiction; see D. Ussishkin, 'The Level V "Sanctuary" and "High Place" at Lachish', in *Saxa Loquentur: Studien zur Archäologie Palästinas/Israels: Festschrift V. Fritz* (AOAT 302; ed. C. G. den Hertog, U. Hübner and S. Münger; Münster:

second that the religious traditions of the LB Age and Iron Age I highlands now entered the new cities with the people who came to settle in them. As a result, the diverse local and familial worship traditions of the families, clans and tribes continued to be practised by the leaders of these groups at their homes or at the local sanctuaries. The fact that, in Iron Age IIA, cultic objects for the performance of sacrificial offerings are frequently found in domestic contexts (Beth-Shan, Taanach, Jabneh) fits well with this picture.[78] Incense bowls and clay statue shrines, decorated in the local → *iconographic* traditions, are often found.

Expensive metal figurines are absent in local cult, with the result that male deities are significantly less frequent in the iconographic findings, since only seldom were they replaced by cheap clay figurines. The clay statuary belongs firmly in the hand of the goddesses (mostly represented in the round). Miniature terra-cotta shrines for cultic images of goddesses (identified by their surrounding iconography) became increasingly popular from Iron Age IIA on[79] and continue to be found until ca. 600 BCE. All in all, these findings do not indicate that in Palestine during this period there were any inhibitions about representing deities in → *anthropomorphic* shape.[80] The beginnings of hostility to images, as propagated by the OT in the prohibition of idols and the polemics of the prophets against idols, cannot be projected back into Iron Age IIA, whose iconographic findings confirm the survival of traditional motifs (goddesses holding their breasts, goddesses with a child) as well as the appearance of new motifs.

The relationships of the various local deities of the families, clans and tribes among themselves would have come to play a role when the clans joined into tribes or the tribes joined into tribal-confederations and thus

Ugarit-Verlag, 2003), 205–11. The cult objects found in a pit (not an active sanctuary) belong to stratum IV (9th/8th cent.).

78. C. Frevel, 'Eisenzeitliche Kultständer als Medien in Israel/Palästina', in *Medien der Antike: Kommunikative Qualität und normative Wirkung* (ed. H. von Hesberg; Köln: Lehr- und Forschungszentrum für die antiken Kulturen des Mittelmeerraumes, 2003), 147–202. See also the recently discovered hoard of cult stands from the 9th cent. BCE found in Jabne, G. Dolev, ed., *In the Field of the Philistines: Cult Furnishings from the Favissa of a Yavneh Temple* (Tel Aviv: Eretz Israel Museum, 2007); R. Kletter *et al.*, *Yavneh I: The Excavation of the 'Temple Hill' Repository Pit and the Cult Stands* (OBO Series Archaeologica 30; Fribourg: Academic Press/Göttingen: Vandenhoeck & Ruprecht, 2010).

79. O. Keel and C. Uehlinger, *GGG*, § 100–101 and Ill. 188ab.

80. Contrary to O. Keel and C. Uehlinger, *GGG*, § 108–109.

had to face the question of choosing a *common* divine patron. Similar to the way the human leaders of various clans or tribes were brought together into genealogical relationships, one could relate their clan and tribal deities to each other so that they would reflect similar family relationships on the divine level. In this case, the god of the leading family or the predominating tribe came to enjoy special honour. The divine couple of the family or the clan of the tribal chieftain or king (the transition was fluid) became the head (= parents) of the subordinate clans and their gods. When tribes united into tribal-confederations under a chieftain or king, the tribal deity of the chieftain usually came to dominate the pantheon. Correspondences in the strength of the component clans or tribes could be expressed by the identification of the various deities of the new community with each other. In the course of the transformation of tribal chieftains via tribal-confederation kingdoms into centrally organized territorial states (consisting of various tribes and cities), a corresponding development also took place among the gods. The tribal god of the strongest tribe, whose chieftain had brought about the amalgamation and given the name of his tribe to the tribal-confederation, became the patron god of the new entity. In this way, the god (with his consort) of the dominant tribe rose, together with his tribe, from being a mere local figure to become the lord over several tribes and later over a territorial state. This god, who in the states on the western and eastern sides of the Jordan was male without exception, remained closely linked with the ruling family and its territorial claims (see the Mesha Stela). In the course of becoming lord of a territorial state, this god became the highest god, whereas the other gods of the united tribes and settlements continued to be the locally predominant deities and were subordinated to the god or divine couple ruling the whole entity either genealogically and/or within the framework of a heavenly divine assembly, whereby this assembly was conceived in analogy to the assembly of the clan or tribal heads (elders) around the chieftain or tribal-(confederation) king. In this way, the local deities and the gods of the ruling house came either to be hierarchically related to each other or, at times, to be identified with each other. When a chieftain expanded his court by building a palace in the urban seat of his power base (i.e. when he established an urban residence), he built also a sanctuary for the god of his ruling family in the immediate vicinity. As in the Bronze Age, the result was often the creation of an acropolis with both palace and temple side by side.

Such developments, sketched here generally for Iron Age IIA, can be observed for the 9th cent. BCE in the inscription of Mesha of Moab,[81] though they appear there not in terms of the beginnings of the development but rather in terms of its results. Mesha's territorial claims are based on Dibon/Qərīḥō with its heartland and are theologically guaranteed by his god Chemosh. Chemosh was the god of the ruling house and the local god of Dibon. Through the actions of his king Mesha, who consecrated a sanctuary (*bmt*) to him in Dibon/Qərīḥō, Chemosh more and more became the leading god over an expanding territorial state composed of diverse tribes (e.g. the Gadites) and cities (e.g. Nebo, Atarot, Jahaz), who had their own cultic traditions (in Atarot, perhaps the god Dōd; in Nebo, Yhwh). The conquests were made under the battle cry 'For Chemosh and for Moab' (l. 12). Chemosh and the king formed a single acting unity that constituted the state of Moab and legitimated the actions of the king. Mesha presupposed this unity of action in dealing with the places conquered together with their local deities. When he conquered the Israelite Nebo, the defeat of the town went hand in hand with the defeat of the god Yhwh, who dwelt there and whose cultic equipment was plundered and placed before the victorious god Chemosh for him to take possession of them (l. 18). The superiority of Chemosh was thus made manifest. It corresponds with the development of Moab into a territorial state centred on Dibon and to the close relationship between the ruling house and the ruling god, that Mesha erected an acropolis in Dibon/Qərīḥō with both a palace and a temple. As the god of the dynasty, of the tribal-confederation and of the capital city/residence, Chemosh dwelt beside his king. The king's victories were his victories!

## The Name YHWH[82]

→ *Epigraphically*, the Tetragram YHWH (with unknown vocalization) is well attested beginning with the inscription of the Moabite Mesha (9th cent.). It is likewise attested for the following centuries: inscriptions from Kuntillet ʿAjrûd (early 8th cent.) and Khirbet el-Qôm (8th cent.), → *ostraca* from Arad and Lachish (8th–6th centuries), inscriptions from Ḫirbet Bēt Layy (7th cent.), amulets from Ketef Hinnom (5th/4th centuries). Various short forms of the name are also known: YHW = Yaho/Yahu, YW = Yaw/Yau//Yo, YH = Yah and YHH = Yaho, which especially appear in personal names (e.g. Isa-iah, Josh-iah, Jo-natan). Whether the short version YHW is the older form, from which the Tetragram was later derived, or whether the development started with the Tetragram, is a question that cannot at present be decided.

⇨

81. *COS* II, 137–8; *ANET*, 320–1.

82. M. Weippert, 'Jahwe', *RlA* 5:246–53, reprinted in *Jahwe und die anderen Götter: Studien zur Religionsgeschichte des antiken Israel in ihrem syrisch-palästinischen Kontext* (FAT 18; Tübingen: Mohr Siebeck, 1997), 35–44; K. van der Toorn, 'Yahweh', in *DDD*², 910–19.

Significant is the question of the meaning of the name. According to Exod. 3.14 in the → *masoretic* vocalization, it derives from the Hebrew root HYY 'to be' 'to become' (Qal); however, since the work of Julius Wellhausen, a derivation from the Arabic root HWY 'to blow' is thought to be more plausible, because, among other reasons, it better fits the theological profile of Yhwh as originally a weather-god (compare Judg. 5.4-5; Hab. 3.3; Ps. 68.8-9 [NRSV 69.7-8]; Deut. 33.2). Philologically, both derivations are possible from the root HWY. From this form, the name Yhwh can be understood as a finite verb form of the long imperfect, 3rd pers., masc. sing. in the G-stem/Qal, meaning either 'he will be/is' or 'he will blow/blows'. The consonant sequence YHW is the corresponding form in the short imperfect or the jussive, meaning 'he should/shall be' or 'he should/shall blow'. If one assumes the causative instead of the G-stem/Qal, further possibilities of interpretation open up (Yhwh: 'causes to be' or 'creates' (see W. F. Albright) or 'causes to blow' or 'lets blow'). The LXX interpretation of Exod. 3.14 'I am the one who is' is based on Greek ontology. Out of fear of profaning the divine name, it was less and less pronounced in post-exilic (→ *exile*) times and more and more replaced by other → *epithets ('adōnāy; haš-šēm* = the Name). The LXX usually writes *'kyrios'* (= lord). The Masoretes vocalized the Tetragram with the vowels of the Hebrew word *''adōnāy'* (= my Lord) or (when written next to *'adōnāy*) with the vowels of the word *''ĕlōhîm'* (= God). The most frequently used form today, 'Yahweh' rests on efforts to recover the pronunciation on the basis of isolated testimony of late antiquity (e.g. Clement of Alexandria, 3rd cent. CE).

Because there is no evidence for a Yhwh cult outside of Israel/Judah in the Syro-Palestinian sources, it is generally concluded that he did not belong to the traditional pantheon of the region. Extra-biblical sources from Egypt dating to the 14th to 13th centuries BCE mention a place called 'Yahu (used as place name) in the land of the Shasu-nomads' and point to the northwestern part of the Arabian Peninsula. Since there are no other extra-biblical sources for the history of Yhwh before his encounter with 'Israel', scholars argue for an origin in the desert South of Palestine and for his connection with his divine seat mount Sinai, whose location, however, is not agreed upon (Sinai Peninsula, Arabian Peninsula). How the various tribes, which, as the name 'Isra-el' would indicate, were originally attached to the god El, came to worship Yhwh, is also a disputed question. It is thought that the Yhwh cult was transmitted to the tribes of Palestine by a particular group that gradually, in the course of history, became absorbed into 'Israel'. In this connection, various possibilities are under discussion. The classical Kenite or Midianite hypothesis offered the explanation (proposed by Bernhard Stade, Werner H. Schmidt), that Moses and his Midianite father-in-law, the priest Jethro/Reguel (Exod. 2.16; 3.1; 18.1, 10-12) transmitted the Yhwh cult to the whole people 'Israel', which had fled from Egypt, and that they in turn introduced it into Palestine. Because, however, a general agreement now prevails that 'Israel' had arisen within Palestine itself rather than having migrated into it, the Kenite hypothesis has been modified to the effect that no longer the whole people, but only a small band of exodus refugees encountered Yhwh while passing through the settlement area of the Kenites/Midianites in the southern desert. This fugitive group, which later dissolved into the Palestinian tribal-confederations, then introduced the Yhwh cult into their new homeland. It has also been proposed to turn the direction of migration around, so that, instead of 'Israelites' passing through Midian, it was Kenites/Midianites themselves, who, as merchants for example, brought their god into central Palestine. None of these hypotheses can be proven, and so it remains historically unclear, how a southern Semite deity rose to become the state god of two central Palestinian states.

As originally a weather-god, Yhwh (like the Edomite Qōs/Qaus or the Moabite Chemosh) belonged to the deities of the Baal-Hadad type, which is well documented in the Near East. Whereas at the beginning of the 2nd millennium, the god El still played the leading role in the Syro-Palestinian pantheons, he had to surrender this position to the deities of the Baal-Hadad type at the latest toward the end of the 2nd millennium. Thus, at the beginning of the Iron Age, worship of gods of this type rather than of El constituted the prevailing practice. This could explain the absence of biblical polemics against El – whose name became merely a term for 'god' or 'personal god' – (so Karel van der Toorn) just as well as the older hypothesis of an original essential similarity and early identification between Yhwh and El.[83] In the course of El's decline, his theological responsibilities and characteristics (creation, wisdom, age etc.) shifted to his more dynamic heirs of the Baal-Hadad type in their local forms. In the territory of the later northern kingdom Israel and the southern kingdom Judah, these were the local manifestations of the weather-god Yhwh, so that theologoumena concerning El can be found also in connection with Yhwh (e.g. Deut. 32.6-7). A further connection between Yhwh and El consisted in the choice of his female consort, the goddess Asherah, who had long been indigenous to the region.[84] In the texts from Kuntillet ʿAjrûd and Khirbet el-Qôm from the 8th cent., she is documented as his consort,[85] and, in both the north and the south, Yhwh and Asherah appear to have been the principal divine couple.[86] Epigraphically, Anath is also attested as Yhwh's consort, though only in the texts from Elephantine dating to the 5th cent. BCE (Anath-Yahu; compare Ch. 4.3.2.2). These findings are handled controversially in the scholarly discussion. It can, for instance, be interpreted as a local difference in the traditions, so that, in Judah, Yhwh is paired with Asherah, in the northern kingdom Israel, by contrast, with Anath. At the earliest, this could

⇨

83. For a critical appraisal of this thesis, see H. Niehr, *Der höchste Gott: Alttestamentlicher JHWH-Glaube im Kontext syrisch-kanaanäischer Religion des 1. Jahrtausends v.Chr.* (BZAW 190; Berlin: de Gruyter, 1990), 4–6.

84. In the OT, 'asherah' generally refers to a cult object made of wood, which could be set up or pulled down, cut down and burned. It is usually pictured as a tree or a stylized tree or a post.

85. *COS* II, 171–3; 179. In the Bible, Asherah is mentioned 40 times, sometimes as a goddess, but often materialized as a cult object.

86. However, a question has been raised about the extent to which inscriptions from Kuntillet ʿAjrûd and Khirbet el-Qôm allow conclusions to be drawn about the official cult in the northern and southern kingdoms, since they belong primarily to the area of private religiosity.

have been the case from the 8th to 7th centuries on, since, for the north, a connection with Asherah is also known from Kuntillet ʿAjrûd (Herbert Niehr, Karel van der Toorn).[87] The findings concerning the different epigraphically attested partners of Yhwh can also be interpreted, however, as a purely diachronic development.[88] But this interpretation (especially in the sequence proposed by Manfred Weippert, namely that initially Yhwh had been joined with Baal's Anath and only later, after his rise to become the highest god in El's place, did he become linked with Asherah) only sharpens the basic problem that Anath on Yhwh's side is documented only in later texts. In addition, the presupposed fixed connections of Baal/Hadad with Anath and of El with Asherah are untenable at least in this form.[89]

It is evident that the history of Yhwh in the 10th cent. BCE in an 'Israel' and Judah described in the categories of a disparate and only occasionally centralized tribal society, must have taken quite a different form than the one suggested by the biblical account, which describes an aniconic Yhwh as the sole midpoint of the official temple cult of an organized Davidic-Solomonic state having its seat in Jerusalem. Whereas in the first scenario, a god with the name Yhwh (together with other local deities; see below) can very well have been worshipped as a tribal or tribal-confederation god at various local tribal sanctuaries and later in the urban residences of the leading families, the OT view presupposes a well-organized urban cult from the time of Solomon on. Although one might expect that the task of building a temple for the god of the newly established state would have fallen to the first king of that state, the → *Deuteronomistic history* does not ascribe this action to either Saul or David, the first persons to whom it gives the name 'king', but instead entrusts Solomon with this measure (1 Kgs 5–6), which was of such central importance for Jerusalem (see below). For the temple(s) of the official cult of the northern kingdom,

87. H. Niehr, 'The Rise of YHWH in Judahite and Israelite Religion: Methodological and Religio-Historical Aspects', in *The Triumph of Elohim: From Yahwisms to Judaisms* (CBET 13; ed. D. V. Edelman; Kampen: Pharos, 1995), 45–73; K. van der Toorn, 'Anat-Yahu, Some Other Deities, and the Jews of Elephantine', *Numen* 39 (1992): 80–101.

88. So M. Weippert, 'Synkretismus und Monotheismus. Religionsinterne Konfliktbewältigung im alten Israel (1990)', in *Jahwe und die anderen Götter. Studien zur Religionsgeschichte des antiken Israel in ihrem syrisch-palästinischen Kontext* (FAT 18; Tübingen, Mohr Siebeck, 1997), 1–24, here 15–17.

89. See P. L. Day, 'Anat', in *DDD*², 36–43; N. Wyatt, 'Astarte', in *DDD*², 109–14, here 110.

there are no parallel stories, since the biblical authors and redactors regard the Jerusalem temple as the only legitimate place of worship for both the northern and the southern kingdoms, and they treat the cult of the northern kingdom as an illegitimate schism, as an apostasy. Consequently, one finds in 1 Kgs 12 only a polemical account of the efforts of Jeroboam I to establish bull worship of Bethel and Dan as an alternative to the Jerusalem cult,[90] whereby the despotic and sacrilegious character of these efforts as described in 1 Kgs 12 contrasts sharply with the ideal scenario of 1 Kgs 5–6. As the 'sin of Jeroboam', this action plays a central role in the ductus of the OT accounts of the northern kingdom and is intended to show that, from the beginning, the northern kingdom bore within itself the seeds of its destruction.[91] The religious schism described in 1 Kgs 12 should thus be seen as a paradigmatic rather than a historical event. Official bull worship of the northern kingdom in Dan during the 10th to 9th centuries BCE and thus during the reign of Jeroboam I, is historically most unlikely, if for no other reason than the fact that the whole region at this time was in the hands of the Aramaeans!

### The First Jerusalem Temple up to the Time of the Exile

For the OT, the Jerusalem temple ranks as *the* sacred building of the Judean state, having been erected by Solomon (1 Kgs 6–7; 2 Chr. 2–4) for Yhwh as the state god of the united monarchy. Due to the lack of opportunities for excavation, neither its exact location nor the existence of a preceding temple can be established; presumably it was located to the north of the present Dome of the Rock. For well-known reasons, archaeological research is not possible, so that this temple's architecture, furnishings and iconography can only be deduced from the OT texts handed down in 1 Kgs 6–7 resp. 2 Chr. 2–4, which, however, have been revised more than once. The history and date of these texts is actually debated. The temple plan of Ezekiel (Ezek. 40–42) is a fiction, which indeed rests on conditions of the pre-exilic temple but is, for the most part at least, determined by theological considerations (e.g. the Eastern Gate). The OT description of the first temple is historically/archaeologically unverifiable, but, because it corresponds structurally

⇨

90. Bull iconography is attested in Palestine since the earliest times. In the LB Age and Iron Age I, bulls could be linked with a weather-god or with El. Bovines are found in both the northern and the southern kingdom and thus are not a specific characteristic of the cult in the north.

91. A. Berlejung, 'Twisting Traditions: Programmatic Absence-Theology for the Northern Kingdom in 1 Kgs 12:26-33* (the "Sin of Jeroboam")', *JNSL* 35/2 (2009): 1–42.

to the Syro-Palestinian building traditions for city temples (long-room buildings since the MB Age II), it enjoys a certain plausibility. Customarily, scholars assign the Jerusalem temple to the Syrian long-room type, consisting of an atrium, a hall/antecella, and a 'holy of holies', a 'cella'. Recently, Jens Kamlah has proposed connecting the first temple with the Iron Age temples built in pillar constructions, which might have constituted an → *autochthonous* building type of the Levant. Unfortunately his (few) parallels are not convincing enough to support this idea. According to the OT account, the first temple was enclosed by a surrounding passage and decorated with the two pillars bearing the names Jachin and Boas (1 Kgs 7.21) at the entrance (**fig. 4**, see above). In the interior of the cella, stood the empty cherubim throne under which Solomon caused the ark of the covenant[92] to be placed (1 Kgs 6.19; 8.1-9). The Deuteronomistic history knows nothing of a cultic image of Yhwh. The temple and the palace area was surrounded by an enclosing wall (1 Kgs 7.9-12) and formed a linked territory, which identified the temple within the palace compound as the sanctuary of the ruling royal dynasty (so documented already since the MB Age in Shechem and Hazor among other places). In accordance with Ancient Near Eastern customs, the temple service was instituted by the king (1 Kgs 7.51; 8.62-65), who also claimed sacerdotal functions for himself (2 Sam. 8.18; 1 Kgs 8; 12.33). Because of the build-up of smoke, the altar of burnt offerings was located in the forecourt (1 Kgs 8.64; 9.25; 2 Kgs 16.10-16). According to 1 Kgs 15.13, 2 Kgs 21.7; 23.6 (Asherah), 2 Kgs 18.4 (Nehushtan), 2 Kgs 21.5; 23.12 (the army of heaven), 2 Kgs 23.11 (the sun-chariot), Ezek. 8.14 (Tammuz), 8.16 (the sun), other deities were also worshipped in the temple, so that, according to the Deuteronomistic account, it had to be cleansed on a number of occasions. In 587/586 BCE, the temple, together with the palace, was plundered and destroyed by the Babylonians (2 Kgs 25.9); however, according to Jer. 41.4-5 and Ezek. 33.24-29, this did not mean the end of the Yhwh cult in the land.[93]

T. A. Businck, *Der Tempel von Jerusalem von Salomo bis Herodes. I & II*. Leiden: Brill, 1970/1980; J. Kamlah, 'Die Tempel und Heiligtümer Phöniziens: Kultstätten im Kontext der eisenzeitlichen Stadtkultur in der Levante'. Pages 83–100 in *Phönizisches und punisches Städtewesen*. Edited by S. Helas and D. Marzoli. Mainz: Zabern, 2008.

92. Regarding this chest, there are various hypotheses concerning its function (as a divine throne, a throne substitute, a military palladium, a container for the transport of cult objects, a transportable sanctuary, or a sacral symbol) and about its content (→ *baetylus*, cult images, a bull-image of Yhwh, oracle stones, tablets of the law, see 1 Kgs 8.9). See T. Staubli, *Das Image der Nomaden im Alten Israel und in der Ikonographie seiner sesshaften Nachbarn* (OBO 107; Fribourg: Academic Press/Göttingen: Vandenhoeck & Ruprecht, 1991), 131–2, 222–9.

93. A. Berlejung, 'Notlösungen: Altorientalische Nachrichten über den Tempelkult in Nachkriegszeiten', in *Kein Land für sich allein: Studien zum Kulturkontakt in Kanaan, Israel/Palästina und Ebirnâri: FS M. Weippert* (OBO 186; ed. U. Hübner and E. A. Knauf; Fribourg: Academic Press/Göttingen: Vandenhoeck & Ruprecht, 2002), 196–230, here 224–5.

The biblical connection of the royal dynasty 'house of David' with the residence Jerusalem and the dynastic god Yhwh would seem to indicate that Yhwh only entered the City of David with the dynasty's founder, David, (as tribal chieftain, leader of an armed band, or as tribal king). In this way, a tribal god became a city god. It is hardly possible to clarify what god(s) may have been worshipped in Jerusalem before Yhwh, whether, from the beginning, he was placed at the peak of the already existing pantheon, or where and how (i.e. in what visible form) he was integrated into the local cult. According to the OT account, no construction measures for his cult were carried out when the city was turned into the dynastic seat. That David, (according to 2 Samuel, see esp. 2 Samuel 24) undertook no such works, evidently created a problem for the OT, which was only solved in 1 Chr. 28–29. In terms of material culture, the 10th cent. BCE, as already indicated, emerges as a time of diverse local cultic traditions on a modest financial level. Thus the erection or enlargement of an urban temple in Jerusalem in the 10th cent. BCE by a local city prince ruling over some 1,000 souls may not be void of any plausibility, but such a temple could hardly have contained the riches that 1 Kgs 5–6 says were to be admired in it. Because the official cult of the ruling house of the residence was, as such, nothing more than the house cult of the royal family, when it was introduced, nothing changed for the house cult of 'normal' families or for the local cult of other locations. Thus the 10th cent. BCE is by no means marked by a reduction of the world of gods and goddesses or by any other drastic cultic paradigm shift (e.g. → *aniconism*, → *monotheism*, disappearance of goddesses).

Alongside the above-mentioned terra-cotta goddesses in house and local cult, attention is called to the seal iconography of local production in Palestine, where in addition to the suckling mother animal, capridae with branches, and worshippers around a holy tree/tree sanctuary, one finds the 'lord of the ostriches', an → *autochthonous* figure, which should be associated with divine rule over the animals of the steppe. Newly documented on seal amulets of steatite is an angularly stylized enthroned god with a sun-disk, which goes back to Egyptian traditions. The seal and amulet iconography in Iron Age IIA generally continues to show strong Egyptian influence (Amun Re), which is not confined to the coast or the southern territories but also includes the northern interior. A vigorous exchange of neighbouring religious symbol systems is also revealed by imports from northern Syria (seal amulets of haematite and quartz with animal figures, mostly cattle symbolism and the moon-crescent), as well as from Cyprus, and Phoenicia.

The presence of Aramaeans in northern Palestine, especially around the Sea of Galilee, which goes back to ca. 1200 BCE and is tangible in the 10th and 9th centuries, should not be underestimated. From ca. 1050 BCE on, the religious centre of the Aramaeans was Haran in northwestern Mesopotamia, where, at least since the 18th cent. BCE, a place of worship for the moon-god Sin was located. His symbolism (moon-crescent standard with bells, bull iconography) and the lunar elements associated with him thus found early entrance into Palestine and in subsequent times continued vehemently to assert themselves (see e.g. Beth-Saida).

*3. Iron Age IIB (926/900–722/700 or 800/785/748–722/700 BCE[94]).* In this epoch, with the rise to statehood, the development of the former local deities of individual clans and tribes into dynastic gods, then into urban residence gods, and finally into (territorial) state gods reached its term. In the course of this process, Milcom of Ammon, Chemosh of Moab, Qōs/Qaus of Edom, Yhwh of Israel/Samaria, and Yhwh of Judah/Jerusalem evolved into supreme gods of the pantheon of the corresponding territorial states, which from then on ranked as belonging to them. Thus the religio-historical evolution of Yhwh and his rise to the supreme god and king in the 10th–9th centuries BCE should be seen against this background as part of an (on the whole uniform but regionally differentiated) Syro-Palestinian religious history, which terminated in the emergence of a limited number of local state gods. Accordingly, Yhwh, initially a local god of the two tribal-confederations 'Israel' and 'Judah' – with the rise of 'his' tribes and their leading clans to become dynasties ruling over the tribal-confederation kingdoms they had founded – rose himself to become the leading god of the two royal dynasties, of their residences, and of their kingdoms in the north and in the south.

## The Rise of Yhwh

Even when much remains open to discussion: The rise of Yhwh to become the highest god in the northern kingdom must have taken place in the course of the development to statehood, for, already in the 2nd half of the 9th cent. (Mesha Stela), he is attested as the god of the northern kingdom Israel with valuable

94. Concerning the demarcation from Iron Age IIB, see Ch. 2.2.

possessions in Nebo, which were worth plundering, and, from the early 8th cent. on, he is documented in blessing formulae on inscriptions of the South (Kuntillet ʿAjrûd).[95] In the period of the kings, Yhwh is without question the most important and highest god (though not the only one!) of the official cult in both of the northern and the southern kingdoms. This is well documented not only biblically but also extra-biblically by the theophoric personal names of members of the ruling classes.[96] According to both extra-biblical and biblical textual sources, however, the cultic reality consisted of → *polytheism* (Baal,[97] Asherah, Bes, Horus[98]) and → *poly-yahwism* and found expression in the most disparate local manifestations: the Yhwh of Samaria with his Asherah (Kuntillet ʿAjrûd, early 8th cent.), the Yhwh of Teman with his Asherah (Kuntillet ʿAjrûd, early 8th cent.), Yhwh as the god of Jerusalem with claims to the highlands of Judah and the whole land (Ḫirbet Bēt Layy, 7th cent.),[99] the Yhwh of Zion (Ps. 99.2) and the Yhwh of Hebron (2 Sam. 15.7).[100] At the earliest after the end of the statehood of the northern kingdom but more likely only after the end of Judah in the 6th cent., there came an identification, or at least to the theological construct of an identity, between the Yhwh worship in the southern and that in the northern kingdom. This opened the way (by eliminating the divine consort(s) of Yhwh, Asherah [and Anath] step by step) for the exclusive worship of Yhwh in the form he would later take in the Second Jerusalem Temple, and thus ultimately for monotheism.

Alongside the reigning dynasty's official cult of the ruling god of the northern and of the southern kingdoms, the diverse local or familial worship traditions of families, clans and tribes survived in Iron Age IIB and continued to be practised at home or in the local sanctuary. Into this picture fits the fact that, just as in Iron Age IIA so also in Iron Age IIB, cultic objects are frequently found in domestic context: clay statue shrines, terra-cottas, and clay plaques of goddesses are well documented.

95. See the large discussion in Z. Zevit, *Religions*, 370–405, with the critical remarks of M. Smith, 'Review Article', *Maarav* 11 (2004): 143–218, here 188–91.
96. Names containing Yhwh are found in the → *ostraca* of Samaria and Arad from the 1st half of the 8th cent.
97. Among members of the upper class, names containing Baal are found on ostraca from Samaria in the 1st half of the 8th cent. On the relationship between Baal and Yhwh see the following.
98. Bes and Horus are also found on ostraca from Samaria.
99. Z. Zevit, *Religions*, 417–27, 692–3.
100. On the construction of divine name + b + with the place-name as an indication of a local divine manifestation, see K. van der Toorn, 'Yahweh', in *DDD*[2], 919.

*The northern kingdom Israel*: In northern Palestine, the religio-historical development in the 10th to 9th and the 8th centuries is no less complex than the political development, with which it is closely linked. The local extension of the Yhwh cult of Israel/Samaria must be seen in connection with the area ruled by the kings of the northern kingdom. Against the background of the Aramaean expansion in the Jezreel Valley and Galilee in the 10th and early 9th centuries, there is little room for a very large sphere of influence for the god of the northern tribes. Both regions formed an intermediate area between the religious symbol systems of the Aramaeans and that of the 'Israelite' tribal groups as well as that of the Phoenician coastland, so that this area cannot be ascribed simply to the influence sphere of Yhwh. Megiddo, the Jezreel Valley, the Beth-Shan Plains and Galilee (Kinneret, Hazor, Dan) were subjected to various cultic-religious influences parallel to their political fate, whereby one must also reckon with the existence of a local cult that had survived all the transformations unscathed[101] or which managed to integrate the successive in-flowing religious notions into its own local traditions (see, for example, the amalgamation of the local weather-god and the Aramaean moon-god at Beth-Saida). Yhwh was at first only the highest god of the tribal-confederation state of a central Palestinian society composed of highland peasants and herders – in short, the state god of a mini-state in the highlands (see also 1 Kgs 20.23, 28). The location of his official cult initially shifted with the various royal residences. Only under Omri and his successor, did the god of the highland state 'Israel' emerge out of this heartland to lead the tribal-confederation of the north to become the territorial state 'Israel' extending into Transjordan, the Jezreel Valley, and Galilee. In this way, the influence sphere of the Israelite state god varied with the political and military successes and failures of his kings. According to the Mesha Inscription, in the context of the expansion of the Omrides into Transjordan in the 9th cent. BCE, Yhwh was worshipped in

101. Local pantheons continued to exist in Transjordan during the period of the monarchy. The Gileadite inscription from Tell Deir ʿAlla (M. Weippert, 'The Balaam Text from Tell Deir ʿAlla and the Study of Old Testament', in *The Balaam Text from Deir 'Alla Re-Evaluated: Proceedings of the International Symposium held at Leiden 21-24 August 1989* [ed. J. Hoftijzer and G. van der Kooij; Leiden: Brill, 1991], 151–84) belongs to the end of the 9th or the 1st half of the 8th cent. and provides evidence for the → *autochthonous* tradition of a vision of the seer Balaam, son of Beor (Numbers 22–24), in which various deities played a major role. Presumably, they belonged to the local pantheon of the place in Transjordan: Šagar, ʿAštar, deities ('lhn), Šadday-deities and (according the (re-)construction of the text), perhaps also El.

Nebo, and, by plundering his furnishings, Mesha damaged or even ended his cult there. A similar situation can be assumed for the Jezreel Valley and the Beth-Shan Plains as well as for Galilee. These places were under the influence of the kings of Samaria and their god for only short intervals, 880–840/837 BCE (Omri to Jehoram/Joram) and 800–738/732 BCE (Joash to Pekah). Prior to Omri and from ca. 840/837 to 800 BCE, they were, not only in political but also in religious regard, under Aramaean influence. After 738/732 BCE, they fell to the Assyrians. Thus Israelite hegemony in this region lasted only ca. 40 plus 70 years, with a 40-year interruption in between, and it can hardly be expected that the local population exchanged its gods with every shift of political sovereignty. To what extent the shifting of the gods of the official cult from Hadad/Baal to Yhwh (or in reverse) was systematically carried out by the respective rulers or was even noticed by the people, is difficult to say. Whether the worship of Yhwh, in contrast to Hadad/Baal, was able to take root at all in these places, is so very difficult to decide, because, as weather-gods, the two deities were already very closely related and thus could easily be identified. It is questionable, therefore, if/to what extent the cult of Yhwh in Dan, a traditional sanctuary at a spring of the Jordan, could have gained a foothold during the short time of Israelite hegemony. According to Amos 8.14, the local god was known as the 'god of Dan' without a proper name and as the nameless 'god of Dan' he is attested much later in a → *Hellenistic* votive inscription.[102] How far the influence of the Aramaean religious symbol system extended into the Israelite heartland and to the south, is also difficult to say. In 2 Kgs 23.8; Ezek. 8.3-5, a 'cult at the gates', as archaeologically documented in Dan and Beth-Saida, is mentioned at Jerusalem and is branded as an illegitimate worship of false gods, whereby it is no longer possible to determine to what deity it might have been addressed in the Judean capital. When Dan by and large is eliminated as a location of the official cult of the northern kingdom except for the brief intervals of 40 plus 70 years mentioned above,[103] two other sanctuaries of the northern kingdom with supra-regional significance are named in the OT: Samaria and Bethel.

102. A. Biran and V. Tzaferis, 'A Bilingual Dedicatory Inscription from Tell Dan', *Qad* 10 (1977): 114–15.

103. Dan played almost no role in the prophetic criticism of Amos and Hosea. For this reason, C. Dohmen, *Das Bilderverbot: Seine Entstehung und Entwicklung im Alten Testament* (BBB 62; 2nd ed.; Frankfurt: Athenäum, 1987), 145–6 has proposed the hypothesis that the bull of Dan was a Deuteronomistic expansion (with 2 Kgs 10.29).

In *Samaria*, as the seat of the ruling dynasty since Omri, a temple of the dynastic god for the official cult could be expected. The OT indeed speaks of building measures for the official cult, but only by Solomon; whereas there is no mention of activities on Omri's part in this direction. In terms of the general ductus of the → *Deuteronomistic* history from 1 Kgs 12, there is no need to do so, for with the mention of the 'sin of Jeroboam', i.e. his patronage of bull worship in Bethel and Dan in 1 Kgs 12.26-33, the cult of the northern kingdom is characterized as the worship of idols and foreign gods.[104] Only under Ahab, is mention made in 1 Kgs 16.32 of the erection of a temple in the Omridic residence Samaria, which, it is claimed, was consecrated to Baal and also contained (the) Asherah (1 Kgs 16.33; 2 Kgs 13.6). According to 2 Kgs 10.18-27, the Baal temple and the Asherah were destroyed by Jehu in a large-scale operation, although, according to 2 Kgs 13.6, at the time of Joash of Israel, the Asherah continued to stand. The attribution of this temple to Baal and Asherah like the account of its destruction is → *Deuteronomistic*,[105] so that from these texts no historical certitude can be won concerning the existence of a temple for these deities or concerning their relationship to Yhwh (competition or identification between Yhwh and Baal?). In any case, → *ostraca* from Samaria show names containing Yhwh and thus document Yhwh's presence there. At the same time names containing Baal are attested. That says nothing, however, about the relationship between Yhwh and Baal. They may have been two distinct, even rival gods in Samaria, or they may refer to one and the same god, since Yhwh was none other than the local Baal (= ruler). The → *Deuteronomistic* narrative fails to acknowledge the existence of a really legitimate Yhwh temple for the northern kingdom either in Samaria or anywhere else, but this can be interpreted as tendentious polemics and historically questioned. → *Epigraphically*, the cult of Yhwh and Asherah is documented in Samaria of the early 8th century BCE by the mention of the Yhwh of Samaria and his Asherah on Pithos A in Kuntillet ʿAjrûd; but this has not been otherwise archaeologically proven. According to the Nimrud prism of Sargon II,[106] → *anthropomorphic* cult statues were found in the local temple of the Yhwh of Samaria,[107] and these were then carried off by the Assyrians.

104. See the extensive discussion in A. Berlejung, *Die Theologie der Bilder: Das Kultbild in Mesopotamien und die alttestamentliche Bilderpolemik unter besonderer Berücksichtigung der Herstellung und Einweihung der Statuen* (OBO 162; Fribourg: Academic Press/Göttingen: Vandenhoeck & Ruprecht, 1998), 325–34.

105. Ahab was described in the → *Deuteronomistic* narrative as the predecessor of the sacrilegious Manasseh (backwards reference in 2 Kgs 21.3), so that his cult measures in 1 Kgs 16.32-33 are closely connected with 2 Kgs 21.3-7.

106. *COS* II, 259–60.

107. B. Becking, 'The Gods in Whom They Trusted… Assyrian Evidence for Iconic Polytheism in Ancient Israel?' in *Only One God? Monotheism in Ancient Israel and the Veneration of the Goddess*

Nothing is known about the outer appearance of such statues (and thus of the Yhwh of Samaria). Occasionally, it has been proposed to relate the drawings on the Pithos A of Kuntillet ʿAjrûd to the inscription in such a way that a representation of the two deities Yhwh and Asherah is seen therein. However, this opinion has failed to convince for a variety of reasons, among them that the two male figures should be interpreted as representations of Bes and the depiction of three persons, instead of two, shows that they cannot correspond to the inscription as an illustration.[108]

*Bethel* likewise counts as a supra-regionally significant sanctuary of the northern kingdom (1 Kgs 12.26-33; Hos. 4.15; 6.10; 10.5; Amos 4.4; 5.5; 7.10-17), which perhaps was maintained by the kings as a border sanctuary towards the south[109] (Amos 7.10-17). Occasionally, it has been argued that, with the erection of a bull image in Bethel (1 Kgs 12.26-33), Jeroboam I tied into older cult traditions[110] and thus raised Bethel from the status of a local sanctuary to that of a royal state temple (Amos 7.13). The OT connects both pilgrimages and schools of prophets with the place (2 Kgs 2.2-3, 23; Amos; Hosea), which evidently lost its moveable cult furnishings to the Assyrian conquest in 722/721 BCE (Hos. 10.5-6), though immoveable objects like → *mazzeboth* (if according to Gen. 28.10-22 a mazzebah really existed there) undoubtedly remained in place. Archaeologically, none of this can be verified. The Bethel of Iron Age II appears to have been a relatively modest place.[111] The local sanctuary, which has not been clearly identified (perhaps it was on the Burj Beitin, east of Beitin), may have stood outside the settlement since the LB Age, and, according to 2 Kgs 23.15, it continued to exist into the times of Josiah despite the Assyrian plundering.

According to 1 Kgs 12.26-33; Hos. 8.5-6; 10.5; 13.2, the bull cult prevailed in Samaria, Bethel and Dan, whereby the bulls, according to the exodus formula in 1 Kgs 12.28 counted as real representatives of Yhwh and not

*Asherah* (ed. idem *et al.*; Sheffield: Sheffield Academic Press, 2001), 159–63; S. Timm, 'Ein assyrisch bezeugter Tempel in Samaria?' in *Kein Land für sich allein: Studien zum Kulturkontakt in Kanaan, Israel/Palästina und Ebirnâri: FS M. Weippert* (OBO 186; ed. U. Hübner and E. A. Knauf; Fribourg: Academic Press/Göttingen: Vandenhoeck & Ruprecht, 2002), 126–33.

108. For the discussion, see the extensive treatment in C. Uehlinger, 'Anthropomorphic Cult Statuary', 142–6 (above, Ch. 3 n. 18).

109. H. M. Niemann, *Herrschaft, Königtum und Staat: Skizzen zur soziokulturellen Entwicklung im monarchischen Israel* (FAT 6; Tübingen: Mohr Siebeck, 1993), reckons with religio-political measures of the northern kingdom in Bethel and Dan.

110. So for example K. Koenen, *Bethel: Geschichte, Kult und Theologie* (OBO 192; Fribourg: Academic Press/Göttingen: Vandenhoeck & Ruprecht, 2003), 42–8.

111. I. Finkelstein and L. Singer-Avitz, 'Reevaluating Bethel', *ZDPV* 125 (2009): 33–48.

simply as his pedestal.[112] The value of these texts as a historical source has been widely discussed, and the proposed evaluations range over the whole spectrum of possibilities from historical fact to unhistorical fiction. While a consensus appears to be forming, that, before Hosea (i.e. before the 2nd half of the 8th cent.), the worship of Yhwh in the shape of a bull or a → *mazzebah* posed no problem, on the basis of the redactional-historical problematic of the book of Hosea, it is hardly possible to decide whether the polemic against foreign gods and idols in fact began with Hosea himself[113] or only later came to be inserted redactionally into the collection of his sayings.[114] For the prophets of the 8th century, Asherah was apparently still no problem, for they indeed contain polemics against Baal (Hos. 2.10, 15, 18-19 [NRSV 2.8, 13, 16-17]; 9.10; 11.2; 13.1), but not against Asherah.

## Yhwh, Baal and the Sun-God in the Northern Kingdom

The OT is marked in many parts by sharp polemics against Baal (Elijah and Elisha stories: see 1 Kgs 18; 2 Kgs 10; Hosea, Num. 25.1-5, Deut. 4). It repeatedly calls upon Israel to decide for Yhwh over Baal and thus constructs an irreconcilable opposition between the two gods. The religio-historical interpretation of this opposition is controversial. Sometimes it is argued that Baal represented a danger for Yhwh, because the notions of fertility connected with him were not compatible with Yhwh belief. In this case, unlike the relationship between Yhwh and El, identification between Yhwh and Baal would not have been possible. In the meantime, however, it has become clear that Yhwh and Baal are very closely related to each other and as weather-gods shared similar competencies. In Iron Age II, a further aspect enters the scene. Arguing from the Phoenician religion since the 10th cent. BCE, in which neither Baal nor El, but rather Baal-šamēm (Baal of the Heavens/Lord of the Heavens) was worshipped as the tutelary god of the king, as the weather-god of the heavens, and as the supreme god (or at least identified with the locally supreme

112. On the debate, see A. Berlejung, Theologie, 328–9 (above, n. 104).

113. H. D. Preuss, *Verspottung fremder Religionen im Alten Testament* (BWANT 92; Stuttgart: Kohlhammer, 1971), 120–9; E. Bons, *Das Buch Hosea* (Neuer Stuttgarter Kommentar AT 23/1; Stuttgart: Katholisches Bibelwerk, 1996), 107–8, 160–1.

114. M. Nissinen, *Prophetie, Redaktion und Fortschreibung im Hoseabuch: Studien zum Werdegang eines Prophetenbuches im Lichte von Hos 4 und 11* (AOAT 231; Neukirchen-Vluyn: Neukirchener, 1991); J. Jeremias, 'Hosea/Hoseabuch', *TRE* 15:586–98, esp. 592–3.

god). Herbert Niehr,[115] following Otto Eissfeldt, has called attention to the fact that not only the Phoenician and the Aramaean Baal/Hadad but also the northern Israelite Yhwh of the Omrides (i.e. the official cult) was conceived with solar and celestial connotations, so that Yhwh in Samaria was understood as Baal-šamēm. In fact, it can be shown on the basis of → *iconography* that the widespread tendencies toward solar and celestial symbolism of the Levantine deities also put their stamp on the religious symbolism of Israel and later Judah. This suggests that Yhwh too moved into this role and assumed heavenly and solar traits,[116] so that, in the northern kingdom since the 9th cent. BCE, he was increasingly understood as solar Baal-šamēm. The iconographically documented symbolism of the sun and the heavens had come from Egypt and through Phoenician mediation, become native in Israel. Analogously to the political and economic orientation of the northern kingdom toward Syria and Phoenicia, its iconography is likewise characterized by close relationships to Phoenician art. The religious symbolism of the sun and of a protecting power (winged creatures) entered Israel through Phoenician mediation from the 9th cent. on (most productively in the 8th cent.) and thus was received earlier and more intensively than in Judah, where this development began only in the 2nd half of the 8th cent. The uranisation and solarization of Yhwh is tangible in epigraphic and OT sources (e.g. Hos. 6.3-5).

The official cult of Yhwh in the northern kingdom, like that of other deities, seems to have taken place for the most part in sanctuaries outside the cities. The archaeological findings of Iron Age IIB point to few city temples (an exception is the southern temple of Beth-Shan V[117]). Not even the religious policy of the Omrides, which established numerous cities as places with state functions, appears to have put special emphasis on the erection of city temples (with the exception of the chapel in Samaria). In Omridic administrative centres like Hazor (Stratum X), Megiddo (Stratum VA–IVB),[118] Jezreel and perhaps Gezer (Stratum VIII), no city temples have yet been

115. H. Niehr, 'JHWH in der Rolle des Baalšamem', in *Ein Gott allein? JHWH-Verehrung und biblischer Monotheismus im Kontext der israelitischen und altorientalischen Religionsgeschichte* (OBO 139; ed. W. Dietrich and M. A. Klopfenstein; Fribourg: Academic Press/Göttingen: Vandenhoeck & Ruprecht, 1994), 307–26.
116. O. Keel and C. Uehlinger, GGG, 164.
117. The temple there was in service from the 11th to the 9th centuries BCE.
118. Toward the end of the 10th cent. or in the early 9th cent., a modest village had again arisen in Megiddo (stratum VB), which in the 1st half of the 9th cent. was expanded into a settlement with public buildings for the local administration. Strata VA–IVB were fortified, the outer walls of the houses forming a closed front. City walls of this type required very little state coordination

identified. Nevertheless, the plundering of the cultic equipment of Yhwh in Transjordanian Nebo by Mesha of Moab (Mesha Inscription from the mid 9th cent) indicates that, in the Israelite territories, the cult of the state god Yhwh also existed outside the capital/residence. The general absence of city temples in Palestine of the Iron Age makes it hardly possible to (re-)construct an → *autochthonous* 'Israelite' (or 'Judean') building tradition. The recent finding of city temples in Beth-Shan V and in Philistine Ekron (7th cent.) do not change this situation. These buildings with three naves in pillar construction, with rooms at the sides (and eventually at the back) can hardly be viewed as an indigenous Levantine temple type of the Iron Age, since these two temples are not located in the Israelite-Judean heartland.[119]

> The material findings of Iron Age IIB show only a small number of → *anthropomorphic* metal statues of gods of the standing/smiting or enthroned types. Much more frequent are clay statues (e.g. Dan), terra-cottas of feminine (e.g. Beth-Shan V, Samaria) or masculine deities (Transjordan, Beth-Saida), plaques of naked goddesses, faience figures mostly imported from Egypt, larger limestone statues (Transjordan), and smaller stone statuettes of Cisjordan (Gezer, Megiddo). The state gods of the Transjordan region were evidently pictured as bearded men with the Egyptian atef-crown (Amman) in a long robe; their consorts were pictured as clothed female rulers, who expressed their nurturing aspect by holding their breasts.[120] In the Iron Age, → *mazzeboth* continue to be found as signs of the presence of the gods or the ancestors (e.g. Arad, Lachish, Megiddo), which, in the Yhwh cult of the pre-deuteronomistic period, were (just as cultic images) not found objectionable (a different attitude is reflected only in Deut. 16.22; 2 Kgs 18.4).

All in all, the → *glyptic* and the artistic craftsmanship of the northern kingdom show it to be a region which had taken up various religious symbol systems but also held fast to its local tardyons. The → *iconography*, the handicraft (ivories, seals), and the material remains of northern Palestine all show a strong affinity to Phoenicia and Syria. The Egyptian religious symbol system continues, however, to be present in both the north and the south

and investment. This frontage-wall was replaced by a uniformly constructed city fortification in stratum IVA.

119. Contra J. Kamlah, 'Der salomonische Tempel: Paradigma der Verknüpfung von biblischer Exegese und Archäologie für eine Rekonstruktion der Religionsgeschichte Israels', *VF* 53 (2008): 40–51.

120. C. Uehlinger, 'Cult Statuary', 112–23 (above, Ch. 3 n. 18).

(amulets). In the 9th and even more in the 8th cent. BCE, both the Israelite and the Judean societies, especially the ruling classes, were unquestionably fascinated by the power of Egypt, its religious traditions (sun-god, sun-disk, → *scarab*, → *uraeus*), and their connection with the royal ideology (pharaoh as the earthly representative of the sun-god, the conqueror of the enemies). Especially the Egyptian sun-god, who had achieved a predominant position in the New Empire, or at least elements belonging to his sphere (winged Sphinxes, greifs, uraeuses, falcons, the falcon-headed god with the sun-disk) found considerable echo in Palestine. Alongside these imported motifs, however, one continues to encounter in the → *glyptic* of both Israel and Judah the 'Lord of the Ostriches' (Megiddo, Lachish, Mizpah), while the 'Lord of the Capridae' is encountered especially in the north (Dan, Samaria, Hazor).

*The South:* In the south, since the time of David, the tribal kings/chieftains of Judah had had their seat in Jerusalem and were thus simultaneously city kings ruling over an urban centre with a state temple, in which Yhwh was worshipped as the state god of the mini-state of the highlands. Analogous to the political history and to the shifting extension of the Judean state in Iron Age IIB, the question of Yhwh's sphere of influence poses a problem calling for different answers for the different periods of time. The boundaries of the Yhwh cult to the north are of special interest, because, in the border area between the northern and southern kingdoms, the initial opportunities for an amalgamation of the Yhwhs of the north and the south were to be found. However, significant differences seem to have existed between the two cults. Unlike in the north, Yhwh in the south was linked with *only one* royal dynasty, thus making him perhaps more strongly the god of the king's family. Perhaps the Yhwh of the north was also more strongly conceived as Baal/Baal-šamēm, whereas the Yhwh of the south had received the characteristics of the Jerusalem city god (perhaps a sun-god[121]). To the west, in accordance with the shifting western boundaries of Judah, the Yhwh cult likewise had to confront the cults of the Philistine cities. For the inter-cultural border regions of the Shephelah and the territory of the tribe of Benjamin, it is probable that they retained their local religious traditions independently of whatever power claimed or actually exercised hegemony or that they at least integrated the newly introduced deities (no problem in → *polytheism*) into their already existing pantheons (so for example in Ekron).

121. O. Keel and C. Uehlinger, 'Jahwe und die Sonnengottheit von Jerusalem', in *Ein Gott allein?* (ed. W. Dietrich and M. A. Klopfenstein), 269–306 (above, n. 115).

Concerning the religious policy measures of the kings of Judah until the end of the 8th cent. BCE, the → *Deuteronomistic* history (and the Chronicles; 23) narrate very little, and the historicity of even this meagre information is doubted. Michaiah/Maacha, the mother of the king, is said to have caused an Asherah to be erected in the Jerusalem temple, which cost her position (1 Kgs 15.13). Joash is said to have taken up a collection to renovate the Jerusalem temple (2 Kgs 12). Ahaz is said to have caused an altar to be built on the Damascene model and set up in the temple (2 Kgs 16.10-16).[122] Hezekiah (in this context, under the impression made by the fall of the northern kingdom) is said to have carried out a cultic reform directed against the cults of the local high places, the → *mazzeboth*, the Asherah posts, and the Nehushtan (2 Kgs 18.4), which prefigured the cult reform of the Deuteronomistic ideal king Josiah in 2 Kgs 22–23 (→ *Josiah's reform*).[123] Further cultic measures outside Jerusalem (with the exception of the stereotyped references to the worship at the high places, e.g. 2 Kgs 15.4, 35; 16.4 etc.) are not mentioned in the Bible. The cult of the non-Judean neighbouring city Ekron is mentioned in 2 Kgs 1, because King Ahaziah of Israel chose to consult the Baal-Zebub of Ekron for an oracle concerning his illness rather than Yhwh. The 2nd half of the 8th cent. was also the time of the Judean prophets Isaiah and Micah, who took different positions regarding Jerusalem and → *Zion*, though both focused on the capital city in their preaching. If the corresponding texts are authentic, for the rural Judean Micah, the economically prospering Jerusalem was a hotbed of corrupt judges, priests and prophets, which for this reason was doomed to destruction (Mic. 3.9-12). By contrast, the Jerusalemite Isaiah was apparently a prophet at the court of the kings Uzziah to Hezekiah, who realistically appraised the foreign political situation of Aram, Israel (Isa. 8.1-4), Philistia (Isa. 20), and Judah in the 2nd half of the 8th cent.; he warned about preparations for war (Isa. 22.8-11), and deceptive alliances with Egypt (Isa. 18.1-19.15; 20), and predicted the survival of Jerusalem despite Judah's drastic territorial losses and repeated imperilment (Isa. 1.7-8).

The material culture of Judah shows no signs of a city temple except in Jerusalem. In the late 8th cent., the remains of a sanctuary with an alcove and

122. The text of 2 Chr. 28.2 can be seen as a fiction of the Chronicler.

123. The Deuteronomistic account of Hezekiah's cult reform has been worked over several times, so that it is extremely difficult to cull from it what Hezekiah actually did. Although many regard the whole reform as a Deuteronomistic fiction (H.-D. Hoffmann), most see the historical kernel as consisting in the destruction of the serpent Nehushtan (e.g. H. Donner, *Geschichte*, 363–4).

a court with a sacrificial altar have been found only in the Negev fortress Arad. Disparate signs of cult activity appear to be found in Beer-sheba (horned altar, vessel with dedicatory inscription), Hazor and Tell Bēt-Mirsim. As the Arad finds show, this does not necessarily point to cult in a city temple complex. Cultic shrines can mainly be expected within palaces and fortresses or in open-air sanctuaries.

The altar in Arad was built up of layered quarry stones and covered with a plate of flintstone with channels for the runoff of the sacrificial blood. In the surrounding deposits, figurines of goddesses of the typically Judean type of the pillar-figurine (**fig. 5j**) were found, which should be assigned to the realm of private religiosity.[124] These clay figurines originated in the 2nd half of the 8th cent. and gained great popularity in the 7th cent. They depict a goddess in a flared skirt, whose name cannot be identified (Asherah?); she is holding her breasts. In the holy of holies of the temple at Arad (**fig. 5i**), there was a → *mazzebah* (or two)[125] and two incense altars. → *Mazzeboth* and the pillar-figurines make clear that various deities were worshipped and that they were represented in different forms (→ *aniconic* as mazzebah, → *anthropomorphic* as a feminine figure holding her breasts, and even zoomorphic).[126] The findings argue against making generalizing conclusions about the genuine aniconic character of the religion of (Israel) and Judah.[127] The end of this sanctuary used to be dated to the late 7th cent. and to be connected with the cult reform of Josiah, but now it is more often attributed to the Babylonian or Edomite destruction of the entire fortress in the early 6th cent.[128]

In the Judean → *iconography*, from the 9th cent. on, a strong reception of Egyptian symbols of lordship is in evidence, leading to the conclusion that the royal ideology there was strongly influenced by Egypt. Evidently, the king of Jerusalem took his bearings from the Egyptian pharaoh. As in earlier times, Egypt counted for the Judeans as the predominating and most attractive

124. Clay figurines of the naked goddess are found in the Philistine coastal region and the Shephelah in the 2nd half of the 8th cent.
125. On this problem, see. T. N. D. Mettinger, *No Graven Image? Israelite Aniconism in its Ancient Near Eastern Context* (ConBOT 42; Stockholm: Almquist & Wiksell, 1995), 143–9.
126. R. Kletter, *The Judean Pillar-Figurines and the Archaeology of Asherah* (British Archaeological Reports: International Series 636, Oxford: Tempus Reparatum, 1996), Nr. 442, 446 and 448. See also fig. 35.
127. Arad is often cited as the prime example of aniconic religious practice or even of an explicit prohibition of images, see, for example, T. N. D. Mettinger, 'Israelite Aniconism: Developments and Origins', in *The Image and the Book*, 173–204, esp. 203 (above, n. 18).
128. Compare e.g. Z. Zevit, *Religions*, 161–2.

political and cultural power and as a role model. In this connection, the divine protection of the monarchy played a major role and was taken up as an iconographic theme of the New Kingdom. In the OT as well, the theocratically inflated Egyptian royal ideology is reflected, when the king appears as the son of Yhwh (Ps. 2; 110). The widespread solarizing of the local pantheons reached Jerusalem and Judah in the early 1st millennium BCE. With a time lag in comparison to the north, Egyptian or egyptianizing motifs appear on name seals or royal seals produced in Judah only toward the end of Iron Age IIB. The integration of the religious sun symbolism of Egyptian character became more explicit than ever in the last third of the 8th cent. Judah stood under the spell of the Egyptian symbol system: winged uraeuses (with four wings) and sun symbolism (the pharaoh as sun-god, winged scarabs, the sun-disk) are widely attested. The Yhwh of Jerusalem took on distinctly solar characteristics, which also find expression in texts like Deut. 33.2; Hab. 3.3-13; Zeph. 3.5. Further *loci classici* of the solar elements in the Yhwh faith (and their links with Jerusalem) are Pss 46; 72; 84.12 (NRSV 84.11); Isa. 1.26; 18.4; 59.9; 60.1-3 and Mal. 3.20 (NRSV 4.2). It should be emphasized, however that the OT preferentially takes over those characteristics of the Near Eastern sun-god for Yhwh, which concern his actions of judging and punishing, saving and healing, whereas → *chthonic* aspects were taken up only much later. Solar symbolism continued into the following period as well, even though, under Assyrian and Aramaean influence, the cult of the moon-god and of the stars (esp. Venus) likewise led to a lunarization and astralization of the religious symbol system.

*4. Iron Age IIC (722/700–587/586 BCE)*. In Palestine, this was a time of shifting hegemony (Assyrians, Egyptians, Babylonians), all of which left their traces in the religious symbol system, without prejudice to the local traditions, which were not and needed not be abandoned (see below). The result was that deities of the most disparate provenience were often worshipped alongside or mingled with each other in a single place. In addition, from the 7th cent on, luxury ware from all parts of the contemporary world were imported into Palestine, including a growing number of Greek trade goods and pointing to the presence of Greek mercenaries and merchants, who undoubtedly brought their gods with them. The increasing economic and cultural internationalization led to an accretion of the Palestinian pantheon through imports from formerly distant lands. City temples remain the exception (e.g. Ekron) in this period, so that it continues to be impossible to identify a typical architecture for the Iron Age urban sacral buildings. The former northern kingdom and Judah, existing since 701 BCE only as a rump state, continued to go different ways in terms of religious history, although in Jerusalem the theological traditions of the north apparently found increasing acceptance; a process of theologically coming to terms with the downfall of the northern kingdom began, and controversies about the correct form of the state/official Yhwh cult broke out.

The former *northern kingdom* was now organized as an Assyrian province with provincial seats in Megiddo and Samaria, where Israelites and Assyrians mingled, together with their gods. The official cult of the northern kingdom and its royal house had now ended with the political end of the kingdom around Samaria, but Israelites continued to dwell in the land (contrary to 2 Kgs 17), and they could have continued to practise the Yhwh cult in local sanctuaries and in their homes. In connection with the downfall of the northern kingdom, it is often thought that the Israelite ruling class, which would have been the bearers of the kingdom's religious traditions, sought refuge in Jerusalem, which could explain, for example, how the basic substance of the books of Amos and Hosea came to Jerusalem. When, however, a historical fact underlies 2 Kgs 23.15 (Josiah's raid against Bethel), then the sanctuary of Bethel must have existed during the period of Assyrian dominion at least until ca. 612 BCE, so that it is quite possible that Bethel continued as a local centre of the Yhwh cult despite Assyrian presence and that the collections of Amos and Hosea were part of the library there.

In the Assyrian vassal kingdom of *Judah*, in contrast to the north, the official Yhwh cult continued to be practised in the temple. Although the state territory of the state god of the south was reduced after 701 BCE to the mountain region and the Negev, (Judean until ca. 600 BCE), the links with the seat in Jerusalem and the Davidic Dynasty remained intact. The religio-historical development in the intermediate areas (Shephelah, the tribal area of Benjamin, the Negev), which over the course of time belonged to very different, shifting economic, political and cultural spheres of influence and which continued to practise their old indigenous religious traditions alongside their reception of new elements, is very difficult to get hold of. The complex, locally divergent cultic histories can only be briefly sketched here in very simplified and schematic form. In the *Shephelah*, one must reckon with influences coming from the Philistine and Phoenician coastal cities, increasingly also from Greece. The coastland and the vassal kings of Ashdod, Ekron and Gaza profited from the *pax assyriaca*. What the pantheon in these internationally intertwined cities might have looked like, can be (re-) constructed on the basis of Ekron, which cooperated economically with Judah at the time of Manasseh, so that Judeans came into contact with the world of gods prevailing there[129] (composed of Assyrian, Egyptian, local divinities). In the *Negev*, alongside local traditions, growing Edomite and Arabian influences are in evidence. Although the individual regions of southern Palestine had always been conditioned by influences flowing in from neighbouring cultures, *all of Palestine* continued to be under the strong influence of the Egyptian symbol system in Iron Age IIC, which is recognizable in the increasing solarization and the presence of numerous Egyptian deities in the glyptic of the south (at least on the coast). The period of Assyrian domination was also a time in which Assyrian influence penetrated all areas of life not only in the former northern kingdom but also in Judah: this is evidenced in the expressions of material culture (tombs, ceramics, → *glyptic*) inter alia. Even if the Assyrians did not promote a deliberate assyrianization, the cultural contact and the presence of Assyrian officials and traders changed the world. But the result of Assyrian domination was the internationalization, not the assyrianization of Judah and Jerusalem.[130] In Iron Age IIC, *Jerusalem* was a flourishing city in which, alongside different languages, also different religions came to meet.[131]

If one can believe the presentation of 2 Kings, there must have been different groups within the Jerusalem ruling classes, the one pro-Assyrian (and thus anti-Egyptian), e.g. Manasseh, Amon and their counsellors, and the other anti-Assyrian (and therefore ostensibly 'nationalistic', but also pro-Egyptian), e.g. Josiah and his counsellors. The deuteronomistic interpretation of the events of the 7th cent. BCE is written out of hindsight after the fall of Judah and from the perspective of the anti-Assyrian and 'nationalistic' group, which appealed to Yhwh and the principles of cultic unity. In a mixture of political and religious argumentative strategies, the representatives of the pro-Assyrian opposition party are associated with worship of idols and false gods, although it can hardly fit the historical facts that a Davidic king (like

129. On the temple and pantheon of Ekron, see J. Kamlah, 'Tempel 650 in Ekron und die Stadttempel der Eisenzeit in Palästina', in *Saxa Loquentur*, 101–25 (above, n. 121).

130. Contra S. Parpola, 'Assyria's Expansion in the 8th and 7th Centuries and its Long Term Repercussions in the West', in *Symbiosis, Symbolism, and the Power of the Past* (ed. W. G. Dever and S. Gitin; Winona Lake, Ind.: Eisenbrauns, 2003), 99–111.

131. B. Sass, 'Arabs and Greeks in Late First Temple Jerusalem', *PEQ* 122 (1990): 59–61.

Manasseh) would have subverted the cult of his own dynastic god Yhwh. Nevertheless, the pro-Assyrian politics of Manasseh (694–640 BCE) in 2 Kgs 21 earned him an unimaginably poor reputation in the → *Deuteronomistic* history.

In sharp contrast to the positively rated Hezekiah (and the idealized Josiah), Manasseh is said to have carried out a kind of negative cult reform by reversing the reforms of his father Hezekiah and conducting himself as a kind of second Ahab. The explicit reference from Manasseh back to Hezekiah and Ahab in 2 Kgs 21.3 and to David and Solomon in 2 Kgs 21.7 and the explicit reference back to Manasseh in 2 Kgs 23.12 indicate the central significance of the repeatedly worked over chapter 2 Kgs 21 within the general structure of the → *Deuteronomistic* history. The existing literary presentation leaves out not a single religious offence (measured in terms of the Deuteronomistic programme of cultic unity and purity) that is not ascribed to Manasseh: he restored the cult of the high places; he built altars for Baal and an asherah for Asherah; he worshipped the hosts of heaven; and in the Jerusalem temple put up asherahs and altars for the heavenly hosts next to Yhwh. The list of his vices has been enriched with stereotypes of religiously motivated polemics against the enemy, when it says that he sacrificed his son by fire (= Moloch cult[132]) and caused witchcraft, divination, and necromancy to be practised (2 Kgs 21.6). The historicity of the religious policy measures of Manasseh described in 2 Kgs 21 is a subject of controversial discussion among scholars. Depending on how the literary analysis of individual texts turns out, the stories of Manasseh's cult measures will be treated as fact or fiction.

Against the background of the long history of the indigenous worship of the goddess Asherah (and of Baal or of Yhwh as Baal), measures of the king in favour of the goddess (or for Baal), if they really took place, would have been nothing really new. Even when the → *Deuteronomistic* rhetoric in 2 Kgs 21 does its best to express the opposition between Yhwh and Asherah, the complete silence of the pre-exilic prophets about Asherah[133] indicates that the presence of this goddess alongside Yhwh only much later became a problem, namely for the Deuteronomic/Deuteronomistic theologians of the → *exile*. Standing out from the stereotyped Deuteronomistic polemic against Baal and Asherah is the mention of the cultic worship of the heavenly hosts (= astral cult) in the temple (v. 5),

132. More and more scholars are convinced that the Moloch-cult did not involve child-sacrifice, as the biblical text suggests, but rather consisted in a rite of consecration of children to the royal weather-god Baal/Hadad.

133. C. Frevel, *Aschera und der Ausschließlichkeitsanspruch YHWHs: Beiträge zu literarischen, religionsgeschichtlichen und ikonographischen Aspekten der Ascheradiskussion* (BBB 94; Weinheim: Beltz, 1995), 251–4, 514–17.

> which for this reason is sometimes treated as a historical note. It fits well into the picture that one can create on the basis of the material culture of Iron Age IIC for the whole of Palestine. The religious symbol system was marked by progressive astralizing and lunarizing tendencies of the local pantheons (see below) derived from Aramaean and Assyrian influences. The cult of the sun, the moon and the stars enjoyed enormous popularity. Perhaps Manasseh wanted to comply with this development on the level of the official cult. This too, however, was not a real innovation, for astral and lunar cults were known in Palestine from much earlier periods and needed only an impulse (from without) to revive in Iron Age IIC.

The text of 2 Kgs 21.19-26 mentions no religious measures on the part of Manasseh's son Amon and rests content with a generic negative evaluation of this king, who according to the context was assassinated as a result. However one may judge the biblical account of Judah under Assyrian hegemony, it is clear, inter alia through the murder of Amon, that there were serious conflicts within the Jerusalem ruling classes, in which political and religious policy attitudes played a role. These conflicts were triggered essentially by the Assyrian presence in southern Palestine, which intensely influenced not only the politics but also the Judean-Jerusalemite religion to such an extent that segments of Jerusalem's ruling classes became caught up in an identity crisis and thought the time had come for an urgently needed fundamental protection of identity.

### The Assyrian Crisis of the Judean Religion?

Whereas earlier studies assumed that the Assyrians forced the worship of Assyrian deities upon their vassals, or at least in their provinces, by causing Assyrian cult images to be set up in the temples of the conquered territories, more recent studies have shown that this was the case only in exceptional situations.[134] With the exception of the deportation of temple goods and cultic images, no direct interference with the cults of the conquered peoples is documented. Faith in the Assyrian gods was not demanded, only submission to the Assyrian royal ideology. Thus the Assyrian king is more clearly present in the material culture than Assyrian deities. While therefore no direct coercive cultic measures on the part of the Assyrians should be assumed, the fact remains that in the conquered territories the Assyrian presence led to changes in the religious symbolic system and everyday life. But the peoples of Palestine had the possibility to make their own choice and to decide if they wanted to venerate Assyrian deities. Consequently, in the → *glyptic*, for example, Assyrian motifs play a rather unimportant role. Only a few Assyrian deities are attested (Ishtar, Ninurta,

134. On the debate, see A. Berlejung, *Theologie*, 343–6 (above, n. 104).

Adad, Gula, on amulets the demons Pazuzu, Lamaštu). Above all, the Assyrian goddess Ishtar as the Queen of Heaven (represented by the evening star) appears to have exercised a strong attraction. Occasionally, it has been assumed that she stood behind the cult of the Judean Queen of Heaven in the early 6th cent. (Jer. 7.16-20; 44),[135] but it rather appears that the local Asherah integrated characteristics of Ishtar. To what extent the astralizing of Asherah affected the official cult in Jerusalem, can no longer be determined. If Manasseh really did introduce astral and lunar symbolism into the Jerusalem temple, this occurred voluntarily and was hardly intended to introduce new deities but rather to translate the traditional gods Yhwh and Asherah into contemporary categories. Nevertheless, these measures could well be understood by the anti-Assyrian, 'nationalistic' factions as a surrender of political and religious identity and thus as a provocation. What exactly constituted the proper observance of the Judean/Jerusalemite Yhwh cult was evidently the subject of controversial discussion in the 7th cent., whereby all parties claimed to speak for Yhwh. In any case, the fact remains that the presence of the Assyrians in Palestine left strong traces in the religious history of the region.

With 2 Kgs 22–23, the anti-Assyrian and 'nationalistic' King Josiah, whom the → *Deuteronomistic* tradition has idealized, appears on the scene. According to the Deuteronomistic presentation in its present form (which has been worked over and expanded at least several times), his religious policy measures (at last) achieved the Deuteronomistic goal of cult unity and purity. According to 2 Kgs 22, the reform began with the renovation of the Jerusalem temple, in the course of which the high priest Hilkiah found a 'book of law', which the scribe Shaphan read to the king. After obtaining an oracle from the prophetess Huldah announcing Yhwh's anger over Judah, the book was then read in public and a → *covenant* was made between Yhwh, the king, and the people (2 Kgs 23.1-3). Only thereafter did the cult reform as such begin (2 Kgs 23.4-27), ending in the celebration of a solemn → *Passover* feast (2 Kgs 23.21-23).

## Josiah's Reform (622/621 BCE)

The religion of Israel and Judah was → *polytheistic* and → *poly-yahwistic* in the pre-exilic period. The propagation of an exclusive Yhwh worship perhaps began

⇨

135. See O. Keel and C. Uehlinger, *GGG*, § 171. Further candidates for the Queen of Heaven are Astarte, Asherah, Anath, Qudšu and Hathor, see ibid., § 197.

with Elijah in the 9th cent. BCE or with Hosea in the 8th cent. BCE, but, in the light ofthe redaction-historical problems of the Elijah-Elisha stories (Ch. 7.6.3.6) and of the book of Hosea (Ch. 12A), this cannot be taken to be certain: too much has been inserted here at a later date. With the cult reform of Josiah at the end of the 7th cent. BCE, scholars have thought to find a historical benchmark on which to fix the point of transition of the official Judean-Jerusalemite religion into exclusive Yhwh worship (→ *monolatry*) as well as → *cult centralization* in Jerusalem and the introduction of → *aniconic* divine worship. The OT presentation in 2 Kgs 23.4-27 does indeed name extensive measures ordered by Josiah in matters of cult practice. They aimed to enforce the exclusive cultic veneration of Yhwh, to eliminate non-yahwistic cults, and to make Jerusalem the only legitimate and operative place of worship. On closer attention, however, it becomes apparent that the cultic changes mentioned in 2 Kgs 23 are essentially of a destructive rather than a constructive nature; that they have evidently been redactionally expanded several times, and that they constitute a kind of literary bracket construction by being referenced to other texts within the books of Kings (e.g. 2 Kgs 23.13 with 1 Kgs 11.7-8; 2 Kgs 23.14 with 1 Kgs 14.23; 2 Kgs 23.15-20 with 1 Kgs 12.31-1 Kgs 13). Alongside the question of whether the reform in fact really took place, and, if so, in what form, scholars discuss the relationship of the book that allegedly had been found to the reform itself (a work commissioned by Josiah, an authentic find?) and above all the identity of the book. Regarding the last question, it has been proposed that it might have been the → *Covenant Code* or a basic version of the book of Deuteronomy. However, the affinity between 2 Kgs 22–23 and Deuteronomy can not be overlooked (cf. 2 Kgs 23.3 and Deut. 6.5; 2 Kgs 23.21-23 and Deut. 16.1-8; 2 Kgs 22.16-17, 19-20 and Deut. 28 [blessing by obedience, curse by disobedience]; 2 Kgs 23 and Deut. 12 [cult centralization at a chosen place]; 2 Kgs 23.5 and Deut. 17.3 [cult purity, exclusive worship of Yhwh]). The story of the unexpected discovery of the book, lends the 'book of law' a miraculous and authoritative character as well as conferring on its provisions both the dignity of age and deep roots in the tradition, and, in doing so, defines Josiah's cult measures based upon it as a programme of restoration (see esp. 2 Kgs 22.13). When, however, one considers the reforms narrated in the context of the de facto religious traditions of Palestine or even of Judah alone since achieving statehood (as these are manifested in the material culture), then it becomes clear that the 'reforms' represent modernizing novelties without roots in the society as a whole. The disguising of modernization as a restoration can often be found in the Ancient Near East and corresponds to the Near Eastern mentality, according to which only what goes back to old traditions can claim validity and authority. There is no archaeological evidence of this reform;[136] the material findings in Judah point instead to a survival of iconic traditions (e.g. the pillar-figurines etc.) and to the presence of other deities, although it can also be observed, that

136. On Arad and Beer-sheba, which have repeatedly been cited erroneously as proofs for Josiah's cult reform, see above, p. 163 and O. Keel and C. Uehlinger, *GGG*, § 215 with footnote 399.

increasingly → *aniconic* motifs do appear (likewise, however, in the neighbouring cultures of Judah!). Even in terms of the Bible itself, Josiah's reform remained but an episode and found no echo among Josiah's contemporaries Zephaniah, Nahum and Jeremiah. Thus, if one wants to hold fast to their historicity in general, one can only look for a 'well-founded minimum' (transl.).[137] This could have been that the exclusive worship of Yhwh, that till then had been the concern of only a small opposition group – a 'Yhwh-alone-Movement', that is perhaps reflected biblically in the Covenant Code (Exod. 20.24–23.19*) of the late 8th or early 7th centuries and in parts of the Deuteronomic Law – now, for the first time, gained broader social influence through a king, who, with 'national' ambitions, made this programme his own. This programme of exclusive Yhwh worship was still a matter of monolatry; only in exilic times was it spelled out as a theoretical monotheism, and only in the post-exilic period was it able to assert itself as the norm.

With the collapse of Assyria, Josiah and his party thought the time had come to realize their program. In the name of Yhwh, whom his counsellors – the ancestors of the later Deuteronomists (→ *Deuteronomism*) – had conceived after the pattern of the Assyrian god Ashur, Josiah had freed Judah/Jerusalem from Assyrian control and even expanded its territory. He now invaded Assyrian territory in the province of Samaria and took possession of its religious traditions (Hosea, Amos), perhaps in Bethel (if these had not already come to Jerusalem with the refugees in 722/721), thereby staking his claim to assume the heritage of the northern kingdom. Perhaps, however, Josiah had much more pragmatic political motives in mind, namely the stabilization of his dominion over his inhomogeneous territories. When one considers his territorial gains (the Shephelah and some parts of the former northern kingdom), one could also imagine that he wanted to tie these problematical intermediate zones more closely to Jerusalem and therefore used the concentration on the Jerusalem cult as an instrument of control and integration to construct a common 'national'-religiously grounded identity. As a political, religious and cultural centre for his kingdom, Jerusalem alone came into question. Political pragmatism and religious motivation by no means exclude each other. The unity in action between the king and his dynastic and state god was an integral part of the Ancient Near Eastern kingship ideology. Wherever

137. See C. Uehlinger, 'Gab es eine Joschijanische Kultreform? Plädoyer für ein begründetes Minimum', in *Jeremia und die 'deuteronomistische Bewegung'* (BBB 98; ed. W. Groß; Weinheim: Beltz, 1994), 57–89.

one draws the boundary between historical facts and Deuteronomistic fiction, no fundamental paradigm shift to → *monolatry*, to → *aniconism*, or to → *cult centralization* in Jerusalem is recognizable in the material culture of Palestine at the time of the transition from the 7th to the 6th centuries. The biblical presentation largely passes over the fact that Josiah's activities and territorial expansion in the Shephelah depended upon and was limited by the pharaohs of the 26th Dynasty. His anti-Assyrian programme was only possible as a pro-Egyptian programme. Both Josiah and his successors were Egyptian vassals and the Egyptian renaissance left its traces inter alia in the → *iconography* of the 7th cent. BCE (see above). Alongside and at times together with the Egyptians, Greeks increasingly appear in Palestine in the 7th cent. Greek mercenaries served in the Saite armies, where they were especially valued as special units for their phalanx tactics. To the period of Egyptian pre-eminence in Palestine in the later 7th cent. BCE belong Judean contacts with Greek mercenaries and merchants (Məṣad Hăšavyāhū), who penetrated into the hinterland from the Mediterranean coastal area. The meeting of the Greek and the Judean spheres of influence intensified in the following period, not least due to the presence of Greek mercenaries in Judean service (→ *ostraca* from Arad ca. 600 BCE).

After the end of Egyptian vassaldom and the shift to Babylonian vassaldom around 605 BCE at the time of Jehoiakim (and his successor), the conflict between a pro-Egyptian/anti-Babylonian party and an anti-Egyptian/pro-Babylonian party broke out anew, with both sides claiming to serve state interests and evidently basing their arguments on the will of Yhwh (Jer. 28). According to the book of Jeremiah, different groups of prophets (each appealing to Yhwh) played a central role in these conflicts at the court of the king, who thus became caught in a conflict about true and false prophecy (Jer. 37.17-21; 23.9-40).[138] Since the difference between true and false prophecy can only be decided after the fact (Deut. 18.21-22), the Judean kings found little help in their predicament. The anti-Babylonian (pro-Egyptian) party initially set the political course, but the catastrophe of 598/597 and 587/586, which followed the senseless rebellion against Babylon, proved the protagonists of the pro-Babylonian (anti-Egyptian) opposition party to be in the right, so that their fulfilled prophecies of doom led Jeremiah and Ezekiel to be recog-

138. F. L. Hossfeld and I. Meyer, *Prophet gegen Prophet: Eine Analyse der alttestamentlichen Texte zum Thema: Wahre und falsche Propheten* (BibB 9; Fribourg: Schweizerisches Katholisches Bibelwerk, 1973).

nized as true prophets. This led in turn to the preservation of their sayings. The sayings of the prophets of the opposite party, who had advised rebellion against Babylon, by contrast, were handed down only as false prophecies and at best as a foil for the true prophecies (Jer. 27-29). After the fact, their authors were branded as idolaters (Deut. 13; 18.9-22).

As the cult of the royal residence and dynasty, the official cult of Yhwh in Jerusalem met an abrupt end with the fall of the Davidic monarchy, but the cult of Yhwh survived as the religion of those who remained in the land and who continued to practise it in the temple ruins of Jerusalem, in local sanctuaries (Mizpah, Bethel?) and at home. With the end of Judah's political independence, the worshippers of Yhwh split into four groups. According to the OT, these were:

- the Yhwh worshippers, who remained in the Babylonian province of Judah (now reduced by the splitting off of the Negev (in Edomite hands) and the southern Shephelah). It appears that they rather quickly were able to renew the cult in Jerusalem. One can also imagine a continuation of the Yhwh cult in Mizpah or Bethel (Jer. 41.5);
- those segments of the ruling classes who were carried off into Babylonian → *exile* in the course of the various deportations. They were the bearers of the religious traditions (e.g. Ezekiel) and were evidently in possession of books that they had been able to salvage from the temple library and to take with them;
- those segments of the ruling classes (including Jeremiah) and the general population, which had fled to Egypt (Jer. 41–44; 2 Kgs 25.26);
- those segments of the ruling classes (e.g. the Davidide Ishmael) and the population that had taken refuge in Transjordan (Jer. 40.11; 41.15).

In the material culture of the 7th and early 6th centuries, there are clear signs of different cultures living side by side on Palestinian soil. According to texts from Gezer, which belonged to the Assyrian province of Samaria, people with Egyptian, Aramaic, Akkadian, Hebrew, and non-Semitic names not only lived together but also worked together. As indicated by the seal → *iconography*, diverse religious symbol systems could be combined with each other (Egyptian ankh-symbols with the Aramaean-Assyrian moon-crescent, the eight-pointed star and an → *anthropomorphic* deity: see **fig. 13**). Already mentioned is the tendency towards astralizing and lunarizing local pantheons that goes back to Aramaean and Assyrian influences and which is clearly evident in the material culture of the epoch. The texts of 2 Kgs 21–23; Jer. 7; 44; and Zeph. 1.5 point to it as the dominant current of the 7th to 6th centuries. In the iconography of Iron Age IIC, the Egyptian and egyptianizing iconography on locally produced products is increasingly replaced by pieces with Assyrian or Aramaean inspiration. In particular, the stars, the evening star, and the moon take an outstanding position, and even traditional motifs of local artwork (e.g. the suckling mother animal, anthropomorphic deities, scenes with worshippers) are often combined with the moon-crescent and the stars. In the Palestinian → *glyptic*, the moon-god appears in the 7th cent. in the form of the cult standard of the moon-god from Haran, who ranked for the Assyrians as the highest god of the West. Moon-standards are likewise documented on seals, → *scarabs*, and other image-bearing objects. Their cultic use is obvious in the top of a standard which has been found in an Assyrian fortress (Tell eš-Šerīʿa). However, the moon-god could also be represented in anthropomorphic shape.

**Fig. 13:** Seal with different religious symbols: 8-ray star, Aramean-Assyrian moon-crescent, Egyptian 'Ankh' character and anthropomorphic deity.

Especially in the specifically inner-Palestinian local traditions around Jerusalem (though also in the former northern kingdom and in northern Transjordan), one finds representations of the mood-god in anthropomorphic form as a bearded, enthroned figure sitting in a boat and conferring blessing (sometimes with the name of the Judean owner of the seal). This find has been interpreted[139] as an indication that the local supreme gods in Palestine had assumed lunar characteristics, i.e. that in Judah of the 7th cent BCE Yhwh was worshipped as a moon-god (according to Keel/Uehlinger as the uranic-lunar El[140]) or that the characteristics

139. G. Dalman, 'Ein neu gefundenes Jahvebild', *PJ* 2 (1906): 44–50, esp. 49.
140. O. Keel and C. Uehlinger, *GGG*, § 180.

of a local Palestinian god (in Judah therefore of Yhwh) were transferred to the Aramaean-Assyrian moon-god of Haran.

The growth of astral and lunar cults in the 7th cent. can be viewed as the worship of distant powers, whereby the heavenly bodies, as the guarantors of the eternal order, provided a feeling of stability in the newly arisen multicultural and international world.[141] At the same time, one should recall that the celestial bodies can everywhere be seen in the heavens and can thus be invoked from every place on earth, so that their worship can be practised independently of any presence in a sanctuary, since they are present everywhere. The internationalization of the world and the confluence of diverse cultures may well have given new impetus to questions about the creation of the world (see Jer. 27.5) and its creator. In this connection, a fragmentary inscription from Jerusalem mentioning the '*'l qn 'rṣ*' = 'god – creator of earth' deserves mention. It could be an indication that in Jerusalem the theologoumenon of the creation of the world was connected with Yhwh. Iconographic traditions of earlier times likewise survive in southern Palestine of the 7th cent., but also new traditions establish themselves:

In the 7th cent. BCE, in Jerusalem and Judah (esp. Mizpah, Lachish), the pillar-figurines already known from the 8th cent., continue to be found. They were produced locally and show a local goddess important in private religiosity (house cult, tombs). Similar figurines are attested in northern Israelite, Phoenician, Philistine, and Transjordanian regions, so that they need not point to the same goddess. In Judah, the statuettes probably were identified with Asherah. The goddess figurines disappeared only in the 6th cent. BCE (i.e. in no case in conjunction with Josiah's reform). Especially in places not affected by the Babylonian conquests of 598/597 and 587/586 BCE (e.g. Mizpah), they seem to have fallen out of use only in the Persian Period. Clay figurines of doves are found in funeral (esp. Lachish, Jerusalem) and occasionally in domestic contexts. They should be seen as representations of the → *autochthonous* Asherah. To date, the frequently found horse and rider figurines that comprise a large number of terra-cottas from both the former northern kingdom and Jerusalem-Judah in Iron Age IIC have not been clearly explained. They evidently belong to the realm of domestic religiosity, but it has not been determined, whether they represent a deity (sun-god, warlike weather-god, warlike supreme god) or some kind of protective spirit (representative of the heavenly hosts).[142]

141. O. Keel and C. Uehlinger, *GGG*, § 184.

142. O. Keel and C. Uehlinger, *GGG*, § 200–1.

# 4.3 The Babylonian-Persian Period (587/586–333/332 BCE)

Bibliography 6.3 Archaeology and Iconography; 7 The History of the Ancient Near East and its Religions (P. Briant, *Cyrus*); 8 The History of Ancient Israel and Judah (G. Ahlström, *History*, 804–906; P. Sacchi, *History*). Further: E. Stern, *Material Culture of the Land of the Bible in the Persian Period 538–332 B.C.* Warminster: Aris Phillips, 1982; D. S. Vanderhooft, *The Neo-Babylonian Empire and Babylon in the Latter Prophets*. HSM 59. Atlanta: Scholars 1999; 9: History of Religion of Ancient Israel (L. L. Grabbe, *Judaic Religion*; O. Keel/C. Uehlinger, *GGG*, 216–27). Further: I. Eph'al, 'Changes in Palestine During the Persian Period'. *IEJ* 48 (1998): 106–19; R. Albertz, 'The Thwarted Restoration'. Pages 1–17 in *Yahwism After the Exile: Perspectives on Israelite Religion in the Persian Era: Papers read at the First Meeting of the European Association for Biblical Studies, Utrecht 6-9 August, 2000*. Studies in Theology and Religion 5. Edited by idem and B. Becking. Assen: Royal Van Gorcum, 2003; L. L. Grabbe (ed.), *Leading Captivity Captive: 'The Exile' as History and Ideology*. JSOTSup 278. Sheffield: Sheffield Academic Press, 1998; M. Heltzer, *The Province Judah and the Jews in Persian Times*. Tel Aviv: Archaeological Center Publication, 2008.

## 4.3.1 Society and Economy: The Times of the Exile, the Partial Return, the New Beginnings and the Conflicts with the Inhabitants of the Country

*1. General Survey:* With the conquest of Jerusalem by Nebuchadnezzar II in 598/597 (resp. 587/586 BCE), the Babylonian Period began for Judah, that only some 50 years later, with the last Neo-Babylonian king Nabonidus (556–539 BCE) and his son and coregent Belshazzar rapidly came to an end. Nabonidus's policy of putting the empire on a new, more decentralized basis and giving it a comprehensive, international religious identity with the moon-god Sin was strongly opposed by the traditionalists of his times, and led to rebellions, to the defamation of Nabonidus in corresponding propagandistic writings, and ultimately to the collaboration of the Babylonian Marduk priesthood with Cyrus II. Cyrus, who stemmed from the Achaemenid Dynasty, succeeded in defeating Astyages, the king of the Medes, around 550 BCE and thus began his unimpeded rise to power. While Nabonidus was still busy with the stabilization of his empire, Cyrus defeated Croesus of Lydia, extending his dominion to the West coast of Asia Minor (547/546 BCE) and leaving him free to attack Babylonia. Babylonia was taken in 539 BCE with little resistance, and Cyrus was celebrated as a liberator by the Marduk priests, who thereby secured their privileges.[143] Thus the short-lived Neo-Babylonian Empire was definitively succeeded by the Persian Empire, which, by contrast, would endure some 200 years, so that – much more strongly than the Neo-Babylonian Empire – it managed to put its stamp on the Near East, before it met its end through the successful campaigns of the Macedonian Alexander the Great in 333/332 BCE.

After an initial series of Achaemenid political successes, the Persian Period was shaken internally by repeated rebellions of the Persian tribal aristocrats, satraps, or subordinated regions, while externally (especially after Xerxes) it had to face military conflicts with the Greeks (Athens, Sparta, later Macedonia). The Persian Empire was divided into large and subordinate satrapies and comprised provinces and vassal kingdoms as well. The number and size of these regions varied according to the succession of the various kings, who moved from residence to residence (Susa, Ekbatana, Persepolis, Pasargadae) according to a palatinate system. Like the Babylonians before him, Cyrus II (558–530) took over the administrative structures of the newly conquered territories. Thus the satrapy 'Babylonia and the territories beyond the River (= Trans-Euphrates)', which he conferred on the Iranian satrap Gubaru/Gobryas in 535 BCE, was purely and simply the former Neo-Babylonian Empire. A major shift took place in the politics and the religious policy of the Persians by comparison to the Babylonians: Cyrus revoked the cultic measures of Nabonidus in Babylonia and proceeded to refurbish the temples and cities in strategically important regions. As far as possible, existing local rulers, legal traditions, and traditional → *autochthonous* cults were supported, so that the Persian Empire took the form of a confederation. The much praised Persian tolerance of non-Persian religions and cultures was thus a consequence of their conservative-traditionalistic regional policies in the service of their overall interests. From the support of religious and cultural regionalism in combination with simultaneous subordination to the imperial interests of the whole Persian Empire emerged the character, so typical of the epoch, of a combination of regional particularism and simultaneous → *universalism* oriented to the empire as a whole. Cyrus's son Cambyses (530–522 BCE) continued the military successes of his father by conquering Egypt in 525 BCE and causing himself to be installed as pharaoh of the 27th Dynasty. His sudden death in Syria (Herodotus, *Hist. III*, 61–66) led to the coronation of the rebel Gaumata, who pretended to be Bardiya

143. *ANET*, 306–7; *COS* II, 314–16.

(Greek: Smerdes), the secretly murdered brother of Cambyses. A conspirative group of Persian tribal noblemen, who saw their share of riches and power threatened by the reforms of the new king, assassinated Gaumata, which in turn led to new rebellions (inter alia in Babylon). Darius I Hystaspes (522–486 BCE), who ultimately successively claimed the throne for himself, needed three years to consolidate his rule and to pacify the empire (522–519 BCE). Thereafter, he tackled the administrative and tax reforms so urgently needed to stabilize the empire economically and politically, without cutting back the privileges of the still dangerous tribal nobility.

According to Herodotus, *Hist. III*, 89–94, Darius divided the empire into 20 satrapies, separating Babylon and Trans-Euphrates. This does not fit the historical facts, however. The large satrapy 'Babylonia and Trans-Euphrates' continued to exist and was apparently conferred upon the satrap Uštānu in 521–516 BCE. The western region Trans-Euphrates was a sub-satrapy of this large satrapy, and its first known sub-satrap was Tattenai (Ezra 5.3, 6; 6.6, 13); he ruled from 520 to 502 BCE and was subordinated to Uštānu. In any case, the large satrapy continued to exist in 486 BCE under the satrap Ḫuta-x-x-', son of Pagakanna.[144] For the most part, it is assumed that the large satrapy 'Babylonia and Trans-Euphrates' was later divided into two satrapies of equal rank, but this cannot be pinned down to a particular date (perhaps under Xerxes or later, in any case before 420 BCE) (**fig. 14**). According to Herodotus, *Hist. III*, 90–97, under Darius I, every satrapy was assigned a fixed taxation sum (for Trans-Euphrates, 350 talents of silver), which it had to pay in precious metal (independently of the actual harvest for the year). Darius I did not really introduce coinage, since the gold coin he introduced, the Daric with a weight of 8.42g gold, was too large a unit to play much of a role except in trade with the Greeks. In day to day commerce, coins of lesser denominations were needed (in the small provinces of Samaria and Jehud, they are found only in the 4th cent. BCE). Darius I organized the collection of local legal texts (e.g. in Egypt), protected the privileges of the local priesthoods, and ordered the composition of multi-lingual propaganda texts.[145] His inscriptions reflect the

144. M. W. Stolper, 'The Governor of Babylon and Across-The-River in 486 B.C.', *JNES* 48 (1989): 283–305.

145. Bisitun-Inscription, see J. C. Greenfield and B. Porten, *The Bisitun Inscription of Darius the Great: Aramaic Version, Corpus Inscriptionum Iranicarum, Part I. Inscriptions of Ancient Iran, Vol. V. The Aramaic Versions of the Achaemenian Inscriptions, etc., Texts I.*, (London: Lund Humphries, 1982); B. Porten and A. Yardeni, *TADAE*, C2.1; C.-H. Bae, *Comparative Studies of King Darius's Bisitun Inscription* (Ann Arbor, Mich.: UMI, 2001); R. Schmitt, *The Bisitun Inscriptions of Darius the Great: Old Persian Text* (London: School of Oriental and African Studies, 1991); E. N. von Voigtlander, *The Bisitun Inscription of Darius the Great: Babylonian Version. Corpus*

Persian royal ideology, according to which the king was the perfect guarantor of the interests and traditions of the Persians and the other parts of the empire, and the firm supporter of all the gods and their priesthoods (who in turn supported him): for the Egyptians, he was the pharaoh recognized by the Egyptian gods; for the Persians, he was the king installed by Ahura Mazda.

Darius I was also the first ruler to come into severe conflict with the enemy that in the following years would increasingly challenge the Persian Empire, namely the Greeks (490 BCE, the battle of Marathon). His successor Xerxes (486–465/464 BCE) met his death through murder, and turmoil concerning the succession to the throne broke out. Xerxes' son Artaxerxes I Longimanus (465/464–425 BCE) managed to put down rebellions in Egypt supported by Athens and to ward off other Greek attacks. After him, however, turmoil again marked the royal succession, until Darius II (424–404 BCE) ascended the throne. He too saw himself confronted by the Greek city-states. Continuing conflicts, especially (together with Sparta) with Athens marked his reign. At the end of his reign or at the beginning of the reign of his successor Artaxerxes II Mnemon (404–359/358 BCE), revolts took place in Egypt, leading to the loss of this profitable satrapy for the Persians in 404 BCE. The king also found himself confronted with revolts of the satraps of Asia Minor, and he was unable to achieve any significant results against the 28th to 30th dynasties that rapidly followed each other in unstable Egypt. Moreover, in 360 BCE, with the support of Sparta and Athens, pharaoh Tachos of the 30th Dynasty dared to invade Palestine, but a revolt in his homeland forced him quickly to withdraw. Artaxerxes III Ochos (359/358–338 BCE) managed once more to decide for Persia the power game, which had arisen between the Persians and Phoenicians on the one side and the Egyptians and the quasi omnipresent Greeks (as mercenaries in armies, as naval support for Egypt, or as refuges for rebellious satraps) on the other. He put an end to the rebellions of the satraps and recovered Egypt (343/342) after putting down the rebellion of Tennes of Sidon (349/348 BCE), which had been instigated by Egypt. During his rule, trade and the monetary economy expanded. The minting of coins (including now small coins in silver and bronze) enjoyed an enormous upswing. It turned out to be a grave political mistake, that in

*Inscriptionum Iranicarum. Part I. Inscriptions of Ancient Iran. Vol II. The Babylonian Versions of the Achaemenian Inscriptions. Texts I* (London: Lund Humphries, 1978).

the battle of Perinthus in Thrace (340 BCE) he remained content merely to repel the Macedonian Philip II (359–336 BCE) defensively without definitively putting him down, for Philip in these years already planned a war of conquest against Persia, a plan that his son and successor Alexander III would put into action. The circumstances of the murder of Artaxerxes III Ochos by Bagoas are unclear. Briefly Artaxerxes IV ('Arses'; 338–336 BCE) ascended the throne, to be followed, after his assassination, by Darius III Codomannos (336–331 BCE). Darius III was defeated by Alexander III of Macedonia in the battle of Issos (333 BCE). After the last Persian satrap had surrendered Egypt to Alexander without a battle (332 BCE) and Darius III was definitively beaten in the battle of Gaugamela in 331 BCE, the → *Hellenistic* Period began for the Ancient Near East.

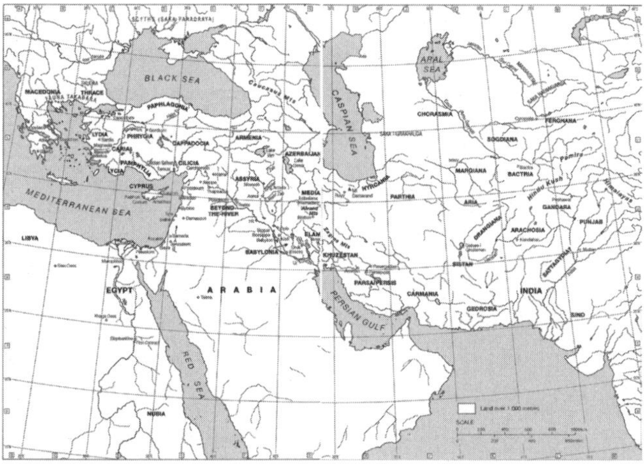


**Fig. 14a:** Map of the Persian Empire.

In its economy, culture, religion, arts and society, the Babylonian-Persian Period was marked by a pronounced internationalization and cultural mixture, recognizable inter alia by the fact that economic and cultural goods, → *iconographic* motifs, and deities can be found well outside their places of origin. At the same time, it is a period in which, under the aegis of the Babylonians, the political and economic rise of the Phoenician coastal cities rapidly accelerated to attain outstanding significance in the Persian Period, whereas the hinterland only slowly recovered from the raiding policy of the Babylonians. The career of the Phoenician cities was based on the fact that the Babylonians, and even more so the later Persians, needed the fleet of the Phoenicians for their military undertakings in the west, so that they treated the Phoenicians

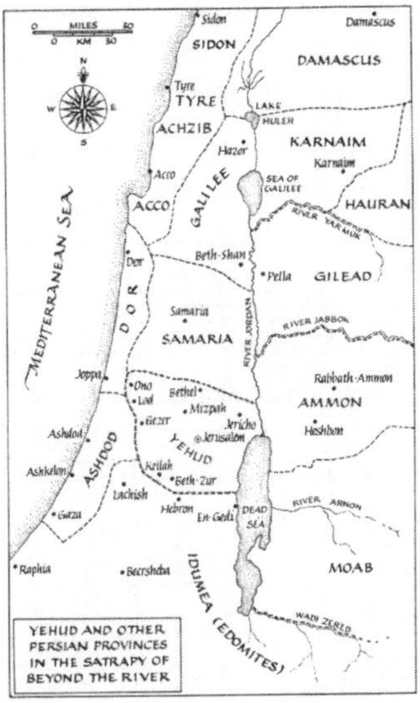


**Fig. 14b:** The Persian province Yehud and neighboring provinces.

with care. After the Greek navies gained increasing importance in the battles between the Persians, Egyptians and the Greeks, the Persian support of the Phoenician cities served the self-interests of the Persians in the region. In multiple ways, the Persian Empire profited from the empires to which it had succeeded. Thus it was to the advantage of this international empire, which in its greatest extension reached from the Indus to the Greek mainland and from Armenia to Egypt, that Aramaic had meanwhile established itself as the *lingua franca*. There were no communication/language limits to the trade, the economy, and even the propaganda of the Achaemenid royal ideology. With the introduction of coinage by the Persians, a Mediterranean global economy of hitherto unknown dimensions was able to develop. Alongside the internationality of the economy and the culture characterizing the Mediterranean world during the Babylonian and even more strongly the Persian Periods, however, a regionalism can also be observed, which becomes evident inter alia in the landscape of Palestine, which was parcelled out into small units. Thus, as in the preceding periods, different individual regions each with its own distinctive characteristics can be distinguished. The coastal region and Galilee, which clearly belonged to the hinterland of Phoenicia, were under Phoenician influence. With the conveyance of Dor, Jafo and the Sharon Plain to the king of Sidon by the Persian emperor in the 6th to 5th centuries, direct

Phoenician influence in Palestine gained momentum. The political affiliation of this region to Phoenicia had very positive effects on the material culture. The architecture (storage buildings, industrial facilities for glass production, dyeing fabrics, and metalworking), pottery, and small objects found are all signs of an economic upswing, of international linkups, and of the opening toward the West. Settlements on the coast and on important traffic routes reveal high quality architecture in the form of fortifications, palaces and fortified buildings. This development of urban construction passed by the Samarian and Judean highlands, because they were not directly involved in the international trade. For the same reason, the economic situation there remained modest. It was the Phoenicians basically, who transmitted the Egyptian culture (and religion) both to the regions under their control and to their neighbours. Egyptian imports grew more abundant and, via Phoenician trade, came to circulate in the region. The cultural, economic, and religio-historical conditions on the coast and in Galilee should thus be interpreted against the background of the Phoenician presence and can hardly be compared with the situation in Samaria or Jerusalem. By the same token, local preferences in matters of economy, culture and worship prevailed in Transjordan, in southern Palestine, which later became Idumea (esp. Negev and the southern Shephelah) and where Edomite/Arabian influence prevailed. Gaza too enjoyed a special status, because it served the Arabians as the port at the end of the Incense Route.

*2. Palestine in the Babylonian Period*: In the time after the first appearance of the Babylonians in the west, Palestine became the theatre of the conflict between the Babylonians and the Egyptians for the Assyrian legacy, which had cost Judah its political independence. How Nebuchadnezzar II, who ranks as the architect of the Neo-Babylonian Empire (605–562 BCE), organized the administration of his territorial gains, has only recently become clearer. In contrast to the Assyrians, the Babylonian kings evidently had no particular interest in imposing elements of their royal ideology in the marginal areas of their kingdom or in developing a comprehensive, systematically efficient imperial bureaucratic structure or a provincial organization for their vast empire, i.e. an organization which would have enabled them systematically to restructure the conquered territories, to develop their economies, to control them, and to exploit them. From the finds of Dūr-Katlimmu, it becomes evident that the Babylonians relied upon the structures of empire that had been prepared by the Assyrians before them, even though the Babylonian administration may not everywhere have developed the same intensity of bureaucracy as the Assyrians. Wherever possible, they took over the Assyrian provincial organization and left intact the structures they found in place.[146]

How little needed to be changed under Babylonian dominion is shown, for instance, by the city-states of the Levantine coastal plain, which in part at least had already entered into arrangements with the Assyrians and which under their new sovereigns lost neither their (partial) independence nor their control over their territories. The disinterest of the Babylonians in creating a uniformly administered, homogeneous empire with political stability, economic recovery, and general prosperity even in the marginal regions shows itself among other things in their deportation policy: they deported only segments of the population of the peripheral territories into the Babylonian heartland, but made no efforts to refill the vacated regions with new population groups. Corresponding to this 'one-way-street' approach and predatory raiding policy, the focus of economic contacts between Babylon and the western territories (at least according to Babylonian propaganda) lay in the one-sided withdrawal of goods from the periphery into the heartland (in the form of tribute and booty).

Due to the repeated invasions between 604 and 587/586, which were intended on the one hand to repel the Egyptians and on the other to carry off booty, the Babylonian territories in the west were unable to regain economic stability. Thus many economically prosperous centres of the Assyrian Period (Ekron, for example) were abandoned after the Babylonian expeditions and only re-settled in the Persian Period (Rāmat Rāḥēl). Judah too was evidently not systematically transformed into a province: no clear traces of permanent Babylonian administrative structures are found either in the OT or in the archaeological remains in the territory. Thus one can interpret the OT account of Gedaliah in the undestroyed city of Mizpah as a Babylonian attempt to leave Judah under autonomous administration in Mizpah. Whether Gedaliah had been installed as a vassal king of the rump state or merely as a vice-regent, or at least was seen as such by the Judeans, was of no consequence. One way or the other, tribute payments were called for.

The conquests of Nebuchadnezzar II were not as drastic as the OT account would lead one to believe. The biblical authors, after the catastrophes of 598/597 and 587/586, took it as demonstrated, that God had rejected his

146. H. Kühne, 'Vier spätbabylonische Tontafeln aus Tall Šēḫ Hamad, Ost-Syrien', *SAAB* 7.2 (1993): 75–107, esp. 84–5.

> people, that the gift of the land to his people had been forfeited, and that the land itself had become an empty desert. This theologically motivated view is contradicted by the archaeological findings, which show that the Babylonian destruction by no means had affected all of Palestine, so that the cultural break was kept within bounds.[147] The territories of Samaria and Galilee, and above all the tribal area of Benjamin north of Jerusalem were notable exceptions to the devastation, so that Mizpah in fact was spared (Jer. 40.6, 8 *et al.*). Other cities north of Jerusalem like Bethel and Gibeon likewise remained intact and were inhabited in the Babylonian-Persian Period. By contrast, the destructions evidently affected the Shephelah (Lachish II) and places in the Judean mountains (Rāmat Rāḥēl V, Jerusalem X). The interpretation of the numerous destruction layers around 600 BCE in the Negev (Arad VI, Kadesh-barnea), is unclear, since it has not been determined whether they all go back to the Babylonians: Egyptians, Edomites and Arabs also come into question as potential agents. Similar problems are raised by the findings in the coastal area. The coastal cities quickly recovered their partial independence as semi-autonomous city-states, so that they could continue to maintain their international Mediterranean trade and continued to exist as trade centres for cultural and economic exchange. Thus the two Babylonian conquests of Jerusalem 598/597 and 587/586 did not mark a break of equal importance in all the regions of Palestine: many had been taken years before, and others were completely spared. Even in Jerusalem, as indicated by the findings of Ketef Hinnom, life went on normally or quickly revived in the 6th cent. without a material interruption. Jerusalem was by no means a ghost-town in the exilic period: it was inhabited,[148] and it even housed an upper class that was rich enough to afford luxury wares.

The events around 600 BCE led to decisive territorial losses for Judah. First the Negev, then the southern Shephelah and the southern parts of the Judean highland came under the dominion of the Edomites and the Arabian tribes. The latter controlled the long-distance trade on the Incense Route and thus had come to conspicuous prosperity. Probably, these southern territories were incorporated into the large Neo-Babylonian province of Arabia in 553/552 BCE Judah, in Babylonian times, consisted only of the mountains and the northern Shephelah.

147. H. M. Barstad, *The Myth of the Empty Land* (SOSup 28, Oslo: Scandinavian University Press, 1996), esp. 8, 47–55.

148. See O. Lipschits, *Fall*, and the various articles in Idem and J. Blenkinsopp, eds, *Judah*.

## The various Exiles and Migrations of the Inhabitants of the Southern Kingdom of Judah

1. Assyrian deportation: In connection with Sennacherib's campaign of 701 BCE, Judean people were deported from the Shephelah. Their fate can be read on the pictures in room XXXVI of Sennacherib's SW palace in Nineveh. Further reliefs[149] show that the exiled Judeans served the Assyrians as forced labourers, as freight carriers, or as soldiers in the royal guard.

2. Babylonian deportations: Apparently, there were three deportations of Judeans by the Babylonians (598/597, 587/586, 582 BCE, see Jer. 52.30; 40.5–43.7). In contrast to the Assyrian deportation practice, according to which the depopulated territories were subsequently repopulated with people from other regions of the empire (Babylonians, Elamites, Arabs), after the Babylonian deportations the territories were left to those who remained behind. Concerning the number of those deported, the OT gives conflicting information, which has been evaluated in different ways among the scholars. Nevertheless, a general consensus now agrees that about 20 per cent of the population was affected. Those deported were settled in closed settlements in Babylonia, where places like āl-Jāḫudu (city Judah = New-Jerusalem, perhaps near Nippur, Borsippa or Sippar[150]), Tel-Abib (Ezek. 3.15) near Nippur, Tel-Melach, Tel-Harsha, Kerub-Addon, Immer (Ezra 2.59), Kasifiah (Ezra 8.17), later still Nehardea (Josephus, *Ant. XVIII*, 311.314.369.379), Pumbedita, and Sura are attested. The exile communities were evidently organized around elders (Jer. 29.1; Ezek. 8.1; 14.1; 20.1), which made a certain degree of local autonomy possible and allowed forms of tribal organization once again to come to the fore. In addition, priests and accepted prophets seem to have exercised functions of leadership (Ezekiel). Nevertheless, the community of exiles evidently continued to feel attached to their last legitimate king, Jehoiakim of Judah, whose fate in Babylon (pardoned in 562; see 2 Kgs 25.27-30; Jer. 52.31-34) was closely watched.[151] He was no longer king of Judah, but he did not cease to be the king of the Judeans. The exiles apparently lived in lineage groups (houses of the father(s)

⇨

149. C. Uehlinger, 'Bildquellen und "Geschichte Israels": grundsätzliche Überlegungen und Fallbeispiele', in *Steine – Bilder – Texte* (ed. C. Hardmeier), 57–61.

150. F. Joannès and A. Lemaire, 'Trois tablettes cunéiformes à onomastique ouest-sémitique', *Transeu* 17 (1999): 17–34 (treaty of the year 498 BCE). The presence of Judeans in Sippar, Borsippa and Nippur is attested in cuneiform tablets, which contain Judean names, see e.g. L. E. Pearce, 'New Evidence for Judeans in Babylonia', in Judah (ed. O. Lipschits and M. Oeming), 399–411.

151. The king and his family lived well at the Babylonian court. Cuneiform tablets note his provisioning by the Babylonians, who unconditionally recognized his royal status, see E. F. Weidner, 'Jojachin, der König von Juda, in babylonischen Keilschrifttexten', in *Mélanges syriens offerts à Monsieur R. Dussaud* II (Bibliothèque archéologique et historique 30; Paris: Geuthner, 1939), 923–35.

= 'Vaterhäuser'; family associations) in the places of their residence (Ezra 2; Neh. 7.5-72) or were sorted by profession. The importance of the continuity of familial relationships played a major role, and would serve as the basis of a new beginning in the construction of self-identity in the post-exilic period. For the Davidides from Jehoiachin to Zerubbabel, familial continuity was asserted until after the exile, just as for Jerusalem's last high priest Seriah (2 Kgs 25.18) through his exiled son Jehozadak (1 Chr. 5.40-41 [NRSV 6.14-15]) to Joshua, who became the first high priest of the Second Temple. The political and cultic-religious new beginning after the exile under the leadership of Zerubbabel and Joshua was thus anchored in the continuation of pre-exilic familial traditions. All in all, the extra-biblical texts show that the Judeans led a comfortable life in Babylon, where they were able to purchase moveable and immoveable goods and slaves, to participate in economic enterprises[152] and to exercise their trades. In their legal status, they were set on the same level as the Babylonians, and they were able to practise their religion without hindrance. The collections for Jerusalem (Zech. 6.10-11; Ezra 2.69; 8.25-30) show that the exiles prospered economically, so that it is no surprise that only a limited number were prepared to return to Judah. In the exile community, prophets repeatedly appeared on the scene (Ezekiel), whereby the anonymous prophet → *Deutero-Isaiah* and his disciples anticipated the end of the Neo-Babylonian rule and the end of the exile with the advent of Cyrus (Isa. 41.2; 44.28a; 45.1-7; 46.11) and thus awakened new hopes of salvation. Anti-Babylonian (Isa. 47) and respectively pro-Persian oracles evidently laid the foundations for the good relationship between the Judean exiles and the Persians, which would pay out in the following period. The question of why the Judean exile community, unlike the deportees from the northern kingdom did not assimilate into the mixture of so many diverse peoples in their new homeland, but instead created for themselves a new identity that set them off outwardly and consolidated them inwardly, has various answers been met with:

- On the whole, the Judean kingdom had existed longer than the northern kingdom and was culturally more homogeneous, so this could explain why the Judean community of exiles by and large held together more strongly than the Israelites.[153]
- Important was the fact that the Davidic royal house continued to exist and was recognized in the exile community as a bearer of political hopes.

152. This is made clear by texts from the trading house of Murašu in the area of Nippur, which shed light on the situation in the years 455–403 BCE and attest to the vital participation of Judeans in the affairs of the enterprise, see M. W. Stolper, *Entrepreneurs and Empire: The Murašû Archive, the Murašû Firm and the Persian Rule in Babylonia* (Uitgaven van het Nederlands Historisch-Archaeologisch Instituut te Istanbul 54; Istanbul: Nederlands Historisch-Archaeologisch Instituut, 1985).

153. Assimilation processes can be observed here too: people with personal names containing Yhwh often named their children after traditional Babylonian deities. Contracts between Judeans and their descendants and other peoples were put under the protection of Babylonian gods.

- The redactional history of the prophetic books of Isaiah, Jeremiah, and Ezekiel suggests that the exiles took books with them and thus preserved their cultural identity. In addition, they corresponded by letter with those who had remained behind in the land (Jer. 29.1-3; 51.59-60).
- The institutional framework for the cohesion of the Judeans in Babylonia was more favourable than that in Assyria, so that it was easier for them to maintain their identity.

3. Voluntary migration to Egypt: According to Jer. 43.7–44.30, Judeans fled to Egypt in 582 BCE There they settled in Tachpanhes (Daphne) in Lower Egypt. According to Jer. 44.1, there already existed Judean settlements in Migdol (a border fortress in the eastern Nile Delta), Nof (Memphis), and Patros (= Upper Egypt). Evidently, Judeans had already taken refuge in Egypt before Nebuchadnezzar's ravages in Palestine, either having immigrated there or having gone there as mercenaries or merchants, only to take roots there. Archaeologically and in extra-biblical texts, the presence of Judean communities in Egypt can be documented, though it is not always certain when the immigrants actually settled down in the new homeland. This is the case, for instance, for the 'Judean' military colony in Elephantine (a Nile island near Assuan), whose inhabitants evidently already had before 525 BCE erected a Yhwh-temple there.[154] The origins of this colony of mercenaries, whose existence is well documented in the 5th cent. BCE, are a topic of numerous hypotheses, among them proposals that link the beginnings of the settlement to the destruction of Samaria (722/721 BCE) and to refugees from the northern kingdom. Other options suggest an emigration of Judeans in connection with military service for the Assyrians at the time of the Assyrian vassalage of the kings Hezekiah or Manasseh or in connection with a flight before the Babylonian conquests of 597/596, 587/586 and 582 BCE. The community of Elephantine stood in Persian service and was a ḫaṭ[ā/ī]ru-community, i.e. a corporation with certain civil and religious rights and thus capacities for a restricted self-government.[155] It had to endure several conflicts with the local Egyptian priesthood, but the settlers remained there and did not return to Palestine. Their traces are lost only around 400 BCE, apparently when the colony perished in the course of the Egyptian rebellions against the Persians (on the religion of Elephantine, see below Ch. 4.3.2.2).

It is striking that the OT gives no continuous account of the exile period. It is only narrated how it came to the forced Babylonian exile and the voluntary Egyptian → *diaspora* (2 Kgs 24–25; Jer. 39–43; 2 Chr. 36) and how the exile came to an end (Ezra). For the time in between, it is only recounted how Jehoiakim of Judah was pardoned by Nebuchadnezzar's son Amel-Marduk/ Evil-Merodach (562 BCE) (2 Kgs 25.27-30; Jer. 52.31-34) and how the

154. B. Porten and A. Yardeni, *TADAE*, A4.7.

155. Diaspora communities of ethnically defined population elements could establish themselves in this way in the Persian Empire.

conquest of Egypt by Nebuchadnezzar II was expected (Jer. 43.8-13; 46.13-26; Ezek. 29.17-21; 30-32), though it did not take place. The siege of Tyre by Nebuchadnezzar II is also mentioned (Ezek. 29.17-18; Josephus, *Ant. X*, 228), although it ended in 572 BCE – contrary to Ezek. 26.7–28.19 – not with the destruction of the city but with an agreement. According to the OT presentation, the 'history' which had come to a standstill in the Babylonian Period, resumed only in 539 BCE with the books of Ezra and Nehemiah. Concerning the period in between, the OT offers different conceptions and evaluations. When one compares 2 Kgs 24–25, Jer. 39–43, and 2 Chr. 36, contradictory but also complementary pictures emerge:

1. The books of 2 Kgs and Jeremiah differ in their judgements about the situation after the Babylonian conquest. In 2 Kgs, the history of Israel and Judah comes to an end with the exile; thus the exile is seen there only as a negative sign marking God's final judgement and the end of history. In the general perspective of doom, it is suggested that the royal house had not only been exiled, but also that Jerusalem with its palace and temple had been totally destroyed and that the city together with all of Judah had been stripped of its population (2 Kgs 25.21b) – with the exception of a few vintners and farmers (2 Kgs 25.12). Jer. 39–43 presents a different picture of the first days after the Babylonian conquest: the Babylonians clearly knew who had been for them and who against them and accordingly dealt with the population and the ruling classes quite differently. So the pro-Babylonian party around Gedaliah and Jeremiah were granted a real chance of life in Mizpah, but this was undone by the Davidide Ishmael. The verse 2 Kgs 25.12 mentions only briefly, a Babylonian measure that Jer. 39.10 strongly emphasizes: Nebusaradan distributed the confiscated goods of the deportees among the people who remained in the land. Since the Babylonians in the main deported only members of the anti-Babylonian (= pro-Egyptian, 'nationalist') upper class, it was the pro-Babylonian (anti-Egyptian) upper class who profited from this measure (and gave work to the peasants and vintners). These people evidently had their centre in Mizpah, which according to archaeological findings experienced no wartime destruction.
2. Contrary to 2 Chr. 36.20-21 and 2 Kgs 25.21b, the country was neither wasted nor depopulated. This is shown already by Jer. 39–43, where – contrary to the view that only the lower classes were left behind (2 Kgs 24.14; 25.12) – members of the upper class belonging to the pro-Babylonian party represented by Gedaliah and Jeremiah were allowed to remain in the land (Jer. 40.7-8, 11-12); some of them later fled to Egypt in 582 BCE (Jer. 43.5-7) or fell victim to the third deportation (Jer. 52.30).

The year 582 BCE was evidently a critical year for Judah, for the assassination of Gedaliah destroyed the hopes of both the Babylonians and the Judeans that the land had come to rest. Here too, many unresolved questions remain for the historians, but, in general, it would appear that the situation of the Judeans deteriorated. Perhaps it was only at this time that Judah was turned into a Babylonian province (with its centre in Mizpah), or perhaps it was ruled from Samaria and in this form fell into the hands of the Persians in 539 BCE.

3. *Palestine in the Persian Period*: The fall of Babylon in 539 BCE was not the kind of decisive break indicated by 2 Chr. 36.22-23. Palestine was only a marginal territory within the enormous large satrapy of 'Babylonia and Trans-Euphrates' and it only became strategically important around 525 BCE, when Cambyses marched against Egypt. Once more, the Levantine corridor witnessed the passage of an army that intended to attack Egypt, and, as a tactical outpost fronting Egypt, Palestine was able to profit from this situation. Thus it is generally assumed that the real break in the culture of Palestine only occurred around 520 BCE with the reign of Darius I, when new administrative and economic structures were created. Increasingly, however, attention has been called to the fact that the real changes in the material culture of Jehud with respect to the number and size of the settlements only date to around 450 or even 400 BCE, so that the Persian Period should be divided into a Persian Period I (539/538–450/400 BCE) and a Persian Period II (450/400–333/332 BCE).[156]

In the middle of the 6th cent. BCE, numerous settlements with a mixed Phoenician-Persian culture arose in the northern coastal line around Akko. Their sphere of influence extended into the Galilean backcountry. This hinterland functioned as a supplier for the coastal cities, which were endowed by the Persians with political and economic privileges. The global economic system of the Persians flourished, and the Phoenicians had a most important share in it. The cities of the Mediterranean coast experienced an upswing, large administrative buildings were erected, port facilities were expanded. The quantity of imports from Greece indicates the extent of international

156. For a division only around 400 BCE speaks the fact that in ca. 404 BCE the Persian rule over Egypt came to an end, so that southern Palestine became the southern border of the Persian Empire. This led to the construction of fortified administrative centres (e.g. Lachish IB) and massive Persian presence. On this topic, see A. Fantalkin and O. Tal, 'Redating Lachish Level I: Identifying Achaemenid Imperial Policy at the Southern Frontier of the Fifth Satrapy', in *Judah* (ed. O. Lipschits and M. Oeming), 165–97.

connections. This upswing reached the Palestinian backcountry only with some delay. But from the Persian Period on, here too new settlements were founded and previously abandoned places were resettled: as suppliers for the coast, however, they depended on the markets there. A significant upswing in population density and structure is archaeologically and demographically only observable with the beginning of Persian Period II. Corresponding investigations have shown that (in comparison to Iron Age II) Jehud was settled only very sparely and humbly in the Babylonian times and in Persian Period I. Jerusalem was a small rural town of some 500 inhabitants; in all of Jehud there lived only some 13,000 people. This situation changed only around 460/450 BCE, though conditions remained modest: Jerusalem is estimated to have had then some 1,500 inhabitants and all of Jehud only some 20,000–25,000 inhabitants. The urban centres of the time lay outside of Jehud, in the Shephelah, Galilee and on the coast. Recently, a continuity of settlement has been established for the city of Samaria (and its neighbourhood) from the late 8th cent. BCE through to the Persian times, so that Samaria in the Persian Period should be seen as a flourishing urban centre. By contrast to Jehud, the population of the province of Samaria has been estimated at ca. 60,000–70,000 inhabitants.

Palestine belonged to the legacy of the Neo-Babylonian Empire and was a part of the large satrapy of 'Babylonia and Trans-Euphrates', which had been carved out of it. In this large satrapy, there were provinces with governors (Karnaim, Hauran, Gilead, Ammon, Moab, Galilee, Samaria) and vassal kingdoms with their kings (e.g. Sidon). Judah belonged to the first category, though there are some indications that the latter might not be excluded. For this reason, the scholars debate the administrative status of Judah in Persian Period I.

The following scenarios are possible:

- Judah was from the beginning a part of the province Samaria and was administered from there. Only with Nehemiah was the independent Persian province Jehud created and Nehemiah served as its first governor (A. Alt; H. Donner[157]). Against this position speaks the fact that already before Nehemiah governors are mentioned (see below and Neh. 5.15).
- Judah was a vassal kingdom after the fashion of the Phoenician city-states. The Davidide Zerubbabel/Ṣemaḥ (Zech. 3.8; 6.12; 1 Chr. 3.19) and before

157. H. Donner, *Geschichte*, 454–6.

him Sheshbazzar[158] were Judean vassal kings (Paolo Sacchi, Herbert Niehr[159]). Against this view speaks the fact that they are never spoken of in the OT as kings but only called governors (Ezra 5.14; Hag. 1.1, 14; 2.2, 21).

- Jehud, at least from the beginning of the Persian Period, was a separate province with its own governor. If one takes Hag. 1.1, 14; 2.2, 21 at face value, then Zerubbabel was the first (Persian) governor of the province Jehud, whereby it remains unclear, whether this province already existed in Neo-Babylonian times or was only erected by the Persians. The role of Sheshbazzar can no longer be more exactly defined. He is called the 'the Prince for Judah' (Ezra 1.8), but, as an official title in relation to his equally proclaimed governorship (Ezra 5.14), it is unclear what is meant thereby. Sometimes it is argued that Jehud already with Sheshbazzar was an autonomously administered Persian province.[160] According to his name (without mention of his father), he was a Babylonian, who might have been confirmed by Cyrus in office as the last Babylonian governor of Judah and the first Persian governor of Jehud. According to a combination of biblical and → *epigraphic* evidence, the list of governors of the Persian province of Jehud would then be as follows: Sheshbazzar? (538 BCE), Zerubbabel (520/515 BCE), Hananiah? (perhaps a son of Zerubbabel?), Elnatan (perhaps the son-in-law of Zerubbabel, but not a Davidide), Jeho῾ezer, Aḥzai, Nehemiah (445–433 BCE), followed later by Bagohi/Bagoas (410–407 BCE) and Jeḥizqiah (ca. 330 BCE).
- Governors of the Persian province of Samaria were members of the family of the Sanballatides: Sanballat I, Delaiah (Shelemiah; 407–401 BCE), Sanballat II, Isaiah, Hananiah (ca. 375–332 BCE) and Sanballat III (around 330 BCE). The status of the two independent Persian provinces of Samaria in the north and Jehud in the south is well documented in the material culture from the middle of the 5th cent. (Persian Period II).[161]

158. As to Sheshbazzar, questions have been raised about a possible identification with Shenazzar in 1 Chr. 3:18 and a possible identification with Zerubbabel, see J. Lust, 'The Identification of Zerubbabel with Sheshbassar', *ETL* 63 (1987): 90–5. Both are etymologically improbable.
159. Compare P. Sacchi, *History*, 51–8; H. Niehr, 'Religio-Historical Aspects of the "Early Post-Exilic" Period', in *The Crisis of Israelite Religion: Transformation of Religious Tradition in Exilic and Post-Exilic Times* (OtSt 42; ed. B. Becking and M. C. A. Korpel; Leiden: Brill, 1999), 228–44.
160. C. E. Carter, *The Emergence of Yehud in the Persian Period: A Social and Demographic Study* (JSOTSup 294; Sheffield: Sheffield Academic Press, 1999), 52.
161. Among the sources, seals and papyri from Wādī d-Dāliye north of Jericho deserve mention, see D. M. Gropp, *The Samaria Papyri from the Wadi ed-Daliyeh: The Slave Sales* (Cambridge: Harvard University Dissertation, 1986); these are private legal documents according to Neo-Babylonian formulars, which were issued in Samaria around 334–331 BCE. Further sources are Elephantine-Papyri (B. Porten and A. Yardeni, *TADAE*, A4.7; A4.8. and A4.9.) and coin finds. Clay seals and jar stamps with the word Jehud appear from the middle of the 5th cent. until the early 3rd cent. BCE. These stamp impressions on jars and bullae with the legend 'Jehud + personal name', 'Jehud

> André Lemaire has pointed out that the forms of address as vassal kingdom or king and province or governor need not exclude each other,[162] and that one can reckon with the possibility that the Persians appointed the Davidide Zerubbabel as governor with the intention of restoring the royal dynastic succession. Perhaps they may not themselves have had this intention, but with the choice of a Davidide as governor, they raised hopes among the Judeans of the restoration of the Davidic monarchy. In any case, the Persian and Judean attempts to re-establish a Davidic monarchy (Hag. 2.20-23; Zech. 4.6-10a) failed in the long run, and thus Jehud was placed under a mere provincial governor, who had no Davidic origin or claims (Nehemiah; Neh. 5.14; 12.26).

The economy of Jehud, which as in the past rested on agriculture (oil, wine, grain), functioned on a → *subsistence* level during Persian Period I and served only to supply Jerusalem. It did not produce enough for export, so it had no share in the economic opportunities of the new international markets of the Persian Period. In comparison to neighbouring provinces, Jehud was poor, so it is hardly surprising that Jehud only really becomes tangible as a separate province in the material culture of Persian Period II. In all periods, however, there existed a local upper class (see the finds from Ketef Hinnom). Alongside the governor, a local administration took care of regional needs in the interest of the Empire. Native institutions like the elders continued to function. After the end of the unsuccessful restoration of a Davidic monarchy around 520/515, the new office of the high priest grew in influence, because here the pre-exilic familial continuity endured, and the Second Temple (unlike the pre-exilic temple, which had been mainly in the control of the king) was now exclusively under the control of the priests. Successively, the priests succeeded in expanding their status, as is evident, for instance, in a papyrus from Elephantine, in which a Judean → *diaspora community* in Egypt (toward the end of the 5th cent.) appealed to the rulers of the province Jehud for instructions and assistance. To this end, they wrote (i.a.) to the high priest Johanan and the Jerusalem priests, who are named before Ostanes and the 'nobles of the Jews', a fact that one can interpret as a sign of a hierarchical pre-eminence of the priesthood. From the text, it becomes clear that the internal self-government of the province Jehud consisted of a priestly

+ personal name + the governor' or 'personal name + the governor' or stamp impressions which contain only 'Jehud' represent a new genre.

162. A. Lemaire, 'Zorobabel et la Judée à la lumière de l'épigraphie (fin du VIe s. av. J.-C.)', *RB* 103 (1996): 48–57.

and an aristocratic ruling council with presiding officers (cf. Neh. 5.7).[163] Evidently, the returning exiles quickly laid claim to the political, economic and religious leadership. According to the OT account, for the purpose of consolidating Jehud as an independent entity in the succession of Judah and of the northern kingdom Israel and of setting it apart from the surrounding world of so many different peoples, various mechanisms were introduced to hold the influence of foreign surroundings at bay: these were the same mechanisms that had been developed in the exile communities, e.g. organization in houses of the father(s) ('Vaterhäuser') or family associations, circumcision, rules concerning eating and foodstuffs, Sabbath rest, prohibition of mixed marriage (Ezra 10; Neh. 13.23-28); they were imported to Jehud and imposed with Persian help as measures of restoration, though in fact they represented modernizing innovations. With these ritual/religious commandments, which so strongly influenced the life of the individual and forced him to take a personal stand (acceptance and observance or not), the problem of self-definition was put before every single Judean/Jehudean and brought to their conscious awareness. This was as much a problem in Palestine as it had been in Babylonia, since an exile, who no longer found himself among Babylonians, now found himself surrounded by Greeks, Arabs and Phoenicians.

The size of the Persian province Jehud is relatively well known. By and large, it corresponded to the scope of the former Babylonian province: to the north, the border ran somewhat north of Bethel; to the east, it ran along the Jordan and the Dead Sea, to the west, Jehud's territory ended behind Gezer and Azekah (i.e. portions of the northern Shephelah belonged to Jehud); and in the south it ended behind Beth-Zur (**fig. 14b**).

There Jehud bordered on the former Neo-Babylonian province of Arabia, which, after the Persian conquest of Babylon evidently enjoyed the status of a confederate state and was under Arabian control.[164] The Arab Geshem/Gashem was in fact a neighbour to Nehemiah, the governor of the province Jehud (Neh. 2.19; 6.1-2, 6). The king of the Arabs (= the kingdom of Kedar) had joined the rebellion of Egypt and Cyprus against the Persian Empire around 387/385 BCE (Diodorus XV, 2,4). This led, in connection with the attempt of the Persians to reconquer Egypt (385 or 373 BCE), eventually to the elimination of the Arabian royal family. The

163. B. Porten and A. Yardeni, *TADAE*, A.4.7; A.4.8.

164. Concerning the texts that demonstrate this, see A. Lemaire, 'Der Beitrag idumäischer Ostraka zur Geschichte Palästinas im Übergang von der persischen zur hellenistischen Zeit', *ZDPV* 115 (1999): 12–23, esp. 17.

Persians regained control of southern Palestine and created (between 385/373 and 360 BCE) the Persian province of Idumea (Edom), in which, toward the end of the 4th cent. BCE, the Idumeans and the Nabateans set the tone. In 332 BCE, the whole region came under the control of Alexander the Great.

The Persian Period – as the time after the exile – was marked (according to the OT) by (1) the permission of the Persian king (Cyrus II or Darius I) to return to Palestine; (2) the rebuilding of the Jerusalem temple and its re-consecration in 520–515 BCE; (3) the construction of the city wall in 445–444 BCE; (4) social reforms; and (5) religious reforms. All of these measures belonged to the basic programme of restoring Jehud as a part of the Persian Empire, which in turn must be seen in the larger context of the Persian confederation policy. The multi-national Persian Empire encouraged political self-organization and local, juridical, administrative, religious and cultural independence of the individual regions as long as they did not endanger the empire as such. Privileges of all types had their politically pragmatic background. Regionalism was promoted as long as this policy secured the loyalty of the diverse small groups to the empire as a whole. Loyal local elites were granted privileges; disloyal groups were eliminated. This held for Jehud as well. The rise of an elite there that was loyal to the Persians was due to the strategically important position that the territory enjoyed since Cambyses's successful invasion of Egypt. The loyalty of the elite of the southern province on the border of Egypt was secured by recruiting them from the Judean exile community in Babylonia and endowing them with riches and privileges. This imported an upper class, whose loyalty to the Persians could be relied upon, and who counted for the emperors as a representative population that could serve as a cornerstone for the development of the empire in the West. In this way, many a Davidide was initially re-called into action.

*(1.) The permission to return.* The Bible contains two divergent traditions concerning the return of the exiles from the exile and the reconstruction of the temple. One is connected with Sheshbazzar and the year 538, i.e. with Cyrus II (Ezra 1.7-11; 5.14-16), the other with Zerubbabel and Joshua in 520/515, i.e. with Darius I (Ezra 2.2; 3.2-3, 8-9). What exactly Sheshbazzar did, is historically no longer ascertainable. Perhaps he led the first group of repatriates; perhaps he was the last Babylonian governor or vassal king,[165] who was then confirmed in office as the first Persian governor by Cyrus; perhaps he was only deputed

165. So P. Sacchi, History, 60–1.

to return the temple furnishings to Jerusalem (Ezra 1.8-11). In accord with the prophetic testimonies of the OT (Hag. 1.11-12; Zech. 4.9; see also Ezra 5.1-2; 6.14 against Ezra 5.14-16), the erection of the temple is generally not attributed to him but to Zerubbabel.[166] Likewise, it is generally thought that a larger party of repatriates only arrived in Jerusalem with Zerubbabel in 520 BCE (Ezra 2). In favour of the dating under Darius I speaks the fact that Jehud only came into the Persian king's field of interest in connection with the Persian activities in Egypt, so that only then can one reckon with a reconstruction of Jehud with Persian support and corresponding privileges, when namely the region had become tactically important. The association of the construction of the temple with Sheshbazzar can be viewed as a theologically motivated re-projection, which sought to link the political and religious new beginning directly with Cyrus's accession to power. It is certain that the return took place in several waves (Ezra 1.11; 2 = Neh. 7.6-68; Ezra 7.6; 8; Neh. 2.7-9); but the numbers of repatriates given in the biblical texts are completely unrealistic in terms of the archaeologically established population density (see above).

*(2.) The building of the temple.* According to the concept of the books of Ezra and Nehemiah, the end of the exile began under Cyrus in 539 BCE: already in the first year of his reign, Cyrus is said to have issued an edict allowing the exiles to return to Jerusalem and to rebuild the temple, though 18 years passed before this took place (Ezra 4.1-24). This edict is cited in the Bible in two Hebrew versions (Ezra 1.2-4 = 2 Chr. 36.23) and two Aramaic versions (Ezra 6.3-5; 5.14). The question of the historical credibility of these traditions is given different answers among the scholars.[167] Generally, Ezra 6.3-5, which speaks of the return of the temple furnishings and the commission to rebuild the temple, is taken to be more reliable than Ezra 1.2-4,[168] which suggests a general permission to return to Palestine for the whole exile community. In all the biblical versions, the edict is ascribed to Cyrus, although among many scholars, the current tendency is to see a possible decree of Cyrus as being restricted to the return of the temple furnishings, whereas the edict concerning the permission for the exiles to return and to reconstruct the temple would have been granted only under Darius I in 521 BCE.[169] The engagement of Darius I in Egypt appears to have moved him to permit the return of the Judeans loyal to Persia in order to stabilize the situation through the Davidic governor or vassal king Zerubbabel and the priest Joshua.

166. So, for example, A. Meinhold, 'Zerubbabel, der Tempel und die Provinz Jehud', in *Steine – Bilder – Texte* (ed. C. Hardmeier), 193–217; P. R. Bedford, *Temple Restoration in Early Achaemenid Judah* (JSJSup 65; Leiden: Brill, 2001), 180–1.

167. Negative by P. Sacchi, *History*, 59; positive by J. Schaper, *Priester und Leviten im achämenidischen Juda* (FAT 31; Tübingen: Mohr Siebeck, 2000), 67–75.

168. So H. Donner, *Geschichte*, 439–42; R. Albertz, *Israel*, 119–20.

169. R. Albertz, *Israel*, 119–32. But see now D. V. Edelman, *The Origins of the 'Second' Temple. Persian Imperial Policy and the Rebuilding of Jerusalem* (London: Equinox, 2005).

One of their first measures was to restore the altar of burnt sacrifice (Ezra 3.2-3), whereby the OT emphasizes the new beginning of cultic-religious life in Jerusalem marked by this action. Against this position, one must recall Jer. 41.5; Lam. 1.4; Zech. 7.2-3; 8.18-19, which point to the continuity of the Yhwh cult in Jerusalem. On more than one occasion, Zerubbabel and the high priest Joshua are described as the persons on the side of the Judeans who were mainly responsible for the building of the temple[170] (Zech. 4.9; Hag. 1.14; Ezra 3.6; 4.2-3) and not Sheshbazzar (cf. Ezra 5.14-16). Despite diverse difficulties, the building went forward. It would appear that the Jerusalemites themselves opposed the rebuilding of the temple, having more existential concerns (Hag. 1.2-11). In Ezra 4.1-5, the 'adversaries of Judah and Benjamin' and the 'people of the land' are mentioned, whose origins, according to v. 2, went back to Assyrian settlers under Esarhaddon. Ezra 4.3 recounts their hostility, which arose because they wanted to participate in the building of the temple.[171] Because Zerubbabel refused their cooperation, the Second Temple became an undertaking of the Persians and the exile community in Jehud and thus excluded a large portion of the population of the land and the province of Samaria. Those who built and paid for the temple would later have the say over the cult and who could participate in it. Thus the construction of the temple is said to have come to a standstill and only resumed with the double legitimation of Cyrus II (historically improbable) and Darius I (Ezra 6), so that it was finished only in 515 BCE (Ezra 6.15). Darius I is said to have granted financial aid, inter alia for the sacrificial cult (Ezra 6.6-11) and requested a sign of loyalty in the form of regular prayers for himself and his sons (Ezra 6.10). Thus, the Second Temple, like its predecessor, was the centre of an official cult and was closely tied to the political overlordship (Ezra 6.10-12; 7.23). Because the Persians supported the construction financially, they enjoyed the right to have a say in the cult and to claim the loyalty of the priests and of the god Yhwh worshipped there. According to the idealizing OT account, the temple came into being through the cooperation between a Davidide, a priest of an ancient family, two prophets (Ezra 6.14), the Persian sovereignty, the elders, and the people, so that it de facto became a Persian imperial sanctuary and an instrument of Persian imperial rule, that united the people and their new rulers descended from ancient lineages. Thus, for the temple, a story of its foundation was created, that bundled all the prevailing political structures of the post-exilic period. The temple became the sign of collective identity and, according to the account of Ezra and Nehemiah, the crystallization point for the province of Jehud, the consolidation of which had begun with the temple (Ezra 1–6) and reached its term with the fortification of Jerusalem (Neh. 1.1–7.4; 11.1–12.47).[172] At the

170. Both are mentioned in Ezra 2 = Neh. 7, suggesting that they both left Babylon in 538 with Sheshbazzar.

171. On Ezra 4.6-23, see below.

172. T. Willi, *Juda – Jehud – Israel. Studien zum Selbstverständnis des Judentums in persischer Zeit* (FAT 12; Tübingen: Mohr, 1995).

consecration of the temple (Ezra 6.15-18), Joshua and Zerubbabel no longer play a role and nothing is known about their fate or whereabouts.

*(3.) The construction of the wall.* The construction of the city wall around Jerusalem is associated with Nehemiah. From Neh 1.1; 13.6, it is surmised that there were two missions of Nehemiah, one in 445/444 and a second after 433 BCE: his tasks – construction of the Jerusalem wall, debt relief (Neh. 5), and establishment of the city compact (Neh. 10) – are generally regarded as belonging to the realm of political pragmatism. According to Neh. 3.33–4.17 (NRSV 4.1-23) and Ezra 4.6-23,[173] disruptive action against the construction of the wall was taken under Artaxerxes I Longimanus (465/464–425 BCE), but in the end it was completed (the exact course has yet to be archaeologically established). Governor Sanballat of Samaria, governor Tobiah of Ammon and the Arab king Geshem are identified as the instigators of the activities against Jerusalem. The appearance of Nehemiah in Jerusalem and the Persian interest in fortifying Jerusalem fits well into the political situation of the Persian Empire, which from 460/450 and esp. 404 BCE increasingly sought new ways to control its western provinces more strongly. These measures were directed against the Greeks and the Egyptians, so that securing the borders of the outer territories lay very much in the imperial interests. Because the Persians also had to fear that Jehud, Samaria and other areas might join in the rebellions, it was important for them to maintain peace in the border provinces. At the same time, the Persians built up an efficient network of fortresses in the Levant, which were meant to control the important highways. According to Neh. 7.4-5; 11.1-2, people from elsewhere were resettled in Jerusalem, a fact often discussed under the term 'synoikismos'. Archaeological test pits show that Jerusalem, relatively unchallenged, was the only walled town in Jehud during the Persian Period (possible exceptions are Mizpah and Rāmat Rāḥēl).[174] Essentially, the province consisted of unfortified villages and hamlets.

*(4.) Social reforms.* With the return of the exiles from Babylonia, various social problems arose in Jehud. The repatriates had to be resettled, their property rights clarified. The latter task proved complicated, because the claims of the repatriates to their former land holdings had to be regulated and clarified with respect to the people who had meanwhile settled and worked these properties (2 Kgs 25.12; Jer. 39.10; Ezek. 11.15; 33.24). Apparently, the principle of restoration rather than compensation prevailed, with the result that many people were driven from the holdings that had been assigned them since 587/582 BCE. Once more, one should recall that Jehud during Persian Period I did not count more than 13,000 persons and in Persian Period II it contained only about 20,000–25,000 persons, so that the OT numbers of those who returned are quite unrealistic. Alone this

173. Ezra 4.6-23 is anachronistic and unhistorical in the present context of the construction of the temple.

174. See C. E. Carter, *Emergence*, 215 (above, n. 160).

very small population constituted the post-exilic community that was affected by the measures of Nehemiah and Ezra (to the extent that they are historical). The statements of Hag. 1.6, 9-12 and Zech. 8.10 describe the economic situation as desolate, this being attributed prophetically to the absence of the temple, whose reconstruction was thus theologically motivated. The economic situation of Jehud in Persian Period I was tense. In reality, it was the Persian financial policy of collecting property and poll taxes in coin, which led to the impoverishment of the peasants and the lower classes. In Jehud, → *subsistence economy* prevailed and this failed to produce enough surpluses to be sold for money. In addition, it should be recalled that the immigration of the wealthy exiles into Palestine upset the social equilibrium there. Thus social tensions were sharpened. According to Neh. 5, one of Nehemiah's most important tasks was to end the social unrest. To this end, he ordered the cancellation of debts and the return of mortgaged or alienated landed property (Neh. 5.1-13). Neh. 13 ascribes to Nehemiah further cultic-religious reforms, for instance his actions against mixed marriages (Neh. 13.23-27), measures for the support of the levites (Neh. 13.10-14), and provisions for the observation of the Sabbath rest (Neh. 13.15-22), which are the subject of discussion in their connection with Nehemiah (rather than Ezra). Only in Persian Period II did the economic situation improve somewhat. It is noteworthy that, according to the material findings, metal and precious metals again become available in larger quantities and that the production of bronze gains new impetus.

*(5.) Cult reforms.* With the person of the priest Ezra, who according to Ezra 7.12, 21 bore the title 'the scribe of the law of the God of heaven', various problems are connected. On the one hand, his actions are artfully interwoven and synchronized with those of Nehemiah in the books of Ezra and Nehemiah (on the dating of Ezra and Nehemiah see Ch. 22.1). On the other, the question has been raised, whether Ezra appeared on the scene before or after Nehemiah. In the meantime, on the basis of a critical reading of the books of Ezra and Nehemiah, this question has been resolved in favour of the second option. According to Ezra 7.12-26, the mission of Ezra in 398 BCE consisted in establishing the law of the God of heaven in Jehud and Jerusalem. The question is, what is meant by this law. In the past, the following answers have been proposed: 1. a form of Deuteronomy (Ulrich Kellermann and others) 2. the → *Priestly Document* (P; Abraham Kuenen inter alia) 3. an early edition of the → *Pentateuch* (Julius Wellhausen inter alia) 4. legal materials which later came to be incorporated into the Pentateuch (Rudolf Kittel, Gerhard von Rad and others). 5. Persian imperial law (aram. *dāt*), that only later on the redactional level came to be identified with the Torah (Rolf Rendtorff inter alia) (→ *Persian imperial authorization*). According to Ezra 7, Ezra negotiated privileges for the Jerusalem temple, organized its finances, and pushed through the tax exemption of the cult personnel. Furthermore, he dissolved the mixed marriages (Ezra 9.1–10.44) and thus regulated priestly affairs in the province of Jehud. The period from ca. 400 to ca. 300 BCE is rather poorly documented for Jehud, so that little can be said about the historicity of these measures. Since

the OT with regard to mixed marriages, for instance, also takes more positive positions (Ruth for example), the last word had evidently not yet been spoken at this time. It likewise remains unclear, whether the province took part in the various anti-Persian revolts (387/385 and 349/348 BCE) and even whether the people in Jerusalem, preoccupied with the construction of their own identity, took notice of the arrival of the Macedonians and recognized the signs of a new era.

## 4.3.2 Religion and Cult: Tradition and Innovation

As mentioned above, the Mediterranean world of the Babylonian and Persian Periods was marked by cultural internationality, although at the same time the revival of regional and local traditions can be observed. Palestine, in this epoch, was once again a region that was divided into many individual districts, all of which shared in the internationalization of the world of the gods, though each district cultivated and developed its own locally specific religious traditions: Galilee and the coast belonged to the Phoenician sphere of influence and thus shared in the Phoenician culture and religion. However, the Phoenician religion of the Persian Period was strongly egyptianized, as one can see in the sacral architecture and the use of Egyptian names for the gods in inscriptions and in personal names. It is no wonder, therefore that the numerous indications of religious cults in the coastal region and in Galilee reveal strong Egyptian influence mediated by the Phoenicians. Local preferences also appear in southern Palestine, the later Idumea, where Edomite and Arab influences increasingly find expression. The cultural and religious conditions in these territories can hardly be equated with those in Samaria or Jerusalem. In both places, Yhwh continued to be worshipped. Through the exiles, his cult found its way to Babylonia, where it underwent important modifications, which were imported back to Jehud in the Persian Period with the return of a portion of the exiles. Because many descendants of the exiles chose to remain in Babylonia, they laid the foundations there for the → *diaspora communities* which emerged there. Fleeing Judeans, mercenaries and merchants likewise found their way to Egypt, where they settled down. Of central importance for the religious history of the Persian Period is the Yhwh-temple on the Nile island of Elephantine in Egypt, which during the Persian Period was maintained by the military colony there. Little is known about the religious communities of the refugees in Transjordan, and they will not be discussed here. On the basis of this dispersal of the Yhwh worshippers, a religious history must now leave the exclusively Palestinian perspective to sketch developments in the various communities elsewhere. These communities lived in different contexts, each of which put their stamp on the religious ideas and cultic practices of the region. In what follows, we shall briefly describe the situations in (1) the coastal areas, Galilee and Samaria; (2) Egypt/Elephantine; (3) Babylonia; and (4) Judah/Jehud.

*1. The Coastal Areas, Galilee and Samaria:* On the Phoenician coast in the west, in the Phoenician hinterland of Galilee in the north, in the Edomite/Arab south, and in the Transjordanian east, people cultivated very diverse religious and cultic traditions, which need not be described here. In general, it should be noted that the presence of the Babylonians in the land is hardly evident in the material culture. In terms of → *iconography*, they evidently had no lasting influence on the religious history of Palestine. Of the Babylonian deities, it is Marduk/Merodach and Nabu/Nebo, who are documented in the context of cult scenes in the form of their divine symbols (spade and stylus) on → *conoids* (sometimes combined with astral symbolism). These were in use well into the 5th cent. BCE and presumably belonged to Babylonian or babylonianizing and later to Persian administrative officials. As to temple complexes, the Palestinian findings are modest: the Babylonian Period as a whole is poorly represented, and even for the Persian Period there is hardly a single ground plan that, without question, can be treated as a candidate for a sacral edifice.

As possible candidates for a temple of the Persian Period, some structures in Dan deserve mention. There the excavators thought to recognize a cult area with a broad room structure (the plan is not clear). In addition, in Lachish, a building with a limestone altar (grid squares R/Q/S.15/16:10–21) and the 'solar shrine' deserve mention, although it is questioned whether the latter was founded already in the Persian Period or only in the Hellenistic Period. Possible sanctuaries of the Persian Period have also been proposed in Dor, Makmish, Jaffa and Nebī Yūnis. However, whether the buildings there were in fact sanctuaries or not, it should be noted that all of them lay *outside* the boundaries of Judah/Jehud. Two *clear examples* of Persian Period temples, though again outside of Jehud, have only recently been identified in Galilee (Miṣpe Yammīm) and the Sharon Plain (ʾElyāḵīn).[175]

175. J. Kamlah, 'Zwei nordpalästinische "Heiligtümer" der persischen Zeit und ihre epigraphischen Funde', *ZDPV* 115 (1999): 163–90.

## The Temple on Mount Gerizim

Recent excavations on Mount Gerizim have confirmed that the north had its own centre for the worship of Yhwh. Easy to recognize are the remains of a temple dating to the 5th cent BCE, with individual finds pointing to an earlier predecessor building. According to Y. Magen, the Persian ground plan of the building complex reflects Ezek. 40–48. Bone finds of goats, sheep, cattle and doves from the 5th cent. BCE point to an extensive sacrificial cult. In Hellenistic times, the temple was expanded, and it evidently represented the religious centre for 'Samaritan' → *diaspora communities*, to which they turned and for which they made financial contributions. Inscriptions from Delos from the time around 250–175 and 150–128 BCE attest payment of firstfruits offerings of the local synagogue to the Gerizim sanctuary (compare the regulations for the Jerusalem temple in Neh. 10.36-38 [NRSV 10.35-37]; 13.31). The investigation and analysis of similarities and differences between Yhwh worshippers on Mt. Gerizim and Mt. Zion during the Persian and Hellenistic Periods are the subject of recent studies, which shed new light on the interpretation of 1 and 2 Chronicles, the books of Ezra and Nehemiah, and the formation and canonization of the Pentateuch.

G. N. Knoppers, 'Revisiting the Samarian Question in the Persian Period'. Pages 265–89 in *Judah and the Judeans in the Persian Period*. Edited by O. Lipschits and M. Oeming. Winona Lake, Ind.: Eisenbrauns, 2006; Y. Magen, H. Misgav and L. Tsfania, *Mount Gerizim Excavations*. Jerusalem: Israel Antiquities Authority, 2004.

The world of the gods in the Persian Period reveals both the survival of → *autochthonous* traditions and the growing popularity of Egyptian, Phoenician and Greek deities.[176]

Stone and bronze statues of deities of the local types (weather-god, enthroned god), but above all statues of Egyptian provenience are well documented in Palestine, but the distribution of the finds shows that the majority comes from territories which no longer belonged to Jehud or Samaria, namely the coastal region, the Shephelah, and Galilee. A hoard finding in Ashkelon dating to the 5th/4th cent. BCE contains Egyptian bronze statues of Egyptian deities (Osiris, Isis, Horus/Harpocrates, Amun, Thot, Anubis, Bastet/Sechmet, Renenutet, Apis-Bull) as well as cultic inventory imported from Egypt for the performance of libations within the Isis cult (situlae); however male gods of the local Palestinian style also appear. Since there is no evidence of local manufacture in Ashkelon, these

176. On the epigraphical evidence, see A. Lemaire, 'Épigraphie et religion en Palestine à l'époque achéménide', *Transeu* 22 (2001): 97–113.

objects evidently were imported, to be bought and sold in Palestine. The *aegyptiaca,* like the religious notions associated with them, were spread by Phoenician trade reaching as far as Mesopotamia. In the material culture of the goddess iconography (seals, terra-cottas), it strikes the eye that although the figure of the naked goddess holding her breasts continued to find its adherents, the role of the goddess as nursing mother with child (Isis *lactans*) or as the pregnant mother gained in importance. Isis with the child Horus was an Egyptian theme that, in Palestine was only occasionally adapted locally,[177] since there was no → *autochthonous* tradition of a divine child. Among the clay figurines of the 5th to 4th centuries, the figurine of the '*Dea Tyria*' strikes the eye, a seated pregnant goddess, with a hand lying on her abdomen. She is known in Phoenicia, in Cyprus, in the Punic world, and in Palestine. In the coastal cities of Gaza and Ashkelon, Astarte had become the dominant goddess, having merged with Atargatis and Aphrodite and assumed the position of Tyche and the highest city goddess. In the Persian Period generally, Astarte was one of the most popular goddesses.

In the → *glyptic*, the internationalization of society is also reflected. Babylonian, Persian, Egyptian and Greek seals and signet rings are found; in the local glyptic, the multi-cultural influences are evident in the decidedly mixed style. In the Phoenician repertoire, Greek deities increasingly take their place alongside Egyptian deities. Above all, Heracles (the patron of soldiers and merchants) exercised a fascination that extended even into the hinterland (e.g. Lachish, Samaria). By contrast, Persian motifs were only sparely adopted in the glyptic of Palestine.

Seal impressions from Wādī d-Dāliye[178] (4th cent.) show a colourful hodgepodge of motifs, reflecting well the internationality of Samaria and the adoption of the Persian royal ideology. The fighting (royal) hero and the royal Sphinx belong to the Persian symbol system. Greek influence is evident in the athletic naked male figures (athletes, Heracles, Hermes, Perseus); in addition, animals and hybrid creatures are found. Egyptian motifs play nearly no role at all. Goddesses (Nike) play a subordinate role. On the basis of the find of fragments of a throne in Samaria, which unquestionably belonged to a Persian state official, one must reckon with a strong presence of the Persian power there.[179] On the whole, representations of the king played little role in the Babylonian iconography, so that they need not be expected in Palestine. Only in the Persian Period, did they

177. Already in Lachish in the 7th cent. BCE, see O. Keel and C. Uehlinger, *GGG*, Ill. 328.

178. M. J. W. Leith, *Wadi Daliyeh 1: The Wadi Daliyeh Seal Impressions* (DJD 24; Oxford: Clarendon, 1997).

179. M. Tadmor, 'Fragments of an Achaemenid Throne from Samaria', *IEJ* 24 (1974): 37–43.

find their way into the glyptic (the hero in combat with lions or hybrid creatures) of Palestine (Gezer, Samaria, Wādī d-Dāliye).[180] The Persian royal ideology found expression in a new medium, namely the iconography of the coins. The Samarian coins of the 4th cent. show the king in diverse poses, all of them representing him as the guarantor and upholder of order.

On the level of personal piety, there are signs of change. In the 6th to 4th centuries BCE, dedicatory inscriptions and votive offerings become more numerous. There was extensive commercial trade in votive objects. The growing demand for such objects reflects the fact that the relationship of the individual to his personal deity became increasingly important. Donation and dedication were acts of communication that bonded the giver and the receiver. At the same time, the individual, by his act of donation, takes his place within the order of the cult community to which he feels a sense of belonging. His gift thus takes on the character of a confession of faith. A new cult practice is documented by the appearance of limestone box-like incense altars (Lachish, Megiddo, Mizpah *et al.*), which served for the cultic burning of incense on all levels; incense reached Palestine in large quantities via the Incense Road from South Arabia.

*2. Egypt/Elephantine:* The religion of the Jewish colony on Elephantine (on the origin of the settlers see Ch. 4.3.1.2) was → *polytheistic*, and it connected Yhwh (called Yaho there) with various Egyptian deities,[181] as well as with deities that had been brought there from Palestine (Anath-Yaho[182], Ḥēræm-Bethel,[183] ʾAšim-Bethel, Anath-Bethel). According to a financial list from Elephantine, which gives account of temple income for the Yaho/Yhwh temple, there existed alongside Yaho/Yhwh the deities ʾAšim-Bethel and Anath-Bethel,

180. C. Uehlinger, '"Powerful Persianisms" in Glyptic Iconography of Persian Period Palestine', in *The Crisis of Israelite Religion: Transformation of Religious Tradition in Exilic and Post-Exilic Times* (OtSt 42; ed. B. Becking and M. C. A. Korpel; Leiden: Brill, 1999), 134–82.

181. B. Porten and A. Yardeni, *TADAE*, D7.21:3 ('I have blessed you by Yhh and Khnum'). Babylonian gods were also worshipped in Elephantine: Marduk/Merodach, Nabu/Nebo, Šamaš and Nergal are all named in a blessing formula for a man named Haggai, see B. Porten and A. Yardeni, *TADAE*, D7.30:3.

182. The interpretation of 'Anath-Yaho' as 'Anath, (consort of) Yaho' can be contested, and 'Anath' can be read as a noun; on this point, see P. L. Day, 'Anat', in *DDD*$^2$, 41.

183. B. Porten and A. Yardeni, *TADAE*, B7.2–3.

whereby the last received almost as much silver as Yaho/Yhwh[184] and probably should be seen as his consort.

> Significant from a religio-historical point of view is a papyrus that contains a copy of a petition sent to governor Bagohi/Bagoas of Jehud. In a postscript to the request, it is noted that the petition was also addressed to the Jerusalem high priest Johanan (see Neh. 12.22) and the priests of Jerusalem, as well as to Ostanes and the 'nobles of the Jews', but that it had not been answered. It also reached the Sanballites Delaiah and Shelemiah of Samaria.[185] The petition posed the question, whether the island temple of Yaho/Yhwh, which had been destroyed around 410 BCE, could be rebuilt (407 BCE), and thus indicates that the people of Elephantine respected the instructions of the governors of Samaria and Jehud and of the Jerusalem priesthood. The petition was answered positively by both governors,[186] so that the Deuteronomic-Deuteronomistic commandment of → *cult centralization* was not applied. Concerning the reasons for this exception, one can only speculate. It is possible that the commandment did not yet exist, that it was ignored, or that it only held for Jehud. Evidently a second temple was rebuilt on Elephantine, though restrictions were imposed in the practice of making offerings: offerings of food and incense were allowed, but not animal burnt offerings. Likewise significant is the 'Passover/Pesach Letter' of Darius II (419 BCE), which speaks of the celebration of the → *Passover/Pesach* and the Feast of Unleavened Bread,[187] the correct ceremonial agenda for which was evidently not known to the → *diaspora community* of Elephantine. The notion of Passover was evidently well known, but the date was flexible.[188] Likewise the Sabbath is attested as an element of counting time, but it was not clear what activities were permitted or forbidden on this day. According to an → *ostracon*,[189] there was no problem about engaging in trade on this day.

Despite all the agreements with elements of the Yhwh cult as described in the OT, significant differences must be mentioned at least briefly. Aside from polytheism, many elements that according to the OT were of central importance for the faith in Yhwh and the identity of the Yhwh community, e.g. circumcision, are lacking here in Elephantine. Not a word is said about the patriarchs, David, Moses, 'Israel' (however understood), or the exodus (which

184. B. Porten and A. Yardeni, *TADAE*, C3.15.

185. B. Porten and A. Yardeni, *TADAE*, A.4.7; A.4.8.

186. B. Porten and A. Yardeni, *TADAE*, A.4.9.

187. B. Porten and A. Yardeni, *TADAE*, A4.1.

188. B. Porten and A. Yardeni, *TADAE*, D7.6:8–10; D7.24:5.

189. B. Porten and A. Yardeni, *TADAE*, D7.16; see further 7.10:5; 7.12:9 and often elsewhere.

the Elephantine community itself had carried out by moving into Egypt rather than out of Egypt!). Although one can explain these deficits in the letters and documents on the basis of their textual → *genre*, the problem remains that there evidently existed a collection of literary works in Elephantine, none of which can be connected with the Torah, the Prophets or the Writings. Among the literary texts found in the archives, were the story and sayings of Ahikar[190] as well as an Aramaic translation of the Bisitun inscription of Darius I.[191] All in all, the cult practice in Elephantine shows that Yaho/Yhwh was worshipped there as the supreme god (with his consort), but that no dynamism developed there to make him the sole god.

3. *Babylonia:* The Babylonians did not interfere with the religion of the exiles in Babylonia or of the populations of the conquered territories. For the exile communities, which were settled in the territories assigned them, the possibility of practising their personal religion and of erecting sanctuaries for the common local practice of the cult of their traditional gods continued to exist. Whether the Jewish exiles made use of this possibility has not been demonstrated before (against this speaks Ezek. 20.30-32), but it cannot be excluded (hints in āl-Jāḫudu). In the multi-cultural and multi-religious world of Babylonia, the exiled Judeans found themselves in a situation in which the diverse deities they encountered exercised a strong attraction, and many of them named their children after Babylonian or Aramaean gods and put their business dealings under the protection of such deities. Alongside such possible integration of new deities into the personal piety of a portion of the Judeans, for others there evidently existed a need to separate themselves from the domination of the Babylonian gods in particular and to set themselves against a possible assimilation into the Babylonian mixture of diverse peoples. These efforts were borne up by the hope and the confidence that a return to Judah might become possible in the foreseeable future. In this connection, during the exile, historical reflections on a large scale were carried out by members of the upper class elite: these were designed to cope with the past and to interpret it in such a way as to derive from it prospects for the future. Such reflections concentrated on the question, why God had rejected his king, his people, his temple, and his city Jerusalem, and, on the whole, the relatively unanimous (and for the Ancient Near East conventional) answer was given

190. B. Porten and A. Yardeni, *TADAE*, C1.1.

191. B. Porten and A. Yardeni, *TADAE*, C2.1.

that this was God's punishment for earlier human misconduct. In this context, earlier impulses critical of the kings and the social order (e.g. the prophecies of judgement) were integrated as important ingredients of the group's religious tradition, since they pointed to culpable faults. The other questions; what should become of the monarchy and the Davidides and what should become of the Jerusalem temple and its cult, were treated more controversially. On the one hand, there was the pro-Davidic, 'national'-religious upper-class group, which perhaps had gathered around the Davidides in Babylon and which can be regarded as the → '*Deuteronomists*'. On the other hand, there were the priestly (and → '*Priestly Document*') circles (originally perhaps around Ezekiel), which had reservations about the monarchy or were even expressly anti-monarchical. → *Deutero-Isaiah* and his disciples ultimately separated the expectations of a future king from any human pretender and looked forward to the royal rule of Yhwh himself (Isa. 40.9-11; 52.7-10), which would know no more regional boundaries. This divine rule over the world thus came to be separated from political dominion and to be extended to embrace the whole of the world (Isa. 45.20-25).

The older OT connection between the dynastic god Yhwh and his king was dissolved in favour of Yhwh's connection with his whole people and ultimately extended to embrace all peoples of the earth. Out of the conviction that Yhwh determines the history of his people Israel and indeed of all the peoples of the earth and that he rules over foreign kings like Cyrus as well, in order to exercise his dominion and to realize his plan for history (Isa. 41.22-23), was born the concept of Yhwh's uniqueness. For the first time in the religious history of the Judean religion, the call for → *monotheism* found explicit and consistent expression (Isa. 45.5-6). Concerning the reasons for this development, there has been much speculation. On the one hand, external impulses have been proposed (e.g. the Sin-monolatry [→ *monolatry*] of the last Neo-Babylonian king Nabonidus or the influence of the → *Zoroastrian* religion),[192] which could have given the impetus toward the development

192. H. Vorländer, 'Der Monotheismus Israels als Antwort auf die Krise des Exils', in *Der einzige Gott: Die Geburt des biblischen Monotheismus* (ed. B. Lang; München: Kösel, 1981), 84–113; M. Albani, *Der eine Gott und die himmlischen Heerscharen: Zur Begründung des Monotheismus bei Deuterojesaja im Horizont der Astralisierung des Gottesverständnisses im Alten Orient* (Arbeiten zur Bibel und ihrer Geschichte 1, Leipzig: Evangelische Verlagsanstalt, 2000).

of monotheism. On the other hand, an inner-Judean development has been proposed, which could have been rooted within the Yhwh faith as such.[193]

In the face of the superiority of the Babylonian rule and the Babylonian gods, the concept of monotheism contained the potential for a criticism of dominion as such, because it denied to the Neo-Babylonian Empire its religious foundation (Marduk/Merodach was the king of the gods) and placed it within a universal plan of history which was drawn up by Yhwh, so that the political rule of the Babylonians was seen as only one building block within Yhwh's universal plan and it was expected that it would later be replaced by another building block. For the → *Deutero-Isaiah* group, the long awaited new stage in God's plan, which was foretold in the oracles of salvation, was connected with the advent of the Persian king Cyrus (Isa. 44.28; 45.1-4), thus identifying the authors of this conception as representatives of the pro-Persian policy (i.e. in Babylonian eyes, an anti-Babylonian cabal). In the exile, it evidently came to confrontations of various groups with the Babylonian image cult (see Ezekiel and the exilic Deuteronomists), which apparently was experienced as both fascinating and oppressive. As a consequence of the formulation of Yhwh's exclusivity, it would appear that the programmatic → *aniconism* of the Yhwh cult developed in Babylonia, where its full potential for setting off the Yhwh worshippers on the outside and securing their identity on the inside was recognized and thus pushed through. For the practical maintenance of the community, the elders, priests and prophets of the exile community thus developed a set of survival strategies designed to consolidate the community.

> Among these were the already mentioned organization in houses of the father(s) ('Vaterhäuser'), which gave the individual communities of exiles dispersed in the land a clear identity and an ethnic continuity spanning the generations. The rite of circumcision was introduced for young boys, which set the male descendants off from their Mesopotamian surroundings, where (in contrast to Egypt, Edom, Ammon and Arabia) circumcision was not practised. Every act of circumcising one of his sons became for the individual family father's a public confession of his relationship to Yhwh and a sign of hope for the future, i.e. for the next generation. Because eating in common belongs to the identity-creating events of a community, it is no wonder that the community laid down rules about what they ate and did not eat. Likewise the introduction of the Sabbath as a day of rest

193. A short summary with his own proposal is offered by R. Albertz, 'Der Ort des Monotheismus in der israelitischen Religionsgeschichte', in *Ein Gott allein?* (ed. W. Dietrich and M. A. Klopfenstein), 77–96 (above, n. 115).

belongs in this context (Ch. 3.3 excursus). All of these measures had profound effects on the day-to-day life Ch. 3.3 of the people, who thus proclaimed their membership in the community defined by such practices. Circumcision, Sabbath and dietary laws forced each individual to make decisions and to conduct himself accordingly. Confession and obedience to these ritual demands gave rise to a state of belonging; refusal and disobedience (as established by social control) led to exclusion (Gen. 17.14; Lev. 7.20-21, 27; Exod. 31.14).

In the exile, the personal religiosity of the individual and his family group assumed the function of securing the identity of the group, which was now defined by religious-ritual regulations. Concerning the form of common worship, little information is available. Evidently, praying in the direction of Jerusalem became the practice (Dan. 6.11-12 (NRSV 6.10-11); 1 Kgs 8.48). But regarding the rise of synagogues as houses of assembly and prayer in Babylonia, nothing can be said with certainty. The first clearly identified synagogues are found in → *Hellenistic* Egypt and Delos.[194] A portion of the exilic community evidently connected hopes for a return to Judah with the end of the Babylonian rule, and in the Persian Period various groups of repatriates actually set off for Judah. Others, however, remained gladly and willingly in Babylonia, where a flourishing → *diaspora community* took form.

4. *Judah/Jehud:* As noted above, the Babylonian destructions by no means affected the whole of Palestine, so that the break in traditions remained within limits. This applies especially to the areas and places north of Jerusalem. There the local religious traditions continued to be cultivated, although almost no extra-biblical sources for this practice exist.[195] Mizpah and the cult in Bethel gained supra-regional significance in the exilic period.[196] The texts of Ezek. 33.24-29 (polemics against the cult in the land during the time of the exile) and Jer. 41.4-5 (intended sacrifices at a Yhwh temple in Mizpah, Bethel, or Jerusalem) point to the revival and continuation of pre-exilic cultic traditions in the land. This holds also for the book of Lamentations, whose *Sitz im Leben*, in analogy to the Babylonian lamentations, should perhaps be seen in the

194. M. Trümper, 'The Oldest Original Synagogue Building in the Diaspora: The Delos Synagogue Reconsidered', *Hesperia* 73 (2004): 513–98.

195. From Mizpah, during the Babylonian period, there is, for instance, a vessel for libations, which attests to the practice of making libation offerings.

196. J. Blenkinsopp, 'The Judean Priesthood during the Neo-Babylonian and Achaemenid Periods: A Hypothetical Reconstruction', *CBQ* 60 (1998): 25–43.

ritual context of a resumption of cultic worship rather than in regular worship services in the ruins of the temple.[197] The religious situation in the country was by no means such that a religious vacuum ensued. Depression and lethargy remained within bounds: they were less an element of actual life in this time, than a matter of life's interpretation. Even the temple cult in Jerusalem, at least up to a point, could quickly be resumed.[198] The destruction of the sanctuary remained a theological problem, even though the daily routine had long been restored by the erection of an altar in the ruins of the temple or by the cult practice in Bethel (or Mizpah). The *cultic reality* in its various facets (local or private worship) with the option of stopgap solutions stood over against the *theological interpretation of the cultic situation,* which produced a whole spectrum of coping models as *interpretations* of the (dramatized) situation.

The Persian Period I did not mark a real break in the material culture of Jehud. Large bodies of people from Babylonia did not arrive in Jehud: no significant population increase can be demonstrated. The exile had affected only a small part of the people, so that (contrary to the OT presentation) 'exile and return' should be viewed as a central theme only for a small minority. Concerning the religion of the majority, little can be said with certainty, since the sources are too sparse. The religious-historical situation in Jehud at the beginning of Persian Period I hardly differed from that of the Babylonian Period. Noteworthy, however, is that solar elements continued to play a role and that official Jehud of Persian Period I saw itself represented by the aggressive lion.[199] The small finds from Jehud attest influences from Phoenicia, Greece (Pallas Athena, naked athletes) and Egypt (Isis-Osiris-Horus-cycle), that had reached the hinterland. With the return of a small group from Babylonia that had in mind the project of rebuilding the temple, the situation in Jehud changed according to the OT account: once more the official cult in the Jerusalem temple had a centre point, from which the political restoration also was meant to take its start. It is no wonder, therefore, that on this point

197. For a critical discussion, see C. Frevel, 'Zerbrochene Zier: Tempel und Tempelzerstörung in den Klageliedern (Threni)', in *Gottesstadt und Gottesgarten: Zu Geschichte und Theologie des Jerusalemer Tempels* (QD 191; ed. O. Keel and E. Zenger; Freiburg: Herder, 2002), 99–153.

198. So P. Machinist, 'Palestine, Administration of', *ABD* 5:69–81, here 79.

199. From Jerusalem, Mizpah, and other places, jar handles from the Persian Period I are known, which show an aggressive lion, sometimes with a sun-disk. This appears to have been an emblem standing for Judah/Jehud, which in the middle of the 5th cent was replaced by seals with the name of the province Jehud.

diverse fundamental questions arose, since important decisions were made regarding the course for the future. The conflicts surrounding the rebuilding of the Second Temple indicate that a large segment of the resident population of the land and of the rural upper classes (Hebr. *ʿam haʾareṣ* = 'people of the land') were excluded from the cult, which was financed and shaped essentially by members of the exile group and by the Persians, and that the thus excluded segment of the population had no say in the decisions to be taken.

(1.) With the dedication of the Jerusalem temple, the question was raised, in what form the presence of Yhwh in the temple should be represented. → *Aniconism* had been promoted by the returned exiles as the only legitimate form of Yhwh worship, and this led to an internal religious controversy with other population groups in Jehud. The Deuteronomistic circles had developed a theology of the name, according to which Yhwh is enthroned in heaven and lets his name dwell on earth in the place he has chosen. Ezekiel and the Priestly circle developed the *Kābōd* theology, according to which the 'glory' of Yhwh fills the temple, where he takes up residence. Both theologies solved the problem of the presence of Yhwh in the temple without a cult image by resort to abstract concepts. The demand for aniconism in the Yhwh cult in fact came to prevail in the temple cult in the course of post-exilic times, but not everywhere and not immediately. Concerning the worship of Asherah in Jehud of the Persian Period, hardly any information is available. In connection with the Second Temple, she is not mentioned. The goddess was consciously eliminated from the biblical writings only by the Chronicler, which, depending on the dating of his work, would mean in the 4th to 3rd centuries BCE. Of the eliminated goddess, only traces remain, namely in the personified feminine Wisdom (Prov. 8.22-31; Wis. 9.1-11).

(2.) The Second Temple counted as the dwelling place of Yhwh. Concerning his theological profile in this period, the post-exilic texts provide some information. It is striking that the solarization of Yhwh continues to be productive (Isa. 59.9; 60.1-3; Mal. 3.20 [NRSV 4.2]; Wis. 5.6). A further element is the theology of heaven, which becomes tangible in the title 'God of heaven'. Here the Persian religion provides the decisive model. Although the Persians did not impose their god Ahura Mazda on their subjects, this god exercised a strong attraction on their subject peoples, so that, in the wake of Persian cultural pressure, these peoples shaped their own local supreme god to resemble the supreme god of their rulers. The Achaemenid god was a creator of all things, a god of the absolute beginning, and perhaps, from the Persian 'internal' perspective, he was not really a heavenly god, but from the non-Persian 'outer' perspective (Herodotus, *Hist. I*, 131) he was perceived as such (see the 'winged god' of the Achaemenid → *iconography*), Since Yhwh too in the Elephantine papyri, in the books of Ezra, Nehemiah and Daniel is titled the 'God of heaven', it would seem plausible that the Yhwh title 'God of heaven' was chosen in the Persian Period in order to match him to Ahura

Mazda.[200] The theology of heaven which thus developed made it possible to claim that the worship of all the peoples of the world was directed to one and the same God, who dwelt in the heavens which were everywhere visible. This theology entailed a religious → *universalism* that was opposed to the 'nationalistic'-particularistic notions of the Deuteronomic-Deuteronomistic school.

(3.) Concerning the temple theology which finds expression in the works of → *Trito-Isaiah*, Haggai, and Zechariah, it is clear that the pre-exilic → *Zion*-theology with its notion of the temple as the dwelling place of Yhwh in his city was taken up again. However, it was now expanded in a universalistic manner to mean a kingship over all 'nations' (e.g. Zech. 4.14; 6.5). The theme of Zechariah's third nocturnal vision of the post-exilic Jerusalem as an open residential city of Yhwh, which (in the reception and outdoing of the Persian notion of city construction) needs *no* encompassing wall,[201] fits well into this conception. By contrast, behind the books of Ezra, Nehemiah and Chronicles, a party can be identified, which held 'national'-particular notions of the temple.

(4.) The abolition of the state cult connected with the king gave reason to reflect on the financing of the sacrifices and the support of the priesthood. For both, duties were imposed on the people (Num. 18; Lev. 7; Neh. 10), which increased the tax burden on the one hand but established the economic importance of the temple on the other. Because the Persian rulers contributed to the building of the temple, made other financial contributions as well, and granted tax exemption to the temple personnel, once again no separation of 'throne and altar' took place.

(5.) The fundamental priestly distinction between the holy and the profane gained importance in the post-exilic period. In the future, the temple needed to be preserved from any form of profanation, so that Yhwh never again should be forced to abandon it (Ezek. 8–11). As a consequence, the laity was excluded from any form of contact with the holy, and the cult was placed exclusively in professional hands. From within the Ezekiel group, clear boundaries were drawn, that divided the cult personnel into different levels of holiness: the service of the altar and all the cult actions which took place in the inner court and in the temple building itself were reserved to the Zadokites (Ezek. 40.46b; 44.15-16; 48.11); activities in the outer court, the oversight of the gates, the slaughter of the offerings of the laity, and other services for the laity (Ezek. 44.11-13) fell to the responsibilities of the levites. This division of responsibilities and the downgrading of the levites did not go without controversy (see the → *Priestly Document* and the Chronicles history). From the priestly point of view, purification rituals were

200. A different position is taken by H. Niehr, *Der höchste Gott*, 43–55, who traces the title to the connection of Yhwh with the Phoenician-Aramaean Baal-šamēm.

201. See R. Lux, 'Das neue und das ewige Jerusalem: Planungen zum Wiederaufbau in frühnachexilischer Zeit', in *Ein Herz so weit wie der Sand am Ufer des Meeres: FS G. Hentschel* (ETS 90; ed. S. Gillmayr-Bucher *et al.*; Würzburg: Echter, 2006), 255–71.

> meant to permeate the daily life of the laity in increasing measure (Lev. 12; 14; 15), and. from the same point of view, the cult was increasingly interpreted as the prevention of guilt or reparation for it, i.e. as → *atonement* (Lev. 16; the list of feasts in Lev. 23).

The cultic-religious new beginning carried out, after the exile, by (Zerubbabel and) Joshua was legitimated by the returned exiles as the continuation of pre-exilic traditions, but already the introduction of the new office of the high priest is an indication that profound changes had taken place. With the columns of the returning exiles, the Babylonian calendar and the forms of Yhwh worship and Yhwh cult developed in Babylonia were imported into Jehud: circumcision, Sabbath observance, dietary laws, perhaps the prohibition of mixed marriage, → *monotheism*, and → *aniconism* were meant to define the community centred on the Second Temple. With respect to the form of Yhwh worship which until then prevailed in the land and which appeared pagan and archaic to the repatriates, these measures represented innovations, which (with the help of foundation stories) were proclaimed to be in reality the restoration of ancient cult practices and the implementation of indications of the divine will. Although the thoughts about the political and religious reorganization of Judah/Jehud that had been elaborated during the exile had by and large been merely theoretical, the return of the adherents of various 'schools' of thought to Jehud meant that they imported different programmes, and this led to substantial conflicts when it came to their realization and implementation. The threatening split between the diverse groups, parties and schools (Priestly, Deuteronomic-Deuteronomistic, Prophetic and → *Wisdom/sapiential*) which is palpable in the OT, led to a compromise and to an initial canonization (→ *canon*) of diverse writings into the → *Pentateuch*. This came to be seen as the collection of the texts which were foundational for the new community: it incorporated, however, the diversity of theological currents of the time. These currents at times competed with each other, at other times they cooperated. Together they struggled for influence within the diverse institutions of local self-government (assemblies of elders, of priests) or with the Persian ruling class when it came to restructuring the province of Jehud. Although the real situation was certainly more complex and the individual groups certainly more fragmented, two major trends can roughly be distinguished: on the one hand, the → *Deuteronomists* interested in the restoration of the monarchy under new auspices; on the other, the priestly circles working for a kingless rule of the priests (theocracy, hierocracy).

Theologically, the desolate situation in Jehud after 539/538 and 515 BCE raised the problem that the prophecies of salvation represented by → *Deutero-Isaiah*, → *Trito-Isaiah*, Haggai and Zechariah threatened not to match up to reality. In this context, the prophecies were increasingly transformed into → *eschatological* oracles by redactional correction during the post-exilic period. The overthrow of the existing conditions by Yhwh was no longer expected within history but only at the end of history. This trend toward eschatologization (eschatology = the teaching about the last things) found its endpoint in → *apocalyptic literature*, which would prove enormously productive in the → *Hellenistic* Period. In the book of Daniel, one finds for the first time the notion that historical time will come to an end and a new era will begin (Dan. 2.28; 8.17, 19). Toward the end of the Persian Period, a quantitative leap in the belief in angels and demons can be observed and these are increasingly organized into hierarchies (angels under God, demons under Satan/the devil). The latter is for the first time mentioned as the heavenly accuser in Zech. 3.1-2; whereas in Job 1.6–2.7 he belongs to the sons of god and so disencumbers Yhwh of possible inhuman and capricious traits. Angels and demons approach individual human beings as helpers or as enemies, and experience a real boom in the Hellenistic Period; among other things this could be attributed to the explicit dualism that increasingly defines the notion of the world. Its origins are the subject of controversy, but they are often seen in connection with Zoroaster.

## Zarathustra and the Zoroastrian Religion

Zarathustra, the founder of the Zoroastrian religion, evidently lived in Central Asia between 1400 and 1200 BCE. Because his teachings initially were handed down only by word of mouth, their content and later developments are difficult to (re-) construct. He appears to have taught an explicit dualism, in which the supreme (and good) God Ahura Mazda, who bore → *monolatric*, or perhaps even → *monotheistic* traits, had an antagonist in an evil spirit (Angra Mainyu, later Ahriman). The supreme God was surrounded by angels, just as his adversary was surrounded by demons. An end of the world, a bodily resurrection of the dead, and an apocalyptic renewal of the world marking the final victory over evil belonged to the end-times scenario of the Zoroastrian religion. The influence of these ideas on the exilic and post-exilic religion of Judah/Jehud/Judea has long been controversially discussed. As the elements described here indicate, there are characteristic agreements between the late biblical and extra-biblical Jewish writings and the Zoroastrian teachings, but also significant differences. A hint of Jewish-Zoroastrian cultural contacts is found in the book of Tobit, for, according to Tob. 4.20; 9.2, there were Jews living in the Median city Rages, which was a centre of Zoroastrianism (compare Ch. 22.4).

Alongside the notions of angels and demons, which played a role particularly in personal piety and perhaps served as a substitute population for the heavens which had been emptied of their gods by monotheism, a 'theological wisdom' gained increasing importance in the post-exilic period, especially in upper-class circles: this wisdom finds expression in the book of Job and in Proverbs 1–9. Personal trust in God and a perfect way of living provided the maxims for a successful life, to which, for the wealthy, alms-giving and the care of the poor were intended to have their place. Because this traditional connection between what one does and what one experiences is often contradicted empirically good (trust in God) and evil (unbelief) are not always rewarded or punished in real life, thus wisdom theology became caught in a crisis that is most clearly reflected in the books of Job and Qoheleth (Chs 14 and 18).

## 4.4 The Hellenistic Period (333/332–63 BCE)

Bibliography 8 The History of Ancient Israel and Judah (L. L. Grabbe, *History*; P. Sacchi, *History*; E. Schürer, *History*); 9: History of Religion of Ancient Israel (L. L. Grabbe, *Judaic Religion*); further: J. Sievers, *Synopsis of the Greek Sources for the Hasmonean Period: 1–2 Maccabees and Josephus, War 1 and Antiquities 12–14*. SubBi 20. Rome: Pontificio Istituto Biblico, 2001; A. Berlin, 'Archaeological Sources for the History of Palestine Between Large Forces: Palestine in the Hellenistic Period'. *BA* 60 (1997): 2–51; J. H. Hayes and S. R. Mandell, *The Jewish People in Classical Antiquity: From Alexander to Bar Kochba*. Louisville: Westminster John Knox, 1998.

### 4.4.1 Society and Economy: Between Assimilation and Revolution

The Hellenistic Period is defined by two successful conquerors: at the beginning of the period, stands the Macedonian Alexander the Great, who seized Palestine and Egypt in 332 BCE and thus founded the dominion of the 'Greeks' there: at the end of the period, stands the Roman general Pompey, who in 63 BCE conquered the temple area and thus began the Roman epoch (63 BCE–324 CE). In the Near East, the time between these two military figures was marked by the Ptolemies as the successors of the Egyptian pharaohs and the Seleucids as the successors of the Achaemenids. The Ptolemies (with their centre in Alexandria) ruled over Egypt and had no intention – any more than the pharaohs before them – of giving up their Asiatic forefield, a policy that brought them into repeated conflicts with the Seleucids. Ptolemy I Soter (satrap 323–306; king 305–283/282 BCE) founded the cult of Alexander the Great in Alexandria (around 290 BCE), which later became the Ptolemaic dynastic cult under Ptolemy IV Philopator (221–205 BCE). The Seleucids (with their centre in Antioch) derived from the Macedonian nobility and attempted to legitimize their power through claims of descent from Apollo. The founder of this Hellenistic dynasty was Seleucus I Nikator (satrap 320/312–306; king 305–281 BCE). In the prolonged competition with the other Hellenistic ruling houses, especially the Ptolemies, the Seleucids ruled over the eastern part of Alexander's empire. Under Antiochus III Megas (223–187 BCE), the Seleucid Empire comprised the region extending from the Hellespont in the west and India in the east, together with parts of Egypt. After its defeat by the Romans at Magnesia in Asia Minor (190 BCE), Antiochus III agreed in the Peace of Apamea (188 BCE) to vacate Anatolia up to the Taurus. After Antiochus III Megas, the Seleucid state was divided by the political claims of his two sons, Seleucus IV and Antiochus IV, who in the course of the following generations alternately prevailed. Internally, the Seleucid Empire was weakened by these internal conflicts, and externally it was gradually rubbed out between the Roman Empire and the Parthians (a Eurasian group of mounted nomads). The Parthians took over the eastern part of the former Achaemenid Empire including Babylonia in 130/129 BCE, and in 64 BCE the remainder of the Seleucid Empire was incorporated into the Roman Empire by Pompey.

With the beginning of the Hellenistic Period, the former Persian province Jehud came to be called Judea. After Alexander's conquests in the Levant, which in essence were only a side product of his successful move into Egypt, Macedonian military colonies were established only on the Palestinian coast, so that in the hinterland at first little changed. Alexander granted the Jews religious freedom (Josephus, *Ant. XI*, 337–338) and relied on continuity in the former Persian territories, which he took over with no significant changes. The regent for the former satrapy of Trans-Euphrates was his general Parmenio. However, against cities that resisted his claims (Tyre, Gaza, Samaria), Alexander took vigorous action. In Samaria, after a rebellion against the governor Andromachus and the flight of a part of the population (see the texts from the Wādī d-Dāliye), a Macedonian colony was established. In Alexander's lifetime, the monetary system for the whole empire was unified, though the local small silver coins of Jehud/Judea were not initially affected by the monetary reform, since they represented only small local currency.

After Alexander's death (323 BCE) in Babylon, numerous armies passed through the Levant as a result of the power struggles which broke out among his generals (the diadochi). The events of the following period are marked primarily by the conflicts between the two great Oriental diadochic empires, the Ptolemies and the Seleucids. In the course of these struggles, Palestine and the Phoenician coast initially fell to the Ptolemies (312/301–200/198 BCE), after Ptolemy I Soter managed to defeat Demetrius Poliorcetes at Gaza in 312 BCE and his father Antigonus at Ipsos in 301 BCE. Ptolemy conquered Jerusalem as well (301 BCE) and deported a portion of the population to Egypt (Josephus, *Ant. XII*, 3–9).This conquest may have served as the trigger for many other Jews to migrate voluntarily to Alexandria, where they proceeded to form a flourishing colony. It is possible that already under Alexander a small Jewish mercenary colony had existed there, which had achieved equal legal standing with the Greeks (Josephus, *Bell. II*, 487).

In Alexandria, there were → *proselytes* ('those who came near'). This indicates that the Jewish communities there were open; they received people as converts, who had no Jewish ancestors, provided they were willing to follow the duties of the → *covenant* (circumcision, keeping the Sabbath, following the dietary rules). The presence of the proselytes and the fact that Greek was the *lingua franca* in Alexandria had the effect of making Greek the language of the Jewish community in the city (concerning the translation of the Torah into Greek see Ch. 1.2.1.2), which perhaps already under Ptolemy VI Philometor (180–145 BCE) had been organized as a semi-autonomous community with an ethnarch (= local ruler with limited responsibilities). From the time of Ptolemy III Euergetes (246–221 BCE), the first indications of Jewish synagogues (i.e. assembly buildings of the Jews) are found in the Nile Delta and in the Faiyum (a Jewish military colony there).

By contrast, in Judea itself, it would seem, Jerusalem remained a closed community. During the Ptolemaic Period, many cities flourished and older places were resettled (often with new names), and often they contain characteristic Hellenistic building types (e.g. gymnasia), Jerusalem too evidently prospered, but no buildings of the Hellenistic type were erected there (not yet at least). In the Ptolemaic Period, Judea belonged to the Ptolemaic province of 'Syria and Phoenicia' or 'Coele-Syria' and was centrally administered from Alexandria. This large province (roughly corresponding to the former Persian satrapy) was divided into hyparchies or eparchies (corresponding roughly to the Persian provinces), which could be further subdivided into small districts or toparchies. The large province could also contain Greek colonies, mostly in the cities, which were included within a hyparchy/eparchy or were made independent units (*polis*) by the grant of a city charter. Autonomous cities existed on the coast (Ashkelon, Gaza) and Dor was a royal fortress with its own rules.

## Important Hyparchies in Palestine

- *Judea* consisting of the city Jerusalem (under the local government of the high priest) as well as the population of the vicinity and the cultic centre of the Jerusalem temple.
- *Samaria* consisting of the Greek municipal colony together with the population of the vicinity and the cultic centre of the temple on Mount Gerizim.
- *Galilee* with the autonomous Greek municipal colony of Skythopolis (Beth-Shan).
- *Idumea* consisting of eastern Idumea with Adoraiim and western Idumea with Maresha, where a Sidonian colony existed.
- *Ashdod* being a hyparchy of the Philistine territory with its centre in Jamnia/Jabneh.
- *Ammonitis* being a hyparchy in Transjordan, where the family of the Tobiads set the tone.

The Hellenistic Period in Judea is distinguished from the preceding Persian Period II above all by the enormous growth of settlement density and structure in the former tribal area of Benjamin (a growth of 320 per cent!). The Judean highland was also increasingly settled in the Hellenistic Period, though the growth in the number of settlements there is more moderate (an increase of 13 per cent).[202] The progressive urbanization of Palestine in the Hellenistic Period went hand in hand with an economic upswing, which however did not improve the condition of all parts of the population and thus led to strong social fragmentation. Owing to the economic and tax systems of the Ptolemaic (see Zenon archive) and later the Seleucid rule, social tensions increased. The economy had now been monetarized, since small denomination copper coins were now available. The indigenous upper classes had their share in the economic upswing and were able to amass enormous riches through the system of tax farming. This system functioned as follows: the tax farmer made a bid for the taxes of a city and then received a contract for a specified sum, which he proceeded to collect from the inhabitants of the district. He needed to deliver up to the king only the fixed sum agreed upon, (together with possible bribes); everything that he managed to press out of

202. Percentages according to C. E. Carter, *Emergence*, 235–6 (above, n. 160).

the population beyond this sum, he could keep as his own profit. In the Ptolemaic Period, the tax contract lay in the hands of the high priest; later it passed to the Tobiads. The shift to Seleucid dominion evidently brought only temporary relief. For the Hasmonean Kingdom, Simon obtained tax exemption from Demetrius II in 141 BCE (1 Macc. 13.39).

In the course of the 3rd cent. BCE, five Syrian wars took place, in which the Ptolemies managed to maintain their claims to power in the Levant.

In the last decade of the Ptolemaic rule in the Levant, it would appear that Onias II was the high priest in Jerusalem. He was clothed with *timē archieratikē* = 'high priestly dignity' and *prostasía tou laóu* = 'leadership of the people' and thus enjoyed the highest authority. Around 221 BCE, he seems to have used the transfer of rulership from Ptolemy III Euergetes to Ptolemy IV Philopator and the turmoil of the 4th Syrian War to stop the tax payments to the Alexandrians. Through his rebellion against the Ptolemaic tax policy, he acted in an anti-Ptolemaic and thus pro-Seleucid manner, which proved rather premature. His action led to threats of massive punitive measures by the Ptolemaic ruler and to conflicts in Jerusalem, where the pro-Ptolemaic party put him under pressure. Onias II was forced to transfer the political power to his nephew, the Tobiad Joseph. Joseph assumed the title *prostasía tou laóu* (Josephus, *Ant. XII*, 167) and therewith a portion of the ruling power.

From the Ptolemies, he received for himself both the right and the needed military support to collect the taxes from all the territories of Coele-Syria (Josephus, *Ant. XII*, 175). As the Ptolemaic financial administrator of the Levantine province, he was also the head of the Ptolemaic party in Jerusalem.

With the battle of Paneas (later Caesarea Philippi) between Antiochus III Megas (223–187 BCE) and Ptolemy V Epiphanes (205–180 BCE) in the year 200 or 198 BCE, the situation changed, and Judea shifted from the Ptolemaic to the Seleucid domain. This entailed a policy shift, for the Seleucids pursued the hellenization of their dominions with much more vigour than the Ptolemies, and only under this condition were they prepared to foster local autonomy. After the sovereignty over Syria-Palestine had fallen to the Seleucids, disputes about the royal succession broke out among them, and the conquered territories made use of these disputes in the course of their shifting coalitions. In addition, the enemies of the Seleucids, the Ptolemies, the Parthians, and later the Romans were drawn into the various conflicts, often by the rival parties themselves in order to gain an advantage. The situation in Jerusalem and Judea in these times is marked by these conflicts, which had concrete consequences for Jerusalem especially when the various parties within the upper class made use of every means at their disposal to secure positions of leadership for their own candidates. The most important office in Jerusalem in this period was that of the high priest, and repeatedly conflicts broke out about his succession.

## The High Priest

The head of the Jerusalem priesthood and of the temple service was called the 'chief priest' (*hak-kōhēn/kōhēn hārō'š*), in pre-exilic times, whereas the notion of the 'high priest' (*hak-kōhēn hag-gādōl*) arose only in the post-exilic period as a new title, which quickly gained in importance. The political influence of the office was limited at first (Joshua alongside Zerubbabel); his cultic duties are described in the → *Priestly Document* in connection with the person of Aaron. His vestments, ornaments, diadem and anointing (Exod. 28–29) indicate that he was promoted to royal status. His most important function was the absolution of the people on the Day of → *Atonement* (Lev. 16). Special purity requirements applied to the high priest (Lev. 21.10-15). The office was hereditary and was conferred for life; the officeholder had to be male and to stand in the Zadokite lineage. Through the person of the high priest Joshua, who was present at the resumption of the cult of the Second Temple (Hag. 1.1, 12; Ezra 2.2 *et al.*), continuity with the pre-exilic cult was established. At the same time, he was the ancestor of the subsequent high priests. Under the Ptolemies and the Seleucids, the high priest of Jerusalem rose to the status and function of an ethnarch, with corresponding duties to pay taxes to the sovereign and corresponding powers to collect them from the subjects. Tax exemption was an occasional privilege, which could be granted for a limited period of time (1 Macc. 10.29-31; 11.33; 13.39). The Zadokite lineage was interrupted in Seleucid times (around 173 BCE) by the appointment of Menelaus, who had purchased the office; the Zadokites then fled (see below). In the turmoil of the Maccabean revolt, the Maccabee Jonathan assumed the office; though not a Zakodite, he came from a priestly family. During the Hasmonean Period, the office of the high priest was connected with that of the worldly ruler (ethnarch or king). In the Roman Period, the principles of heredity and life-long office were abolished. The high priest was appointed by the Roman overlord.

D. W. Rooke, *Zadok's Heirs: The Role and Development of the High Priesthood in Ancient Israel*. Oxford: Oxford University Press, 2000.

The Seleucid Antiochus III Megas wanted above all to pacify his new territories in Palestine, since he was arming against Rome (190 BCE, the battle of Magnesia). Evidently, he promised Jerusalem reconstruction measures (Josephus, *Ant. XII*, 138-39; 143), guaranteed privileges such as the delivery of sacrificial offerings, cost-free tree trunks, tax exemption for the priests and the upper class, and three years free of taxes for anyone who settled in Jerusalem.

The southern boundary was pacified by means of a political wedding: Antiochus III gave his daughter Cleopatra I (ca. 193 BCE) to Ptolemy V Epiphanes in marriage and thus sealed the alliance with the former adversary. The presence of the Seleucid Empire in the west, however, soon gave rise to conflicts with the Romans, who in subsequent times would more and more enter the Near Eastern theatre as a force in themselves. Thus, in 190 BCE, it came to a battle between Antiochus III and the Romans at Magnesia in Asia Minor, which Scipio Asiaticus decided in favour of Rome. By the treaty of Apamea (188 BCE), Antiochus III had to abandon his European and Anatolian territories; he was forced to make enormous payments to Rome and to send his son, the later Antiochus IV Epiphanes to Rome as a hostage. In any case, the pro-Seleucid policy of Onias II, which was followed by his son Simon II at the time of Antiochus III, appears to have paid off. The high priest Simon II acted together with a portion of the now pro-Seleucid Tobiad family (which had changed sides in the meantime) and with the Seleucids against the Tobiad Hyrcanus, the son of Joseph, who had replaced his father as the tax collector of the Ptolemies. Hyrcanus was evidently forced to leave Jerusalem and settled in Transjordan. He resided there in the traditional Tobiad family seat in Transjordanian Tyrus (17 km west of Amman), where he built for himself a fortified palace. His elder brothers remained in Jerusalem, so that the family of the Tobiads split into a pro-Ptolemaic and a pro-Seleucid segment.

The estrangement within the Jerusalem upper class between the supporters of the Ptolemies and the supporters of the Seleucids reached a new tragic high point under the rule of Seleucus IV Philopator (187–175 BCE). Like his father, Seleucus IV attempted to confiscate temple treasures to cover his financial needs. This picture is confirmed by the so-called 'Heliodorus-Stela', which documents a correspondence between Seleucus IV and Heliodorus, in which the king announces in August 178 BCE the appointment of an administrator who was to be responsible for the sanctuaries of the province Coele-Syria and Phoenicia.[203] The goal of this measure was certainly to back up the seizure of temple finances. 2 Macc. 3 recounts a story about how Heliodorus intended to confiscate a portion of the Jerusalem temple treasures. The reigning high priest Onias III, son of Simon II, successfully resisted him with the aid of a divine

203. H. Cotton-Paltiel and M. Wörrle, 'Seleukos IV to Heliodoros: A New Dossier of Royal Correspondence from Israel', *ZPE* 159 (2007): 191–205.

wonder. However, serious doubts are raised against the historicity of this tale, among other reasons because it is by no means evident, why Hyrcanus, the friend of the Ptolemies living in Transjordan would have deposited money in the Jerusalem temple (2 Macc. 3.11).

The troubles associated with throne successions in Antioch were particularly well suited for parties in Jerusalem to change the power situation there to their own advantage by professing loyalty to the most promising throne pretender. Despite all the rivalries, for the appointment of the Jerusalem high priest, the Seleucid rulers in Antioch were ultimately responsible, so that the upper-class parties in Jerusalem left out no opportunity for intrigue (2 Macc. 3–4), to fill the office according to their own pleasure. After Seleucus IV was murdered by Heliodorus in 175 BCE, his younger brother Antiochus IV Epiphanes (175–164 BCE) became king, needing both money and allies to hold his position. Offering both money and loyalty, the Tobiads – shortly after the change of government in Antioch – managed to persuade Antiochus IV Epiphanes to depose Onias III as high priest (perhaps under the charge of pro-Ptolemaic cabal) in 174 BCE (2 Macc. 4.8-9) and to replace him with his brother Joshua, also a son of Simon II. It remains unclear, whether Onias III was murdered or perhaps fled to Egypt, where either he or his son Onias IV founded a Yhwh temple in Leontopolis with Ptolemaic assistance.[204]

The new high priest Joshua hellenized his name to Jason. There was nothing unusual about his buying the office of the high priest directly from the Seleucid king: after all, he was descended from the priestly family of the Oniads. However, in principle, the office of the high priest was held for life, so that the appointment of a successor during the lifetime of a still-reigning predecessor did not correspond to prevailing practice and thus raised doubts about the legitimation of the new officeholder. At the time of Jason, the situation in Jerusalem increasingly got out of control, because the new high priest had chosen to make deliberate further hellenization his goal. The city was to be turned into a *polis* and ultimately to be modernized.

The construction of a gymnasium (= athletic exercise and training centre) became the symbol of a new upper-class mentality in Jerusalem, which took its orientation from Greek ideals (including ideals of the human body!) (2 Macc. 4.12, 14; 1 Macc. 1.14-15). According to 1 Macc. 1.15, circumcision was no longer regularly practised and efforts were even made to disguise it. In

204. See on this point G. Bohak, 'CPJ III, 520: The Egyptian Reaction to Onias' temple', *JSJ* 26 (1995): 32–41.

addition, new gods entered the land: above all, the muscular Heracles found adherents. According to 2 Macc. 4.19, Jason himself sent Antiochus IV money for a sacrifice to Heracles. Jason was quickly deposed by the Seleucid ruler, and in 173 BCE he was replaced by Menelaus, who, unlike his predecessors, could not point to any Zadokite ancestry (2 Macc. 4). The end of the Zadokites in the high-priestly office in Jerusalem resulted in the flight of the Zadokite priests, who had resisted hellenization, into the desert – an event which is presumably connected with the origins of the → *Qumran* community. The struggle for the office of the high priest between Jason and Menelaus caused the Seleucid Antiochus IV Epiphanes, upon his return from an Egyptian campaign in 169/168 BCE, to intervene in favour of Menelaus. He conquered Jerusalem and built up the acra (whose beginnings went back to Ptolemaic times) into a stronghold with a Seleucid garrison; he proceeded to plunder the temple, to desecrate the altar, to forbid observance of the Torah, and to erect an altar to Zeus (?) in the place of the altar of holocausts (or upon it?) in the temple (the 'abomination of desolation'[205]; 1 Macc. 1.41-49; 2 Macc. 6; Dan. 9.27; 11.31; 12.11). The Yhwh temple on Mt. Gerizim was dedicated to Zeus Xenios/Hellenios (2 Macc. 6.2; Josephus, *Ant. XII*, 262–263). This forced imposition of the hellenization of the Jerusalem and Samaritan worship of Yhwh, who was now identified in the official cult with Zeus, provoked the opposition of the priest Mattathias, son of Hasmon (hence the family of the 'Hasmoneans'), who, followed by his sons, dared to rebel against the Seleucids and Menelaus in order to roll back the cultic measures of Antiochus IV and, according to 1 Macc. 2.1-26, to make Jewish life according to the Law once again possible. Because the measures of Antiochus IV Epiphanes concerning the Jewish observance of the Law were not extended to the whole empire, in which many Jews also lived, his actions were evidently confined to Jerusalem and Judea. The fact that Menelaus remained high priest in Jerusalem and himself officiated at the rededication of the temple in 164 BCE indicates that the Seleucid religious policy was not intended to eradicate Judaism as such or extinguish the cult of Yhwh.

The rebellion of the Maccabees (an appellation derived from the surname of Judas Maccabaeus) combined religious with social motives: it can be interpreted as a revolt of the traditionalistic rural folk against the hellenistically acculturated

205. The identity of the 'abomination of desolation' is debatable. Proposals include a Zeus statue, one or more → *Mazzeboth*, an altar construction for the sacrifice of pigs, or an altar to Zeus, see O. Keel, *Geschichte Jerusalems*, 1193–1201.

upper class of the city. The aim was not to overthrow the prevailing social system as such, but only to return to observance of the former standards of social order. Thus the Maccabees quickly found many supporters in their fight for traditional Jewish life in the sense of the Torah (and its social regulations) and the purification of the temple. According to 1 Macc. 2.42, they were joined by the group of the Hasideans/Hasidim (the 'pious'), who were concerned with the fulfilment of the Torah in daily life. The author of 1 Maccabees interprets the Jewish Civil War from 167 to 143/142 BCE as a war of liberation from foreign rulers, who had used Hellenism as a means to destroy the Jewish society and identity. However, from 1 Macc. 1.11-15 it is clear that many Jews of the urban upper class had acquired a liking for Hellenistic ideas and the new style of life, so that the actions of the Maccabees were directed not just against the Seleucids and Menelaus, but also against their hellenized Jewish coreligionists. Thus the whole affair was from the beginning also an inner-Jewish conflict between the traditional and the hellenized Jewish styles of life (which went back to the hellenizing policies of the Seleucids, who had fostered the self-hellenization of their subjects). The Jerusalem upper class lived a life which was oriented to Hellenistic standards (e.g. import of Hellenistic luxury goods) and was working for the transformation of Jerusalem into a Greek *polis*; this ran contrary to the principles of the conservative rural upper class.

The armed revolt began with Mattathias (1 Macc. 2.15-28) as a civil war and later became a war of liberation when the Seleucids supported Jerusalem's high priest Menelaus. Mattathias died in 166 BCE, and his son Judas Maccabaeus continued the fight. He won various battles against the Seleucid armies and entered Jerusalem in 164 BCE, where he reached an agreement with Menelaus. The temple was reconsecrated (this was commemorated in the → *Hanukkah*); Menelaus remained the high priest (2 Macc. 11.13-38). Life according to the Torah was once again permitted in Jerusalem, but the Hellenistic lifestyle was left untouched. While Antiochus IV was preoccupied with wars against the Parthians, in which he ultimately lost his life, Judas Maccabaeus undertook successful campaigns into Galilee, Idumea, Gilead and the coastal plain (163 BCE). According to the account given in the books of Maccabees, the aim was to establish the Torah there, to combat Hellenism, and to free the Jews. But the course of events shows that, at least in addition, the Maccabees intended thereby to enlarge the sphere of their power. Judas built a fortress in Jerusalem opposite to the Hellenistic acra of Menelaus and the Seleucids (1 Macc. 4.60).

On the Seleucid side, Lysias had to intervene when the Seleucid garrison in the acra was besieged by Judas (1 Macc. 6). Lysias defeated Judas, who, however, escaped a worse fate thanks to the intervention of Philipp (a challenger the claims of Antiochus V Eupator to the Seleucid throne) and to the general internal struggles for the Seleucid throne. Menelaus was executed for unknown reasons (2 Macc. 13.4-7). Meanwhile the struggle for the throne in Antioch had been decided by Demetrius I, the son of Seleucus IV. Demetrius I gave the office of the high priest to Alcimus, who according to 2 Macc. 14.3 already held the office and apparently had been appointed by Lysias as the successor to Menelaus (1 Macc. 7.9-10; 2 Macc. 14.3-14; Josephus, *Ant. XII*, 385; 391). Alcimus was expected to settle the situation in Judea. The Hasideans accepted him in the basis of his Aaronide lineage, and Judas Maccabaeus had to fight on alone (1 Macc. 7.12-16; Josephus, *Ant. XII*, 396–398). Alcimus promised the traditionalists to respect the Torah-oriented way of life. But the conflict with Judas Maccabaeus continued, leading to warlike altercations and a Seleucid intervention, in which Judas met his death in 160 BCE at Beth-Horon. Judas's successor Jonathan had to withdraw into the desert in defeat; the cities were all in the hands of Alcimus and the Seleucids. Then however, Alcimus died unexpectedly. According to 1 Macc. 9.54-55; Josephus, *Ant. XII*, 413, he had offered to tear down the wall of the inner court of the temple, an act which can be interpreted as the abrogation of the separation between the priests and the laity in the sense of a laicization of the cult or a sacralization of the laity.[206] After the death of Alcimus, the Hellenists evidently could present no suitable successor, and the city remained seven years without a high priest (Josephus, *Ant. XX*, 237 against *XII*, 414; 419; 434).[207] Jonathan seized the opportunity (1 Macc. 10) offered by the ascent of Alexander I Balas (150–145 BCE) to the Seleucid throne in 150 BCE and offered to support Alexander. In exchange, Jonathan was appointed high priest, thus marking the beginning of the end of the Hellenistic party and the laying of the foundations for the Hasmonean monarchy. Here at the latest, it became clear that the Maccabees were not only interested in pursuing cultic-religious goals, but also that they intended to establish their own Jewish state that would be separated from the hellenized world and in which they themselves would exercise both the political and the religious power. Alexander Balas ruled until 145 BCE when two different pretenders laid claim to the throne: Demetrius II (145–139/138) and Antiochus VI (145–142). Jonathan allowed himself to become involved in these quarrels and died in an ambush in 143 BCE. He was succeeded by his brother Simon Maccabaeus, who made Judah an independent state.

206. P. Sacchi, *History*, 245.

207. Flavius Josephus contradicts himself in this matter, since elsewhere he calls Judas the successor of Alcimus.

Demetrius II confirmed Simon in the office of the high priest (1 Macc. 14.38), guaranteed him exemption from taxes, and accorded him the right to build fortresses. Although he never called himself king, Simon had in effect achieved sovereignty for the territories he ruled from 141 BCE on. Dating was done according to the years of his rule (Josephus, *Ant. XIII*, 214; 1 Macc. 13.41-42). Simon systematically expanded his new power by smashing the Hellenistic party in Jerusalem and, like his brother before him, seeking alliances with Rome and Sparta (1 Macc. 12; 14.16-24). The text of 1 Macc. 14.41-42, 47 describes Simon as a high priest (*archiereús*), ethnarch (*hegoúmenos*) and military leader (*strategós*) for his lifetime 'until a trustworthy prophet shall arise'. According to 1 Macc. 14.28, he was appointed by an assembly of the priests and the laity, whereby the latter consisted of the leaders of the people in Jerusalem (= the urban elite) and the elders of Judea (= the rural elite). Evidently, Simon had succeeded in uniting the clergy and the upper class of Jerusalem with the upper classes of the other cities and the countryside. It remains unclear, whether this assembly should be seen as a fixed governmental body or was simply a onetime or spontaneous gathering.

Beginning with the first year of Simon Maccabaeus, one no longer speaks of the Maccabees but rather of the Hasmonean kings. This was the first royal house on Judean soil that *did not have* Davidic roots. Although the Maccabees had fought against Hellenistic ideas, in fact they had themselves taken over such ideas to a large extent. In his home city Modein, Simon built a monumental tomb-complex for himself and his family (like Hellenistic kings). Novelties were represented, for example, by the columns with victory trophies (1 Macc. 13.25-30) but also his mercenary armies (1 Macc. 14.32). Simon was murdered by his son-in-law Ptolemy (1 Macc. 16.11-17). A son of Simon, Johannes Hyrcanus escaped the butchering of his family and was confirmed in office by Antiochus VII after promising military aid against the Parthians. Antiochus VII died in 129 BCE, and Demetrius II again became king. Hyrcanus returned to Jerusalem and ruled like his father Simon with Seleucid acquiescence (135/4–104 BCE). He hired mercenaries of many different nationalities (Josephus, *Ant. XIII*, 249), using them to realize his far-reaching expansionistic ambitions. These led him into Transjordan and to Shechem in 129/128, where he destroyed the temple on the nearby Mt. Gerizim (see above). Contrary to 1 Macc. 15.6, it was not Simon, but Johannes Hyrcanus who was the first Hasmonean to mint coins.[208] The iconography of his coins was borrowed from Hellenistic models (e.g. the double cornucopia,

208. So with S. Ostermann, *Die Münzen der Hasmonäer: Ein kritischer Bericht zur Systematik und*

see **fig. 18a**), which were slightly modified (pomegranate and ears of grain).[209] The inscriptions on the coins indicate that he was not only the high priest, but also bore the title 'head' or 'chief' (*rōš*).[210] In 112/111 BCE, he annexed Idumea, whose inhabitants he compelled to undergo circumcision and to observe the Torah (Josephus, *Ant. XIII*, 257–58); this led to a flight of refugees into the Nabatene and to Egypt. Finally, Hyrcanus turned to Samaria, which after a long war was destroyed. In terms of internal politics, the situation, however, became destabilized because the Hasmoneans in repeated conflicts lost the support of the Hasideans, who in the meantime had become the Pharisees, and had to rely on the Sadducees (= hellenized Zadokites) (Josephus, *Ant. XIII*, 288–92). Johannes Hyrcanus died in 104 BCE and was succeeded by his son Aristobulus I, who, according to Flavius Josephus, *Ant. XIII*, 301, was the first to claim the title of king, though this is not confirmed by the coins of his reign. In his short reign (104–103 BCE), Aristobulus I continued the wars of his father and reached out toward Galilee, where Iturean tribes dwelt; he forced them to undergo circumcision and to observe the Torah. He was succeeded by his brother Alexander Jannaeus (103–76 BCE), who had to struggle against both internal (the Pharisees) and external political enemies.

In the course of his shifting wars, he came into possession of parts of Transjordan, the coastal plain, and Galilee, which in the course of Jewish colonization now changed its character. With the already annexed Idumea, the Hasmonean state under Alexander Jannaeus (103–76 BCE) reached its greatest extension. Alexander Jannaeus too minted his own coins (**fig. 18b**), whereby it is striking that there was a 'high-priestly' and a 'royal' series: in the first, he was titled 'high priest', in the second 'king', but the two titles were never combined.[211] Alexander's position as high priest in Jerusalem, however, proved unstable. While exercising his office in the temple at the → *Feast of Tabernacles*, he was attacked by a rebellion (Josephus, *Ant. XIII*, 372–73); his adversaries charged him with being of unworthy descent

*Chronologie* (NTOA 55; Fribourg: Academic Press/Göttingen: Vandenhoeck & Ruprecht, 2005), 6–7, 20.

209. S. Ostermann, *Münzen*, 19 (above, n. 208). On the coins, see also http://www.menorahcoin-project.org/index.htm

210. S. Ostermann, *Münzen*, 55–6 (above, n. 208).

211. S. Ostermann, *Münzen*, 57 (above, n. 208). On the coins of Alexander Jannaeus, see also now I. Shachar, 'The Historical and Numismatic Significance of Alexander Jannaeus's Later Coinage as Found in Archaeological Evidence', *PEQ* 136 (2004): 5–33; D. Ariel and Y. Hirschfeld, 'A Coin Assemblage from the Reign of Alexander Jannaeus (104–76 BCE) Found on the Shore of the Dead Sea', *IEJ* 55 (2005): 66–89.

and thus unsuited for the office of high priest. The revolt was suppressed by Alexander's mercenaries in a most bloody manner, and a civil war broke out (exact date unknown). When the Pharisees realized that they had no chance against Alexander's soldiers, they sought the help of the Seleucid Demetrius III (95–88 BCE). Alexander was defeated, but Demetrius III had to turn to affairs in Syria before he could establish a new order in Jerusalem. Alexander's revenge on the Pharisees was brutal (Josephus, *Ant. XIII*, 376–80) and brought death and executions. Having so stabilized his position, the Hasmonean king (the title on his coins) returned to the conduct of war and attacked once again the Nabateans (Aretas III; 85–63/62 BCE). A battle took place at Lydda, which ended in Alexander's defeat.

According to Flavius Josephus, *Ant. XIII*, 399–404, Alexander, before his death, had directed his wife Alexandra Salome/Salina to seek an accord with the Pharisees: evidently she succeeded. Alexandra reigned as queen and military leader from 76 to 67 BCE and was supported by the Pharisees (Josephus, *Ant. XIII*, 408). During her reign, the Pharisees evidently gained considerable political influence, but they quickly lost it again under Aristobulus II and became a purely religious party in the times following. Alexandra made her weaker son Hyrcanus II high priest and her more active son Aristobulus II commander of the military and the fortresses. When Alexandra died in 67 BCE, Rome was already in Syria. Her two sons, Aristobulus II with the Sadducees at his side and the high priest Hyrcanus II supported by the Pharisees, fought for control of Judea. Hyrcanus II claimed the title of king, but had to fight a battle at Jericho and was defeated (Josephus, *Ant. XIV*, 4–7). Antipater the Idumean had persuaded the Nabatean king Aretas III to help Hyrcanus II to regain the throne at the cost of surrendering Transjordanian territories. Aristobulus II was defeated and barricaded himself in the Jerusalem temple with the rest of the loyal Sadducees. The Roman general Pompey, who had been wintering with his army in Damascus, was drawn into the conflict between the two princes: he decided in favour of Hyrcanus II and Antipater. Pompey took Aristobulus II prisoner in an opportune moment and then moved toward Jerusalem. The populace of the city appears to have opened the gates to the approaching Roman army: only a minority of the Sadducees remained in the temple complex and had to be expelled by force (63 BCE). On the next day, the temple was purified and returned to service. Pompey had no interest in upsetting the established order. Hyrcanus II was reinstated as high priest and received the title of ethnarch (Josephus, *Ant. XIV*, 244). Judea was no longer independent, but now stood under Roman control. The Hasmonean state was reduced in size: parts of Transjordan as well as the Hellenistic cities (among them Samaria) were separated from it. The cult on Mt. Gerizim was allowed to resume.

Judea continued to hold both eastern Idumea and Galilee (without the Plain of Megiddo), as well as Perea consisting of a small corridor between Amathus and Machaerus. With Hyrcanus II, a Hasmonean remained in office, but, for the time being, the dream of an independent kingdom of Judea was over.

## 4.4.2 Religion and Cult: Greek Gods and the '*Interpretatio Graeca*' of Autochthonous Deities

The religious history of the Hellenistic Period is marked, on the one hand, by the strong presence of Greek gods and heroes in Palestine (Pallas Athena, Aphrodite, Artemis, Zeus, Dionysos, Hermes, Perseus, Heracles) and by the *interpretatio graeca* of local → *autochthonous* deities and, on the other hand, by the practice of the Greek emperor cult.

The **emperor cult** appears to have had two roots: the one derived from the Egyptian notion of the pharaoh as the son of god; the other was rooted in the hero cults, which were widespread in the Greek world. These were directed to historical personalities, who during their lifetime had performed outstanding deeds and therefore came to be venerated *after their death.* The idea was that the deceased hero had been received into the world of the gods after his death; in the hierarchy, however, the heroes were below the gods though above other human beings. With Alexander the Great, the Alexander cult was founded, which had its principal seat in Alexandria. Ptolemy II Philadelphos (283/282–246 BCE) divinized *posthumously* the first Ptolemean couple, Ptolemy I Soter and Berenice I, and connected himself and his sister-spouse Arsinoe II with the Alexander cult. After her death in 270 BCE, Arsinoe II was proclaimed an Egyptian and Greek goddess. In the years that followed, various priestly bodies in Egypt ordered the celebration of Old-Egyptian cultic honours and feasts for the reigning royal couple. The Alexander cult in the expanded form established by the various Ptolemaic royal couples was definitively made the official Ptolemaic dynastic cult by Ptolemy IV Philopator (221–205 BCE). The Seleucids too were offered cultic worship in various cities: their alleged descent from Apollo found iconographic expression on their coins and was manifested in their special relationships to the more important Apollo sanctuaries (Delphi, Delos, Didyma, Klaros). To celebrate the birthday of Seleucid kings, it appears that monthly banquets were held. Participation in these banquets was impossible for conservative, Torah-observing Jews (2 Macc. 6.7).

In their religious policy, the Hellenistic rulers, like the Persians before them, were tolerant as long as taxes were paid. The measures undertaken by Antiochus IV Epiphanes in 169/168 BCE to hellenize the Judeans and the city Jerusalem appear to have been provoked by special internal and external political circumstances (see above) and to be locally confined, exceptional phenomena. Greek language, ideas, philosophies, gods and life-style, however, pervaded the whole Near East. The Phoenician cities transformed themselves into Greek *poleis* and regained their independence. Since they had long maintained trade and other contacts with the Greek world, an *interpretatio graeca* of diverse Phoenician deities had already taken place during the Persian Period (e.g. identification of Astarte with Aphrodite, Melqart with Heracles, Baal-šamēm with Zeus). Samaria, where already in the Persian Period a strong reception of Greek gods had been in evidence (see above), was colonized as a Greek city under Alexander the Great, so that here as in other *poleis* (Dor, Beth-Shan/Skythopolis) temples were erected in the Hellenistic tradition. At the source of the Jordan there was a sanctuary of Pan (Paneas). According to 1 Macc. 5.43-44; 2 Macc. 12.26, a sanctuary of Atargatis existed at Karnaim in Hauran.[212] In the southern and southwestern vicinity of Judea, various temples are in evidence (e.g. Beer-sheba, Lachish), and there too the identification of local and Greek deities was productive (Qōs/Qaus = Apollo).

In Judea, the Hellenistic Period was not only politically but also in terms of religious history an extremely chequered epoch, marked on the one hand by the hellenization of segments of the upper class and on the other by increasing resistance to what was perceived as a creeping 'domination of foreign influences'. This resistance broke into an open revolt of the conservative, Torah-observing faction in the face of Antiochus IV Epiphanes' efforts to impose hellenization by force. According to Flavius Josephus, the books of Chronicles and Maccabees, the books of Daniel and Qoheleth, the various → *apocalypses*, and diverse other texts, various topics were discussed in Jerusalem in an extremely controversial manner:[213]

(1.) The identification of Yhwh with Zeus, the supreme Greek god. Zeus had his dwelling on Mt. Olympus, a fact that evidently eased his identification with Palestinian weather-gods, to the extent that they also dwelt on mountains. In the course of the increasing hellenization of portions of the upper class, groups emerged among the Jews of Jerusalem (and Samaria), which interpreted the

212. The goddess is attested since the 4th/3rd cent. BCE. The name goes back to an amalgamation of the warlike Anath with the related goddess Astarte. She was a goddess of the life-force (often represented with fishes, doves, or lions) and the tyche of the city (= a personification of the city's well-being, in this function often represented with a wall-crown).

213. Compare P. Sacchi, *History*, 316–484.

Yhwh of → *Zion* (and of Gerizim) in the categories of Greek religion as the chief of the gods, Zeus Olympius (in Samaria Xenios/Hellenios). In Jerusalem, the conservative, Torah-observing groups, who were likewise 'nationalistically'-particularistically oriented, were unable to follow such thinking. This led to a division of the upper class into conservative and Hellenistic factions. The conflict between the two factions led to quarrels about the office of the high priest, so that what was primarily an inner-Jewish conflict came to link religious with political interests and lines of argumentation (see above). But, the fragmentation of Judean society into diverse splinter-groups was not exhausted by the division into conservatives versus Hellenists; there were other groups as well. Among them were the Hasideans/Hasidim (the 'pious'), who developed into the Pharisees. Further there was the group of the Sadducees, who were perhaps the descendants of the hellenized priests, who had cooperated with Menelaus and Alcimus. From the 3rd cent. BCE on, apocalyptic circles are increasingly in evidence. In a society marked by such political, religious and social fragmentation, the announcement of a coming → *messiah*, who would bring cosmic changes and a bold reordering of the situation, represented a promising hope which many people could follow. A messianism founded on the Davidic tradition could also constitute a critical counterweight to the Hasmonean royal ideology, since that family could not point to any Davidic roots. Against this background, → *apocalyptic* scenarios could have a direct anti-Hasmonean impact, when they taught that Yhwh himself would assume the office of king at the end of time and rule in the circle of his elders (Isa. 24.23).

(2.) The architecture and character of the temple. According to 2 Macc. 3.3; 13.23; 1 Macc. 10.39-44, the Seleucids made payments to the Jerusalem temple, which were only interrupted when the relationships between the Seleucids and Jerusalem were tense (Antiochus IV Epiphanes). Costs for repairs and further developments, which were to be organized by the high priest, were also covered by the Seleucids (Sir. 50.1-3). Concerning the outer appearance of the temple, there were quarrels between the Hellenists and the conservatives, e.g. the construction or destruction of walls in the temple area, which separated the priests and the laity (Alcimus; 1 Macc. 9.54-55; Josephus, *Ant. XII*, 413). Conflicts of this type were ignited by the problem of the defilement of the temple by unclean persons, objects, ways of life, or actions. Worship in profaned or defiled places was rendered impossible and regarded as an occasion of divine wrath, which once again required retribution (requiring → *atonement*). The categories of clean/unclean (as defined by priests) enjoyed highest priority in the temple cult, as was the case throughout the Ancient Near East. A state of pollution, however, could at any time be undone by purification rites and re-consecration. This became necessary after the compulsory hellenization measures of Antiochus IV Epiphanes (1 Macc. 1.16-24; 2 Macc. 5.11–6.11) had defiled the temple and the altar in 169/168 BCE (the 'abomination of desolation'), and the corresponding rites were carried out with full publicity.

(3.) The character of the cult. Quarrels about the continuation or the cessation of the Zadokite line in the office of the high priest led to the withdrawal of the

Zadokites around 169–164 BCE into the wilderness (→ *Qumran*) or to Leontopolis (Onias III/IV, see above), where they could continue to practise their ideal of the correct cultic worship of Yhwh, which could no longer be realized in Jerusalem. Concerning the Yhwh cult in Leontopolis, little is known. The programme of the Qumran community, by contrast, is well documented by the texts found in the caves there. Particularly striking is the expansion of the cultic categories of pure/impure, which according to the Qumran texts were to define the life of the individual in much greater measure than according to the biblical texts. Quarrels about the right calendar to be used (solar calendar in Qumran, luni-solar calendar in Jerusalem) apparently played a role, because they concerned the determination of the feast days (Ch. 3.3 excursus). In contrast to the temple on Mt. Gerizim (concerning the schism, see Ch. 3.2.1) and in Leontopolis, the Qumran group did not erect a temple with their own cult practice, but instead replaced the sacrifices in Jerusalem with liturgies and prayer. They developed an elaborate order of service for the priests (4Q259; 4Q320–330) and concepts for the functions of the priests in the → *'Holy War'* (1QM), in which the Zadokite priests would play the leading role. The ideal of the priesthood and of purity according to the conception of Exod. 19.6 was extended to the whole community, which was to become a kingdom of priests and a holy people (1QS par. 4Q255–264; CD par. 4Q266–273). This programme served both the assertion of the group's identity and its outward demarcation.

In the territories they conquered, the Maccabees, and later the Hasmoneans, evidently pursued with force a policy of coerced conversion to Judaism and claimed for themselves the power to determine what constituted normative Judaism, among them: exclusive → *monotheism*, strict prohibition of images (not just cult images, cf. 1 Macc. 5.68; 13.47; 2 Macc. 10.2), circumcision, Sabbath-keeping, observance of the dietary laws, and the celebration of the feast days. Amulets, which had not been explicitly forbidden in the OT and thus were frequently mentioned there without further thought, now became a problem (2 Macc. 12.40) and they were now associated with the worship of false gods. The Torah rules thus became an instrument of domination, which was used to restructure the territories claimed by the Hasmoneans and to give them a new character. For the Maccabees, evidently, a martial ideology of war constituted a part of the Yhwh religion, leaving the dissenters only the choice between forced conversion or death. Within the theological → *wisdom* tradition, more open conceptions were developed. There, thinkers opened themselves to Hellenistic influence, e.g. the problems of human cognition and the relationship between tradition and empiricism (Qoheleth). Likewise, in the theological wisdom tradition, the culticly defined notions of purity, which were meant to permeate (and complicate) people's daily lives, were reinterpreted. Here purity was identified with justice (Job 17.9), and the possibility of being pure in God's sight (Prov. 20.9; Job 4.17), indeed the distinction between pure and impure itself, was called into question (Qoh. 9.2; cf. Job 14.4). Alongside outer (cultic) purity, inner purity (Ps. 51.4, 9, 12 [NRSV 51.2, 7, 10]) was now called for: this concerned the individual relationship to God and the model ethic oriented to the Torah. In optimal obedience to the Torah, external and internal purity were meant to coincide, and this merger became the object of → *eschatological* expectations (cf. Ezek. 18.5-9; 36.25, 26-27). In addition to the interiorization of the Torah requirements, with their individualized ethical practice and the individual relationship to God, which now stood in the centre, one can now observe the growth of an intensive study of the Torah, which even took on erotic qualities (Ps. 119.131) and (perhaps in compensation for the suppressed goddess) came to be seen as the ideal (feminine) partner in life.

# Part III

## The Literature of the Old Testament: Torah and Former Prophets

# 5

# The Overall Context of Genesis–2 Kings

(Jan Christian Gertz – Translation by Peter Altmann)

## Chapter Outline



Overviews: R. G. Kratz, *Die Komposition der erzählenden Bücher des Alten Testaments: Grundwissen der Bibelkritik*. Göttingen: Vandenhoeck & Ruprecht, 2000 (ET *The Composition of the Narrative Books of the Old Testament*. Transl. by J. Bowden. London: T&T Clark, 2005); M. Noth, *Überlieferungsgeschichte des Pentateuch*. Stuttgart: Kohlhammer, 1948, 3rd ed., Darmstadt: Wissenschaftliche Buchgesellschaft, 1966 (ET *A History of Pentateuchal Traditions*. Transl. by B. W. Anderson, Englewood Cliffs, N.J.: Prentice-Hall, 1972, repr., Chico, Calif.: Scholars Press, 1981) (=HPT); idem., *Überlieferungsgeschichtliche Studien*. Halle (Saale): M. Niemeyer, 1943; 2nd ed. Darmstadt: Wissenschaftliche Buchgesellschaft, 1957 (ET Part I *The Deuteronomistic History*. JSOTSup 15. Sheffield: Sheffield University Press, 1981; Part II *The Chronicler's History*. JSOTSup 50. Transl. by H. G. M. Williamson, with an introduction, Sheffield: Sheffield University Press, 1987) (= DH/CH); H.-C. Schmitt, 'Das Spätdeuteronomistische Geschichtswerk Genesis I–2 Regum XXV und seine theologische Intention', Pages 277–94 in *Theologie in Prophetie und Pentateuch: Gesammelte Schriften*. BZAW 310. Berlin/New York: de Gruyter, 2001.

Commentaries: *1. Genesis:* G. W. Coats (FOTL 1. Grand Rapids, Mich.: Eerdmans 1983); H. Gunkel (4th ed., HKAT I/1. Göttingen: Vandenhoeck & Ruprecht 1917 = 9th ed., 1977; ET Transl. by M. E. Biddle, foreword by E. W. Nicholson. Macon, Ga.: Mercer University Press, 1997); R. W. L. Moberly (Gen 12–50. OTG. Sheffield: JSOT

Press, 1992); G. von Rad (12th ed., ATD 4/2, Göttingen: Vandenhoeck & Ruprecht, 1987; ET OTL. Transl. by J. H. Marks. 2nd rev. ed. Philadelphia: Westminster, 1972); J. W. Rogerson (Gen 1–11. OTG. Sheffield: JSOT Press, 1991); E. A. Speiser (AB 1. repr., London: Yale University Press, 2008 [1964]); – 2. *Exodus:* B. S. Childs (OTL. Philadelphia: Westminster, 1974); G. W. Coats (Exod 1–18. FOTL 2a. Grand Rapids, Mich.: Eerdmans, 1999); C. Houtman (4 vols. Historical Commentary on the Old Testament. Kampen: Kok Publishing House: 1993–2000); W. Johnstone (OTG. Sheffield: JSOT Press, 1990); M. Noth (ATD 5. Göttingen: Vandenhoeck & Ruprecht, 1958; ET OTL. Transl. by J. S. Bowden. London: SCM Press, 1962); W. Propp (2 vols. AB 2. New York: Doubleday, 1999–2006); – *3. Leviticus:* E. S. Gerstenberger (ATD 6. Göttingen: Vandenhoeck & Ruprecht, 1993; ET OTL. Transl. by D. W. Stott. Louisville, Ky.: Westminster John Knox, 1996); L. E. Grabbe (OTG. Sheffield: JSOT Press, 1993); J. Milgrom (3 vols. AB 3. New York: Doubleday, 1991–2001); – *4. Numbers:* R. P. Knierim and G. W. Coats (FOTL 4. Grand Rapids, Mich.: Eerdmans, 2005); B. Levine (2 vols. AB 4. New York: Doubleday, 1993–2000); M. Noth (ATD 7. Göttingen: Vandenhoeck & Ruprecht, 1966; ET OTL. Transl. by J. D. Martin. London: SCM Press, 1968); L. Schmidt (ATD 7/2. Göttingen: Vandenhoeck & Ruprecht, 2004); G. J. Wenham (OTG. Sheffield: Sheffield Academic Press, 1997); – *5. Deuteronomy:* R. E. Clements (OTG. Sheffield: JSOT Press, 1989); S. R. Driver (ICC. Edinburgh: T&T Clark, 1896); R. D. Nelson (OTL. Louisville, Ky.: Westminster John Knox, 2002); A. D. H. Mayes (NCBC. Grand Rapids, Mich.: Eerdmans, 1981); M. Weinfeld (Deut 1–11. AB 5a. New York: Doubleday, 1991); T. Veijola (Deut 1–16. ATD 8/1. Göttingen: Vandenhoek & Ruprecht, 2004); – *6. Joshua:* V. Fritz (HAT 1/7. Tübingen: Mohr Siebeck, 1994); R. D. Nelson (OTL. Louisville, Ky.: Westminster John Knox, 1997); M. Noth, *Das Buch Josua* (2nd ed. HAT 1,7. Tübingen: Mohr Siebeck, 1953); – *7. Judges:* W. Groß, *Richter* (HThK. Freiburg: Herder, 2009); A. D. H. Mayes (OTG. Sheffield: JSOT Press, 1985); S. Niditch (OTL. Louisville, Ky.: Westminster John Knox, 2008); – *8. Samuel:* S. Bar-Efrat, *Das Erste Buch Samuel: Ein narratologisch-philologischer Kommentar* (BWANT 176. Stuttgart: Kohlhammer, 2007); A. F. Campbell (FOTL 7–8. Grand Rapids, Mich.: Eerdmans, 2003, 2005); R. P. Gordon (OTG. Sheffield: JSOT Press, 1984); P. K. McCarter, Jr. (AB 8–9. repr., New Haven, Conn.: Yale University Press, 2007); – *9. Kings:* M. Cogan (1Kgs. AB 10. New York: Doubleday, 2001); V. Fritz (ZBK 10.1–2. Zurich: Theologischer Verlag, 1996, 1998); J. Gray (OTL. 3rd ed., fully rev., London: SCM, 1977); B. O. Long (FOTL 9–10. Grand Rapids, Mich.: Eerdmans, 1984, 1991); I. Provan (OTG. Sheffield: Sheffield Academic Press, 1997); M. Sweeney, *First and Second Kings* (Louisville, Ky.: Westminster John Knox, 2007); E. Würthwein (ATD 11/1. 2nd ed., Göttingen: Vandenhoek & Ruprecht, 1984).

# 5.1 Biblical Context

## 5.1.1 Structure

'In the beginning God created the heaven and the earth' – this sentence opens the first book of the Old Testament as well as the first part of the → *canon*,

| | | | |
|---|---|---|---|
| **Torah** | **Gen. 1–11** | **Primeval History** (see Chs 7.1; 7.3) | |
| | **Gen. 12-36, 38** | **Ancestral Narratives (Patriarchal History)** (see Chs 7.1; 7.4) | |
| | | Gen. 12–25.26: Abraham/Sarah – Isaac/Rebecca | |
| | | Gen. 25–36.38: Jacob/Leah and Rachel | |
| | **Gen. 37, 39–50** | **Joseph and his brothers** (see Ch. 7.5) | |
| | **Exod. 1–Josh. 24** | **Exodus and the Conquest of the Land** | |
| | | Exod. 1–Deut 34: Moses (see Chs 6; 7.1; 7.2; 7.6) | |
| | | Exod. 1–15 | Israel in Egypt; Exodus |
| | | Exod. 16–18 | Israel in the Desert |
| | | Exod. 19–Num. 10 | Israel at Sinai |
| | | Num. 10–20 | Conquest of the Land East of the Jordan |
| | | Deut 1–34 | Moses' Farewell Address in Moab |
| | | Deut. 34 | Moses' Death |
| **Former Prophets** | | **Josh. 1–24: Joshua** (see Ch. 7.6) | |
| | | Josh. 1 | Commissioning of Joshua |
| | | Josh. 2–12 | Conquest of the Land West of the Jordan |
| | | Josh. 13–23 | Division of the Land |
| | | Josh. 23–24 | Joshua's Farewell Addresses, Death, and Burial |
| | **Judg. 1–21** | **Stories of the Judges** (see Ch. 7.6) | |
| | **1 Sam.–1 Kgs 11** | **Narratives of Saul, David, and Solomon** (see Ch. 7.6) | |
| | | 1 Sam. 1–7 | ***Samuel*** |
| | | 1 Sam. 8–15 | Samuel and ***Saul*** |
| | | 1 Sam. 16–31 | Saul's Descent, ***David's*** Ascent |
| | | 2 Sam. 1–1 Kgs 2 | ***David*** |
| | | 1 Kgs 2–11 | ***Solomon*** |
| | **1 Kgs 12–2 Kgs 25** | **Narratives of the Kings of Judah and Israel** (see Ch. 7.6) | |
| | | 1 Kgs 12–2 Kgs 17 | The Divided Kingdoms |
| | | 2 Kgs 18–25 | Judah from 722–587 BCE |
| | | 2 Kgs 25 | Pardon of Johoiachin, 562 BCE |

which is generally called the Pentateuch in scholarly terminology. The term 'Pentateuch' is the latinized form of the Greek *hē pentateuchos biblos,* 'the five-part book'. The Jewish tradition uses the designation 'Torah' (*tôrâ*), in English 'Teaching'. In the Bible translations of the Protestant traditions they are commonly designated the five books of Moses and 'the Law'. The designation 'Law' is based on the translation of the Hebrew *tôrâ* with *nomos* in the ancient Greek translation of the Old Testament, the → *Septuagint* (LXX).

In the Jewish tradition the names of the individual books of the Torah correspond to the introductory words of each book, while the titles in the Greek and Latin tradition generally reflect the content of each book.

| | |
|---|---|
| 1. *běrē'šît* 'In the beginning' | = Genesis (Gen.) 'Creation Beginning' |
| 2. *šěmôt* 'Names (of the Israelites in Egypt)' | = Exodus (Exod.) 'Departure (from Egypt)' |
| 3. *wayyiqrā'* 'And called (Yhwh to Moses)' | = Leviticus (Lev.) 'The Levitical Law' |
| 4. *běmidbar* 'In the desert' | = Numbers (Num.) 'Numbers (of the Israelites)' |
| 5. *děbarîm* 'Words (of Moses to the Israelites)' | = Deuteronomy (Deut.) 'The Second Law' |

The Pentateuch is a highly complex and sometimes bewildering tapestry. This results from its multi-staged developmental process. However, its final form also appears as a thoughtfully formed composition, such that an interpretation of the final form of the whole work – a so-called 'close reading' also makes sense. How can this final form be described? At first sight the naming of the Pentateuch as Torah ('teaching') or as Law suggests a concentration on the legal ordinances and collections in the books of Exodus–Deuteronomy. An alternative option would be to concentrate on the narrative that begins with creation and extends to the death of Moses on the evening before the entry into the Promised Land. Upon closer examination both perspectives should be taken into account. The Pentateuch manifestly provides a narrative concerning the origins of the people of Israel. Nevertheless, enmeshed in the themes that extend beyond the bounds of each book are also religious laws and ritual instructions. These instructions grow out of the events displayed in the narratives while at the same time determining their progression. This is clearly recognizable in the case of the → *Decalogue* (Exod. 20). Its starting point is the declaration of the previously narrated act of deliverance by

Yhwh (Exod. 1–15), which forms the foundation for the relationship with God, which then unfolds into the demands of this God.

With regard to its narratival sequence one can read the Pentateuch as the biography of Moses. Moses appears as the central human character in four of the five books – beginning with the story of his birth in Exod. 2 and ending with his death and the conclusion that no prophet compares to Moses in Deut. 34. If the Pentateuch is read as the biography of Moses, then the narratives of Genesis to some degree describe his prehistory. However, the focus may also be on the emergence and fate of the people of Israel and the promise of its land, which constitute the fundamental motifs of the narrative from the command to Abraham to leave the land of his ancestors from Gen. 12 onwards. Read in this manner, the Pentateuch describes Israel's difficult path to the promised land. After the creation of the world (Gen. 1–11) Genesis portrays the journeys of the ancestors and ancestresses Abraham and Sarah, Isaac and Rebecca, as well as Jacob, Rachel and Leah in the land that is both foreign and promised (Gen. 12–36). Finally the Joseph story depicts the relocation of the future Israelites to Egypt (Gen. 37–50). The portrayal of the time of Moses follows: Moses frees Israel's children (who have now become a nation) at the command of Yhwh, familiarizes them with the will of Yhwh on the mountain of God and leads them as far as the land east of the Jordan (Exod.–Num.). There Moses gives his farewell address, essentially laying out the laws for life in the promised land, which the dying Moses is allowed to see but is not allowed to enter (Deut.).

While Moses' glimpse of the promised land and his death certainly provide a break in the narrative sequence, they do not constitute its conclusion. Joshua is designated as Moses' successor while the latter is still alive (Num. 27.18, Deut. 34.9), and the book of Joshua depicts his leading the subsequent conquest of the land. The book of Joshua is also closely bound with the subsequent book, Judges, which portrays the final period of the pre-state era in which charismatic leaders, the judges of Israel, secure the life of the people through military means. Conflicts stemming from the period of the Judges lead to the establishment of the monarchy in Israel through the final judge, Samuel. Samuel first anoints Saul as king and after Saul's failure supports David, who rises up to become king over the northern and southern tribes of Israel (1 Sam. 1–2 Sam. 5). Despite the conflicts surrounding succession to his throne (2 Sam. 9–1 Kgs 2), King David becomes the Archimedean point for the portrayal of the monarchy, first for the United Monarchy under Solomon (1 Kgs 2–1 Kgs 11) and then for the divided kingdoms of Israel (1 Kgs 12–2 Kgs 17) and Judah (1 Kgs 12–2 Kgs 25). The presentation of the history of the people of Israel, its conquest of the land, and its kingdoms ends with the final report of the pardoning of Jehoiachin by Amel-Marduk in Babylon (2 Kgs 25).

From this vantage point the narrative of the Pentateuch points far beyond itself. More precisely, it constitutes the fundamental part of the story of the people of Israel and its land extending from creation to the demise of the kingdom of Judah and the beginning of the Babylonian → *exile*. Within this story, a basic separation into two parts can be clearly noticed (even though each part contains aspects of the other as well): The theme of the books of Genesis–Joshua is salvation history (*Heilsgeschichte*), which displays the normative ideal time of the relationship between God and nation. The theme of the books Judg.–2 Kgs is the history of calamity (*Unheilsgeschichte*), which leads to the loss of land and state.

| | |
|---|---|
| Gen.–Num. | Tetrateuch |
| Gen.–Deut. | Pentateuch |
| Gen.–Josh. | Hexateuch |
| Gen.–2 Kgs | Enneateuch |

Biblical scholarship has come to refer to the entire narrative of the nine books Genesis–Deuteronomy, Joshua, Judges, (1–2) Samuel, and (1–2) Kings as the *Enneateuch*. When referring to the close connection between the six books of Genesis–Joshua, then the term *Hexateuch* is used, while *Pentateuch* without the somewhat separate and self-contained Deuteronomy is termed *Tetrateuch*.

## 5.1.2 The Redactional Structure Overlapping Individual Books

The unity of Genesis–2 Kings and the portrayal of the history of the people of Israel from the creation of the world until the Babylonian exile results not only from the chronological order and the generally coherent thematic treatment. There are also a number of redactional connections which, while not stretching through the whole work, bind together and structure individual compositions or link neighbouring compositions.

An overview of these overlapping connections will begin with *Genesis*. First off, there are the promise texts that anticipate the Exodus of the people from Egypt, the most prominent being the narrative of Yhwh's → *covenant* with Abraham in Gen. 15. It includes a small outline of the salvation history that will befall the people of Israel in Egypt (vv. 13–16) and alludes to the Sinai →

*theophany* and the → *conquest* of the land thus turning the Abraham narrative into a prolepsis. So the whole salvation history of Israel to be later narrated in the book of Exodus is foreshadowed in the figure and narrative of Abraham. A similar foreshadowing can be observed in the account of the ancestress endangered by sexual advances from the foreign ruler as given in Gen. 12.10-20. The narrative begins with the trip to Egypt as a result of famine, then uses the motifs of plague and release by Pharaoh. In this way Abraham and Sarah perform the story of the later people of God ahead of time. Likewise, the glue that holds the ancestor and ancestress narrative (Patriarchal History) and the Exodus narrative together is provided by the promise to Jacob en route to Egypt (Gen. 46.1-5a) that his descendants will grow into a nation there and later return to the promised land. Perhaps somewhat bizarre is the connection of Jacob's purchase of land in Shechem (Gen. 33.19), Joseph's request that his bones accompany the return out of Egypt (Gen. 50.25), the preparation and mummification of Joseph's corpse (Gen. 50.26b), the note that the coffin accompanies the exodus (Exod. 13.19), and the concluding report of Joseph being laid to rest in the plot purchased by his father in Shechem (Josh. 24.32).

The structuring texts of the Priestly Document (P), a source document (Ch. 7.1) taken up into the overall work as a whole, present a special case. Its revelatory theological structure leading from Creation (Gen. 1), Noahic and Abrahamic covenants (Gen. 9, 17), calling of Moses (Exod. 6), Sinai revelation, and entering of the holiness (heb. *kābôd*) of Yhwh into the → *tabernacle* (Exod. 25–40*) requires special treatment, even though the connections between these texts remain noticeable at the level of the final form and consequently play a linking function in their later final form context.

The threads of Genesis are especially taken up in the books of Exodus–2 Kings wherever the triad of the ancestors, Abraham, Isaac and Jacob is named. Foundational here is the calling of Moses according to Exod. 3–4 and 6. Moses and the liberation of Israel from Egypt are placed in continuity with Yhwh's treatment of the ancestors: he is the God of the fathers, who remembers his covenant with the fathers (Exod. 2.24; 6.2-8; cf. Gen. 17) and for this reason will deliver the people of Israel and will lead them out of Egypt through Moses and then bring them into the land promised to the fathers (Exod. 3.6-8; 6.6-8). This anticipation of the Exodus and the conquest of the land – linked back to the events in Genesis – corresponds to the salvation historical summary that Joshua gives in his farewell address (Josh. 23–24) after having closely followed Moses' legacy in leading the conquest of the land. He begins with a glance back at Abraham leaving the land on the other side of the Euphrates, proceeds to review the salvation history begun in Genesis and continues on to the successful conquest and parcelling out of the land as its fulfilment (Josh. 24.2-13). In this way Moses and Joshua, Exodus and Conquest stand in thematic and literary continuity to the ancestors.[1] Wherever else Deuteronomy–2 Kings speak of 'fathers', the reference originally referred only to the generation that took part in the Exodus from Egypt and the wilderness wandering; however, in the context of the work as a whole these notices can be read as including the ancestors as well.

The book of *Exodus* itself contains a trace leading towards the events of the books of Kings. The narrative of the golden calf in Exod. 32–34 formulates the archetypal picture of 'Israel falling away from Yhwh', whose reproduction is found in the → '*Sin of Jeroboam*' of 1 Kgs 12, which determines the historical progression of the northern kingdom of Israel until its demise (2 Kgs 17.22). Just like Aaron and the people of Israel did back at Sinai, Jeroboam has cult objects made for the sanctuaries in Bethel and Dan and says regarding them 'Here are your gods, O Israel, who brought you up out of the land of Egypt' (1 Kgs 12.28; Exod. 32.4). Viewed from the other direction, the portrayal in 1 Kgs 12 refers back to the book of Exodus – one of many references to this book within Joshua–2 Kings. Joshua repeatedly remembers Yhwh's acts of salvation, especially the miracle at the Sea of Reeds (Josh. 2.8-11; 5.1; 24.2-8). Similarly the elders of Israel, the Yhwh-prophets, the messenger of Yhwh, Samuel, and even the enemies of Israel appeal to the Exodus in rather diverse contexts.[2] Parallel narrative structures and shared motivations reveal connections to the book of Exodus. For example, the portrayal of the Solomonic period with the enforced labour placed on the northern tribes, Solomon's building projects, and Jeroboam's rebellion (1 Kgs 5–12) acts as a distant reminder of Israel's oppression in Egypt and liberation through Moses (Exod. 1–12). Furthermore, God's appearance to Elijah, who flees to the mountain of God in despair (1 Kgs 19), must be understood in the context of the revelation that happened to Moses on Sinai (Exod. 19).

The most prominent role in holding the entire work together is held by the book of *Deuteronomy*. It completes the Mosaic period and provides the theological criteria for the historical presentation of the post-Mosaic era. This era's downward journey towards destruction is evaluated by the degree to which Israel and its kings are obedient or disobedient to the directives for life in the land given in the Deuteronomic Law (Deut. 12–26). The degree to which Israel falls away from Yhwh or, as it is formulated there, 'does right in the eyes of Yhwh' (Judg. 2.11-13; 2 Kgs 17.7-23; etc.), in the subsequent books is especially determined in

1. See also Deut. 1.8; 6.19; 9.5,27; 29.12; 30.20; 34.4; 1 Kgs 18.36; 2 Kgs 13.23.

2. Judg. 2.1; 6.8-9; 10.11; 1 Sam. 4.8; 8.8; 10.18; 2 Sam. 7.6; 1 Kgs 9.9; 2 Kgs 17.7, 26, etc.

accord with Deuteronomy's law to worship Yhwh alone, (Deut. 5.7; 6.4-5) and to restrict Yhwh's cultic worship to one legitimate sanctuary (Deut. 12).

## 5.1.3 The Separation into Individual Books

In the final form of the Old Testament the books of the Pentateuch and the books from Joshua–2 Kings fall into two different sections of the canon. The Jewish tradition speaks of the Torah and the Former Prophets. The separation of the Torah from the entirety of the Great Historical Opus is appropriate in light of the Old Testament canon and also has support from the text itself. As already pointed out, the Pentateuch can also be read as a biography of Moses. In this sense the end of Deuteronomy marks a clear break, which is also underlined by its epoch-changing character. No new laws may be promulgated once Moses has died; Moses' death therefore ends the incomparable story of Israel's origins. Thus states the so-called Moses epitaph (grave inscription) in the final verses of the Pentateuch:

> Never since has there arisen a prophet in Israel like Moses, whom Yhwh knew face to face. He was unequaled for all the signs and wonders that Yhwh sent him to perform in the land of Egypt, against Pharaoh and all his servants and his entire land, and for all the mighty deeds and all the terrifying displays of power that Moses performed in the sight of all Israel. (Deut. 34.10-12)

Moses' successor, Joshua, is explicit in not seeking this kind of special role for himself. Thus the beginning of the book of Joshua looks back at the Pentateuch as a completed entity:

> This book of the law shall not depart out of your mouth; you shall meditate on it day and night, so that you may be careful to act in accordance with all that is written in it. For then you shall make your way prosperous, and then you shall be successful. (Josh. 1.8)

It can be concluded at this point (and will be discussed in later sections) that the separation of the Torah as a work *sui generis* stands as a relative end point for the textual development of the books of Genesis–2 Kings. It could occur only after the main portions of the Great Historical Opus of the beginnings of Israel had been put together. Biblical scholarship often places the delimitation of the Torah in connection with the institution of law by the 'Persian Imperial Administration' towards the end of the fourth century BCE.

### The 'Persian Imperial Administration'

The Persian emperors considered themselves called to rule over and provide peace for many peoples. Therefore, in contrast to the preceding empires, the Persians allowed numerous cities, tribes and nations to have a comparably large degree of legal, religious and cultural autonomy within the empire. They did this by acknowledging local norms through instances of imperial administration, thereby raising the locally valid laws to imperial law – as long as these local laws were in line with imperial interests. Such an 'Imperial Authorization' process can also be seen behind the equation of the law of the Jewish God, the Torah, with that of the Persian emperor in Ezra 7.25-26 – the authenticity of which is debated (but not its recognition of the legal relationships). It remains problematic that there are no known comparable authorizations of such a complex and elaborate form like the Pentateuch.

P. Frei, 'Die persische Reichsautorisation: Ein Überblick', *ZABR* 1 (1995): 1–35; J. W. Watts, ed., *Persia and Torah: The Theory of Imperial Authorization of the Pentateuch*. SBLSymS 17. Atlanta, Ga.: Society of Biblical Literature, 2001.

The separation of the Torah from the Former Prophets is a different matter from the separation of books within the Torah from one another. Within the Torah the separations take place because of practical necessity, namely that the text was too extensive to fit a single scroll. Nevertheless, content also played a role in the division of the scrolls, which is apparent from the various lengths of the individual books. It is remarkable that only Deuteronomy has a book heading, a feature otherwise found in the prophetic books and the → *wisdom* texts. Some book boundaries are marked by 'catchlines', with the respective book beginnings reaching back to the previous book's conclusion, sometimes verbally and other times in terms of content. In this manner Exod. 1.6 repeats the death of Joseph from Gen. 50.26; Lev. 1.1-2 calls up the tabernacle from Exod. 40.34-35; Num. 1.1-2 recalls the → *colophon* in Lev. 27.34; and Deut. 1.1-5 alludes to the one in Num. 36.13. The double recording of Joshua's death in the Former Prophets at Josh. 24.30-31 and Judg. 1.1 marks the transition from the book of Joshua to the book of Judges. The progression from the book of Judges is set off by the summary notice in Judg. 21.25 'in that time there was no king in Israel' from the subsequent books of Samuel and Kings, where kingship is the dominant theme. In contrast, the books 1 Samuel–2 Kings were largely transmitted as a unity. The Septuagint calls the books *basileiōn a–d* (1–4 Kingdoms), while the boundaries of each book gradually solidified in the tradition. The separation of the books of Samuel and Kings into four first penetrated the Jewish tradition in the 15th/16th century CE. Accordingly, the book ending Masorah are missing in the → *Masoretic Text* at the ends of 1 Sam. and 1 Kgs.

# 5.2 Textual Issues and Major Issues in the History of Critical Interpretation

Bibliography 5 Introductions and Histories of Literature.

The corpus as a whole: D. M. Carr, '"Empirical" Comparison and the Analysis of the Relationship of the Pentateuch and the Former Prophets', in *Pentateuch, Hexateuch, or Enneateuch: Identifying Literary Works in Genesis through Kings.* Ed. by K. Schmid and T. Dozeman. Atlanta, Ga.: Society of Biblical Literature, 2011; O. Kaiser, 'Pentateuch und Deuteronomistisches Geschichtswerk', Pages 70–133 in *Studien zur Literaturgeschichte des Alten Testaments.* Forschungen zur Bibel 90. Würzburg: Echter, 2000; K. Schmid, *Genesis and the Moses Story: Israel's Dual Origins in the Hebrew Bible*, Winona Lake, Ind.: Eisenbrauns, 2010: 16–49; further: R. Achenbach, 'Tetrateuch, Hexateuch, und Enneateuch: Eine Verhältnisbestimmung', *ZABR* 11 (2005): 122–54; T. Römer and K. Schmid, eds, *Les dernières redactions du Pentateuque, de l'Hexateuque et de l'Enneateuque: Le question des grands ensembles littéraires en Genèse à Rois; Die Frage literarischer Werke in Genesis bis Könige.* BETL 203. Leuven: Peeters, 2007.

Pentateuch: J. Blenkinsopp, *The Pentateuch: An Introduction to the First Five Books of the Bible.* 2nd ed. New York: Doubleday, 1992; C. Houtman, *Der Pentateuch: Die Geschichte seiner Erforschung neben einer Auswertung.* Kampen: KOK Pharos, 1994; E. Otto, 'Kritik der Pentateuchkomposition', *TRu* 60 (1995): 163–90; idem, 'Neuere Einleitungen in den Pentateuch', *TRu* 61 (1996): 332–41; A. de Pury, ed., *Le Pentateuque en question: Les origins et la composition des cinq premiers livres de la Bible à la lumière des recherches récentes.* Monde de la Bible 19. 3rd ed. Geneva: Labor et Fides, 2002; T. Römer, 'Hauptprobleme der gegenwärtigen Pentateuchforschung', *TZ* 60 (2004): 289–307; L. Schmidt, 'Zur Entstehung des Pentateuch: Ein kritischer Literaturbericht', *VF* 40 (1995): 3–28; J. Van Seters, *Prologue to History: The Yahwist as Historian in Genesis.* Zurich: Theologischer Verlag, 1992: 1–23; J.-L. Ska, *Introduction to Reading the Pentateuch.* Winona Lake, Ind.: Eisenbrauns, 2006.

Former Prophets: M. Witte *et al.*, eds, *Die deuteronomistischen Geschichtswerke: Redaktions- und religionsgeschichtliche Perspektiven zur 'Deuteronomismus'-Diskussion in Tora und Vorderen Propheten.* BZAW 365. Berlin/New York: de Gruyter, 2006 (with an extended bibliography); C. Frevel, 'Deuteronomistisches Geschichtswerk oder Geschichtswerke'. Pages 60–96 in *Martin Noth – aus der Sicht der heutigen Forschung*. Biblisch-theologische Studien 58. Ed. by U. Rüterswörden. Neukirchen-Vluyn: Neukirchener, 2004; M. P. Graham and S. L. McKenzie, eds, *The Heritage of Martin Noth*. JSOTSup 182. Sheffield: Sheffield Academic Press, 1994; A. de Pury, T. Römer and J.-D. Macchi, eds, *Israel Constructs Its History: Deuteronomistic Historiography in Recent Research*. JSOTSup 306. Sheffield: JSOT Press, 2000; G. N. Knoppers and J. C. McConville, eds, *Reconsidering Israel and Judah: Recent Studies on the Deuteronomistic History*. Sources for Biblical and Theological Study 8. Winona Lake, Ind.: Eisenbrauns, 2000; T. Römer, *The So-Called Deuteronomistic History: A Sociological, Historical and Literary Introduction*. London: T&T Clark, 2007; T. Veijola, 'Martin Noths "Überlieferungsgeschichtliche Studien" und die Theologie des Alten Testaments', Pages 11–28 in *Moses Erben: Studien zum Dekalog, zum Deuteronomismus und zum Schriftgelehrtentum*. BWANT 149. Stuttgart: Kohlhammer, 2000.

## 5.2.1 Introduction

The Jewish and the Christian traditions ascribed the authority behind the individual books of the Great Historical Opus to multiple 'authors'. According to the Babylonian → *Talmud*, Moses wrote the Torah, while Joshua and Samuel wrote the books bearing their names. Samuel was also considered the author of the book of Judges (and the book of Ruth), while the books of Kings (in addition to Lamentations and the book of Jeremiah) could be traced back to the prophet Jeremiah (Baba Batra 14b). These ascriptions were only claimed under certain conditions: Moses and Samuel could only with difficulty have written about their own deaths and beyond unless these men possessed supernatural visionary abilities – a suggestion pronounced in antiquity by Philo of Alexandria (13 BCE – 45 CE) (*De vita Mosis* II, 291) and Josephus (37–100 CE) (*Ant. IV*, 326) for Moses. For this reason the Babylonian Talmud points to Joshua for the final verses of the Torah (Deut. 34.5-12) and to the prophets Gad and Nathan for the portrayal of the time after Samuel's death (1 Sam. 28.3). These simple examples reveal the double problem that marks the beginning point for all historical research of the formation of the Old Testament: the questionable nature of the authenticity of the traditional ascriptions of authorship on the one hand and the unity of the Old Testament books on the other.

Because of the highly complex subject matter the historical research of the formation of the Old Testament deals with, the above-named difficulties did not remain the only ones. A reading of the first chapters of the Bible independent of the traditional guidelines already suggests the multiple layers of the historical-critical issues. The report of the creation of the world in Gen. 1.1–2.3 is followed by the Paradise narrative of 2.4–3.24. Both texts deal with the theme of God's creation activities, but they contradict one another in both general scenery and sequence. Gen. 1.1–2.3 describes the original and primitive state of the world with an image of a flooded surface out of which a sheet of land appears. Vegetation begins to sprout upon this land, and as time goes on the land is populated by animals and then people. 'Elohim' (God) creates humanity at the end of his creative work, and humanity appears like the animals from the beginning as having both male and female specimens of a single species. In contrast, according to Gen. 2.4–3.24 the original and primitive form of the world is a dry steppe. After watering the ground, 'Yhwh-Elohim' (Yhwh-God; NRSV: Lord-God) forms a human being out of dust. The creation around the human being is then laid out as a garden. Significantly later, the creation of the woman follows. With regard to the thematic and terminological differences, such as in the portrayals of God, the two narratives use different narrative styles that can be traced even in modern translations.

While the competing texts of Gen. 1–3 have been placed next to one another, the corresponding versions of the flood in Gen. 6–9 were knit together. Nevertheless the tensions in this section can also be clearly observed.

Following the narrative progression, one encounters several and quite distinct versions of the endangerment of the ancestress through the sexual advances of a foreign ruler (Sarah: Gen. 12.10-20, 20.1-8; Rebecca: 26.1-11), the calling of Moses (Exod. 3, 6) or the events at the Sea of Reeds (Exod. 14), in the desert and on Sinai (Exod. 19ff.). The beginning of the monarchy is also reported in multiple and decidedly different ways (1 Sam. 8–12). Finally the books of Joshua and Judges provide competing pictures of the premonarchic period.

What these and many other narratives show is also the case for the legal texts. The co-existence of three large legal corpuses – the → *Covenant Code* (Exod. 20.22–23.33), the Deuteronomic Law (Deut. 12–26), and the Holiness Code (Lev. 17–26) – is striking, especially with several subject matters being treated multiple times and with different purposes in mind in each instance. The material itself shows that the Old Testament legal texts come from quite divergent historical contexts. It is not possible that they all go back to a single lawgiver (Ch. 6).

Since the 18th cent. the observation of thematic, terminological and grammatical tensions and fractures, of repetitions and doublets, as well as of competing ideas and claims has led to reconstructions of the Old Testament's history of development. This process has led to scholarship's growing separation from traditional views. Historical-critical work has not yet reached its goal and the partial conclusions thus far remain debated. However, two points have achieved a basic consensus in the theological and historical treatments of the books of Genesis–2 Kings:

- The 'Great Historical Opus' and its constitutive parts result from a long, multi-staged process of deveopment that mirrors Israel's wrestling with its identity.
- The image that Israel projects of its history in the 'Great Historical Opus' is not identical with the historical process itself, but neither is it completely fictional. Rather, it attempts to provide an interpretation of its present in the mode of a narrative testifying to Israel's belief in God's involvement in history.

In scholarship up to the present moment the history of textual development of the Tetrateuch or Pentateuch is generally treated separately from that of the Former Prophets or the books of Deuteronomy–2 Kings. Since the following explication of the issue is focused on the history of scholarship, the difficulties with this differentiation will for now go unmentioned.

## Basic Approaches to the Pentateuch in the 18th and 19th Century

1. Early Source-Critical (Documentary) Hypothesis (Early 18th cent.): Henning Bernhard Witter (1683–1715) (Textual basis: Gen. 1–3); Jean Astruc (1684–1766) (Textual basis: Gen.–Exod. 1–2). The differences in the titles for God in the creation narratives (Gen. 1.1–2.3: Elohim; Gen. 2.4–3.24: Yhwh, read at that time as 'Jehovah') led to the conclusion of two sources, the Elohist and the Jehovist. Astruc concluded that Moses had these two sources as well as ten further fragmentary sources in front of him, which he then combined into four columns. A later edition put these four columns together thus mixing them up. Astruc's model was taken up and modified by Johann Gottfried Eichhorn (1752–1827) and Karl David Ilgen (1763–1834).

| | | | | | |
|---|---|---|---|---|---|
| *J. G. Eichhorn:* | E | + | J | + | Fragmentary Sources |
| *K. D. Ilgen:* | $E_1/E_2$ | + | J | | |

2. Fragmentary Hypothesis (Early 19th cent.): Because of the loose connections between the legal passages and their narrative context Alexander Geddes concluded that they were fragments from different circles of tradition. According to Johann Severin Vater (1771–1826) (Textual basis: Genesis–Deuteronomy) the Pentateuch consisted of 39 fragments coming from two authorial circles ('E' and 'J'), with Deuteronomy as their core.

*J. S. Vater:* 39 Fragments (of 'E' and 'J' material) with Deuteronomy as core

3. Supplementary Hypothesis: (1st Third of 19th cent.): Wilhelm Martin Leberecht de Wette (1780–1849) and Georg Heinrich August Ewald (1803–1875) (Textual basis: Pentateuch) promulgated a combination of the documentary and the

fragmentary hypotheses in which the Elohistic source (= 'Elohist Epic') stands as the foundation of the Pentateuch into which numerous 'Jehovah' fragments (= Eichhorn's disintegrated Jehovist) are inserted as explanations. The 'Jehovah' fragments prefer the saga style and are later.

| | | | |
|---|---|---|---|
| *W. M. L. de Wette:* | Elohist: Original document | + | 'Jehovah' fragments as additions |
| *H. Ewald:* | Elohist: Original document | + | Law and Kings' book; 'Jehovah' fragments; Deuteronomic source |

4. Newer Source-Critical (Documentary) Hypothesis (2nd half of 19th cent.): Hermann Hupfeld (1796–1866) recognized three sources in Genesis – the Elohistic foundation (= Priestly document [P]; separated out by Theodor Nöldeke [1836–1930]), the Elohist and the Jehovist. From these the editor is to be strictly differentiated. W. M. L. de Wette and Eduard Riehm (1830–1888) demonstrated the independence of Deut.

P + E + J + Deut.

4.1 The Literary and Religious Historical Setting of P (late 19th cent.): Building on the earlier work of Eduard Reuss (1804–1891) and Wilhelm Vatke (1806–1882), the sources of the Pentateuch were redated by Karl Heinrich Graf (1815–1869), Abraham Kuenen (1828–1891), and Julius Wellhausen (1844–1918). Wellhausen's late dating of P and early dating of J revolutionized the understanding of the development of the Pentateuch and with it the related history of Israel. Graf recognized that the laws in Leviticus–Numbers were later than Deuteronomy. The religious history provided by Chronicles, which is in line with P, is viewed as suspect for reconstructing the history of Old Testament cult. Kuenen demonstrated the connection between the P laws and the P narratives, which implied that the narratives were to be dated late along with the laws. Wellhausen recognized that P (Wellhausen: Q[3]) assumes the → *cult centralization* that is called for in Deuteronomy but not yet known in J/E or the prophets (except for Ezek.). The views in J/E are in general older than those in Deuteronomy. Apart from Deut. 34, Deuteronomy is an independent work.

J + E + Deut + P

3. Wellhausen called the priestly document *liber quattuor foederum* (Q for *quattuor*) 'Book of Four Covenants', in which the three covenants made with Adam (Gen. 1:28–2:3; sign of the covenant: Sabbath), Noah (Gen. 9:1-17; sign of the covenant: rainbow), and Abraham (Gen. 17; sign of the covenant: circumcision) function as precursors to the Sinai Covenant. However, it was rightfully objected to Wellhausen that P speaks of covenants explicitly only with regard to Noah and Abraham (Heb., *bĕrît*). The Book of Four Covenants combined with the law Wellhausen called the 'Priestly Code'.

## 5.2.2 The Question of Sources in the Pentateuch

The tradition and its modern version, 'general opinion', ascribe Moses as author of the Pentateuch. The ineradicable title '1st–5th Books of Moses' in many modern Bible translations suggests to this day that Moses was the author. Yet Mosaic authorship and the unity of the Pentateuch have been given up entirely in scholarly treatments on the basis of two hundred years of historical-critical work. Instead a number of hypotheses for the developmental history have emerged in order to explain the complex critical observations. They lead back to three basic models (Erich Zenger) and various combinations thereof: the *Foundational Document Hypothesis* (also *Supplementary Hypothesis*), the *Documentary Hypothesis*, and the *Fragmentary Hypothesis*.

### Basic Models for Explaining the Development of the Pentateuch

- The Foundational Document Hypothesis (also Supplementary Hypothesis) assumes that the essential parts of the Pentateuchal narratives can be traced back to a single work. This foundational document was then expanded during the transmission and traditioning process, either through the incorporation of written or oral texts or through limited interpretative comment. The foundational document is often equated with the priestly document of the documentary hypothesis.
- The Documentary Hypothesis recognizes various original documents ('sources') in the Pentateuchal narratives especially through doublets. These original documents come from different historical contexts and offer more or less extensive but to a large degree parallel portrayals of the prehistory and early history of Israel. The original documents were successively placed together by redactors (editors). The degree to which these redactors edited the texts is debated.
- The Fragmentary Hypothesis separates the Pentateuchal narratives into a number of originally stand-alone themes (creation and flood, Abraham, Jacob, Exodus, Sinai, wilderness wandering, conquest): in the process of tradition and transmission the individual themes were combined into chains of narratives or blocks, which were passed on and updated independently from one another for a lengthy period of time until they were brought together to make up the whole of the Pentateuch by one or more redactors.

The classic Pentateuch model that possessed an unquestioned validity for a long period is the New Documentary Hypothesis. It received its decisive form from Julius Wellhausen (1844–1918) and was later modified by Martin

Noth (1902–1968).[4] The New Documentary Hypothesis recognized four originally independent literary works in the Pentateuch – the Yahwist (J), the Elohist (E), the Priestly Document (P), and Deuteronomy. The three first are Pentateuchal sources in the strict sense, meaning that they comprise the main themes of the Pentateuchal narrative each in their distinct form. Deuteronomy, however, is a work of a different sort, in that only its final chapter reveals traces of the Pentateuchal sources. The separation of sources was based mainly on the criteria of the alternating use of the names for God 'Elohim' (God) and 'Yhwh'[5] as well as the aforementioned doublets in the narratives. The four sources were assembled together by redactors, who today are increasingly viewed as having themselves added to the sources autonomously.

The Yahwist (J), reaching from the Paradise and creation account of Gen. 2.4b–3.24 to the → *conquest,* is deemed the oldest source text. It included elaborate portrayals of the Primeval History (Gen. 2–4; 6–8*; 9.18-27; 11*), the time of the ancestors/ancestresses (Gen. 12–13*; 18–19*; 24; 28.10-22*; 32.23-33; 37–50*), and the exodus from Egypt (Exod. 1–17*). However, little of the Sinai pericope (Exod. 19–Num. 10) is ascribed to the Yahwist (Exod. 19*; classically also the 'Cultic → *Decalogue*' in Exod. 34). The origins of the Yahwistic document, which has received its name from its use of the divine name Yhwh, have often been brought into connection with the Solomonic Empire in the middle of the 10th cent. BCE.[6] It is difficult to accept that a single stroke brought about the conception and writing down of such a multilayered textual complex comprising multiple traditions. Therefore one should assume a longer developmental history of the work. Dating the Yahwistic document in the Solomonic period thus implies that the actual formation of Pentateuch traditions happened in the pre-monarchic period. The period of formation and the extent of

4. J. Wellhausen, *Die Composition des Hexateuchs und der Historischen Bücher des Alten Testaments* (3rd ed. Berlin: Reimer, 1899); M. Noth, *HPT (History of Pentateuch Traditions)*; idem, *DH (The Deuteronomistic History)* and *CH (The Chronicler's History).*

5. On these overused original criteria for separating the sources, see E. Blum, 'Der vermeintliche Gottesname Elohim', in *Gott Nennen: Gottes Namen und Gott als Name* (ed. I. U. Dalferth and P. Stoellger; Religion in Philosophy and Theology 35; Tübingen: Mohr Siebeck, 2008), 97–119.

6. Wellhausen dated the Yahwist to the later pre-exilic period (9th/8th cent. BCE). The connection with a spiritual blossoming during the reign of Solomon (so-called 'Solomonic Enlightenment') essentially goes back to Gerhard von Rad.

the text of the Yahwist are controversial among those supporting the New Documentary Hypothesis. Their basic consensus is that the Yahwist was the first to present an overall picture running from the Primeval History and the history of the ancestors of Israel until their eventual immigration into Palestine.

The second oldest source according to the New Documentary Hypothesis is the Elohist (E). Its origin is placed in the northern kingdom directly before the rise of classical prophecy in the 8th cent. BCE (Hosea). The name goes back to the almost exclusive use of the *genus*-term 'Elohim' (God): according to the Elohistic presentation the divine *name* Yhwh is first revealed in the context of the call of Moses (Exod. 3.14). The plot of the Elohist generally runs parallel to J, yet E lacks a Primeval introduction. The inventory of texts found in the final form of the Pentateuch is much smaller, especially for the depiction of the Mosaic period where it is almost impossible to differentiate E from J. Prominent texts ascribed to the Elohist include the covenant with Abraham in Gen. 15 (→ *covenant*), the sacrifice of Isaac in Gen. 22, the call of Moses and revelation of the divine name Yhwh in Exod. 3*, as well as parts of the Bileam tradition in Num. 22–24*.

The third source document of the New Documentary Hypothesis is the Priestly document (P) from exilic or early postexilic times (6th/5th cent. BCE). It begins with Gen 1 and is almost completely preserved. The origin of the fourth source, Deuteronomy, is brought into connection with the report of → *Josiah's reform* of 622 BCE in 2 Kgs 22–23. Extensive expansions of Deuteronomy took place in the subsequent period.

The hypothesis assumes that the combination of the sources began in the wake of the demise of the northern kingdom (722/1 BCE) when the Elohist and Yahwist were interwoven. The resulting Jehovistic Work (JE) would then be integrated into the Priestly document in the postexilic period. Whether Deuteronomy (or with Martin Noth the Deuteronomistic History [Deut.–2 Kgs]; cf. Ch. 5.2.3) was already united with the Jehovistic Work before the latter was combined with the Priestly document or afterwards is debated by the supporters of the New Documentary Hypothesis. Assuming that the redactions always used one source as the basis and then added parts of another source to it allows for an explanation of why the Elohistic source is so fragmentary while the Priestly document is nearly complete:

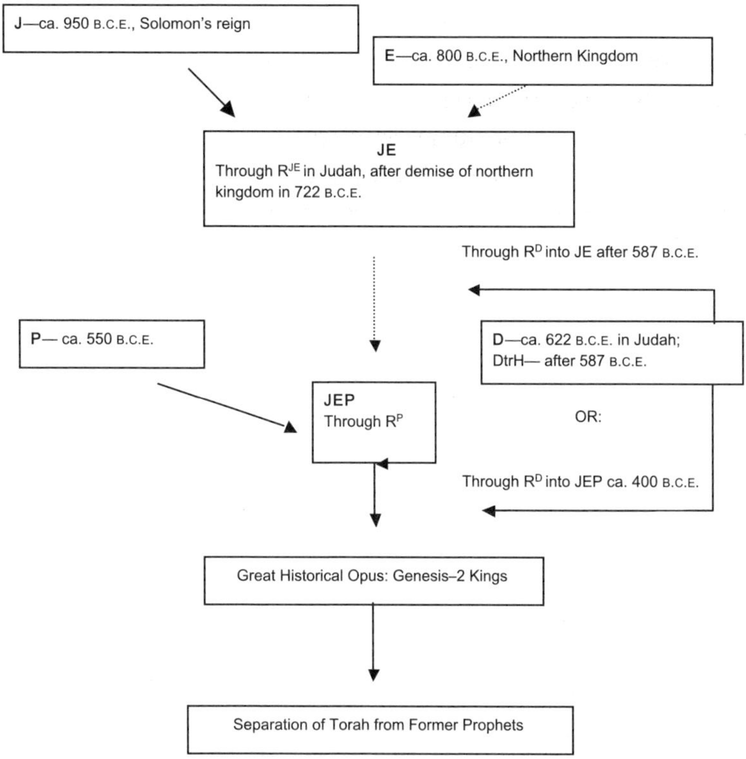


The New Documentary Hypothesis has recently come under fire.[7] Only the separation and the historical classification of the Priestly texts as well as the basic determination of Deuteronomy as coming from the late pre-exilic period and its special position in the entirety of the Pentateuch have stood the test of time. These theses continue to find support in scholarship independent of scholars' view of the New Documentary Hypothesis. They will be treated separately (Chs 7.1 and 7.2). As far as the other source documents, the Yahwist and the Elohist, the state of the discussion is quite different. It is safe to say that the source-critical separation and historical placement of the non-priestly texts in the → *Tetrateuch* are burdened with considerable uncertainty. By no later than the beginning of the Sinai pericope a differentiation of sources beyond the rough division in Priestly and non-priestly texts is nearly impossible. It is symptomatic that there is great uncertainty about the endings of each source (including the Priestly document!).

7. It also continues to receive support. Cf. as a prominent example advocating an opposing view of what follows: W. H. Schmidt, *Einführung/Old Testament Introduction*.

The notion of an *Elohistic Source*[8] is especially problematic. The existence of an Elohist is not only debated among critics of the New Documentary Hypothesis, but even supporters of this view see it as a weakness of the model. The criticism can be summarized briefly: the Elohistic source contains neither a clear beginning nor a clear ending; neither does the Elohist offer a continuous plot nor a unified perspective. The texts instead come from rather different periods of the Old Testament history. Core texts of the supposed source such as the sacrifice of Isaac in Gen. 22 and the 'Elohistic' portion of the call of Moses in Exod. 3 prove to be additions to their literary contexts, which in the New Documentary Hypothesis lead back to the Yahwist or already assume the Priestly document.[9] It may be possible to entertain the notion that the narratives of Abraham and Abimelech in Gen. 20.1b-18; 21.22-34 are fragments taken from a once larger document. However, these narratives belong to a historical level that is different from the rest of the supposed Elohistic texts.

The hypothesis of a *Yahwistic Source* finds considerably more support at first glance. This impression is misleading, however, since almost everything about the Yahwist is currently under review – age and extent, inner coherence, and theological perspective. As a result, the term 'Yahwist' has come to mean quite different literary entities.[10] A common denominator is at best the assumption that the source is found throughout the Tetrateuch. Especially the dating of the

8. The fundamental criticism was already formed by P. Volz and W. Rudolph, *Der Elohist als Erzähler: Ein Irrweg der Pentateuchkritik an der Genesis erläutert* (BZAW 63; Giessen: Töpelmann, 1933); W. Rudolph, *Der 'Elohist' von Exodus bis Josua* (BZAW 68; Berlin/New York: de Gruyter, 1938). For a different interpretation see A. Graupner, *Der Elohist* (WMANT 97; Neukirchen-Vluyn: Neukirchener, 2002); J. S. Baden, *J, E, and the Redaction of the Pentateuch* (FAT 68; Tübingen: Mohr Siebeck, 2009).

9. See for example the treatment of Gen. 22 by T. Veijola, 'Das Opfer des Abraham – Paradigma des Glaubens aus dem nachexilischen Zeitalter', *ZTK* 85 (1988): 129–64.

10. See the quite different positions regarding the Yahwist in W. H. Schmidt, 'Ein Theologe in salomonischer Zeit? Plädoyer für den Jahwisten', *BZ* 25 (1981): 82–102; J. Van Seters, *Der Jahwist als Historiker* (ThSt 134; Zurich: Theologischer Verlag, 1987); idem, *Prologue*; idem, *The Life of Moses: The Yahwist as Historian in Exodus–Numbers* (Louisville, Ky.: Westminster John Knox, 1994); C. Levin, *Der Jahwist* (FRLANT 157; Göttingen: Vandenhoeck & Ruprecht, 1993); idem, 'Das israelitische Nationalepos: Der Jahwist', in *Große Texte alter Kulturen: Literarische Reise von Gizeh nach Rom* (ed. M. Hose; Darmstadt: Wissenschaftliche Buchgesellschaft, 2004), 63–85. Critical responses can be found in J. C. Gertz, K. Schmid, and M. Witte, eds, *Abschied vom Jahwisten* (BZAW 315; Berlin/New York: de Gruyter, 2002); T. Dozeman and K. Schmid, eds, *A Farewell to*

Yahwistic work and its parts has been subject to considerable change. This is due to the fact that the historical foundation the notion of a Yahwistic source rests upon has been largely renounced for the early monarchic period. Neither the notion of exclusive worship of Yhwh (→ *monolatry*) assumed in the core texts of the Yahwistic source nor the motive for and conceptual prerequisites of an overarching theology of history as it is ascribed to the Yahwist are plausible for this time period. This is even more the case for the notion of a preceding literary formation in the pre-monarchic period, which must be assumed if the extensive and multi-faceted Yahwistic source is supposed complete in the early monarchic period. The hypothesis that there were the necessary institutions for the collection of traditions in a pre-state tribal society has failed. This is also true for the attempt to demonstrate that the pre-state period was the formative epoch for Israel on the basis of form-critical and tradition-historical queries of oral transmissions. On the contrary, the work as a whole assumes the conception of Yhwh and his people Israel emerging with the prophecy of doom and the demise of the northern kingdom in the 8th cent. BCE. There are composition-critical objections to add to those from religious and institutional perspectives. They deal on the one hand with the literary integrity of the source as a whole and on the other hand with the relative chronology of the Yahwistic texts. Precisely those portions of Exod. and Num. which are held to be core texts of the Yahwistic portrayal of the Mosaic era display both a strong affinity to literature influenced by Deuteronomy and also knowledge of the forms of prophetic writing. These texts, including the elaborate form of the call of Moses in Exod. 3–4, the plague narratives in Exod. 7–11, and the Sinai pericope in Exod. 19–24, 32–34, in part respond already to the Priestly document and come from the exilic period at the earliest. A similar conclusion may be drawn for certain prominent promises to the patriarchs in Genesis. The observation that the most meaningful theological and literary core texts of the assumed Yahwistic source come from a relatively late phase in the history of Old Testament literature also speaks against the often promulgated notion of an 'early Yahwist' that has only been expanded through redactions. Much rather, the source as a whole is affected by the tendency towards late dating. Naturally this late dating does not preclude the possibility that the source has integrated older material. However, this brings up the question of the scope of these earlier stages, and whether one may still speak of them meaningfully as a

*the Yahwist? The Composition of the Pentateuch in Recent European Interpretation* (SBLSymS 34; Atlanta, Ga.: Society of Biblical Literature, 2006).

'Yahwist'. One way or another it can be concluded for the Yahwistic designated texts that they represent diverse, multi-layered literary complexes for which it is difficult to find a common denominator. For this reason there is very little unanimity concerning the profile of the Yahwist: he is considered a theologian from Solomon's court (W. H. Schmidt) or a historian following Greek examples in the exilic period (J. Van Seters). His fundamental orientation can be seen as influenced by Deuteronomism (J. Van Seters) and as anti-Deuteronomistic (C. Levin).

The *Criticism of the New Documentary Hypothesis* has put forth a number of modifications and new approaches. The composition-historical model of E. Blum has been most widely propagated.[11] From the inheritance of the Documentary Hypothesis Blum assumes the separation between texts belonging to P and those not belonging to P in the Pentateuch. He stresses the independent existence of tradition blocks for the texts that are both non- and pre-priestly. In Genesis the narrative compositions of Jacob, Joseph and Abraham-Lot are linked together and extended in multiple steps into a Patriarchal History. A 'life of Moses' that can only be reconstructed rudimentarily is what lies at the base of the books that follow, while the largest portion of the non-priestly texts goes back to a → *Deuteronomistic* composition layer from the early Persian period. At one point Blum thought that certain texts inside the Patriarchal History could also be assigned to this so-called Kᴅ compositional layer, but he later modified this position:[12] the treatment of the pre-priestly Kd covers the 'Life of Moses' in Exod. 1–Deut. 34, while the texts in Genesis earlier assigned to Kd including the non-priestly transition from the Patriarchal History to the Exodus narrative are now judged as post-priestly formations of tradition. As already shown in his earlier work, Kd represents the salvation-historical prologue to the → *Deuteronomistic history* in the books (Deut.) Josh.–2 Kings (see Ch. 5.2.3).

The Priestly document provides a literary structure with distinct contours still noticeable in the final form of the Pentateuch. Blum ascribes it to a

11. E. Blum, *Die Komposition der Vätergeschichte* (WMANT 57; Neukirchen-Vluyn: Neukirchener, 1984); idem, *Studien zur Komposition des Pentateuch* (BZAW 189; Berlin/New York: de Gruyter, 1990).

12. E. Blum, 'Die literarische Verbindung von Erzvätern und Exodus: Ein Gespräch mit neueren Endredaktionshypothesen', in *Abschied* (ed. J. C. Gertz, K. Schmid, and M. Witte), 119–45 (above, n. 10).

Priestly composition layer (KP) which is also responsible for linking the Primeval History and the Patriarchal History as well as (according to the revised version of his theory) the 'Life of Moses'. KP is essentially an extension dependent on KD. However, this composition also includes texts that were conceptualized in and of themselves with allusions to other texts from KP. Thus, according to Blum, what was previously known as the Priestly document is neither a source document nor a redactional level, but rather both at once. Both compositions, KD and KP, are essentially contemporaries. On the road to the final form the work experienced further editing that went beyond the boundaries of the Pentateuch. Among these is the 'Joshua 24-edition', which comprises references from Jacob's land purchase in Gen. 33 to the burial of Joseph in Joshua 24.

The following features of Blum's model are typical for the present state of scholarship: the basic differentiation between the P-texts and the non-priestly texts, the abandonment of source differentiation within the non-priestly inventory of texts, the highlighting of larger tradition blocks, and the relatively late dating of the first sketch of a comprehensive early history of the people of Israel. The most debated current issues are when and how the individual blocks of tradition were combined, the original literary character of the P-texts – as either an independent work or redactional layer – as well as the literary historical relationship between the Pentateuch and Former Prophets. Before addressing these debated points it is important to first lay out the state of scholarship regarding the development of the books of Deuteronomy and Joshua–2 Kings.

### Consensus Opinions and Open Questions in Current Pentateuch and Former Prophets Scholarship

- Considerable unanimity reigns regarding the fundamental difference between Priestly and non-priestly texts. However, the original literary character of the Priestly texts remains debated: source document, editorial layer, or both.
- The distinction between Yahwistic and Elohistic texts within the non-priestly portions has been abandoned in most cases. Instead the pre-history of the non-priestly Pentateuch is increasingly viewed in terms of larger entities/blocks of tradition that each have their own history. It is disputed how much of this process of handing down the traditions can be reconstructed from a redaction-historical perspective. How large the inventory of non-priestly texts assuming P is remains also disputed.

⇨

- Simply assuming, more or less, that nearly *all* non-priestly texts are pre-priestly has generally been given up. In general the narrative substance of the non-priestly texts is older, but their arrangements are commonly later than P (and Deut.).
- The connection of individual blocks of tradition into a continuous portrayal of the early history of Israel is recognized as a comparatively late stage in the formation of traditions. It belongs in the intellectual historical context of (re-) building identity and self-assurance of Yhwh religion during a time of crisis. However, the discussions of the literary historical setting of this process are controversial. Does it belong to the period of the demise of the northern kingdom, or is it essentially a reaction to the complete loss of political independence in the exilic-postexilic period? Furthermore, it is increasingly asked whether the decisive connection between the ancestor/ancestress narrative (Patriarchal History) and exodus or exodus–conquest narrative occurs before or rather in the Priestly Document.
- Clarification about the historical development of the Tetrateuch and Pentateuch cannot be reconstructed independently from that of the books Joshua–2 Kings. It remains disputed whether the representation of history in the books of Joshua–2 Kings should be understood as having occurred one step at a time or rather as an attached sequel to parts of the Pentateuchal story (or rather whether the non-priestly Pentateuchal narrative was an extension composed as prelude to the history in Joshua–2 Kings).

## 5.2.3 The Historical-Critical Problem of Joshua–2 Kings

Older presentations of the New Documentary Hypothesis thought that the recognized source documents in the Pentateuch (more specifically in the Tetrateuch and Deut. 34) continued at least into the book of Joshua. The reformulation of the New Documentary Hypothesis by Martin Noth signified a decisive turning point in this discussion that is still important today. He differentiated between the development of the Pentateuch on the one hand and the development of the Former Prophets including Deuteronomy on the other. While Noth held fast to the formation of the Pentateuch through the combination of comprehensive and generally independent source documents, he explained the development of Deuteronomy–2 Kings with a kind of fragmentary hypothesis, namely the hypothesis of a 'Deuteronomistic History' (DtrH).[13]

A fundamental observation for Noth is that the inner coherence of Deuteronomy–2 Kings results from the use of a number of cross-connections,

13. M. Noth, *DH*.

typical judgements of human actors as well as speeches and other programmatic texts that interpret historical sequences. They are not found on the level of the individual narrative but rather are the result of a redaction influenced by the language and theology of Deuteronomy that is therefore called 'Deuteronomistic' (= Dtr).

## The Inner Connections of the Deuteronomistically Redacted History Books/ the Deuteronomistic History (DtrH)

- Intertextual connections: i.e., Joshua's curse of whoever would rebuild Jericho (Josh. 6.26) and the fulfillment of this curse in 1 Kgs 16.34.
- The judgement of human actors: 'did evil in the eyes of Yhwh' in Judg. 2.11; 3.7,12; 4.1; 6.1; 10.6; 13.1 of the Israelites and then the monotone judgement with relatively few exceptions of the kings beginning with Solomon in 1 Kgs 11.6 and concluding with Zedekiah in 2 Kgs 24.19.
- Programmatic texts marking turning points in the narrative: Deut. 1–3 (Moses' retrospective on the forty years of wandering in the wilderness); Deut. 31 (Moses' farewell speech); Josh. 1 (Joshua's call); Josh. 23 (Joshua's farewell speech); Judg. 2.6–3.6 (overview of the time of the judges); 1 Sam. 8 (Samuel's overview on the monarchy); 1 Sam. 12 (Samuel's farewell speech); 2 Sam. 7 (The promise of Nathan); 1 Kgs 8 (Solomon's temple dedication); 2 Kgs 17 (Reflection on the demise of the northern kingdom).
- The use of Dtr type language in the interpretative passages.
- The structuring of individual epochs according to thematic points of view that follow the commands of Deuteronomy. One example is the systematic ordering of the appearances of Asherah in Kings: the cult of Asherah forbidden in Deuteronomy (16.21) frames the history of the northern kingdom from the 'partition' (1 Kgs 14.15) until its destruction (2 Kgs 17.10) and provides the negative foil for → *Josiah's reform* and the success of exclusive worship of Yhwh (2 Kgs 23.14).

For Noth the uncontroversial findings pointed towards the conclusion that Deuteronomy–2 Kings represent a methodically constructed work, that of the Deuteronomistic History (DtrH). Noth saw DtrH as the work of a single Dtr author from the exilic period who bound together individual texts into a historical work in such a way as to allow the handed-down sources to retain their voices, but now as part of a larger whole. The sources include the outside frame of Deuteronomy (Deut. 1–4*; 31–34), collections of sagas about the conquest and the judges, a Samuel-Saul-David history, a history of Solomon, → *annals* of the kings of Israel and the kings of Judah, as well as narratives from the prophets Elijah, Elisha and Isaiah. The causal relationship between obedience to the will of Yhwh and the fate of the people served as glue holding the sources together and reconstructing the history in DtrH. In this way the varied fate of Israel from the time of the conquest until the exile is interpreted according to the demand of Deuteronomy to worship Yhwh exclusively, and this only at the place he chooses (Deut. 6.4-5; 12). In this way DtrH functions as an explanation for the eventual religious and national catastrophe of the exile.

The notion of an essentially unified DtrH cannot be maintained in spite of repeated defences.[14] As the discussion has progressed terminological differences and theological accentuations within the Dtr texts have called for more differentiated models. The (so-called *Göttingen*) *Layered Model* reckons with different redactions that go throughout the DtrH.[15] After the DtrH was written before the middle of the 6th cent. BCE by a Deuteronomistic Historian (DtrH), there were several prophetically oriented theological redactors (DtrP), and finally a group of further redactors who shared a certain focus on law (*nomos;* DtrN).

The *Block- or Step Model* (followed especially in the Anglo-American discussion) in contrast speaks of a pre-exilic and a (post) exilic edition of the DtrH.[16] The observation that the Dtr appraisals of the final four kings differentiate from those of the earlier ones led to the conclusion of an earlier work ending with Josiah's death (2 Kgs 23.25). This work would have functioned as propaganda in support of the reform efforts of Josiah (639–609 BCE; cf. 2 Kgs 22–23). The second edition of the DtrH was then completed by an exilic redactor who added the final four kings and judged them entirely negatively.[17] It thus intended to prove that the demise of Judah represented the final judgement over the people's abandonment of the path laid out in Deut.

14. J. Van Seters, *In Search of History* (New Haven: Yale University Press, 1983); R. Albertz, 'Die Intentionen und die Träger des Deuteronomistischen Geschichtswerks', in *Schöpfung und Befreiung: FS C. Westermann* (ed. R. Albertz; Stuttgart: Calwer, 1989), 37–53.

15. An overview of the foundational works of R. Smend, W. Dietrich and T. Veijola can be found in R. Smend, *Die Entstehung*, 111–125.

16. F. M. Cross, 'The Themes of the Book of Kings and the Structure of the Deuteronomistic History', in *Canaanite Myth and Hebrew Epic: Essays on the History of the Religion of Israel* (Cambridge, Mass.: Harvard University Press, 1973), 274–89; B. Halpern, *The First Historians: The Hebrew Bible and History* (University Park, Penn.: Pennsylvania State University Press, 1996). Compare the contrary position recently in E. Aurelius, *Zukunft jenseits des Gerichts: Eine Religionsgeschichtliche Studie zum Enneateuch* (BZAW 319; Berlin/New York: de Gruyter, 2003).

17. Regarding the first Dtr edition of the books of Kings in the pre-exilic period see already J. Wellhausen, *Composition*, 297–300 (above, n. 4).

The idea that the DtrH should be understood as the result of secondary redactional links or gradual inclusions of the conquest, judges, and monarchical traditions that were all already edited by Dtr could likewise be termed a block model.[18] These considerations defer to the present scholarship on the Pentateuch, which is becoming increasingly separated from the notion of sources limited to the Tetrateuch, and also highlights the independence of various blocks of tradition as well as connects the Pentateuchal narratives with the narratives of the subsequent books.

## 5.3 Origins of Genesis–2 Kings

The understanding of the origin of the Great Historical Opus in the books Genesis–2 Kings supported in this book begins from the assumption that the unification and smoothing out of the history of origins of Israel, as it appears in the Great Historical Opus, emerged first as the result of a retrospective formulation, for which the multiplicity and contradictory nature of the individual traditions appeared problematic. The historical beginnings of this process are to be found in the crisis experiences brought on by the demise of the nations of Israel (722/1 BCE) and Judah (587/6 BCE). Thus the synopsis is to be late dated and is clearly secondary to the individual blocks of tradition and narratives. While there is a considerable agreement with regard to this new conception, the question of who should be considered responsible for the first overarching conception of the Pentateuchal narratives continues to be subject to great controversy. This question is an area that received little discussion during the reign of the New Documentary Hypothesis since this theory concluded that the first comprehensive narrative comprising the main themes of the Pentateuch was formed prior to the Priestly composition – regardless whether one spoke of an early or late Yahwist or a differently named work.

In order to test this assumption we will examine what is perhaps the most decisive thematic link, namely the placement of the ancestral history before

18. N. Lohfink, 'Kerygmata des deuteronomistischen Geschichtswerks', in *Studien zum Deuteronomium und zur deuteronomistischen Literatur 2* (SBAB 12; Stuttgart: Katholisches Bibelwerk, 1991 [original publication 1981]), 125–42; E. Würthwein, 'Erwägungen zum sog. Deuteronomistischen Geschichtswerk', in *Studien zum Deuteronomistischen Geschichstwerk* (BZAW 227; Berlin/New York: de Gruyter, 1994), 1-11; R.G. Kratz, *The Composition of the Narrative Books of the Old Testament* (transl. by J. Bowden; London: T&T Clark, 2005), 153–215.

the Exodus narrative.[19] The fact that this connection is not original (despite a seemingly coherent chronology)[20] is widely acknowledged and can be ascertained quickly through the divergent literary forms. Genesis (apart from the special example of the Joseph story) consists of individual sagas placed together into a narrative chain. In contrast, the exodus narrative in Exod. 1–15 deals with a well-conceived narrative thread to which further stories and themes are subsequently added to the end. In addition, there are theological differences. While the ancestral history includes a thoroughly peaceful picture that points towards the goal of religious integration, the generally militant exodus narrative propagates a religion inclined towards segregation and elimination of other religions. Inquiring into when the coupling of these highly divergent works of literature took place shows that the content and verbal connections appear first in the Priestly level of the text. The Priestly version of the call of Moses in Exod. 6 specifically refers back to the → *covenant* between Yhwh and Abraham in Gen. 17 (cf. Exod. 6.4 and Gen. 17.7, 8, 19). Furthermore, the growth of Jacob's family into a nation in P appears analogously to the fulfilment of the promises of fruitfulness found in the Priestly creation story (cf. Exod. 1.7 and Gen. 1.22, 28; 8.17; 9.1, 7; 17.2, 6, 20; 28.3; 35.11). These connections are then significantly extended in the later stages of the developmental history of the Pentateuch through further intertextual allusions. The pre-priestly texts on the other hand do not exhibit any recognizable connections between the exodus narrative and the portrayal of the ancestral epoch. The original beginning of this pre-priestly Exodus narrative has been lost, and has instead been replaced with the transitional notice (Exod. 1.8) 'Now a new king arose in Egypt, who did not know Joseph,' which serves to neutralize the whole of the Joseph story. On the other hand, the Joseph story

19. See K. Schmid, *Genesis and the Moses Story: Israel's Dual Origins in the Hebrew Bible* (transl. by J. D. Nogalski; Winona Lakes, Ind.: Eisenbrauns, 2009); J. C. Gertz, *Tradition und Redaktion in der Exoduserzählung: Untersuchungen zur Endredaktion des Pentateuch* (FRLANT 186; Göttingen: Vandenhoek & Ruprecht, 2000), 330–88; cf. the opposing positions in the essays of K. Schmid, J. C. Gertz, C. Levin, D. M. Carr in *A Farewell to the Yahwist?* (ed. T. Dozeman and K. Schmid; above, n. 10).

20. Close analysis of the chronological details actually reveals some inconsistencies. According to Gen. 15.13 (cf. Acts 7.6) the Israelites remained in Egypt for 400 years, while Exod. 12.40-41 reports a stay of 430 years. The combination of the reports in Exod. 1.8 and 2.1 where Moses appears as a grandchild of Levi through his mother (cf. Exod. 6.20) only allows for three generations between Jacob and Moses.

(disregarding the later insertions) does not give off the impression that it was originally conceived to be a literary bridge between the ancestors and Moses (Ch. 7.5). This conclusion corresponds with the observation that very late texts in Genesis emphasize the separation and independence of the ancestors from Moses and the Exodus (cf. Gen. 12.10-20; 15 [without the addition in vv. 11, 13-16]; 16). One may draw the redaction-historical conclusion from these observations – which correspond to similar findings for the transition from the Primeval History to the history of the ancestors – that the Priestly Document (Ch. 7.1) was the first to conceive of a salvation history of Israel beginning with the creation of the world and the first to shift the history of the ancestors to its place as pre-history to the portrayal of the Moses period. The Priestly Document therefore represents the first and only comprehensive text layer in the Pentateuch (more specifically Gen.–Exod. [–Lev.]). In contrast the pre-priestly versions of the history of the ancestors and the exodus narrative are two competing models of the history of the origins of Israel. Like the pre-priestly Primeval History, they too became part of the Great Historical Opus only through their connection with the Priestly Document.

The pre-priestly versions of the Primeval History, the history of the ancestors, and the exodus narrative grew and were passed on independently from one another for a long period of time. The exodus narrative at first comprised the period from the departure from Egypt until the → *conquest* and may even have originally concluded with the deliverance of Israel at the Sea of Reeds. It was then extended through a Dtr edited version of the periods of the Judges and the monarchy which eventually resulted in a Dtr composition of the history of the people of Israel from the exodus out of Egypt until the → *exile* (Ch. 7.6). These stand-alone works of literature never formed a cohesive narrative complex akin to something like a Yahwist or another similar hypothesized source. They were first worked into the Priestly Document in the postexilic period. The Priestly Document itself was an originally independent source document whose plot of the history of Israel's origins was the first to consist of the sequence of creation, ancestors and exodus (Ch. 7.1). After the non-priestly literary works and the Priestly Document had been united this Great Historical Opus experienced further additions, one of the final redactional steps being the separation of the Torah from the Former Prophets.

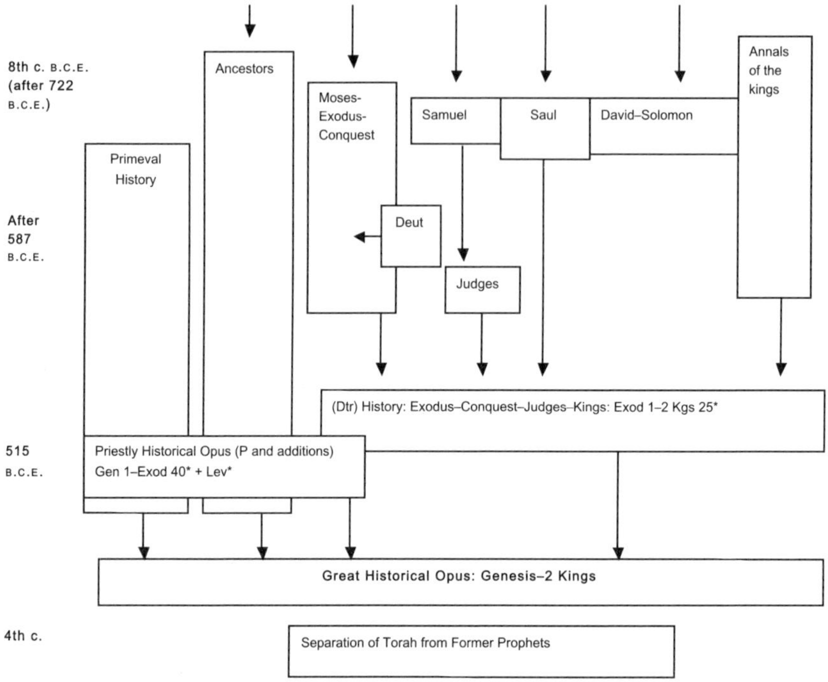


# 5.4 Theology of the Complex as a Whole

The Old Testament deals in large part with the history of the people of Israel. This is shown already by the reach of the Great Historical Opus in the books of Genesis–2 Kings and its interpretation in Chronicles (Chs 22 and 23), which reveals a process of interpretation lasting until the → *Hellenistic* period. From the perspective of the final form of the Old Testament one can generally agree with Gerhard von Rad's assessment that 'the faith of Israel… always [referred] to events, to a divine self-manifestation in history',[21] which does not negate the fact that other and older conceptions of theology can also be found in the OT.

As a result of crisis experiences, such as those caused by the demise of both nations, the historical traditions of the Old Testament reflect the divine-human relationship such that Yhwh is the God of Israel and Israel is the

21. G. von Rad, 'Aspekte alttestamentlichen Weltverständnisses', *EvT* 24 (1964): 57–73 (here p. 57).

people of Yhwh. Yet the use of the term 'history' to describe the material is somewhat unclear. On one hand it concerns 'believed history' (von Rad), meaning that the historical experiences and their interpretation as the history of Yhwh with Israel are inseparably connected to one another in the Old Testament portrayal and have undergone mutual interpenetration. Naturally, to the Old Testament writers it was uncontroversial that the historical events really – or at least most likely – happened that way. Yet the narratives were not passed on solely for archaeological or archival interests, but because of their significance for the theological interpretation of history at that time. The term 'history' is also unclear because of the various functions played by the historical traditions in the Old Testament. 'Believed history' is itself a historical phenomenon, with each epoch interpreting in its own way and for its own purposes the salvation events handed down by tradition. The salvation-historical origins of Israel in Genesis–Deuteronomy/Joshua can be roughly differentiated from the judgement-historical → *aetiology* of the → *exile* in Joshua/Judge–2 Kings as well as from the theology of history explanation for a theocratic ideal in literature of Chronicles.

The overarching theme of Genesis–Deuteronomy/Joshua is the salvation-historical explanation of the origins of Israel. It brings together highly divergent conceptions of the reasons behind Israel's existence in the land and arranges them into a linear sequence. This sequence allows for a uniform and unified foundational narrative reaching from the ancestors to the exodus, the wilderness wandering, the stay at Sinai with the reception of the Law, as far as the → *conquest*. It is also connected to the history of the world as a whole 'from the beginning' by the insertion of the Primeval History. This Primeval History serves as the prelude to the history of the people of Israel in the land and to the judgement-historical aetiology of the exile in Joshua/Judge–2 Kings. The latter rests on two conceptual pillars: 1. The early form of the theology of the prophetic traditions explains that Yhwh's history with Israel should be understood as punishment for Israel's guilt. According to prophetic theology, rejection of the divine gifts of Law and justice lead to Yhwh's judgement on Israel carried out by foreign nations. 2. This conception is brought into connection with the notion of 'covenant' and the demand for exclusive Yhwh worship as explicitly found in the 1st Commandment of the → *Decalogue*. This second pillar of the judgement-historical aetiology arises from the concept according to which Yhwh's → *covenant* (Heb. *bĕrît*) with Israel and the demand of the 1st Commandment are anchored deeply in the foundational narrative. As a result the keeping or breaking of the covenant in the form of observance or neglect of the 1st Commandment becomes the decisive criterion by which the history of Israel is measured in this aetiology of judgement history.

The differences in function and purpose between the two concepts, namely the salvation-historical establishment of the origins of Israel and the judgement-historical aetiology, are not resolved in the Great Historical Opus yet are incorporated in an overall theology of history. Thus a line is drawn from the narrative of the origins to the present moment of address which is defined by the experience of exile: in other words it provides a justification for the Persian period and also the later Hellenistic Israel's existence in the land ruled by foreign powers as well as its life in the → *diaspora*. However, the foundational period is clearly structured. The 'myth of Israel' in Genesis–Joshua depicts an ideal relationship between God and people. This certainly does not occur in the sense of an untarnished harmony, but rather through the possibility of divine presence through cultic → *atonement* or through the mediation of Moses, all beginning in the Mosaic period. The subsequent history of decline begins no later than the book of Judges, but the transition is not sharp. The portrayal of the miracle at the Sea of Reeds (Exod. 14) and the murmuring narratives during the wilderness wanderings (Exod. 15ff.; Num. 11ff.) already hint that Yhwh's salvific treatment could be gambled away by Israel's lack of trust and rebellion. Since the history of decline in Judge–2 Kings together with Joshua now forms part of the *corpus propheticum* (Josh.–Mal.) this must be accounted for in the overall context in that the writing prophets are to be read against the background of the Great Historical Opus. From this perspective they function as signs towards a new salvation history in which 'God as the foundation of history changes the human and societal structure to such an extent that a renewed time of salvation could not possibly "tip over" into a period of decline.'[22] The larger context of Genesis–Malachi, that is the Torah and the prophetic books, form a three-step work extending from the earlier salvation history (Gen.–Josh.), to judgement history (Judg.–2 Kgs), and finally to a new salvation history (Isa.–Zech./Mal.). From this perspective, the recipients of the Great Historical Opus have the judgement in 2 Kgs 25 behind them and look forward to the salvation history to come. So while the promises to the

22. K. Koch, 'Qädäm: Heilsgeschichte als mythische Urzeit im Alten (und Neuen) Testament', in *Vernunft des Glaubens: Festschrift for W. Pannenberg* (ed. J. Rohls and G. Wenz; Göttingen: Vandenhoek & Ruprecht, 1988), 253–88 (here p. 283).

ancestors were fulfilled through the conquest under Joshua (Josh. 21.45), for the recipients of the final form and their situation the promises (formulated after the land had already been lost!) point beyond this qualified fulfilment – even though in a perspective of a strict connection between obedience to the commandments and future deliverance.

## 5.5 Notes on the History of Reception

Bibliography 12: History of Exegesis and Reception of the Bible.

*Preliminary Remarks:* Christianity first spread by following the tracks of the Jewish diaspora communities and then later on its own throughout the entire Mediterranean and neighbouring regions as far as Ethiopia and parts of India. It then developed into a world religion. Through Christianity the Bible attained different levels of influence in the various regions of the world, each with their own cultural histories and experiences with Christianization. When considering the history of reception of the Old Testament, one must keep in mind that it functions simultaneously as holy scripture for both Judaism and Christianity. Both Christianity and Judaism and their handling of the Bible influenced culture throughout the world. This volume will, out of necessity, limit its remarks to the history of reception in the Western tradition where the Bible has unquestionably been the most important book. No other work of literature has influenced religion and culture as much as the Bible. Given this reality it is hardly possible to provide more than individual and exemplary literary works in the 'Notes on the History of Reception' section with hopes that they will provide stimulation for further study.

The Old Testament has influenced Western culture in various ways. Personal names, expressions, sayings and sagas all reflect the general mediation of ancient Jewish and ancient Near Eastern approaches to life in the West. The history of Western art, literature and music owe a large number of their motifs to the Bible, and especially to the rich portrayals of the Old Testament. The Bible was taken as the model for (almost) all other literature. Furthermore, many of the foundational convictions of Western law and societal order can only be understood as part of the history of reception of Christianity and therefore also indirectly of the Bible: the Old and New Testament.

Turning to the books of Genesis–2 Kings, the following aspects of the history of reception (in terms of ideal types as well as examples) can be differentiated: literary, musical and cinematic interpretations, individual motifs used in literature, music and visual arts, as well as theological and intellectual historical impulses.

Reinterpretations of the Great Historical Opus already appear within the biblical material itself such as the historical summary of Neh. 9 and the books of Chronicles (Ch. 23). The Jewish historian Flavius Josephus continues the representation of the biblical history into his own time of the 1st cent. CE in his 'Jewish Antiquities' (Antiquitates Judaicae). The Book of Jubilees from ca. 150 BCE provides a historical portrayal paraphrasing Gen.–Exod. 14 ('rewritten Torah').

The majority of the literary, musical and cinematographic receptions concentrate on smaller portions of the Great Historical Opus, and a limited number of them will receive mention in the appropriate 'Notes on the History of Reception' sections. The individual motifs in the visual arts, literature and music will also be discussed there. It is enough at this point to mention that Western art history has until recently taken up motifs primarily from biblical themes. By the beginning of the classical modern period at the latest, however, the use of biblical motifs as sources for inspiration has increasingly been confined to religious art only.

With regard to the theological and intellectual historical effects of the Great Historical Opus, its portrayal provided the decisive picture of the history of 'Israel' and the entire ancient Near East until the modern era. Correctives of this picture first began to appear as a result of detailed historical-critical analysis of the biblical texts and – more prominently in popular culture – through the discovery of original ancient Near Eastern source documents. These discoveries brought on the early 20th cent. 'Babel–Bible Controversy',[23] which intermingled the questions of historicity, uniqueness, and age of the Old Testament traditions on the one hand and the normative role of the Old Testament for Christianity and its cultural significance on the other. The result was a – sometimes harsh – rejection of

23. Cf. R. G. Lehmann, *Friedrich Delitzsch und der Babel-Bibel-Streit* (OBO 133; Fribourg: Academic Press/Göttingen: Vandenhoeck & Ruprecht, 1994); R. Liwak, 'Bibel und Babel: Wider die theologische und religionsgeschichtliche Naivität', *BTZ* 15 (1998): 206–33.

the Old Testament. The continued release of cinematographic portrayals of Old Testament material as well as popular science reports dealing with the 'historicity' of biblical stories such as the Flood may serve as an indicator of the deep roots of the biblical presentation of history and of its continued influence. Besides, the salvation-historical conceptualization of the Great Historical Opus has directly or indirectly operated as an archetype of all Western attempts to systematize some sort of theology (or philosophy) of history.

# 6

# The Legal Texts of the Pentateuch

(Jan Christian Gertz – Translation by Peter Altmann)

## Chapter Outline




H. J. Boecker, *Law and the Administration of Justice in the Old Testament and Ancient East*. Transl. by J. Moiser. London: SPCK, 1980; F. Crüsemann, *The Torah: Theology and Social History of Old Testament Law*. Transl. by A. W. Mahnke. Edinburgh: T&T Clark, 1996; M. Noth, 'The Laws in the Pentateuch'. Pages 1–107 in *The Laws in the Pentateuch and Other Studies*. Transl. by D. R. Ap-Thomas. Introduction by N. W. Porteous. Edinburgh: Oliver & Boyd, 1966 (1940); E. Otto, *Theologische Ethik des Alten Testaments*. Theologische Wissenschaft 3/2. Stuttgart: Kohlhammer, 1994; T. Veijola, ed., *The Law in the Bible and in its Environment*. Helsinki: Finnish Exegetical Society/Göttingen: Vandenhoeck & Ruprecht, 1990; R. Westbrook/B. Wells, *Everyday Law in Biblical Israel: An Introduction*, Louisville, Ky.: Westminster John Knox, 2009.


## 6.1 Biblical Context

In addition to the narrative threads that go beyond the individual books, the Pentateuch typically imbeds theocratic-legal and cultic ordinances within narrative contexts. The ordinances often contain connections to the particular narrative. Such texts can be found as follows:

| | | |
|---|---|---|
| .oah | Gen. 9.4-5 | Prohibition on Consuming Blood |
| Abraham | Gen. 17.10-11 | Command to Circumcise All Males |
| Moses/Israel in Egypt | Exod. 12.1-28 | Passover-Massot Ordinances |
| | Exod. 13.1-16 | Dedication of Firstborn and Massot Ordinances |
| Moses/Israel at Sinai | Exod. 20.2-17 | Decalogue |
| | Exod. 20.22–23.33 | Covenant Code |
| | Exod. 25–31 | Provisions for Building the Tabernacle |
| | Exod. 34.10-28 | New Copy of the Tablets (*Yahweh's Privilegrecht*) |
| | Lev. 1–7 | Offering Laws |
| | Lev. 11–15 | Purity Laws |
| | Lev. 16 | Day of Atonement |
| | Lev. 17–26 | Holiness Code |
| | Lev. 27 | Vow and Tithe Ordinances |
| | Num. 5 | Purification Sacrifice and Washing |
| | Num. 6 | Nazarite Laws |
| | Num. 8.5-19 | Dedication of the Levites |
| Moses/Israel in the Desert | Num. 18 | Duties and Privileges of the Priests and Levites |
| | Num. 19 | Purification Water from the Ashes of the Red Heifer |
| | Num. 27.6-11 | Law Regarding the Inheritance of Daughters I |
| | Num. 28–29 | Laws for Daily and Festival Offerings |
| | Num. 30 | Vow Ordinances II |
| | Num. 35 | Laws for Levitical Cities and Cities of Asylum |
| | Num. 36 | Law Regarding the Inheritance of Daughters II |
| Moses/Israel in the Land of Moab | Deut. 5.6-21 | Decalogue (Reminder of the Laws from Horeb) |
| | Deut. 12-26 | Deuteronomic Law (Reminder of the Laws from Horeb; cf. Ch. 7.2) |
| | Deut. 27.1-8 | Command to Construct the Law Stela and Altar on Mt. Ebal |
| | Deut. 27.15-26 | Deuteronomic Curse (Do)decalogue |

Since the Pentateuch largely presents its legal texts as the law of God mediated by Moses, it dates the disclosure of the theocratic-legal and cultic ordinances with the exceptions of Gen. 9 and Gen. 17 to the Mosaic period. For the most part the legal texts are divided into three collections, the → *Covenant Code* in Exod. 20.22–23.33, the Holiness Code in Lev. 17–26, and the Deuteronomic Code in Deut. 12–26. In addition there are the provisions for building the → *tabernacle* in Exod. 25–31, which are, however, oriented towards a one-time event and therefore do not constitute a legal text in the strictest sense. The concentration of law on Sinai, or Horeb as the mountain of God is called in the Deuteronomic and Deuteronomistic Literature (→ *Deuteronomism*), is especially conspicuous. As a result Sinai/Horeb becomes the pre-eminent location for the self-revelation of God.

The collections of legal texts given on Sinai (Exod. 20–Num. 8) or Horeb (Deut. 5; 12–27) each begin with the → *Decalogue* (Exod. 20.2-17 // Deut. 5.6-21), underlining its fundamental importance for understanding Old Testament 'Law'. Within the Sinai narrative this is also enhanced by the fact that the Decalogue alone is received by the people directly from God. In their final form at least the subsequent law corpuses, the Covenant Code and the Deuteronomic Law, are meant to be read as explication of the laws of the Decalogue. Conversely, the Decalogue is meant to be understood as a summary of the Torah. Within the Decalogue itself everything again depends on the First Commandment, with its demand for exclusive worship of Yhwh, and on the preamble telling of Yhwh's act of deliverance in Egypt. Together these formulate the inseparability of Yhwh's salvific actions and the subsequent claim and consolation to be the God of the Israelite people, undergirding the foundational structure for Old Testament law: 'I am Yhwh, your God, who brought you out of the land of Egypt, out of the house of slavery. You shall not have any gods besides me' (Exod. 20.2-3 // Deut. 5.6-7). This foundational structure is also highlighted through the textual context that presents the Covenant Code and Deuteronomic Law as documents of a → *covenant* of Yhwh with Israel, shown explicitly in the report of covenant making at the conclusion of each (cf. Exod. 24.4-8; Deut. 26.16-19).

## 6.2 Textual Issues and Major Issues in the History of Critical Interpretation

One of the basic observations in Old Testament scholarship is the fact that the legal texts in the Pentateuch repeatedly treat the same material in diverse ways. A historical comparison of the texts reveals that the differences occur as a result of their origins in various time periods in ancient Israel. This perspective is quite important for the reconstruction of the compositional history of the Pentateuch. It implies that the legal texts of the Pentateuch stem from divergent authors from different times. Furthermore, the correlation of the legal texts and the narrative material that belongs with them allows for a relative chronology of narratives and laws on the basis of legal history and institutional history. In this regard Julius Wellhausen's *Prolegomena to the History of Israel*[24] has been epoch-making in its determination of the relationships between the → *Covenant Code*, the Deuteronomic Law, and the legal texts from the milieu of the → *Priestly Document* (P) including especially the provisions for building the → *tabernacle*, the Holiness Code and the legal texts found in the book of Numbers. One may briefly summarize Wellhausen's results as follows: the cultic ordinances of Deuteronomy elevate the demand of exclusive worship of Yhwh at a single chosen Jerusalem sanctuary (cf. Deut. 12; → *cult centralization*).[25] While the demand for

**Historical Comparison within the Pentateuchal Legal Collections: Ordinances Regarding the Release of Hebrew Slaves in the Covenant Code and Its Reformulation in the Deuteronomic Law**

Exod. 21.2-7: When you buy a male Hebrew slave, he shall serve six years, but in the seventh he shall go out a free person, without debt. If he comes in single, he shall go out single; if he comes in married, then his wife shall go out with him. If his master gives him a wife and she bears him sons or daughters, the wife and her children shall be her master's and he shall go out alone. But if the slave declares, 'I love my master, my wife, and my children; I will not go out a free person,' then his master shall bring him before God. He shall be brought to the door or the doorpost; and his master shall pierce his ear with an awl; and he shall serve him for life. When a man sells his daughter as a slave, she shall not go out as the male slaves do.
Deut. 15.12-18: If a member of your community, whether a Hebrew man or a Hebrew woman, is sold to you and works for you six years, in the seventh year you shall set that person free. And when you send a male slave out from you a free person, you shall not send him out empty-handed. Provide liberally out of your flock, your threshing floor, and your wine press, thus giving to him some of the bounty with which Yhwh your God has blessed you. Remember that you were a slave in the land of Egypt, and Yhwh your God redeemed you; for this reason I lay this command upon you today. But if he says to you, 'I will not go out from you,' because he loves you and your household, since he is well off with you, then you shall take an awl and thrust it through his earlobe into the door, and he shall be your slave forever. You shall do the same with regard to

24. J. Wellhausen, *Prolegomena to the History of Israel* (transl. and preface by W. R. Smith; Atlanta, Ga.: Scholars Press, 1994; transl. of *Prolegomena zur Geschichte Israels* [6th ed., Berlin/New York: de Gruyter, 1927; Student edition, 2001; 1st ed. 1878 under the title *Geschichte Israels I*]).

25. The fact that the place of the legitimate sanctuary remains unnamed in Deuteronomy arises from the fiction of Mosaic authorship.

your female slave. Do not consider it a hardship when you send them out from you free persons, because for six years they have given you services worth the wages of hired labourers; and Yhwh your God will bless you in all that you do.

## Deuteronomy's *Legal* Differences with the Covenant Code

- The released debt slave should be given provisions so that he will be able to provide for himself.
- Male and female slaves should be treated in the same manner, which amends the differentiation between genders found in the Covenant Code (showing a more developed understanding of women and family).
- The special rule governing a wife and children received during the period of debt slavery is dropped (also showing a more developed understanding of women and family).
- The ceremony of the nailing of the ear with an awl is moved from the local sanctuary to the houses of the local villages and is de-sacralized (as a result of cult centralization).

## Deuteronomy's *Ethical* Differences with the Covenant Code

- The debt slave is called 'brother', so that the ethical demands attached to family members apply to him.
- The ordinance contains a → *parenetic* rationale in which the experience of debt slavery is brought into relationship with Yhwh's act of deliverance in Egypt and the experience of the people in Egypt as oppressed and then freed by Yhwh.
- An appeal is made to ethical insight and a promise of blessing is provided.

cult centralization was still unknown in the Covenant Code, it is taken for granted and assumed in P and the cultic laws related to P. The resulting relative chronology of Covenant Code, Deuteronomic Law, and Priestly ordinances can be anchored historically through the connection of the Deuteronomic Law with the document found in → *Josiah's reform* of 622 BCE as reported in 2 Kgs 22–23. Wellhausen's determination of the relations between legal corpuses (and their connected narratives) has generally been maintained, even if certain updates have become necessary. In contrast to Wellhausen, there are Deuteronomistic additions found in the Covenant Code, and P did not simply replace Deuteronomy. Rather, the Deuteronomic-Deuteronomistc texts and perspectives continued to be taken into consideration in later texts alongside P and were – at times independently and at times with the interpenetrating influence of P – updated. Finally, the historical veracity of the reforms in 2 Kgs 22–23 remains a point of contention.

In addition to the historical comparison of the Old Testament legal collections and their individual ordinances, attempts have also been made to detect the various legal → *genres* within the legal collections. This approach has contributed considerably to a differentiated understanding of the texts. Following Albrecht Alt (1883–1956) one may determine the formal differences in the Old Testament between casuistic and apodictic legal statements.[26]

A casuistic law states which legal consequences arise from particular actions. Its introductory statement (protasis) begins with 'if' (*kî*) and describes the behaviour. This action can be given further conditions (introduced by the Hebrew *'im* 'if/when'), and subsets to these conditions beginning with *wĕ'im* ('and if'). The consequence (apodosis) lays out what is to happen when the named action has taken place.[27] The legal clauses are formulated in the 3rd person and were originally found in so-called village gate judgement settings.

## Excursus: The Nature of Law in Ancient Israel and Judah

The administration of justice was not centrally organized long into the period of the monarchy. Within the extended family the jurisdiction – including the responsibility for determining a death sentence or exclusion from the family – lay with the *pater familias* (Gen. 16.5-6; 31.25-54; 38.24-26). The most important matter of justice for the extended family or tribe was the responsibility to carry out blood revenge when someone was killed by a person from outside the tribe. Revenge was confined by the *ius talionis* ('Life for life'; Exod. 21.22-25) applying to bodily harm with fatal consequences and by the provision of asylum at the sanctuary that made possible an objective investigation of whether a homicide was wilful or not (with only the former deserving a death sentence) (Exod. 21.12-14; Deut. 19.1-13). Inter-tribal disputes were settled through the **justice of the gate**, in

26. A. Alt, 'Die Ursprünge des israelitischen Rechts', in *Kleine Schriften zur Geschichte des Volkes Israel I* (4th ed.; Munich: Beck, 1968; [1934]), 278–332 (ET 'The Origins of Israelite Law', in *Essays on Old Testament History and Religion*, transl. by R. A. Wilson; Sheffield: JSOT Press, 1989, 79–132).

27. In English one might expect the apodosis to begin with 'then', though this is generally not reflected in English translations of the Bible. These translations reflect the fact that in Hebrew the apodosis simply begins with a converted perfect (*wĕ* + perf.) or impf. verb.

which the free men of the place would try the case. The justice of the gate was constituted in response to the accusation by the aggrieved party or by witnesses; it did not prosecute 'automatically' as in modern criminal offences liable to public prosecution. The process reached its conclusion with the determination of guilt or innocence of the defendant. If the normal means such as evidence, testimonies from (Deut. 19.15-21: at least two) witnesses, or confessions were not sufficient for reaching a verdict, then the case would be transferred to the religious court of the priests at the local sanctuary. In this case the defendant would declare their innocence through an assertoric statement, namely an oath ensuring innocence (Exod. 22.7-10; 1 Kgs 8.31-32) or an ordeal (Num. 5.11-31). The justice of the gate provided the institutional background for the Covenant Code. The socio-economic differentiations within the villages recognizable in the Covenant Code had negative consequences for justice according to the prophetic texts (Amos 5.10, 12), since jurisdiction was based on the assumption of people having equal rights. Judges first arose throughout the land in the late monarchical period (the administration of justice of the 'judges for all Israel' in → *DtrH* is a late fiction). At this time Josiah extended the judicial practices of the capital (Isa. 1.26, 3.2, Zeph. 3.3) to all of Judah and professionalized the justice of the gate through the installation of judges and court secretaries (Deut. 16.18). He also restricted the cultic administration of justice to the central sanctuary (Deut. 17.8-13) and provided the cities of asylum as a replacement for the local sanctuaries (Deut. 19.1-13). After the collapse of the monarchy the elders of the villages (again) became the administrators of justice for the familial groups which alone remained intact (Deut. 21.18-21; 22.13-21; 25.5-10). Ruth 4 gives an example of a postexilic judicial process. These judicial processes were superimposed with those of the Persian governor and his officials (Ezra 7.25-26). In the event of a capital offence an assembly of the family groups was required in addition to the elders (Num. 35.24), from which the judicial procedures of the synagogue during the → *diaspora* developed. The influence of the Jerusalem priesthood on judicial proceedings increased during the postexilic period (Deut. 21.5; Ezra 7.26; Neh. 8) and became even stronger in the post-Persian period because of the heightened political importance of the high priest (Num. 35.25, 28). In the Hellenistic period the administration of justice and legal interpretation was transferred to the gerusia (a council of aristocrats made up of laity, priests and scribes) which later became the Sanhedrin. The Sanhedrin and the synagogue carried out the administration of justice in Judea as well as in the diaspora during the imperial period for the *imperium romanum,* though the Roman magistrate could intercede on behalf of Roman interests.

B. S. Jackson, 'Ideas of Law and Legal Administration'. Pages 184–202 in *The World of Ancient Israel*. Ed. by R. E. Clements. Cambridge: Cambridge University Press, 1989; H. Niehr, *Rechtsprechung in Israel.* SBS 130. Stuttgart: Katholisches Bibelwerk, 1987.

Collection, arrangement, redaction and transmission of casuistic legal collections belonged to the domain of the scribal schools. A glance at the cuneiform legal collections, such as the famous Code of the Babylonian king Hammurabi (1728–1686 BCE; *ANET*, 163–180, [abbreviation CH]), demonstrates that the genre is not limited to the Old Testament. Instead, ancient Israel took part in a highly developed ancient Near Eastern legal culture.

### Casuistic Law in the Covenant Code and in the Code of Hammurabi (CH)

Exod. 22.7-8: 'When someone delivers to a neighbour money or goods for safekeeping, and they are stolen from the neighbour's house, then the thief, if caught, shall pay double. If the thief is not caught, the owner of the house shall be brought before God, to determine whether or not the owner had laid hands on the neighbour's goods.'

CH §§ 122–125: 'If any one give another silver, gold, or anything else to keep, he shall show everything to some witness, draw up a contract, and then hand it over for safe keeping. If he turn it over for safe keeping without witness or contract, and if he to whom it was given deny it, then he has no legitimate claim. If anyone deliver silver, gold, or anything else to another for safe keeping, before a witness, but he deny it, he shall be brought before a judge, and all that he has denied he shall pay in full. If any one place his property with another for safe keeping, and there, either through thieves or robbers, his property and the property of the other man be lost, the owner of the house, through whose neglect the loss took place, shall compensate the owner for all that was given to him in charge. But the owner of the house shall try to follow up and recover his property, and take it away from the thief.'

In contrast to the casuistic laws, the apodictic law texts command and forbid unconditionally. According to Alt a further mark of apodictic law is their sequential formation. The most prominent representative of apodictic law is the → *Decalogue.*[28] The commandments are formulated in the 2nd person singular, and the weight behind the directive to the Israelite 'you' is the 'I' of Yhwh himself. Alt argued that apodictic law was *the* genuine Israelite Yhwh law from the earliest period of Israel, while casuistic law was an inheritance from Canaan that Israel adopted in the → *conquest* and settlement in Palestine. This argument based on form criticism and the history of law was interpreted theologically in subsequent

28. Alt goes on to name the curse sequence in Deut. 27.15-26, a listing of prohibited sexual relationships with relatives in Lev. 18.7-17, as well as the incomplete or scattered sequences concerning capital crimes (Exod. 21.12, 15-17; 22.18-19; 31.15b; Lev. 20.2, 9-13, 15-16, 27; 24.16-17; 27.29), and the commands governing the treatment of specific persons (Exod. 22.17, 20*, 21, 27) or judicial procedures (Exod. 23.1-3, 6-9).

scholarship to mean that apodictic law functioned as an expression of → *covenant* behaviour from the earliest period of Israel's history that separated Israel from the surrounding cultures. It seemed that with apodictic law one had struck the genuine Israelite kernel in the Old Testament, which scholarship increasingly viewed as embedded in ancient Near Eastern religious and legal traditions. This apodictic law was therefore seen as demonstrating Israel's revelatory uniqueness within history.

This position is no longer supported in the present scholarly discussion because Alt's form-critical and legal-historical thesis needs correction and increased precision. The determination of apodictic law as Israelite Yhwh law and casuistic law as Canaanite inheritance has been widely rejected. This rejection has occurred as a result of considerable change in the understanding of the history and history of religion of the early period in Israel rendering a strict opposition between Israel and Canaan no longer justifiable (Ch. 3.1). Form-critical objections to Alt can be made in light of the fact that (1.) the impression of the uniformity of apodictic law arises essentially from its contrast with casuistic law. In fact, apodictic ordinances appear in quite diverse forms, which originate from (2.) different legal spheres and (3.) are not genuinely Israelite. Furthermore, contra Alt (4.) individual laws are now judged as more ancient while their formation into sections is seen as a later stage.

# 6.3 Origins of the Legal Texts in the Pentateuch

## 6.3.1 Basic Approach to the Development of Law in Ancient Israel

The legal traditions of the Old Testament are presented as divine law mediated by Moses. However, this conceptualization resulted from a multi-layered process that was decisively influenced by the judicially trained authors of Deuteronomy and the Dtr scribes. This process may be described in simplified form as follows: as the legal traditions were passed on, the basically religious → *Privilegrecht* of Yhwh and a collection of the (not explicitly religious) tribal law from the pre and early monarchical period and the law of the village gate from the monarchical period were subsequently joined and given a salvation-historical perspective until they finally came to be understood as all having the authority and sanction of Yhwh.

The apodictic laws can be separated formally into commands and prohibitions. The tribal or social laws can be differentiated from the sacral laws in terms of content. Obligations to Yhwh, such as the sanctification of the firstborn to Yhwh (Exod. 22.28-30) order the religious and cultic duties of Yhwh worshippers. In contrast, profane prohibitions ensure the ethical norms of the families and tribes. In this group belong for example the prohibitions against killing, stealing and adultery (Exod. 20.13-15) taken up into the → *Decalogue.* In the → *Covenant Code*, parallels to these commandments are found in the so-called capital crimes. These crimes, for which a death sentence is mandated, have the apodosis 'he must certainly be put to death' and are therefore referred to as *Mot-yumat*-laws (Exod. 21.12, 15, 17). These legal rules provide a code of practice for borderline situations within the family and individual tribes. This is especially clear for the offences against one's own parents. The *Mot-yumat*-laws are meant to help prevent the violation of fundamental norms of inner-familial solidarity through the deterrent of a death sentence. These laws originally have nothing to do with a → *covenant* relationship between Yhwh and Israel or a systematization of the divine will. This is also the case for the legal curses, which primarily served to exclude a perpetrator from family and tribe as well as to protect the purity of the cultic community from the guilt coming from the religious and social trespass (Deut. 27.15-26). The premise of the curses, especially in the light of unknown or unexplainable trespasses, is the conviction that an injury to the legal order of society by an individual can have negative effects for the entire community.

The *ius talionis*, which is commonly viewed as *the* legal principle of the Old Testament, regulates inter-tribal offences dealing with bodily harm. Its well-known demand to repay in like form ('Eye for an eye …'; Exod. 21.23; Lev. 24.19-20; Deut. 19.21), served to confine revenge as well as equalize damages between individual tribes. It is impossible to miss the profane origin of the casuistic formulated laws coming from the judicial procedures of the courts in the individual village gates, which deal primarily with disputes between different families or tribes.

The linking of these laws, all from various backgrounds, can first be observed in the Covenant Code, in that the apodictic social norms for inner-tribal dealings are brought together here with laws governing relationships between tribes.[29] In addition, the Covenant Code is the first to reveal the move towards the theologization of law, as found in the ordinances of Exod. 22.20-26 that provide protection for the foreigner, widow, and orphan. By placing these figures under Yhwh's

29. The inner-familial norms (Exod. 21.12, 15, 17) provide a frame around the ordinances for inter-tribal conflicts (Exod. 21.13-14, 16), which leads to the linking of apodictic (v.12) and casuistic formulations (vv. 13-14).

protection the process towards *theologization* of profane law – very important for reception history – takes place and secures divine advocacy for the rights of the oppressed. In the face of considerable social differentiation it had become apparent that the civil justice system did not provide sufficient protection for the lowly. The earlier named foreigners, widows and orphans were easily made into victims of foreign interests because they had no individual voice in the judicial proceedings at the village gate. Therefore it was necessary to deter possible perpetrators with the concept of divine retribution: there is a compassionate God who hears the cries of the poor and listens to the foreigner, widow, and orphan as well. Also, the interweaving of Yhwh's *Privilegrecht* with profane law[30] added to the theologization of law in the Covenant Code.

The second characteristic of Old Testament law is its *historicization*. This feature is directly linked to the law's theological nature: Yhwh's acting in history and the formulation of law as an expression of his divine will are tied together in that the entire promulgation of law is assigned to a certain place within Israel's salvation history. This can be seen for instance when Deuteronomy for the first time provides a rationale for the Israelite feasts (which covers over and removes them from their origins in the agricultural year and the related cultic celebrations) making them remembrances of the salvation history rather than celebrations of the agrarian annual cycle and related religious meaning (cf. Deut. 16). The promulgation of the law, that is its publication within a particular historical (salvation-historical is more precise) setting marked the completion of the historicization of the law. What is meant here is the concentration of the legal promulgations on Sinai/Horeb especially apparent in Deuteronomy and the → *Dtr* redactions of the Sinai pericope.

Having outlined the major lines of thought that lead to the notion of a divine law mediated by Moses, the following sections will address the most important questions concerning the compositional history of the various legal text corpuses – with the exception of the Deuteronomic Law, which will be addressed in the context of the later treatment of Deuteronomy. (Ch. 7.2).

## 6.3.2 The Covenant Code (Exod. 20.22–23.33)

gets its name from Exod. 24.7, where Moses, looking back at the preceding revelation of the divine will, speaks of 'the Book of the Covenant' (*seper ha-bᵉrît*)

30. As found in the interweaving of the profane laws on the judicial process (Exod. 23.1-9) with the laws on divine privileges (Exod. 22.27-30 and 23.10-19); cf. E. Otto, Ethik, 99–103.

to which Israel will be bound. The core of the Covenant Code is found in Exod. 20.24–23.29, its original starting point is marked by the altar law of Exod. 20.24-26 that limits Yhwh worship to only those locations that meet specific requirements. Comparison with the Deuteronomic law of the early 7th cent BCE shows that the core of the Covenant Code is older. The → *terminus post quem* for the composition of the Covenant Code is more difficult to pinpoint and as a result suggested dates are controversial. The systematic collection of law from different provenance assumes a certain degree of institutionalization and therefore suggests a connection with the state. The Covenant Code contains the first tangible theologization of law and may thus be understood as a reaction to the growing social stratification of ancient Israelite society that is reflected by the social criticism of the classical prophets as well. With that in mind the core of the Covenant Code can be dated in the 8th cent BCE at the earliest and the 7th cent BCE at the latest. The frame (Exod. 20.22-23; 23.20-33), however, can be traced to Dtr editors that also left their imprint within the legal corpus itself. In particular they separated the altar law (which reckoned with more than one sanctuary) from the core of the law corpus and provisionally adapted it to the demand of Yhwh worship at one exclusive sanctuary. It is currently debated whether or not late Dtr redactors were also responsible for inserting the Covenant Code into the Sinai story or whether they already found the Covenant Code in that setting. The latter is more likely because it is difficult to explain why the Dtr redactors should have referred to an older law text that at times contradicted their own intentions and was difficult to incorporate into a unified picture with the Deuteronomic Law.

## 6.3.3 The Decalogue (Exod. 20.2-17; Deut. 5.6-21)

is the most famous body of laws in the Old Testament. In accordance with the mention of the two tablets Moses or Yhwh wrote on (Exod. 24.12; 31.18; 34.1-4; Deut. 5.22; 10.1-5), it is organized into the first tablet concerning obligations to God and the second containing social and ethical obligations. The obligations to God include the ban on foreign gods and images, the prohibition against misuse of the divine name and the Sabbath law. After these follow ordinances designed to safeguard the human community. One is inclined to conclude that the tradent responsible for assembling the Decalogue saw the social ordinances on the second tablet as developments unfolding the obligations to God on the first tablet. The tablets are bound together through the command to honour parents. The content of this commandment 'You shall honour your father and mother' belongs to the realm of social obligations but its subsequent rationale 'that you may have long life in the land that Yhwh your God will give you' points back to the obligations to God. Read as a complete unit the Decalogue summarizes the divine will.

## The Numbering of the Ten Commandments

The Greek expression Decalogue ('ten word') originates from the reference to 'ten words' in Deut. 4.13 and 10.4. It does not appear within the Decalogue itself, however, and neither does the Decalogue include a numbering of the individual commandments. This fact and the difficulty with identifying the individual units of meaning in the slightly different versions of the Decalogue explain why in the history of interpretation the numbering of the commandments has varied. Besides, the history of interpretation has highlighted different aspects of the divine will at different times. The Roman Catholic and Lutheran traditions follow Augustine (354–430 CE) in seeing the 1st Commandment as the combination of the prohibition on foreign gods and the image prohibition – the latter having been increasingly left out since the 13th cent. In order to retain the number ten the prohibition on coveting (Exod. 20.17; Deut. 5.21) has been split to form the 9th and 10th Commandments. This division is made possible by the repetition of the verb 'covet'. The Reformed tradition, following a tradition found as early as Philo (1st cent. CE), counts the prohibition on foreign gods and images as the 1st and 2nd Commandments, making a division of the prohibition on coveting superfluous. A similar approach is taken by Orthodox Judaism, which counts the preamble to the Decalogue as the 1st Commandment and fuses the prohibitions on foreign gods and images into the 2nd Commandment.

The two formulations of the Decalogue contain more than 20 differences with the clearest ones coming in the Sabbath command. Exod. 20.10-11 grounds the Sabbath commandment in the priestly document's creation story ('Rest on the seventh day'), while Deut. 5.15 connects the commandment with the memory of oppression in Egypt. The non-uniformity in terms of form and legal-historical origins allow for the recognition that the Decalogue is a secondary composition. The evidence for this is found in the change from God as first person speaker to speech about God as well as the different lengths and varying degree of elaboration of the commandments. The two first commandments (prohibitions of foreign gods and images) open the Decalogue with God speaking in the first person, but the prohibition on the misuse of the divine name and the Sabbath commandment already change to speaking about God in the third person. This is also the case for the subsequent commandment about parents, which is the only commandment formulated as a positive command. The subsequent commandments do not mention Yhwh. In Commandments 6–8 a small series of short prohibitions deal with the protection of life, marriage, and neighbour's property. The Ninth Commandment, which prohibits false testimony in court, is somewhat longer. The very detailed Tenth Commandment covers the coveting of a neighbour's possessions and estate that appeared as the subject matter in previous commandments and thereby formulates a transition from law to ethics.

The variety of the forms has continually led to attempted reconstructions of an 'original Decalogue', but these attempts have not been persuasive. One should instead assume that the Decalogue developed through the collecting and choosing of commandments as well as conscious literary arrangement. Individual laws from various origins or even smaller collections like the short prohibitions in the 6th–8th Commandments were brought together under the guiding principle of the commandment to not worship any god besides Yhwh to form a summary of the divine will. This foundational First Commandment as well as the preamble are clearly shaped by Deuteronomic theology (cf. Deut. 6.4), meaning that the Decalogue could not have emerged before the 7th cent. BCE This dating is also supported by the fact that there are no allusions to the Decalogue in earlier periods. The oft-cited evidence of Hos. 4.2 (cf. Jer. 7.9) more likely represents the prehistory of the Decalogue. Certainly, some religious and ethical elements of the Decalogue have a prehistory reaching back to an earlier period. Finally, the Decalogue was only secondarily inserted into the Sinai pericope, and neither does it belong to the earliest layer of Deuteronomy. Scholarship continues to debate which version of the Decalogue was first inserted into its present literary position.

Perhaps the question should not be answered within the strict category of an 'either-or'. It is conceivable that the Decalogue was inserted into the Sinai pericope in Exod. 20 first, but that it was formulated with knowledge of Deuteronomy (without the Decalogue of Deut. 5). Subsequently, attempts to align Deuteronomy and the Covenant Code would have led to a similar inclusion of the Decalogue in Deut. 5 at the beginning of the law corpus to match its position in Exod. 20 before the Covenant Code. This later version may then in turn have brought about additions in Exod. 20. In either case, by the time it was inserted in its present context the Decalogue – or its earlier version – already represented a citable text.

M. Köckert, *Die Zehn Gebote*. Munich: Beck, 2007; P. M. Miller, *The Way of the Lord: Essays in Old Testament Theology*. FAT 39. Tübingen: Mohr Siebeck, 2004; W. H. Schmidt, H. Delkurt, and A. Graupner, *Die zehn Gebote im Rahmen alttestamentlicher Ethik*. EdF 281. Darmstadt: Wissenschaftliche Buchgesellschaft, 1993; B.-Z. Segal and G. Levi, eds, *The Ten Commandments in History and Tradition*. Jerusalem: Magnes Press, 1990.

### 6.3.4 The Holiness Code (Lev. 17–26)

This was first marked off from its context as a self-contained text by August Klostermann (1837–1915) in 1877. Its name reflects the overarching motif appearing in the command 'You should be holy because I, Yhwh your God am holy' (Lev. 19.2 etc.). This formulates the ethical basis that Yhwh's nearness demands as well as allows for the people's holiness: because Yhwh is holy and lets the Israelites participate in his holiness, Israel can – as the people of Yhwh – be holy. It is undisputed that this concept originated in priestly thought. The Holiness Code forms a relatively self-contained unity within the Priestly theology in the broader sense, but the process of its compositional development remains unsure. It is generally acknowledged that the Holiness Code represents a historical development that consciously carries further and corrects Deuteronomy, even if some individual laws from the Holiness Code affected later editions of Deut. More controversial is whether the Holiness Code was an earlier-formed independent legal corpus that was secondarily inserted into P (A. Klostermann) or if it was formed from various materials as an addition composed specifically for insertion into its current literary context (E. Otto), or finally if the Holiness Code was never conceived as an independent entity, but was composed along with its priestly context (F. Crüsemann, E. Blum).

## 6.4 Theology of the Pentateuchal Legal Texts

The legal traditions in the Old Testament display significant similarities in form and content with their counterparts from the ancient Near Eastern environment. In addition, the Old Testament holds in common with the entire ancient Near East the conviction that successful community life is only possible when a society keeps in step with the divinely ordained world order and that damage to this order by an individual can have negative consequences for the entire community. Therefore the prologues and epilogues of the ancient Near Eastern legal corpuses, which contain fewer positive commands than negative ones like the Old Testament legal collections, name the establishment and maintenance of law and justice as the primary task of the king. In this respect the Old Testament differs from its surrounding cultures in a characteristic way. For according to the Old Testament the foundation and enforcement of law takes place rather independently from the king (but compare Ps. 72). This resulted on one hand from the relatively late establishment of national structures, especially those of a legal nature, in Israel. The main reason for this idiosyncrasy in the Old Testament, however, was that Judah did not exist as a state anymore when the formation of its legal collections took place, namely in the → *exilic* and postexilic periods. The theologization of law certainly had already begun in the Covenant Code written during the monarchy. However, its peculiar dynamic first gains steam in connection with the historization of law in the Deuteronomic law at the end of the monarchy and then especially in the → *Deuteronomism* of the exilic period. The final formation of the legal traditions in which the promulgation of law is almost completely concentrated on Sinai/Horeb – outside of the land and the state – occurs in the postexilic period. For the redactors responsible for this conceptualization the legal traditions represent the sum

**Torah,** Heb. *tôrâ,* generally means 'instruction'. The specific connotations of the term are understood according to its context. So Torah in theological contexts means divine instruction given through the mediation of a priest or a prophet, which through a number of steps came to signify the entirety of God's instructions. The roots of the appellation of the entire law as Torah or as the book of the Torah of Moses lie in the → *Dtr* edition of Deuteronomy, where the expression denotes the warnings, ordinances and judgements of the Deuteronomic law (Deut. 4.44-49). This Torah is available to Israel as a book (Deut. 30.10), meaning that it exists in written form and as such persists over generations. Ps. 1.2 (and possibly also 1 Chr. 22.12) refers to the extended meaning of Torah, namely as a designation for the Pentateuch and its collected legal traditions. This meaning conforms with the usage in the synoptic gospels when referring to the law and the prophets (Mt. 7.12, etc.).

of Yhwh's salvific care for Israel and of the revelation of the divine will as it is written down in the Torah.

The value of the Torah can be seen in the very late sermon of Deut. 4.1-40 where Moses asks:

> 'And what other great nation has statutes and ordinances as just as this entire law that I am setting before you today?' (v. 8)

Israel is different from all other nations because it possesses the Torah:

> 'You must observe them (the laws and the statutes) diligently, for this will show your wisdom and discernment to the peoples, who, when they hear all these statutes, will say, "Surely this great nation is a wise and discerning people!"' (v. 6)

Israel's greatness as a nation lies in the fact that Yhwh is close to his people through the gift of the Torah, which is a claim that other nations cannot make. Both as the Israel standing on the banks of the Jordan before becoming a political entity as the narrative of Deuteronomy portrays the Moses speech and also as the Israel which is a politically unimportant land under foreign dominion to whom Deuteronomy is oriented, God's presence is promised to Israel from wherever Israel calls to him. The central meaning of the Torah, which in fact draws on very divergent legal material, is found in the → *Decalogue* (v. 13), whose primary focus is on the exclusive worship of Yhwh that in turn becomes the central pillar for all remaining commandments. The demand of the First Commandment does not simply appear without reason, but itself depends on the deliverance of Israel from slavery in Egypt found in the Decalogue's preamble. The gift of the Torah therefore includes both Yhwh's care and the call to keep his commandments. From this perspective the obedience that is both a demand and a path towards deliverance is a response to the experience of Yhwh's actions on behalf of Israel that secured Israel's existence in the first place. This conceptualization is articulated in the formulation of the → *Šĕmaʿ yiśrāʾēl.*

> 'Hear, Israel, Yhwh is our God, Yhwh alone! And you shall love Yhwh your God with all your heart, with all your soul, and with all your strength,' (Deut. 6.4-5).

The fact that the Torah provides the criteria for the presentation and evaluation of the historical development in the books of Judges–2 Kings has already been explicated (Ch. 5.4). In addition the Torah also serves as the interpretative guideline for the reading of the Old Testament as a whole according to a number of texts. For example, the prophetic corpus ends with a reference to the Torah of Moses:

> 'Remember the teaching of my servant Moses, the statutes and ordinances that I commanded him at Horeb for all Israel' (Mal. 3.22 [NRSV 4.4]).

This remark should be read in conjunction with the ending of the Torah in Deut. 34.10-12:

> 'Never since has there arisen a prophet in Israel like Moses, whom Yhwh knew face to face. He was unequalled for all the signs and wonders that Yhwh sent him to perform in the land of Egypt, against Pharaoh and all his servants and his entire land, and for all the mighty deeds and all the terrifying displays of power that Moses performed in the sight of all Israel.'

Both remarks frame the prophetic corpus and clearly demand that the prophets be read according to the Mosaic guidelines, which according to the final form of the text means according to the demands of the Mosaic Law (cf. Deut. 18.15). This interpretative guideline of Torah-regulated reading is extended to also include the portion of the → *canon* called the writings, which begin in Ps. 1 with a Torah Psalm. It is in keeping with the meaning of texts such as Ps. 1 that the Torah is said to be the chief part of the Old Testament. While this edition of the Hebrew Bible which is oriented towards the Torah is presumably the latest version, it is not the only version with a ongoing claim to truth. This fact is seen through comparison with the very differently structured → *Septuagint* (LXX). The editors of this version placed the prophetic corpus at the end so that it would be seen as the climax.[31] This understanding mirrors an → *eschatological* orientation with a different emphasis than the Torah emphasis of the later Rabbinic period. The traditional order of the LXX stems from the Christian reception of the Hebrew Bible. However, the different emphasis in the LXX was not only important for early Christianity, but is also representative for further Jewish groups in the Hellenistic period (→ *Hellenism*). Thus the Torah is certainly one, if not *the* centre of Old Testament faith. However, an exclusive orientation towards the Torah runs the risk of ignoring the diverse ways in which the Old Testament speaks of God. The theology of the legal traditions is therefore not *the only*, but rather *one of many theological conceptions* in the Old Testament.

## 6.5 Notes on the History of Reception

As already found in the Old Testament itself, the promulgation and mediation of divine law in the Jewish and Christian traditions are inseparably connected

31. However, the handwritten transmission of the Septuagint is not uniform in this respect.

to the person of Moses. Moses is the lawgiver who reveals the will of the one God Yhwh to Israel and records it in the Torah – the Torah, which is deemed directly or indirectly as the work of Moses and influences all aspects of Jewish life. Accordingly the reception in art, literature and film is concentrated around 'Moses the lawgiver'. The visual arts have especially received the portrayal of Moses with the stone law tables, as seen in Rembrandt's 'Moses destroying the Tablets of the Law' (1659).[32] The enactment of the moral law by Moses and the Jewish people is the subject treated by Thomas Mann in the novel, *Das Gesetz* (1944), where the Ten Commandments are called the 'ABC's for human behavior.'[33] The range of reception history in film can be seen in the epic film 'The Ten Commandments' directed by Cecil B. DeMille (1923, also in 1956 starring Charlton Heston and Yul Brunner) and the ten-part television series 'Decalogue' (1987/1988) by Krzysztof Kieslowski, which investigates the question of the validity of the ethical canon of the Ten Commandments for the present day through examples set in a Polish apartment complex. Beyond those examples the legal texts largely defy illustration or paraphrase.

Turning to reception in theology and the wider intellectual history, the legal texts of the Pentateuch have had very different receptions in Judaism and Christianity. The Torah is indisputably the centre of Jewish religion, and all other writings are seen as attempts at interpretation of the Torah. The reason for this uncontested position of the Torah is the conviction that Yhwh revealed himself and fundamentally bound himself to Israel on Mount Sinai. The 613 *Mitswot* (248 commands and 365 prohibitions) mediated by Moses according to Jewish tradition cover everything needed for a successful life before God. The process of explaining and adapting them in the → *Mishnah*, → *Talmud*, and commentaries is called 'oral Torah'. Christianity, on the other hand, has often understood the Torah (and the Old Testament as a whole) as 'Law' opposed to the 'Gospel'.[34] However, while Paul calls the Old Testament

32. The common portrayal of the 'horned Moses' in Medieval art but still found in Marc Chagall stems from a translation mistake in the → *Vulgate* of Moses' radiant face after receiving the Tablets of the law (Exod. 34:29, 35) as '*cornutus*'.
33. T. Mann, 'Das Gesetz', in *Der Tod in Venedig und andere Erzählungen* (Frankfurt: Fischer, 1992), 261–329, esp. 328 (ET *The Tables of Law*, transl. by M. Faber and S. Lehmann, Philadelphia: Paul Dry Books, 2010).
34. A short introduction to the interpretation of the Old Testament as Law and an investigation of law in the Old Testament can be found in M. Köckert, *Leben in Gottes Gegenwart: Studien zum Verständnis des Gesetzes* (FAT 43; Tübingen: Mohr Siebeck, 2004), 3–15.

as a whole 'Law' (*nomos;* cf. 1 Cor. 14.21; Rom. 3.19), he also refers to the scriptures as announcing the 'Gospel' (Gal. 3.8) and cites the Law as the word of righteousness against the Law as path to salvation (Rom. 10.6-8 with allusion to Deut. 30.11-14).[35] It has also been noted that the opposition of 'Law' and 'Gospel' quickly leads to the separation of the 'Law' from its narrative context and thereby ignores Yhwh's acts of deliverance that precede any demand.[36] Aside from the matter of the Law v. Gospel, the → *Decalogue* could easily be the most well-known text of the entire Bible, and in connection with Martin Luther's explanation in the Shorter Catechism (1529) serves as an embodiment of Lutheran ethics. Luther also provided a musical version of the Decalogue for catechetical purposes. Finally, one should remember that Western legal history has been shaped by (the Christian reception of) Old Testament law.

35. Also Luther is more subtle than often understood: 'Luther neither simply identifies the living voice of the gospel with the scriptures nor the gospel with the New nor the Law with the Old Testament' (Ibid, 3–4 and note 3).
36. Cf. especially W. Zimmerli, 'Gesetz im Alten Testament', in *Gottes Offenbarung: Gesammelte Aufsätze zum Alten Testament* (TB 19; Munich: Kaiser, 1963), 249–76.

# 7

# The Partial Compositions

(Jan Christian Gertz – Translation by Peter Altmann)

## Chapter Outline



## 7.1 The Priestly Document

Bibliography to Ch. 5 and 5.2. Further: I. Knohl, *The Sanctuary of Silence: The Priestly Torah and the Holiness*. Minneapolis, Minn.: Fortress Press, 1995; M. Köckert, 'Leben in Gottes Gegenwart: Zum Verständnis des Gesetzes in der priesterschriftlichen Literatur', *Jahrbuch für Biblische Theologie* 4 (1989): 29–61; S. Shectman and J. S. Baden, eds, *The Strata of the Priestly Writing: Contempory Debate and Future Discussion*. ATANT 95. Zurich: Theologischer Verlag, 2009; O. H. Steck, 'Aufbauprobleme in der Priesterschrift'. Pages 287–308 in *Ernten, was man sät*. Ed. by D. R. Daniels; Neukirchen-Vluyn: Neukirchener, 1991; E. Zenger, *Gottes Bogen in den Wolken*. SBS 112. 2nd ed. Stuttgart: Katholisches Bibelwerk, 1987.

Preliminary remark: The following section will further develop the introductory comments on the Priestly Document provided in the model sketched above for the development of the Great Historical Opus of Genesis–2 Kings (Ch. 5.3).

## Basic Data on the Priestly Document

- Priestly Document (P) is a formerly independent source document that was later combined editorially with the core compositions of the older non-priestly compositions (Primeval History, ancestral story, Moses-exodus-conquest narrative).
- Since the individual non-priestly compositions, before being combined with P, never formed a thoroughgoing Pentateuchal narrative extending from creation to conquest, P represents the first and only continuous source document.
- P begins with the creation report of Gen. 1.1–2.3. It unquestionably continues as far as the entrance of Yhwh's glory into the sanctuary/tent of meeting in Exod. 40.16-17, 33b, 34. Whether the text of P originally continued on and contained the dedication of Aaron and his sons to the priesthood and the beginning of the sacrificial offerings found in Lev. 8–9 is less sure.
- P was gradually expanded, but these expansions to the still independent source document should be differentiated from those expansions of (post-) priestly style that already assume P's combination with the various non-priestly compositions.
- P assumes the centralization demand (→ *cult centralization*) of the late pre-exilic Deuteronomy and should be dated to the late exilic or (more probably) the early postexilic period.

# 7.1.1 Biblical Context

| Texts[1] | Original Core of Formerly Independent P ($P^g$) | Additions to Independent P (PS) |
|---|---|---|
| | **Creation/Elohim** (*'elōhîm)*<br>Blessing; Mandate to Rule: Gen. 1.28 | |
| Gen. 1.1–2.3 | Toledot of Heaven and Earth | |
| Gen. 5 | Toledot of Adam | |
| | **Flood and Noahic Covenant** | |
| | Blessing; Mandate to Rule: Gen. 9.1-7, 8-17 | |
| Gen. 6–9 | Toledot of Noah | |
| Gen. 10 | Toledot of Noah's Sons | |
| Gen. 11.10-26 | Toledot of Shem | |
| Gen. 11.27–25.11 | Toledot of Terah | |
| Gen. 17 | **Covenant with Abraham/El Shadday** (*'ēl šadday*)<br>Promise of Divine Presence and Gift of Land: Gen. 17.7-8 | |

1. The information of the larger text blocks does not differentiate between the various layers within P and at times also pockets of non-priestly texts.

| | | |
|---|---|---|
| Gen. 25.12-17 | Toledot of Ishmael | |
| Gen. 25.19–35.29 | Toledot of Isaac | |
| Gen. 36 | Toledot of Esau | |
| Gen. 37.2–Exod. 40.34 | Toledot of Jacob | |
| Exod. 1.7, 13–14 | Israel in Egypt | |
| Exod. 2.23-25; 6.2-8 | **Call of Moses/Yhwh**<br>Yhwh Remembers His Covenant with the Ancestors: Exod. 2.24; 6.5<br>Promise of Divine Presence and Gift of Land: Exod. 6.7-8 | |
| Exod. 7–13 | Plagues and Exodus | |
| Exod. 14 | Miracle at the Sea | |
| Exod. 19; 25–29 | **Foundation of the Cult at Sinai**<br>Directives for the Building of the Tabernacle on the 7th Day: Exod. 24.16<br>Covenant Formula and Promise of Divine Presence; Reminder on the Exodus: Exod. 29.44-46 | |
| Exod. 30–31 | | Incense Altar, Sabbath Celebration |
| Exod. 35–39 | | Report of Completion of Directives from Exod. 25–31 |
| Exod. 40.16-17, 33b, 34 | **Building of the Tabernacle**<br>**Entrance of Yhwh's Glory into the Sanctuary** | |
| Lev. 1–15 | | Cultic Laws |
| Lev. 16 | | Day of Atonement |
| Lev. 17–26 | | Holiness Code (H) |

In addition to its uniform language, P also features a well-ordered and carefully planned structure. Its most conspicuous structural characteristic is the so-called *Toledot formula:* 'This is the genealogy/story (Heb. *tôlĕdôt* from *yālad* 'to bear') of so-and-so.' This formula could have been a feature that P took over from earlier material. At least this seems to be the case for the formulation in Gen. 5.1, the first occurrence of the formula in the original layer of P, which instead of using the normal formula instead speaks of a '*book* of the genealogy/story'.[2] In the ongoing

2. The occurrence in Gen. 2.4a is secondary and is inserted as an editorial transition combining

narrative the formula appears an additional eight times within the original P composition always to introduce a family tree (Gen. 6.9; 10.1; 11.10, 27; 25.12,19; 36.1, 9; 37.2). The formula is limited to the priestly Primeval History and ancestral narratives, while the history of the people of Israel is apparently part of the genealogy of Jacob, who receives the name Israel in the progression of the narrative.

In addition to the Toledot formula, structure is also provided by an overlapping system of cross-references. These cross-references link the central theological texts, thereby forming the message of the work as a whole. The beginning point for this interpretative and structuring framework is in many ways the *Priestly Primeval History.* After the creation of humanity God/Elohim blesses the human beings and sets them up as his representatives to rule over the earth and its creatures (Gen. 1). After the flood God/Elohim blesses the human beings again and sets up a → *covenant* with them (Gen. 9). The motif of blessing and covenant are again taken up and developed in connection with Abram/Abraham and his descendants: God/Elohim[3] reveals himself to Abraham as *ʾēl šadday* ('Almighty') and sets up a covenant with him and with his descendents. Abraham will become the father of many nations, but will especially become the founding ancestor of the nation of Israel to whom the covenant commitment and promise of divine presence and gift of land apply (Gen. 17). It is this covenant that God/Elohim remembers when Israel is oppressed in Egypt (Exod. 2.24). Because of this covenant God reveals himself to Moses under the name Yhwh thereby repeating the covenant promise made to Abraham and his descendants (Exod. 6.2-8). The promise of the covenant and the divine presence – as well as the work as a whole – find their completion in Yhwh's entrance into the sanctuary on Sinai in the midst of his entire people (Exod. 25.8; 29.45-46; 40.34). While the connections between covenant and blessing in the individual stages of the narrative already make clear how creation and history stand together in a thoughtful entirety, the two poles of the priestly portrayal – creation and temple – are set in relation so that the creation report and the beginning of the Sinai revelation appear as reciprocal events. God's six days of speaking and seventh day of silence in creation (Gen. 1.1–2.3) contrast the six days of silence followed by God's speaking on the seventh day of the Sinai revelation (Exod. 24.15b–25.1).

the 'creation accounts' of Gen. 1.1–2.3 and Gen. 2.4b–3.24. The occurrence in Num. 3.1 is also secondary.

3. P's only use of Yhwh before Exod. 6.2 is in Gen. 17.1. This use of the divine name is either redactional or (more likely) a signal from P to the reader that Yhwh (and no other deity) appeared to Abraham as *ʾēl šadday*.

## 7.1.2 Textual Issues and Major Issues in the History of Critical Interpretation

The determination of texts generally belonging to P – disregarding numerous debated details – has remained more or less undebated since Theodor Nöldeke (1836–1930).[4] This level of consensus, which is quite rare in modern scholarship, rests primarily on the peculiarity of the Priestly texts with regard to their verbal characteristics and content, which make it possible to identify them in their present context. When compared with the parallel non-priestly narrative texts, P's treatments are sparser, leaving out those details that give the stories their colour and avoiding ambiguity in characterizations. P instead employs stereotypes, emphasizing theological explanation over narrative buildup. Cultic, chronological and genealogical details are listed with great care. While P's rhetorical character may seem pedantic and uncreative, it is not only the Priestly creation report in Gen. 1 that conveys 'the aesthetic impression of controlled power and lapidary immensity' (Gerhard von Rad). P's style is not beneath that of the other authors of the Pentateuch, but instead just rather different. The care with which P portrays the divine order through structural elements in nature and history are unmistakable. This includes the exact correspondence between command and execution of divine orders, which allows for the recognition of a nearly sacramental theology of language.

The broad consensus concerning the basic determination of Priestly texts is matched by disagreement in present scholarship with regard to understanding the composition-historical differences within P. As a general rule: (1) if P is viewed as an independent source text, then the original textual layer ($P^g$) is generally differentiated from later additions to this still independent source text ($P^s$) and later post-priestly additions. These post-priestly additions either come after the combination of P with the non-priestly layers of the Pentateuch or as part of this combination ($R^P$). On the other hand, (2) if P is viewed as a redactional layer rather than an independent source, then the evidence is understood differently. In this case there is no need for assuming a redactional layer $R^P$, and the texts that – according to model (1) – might be seen as connecting P with the non-priestly texts are counted as part of the basic layer of P-texts. Both positions generally agree that P does not stem from one hand. Debated is the identification of the parties involved, which in turn affects the appraisal of the literary character and historical

4. T. Nöldeke, 'Die sogenannte Grundschrift des Pentateuchs', in *Untersuchungen zur Kritik des Alten Testaments* (Kiel: Schwers, 1869), 1–144.

and sociological location of P: there are Priestly texts that are comprehensible when completely independent from their non-priestly parallels and whose individual profile can first be clarified when they are read on their own. Such texts include the Priestly portions of the Primeval History and the Priestly complex of the call of Moses, the plagues, and the exodus. If the original inventory of P is limited to such texts, then P can easily be understood as an independent stand-alone source. However, there are also Priestly texts that are closely bound to their non-priestly context and that cannot be understood easily without this context. If these texts also belong to the core of the Priestly tradition, then P should be seen as a redactional layer. The questions of P's end and its socio-historical location and also the question of its original status as either source document or redactional layer are inseparably related to the delimitation of P's core texts from its later additions. The larger the basic core and the more numerous the Priestly texts alluding to late non-priestly texts, the later P must be dated in the postexilic period (→ *exile*).

## 7.1.3 Origins of the Priestly Texts of the Pentateuch

### *7.1.3.1 An Originally Independent Source Document or a Redactional Layer?*

Discernment regarding P's original literary character begins by setting aside the texts that were clearly written to fit in the context of the surrounding non-priestly texts, yet whose affiliation with $P^g$ is debated. Arguments against the theory that P was originally an independent source document focus especially on those observations that seem to prove that the supposed source document was never complete and is only sensible when brought into connection with non-priestly texts: (1.) The story line of $P^g$ incorporates texts with rather different narrative techniques. While individual passages such as the creation story (Gen. 1.1–2.3), the → *covenant with Abraham* (Gen. 17), the call of Moses (Exod. 2.23-25; 6.2-8), and the plagues (Exod. 7–9*) are made of sweeping narratives and speeches, the Priestly sections dealing with the rest of the ancestors are reduced to mere fragmentary notices. (2.) The absence of a Priestly introduction of Moses, who is the most important character, is striking. (3.) Finally, some theologically important themes found in the non-priestly traditions have no parallel in P, such as the narratives of the fall and the covenant at Sinai.

These observations do not all carry the same weight. Essentially they establish that P both narrates in manners and possesses narratives that are different from the non-priestly texts. This is especially the case for the ancestral narratives for which P limits detailed development to the covenant ceremony with Abraham, while typically handling the rest in genealogies. The fact that P chooses to tell the plagues in great detail can be sufficiently explained by the notion that P claims Yhwh's total superiority over history, which completely contradicts normal human experience of historical reality. The absence of an introduction of Moses may instead be explained through the redaction history: in the redactional connection with the dramatic portrayal of Moses' beginnings according to the non-priestly exodus narrative there was no space for the likely short genealogical notice about Moses in P. For this reason it was simply left out. The absence of the narratives of the fall and the Sinai covenant ceremony should not be held against P. The transition from the good creation to the flood is sufficiently depicted through the ongoing reduction of the life spans of the generations between Adam and Noah as a result of increasing distance from God and the observation of the complete depravity of all flesh (Gen. 6.12). The Sinai covenant has no place in P because the foundational relationship with God was put in place by the covenant with Abraham and is completed by Yhwh's glory (Heb. *kābôd*) entering into the sanctuary, Yhwh's presence with Israel, and the initiation of the sacrificial cult (cf. Exod. 29).

In addition to the fact that the objections to the theory of an originally independent P source document are not persuasive, there are also important arguments that support the theory of its original independence. (1.) The compositional shape and the theology of a number of Priestly texts can only be recognized when they are separated from their current context in the midst of non-priestly texts. This is the case for the call of Moses (Exod. 2.23-35; 6.2-8) and the five-part plague cycle that – when read sequentially – demonstrates an intended logic of escalation. This escalation is no longer visible when the individual scenes are pulled apart as they are in their present context. (2.) The ongoing intertwining of the non-priestly and Priestly passages in the narratives of the flood and the crossing of the sea (Gen. 6–9; Exod. 14) cannot be explained by the theory of P as a redactional stratum. The Priestly portions offer a complete narrative in and of themselves, and no editor would have created the tensions of content that can be found especially in rather marginal details and that exhibit no redactional purpose. This evidence can only be explained as the combination of previously independent texts. (3.) The same is the case for the juxtaposition of texts that deal with the same topic but contradict each other massively. Illustrative of this aspect is the above comparison between the Priestly creation report and the non-priestly paradise narrative (Ch. 7.3). (4.) Even relatively smooth text complexes like the call of Moses reveal that P was first combined with its non-priestly context through a redaction. The Priestly version's introduction (Exod. 2.23-25) now functions as the introduction to the whole complex, and its climax (Exod. 6.2-8) can be understood in the present context as an affirmation of the non-priestly parallel (Exod. 3–4). It has therefore been placed after the intensification of the slave labour and Moses' complaint (Exod. 5.1–6.1) as God's reaction. Even though a coherent narrative results, it is quite conspicuous that the supposed affirmation of Moses' call never refers to the earlier parallel.

Regardless of whether P was originally a source text or a Priestly redaction, which first formulated its traditions independently and then combined them with the received non-priestly text (Blum, cf. Ch. 5.2.2), the following can be said: It is beyond doubt that P was familiar with the older traditions that have in part been passed on in the non-priestly material of the Pentateuch and that P reacted (critically) to these texts.

### *7.1.3.2 The Length and Ending of P*

While there is no debate about the beginning of P as Gen. 1.1–2.3, the question of P's original ending is quite controversial. P's end has generally been seen in Deut. 34.1aα, 7-9 so that P reached from the creation of the world until the death of Moses and concluded with a view of the land. However, more recent scholarship has developed sound objections to this position: Deut. 34* is not particularly well connected with the overall context of P, and especially allusions to the beginning of the Primeval History are lacking. The language of Deut. 34* is not genuinely Priestly but instead is influenced equally by P and Deut.–Dtr language (→ Deuteronomism), a feature typical for the final redaction(s) of the Pentateuch.[5] The (partial) verses attributed to P in Deut. 34 never speak of Moses' death; instead they reveal a reaction to the events portrayed in the non-priestly content of the chapter. Also unlikely is the earlier theory that saw P reaching into the book of Joshua. It is less than convincing to interpret linguistic correspondences between Gen. 1.28 and Josh. 18.1; 19.51 on the premise that of all the announcements made in Gen. 1.28 the possession of the land is the only one yet to be fulfilled. The possession of the earth by humanity mentioned in Gen. 1.28 is something quite different than the occupation of the land by the Israelites. Furthermore, if Deut. 34* is bracketed out, then there are no certain textual connections between Josh. and $P^g$ in the → Tetrateuch. As is the case in Deut. 34*, it is more likely that later redactions in Josh. have mixed Dtr and Priestly language.

5. Cf. L. Perlitt, 'Priesterschrift im Deuteronomium?' in *Deuteronomium-Studien* (FAT 8; Tübingen: Mohr Siebeck, 1994): 123–34.

The differentiation between $P^g$ and later additions can be pursued reasonably only as far as the Sinai pericope. This pericope suggests itself as P's original ending for the following reasons: the construction of the sanctuary at Sinai and Yhwh's entrance into the sanctuary are clearly the climax and goal of the Priestly narrative as shown through the cross references (see above Ch. 7.1.1). Therefore the originally independent P likely ended with Exod. 40.16-17, 33b, 34 ($P^g$) and was then extended step by step to Lev. 9 and then 26 ($P^s$), while various religious-legal and cultic material was also incorporated (Exod. 30–31; 35–39; 40*; Lev. 1–16; 17–26). The Priestly passages in the following books all presume the combination with non-priestly texts ($R^P$).

### *7.1.3.3 Dating P*

Regardless of the fact that P reckons with rituals and approaches to ritual that have their roots in the cult of the First Temple, there is no doubt that it should be given a late exilic-early postexilic date (→ *exile*). Knowing the versions of the Primeval History, the ancestor narrative, and the exodus narrative that are non-priestly as well as pre-priestly, P presents its own account as a coherent whole. Furthermore, P assumes the stipulation of late pre-exilic Deuteronomy to only worship Yhwh at one chosen cultic location. This stipulation is the unquestioned backdrop to the grandiose story of the sanctuary that was established as early as the wilderness wandering. Also P represents a thoroughgoing → *monotheism*, which appears outside P first in the Deutero-Isaian texts of the book of Isaiah – but with different accentuation (Ch. 9B). P also displays a number of linguistic and thematic connections with Deuteronomism and with 'Deutero-Isaiah', as well as with the second great exilic prophet, Ezekiel. The → *universalism* of the Priestly Primeval History mirrors the intellectual and political circumstances of the Achaemenid Empire (Ch. 4.3). Finally, the thematic connection between the Priestly provisions for the building of the → *tabernacle* at Sinai and the Second Temple, which was dedicated in 515 BCE as the replacement building for the 'Solomonic' temple destroyed by Nebuchadnezzar in 587/6 BCE, are also important for the dating of P. However, the equally → *aetiological* and programmatic character of the tabernacle makes the relative historical placement of the Priestly account of the building difficult. It is possible that the stipulations for building the tabernacle and therefore P as a whole are meant to be read as a 'critical and utopian' contribution for the as yet unfinished temple or instead as a founding legend for the Jerusalem temple and its cultic community that was re-established in 515 BCE. The latter is more probable, but in either case the author is to be found in priestly circles.

### 7.1.4 The Theology of the Priestly Document

The Priestly document is the first and only continuous source document of the → *Pentateuch.* Its salvation-historical portrayal extends from creation until the installation of the cult and Yhwh's entrance into the → *tabernacle*, the archetype of the Second Temple. P includes an → *aetiology* of the Second Temple and of postexilic Israel from a universal perspective.

P arranges the salvation history of the Primeval History, ancestral stories, and exodus narrative into three sequential epochs, the first of which extends from the creation until the flood. The second epoch begins with the Noachic covenant (Gen. 9) and uses genealogical lists to depict the dispersal of the descendants of Noah, from whom the Terah-Abraham line is separated out. The third epoch begins with the Abrahamic covenant (Gen. 17) and in the first edition of P ($P^g$) extends as far as the entrance of Yhwh's glory (Heb. *kābôd*) into the tabernacle (Exod. 40.16-17, 33b, 34). A basic three-part partitioning is also recognizable in the narrative of the revelation of the divine name: after the use of the term *Elohim* 'God' from the beginning until the time of the descendants of Noah, then *ʾel šadday* is revealed to the ancestors, and finally there is the revelation of the name Yhwh (Exod. 6.2-3). Creation and Sinai form the frame around the salvation history comprised of the above structure, as the allusion to the temporal structure of the creation into six days and one day (Gen. 1.1–2.3) in the beginning of the Sinai revelation (Exod. 24.15b–25.1) shows. The frame and inner structure of the salvation history clearly set the construction of the sanctuary by the people of God – the Israelites chosen through the covenant with Abraham and liberated by the exodus – as the goal of creation. More precisely, creation reaches its purpose with the atoning cult (→ *atonement*) and the presence of Yhwh in his sanctuary. In the period between creation and the Sinai revelation instructions are given for Jewish life in the midst of a pagan environment, including the permission to slaughter along with the basic prohibition against eating blood (Gen. 9), the command to circumcise everything male (Gen. 17), and the → *Passover* stipulations (Exod. 12). Israel is also made aware of the holiness of the Sabbath at this time (Exod. 16: $P^S$), even though the Sabbath command first appears in the context of the Sinai revelation (Exod. 31.12-17; $P^S$).

The salvation history is furthered by Yhwh's pre-planned action, which is apparent in both the ordering of the world and the structuring of history. Through these Yhwh reveals himself as lord of creation and of history. Universalism and the omnipotence of the creation God are uncontested presuppositions of the Priestly creation report: the transcendent God created the cosmos, nature, and humanity (Gen. 1). The notion of the universality of God corresponds to the proposition of the unconditional election of Abraham and his descendants, for whom alone the covenant promises are intended (Gen. 17). The omnipotence of God appears in the course of history especially when foreign rulers seemingly attempt to set themselves against the will of Yhwh. Thus the hardening of Pharaoh's heart demonstrates Yhwh's supremacy, in that the antagonists of Israel and its God are made to obey unwillingly (Exod. 7–14*). P's theology amounts to a pure theology of grace, for it is Yhwh himself who establishes the election of Israel – an election that is unconditional and irreversible, even in the face of massive human guilt. At the same time, amidst the bitter experiences of the exilic and postexilic period it proclaims Yhwh as the universal God, which works as a protest against the normative powers of the actual course of history.

From the many theological statements that P makes in passing and that nevertheless form part of a coherent whole, brief mention should be made of its conception of humans as the image of God, the *imago dei* (Gen. 1.26-27), and commissioning of humanity to dominion, the *dominium terrae* (Gen. 1.28).[6] They are rooted in the royal ideology of the ancient Near East, yet now the right and power to good and just dominion is extended and universalized to all humanity. Just as in provinces that he did not personally visit the human sovereign set up an image of himself as a sign of his dominion, so also humanity is set up as the image of God on the earth as a sign of God's sovereignty. Humanity is the representative of God and is called, sort of like a cultic image of God, to protect and carry out God's authority on earth.

## 7.1.5 Notes on the History of Reception

The reception of the Old Testament rarely takes the textual developments and corresponding source or redactional differentiations into consideration. As a result these reception-historical notes are limited to texts in which the Priestly content is generally unconnected to non-priestly texts. Passages that connect the Priestly texts with non-priestly material into a new portrait of the whole (flood, exodus narrative, Israel's stay at Sinai) or passages that have only minimal Priestly portions (ancestor and Joseph stories) will instead be considered in the 'Notes on

6. Cf. B. Janowski, 'Die lebendige Statue Gottes', in *Gott und Mensch im Dialog* (BZAW 345/1; ed. M. Witte; Berlin/New York: de Gruyter, 2004), 183–214; H.-P. Mathys, ed., *Ebenbild Gottes – Herrscher über die Welt: Studien zu Würde und Auftrag des Menschen* (Biblisch-theologische Studien 33; Neukirchen-Vluyn: Neukirchener, 1998).

the History of Reception of the Non-Priestly texts'. The history of reception of the legal texts within the Priestly document can be found in the preceding chapter (Ch. 6). As a whole the Priestly Document has been influential in that it was the first to combine the Primeval History, ancestor narratives, and exodus story into one salvation-historical scheme. The Great Historical Opus of Genesis to 2 Kings and with it the biblical picture of the history of 'Israel' follow the scheme of the Priestly Document, whose concept – once conceived – was taken to be true to the historical events and to be the implicit theological meaning of all earlier concepts.

The reception history of the Priestly texts reveals a particular focus on the creation account in Gen. 1. Gen. 1 has influenced the understanding of the origin of the world up to modern history. The description of the previous state of the world as '*Tohuwabohu*' is proverbial. In addition the importance of the chapter for → *anthropology* can hardly be overestimated. The teaching that humans are in the image of God (*imago dei*), namely that humans in their physical and spiritual constitution are placed between the visible and invisible creation, appeals first and foremost to Gen. 1.26-27. The mandate of human dominion (*dominium terrae*) formulated in Gen. 1.28 has worked considerably to 'demystify' the world and thereby provided an essential presupposition for the nature of human interaction with the world. As mentioned earlier, the notion of humans being made in the image of God and the mandate of human dominion originate from ancient Near Eastern royal ideology according to which the king was the representative of the deity. Gen. 1 reformulates this notion into a foundational statement about human nature. Both concepts, *imago dei* and *dominium terrae*, thereby gain emancipatory meaning, which is why biblical justifications of human rights usually refer to Gen. 1. Against the accusation that biblical 'demystification' of the world has promoted environmental destruction, increasing reference is made to the fact that P does not put violence in the forefront of its notion of dominion, but rather just and religiously limited authority as well as caring on the part of the royal humans.[7] The dogmatic teaching of the creation out of nothing (*creatio ex nihilo*), in which the unconditionality of the divine action in creation is emphasized, also refers to Gen. 1. Contrary to a long history of interpretation, however,

7. Cf. C. Amery, *Das Ende der Vorsehung: Die gnadenlosen Folgen des Christentums* (Reinbek: Rowohlt, 1972); K. Koch, 'Gestaltet die Erde, doch hegt das Leben! Einige Klarstellungen zum dominium terrae', in *Wenn nicht jetzt, wann dann?* (ed. H.-G. Geyer *et al*; Neukirchen-Vluyn: Neukirchener, 1983), 53–68; B. Janowski, 'Herrschaft über die Tiere: Gen 1,26–28 und die Semantik von רדה', in *Biblische Theologie und gesellschaftlicher Wandel* (ed. G. Braulik; Freiburg: Herder, 1993), 183–98.

this position originates from → *Hellenistic* thought and not from Gen. 1.1-2. At best biblical evidence for this teaching can be found in 2 Macc. 7.28.

In painting, the six-day work of creation is usually divided into several scenes, or else one specific day of creation is portrayed, as in Hieronymos Bosch's 'The World on the Third Day of Creation' (1503/04) or Tintoretto's 'The Creation of the Animals' (ca. 1550). The creative acts of God are usually expressed through the eye or hand of God. At times, as in 'The Origin of the World' (1824) by William Blake, God is portrayed as an architect determining the dimensions of the world with a compass. The first two parts of Joseph Haydn's oratorio 'The Creation' (1798) are dedicated to the six days of creation, with the 'representation of chaos' appearing in the place of the traditional overture. The comical and satirical adaptation in the seven-minute animation film 'The Creation' (1994) by Thomas Meyer-Hermann provides an unusual ending. From the Priestly Primeval History the rainbow (the covenantal sign after the flood; Gen. 9) has enjoyed an unbroken and frequent reception as a result of its rich symbolic potential. In addition to 'biblical' portrayals such as the 'Viennese Genesis' (6th cent. CE) and the pen-and-ink drawing 'Noah with the Rainbow' by Marc Chagall (1956), the rainbow is especially prominent as a sign for peace and environmental movements.

# 7.2 Deuteronomy

Bibliography see Ch. 5 and Ch. 5.2. Further: B. M. Levinson, *Deuteronomy and the Hermeneutics of Legal Innovation*. Oxford: Oxford University Press, 1997; N. Lohfink, *Studien zum Deuteronomium und zur deuteronomistischen Literatur 1–5*. SBAB 8, 12, 30, 31, 38. Stuttgart: Katholisches Bibelwerk, 1990, 1991, 1995, 2000, 2005; E. Otto, *Gottes Recht als Menschenrecht: Rechts- und literarhistorische Studien zum Deuteronomium*. Beihefte zur Zeitschrift für altorientalische und biblische Rechtsgeschichte 2. Wiesbaden: Harrassowiz, 2002; L. Perlitt, *Deuteronomium-Studien*. FAT 8. Tübingen: Mohr-Siebeck, 1994; A. Rofé, *Deuteronomy, Issues and Interpretation*. OTS. London: T&T Clark, 2002; T. Veijola, 'Deuteronomismusforschung zwischen Tradition und Innovation', *TRu* 67 (2002): 273–327, 391–424.

## 7.2.1 Biblical Context

According to the narrative of the outside 'frame' chapters, Deuteronomy deals with the events on the day of Moses' death in the land of Moab, east of the Jordan, and thus at the entrance to the promised land. A number of speeches and the Deuteronomy law corpus (Deut. 12–26) are bound together by this short narrative frame, which in their current form are to be read as *one* large farewell speech delivered by Moses. Moses' last day comes in the fortieth year after the exodus and on the evening before the crossing of the Jordan and the conquest of the land by the Israelites. It therefore represents a deeply symbolic date, marking an epochal change within the historical narrative presented in the books Genesis–2 Kings: the Moses narrative and the story of Israel outside the land come to an end and are followed by the 'post-Mosaic period' and 'the time in the land'.

Through its stylization as the farewell speech of Moses on the day of his death, Deuteronomy claims the special dignity of being Moses' testament. It is intended to be read as the final valid proclamation and interpretation of the will of God as mediated by Moses, which means nothing other than that Deuteronomy should function as the recorded standard of Torah for all subsequent disclosures of the will of God. The implementation of this claim is shown by the → *Dtr* portrayal of history in the books of Joshua–2 Kings. The First Commandment of Deuteronomy, the command to worship Yhwh alone and to love God (Deut. 5.7; 6.4-5), as well as the Foundational Command of Deuteronomy, the limitation of the Yhwh cult to one legitimate cultic location (Deut. 12), function in these books as the criteria determining whether Israel does – as it says – 'what is right in the eyes of Yhwh', or whether Israel has fallen away from Yhwh.

## Structure of the Book of Deuteronomy

| Moses' Speech in Deut. 1–30 | | | |
|---|---|---|---|
| 1.1-5 | Book Heading | | |
| 1.6–4.43 | First Speech. Look Back at the 40-Year Journey from Horeb to Moab in chs. 1–3 and Parenesis Concerning the Ban on Images in 4.1-40 [4.41-43: Asylum Cities in the Transjordan] | | |
| 4.44, 45-49 | Superscription and Introduction to the Second Speech | | |
| 5.1–11.32 | Second Speech: Decalogue in ch. 5; *Šĕma' yiśrā'ēl* and Parenesis Regarding the First Commandment in chs. 6–11 | | |
| 12.1 | Superscription to the Law Corpus | | |
| 12.1–26.15 | Law Corpus | | |
| | | 12.1–16.17 | Cult Centralization and Yhwh's Privilegrecht; Social Ordinances |
| | | 16.18–18.22 | So-Called Laws of Officials (Judges, Kings, Priests, Prophets) |
| | | 19.1–26.15 | Legal, Social and Taboo Ordinances with a Cultic Appendix in 26.1-15 (Including the 'Short Historical Creed' [vv. 5-9]) |

| | |
|---|---|
| 26.16-19 | Transition to the Summary Parenesis |
| 27–30 | Summary Parenesis with Blessings and Curses in ch. 28; Moab Covenant in ch. 29 (Superscription or Summary Statement in 28.69) |
| Concluding Frame of the Pentateuch/the Torah in Deut. 31–34 | |
| 31–34 | The Appointment of Joshua in ch. 31; Song of Moses in ch. 32; Blessing of Moses in ch. 33; Death of Moses in ch. 34. |

The farewell address is a complicated tapestry and comprises Deut. 1–30 (exceptions: the setting aside of cities of asylum in the Transjordan in Deut. 4.41-43, the instructions of Moses, the elders of Israel, and the Levitical priests in Deut. 27.1-10). The juxtaposition of predominantly legal texts in Deut. 12–26 and → *parenetic* frame chapters in Deut. 1–11 and 27–30 is striking. In addition, the speech is divided into different sections by a number of superscriptions (Deut. 1.1-5; 4.44, 45; 6.1; 12.1; 28.69; cf. 33.1).

In the first speech section Moses looks back over the events that have taken place since breaking camp at Horeb, which is the Deuteronomic-Dtr tradition's name for Sinai (Deut. 1–3). The historical review, whose motifs are also the subject matter in the books of Exodus and Numbers, leads to an exhortation concerning the ban on images in the present form of the text (Deut. 4.1-40). The centre of the subsequent section is the admonition to keep the Deuteronomic First Commandment, which is the double command concerning exclusive Yhwh worship and love of God (Deut. 5–11). The First Commandment begins the → *Decalogue* in Deut. 5, and is the subject matter of the *Šĕma῾ yiśrā῾ēl* in its present form.

The *Šĕma' yiśrā'ēl* in Deut. 6.4, together with the Decalogue, is surely the most well known and has definitely been the most important text of Deuteronomy. in the history of interpretation. In the present form of the text it follows the disclosure of the Decalogue and is intended to be read in the spirit of the 1st Commandment as Israel's profession to the exclusivity of Yhwh: 'Hear O Israel: Yhwh is our God, Yhwh alone!' This translation is problematic, but its understanding of the text has become prevalent already in the OT (Zech. 14.9) and NT (Mk 12.28-34). It does not, however, likely express the original intention of the *Šĕma' yiśrā'ēl*. Before the secondary addition of the Decalogue and the command to love God in Deut. 6.5 ('You shall love Yhwh your God with all your heart, and with all your soul, and with all your might') the *Šĕma' yiśrā'ēl* was the introduction to the Deuteronomic Law. In the context of the demand for centralization (→ *cult centralization*) it was directed against the existence of various local and national manifestations of Yhwh – a fact

⇨

documented by inscriptions (Ch. 4.2.2.3 'The Rise of Yhwh'). These manifestations shaped the competition between the two states Israel and Judah, who often went to battle against each other under the protection and with the assistance of 'their' Yhwh. There should now only be one Yhwh, namely the one residing in the chosen place. The *Šěma' yiśrā'ēl* should therefore be translated: 'Hear O Israel, Yhwh is our God, Yhwh is one!' This → *mono-yahwism* does not serve as a foundation for the demand for cult centralization. Nevertheless, Mono-Yahwism and cult centralization can be seen as interrelated demands. It was only in the course of its actual enforcement and its connection with the Decalogue and law of love for God that the Mono-Yahwistic proclamation developed further into a demand for exclusivity.

In present day Judaism the *Šěma' yiśrā'ēl* is recited as part of the daily morning and evening prayers. Furthermore, the section Deut. 6.4-9 is used in the custom of Tefillin and Mezuzot. Tefillin are prayer bands worn on the forehead and arm with small capsules for parchment rolls containing biblical texts. Mezuzot are capsules hanging on the right doorpost of apartments and houses that also contain a parchment roll inscribed with biblical texts and that are attributed → *apotropaic* powers. The text of modern Tefillin comes from Exod. 13.1-10, 11-16; Deut. 6.4-9; 11.13-21, while that of Mezuzot comes from Deut. 6.4-9; 11.13-21. This textual grouping became binding around 100 CE. Before this point there was greater diversity. For the time of Deuteronomy one can postulate that there were arm and headbands, amulets, and small inscriptions. If the instructions in Deut. 6.8-9 date from the pre-exilic beginnings of Deut., then it would be conceivable that they were originally meant as instructions for the followers of Deuteronomic theology, who – being a marginal minority at first – were prompted to proclaim their views publicly.

T. Veijola, 'Das Bekenntnis Israels: Beobachtungen zur Geschichte und Theologie von Dtn. 6.4-9', *TZ* 48 (1992): 369–81 (according to Veijola it was originally a → *monolatric* text).

Also, the First Commandment is the focus of the extensive review of the golden calf episode, which represents the archetype of apostasy from Yhwh (Deut. 9–12). After the wide-reaching exhortation regarding the First Commandment and the subsequent superscription comes the law corpus itself (Deut. 12–26). Its structure can be understood as follows: Deut. 12.1–16.17 contains the → *Privilegrecht* of Yhwh and the social laws. At their head is the Foundational Command of Deuteronomy, exclusive worship of Yhwh at the place that Yhwh chooses. Deut. 16.18–18.22 is often described as the draft constitution of Deuteronomy since it deals with a collection of laws and ordinances concerning officers as diverse as the judge, the king, or priests and prophets. Deut. 19.1–26.15 by and large offers legal, social, and taboo ordinances concluded by an appendix dealing with sanctuary contributions. The subsequent conclusion focuses on the promises of blessing and threats of curses (Deut. 27–30): blessings for those that follow the laws and curses for those who act contrary to them.

The Song of Moses (Deut. 32) and the Blessing of Moses (Deut. 33) fall somewhat outside the notion of the farewell speech, while the dedication of Joshua as Moses' successor and the death of Moses (Deut. 34) pick back up the theme of the frame story.

### 7.2.2 Textual Issues and Major Issues in the History of Critical Interpretation

Deuteronomy reveals a number of idiosyncrasies that set it apart from the other books and textual complexes of the Pentateuch as an entity that is *sui generis:* (1.) Deuteronomy is only loosely connected with the Pentateuchal narrative through its frame story; (2.) it is almost completely formulated as the farewell address of Moses; (3.) it has a peculiar verbal and theological diction; (4.) it evinces connections in its form and content to ancient Near Eastern treaties. The demands of Deuteronomy correspond to cult reform measures taken – according to the portrayal of 2 Kgs 22–23 – by King Josiah in 622 BCE following the discovery of a book in the temple (→ *Josiah's reform*). Early on in the history of interpretation this correspondency led to the identification of this book with Deuteronomy. The well-grounded thesis that Deuteronomy is hardly older than the situation in which it plays its first historical role goes back to Wilhelm Martin Leberecht de Wette (1780–1849). While the exact determination of the limits of this Josianic book (*Ur-Deuteronomion*) has been debated ever since within scholarship, the connection of Deuteronomy with this historical location provided an essential point of reference for the historical-critical analysis of the Pentateuch and the Former Prophets. Difficulties remain in the details and especially in the compositional layers of the book, its literary connections with other texts, and the historicity of the Josianic reform pictured in 2 Kgs 22–23.

The signs of a multi-levelled compositional history of Deuteronomy are especially conspicuous in Moses' addresses to the Israelites. Next to sections where Moses almost exclusively uses the 2nd person singular appear sections which employ 2nd person plural, and at times the change from one to the other takes place within a text or sentence more than once. Besides, an explication is needed for the varying uses and uneven scattering of stereotypical expressions, as well as for the observation that some passages assume the frame story of a Mosaic farewell address on the evening before the → *conquest* while others do not seem aware of this situation or else seem to have this perspective added later.

This is only to name the source-critical and redaction-critical findings typical of Deuteronomy. In addition there are numerous disruptions to the verbal and thematic coherence. Apart from these observations within the book itself there are thematic congruities and differences with the Sinai pericope and the legal texts attached to it, which indicate a complex composition-historical relationship between Deuteronomy and these texts. While at first scholars attempted to explain these findings through the theory of parallel editions of Deuteronomy and their later conflation (J. Wellhausen),[8] several theories currently compete with one another: the theory of the joining of larger blocks (G. Braulik; N. Lohfink),[9] that of a continual editing of a foundational text (L. Perlitt; T. Veijola),[10] as well as a mediating model (E. Otto).[11] Nearly all models agree in that they assume pre-Deuteronomic traditions, a larger inventory of genuine Deuteronomic texts, and a more or less multi-layered and extensive Dtr redaction.

## Excursus: Deuteronomism

The attributions of 'Deuteronomism' or 'Deuteronomistic' (Dtr) are among the most used terms in Old Testament exegesis. There is, however, lack of clarity about what they mean precisely. Generally speaking, those concepts and expressions are referred to as Dtr that have evolved under the influence of Deuteronomy and its verbal and intellectual world. This is especially the case for the Dtr literature narrowly defined, which includes the frame and current context of Deuteronomy, the Dtr edited historical books Joshua–2 Kings, as well as the corresponding revisions in the book of Jeremiah. In addition there is Dtr editing in the → *Tetrateuch,* which becomes more widespread beginning with the book of Exodus, as well as in most of the remaining prophetic books and several Psalms.

8. J. Wellhausen, *Die Composition des Hexateuchs und der historischen Bücher des Alten Testaments* (3rd ed. Berlin: Reimer, 1899) 186–208, 353–63

9. G. Braulik (NEchtB 15; Würzburg: Echter, 1986); idem (NEchtB 28; Würzburg: Echter, 1992); N. Lohfink, 'Die Sicherung der Wirksamkeit des Gotteswortes durch das Prinzip der Schriftlichkeit der Tora und durch das Prinzip der Gewaltenteilung nach den Ämtergesetzen des Buches Deuteronomium (Dt 16,18–18,22)', in *Studien I*, 305–53; idem, 'Kerygmata des Deuteronomistischen Geschichtswerkes', in *Studien II*, 125–42.

10. L. Perlitt, Dtn-Studien; M. Rose (ZBK 5; Zurich, Theologischer Verlag, 1994); T. Veijola (ATD 8/1; Göttingen: Vandenhoeck & Ruprecht, 2004); idem, 'Bundestheologische Redaktion im Deuteronomium (1996)', in *Moses Erben: Studien zum Dekalog, zum Deuteronomiusmus und zum Schriftgelehrtentum* (BWANT 149; Stuttgart: Kohlhammer, 2000), 153–75.

11. E. Otto, *Das Deuteronomium: Politische Theologie und Rechtsreform in Juda und Assyrien* (BZAW 284; Berlin/New York: de Gruyter, 1999).

The determination of Dtr passages within Deuteronomy. clearly reveals the vagueness of the concept of Dtr. Texts *within* Deut. cannot really be said to have come *from* Deuteronomy. In this case Dtr is used to distinguish within Deuteronomy a 'Deuteronomic' (Dtn) original layer of text from other 'Dtr' layers that integrate Deuteronomy into a larger context, namely the Dtr historiography in the books Deuteronomy–2 Kings (or Exodus–2 Kings) – or that already assume this integration. Furthermore, Dtr literature shares certain peculiarities in language and content that cannot be traced back to Deuteronomy itself. Nevertheless they are referred to as characteristics of Dtr language and concepts. Thus phenomena can be characterized as Dtr although they do not yet appear in Deuteronomy itself. Finally, the term can also be used sociologically for the groups who pass on the Dtr texts, redactions and literary works. Here one speaks of Deuteronomists, Dtr editors, a Dtr school or a Dtr movement.

It is obvious that the identification of Dtr language and Dtr concepts as described above has led to a very broad understanding of the term 'Dtr'. In addition one must note the temporal reach of the texts characterized as Dtr. Yet the broader a historical-critical category is defined, the less powerful its explanations become. For this reason different stages and forms are distinguished within Deuteronomism itself, as in the models of the formation of the → *DtrH*. Furthermore, it is becoming increasingly accepted that a number of texts that have been named Dtr originated at a time in the Old Testament period when Dtr language and perspectives had already become general knowledge, and therefore can no longer be traced back to a sociologically limited group of Dtr authors or editors.

📖 M. Weinfeld, *Deuteronomy and the Deuteronomic School*. Oxford: Clarendon, 1972, 320–65 (with a good collation of Dtn-Dtr phraseology); L. S. Schearing and S. L. McKenzie (eds), *Those Elusive Deuteronomists: The Phenomenon of Pan-Deuteronomism*. JSOTSup 268. Sheffield: Sheffield Academic Press, 1999.

Apart from the source-critical and redaction-critical issues of individual texts the historical placement of the recognized layers is considerably debated. This is the case even for the original inventory of Deuteronomy. The majority opinion in scholarship has concluded that the original layer had its beginnings towards the end of the monarchical period. However, an opposing thesis stating that Deuteronomy originated as an exilic model for the restitution of Israel for the time after the → *exile* has found supporters for almost 100 years.[12] This position profits from the historiographical difficulties connected to the assumption of a Josianic Reform.

12. G. Hölscher, 'Komposition und Ursprung des Deuteronomiums', *ZAW* 40 (1922): 161–255; more recently R. G. Kratz, *Die Kompostition der erzählenden Bücher des Alten Testaments: Grundwissen der Bibelkritik*. Göttinger: Vandenhoeck & Ruprecht, 2000 (ET *The Composition of the Narrative Books of the Old Testament*. Transl. by J. Bowden. London: T&T Clark, 2005)., 114–33.

The question regarding the historicity of the Josianic Reform reported in 2 Kgs 22–23 is both a source-critical and an archaeological problem. The evidence at first glance is rather sobering, which leads to the conclusion that the historical location of Deuteronomy should not be based primarily on its connections with 2 Kgs 22–23. The report in 2 Kgs 22–23 is clearly in a Dtr redacted form, which diminishes its historical value and raises the suspicion that it was created as a legend inspired by Deuteronomy itself to legitimate Deuteronomy's authority. Archaeological evidence for the individual reform measures have not been found, and evidence used earlier to support the reform has since received alternative interpretations (Ch. 4.2.2.4 'Josianic Cult Reform').

## 7.2.3 The Origins of Deuteronomy

Fundamental for analysis of Deuteronomy is the differentiation between the → *parenetic* frame chapters and the legislative core in Deut. 12–26. The thematic and composition-historical differences are already mentioned in the book itself where Moses keeps announcing the proclamation of the legal ordinances in the introductory parenesis and looks back over the proclamation in the concluding parenesis. The parenetic frame is therefore characterized within the book as prologue and epilogue to the law. Besides, in the parenesis the law is described as a repetition of the promulgation at Horeb, which indicates different origins for parenesis and law respectively. Yet even apart from all that the differences between the two are noticeable. Although still inviting the inner agreement of its target group the Deuteronomic Law in Deut. 12–26 features judicial terminology predominantly whereas parenetic aspects recede. Most notably, Moses is no longer explicitly mentioned as speaker in the law. While the frame and law are woven together in multiple ways, it is conspicuous that the connections between the law and frame chapters can generally be identified as later additions. Taking into account that the law can stand alone without the frame, while the frame, on the other hand, leans heavily on the law, one can conclude from the perspective of content and compositional history that the core of Deuteronomy is to be found in Deut. 12–26.

### *7.2.3.1 The Deuteronomic Law in Deut. 12–26 and Its Original Beginning in Deut. 4.45*; 5.1aα; 6.4*

The Deuteronomic Law itself is compositionally uneven in that the basic inventory can be contrasted with a multi-layered → *Dtr* redaction and even later supplements.

## The Prehistory and Aftermath of the Foundational Command of Cult Centralization in Deut 12

The editing process of the Deuteronomic Law can be shown best through the present text of the Foundational Command of cult centralization in Deut 12. Its stipulation, that the Yhwh cult should be limited to *one* cultic location is similarly elevated three times (vv. 5-6, 11, 14). Each is preceded by a negative ordinance decreeing that either the cult installations that the earlier residents of the land made for their gods shall be destroyed (vv. 2-3), or that the cultic practices followed before the possession of the land should be abandoned (vv. 8-10), or simply that sacrifice should not take place in just any place (v.13). In each case a command to enjoy the cultic offerings with one's entire household follows the centralization law (vv. 7, 12, 18b). One of the consequences of cult centralization is the permission for profane slaughter in the villages: to this point every slaughter had been a sacred act, so for practical reasons the concentration of the cult also demanded a redefinition of sacrifices. The allowance of profane sacrifice is mentioned twice (vv.15, 21); each time it is noted that the slaughtered animal's blood requires special treatment (vv.16, 23).

The evidence is clear. Within Deut. 12 three separate prescriptions can be identified: Deut. 12.2-7; 12.8-12, and 12.13-28, while a doubling occurs within the final section in vv. 15-19 and vv. 20-27. The corresponding conclusion of a multilevel compositional history of the chapter is supported by the *Numeruswechsel* (change of address between 2nd singular and 2nd plural) as well as the divergent references to the frame of the chapter: vv. 1-12 contain mostly plural forms and assume the Dtr conception of Deuteronomy as Moses' farewell address on the night before the conquest (cf. v.10). These verses are therefore of Dtr origin themselves. Since doubling is found also in vv.1-12 one may assume that there are two Dtr redactions (apart from the Dtr superscript in v.1). The older Dtr redaction includes vv. 8-12 and is concerned with connecting the law to the narrative frame. The latter Dtr redaction assumes this connection and is primarily concerned with Israel's separation from other peoples. This theme of vv. 2-7 is taken up in vv. 29-31, which belongs to the same redaction in spite of its singular forms. In the later Dtr additions the addressees can fluctuate between singular and plural according to context. The inventory of the oldest layer of the chapter is therefore to be found in vv. 13-28, even if later additions may be found here as well (vv.14b, 20-28).

The oldest textual layer of Deut. 12 focuses on the reformulation of the altar law in the older → *Covenant Code,* whose text is explicitly cited:

'Take care that you do not offer your burnt offerings *at any place* you happen to see. But only at the place that Yhwh will choose in one of your tribes – there you shall offer your burnt offerings' (Deut. 12.13-14b).

'You need make for me only an altar of earth and sacrifice on it your burnt offerings and your offerings of well-being, your sheep and your oxen; *in every place* where I cause my name to be remembered I will come to you and bless you' (Exod. 20.24).

While the altar law of the Covenant Code legitimizes various cult locations by mention of the name of Yhwh, to Deuteronomy the multiplicity of cult locations is the result

⇨

of arbitrary human choice. Therefore, the legitimizing relative clause of the Covenant Code is replaced by the centralization formula 'in the place that Yhwh will choose'.

B. M. Levinson, *Deuteronomy and the Hermeneutics of Legal Innovation*. Oxford: Oxford University Press, 1997.

The most important *criterion for identification of Dtr redactions* – besides the references to the frame chapters and their stylization of Deuteronomy as Moses' farewell address on the evening before the conquest – is the *Numeruswechsel*. The 2nd plural is secondary to the 2nd singular. However, not every singular passage belongs to the original text, since it has also been supplemented with singular additions. In the later Dtr redactions the *Numeruswechsel* functions almost as a stylistic tool.

A relatively safe *criterion for classification of the Deuteronomy original text inventory* is the *reception of the Covenant Code*. However, one must proceed with caution since the Covenant Code also contains Dtr additions, so in a few places one can assume reciprocal influence. Finally, Deuteronomy also contains various provisions for which no corresponding section may be found in the Covenant Code. A further criterion for identification of the original text is the ideological tendency which places the legislation under the stipulation of *cult centralization*. This centralization proves to be Deuteronomy's specific difference from the Covenant Code and the ancient Near Eastern legal tradition. It was possibly also the decisive motive leading to the amendment of the older Covenant Code and the norm that regulated the changes made. Certainly not all of the innovations of the Deuteronomic Law flow from the centralization law. This is the case even for the centralization laws themselves, whose innovations are in part also due to the development of judicial terminology or to an interest in making the legal system uniform. For this reason it is almost an axiomatic statement when scholarship limits the original text of Deuteronomy to the centralization laws in their narrowest sense.

As mentioned earlier, the composers of the Deuteronomic Law used the Covenant Code (Exod. 20.22–23.33) as a model. Historical comparison of these two law corpuses shows that individual ordinances of the Covenant Code were reformulated mostly under the guiding principle of cult centralization (see above Ch. 7.2.2).

The **Foundational Inventory of the Deuteronomic Law** included at least the following provisions: The Foundational Command of cult centralization (Deut. 12.13-28*); provisions for the tithe (Deut. 14.22-29*), for the year of jubilee and release of slaves (Deut. 15.1-18*), for the firstborn (Deut. 15.19-23*), as well as the festival calendar (Deut. 16.1-17*), and the standardization and reformulation of the judicial process (Deut. 16.18*; 17.8-13*; 19.1-13*, 15-21*; 21.1-9; 25.1-3*). In addition Deut. 6.4 functioned as the original introduction with the programmatic invocation of the → *Šĕma' yiśrā'ēl* 'Hear O Israel, Yhwh is our God, Yhwh is one' together with the speech introduction and superscription in Deut. 4.45* (without 'the instructions and...' [*hā-'edot wĕ ...*]); 5.1aα* ('And Moses called to all Israel and said to them').

These reformulations reveal the attempt to find practicable solutions for cult centralization and its implications for everyday life. Apart from allowing profane slaughter in the individual villages (Deut. 12), this includes the transfer of the commitment ceremony of a slave from the local sanctuary (Exod. 21.6) to the household of the owner (Deut. 15.17) and the establishment of cities of asylum (Deut. 19.1-13*) as a replacement for the loss of sanctuary asylums in the local sanctuaries (Exod. 21.12-14). In addition further development in various judicial and ethical ideas are found in Deuteronomy's reformulation of the Covenant Code, so the Deuteronomic composers cannot be understood simply through the notion of cult centralization alone. This is especially apparent in the new organization of the judicial system, which rearranges the ordinances and institutions of the Covenant Code. While the relocation of the cultic court is clearly regulated by the notion of centralization in the new structure (Deut. 17.8-13*), the introduction of a professional court system is not subject to this idea (Deut. 16.18*). Instead, here the concern for a uniform and functioning judicial system and the administration of the land prove decisive. As a source for Deuteronomy the Covenant Code represents a known text corpus, while other pre-existent texts used by Deuteronomy can only be identified through source-critical analysis of the earliest Deuteronomic text. The existence, extent and form of such earlier texts are therefore less sure. However, one may suppose that such a festival calendar text from the period existed that was then reworked under the perspective of cult centralization and included in the Deuteronomic law (Deut. 16.1-17*).

### *7.2.3.2 The Frame of Deut. 1–4, 31–34 and 5–11, 27–30*

Moses announces the proclamation of the law and the demand for obedience to the law unceasingly and with a certain redundancy in the frame chapters of Deuteronomy. The repetitions, the *Numeruswechsel*, and the repeated superscripts show that the frame chapters were not all written in one fell swoop. On closer inspection the later outer frame of Deut. 1–3, 4 + 31–34 can be separated from an older inner frame in Deut. 5–11+ 27–30, though both frames are the result of a multi-staged growth process.

The most conspicuous mark of the outer frame is the elaborate review of the events that occurred after leaving Horeb, which is generally seen as the beginning of the → *DtrH*. This assumption is supported by a number of allusions forwards and backwards that connect Moses' farewell speech in Deuteronomy with the portrayal of the conquest under Joshua (Deut. 3.21-28; 31.1-8; 32.45-52; Josh 1.1-3). Scholars sceptical about the DtrH beginning with Deut. 1–3 view these chapters as interpretative recapitulations of the preceding narrative that are formulated in response to the insertion of Deuteronomy into the narrative sequence of exodus and the conquest.[13] In any case, the elaborate parenesis about the ban of images in Deut. 4 belongs to the latest chapters of the book and is already familiar with P. The Song of Moses and Blessing of Moses in Deut. 32–33 are late material in archaistic linguistic form.

The inner frame of Deuteronomy is deeply influenced by the linking of Deuteronomy with the Sinai pericope. The → *Decalogue* with its parenetic frame in Deut. 5.1–6.3 (cf. Exod. 20) was inserted for that purpose, as well as the explicit recapitulation of the events surrounding the golden calf from Exod. 32–34, which itself exerted influence on the further arrangement of these chapters. Placing the Decalogue at the beginning of the Deuteronomic Law allows for the law in its current context to be read as further explanation of the Decalogue. However, since a detailed attribution of the individual ordinances or thematic groups to the Decalogue provisions remains difficult, the Decalogue serving as the ordering principle behind the Deuteronomic Law ought to be viewed as an idea emerging in the later stages of the text's compositional history. On the other hand, placing the Decalogue at the beginning of the Deuteronomic Law leads to the notion of Deuteronomy as a → *covenant* document, thereby relating the conception of

13. J. C. Gertz, 'Kompositorische Funktion und literarhistorischer Ort von Deuteronomium 1–3', in *Die deuteronomistischen Geschichtswerke* (BZAW 365; ed. M. Witte et al; Berlin/New York: de Gruyter, 2006), 103–23. A critical appraisal can be found in E. Blum, 'Pentateuch–Hexateuch–Enneateuch? Oder: Woran erkennt man ein literarisches Werk in der hebräischen Bibel?' in *Les dernières rédactions du Pentateuque, de l'Hexateuque et de l'Enneateuque: La question des grands ensembles littérairs en Genèse à Rois: Die Frage literarischer Werke in Genesis bis Könige* (BETL 203; ed. T. Römer and K. Schmid; Leuven: Peeters, 2007), 67–97.

Deuteronomy clearly to the ancient Near Eastern treaty tradition. The central texts for this covenant theology interpretation and redaction of Deuteronomy lie in the addition of the command to love God in Deut. 6.5 to the *Šĕma῾ yiśrā῾ēl* in 6.4 as well as in the covenant theology chapter Deut. 7.

### *7.2.3.3 Dating the Origins of Deuteronomy in the Waning Moments of the Monarchical Period*

Dating Deuteronomy on the grounds of its obvious similarity to → Josiah's reform of 622 BCE portrayed in 2 Kgs 22–23 is problematic on account of the historiographical difficulties connected to this reform. However, there are still good reasons supporting the conclusion that the historical origins of Deuteronomy belong in late pre-exilic Judah under King Josiah (638–609 BCE): the portrayal of the Josianic reform in 2 Kgs 22–23 represents a Dtr edition which strongly depicts the extent of the reform and its connection to Deuteronomy. Yet even the (pre-Dtr) groundwork of this Dtr edited text allows for the recognition of a certain interest in cult-political measures that correspond to the intention of Deuteronomy. Besides, the imagination of the Dtr editors responsible for the first edition of the DtrH in the exilic period (→ *exile*) was restricted by the fact that their audience included contemporary witnesses of the late pre-exilic period. Thus their portrayal of this time could not deviate too much from the historical 'reality'. In addition, there are a number of signs indicating religious-historical changes at the end of the monarchic period that allow for the setting of the innovative features of Deuteronomy within a larger religious-historical framework.[14] Seals from the 7th cent. BCE display a strong tendency towards astralization, which then clearly receded in the 6th cent. BCE (Ch. 4.2.2.4 'The Assyrian Crisis of Judahite Religion?'). Similarly, there are → *epigraphic* finds from the period between King Hezekiah (723–695 BCE) and the exile which display an increase of Yhwh's responsibilities, first to include those of the Near Eastern sun god and later also → *chthonic* elements. In this way Yhwh, the high deity of Jerusalem, moved into areas that used to be reserved for other deities (Ch. 4.2.2.3 'The rise of the god Yhwh'). In addition to the developments in the religious sphere one may add the political developments: since Tiglath-Pileser III (745–726 BCE) Judah had been firmly integrated within the network of Neo-Assyrian vassal states and had to pay Sennacherib dearly for

14. C. Uehlinger, 'Gab es eine joschijanische Kultreform? Plädoyer für ein begründetes Minimum', in *Jeremia und die 'deuteronomistische Bewegung'* (BBB 98; ed. W. Gross; Weinheim: Beltz Athenäum, 1995), 57–89.

its attempt to free itself from this Assyrian hegemony under Hezekiah. At the time of Josiah's predecessors, Manasseh (694–640 BCE) and Amon (640–638 BCE), the dominance of the Neo-Assyrian Empire in Mesopotamia and Syria-Palestine was complete. At the death of Ashurbanipal in the year 628/7 BCE the surprisingly quick demise of the Assyrian Empire began (Nineveh fell in 612 BCE). Assyria likely pulled back from Syria-Palestine around 640 BCE already. Nominal supremacy returned to Egypt, and Josiah became vassal to pharaoh. However, this dominance replicated the conditions and claims of the Late Bronze Age and was only exercised at a distance. It is therefore likely that after the end of Neo-Assyrian control Josiah had the freedom to tackle the necessary political reorganization, and the removal of hegemony in the ancient Near East always also carried religious implications. It is enough here to mention the evidence that vassal treaties, for instance, stood under the protection of the deities of both of the treaty partners. And naturally, political hegemony in one way or another also meant cultural dominance, and thereby also religious influence. The time of King Josiah marks a political change that should not be underestimated, which by all appearances brought on the necessity and also the possibility for the reorganization of the kingdom in Judah.

The findings in the religious-historical and political conditions correspond to those in the Deuteronomic laws, in which → *Mono-Yahwism* and the Foundational Command of cult centralization mark a turning point in the history of religion, and in which the provisions for the judicial system reveal the desire to reorganize the society. One should also take into account that the ordinances of Deuteronomy were already common knowledge by the time of the (early post) exilic → *Priestly Document*, even if they were not always carried out in practice (Ch. 4.3.2.1). Besides, a Neo-Assyrian influence cannot be missed. In fact this influence is also visible in the Dtr passages of Deuteronomy, which means that a reception of Neo-Assyrian expressions and concepts can also be expected after the demise of the Neo-Assyrian Empire. This is especially true for the orientation of the Dtr covenant theology towards the ancient Near Eastern vassal treaties, which results in the use of legal categories of the treaty law to serve as an interpretation of the First Commandment.[15] The various Dtr redactions begin in the Exile and continue well into the postexilic period.

15. *ANET*, 532–41. For the discussion compare the articles of C. Koch, J. Pakkala, K. Radner, and H. U. Steymans in *Die deuteronomistischen Geschichtswerke* (ed. M. Witte *et al*; above, n. 13). For neo-Assyrian influence upon the legal corpus of Deuteronomy, see B. M. Levinson, *The Right Chorale: Studies in Biblical Law and Interpretation* (Winona Lake, Ind.: Eisenbrauns, 2011), 112–194.

## 7.2.4 Theology of Deuteronomy

Deuteronomy marks a decisive turning point in the Old Testament history of religion, which – simply stated – represents the change from the ancient Israelite religion of the independent states of Judah and Israel into Judaism: (1.) The First Commandment of exclusive Yhwh worship pronounced repeatedly in the introductory speeches as well as the Foundational Command of → *cult centralization* in Deut. 12 was not only determinative for the religion and history of postexilic Judaism but also prepared the way for the biblical → *monotheism* first extant in the exilic period. This monotheism has then been developed in different manners in the Christian and Islamic traditions. (2.) The → *Dtr* interpretation of Deuteronomy as a → *covenant* document valid for Israel in every time and place shaped Israel's conception of its relationship with God in subsequent epochs. This so-called covenant theology can be summarized by the following formula: Yhwh is the God of Israel and Israel is the people of Yhwh ('covenant formula'). As a people belonging to Yhwh, Israel is bound to keep all commandments given by God. This reciprocal relationship receives its classical formulation in the covenant-making narrative on Horeb in Deut. 7:

> '...Yhwh your God has chosen you out of all the peoples on earth to be his people, his treasured possession. It was not because you were more numerous than any other people that Yhwh set his heart on you and chose you ... It was because Yhwh loved you' (Deut. 7.6-8*).

The God who became Israel's God and who can claim Israel as his possession as a result of the deliverance from Egypt gives the following commands:

> 'Know therefore that Yhwh your God is God, the faithful God who maintains covenant loyalty with those who love him and keep his commandments, to a thousand generations, and who repays in their own person those who reject him. He does not delay but repays in their own person those who reject him. Therefore, observe diligently the commandment – the statutes, and the ordinances – that I am commanding you today' (Deut. 7.9–11).

(3.) The Dtr identification of Moses' oral law promulgation with the book of the Torah made it possible for Judaism to develop from a cultic-oriented to a book-oriented religion and allowed for the related formation of a collection of holy books interpreting the Torah. Deuteronomy not only influenced Judaism in this manner but also Christianity and Islam. (4.) Not to be underestimated are the ethical and judicial developments that can be observed when comparing Deuteronomy with the Covenant Code. (5.) Finally, through its afterlives in the Dtr school Deuteronomy has significantly moulded the conceptions of the history and prophecy of Israel until the present day. The Dtr perspective understands prophets as those who make known future events and as preachers who call for repentance and a return to following the laws of God.

## 7.2.5 Notes on the History of Reception

Deuteronomy has had an immense impact throughout history in theological and other intellectual disciplines. Within the Old Testament itself the previously mentioned → *Deuteronomism* has probably been the most influential current of thought. The interweaving of legal texts with exhortative instructions (parenesis) has deeply influenced Jewish piety. An early paraphrase may be found in the Temple Scroll from → *Qumran* (11QTR; 1st cent. CE).[16] The most important liturgical text of Deuteronomy is the → *Šĕma´ yiśrā´ēl* in Deut. 6.4-5, whose command to love God is connected with the command to love one's neighbour from Lev. 19.18 to form the highest commandment by Jesus according to Mk 12.28-34, Lk. 10.25-37, and Mt. 22.34-40. Further notes on the reception history of the legal texts may be found in the corresponding notes in Ch. 6.5.

The parenesis and legal corpus of Deuteronomy are generally absent from visual and musical works. One exception is the death of Moses, which is often included in cycles portraying scenes from the life of Moses. The wall painting 'The Testament and Death of Moses' (1482) by Luca Signorelli in the Sistine Chapel brings together the events of his last day including Moses' appointment of Joshua, the reading of the laws, and his viewing of the Promised Land. The → *ark of the covenant* mentioned in Deut. 10.1-5 and its subsequent disappearance (during the destruction of the Temple in 587/6 BCE?) has provoked brisk imaginations like the adventure film 'Raiders of the Lost Ark' of the Indiana Jones trilogy by Steven Spielberg and George Lucas (1981). One should also make note of the Islamic tradition maintaining that the 'until today' unknown grave of Moses (Deut. 34.6) lies at Nebī Mūsā on the west side of the Jordan, approximately 8 km south of Jericho on the edge of the Judean desert. A chapel or shrine was built there in the 13th cent. BCE to mark the assumed grave of Moses.[17]

16. Cf F. García Martínez and E. J. C. Tigchelaar, *Dead Sea Scrolls I–II*.

17. Cf. O. Keel *et al.*, OLB 2, 477–8.

# 7.3 The Non-Priestly Primeval History

Bibliography see Chs 5 and 5.2. Further: D. M. Carr, *Reading the Fractures of Genesis: Historical and Literary Approaches*. Louisville, Ky.: Westminster John Knox, 1996; K. Schmid and C. Riedweg, eds, *Beyond Eden*. FAT II/34. Tübingen: Mohr Siebeck, 2008; J. Jeremias, 'Schöpfung in Poesie und Prosa des Alten Testaments: Gen 1–3 im Vergleich mit anderen Schöpfungstexten des Alten Testaments', *Jahrbuch für Biblische Theologie* 5 (1990): 11–36; H. Spieckermann, 'Ambivalenzen: Ermöglichte und verwirklichte Schöpfung in Gen 2f.', Pages 49–61 in *Gottes Liebe zu Israel*. FAT 33. Tübingen: Mohr Siebeck, 2001.

## 7.3.1 Biblical Context

### Structure of the Biblical Primeval History and Its Components

| The Text as a Whole | The Primeval History According to P | The Non-Priestly Primeval History[18] |
|---|---|---|
| **Creation** | | |
| | Toledot of Heaven and Earth (Gen. 1.1–2.3) | |
| | | **Paradise Narrative** (Gen. 2.4–3.24) |
| | | **Cain and Abel** (Gen. 4.1-26) |
| | Toledot of Adam: Genealogy of Adam to Noah (Gen. 5.1-32*) | |
| **Flood** | | |
| | | Angelic Marriages (Gen. 6.1-4) |
| | Toledot of Noah: Flood Narrative (Gen. 6.9–9.29*) | **Flood Narrative** (Gen. 6.5–9.29*) |
| **Interlude** | | |
| | Toledot of the Sons of Noah: (Gen. 10*) | |
| | | Table of Nations (Gen. 10*) |
| | | Tower of Babel (Gen. 11.1-9) |
| | Toledot of Shem: Genealogy from Shem to Terah (Gen. 11.10-26*) | |
| **Time of the Ancestors** | | |
| | Genealogy from Terah to Abram (Gen. 11.27-32*) | |

18. The components of the originally independent non-priestly primeval history are in bold.

The structure of the biblical Primeval History in its present form has, on the one hand, been determined by the Priestly → *toledot formulas.* According to this structure the time of the ancestors begins with the genealogy of Terah in Gen. 11.27 (Ch. 7.1), which leads to Abraham. On the other hand, the structure of the Primeval History is also influenced by a separation already recognizable in the pre-priestly (and non-priestly) version. Analogous with ancient Near Eastern texts whose 'Primeval History' comprises creation and flood,[19] the biblical Primeval History reaches its conclusion with the end of the flood. From this perspective the theme of 'creation' includes the flood and the deliverance of Noah and his children. The genealogies of Noah's sons and of Shem (Gen. 10.1–11.26) are then best viewed as an 'Interlude'.

## 7.3.2 Textual Issues and Major Issues in the History of Critical Interpretation

Critical analysis of the Pentateuch began with the observation that Gen. 1–3 contains two markedly different reports of creation. The foundation for further discussion is based on the assumption that Gen. 1–11 contains two originally separate and independent versions that were first combined in a later redaction step. One of the two versions, the Priestly Primeval History (→ *Priestly Document*), belongs to a larger salvation-historical plot that begins with creation and continues until Yhwh's entrance into the → *tabernacle* found in Exod. 40 (Ch. 7.1). The second version, which is both non- and pre-priestly, contains both creation and flood, themes also belonging together in the ancient Near Eastern parallels. According to the model proposed by the Documentary Hypothesis these texts were attributed to the → *Yahwist.* Both versions were then worked together through a redaction that understood the meaning of the two texts to be complementary.

**The Complementary Understanding of the Redactors of the Primeval History** can be illustrated easily by looking at the juxtaposition of the two creation accounts. From the perspective of this redaction both texts are 'true' and speak of the actions of the same God, and therefore complement one another. If one reads P alone but with the non-priestly paradise narrative in Gen. 2.4–3.24 in mind, then the impression arises that something is missing from P: In comparison to the non-priestly account, P does not explain how the original peace state found in the good creation could have

19. As seen in the Sumerian Flood Story (*ANET*, 42–4) and the Old Babylonian Atrahasis Epic (*COS* I, 450–3).

> been destroyed to the point that a great flood became necessary. In the present text the non-priestly paradise narrative offers the missing explanation. It adds that it was humanity that corrupted the good creation.

These basic assumptions of literary analysis of the Primeval History have not gone unchallenged in biblical scholarship. In addition to the question of whether P was originally an independent source text or rather a redaction (Ch. 7.1), the literary character of the non-priestly texts has recently become controversial. Objections have been raised to the idea of a Yahwist in the sense of a pre-priestly narrative consisting of the overall plot of the Pentateuch (cf. Ch. 5.3). The opinion is often voiced that the non-priestly texts represent a redaction of P.[20] This thesis, which seems unusual at first, has been developed mostly with regard to the non-priestly Paradise narrative of Gen. 2.4–3.24. It is not viewed as a second creation account set in juxtaposition to the P report in Gen. 1, but rather as a midrash-like (→ *Midrash*) reflex that stems from a → *wisdom* perspective and seeks to correct the optimistic view of the Priestly Primeval History in light of Israel's historical experiences. Its intent is to provide an explanation for how the good creation ('God saw everything that he had made, and look, it was very good,' Gen. 1.31) could become so corrupted that Yhwh found it necessary to throw it back into a primordial chaos.

Controversial as well are the determination of the ending and therefore the exegetical context of the non-priestly Primeval History: did it only include creation and the flood or was it always connected with subsequent ancestor stories? Both questions – the original literary form of the non-priestly texts and the original ending of the non-priestly Primeval History – remain necessarily connected to the much-discussed questions of redactional layers within the non-priestly texts.

20. Cf. J. Blenkinsopp, *The Pentateuch: An Introduction to the First Five Books of the Bible* (2nd ed.; London: T&T Clark, 1992), 54–99; J. L. Ska, 'El relato del diluvio: En relato sacerdotal y algunos fragmentos redaccionales posteriores', *EstBib* 52 (1994): 37–62; E. Otto, 'Die Paradieserzählung Genesis 2–3', in *'Jedes Ding hat seine Zeit...': Studien zur israelitischen und altorientalischen Weisheit* (BZAW 241; ed. A. A. Diesel *et al*; Berlin/New York: de Gruyter, 1996), 167–92.

## 7.3.3 Origins of the Non-Priestly Primeval History

### *7.3.3.1 Source Texts or Redaction in the Biblical Primeval History*

For an orientation to the discussion about the original literary character of the Priestly and non-priestly texts – redaction or independent version of the Primeval History – it is sufficient to recall the foundational observations of the differentiation of sources in Gen. 1–3.

#### Foundational Observations for Differentiating between Sources in Gen. 1–3

The Priestly creation account in Gen. 1.1–2.3 and the non-priestly paradise narrative are:

1. two self-contained narratives, which
2. both in their own way thematize God's creative deeds, but
3. which contradict one another in their overarching scenery and order of events:
   - Human beings are created twice. In Gen. 1.26-27 as male and female at the end of the acts of creation, namely after the earth has been thoroughly populated with animals. In Gen. 2 the human being is first created as person/man and later clearly temporally separate – also as woman. The creation of the man occurs before his surrounding world, including plants and animals, while the woman's creation occurs afterwards. So in Gen. 1 the first human pair is placed into the finished world, while in Gen. 2 the world is built up around the first man.
   - The original or primordial state of the world is reported twice. Gen. 1.1–2.3 describes the original and primordial state of the world as a flooded surface out of which the slab of earth emerges. Then vegetation begins to grow and the earth is subsequently populated. According to Gen. 2.4–3.24 the original and primordial state of the world resembles a dried-out steppe.
   - While each act in Gen 1 is identified as 'good', Gen. 2 presents a narrative dynamic in which something is always missing: First the man who tills the ground and then later his counterpart, which – after the well known detour – leads to the creation of the woman.
   - Gen. 1.1–2.3 speaks consistently of 'God' (Elohim), while Gen. 2.4–3.24 uses 'Yhwh-God' (Yhwh Elohim). This change occurs without any recognizable intention.
   - Gen. 1.27 sees the nature of humanity as made in the image of God as a given, but according to Gen. 3.22 'being like God' is the consequence of the transgression of the divine prohibition against eating from the Tree of Knowledge (2.17).
4. Both narratives are combined through the redactional → *toledot formula* in Gen. 2.4a thus classifying 2.4–3.24 as explication of the previous creation account.

These findings can hardly point to any other conclusion than that Gen. 1–3 were originally two independent texts that were passed on separately and later combined redactionally. Instead of understanding the non-priestly paradise narrative as a redactional addition that intends to correct the optimism of the Priestly creation account, this intention is rather to be attributed to the redaction that brought both texts together. In fact, the redaction also left traces in the texts themselves in order to connect them to one another. These intertextual connections, which have repeatedly been taken as proof for the redactional origin of the Priestly or non-priestly texts as a whole, can instead be separated from each of the independent versions as secondary additions.

#### *7.3.3.2 The Extent and Ending of the Originally Independent Non-Priestly Primeval History*

The question of the ending and the extent of the exegetical horizon of the non-priestly Primeval History cannot be answered unequivocally. The scholarly approach stemming from Gerhard von Rad spread widely the notion that the non-priestly Primeval History was always connected with Abraham as the beginning of the history of Israel and had its immediate climax in the call of Abraham:

> Now Yhwh said to Abram, 'Go from your country and your kindred and your father's house to the land that I will show you. I will make of you a great nation, and I will bless you, and make your name great, so that you will be a blessing. I will bless those who bless you, and the one who curses you I will curse; and in you all the families of the earth shall be blessed.' (Gen. 12.1-3)

This text is then understood as the positive answer corresponding to the annulment of the curse on the earth in Gen. 8.21-22 and is viewed as one of the → *Yahwist's* counteracting movements against his portrayal of the Primeval History as a story of curse, which is now followed by a story of blessing. However, several observations support the conclusion that the Primeval History with the themes 'creation' and 'flood' first developed as an independent narrative cycle and was only later inserted into the history of Israel's beginnings.[21] (1.) The non-priestly Primeval History can be read as a self-contained

21. Cf. F. Crüsemann, 'Die Eigenständigkeit der Urgeschichte: Ein Beitrag zur Diskussion um den "Jahwisten"', in *Die Botschaft und die Boten* (ed. J. Jeremias and L. Perlitt; Neukirchen-Vluyn: Neukirchener, 1981), 11–29; M. Witte, *Die biblische Urgeschichte: Redaktions- und theologiegeschichtliche Beobachtungen zu Genesis 1,1–11,26* (BZAW 265; Berlin/New York: de Gruyter, 1998), 192–205.

narrative. (2.) The non-priestly Primeval History does not allude to other texts in Genesis beyond its boundaries. Also, in the pre/non-priestly narrative texts following the Primeval History no clear allusions are made back to it. Especially striking is the lack of such an allusion in Gen. 12.1-3 – the supposed climax and goal of the non-priestly Primeval History – when compared to the network of allusions within the non-priestly Primeval History. There is also no literary bridge between Gen. 8.22 and Gen. 12.1-3. (3.) The concentration on the themes of 'creation' and 'flood' is found repeatedly in the texts of the ancient Near Eastern environment to which the Primeval History is also otherwise closely related. (4.) As regards content, 'the human' is described in the Primeval History as a farmer (cf. Gen. 2.5; 3.23) with a strong connection to his soil (cf. the nature of the curse against Cain in Gen. 4). On the contrary the ancestral narratives portray the ideal life as semi-nomadic. Even the goal of the exodus, settling in a 'land flowing with milk and honey', is not characterized as overcoming the curse of Gen. 3–4. (5.) The tradition-historical background of Gen. 12.1-3 arises from the ancient Near Eastern and Old Testament royal theology, whose formulas are transferred to Abraham and the nation descending from Abraham – Israel – as in postexilic prophecy (Isa. 19.24; Zech. 8.13, 23). Unlike the future expectations of the postexilic prophecy, the idea that Israel appears as a blessing for the nations represents an expectation projected onto Isreal's prehistory in Gen. 12.1-3. The non-priestly Primeval History, however, contains neither an → *aeschatology* nor any notion of an Israelite salvation history. Because of its general → *etiology* for humanity and explanations for the characteristics of human existence, its focus is much more on the present; it is oriented towards → *anthropology* and creation theology. It conceives not of Abraham, but already of Noah as the 'new human being'.

The non-priestly Primeval History therefore was originally comprised of the themes 'creation' and 'flood'. It begins with the paradise narrative in Gen. 2.4–3.24 and continues with the fratricide story in Gen. 4.1-26 and the flood narrative in Gen. 6.5–8.22. The table of nations in Gen. 10* and the narrative of the building of the city and tower of Babel in Gen. 11 are later additions. The originally separate and independent tradition of the non-priestly Primeval History therefore consists of a self-contained, though not compositionally uniform, narrative. This can be seen in the often noted and difficult to explain tensions within the paradise narrative in Gen. 2.4–3.24. While the Tree of Life likely represents a later addition, other tensions in the text rather arose from the attempt by the author of the paradise narrative to bring together motifs of various origins – the world tree, the divine garden, the *formatio* of humanity, etc.

#### *7.3.3.3 The Date of the Non-Priestly Primeval History*

Being oriented towards human corruption the Primeval History moves from depicting the formation of human beings – with a special focus on cultural history – (anthropogony) to presenting a theological doctrine of human nature (anthropology) and finally to a narrative doctrine of sin (hamartiology). It narrates the creation of humanity, the disobedience of the original human couple against Yhwh's prohibition, the fratricide, the growth of human desire for revenge and murder, as well as the flood. It ends with the prospect of constancy of the cosmic order and the human condition watched over by the just creator God. All in all the non-priestly Primeval History is a breathtaking attempt to conceive of the various perceptions of Yhwh together as one Yhwh: the good creator God, the punishing and providing God, the God who delivers because of his merciful nature, the God who imposes limits on himself in the face of human evil. This juxtaposition of the various perspectives in a single deity Yhwh is difficult to imagine for the early periods of the religious and literary history of ancient Israel. The hamartiological orientation of the non-priestly Primeval History assumes the unconditional judgement proclamations of the eighth and seventh-century BCE prophets, but is likely older than P. The later tower of Babel story mirrors a Persian-period context.

### 7.3.4 Theology of the Non-Priestly Primeval History

The portrayal of primeval events in the Old Testament, like in the ancient Near East in general, is not attempting to give a historically true account of the early prehistory of humanity, but rather to make a statement about the nature of human reality and the fundamental world order. Therefore, the non-priestly Primeval History should be described as an → *aetiology*, a teaching seeking to explain the present circumstances through a description of how the present order came to be. Consequently, the biblical Primeval History speaks of a past situation that determined the present. In the truest meaning of the word, the paradise narrative of Gen. 2.4b–3.24 is foundational. Its topic is the basic religious interpretation of human life: 'Humans are human and not divine.' In the development of this statement the paradise narrative is shot through with a peculiar ambivalence. On the one hand it reports the creation of human beings, their procreation, and cultural development with untroubled self-confidence. On the other hand the aspiring development is tarnished by the humans' growing distance from God. Thus the insight regarding the distinction between God and human beings unfolds into the ambivalence experienced in human existence. The change of tone from untroubled self-esteem to the experience of distance from God in the Primeval History functions to explain the ambivalence of life experienced in the present. Thus the human being acquires what makes him essentially human, namely the knowledge of what supports life and what hinders it ('the knowledge of good and evil'), specifically by transgressing a divine command. This transition marked by knowledge is illustrated with regard to human nakedness. The acquisition of knowledge is portrayed as a step from childlike naiveté into adult consciousness. The episode of the fall depicts the progression from pre-humanity into humanity, or from nature to culture, and thereby into reality as it is experienced. The motif is also found in extra-biblical texts in connection with sexual connotations. However, characteristic of the biblical Primeval History is that the acquisition of knowledge and the birth of civilization receive a negative connotation: the knowledge of good and evil, which paves the way for the development of civilization, is dependent on the transgression of the divine command and thereby makes the subsequently depicted cultural achievements into products of the fall. The manner in which sin leads to violence and in precisely this way brings about the development of law, community life, and culture is portrayed through the narrative of Cain's murder of his brother Abel in Gen. 4. The descendants of the fratricidal Cain are heroes of cultural history. Yet they are the descendants of Cain, who killed his brother Abel and for this reason had to leave his ancestral field and found a new society. This development of culture therefore appears as the consequence of an evil deed. This is explicitly the case also for law, which develops as a protection for the offender in the form of the Cain symbol.

The biblical Primeval History portrays the development of sin – the ever-increasing distance from God – as an individual destiny, so that each individual must take responsibility. However, it also offers a fundamental statement about the human tendency towards violence. This is already implicit in the → *genre* primeval history. It is made explicit especially in the rationale for the flood, which points to the evil and violence of humanity:

> Yhwh saw that the wickedness of humankind was great in the earth, and that every inclination of the thoughts of their hearts was only evil continually. And Yhwh was sorry that he had made humankind on the earth, and it grieved him to his heart. (Gen. 6.5-6)

The tone of these statements about the corruption of humanity recalls the judgement proclamations of the prophets, though they are now maximized into fundamental statements about humanity and shifted to the Primeval History. The maximization also affects the nature of the judgement. Unlike the calamity proclaimed by the prophets, the flood does not merely lead to the → *exile* of the people, but rather to the return of chaos into the world and, therefore, also to a revocation of creation. The non-priestly Primeval History in its narrative hamartiology takes up the early judgement prophecies and proclamations of calamity responding to Israel's transgressions and transfers them into an → *anthropological* statement about the tendency of humanity towards evil. This tendency is confirmed by the result of the flood, which – with regard to human nature – turns out to be no result at all, for even after the flood God has to conclude:

> I will never again curse the ground because of humankind, for the inclination of the human heart is evil from youth; nor will I ever again destroy every living creature as I have done. (Gen. 8.21)

If even the flood was not able to remove the human inclination towards evil from the world, then there is no possible abrogation of this fate in the world. It remains a comforting piece of information that God has changed himself and from then on will forego his just right to punish.[22] It is with this statement that the original biblical Primeval History came to an end.

The later additions of the building of the city and tower of Babel (Gen. 11) depict an unsuccessful attempt by humanity to preserve its unity previously lost on account of its violence through the cultural achievement of a building. At the same time the narrative provides an aetiology for the diversity of peoples, languages and cultures. In this way it prepares the way for the election of Abraham, through whom all tribes on the earth should receive blessing (Gen. 12.1-3).

## 7.3.5 Notes on the History of Reception

The biblical Primeval History deals with the large themes of humanity – the question of the origins of the world, where humans come from, humanity's

22. Cf. J. C. Gertz, 'Noah und die Propheten: Rezeption und Reformulierung eines altorientalischen Mythos', *Deutsche Vierteljahrschrift für Literaturwissenschaft und Geistesgeschichte* 81 (2007): 514–22.

ability to develop culture and humans' reliance on culture, and human imperfection. Accordingly, the reception history of the biblical Primeval History is variegated and multitudinous. The rich symbolic power of its motifs continues to be influential even when the biblical context is largely left behind, such as the widely used apple (which does not appear in Gen. 3!) in commercials, the sign of Cain, the use of the ark as a brand name, and the use of the dove with olive branch (Gen. 8.8-12) – portrayed repeatedly by Picasso amongst others – as well as the rainbow (Gen. 9.1-17 [P]) as symbols by the peace movement. Common sayings have been made from such notions as 'naked as when God made them', the 'lying snake', 'rain like the flood', and a 'Babylonian confusion of tongues'.

The earliest retellings and receptions include the 'Life of Adam and Eve' (*vita adae et evae*), likely from the first century CE, which narrates the fall, the banishment from paradise and the resulting consequences such as disease, threats from wild animals, the loss of the original glory, and death. Also reported is God's forgiveness of Adam after his death. In his use of the Adam-Christ → *typology* (Rom. 5), Paul sets Adam as the originator of sin and death over against Christ as the new Adam who justifies humanity and reconciles humans with God. The church fathers considered Gen. 3.15 to be a prophecy of Christ's victory over the Satan (*proto-evangelium*). The short notice of the assumption of Enoch (Gen. 5.21-24) experienced a rich afterlife in the → *apocalyptic* Enoch books and in Jewish mysticism (Hechalot literature). Noah already functions inner-biblically as an exemplary righteous and pious man (Ezek. 14.14, 20; Sir. 44.17-18; Wis. 10.4; 2 Pet. 2.5; Heb. 11.7), who acts justly in the face of coming calamity (Mt. 24.37-44). In early Judaism the minimal legal and cultic requirements for non-Jews are traced back to Noah in order to establish their universal validity. These so-called Noachic laws (abstention from profanation by idols, abstention from fornication, from strangling, and from blood) are also the subject matter for the 'Apostolic decree' (Acts 15). The confusion of languages from Gen. 11 is overcome in the depiction of the Pentecost story (Acts 2).

Adam and Eve appear quite early in painting. The scene of the fall with Eve, the snake, and the Tree of Knowledge has until the early modern period often been the only opportunity to depict nudity. The oldest known representation is found in the catacomb of San Genaro in Naples (3rd cent.), later representations include Hugo van der Goes (1470), Albrecht Dürer (1504), Lucas Cranach the Elder (1526), Tintoretto (1550) and Peter Paul Rubens (1628). Important as well are the representations of paradise (such as Hieronymus Bosch 1503/04, Jan Bruegel 1610, Jacopo Bassano ca. 1570). The paradise and fall scenes were a mainstay of the medieval religious theatre, while the social aspects became important during the German Peasants' War in the 16th century ('As Adam dug and Eve spun, where was there the nobleman?'). The problem of the freedom of the will moves to the forefront in John Milton's *Paradise Lost* (1667). Amongst the musical interpretations, the third part of Joseph Haydn's oratorio 'The Creation' (1798) deserves special mention. Cain's murder of Abel, and also (not portrayed in Gen. 4!) Adam and Eve's crying over their stricken son, appears multiple times in painting and literature, including the 20th cent. painting 'Cain, or Hitler in Hell' by George Grosz (1944) and the novel *East of Eden* (1952; film starring James Dean) from John Steinbeck. For the flood narrative at least an early portrayal of Noah and the ark in the Priscilla catacomb in Rome and Michelangelo's fresco in the Sistine Chapel (1512–15) as well as the poem 'Flutender' (1967) by Paul Celan should be mentioned. The building of the tower of Babel is a popular motif in visual arts (Pieter Bruegel the Elder, 1563) and has increasingly become a symbol for the ambivalence of cultural progress (i.e. Friedrich Dürrenmatt, 1952; Pierre Brauchli, 1979).

## 7.4 The Non-Priestly Ancestral Story

Bibliography see Chs 5 and 5.2. Further: E. Blum, *Die Komposition der Vätergeschichte*. WMANT 57. Neukirchen-Vluyn: Neukirchener, 1984; D. M. Carr, *Reading the Fractures of Genesis: Historical and Literary Approaches*. Louisville, Ky.: Westminster John Knox, 1996; R. G. Kratz and T. Nagel, eds, *'Abraham unser Vater': die gemeinsamen Wurzeln von Judentum, Christentum und Islam*. Göttingen: Vandenhoek & Ruprecht, 2003; C. Levin, *Der Jahwist*. FRLANT 157. Göttingen: Vandenhoek & Ruprecht, 1993; A. de Pury, 'Situer le cycle de Jacob: Quelques réflexions, vingt-cinq ans plus tard'. Pages 213–41 in *Studies in the Book of Genesis: Literature, Redaction and History*. BETL 155. Ed. by A. Wénin. Leuven: Peeters, 2001; T. C. Römer, 'Recherches actuelles sur le cycle d'Abraham'. Pages 179–211 in *Studies in the Book of Genesis: Literature, Redaction and History*. BETL 155. Ed. by A. Wénin. Leuven: Peeters, 2001.

### 7.4.1 Biblical Context

| The Narratives of the Patriarchs and Matriarchs of Israel in Genesis 12–26 | |
|---|---|
| **12–25** | **Abram/Abraham and Sarai/Sarah** |
| | 11.10-32 Genealogical Introduction of Abram |

| | | | |
|---|---|---|---|
| | 12 | Abram's Journey to Canaan | Promise |
| | | Abram and Sarai in Egypt: Endangerment of the Ancestress (I) | |
| | 13 | Abram's Separation from Lot | Promise |
| | [14 | Abram and Melchizedek] | |
| | 15 | Covenant with Abram | Promise |
| | 16 | Hagar; the Birth of Ishmael | Promise |
| | [17 | Covenant and Circumcision (P) | Promise |
| | | Name Change: Abram → Abraham, Sarai → Sarah] | |
| | 18 | Appearance of the Three Men in Mamre/Hebron | |
| | 19 | Destruction of Sodom and Gomorrah, Deliverance of Lot | |
| | | Lot's Daughters: Ammonites and Moabites | |
| | 20 | Abraham and Sarah with Abimelech: Endangerment of the Ancestress (II) | |
| | 21 | Birth of Isaac; Banishment of Hagar and Ishmael | Promise |
| | | Abraham's Covenant with Abimelech | |
| | 22 | Binding of Isaac – the Sacrifice on Moriah | Promise |
| | 23 | Sarah's Death; Purchase of the Grave Site in Hebron | |
| | 24 | Search for a Bride for Isaac; Rebecca | |
| | 25 | Death of Abraham; Ishmael's Descendants | |
| **24–26** | | **Isaac and Rebecca** | |
| | 24 | Courtship | |
| | 25 | Birth of the Twins Esau and Jacob | |
| | 26 | Isaac and Rebecca in Gerar: Endangerment of the Ancestress (III); | Promise |
| | | Isaac's Covenant with Abimelech | |
| **25; 27–36** | | **Jacob, Leah, and Rachel** | |
| | 25 | Birth of the Twins Esau and Jacob | |
| | | Jacob Buys the Right of the Firstborn | |
| | 27 | Jacob Obtains the Blessing by Trickery | |
| | 28 | Jacob Flees from Esau; Dream in Bethel | Promise |
| | 29–31 | Jacob Serves Laban for Leah and Rachel | |
| | | Jacob's Children | |
| | | Leah: Reuben, Simeon, Levi, Judah, Issachar, Zebulun, Dinah | |

| | | |
|---|---|---|
| | Leah's Servant Zilpah: Gad, Asher | |
| | Rachel: Joseph, Benjamin | |
| | Rachel's Servant Bilhah: Dan, Naphtali | |
| | Jacob's Flight from Laban | |
| 32–33 | Jacob and Esau | |
| | Struggle at the Jabbok with Name Change: Jacob Renamed 'Israel' | |
| 34 | Rape of Dinah by Shechem | |
| 35 | Jacob in Bethel | Promise |
| | Benjamin's Birth; Rachel's Death; Isaac's Death | |
| 36 | Esau, Progenitor of the Edomites | |
| | 38: Judah and Tamar; 46–50: Jacob in Egypt, His Blessing and Death | |

At first glance Gen. 12–36 narrates the story of a patriarchally organized family.[23] Abraham (Gen. 12–25), Isaac (Gen. 21, 22, 24–26), and Jacob (Gen. 25, 27–36) are grandfather, father, and son. The individual episodes that influence the text complex as a whole and set its tone are concerned with events that are fundamental for the life and continuing existence of a family: courtship and wedding (Gen. 24; 29), the birth of sons (Gen. 16, 21, 25, 29–30), as well as jealousy and conflict within the family (Gen. 13, 16, 29–31) including confrontation about inheritance (Gen. 27). The familial relationships include the neighbours of Israel and Judah: Abram and Lot, to whom the Moabites and Ammonites trace their roots (Gen. 19), are uncle and nephew. Isaac and Ishmael are brothers, just like Jacob and Esau, the latter being portrayed as the progenitor of the Edomites (Gen. 25). Jacob's uncle and father-in-law Laban is an Aramaean. The goal of this genealogy is reached in the birth of Jacob's sons, including Judah (Gen. 29–30), and the changing of Jacob's name to Israel (Gen. 32). The genealogy corresponds to the geography of the narratives, whose considerable geographical distribution is noteworthy, covering the states of Israel and Judah as well as the bordering regions. The genealogies and geography make it clear that the narratives are more than a family history: they are concerned with the history of a people told through the mode of a family history.

23. Cf. the characterization in C. Levin, *The Old Testament*, 63.

**The Geography of the Ancestral History:** Abraham and Sarah first settle south of Hebron in the Negev (Gen. 12.9) and then move to the southwest coastal plain near Gerar (Gen. 20.1). Isaac is connected with the southern location of Beer Sheba (Gen. 26.23). Their relatives live near the Dead Sea (Gen. 13, 19) and in northern Syria. It is in Syria that Abraham searches for a wife for his son Isaac (Gen. 24) and where Jacob flees from his brother Esau (Gen. 29). Otherwise, the geographic focus of the Jacob narratives is in the region of the northern kingdom Israel. Jacob establishes the sanctuary in Bethel/ Luz (Gen. 28), gives the mountains of Giliad their name (Gen. 31), founds Mahanaim in the Transjordan (Gen. 32), and buries his wife Rachel in Ephrata, the later Bethlehem (Gen. 35). Grandfather, father and son are connected to one another geographically through something of an itinerary or list of stops. After setting out from the east Abram/Abraham wanders through the whole land, from Shechem (Gen. 12.6) southwards (Gen. 12.9), and then again in the area between Bethel and Ai (Gen. 13.3-4). After separating from Lot he makes a stop at the oaks of Mamre, a site near Hebron (Gen. 13.18). Isaac is born to him in the south (Gen. 20.1; 21.1-8). Later Isaac moves to Gerar and Abimelech and from there to Beer Sheba (Gen. 26.23). Beer Sheba is the location from which Jacob begins his journey to Laban in Haran, where he remains until the birth of his eleventh son Joseph (Gen. 30.23-24) and until the point when he returns to the promised land. With this return Jacob, who has received the name Israel in the meantime, and his sons take possession of the land that Yhwh promised to the fathers.

The inner unity of the ancestral story is formed theologically through the *promise texts.* These texts set the tone for the narrative as a whole. The beginning is marked by Yhwh's command to Abram/Abraham to venture out into the unknown under Yhwh's direction. Connected with this command is the *promise of descendants*, protection and blessing. In addition, Yhwh connects his treatment of the nations to their treatment of Abraham (Gen. 12.1-3). As soon as Abraham is in the land, the *promise of land inheritance* (Gen. 12.7) follows. This theme reappears in God's speech to Abraham localized in Bethel (Gen. 13.14-17), and it is then repeated in connection to Isaac (Gen. 26.2-5*) and Jacob (Gen. 28.13-15). The essential significance of the promise texts lies in the fact that Israel's existence, land, and life in the land are all dependent on the actions and leading of Yhwh. Correspondingly, the contents of the promises are those things which make a nation into a nation – descendants, land, and blessing.

## 7.4.2 Textual Issues and Major Issues in the History of Critical Interpretation

The unity found in the present text and its significance are constructed by the genealogy, the geography and the theology in the form of the promise speeches. What is true for the text complex as a whole is also the case in the individual texts and partial compositions – although characteristic accentuations can be noted. The genealogical orientation, the local character of the narratives, as well as the motifs of blessing and promise belong to the entire narrative material in one form or another with various emphases. They cannot be separated generally or completely from the narratives as later redactions. However, it is clear that the genealogy of grandfather, father and son – Abraham, Isaac and Jacob – is secondary. The interconnected promise texts in particular do not belong to the 'ground floor' of the ancestral story, but are rather later compositional elements that hold together the multiplicity of narratives and narrative strands. Scholarship is generally in agreement that the originally individual traditions concerning the various patriarchs and corresponding matriarchs were only later assembled and connected with one another through genealogy and geography.

Also certain is that the genealogy, geography and theology of the narratives of the ancestors are intended to provide a justification for the existence of Israel in the land. They reflect the relationships with the neighbouring nations such as Moab, Ammon, Edom and Aram. The God of the fathers is unquestionably Yhwh, the national and dynastic deity of Judah and Israel. Therefore, it can be concluded that the ancestral stories generally narrate the history of Israel's origins from the perspective of the period of the nation's existence. This insight is not new. Julius Wellhausen already recognized that these narratives did not emerge from the pre-state epoch of which they speak, but are in their core projections back from the period of national existence. The present text as a whole concerning the ancestors of Israel should therefore be differentiated from the originally independent narrative complexes of Abram/Abraham and Sarai/Sarah (Gen. 12–25), Isaac and Rebecca (Gen. 24–26), as well as Jacob, Leah and Rachel (Gen. 25; 27–36). *The complex as a whole reflects the circumstances of the period of national existence and the post-state period of Israel.*

Controversial are the age, original literary form and form of transmission, and religious-historical background of the individual narratives and partial compositions of the ancestral story. Turning points in the history of scholarship have been the Genesis commentary of Hermann Gunkel (1862–1932)[24] and Albrecht Alt's (1883–1956) thesis concerning the 'God of the fathers'.[25] Gunkel's famous characterization, 'Genesis is a collection of *legends*,'[26] describes the development of the ancestral story as a compilation of earlier self-contained individual narratives, first into strands of legends, and then into the present whole. The individual narratives represent sagas that were originally handed down orally. Characteristic for such legends, according to Gunkel, is their lack of context or need for previous knowledge on the part of the reader. They possess a clear and tight structure containing few scenes and few people, the latter being characterized more through their actions than through description. They also display the rich use of direct speech and often deal with → *aetiologies.*

**Aetiologies** are legends that depict the origin or cause (Gk. *aitia*) of a particular situation and explain why a certain custom, linguistic convention, or something abnormal is the way it is rather than otherwise. Because its goal is explanation, the aetiology deduces the current state from events taking place in the past that brought about the current state, as is typically said, 'until this very day'. This type of narrative is generally found in connection to striking phenomena, such as the bizarre rock formations around the Dead Sea (Gen. 19) or a pile of stones (Josh. 8). In other words they originate from a specific locale that they attempt to explain. They can also be stories that parents tell their children to explain the ways of the world.

Gunkel thought it still possible to reconstruct the oral forms of the legends as they were passed on, and claimed that the legends did not originally deal with Israel and Yhwh. Alt's thesis is connected to this assertion: in the legends of Genesis one can still recognize a discrete form of genuine nomadic religion, that of the 'God of the fathers' (cf. Gen. 31.5, 42, 53). A specific mark of this type of religion is the connection to a person who received a revelation

24. H. Gunkel, *Genesis* (HKAT I/1; Göttingen: Vandenhoeck & Ruprecht, 1901; 9th ed., 1977; ET *Genesis*, transl. by M. E. Biddle, foreword by E. W. Nicholson; Macon, Ga.: Mercer University Press, 1997).

25. A. Alt, 'Der Gott der Väter' (1929), in *Kleine Schriften zur Geschichte des Volkes Israel I* (4th ed.; Munich: Beck, 1968), 1–78 (ET 'The God of the Fathers' in *Essays on Old Testament History and Religion*, transl. by R. A. Wilson; Sheffield: JSOT Press, 1989, 1–77).

26. H. Gunkel, *Genesis*, vii (above, n. 24; italics mine).

(i.e., Jacob). In contrast to the El-deities of the settled groups of nations (Canaanites), this type of religion concerns a deity that travels with its people, and who is marked by his protective and life-giving provision for the family and clan. Alt argued that the identification of various gods of the fathers with Yhwh occurred first with the writing and collection of the stories that took place in connection to the settlement. An important implication of this thesis concerns the religious-historical source value of the legends: since the ancestral story was first written down during the time of the monarchy, the written tradition therefore gives no information about the pre-state period. Biblically speaking it provides no information about the pre-Mosaic time of the fathers. If it is possible, however, to reconstruct an oral tradition, then these legends may reach back into the pre-history of Israel. The inquiry into the oral transmission of the story makes possible such an inquiry into the pre-state and pre-Israelite form of the individual narratives.

Gunkel and Alt's widely accepted theses about the origin and religious-historical background of the ancestral story have been subjected to increasing critique in the past two decades. On the one hand, scepticism has grown with regard to the possibility of reconstructing the oral prehistory of the texts. This scepticism is in large part due to comparative evidence with present-day non-literate cultures, which has shown that the oral transmission is considerably less consistent than Gunkel and Alt assumed. On the other hand, when turning to the written traditions, there is hardly any narrative in the ancestral story in which one could demonstrate that there has been a stage that did not concern Yhwh and Judah or Israel. It has also been proven that the particularly important promise texts belong to the textual level that connected the narrative cycles of the individual patriarchs together in the literary rather than the pre-literary stage of religion. Finally, Alt's thesis concerning the 'God of the fathers' is no longer accepted.[27] The type of religion described by Alt is not genuinely nomadic, but instead can be seen from the ancient Near Eastern comparative evidence to belong to the realm of personal religiosity in settled cultures (Ch. 4.2.2.1). The observed differences between the religion of the patriarchs and the religion of the exodus narrative can be better explained from the perspective of the sociology of religion: since the ancestral story portrays the origins of Israel through the picture of a family story, its religion corresponds to those religious forms found in family religion. Therefore,

27. M. Köckert, *Vätergott und Väterverheißungen: Eine Auseinandersetzung mit Albrecht Alt und seinen Erben* (FRLANT 142; Göttingen: Vandenhoek & Ruprecht, 1988).

emphasis is placed on God who provides for the individuals and the family. Even if it deals with Israel the depiction is not of the political realm, but rather of the familial realm. However, it need not be doubted that the God of the fathers in the texts is nevertheless Yhwh, the God of Israel and Judah.

## 7.4.3 Origins of the Non-Priestly Ancestral Story

The ancestral story is structured by its male protagonists into three narrative cycles, the Abraham-Lot cycle that emerged in the south, the Jacob-Esau-Laban cycle at home in the north, and the narratives about Isaac that also belong to the south. The narrative cycles were originally passed on independently from one another, after which they were gradually combined into the ancestral story and expanded further. The basic material is made up of the narratives surrounding Jacob. He is the patriarch of patriarchs because he receives the name Israel and the twelve tribes of Israel are traced to his sons. The Jacob-Esau-Laban narrative cycle was expanded to include first the Isaac narratives after the demise of the northern kingdom in the year 722/1 BCE and later the Abraham-Lot narrative cycle. While Abraham is presented as the first of the three patriarchs, he is 'perhaps the youngest figure in this company, and it was probably at a comparatively late period that he was put before his son Isaac'.[28]

### *7.4.3.1 Jacob*

Within the Jacob-Esau-Laban narrative cycle the narratives concerning Jacob and his brother Esau (Gen. 25.19-34; 27.1-45 [46; 28.1-9], and Gen. 32.4-22; 33.1-20) can be separated out from the narratives concerning Jacob and Laban (Gen. 29.1–32.2a). Jacob's conflict with his brother Esau is placed as a frame around the stay with Laban. The two narrative complexes are interlocked by the double motif of Jacob's flight from Esau with Laban as his destination and Jacob's later flight from Laban with Esau as his destination. It is likely that the older material may be found in the narratives concerning Jacob and Laban. These narratives depict Jacob as the progenitor of a large family and successful shepherd, reporting the separation of his family from Laban's family as well as an agreement between the two families. These narratives only became national narratives later, after their connection with the narratives concerning Jacob and Esau by way of the genealogy of the tribes. The narrative complex dealing with the conflicts between the brothers Jacob and Esau is only

28. J. Wellhausen, *Prolegomena*, 353 (German ed., 323 = Studienausgabe, 317; above, Ch. 6 n. 24).

slightly younger. One can also assume that the individual episodes within this narrative complex or at least their separate parts were originally passed on independently. This is especially the case for the narratives of the birthright (Gen. 25) and the stealing of the blessing (Gen. 27). The latter narrative in its present form clearly assumes the knowledge of a larger context because it is composed with a view to the events concerning Jacob and Laban. Other separate narratives, such as the dream revelation in Bethel (Gen. 28) and the wrestling with God at the Jabbok (Gen. 32), were worked into what had become the combined Jacob-Esau-Laban block of narrative tradition. Jacob and his narratives belong according to their middle Palestinian locales in the northern kingdom and perhaps originally even in the Transjordan. After the demise of the northern kingdom in 722 BCE the narratives arrived in the south. Once there they were extended to form the northern and southern Israelite ancestral story by placing before the Jacob-Esau-Laban block first the Isaac narratives and later the Abraham-Lot narratives.

#### *7.4.3.2 Isaac*

In terms of breadth of material Isaac does not equal the other two patriarchs, especially since Gen. 26, comprising most of the Isaac tradition, largely offers variations to narratives treating Abraham and Sarah. However, in the case of the endangered ancestress (Gen. 12; 20; 26) and the covenant with Abimelech concerning water rights (Gen. 21; 26), the Isaac narratives were likely earlier. It is probable that Abraham, the later more beloved and more important patriarch figure, attracted narrative elements to himself that did not originally belong to him. In Gen. 26 there is a kernel of an originally independent and self-contained tradition about the ancestral figures Isaac and Rebecca, which is bound geographically to the boundary region between southern Judah and the Philistines.

#### *7.4.3.3 Abraham*

The narratives concerning Abraham and Sarah are structured into episodes more than those of Isaac and Jacob. The literary kernel is found in the Abraham-Lot cycle (Gen. 13.1-13*, 18; Gen. 18-19*; 21.1-7*), which constitutes a distinct narrative complex to which other texts were joined over time in the course of the compositional history. Within the Abraham-Lot cycle itself the story of the three visitors at Mamre (Gen. 18) and the story of Sodom and Gomorrah (Gen. 19) are the most likely candidates for once having been independent narratives. The Abraham-Lot cycle belongs geographically to the region of Hebron, therefore in the territory of Judah.

However, the larger part of the narratives concerning Abraham and Sarah is the result of a replenishment, which most probably took place after the transfer of the Jacob narratives to the south and therefore no earlier than the end of the monarchical period. It was first in this layer of the compositional history that the story of Abraham and Sarah was started with Yhwh's command to leave the ancestral homeland for the promise of becoming a nation and a blessing (Gen. 12.1-3). This text, like the other connected promise texts that also deal with the possession of the land, offers an answer to the experience of the demise of Judah and Jerusalem in the year 587/6 BCE that radically questioned the highlighted contents of salvation (land, nation, blessing, and presence of Yhwh). The multiple allusions to the exodus as they appear especially in the narratives concerning Abraham and Sarah also belong to this context. Thus Abraham, as first receiver of the revelation of the faith of Yhwh, is portrayed as a counter model to Moses (Gen. 12.10-20; 15; 16). The great attractiveness of the figure of Abraham as someone with whom to identity in the postexilic period (→ *exile*) is apparent in the many late additions to the Abraham-Sarah story, especially the courtship of Rebecca (Gen. 24), the intercessions of Abraham for Sodom (Gen. 18) and Abimelech (Gen. 20), as well as the sacrifice of Isaac (Gen. 22).[29]

## 7.4.4 Theology of the Non-Priestly Ancestral Story

The ancestral story portrays the beginnings of the nation of Israel in the literary form of a family narrative as a colourful life story of men, women and children. The inner unity of the variegated material is constituted by its theology that is through the connective framework of the so-called promise to the fathers. The promise texts, which can hardly have been part of the 'ground floor' upon which the narratives were built but instead constitute later composition elements, display a clear message: Israel is completely dependent on the actions and leading of Yhwh for its existence in the land. The objects of the promise are those goods needed to constitute a nation and to maintain a nation – descendants, land and blessing.

29. Cf. also the allusions to Abraham that are all very late in Isa. 41.8; 51.2; Jer. 33.26; Ezek. 33.24; Ps. 47.10; 105.6, 9, 42; Neh. 9.7 and the discussion in A. Mühling, *'Blickt auf Abraham, euren Vater:'Abraham als Identifikationsfigur des Judentums in der Zeit des Exils und des Zweiten Tempels* (FRLANT 236; Göttingen: Vandenhoeck & Ruprecht, 2011).

**The Programme of the Promise Texts of the Ancestral Story:** The story of the ancestors begins with Yhwh's command to Abraham to set out and follow his leading into the unknown. As a result Abraham is promised descendants, protection and blessing. He also receives affirmation from Yhwh that Yhwh will treat other peoples in accordance with how they treat Abraham (Gen. 12.1-3). Missing at this point is the promise of land. It first follows, understandably from the narrative, when Abraham is in the land (Gen. 12.7). This theme which begins here is again addressed in the divine speech localized at Bethel where it reaches its first climax (Gen. 13.14-17). Abraham now sees the land that Yhwh had said he would show him. At this point there is also a legally binding transfer that takes place through the double rites of overlooking and walking through the land. Additionally, the contents of the promise are increased. Abraham will become such a great nation that his descendants will become innumerably many, and the land given to him will be as large as he can see. The promises of this programmatic prelude to the ancestral story are then repeated with regard to Isaac (Gen. 26.3-4) and Jacob (Gen. 28.13-15). The focus in the wide-reaching narratives concerning Jacob is in fact on the theme of blessing, but blessing and promise are not unconnected from the perspective of the ancestral story in its latest independent form. Thus in the course of the story the promise passes from Abraham (Gen. 12.1-3, 7; 13.14-17) to Isaac (Gen. 26.3-4), then to Jacob, first in the form of a blessing obtained through trickery (Gen. 27.27-29), only to be confirmed again through a promise that is rhetorically and thematically closely connected to Gen. 12–13: 'I am Yhwh, the God of Abraham your father and the God of Isaac; the land on which you lie I will give to you and to your offspring; and your offspring shall be like the dust of the earth, and you shall spread abroad to the west and to the east and to the north and to the south; and all the families of the earth shall be blessed in you and in your offspring,' (Gen. 28.13-14). Closing the line of programmatic promise texts this text comprises the promises of land, increase, and mediation of blessing, like in Gen. 12–13, but this time all concentrated in a single speech.

The ancestral history narrates a promise story that ends with success. However, delays and dangers to the promise do not go without mention, so that the story of the bearers of the promise is portrayed as a progression of detours and obedience. The narrators, who operated from the theological premise that Israel exists only as a result of Yhwh, chose narratives that clearly led to such an understanding. Sarah is able to bear a child long after the human possibility of such fertility would have passed. Rebecca bears the children Esau and Jacob only after Isaac's intercession. The blessed Jacob is in danger from Esau, who only lost the blessing by trickery. Rachel's barrenness triggers first the rivalry of the wives and their servants Bilhah and Zilpah and then is overcome through Yhwh's intervention, all so that in the end the 12 forefathers of the tribes of Israel are born. Keeping with the notion of a national history in the form of a family narrative, membership to Israel is determined genealogically. The question of belonging to Israel is decided by determining membership to one of the 12 tribes, whose forefathers are the sons of Jacob. Behind this genealogical conception stands an already existing communal consciousness that derives from a number of social, cultural, geographic, and economic factors, and that seeks to affirm itself through recourse to the foundational origins in earliest times. This is why with regard to the ancestral story one can also speak of a myth.

Although presenting a national history in the mode of a family narrative the literary form nevertheless opens the possibility for self-identification with the portrayed characters. This is the reason for the polyvalence in the narratives of the fathers and mothers of Genesis that has been noted numerous times. It provides many points of connection to an incalculable number of different significances and meaning dimensions that are easily integrated in familial religion. Pertinent themes (which, incidentally, are not at all secondary themes in terms of the significance of the text) are descendants, the preservation of the group/family in danger, and protection from more powerful groups. More extensive themes from the complex consist, for example, of the narrated realization of the theme of blessing in the Jacob narrative and Abraham's numerous paradigmatic actions. To the degree that the national history is presented as a family story, the national story is therefore also always an exemplary narrative for foundational human experiences in the realm of tribe and family – and the inverse as well. Finally, such a reading also prohibits the widespread exegetical perception that bifurcates the meaning such that the narratives of the patriarchs are interpreted as highly political and highly theological national history, while the narratives in which the matriarchs stand in the foreground, serve as idyllic and generally trivial 'little family histories'.[30]

## 7.4.5 Notes on the History of Reception

Abraham serves as the progenitor of faith for Judaism, Christianity and Islam. He is therefore a central figure of identification in many modern-day

30. Regarding the call for a 'gender fair' exegesis, see I. Fischer, 'Das Geschlecht als exegetisches Kriterium: Zu einer gender-fairen Interpretation der Erzeltern-Erzählung', in *Studies in the Book of Genesis: Literature, Redaction and History* (BETL 155; ed. A. Wénin; Leuven: Peeters, 2001), 135–52.

approaches to interreligious dialogue between these three religions.[31] Rare and thoroughly post-exilic are the appearances of Abraham outside of Genesis, though prophetic texts allow for the recognition that Abraham was a figure with whom one could identify during crises (Ezek. 33.24; Isa. 51.1-2). Within the NT there are references to Abraham's faith (Rom. 4) and – with anti-Pauline overtones – of his works (Jas 2.21–24). Abraham is perceived as 'the friend of God' (Jas 2.23). For the author of the letter to the Hebrews Abraham embodies faithfulness, since he left his home for a heavenly home and was even ready to sacrifice his son (Heb. 11). The so-called sacrifice of Isaac, which in the Jewish tradition is termed the 'binding' (*Aqedah*), plays a central role in all three Abrahamic religions: it is given special honour and serves as the highest expression of piety. Immanuel Kant levied this appraisal with strong protest in his writing *The Conflict of the Faculties* (1798),[32] but the inner-Jewish religious discussions concerning the Shoah repeatedly reference the *Aqedah*. The Koran mentions Abraham in 25 Suras and views him as the first Muslim monotheist (Hanīf; Sura 16.120-23), on which Islam makes its claim to conserve a pure → *monotheism* free from later Jewish and Christian distortions (Sura 2.135). Abraham, together with his son Ishmael, founded the *Ka'ba* (Sura 2.124–26). In the visual arts Abraham often appears as a white-bearded old man with a knife (Gen. 22). The oldest preserved portrayal of Abraham is likely from the Synagogue of Dura-Europos (3rd cent. CE), which shows Abraham receiving the promise. A further fresco portrays the 'sacrifice of Isaac'; a scene found in every art-historical period: including on the mosaic floor of the synagogue in Beth Alfa (6th cent.), Lorenzo Ghiberti (1401/02), Marc Chagall (1960–66) and Richard McBee (1996; 2001). This topic has been taken up musically by Marc-Antoine Charpentier (ca. 1685) for example. Other important scenes in painting are the greeting and serving of the meal to the three men (Gen. 18), first in Dura-Europos (3rd cent.) and in the catacombs on the Via Latina in Rome (4th cent.), as well as Abraham and Melchizedek (Gen. 14) among others by Peter Paul Rubens (1675). Often taken up is the courtship of Rebecca according to Gen. 24, which was treated by Nicolas Poussin (1648), Francesco Solimena (ca. 1700), and Marc Chagall (1977/78; glass window in the church of St. Stephen in Mainz, Germany).

31. Cf. K.-J. Kuschel, *Abraham: Sign of Hope for Jews, Christians, and Muslims* (transl. by J. Bowden; New York: Continuum, 1995).

32. On the reception and exegesis of Gen. 22 see T. Veijola, 'Das Opfer des Abraham' (above, Ch 5 n. 9).

While the question of the identity of the people of God, the Israelites, is connected to the character of Jacob more than any other within the Old Testament, Abraham overtakes him in importance in the history of reception. Jacob is repeatedly perceived as the tricked trickster. A critical reflection on the Jacob narratives is found as early as Hos. 12. Of the literary adaptations pride of place should be given to the first volume *The History of Jacob* (1933) from Thomas Mann's four-part *Joseph and His Brothers*. In Jurek Becker's novel *Jacob the Liar* (1969), which takes only – although fittingly – its title from Genesis, Jacob's lie to the people surrounding him in the ghetto turns into the blessing of an illusionary hope. Well-known motifs of biblical → *iconography* from the Jacob cycle include the dream of the heavenly ladder – such as the fresco in Dura-Europos (3rd cent.), a wall painting in the catacomb on the Via Latina (4th cent.), William Blake (1790), and repeatedly Marc Chagall. Finally there is 'Jacob's wrestling with the angel' by Rembrandt van Rijm (ca. 1600), Eugène Delacroix (1855–1861), Paul Gaugin (1888), and Marc Chagall (1889–1985).[33]

# 7.5 The Non-Priestly Joseph Story

Bibliography see Chs 5 and 5.2. Further: W. Dietrich, *Die Josephserzählung als Novelle und Geschichtsschreibung: Zugleich ein Beitrag zur Pentateuchfrage*. Biblisch-theologische Studien 14. Neukirchen-Vluyn: Neukirchener, 1989; Konrad Schmid, 'Die Josephsgeschichte im Pentateuch'. Pages 83–118 in *Abschied vom Jahwisten*. BZAW 315. Ed. by J. C. Gertz, K. Schmid, and M. Witte. Berlin/New York: de Gruyter, 2002).

## 7.5.1 Biblical Context

**The Joseph Story in Genesis 37, 39–50**

| | | |
|---|---|---|
| 37 | Exposition: Joseph's Dreams | |
| | 38 | Judah and Tamar |
| 39–41 | Joseph's Rise in Egypt | |
| | 39 | Potiphar |
| | 40 | Joseph in Prison; Dream Interpretations |
| | 41 | Pharaoh's Dreams; Joseph's Exaltation |

33. Cf. H. Spieckermann (in collaboration with S. Dähn), *Der Gotteskampf: Jakob und der Engel in Bibel und Kunst* (Zurich: Theologischer Verlag, 1997).

| | | |
|---|---|---|
| 42–45 | Joseph and His Brothers | |
| | 42 | First Trip of the Brothers |
| | 43–44 | Second Trip of the Brothers |
| | 45 | Joseph Reveals His Identity; First Reconciliation |
| 46–49 | Jacob in Egypt | |
| | 46 | Jacob Travels to Egypt |
| | 47 | Jacob's Audience with Pharaoh |
| | 48 | Jacob Blesses Ephraim and Manasseh |
| | 49 | Jacob's Blessing and Death |
| 50 | Conclusion | |
| | 50.1-14 | Jacob's Burial |
| | 50.15-21 | Final Reconciliation Among the Sons of Jacob/Israel |
| | 50.22-26 | Joseph's Death and Embalmment |

| The Dreams in the Joseph Story | | |
|---|---|---|
| 37.7-8 | Joseph's First Dream (Sheaves) | |
| 37.9-11 | Joseph's Second Dream (Stars) | |
| | 40.9-15 | The Cupbearer's Dream |
| | 40.16-19 | The Baker's Dream |
| | 40.20-21 | The Cupbearer's Dream Fulfilled |
| | 40.22 | The Baker's Dream Fulfilled |
| | 41.1-4 | Pharaoh's First Dream (Cows) |
| | 41.5-7 | Pharaoh's Second Dream (Ears of Grain) |
| | 41.47-49 | Pharaoh's Dreams Fulfilled |
| | 41.53-57 | Pharaoh's Dreams Fulfilled |
| 42.6-8 | Joseph's First Dream Fulfilled | |

The story concerning Joseph and his brothers is comprised of Gen. 37, 39–50. Chapter 37 offers an exposition of the following events: Jacob favours Joseph, who is at that point his youngest son and the only son of his beloved Rachel. This favouring leads to Joseph's overblown confidence in himself (seen here in the form of dreams) and the enmity of his brothers, which together determine the progression of the story. Thus the brothers sell Joseph to Egypt, which becomes the location for the following events. These include Joseph's miraculous rise and his reconciliation with his brothers. The rise of Joseph to the deputy of Pharaoh is depicted in chs. 39–41. Chapters 42–45 describe the long road to the brothers' reconciliation, and chs. 46–47 portray the way to reunion with his father. The testament and death of Jacob follow in chs. 48–49, followed in ch. 50 by Jacob's interment. Afterwards follows a conclusion containing a second, final reconciliation between the brothers (50.15-26) and the death of Joseph.

## 7.5.2 Textual Issues and Major Issues in the History of Critical Interpretation

In contrast to the ancestral story, the Joseph story is thoroughly novella-like, namely a prose narrative that tells of an 'unprecedented event'.[34] Different than in a legend, it treats an event that can be imagined as real and contains a central conflict. In the centre of the Joseph story is the conflict between the brothers, which is the catalyst behind and reason for Joseph's rise. In terms of form a novella is characterized by a terse, usually one-stranded progression of events, though nevertheless artfully constructed and designed. These features can also be easily observed in the Joseph story. Apparent is its unity with a single dramatic arc consisting of more than ten chapters, sometimes including interludes and retarding elements, and developing complicated psychological situations.

Irrespective of the thematic consistency, the Joseph story long served as an exemplary example for the separation of the sources 'J' and 'E'.[35] Evidence for this assumption is supposed to be found in the alternations between Judah and Reuben as spokesman for the brothers already in Gen. 37 and the varying identification of the caravan leaders as either Ishmaelites or Midianites.[36] Within the Joseph story there is also a change in the name of the father from Israel to Jacob. In this manner a Judah-Israel-Ishmael layer was identified with 'J' and differentiated from a Reuben-Jacob-Midianite layer attributed to 'E'.[37]

34. J. W. v. Goethe, 'Then what is a novella except for the occurrence of an unprecedented event', (Conversation with Eckermann, January 29, 1827).

35. Cf. most recently, L. Schmidt, *Literarische Studien zur Josephsgeschichte* (BZAW 167; Berlin/New York: de Gruyter, 1996), 121–297.

36. Judah: 37.26-27; further 43.8-10; 44.14-34 and 46.12, 28; 49.8-12; Reuben: 37.21-22; further 42.22, 37-38 and 46.9; 48.5; 49.3-4; Ishmaelites: 37.25, 27, 28b; Midianites: 37.28a, 36.

37. The dream narratives are also generally attributed to 'E' since dream revelation is considered a mark of this source document.

However, the distinction of sources within the Joseph story is questionable because of its thematic and formal consistency. Furthermore, interludes and retarding elements to which the supposed doublets belong are part of the novella genre and can therefore be explained easily as stylistic devices:

> The Joseph novella has a conspicuous fondness for the number two. [. . .] Joseph's dreams in the presence of his brothers, the dreams of the palace officials in prison, and the dreams of Pharaoh all appear in pairs. Joseph is taken captive twice – in the cistern and in the Egyptian prison. The brothers travel to Egypt twice. Two attempts are made to bring the youngest brother, Benjamin, to Egypt. The silver for the grain is put back in the brothers' grain sack twice. In both of the brothers' stays in Egypt they have two audiences each with Joseph. Jacob and his sons are [. . .] invited to relocate to Egypt twice.[38]

Furthermore, the divine name cannot be used categorically as a criterion to differentiate between sources in the Joseph story because the change occurs for distinct reasons in the narrative itself, so that in the foreign land of Egypt only 'Elohim' is used. The formal and thematic consistency of the Joseph story supports the increasingly accepted conclusion that it is in large part a self-contained literary unit.[39] The unmistakable tracks of literary growth can then be understood appropriately through redactional-historical explanations that do in part differentiate between a Judah-Israel-Ishmael original narrative and a Reuben-Jacob-Midian redactional layer.[40] Dating suggestions for the Joseph story range from a Solomonic

38. H. Donner, 'Die literarische Gestalt der alttestamentlichen Josephsgeschichte', in *Aufsätze zum Alten Testament aus vier Jahrzehnten* (BZAW 224; Berlin/New York: de Gruyter, 1994), 76–120, here 106–7.
39. Ibid.; C. Westermann, *Genesis 37-50: A Commentary* (transl. by J. J. Scullion; London: SPCK, 1987); E. Blum, Komposition, 229–44 (Bibliography, Ch. 7.4); K. Schmid, 'Josephsgeschichte' (Bibliography, Ch. 7.5).
40. Cf. H.-C. Schmitt, *Die nichtpriesterschriftliche Josephsgeschichte* (BZAW 154; Berlin/New York: de Gruyter, 1980); idem, 'Die Josephsgeschichte und das Deuteronomistische Geschichtswerk', in *Theologie in Prophetie und Pentateuch* (BZAW 310; Berlin/New York: de Gruyter, 2001), 295–308. Exactly the opposite assignment of a Reuben-Jacob-Midian layer and Judah-Israel-Ishmael layer is found in W. Dietrich, *Josephserzählung*. Arguments against Dietrich's theory include the fact that unlike the Judah passages the Reuben passages do not have a decisive function, and that only the notes about the Ishmaelites allow for the reconstruction of a coherent text. The Midianites owe their later mention to the exculpation of the brothers: the sale of a brother is a crime punishable by death (cf. Exod. 21.16); therefore according to the present text complex it is no longer the brothers that sell Joseph to the Ishmaelites (37.27-28*), but rather the Midianites (37.28). Also, the later positive portrayal of the firstborn Reuben exonerates the brothers.

'J' in the tenth century BCE to the northern Israelite court of the ninth or eighth century, as far as the Persian → *diaspora* of the fourth century BCE.[41]

## 7.5.3 Origins of the Non-Priestly Joseph Story

In its present form the Joseph story appears as an elaborate connection piece between the ancestral story and the Mosaic history. The assumption that the Joseph story was originally conceived to explain how and why the forefathers of the tribes of Israel came to Egypt only matches the textual material with difficulty. As a whole the narrative moves towards this assumed goal with too little single-mindedness. According to Gen. 50.7-13 the Jacob clan is again in Palestine. The renewed relocation of the clan to Egypt is reported in a single verse (Gen. 50.14), which does not support the idea that this was the original purpose of the narrative. Besides, the juxtaposition of the Joseph story with the exodus narrative results in tensions that are difficult to settle. Symptomatic is the (redactional) opening notice of the exodus narrative:

> Then Joseph died, and all his brothers, and that whole generation. But the Israelites were fruitful and prolific; they multiplied and grew exceedingly strong, so that the land was filled with them. Now a new king arose over Egypt, who did not know Joseph. (Exod. 1.6-8)

This notice has no other function than to abrogate the effects of the Joseph story so that the events reported in the exodus narrative can begin. The necessity of this redactional operation arises from the discrepancy in the evaluation of the Egyptian kingdom – a well-functioning bureaucratic nation or brutally oppressive state apparatus – and the different characterizations of Israel's ancestors – breeders of flocks and semi-nomads or slave labourers, which in Egypt were primarily made up of war captives. Leaving aside for a moment the redactional notices concerned with the transfer of his bones to Canaan in Exod. 13.19 and Josh. 24.32, Joseph – once second only to Pharaoh – never appears in the progress of the exodus narrative. On the other hand, the Joseph story does not make sense as a (secondary) continuation of the ancestral story either. Support for this conclusion emerges already through consideration of the divergent literary forms: generally speaking additions lean on the literary forms of the text they are adding to.

41. Cf. K. Schmid, 'Josephsgeschichte', 106–12 (see his bibliography and extensive discussion; Bibliography Ch. 7.5).

Therefore it is unlikely that the novella-like Joseph story represents a redactional addition to the narrative cycles forming the ancestral story. In other words, the Joseph story was originally independent from both the ancestral story and the exodus narrative. This assumption is confirmed by the fact that the sparse connections between the blocks of tradition (Gen. 46.1-5a; 50.24-26) are secondary.

Essentially two options are discussed for the scope of the originally independent Joseph story, namely a long and a short version. While formerly the entire narrative thematic found in Gen 37. to Gen. 50 was seen as original, later the discussion limited the original text to Gen. 37–45.[42] At first glance, the motif of Joseph's dreams and the motif complex of clothing, as well as the portrayal of the change of heart of the brothers, which are limited to chs. 37, 39–45, seem to support the 'short version' theory. In addition, the goal of the Joseph narrative, the reconciliation of the brothers found in Gen. 45.5-8, is again treated in Gen. 50.15-21. From a redaction-historical perspective, this double climax points to an original ending to the narrative in Gen. 45.27. Admittedly this version then leaves out Joseph's reunion with his father, which is addressed in the verse immediately following the suggested conclusion (45.28). Without the reunion scene (46.29-30) that is prepared for here, which itself points to the death and burial of Jacob (47.29-31; 50.1-14*), the father-son thematic (itself strongly connected to the motif of Joseph's dreams [37.9-10] and the motif complex of clothing [37.3]) remains without closure. Neither does the reconciliation scene in Gen. 50.15-21 represent a redactional resumption of Gen. 45.5-8. Rather it is the result of the tendency throughout the Joseph story for double reports – though the brothers only know in advance of the second telling that they actually are standing before Joseph. Thus one can only fully speak of reconciliation (and the brothers' change of heart) in the second reconciliation scene. Finally, the impression that chs. 46–50 extend far beyond the frame set by the motif of Joseph's dreams and the motif complex of clothing can be mitigated by the fact that especially these chapters include extensive later additions, so that originally they were considerably shorter than the current text seems to suggest.[43] As a result one should conclude that the original text layer of the Joseph story reached to Gen. 50.21.

42. For discussion cf. the detailed discussion in K. Schmid, 'Josephsgeschichte' (Bibliography Ch. 7.5), who argues for the 'long version'.

43. Additions include Gen. 46.1-5*; 48; 49; 50.22-26. One can conclude that the scope of individual motifs does not necessarily set the outer frame for the Joseph story. This is the case for the postulated 'short version'. The motif of dreams strictly speaking only extends to Gen 43.26-28, but this

Attempts to date the Joseph story are based on its diaspora thematic: the Joseph story takes place in a foreign land where the Israelite protagonist rises to prominence in a foreign court.[44] Egypt is not only the land of the enemy, but also – in contrast with its portrayal in the exodus narrative – at least a place where one can sojourn while survival in the homeland is impossible. Joseph's marriage to the Egyptian Asenath shows that marriage with a pagan foreigner is allowed, which distances the Joseph story far from the → *Dtr* view (dominating from Exod. 1 onwards) and its understanding of the historical identity of Israel. It is difficult to imagine that this motif constellation could be operative without an Israelite diaspora in Egypt. On the other hand, it is difficult to conceive of the choice of a representative of the northern kingdom for a hero during the Persian period, which instead suggests the period after 722/1 BCE. This assumption is supported by the papyri from the Nile island Elephantine (*ANET*, 491–2) which suggest the development of a Jewish colony prior to the Persian period and for which a connection to the former northern kingdom cannot be excluded.

## 7.5.4 Theology of the Non-Priestly Joseph Story

In all its various literary contexts the Joseph story develops the basic notion that God has the ability to make even human guilt serve his salvific plan and action, especially during the conditions of → *diaspora*. Joseph's arrogance and the jealousy of his brothers bring about the attempted murder of the hated favourite son of the father. And yet it is this event that prepares the way for Joseph's rise in Egypt which seems to accelarate after each setback. It is an unspoken presupposition that divine foreordination stands behind and moves the events along. Not until the very end is it revealed that God's salvific deeds lay behind the complicated human events – an insight that is true for the Joseph narrative and the reader's realm of experience alike. It is Joseph who in one of the final encounters with his brothers voices the clarifying insight in → *wisdom* like manner:

> 'Do not be afraid! Am I in the place of God? Even though you intended to do harm to me, God intended it for good, in order to preserve a numerous people, as he is doing today.' (Gen. 50.19-20)

has not led anyone to the conclusion that the subsequent text as far as Gen. 45.27 is therefore secondary.

44. Corresponding rises to prominence are also found in the book of Esther and the Daniel legends (Dan. 1–6).

### 7.5.5 Notes on the History of Reception

The narrative art and richness of motifs in the Joseph story were already animating within ancient Judaism. The romantic composition 'Joseph and Aseneth' (*Jos. Asen.*) moulds the brief notices about the marriage of the hero with the daughter of an Egyptian priest (Gen. 41.45, 50; 46.20) extensively into the form of a → *Hellenistic novel*. The motif of endangerment and exaltation in the diaspora is taken up even innerbiblically in the Esther novella (Ch. 20). Literary adaptations in the twentieth century include Hugo von Hofmannsthal's 'The Joseph Legend' (1914), 'Jud Süß' (1925) by Lion Feuchtwanger, and especially *Joseph and His Brothers* (1933–43) by Thomas Mann.[45]

The first visual portrayal is found in the synagogue in Dura-Europos on the Euphrates and comes from the 3rd cent. CE. Probably the most well-known sets of paintings about Joseph are from Rembrandt van Rijn and Marc Chagall (LCI Bd. 2, 423–34). The musical reception extends from Georg Friedrich Händel's oratorio 'Joseph and His Brothers' (1744), to Richard Strauss' ballet 'The Joseph Legend' (1914), and the musical 'Joseph and the Amazing Technicolour Dreamcoat' by Andrew Lloyd Webber and Tom Rice (1968).

## 7.6 The Deuteronomistic Composition of the History of the Nation of Israel from Exodus to Exile

Bibliography see Ch. 5 and Ch. 5.2. Further: R. Albertz, 'Die Intentionen und die Träger des Deuteronomistischen Geschichtswerks'. Pages 37–53 in *Schöpfung und Befreiung*. Stuttgart: Calwer, 1989; E. Würthwein, 'Erwägungen zum sogenannten deuteronomistischen Geschichtswerk'. Pages 1–11 in *Studien zum Deuteronomistischen Geschichtswerk*. BZAW 227. Berlin/New York: de Gruyter, 1994; as well as the literature mentioned under the explanations in Section C to the individual sections of the history. Commentaries to the individual books are given in Ch. 5.

45. On Thomas Mann's four-part novel series which has itself had an immense history of reception see F. W. Golka, *Joseph – biblische – Gestalt und literarische Figur: Thomas Manns Beitrag zur Bibelexegese* (Stuttgart: Calwer Verlag, 2002).

## 7.6.1 Biblical Context[46]

The narrative threads that are both pre- and non-priestly in the books of Exodus, Numbers, and Deuteronomy report the *formation of the people of Israel outside the land* and independent from national institutions in the foundational experience of the exodus. Their narrative plot leads Israel as far as the edge of the promised land. The books of Joshua–2 Kings depict the *history of the people in the land*, until they once again lose the land. These books report the development of national institutions and end with the pardon of the last Davidic king in the Babylonian → *exile*. Notwithstanding this pardon, Israel at the end of the portrayal is again the people that it was at the beginning: the people of God outside the land and without its own national institutions.

Both parts of the portrayal, the formation of the people of Israel outside the land and the history of the people of Israel in the land, are connected with each other in multiple ways. Worthy of mention are the chronology of the events and the succession of persons: Joshua is Moses' successor; the children and descendants of the ancestral generation of the exodus represent the generations in the land. Additionally, it is in and through the book of Deuteronomy that the two parts are woven into one another. Deuteronomy ends the phase of the formation of the people outside the land. At the same time it points beyond itself in that Moses, the central leader of the exodus and the wilderness wandering, promulgates the divine legal foundation for Israel's existence in the land in the Deuteronomic Law. Moses and Deut. thereby lay the foundation for the inner unity of the subsequent historical narratives, for it is the evaluative orientation towards the demands of Deuteronomy that provide the shared historical perspective and form a historical *work* from the individual narratives. Seen in this way, the entire portrayal in the books Joshua–2 Kings presupposes the Deuteronomic Law. Finally, the intertextual connections within the overarching narrative complex, that is the final form of the Great Historical Opus in the books of Genesis–2 Kings (Ch. 5.1) come to mind. These intertextual connections generally do not belong to the individual narratives themselves but instead are the result of various redactional movements. A large number of these connections is constitutive of the → *Dtr* composition of the history of the people from exodus to exile. However, the intertextual

46. Regarding the structure of the work as a whole see the diagram in Ch. 5.1 (with the exception of Genesis). For the individual sections of the portrayal of the history see the diagrams in the respective subsections in 7.2.1 as well as Ch. 7.6.3 for the outline of Deut.

cross-references vary in their scope and often are limited to certain sections of the whole. This insight also forms a basis for differentiating between individual partial compositions: the Moses-exodus-conquest narrative (Exod. 1–Josh. 12); the Judges narratives (Judg. 3–16); the Samuel–Saul narrative, the Saul-David-Solomon narrative (1 Sam.–1 Kgs 11), as well as the → *annals* and narratives of the kings of Judah and Israel (1 Kgs 12–2 Kgs 25).

## 7.6.2 Textual Issues and Major Issues in the History of Critical Interpretation

While older scholarship maintained the presence of thoroughgoing source documents as well as the Dtr redactions in Genesis–2 Kings (or at least in Genesis–Joshua), since Martin Noth (1943/48) the narrative complex of the → *Enneateuch* has been split into two literary works with different pre-histories. Noth found the 'old sources' only present in the → *Tetrateuch* and in Deut. 34. Deuteronomy and the Dtr edited books of Joshua–2 Kings he instead recognized as the historical work of a Dtr author who collected, arranged, and edited traditions. The difficulties that are connected with this double explanation model of Documentary Hypothesis and the theory of a → *DtrH* have already received mention in this book: the rejection of an → *Elohist* source document and a pre-priestly connection between the ancestral story and the exodus narrative (Ch. 5.3) speak against the assignment of the narrative threads that are both non-priestly and pre-priestly in Genesis–Numbers and Deut. 34 to the 'old sources'. However, one may still speak of a number of texts in the books of Exodus, Numbers, and Deuteronomy that constitute a thoroughgoing narrative plot that is both non- and pre-priestly. Yet the problem arises here that this narrative plot only comes to an end beyond this set of texts. The natural conclusion of the narrative arch beginning with the exodus from Egypt is indisputably the arrival at and possession of the promised land reported first in Josh. 1–12. So if this set of texts is assigned to another literary work (the DtrH beginning with Deut. 1–3), then one is forced to conclude with Noth that the original end of the Tetrateuch was lost when the Tetrateuch was combined with the DtrH. This hypothesis gives the impression of a makeshift solution, especially since an older → *conquest* narrative can be reconstructed in Josh. 1–12 that is tied through its content to both the non- and pre-priestly narrative plot in Exodus, Numbers, and Deuteronomy. The assumption of such a Moses-exodus-conquest narrative in Exod. 1–Josh. 12* naturally cannot be connected with the theory of a DtrH beginning in Deut. 1–3.

Noth's now classic notion of the development of the Torah and the Former Prophets is, however, undermined by textual evidence within the DtrH as well. Subsequent scholarship has shown that the assumption of a single Dtr author and various later additions does not sufficiently explain the redaction-historical evidence. The → *Deuteronomism* within the history books is a many-sided and multilayered phenomenon. Noth's theory has therefore been corrected towards the idea of many Dtr editions of the DtrH. Under discussion are a growth by text blocks within the DtrH, thoroughgoing redactional layers, or both together (Ch. 5.2). In any case the unity of the DtrH has itself been problematized. The problem becomes more grave when one bears in mind that numerous texts that Noth saw as the basic structure of the DtrH have since his time been attributed to later Dtr redactions (Deut. 1–3; Josh. 23–24; Judg. 2–3; 1 Sam. 12; 2 Sam. 7; 1 Kgs 8; 2 Kgs 17). The heterogeneous nature of the DtrH and the ascription of supporting structural elements to later redactional stages also cannot be counterbalanced by the oft-emphasized chronological coherence of Deuteronomy–2 Kings. The note that the building of the temple took place 480 years after the exile (1 Kgs 6.1) plays an important role here. However, the oft-supposed agreement of this note (whose origin is uncertain) with the time specifications in the previous books only results from the choice of particular texts.

In addition there are obvious differences between individual blocks of material in the DtrH. Foundational for the narrative in the book of Judges is the so-called Dtr 'judges pattern': a repeated pattern of events consisting of apostasy, oppression by enemies, cry to Yhwh, and deliverance (cf. Judg. 2.10-19). This cyclical progression has no real correspondence with the linear structure of Kings, which for the northern kingdom portrays the consequences of the → *Sin of Jeroboam* (1 Kgs 12) and for the southern kingdom reckons with increasing apostasy leading to ruin.[47] In addition, the oldest Dtr redaction in Kings focuses interest in the observance of the centralization command (→ *cult centralization*) from Deut. 12. This command is the criterion by which a king is judged to have done 'what is evil in the eyes of Yhwh' or not. Only later Dtr redactions pay special attention to cultic purity and emphasize the apostasy of Israel from Yhwh in favour of foreign deities and thus the violation of the First Commandment. However, in Joshua–Judges the centralization command is not an issue. Here the formula 'do what is evil in the eyes of Yhwh' refers to Israel's apostasy from Yhwh in favour of foreign gods. These observations have led to the supposition that with regard to the oldest Dtr edition of Deuteronomy–2

47. Cf. already G. von Rad, *Theology*, 346–7; G. Fohrer, *Introduction*, 205–15 and 227–37.

Kings one cannot yet speak of a coherent DtrH beginning with Deut. 1–3 or Josh. 1 and continuing to 2 Kgs 25.[48] If one acknowledges a pre-Dtr core in the conquest narratives of Josh. 1–12 that constitutes the original continuation of the non- and pre-priestly Moses-exodus narrative, then the existence of a DtrH with the boundaries postulated by Noth is fundamentally undermined.[49]

Finally, independent from the discussion of the basic nature of the DtrH, the development and origins of the materials later incorporated into the History are also hotly debated. Of course these questions must be answered individually for each text. Two general tendencies can still be detected within scholarship: one reckons with a number of stories that are of post-Dtr origin. In other words, there are a number of narratives that were only later worked into the overall framework of the History. This conclusion has recently been considered for example for the narratives concerning the prophet Elijah (see below, Ch. 7.6.3.6). The other tendency proposes that a number of narratives were already joined together into smaller or larger compositions before Dtr. The most prominent example here is the thesis of a pre-Dtr Saul-David-Solomon narrative (see below, Ch. 7.6.3.4).

## 7.6.3 Origins of the Deuteronomistic Composition of the History of the People of Israel from Exodus to Exile

### *7.6.3.1 The Work as a Whole and Its Dating*

With regard to the formation of the Dtr edited books of Joshua–2 Kings scholarship continues to move away from a sustainable consensus. In general Noth's theory of a → *DtrH* continues to be promulgated in some modified form. Contrary sketches are mostly based on the analysis of particular texts and are still in need of detailed testing for the text complex as a whole. Based on the current state of discussion concerning the formation of the Pentateuch and drawing on the central objections to Noth's theory of a DtrH the following sketch of a Dtr composition in Exodus–2 Kings and of its formation can be given: The Dtr composition of the history of the people of Israel from exodus to the → *exile* is formed around two poles that gradually grew together. The first pole consists of the non- and pre-priestly Moses-exodus-conquest narrative in – Exod. 1–Josh 12. The second pole is the Dtr portrayal of the history of the kingdoms of Judah and Israel including their formation under Saul, David and Solomon in the books of

48. E. Würthwein, 'Erwägungen' (Bibliography Ch. 7.6).

49. K. Schmid, *Genesis*, 147–50 (above, Ch. 5 n.19); R. G. Kratz, *Composition* (above, n. 12).

1 Samuel–2 Kings. While the Moses-exodus-conquest narrative in Exod.–Josh. 12 was gradually expanded through the law, the Dtr portrayal of the monarchical period grew backwards in time. The connection between the two poles was established by a late Dtr redaction that is traceable throughout the entire text complex of Exodus–2 Kings but was especially concerned with the portrayal of the premonarchic period of Israel in the land (Joshua–Judges).

In light of the current state of the discussion, it is appropriate to note that most observations concerning the pre-history of the books Exodus–2 Kings (especially concerning the pre-Dtr text inventory) are only dependent on the large hypotheses with regard to the composition-historical determination of its integration in a larger work and are therefore not significantly impacted by the existence of a DtrH or its denial. This is also the case for the basic deliberations regarding the composition-historical indexing of the edited books. For the work as a whole the → *terminus a quo* is the last reported event, namely the last Davidic king Jehoiachin's pardoning by the Babylonian King Amel-Marduk. This event can be dated fairly precisely to the year 562 BCE. If the work as a whole is the result of the connection of various Dtr partial compositions, then it would correspondingly come from a subsequent date. Either way the late Dtr redactions stretch far into the postexilic period.

Bibliography see Ch. 5 and Ch. 5.2. Further: E. Aurelius, *Zukunft jenseits des Gerichts: Eine religionsgeschichtliche Studie zum Enneateuch*. BZAW 319. Berlin/New York: de Gruyter, 2003.

### *7.6.3.2 Moses-Exodus-Conquest Narrative (Exod.–Josh.)*

The basic content of the non-priestly narrative complex in the books of Exodus–Joshua begins with the oppression and persecution of the Israelites in Egypt. It reports the birth and deliverance of the child Moses, Moses' stay and marriage in Midian, his calling and return to Egypt, as well as the Israelites' flight out of Egypt and the destruction of the Egyptian pursuers at the Sea of Reeds (Exod. 1–14*). Notices preserved in the books of Numbers and Deuteronomy follow. These concern the movements of the Israelites to the oasis of Kadesh and the region of the Moabites, where Moses dies and is buried. The basic layer ends with the depiction of the crossing of the Jordan and the conquest of various cities and districts in the region of the tribe of Benjamin (Josh. 1–12*) including Jericho (Josh. 6*) and Ai (Josh. 8*). The promise issued at the burning bush reaches fulfilment in the → *conquest* under Joshua, thereby concluding the thematic arch begun in Egypt. This older Moses-exodus-conquest narrative does not know of Israel's detour to the mountain of God and the revelation of the law there. Regardless of the theological closeness to the beginnings of Deuteronomy, it is nevertheless older than Deuteronomy and the Dtr portion of the Sinai pericope. Its content treats the origins of Israel, which it locates outside the land and stemming from its election by God occurring without mediation of the monarchy. This supports a formation in either a pre- or postmonarchic context. The literary relationships, such as the narrative of the birth and deliverance of the Moses child (Exod. 2*) to the Akkadian Sargon Legend (ANET, 119), as well as the theological orientation support a Neo-Assyrian date. One may therefore suppose that the beginnings of the narrative of Moses, the exodus, and the conquest passed on to us were formed in the region of the northern kingdom after its demise in the year 722/1 BCE.

| **Exod. 1–Deut. 34: Moses** | | |
|---|---|---|
| Exod. 1–15* | Israel in Egypt and Exodus from Egypt | |
| | Exod. 2* | Birth and Deliverance of the Child Moses |
| | Exod. 3–4* | Call of Moses |
| | Exod. 7–11* | Plagues |
| | Exod. 12–13* | Flight out of Egypt |
| | Exod. 14* | Miracle at the Sea of Reeds |
| | Exod. 15.21 | Song of Miriam |
| Exod. 15–Num. 24* | Israel in the Desert and at Sinai | |
| | Exod. 19* | Theophany at Sinai |
| | Exod. 20* | Decalogue |
| | Exod. 21–23* | Covenant Code |
| | Exod. 32–34* | Golden Calf and Renewal of the Covenant |
| | Num. 10* | Departure from Sinai |
| | Num. 22–24* | Balaam |
| Deut. 1–34* | Moses' Farewell Address in Moab (cf. 7.2) | |
| | Deut. 5* | Decalogue |
| | Deut. 12–26* | Law |
| | Deut. 34* | Death of Moses |

| **Josh. 1–24: Joshua** | |
|---|---|
| Josh. 1* | Joshua's Commissioning |
| Josh. 2–12* | Conquest of the Land |

| | | |
|---|---|---|
| | Josh. 2–8* | Conquest of the Cities of Jericho and Ai |
| Josh. 13–21* | Partitioning of the Land | |
| Josh. 23–24* | Joshua's Last Works | |
| | Josh. 23: Joshua's First Farewell Address | |
| | Josh. 24: Assembly at Shechem; Joshua's Second Farewell Address and Burial | |

The author of the older Moses-exodus-conquest narrative was able in part to draw on traditional material such as the traditions of Moses' stay in Midian (Exod. 2.15-23*; 4.18-20*) and Miriam's famous victory song (Exod. 15.21b). Much easier to detect are the traditions included in Josh. 2–12 that are at their core primarily a collection of → *aetiological* sagas of Benjaminite origins.

The date of these sagas is controversial. With respect to their collection and arrangement it is safe to assume that their shared topic – possession of the land granted through Yhwh – was intended as an antithesis to the experience of loss of the land after the Neo-Assyrian occupation in the 8th cent. BCE.

It is also certain that the sagas concerning the capture of Jericho and Ai (Josh. 2–8) do not provide historical information concerning the period of the Israelites' possession of the land in the 13th/12th cent. BCE. It is fairly certain that Jericho was not inhabited from the 14th cent. into the 12th cent., and there is no trace that Ai was an inhabited city for the whole second millennium. After the Early Bronze Age city protected by strong walls from the middle of the third millennium was abandoned, the location remained uninhabited until the founding of an early Iron Age village. Up to this time it was exactly what its name indicates: a ruin. At the time of Joshua there was neither a city in Jericho nor in Ai that could be conquered.

## Excursus: Moses

The search for the figure of Moses is primarily a problem of the sources and their historical appraisal. Moses is reported exclusively in biblical texts and its dependent traditions. According to the biblical witness Moses is the central figure of the most ancient history and of Israel's classic period of salvation. Outfitted with an authority unrivalled in the Old Testament and privileged with an incomparable closeness to God, Moses frees the people of Israel from Egypt at the charge of the God Yhwh. He then imparts the law to them on the mountain of God and leads them for 40 years through the desert until they reach the boundary of the promised land. In the wake of the biblical portrait the Jewish as well as the Christian tradition has created various images of Moses, though the image primarily found in tradition is Moses the lawgiver who promulgates to Israel the will of the one God Yhwh and records it in the Torah. This traditional picture has not been able to withstand historical enquiry. Pentateuchal scholarship has dated Deuteronomy and later P to the late monarchical period as well as to the exilic and post-exilic periods (Ch. 5.2). Even the → *Decalogue*, whose connection to Moses has been maintained despite the late-dating of Deuteronomy and P, along with the older legal texts all together, can no longer be traced back to Moses (Ch. 6). As a result the historical characterization of Moses as lawgiver no longer possesses any historical basis but is instead the projection of a later period. Neither was it the earliest image of Moses in the Old Testament. However, the charismatic deliverer and leader of the exodus also disappears into the silence of history. This is hardly surprising because the beginnings of the narrative of the exodus under Moses' leadership passed down to us likely stem from the end of the 8th cent. BCE. This is – if the Pharaoh of the oppression was Rameses II – approximately 600 years after the exodus. Yet normally the origins of oral traditions withdraw completely behind the narrative itself within four generations. Therefore the biblical traditions only allow for the culling of historical information about Moses to a very limited degree and through indirect means. The possible historical data include the fact that Moses is an Egyptian name (a short form formed by the loss of the → *theophoric element* of a name like Thutmoses 'the God XY is or has been born') and Moses' connection with Midian. Later fabrications can be excluded in these cases. It is simply impossible to explain why tradition should have given a non-Israelite name to a man it portrayed as the founder of everything genuinely Israelite. The same is the case for his marriage to the daughter of a foreign priest, a union contrary to later religious decorum. All other detailed characterizations of Moses can be considered non-historical, and the more general information at best belonging to the realm of historical possibility. This is the case, for example, for the Egyptian sources of the New Kingdom which document the entry and the commissioning of Semitic tribes in Egypt (cf. the 'Letter of an Egyptian border officer' from the early 12th cent. BCE in TGI[3], 40–1). It is also the case for the depiction of the semi-nomadic milieu, and finally for the fact that military victories such as the one reported in Exod. 14 were attributed to the delivering action of Yhwh.

📖 J. Assmann, *Moses the Egyptian: The Memory of Egypt in Western Monotheism*. London/Cambridge, Mass.: Harvard University Press, 1997; M. Buber, *Moses: The Revelation and the Covenant*. With an introduction by M. Fishbane. Atlantic Highlands, N.J.: Humanities Press International, 1988; R. Smend, 'Mose als geschichtliche Gestalt', *Historische Zeitschrift* 260 (1995): 1–19; repr. in *Bibel, Theologie, Universität*. Göttingen: Vandenhoeck & Ruprecht, 1997, 5–20.

The older Moses-exodus-conquest narrative was enlarged considerably as the tradition continued to be handed down. Expansions include narrative material such as the non-priestly plague narratives (Exod. 7–11*) and the Balaam pericope (Num. 22–24*), as well as legislative texts, like the → *Covenant Code*

(Exod. 21–23*), the Deuteronomic Law (Deut. 12–26*), and the → *Decalogue* (Exod. 20; Deut. 5). The Dtr redactions of the older Moses-exodus-conquest narrative began no later than the incorporation of the already → *parenetically* framed Deuteronomic Law in the exilic period. These redactions are responsible in particular for the formation of the non-priestly Sinai pericope, the arrangement of the framing chapters of Deuteronomy, as well as the orientation of the book of Joshua towards the command to exclusively worship Yhwh (Josh. 1; 23; 24). The Dtr editors used list material from the late monarchical period that chronicled place-names and boundaries for the portrayal of the partitioning of the conquered land (Josh. 13–21*). With regard to the discussion of the DtrH one should highlight that the Dtr redactions in the book of Joshua have in view the complete work of the history of the Israelite people from exodus to exile. They therefore clearly belong to one of the later Dtr redactions.

The book of Numbers posts a very unique question that shall be addressed briefly here. The heterogeneous non-priestly texts appear almost entirely to consist of multiple layers of additions to the priestly passages that themselves can hardly have belonged to the original layer of P (Ch. 7.1). At the same time, however, the non-priestly narratives contain material that is assumed by the Deuteronomic recapitulation of the wilderness wandering; in fact it is assumed in a state not yet combined with the priestly material. Therefore, it is possible to consider Deut. 1–3 a relatively free adaptation of a tradition also drawn on by Num. 13–14. However, in Num. 13–14 the tradition appears in a form that is both post-priestly and influenced by Deut. 1–3.[50]

A. G. Auld, *Joshua Retold: Synoptic Perspectives*. OTS. Edinburgh: T&T Clark, 1998; K. Bieberstein, *Josua–Jordan–Jericho: Archäologie, Geschichte und Theologie der Landnahmeerzählungen Jos 1–6*. OBO 143. Fribourg: Academic Press/Göttingen: Vandenhoeck & Ruprecht, 1995; J. C. Gertz, 'Mose und die Anfänge der jüdischen Religion', *ZTK* 99 (2002): 3–20; E. Noort, *Das Buch Josua: Forschungsgeschichte und Problemfelder*. EdF 292. Darmstadt: Wissenschaftliche Buchgesellschaft, 1998.

### *7.6.3.3 Narratives of the Judges (The Book of Judges)*

The book of Judges receives its name from the army leaders and clan heroes that

50. For Num 13–14 cf. E. Blum, *Pentateuch* (above, Ch. 5 n. 11), 180–1; E. Otto, *Das Deuteronomium im Pentateuch und Hexateuch: Studien zur Literaturgeschichte von Pentateuch und Hexateuch im Lichte des Deuteronomiumrahmens* (FAT 30; Tübingen: Mohr Siebeck, 2000). For analysis of the book of Numbers cf. T. Römer, 'Das Buch Numeri und das Ende des Jahwisten', in *Abschied* (ed. J. C. Gertz, K. Schmid, and M. Witte), 215–31 (esp. no. 10; above, Ch. 5 n. 10).

determined the fate of Israel according to the portrayal of Judg. 2.6–16.31 in the time between the possession of the land and the formation of the state. They are the so-called judges (Heb. *šopĕṭîm*), better: chiefs, or local rulers. The book is structured in three parts – the introduction (Judg. 1.1–3.6), the main body with the narratives of the judges (Judg. 3.7–16.31), and individual narratives (Judg. 17–21). The introduction begins with an excerpt from Josh. 14–19. This excerpt highlights the incomplete possession of the land by the tribes in the south under Joshua while the following negative account of possession suggests that the possession of land was also incomplete in the rest of the tribes. Afterwards comes the notice reporting the death of Joshua (cf. Josh. 24.29-30) again, which can be explained to have come about as a result of the book division between Joshua and Judges. The most important text in the introduction is the Dtr judges pattern, which lays out the theology of history that plays a leading interpretative role for the book (Judg. 2.10-19): Israel's apostasy from Yhwh brings about Israel's affliction by its enemies. In their distress the people cry out to Yhwh, who then allows the judges to emerge to deliver the people from their enemies. It does not take long after the death of a respective judge before Israel again falls into apostasy so that the events repeat themselves.

| The Book of Judges | | |
|---|---|---|
| Judg. 1.1–2.5 | Appendix to the Conquest of the Land | |
| Judg. 2.6–3.6 | Prologue: Prospective Look at the Time of the Judges | |
| Judg. 3.7–16.31 | Narratives of the Judges | |
| | Judg. 3 | Othniel; Ehud |
| | Judg. 4–5 | Deborah and Barak |
| | Judg. 5 | Song of Deborah |
| | Judg. 6–8 | Gideon |
| | [Judg. 9 | Abimelech's Kingdom; Jotham's Fabel] |
| | Judg. 10–12 | Jephthah |
| | Judg. 13–16 | Samson |
| Judg. 17–18 | Micah's Divine Image/ the Danites' Migration | |
| Judg. 19–21 | The Sacrilege of the Benjaminites | |

The judges pattern appears at the very beginning of the main section as a

### The Pattern of the Judges (Judg. 3.7-11; cf. Judg. 2.10-19)

| | |
|---|---|
| Declaration of Sin | And the Israelites did what was offensive to Yhwh, and forgot Yhwh their God and served the Baals and the Asherahs (v. 7). |
| Yhwh's anger | Then the anger of Yhwh burned against Israel (v. 8). |
| Handing over | And he sold them into the hand of Cushan-rishathaim, the king of Mesopotamia (v. 8). |
| Duration | And so Israel served Cushan-rishathaim for eight years (v. 8). |
| Cry | Then the Israelites cried to Yhwh (v. 9). |
| Rise of a deliverer | And Yhwh aroused for them a deliverer that would deliver them, Othniel, the Kennizzite, the younger brother of Caleb. And the spirit of Yhwh came upon him, and he became a judge in Israel and went out to war. And Yhwh gave the king of Mesopotamia, Cushan-Rishathaim, into his hand (vv. 9–10a), |
| Declaration of subservience* | So that his hand became strong against him (v. 10b) |
| Peace declaration | Then the land was at peace for forty years (v. 11a) |
| Declaration of death | And Othniel the Kenizzite died (v. 11b). |

*Meaning: PN bowed on that day under the hand of Israel (cf. Judg. 3.30).

paradigm in the story of the Judahite judge Othniel (Judg. 3.7-11), which is a purely redactional story. Following this example piece comes a complex dealing with the heroic deeds of the so-called major judges – Ehud from Benjamin (Judg. 3.12-30), Deborah from Ephraim and Barak from Naphtali (Judg. 4–5), Gideon from Manasseh (Judg. 6–8), Jephthah from Gilead (Judg. 10.6–12.7), and Samson from Dan (Judg. 13–16). Additionally there is an episode concerning Abimelech's failed attempt at establishing a kingdom in Shechem (Judg. 9), which shares its anti-monarchical orientation with the Gideon story. The individual hero stories are bound together through the judges pattern. Short list-like notices concerning the so-called minor judges are worked into the larger complex (Judg. 10.1-5; 12.8-15). According to the Dtr conception the minor judges have the same role as the major ones – though the exact nature of this role is not completely clear. On the one hand the judges are described as charismatics gifted with the spirit of God (cf. Judg. 3.10; 6.34; 11.29) that deliver the people of Israel from distress. On the other hand they also appear to be bearers of an office responsible for leading all Israel (Heb. *šāpaṭ* 'judge, rule'; cf. Judg. 3.10; 4.4-5; 10.1-5; 12.7-15; 15.20; 16.31). This coexistence and intertwining of functions is intentional in the Dtr edition of Judges and has arisen as a result of the Dtr notion of 'Israel' as a united people and polity already in the premonarchic period. Hence, pre-Dtr are at best the charismatic leaders; the notion of a premonarchic 'all Israel' is the historical construction of Dtr. The individual narratives in the third part of the book (Judg. 17–21) create a negative image of the religious and social circumstances of the time of the Judges. They are held together by the refrain 'In those days there was no king in Israel; all the people did what was right in their own eyes' (Judg. 17.6; 21.25; cf. 18.1; 19.1). This refrain also points to an idiosyncrasy of the book of Judges, namely its divergent evaluations of the monarchy.

The portrayal of the premonarchic period after Moses and Joshua found in the book of Judges can also be read as offering an alternate view to a state-organized Israel. While the drawbacks in the third part of the book call to mind the ordering functions of the monarchy on political, cultic and legal levels, in one of the Dtr formulated speeches of the book Gideon openly rejects the royal dignity offered to him. According to him, the monarchy clearly contradicts the theocratic ideal of Yhwh's royal authority over Israel (Judg. 8.22-23). The episode concerning Abimelech (Judg. 9) also views the monarchy quite sceptically. In the Jotham fable, only the completely unsuitable thorn bush is willing to take part in the experiment, while the elites reject the office of king. Accordingly, in the subsequent narrative Abimelech also proves to be unsuitable. His violent seizure of power leads to increasing violence and fails. These incompatible views of the monarchy – also in the portrayal of the formation of Saul's kingdom (see below, Ch. 7.6.3.4) the voice of rejection (1 Sam. 7–8; 10.17-27; 12.1-25) stands next to pro-monarchic passages (1 Sam. 8*; 9.1–10.16; 11.1-15 – mirror a debate that began with the demise of the northern kingdom and continued for a long duration. Its perspective includes the collapse of the kingdom as well as hope for its renewed establishment after the end of the exile.[51]

The narrative core of the book is often identified with individual tribal legends that were passed on independently from one another, all narrating the oppression by enemies and liberation by heroes. However, differentiation is called for at this level: apart from the purely redactional Othniel, the Samson stories (Judg. 13–16) are also considered (still later) additions. It is controversial whether the older individual sagas were already put together into a

51. Cf. T. Veijola, *Das Königtum in der Beurteilung der deuteronomistischen Historiographie: Eine redaktionsgeschichtliche Untersuchung* (AASF 198; Helsinki: Suomalainen Tiedeakatemia, 1977); R. Müller, *Königtum und Gottes Herrschaft: Untersuchungen zur alttestamentlichen Monarchiekritik* (FAT II/3; Tübingen: Mohr Siebeck, 2004).

pre-Dtr 'book of deliverers'[52] or rather if the collection first took place in the Dtr redaction.[53] Either way one will hardly find sources of the premonarchic period in the individual narratives. This is likely also the case for the Song of Deborah (Judg. 5), which according to a long-held opinion represents the only truly authentic source from the premonarchic period at least in its core. The song underwent a wide-reaching redaction through which a battle at the waters of Megiddo, which according to the original layer only included Naphtali and Zebulun, became stylized into a conflict between Canaan and 'all Israel', though Judah (still?) remains unmentioned. The conception of a 'period of the Judges' by all means represents the work of the Dtr editors, since the portrayal is clearly dependent on the pattern of the judges and the individual narratives (which, taken for themselves, are rather profane stories) are subject to the theological question of exclusive Yhwh worship. Both are certainly due to Dtr redaction. Also certain is that there are composition-historical differences within the Dtr redaction. Critics of the DtrH theory highlight the fact that the first Dtr edition of the book is basically critical of the monarchy and is thus in agreement with later Dtr redactions in 1 Samuel–2 Kings. This could support the notion that the Dtr portrayal of history in the block Judges–2 Kings grew from the end back towards the beginning. However, the composition-historical classification of the clearly pro-monarchic texts is controversial at this time.

Bibliography 8 The History of Ancient Israel and Judah; P. Guillaume, 'From a Post-Monarchical to the Pre-Monarchical Period of the Judges', *BN* 113 (2002): 12–17.

### *7.6.3.4 Narratives of Saul, David and Solomon (1 Sam.–1 Kgs 11)*

| **Samuel (1 Sam. 1–7)** | |
|---|---|
| 1 Sam. 1 | Samuel's Birth |
| 1 Sam. 2 | Hannah's Song of Praise |
| 1 Sam. 3 | Call of Samuel |

52. W. Richter, *Traditionsgeschichtliche Untersuchungen zum Richterbuch* (rev. ed.; BBB 19; Bonn: P. Hanstein, 1966); idem, *Die Bearbeitungen des 'Richterbuches' in der deuteronomischen Epoche* (BBB 21; Bonn: P. Hanstein, 1964).

53. M. Noth, *DH*; U. Becker, *Richterzeit und Königtum* (BZAW 192; Berlin/New York: de Gruyter, 1990).

| | | | |
|---|---|---|---|
| | 1 Sam. 4–6 | *Story of the Ark I: Loss and Later Return of the Ark from the Hand of the Philistines* | |
| 1 Sam. 7 | Samuel's Function as Judge | | |
| **Samuel and Saul: the Formation of the Monarchy (1 Sam. 8–15)** | | | |
| 1 Sam. 8 | Israel Desires a King | | Negative |
| 1 Sam. 9–10 | Saul Looks for Donkeys and Is Anointed King | | Positive |
| 1 Sam. 10 | Drawing of Lots | | Negative |
| 1 Sam. 11 | Appointment of Saul as King after His Victory over the Ammonites | | Positive |
| 1 Sam. 12 | Samuel's Farewell Address | | Negative |
| 1 Sam. 13–15 | Saul's Kingdom; His Rejection | | |
| **Saul's Descent and David's Ascent (1 Sam. 16–31)** | | | |
| 1 Sam. 16–20 | David at Saul's Court | | |
| | 1 Sam. 17 | David and Goliath | |
| 1 Sam. 21–31 | David as Army Captain | | |
| | 1 Sam. 31 | Saul's death | |
| **David's Kingdom (2 Sam. 1–1 Kgs 2)** | | | |
| 2 Sam. 1–5 | David Becomes King in Hebron, First over Judah, Later Also over Israel (2 Sam. 5), and Conquers Jerusalem (2 Sam. 5) | | |
| | *2 Sam. 6* | *Story of the Ark II: Transport of the Ark to Jerusalem* | |
| 2 Sam. 7 | Nathan's Promise | | |
| 2 Sam. 8 | David's Wars and Officials | | |
| 2 Sam. 9–1 Kgs 2 | Arrangement of the Succession to David's Throne | | |
| | 2 Sam. 11 | David and Bathsheba | |
| | 2 Sam. 13–19 | Absalom's Revolt | |
| | 1 Kgs 1–2 | David's Death; Solomon's Political Murders | |
| **Solomon's Kingdom (1 Kgs 3–11)** | | | |
| 1 Kgs 3 | Solomon's Wisdom | | |
| 1 Kgs 4 | Solomon's Officials | | |
| 1 Kgs 5–7 | Temple Construction | | |
| 1 Kgs 8 | Temple Dedication Prayer | | |
| 1 Kgs 9–11 | Solomon's Riches; His Wives and Enemies | | |

The editing technique used by the Dtr authors of the books of Samuel and Kings in the portrayal of the formation and consolidation of the monarchy differs decisively from the one used in the portrayal of the two partitioned states Judah and Israel. According to the general information in the Dtr frame notices, the portrayal of the period of the kings beginning with Rehoboam of Judah (1 Kgs 14.21-29) and Nadab of Israel (1 Kgs 15.25-32) is based on the 'journals or → *annals* of the kings of Judah / Israel'. Further narrative material from various origins and of varying historiographic quality has gradually been interpolated into these annals (see below, Chs 7.6.3.4 and 7.6.3.5). The literary features appear somewhat different for the forerunners Saul, Ishbaal, David, Solomon and Jeroboam. Here the Dtr frame notices together with further Dtr passages are inserted into an existing tradition complex. They do not draw upon annals from the early monarchy, nor were there likely any to draw upon. So the particulars of the reigns of the Saulides and of David and Solomon were obviously unknown. In fact, information about Saul's age at the beginning of his reign and the length of his reign seem to have been missing from the beginning (1 Sam. 13.1). The age given for his son is questionable and the unknown data was replaced with round numbers (2 Sam. 2.10). A similar scenario has taken place for the 40 years allotted to the reigns of David (1 Kgs 2.11) and Solomon (1 Kgs 11.42), but here the length is also telling in that 40 years are a symbol for completion and for the time of an entire generation. Nevertheless, the Dtr editors also based the portrayal of the formation and consolidation of the monarchy in Israel and Judah under Saul, David and Solomon on a number of pre-Dtr traditions according to many scholars.

***Vorlagen* for the Deuteronomists in 1 Sam.–1 Kgs 11:** Generally speaking the following individual narrative traditions are considered to have been passed on and then edited by Dtr: a) the → *ark* narrative (1 Sam. 4.1–7.1; 2 Sam. 6.2-23); b) the history of Saul's reign (1 Sam. 9–15); c) the history of David's ascent (1 Sam. 16–2 Sam. 5, 7–8); d) the succession history (2 Sam. 9–20; 1Kgs 1–2); e) the history of Solomon's reign (1 Kgs 3–11).

The exact boundaries and inner relationships between the individual narrative entities as well as their historical value are in fact controversial and in most cases can hardly be determined satisfactorily. One example is the seemingly unending discussion concerning the narrative complex of the succession of David (2 Sam. 9–20; 1 Kgs 1–2). Leonhard Rost's characterization of the succession narrative as a self-enclosed work of literature (1926) has become very influential.[54] Composed by a skilful narrator from the Solomonic royal court '*in majorem gloriam Salomonis*', the narrative was considered for a long time as the beginning and high point of Old Israelite historiography.[55] Yet the interlocking questions concerning the extent, the redaction-history, and the intention of the narrative of the succession to David's throne are not without controversy.[56] The narrative is by some viewed as a massive critique of the Solomonic regime because of its depiction of ruthless power politics at work in the court; others describe it as a pro-royal redaction of a narrative originally taking the opposite view on the kingdom. The topic may also have been something completely different, more a theological → *anthropology* concerned with the human ability to shape one's reality through autonomous action. A special problem lies in the unmistakable literary allusions to the previous traditions of Saul and David. Is it a redactional connection between originally self-contained works of literature or rather the mark of a single larger narrative complex? Finally, the long-held view that the succession narrative is quite ancient has fallen prey to increased questioning. As a result it has recently been argued repeatedly that there was an older tradition concerning Samuel and Saul (1 Sam. 1–14) and a collection of Jerusalem court stories about David and his descendants (2 Sam. 11–1 Kgs 2) that developed separately. The narrative of Saul's rejection (1 Sam. 15) and David's ascent (1 Sam. 16–2 Sam. 8) is then – with varying boundaries – deemed a connecting piece. This connection is in fact concerned with more than simply bringing together narratives. Rather, it is interested in the historical and theological problems surrounding how David, who is historically most likely to have been founder of the dynasty of the southern kingdom, could

54. L. Rost, *The Succession to the Throne of David* (transl. by M. D. Rutter and D. M. Gunn; with an introduction by E. Ball; Sheffield: Almond Press, 1982).

55. G. von Rad, 'Der Anfang der Geschichtsschreibung im alten Israel', in *Gesammelte Studien zum Alten Testament* (3rd. ed.; TB 8; Munich: Kaiser, 1965 [1944]), 148–88 (ET 'The Beginnings of Historical Writing in Ancient Israel', in *The Problem of the Hexateuch and Other Essays*; London: SCM, 1984, 166-204).

56. Cf. the contributions in A. de Pury and T. Römer, eds, *Die sogenannte Thronfolgegeschichte Davids: Neue Einsichten und Anfragen* (OBO 176; Fribourg: Academic Press/Göttingen: Vandenhoeck & Ruprecht, 2000).

also become Saul's legitimate successor and king over the northern kingdom of Israel according to the Old Testament view of history. David's lament over the house of Saul and the punishment of Saul's murderers are highlighted for this reason. The intent is to prove that David does not bear any responsibility for the deaths of Saul, Abner, or Ishbaal, and that he was not a usurper (2 Sam. 1–5).[57] If this analysis is correct, then the formation of this synopsis most likely took place in the period after the demise of the northern kingdom when the Jerusalem dynasty of the Davidides took on the inheritance of Samaria (see below).

## Excursus: David

The Old Testament has more to report about David than about any other king. His unstoppable ascent is closely intertwined with Saul's descent (1 Sam. 16–2 Sam. 5, 7–8). Samuel anoints David, the youngest of the eight sons of Jessie from Bethlehem, to take the place of the sitting king Saul, who had been rejected by Yhwh. 'Skilful in playing, a man of valour, a warrior, prudent in speech, and a man of good presence; and Yhwh is with him' (1 Sam. 16.18) – in this manner he arrives at Saul's court in order to alleviate Saul's anguish with his music. A different narrative reports how David becomes Saul's armour bearer after his victory over the gigantic Philistine warrior Goliath (1 Sam. 17; but cf. 2 Sam. 21.19!). The military and human success of this brilliant hero – who first wins the heart of the king (1 Sam. 16.21) and goes on to win friendship with his son Jonathan (1 Sam. 18.1-4; 20) and to become the king's son-in-law (1 Sam. 18.17-27) – later evokes the king's jealousy. Saul recognizes David as the proclaimed opposing king, which brings David and those around him into mortal danger (1 Sam. 18.5-16; 19-22). David flees and becomes chief of a band of refugees and privateers (1 Sam. 22.2) that sometimes serves the Philistines (1 Sam. 27). He is, however, able to avoid taking part in the Philistine actions against the 'Israelites' (1 Sam. 29), instead sharing his war booty with them (1 Sam. 30.26-31). Twice David spares Saul when Saul is in his hands (1 Sam 24; 26). Saul and three of his sons, one of them Jonathan, fall in the battle of Gilboa in the war against the Philistines (1 Sam. 31). Then David returns from his exile with the Philistines and is appointed king over Judah in Hebron (2 Sam. 2). When the last Saulides able to rule die a violent death (without David's involvement or approval), David also becomes king over Israel (2 Sam. 5). After conquering Jebusite Jerusalem, David becomes city-king over the 'City of David' (2 Sam. 5), thereby combining in himself sovereignty over three legally and historically different entities. As the story progresses it narrates how David brings the → *ark* to Jerusalem – which the Old Testament recognizes as the decisive push towards the later building of the Temple under Solomon (2 Sam. 6) – and how he establishes

57. A. A. Fischer, *Von Hebron nach Jerusalem: Eine redaktionsgeschichtliche Studie zur Erzählung von König David in II Sam 1–5* (BZAW 335; Berlin/New York: de Gruyter, 2004).

an empire through military and diplomatic skill. He subdues the Aramaeans and the Transjordanian 'states' (2 Sam.8; 10; 12.26-31) and establishes covenants with the Phoenicians (2 Sam. 5.11), while expelling the Philistines (2 Sam. 5.17-25; 8.1; 21.15-22). The second part of the narrative of David treats the disturbances that occur with regard to succession to the dynasty founder's throne among his 17 sons and are decided in Solomon's favour (2 Sam. 9–20; 1 Kgs 1–2). These narratives describe David as both exemplary and fallible, as a man who is met by temptation and who is sustained through and in spite of it. It is narrated in detail how his beloved son Absalom contests his rule (2 Sam. 15–19). David's affair with Bathsheba, Solomon's mother, whose husband Uriah is sent by David to his death to cover up the adultery (2 Sam. 11), weighs especially heavy. Yet David appears remorseful and thereby grows in stature as one who is repentant (2 Sam. 12).

Even though the shadow of the scrupulous power politician laden with heavy guilt weighs on the image of the brilliant ascent of the young shepherd and singer to architect and ruler of an empire, David remains the ideal king in the biblical tradition. Through divine assistance David remains successful and in that becomes the benchmark for later kings. Promises of sovereignty in the Prophetic Books – setting before the harried Israel of the exilic and postexilic period an existence in freedom and justice (Isa. 9.1-6; 11.1-8; Mic. 5.1-4; Zech. 9.9-10) – derive from Yhwh's promise of an eternal existence of David's dynasty (2 Sam. 7). The tradition ascribes 73 (→ *Septuagint:* 88) psalms in the Psalter (Pss 3–41; 51–71 [without 66; 67; 71]; 86; 101; 103; 108–110; 138–145) to the singing and praying David (2 Sam. 1.17-27; 7.18-29; 22 = Ps. 18; 23.1-7). The scrolls from → *Qumran* note 4050 psalms and songs (11 QPs$^a$ 27.2-11).

The historical David, on the other hand, is quite elusive. Even the information about his 40-year reign (first 7½ years in Hebron, then in Jerusalem as king over Judah, Israel and Jerusalem; 2 Sam. 5.4-5) is completely uncertain. In this text the Old Testament replaces the historically unknown with a round number. Extra-biblical and archaeological witnesses are completely absent. The 'House of David' appears first in the second half of the ninth century in an Old Aramaic inscription from Dan.[58] As a result one can conclude that at *this* time there was a tribal state in the south to go along with the Omride northern kingdom. The southern state was a local entity, focused on its central city and a strong leading personality, namely David and his clan. This picture agrees with the nature of territorial dominions in Palestine in the tenth and ninth centuries that were based on small city kingdoms with a relatively small yet professionally operating army (Ch. 4.2.1.2). This data agrees in turn with the (critically viewed) Old Testament portrayal of the beginnings of the monarchy under Saul and David as well as with David's successful attempt to gain some sort of hegemony over the region belonging to the Benjaminites which was ruled by the Saulides.

D. M. Gunn, *The Story of King David*. Sheffield: Dept. of Biblical Studies Press, 1978; S. L. McKenzie, *King David: A Biography.* Berlin/New York: de Gruyter, 2002.

58. *COS* II, 161–162.

As a source for the portrayal of the Solomonic period (1 Kgs 1–11) the Dtr editors point to 'the book of the history of Solomon' (1 Kgs 11.41). It is not totally impossible that this book title is a Dtr creation. The Dtr editors would then have asserted a corresponding source for the period of the united monarchy analogous to the annals of the kings of Judah and Israel. However, the book is not characterized explicitly as a set of 'annals or journals'. It is therefore more probable that the title belongs to an older text still recognizable within the present form of the account of the Solomonic reign.[59] The content of this pre-Dtr literary work focuses on glorifying Solomon, making him appear a wise and (as a result) powerful ruler. The book of Solomon's history can in this case be seen as a document of court literature. The pegs for dating the book and its image of Solomon historically come from the portrayal of Solomon's trade relationships (with the Phoenicians among others) and the cultural contact with Egypt that is taken for granted throughout the text. Both support the time of Hezekiah of Judah (725–697 BCE) as the temporal background for the authors.[60] The historiographic investigation behind the book of Solomon's history in the eighth century BCE is of course littered with uncertainties. Source material from the Solomonic period is generally posited for the portrayal of the palace and temple building (1 Kgs 6–7), in a number of building notices (1 Kgs 9), as well as in the administrative lists (1 Kgs 4).[61]

As has been shown above, the Dtr editors likely did not take the traditions as individual and isolated entities into their work. Material parentheses hold the entirety of the pre-Dtr text complex together and clearly did not originate first from the Dtr redactions. This suggests that a larger text complex comprising the stories about Saul, David and Solomon and thus narrating the origins of the monarchy had already been formed prior to any Dtr redaction. The intention of this narrative work can be recognized in the fact that the history of the first three kings of Israel is bound together by the transfer of authority first from Saul to the non-Saulide David and then from David to the Davidide Solomon in such a way that it seems comprehensible, unavoidable, and even legitimate and divinely intended (W. Dietrich). In other words, it is concerned with the legitimacy of the Davidide monarchy for all

59. See already M. Noth, *DH*, 92.

60. B. U. Schipper, *Israel und Ägyten in der Königszeit: Die kulturellen Kontakte von Salomo bis zum Fall Jerusalems* (OBO 170; Fribourg: Academic Press/Göttingen: Vandenhoeck & Ruprecht, 1999).

61. Cf. the critical survey in J. C. Gertz, 'Konstruierte Erinnerung: Alttestamentliche Historiographie im Spiegel von Archäologie und literarhistorischer Kritik am Fallbeispiel des solomonischen Königtums', *BTZ* 21 (2004): 3–29.

Israel after the demise of the northern kingdom. The author would most likely have been found in the environment of the Jerusalem court.

The Dtr redaction in the texts of 1 Sam.–1 Kgs 2 is not of one piece. This fact appears in the divergent appraisals of the monarchy in the texts attributed to Dtr. The depiction of the emergence of the monarchy in 1 Sam. 7–11 displays two different Dtr strands. The older strand, likely dating from the early exilic period, builds on the pre-Dtr narrative and is generally pro-monarchy. It reports how Saul went out in order to find his father's donkey and instead found a kingdom, how the hero was first secretly anointed by Samuel and his reign only began publicly after his successful battle (1 Sam. 9.1–10.16; 11.1-15). The later strand of the Dtr portrayal judges the monarchy critically and reports that Saul's proclamation to kingship occurs through the drawing of lots. Here the formation of the monarchy is bound together with the demand of the people and numerous speeches by Samuel that evaluate the monarchy as an emergency solution or (in still later Dtr layers) as a revolt against Yhwh's kingdom (1 Sam. 7–8; 10.17-27; 12.1-25).[62]

Bibliography 8 The History of Ancient Israel and Judah (Dietrich, *Early Monarchy*); idem, *Von David zu den Deuteronomisten: Studien zu den Geschichtsüberlieferungen des alten Testaments*. BWANT 156. Stuttgart: Kohlhammer, 2002; C. S. Ehrlich and M. C. White, eds, *Saul in Story and Tradition*. FAT 47. Tübingen: Mohr Siebeck, 2006; T. Veijola, *David: Gesammelte Studien zu den Davidüberlieferungen des Alten Testaments*. Publications of the Finnish Exegetical Society 52. Helsinki: Finnish Exegetical Society, 1990.

### *7.6.3.5 Narratives of the Kings of Judah and Israel (1 Kgs 12–2 Kgs 25)*

| | |
|---|---|
| **1 Kgs 12–2 Kgs 17:** | **The Divided Monarchy** |
| 1 Kgs 12 | 'The Division of the Kingdom' and the 'Sin of Jeroboam' |
| 1 Kgs 17–19; 21; 2 Kgs 1 | Elijah Narratives |
| 2 Kgs 2–9; 13 | Elisha Narratives |
| 2 Kgs 17 | Destruction of Samaria by the Assyrians; Demise of the Northern Kingdom; Deportation to Assyria |
| **2 Kgs 18–25** | **Judah from 722 to 587 BCE** |
| 2 Kgs 18–20 | Hezekiah (+ Isaiah) |

62. Cf. above Ch. 7.6.3.3 for the divergent evaluations of the monarchy in the book of Judges.

| | |
|---|---|
| 2 Kgs 22–23 | Josiah and → *'Josiah's reform'* |
| 2 Kgs 24–25 | The Babylonian Conquest of Jerusalem; Deportation to Babylon |
| 2 Kgs 25 | Pardon of Johoiachin 562 BCE |

The books of Kings depict the history of the united kingdom under Solomon (1 Kgs 1–11), then the history of the two kingdoms until the demise of Samaria, the capital city of the northern kingdom Israel (1 Kgs 12–2 Kgs 17), and finally the remainder of the history of the southern kingdom Judah (2 Kgs 18–25). Beginning with the history of the divided monarchy the portrayal is held together by Dtr framing notices to the individual kings. They provide the basic structure into which further narrative material from various origins was inserted. The Dtr editors can therefore be seen as the essential authors of the history of the kingdoms of Israel and Judah. The Dtr framing notices provide dates for the kings of the northern kingdom in terms of their relationship to the southern kings and vice versa (a). They also provide the length of a king's reign (b), for the southern kingdom the king's age at the beginning of his reign (c), as well as the name of the king's mother (d), and a judgement about whether the kings did what was right or what was evil in the eyes of Yhwh (e). In addition there is a reference to the 'journal', that is to the chronicle or annals of the respective kingdom (f), a note concerning death and burial (g), as well as the name of the successor (h).

### The Dtr Framing Schema in the Books of Kings

*Northern kingdom of Israel (i.e., 2 Kgs 13.10-13):* 'In the thirty-seventh year of King Joash of Judah, Jehoash son of Jehoahaz began to reign over Israel in Samaria (a); he reigned sixteen years (b). He also did what was evil in the sight of YHWH (e); he did not depart from all the sins of Jeroboam son of Nebat, which he caused Israel to sin, but he walked in them. Now the rest of the acts of Joash, and all that he did, as well as the might with which he fought against King Amaziah of Judah, are they not written in the Book of the Annals of the Kings of Israel (f)? So Joash slept with his ancestors (g), and Jeroboam sat upon his throne; Joash was buried in Samaria with the kings of Israel (g).'

*Southern kingdom of Judah (i.e., 2 Kgs 15.32-38):* 'In the second year of King Pekah son of Remaliah of Israel, King Jotham son of Uzziah of Judah began to reign (a). He was twenty-five years old (c) when he began to reign and reigned sixteen years in Jerusalem (b). His mother's name was Jerusha daughter of Zadok (d). He did what was right in the sight of Yhwh (e), just as his father Uzziah had done. Nevertheless the high places were not removed; the people still sacrificed and made offerings on the high places. He built the upper gate of the house of Yhwh. Now the rest of the acts of Jotham, and all that he did, are they not written in the Book of the Annals of the Kings of Judah (f)? In those days Yhwh began to send King Rezin of Aram and Pekah son of Remaliah against Judah. Jotham slept with his ancestors, and was buried with his ancestors in the city of David, his ancestor (g); his son Ahaz succeeded him (h).'

As the Dtr frame notices with their reference to the journals of the kings of Israel and Judah themselves indicate, they go back to king lists. Similar to the roughly contemporary Neo-Babylonian chronicles these 'journals / annals of the kings of Judah / Israel' (cf. 1 Kgs 14.29; 15.31, etc.) record the dates of rulership of the respective kings and a number of important events (*COS* I, 467–468). Their historical reliability has generally been confirmed by extra-biblical sources, as in the case of the Palestinian campaign by Pharaoh Shishak I (1 Kgs 14.25-26; cf. Ch. 4.2.1.3).

As expected the judgements passed by the Dtr authors reveal their historiographical and theological intention particularly plainly. Yet it is striking that every king of the northern kingdom receives poor grades. The reason for this evaluation lies in the 'sin of Jeroboam', namely the perpetuation of the cults (allegedly) initiated by Jeroboam in Bethel and Dan (1 Kgs 12; 2 Kgs 17) after the division of the kingdom. As many as eight of the kings of Judah did 'what was right in the eyes of Yhwh', though with the exception of Hezekiah and Josiah they did not destroy the local open-air sanctuaries (high places) where the people continued to offer sacrifices. As in the case of the northern kingdom and the sin of Jeroboam, the evaluations of the southern kings are also oriented towards the → *cult centralization* stipulations in Deut. Another matter is the negative evaluation of kings of Judah: Where a reason is provided for a negative evaluation it gives the impression that it is a later addition concerned with the problem of exclusive worship of Yhwh (2 Kgs 16.2-4; 21.2-16). Whenever no reason is given, the kings in question are always those in times of political crisis. From these differences in the Dtr frame notices one can conclude that the original Dtr layer was oriented historiographically and theologically towards the stipulation of cult centralization and the corresponding negative example of the 'sin of Jeroboam'. Accordingly, only the demise of the northern kingdom provided the occasion for a detailed Dtr commentary (2 Kgs

17), while the southern kingdom disappears almost without commentary. The attribution of guilt according to the standard of exclusive worship of Yhwh on the other hand can be traced to later Dtr redactors.

In any case, the Dtr author and later Dtr redactors of the books of Kings worked further materials such as the narratives of Jehu's revolt (2 Kgs 9–10) and the prophetic legends concerning Elijah (1 Kgs 17–19; 21; 2 Kgs 1) and Elisha (2 Kgs 2–9; 13) into the basic structure of the frame notices. It remains difficult, however, to separate the Dtr redaction from the older source material in the individual texts as is demonstrated by the unending discussion regarding the composition-history and historiographic reliability of the report of → *Josiah's reform* in 2 Kgs 22–23.

Bibliography 8 The History of Ancient Israel and Judah; C. Levin, *Der Sturz der Königin Atalja*. SBS 105. Stuttgart: Katholisches Bibelwerk, 1982; S. L. McKenzie, *The Trouble with Kings: The Composition of the Book of Kings in the Deuteronomistic History*. Leiden/Boston: Brill, 1991.

### *7.6.3.6 Narratives about the Prophet Elijah (1 Kgs 17–19; 21; 2 Kgs 1)*

According to the portrayal in the books of Kings the prophet Elijah appeared in the second half of the 9th cent. BCE in the northern kingdom. The texts speaking of him belong to the most detailed and prominent prophetic narratives in the Former Prophets.[63] According to this composition Elijah was a champion of exclusive worship of Yhwh and, therefore, a critic of the Samarian court. This places him, like his successor Elisha, in terms of content in close proximity to the writing prophets of the 8th cent. BCE and makes him into a 'bird that sings before morning'.[64] However, as in the similar cases of Moses, David and Solomon, the biblical and historical figures need to be distinguished.

Amongst the narratives concerning Elijah, the ones about Naboth's vineyard (1 Kgs 21) and Elijah's ascension into heaven (2 Kgs 2.1-18) have an exceptional position. 1 Kings 21 is a narrative coloured by Dtr ideology that picks up an anonymous prophetic word of judgement from 2 Kgs 9.26, originally directed

63. Further prophetic narratives in 1 Sam.–2 Kgs: Nathan and Gad (2 Sam. 7; 12; 24); Ahijah from Shiloh (1 Kgs 11.29-39; 14); a man of God from Judah traveling to Bethel (1 Kgs 13; cf. Amos 7.10-17); an unnamed prophet before King Ahab (1 Kgs 20); Micaiah son of Imlah and the 400 (false) prophets (1 Kgs 22); Elisha (1 Kgs 19; 2 Kgs 1–9; 13.14-20); Isaiah (2 Kgs 18–20; cf. Isa. 36–39).

64. J. Wellhausen, 'Israelitisch-jüdische Religion', in *Grundrisse zum Alten Testament* (TB 27; ed. R. Smend; Munich: Kaiser, 1965 [1905]), 65–109, here p. 90.

towards King Joram of Israel (851/0–845/4 BCE) and transfers it to the colourfully painted conflict of the Elijah cycle between Elijah on the one hand and King Ahab of Israel (871/0–852/1 BCE) and his wife Jezebel on the other. To the degree that 2 Kgs 2.1-18 regulates Elijah's succession this narrative of the assumption of the prophet, like the previous narrative of the call of Elisha (1 Kgs 19.19-21), belongs more to the Elisha cycle. It likely rests on popular traditions holding that Elijah, the powerful champion of God, did not die, but was instead taken away by God. Genesis 5.24 knows of a similar incident with respect to Enoch who walked with God. For the contents of 1 Kgs 17.1–19.18 tensions have repeatedly been noted. This is especially the case for the narrative of Elijah on Horeb (1 Kgs 19), which is clearly geared as an antithetical reception of the portrayal of the Sinai → *Theophany* in Exod. 19. To the degree that the narrative concerns Elijah's suffering and persecution by the royal house and the collective apostasy of the people from Yhwh, the less it fits with the immediately preceding triumph by the prophet in the sacrificial challenge on Mount Carmel (1 Kgs 18). This discrepancy is intensified by the fact that the drought, which had initiated the events culminating on Mount Carmel, has ended with Elijah's success. The Dtr interpretations of the depicted events can also be lifted easily from the substantial core of the narratives. This has led to the theory that the Elijah cycle (like the texts in the Elisha cycle as well) had a distinct pre-history outside of and a history of reception within the Dtr books of Kings. The core of the tradition is often located in an older drought cycle,[65] which was subsequently combined with further individual narratives and supplemented by redactional passages. Yet 1 Kgs 17.1–19.18 can just as well be read as a coherent, episodic narrative, which goes back to an author that integrated a number of earlier texts and material.[66] The received material originates from a larger body of Elisha legends that are in part passed on in sections of 2 Kgs 4.[67] The theme of the Elijah narrative is the retrospective dispute over right and wrong of the prophecy of doom. While 1 Kgs 19 makes it clear that if the prophecy of doom comes true it means the ruin of Israel, the previous drought narrative in 1 Kgs 17–18 and its positive ending shows that if Israel embraces Yhwh and the prophets' repentance

65. Cf. the representative position of O. H. Steck, *Überlieferung und Zeitgeschichte in den Elia-Erzählungen* (WMANT 26; Neukirchen-Vluyn: Neukirchener, 1968): 1 Kgs 17,1-6; 18,1-2a, 17-18a . . . 41-46.

66. E. Blum, 'Der Prophet und das Verderben Israels: Eine ganzheitliche, historisch-kritische Lektüre von 1 Reg XVII–XIX', *VT* 47 (1997): 277–92.

67. Cf. 1 Kgs 17.10-16 with 2 Kgs 4.1-7; 1 Kgs 17.17-24 with 2 Kgs 4.8-16, as well as 1 Kgs 18.3, 12b with 2 Kgs 4.1 and 1 Kgs 18.12 with 2 Kgs 2.16.

teaching, then the future could turn out well. This kind of apologetic text for judgement prophecy looks back at least on the destruction of Samaria in 722/1 BCE, if not on the demise of Jerusalem and Judah in the year 587/6 BCE as well. However large the extent of the corpus of traditions reaching back to the time of Elijah (Elisha) may be, their beginnings seem to lie with a miracle worker and rain maker who first in the course of (post-) Dtr reception history became a paradigmatic Yhwh prophet whose words always came to pass.

F. Crüsemann, *Elia – die Entdeckung der Einheit Gottes: Eine Lektüre der Erzählungen über Elia und seine Zeit (1 Kön 17–2 Kön 2)*. Gütersloh: Kaiser, 1977; M. Köckert, 'Elia: Literarische und religionsgeschichtliche Probleme in 1Kön 17–18'. Pages 111–44 in *Der eine Gott und die Götter: Polytheismus und Monotheismus im antiken Israel*. AThANT 82. Ed. by M. Oeming and K. Schmid. Zurich: Theologischer Verlag, 2003; S. L. McKenzie, 'Prophets Come Lately', Pages 81–100 in *The Trouble with Kings*. VTSup 42. Leiden/Boston: Brill, 1991.

## 7.6.4 Theology of the Deuteronomistic Composition of the History of the People of Israel from Exodus to Exile

The Dtr composition of the history of the people of Israel from exodus to exile corresponds to the work of the Great Historical Opus in the books Genesis–2 Kings (of which it forms part), in that it provides a basic two-part schema of salvation history: the normative idyllic time for the relationship between God and the people in the epoch outside the land and the history of the people's demise beginning no later than the book of Judges. This salvation-historical structure holds true for the entirety of the work and does not need to be repeated here (Ch. 5.4). This is also the case for the fundamental significance of Deuteronomy, whose First Commandment with exclusive worship of Yhwh and the Foundational Command of → *cult centralization* serve as the measuring rod for the portrayal of the historical course of events in the books Joshua–2 Kings (Ch. 7.2.4).

To the degree that the Dtr composition portrays the history of the people of Israel from its salvation-filled beginnings until the end of the independent states of Israel and Judah and – drawing on the stipulations of the Deuteronomic Law – demonstrates why both states had to come to an end it offers an → *aetiology* for the existence of the people of Israel in exile. From this perspective the origins of the people of Israel in Egypt and their present in the Babylonian exile fall together: just as the origins of the people of Israel according to the portrayal of the exodus narrative lie outside the land and prior to the establishment of an independent political polity, the portrayal of the history of the people of Israel also returns to this situation in its end. Thus, after the loss of the land and the monarchy history returns to its beginnings. The narrative of the beginnings of the people of Israel in the exodus from Egypt therefore describes more than just the beginnings of the national history: it in fact determines the identity of the people of Israel beyond the loss of state and land.

But what determines Israel's identity according to the fundamental narrative of the beginnings of the people? 1. The people of Israel come from outside into the land. Contrary to the Israel of the ancestral story,[68] which is essentially → *autochthonous*, meaning that it has always been settled in the land, it is therefore → *allochthonous*. The Dtr Israel only attains its ethnic and cultural identity through the fact that Yhwh made its liberation from Egypt successful. Yhwh's victory over the Egyptians on behalf of Israel at the Sea of Reeds constitutes the beginning of the national history of Israel. 2. The original datum of the national history, determined in this religious manner, comes forth from a peculiar conception of God. The aspect that a deity stands militarily by those that honour him is conventional. However, according to the portrayal of the exodus narrative, Yhwh is a deity that first binds himself to Israel in the liberation of Israel from Egypt, and does this completely voluntarily. Yhwh is therefore not a tribal deity nor the god of a king that resides in the midst of its people and then powerfully acts against the enemies, but he is instead God by election. This means that the human-divine relationship between Israel and Yhwh does not come about quasi-naturally from the land or from the function of Yhwh as protector of the king and the nation. The divine-human relationship instead rests on Yhwh's salvific deeds and is implemented through a mutual promise that is then in Deut. connected to the term covenant.

**Covenant** (Heb. *bĕrît*) was originally a legal term for a reciprocal agreement between equal partners in a treaty (cf. 1 Kgs 5.26b; 15.19) or the grant or imposition of a (self-) obligation in a dependent relationship (1 Kgs 20.34; Hos. 12.2; Ezek. 17.13-18; cf. Deut. 7.2). In theological terms it designates the relationship of the deity Yhwh with his people 'Israel', for which the so-called covenant formula 'Yhwh the God of Israel, Israel the people of Yhwh' is used (cf. Deut. 26.17-18). The accent is clearly laid on the side of the divine self-obligation: Yhwh does not engage in some sort of a reciprocal covenant, but instead grants the covenant and commits himself and those on whom he imposes his covenant. The conception of a covenant granted to Israel by Yhwh (Exod. 19; 24; 34; Deut. 7) ⇨

68. The short Mesopotamian prelude in Gen. 11.27-32* belongs to the very late expansions of the ancestral story.

has an exceptional significance among the theological concepts of the Old Testament and developed a significant theological and intellectual reception, as seen in the later promise of a new covenant (Jer. 31) and the Priestly mention of the Noachic covenant (Gen. 9). Nevertheless, it has never been the exclusive nor was it the earliest conception of the human-divine relationship. Its considerable concentration in Deuteronomy and the Dtr literature as well as the 'covenant silence' of the eighth-century prophets clearly support the conclusion that the theological usage of 'covenant' first came about in the crisis experience at the end of the monarchy and in the exile. As such it expressed the continuing connection between Yhwh and 'Israel' when this notion became increasingly questionable as a result of the people's historical experience. By tracing this connection back to a particular covenant pact, the catastrophe of the exile could be understood as a consequence of Israel's covenant transgression, especially its neglect of the First Commandment. Furthermore, trust in Yhwh's covenant loyalty opened the possibility of hope for a continuation of the divine-human relationship beyond the exile.

J. C. Gertz, 'Bund'. Pages 1862–5 in vol. 1 of *RGG*. 4th ed. Tübingen: Mohr Siebeck, 1997; ET: 'Covenant'. Pages 526–8 in vol. 3 of *Religion Past & Present*. Leiden/Boston: Brill, 2007; E. W. Nicholson, *God and his People: Covenant and Theology in the Old Testament*. Oxford: Clarendon Press, 1986; L. Perlitt, *Bundestheologie im Alten Testament*. WMANT 36. Neukirchen-Vluyn: Neukirchener, 1966.

The implications of the depicted determination of Israel's identity and its foundational conceptualization of God are immense. They appear on the one hand in Yhwh's claim for uniqueness. The human-divine relationship rests on the two-sided choice and through the mutual promise aims to give priority to the 'covenant God' over and against all deities that compete with him. This is the exclusive nature of the 'exodus religion' that is later formulated in the First Commandment. On the other hand, the theological conceptualization of an electing deity, a foreign and in principle intangible God binding himself to a people, brings up the question of the implementation of such a divine-human relationship. The conceptualization thus has ethical implications. More than other deities which 'are there' in the land or 'are there' to protect the dynasty, etc., Yhwh is rather demanding with regard to the fulfilment of particular commands and social-ethical everyday norms. It is not accidental that the legal ordinances were incorporated into the narrative progression of the Moses-exodus-conquest narrative (Ch. 6.4). The conceptualization of God described above therefore leads to an *Ethicalization of Yhwh religion*. This feature is strengthened by the fact that the covenant is made with Yhwh himself. Yhwh is not only – as is generally found in ancient Near Eastern treaty law

– a guarantor of the covenant, but any transgressions of the treaty violate his very own legal claims. When the divine-human relationship rests on mutual election, then it appears at first glance rather unstable and constantly threatened by the possibility of 'covenant breaking'. Nevertheless the notion that keeping the promise sworn to Yhwh represents a condition of the covenant is a sustainable basis for the further continuity of Yhwh religion even beyond the cultural and political threat of the exile. The exile can be interpreted as a consequence for breaking the covenant, which alleviates the theological crisis brought about by the exile. On the other hand, after the loss of the monarchy and sovereignty the demand for covenant loyalty serves as a mark of Israelite identity. So in the end covenant is the binding bracket of the time before and the time to come.

## 7.6.5 Notes on the History of Reception

In order to limit the immense amount of material, the following remarks will focus on the primary protagonists presented in Ch. 7.6.3. The history of reception of the Great Historical Opus as a whole can be viewed above in the corresponding section Ch. 5.5. It remains to add here that the biblical presentation of history was received by non-Jewish historians of the → *Hellenistic* period (Hecataeus of Abdera, Manetho, Lysimachus of Alexandria, and Apion). They largely concentrated on the Moses story and drew a relatively uniform, in part quite polemic picture of Israel's origins in Egypt, generally identifying Moses as an Egyptian (ex-) priest who started a religion, founded a state (!), and promulgated the law.[69] For the NT, the establishment of the → *Passover* Festival among the events of the exodus plays an especially important role as the chronological and theological frame for the passion of Jesus.

*Moses*' reception in the Jewish as well as the Christian tradition has been especially as the giver of the law who makes the will of the one God Yhwh known to Israel (cf. Ch. 6.5 and Ch. 7.2.5). However, the biblical portrayal of his life and deeds beyond the promulgation of the law has also inspired later generations. According to the data in the church fathers, there appears to have been a rich body of Moses literature consisting in particular of → *apocalyptic* content such as the 'Assumption of Moses' (1st cent. CE; *OTP* I) in which Moses reveals to Joshua the future history of Israel. The Hellenistic Jewish writer Artapans (2nd cent. BCE; *OTP* II) describes Moses as the bringer of culture. The Hellenistic Jewish philosopher Philo of Alexandria, similar to Flavius Josephus, places Moses in the combined

69. A short overview can be found in K. Schmid, *Genesis*, 321–5 (above, Ch. 5 n. 19).

role of the king, philosopher, giver of the law, and prophet (*De vita Mosis II:* 1–7). Moses' primary props in the visual arts are the tables of the law and the staff. The frescos of the synagogue in Dura-Europos (3rd cent. BCE) already display a quite developed Moses cycle including his discovery in the Nile, the burning bush, the exodus from Egypt, and the transmission of the law on the mountain of God to a young Moses in a tunic and pallium. These and a number of further scenes appear throughout art history; a synopsis is offered in the 'Events From the Life of Moses' by Sandro Botticelli in the Sistine Chapel (1482). Musical versions include the opera 'Moses in Egypt' (1818) by Gioacchino Rossini and 'Moses and Aaron' (1957) by Arnold Schönberg. The latter is incidentally limited to Exod. 3–4 and Exod. 32. The intellectual and theological history has been especially impacted by the picture of Moses as the founder of a → *monotheistic* religion. An interesting sideline to this is the notion that can be traced back to Acts 7.22 and elsewhere that Moses did not receive his insights into 'true religion' from the revelations of the burning bush and Sinai, but rather from Egyptian mystery religion. This notion has been especially taken up by the deists and the Freemasons, as well as the philosophers and theologians of the Enlightenment.[70]

The book of *Joshua* and the narratives concerning the conquering of the land have had an ambivalent history of reception. The Rabbis already discussed the moral problems of a war of conquest. In Christianity the portrayal of the violent deeds commanded by Yhwh such as destruction of the defeated enemies, the so-called ban, has repeatedly led to the question of reconcilability of the Old and New Testament conceptions of God – regardless of one's own political behaviour. The most radical position, even though largely unsuccessful, is found in Marcion (ca. 85–160 CE), who called for a separation between the two. → *Allegorical* interpretations following the tradition found in Origen (ca. 185–253) view the cities to be conquered in the Cis-Jordan as a picture of the soul and the (spiritual) battle for freedom from sin. Others point to the practices of war at the time and the narrator's distance from the (fictive) events or emphasize the context of the historical picture as a whole in which the narratives of the conquest of the land stand in juxtaposition to the experience of the loss of land.[71] The motif of the conquest of Jericho is especially beloved in art, literature and music.

The colourful sagas of the heroes of the book of *Judges* with their wars,

70. Cf. J. Assmann, *Moses the Egyptian: The Memory of Egypt in Western Monotheism* (Cambridge, Mass.: Harvard University Press, 1997).

71. Cf. the range of problems noted in E. Noort, *Das Buch Josua: Forschungsgeschichte und Problemfelder* (EdF 292; Darmstadt: Wissenschaftliche Buchgesellschaft, 1998), 15–24.

violence and burlesques have inspired the visual arts, literature and music more than theological debate. Georg Friedrich Händel draws on Judg. 4–5 for his oratorio 'Deborah'. Jephthah's dramatic conflict, in which he must sacrifice his daughter (Judg. 10–12) is recalled by William Shakespeare's Hamlet (Act 2, scene 2; 1602): 'Jephthah, judge of Israel – what treasure have you?' Further receptions include an oratorio by Händel (1752), the early opera 'Jephthah's Vow' by Giacomo Meyerbeer (1812), Lion Feuchtwanger's novel *Jephthah and His Daughter* (1957), and the expressionist drama 'Jephthah' (1919) by Hermann von Boetticher. The narrative of *Samson and Delilah* has been extraordinarily popular since the 17th cent. In addition to the portrayals by Peter Paul Rubens (1609), Rembrandt van Rijn (1636), and Lovis Corinth (1912), it also appears as the opera 'Samson and Delilah' (1877) by Camille Saint-Saëns and in 'Old Testament Epic' films like those by Alexander Korda (Austria, 1922), Cecil B. DeMille (USA, 1949), and Gianfranco Parolini (1961).

The biblical depiction of the early monarchy is energized by the contrast between *Saul* and *David:* the former rejected, failing tragically, and hopeless; the latter chosen, brilliant and successful. The history of reception carries this contrast forward. Saul is subjected innerbiblically to a kind of *damnatio memoriae.*[72] In contrast, even within the Old Testament David is increasingly stylized as the ideal king exhibiting exemplary piety (Ch. 7.6.3 Excursus: David). The New Testament emphasizes the → *messianic* features of the David picture and the Davidic lineage of Jesus. The interest of the visual arts in Saul has been especially focused on his end and his fight with David as seen in 'David and Saul' (1658) by Rembrandt van Rijn and 'The Ghost of Samuel Appears to Saul' (1650–60) by Bernardo Cavallino. Georg Friedrich Händel's oratorio 'Saul' (1738) shows how Saul perishes as a result of his inner ambivalence. Only Voltaire in his tragedy 'Saul' (1763) is able to perceive in the king that falls short of Yhwh's expectations a pioneer of anti-clericalism. David appears often in the pictorial arts (with and without Saul), including repeatedly in Marc Chagall, as a sensitive and peace-loving singer and harpist or as the brilliant victor over Goliath such as in Caravaggio (1599). Likely most famous is Michelangelo's marble statue in Florence (1501–04). Stefan Heym critiques the classic picture of David in his novel *The King David*

72. In the OT Saul only appears in the pertinent narratives of Samuel, the parallel reports in Chronicles, and three redactional superscriptions in the Psalms that point to David's persecution by Saul (Pss 52; 54; 57). The sole New Testament record of him is in a historical retrospective that mentions him as both the first and the rejected king (Acts 13.21-22).

*Report* (1972). An ironic stance that projects new accentuations on the role of Bathsheba is taken up by the novel bearing the same name by Torgny Lindgren (1984). Musical interpretations such as Arthur Honegger's oratorio opera 'King David' (1928) have also appeared.

The cornerstones for the reception of the figure of *Solomon* were already in place by the 2nd cent. BCE: Jesus ben Sira provides a description of David's successor in the so-called 'Praise to the Fathers' as the rich, extremely wise king of peace, though ruled by his sensuality. The books of Proverbs (Ch. 15), Song of Songs (Ch. 17), and Ecclesiastes (Ch. 18) are also attributed to him (Sir. 47.12 [14]-21 [23]). The → *wisdom* attributed to Solomon developed to legendary proportions in the subsequent period. The beginnings of this development and also of the image of Solomon as a binder of demons are already found in Josephus (*Ant.* VIII). The reception of Solomon's wisdom includes the tales from 'One Thousand and One Nights' and the libretto of Georg Friedrich Händel's oratorio 'Solomon'. In Christian → *iconography* Solomon appears as a → *typological* prototype of Christ and takes on the guise of a just king carrying the sword of the Last Judgement. Well-loved subjects such as the 'Visit of the Queen of Sheba' are taken up by Konrad Witz (1435), Pierro della Francesca (1455/56) and the Hollywood production by King Vidor starring Yul Brynner and Gina Lollobrigida (1961), as well as the depiction of Solomon's harem as an illustration of 'Solomon's Idol Worship' by Mattia Pret (1675) among others. Finally, mention should be made of the Kebra-Nagast saga ('Book of the Glory of Kings') from Christian Ethiopia, which knows of a liaison between Solomon and the Queen of Sheba identified here as Makeda of Axum. Descendants of their son and successor to Makeda of Axum, Melenik I, brought the → *ark* to Axum according to the legend. The legend continued to provide dynastic legitimation until the 20th cent. emperor Haile Selassie and his dynasty and plays an important role in Rastafarian religion.

The reception of the prophet *Elijah* begins within the Old Testament itself in Mal. 3.22-24 (Ch. 12). The expectation mentioned there of Elijah's return touches the narrative of his assumption (2 Kgs 2.1-18) and has a considerable reception in the New Testament (Mk 9.11-13; Mt. 17.10-13; Lk. 1.17). It has also promoted the creation of legends in Judaism and Islam. Elijah plays the role of helper for those in need and miracle worker in all three religions. The oldest-known visual depiction comes from the synagogue in Dura-Europos (3rd cent. BCE). Prevalent are portrayals of the angel feeding Elijah. Of the music interpretations one should highlight the oratorio 'Elijah' (1846) by Felix Mendelssohn-Bartholdy.

# Part IV

## The Literature of the Old Testament: The Latter Prophets (Nevi'im)

# 8

# The Canonical Prophets: Isaiah to Malachi

(Konrad Schmid – Translation by Jennifer Adams-Maßmann)

## Chapter Outline



J. Blenkinsopp, *A History of Prophecy in Israel*. Rev. ed. Louisville, Ky.: Westminster John Knox, 1996; K. Koch, *The Prophets*. 2 vols. Transl. by M. Kohl. Philadelphia: Fortress, 1983–4; R. G. Kratz, *Die Propheten Israels*. Munich: Beck, 2003; O. H. Steck, *The Prophetic Books and Their Theological Witness*. Transl. by J. D. Nogalski. St. Louis, Mo.: Chalice, 2000.

## 8.1 Biblical Context

### 8.1.1 The Place of the Prophetic Books within the Canon

Within the three-part → *canon* of the Hebrew Old Testament (Torah ['Law'], Nevi'im ['Prophets'], Ketuvim ['Writings']), the prophetic books (Isaiah, Jeremiah, Ezekiel and the Twelve: Hosea–Malachi) are found in the *Nevi'im* ('Prophets') made up of the books Joshua–2 Kings and Isaiah–Malachi, known respectively as the 'Former Prophets' and the 'Latter Prophets'. The decision to combine the historical books Joshua–2 Kings with the prophetic books Isaiah–Malachi into their own canonical section of the *Nevi'im* ('Prophets') makes sense only when we consider the formation of the Torah (Genesis–Deuteronomy Ch. 5). On the one hand, the Torah presents Moses as the prophet par *excellence* (Deut. 34.10), superior to all other prophets. On the other hand, Israel is promised a succession of prophets after Moses who will teach Israel (Deut. 18.15-18). This chain of succession begins with Joshua, continues with figures such as the judges (Ch. 7.6.3.3), Samuel and Ahijah of Shiloh as recounted in the books of Judges, Samuel and Kings, and finally includes Isaiah through Malachi. Thus, Joshua–Malachi constitutes a unified block as *Nevi'im* ('Prophets') alongside the Torah ('Law').

According to the logic of the Hebrew canon, the prophets of the Old Testament were preachers and interpreters of the Mosaic Law, which is how they were viewed for centuries. Viewed historically, however, this description is inaccurate.

Julius Wellhausen (1844–1918) developed the seminal thesis that the prophetic books originated independently from the Torah and were gradually incorporated and reworked as the Torah emerged as the most important tradition in the Hebrew Bible. Before the Former Prophets were read entirely in light of the Torah, they had been part of the larger context of Genesis–2 Kings, and as such, offered a theologically and historically nuanced view of salvation in which they continued the story of salvation (Genesis–Joshua) and disaster (Judges–2 Kings) that had ended with a theological low-point at the end of Kings. At the same time, they provided a glimpse ahead of a new story of salvation.

A monumental reorganization of the prophetic books was undertaken in the → *Septuagint* (LXX), the Greek translation of the Old Testament, the current order of which is likely of Christian origin.[1] In the standard order of the LXX, the prophetic books are placed at the very end of the Old Testament canon so that the New Testament, which follows immediately afterwards, can be read as the fulfilment of the prophetic books and their Messianic promises (→ *messiah*). The integration of the book of Daniel into the *corpus propheticum* – culminating in the vision of the Son of Man in Dan. 7 (Ch. 21) – underscores this teleology towards the New Testament.

1. Both the prologue to the book of Jesus Sirach as well as texts from Philo from Alexandria show that Alexandrian and Palestinian Judaism possessed the same three-part canon ('Law', 'Prophets', and 'Writings'). The book order passed down in the Septuagint-Codices primarily reflects Christian interests.

## Definition and Manifestations of Prophecy

This sweeping Christian interpretation of the prophets, seen through the lens of the Septuagint in particular, promoted and virtually cemented the widespread view of a prophet as someone who predicts future events. Yet even the Greek term *prophētēs* used by the LXX consistently to translate the Hebrew word *nābî'* ('Called' or 'Chosen One') did not originally mean 'foretell', but rather conveyed the sense of 'public proclamation'. In addition to *nābî'*, the Hebrew Old Testament uses other terms to describe the prophets such as *rō'eh* ('Seer'), *ḥozēh* ('Visionary') or *'îš hā 'ĕlōhîm* ('man of God'). How should we interpret such prophetic figures? Historically speaking, the 'prophets' are quite a diverse group. Certainly, the development of the prophetic tradition over a longer period increasingly made them into foretellers of the future, yet in this respect, the prophets are mainly the product of their books. Of course, they also announced salvation and disaster in the near future, but they did not have an overview of the entire course of world history, unlike the canonical Isaiah who, from his historical position in the 8th century BCE, made predictions about the centuries that followed extending all the way to the re-creation of heaven and earth. The historical prophets performed → *symbolic actions*, which provided a critique of contemporary society and the cult, while also lifting up lamentations. Their message was neither primarily nor consistently determined by glimpses of the future. Therefore, Manfred Weippert was correct to leave out that aspect when suggesting the following definition of prophecy, which takes into account both ancient Near Eastern and Old Testament sources:

> A prophet is a male or female person who (1) experiences the revelation of one or multiple deities by means of a cognitive form of communication, a vision, audition, dream or something similar, and (2) considers him- or herself to be commissioned by the deity or deities concerned to impart this revelation in linguistic or metalinguistic form (symbolic actions) to a third person or group to whom it is actually addressed.[2]

Various forms of prophecy can be identified in Old Testament times:

1) First, the *bands of prophets*, who sought contact with the divine in ecstatic states through music and dance (1 Sam. 10.5-12; cf. 1 Sam. 19.18-24.). This form of 'prophecy' could apparently take place without linguistic communication and thus made use of metalinguistic forms of communication (dance).
2) *Temple and cultic prophets* were active at the sanctuaries where they were employed. Their task consisted primarily in providing cultic advice about the acceptance of sacrifices, intercessions and petitions, or issuing oracles about salvation (cf. Lam. 3.57). In most cases, these are the prophets whom the canonical prophetic tradition had in mind when they spoke critically of 'priests and prophets' (e.g., Isa. 28.7; Mic. 3.11; Jer. 2.8). Figures such as Hananiah in Jer. 28 could also be included in this group of prophets.

⇨

2. M. Weippert, 'Aspekte israelitischer Prophetie im Lichte verwandter Erscheinungen des Alten Orients', in *Ad bene et fideliter seminandum: Festschrift für K. Deller* (AOAT 220; ed. G. Mauer and U. Magen; Neukirchen-Vluyn: Neukirchener, 1988), 287–319, here 289–90.

3) In addition to the sanctuaries, the king also had prophetic officers at his disposal, the so-called *court prophets*. The most famous of these are Nathan (2 Sam. 7; 12) and Gad (2 Sam. 24). According to 1 Kgs 22.6, the King of Israel appears to have hired as many as 400 of such prophets at the time (literally: 'the king's prophets'), who were supposed to use divination to advise him on political matters.

4) Finally, one must mention the primarily oppositional *individual prophets* who are responsible for the existing prophetic books. The prophets named in (1) – (3) approached their work 'inductively', developing their oracles through specific techniques (e.g., incubation [= sleeping at holy sites], haruspicy (examining liver entrails), bird augury, or ecstatic states so their insights could be initiated on request (up to a point). The oppositional prophets, in contrast, could be characterized as 'intuitive', as their insights occurred spontaneously and apparently outside the parameters of established institutional contexts.

Although this last form of prophecy has strongly influenced how the term has been understood over the years, historical evidence suggests it was initially a highly marginalized phenomenon. Above all, such prophecy may be attributed primarily to a societal subculture and was not appropriated by the official religion until the prophecies of doom and disaster came true when the northern and southern kingdoms were destroyed (722 BCE and 587 BCE respectively). As a result it eventually came to be seen as the essence of prophecy.

## True and False Prophecy

The Old Testament does not provide for a general definition of 'true' and 'false' prophecy. Deut. 18.21-22 clearly expresses an awareness of the problem: 'You may say to yourself, "How can we recognize a word that Yhwh has not spoken?" If a prophet speaks in the name of Yhwh but the thing does not take place or prove true, it is a word that Yhwh has not spoken.' (Deut. 18.21-22; cf. Jer. 28.9).

While this criterion may seem sufficiently unambiguous, it also shows that at the moment when a prophecy is uttered there is no means of judging with certainty whether a prophecy is 'true' or 'false'. Thus, in the portrayal of the conflict between Jeremiah and Hananiah in Jer. 28, Hananiah is still accorded the title of 'prophet'. Given the acute danger Babylon posed for Judah, this prophetic conflict revolved around the question whether Babylonian power would end soon and the temple apparatus that had been taken to Babylon in 598/7 BCE would be repatriated (as Hananiah claimed) or whether this would not come to pass (as Jeremiah argued). Only the → *LXX* consistently calls Hananiah *pseudoprophētēs* ('prophet of lies'). The conclusion of the story – in which Hananiah died in the very same year as Jeremiah had predicted (28.16-17) – and the subsequent chain of events finally reveal Jeremiah as the true prophet sent by God.

Nevertheless, the criterion formulated in Deut. 18.21-22 and Jer. 28.9 to determine the truth of prophetic words based on their fulfilment is not applied in a formalized way in the Old Testament. The prophetic books accepted into the canon include a series of pronouncements that did not take place (and which are likely authentic for that reason as they are not → *vaticinia ex eventu*). An example is the pronouncement to King Jehoiakim in Jer. 22.13-19, especially vv. 18-19, in which the prophet declares that Jehoiakim will not have a normal burial (Ch. 10.3). A note in 2 Kgs 24.6 to the contrary indicates he was buried and there is no reason to doubt its historical veracity. One can therefore assume the book of Jeremiah's prediction was not fulfilled in this respect, suggesting the 'truth' of this prophetic logion for the tradents apparently did not derive primarily from any correspondence between the announcement and historical reality, but from Jeremiah's critique of the king. We can also make a comparable assertion about the long-term process of recording the prophetic books (see below Ch. 8.3): namely, that the editorial additions to these books show how concrete, predetermined expectations from older texts were continually adapted and assimilated. The Old Testament prophetic tradents were not waiting transfixed for prophetic words to be fulfilled literally, but rather they updated and reconfigured these words themselves in light of new historical experiences. The criterion for the fulfillment of prophecy was applied retroactively, in part, to particular prophetic announcements.

J. Jeremias, '"Wahre" und "falsche" Prophetie im Alten Testament: Entwicklungslinien eines Grundsatzkonfliktes'. *TBei* 28 (1997): 343–9; G. T. Sheppard, 'True and False Prophecy within Scripture'. Pages 262–82 in *Canon, Theology, and Old Testament Interpretation: Essays in Honor of Brevard S. Childs*. Ed. by G. M. Tucker. Philadelphia: Fortress, 1988.

## 8.1.2 The Framing of Jeremiah/Ezekiel by Isaiah/The Book of Twelve

Both the external integration of prophecy into the canon and its internal organization are theologically significant. Judged by the standards of ancient book production, there are four prophetic books in the Old Testament: Isaiah, Jeremiah, Ezekiel and the Book of Twelve (Hosea–Malachi). The so-called twelve Minor Prophets were united on one scroll and thus counted as one book (Ch. 12). If we consider the canonical sequence in the Hebrew Old Testament in which the four prophetic books appear in a particular order, then the books of Jeremiah and Ezekiel appear to be framed by Isaiah and the Book of Twelve (XII).

| | | | |
|---|---|---|---|
| Isa. 1–39: Assyria | | | Hos., Joel, Amos, Jonah, Mic., Nah.: Assyria |
| Isa. 36–39: Assyria/Babylon | Jer.: Babylon | Ez.: Babylon | Hab., Zeph., Obad.: Babylon |
| Isa. 40–66: Babylon/Persia | | | Hag., Zech., Mal.: Persia |

Jeremiah and Ezekiel deal with a relatively limited period in the history of Israel, addressing the time immediately before and after the catastrophe of Jerusalem and Judah in 587–6 BCE (the capture of Jerusalem and Judah by the Babylonian army under Nebuchadnezzar II). By contrast, Isaiah and the XII provide information about a much broader swath of Israel's history, beginning with the Assyrians and extending all the way to the Persian period. Isaiah even ends with a glimpse of a new heaven and earth (Isa. 65–66).

## 8.1.3 Isaiah as the Leader of the Prophets

Isaiah is accorded an implicit leadership function among the prophets given its placement at the beginning of the prophetic books in the → *Masoretic* tradition as well as the Babylonian → *Talmud* BB 14b + 15a [Jeremiah, Ezekiel, Isaiah, The Book of Twelve]), although this is not the case for the order of the → *Septuagint* traditions [The Book of Twelve, Isaiah, Jeremiah, Ezekiel, Daniel]. In this way, Isaiah sets the tone for the prophets, providing an overview of the entire course of the history of Yhwh and Yhwh's people as recorded in Isaiah's book. Evidence that the book of Isaiah was understood as a comprehensive prophecy of history is provided in the deuterocanonical book of Sirach (190/180 BCE):

> By his dauntless spirit [Isaiah] saw the [end times], and comforted the mourners in Zion. He revealed what was to occur to the end of time and the hidden things before they happened. (Sir. 48.24-25).

For Jesus Sirach, Isaiah speaks not only of his own time but presages the entire course of world history – at least in the current version of the book of Isaiah (chapters 1–66). Isaiah's rise to this position is due to his prominent eponymous authority and position at the beginning of the history of Israel's writing prophets, as well as the early historical evidence for the truth of his message (Isa. 7.4: 'Take heed, be quiet!') which helped preserve → *Zion* from the Assyrians in 701 BCE. Isaiah documents this in chapters 36–39, although the book fails to mention the high ransom Hezekiah had to pay, otherwise noted in both 2 Kgs 18.14-16 and Assyrian sources (*COS* II, 302–3).

# 8.2 Historical-Critical Analysis and Major Issues in the History of Critical Interpretation

U. Becker, 'Die Wiederentdeckung des Prophetenbuches: Tendenzen und Aufgaben der gegenwärtigen Prophetenforschung'. *BTZ* 21 (2004): 30–60; K. Schmid, 'Klassische und nachklassische Deutungen der alttestamentlichen Prophetie'. *Zeitschrift für neuere Theologiegeschichte* 3 (1996): 225–50; D. L. Petersen, 'Defining Prophecy and Prophetic Literature'. Pages 33–44 in *Prophecy in its Ancient Near Eastern Context: Mesopotamian, Biblical, and Arabian Perspectives*. SBLSympS 13. Ed. by M. Nissinen. Atlanta, Ga.: SBL, 2000; idem, *The Prophetic Literature: An Introduction*. Louisville, Ky.: Westminster John Knox, 2002.

## 8.2.1 The Genesis of the Traditional View of the Prophets in the Wake of Idealism and Later Source-Critical Hypotheses

Both the church and larger public have embraced the definition of the essence of Old Testament prophecy as presented in historical-critical research, especially in the 19th century – one of the few times, in fact, when the results of Old Testament studies have been accepted in this way with virtually no qualification. When people speak of the 'prophets' today, they usually envision a picture of the prophets as painted by modern Old Testament exegetes based on the books carrying each prophet's name: they imagine spiritually gifted, brilliant individuals who experience God's will directly and impart this to the addressees without compromise or conditions. Such a picture of the prophets developed when the original logia of the prophets were separated from secondary editorial additions. The exegesis of the prophetic books consisted largely in distinguishing between 'authentic' and 'inauthentic' textual material with the result that the prophets were presented as religious geniuses.

In terms of intellectual history, this traditional image of the prophet as a religious genius was especially inspired by Idealism and the Romantic Movement and predominated in the 19th century. The theory was considerably advanced by the late dating of the law *after* the prophets *(lex post prophetas)* by Julius Wellhausen,[3] so that the prophets no longer had to be seen as interpreters of the law. Because the characterization of the prophetic message as 'not of this world' was very congenial to proponents of so-called Dialectical Theology, this idea continued to have adherents into the 20th century. Yet even Gerhard von Rad (1901–1971), in his seminal work *Old Testament Theology,* sees the central trait of the prophets in their discontinuity.[4] According to von Rad, prophecy cannot simply be combined with Israel's beliefs, so he had to handle it separately from other biblical written traditions in its own second volume.

## 8.2.2 The Emergence of Redaction Criticism

Aside from this classical strand of research emphasizing the uniqueness of the prophets and the prophetic figures themselves, other tendencies in the first half of the 20th century intentionally did not focus exclusively on the prophets and their 'authentic' words. Some scholars focused on the secondary editorial additions for their own sake, arguing they reflected a process of inner-biblical interpretation.

Known as redaction criticism (Ch. 2.1.1), this approach eventually gained acceptance within Old Testament research, particularly due to Walther Zimmerli's (1907–1983) commentary on Ezekiel[5] and has since become one of the dominant approaches in prophetic scholarship. Scholarship no longer focuses solely on the prophetic proclamation itself but also on the various emphases and trajectories in the prophetic books, taking the literary repercussions of the recorded sayings of the prophets into consideration.

3. Cf. J. Wellhausen, *Prolegomena to the History of Israel* (transl. and preface by W. R. Smith; Atlanta, Ga.: Scholars Press, 1994; transl. of *Prolegomena zur Geschichte Israels* [6th ed., Berlin/New York: de Gruyter, 1927; Student edition, 2001; 1st ed. 1878 under the title *Geschichte Israels I*]).
4. G. von Rad, *Theology*.
5. W. Zimmerli, *Ezekiel* (Hermeneia; 2 vols. transl. by R. E. Clements *et al.*; Philadelphia: Fortress, 1979–83). A most helpful overview on the topic of innerbiblical exegesis is provided by B. M. Levinson, Legal Revision and Religious Renewal in Ancient Israel (Cambridge: Cambridge University Press, 2008), 95–181.

Prophetic interpretation in the late 19th and 20th centuries can be characterized as seeking to reclaim the texts for the prophets for whom they were named, while reducing the prophetic books only to those texts whose authorship was certain through 'critical' analysis. They sought to preserve the essence of personal testimony – i.e., the book of Isaiah came from 'Isaiah' and the book of Jeremiah was written by 'Jeremiah', etc. Today, on the other hand, the emphasis has shifted away from the prophets as individuals to their writings. Correspondingly, the emphasis has moved further away from their oral sayings to focus on the written texts of each book. The prophetic books are increasingly seen as meaningful unities and no longer as accidental compilations of 'small units', each with its own theological merit. At this stage in prophetic scholarship, one could almost speak of a paradigm shift, although the older approach should not be completely abandoned as the search for original prophetic logia still has its relative merits. Without this search, for example, it would be impossible to paint an historically accurate picture of oral prophecy, although the results of this research can vary greatly and are sometimes questionable (see Ch. 8.3).

## Genres of prophetic speech and traditions

In the search for original prophetic logia, form criticism offers an approach (Ch. 2.1.1) that provides revealing insights. In many cases one can only grasp the point of diverse prophetic texts by recognizing the standard → *genre* of oral speech being adopted and transformed. Prophecy in certain cases can best be described as alienation or even as a parody of existing genres. In Amos 5.1-2, for instance, a pronouncement of judgement against the northern kingdom is formulated in the style of a lament (*qînâ*): 'Hear this word that I take up over you in lamentation (*qînâ*), O house of Israel: Fallen, no more to rise, is maiden Israel; forsaken on her land, with no one to raise her up.' Two things are notable. First, Amos 5.1-2 refers to a collective (Israel) and not an individual, and this collective is presumed to still exist ('hear'). Second, the lament is intoned over an existing entity which is reproached for its propensity to death. This double transformation of the traditional lament form lends Amos 5.1 its prophetic stridency as a word of judgement. The prophetic words of 'woe' (cf. Isa. 5.8-24; 28-31; Amos 5.18; Hab. 2.6-20) can be interpreted along the same lines: They also adopt the cries of 'woe' from the lament form and apply them to Israel and/or Judah.

One might compare this with Isa. 5 which begins with a love song ('Let me sing for my beloved my love-song concerning his vineyard') before abruptly turning into a pronouncement of judgement against Israel and Judah. In this situation an existing genre ('love song') is adopted and prophetically transformed.

⇨

We can also assume an analogous process for the prophetic disputation (cf. Amos 3.3-6, 8; Jer. 13.23; 23.23-24; Isa. 40,*12-31 and other examples in Isa. 40-66) and the warnings (Joel 2.13; 4.4 [NRSV 3.4]), which should probably be understood in terms of the → *wisdom* school tradition.

Prophecy also gave rise to other genres. Aside from smaller formulas such as the one introducing a new oracle ('And the word of YHWH came to X') or the divine messenger formula ('thus says YHWH'), the *prophetic judgement* directed to individuals or a collective is important and its use is widespread. It is made up of two parts generally consisting of an accusation (*Scheltwort*: 'abusive word') and a pronouncement of judgement ('threat'), connected with the particle 'thus' (*lākēn*) and the so-called divine messenger formula ('thus says Yhwh') in order to distinguish clearly the prophetic discourse from God's speech. A perfect example is 1 Kgs 21.17-19 in the narrative of Naboth's vineyard, which King Ahab has seized after having Naboth killed unjustly. The prophet Elijah addresses Ahab: 'Thus says Yhwh, "Have you killed, and also taken possession?" You shall say to him, "Thus says Yhwh: In the place where dogs licked up the blood of Naboth, dogs will also lick up your blood."' As in this example, one can often recognize inner connections between the accusation and pronouncement of judgement (e.g. 'licking up the blood').

When turning to the narrative passages, the reports of so-called → *symbolic actions* appear as a key characteristic of prophecy (Hos. 1, 3; Isa. 8, 20; Jer. 13, 16, 19, 32; Ezek. 4–5, etc.). They often follow a certain format: an instruction to be carried out, a report to be given on how the instruction was executed, and then the interpretation of the symbolic action. It is perfectly conceivable – even quite likely – these symbolic acts have a basis in real historical events. In some cases no claim is made, however, that these were ever performed in public (cf. Jer. 13) so the literary purpose takes precedence over any historical reality. As such they can apparently no longer be interpreted as nonverbally communicated prophecies.

The form-critical approach also allows for understanding of those passages 'updating' the prophetic books which may only have existed in written form. As written texts, these products of scribal prophecy often borrow from the conventions of certain genres of oral communication, although from the outset they have also been shaped and influenced by written genres (cf. for example, the genre 'prophetic book').

Caution is nevertheless advisable: While the call stories and reports of visions in the prophetic books share striking similarities in terms of composition and style, the close literary connections are more likely due to a common editorial relationship than to the nature of the genre.

As newer trajectories in prophetic scholarship make sufficiently clear, form criticism must involve something more than isolating and interpreting the putative, 'original' logia of the prophets. Increasingly, exegesis of prophetic passages long seen as inauthentic suggests these are more than → *glosses* and textual errors, but in many cases – or even most cases – they should be construed as meaningful (later) interpretations of existing textual material. 'Amenders' are not merely bumbling glossators, but knowledgeable scribes acting as editors. In this respect, these editors also qualify as 'prophets', since their scribal activity reveals an astonishing ability to innovate theologically which could be considered 'prophetic'. Furthermore, they conceived of themselves as prophetic, given their willingness to work anonymously under the name of the eponymous figures whose biblical books they were editing.

## 8.3 Origins of the Prophetic Books

Prophecy is no longer viewed exclusively as a historical phenomenon limited to a particular time and place and attached to individual figures responsible for writing certain books. It is increasingly viewed as a collective phenomenon unfolding over time. This view consciously takes the prophecy of scribal tradents into account; some scholars now find it difficult to imagine or reconstruct individual, historical prophetic figures precisely or with confidence. Comparable ancient Near Eastern texts provide some evidence of prophetic activity elsewhere, notably from Mari (18th century BCE [*ANET*, 623–6 and 629–32]) and Assyria (7th century BCE [*ANET*, 449–52 and 605–7]). Yet as tempting as it may be to look for the origins of Israelite and Judean prophecy in these historical parallels from other religions, it is possible there are no analogous prophets similar to those in Israel and Judah to whom the prophetic books are attributed.

The search for the origins of prophecy should not be abandoned as a result, but a more sophisticated approach needs to be employed. Not all prophecy originated in oral form; large parts of the prophetic books only ever existed in written form (e.g., Isa. 56–66; Jer. 30–33). In the case of individual prophetic books such as Joel, Obadiah, Jonah or Malachi, one must consider the possibility that they are entirely products of scribal activity. Presumably, there is no single prophetic figure behind these texts whose proclamations have been written down as a foundation upon which a later redactional history has been built. On the contrary, these books appear to be the prophetic product – from start to finish – of scribal tradents.

When asking how the process of interpreting and updating the prophetic books played out concretely, one must keep in mind that a limited number of books were in circulation in Old Testament times and the setting in which writing was produced, at least in postexilic Judah (→ *exile*), was presumably limited to one location: Jerusalem. Due to their short shelf life, the books of the Old Testament had to be repeatedly recopied, and keeping the traditions alive included not just preserving the text itself but also its meaning, often reflected in the productive further development of the text (*Fortschreibung*). Because this process involved explicating the meaning found in the original text, it is not identified or labelled as commentary but simply flows into the text of the named prophet as pseudonymous prophecy.

The **interpretation of the prophetic traditions by scribes** varies greatly. Below are examples of different approaches to the process:

1. *Initial recording of oral traditions and → compilation of pre-existing texts:* Exegetical work begins with the *initial recording* of oral logia, itself an act of interpretation as the oral communication has been removed from the original situation in which it was spoken.

   The process continues with the *compilation* of these individual texts before the editor adds any other phrases or formulas. How the editor arranges the texts can result in a particular trajectory of meaning, as Jörg Jeremias[6] demonstrated for the books of Hosea and Amos. This is also the case for the tablets of Neo-Assyrian prophecy (*ANET*, 449–52 and 605–7).The lack of subheadings in Hos. 4–14, for instance, signals that the collected texts should not be read on their own but in relation to one another. One might go a step further and say: there are no 'authentic' prophetic words as such in the Old Testament since the process of writing down oral *logia*, as well as the selection and compilation of various 'smaller units'. are irreversible interpretative acts.
2. *Small-scale written changes:* One can also detect *small-scale* written developments affecting only the immediate context, such as a single pericope made up of several verses. Some scholars argue that scribal interpretative work on the prophetic books involved only such individual changes and additions and that evidence of more extensive levels of editing cannot be substantiated. The literary growth of the prophetic books in this case should be compared to that of an 'unsupervised forest' (Bernhard Duhm) or an avalanche that continues to grow in size as it moves downhill (Otto Kaiser: 'snowball hypothesis'). It must be pointed out, however, there are some texts within the prophetic books in which particular parts of a book or even entire books (presumably even series of books) have been edited to give larger sections of text a new redactional meaning.

6. J. Jeremias, *Hosea und Amos: Studien zu den Anfängen des Dodekapropheton* (FAT 13; Tübingen: Mohr Siebeck, 1996).

3. *Global redactions spanning an entire book:* An example of such texts can be found in Isa. 35: this bridge text, which comes from the early Diadochan period (Ch. 9.1.3), arguably brings together the previously independent traditions of → *Proto-Isaiah* and → *Deutero-Isaiah* into one larger Isaiah book and provides new meaning within the context of further statements in Proto- and Deutero-Isaiah. As details of the text suggest, Isa. 35 was created by conflating formulations from Isa. 34 and Isa. 40–62, thus providing a transition from Proto- to Deutero-Isaiah.[7]
4. *Overarching redactional links:* Finally, there are also *overarching editorial links extending beyond individual books* that apparently helped shape a coherent *corpus propheticum* (Isaiah–Malachi) and even helped constitute the canonical section (→ *canon*) of the Nevi'im (cf. the inclusion of Josh. 1.7 / Mal. 3.22-24 [NRSV 4.4-6]). For example, one finds corresponding editorial perspectives in Isaiah and the XII, as well as conspicuous duplicates such as Isa. 2.2-4/Mic. 4.1-3 and Jer. 49.7-22/Obad.

# 8.4 Theology of the Prophetic Books

This newer approach, which understands the prophetic books as interpretative literature that evolved largely through the further development of existing textual materials, has both historical and theological implications.

## 8.4.1 Productive Exegesis of Pre-Existing Traditions

'Tradition is not the worship of ashes but the preservation of fire,' as Gustav Mahler supposedly once said. This also applies to the inner-biblical handling of the prophetic traditions: the tradents of the prophetic tradition did not preserve the textual material handed down to them by always keeping the exact wording (and only this wording) in the spirit of a *fides historica*, but rather continually sought to understand and explicate the current relevance of the prophetic word.

Paying attention to this dynamic inner-biblical approach to the prophetic traditions, a biblicistic understanding of prophetic statements is clearly not possible. The theological essence of the prophetic books does not derive from concrete individual statements – the Old Testament itself reflects

7. O. H. Steck, *Bereitete Heimkehr: Jesaja 35 als redaktionelle Brücke zwischen dem Ersten und Zweiten Jesaja* (SBS 121; Stuttgart: Katholisches Bibelwerk, 1985).

this awareness that each statement is historically contingent and requires interpretation – but the overall trajectory of the interpretation is revealed in the inner-biblical process of further editing and development. In this respect, prophetic interpretation has shaped the prophetic tradition from the beginning, suggesting a way to approach Old Testament prophecy today.

## 8.4.2 The Essence of Prophecy in Israel and Judah

Even writers in the Old Testament express an awareness that the Israelite and Judean prophets are not unique in the ancient Near Eastern world (cf. 1 Kgs 18.19; Jer. 27.9). Well-known examples include especially the Mari texts (ANET, 623–6 and 629–32) and the library of King Ashurbanipal (ANET, 449–52 and 605–7).

Yet ancient Near Eastern prophecy is of a somewhat different nature; it is institutionally bound to a particular royal court and generally friendly towards the king.[8] It promises military success in domestic and international affairs and is fundamentally hostage to the concerns and perspectives of its own time.

From an Assyrian tablet with prophecies from the time of Esarhaddon (681–669 BCE): '(This oracle is) from the woman Ishtar-la-tashiat of Arbela: O king of Assyria, fear not! The enemy of the king of Assyria I will deliver to slaughter.' (*ANET*, 605).

Here an essential difference compared to the Old Testament tradition of canonical prophecy appears: the long-term, written transmission and reinterpretation of prophecy in the Old Testament expresses a conviction that the relevance of the prophetic words is not exhausted in their original time and setting, but can be valid for successive generations. For this reason they were written down and updated as appropriate.[9] Old Testament prophecy has

8. Cf. however, M. Nissinen, 'Prophecy against the King in Neo-Assyrian Sources', in *Lasset uns Brücken bauen...: Collected Communications to the XVth Congress of the International Organization for the Study of the Old Testament (Cambridge 1995)* (BEATAJ 42; ed. K.-D. Schunck and M. Augustin; Frankfurt/Main: Lang, 1998), 157–70.

9. Neo-Assyrian prophecy appears to have experienced a similar phenomenon in a rudimentary way: under Esarhaddon (681–669 BCE) words that served to legitimate an heir to the throne outside

only been preserved to the present day by being passed down repeatedly. Without the written process of transmission, the prophetic books would have decomposed and been forgotten long ago, much like the prophetic texts in Mari and Assyria had they not been written on durable materials (such as clay tablets).

### 8.4.3 The End of the 'Theory of Prophetic Connection'

Given the classical view of the prophets as religious geniuses, seeing a close correlation between the Old and New Testaments was also common among scholars, characterized by Klaus Koch somewhat polemically as the 'theory of prophetic connection'.[10] This theory argued that, after a five-hundred-year period of spiritual decline shaped by mediocre, second-rate prophets, Jesus of Nazareth joined the ranks of the great prophets, a designation that had previously ended with Jeremiah or perhaps at best → '*Deutero-Isaiah*', although the latter's anonymity made him suspect. Since these last great prophets, the once spiritually rich Israelite religion had slid into a form of Jewish legalism from which it was liberated once again by Jesus. Conversely, the rejection of Jesus of Nazareth by Judaism could be attributed to this decline in prophecy in Israel.

Understanding the further development of the prophetic books by later editors has made it clear, however, that such a crude distinction between the brilliant individual prophetic figures and the subsequent editors of the prophetic books does not adequately grasp the nature of exilic and postexilic religious history. Rather, the literary process by which the prophetic books grew was continuously shaped in a prophetic manner.

Strictly speaking, the *biblical* prophets are constructs of their own books that need to be examined critically. This critical inquiry reveals that Old Testament prophecy is a long-term literary phenomenon developed via inner-biblical interpretative work, and its theological merit may be due to the

of the regular dynastic order were then republished for the same purpose under Ashurbanipal (668–631 BCE). In this case, however, there is no evidence of any productive literary processes but only a process of compilation. For more on this problem, see J. Jeremias, 'Das Proprium der alttestamentlichen Prophetie', *TLZ* 119 (1994): 483–94; idem, *Hosea und Amos* (FAT 13; Tübingen: Mohr Siebeck, 1996), 34–54.

10. K. Koch, *The Rediscovery of Apocalyptic: a Polemical Work on a Neglected Area of Biblical Studies and its Damaging Effects on Theology and Philosophy* (transl. M. Kohl; London: SCM Press, 1972), 36–8.

richness of experiences gathered over time. So the five-hundred-year gap in revelation between Jeremiah and → *Deutero-Isaiah* and Jesus – a distinction that also divides the history of Israel and Judah into an original, pre-exilic Hebraism and a legalistic, postexilic Judaism – is a scholarly construct, neither supported by historical evidence nor theologically useful.

The literary process by which pre-existing prophetic tradition is reinterpreted also points to a new approach for integrative rather than isolationist relationships between the two testaments: the Old Testament is not primarily a witness to discrete moments of contact with God by brilliant individuals. Rather, it is the literary deposit of a long-term exegetical engagement with the Scriptures and experience. This movement is then continued in the New Testament, which is one (but not the sole) outcome of the Old Testament (Ch. 34).

# 9

# The Book of Isaiah

(Konrad Schmid – Translation by Jennifer Adams-Maßmann)

## Chapter Outline



Cf. Chs 9.6 and 9.10. Further: J. Blenkinsopp, *Opening the Sealed Book: Interpretations of the Book of Isaiah in Late Antiquity*. Grand Rapids, Mich.: Eerdmans, 2006; M. A. Sweeney, 'Reevaluating Isaiah 1-39 in Recent Critical Research'. *CurBS* 4 (1996): 79–113.

German Classic: B. Duhm, *Das Buch Jesaja*. HKAT III/1. 5th ed. Göttingen: Vandenhoeck & Ruprecht, 1968.

Gerhard von Rad described Isaiah's proclamation as the most formidable theological phenomenon in the entire Old Testament.[1] Although such superlatives reflect a subjective impression, it is nevertheless clear that the book of Isaiah is not only one of the longest and most complex books of the Old Testament, but also one of the most theologically significant. These traits are related: the book's long developmental history is partly responsible for its theological richness.

# 9.1 Biblical Context

## 9.1.1 The structure of Isa. 1–66

If we view Isaiah as a whole, following the book's own logic as we read it, then we can begin by dividing the book into three major sections (unequal in length). (For more on the internal outline of these sections, see below Ch. 9.6 and Ch. 9.7).

| | | |
|---|---|---|
| 1–35 | | The oracles of Isaiah, principally pronouncements of judgement |
| | 1–12 | Composition around the 'memoir' (*6–9) with conclusion (12) |
| | 13–23 | Oracles about foreign peoples |
| | 24–27 | 'Apocalypse of Isaiah' |
| | 28–35 | 'Assyrian Cycle' (28–32) and bridge texts to Isa. 40–66 (33–35) |
| 36–39 | | 'Stories about Isaiah' |
| | 36–39 | Hezekiah-Isaiah stories (2 Kgs 18–20) |
| 40–66 | | The oracles of Isaiah, principally pronouncements of salvation |
| | 40–48 | Jacob as a redeemed people/Cyrus as 'Messiah' |
| | 49–55 | Return to Zion |
| | 56–59 | Renewed warnings |
| | 60–62 | Glorification of Zion |
| | 63–66 | Eschatological salvation for the pious |

## 9.1.2 The Caesura caused by the Stories of Isa. 36–39

The most striking structural characteristic of the book of Isaiah is the insertion of the Hezekiah-Isaiah stories (36–39) in the middle, separating the two words of 'Isaiah' in 1–35 and 40–66. After the declarations in 1–35, which predominantly contain pronouncements of judgement as well as conditional promises of salvation in 1–35, the stories in 36–39 portray the fundamental desire of

1. *Old Testament Theology* 2, 147.

Yhwh, the God of → *Zion*, for salvation through the wondrous preservation of Jerusalem from Sennacherib in 701 BCE. They provide the substantive basis for the ensuing proclamation of salvation by 'Isaiah', which goes even further in 40–66 and which is introduced with what could be seen as a 'second call' (40.1-8). The fact that events in 701 BCE in chapters 36–39 are presented as segueing directly into chapter 40 – essentially skipping over the Babylonian → *exile* in the sequence of events in the book – reflects a compositional decision with a clear agenda: Isaiah proclaims Yhwh's fundamental and steadfast desire for Zion's salvation. The destruction of Jerusalem by the Babylonians is mentioned only in reference to past and future events.

### 9.1.3 Insertions of Entire Books between Isa. 1 and 66

Striking verbal similarities (in terms of content and vocabulary) link the first and last chapters of Isaiah, which together could be seen as an inclusio wrapping around the entire book.[2] This feature clearly establishes that Isaiah as a whole was not simply compiled as a *florilegium* using existing materials without further thought about its structure and selection, but was conceived as a redactional unit (even as it was being developed).

The noticeable theological shift of themes between Isa. 1 and 66 – in which a prophecy of judgement against Israel (Isa. 1) is transformed into a prophecy of salvation for the pious (Isa. 65–66) – is a sign that the book as a whole develops a certain reading sequence which ought to be appreciated as such. The book of Isaiah provides an overview of the history of the sinful people of God from the Assyrian hegemony via the Persian rule to the consummation of God's reign over God's pious servants.

2. Cf. iniquities in 1.2 (Israel) vs. 66.24 (Yhwh's enemies); Zion has been abandoned in 1.8 vs. Zion as full of children in 66.8, 10; false 'new moons' and 'Sabbaths' in 1.13-14 vs. adoration of Yhwh by the peoples 'from new moon to new moon' and 'from Sabbath to Sabbath' in 66.23; false worship 1.11-13 vs. correct worship 66.20-21; the nations stream to Yhwh's house ('swords') 2.2-4 vs. 66.12, 16; judgement by fire against Judah 1.31, cf. 1.7 vs. judgement by fire against Yhwh's enemies 66.15-16, 24.

# 9.2 Historical-Critical Analysis and Major Issues in the History of Critical Interpretation

## 9.2.1 The Three-Book Hypothesis

One of modern biblical scholarship's earliest insights was that not all of the 66 chapters of the book of Isaiah could have originated from the Isaiah of the 8th cent. BCE, but that one could only expect to find the sayings of the real Isaiah in chapters 1–39. The historical setting of the book appears to change completely after chapter 40 and shifts to a period 200 years later (Ch. 9B). After Isa. 55, many often identify a further break as the prophecy of salvation is again interspersed with words of judgement (Ch. 9.11.1). For this reason, scholars generally followed the lead of Bernhard Duhm[3] (1847–1928) in dividing the book into three autonomous parts (1–39; 40–55; 56–66), each of which could be attributed to a different prophetic figure and era. Chapters 1–39 were said to contain the words of Isaiah ('Proto-Isaiah'); the original content of 40–55 was ascribed to an anonymous person active in the Babylonian exile with the pen name 'Deutero-Isaiah', while the textual groundwork from 56–66 was traced back to a third anonymous figure dubbed 'Trito-Isaiah'. Because scholars believed each of these books could be read alone without considering the other two, editorial structures spanning the entire book were hardly noticed. In contrast to such a division of the book of Isaiah based on the likely historical genesis, one must first distinguish between a diachronic history of origins and a synchronous book structure and then engage in a sophisticated synthesis using literary and historical criteria.

Classical research methods, which relied on the thesis of a three-part book as well as a high regard for the authentic individual *logia*, were largely indifferent to the question of the overall composition of the book of Isaiah. When they did analyse the book's origins historically, they generally assumed the process began with individual texts and collections, first assembled into the Proto-, Deutero- and Trito-Isaiah books, and then joined together into one large Isaiah book. Scholars imagined the consolidation of the three parts of the book in one of two ways: either chapters 40–66 were written as anonymous prophecies on the same scroll as 1–39 and thus took on the name of 'Isaiah', or scholars claimed 'Deutero-Isaiah' and

3. B. Duhm, *Jesaja*, V–XIX.

'Trito-Isaiah' emerged from an 'Isaiah School' active for hundreds of years with a written literary legacy so they could circulate under the name 'Isaiah'.

## 9.2.2 Recent Developments

More recent research has modified the earlier prevailing interest in 'authentic texts' (including a differentiated biographical classification according to various periods of proclamation). Opinion has now shifted towards an integrative notion of original and secondary sections of text. Additionally, scholars have turned their attention from the exegesis of individual texts to a contextual appreciation of the various sections in Isaiah. Two related consequences ensue for the exegesis of Isaiah: on the one hand, significantly more latitude is given when determining the historical period of Isaianic texts. The basic textual material no longer has to fit within the framework of the prophet's biographical details, but could have been produced some time between the 8th and 2nd cent. BCE. Furthermore, the focus when considering context is on the overall arc of meaning within the perspective of the entire book of Isaiah or the books of the Latter Prophets.

Current scholarly approaches to the formation of the entire book can be divided into two principal camps, at least if we exclude the increasingly unlikely assumption that Trito-Isaiah originated independently (and not through redaction) (Ch. 9.11) and limit ourselves instead to determining the relationship between the First (I Isa.: 1–39) and Second Isaiah (II Isa.: 40–66).

(1) The theory supported by the majority of researchers is that I Isa. and II Isa. trace back to two different prophetic figures ('Isaiah' from the 8th century BCE and 'Deutero-Isaiah' from the 6th cent. BCE). These corpora existed first as separate literary entities alongside one another and were only later linked together. Earlier research tended to see the formation of one large Isaiah book as occurring due to a coincidental technical matter related to the book's creation, but current scholarship assumes that I Isa. and II Isa. were connected by means of a redactional process moulded by theological concerns. The most important literary bridge text can be found in Isa. 35. Evidence of insertions by the same hand can also be found in 11.11-16; 27.12-13; 51.1-11* and 62.10-12.[4] Occasionally, Isa. 33 is also seen as an earlier bridging text.[5]

4. Cf. O. H. Steck, *Bereitete Heimkehr* (above, Ch. 8 n. 7).

5. See U. Berges, *Das Buch Jesaja: Komposition und Erdgestalt* (Herders Biblische Studien 26; Freiburg: Herder, 1998), 242–8.

(2) Another strand of scholarship sees I Isa. and II Isa. as significantly more closely related with II Isa. as a virtual continuation of I Isa.[6] Accordingly, they argue II Isa. never existed independently of I Isa., nor did an individual prophet 'Deutero-Isaiah'. The prophecy of II Isa. is a theological development of the themes in I Isa., especially given the dependence of Isa. 40 on Isa. 6 (though limited in Isa. 40 to vv. 6-8) and the anonymity of II Isa. The visible connections between I Isa. and II Isa. need not be analysed within the framework of a model of further written development (*Fortschreibung*); it may simply be a matter of a literary reference within a series of prophetic books.

Both theories agree on the fundamental distinction between I Isa. and II Isa., while the traditional three-book hypothesis has lost support. Whether or not one should go back to a two-book hypothesis depends on whether II Isa. is originally separate from I Isa. – that is, whether it originally developed independently or in connection with Jeremiah (see below Ch. 9.3). This option still appears best able to explain statements in II Isa. that do seem to point to oral proclamation by a particular prophetic figure. References in II Isa. to I Isa. could then be interpreted as editorial additions.

## 9.3 Origins of the Book of Isaiah (Isa. 1–66)

As there is not enough evidence to determine whether the second major section of Isaiah (Isa. 40–66) is a written continuation and development of I Isa. – the references are too inconsistent and the independence of the materials is too pronounced – we must assume that I Isa. and II Isa. originated separately and were joined together at a later stage.

Possible evidence against the independent existence of II Isa. includes the fact that the beginning of II Isa. in Isa. 40 does not have the heading one finds in other prophetic books, nor is it at all clear who is speaking with whom. Perhaps II Isa. did not originate as a completely independent literary entity, but from the outset was written with the book of Jeremiah in mind, rather than Isaiah. This thesis is supported by two important observations: first, 2

6. See, for example, R. Albertz, 'Das Deuterojesaja-Buch als Fortschreibung der Jesaja-Prophetie', in *Die Hebräische Bibel und ihre zweifache Nachgeschichte: Festschrift für R. Rendtorff* (ed. E. Blum *et al.*;Neukirchen-Vluyn: Neukirchener, 1990), 241–56; R. E. Clements, 'Beyond Tradition History: Deutero-Isaianic Development of First Isaiah's Themes', *JSOT* 31 (1985): 95–113.

Chr. 36.22-23 attributes to Jeremiah the predictions from Isa. 44.28 and 45.1, in which Cyrus is seen as the king appointed by Yhwh as well as the builder of the Jerusalem Temple:

> In the first year of King Cyrus of Persia, in fulfilment of the word of Yhwh spoken by Jeremiah, Yhwh stirred up the spirit of King Cyrus of Persia so that he sent a herald throughout all his kingdom and also declared in a written edict: 'Thus says King Cyrus of Persia: Yhwh, the God of heaven, has given me all the kingdoms of the earth, and he has charged me to build him a house at Jerusalem, which is in Judah. Whoever is among you of all his people, may Yhwh his God be with him! Let him go up.'(2 Chr. 36.22-23).

Apparently, the writer of Chronicles (Ch. 23) saw II Isa. as a prophecy by Jeremiah (although Cyrus is not actually named in the book of Jeremiah). Furthermore, the lack of clarity about who is speaking in Isa. 40 can be understood easily if it is read as a continuation from the last chapters of the book of Jeremiah (Jer. 50–51).[7]

II Isa. appears to have been joined to the book of Isaiah in the early Diadochan era.[8] The redactional connection is based on Isa. 35, a scribal prophetic text written solely as a bridge between I Isa. and II Isa. since it connects Isa. 34 to Isa. 40. The post-Persian dating arises from the fact that this text discusses the judgement of the whole earth, which appears to assume the global Persian Empire has collapsed.

## 9.4 Theology of the Book of Isaiah

Determining the theology of the book of Isaiah involves analysing both the elementary sections of I Isa. and II Isa. (Ch. 9.9 and Ch. 9.13) as well as examining the book as a whole. Each of the individual theological themes will be considered in depth within the context of their compositional development as part of the overall book.[9]

7. Cf. R. G. Kratz, 'Der Anfang des Zweiten Jesaja in Jes 40:1f. und das Jeremiabuch', *ZAW* 106 (1994): 243–61.
8. Cf. O. H. Steck, *Bereitete Heimkehr* (above, Ch. 8 n. 7).
9. Cf. K. Schmid, 'Herrschererwartungen und -aussagen im Jesajabuch,' in *The New Things: Eschatology in Old Testament Prophecy: Festschrift for Henk Leene*, (ACEBT 3; ed. F. Postma *et al.*; Maastricht: Shaker, 2002), 175–209; repr. in K. Schmid, ed., *Prophetische Heils- und Herrschererwartungen* (SBS 194; Stuttgart: Katholisches Bibelwerk, 2005), 37–74.

However, a general issue needs to be addressed first: the pre-eminent theological importance of fusing together I Isa. and II Isa. for the prophetic books of the Old Testament as a whole. This step allows the Jerusalem prophet Isaiah from the 8th cent. BCE to become a great visionary of world history who sees beyond his own time of judgement as far as the re-creation of heaven and earth. We cannot overestimate the influence of this literary technique on the traditional perception of prophecy as foretelling even the very distant future. Understanding prophecy this way arises from the editorial development of the prophetic books, not the historical prophetic figures themselves.

## 9.5 Notes on the History of Reception

J. Blenkinsopp, *Opening the Sealed Book: Interpretations of the Book of Isaiah in Late Antiquity*. Grand Rapids, Mich.: Eerdmans, 2006; C. C. Broyles and C. A. Evans, eds, *Writing and Reading the Scroll of Isaiah: Studies of an Interpretive Tradition*. VTSup 70. Leiden: Brill, 1997; B. S. Childs, *Isaiah: A Commentary*. OTL. Louisville, Ky.: Westminster John Knox, 2001.

The reception of the book of Isaiah begins in the Old Testament itself before the book of Isaiah was even completed. In fact, the literary growth of the Isaiah tradition can be described as a product of the reception history of earlier Isaiah texts. Aside from explicit references to the prophet Isaiah in 2 Kgs 18–20 (a parallel to Isa. 36–39) as well as in 2 Chr. 32.32 and Sir. 48.17-23, further indication of Isaiah's influence can be found in the textual development of the Book of Twelve. This book appears to have been repeatedly harmonized by editors to correspond to the authoritative Isaiah tradition, which was expanding and developing at the same time.

In the discoveries at → *Qumran*, the book of Isaiah was the third best-attested book with 20 scrolls after the Psalms and Deuteronomy. The Qumran community's high regard for the book is likely due to Isaiah's final passages which argue for an internal division of Israel and see future salvation as applying only to the pious.[10] The community at Qumran understood this text as referring to them.

Meanwhile, → *deuterocanonical literature* includes numerous implicit references to sayings from the book of Isaiah, and the figure of Isaiah plays a

10. See D. Parry and E. Qimron, eds, *The Great Isaiah Scroll (1QIsa^a): A New Edition* (Leiden: Brill, 1999).

prominent role in the so-called 'Martyrdom of Isaiah'.[11] This short narrative was passed down as part of the Christian apocryphal text known as the 'Ascension of Isaiah' (→ *apocrypha*), but was probably of Jewish origin and may have previously circulated on its own. It tells the story of how Isaiah is denounced by a false prophet named Belkira in front of King Manasseh who then has him sawed in pieces.

After the Psalter, the book of Isaiah is the most cited Old Testament book in the New Testament (Ch. 13). Isaiah is quoted explicitly no fewer than 22 times, and there is roughly the same number of implicit allusions. Isaiah is presented as the prophet who most prominently predicted the Christ, a conviction presented most notably in Matthew's Gospel (Mt. 3.3; 4.14; 8.17; 12.17; 13.14; 15.7).

In rabbinical literature, Isaiah is seen as related to King David and thus of royal descent (b. Sotah 10b; b. Megillah 10b; cf. Leviticus Rabbah 6:6); he allegedly became the father-in-law of King Hezekiah (b. Berakot 10a). He is particularly respected for the vision described in Isaiah 6, sometimes leading the rabbis to place him on the same level as Moses (cf. Deuteronomy Rabbah 2:4).

Aside from the call vision in Isa. 6, the multilayered reception of Isaiah in Christian history has particularly emphasized the Suffering Servant passages and the Immanuel promise in 7.14. Thanks to the translation in the → *LXX* (Hebr. *ʿalmâ* 'a young woman who is able to marry' is translated in Greek as *parthenos*, 'virgin'), the latter has become a central passage supporting the doctrine of the Virgin Birth. The fourth song of the Suffering Servant in Isa 53 virtually developed into a central source for the interpretation of the suffering of Christ in early Christianity.[12] The portrayal of Isaiah in Christian→ *iconography* focuses on the themes of the → *messianic* prophecies, the Temple vision, and the concept of the pantocrator (Isa. 66.1), as well as the apocryphal 'Martyrdom of Isaiah' (the sawing of the prophet in two).

11. J. H. Charlesworth, *OTP* II, 143–76.

12. J. Blenkinsopp, 'The Servant and the Servants in Isaiah and the Formation of the Book', in *Writing and Reading the Scroll of Isaiah: Studies of an Interpretive Tradition* (vol. 1; VTSup 70,1; ed. C. C. Broyles and C. A. Evans; Leiden: Brill, 1997): 155–75; P. Stuhlmacher and B. Janowski, eds, *The Suffering Servant: Isaiah 53 in Jewish and Christian Sources* (Grand Rapids, Mich.: Eerdmans, 2004).

# A First Isaiah (I Isa.: Isa. 1–39)

Commentaries: W. A. M. Beuken (HTKAT. Freiburg: Herder, 2003); idem, (Isa. 28–39. Historical Commentary on the Old Testament. Leuven: Peeters, 2000); J. Blenkinsopp (AB 19. New York: Doubleday, 2000); O. Kaiser (Isa. 1–12. OTL. 2nd ed. Transl. by J. Bowden. Philadelphia: Westminster, 1983); idem, (Isa. 13–39. OTL. Transl. by R. A. Wilson. Philadelphia: Westminster, 1974); H. G. M. Williamson (Isa. 1–5. ICC. London: T & T Clark, 2006). K. Schmid (Jes 1–23. ZBK 19.1. Zurich: TVZ, 2011)

M. Köckert, U. Becker and J. Barthel, 'Das Problem des historischen Jesajas'. Pages 105–35 in *Prophetie in Israel: Beiträge des Symposiums 'Das Alte Testament und die Kultur der Moderne' anlässlich des 100. Geburtstags Gerhard von Rads (1901–1971).* Altes Testament und Moderne 11. Ed. by I. Fischer *et al.* Münster: Lit Verlag, 2003.

## 9.6 Biblical Context

In I Isaiah there are three prominent independent composite sections. Chapters 13–23 constitute one collection as seen in its form and content, based on the use of the *maśśā'* ('sentence/dictum') headings and the thematic focus on foreign nations. Also notable is the so-called Isaiah Apocalypse in chs. 24–27 (→ *apocalyptic literature*) and the narratives in 36–39. The resulting divisions of the book are chs. 1–12, 13–23, 24–27, 28–35 and 36–39.

| | | |
|---|---|---|
| 1–12 | 1 | Introduction |
| | 2.1,2–4,5 | Pilgrimage of the peoples to Zion |
| | 3-4 | Oracle of judgement against Jerusalem and Judah |
| | 5.1-7 | Song of the Vineyard |
| | 5.8-24 | 'Woes' |
| | 5.25-29 (30) | Poetic refrain I |
| | 6–8 (9.1-6 [NRSV 9.2-7]) | 'Isaianic Memoir' |
| | 9.7-20 (NRSV 9.8–21) | Poetic refrain II |
| | 10.1-4 | Woes |
| | 10.5-34 | Woes over Assyria |
| | 11.1-5 (6-16) | Prince of Peace |
| | 12 | Song of Thanksgiving |
| 13–23 | 13.1–14.23 | Oracles against Babylon |

| | | |
|---|---|---|
| | 14.24-27 | Oracles against Assyria |
| | 14.28-32 | Oracles against Philistia |
| | 15–16 | Oracles against Moab |
| | 17 | Oracles against Damascus and Israel (northern kingdom) |
| | 18–20 | Oracles against Ethiopia (Cush) and Egypt |
| | 21 | Oracles against Babylon, Edom, Arabia |
| | 22 | Oracles against Jerusalem and court officials |
| | 23 | Oracles against Tyre and Sidon |
| 24–27 | 24 | Yhwh as judge over the whole world |
| | 25–27 | Deliverance of God's people amidst the judgement of the world |
| 28–35 | 28–32 | 'Assyrian Cycle' |
| | 33 | Judgement against destroyers; Restoration |
| | 34 | Judgement against Edom/Judgement of the whole world |
| | 35 | Return of God's people to Zion |
| 36–39 / 2 Kgs 18–20 | 36–37 | Siege of Jerusalem by the Assyrians (701 BCE) |
| | 38 | Hezekiah's illness |
| | 38.9-20 | Hezekiah's psalm |
| | 39 | Envoys from Babylon |

# 9.7 Historical-Critical Analysis and Major Issues in the History of Critical Interpretation

## 9.7.1 Evidence for the Successive Genesis of Isa. 1–39

Isa. 1–39 is indisputably a text that grew over time. No material from the oldest compositional stratum appears in chs. 24–27 and 36–39. Isa. 24–27 is clearly distinct from the surrounding context because of its unique conception of a judgement encompassing the entire world. Furthermore, a multiplicity of extensive intertextual references (for instance, references to the flood from Gen. 6–9) makes it clear that these are scribal texts that presuppose an advanced stage in the literary development of the Old Testament.

The narrative form of chs. 36–39 distinguishes them from the oracles in Isa. 1–35. The existence of a parallel text in 2 Kgs 18–20, which serves as the source for Isa. 36–39, shows that another author is responsible for this section.

Neither does the residual material in Isa. 1–12, 13–23, 28–35 present a unified text, but it too is the result of multiple stages of development. Given the process of literary formation in ancient Israel and Judah, this is not unusual but rather should be expected. The existence of a duplicate book heading in 1.1 and 2.1 suggests that someone worked over the introduction, which has had a decisive influence on how the book is read. In addition, the poetic refrain of 5.25-29, (30); 9.7-20 (NRSV 9.8-21) – so-named because of the recurring refrain, 'For all this his anger has not turned away, and his hand is stretched out still' (5.25; 9.12, 16 [NRSV 9.13, 17]) – has probably been separated in two in order to frame the coherent block of material found in 6.1–9.6 (NRSV 9.7).

One can assume that Isa. 1–12, 13–23, 28–35 contain older textual material that can presumably be traced back to the historic Isaiah at least in some basic, early form, yet the text's current shape shows considerabe editing and expansion. Reconstructing the literary development of I Isaiah in a way that receives widespread scholarly approval is impossible at this time nor is it likely in the foreseeable future, since it must be based solely on internal evidence, the analysis of which remains a fundamental matter of controversy. Thus, we can do no more than describe the basic trajectories.

## 9.8 Origins of First Isaiah

### 9.8.1 Isaiah 1–12 and the Problem of an Isaianic Memoir from the Syro-Ephraimite War

The traditional assumption has rightly been that the Isaiah tradition emerged from two cores (chs. *6–8; *28–31), although how to delineate those sections has varied. The notes on the recording of the revelations, which appear in 8.16-18 and 30.8, have played an important role in shaping this assumption. The most controversial problem in Isa. 1–12 is what Karl Budde (1850–1935) termed the Isaianic 'memoir'.[13] Isaiah's 'memoir' of the Syro-Ephraimite war (Ch. 4.2.1.3) was supposedly assimilated into chs. *6–8. The texts in these chapters stand out

13. *Jesaja's Erleben: Eine gemeinverständliche Auslegung der Denkschrift des Propheten (Kap. 6,1-9,6)* (Bücherei der christlichen Welt 23; Gotha: Klotz, 1928).

for their attention to the beginning of Isaiah's prophetic activity. They are largely preserved in the 1st person singular (since Bernhard Duhm, scholars often replace the 3rd person singular in Isa. 7 with 1st person singular) and are closely connected in their content and language. Do chs. *6–8 constitute a carefully constructed, authentic block of text documenting the effectiveness of the task of hardening hearts (6.9-11), first in the court (ch. 7) and then among the people (ch. 8), thereby reflecting the futility of Isaiah's proclamation? Should ch. 7 be seen as a more recent insertion into chs. 6–8 that can be removed, or is ch. 7 actually the core of the late development of the tradition in chs. 6–8, making the memoir hypothesis less likely? Analysing the existing text makes clear that chs. 1–11 have been shaped by editors into a ring composition with chs.*6–8 as the centre and with their apparent connection to the book of Amos.[14] Another indicator that the text was composed at an early date is the assumption that readers have extensive knowledge of the historical situation of the Syro-Ephraimite war because this is not self-explanatory for later generations of readers.

The placement of the commissioning vision in Isa. 6 just before the mandate to harden the people's hearts in Isa. 6.9-11 rather than at the beginning of the book creates a shift in emphasis. This composition portrays the previous chapters 1–5 as a call to a repentance that is still possible.

### 9.8.2 The Oracles against the Nations in Isa. 13–23

The collection of oracles about foreign nations in chs. 13–23, now joined to chs. 1–12, was probably originally a collection of its own. In its current guise, however, it has been heavily revised and reworked, as is evident by the opening with the Babylonian oracle in ch. 13, which does not reflect the actual constellation of problems in the Assyrian period. Isaianic material can be found in ch. *17, and possibly also in *14.4b-23 and chs. *18–20. The universal prophecy of salvation in 19.16-25 is theologically significant, as Egypt and Assyria are now included among the 'people of God' in 19.24-25.

### 9.8.3 The So-Called 'Isaiah-Apocalypse' in Isa. 24–27

With their cosmic orientation, chs. 24–27 should be seen as part of the tradition of the judgement of the whole earth that emerged after the collapse of the Persian Empire. Such declarations also appear elsewhere in the *corpus*

14. E. Blum, 'Jesajas prophetisches Testament', *ZAW* 108 (1996): 547–68; 109 (1997): 12–29.

*propheticum*, and the later genre of → *apocalyptic literature* drew crucial inspiration from these cosmic declarations of judgement. The loss of a certain all-encompassing political order by the Persian Empire appears to have influenced the prophetic tradition strongly. It remains doubtful whether any portions of chs. 24–27 originated before the Diadochan era.[15]

## 9.8.4 The 'Assyrian Cycle' in Isa. 28–32 and Chapters 33–35

Within the block of material found in chs. 28–35, chs. 34 and 35 should be singled out: ch. 35 is a purely redactional text linking I Isa. and II Isa.,[16] and ch. 34 has been revised in accordance with this insertion. Whether ch. 33 is rightly categorized as an older bridge between I Isa. and II Isa.[17] is also questionable given its much stronger connection to I Isa.

In chs. 28–32, often called the 'Assyrian Cycle', some texts presumably do trace back to the time of Isaiah himself. These may reflect either the circumstances at the time of the failed Philistine uprisings in 711 or the invasion of Sennacherib in 701 BCE.

## 9.8.5 The Isaiah Narratives in Isa. 36–39

Chapters 36–39 used to be interpreted as an historical appendix similar to the function of Jer. 52 in the book of Jeremiah. While this block of text is essentially identical to 2 Kgs 18–20, some characteristic differences remain (cf. esp. Isa. 38.9–20 and 2 Kgs 18.14-16). Given the overwhelming similarities in vocabulary and style, Isa. 36–39 probably derived from 2 Kings initially and was later integrated into the book of Isaiah.[18] An appealing hypothesis[19] is that these chapters reflect the historical situation between 597 and 587 BCE in Jerusalem. In their new context they serve as a reminder of God's miraculous protection during the Assyrian siege of Jerusalem several hundred years earlier. Precisely

15. O. Kaiser, *Isaiah* 13-39, 173–8.

16. O. H. Steck, *Bereitete Heimkehr* (above, Ch. 8 n. 7).

17. U. Berges, *Jesaja*, 242–49 (above, n. 5).

18. A different account can be found in C. R. Seitz, *Zion's Final Destiny: The Development of the Book of Isaiah: A Reassessment of Isaiah 36–39* (Minneapolis: Fortress Press, 1991).

19. Cf. C. Hardmeier, *Prophetie im Streit vor dem Untergang Judahs* (BZAW 187; Berlin/New York: de Gruyter, 1990).

because of this historical profile, they fulfill a decisive compositional function (Ch. 9.1.2) within the framework of the larger book of Isaiah.

### 9.8.6 Global Edits

I Isaiah has been comprehensively reworked multiple times. A broadly accepted theory is the 'Assur' redaction in 8.23b–9.6 (NRSV 9.1-7); 14.24-27; 30.27-33 from the time of Josiah.[20] This redaction interpreted the earlier perspective on salvation as fulfilled as a result of the decline of the Assyrian superpower and presumably was the first redaction to bring together *1–32 into one book. Further edits in 1–39 focused especially on the relation between the processes of judgement through and against Assyria and Babylon. Still later redactional work, found above all in ch. 35 (also 11.11-16; 27.12-13), establishes a connection between I Isa. and II Isa. or rather presupposes its existence and thus reflects the wider extent of the entire book of Isaiah. Because of its orientation towards → *Zion Theology*, I Isa. appears by and large not to have been subject to a → '*deuteronomistic*' interpretation.

### 9.8.7 The Problem of the Historical Isaiah

Disagreement among scholars about how to understand the historical figure of Isaiah cannot be resolved conclusively. Neither the material about Isaiah reported in Isa. 36–39 and its parallel in 2 Kgs 18–20 (cf. additionally Isa. 7 and 20 as well as 2 Chr. 26.22; 32.20; 32.32) nor the book's poetic texts can be considered reliable sources of information about the historical Isaiah and his message, so that the figure of Isaiah can only be reconstructed based on the texts' own development. The exact amount and content of textual material providing answers about the historical Isaiah remains controversial, so reconstructed portrayals of Isaiah range from an explicit or implicit prophet of salvation to a prophet mostly of doom based on the book of Isaiah itself with some elements of salvation in his proclamation, all the way to portraying him only as a prophet of judgement. Biographical changes have also been considered. So the question remains: Who was Isaiah?

Of paramount importance for answering this question is the interpretation of the so-called 'memoir' of Isaiah. The various stages in the development of

20. H. Barth, *Die Jesaja-Worte in der Josiazeit: Israel und Assur als Thema einer produktiven Neuinterpretation der Jesajaüberlieferung* (WMANT 48; Neukirchen-Vluyn: Neukirchener, 1977). For the image of Assyria in Isa. 1–29, see P. Machinist, 'Assyria and Its Image in the First Isaiah,' *JAOS* 103 (1983): 719–737)

8.1-4, 5-8 reveal how Isaiah first declared God's judgement only against the Syro-Ephraimite coalition (Ch. 4.2.1.3) (cf. 17.1-6), meaning the theologized proclamation of judgement against Judah in 8.5-8 was secondary.

> The stages in the development of Isa. 8.1-4 and 5-8 are recognizable by observing formal aspects in the introduction of the speech in 8.5 and more importantly with the extension of the oracle of judgement against Damascus and Samaria to Judah and Jerusalem.
>
> (1) Then Yhwh said to me, 'Take a large tablet and write on it in common characters, "Belonging to Maher-shalal-hash-baz" (roughly translated as "Hurrying to the spoil, rushing to the plunder"; in Hebrew *mahēr-šālāl-ḥāš-baz*) (2) and have it attested for me by reliable witnesses, the priest Uriah and Zechariah son of Jeberechiah.' (3) And I went to the prophetess, and she conceived and bore a son. Then Yhwh said to me, 'Name him "Hurrying to the spoil, rushing to the plunder" (*mahēr-šālāl-ḥāš-baz*); (4) for before the child knows how to call "My father" or "My mother", the wealth of Damascus and the spoil of Samaria will be carried away by the king of Assyria.'
>
> *(5) Yhwh spoke to me again: (6) Because this people has refused the waters of Shiloah that flow gently, and melt in fear before Rezin and the son of Remaliah; (7) therefore, Yhwh is bringing up against it the mighty flood waters of the [Euphrates] River, the king of Assyria and all his glory; it will rise above all its channels and overflow all its banks; (8) it will sweep on into Judah as a flood, and, pouring over, it will reach up to the neck; and its outspread wings will fill the breadth of your land, O Immanuel.*

If this editorial expansion in 8.5-8 relates to the circumstances in 701 BCE, then Isaiah would have transformed himself into a prophet of judgement for Judah. If it was a reaction to the downfall of Judah and Jerusalem in 587 BCE, then Isaiah was not against Judah until the scribal tradents saw him as such; the 'Isaiah' of the narratives (36–39) would stand closer to the historical prototype than the 'Isaiah' of the oracles in 1–11 and 28–31. The claim that Isaiah preached only disaster as in 6.9-11 cannot be valid if for no other reason than that the 'Assyria' redactions from the seventh century BCE already presuppose the prospect of salvation in the Isaiah tradition. Chapters 36–39 show that Isaiah could have had direct access to the king (cf. ch. 7); similarly, Jerusalem nobles acted as witnesses for Isaiah in 8.2. Even if these references are not necessarily historical, they may be reflections of Isaiah's high social position. Isaiah's roots in Jerusalem are almost indubitable, and are also reflected in his proclamation: The older strata of the book clearly developed within the theological and historical context of the Jerusalem cultic tradition and specifically focus on Zion as the place of Yhwh's holy presence.

# 9.9 Theology of First Isaiah

## 9.9.1 The Relationship between Judgement and Salvation and 'The Hardening of Hearts'

The relationship between judgement and salvation with which I Isaiah grappled presumably holds clues to understanding the biography of the historical Isaiah. If Isaiah actually went through a phase of proclamation in which he was at least implying salvation (by proclaiming judgement against enemies including Damascus and Samaria, cf. 8.1-4) – on analogy with other forms of ancient Near Eastern prophecy – then the proclamation of judgement is neither the sole nor the original subject of Isaianic prophecy. Instead, it seems to have developed out of the original prophecy of salvation. It is almost impossible to clarify whether the historical Isaiah or later writers were responsible for this development, and such a determination depends largely on the interpreter's exegetical methodology.

The well-known call to harden the people's hearts in 6.9-11 is a concrete reflection on the topic of the prophecy of judgement, although controversy exists about where to place this passage historically based on its literary development:

> And [Yhwh] said, 'Go and say to this people: "Keep listening, but do not comprehend; keep looking, but do not understand." (10) Make the mind of this people dull, and stop their ears, and shut their eyes, so that they may not look with their eyes, and listen with their ears, and comprehend with their minds, and turn and be healed.' (11) Then I said, 'How long, O Lord?' And he said: 'Until cities lie waste without inhabitant, and houses without people, and the land is utterly desolate.'

The call to harden the people's hearts, pointless within the framework of the prophetic proclamation, is a theological construction that views the prophecy of judgement in conjunction with its effect on its hearers. The rejection of the prophecy of judgement is presented as the author's intention from the very beginning, clearly showing how prophetic books were understood even in antiquity not as pedagogical texts but rather as theological reflections on history, meaning they are not primarily designed to motivate people to better behaviour, but as a way to process and reflect on the historical experience of disaster.

## 9.9.2 Zion

If we can trust the information provided in the book named after him, the historical person Isaiah came from priestly circles in Jerusalem. The important role that → *Zion Theology* plays in the book of Isaiah – Zion theology was the ruling concept of theology at the Jerusalem Temple which can be reconstructed, for example, from certain psalms (Ps. 46 and 48) – only reinforces this theory. The prominence of Zion theology can be explained most easily as the spiritual tradition Isaiah and the later Isaianic tradents embraced.

In this view Zion is the impregnable mythological cosmic mountain (also representing the connection between heaven and earth) on which Yhwh, presented as a king, is enthroned. Saying that Zion can be considered a cosmic mountain must be understood theologically rather than topographically; even the nearby Mount of Olives is taller than the Zion of Old Testament times (located on the southeast corner of Jerusalem and not to be confused with today's 'Mount Zion' on the southwest corner). The presence of Yhwh lends stability and security to Zion to such a degree that, while the prophecy of judgement in Isaiah involves various destructive actions of God, it does not contain the destruction of Zion itself, in contrast to the words of Micah of Moresheth, a Judean from the country (Mic. 3.12: 'Therefore because of you Zion shall be ploughed as a field; Jerusalem shall become a heap of ruins, and the mountain of the house a wooded height').

The book of Isaiah makes it clear both in individual statements and throughout the book's structure as a whole that Israel's hope and confidence rest in Zion. Thus, the depiction of Jerusalem's preservation during the siege of the Assyrian King Sennacherib in 701 BCE (Isa. 36–39) should be seen within the book's flow as a paradigm of salvation, documenting God's fundamental desire to save Zion.

## 9.9.3 The Kingship of God

The recurring image of God as king throughout Isaiah (cf. for example 6.5; 24.23; 33.22; 37.16, 20; in the later portions of the book 40.11; 41.21; 43.15; 44.6; 52.7; 66.1) presumably relates to the proclamation of the historical Isaiah who claims to look at 'King' Yhwh in Isa. 6.5. The kingship of God is a central component of the Zion theology in which I Isa. is steeped, so that the appearance of such a theological statement is significant for Isaiah (the prophet) and the book of Isaiah overall. One should keep in mind when considering the so-called → *messianic* prophecies from I Isa. (7.10-14;

8.23–9.6 [NRSV 9.1-7]; 11.1-5) that the ruling figures he envisions remain integrated within the larger framework of the kingship of God.

### 9.9.4 Messiah

Especially the so-called messianic prophecies in Isaiah (7.14; 8.23–9.6 [NRSV 9.1-7]; 11.1-5) have attracted particular attention in the Christian tradition. Historically speaking, one should be cautious when using the classification 'messianic prophecies'. On the one hand, not all of these texts can be properly termed 'prophecies' (the use of primarily the perfect tense in 8.23–9.6 [NRSV 9.1-7], for example, derails this classification), nor is every case concerned with the 'Messiah', that is, with an eschatological, royal and salvific figure.[21]

Of the three texts, the famous Immanuel promise in 7.14 presumably foreshadows the figure of Hezekiah (cf. chs. 36–39) early on in the first section of the book. The statements in the perfect tense in 8.23–9.6 (NRSV 9.1-7) likely reflect a historical review of the birth of Josiah; only 11.1-5 may be an authentic prophecy of a coming ruler. However, one could also argue in this case that the image of the offshoot from the stock of Jesse (that is, from the *father* of David) indicates the Davidic dynasty has already been broken.

## B Second Isaiah (II Isa.: Isa. 40–66)

📖 Commentaries: U. Berges (HTKAT. Freiburg: Herder, 2008); J. Blenkinsopp (AB 19A. New York: Doubleday, 2002); K. Elliger (BKAT 11:1. Neukirchen-Vluyn: Neukirchener, 1989).

📖 M. Albani, *Der eine Gott und die himmlischen Heerscharen*. Arbeiten zur Bibel und ihrer Geschichte 1. Leipzig: Evangelische Verlagsanstalt 2000; H.-J. Hermisson, 'Einheit und Komplexität der Verkündigung Deutero-Jesajas'. Pages 132–57 in *Studien zu Prophetie und Weisheit*. FAT 23. Tübingen: Mohr Siebeck, 1998; O. H. Steck, *Gottesknecht und Zion: Gesammelte Aufsätze zu Deutero-Jesaja*. FAT 4. Tübingen: Mohr Siebeck, 1992.

One of the oldest and most enduring insights from historical-critical biblical studies is that the most profound break in the book comes between Isa. 39 and Isa. 40. The tenor of theological argumentation changes completely. While oracles of judgement predominate until chapter 39, starting with chapter 40 proclamations

21. The title 'Messiah' is only used once in Isaiah: namely, in Isa. 45.1 where it refers to a historical figure, the Persian king Cyrus ('my anointed').

of salvation are normative. The historical setting has also clearly shifted. The narrative setting of Isa. 1–39 is largely the 8th cent. BCE, while the setting of Isa. 40–66 presupposes a completely different situation: both Israel and Judah have ceased to exist as sovereign kingdoms, and the Persian king Cyrus, who was ruler almost exactly two hundred years later from 559–530 BCE, is referred to by name (44.28; 45.1). 'Isaiah', however, is no longer mentioned.

For these reasons one can assume that chapters 40–55 trace back to another, later prophetic figure that contrasts with the authentic material in 1–39. Of course, it is also conceivable that a group rather than an individual is responsible for Isa. 40–55. It is unlikely that Isa. 40–66 is a redactional continuation (*Fortschreibung*) developed from Isa. 1–39 without a foundation in its own prophetic proclamation because the texts appear to have been shaped over time from 'small units' of previously independent oral proclamation.

Thus a prophet or a prophetic group ('Deutero-Isaiah') is probably responsible for chs. 40–55, even if the author(s) remains anonymous. This does not necessarily mean that these chapters circulated as a freestanding book, however. The lack of an introduction to chapter 40 is an indication to the contrary. Furthermore, this section may have originally been attributed to Jeremiah (cf. 2 Chr. 36.22), so one should consider the possibility that chs. 40–66 were developed first as an appendix to the Jeremiah tradition (Ch. 9.3).

## 9.10 Biblical Context

The conventional division of II Isa. into chs. 40–55 and 56–66 was based on the observation that chs. 40–55 include prophecies of unconditional salvation while admonitions and even accusations start appearing in ch. 56. While this caesura has a theological basis, the proclamation of salvation for → *Zion* in chs. 60–62 is much more closely related to chs. 40–55 in terms of content than chs. 56–59 and 63–66. So the most elementary outline of II Isa. cannot simply divide chs. 40–55 and 56–66, but must distinguish between chs. 40–55 and 60–62, on the one hand, and chs. 56–59 and 63–66, on the other.

The block of text can be organized in detail as follows:

| | | |
|---|---|---|
| 40–55 | 40.1-11 | Prologue |
| | 40–48/49–55 | Focus on Cyrus / Focus on Zion |
| | 42.1-4; 49.1-6; 50.4-9; 52.13–53.12 | Songs of the Suffering Servant |
| | 52.7-10 | Epilogue to 40.1-11 |

| | | |
|---|---|---|
| 56–59 | 56.1-8 | Admittance of foreigners and those who are mutilated due to accidents with circumcision (contrary to Deut. 23) |
| | 56.9–57.13 | Accusations |
| | 57.14-21 | Words of comfort |
| | 58 | Sermon on fasting |
| | 59 | The sin of the people as a barrier to salvation |
| 60–62 | 60 | The glory of Zion |
| | 61 | The Zion sermon ('I') |
| | 62 | The hastening of the glory of Zion |
| 63–66 | 63.1-6 | Judgement in Edom |
| | 63.7–64.11 (NRSV 64.12) | Prayer of lament |
| | 65–66 | Response to the prayer |

# 9.11 Historical-Critical Analysis and Major Issues in the History of Critical Interpretation

## 9.11.1 'Deutero-Isaiah' and 'Trito-Isaiah'

As obvious and correct as the literary distinction between chs. 1–39 ('First Isaiah') and chs. 40–66 ('Second Isaiah') may be, it is problematic to view the traditional split between chs. 40–55 ('Deutero-Isaiah') and 56–66 ('Trito-Isaiah') as equally fundamental.

It is true that chs. 40–55 certainly offer unconditional prophecies of salvation, while admonitions reappear in ch. 56 and provide conditions for the anticipated salvation the prophet has announced. The texts in chs. 56–66 are thus a reaction to the delayed fulfilment of Deutero-Isaiah's prophecy of salvation for the present. The promised salvation in Deutero-Isaiah was neither fulfilled to the degree nor at the exact moment proclaimed in chs. 40–55. Chapters 56–66 investigate the reasons for this delay and identify barriers to salvation in the behaviour of God's people and warn them of the consequences.

Contrary to the earlier 'Trito-Isaiah' hypothesis, chs. 56–66 are not based on the oral proclamation of an independent prophet ('Trito-Isaiah'). These chapters are examples of scribal tradent prophecy that only ever existed as texts written for inclusion in a book. From the outset, the texts found in chs. 56–66 were editorial developments and expansions (*Fortschreibung*) of the original prophetic tradition, especially of the Deutero-Isaiah tradition in chs. 40–55. Later sections of text presuppose the continuation of I Isa. and II Isa.[22]

| Isa. 40.3: | Isa. 57.14: |
|---|---|
| A voice cries out: | It shall be said, |
| 'In the wilderness prepare | 'Build up, build up, |
| the way of the Lord, | prepare the way, |
| make straight in the desert | remove every obstruction |
| a highway for our God.' | from my people's way.' |

The scribal character of 56–66 can be recognized by the incorporation of 40.3 in 57.14:

In 40.3 the call goes out to make a procession street for Yhwh straight and smooth so that Yhwh can return to → *Zion*/Jerusalem and enter his sanctuary. Verse 57.14 takes this call and reinterprets it based on ethical considerations: the social and religious grievances among the people must be removed so that salvation can break through.

Moreover, within chs. 56–66 a further basic distinction should be made between chs. 56–59 and 63–66 on the one hand, and 60–62 on the other. Conceptually speaking, the only statements that place new conditions on the proclamation of salvation and are therefore 'Trito-Isaianic' sections are chs. 56–59 + 63–66. Chapters 60–62 exhibit a clear and direct relationship to II Isa through their proclamation of unconditional salvation for Zion. There is, therefore, reason to conclude that chs. 60–62 are older than 56–59 + 63–66 and originally belonged to chs. *40–55.

## 9.11.2 Redactions Spanning the Entire Book of Isaiah

In addition to the processes of literary development applicable only to II Isa., one should assume that some texts within 40–66 were written for inclusion into a larger book of Isaiah that already contained I Isa. and II Isa.

These texts do not display uniform literary features and therefore likely have different origins. Some passages within chapters 51.*1-11 and 62.10-12 seem to have the same origin as chapter 35 and were inserted as part of the redactional joining of I Isa. and II Isa. One can even surmise that 62.10-12

22. Cf. O. H. Steck, *Studien zu Trito-Jesaja* (BZAW 203; Berlin/New York: de Gruyter, 1991).

once constituted the conclusion to the first large book of Isaiah. In chs. 65–66 one can find elements of a final redaction of the book of Isaiah which presupposes the joining of I Isa. and II Isa.

# 9.12 Origins of Second Isaiah

## 9.12.1 The First Version of Deutero-Isaiah

Within II Isa. we can still discern the outline of the first draft in *40–48 in particular, framed by 40.1-5 and 52.7-10. These corresponding texts served as the prologue and epilogue respectively (see below, next page).

This first draft differs from all earlier existing examples of written prophecy in Israel because it preaches unconditional salvation. Admittedly, the full impact of this salvation was yet to be realized, but Yhwh made a firm decision and its earthly realization is imminent. The gap between the heavenly decision and earthly realization is expressed linguistically in the so-called 'perfect tense of salvation' in Deutero-Isaiah: chs. 40–55 use the perfect tense to speak of particular saving deeds still pending, because in God their execution has been guaranteed.

Isa. 40.1-5:
'**Comfort, O comfort my people,** says your God. Speak tenderly to *Jerusalem*, and cry to her that she has served her term, that her penalty is paid, that she has received from Yhwh's hand double for all her sins. **Listen**: "*In the wilderness prepare the way of Yhwh, make straight in the desert a highway for our God. Every valley shall be lifted up, and every mountain and hill be made low; the uneven ground shall become level, and the rough places a plain.* Then the glory of Yhwh shall be revealed, <u>and all people shall see it together, for the mouth of Yhwh has spoken</u>."'

Isa. 52.7-10:
How beautiful upon the mountains are the feet of the messenger who announces peace, who brings good news, who announces salvation, who says to *Zion*, 'Your God reigns.' **Listen!** Your sentinels lift up their voices, together they sing for joy; for in plain sight they see *the return of Yhwh to Zion*. Break forth together into singing, you ruins of *Jerusalem*; for Yhwh **has comforted his people**, he has redeemed *Jerusalem*. Yhwh has bared his holy arm before the eyes of all the nations; <u>and all the ends of the earth shall see</u> the salvation of our God.

God's judgement against the people is now past: Deutero-Isaiah sees a new salvation history dawning for Israel quite different from the former one. The most notable difference is that Israel is no longer supposed to have its own king. Instead, integration into the Persian Empire is accepted as a divine act.

The first draft of Deutero-Isaiah was written before Cyrus took Jerusalem without resistance in 539 BCE. Chapters 46–47 indicate as much when they allude to expectations that Babylon will be annihilated without reflecting awareness of the actual events: Babylon was not destroyed during this occupation, but was expanded to become the seat of royal power for the Persian high king. Furthermore, in 45.1-2 one can recognize that the basic foundational text, which in v. 2 was also counting on military action against Babylon ('I [Yhwh] will go before you [Cyrus] and will level the mountains [?], will break the doors of bronze and cut through the bars of iron'), has apparently been corrected in v. 1 to be historically correct ('to open doors before him and the gates shall not be closed'). The corresponding statement in v. 2 should be dated before 539 BCE.

## 9.12.2 Redactional Expansions

The literary history of II Isa. is extraordinarily complex. The number of editorial levels one distinguishes in the text depends largely on one's methodology, causing controversy among scholars. The literary unity of 40–55 has been asserted again recently such that its complexity can be reduced by reading the text as a drama containing many voices and ambiguities.[23] However, most scholars rightly assume that the creation of Isa. 40–66 proceeded in a much more complex manner.

The specific processes of redactional development at work primarily within chs. 40–55 must be distinguished from those that shaped the broader section of chs. 40–66. Finally, there is clear evidence of editorial activity spanning the larger book of Isaiah. Thus, within chs. 40–55 we can say with some certainty that the polemics against idols (40.19-20; 41.6-7; 42.17; 44.9-20; 45.16-17, 20b; 46.5-8) are additions *sui generis*. The Zion texts (→ *Zion*) in 49–55 (esp. 49.14-26; 51.9-11, 17, 19-23; 52.1-2; 54.1) appear to have been introduced successively into the book, and the Suffering Servant songs potentially originated as independent pieces as well. Within the wider section including chs. 40–66, 'Trito-Isaianic' editorial changes and additions to the Deutero-Isaianic book exist in chs. 56–59 and 63–64, while final redactions of the larger book of Isaiah in Isa. 65–66 in particular are designed to bring the entire book of Isaiah to its conclusion. To this end, the final chapters set up an inclusio with ch. 1 (sandwich structure).

23. Cf. K. Baltzer, *Deutero-Isaiah: A Commentary on Isaiah 40–55* (Hermeneia; Minneapolis: Fortress Press, 2001).

## 9.12.3 The Suffering Servant Songs

Based on Bernhard Duhm's commentary,[24] scholars tend to believe that the four linguistically and thematically related texts found in 42.1-4; 49.1-6; 50.4-9; 52.13–53.12 all originated together. These were called the 'Songs of the Suffering Servant' because of the central figure ('my servant' or similar references in 42.1; 49.3-6; 52.13; 53.11). Recent redaction-historical approaches to the prophets, however, may initiate the need to re-examine this thesis of an independent genesis more closely and even lead scholars to abandon it altogether. Nevertheless, the internal connectedness of the texts is striking, even though the fourth song differs from the previous three as it looks back at the death of the servant.

One of the central and enduring questions for exegetes is the identity of the Suffering Servant. Who is this person supposed to be (42.1; 49.3, 6; 53.11), this figure who acts as the most obvious unifying bond in the four songs? One may first distinguish between collective and individual interpretations. The most important collective interpretation sees the servant as representing the people of Israel, a possibility supported by an explicit reference in the Hebrew text in Isa. 49.3: 'And he said to me, "You are my servant, Israel, in whom I will be glorified."' Other references in Isa. 40–48 to the servant of Yhwh also clearly intend Israel (41.8-9; 42.19; 43.10; 44.1f., 21; 45.4; 48.20). Yet aside from this interpretation, individual interpreters have also suggested that the servant represents various particular historical figures, mostly the prophet Deutero-Isaiah himself but also Jehoiachin, Zerubbabel, Cyrus, or other figures from the prophetic tradition such as Moses or Jeremiah.

How can these theories be evaluated? The key lies in the text's redactional history: As the book of Deutero-Isaiah grew, various interpretations were assigned to the Suffering Servant, each of which was then incorporated into the text: It therefore appears that the autobiographical interpretation of the Suffering Servant songs is the oldest, but it was later applied to Cyrus and finally to the people of Israel. Accepting this understanding means not having to choose between false alternatives. It also explains why a clear and unambiguous identification of the servant is apparently neither possible nor intended.

24. Cf. *Das Buch Jesaja* (HKAT III/1; 5th ed.; Göttingen: Vandenhoeck & Ruprecht, 1968), XIII, XVIII.

# 9.13 Theology of Second Isaiah

## 9.13.1 The Election of Cyrus

The fundamental politico-theological decision to proclaim that Cyrus, the Persian king, is Yhwh's 'anointed' (45.1) set the course for the Deutero-Isaianic tradition. This was a novelty within ancient Israelite religious history which previously had not deviated from a national-religious conceptualization in which everything foreign belonged to the realm of chaos. Deutero-Isaiah's view of Cyrus as a legitimate ruler according to God's grace therefore represents a qualitative leap that completely bursts the conceptual framework of conventional religion in the pre-exilic period. Yhwh, the God of Israel, becomes the sole ruler of the world who is also at liberty to establish or, if necessary, depose the Persian high king.

The statements about Cyrus in Isa. 44–45 can be set within the broader spiritual mindset of the period. Certain similarities exist between these texts and the so-called Cyrus Cylinder, a Persian document from the time of the fall of Babylon in 539 BCE when Cyrus had certain information recorded:

> 'Marduk… ordered [Cyrus] to go to his city Babylon. He set him on the road to Babylon and like a companion and a friend, he went at his side. His vast army, whose number, like water of the river, cannot be known, marched at his side fully armed. He made him enter his city Babylon without fighting or battle; he saved Babylon from hardship. He delivered Nabonidus, the king who did not revere him, into his hands… I [Cyrus] relieved [the citizens of Babylon] of their weariness and freed them from their service. Marduk, the great lord, rejoiced over [my good] deeds.'[25]

In the → *Cyrus Cylinder* the Persian king Cyrus is also the chosen one of a foreign god, in this case, the Babylonian high god Marduk; further documents also attest that he was accorded a similar position from a Babylonian perspective.

## 9.13.2 Monotheism

The Deutero-Isaiah tradition advances a very strict monotheism, which acknowledges only Yhwh as God and sees the divinities other peoples venerate as null and void: 'I am Yhwh, and there is no other; besides me there

25. English translation adapted from Mordechai Cogan (*COS* II, 315).

is no god' (Isa. 45.5a). This kind of monotheism can be called exclusive – the category of the 'gods' has been reduced to just Yhwh – in contrast to an inclusive conception such as that of the → *Priestly Source*, which assumes the existence of only one god while clearly admitting that this god can be called upon and worshipped in various guises. This means the category of 'gods' still includes only one element but that god can be called Yhwh (*ʾēl šaddāy* etc.), Ahura Mazda or Zeus, etc.

The monotheism of Deutero-Isaiah designates a profound break in the religious history of ancient Israel; this is the first explicit expression of an exclusive faith in one god (the first commandment of the → *Decalogue*, which forbids worshipping other gods, does not exclude the possibility that others exist – it assumes they do!).

The monotheistic option in Deutero-Isaiah is directly related to the text's notion of sovereignty: If world ruler Cyrus is supposed to rule over Israel as a divinely legitimated king, then this implies Cyrus is God's earthly representative, meaning in turn that God is ruler over the entire world. As a result one can conjecture that the advent of monotheism in the Old Testament is fundamentally associated with shifts in the political situation.

## 9.13.3 Theology of Creation

If Yhwh is the only God and as such the creator and ruler of the world, then this also means that God's activity in the world needs to be rethought in relation to the older literature in the Old Testament. In Deutero-Isaiah all of God's acts qualify as acts of creation in principle. This is particularly striking within the book of Deutero-Isaiah when hymns of praise to the creator God are incorporated at prominent places in the course of the book, thus making clear that divine historical acts are acts of creation (40.12-16, 21-26; 42.5; 43.18; 44.24; 45.7-11,18; 47.13; 49.8; 50.2-3; 51.13; 55.9-10).

## 9.13.4 Old and New Exodus

The historical situation of Deutero-Isaiah after the destruction of Judah and Jerusalem made it necessary to examine critically and rethink the traditions of salvation. Deutero-Isaiah makes it clear that God's action in bringing Israel up out of Egypt no longer has any contemporary relevance for salvation. Apparently, the old exodus from Egypt set in motion a history of disaster for Judah and Jerusalem that culminated in the loss of the land. Israel and its god can no longer look to the exodus event alone as the point when their relationship was established. In contrast, Deutero-Isaiah claims there will be a new exodus, this time from Babylon, far surpassing the first. First Yhwh himself will set forth from Babylon and then the people will follow. Furthermore, this new exodus will establish a new relationship between God and the people such that the old exodus can be confidently laid to rest.

Interestingly, the new exodus will also involve a 'water miracle', although not one that destroys Israel's enemies as in Exod. 14, but rather Yhwh will provide water in the desert so that the people's thirst can be quenched:

> Isa. 43.16-21: '(16) Thus says Yhwh, who makes a way in the sea, a path in the mighty waters, (17) who brings out chariot and horse, army and warrior; they lie down, they cannot rise, they are extinguished, quenched like a wick: (18) Do not remember the former things, or consider the things of old. (19) I am about to do a new thing; now it springs forth, do you not perceive it? I will make a way in the wilderness and rivers in the desert. (20) The wild animals will honor me, the jackals and the ostriches; for I give water in the wilderness, rivers in the desert, to give drink to my chosen people, (21) the people whom I formed for myself so that they might declare my praise.'

## 9.13.5 Israel as the People of the Patriarchs

Deutero-Isaiah handles the stories about the patriarchs quite differently than it treats the exodus tradition. Because the promises related to the land are based on the stories about the patriarchs, these stories represent the sole biblical tradition about salvation with theological relevance for Deutero-Isaiah. Thus, they are adopted and significantly expanded:

> Isa. 41.8-10: '(8) But you, Israel, my servant, Jacob, whom I have chosen, the offspring of Abraham, my friend; (9) you whom I took from the ends of the earth, and called from its farthest corners, saying to you, "You are my servant, I have chosen you and not cast you off"; (10) do not fear, for I am with you, do not be afraid, for I am your God; I will strengthen you, I will help you, I will uphold you with my victorious right hand.'

The people of Israel can be addressed using the names of their ancestors. Deutero-Isaiah thereby activates the promise theology of the ancestral narratives in Genesis that describe Israel as a people to whom the land has been promised unconditionally. Unlike the exodus tradition into which the → *deuteronomistic* theology of the law was incorporated, the stories about the patriarchs provide the people of Israel with an understanding of their new status as exiles (→ *exile*). Applying the patriarchs' names to the people as a whole is connected in Deutero-Isaiah with the similar application of royal statements to the people: The designation of Israel as Yhwh's 'elected' or chosen servant stems from royal ideology as does the standard greeting: 'Fear not!' which is then applied to the people who are now promoted to the privileged position of kings.

# 10

# The Book of Jeremiah

(Konrad Schmid – Translation by Jennifer Adams-Maßmann)

## Chapter Outline



Commentaries: R. P. Carroll (2 vols. Sheffield: Sheffield Phoenix, 2006); W. L. Holladay (Hermeneia. 2 vols. Philadelphia: Fortress, 1986, 1989); G. Fischer (HTKAT. 2 vols. Freiburg: Herder, 2005); G. Wanke (ZBK 20. 2 vols. Zürich: Theologischer Verlag, 1995, 2003).

R. P. Carroll, 'Century's End: Jeremiah Studies at the Beginning of the Third Millennium'. *CurBS* 8 (2000): 18–58.

German Classics: B. Duhm, *Das Buch Jeremia*. KHC 11. Tübingen: Mohr, 1901; S. Mowinckel, *Zur Komposition des Buches Jeremia*. Kristiania: Dybwad, 1914.

## 10.1 Biblical Context

### 10.1.1 Differences between the Hebrew and Greek Versions

The book of Jeremiah has been transmitted in two different versions that display divergent structures.[1] In contrast to the Hebrew version, the old Greek

1. Cf. H.-J. Stipp, *Das masoretische und alexandrinische Sondergut des Jeremiabuches: Textgeschichtlicher Rang, Eigenarten, Triebkräfte* (OBO 136; Fribourg: Academic Press/Göttingen: Vandenhoeck & Ruprecht, 1994).

translation of the book of Jeremiah in the → *Septuagint* (LXX) places the oracles against the nations in the middle of the book rather than at the end.

Hebrew Version:

| 1–25 | 26–45 | 46–51 | 52 |
|---|---|---|---|
| Oracles against Judah and Jerusalem | Narratives including oracles of salvation (30–33) | Oracles against the nations | Historical appendix |

Greek Version (chapter numbering follows the Hebrew version):

| 1–25 | 46–51 | 26–45 | 52 |
|---|---|---|---|
| Oracles against Judah and Jerusalem | Oracles against the nations | Narratives including oracles of salvation (30–33) | Historical appendix |

In addition, the internal arrangement of the oracles against the nations is also different:

| | Hebrew Version: | | Greek Version: |
|---|---|---|---|
| Vision of the cup of wrath | 25.15-38 | Elam | 25.14-19 |
| Egypt | 46 | Egypt | 26 |
| Philistia | 47 | Babylon | 27–28 |
| Moab | 48 | Philistia | 29.1-6 |
| Ammon | 49.1-5(,6) | Edom | 29.8-23 |
| Edom | 49.7-22 | Ammon | 30.1-5 |
| Damascus | 49.23-27 | Kedar, Hazor | 30.6-11 |
| Kedar, Hazor | 49.28-33 | Damascus | 30.12-16 |
| Elam | 49.34-39 | Moab | 31 |
| Babel | 50–51 | Vision of the cup of wrath | 32 |

In addition to differences in the order, the amount of text also varies. Altogether, the Hebrew version is approximately 3,000 words longer than the Greek one, which is almost one-seventh of the entire book. Given the relatively faithful translation technique used in the Septuagint version of Jeremiah, it is impossible that these differences trace back to the Greek translator. It is much more likely that the Septuagint translator of

Jeremiah was using a different Hebrew original. So the LXX shows that two different versions of the Jeremiah tradition were in circulation in Old Testament times. Confirmation is provided by the → *Qumran* findings: the Jeremiah fragments from Qumran can be arranged in six scrolls of which two (4QJer$^{b}$; 4QJer$^{d}$) are suspiciously close to the LXX and thus show there was a similar Hebrew original used in rendering Jeremiah in the LXX.

Scholars have been aware of the differences between the Hebrew and Greek texts for some time and generally have considered the order and scope of the text in the Greek version to be more original; the Hebrew version in contrast has been seen as containing further editorial development and expansion (*Fortschreibung*). The argument in favour of this view is that the book of Jeremiah seems to be based on an organizational principle in the Greek order also found in the other prophetic books, known as the 'three-part → *eschatological* pattern' (Otto Kaiser). It exists in I Isaiah, Ezekiel and Zephaniah, and organizes the tradition in such a way that the oracles of judgement against one's own people are followed by oracles of judgement against the nations with oracles of salvation for one's own people at the end. However, aside from the fact that Jer. 26–45 can only be seen as oracles of salvation for the people on account of Jer. 30–33, this argument rather suggests that the construction of Jeremiah in the Septuagint is not older but more recent than the Hebrew version: as the tradition is being passed down over time one should count on editorial attempts at harmonization, meaning the more difficult reading is most likely to be original (*lectio difficilior lectio probabilior*).

The question of Jeremiah's structure must be separated from considerations about its size and scope. The majority of scholars have assumed that the shorter Greek text reflects an earlier phase in the text's development than the longer Hebrew text. While this may be true in general, it cannot be assumed across the board. The Greek text, in fact, sometimes includes passages that do not appear in the Hebrew version, and a few (though not many) passages in the Septuagint version of Jeremiah have even been shortened (cf. Jer. 25 and 27).

## 10.1.2 Structure and Content of the Hebrew and Greek Versions

| **Hebrew Version:** | | | **Greek Version:** | | |
|---|---|---|---|---|---|
| 1–25 | 1 | Commissioning of the prophet, Visions | 1–25 | 1 | Commissioning of the prophet, Visions |
| | 2 | Indictments, call to repentance | | 2 | Indictments, call to repentance |
| | 4–6 | Destruction from the north | | 4–6 | Destruction from the north |
| | 7 | Temple sermon | | 7 | Temple sermon |
| | 8–10 | Destruction | | 8–10 | Destruction |
| | 11f.; 15; 17; 18; 20 | Confessions | | 11f.; 15; 17; 18; 20 | Confessions |
| | 13; 16; 18 | Symbolic Actions | | 13; 16; 18 | Symbolic Actions |
| | 21–23 | Oracles against the royal house | | 21–23 | Oracles against the royal house |
| | 23.9-40 | Oracles against false prophets | | 23.9-40 | Oracles against false prophets |
| | 24 | Vision of the fig baskets | | 24 | Vision of the fig baskets |
| | 25 | Oracles of judgement against Judah and Jerusalem; after 70 years God will punish Babylon | | 25 | Oracles of Judgement against Judah and Jerusalem |
| | 25.15-38 | Vision of the cup (of God's) wrath | | | |
| 26–45 | 26 | Temple sermon | 25–32 | 25.14-19 | Elam |
| | 27–28 | Yoke narrative; Conflict with Hananiah | | 26 | Egypt |
| | | | | | Babylon |
| | 29 | Letter to the *Golah* (exiles) | | 27–28 | Philistia |
| | 30–33 | Words of salvation | | 29.1-6 | Edom |
| | 34 | Liberation of the slaves | | 29.8-23 | Ammon |
| | 35 | Rechabites | | 30.1-5 | Kedar, Hazor |
| | 36 | Dictation, Destruction and replacement of the scroll with Jeremiah's words | | 30.6-11 | |
| | 37–44 | Siege and Fall of Jerusalem, Gedaliah, Flight to Egypt, Jeremiah is carried off A word of comfort to Baruch | | 30.12-16 | Damascus |
| | 45 | | | 31 | Moab |
| | | | | 32 | Vision of the cup (of God's wrath) |

| | | | | | |
|---|---|---|---|---|---|
| 46–51 | 46 | Egypt | 33–51 | 33 | Temple sermon |
| | 47 | Philistia | | 34–35 | Yoke narrative; Conflict with Hananiah |
| | 48 | Moab | | 35 | Letter to the Golah |
| | 49.1-5(, 6) | Ammon | | 36–39 | Words of salvation |
| | 49.7-22 | Edom | | 40 | Liberation of the slaves |
| | 49.23-27 | Damascus | | 41 | Rechabites |
| | 49.28-33 | Kedar, Hazor | | 42 | Dictation, Destruction and Replacement of the scroll with Jeremiah's words |
| | 49.34-39 | Elam | | 43–50 | Siege and Fall of Jerusalem, Gedaliah, Flight to Egypt, Jeremiah is carried off |
| | 50–51 | Babylon | | 51 | A word of comfort for Baruch |
| 52 | | Destruction of Jerusalem | 52 | | Destruction of Jerusalem |

# 10.2 Historical-Critical Analysis and Major Issues in the History of Critical Interpretation

Twentieth-century research on the book of Jeremiah has been largely shaped by the commentary of Bernhard Duhm (1901) and a succinct study by Sigmund Mowinckel (1884–1965) from 1914.[2]

Duhm delineated three stages in the development of the book. He believed the oldest section was composed of the poems of Jeremiah, found especially in Jer. 1–25. He identified the second element as the book of Baruch – named after the scribe Baruch (Jer. 32, 36, 45) – in Jer. 26–45; later additions pervade the entire book.

Duhm's commentary was groundbreaking because he broke with the prevailing view that Jeremiah was essentially the author of his own book. Duhm radically cropped the proclamation of the prophet: 'The poems of Jeremiah comprise … about 280 masoretic verses … while the sections from Baruch's book are about 220, coming to about 500 for both: the remaining 850 verses can be attributed

2. B. Duhm, *Jeremia*; S. Mowinckel, *Jeremia*.

to editors' (p. XIX). Such an appraisal shocked Duhm's contemporaries. Yet this allowed Duhm to prepare the way for a historical evaluation of the prophet's message, since his approach did not begin by assigning the various messages to diverse periods in the life of the prophet. Instead, he assumed that the texts in the book were created over a significantly longer period of time, which is appropriate from a historical point of view. Thus, Duhm's commentary on Jeremiah was the first commentary to slash the amount of authentic material from the prophet to less than a quarter of the entire book.

Because many interpreters found this approach too radical, another work became the definitive standard for German-speaking Jeremiah research: Sigmund Mowinckel, *Die Komposition des Buches Jeremia* (1914). According to Mowinckel, the book of Jeremiah was pieced together from the four sources he called A, B, C and D:

A: The words of Jeremiah
B: Narratives about Jeremiah
C: Prose speeches in the → *Deuteronomistic* style
D: Words of salvation in Jer. 30–31

This source model, which was clearly inspired by Pentateuchal research (→ *Pentateuch*), was widely embraced. Even the commentary by Wilhelm Rudolph[3] (1891–1987) was based on Mowinckel's interpretation. More recent research has shown, however, that this source model for the book of Jeremiah is not sustainable. Most likely, the narratives (Jer. 26–45) originated independently from the oracles (Jer. 1–25). Winfried Thiel[4] has proved that the texts Mowinckel assigned to source C did not derive from a separate source but were the result of editorial additions: in other words, they were not developed independently from their context but presume that context and seek to develop it further. Thiel attributed both the great → *Deuteronomistic* prose speeches (esp. Jer. 7, 11 and 25) as well as smaller Deuteronomistic texts interspersed within the book to a unified Deuteronomistic redaction ('D') from the exilic period, essentially creating a three-stage model for Jeremiah's development:

3. *Jeremia* (HAT I/12; 3rd ed.; Tübingen: Mohr Siebeck, 1968).
4. W. Thiel, *Die deuteronomistische Redaktion von Jer 1–25* (WMANT 41; Neukirchen-Vluyn: Neukirchener, 1973); idem, *Die deuteronomistische Redaktion von Jer 26–45* (WMANT 52; Neukirchen-Vluyn: Neukirchener, 1981).

1. Texts from Jeremiah
2. Deuteronomistic redactional texts ('D')
3. Post-Deuteronomistic redactional texts ('PD')

However, Thiel's analysis includes disparate – sometimes far too disparate – elements lumped together under 'D', especially because Thiel identifies Deuteronomistic texts primarily by means of a so-called linguistic test: the unspoken assumption is that whatever is formulated using Deuteronomistic diction must also be theologically Deuteronomistic. This problematic linguistic test fails to take into account that the use of specific linguistic idioms does not automatically mean specific theological content can be assumed as well. A theologically differentiated approach is required for dealing with Deuteronomistic texts, in particular because Deuteronomistic language is used in Jeremiah for conceptionally diverse editorial activities. To put it another way: Thiel's 'D' is not a unified editorial layer, so one must make fine distinctions within it as well (see below Ch. 10.3.6).

More recently, scholars have come to yet another, completely different conclusion about the origins of the book of Jeremiah.[5] They argue that the book of Jeremiah was not shaped by overarching editorial activity but rather the book grew through small-scale edits. This 'snowball hypothesis' (Ch. 8.3) has its relative merits. Yet we must also take into account some redactions that can be found throughout the entire book. Considering the complexity of the book of Jeremiah, clearly the book was successively shaped and edited as a whole.[6]

# 10.3 Origins of the Book of Jeremiah

## 10.3.1 The Laments of Destruction as the Oldest Texts

The oldest texts in Jeremiah are the poetic sections, Jer. 1–25 and 46–51. The laments in Jer. 4–10 are a particularly noteworthy example as they are not

5. Cf., for example, C. Levin, *Die Verheißung des Neuen Bundes in ihrem theologiegeschichtlichen Zusammenhang ausgelegt* (FRLANT 137; Göttingen: Vandenhoeck & Ruprecht, 1985); W. McKane, *A Critical and Exegetical Commentary on Jeremiah* (ICC; Edinburgh: T&T Clark, 1996).
6. Cf. K. Schmid, *Buchgestalten des Jeremiabuches: Untersuchungen zur Redaktions- und Rezeptionsgeschichte von Jer 30–33 im Kontext des Buches* (WMANT 72; Neukirchen-Vluyn: Neukirchener, 1996).

yet connected to an accusation. It is hard to imagine they could have been recorded at any time other than in the immediate context of the catastrophic destruction of Judah and Jerusalem in 587–586 BCE.

In the current version of the book, the aggregate block of Jer. 4–10 appears to be one large accusation, yet this impression is due to two secondary revisions. One is the placement of the characteristic call to repentance in Jer. 4.3-4 at the beginning so that it serves as the prefix. Second, a particular set of redactional texts (indicated in italics below) produce the corresponding effect that the accusation is directed against an entity addressed with the 2nd person singular feminine, easily identified as Jerusalem (cf. 4.14, see below Ch. 10.3.2):

> Jer. 4.13-15: 'Look! He comes up like clouds, his chariots like the whirlwind; his horses are swifter than eagles – woe to us, for we are ruined!
> *O Jerusalem, wash your heart clean of wickedness so that you may be saved. How long shall your evil schemes lodge within you?*
> For a voice declares from Dan and proclaims disaster from Mount Ephraim.'
> 4.29-30: 'At the noise of horseman and archer every town takes to flight; they enter thickets; they climb among rocks; all the towns are forsaken, and no one lives in them.
> And you, O desolate one, what do you mean that you dress in crimson, that you deck yourself with ornaments of gold, that you enlarge your eyes with paint? In vain you beautify yourself. Your lovers despise you; they seek your life.'

Some disagree that the laments are the oldest texts in the book, arguing that mere laments over the destruction could not have become a foundational part of the tradition. They argue that it is not clear why they were written down; one would expect lamentation to have taken place historically but not to have been documented.

Ps. 48.3-7, 9, 13-15 (NRSV 2-6, 8, 12-14): (2) Beautiful in elevation, is the joy of all the earth, Mount Zion, in the far *north*, the city of the great King. (3) Within its citadels God has shown himself a sure defense. (4) Then the kings assembled, they came on together. (5) As soon as they saw it, they were astounded; they were in panic, they took to flight; (6) trembling *took hold of them* there, *pains as of a woman in labour* . . .
(8) As we have heard, so have we seen in the city of the Lord of hosts, in the city of our God, which God establishes for ever . . . (12) Walk about Zion, go all around it, count its towers, (13) consider well its ramparts; go through its citadels, that you may tell the next generation (14) that this is God, our God for ever and ever. He will be our guide for ever.

Jer. 6.22-26: '(22) Thus says Yhwh: See, a people is coming from the land of the *north*, a great nation is stirring from the farthest parts of the earth. (23) They grasp the bow and the javelin, they are cruel and have no mercy, their sound is like the roaring sea; they ride on horses, equipped like a warrior for battle, against you, O daughter Zion! (24) "We have heard news of them, our hands fall helpless; anguish has *taken hold of us, pain as of a woman in labor*. (25) Do not go out into the field, or walk on the road; for the enemy has a sword, terror is on every side." (26) O my poor people, put on sackcloth, and roll in ashes; make mourning as for an only child, most bitter lamentation: for suddenly the destroyer will come upon us.'

A counterargument may be found in the fact that the oldest laments in the book of Jeremiah represent a distinct theological position, making it plausible that a tradition developed around them: they obviously attack the Jerusalem-based → *Zion Theology*, the dominant theological conception of the First Temple, which assumed Zion was invulnerable because of the presence of Yhwh. The lament as attack becomes particularly clear in the subversive way by which the position of Psalm 48 is incorporated into Jer. 6 (see above).

In Ps. 48, Zion is safe from all attacks. Even the sight of Zion terrifies adversarial kings so much they retreat. In Jer. 6 the terror intended for their enemies descends on the inhabitants of Zion themselves instead, and 'Mount Zion' is turned into 'Daughter Zion', who is rolling in ashes.

Presumably one should also add to the list of the oldest texts of destruction in Jer. 4–10 the laments in the oracles against the nations in Jer. 46–49, as they are closely related both thematically and linguistically to those in Jer. 4–10. Not only Judah and Jerusalem were affected by the destruction which the Babylonians brought but also the neighbouring peoples found in the literary reflexes of Jer. 46–49.

## 10.3.2 From Lament to Accusation

An extraordinarily important step in the development of Jeremiah is the transition from lament to accusation, concretely visible in written editorial expansions (*Fortschreibung*) scattered among the lament texts as well as in the accusations of guilt made against an entity addressed with the 2nd personal singular feminine: Jerusalem. They come from the time around 587–586 BCE; the destruction of Judah and Jerusalem is already partly acknowledged and named (cf. the textual examples mentioned above in Ch. 10.3.1). Jerusalem can be depicted as a prostitute who dresses up and has lovers who turn against her and rape her. These sections addressed to a 2nd person singular feminine figure are interspersed with the laments in Jer. 4–10. This view was recorded in a pointed fashion en bloc, especially in Jer. 2:

> Jer. 2.19-22: 'Your wickedness will punish you, and your apostasies will convict you. Know and see that it is evil and bitter for you to forsake Yhwh your God; the fear of me is not in you, says Yhwh, God of hosts. For long ago you broke your yoke and burst your bonds, and you said, "I will not [be a slave]!" On every high hill and under every green tree you sprawled and played the whore. Yet I planted you as a choice vine, from the purest stock. How then did you turn degenerate and become a wild vine? Though you wash yourself with lye and use much soap, the stain of your guilt is still before me, says Yhwh your God.'
> Jer. 2.32-33: 'Can a girl forget her ornaments, or a bride her attire? ... How well you direct your course to seek lovers! So that even to wicked women you have taught your ways.'

What does this accusation of harlotry and adultery mean? A common set of metaphors in the ancient Near East for a bad policy of alliances,[7] the accusations of harlotry mean the attacks against Jerusalem are directed against Judah's misguided alliances. In the final years of the Judean kings, they were apparently trying to make compromises with the superpowers of Babylon and Egypt (cf. 2 Kgs 24–25; Ez. 17). The accusation of harlotry is aimed at the fact that Jerusalem did not put its trust in Yhwh its god, but instead made pacts with foreign powers and superpowers, who appear in those texts that use the 2nd person singular feminine as the 'lovers' who now reject Jerusalem or even rape her.

7. Cf. A. Fitzgerald, 'The Mythological Background for the Presentation of Jerusalem as a Queen and False Worship as Adultery in the OT', *CBQ* 34 (1972): 403–16; C. Maier, 'Tochter Zion im Jeremiabuch: Eine literarische Personifikation mit altorientalischem Hintergrund', in *Prophecy in Israel: Beiträge des Symposiums 'Das Alte Testament und die Kultur der Moderne' anlässlich des 100. Geburtstags Gerhard von Rads (1901–1971)* (Altes Testament und Moderne 11; ed. I. Fischer *et al.*; Münster: Lit Verlag, 2003), 157–67.

## 10.3.3 The → Symbolic Actions

Aside from the accusations against the 2nd person singular feminine character that were added to the text, so-called prophetic symbolic actions, which already assume the existence of a theology of guilt, were likely added as well. Examples include Jer. 13, 16, 18 (27–28 [in 3rd person singular]), and 32. Jeremiah 13 describes the symbolic action of Jeremiah burying a linen apron which was then destroyed: this is what will also happen to Judah. In Jer. 16 the prophet receives the commission to remain single because sons and daughters will be killed in the coming judgement. In Jer. 19 Jeremiah is instructed to take a pitcher and shatter it – in this way Judah will also be shattered. Finally, in Jer. 32 Jeremiah buys a field, indicating that the people will not be able to use the land for a long time (32.6-14*; v. 15 is a later interpretation). These symbolic actions belong together as shown by the fact that they are all formulated in the 1st person singular.

In the book of Jeremiah, the prophet is otherwise referred to using the 3rd person singular. So these texts probably provide evidence of an older stage of the book which did not yet include any contributions from a perspective other than that of the prophet.

## 10.3.4 Critique of the King

Among the older texts in the book are the statements about the king in chs. 21–23: Jeremiah appeared as a critic in the royal household of the Judean king. Evidence that these texts are, in part, contemporary with the events described can be drawn, for example, from the statement against Jehoiakim, the third-to-last king of Judah:

> Jer. 22.18-19: 'Therefore thus says Yhwh concerning King Jehoiakim son of Josiah of Judah: They shall not lament for him, saying, "Alas, my brother!" or "Alas, sister!" They shall not lament for him, saying, "Alas, lord!" or "Alas, his majesty!" With the burial of a donkey he shall be buried – dragged off and thrown out beyond the gates of Jerusalem.'

The pronouncement that Jehoiakim would not be buried after his death did not come true; a note in 2 Kgs 24.6 reports Jehoiakim's death:

> So Jehoiakim slept with his ancestors; then his son Jehoiachin succeeded him.

The expression 'slept with his ancestors' describes a regular burial. There is no reason to suppose 2 Kgs 24.6 has failed to pass down accurate information. Since Jer. 22.18-19 includes an unfulfilled pronouncement, one can rightly assume this is old. One would have hardly formulated a word of judgement such as Jer. 22.18-19 that contradicts actual historical events – after all, Jehoiakim was properly buried.

### 10.3.5 Narrative Material in the Jeremiah Tradition

Extensive stories have found their way into the book of Jeremiah in Jer. 26–45, although these did not constitute one integrated textual unit from the outset, but were assembled bit by bit. Jeremiah 37–44 is the most comprehensive unified segment, which portrays events beginning shortly before the downfall of Jerusalem all the way to the emigration of a group of refugees to Egypt, that also carried Jeremiah with them. Jeremiah 39–41 potentially began as an independent narrative. Jeremiah 27–28 includes the yoke narrative, which editors reworked to join it with the letter of Jeremiah to the first → *golah* in Babylon in Jer. 29. The two narratives in Jer. 26 and 36 have also been harmonized.

### 10.3.6 The Problem of a Deuteronomistic Redaction

Ever since the work of Winfried Thiel, the theory of a *Deuteronomistic* redaction in the book of Jeremiah has been hotly debated. The obvious issue is that, compared to other prophetic books, the book of Jeremiah includes more extensive passages of text which sound like the well-known Deuteronomistic idiom found in Deuteronomy and Joshua–2 Kings, suggesting some kind of connection. The presence of some Deuteronomistic elements in the book of Jeremiah is likely due to the fact they were written at about the same time, as well as the historical setting: Because Jeremiah appeared as a prophet right at the time of the catastrophe of Judah and Jerusalem, far-reaching interpretations were appended to traditions about him.

As has already been mentioned, the problem of a Deuteronomistic redaction in Jeremiah is more complex than is commonly acknowledged, largely because one needs to differentiate between linguistic and theological Deuteronomistic elements.

A particularly clear example is the passage about the new → *covenant* (Jer .31.31-34). Siegfried Herrmann and Winfried Thiel have ascribed it to a Deuteronomistic redaction of the book of Jeremiah on the basis of the text's diction. The word choice in this passage certainly does reveal striking affinities to Deuteronomistic idiom. At the same time, theological considerations make it impossible to categorize Jer. 31.31-34 as Deuteronomistic. The promise that the Torah will be written on the people's hearts in the end time with its implicit assumption that the written Torah is dispensable is not compatible with the otherwise identifiable theological interests of Deuteronomistic thought, nor is the rejection of mutual admonition (cf. in contrast to Deut. 6.4-9). Jeremiah 31.31-34 may be formulated in a Deuteronomistic way, but its way of thinking is not Deuteronomistic (cf. the extensive discussion on this subject in section D4).

The use of the term 'Deuteronomistic' should be strictly limited to those texts that follow the guiding theological principles of Deuteronomy (unity and purity of the cult) and evidence the linguistic style characteristic of the Deuteronomistic school. The so-called linguistic test by itself is not sufficient to identify reliably which passages come from a Deuteronomistic editor.

When these criteria are followed, then classical 'Deuteronomisms' can be found, especially in Jer. 7–25, not just in larger texts such as Jer. *25 but also in smaller insertions (indicated in the following example in *italics*), such as those recording the accusation of idolatry in its context:

> '"My joy is gone, grief is upon me," my heart is sick. Hark, the cry of my poor people from far and wide in the land: "Is Yhwh not in Zion? Is her King not in her?" – *"Why have they provoked me to anger with their images, with their foreign idols?"* –
> "The harvest is past, the summer is ended, and we are not saved."
> For the hurt of my poor people I am hurt, I mourn, and dismay has taken hold of me.
> Is there no balm in Gilead? Is there no physician there? Why then has the health of my poor people not been restored?
> O that my head were a spring of water, and my eyes a fountain of tears, so that I might weep day and night for the slain of my poor people!' (Jer. 8.18-23 [NRSV 8.18–9.1]).

Many texts assigned to group 'D' by Thiel require further differentiation based on their editorial history. An important example is the vision of the fig baskets in Jer. 24 (Group 'D', according to Thiel), whose language sounds Deuteronomistic, but expresses quite different concerns. Karl-Friedrich Pohlmann[8] spoke of a *Golah*-oriented theology in this case, meaning a concept that clearly divides God's people

8. *Studien zum Jeremiabuch* (FRLANT 118; Göttingen: Vandenhoeck & Ruprecht, 1978).

into the leading elite deported in 597 BCE and their offspring ('good figs'), on the one hand, and the population that remained in the country as well as the refugees to Egypt ('bad figs'), on the other. This stark contrast seeks to limit the divine plan of salvation to only the children of the first *Golah*, the old leading elite. Such a plan was based on conflicts developing in the postexilic period between the people still living in the land and the repatriates.[9]

Such an unambiguous theology in Jer. 24 soon provoked a counterreaction: in contrast to Jer. 24 where only descendants of the first *Golah* under Jehoiachin in Babylon would play a role in Yhwh's future plan of salvation, a series of textual insertions in Jeremiah allowed the worldwide → *diaspora* to express their views. These carefully placed texts expand the original proclamations of salvation which applied only to the Babylonian Jehoiachin *Golah* in Jer. 24 now to include the entire diaspora. So one can rightly speak of a diaspora-oriented theology. These texts also sound 'Deuteronomistic', not because they primarily express the theology of Deuteronomy, but because they take up the language of the *Golah*-oriented passages, albeit with a critical twist.

If we follow the → *LXX*, the statements in Jer. 23.7-8 very likely appeared in the original text just before the *Golah*-oriented passage in Jer. 24:

> Jer. 23.7-8: 'Therefore, the days are surely coming, says Yhwh, when it shall no longer be said, "As Yhwh lives who brought the people of Israel up out of the land of Egypt", but "As Yhwh lives who brought out and led the offspring of the house of Israel out of the land of the north and out of all the lands where he had driven them." Then they shall live in their own land.'

Along these lines, Jer. 29.14 corrects the insertion in Jer. 29.16-19 supporting the *Golah*, which is a quote from Jer. 24. Jeremiah 32.37 constitutes yet another diaspora-oriented text. The historical situation in these passages indicates they come from the Persian period; they are certainly later than the *Golah*-oriented texts whose existence they take presuppose.

Besides the *Golah*- and diaspora-oriented redactional pieces, yet another collection of texts in the book of Jeremiah belongs together and makes use of

9. Jeremiah 24 is related to several other texts (esp. Jer. 29.16-19; 44.11-14) which structure the entire book of Jeremiah together with Jer. 24 according to a *Golah*-oriented purpose: 'both parts of the fig basket vision (Jer. 24.5-7 [salvation for the 'good figs']; 24.8-10 [judgement for the 'bad figs']) anticipate the prophecies of salvation in Jer. 29–33 which are limited to the descendants of the first *Golah* (cf. 29,17), while announcing destruction in Jer. 37–44, which is valid for the people in the land and Egyptian refugees (cf. 44.11-14, 27-28.).

Deuteronomistic diction, although these texts pursue their own theological interests. They announce a universal and comprehensive world judgement, thereby interpreting Jeremiah as a whole in yet another way. The most important passages in this collection are Jer. 25.27-31 and 45.4-5. Jeremiah 25.27-31 displays the firm belief that the coming judgement will be on a cosmic scale, in keeping with the oracles against the nations in Jer. 25 and the vision of the cup of wrath:

> Jer. 25.27-31: 'Then you shall say to them, Thus says Yhwh, Lord of hosts, the God of Israel: Drink, get drunk and vomit, fall and rise no more, because of the sword that I am sending among you. And if they refuse to accept the cup from your hand to drink, then you shall say to them: Thus says Yhwh, the Lord of hosts: You must drink! See, I am beginning to bring disaster on the city that is called by my name, and how can you possibly avoid punishment? You shall not go unpunished, for I am summoning a sword against *all the inhabitants of the earth*, says Yhwh, the Lord of hosts. You, therefore, shall prophesy against them all these words, and say to them: Yhwh will roar from on high, and from his holy habitation utter his voice; he will roar mightily against his fold, and shout, like those who tread grapes, against *all the inhabitants of the earth*. The clamor will resound to the ends of the earth, for Yhwh has an indictment against the nations; he is entering into judgment *with all flesh*, and the guilty he will put to the sword, says Yhwh.'

The statements about the judgement of the nations in Jer. 25 have been expanded by editors to describe a universal world judgement. An analogous process is at play in Jer. 45, visible in the last two verses before the series of oracles against the nations begins in Jer. 46–51. These so-called words of comfort to Baruch proclaim:

> Jer. 45.4-5: 'Thus you shall say to him, "Thus says Yhwh: I am going to break down what I have built, and pluck up what I have planted – that is, the whole land. And you, do you seek great things for yourself? Do not seek them; for I am going to bring disaster *upon all flesh*, says Yhwh; but I will give you your life as a prize of war in every place to which you may go."'

In this case as well, a preliminary pronouncement of judgement 'upon all flesh' is received such that all the successive sayings of judgement against the nations are expanded to imagine a universal world judgement. In terms of the era when it was written, this perspective very likely post-dates the Persian period, belonging to the beginning of the Diadochan period, as this most naturally explains this concept of a universal world judgement. The collapse of the two-hundred year Persian

Empire and the accompanying loss of political stability in the time of Alexander III of Macedon (Battles near Issus and Gaugamela in 333 BCE and 331 BCE) which encompassed the entire ancient world at that time must have seemed like a divine judgement over the entire world.

## 10.3.7 Words of Salvation in Jeremiah

Although the book is dominated by prophecies of judgement, extensive prophecies of salvation have been compiled, especially in chs. 30–33. Scholars previously claimed the core of this chapter in Jer. 30–31 included the early pronouncements of Jeremiah to the northern kingdom; especially the speech to Ephraim in Jer. 31.15-22 (pars pro toto for the northern kingdom, as in Hos.) which was understood in this sense. This text was situated in the time of Josiah (639–609 BCE): Jeremiah was supposed to have announced salvation to the former northern kingdom during a period when King Josiah had been able to expand the southern kingdom partially to include territories in the northern kingdom (cf. Bethel in 2 Kgs 23.4), thus planting the seeds of hope for a reunion of Israel and Judah.

The problem with this view is that Jer. 30–31 not only announced salvation to Ephraim but to Jacob – meaning he did not have the northern kingdom in mind. Jacob is the designation for the 12 tribes, so Israel as a whole is meant here. The consequence, however, is that if Jer. 30–31 is announcing restitution to all Israel, then the downfall of Judah lies in the past for these texts. They therefore cannot be dated to the time of Josiah.

In addition, the texts in Jer. 30–31 apparently adopt and affirm the oracles of judgement from Jer. 2–10 before turning to proclamations of salvation (compare Jer. 30.5-7 with Jer. 6.24 or Jer. 30.13 with Jer. 8.22). Not only are texts from the book of Jeremiah adopted, but Jer. 30 also takes into consideration more distant texts. Jeremiah 30.18, for example, uses Deut. 13.17 (NRSV 13.16) in order to override the regulation that a city which has fallen away from God should not be rebuilt:

| | |
|---|---|
| Deut. 13.16: 'All of [*the city's*] spoil you shall gather into its public square; then burn the *city* and all its spoil with fire, as a whole burnt-offering to Yhwh your God. It shall remain a [*mound*], never to be rebuilt.' | Jer. 30.18: 'Thus says Yhwh: I am going to restore the fortunes of the tents of Jacob, and have compassion on his dwellings; the *city* shall be *rebuilt* upon its *mound*, and the citadel set on its rightful site.' |

Taken as a whole, Jer. 30–31 should be seen as prophecy from scribal tradents who have adopted pre-existing texts from Jeremiah as well as texts from other more or less distantly related biblical passages in order to proclaim salvation after the judgement that has already taken place. In the course of → *exile*, signs of hope were recorded in Jer. 30–31 that help provide the framework within which to imagine anew the restoration of all Israel. These texts in Jer. 30–31 are important because they belong to the first and oldest prophecies of salvation in the Old Testament formulated after the catastrophe.

### 10.3.8 The So-Called 'Confessions of Jeremiah'

In Jer. 11.18-23; 12.1-6; 15.10-21; 17.14-18; 18.18-23; 20.7-18 the prophet complains before God about his calling and the accompanying hostilities he has endured. In terms of form, these stories strongly echo the individual songs of lament in the Psalter (Ch. 13). They have been designated the 'confessions' of Jeremiah along the lines of the Confessions of church father Augustine of Hippo (354–430). The conventional interpretation of the prophets often drew on the confessions to reconstruct Jeremiah's inner life. In light of the comparison with the psalms, however, and the realization these confessions largely follow formal conventions in terms of language and construction, then they can no longer be used to uncover the psyche of the historical Jeremiah. Furthermore, the confessions are strongly shaped by the antagonism between the pious and ungodly, which locates these texts in a period after Jeremiah in terms of Israel's intellectual history. So it is quite unlikely that the confessions of Jeremiah had anything to do with the sufferings of the historical prophet himself; it is more likely these are redactional texts of consolation attached to the person of Jeremiah.[10]

It is worth comparing the confessions of Jeremiah and the Suffering Servant songs of → *Deutero-Isaiah* (Ch. 9.12.3), as these share some affinities.

## 10.4 Theology of the Book of Jeremiah

### 10.4.1 Lament and Accusation

The observations made above about the oldest texts in Jeremiah have deep theological significance: the text's literary development suggests that the first

10. Cf. H. Bezzel, *Die Konfessionen Jeremias: Eine redaktionsgeschichtliche Studie* (BZAW 378; Berlin/New York: de Gruyter, 2007).

reaction to the in-breaking catastrophe was to lament and the second step involved accusations first against Jerusalem and later against the people as well. The theology of guilt in the prophetic books is thus neither an automatic intellectual reflex nor an unquestionably accepted idea but developed gradually. The book of Jeremiah (like Lamentations as well [Ch. 19]) shows that the predominant reaction in ancient Israel was lament. The catastrophe certainly caused traditional orthodoxy (in this case → *Zion Theology*) to collapse, but it did not preclude the possibility that God could speak at all.

## 10.4.2 Repentance

In its current state, the book of Jeremiah documents a missed opportunity for Judah and Jerusalem to repent. Although it presents Jeremiah as a preacher of repentance in the long prose speeches (Jer. 7, 11, 25), the text also shows the ineffectiveness of his sermon with the book's portrayal of judgement. Even Jeremiah first formulates a theology of history that provides an → *aetiology* for the national catastrophe in 587–586 BCE from a prophetic perspective. In terms of the text's literary development, the thematic focus on repentance in the book of Jeremiah as a whole seems later than the proclamations of judgement. Proclaiming judgement is not the result of the actual ineffectiveness of warnings and calls to repentance; instead, it seems the focus on repentance was gradually strengthened in the postexilic period to explain why the proclamation of salvation in Jer. 30–33 remained unfulfilled (see also Isa. 56–66).

## 10.4.3 The Prophet's Suffering

The book expresses the prophet's suffering in a way unlike any other prophetic book, using both prophetic oracle and narrative sections. For instance, the 'confessions' of Jeremiah in Jer. 11–20 appear alongside the portrayal of his 'passion' in Jer. 26–45. It is likely that this emphasis has some relation to the actual life of the historical Jeremiah, although neither the confessions of Jeremiah nor the texts in 26–45 can be interpreted as strictly biographical. The fact that various generations of tradents have adopted and further developed the theme of suffering reveals the wider appeal of these texts.

## 10.4.4 New Covenant

One of the best-known texts in Jeremiah – at least for Christian theology – is the promise of a new *covenant* in Jer. 31.31-34. The author writes that Yhwh will put the law in Israel's heart in the foreseeable future ('The days are surely coming...') so that no one will need to teach anyone else about the law.

Traditionally, researchers analysing this text have seen it as the bedrock of Jeremiah's tradition using the (admittedly dubious) argument that it contains such an 'unbelievable boldness that only one of the greats would have dared to write it'.[11] Bernhard Duhm, on the other hand, saw in Jer. 31.31-34 little more than 'the ramblings of a scribe whose highest ideal is that every member of the Jewish people learn the law by heart and understand it, so that all Jews are scribes'.[12]

Since Siegfried Herrmann and Winfried Thiel, scholars have largely agreed that Jer. 31.31-34 should be categorized as a → *Deuteronomistic* redactional text. The main argument is the corresponding diction in the text. However, close attention to the passage's theological profile leads to a different view. First, Jer 31.31-34 culminates in the statement that God will 'pardon' (*sālaḥ*) Israel's guilt, a concept reflecting Priestly rather than Deuteronomistic thought. Furthermore, Jer. 31.31-34 can almost be read as countering the so-called → *Šĕmaʿ yiśrāʾēl* in Deut. 6.4-9: the idea that the written Torah and mutual teaching of the law would someday come to an end (as Jer. 31.31-34 claims) does not reflect Deuteronomistic theology. Thus, Jer. 31.31-34 expresses an anti-Deuteronomistic theology with Deuteronomistic language. Given its reference to the written Torah, which is presumably complete, this text can be dated to the outgoing Persian period (4th cent. BCE).

## 10.5 Notes on the History of Reception

Examining Jeremiah within the larger biblical context suggests a close interdependent relationship with the book of Ezekiel. These two books have been harmonized multiple times, especially as the books were shaped over time to conform to the needs and concerns of the → *golah* and → *diaspora*. The reason is the comparable historical situation of the downfall of Judah and Jerusalem envisaged in both books: from the perspective of their first recipients, Jeremiah and Ezekiel as prophets of the one God could not contradict one another, so the theology of the prophets' messages was harmonized. The book of Jeremiah has been more strongly shaped to resemble Ezekiel than the other way around due

11. C.-H. Cornill, *Das Buch Jeremia* (Leipzig: Tauchnitz, 1905), 350.

12. *Jeremia*, 255.

to the primacy of the Babylonian *Golah* who considered the message of 'their' prophet Ezekiel to be especially theologically significant and therefore inserted his message into other prophetic books. In addition, Jeremiah's historical position earned him a few mentions in Chronicles (2 Chr. 35.25; 2 Chr. 36.13, [15], 22; the note in 2 Chr. 35.25 apparently misled the → *LXX* to attribute Lamentations to Jeremiah, cf. Lam. LXX 1.1), but especially the attribution of the 70-year prophecy in Dan. 9 is due to Jeremiah's historical position. The author of Dan. 9 from the period of the Maccabeans, historically far removed from the destruction of Jerusalem, asks when the promised 70 years of destruction (cf. Jer. 25.11-12; 29.10) that Jeremiah predicted for Jerusalem will finally be over and receives the heavenly answer that one year actually represents seven years, so that 70 years translates into 7 times 70, meaning 490 years.

In the intertestamental literature, the so-called Paralipomena of Jeremiah as well as the Epistle of Jeremiah were traced back to Jeremiah. His scribe Baruch also grew in prestige so much, that both the Book of Baruch (Ch. 28) originating in the Maccabean period as well as the Syrian Apocalypse (→ *apocalypse*) of Baruch (called thus because the only copy remaining is in Syrian) from the time after the destruction of Jerusalem in 70 CE were attributed to him.

Although there was little further development in the Old Testament of the idea of a new → *covenant* (Jer. 31.31-34), it was widely assimilated into the Damascus Document of the Essenes (CD[13]), a group which saw itself as a congregation of the new covenant. The idea was also adopted in the New Testament, of course. The use of Jer. 31.31-34 in Hebr. 8.8-12 is the longest continuous quotation of the Old Testament in the New. Furthermore, the confessions of Jeremiah were significant for Christian reception, as they allowed him to be portrayed as a prefiguration of Christ in his sufferings. In Christian → *iconography*, Jeremiah is widely depicted as grieving beside Jerusalem. It thus effectively brings together the book's descriptions of judgement with biographical texts while relying on the ascription of the book of Lamentations to Jeremiah (Ch. 19) in the Greek tradition. In the twentieth century, Jeremiah's story has been made into a novel by Franz Werfel (1890–1945), *Hearken unto the Voice* (German original: *Höret die Stimme*, 1937).

13. Text in F. García Martínez and E. J. C. Tigchelaar, *The Dead Sea Scrolls I*, 550–627.

# 11

# The Book of Ezekiel

(Konrad Schmid – Translation by Jennifer Adams-Maßmann)

## Chapter Outline



Commentaries: M. Greenberg (AB 22-22a. 2 vols. Garden City, N.Y.: Doubleday, 1983, 1995); L. C. Allen (WBC 28-29. 2 vols. Waco, Tex.: Word, 1994, 1990); K.-F. Pohlmann (ATD 22. 2 vols. Göttingen: Vandenhoeck & Ruprecht, 1996, 2001).

K.-F. Pohlmann, *Ezechiel: Der Stand der theologischen Diskussion*. Darmstadt: Wissenschaftliche Buchgesellschaft, 2008; R. L. Kohn, 'Ezekiel At the Turn of the Century'. *Currents in Biblical Research* 2 (2003): 9–31.

German Classics: G. Hölscher, *Hesekiel: Der Dichter und das Buch*. BZAW 39. Gießen: Töpelmann, 1924; W. Zimmerli, *Ezechiel*. BKAT 13. Neukirchen-Vluyn: Neukirchener, 1969, 2nd ed. 1979; ET *Ezekiel: A Commentary on the Book of the Prophet Ezekiel*. Transl. by R. E. Clemens. Philadelphia: Fortress, 1979.

# 11.1 Biblical Context

## 11.1.1 Book Structure

The book of Ezekiel is widely and correctly considered the most tightly structured prophetic book of the Old Testament. With the exception of the heading in 1.3 and the note in 24.24, it has been continuously fashioned as a 1st person narrative so that it qualifies as a literary autobiography, though not a historical one.[1]

The text can be divided up into four sections (although the last two are really one) that not only constitute individual thematic units but should be seen as a unified process. After proclaiming judgement against his own people (Ezek. 1–24) and against foreign powers (Ezek. 25–32), he speaks of salvation for his own people (Ezek. 33–39, 40–48). Some scholars have spoken of the so-called 'three-part → *eschatological* pattern' (Otto Kaiser), a compositional principle apparently also at work in I Isa. (Isa. 1–39) and Jer. LXX.

| 1–24 | 25–32 | 33–39 | 40–48 |
|---|---|---|---|
| Oracles of judgement against his own people and against Jerusalem | Oracles of judgement against foreign nations | Promises for his own people | Ezekiel's 'constitutional draft' |

Of course, this order is not followed slavishly, so some oracles of salvation are found in 1–24 and there are oracles of judgement in 33–39. This does not mean, however, that the basic organizational principle is invalid, but rather that this structure was likely imposed upon a text that had grown and developed over time. Other organizational principles certainly exist within the major sections. A brief sketch of each major section is included below:

1. K. Schöpflin, *Theologie als Biographie im Ezechielbuch: Ein Beitrag zur Konzeption alttestamentlicher Prophetie* (FAT 36; Tübingen: Mohr Siebeck, 2002).

| | | |
|---|---|---|
| 1–24 | 1–3 | The commissioning of Ezekiel |
| | 4–5 | Symbolic acts |
| | 8–11 | Vision of the Temple |
| | 16 | Jerusalem allegory |
| | 18 | Reflections on individual retribution |
| | 20/21 | Symbolic act |
| | 23 | Jerusalem allegory |
| | 24 | Symbolic act |
| 25–32 | 25 | Oracles against Moab, Edom, Philistia |
| | 26–28 | Oracles against Tyre and Sidon |
| | 29–32 | Oracles against Egypt |
| 33–39 | 33 | The prophet's role as watchman |
| | 34 | Shepherd allegory |
| | 35 | Mount Seir |
| | 36 | Promises for Israel |
| | 37 | Vision of the dead bones |
| | 38–39 | Gog and Magog |
| 40–48 | 40–42 | New Temple |
| | 43 | Vision of the return of the 'Glory (*kābôd*) of Yhwh' |
| | 44–46 | Regulations for the Temple |
| | 47–48 | Water flowing from the Temple/Division of the land |

The 'three-part eschatological pattern' is accompanied by the theme of the prophet's muteness, which unfolds chronologically: during the periods of Judgement (beginning with the first deportation of the inhabitants of Jerusalem by the Babylonians in 598–597 BCE, which is the date of reference given in 1.2; 33.21; 40.1, and extending to 587–586 BCE, the destruction of Jerusalem and the second deportation) the prophet remains mute, sharing only the messages that God has given him to share. So he does not simply reprove his people (3.26; 24.27). His silence does not end until after the final fall of Jerusalem (33.22). Ezekiel 3 and 33 also correspond in their use of the theme of the prophet's role as watchman (3.16-21; 33.1-9).

Such correspondences using structuring devices also link Ezek. 1–24 and Ezek. 40–48. Ezekiel 1–24 depicts the 'glory of Yhwh' – that is, the presence of God – withdrawing from the Temple in 11.23; within Ezek. 40–48 this corresponds to the return of the 'glory of Yhwh' in the new temple in Ezek 43.1-5. Overall, the design of the new Temple in Ezek. 40–48 is contrasted with the degenerate Solomonic Temple in Ezek. 8–11.

Compared to Jeremiah, there are not extensive differences in the transmission of the text. The Greek translation of the → *Septuagint*, however, does include some significant deviations. Above all, Papyrus 967 shows a different text order in Ezek. 36–39 (36 [without 23bβ-38]; 38–39; 37; 40–48) that may be older than the order in the → *Masoretic Text.*

## 11.1.2 The Use of Formulas in Ezekiel

The coherent impression of the book results not only from its clear structure, but also its striking linguistic use of conventional formulas. We find, for example, the formula introducing a new oracle ('and the word of Yhwh came to me'), the divine messenger formula ('thus says Yhwh'), the formula for a divine saying ('the oracle of Yhwh') and the formula for closing a divine saying ('for I, Yhwh, have spoken'), the formula for a threat ('see, I am against you') or the recognition formula ('that you (or they) may know, that I am Yhwh'). These formulas also occur in other parts of the Old Testament, but are particularly abundant in Ezekiel.

## 11.1.3 Chronology

The book of Ezekiel displays a notable interest in chronological dating (1.1-2; [3.16;] 8.1; 20.1; 24.1; 26.1; 29.1,17; 30.20; 31.1; 32.1,17; 33.21; 40.1). Dates are found throughout the book, beginning with the reference point of the first deportation in 597 BCE (1.2; 33.21; 40.1) and spanning the period from 593 BCE (1.2) to 571 BCE (29.17). They are exact down to the day and generally arranged according to chronological order (excepting 26.1; 29.17; 32.1 within the oracles against the nations).

The reason for this focus on chronology presumably derives from the priestly background of the book, as priests traditionally paid great attention to questions of dating. The older prophetic books include hardly any historical contextualization in their texts (the individual texts in Amos, Hosea and Micah lack any dates; there are only two references to particular years in Isaiah), while dates in Jeremiah are unevenly distributed and jumbled together. The most consistent schemes are found in Ezekiel, Haggai and Zechariah, all of which originated in a priestly context.

# 11.2 Historical-Critical Analysis and Major Issues in the History of Critical Interpretation

The inner coherence of the book of Ezekiel has wrongly led some interpreters to believe the book's literary origins are also uniform. Thus, they either ascertain the book is an autograph of the prophet (Rudolf Smend, Sr., Moshe Greenberg) or claim it is → *Pseudepigraphy* produced by a later writer (Leopold Zunz, Joachim Becker). As applicable as this assessment may seem given the overall appearance of the book, the thesis that the book of Ezekiel did not undergo a process of literary development is untenable. One of the central tasks for the exegesis of Ezekiel is to determine the relationship between the individual texts and the larger framework of the book as a whole.

Johannes Herrmann[2] argued that the book of Ezekiel was assembled out of numerous small, originally independent units with considerable redactional sections, although Herrmann believed these were also primarily from the prophet himself, making Ezekiel author and editor of his own book. This thesis, in which the authentic sections and the products of literary growth are derived from the same source, is not persuasive, however, but simply reflects a desire to preserve the 'authenticity' of the book. Gustav Hölscher, in particular, limited the likely material from Ezekiel himself to include only poetic pieces, thus drastically reducing the scope of authentic material (170 out of 1,273 verses in the entire book).[3] Yet this view has found few proponents. The only scholar to adopt this thesis again and be even more radical was Jörg Garscha in the 1970s, who identified only 17.*1-10 and 23.*2-25 as traceable to Ezekiel.[4]

More recent research has focused less on the distinction between 'genuine' and 'inauthentic' material because 'secondary' texts are no longer automatically categorized as theologically inferior. The main subject of discussion in current scholarship is the literary development of the book as such and the descriptiveness of the theological concepts it contains.

2. J. Herrmann, *Ezekielstudien* (BWA(N)T 2; Leipzig: Hinrichs, 1908).
3. G. Hölscher, *Hesekiel, der Dichter und das Buch* (Gießen: Töpelmann, 1924).
4. J. Garscha, *Studien zum Ezechielbuch: Eine redaktionskritische Untersuchung von Ez 1–39* (Europäische Hochschulschriften Theologie 23; Bern/Frankfurt: Lang, 1974).

The work of Walther Zimmerli[5] on the book of Ezekiel has proved authoritative not only for research on Ezekiel but for the exegesis of the Old Testament in general. He continually encountered phenomena he classified as editorial expansions or elaborations known as *Fortschreibungen*. He shaped the use of this word which has since become a standard term in exegetical work and means existing texts have been gradually expanded through explicit or corrective commentary.

## Editorial expansions in the Book of Ezekiel

Ezek. 5.1-2: 'And you, O mortal, take a sharp sword; use it as a barber's razor and run it over your head and your beard; then take balances for weighing, and divide the hair. One-third of the hair you shall burn in the fire inside the city, when the days of the siege are completed; one-third you shall take and strike with the sword all around the city; and one-third you shall scatter to the wind, and I will unsheathe the sword after them.'

Ezek. 5.3, 4a: 'Then you shall take from these a small number [of your hair], and bind them in the skirts of your robe. From these, again, you shall take some, throw them into the fire, and burn them up.'

The → *symbolic action* in 5.1-2 is a coherent original unit and apparently symbolizes the complete destruction of Jerusalem by fire, the sword, and the scattering of the population. We can recognize the addition in 5:3-4a in that it boldly attempts to reverse the scattering of his hair in the wind by having the prophet weave some of his hair into the seam of his robe. This editorial addition is apparently designed to record a more nuanced theology of a remnant in Ezek. 5, which speaks of those who have been preserved in Jerusalem, although some of them will still be liable to judgement.

Correspondingly, Zimmerli traces a large section of texts from the book of Ezekiel back to the activity of an Ezekiel school.

The book of Ezekiel did not simply originate through small-scale editorial additions, however, but has gone through demonstrable revisions spanning the entire book, as we can see with the 'three-part eschatological pattern' or the correspondence between the 'Glory of Yhwh' leaving and returning, which links the first and last sections of the book in Ezek. 11.23 and 43.1-5. More recent research examining the text's redactional history has pursued Zimmerli's redactional hypothesis and sought to identify editorial layers spanning the book of Ezekiel that shaped and formed the book as a whole.

5. W. Zimmerli, *Ezekiel*.

# 11.3 Origins of the Book of Ezekiel

## 11.3.1 Texts Oriented Towards the Exiles and *Diaspora*

The book of Ezekiel is particularly connected to the Babylonian → *golah* deported in 597 BCE. The prophet is an active member of this group in Tel-abib on the Kebar canal (1.1, 3; 3.10-15; 3.22-23; 37.1). He is raptured to Jerusalem (8.3; 11.1-13, 24; 40.1-2). The book's chronology has been 'calibrated' based on the deportation in 598–597 BCE (see above Ch. 11.1.3). Ezekiel, who was the son of a priest, began working in the → *exile* according to the prophetic book (1.3) at the age of 30 when priests begin their service, five years after the deportation in 597 BCE. His final oracle for the house of Israel (40.1) is dated 20 years later (see also 29.17), at the age of 50 when priests retire. So it is not surprising that the book of Ezekiel became a mouthpiece for the exclusive interests of the first exiles. Karl-Friedrich Pohlmann in particular sought to show that this tendency is probably the result of a targeted reworking of the book. In the judgement texts in Ezek. 12–24, redactional changes sought to make clear that even those who had survived the catastrophe of Jerusalem were rejected and that the land would become a desolation and a waste. Thus Ezek. 14.21-23 (see also 15.8) portrays the survivors of the judgement against Jerusalem in an unusually harsh way as a special example of abomination in order to illustrate the legitimacy of the catastrophe:

> For thus says Yhwh: How much more when I send upon Jerusalem my four deadly acts of judgement, sword, famine, wild animals, and pestilence, to cut off humans and animals from it! Yet, survivors shall be left in it, sons and daughters who will be brought out; they will come out to you. When you see their ways and their deeds, you will be consoled for the evil that I have brought upon Jerusalem, for all that I have brought upon it. They shall console you, when you see their ways and their deeds; and you shall know that it was not without cause that I did all that I have done in it, says Yhwh. (Ezek. 14.21-23).

The focus on the interests of the exiles (*golah* in Hebrew) becomes particularly clear at the beginning of the section dealing with salvation, when in 33.21-29 the author makes a note of the destruction of the land and then states clearly that the words of salvation that follow (Ezek. 33–39, 40–48) apply only to the relatives and descendants of the first exiles.

> In the twelfth year of our exile, in the tenth month, on the fifth day of the month, someone who had escaped from Jerusalem came to me and said, 'The city has fallen'... The word of Yhwh came to me: Mortal, the inhabitants of these waste places in the land of Israel keep saying, 'Abraham was only one man, yet he got possession of the land; but we are many; the land is surely given to us to possess.' Therefore say to them, Thus says Yhwh: You eat flesh with the blood, and lift up your eyes to your idols, and shed blood; shall you then possess the land? You depend on your swords, you commit abominations, and each of you defiles his neighbour's wife; shall you then possess the land? Say this to them, Thus says Yhwh: As I live, surely those who are in the waste places shall fall by the sword; and those who are in the open field I will give to the wild animals to be devoured; and those who are in strongholds and in caves shall die by pestilence. I will make the land a desolation and a waste, and its proud might shall come to an end; and the mountains of Israel shall be so desolate that no one will pass through. Then they shall know that I am Yhwh, when I have made the land a desolation and a waste because of all their abominations that they have committed. (Ezek. 33.*21-29)

Above all, the visions should be considered part of the *golah*-oriented book of Ezekiel: Ezekiel speaks of 'faces of God' (1.1; 8.3; 11.24; 40.2), in Ezek. 1–3 (chariot-throne visions); 8–11 (rapture to Jerusalem); 37 (the resurrection of Israel) and 40–48 ('constitutional draft'). These are probably the most impressive elements of the book of Ezekiel.

Their orientation towards the exiles is shown when the 'glory (*kābôd*) of God' appears to Ezekiel in Mesopotamia (not Jerusalem). At the same time, the iniquities of Jerusalem are emphasized (Ezek. 8.5-18) and the renewal of the people is discussed (Ezek. 37) who, historically speaking, had for the most part survived the exile in the land.

> The visions deal with a plethora of ancient Near Eastern images and thus show how the book of Ezekiel was rooted in Mesopotamia not just geographically but theologically as well.[6] Comparing Ezek. 1 with the typical images featured on an ancient Near Eastern cylinder seal from the time of Ashurbanipal (669–621/629 BCE) illuminates this point (see picture next page).[7] The scene depicts a winged deity in the middle standing on a horse and connected at hip level with a disc being carried by two ox-people. Above left is an eight-pointed star, and above

6. C. Uehlinger and S. Müller Trufaut, 'Ezekiel 1, Babylonian Cosmological Scholarship and Iconography: Attempts at Further Refinement', *TZ* 57 (2001): 140–71.
7. H. Keel-Leu and B. Teissier, *Die vorderasiatischen Rollsiegel der Sammlungen' Bibel + Orient' der Universität Fribourg Schweiz* (OBO 200; Fribourg: Academic Press/Göttingen: Vandenhoeck & Ruprecht, 2004), seal 236.

right a crescent. The image is framed on the left by a priest dressed like a fish and on the right by a person praying who is turned towards the deity. This ensemble makes clear the deity is supposed to be an anthropomorphized (→ *anthropomorphic*) figure of the sun god who is incorporated into the firmament of the heavens, which, in turn, is upheld by chimera (half-human, half-animal beings).

**Fig. 15:** Neo-Assyrian Cylinder seal (7th century BCE).

The concept of the cosmological constellation pictured above apparently influenced the composition of Ezek. 1. Ezekiel sees four-winged living creatures with feet like a calf (Ezek. 1.6) which are carrying the disc of the heavens (Ezek. 1.22), above which the glory of God is enthroned (Ezek. 1.25-28). Like the Neo-Assyrian seal, the book of Ezekiel also reckons with half-human, half-animal creatures who are supporting the disc of the heavens which, in turn, divides the earthly and divine realms. In contrast to the seal, however, the book of Ezekiel does not locate the divine figure on the dome itself, but instead the throne is located above the dome. Nearness and distance are equally characteristic in the artistry of the seal and in the biblical text.

Evidence suggests the *golah*-oriented redaction of the book of Ezekiel is shaped by the same redactional agenda as the book of Jeremiah. Presumably the book of Jeremiah was influenced by the book of Ezekiel, as Ezekiel has a biographical connection to the Babylonian exiles from the outset and was therefore set to become the key figure to support their theological agenda.

As in the book of Jeremiah, however, the *golah*-oriented influence in the book of Ezekiel was expanded in the course of further editing to show that not only the first Babylonian exiles but the diaspora in general would have a place in God's future acts of salvation (cf. Ezek. 20; 36.16-23; 37.15-28).

## 11.3.2 The Search for the Oldest Texts

Deciding what the earliest Ezekiel tradition would have looked like in book form requires first ascertaining whether an earlier form of the book of Ezekiel existed that would have favoured the exiles. Karl-Friedrich Pohlmann, for example, identifies a pre-golah-oriented book in Ezek. *4–7; *11; *12.21-28; *14; *17–19/31; *15 (*sic*); *21; *24; *36.11-14; *31.1-15. This would have followed a two-part pattern of judgement-salvation, although the perspective on salvation in this first book of Ezekiel would still have been quite restrained with limited textual material. Pohlmann argues the oldest individual texts in the book are the poems in Ezek. *19/*31 which lament the catastrophe that has already begun, yet without reference to Yhwh. He attributes these texts to Jerusalem circles associated with the royal court. This oldest book of Ezekiel would have shared a similar theological focus to the early Jeremiah tradition. However, reconstructing the developmental process of the book of Ezekiel is less feasible and, accordingly, remains controversial.

## 11.3.3 Proto-Apocalyptic Editing in the Visions

In the vision texts in Ezek. 1–3; 8–11; 37 and 40–48, we can already observe unique characteristics of later → *apocalyptic* literature: the heavens are opened (1.1) and a mediating figure (cf. 40.3 among others) ensures that the prophet rightly interprets what has been seen. One can thus assume that these texts were still being reworked quite late, namely, in the intellectual context in which apocalyptic literature arose (3rd/2nd cent. BCE). What is unlikely, however, is that the visions as a whole were not recorded in the book until the final phases of its development. For one thing, they are too fundamental to the book's underlying structure; furthermore, their theological perspective points to another, earlier context.

The relationship of an older original text to a more recent redactional change can be illustrated when we look at Ezek. 37: the vision of the resurrection of the dead of Israel. In vv. 7a, 8a-10b, a syntactically peculiar insertion, the idea of the resurrection of the individual, has been added[8]: In v. 9 the prophet is no longer

8. Cf. R. Bartelmus, 'Ez 37.1–14, die Verbform *wᵉqātal* und die Anfänge der Auferstehungshoffnung', *ZAW* 97 (1985): 366–89.

acting as mediator between God and humankind, but rather he conjures 'the spirit' who is supposed to resuscitate the dead, who – in contrast to the rest of the portrayal in Ezek. 37 – are interpreted as those who have been *violently* 'slain'. The notion of the hypostasized spirit as well as the theme of the murder of central individuals suggest this text was revised in the Maccabean period (Ch. 4.4).

> Ezek. 37.1-12: '(1) The hand of Yhwh came upon me, and he brought me out by the spirit of Yhwh and set me down in the middle of a valley; it was full of bones. (2) He led me all round them; there were very many lying in the valley, and they were very dry. (3) He said to me, "Mortal, can these bones live?" I answered, "O Yhwh, you know." (4) Then he said to me, "Prophesy to these bones, and say to them: O dry bones, hear the word of Yhwh. (5) Thus says Yhwh to these bones: I will cause *spirit* to enter you, and you shall live. (6) I will lay sinews on you, and will cause flesh to come upon you, and cover you with skin, and put *spirit* in you, and you shall live; and you shall know that I am Yhwh." (7) So I prophesied as I had been commanded; and as I prophesied, suddenly there was a noise, a rattling, and the bones came together, bone to its bone. (8) I looked, and there were sinews on them, and flesh had come upon them, and skin had covered them; but there was no spirit in them. (9) Then he said to me, "Prophesy to the spirit, prophesy, mortal, and say to the spirit: Thus says Yhwh: Come from the four winds, O spirit, and breathe upon these slain, that they may live." (10) I prophesied as he commanded me, and the spirit came into them, and they lived, and stood on their feet, a vast multitude. (11) Then he said to me, "Mortal, these bones are the whole house of Israel. They say, 'Our bones are dried up, and our hope is lost; we are cut off completely.' (12) Therefore prophesy, and say to them, Thus says Yhwh: I am going to open your graves, and bring you up from your graves, O my people; and I will bring you back to the land of Israel."'

# 11.4 Theology of the Book of Ezekiel

## 11.4.1 The 'Glory' (*kābôd*) of Yhwh

One of the central themes in the book of Ezekiel is God's presence and absence in Jerusalem. A conflict with traditional → *Zion Theology* exists, which in the book of Jeremiah is addressed in the laments of destruction and the transformation of the notion of Zion from an impregnable mountain to a ravished woman ('Daughter Zion'). The book of Ezekiel also must come to terms with the collapse of traditional → *Zion Theology*, which became apparent through the events of 597 and 587 BCE; it does so by saying that the salvific presence of Yhwh is no longer accessible in the Jerusalem Temple. Because of the evildoing of Judah and Jerusalem, the presence of Yhwh (as interpreted by the priests) withdraws its 'glory' from the temple and moves to the Mount of Olives, which is opposite the Temple Mount, leaving Jerusalem and its temple at the mercy of the enemy without protection and salvation. Thus, they fall victim to destruction.

## 11.4.2 Purity and Impurity

For the book of Ezekiel, the categories of 'purity' and 'impurity' play an important role. 'Impurity' recurs as a motif throughout the accusations against the people, and 'purity' is an urgent problem for the prophet himself. Thus in 4.12-15 he is instructed to bake bread on human dung:

> 'You shall eat it as a barley-cake, baking it in their sight on human dung. Yhwh said, "Thus shall the people of Israel eat their bread, unclean, among the nations to which I will drive them." Then I said, "Lord Yhwh! I have never defiled myself; from my youth up until now I have never eaten what died of itself or was torn by animals, nor has carrion flesh come into my mouth." Then he said to me, "See, I will let you have cow's dung instead of human dung, on which you may prepare your bread."'

This motif again highlights the priestly background of the book when the command to remain pure is applied to the people as well as the prophet. The judgement in chapters 16 and 23 is especially caustic in its portrayal of Jerusalem as a woman and castigation of her for harlotry and impurity. These texts are among the harshest prophetic passages anywhere in the Old Testament; they could almost be labelled 'pornographic'.

## 11.4.3 Collective and Individual Retribution

The book of Ezekiel, and particularly chapter 18, has often been regarded as the turning point in ancient Israelite legal history, moving from an older view of collective responsibility for the sins of one's ancestors to a consistent form of individual accountability.

> 'The word of Yhwh came to me: What do you mean by repeating this proverb concerning the land of Israel, "The parents have eaten sour grapes, and the children's teeth are set on edge"? As I live, says Yhwh, this proverb shall no more be used by you in Israel.' (Ezek. 18.1-3)

As with other texts about collective familial or clan responsibility, however, we must keep in mind this text does not relate to human criminal law but divine justice. In the criminal law codes of the ancient Near East and in Old Testament legal codes, hardly any evidence of collective liability can be detected.[9] Individual liability is an inalienable principle of criminal law as old in essence as criminal law itself. The concept of collective responsibility across generations appears when dealing with the idea of divine punishment – generally due to political or cultic breaches – since events such as military defeats, droughts, or natural catastrophes often affected multiple generations and could thus be seen as divine punishment. So when the prophet polemicizes against collective responsibility in Ezek. 18, he is not speaking about legislating new rules in criminal law, but introducing a theological idea about the historical activity of God, which, as Ezek. 18.19-20 shows, runs counter to his listener's expectations:

> 'Yet you say, "Why should not the son suffer for the iniquity of the father?" When the son has done what is lawful and right, and has been careful to observe all my statutes, he shall surely live. The person who sins shall die. A child shall not suffer for the iniquity of a parent, nor a parent suffer for the iniquity of a child; the righteousness of the righteous shall be his own, and the wickedness of the wicked shall be his own.' (Ezek. 18.19-20).

The hearers of the book of Ezekiel unquestionably assume that, in light of the destruction of the nation, the sons are held responsible for the sins of their fathers before God. In contrast Ezek. 18 posits a new principle of individual responsibility in the religious interpretation of historical events, a principle which at all times has been the foundation of criminal law. Notably, Chronicles follows this line of argumentation, replacing the 'history of theology' interpretation of → *Deuteronomism*, which assumes Israel's and Judah's intergenerational propensity to sin.

## 11.5 Notes on the History of Reception

The book of Ezekiel earned an exceptional position among the prophetic books in Old Testament times and was apparently controversial, probably in large part because the design of the temple in the visions in Ezek 40–48 stood

9. Cf. K. Schmid, 'Kollektivschuld? Der Gedanke übergreifender Schuldzusammenhänge im Alten Testament und im Alten Orient', *ZABR* 5 (1999): 193–222.

in competition with the blueprint in the Torah (cf. Exod. 25–40).[10] Recurring discussions related to its → *canonical* authority took place, and Jerome even reported that Jews were not allowed to read Ezekiel before they turned 30.[11] In late Jewish mysticism, on the other hand, the throne-chariot visions ('Merkavah' = chariot) in Ezek. 1 in particular played an important role, and large strands of Jewish mysticism were based on the content of the visions of Ezekiel.

Findings at → *Qumran* include a pseudo-Ezekiel text, although only fragments remain.[12] In this text, the prophet 'Ezekiel' leans heavily on the style and text of the canonical book of Ezekiel.

Although the New Testament never names or quotes the prophet Ezekiel explicitly, the book of Revelation in particular has been influenced significantly by Ezekiel. 'Gog and Magog' from Ezek. 38 (cf. Rev. 20.8-9) in particular were taken up by the church fathers in later political interpretations of the end times. Also well known is the early Christian association of the evangelists with the vision in Ezek. 1–3, such that they were assigned different symbols corresponding to the beginning of each Gospel: Matthew was associated with the human figure, Mark with the lion, Luke with the bull, and John with the eagle.

Finally, in the synagogue of Dura-Europos along the middle Euphrates there is a famous fresco of Ezek. 37 (3rd cent. CE), one of the rare examples of Jewish figurative art based on biblical subjects.[13]

10. This helps explain why the Temple Scroll attempted to reconcile the Torah stipulations with those of Ezekiel (11QT, cf. F. García Martínez and E. J. C. Tigchelaar, *The Dead Sea Scrolls* II, 1128–1307).

11. *Corpus Scriptorum Ecclesiasticorum Latinorum* 54/1, 460–1.

12. 4QPsEzek (Text in F. García Martínez and E. J. C. Tigchelaar, *The Dead Sea Scrolls* II, 766–87).

13. For more on this, see R. von Bendemann, '"Lebensgeist kam in sie …" – Der Ezekiel-Zyklus von Dura Europos and die Rezeption von Ez 37 in der Apk des Johannes: Ein Beitrag zum Verhältnisproblem von Ikonizität und Narrativität', in *Picturing the New Testament: Studies in Ancient Visual Images* (WUNT II/193, ed. A. Weissenrieder *et al.*; Tübingen: Mohr Siebeck, 2005), 253–86.

**Fig. 16:** Fresco based on Ezek. 37 at Dura-Europos (3rd century CE).

# 12

# The Book of Twelve

(Konrad Schmid – Translation by Jennifer Adams-Maßmann)

## Chapter Outline

Bibliography 8 The History of Ancient Israel and Judah (Albertz, *Israel in Exile*); J. Jeremias, *Hosea und Amos: Studien zu den Anfängen des Dodekapropheton*. FAT 13. Tübingen: Mohr Siebeck, 1996; O. H. Steck, *Der Abschluß der Prophetie im Alten Testament: Ein Versuch zur Frage der Vorgeschichte des Kanons*. Biblisch-theologische

Studien 17. Neukirchen-Vluyn: Neukirchener, 1991; P. L. Redditt and A. Schart, eds, *Thematic Threads in the Book of the Twelve*. BZAW 325. Berlin/New York: de Gruyter, 2003; P.-G. Schwesig, *Die Rolle der Tag-JHWHs-Dichtungen im Dodekapropheton*. BZAW 366. Berlin/New York: de Gruyter, 2006; J. Wöhrle, *Die frühen Sammlungen des Zwölfprophetenbuches: Untersuchungen zu ihrer Entstehung und ihrer Komposition*. BZAW 360. Berlin/New York: de Gruyter, 2006; J. Wöhrle, *Der Abschluss des Zwölfprophetenbuches: Buchübergreifende Redaktionsprozesse in den späten Sammlungen*. BZAW 389. Berlin/New York, de Gruyter, 2008.

# 12.1 Biblical Context

The heading 'The Book of Twelve' (XII) may seem strange at first because contemporary Bible editions do not recognize this 'book'. However, if we look at ancient scrolls of the prophetic books (Ch. 8.1) we are reminded the Old Testament did not originally contain fifteen prophetic books (three 'Major Prophets' and twelve 'Minor Prophets' [according to the → *Vulgate*: *prophetae majores* and *prophetae minores*]), but only four books, namely Isaiah, Jeremiah, Ezekiel and XII (Hosea–Malachi). The so-called twelve Minor Prophets were considered *one* book in ancient times for several reasons. First, the manuscript findings from → *Qumran* and from nearby Wadi Murabba'at suggest that Hosea–Malachi were all included on one scroll.[1] Furthermore, Sir. 49.10, written around 180 BCE, already assumes that the 'Minor Prophets' counted as one unit when a sweeping reference is made to the 'twelve prophets'. The → *LXX*, which places the XII as a block before Isaiah, Jeremiah and Ezekiel, also provides evidence that the book of the twelve prophets was viewed as an entity on its own. Finally, the number of books listed for the Old Testament in 4 Ezra 14 ('twenty-four') and in Josephus, *Contra Apionem* I.8 ('twenty-two') unquestionably assumes the XII is counted as one book.

If ancient Judaism treated the XII as one book (comparable to the treatment of I Isa. + II Isa. as one book), then we must consider whether there is an overarching purpose to this composition. Without going into the internal structure of each book (for this, see the individual book sections), one can still begin by investigating the overall logic of the books' order. Here one must distinguish between the Hebrew and Greek versions, as the → *Septuagint* not only places the XII before Isaiah, Jeremiah and Ezekiel, but also orders them differently within this block. The → *Masoretic Text* seems to organize the XII chronologically as it does with

1. Occasionally, variations in the order are assumed, as in the case of 4Q76. See, however, P. Guillaume, 'The Unlikely Malachi-Jonah Sequence (4QXIIa),' *Journal of Hebrew Studies* (2007), http://www.jhsonline.org.

Isaiah, Jeremiah and Ezekiel, while the Septuagint – as with the Septuagint version of Jeremiah – attempts to reproduce the 'three-part → *eschatological* pattern'. In organizing the books chronologically, the → *Masoretic Text* naturally dates each book based on the historical context of each prophet given in the biblical superscriptions, which are at best accurate for the oldest texts within a given book, although even then this is not for sure.

| Order in the Hebrew Bible | | | Order in the Greek Bible | | |
|---|---|---|---|---|---|
| 8th century | Isa. | Hos. | Judgement against Israel | Isa. | Hos. |
| | | Joel | | | Amos |
| | | Amos | | | Mic. |
| | | Obad. | | | Joel |
| | | Jonah | | | Obad. |
| | | Mic. | | | |
| 7th/6th century | Jer. | Nah. | Judgement against the nations | Jer. | Jonah |
| | | Hab. | | | Nah. |
| | | Zeph. | | | |
| 6th century | Ezek. | Hag. | Salvation for Israel | Ezek. | Hab. |
| | | Zech. | | | Zeph. |
| | | Mal. | | | Hag. |
| | | | | | Zech. |
| | | | | | Mal. |

# 12.2 Composition-Critical Observations on the Book of Twelve as a Whole

## 12.2.1 The Book of Twelve as a Redactional Unity

Aside from external indications that the XII is a redactional unity, key words reappear at the beginning and end of individual books that are next to each other on the scroll, creating a loose interconnectedness,[2] as James D. Nogalski

2. Hos. 14.8 (NRSV 14.7) / Joel 1.1, 5, 7, 10, 12; Joel 4.4, 16-17, 19-21 (NRSV 3.4, 16-17, 19-21) /

in particular has pointed out.[3] These literary points of contact can only be explained if we assume they were intentional. This means, however, that the merging of the individual books into the XII took place at a point in time when their textual development was not yet complete. In other words, the compilation of the XII into one scroll is a pre-canonical rather than a post-canonical event (→ *canon*).

Research did not begin to take into account this comprehensive view of the Twelve until the end of the 20th century, however. Before, the book of Amos, for example, would be interpreted as an isolated entity that originated completely on its own. Scholars were interested above all in the prophets themselves and not their books.

Such an approach is no longer possible today. Scholars have noted the prophetic books were harmonized with one another quite early on, and this occasionally influenced how earlier texts in a book were shaped. If Jörg Jeremias is correct, there was never a written version of the book of Amos that was not influenced by the book of Hosea. Although the historical Amos was active before Hosea, the words of Hosea appear to have been fixed earlier and these Hosea oracles supposedly guided the process of the creation of the book of Amos from the very beginning.

## 12.2.2 Evidence of Preliminary Stages

It is likely that the XII was not compiled all at once from the twelve individual texts, but rather that the XII was antedated by older partial collections. Somewhat clear are the close correspondences between Hosea-Amos, Haggai-Zech 1–8 and even Nahum-Habakkuk that show they were either redacted together from the beginning or at least very early on. The Book of the Twelve probably began with at least two 'focal points' from which the current text was composed[4]:

Amos 1.2, 6-12; Amos 9.2-4, 11-13 / Obad. 1-8; Obad. 11-15 / Jonah 1.2, 7-8.; Jonah 2.5-10 (NRSV 2.4-9) / Mic. 1.2-4, 7; Mic. 7.8-15, 17-18 / Nah. 1.2-8; Nah. 3.2-19 / Hab. 1.5-11, 13-14, 17; Hab. 3.3, 6-17 / Zeph. 1.2-3, 10, 15, 18; Zeph. 3.19-20 / Hag. 2.2-6; Hag. 2.20-23 / Zech. 1.6, 8-11 (Malachi appears to have originally been a Fortschreibung of Zechariah; cf. Ch. 12.60).

3. J. D. Nogalski, *Literary Precursors to the Book of the Twelve* (BZAW 217; Berlin/New York: de Gruyter, 1993); idem, *Redactional Processes in the Book of the Twelve* (BZAW 218; Berlin/New York: de Gruyter, 1993); for an overview, see P. L. Redditt, 'Recent Research on the Book of the Twelve as One Book', *CuBS* 9 (2001): 47–80.

4. It is hard to determine the composition-historical development of Nahum/Habakkuk (cf. Chs 12G and 12H); what can be said, however, is that Nah. 3/Hab. 1 are linked. The headings also create parallels between the books.

Hosea/Amos as an older core from the 8th century BCE and Haggai/Zechariah (/Malachi) as a more recent core from the 6th century BCE.

In terms of more recent steps in the transmission of the text, one can surmise that Hosea, Amos, Micah, Zephaniah once constituted a separate unit. In comparison to the others, these texts show evidence of a comprehensive → *Deuteronomistic* revision. Furthermore, their close relationship with one another is supported by their interrelated superscription system ('the word of Yhwh' + date [Amos varies slightly due to theological reasons]).

## 12.2.3 Redactional 'Books' within the Book of Twelve

Certain books within the XII do not appear to trace back to actual prophetic figures at all. It is reasonably clear this is the case for Malachi. Malachi is so similar to Zechariah in terms of language and content that one can conclude that Malachi does not trace back to the individual logia of a corresponding prophet, but instead was culled from the Zechariah tradition by redactors, apparently so they would have twelve Minor Prophets. As a result the three Major and twelve Minor Prophets are analogous to the three patriarchs Abraham, Isaac and Jacob and the twelve tribal ancestors of Israel – that is, the twelve sons of Jacob – who are juxtaposed with the prophets as the first archetypal bearers of the promise. Furthermore, 'Malachi' is not a real name, but represents a pen name ('my messenger'), which may denote the heralded Elijah in Mal. 3.22-24 (NRSV 4.4-6) who is supposed to return at the end of time.

In addition to Malachi, it is possible that Obadiah or Joel are also examples of prophecy based purely on editorial expansions and not on oral sayings of a prophetic individual, although this is a matter of debate. Jonah is 'redactional' in a different sense: this book depicts a prophetic narrative whose main character has been borrowed from 2 Kgs 14.25, although the book of Jonah's message has no connection to the views presented in Kings.

## 12.2.4 Parallels with the Book of Isaiah

More recent research has raised awareness that Isaiah and XII were apparently harmonized with one another in stages in both their language and content. Some of the most obvious examples include the use of comparable superscriptions in Isa. 1.1 and Hos. 1.1: both mention the same four Jewish kings. Furthermore, correspondences exist between Isa. 13 and Joel 2 as well as at the end of each of the 'major books'. Isa. 66.18-24 and Zech. 14.16-21 are so similar that one can conclude that intentional redactional composition was at play. Thus, in the Hebrew ordering of the prophetic books, the first and last of the four prophetic books (Isaiah, Jeremiah, Ezekiel, XII as a whole) correspond in terms of content.

# A The Book of Hosea

Commentaries: J. Jeremias (ATD 24/1. Göttingen: Vandenhoeck & Ruprecht, 1983); H. W. Wolff (BKAT 14/1. Neukirchen-Vluyn: Neukirchener, 1961); F. Landy (Readings: A New Biblical Commentary. Sheffield, Sheffield Academic Press, 1995); E. Ben Zvi (FOTL 21A/1. Grand Rapids, Mich.: Eerdmans, 2005).

S. Rudnig-Zelt, *Hoseastudien: Redaktionskritische Untersuchungen zur Genese des Hoseabuchs*. FRLANT 213. Göttingen: Vandenhoeck & Ruprecht, 2006; R. Vielhauer, *Das Werden des Buches Hosea: Eine redaktionsgeschichtliche Untersuchung*. BZAW 349. Berlin/New York: de Gruyter, 2007.

## 12.3 Biblical Context

Hosea, the opening book in the Book of Twelve, can be clearly divided into two sections: Hos. 1–3 and Hos. 4–14. Within 4–14 chapters 12–14 should be separated out, although this division may be less clear.

The first section, Hos. 1–3, can be further subdivided into three parts, based on the completed progression from disaster to salvation in each part (Hos. 1.2–2.3; 2.4-25 [NRSV 1.2–2.1; 2.2-23] and 3.1-5), the change in the speaker's perspective (1.2–2.3 [NRSV 1.2–2.1] is a third-person report, 2.4-25 [NRSV 2.2-23] presents a speech by God, 3.1-5 finally returns to a personal narrative), as well as the theme of Hosea's marriage-like relationship in Hos. 1.2–2.3 (NRSV 1.2–2.1); 3.1-5. The latter provides a framework for statements about Yhwh's marriage with Israel in 2.4-25 (NRSV 2.2-23).

The second section, chapters 4–11, begins with a prologue (4.1-3) that is not interrupted by intermediary superscriptions. It seems to have been designed to be read as one piece. This section has traditionally been further divided into two large blocks, 4.4–9.9 and 9.10–11.11 due to the shared subject of the historical reviews in Hos. 9.10–11.11. Given the organizing imperatives in 4.1; 5.1, 8; 8.1; 9.1; and 10.12 (see below Ch. 12.5.1) as well as the 'now' statements in 4.16; 5.3, 7; 7.2; 8.8, 10, 13; and 10.2-3, one might consider subdividing the text into a different two blocks (4.4–10.15; 11.1-11) in order to distinguish between the interpretation of the present and proclamation of salvation for the future.[5]

| | | |
|---|---|---|
| Hos. 1–3 | 1.2–2.3 (NRSV 1.2–2.1) | Third-person narrative |
| | 2.4–2.25 (NRSV 2.2–2.23) | God's speech |
| | 3.1-5 | First-person narrative |
| Hos. 4–11 | 4.1-3 | Prologue |
| | 4.4-19<br>5.1-7 | Two parallel compositions of oracles about the 'Syro-Ephraimite' war (4.4-10 / 5.1-2; 4.11-14 / 5.3-4; 4.16-19 / 5.5-7) |
| | 5.8–7.16<br>8.1-14 | Two parallel collections of oracles about events and the results of the war (5.8 / 8.1; 6.1-3 / 8.2; 6.4-6 / 8.3; 6.7–7.16 / 8.4-14) |
| | 9.1–10.15 | Admonitions |
| | 11.1-11 | Retrospective look at history and glimpse of salvation in the future |
| Hos. 12–14 | 12.1-15 (NRSV 11.12–12.14) | Jacob or Moses? |
| | 13.1–14.1 (NRSV 13.1-16 ) | Ephraim's Guilt |
| | 14.2-9 (NRSV 14.1-8) | Closing proclamation of salvation |

# 12.4 Historical-Critical Analysis and Major Issues in the History of Critical Interpretation

The claim that Hosea grew through a complex process of literary development is based on two concrete observations. The most noticeable is the fact that the prophet Hosea appears to have been active in the 8th century in the northern kingdom of Israel, but the existing form of his book is also addressed to Judean readers, evident first in the naming of Judean kings in the book's superscription, and secondly in a series of appended sayings about Judah. Among the most striking are the following texts:

5. Cf. F. Crüsemann, 'עתה – "Jetzt": Hosea 4–11 als Anfang der Schriftprophetie,' in *'Wort JHWH, das geschah…' (Hos 1:1): Studien zum Zwölfprophetenbuch* (Herders Biblische Studien 35; ed. E. Zenger; Freiburg: Herder, 2002), 13–31.

> Hos. 4.15: *'Though you play the whore, O Israel, do not let Judah become guilty. Do not enter into Gilgal, or go up to Beth-aven, and do not swear, "As Yhwh lives."'*

> Hos. 5.5: *'Israel's pride testifies against him; Ephraim stumbles in his guilt; Judah also stumbles with them.'*

> Hos. 6.10-11: *'In the house of Israel I have seen a horrible thing; Ephraim's whoredom is there, Israel is defiled. For you also, O Judah, a harvest is appointed when I would restore the fortunes of my people.'*

The message of Hosea was evidently updated in the text after the downfall of the northern kingdom to apply to Judah,[6] making it impossible for these readers simply to historicize the prophet's words, instead forcing them to relate Hosea to their own situation as well.

In addition, the promises of salvation (see esp. 2.1-3, 18-25 [NRSV 1.10–2.1; 2.16-23]; 3.5; 11.8-11; 14.5-9 [NRSV 14.4-8]) go beyond the tenor of judgement in the rest of the book. They first assume judgement and then continue by developing the theme further. A more sophisticated reflection is suggested in the far-reaching historical retrospectives in chs. 9–10, which base Hosea's message of judgement on Israel's apostasy from the very beginning of its history with Yhwh. Finally, the change in personal pronouns used for the addressee (2nd/3rd person plural) is also an indication of a progressive process of textual development (cf. for example 4.1-6, 7-10; 5.1, 2a-b, 3, 4).

Earlier source criticism was largely satisfied with separating out the later texts updated for Judah and the words of salvation from the book's original material. Hosea 3 was often seen as a secondary interpretation of Hos. 1. Yet the process of the book's literary growth was probably more complex and took place over a longer period of time.

More recently researchers have begun to appreciate more fully the uniqueness of the book of Hosea *as a prophetic book.* Hans-Walter Wolff (1911–1993) – following Scandinavian scholars – argued the individual fragmentary texts with diverse content that remained separate from one another were believed to be 'sermon outlines' with which Hosea would have addressed his circle of disciples.

6. In general, the following statements are seen as Judean updates: 1.1, 5, 7; 2.1-3, 6, 10b, 16-25 (NRSV 1.10–2.1; 2.4, 8b, 14-23); 3.1bβ, 5; 4.1-3, 5aβ, 10, 15; 5.5; 6.10-11; 7.10; 8.1b, 6aβγ, 14; 9.4b; 10.15a; 11.5b, 6b, 10; 12.1b, 2aγ, 3a, 6 (NRSV 11.12; 12.1aγ, 2a, 5); 13.2aβbα, 3; 14.2-9 (NRSV 14.1-8).

In contrast, Jörg Jeremias showed that the textual material from the book's corpus (4–11) does not merely offer clustered compilations of individual pieces of text, but has been inserted into a text that should be read as one continuous, fluid piece. The open and unfinished nature of the text is not due to its original oral context (such as the prophet preaching to his circle of disciples), but derives from the particular literary context. Although Jeremias' diachronic assessment of the book of Hosea also distinguishes various literary layers in the texts predicting disaster, he still identifies these as originating historically close to the same time. Other scholars[7] have drawn considerably sharper distinctions between the historical dating of various textual layers. A consensus on this matter is not imminent.

# 12.5 Origins of the Book of Hosea

## 12.5.1 Hosea *4–9 (10–11)

Very little is known about the historical person of Hosea and his prophetic activity. One likely reason is that the beginnings of the book date from a transitional time from a culture of oral transmission to a written culture. Much in the book of Hosea is not explicated; considerable historical knowledge is assumed on the part of the readers in order to understand the texts. The older texts in the book of Hosea can likely be found in Hos. *4–9 (10–11), which has been designed as a compositionally integrated text despite apparent thematic disparities. Superscriptions and concluding formulas are missing. Furthermore, the book of Hosea generally forgoes using the messenger formula ('thus speaks Yhwh'), while the formula for a divine saying ('oracle of Yhwh') is used solely in 2.15, 18, 23 (NRSV 2.13, 16, 21) and 11.11. The current form of Hosea attaches little importance to the original smaller units. Its overarching shape can be recognized in the imperatives in Hos. 4–9 (10), which provide structure, here grouped under the appropriate themes:

> Proof of Guilt
> Hos. 4.1: 'Hear the word of Yhwh, O people of Israel; for Yhwh has an indictment

7. Cf. M. Nissinen, *Prophetie, Redaktion und Fortschreibung im Hoseabuch: Studien zum Werdegang eines Prophetenbuches im Lichte von Hos 4 und 11* (AOAT 231; Kevelaer: Butzon & Bercker, 1991); H. Pfeiffer, *Das Heiligtum von Bethel im Spiegel des Hoseabuches* (FRLANT 183; Göttingen: Vandenhoeck & Ruprecht, 1999); R. Vielhauer, *Werden*.

against the inhabitants of the land. There is no faithfulness or loyalty, and no knowledge of God in the land.'
Hos. 5.1a: 'Hear this, O priests! Give heed, O house of Israel! Listen, O house of the king! For the judgment pertains to you.'

Judgement
Hos. 5.8: 'Blow the horn in Gibeah, the trumpet in Ramah. Sound the alarm at Beth-aven ...!'
Hos. 8.1: 'Set the trumpet to your lips! One like a vulture is over the house of Yhwh, because they have broken my covenant, and transgressed my law.'

Consequences
Hos. 9.1: 'Do not rejoice, O Israel! Do not exult as other nations do; for you have played the whore, departing from your God. You have loved a prostitute's pay on all threshing-floors.'

[Warning
Hos. 10.12a: 'Sow for yourselves righteousness; reap steadfast love; break up your fallow ground.']

In chapters 4–9 a larger unit (4.4-19; 5.8–7.16) is followed by a matching shorter section (5.1-7; 8.1-13) constructed correspondingly, with the second unit also introducing new aspects of the subject.

## 12.5.2 Hosea 12–14

Hosea 12 distinguishes between the Jacob and Moses traditions as stories about origins which, after the fall of the northern kingdom, each in their own way seek to base Israel's identity in a history which can no longer be taken for granted. Apparently Hos. 12 still presumes these traditions come from separate sources and are in competition with one another in terms of content.[8] Hosea 14 offers a prophetic view of salvation in a style matching the expectations of the Persian period, and a → *sapiential* aphorism ends the book in 14.10 (NRSV 14.9).

8. Cf. A. de Pury, 'Erwägungen zu einem vorexilischen Stämmejahwismus: Hos 12 und die Auseinandersetzung um die Identität Israels und seines Gottes', in *Ein Gott allein? JHWH-Verehrung und biblischer Monotheismus im Kontext der israelitischen und altorientalischen Religionsgeschichte* (OBO 139; ed. W. Dietrich and M. Klopfenstein; Fribourg: Academic Press/ Göttingen: Vandenhoeck & Ruprecht, 1994), 413–39.

## 12.5.3 Hosea 1–3

Scholars disagree whether each of the three chapters in Hos. 1–3 originated and were transmitted separately as has often been assumed. First, this traditional assumption was based on the noticeable fact that each of the three chapters possesses its own secondary conclusion of salvation (2.1-3; 16-25 [NRSV 1.10–2.1; 2.14-23]; 3.5), which could be an indication of the chapters' original autonomy. Secondly, conspicuous differences in form are also apparent: Hosea 1.2-9 is a 3rd person narrative, whose focus is especially on the naming of the children of Hosea, the product of his relationship with the prostitute Gomer: Jezreel, Lo-ruhamah ('No Pity') and Lo-ammi ('Not my people'). Hosea 2.4-15 (NRSV 2.2-13) is one continuous speech by God about the unfaithfulness of Israel, while Hos. 3.1-4 shares a personal narrative of Hosea about his (second?) marriage to an adulteress which is designed to embody the relationship of God and Israel.

If we assume that Hos. 1, 2 and 3 originated separately, this would explain the unclear relationship between Hos. 1 and 3 in the current version of the book: the existing text does not indicate whether Hos. 3 is referring again to Hosea's relationship to Gomer (Hos. 1) or another woman. A differentiation in the text's redaction history could account for the problem: originally, there were two separate events, although the event did not have anything to do with the subject of prostitution evoked in Hos. 1.2. Chapter 1 initially dealt only with the birth of his children and the giving of symbolic names. It was not until after the text had been revised based on Hos. 3 that the wife of the prophet and mother of his children was made into a wife of 'whoredom' and the children were dismissed as 'children of whoredom'. Hosea 1.2 appears to have been revised subsequently in this fashion when Hos. 1 and 3 were linked together by redactors:

> When Yhwh first spoke through Hosea, Yhwh said to Hosea,
> 'Go, take for yourself a wife of *whoredom*
> and have children of *whoredom*,
> *for the land commits great whoredom by forsaking Yhwh.*'

In contrast, more recent examinations based on redactional history (Susanne Rudnig-Zelt; Roman Vielhauer) have interpreted Hos. 1–3 as further redactional interpretations written in stages, inspired by Hos. 4–9, whose literary core is either in Hos. *1 (Rudnig-Zelt) or Hos. *2 (Vielhauer). Hosea 1 operates within the framework of Deuteronomic-Deuteronomistic theology, but intensifies this by condemning Jehu (1.4-5), who is portrayed comparatively more positively in the book of Kings (2 Kgs 9.28-31). Meanwhile, Hos. 3 attempts to transcend this way of thinking by referring to the steadfast love of God.

### 12.5.4 'Amos Language' in the Book of Hosea

The present version of Hosea includes specific echoes of the book of Amos: Aside from the → *doxology* in Hos. 12.6 (NRSV 12.5), which is strikingly similar to the doxologies in Amos, Hos. 4.15; 7.10; 8.14 and 11.10 also stand out. These texts show that the book of Hosea was probably harmonized relatively early on with the message of the book of Amos, which for its part was likely written down from the outset with the linguistic and theological framework of the book of Hosea in mind.[9]

## 12.6 Theology of the Book of Hosea

### 12.6.1 Knowledge of God

The motif of the 'knowledge of God' recurs continually throughout the book of Hosea.[10] Israel's lack of 'knowledge of God' refers to its political relations, its misguided policy of alliances (5.4; 8.2) and the misguided cult (6.6). It is also described as 'forgetting' Yhwh (2.15 [NRSV 2.13]; 4.6; 8.14). The accusation in 4.1 has been generalized as a theological statement, functioning as something of a superscription for chapters 4–14. Mythologized and rooted in the history of origins, the text looks back to the early stages of Israel's salvation history (2.10 [NRSV 2.8]; 11.3; 13.6). Ultimately, the 'knowledge of God' can be announced as a promise to Israel in the time of salvation (2.22 [NRSV 2.20]; 6.3; 10.12; 11.3; 13.4). The subject of 'knowledge', with its various theological emphases, can almost be seen as the leading indicator of the historical development of Hosea's theology.[11]

### 12.6.2 Yhwh-Baal Theme

There can be no doubt the conflict between Yhwh and Baal shaped large parts of the Hosea tradition. Traditionally, this polemic within the book of Hosea

9. Cf. J. Jeremias, *Hosea und Amos*, 38–41.

10. Cf. 2.10, 22 (NRSV 2.8, 20); 4.1; 5.4; 6.3, 6; 8.2; 10.12; 11.3; 13.4; cf. 5.3; 8.4; 14.10 (NRSV 14.9).

11. R. G. Kratz, 'Erkenntnis Gottes im Hoseabuch', *ZTK* 94 (1997), 1–24.

was believed to be related to the particularly strong cultural conflict between 'Canaan' and 'Israel' in the northern kingdom. Hosea defended the Israelite Yhwh against the Canaanite Baal.[12] Historically speaking, Baal and Yhwh were likely much more closely related at the time in question than the Old Testament is willing to admit. Yhwh and Baal were probably two innately different deities, but in Israel at the time of Hosea they could be easily identified with one another. In this respect Hos. 2.16 is illustrative: 'On that day, says Yhwh, you will call me, "My husband", and no longer will you call me, "My Baal."' Another clue are the proper names containing 'Baal' in the → *ostraca* from Samaria,[13] which are probably references to Yhwh.

It is possible that the Baal temple in Samaria (1 Kgs 16.32; 2 Kgs 10.21) was understood by insiders as a Yhwh temple.[14] If so, the polemic against Baal in Hosea could be understood as a form of religious boundary-setting towards the outside, although it really reflects an inner-religious conflict.

## 12.6.3 Marriage Metaphors

The extensive marriage metaphor in Hos. 1–3 used to portray the relationship of God and Israel should be understood against the background of ancient Near Eastern traditions: adultery imagery is commonly used when the relationship between a municipality (city/state) and their assigned deity has gone sour as a result of the community's policy of alliances with foreign powers.[15] So the book of Hosea is not formulating an original idea but recycling a traditional one. His imagery set a precedent, however. The image of the love of God and marriage between God and Israel plays a particularly important role in the books of Jeremiah and Deuteronomy. This image was gradually disassociated from its roots in the history of traditions.

12. Cf. page 158.
13. F. W. Dobbs-Allsopp *et al.*, *Hebrew Inscriptions: Texts from the Biblical Period of the Monarchy with Concordance* (New Haven/London: Yale University Press, 2005), 423–97
14. Based on the naming of a 'Yhwh of Samaria' in the inscriptions from Kuntillet ʿAjrûd (*COS* II, 171–3), we can conclude there was a Yhwh sanctuary in Samaria if we take the term Samaria to mean the city and not the kingdom.
15. Evidence in A. Fitzgerald, 'Background', 403–16 (above, Ch. 10 n. 7).

## 12.7 Notes on the History of Reception

Evidence for the book of Hosea's oldest *Wirkungsgeschichte* can be found in the book itself in the application of the prophet's message to Judah, thus documenting the reception of the book in the southern kingdom after the collapse of the northern kingdom. Furthermore, we can surmise that the book of Hosea, given its focus on and polemics against the northern kingdom, was read in the postexilic period (→ *exile*) as an anti-Samaritan text (Ch. 3.2.1) and may even have been reworked with this in mind.[16]

In addition, traditional research has frequently examined the influence of Hosea on Deuteronomy and the book of Jeremiah. In fact, there are several unmistakable combinations of motifs as well as linguistic similarities between the book of Hosea and these texts (polemics against foreign gods, cults in the high places, profanation of the land, marriage imagery, 'the love of God', and 'repentance'). It must be noted, however, that in contrast to earlier research, scholars now believe not everything in the book of Hosea is 'Hoseanic' in fact, so that one must examine in detail exactly how to date the Hosea texts chosen for these comparisons. In all likelihood some of the tangencies may be traced back to revisions in various books undertaken at the same time or with the same purpose in mind.

In → *Qumran,* Hosea seems to have been highly regarded as attested in various ways by the biblical manuscripts, the pesharim (interpretative commentaries) on Hosea (4Q166 and 167) as well as allusions to Hosea in further Qumran texts such as CD, 1QH, 1QS and 1QM.[17]

In the New Testament and later in the church, the most prominent references to Hosea are the saying in Hos. 6.6 ('For I desire steadfast love and not sacrifice, the knowledge of God rather than burnt-offerings') and the statements about the scandalous marriage in Hos. 1–3.

16. C. Levin (*The Old Testament*, 129–33) dates texts such as Hos. 9,*11–16 to the 5th or 4th century BCE rather than to the time of Hosea: 'Ephraim: Their glory will fly away like a bird. Ephraim: once I saw Ephraim like a young palm planted in a meadow. Ephraim is stricken. Their root is dried up, they shall bear no more fruit.' Levin explains the prominent use of Ephraim terminology by saying that Judah has now claimed the name of Israel for itself, and as a result the northern kingdom moves from being called 'Israel' to 'Ephraim'. Yet it remains questionable whether this interpretation truly reflects the primary meaning of the text or more likely a secondary meaning.

17. The texts can be found in F. García Martínez and E. J. C. Tigchelaar, *The Dead Sea Scrolls*.

# B The Book of Joel

📖 Commentaries: J. A. Crenshaw (AB 24C. New York: Doubleday 1995); J. Jeremias, *Die Propheten Joel, Obadja, Jona, Micha* (ATD 24/3. Göttingen: Vandenhoeck & Ruprecht, 2007); H. W. Wolff, *Joel and Amos* (Hermeneia. Philadelphia: Fortress, 1977).

📖 J. Jeremias, 'Joel/Joelbuch'. Pages 91–7 in vol. 17 of *TRE*. Berlin: de Gruyter, 1998.

## 12.8 Biblical Context

The book of Joel can be divided into two parts, although the exact contours are not easy to sketch. Based on content some have identified two main sections in 1–2 (NRSV 1.1–2.27) and 3–4 (NRSV 2.28–3.21) (corresponding to the later chapter division system): chapter 1–2 (NRSV 1.1–2.27) deals with a locust plague and drought in the past, while 3–4 (NRSV 2.28–3.21) maps out the future with the distinct themes of the pouring out of the spirit and the future judgement of the nations. Distinct linguistic signals in Joel, however, suggest that the second part of the book should also include 2.18-27, which describes the imminent fate of Israel in coming to terms with and overcoming the catastrophe they have experienced:

| | |
|---|---|
| 1.2–2.17<br>Prophetic call for lamentation and repentance | Retrospective look at the plague of locusts and drought<br>*1.14a Refrain: 'sanctify a fast, call a solemn assembly'*<br>Imminent military catastrophe<br>*2.15 Refrain: 'sanctify a fast; call a solemn assembly'* |
| 2.18–4.21 (NRSV 2.18–3.21)<br>God's speech proclaming salvation for Jerusalem and Judah | End of hardship and misery, new blessing<br>*2.27 Refrain: 'You shall know that… I, Yhwh, am your God.'*<br>Redemption and being spared on the 'Day of Yhwh'<br>*4.17 (NRSV 3.17) Refrain: 'So you shall know that I, Yhwh…[am] your God'* |

The placement of Joel in the Hebrew → *canon* between Hosea and Amos is probably due to the prominent references at the end of the book to Amos.[18]

18. Compare Joel 4.16, 18 (NRSV 3.16, 18) with Amos 1.2; 9.13, as well as the theme of the 'day of Yhwh'.

## 12.9 Historical-Critical Analysis and Major Issues in the History of Critical Interpretation

The main literary-historical problem with Joel is determining which of the primary sections originated first. In the traditional structure, the thematic and theological differences almost inevitably caused the → *eschatological* perspective with the outpouring of the spirit and judgement of the nations to appear as an appendix to the prophet's lamentations and message of judgement. Furthermore, scholars often made composition-critical judgements based on supposed differences between locust plague and drought motifs. Once it was observed, however, that the second part of the book developed from the first, more and more scholars have come to accept that the book's development was largely unified but took place at a later date. More recently, Jörg Jeremias' commentary has brought back the concept of a gradual process of textual development. He assumes that Joel 4 (NRSV 3) should be read as a simplified exegesis of the intentionally ambivalent and enigmatic statements in Joel 1–3 (NRSV 1–2). The outpouring of the spirit in Joel 4 (NRSV 3) thereby universalizes the gift of prophecy to the congregation; in the future there will no longer be any need for a particular prophetic office to discern the will of God. Clearly, even the oldest texts in Joel presume the existence of a considerable amount of other Old Testament textual material so that they must have originated at a late stage in ancient Israelite literary history. Some degree of consensus exists that 4.4-8 (NRSV 3.4-8) should be seen as an addendum given its linguistic issues (its use of prose, the way it interrupts the text's flow) and the historical realities it reflects (selling of slaves to the Greeks), although this opinion may need to be revised considering the generally late dating of the book.

## 12.10 Origins of the Book of Joel

Joel was traditionally dated to the pre-exilic period by earlier researchers due to its → *canonical* position between Hosea and Amos, but historical analysis provides no justification for this view. The only concrete evidence for the dating of the book comes from Joel 3–4 (NRSV 2.28–3.21), where the existence of a worldwide → *diaspora* is assumed (3.5; 4.2-3 [NRSV 2.32;

3.2-3]). If we follow Jeremias' approach, these chapters can be interpreted as the gradual written continuation of the original text of Joel 1–3 (NRSV 1–2), but the latter is only slightly older, meaning the earliest it could have originated is the Persian period. The book of Joel is probably even later, however, at least in its final form: the theme of world judgement in Joel 4 (NRSV 3) possibly assumes a situation after the collapse of the Persian empire in the time of Alexander III or the Diadochans (this is the fulfilment of the 'world judgement' predicted by Joel); dated this way, the text may have originated as recently as the 3rd cent. BCE. Numerous textual references in the book of Joel strongly suggest that the book as a whole is scribal prophecy without precursors in oral proclamation.

## 12.11 Theology of the Book of Joel

The theme of 'the day of Yhwh' is central to the theology of the book of Joel (Joel 1.15; 2.1, 11; 3.4; 4.14 [NRSV 2.31; 3.14]). The concept of the 'day of Yhwh' may have traditionally been used in the context of war to denote the intervention of Yhwh in battle in favour of his people. Originally, this term appears to have had a positive connotation, but by the time of Amos it had been reformulated to reflect a judgement prophecy (cf. Amos 5.18-20). As a result, the 'day of Yhwh' is repeatedly employed in written prophecy to express divine judgement against Israel (Isa. 2.12-17; Ezek. 7; Zeph. 1.2-18; 2.1-3; 3.6-8), against other nations (Isa. 13; 34; Jer. 46.2-12; Ezek. 30.1-8), or against the entire world (Isa. 34.2-4; Zech. 14.1-5).

Most importantly for Joel, this theme has been adopted to describe the disastrous present. The 'day of Yhwh' lies not only in the future but begins here and now. The traditionally ambivalent character of the 'day of Yhwh' correlates well with the view of the future developed in the book of Joel insofar as these include the possibilities of both salvation and judgement.

The statement concerning the outpouring of God's spirit in the end times shaped the history of theology, as it makes prophecy into a universal phenomenon in Israel (Joel 3.1-2 [NRSV 2.28-29]). With this statement, the book of Joel aligns itself with those voices in the Old Testament that see salvation for Israel as dependent on anthropological changes (→ *anthropology*), which will be brought about by God's own action (cf. the changes wrought in human hearts in Deut. 30; Jer. 31; Ezek. 36).

## 12.12 Notes on the History of Reception

The dominant theme of the day of Yhwh in the book of Joel is expanded in Joel 4 (NRSV 3) to a comprehensive prophecy of world judgement, an approach adopted in turn by → *apocalyptical literature* (e.g., Rev. 6.12, 17). The locust plague played an important symbolic role which could be combined with the subject of the similar plague in Egypt, as well as the 'valley of Jehoshaphat' (Joel 4.2, 12 [NRSV 3.2, 12]) as the location of the cosmic judgment, often identified with the Kidron Valley next to Jerusalem following the interpretation of Eusebius of Caesarea (†339 CE).

The promise of the outpouring of the spirit in Joel 3 (NRSV 2.28-32) was the main concept from Joel incorporated into the New Testament, notably in the Pentecost text in Acts 2 (cf. Joel 3.1-5a [NRSV 2.28-32a]/Acts 2.17-21). The majority of the church fathers concentrated on this promise in Joel 3 (NRSV 2.28-32) when reading Joel.

# C The Book of Amos

📖 Commentaries: F. I. Andersen and D. N. Freedman (AB 24A. New York: Doubleday, 1989); J. Jeremias (OTL. Louisville, Ky.: Westminster John Knox, 1998); S. M. Paul (Hermeneia. Minneapolis: Fortress, 1991).

📖 A. Schart, *Die Entstehung des Zwölfprophetenbuchs: Neubearbeitung von Amos im Rahmen schriftübergreifender Redaktionsprozesse*. BZAW 260. Berlin/New York: de Gruyter, 1998.

## 12.13 Biblical Context

Within the Book of the Twelve, Amos may have been separated from its original predecessor Hosea at a relatively late date. It can be clearly divided into three sections: 1–2 proclaim judgement against various nations including Israel and Judah; 3–6 offer a collection of shorter oracles; and finally 7–9 bring together a series of visions. The oracles about the nations in 1–2 and the visions in 7–9 correspond closely, thereby framing the oracles of judgement in 3–6.

| Amos 1-2 | Amos 3–6 | Amos 7–9 |
|---|---|---|
| Oracles about the nations | Oracles of judgement | Visions |

The correspondence between the oracles about the nations and the visions arises from the fact that there appears to have originally been four stanzas arranged in pairs in both cycles which were matched with a fifth concluding stanza serving as a climax: the oracles about the nations (Amos 1–2) crescendo as they reach the Israel verse, which is the only verse to specify the named 'four transgressions' that lead to judgement against the relevant nation:

> Amos 2.6-8: 'Thus says Yhwh: For three transgressions of *Israel*, and for four, I will not revoke the punishment; (a) because they sell the righteous for silver, and the needy for a pair of sandals – (2) they who trample the head of the poor into the dust of the earth, and push the afflicted out of the way; (3) father and son go in to the same girl, so that my holy name is profaned; (4) they lay themselves down beside every altar on garments taken in pledge; and in the house of their God they drink wine bought with fines they imposed.'

Similarly, the emphasis in the visions (Amos 7–9) is on the last one in which Yhwh refuses to allow them to enter the sanctuary, thus robbing Israel of its last possibility of salvation.

The existing form of the book has somewhat obscured the exact correlation between Amos 1–2 and 7–9 with editorial additions, particularly in the oracles about the nations (stanzas about Tyre, Edom and Judah). Nevertheless, we can still clearly reconstruct the original scope and sequence of 1–2 and 7–9. In addition, the refrain in 1–2 ('for three transgressions of X, and for four I will not revoke the punishment') cannot be understood at all without the themes in the first vision stanza – the vision of judgement, the prophet's intercessions, the revocation of the judgement by Yhwh: The 'it' which cannot be revoked is apparently the judgement which Yhwh threatened against the people in the visions and which, starting in stanza III, becomes inevitable. In this respect, the only report about the prophet Amos in the book, the narrative inserted in 7.10-17 about Amos' expulsion from the sanctuary in Bethel by the priest Amaziah, plays an important compositional role within the cycle of visions. The official repudiation of the prophet means it is no longer possible to revoke the divine judgement.

| | Sayings about the nations in Amos 1–2 | Visions Amos 7–9 |
|---|---|---|
| Stanzas I & II | **1.3-5: Damascus** | **7.1-3: Plague of locusts** |
| | **1.6-8: Gaza** | **7.4-6: Fire** |
| | *1.9-12*: Tyre, Edom | |

| | | |
|---|---|---|
| Stanzas III & IV | **1.13-15: Ammon** | **7.7-8: Tin** |
| | | *7.9: Harmonization with Hosea* |
| | | *7.10-17*: Expulsion of Amos from the sanctuary in Bethel |
| | **2.1-3: Moab** | **8.1-2: Basket with fruit** |
| | *2.4-5: Judah* | *8.3.4-14: Words of judgement* |
| Stanza V | **2.6-8: Israel** | **9.1-4: Altar** |

The parallel content between the oracles about the nations and visions reflects a particular purpose which emerges in the course of the visions and in the placement of the oracles against the nations at the beginning of the book: the visions, which are largely communicated privately between Yhwh and Amos and do not involve a commission to preach, apparently serve as evidence that Amos's message of judgement has been imposed on him. Amos functions at first as an intercessor, but beginning with the third vision he acknowledges the inevitability of judgement leading towards the 'end of Israel'. Placing the sayings about the nations at the beginning of the book at first obscures the refrain ('For three transgressions of N.N., and for four, I will not revoke it') in the course of the narrative. This arrangement, however, is likely supposed to explicate the guilt of Israel and also its neighbours *before* the proclamation of judgement. Framed by 1–2 and 7–9, the middle section 3–6 has been carefully designed. The superscriptions in 3.1 and 5.1 lend this middle section (3–6) its most elementary structure:

> Amos 3.1: 'Hear this word that *Yhwh* has spoken against you (perfect tense), O people of *Israel.'*
> Amos 5.1: 'Hear this word that *I* take up over you in lamentation (present), *O house of Israel.'*

Amos 3.1 addresses the people of God ('Israelites') with God's oracles which were uttered against Israel in the past, followed by prophetic words in 5.1, directed against the political entity of the 'House of Israel' (= northern kingdom of Israel) in the present and which is immediately declared as a 'funeral lamentation'. Chapters 3–6 thus express that Amos is mourning the downfall of the northern kingdom as a state, because the people of God have completely failed to carry out God's will.

## 12.14 Historical-Critical Analysis and Major Issues in the History of Critical Interpretation

There is no doubt that Amos as a literary entity developed over time. The superscription illustrates this fact:

> Amos 1.1: 'The words of Amos, who was among the shepherds of Tekoa, which he saw concerning Israel *in the days of King Uzziah of Judah and in the days of King Jeroboam son of Joash of Israel*, two years before the earthquake.'

The names of the kings (of Israel and Judah!) contradict the precise dating based on the earthquake, which was probably an original part of the text. It was probably understood as early proof of the Amos prophecy, as the theme of the earthquake has a prominent place in the proclamation in the book of Amos:

> Amos 2.13: 'So, I will press you down in your place, just as a cart presses down when it is full of sheaves.'

> Amos 9.1: 'I saw Yhwh standing beside the altar, and he said: Strike the capitals until the thresholds shake, and shatter them on the heads of all the people; and those who are left I will kill with the sword; not one of them shall flee away, not one of them shall escape.'

Yet the inconsistency in the superscription is just one of many indications suggesting that the book of Amos experienced a longer process of literary growth and development. The correspondence between the oracles against the nations and visions depicted above indicates that three stanzas (concerning Tyre, Edom and Judah in 1.9-12; 2.4-5) were appended to the other oracles against the nations. Conversely, the vision cycle has likewise been expanded with intervening bits of text (7.9, 10-17; 8.3, 4-14). Although Amos 3–6 appears to have a coherent and comprehensive structure, thematic and formal differences suggest these texts were likely united bit by bit into the existing composition. Moreover, the superscription 1.1-2 as well as statements such as 6.1 ('Alas for those who are at ease in Zion') show that, like Hosea, the book of Amos also underwent a Judean redaction.

Furthermore, for some time[19] scholars have presumed the book also was subject to a → *Deuteronomistic* revision which, although not very extensive (e.g., 1.1, 9-12; 2.4-5; 2.10-12; 3.1,7; 5.25-26), was quite marked. This assumption can and will be justified in detail as part of the debate about 'Deuteronomisms'. Amos lent itself to a 'Deuteronomistic' revision as the prophet was active when the northern kingdom was destroyed, just as Jeremiah was during the catastrophe that befell the southern kingdom. Verses 9.9-10 reveal a distinctive perspective within the book: the contrast here between sinners and righteous among the people (9.10a: 'All the sinners of my people shall die by the sword') contradicts the total condemnation of the entire population in the rest of Amos. The separation of Israel into groups is similar to later prophetic texts such as Isa. 56–66.

Finally, the thematic shift towards salvation at the end of the book (9.11-15) is admittedly an addition, which explicitly alludes to the end of the Davidic dynasty, clearly presupposing the events of 587 BCE. In addition, allusions to Deut. 28.30, 33 as well as Jer. 1.10; 24.6; 31.28 show the scribal character of the book's conclusion.

> 'On that day I will raise up the booth of David that is fallen, and repair its breaches, and raise up its ruins, and rebuild it as in the days of old … I will restore the fortunes of my people Israel, and they shall rebuild the ruined cities and inhabit them; they shall plant vineyards and drink their wine, and they shall make gardens and eat their fruit. I will plant them upon their land, and they shall never again be plucked up out of the land that I have given them, says Yhwh your God.' (Amos 9.*11, 14-15).

# 12.15 Origins of the Book of Amos

The prophet Amos, who lived in the first half of the 8th century BCE according to his book, came from Tekoa in Judah but the texts indicate he was active in the northern kingdom of Israel, particularly in Bethel, close to the border with Judah. The full details of his message can be reconstructed only with difficulty. His message was recorded in the book named after him and then shaped and rearranged. Apparently, the oldest written texts from the Amos tradition were reworked in line with the message of Hosea.

According to the superscription in 1.1, Amos was active as a prophet in the

19. W. H. Schmidt, 'Die deuteronomistische Redaktion des Amosbuches', *ZAW* 77 (1965): 168–93.

time of Jeroboam II (785–745 BCE) before the Assyrian threat, which became acute in the Near East when Tiglath-Pileser III ascended the throne. Verses such as Amos 5.27 and 6.2 assume knowledge of the Assyrian practice of mass deportations or allude to concrete Assyrian conquests, so his message was either written down in light of Assyrian conquests from the outset or interpreted accordingly soon thereafter, especially after the fall of the northern kingdom.

> 'Therefore I will take you into exile beyond Damascus, says Yhwh, whose name is the God of hosts' (Amos 5.27).

> 'Cross over to Calneh, and see; from there go to Hamath the great [city]; then go down to Gath of the Philistines. Are you better than these kingdoms? Or is your territory greater than their territory?' (Amos 6.2)

The fact that the book of Amos is decisively shaped by the catastrophe of 722–721 BCE, also means that it was primarily transmitted within Judah, as shown by the naming of the Judean king Uzziah as well as the mention of → *Zion* in 1.1-2 (see Ch. 6.1).

Of the three sections of the book (Amos 1–2, 3–6, and 7–9), Amos 1–2 and 7–9 can hardly have been recorded independently of one another, but rather 1–2 assumes the existence of 7–9, as is clear from the refrain in the oracles against the nations ('For three transgressions of N.N., and for four, I will not revoke it'), which addresses the intercessory setting in Amos 7–9. Jörg Jeremias even argues that Amos 7–9 originally came before Amos 1–2. While the composition of Amos 3–6 unites individual sayings, it possesses some inner coherence and its compositional technique is closely related to Hos. 4–11.

The oldest sections of the book can presumably be found in Amos 7–9[20] and in individual passages in 3–6.[21] In terms of the book's composition, 1–2

20. A different view is taken by U. Becker in 'Der Prophet als Fürbitter: Zum literarhistorischen Ort der Amos-Visionen', *VT* 51 (2001): 141–65, who believes the visions date from the Persian Period; cf. however, J. C. Gertz, 'Die unbedingte Gerichtsankündigung des Amos', in *Gottes Wege suchend: Beiträge zum Verständnis der Bibel und ihrer Botschaft, Festschrift für Rudolph Mosis* (ed. F. Sedlmeier; Würzburg: Echter, 2003), 153–70.

21. It is questionable whether one can agree with R. G. Kratz that the original message of Amos – corresponding to the literary growth of the Jeremiah tradition (Ch. 10) – can be reduced to the fragmentary messages of disaster without any relation to Yhwh. For the details of his position, see his contribution 'Die Worte des Amos aus Tekoa', in *Propheten in Mari, Assyrien und Israel*

and 7–9 were likely together before 3–6 (which in its earliest form was an independent text) was inserted into the present context.

The → *Deuteronomistic* passages (1.10-12; 2.4-5, 9-12; 3.1b, 7; 5.25-26; 6.1*; 9.7-8) have the downfall of Judah and Jerusalem in view. However, the label 'Deuteronomistic' should not imply an unquestionable historical dating of these texts in the first few decades after the destruction of Jerusalem in 587 BCE. Evidence for 'Deuteronomisms' can be found throughout the entire history of theology in the Second Temple period. Later expansions can be found both in the so-called judgement doxologies (→ *doxology*) (1.2; 4.13; 5.8-9; 9.5-6), which praise the righteousness of the judging creator, limiting judgement to the sinners in Israel (9.9-10), as well as in the salvific conclusion in 9.11-15, which promises the re-establishment of the Davidic dynasty and announces that Israel will enjoy an eternal and prosperous existence in the land.

# 12.16 Theology of the Book of Amos

## 12.16.1 Prophecy of Judgement

The theology of the book of Amos should be seen as a presentation and apologia on behalf of judgement prophecy, an emphasis which clearly became explicit at a later stage of the book's formation with the doxologies of judgement (1.2; 4.13; 5.8-9; 9.5-6). Starting with chapter 1, the book of Amos leaves no doubt that the judgement against Israel is inescapable. The correspondence between the oracles against the nations and the visions in the further course of the book, however, is a sign that this irreversible proclamation of judgement is not based on the will of the one who is announcing it. It is not Amos but God who has decided on the coming disaster. The middle section of the book provides factual reasons for the judgement: the main accusations are based on a critique of society and the cult, issues which are certainly related. Due to its social transgressions, Israel is no longer able to establish any contact with God by means of its cultic institutions.

As with written prophecy in general, the function of 'disaster prophecy' in its original historical context is not to bring about repentance. Instead, evidence of guilt, the ineffectiveness of the prophet and – at critical junctures in the text – the in-breaking of judgement are already intertwined. So we

(FRLANT 201; ed. M. Köckert and M. Nissinen; Göttingen: Vandenhoeck & Ruprecht, 2003), 54–89.

might say that, first and foremost, disaster prophecy is motivated by a hermeneutical impetus not an ethical one. Its primary goal is to help the people understand their own history. Later generations also read the book of Amos as a warning, of course, but these are secondary instances of reception.

The short narrative about Amos in Amos 7.10-17 is characteristic as it reveals that Amos apparently did not understand himself as a 'prophet' *(nābî ʾ)* *in the way it was understood at the time.*

> 'And Amaziah said to Amos, 'O seer, go, flee away to the land of Judah, earn your bread there, and prophesy there; but never again prophesy at Bethel, for it is the king's sanctuary, and it is a temple of the kingdom.' Then Amos answered Amaziah, 'I am no prophet, nor a prophet's son; but I am a herdsman, and a dresser of sycamore trees, and Yhwh took me from following the flock, and Yhwh said to me, "Go, prophesy to my people Israel."' (Amos 7.12-15)

We can gather from this episode that Amos obviously sees a 'prophet' *(nābî ʾ)* as formally employed by the royal court or temple, meaning this person had certain dependencies. In contrast, Amos emphasizes that he is not a 'prophet' *(nābî ʾ)* in this sense, but has been independently commissioned by God. Amos' use of the appellation sets a precedent: today we generally understand 'prophets' as figures such as Amos and not as the kind of court prophets familiar from passages such as 1 Kgs 22.

## 12.16.2 Social Critique

In contrast to the book of Hosea, which dramatically spotlights Israel's cultic and worship transgressions, the book of Amos emphasizes Israel's social problems (cf. 2.6-9; 5.12; 6.1-6; 8.4-6, etc.) reflecting a specific historical background. The period when Amos was active in the northern kingdom was fundamentally characterized by economic prosperity that only benefited certain social strata within the population while making others destitute and dependent. The standards for social critique laid out by Amos seem to be quite universal and probably derive from a → *wisdom* background. Seen from a modern, though anachronistic, view they could almost be called humanistic.

It would be a disservice to ignore the theological aspect of Amos' social critique by interpreting it simply as a strict alternative between 'ethics' and 'the cult'. Rather, the goal of his social critique can be seen in the statement that every worship service is worthless given the social corruption in society. Without 'ethics', worship is rendered ineffective *a priori*: God cannot be reached at all.

## 12.17 Notes on the History of Reception

As the oldest prophetic book aside from Hosea, Amos is significant in terms of reception history because of its historical position at the beginning of written prophecy. Together with Hosea, it represents the core of the later Book of the Twelve. Within its biblical context, the book of Amos also seems to have exercised a decisive influence on the nascent Isaiah tradition.[22]

The harsh talk about the 'end' for the people of Israel (Amos 8.1-2) was apparently universalized and incorporated into the narrative of the flood by the → *Priestly* writer (Gen. 6.13).[23] At the same time, the Priestly writer also mitigated Amos' message, asserting that God's definite judgement already occurred in primeval history, so it no longer poses a threat in the current situation.

In the New Testament, the book of Acts quotes Amos' words in Acts 7.42-43 and Acts 15.15-18. For early Christian writers, the → *doxology* in 4:13 as well as the conclusion of the book with its augury of the restoration of the 'booth of David' played a certain role. Overall, however, the book of Amos does not feature prominently in either Jewish or Christian exegesis.

# D The Book of Obadiah

📖 Commentaries: J. Jeremias, *Die Propheten Joel, Obadja, Jona, Micha* (ATD 24,3. Göttingen: Vandenhoeck & Ruprecht, 2007); P. R. Raabe (AB 24D. New York: Doubleday, 1996); J. Renkema (Historical Commentary on the Old Testament. Transl. by B. Doyle. Leuven: Peeters, 2003); H. W. Wolff, *Obadiah and Jonah: A Commentary* (Hermeneia. Transl. by M. Kohl, Minneapolis: Augsburg Fortress, 1986).

📖 E. Ben Zvi, *A Historical-Critical Study of the Book of Obadiah*. BZAW 242. Berlin/New York: de Gruyter, 1996.

## 12.18 Biblical Context

With just 21 verses, the book of Obadiah is extraordinarily succinct. Although

22. Cf. E. Blum, *Jesajas prophetisches Testament*, 12–29 (above, Ch. 9 n. 14).

23. Cf. R. Smend, '"Das Ende ist gekommen": Ein Amoswort in der Priesterschrift', in *Die Botschaft und die Boten: Festschrift für H. W. Wolff* (ed. J. Jeremias and L. Perlitt; Neukirchen-Vluyn: Neukirchener, 1981), 67–72.

its message is communicated at multiple levels with a complex organizational structure, it can still be roughly broken into two main divisions in vv. 1-15 and 16-21, although both sections overlap in v. 15. The first main section deals with the judgement of Yhwh against Edom, while the second speaks about salvation for Israel and → *Zion*. The terse superscription ('Vision of Obadiah') does not help locate the text in a more specific era.

## 12.19 Historical-Critical Analysis and Major Issues in the History of Critical Interpretation

While Obadiah is the shortest book in the Old Testament, it is still replete with textual problems. Determining the relationship between the two main sections is the first difficult issue to address, especially how to interpret the intersection in v. 15. The oracle against Edom in Obad. 1b-4 is very close to Jer. 49.14-16 (cf. also Obad. 5/Jer. 49.9-10), so one should ask whether Obad. as a whole is a redactional prophetic book that was only secondarily associated with a fictional prophetic figure 'Obadiah' (literally: 'adherent of Yhwh') through an addition in verse 1.[24] Furthermore, given the concluding formula in v. 18 and the emphatic focus on the entire people of Israel in vv. 19-21, it seems the view of salvation for Israel and → *Zion* in Obad. 16-21 was not written all at one time but came about gradually (vv. 16-18, 19-21).

## 12.20 Origins of the Book of Obadiah

The dominant theme of judgement against Edom as well as the closeness of Obad. 1b-4 to Jer. 49.14-16 – a probable sign of textual dependency – make it likely that even the oldest texts in Obadiah presuppose the destruction of Jerusalem by the Babylonians in 587 BCE from which Edom probably profited through collaboration (Lam. 4.21-22). A noticeable discrepancy exists between the closeness of Israel and Edom in the patriarchal stories with their tradition about twins Jacob ('Israel') and Esau ('Edom') which links both

24. Contrary to Jewish tradition, Obad. has nothing to with the historical Obadiah from 1 Kgs 18.3-7, as is clear from the different themes as well as their divergent historical and geographical situations.

peoples closely, on the one hand, and the peculiar 'hatred' of Edom in some prophetic texts (such as Obadiah in particular). This discrepancy can best be explained if we accept that Edom was involved or at least given preferential treatment in the course of events leading up to Judah's destruction. It does appear that sections of Judah's southern frontier were taken over by Edom (Ch. 4.4). Verses 16-18 evidently presuppose that Edom was displaced by the Nabateans in the 5th cent. BCE. Verses 19-21 are likely somewhat later.

## 12.21 Theology of the Book of Obadiah

The theology of Obadiah revolves around the relationship between Israel and Edom, expanding the proclamation of judgement which had already afflicted Israel to include a neighbouring people who, if anything, had benefited so far from the destruction. This theology is Zion- and Israel-centred (→ *Zion Theology*), following a broad anti-Edom tendency in the prophetic books (Isa. 34; 63.1-6; Jer. 49; Ezek. 35; Amos 1.11-12; 9.11-12). This is understandable given the historical context in which Israelite prophecy was developed, in which the punishing power of God in human history is applied to non-Israelite peoples as well.

## 12.22 Notes on the History of Reception

The problematic relationship between Israel and Edom, emblematized in Jacob and Esau, has been shaped into a paradigm for election and rejection in Christian theology many times. The first use of this Christian motif can be found already in the New Testament in Rom. 9–11.

# E The Book of Jonah

Commentaries: J. Jeremias, *Die Propheten Joel, Obadja, Jona, Micha* (ATD 24/3. Göttingen: Vandenhoeck & Ruprecht, 2007); J. Limburg (OTL. London: SCM Press, 1993); H. W. Wolff, *Obadiah and Jonah: A Commentary* (Hermeneia. Transl. by M. Kohl. Minneapolis: Augsburg Fortress, 1986).

## 12.23 Biblical Context

Unlike most books in the Book of Twelve, the book of Jonah contains a prophetic narrative (cf. Haggai as well), rather than the proclamation of the prophet Jonah himself. It is thus closer to the prophetic narratives in the book of Kings (1 Kgs 17–2 Kgs 13) as well as the narratives in Isaiah (Isa. 36–39) and Jeremiah (Jer. 26–29, 36–45).

The book tells the story of the prophet Jonah who tries to flee on a ship from his divine commission when he is overtaken by a great storm. As the one responsible for the storm, he is thrown overboard by the sailors. A large fish swallows him up, but after three days the fish spits him out on land again. Jonah then fulfils the divine commission: he goes to Nineveh and preaches to the people who respond and repent, thereby moving God to retract the judgement. As a result, the prophet Jonah becomes extremely angry and expresses the wish to die. God then allows a bush (probably a *ricinus* or 'castor-oil plant') to grow and provide shelter for Jonah, which makes him very happy. Suddenly, however, God allows the plant to wither, causing Jonah to become angry again. The loss of the bush at the end of the story serves as a mirror-image illustration of the preservation of Nineveh.

This narrative can be divided into two corresponding sections in terms of form (1–2 'sea'; 3–4 'land'): in chapters 1 and 3 God, Jonah and the sailors or the Ninevites each act, while in chapters 2 and 4 God and the prophet are alone. Both parts have been constructed with a particular symmetry so that their outcome is based on a command of Yhwh to Jonah and his disobedience or obedience (1.1-3/3.1-3a), which in each case is followed by a depiction of the fear of God (sailors) or the repentance of the Gentiles (Ninevites) (1.4-16/3.3b-4.5). Each section concludes with the reaction of the prophet alone (2.1-11 [NRSV 1.17–2.10]) or of the prophet and God (4.6-11).

## 12.24 Historical-Critical Analysis and Major Issues in the History of Critical Interpretation

The careful structuring and integrated narrative flow of the book of Jonah suggest the narrative was largely unified in terms of its literary development. Widely discussed among scholars is whether the so-called Jonah psalm in Jonah 2 is a subsequent addition, as its language is distinct compared to the rest of the book. Jonah prays using the language of the Psalms to express gratitude towards God, although he would not have had reason to do so in the stomach of the fish. It is certainly conceivable, however, that this prayer of thanksgiving is supposed to provide a critical twist within the context of the book, so that the psalm may also belong to the original book. An argument in its favour is that without Jonah 2 the book's existing compositional harmony would largely disintegrate.

## 12.25 Origins of the Book of Jonah

Despite the Assyrian setting adopted in the book, Jonah likely originated in the Ptolemaic period (3rd cent. BCE). Evidence includes its thoroughgoing scribal character as well as affinities with Greek mythology. Both can be explained briefly: the book of Jonah is a skilfully constructed narrative in which numerous biblical references have been integrated to create a deeper meaning. The central theme of God's repentance and the possibility of his subsequent remorse is clearly borrowed from Jeremiah (Jer. 18.7-8; 26; 36) and Joel. A few verses from Joel are even reproduced verbatim in Jonah (Joel 2.13b/Jonah 4.2b; Joel 2.14a/Jonah 3.9b). Further, the Jonah psalm in Jonah 2 incorporates unmistakable language and theology from the Psalms (cf. Jonah 2.3 [NRSV 2.2]/Ps. 120.1; Jonah 2.3, 5/Ps. 31.23 [NRSV Jonah 2.2, 4/Ps. 31.22]; Jonah 2.6/Ps. 18.5 [NRSV Jonah 2.5/Ps. 18.4]; 116.3; Jonah 2.7 [NRSV 2.6]/Ps. 103.4).

Even more striking than the inclusion of other biblical sayings in Jonah is the motif of being swallowed by a fish and then spat back up again, a plot line taken from a solar myth (the sun is swallowed by a fish at night and spat back up every morning). This connection shows up in Christian → *iconography*: Jonah is usually portrayed as bald because his hair has been burned off by the heat inside the fish. The closest parallels to the biblical Jonah can be found in Greek mythological stories of Heracles and Perseus and in the Arion saga (Arion is saved by a dolphin by riding on his back). Additionally, the Ptolemaic period provides a better background for understanding the motif of the hostile city of 'Nineveh' than the period of Persian rule, which is usually seen very positively in the Old Testament.

The protagonist Jonah, son of Amittai, is mentioned in 2 Kgs 14.25, which is probably the source from which the book borrowed the name of its hero. There is certainly no reference in 2 Kgs 14.25 to a book of Jonah.

## 12.26 Theology of the Book of Jonah

The theology of Jonah cannot be reduced to one purpose, but combines various theologies in dialogue with one another. First, it seems to reflect on Israel's relationship with other peoples and does not view them as *massa perditionis*, but instead finds evidence that they also fear God and practise repentance, suggesting salvation is also possible for other peoples in the world. The 'guilt-punishment syndrome' Jonah advocates is ruptured by the new framework of this inclusive concept: God is not obligated to punish guilt because there is the possibility of repentance. The book of Jonah also expresses misgivings about the inclusion of the innocent in a national judgement (4.11 children and cattle) and raises this as a theological problem. Finally, the book of Jonah can also be read as a theological critique of the prophetic office, implying that the role of the prophet always remains subordinate to the (merciful) freedom of God, for whom preserving God's creatures is more important than the realization of God's mediated prophetic word.

## 12.27 Notes on the History of Reception

In terms of its reception history Jonah is among the most widely received prophetic books in the Bible to the present day. This is partly due to its fanciful plot, which has stimulated interpretative fantasy. Above all, however, the fate of Jonah was seen in conjunction with the mystery of death and resurrection in Christian interpretation. In addition, the theme of repentance figured prominently in the Christian reception. In intertestamental literature Jonah plays a role in the apocryphal (→ *apocrypha)* book of Tobit (Tob. 14.3-4).

In the New Testament, Matthew and Luke cite the sign of Jonah (Mt. 12.39-40; 16.4; Lk. 11.29-30); the days Jonah spent in the belly of the fish are compared to the days the Son of Man spends in the grave. This, in turn, inspired the typological *interpretation* (→ *typology*) of the fish swallowing and spitting up Jonah as a prefiguration of Christ's death and resurrection widely developed in Christian tradition.

Beginning in the 3rd century CE, a relatively stereotypical Jonah-cycle appeared in grave paintings of the Roman catacombs which illustrated three main elements of the story: Jonah being thrown into the sea, spit out by the fish and then resting under the arbour of the bush. In addition, a curious oddity developed in the Baroque period when whale pulpits were built, especially in Silesia in Poland, in which the preacher spoke from the open mouth of the fish. Thus the preacher was cast as Jonah calling the people to repentance and change.

# F The Book of Micah

📖 Commentaries: J. Jeremias, *Die Propheten Joel, Obadja, Jona, Micha* (ATD 24/3. Göttingen: Vandenhoeck & Ruprecht, 2007); R. Kessler (HTKAT. Freiburg: Herder, 1999); W. McKane (Edinburgh: T & T Clark, 1998); H. W. Wolff (Hermeneia. Transl. by G. Stansell, Minneapolis: Augsburg Fortress, 1990).

📖 B. Zapff, *Redaktionsgeschichtliche Studien zum Michabuch im Kontext des Dodekapropheton*. BZAW 256. Berlin/New York: de Gruyter, 1997.

## 12.28 Biblical Context

The composition of the book of Micah is marked by an alternating sequence of oracles predicting disaster and salvation that is repeated three times. Each new beginning is introduced with the call 'Hear' (1.2; 3.1; 6.1). Like the book of Amos, Micah is strongly shaped by prophetic social critique. The book's superscription, 1.1, locates the activity of Micah in the 8th century BCE and he is presented as a somewhat younger contemporary of Isaiah, from the Judean countryside ('from Moresheth').

| | | |
|---|---|---|
| 1.2–2.11 | Disaster | Judgement against Israel and Judah, social critique |
| 2.12-13 | Salvation | Salvation for the remnant of Israel |
| 3.1-12 | Disaster | Zion and Jerusalem as a heap of ruins |
| 4.1–5.14 | Salvation | Pilgrimage of the peoples to Zion, swords to ploughshares, Messiah from Bethlehem |
| 6.1–7.7 | Disaster | Instructional speech, proclamation of disaster against Jerusalem |
| 7.8-20 | Salvation | Salvation for Jerusalem, world judgement |

## 12.29 Historical-Critical Analysis and Major Issues in the History of Critical Interpretation

The three cycles moving from disaster to salvation develop a rhythmic view of history and likely reflect the elementary developmental stages of the book of Micah. Since the 19th century scholars have assumed that only Mic. 1–3 includes authentic material, even though Mic. 1–3 originated after the time of the prophet Micah himself in the time of the Judean king Manasseh (Rainer Kessler) or in the postexilic period (Eckart Otto[25]). Contrary to the interpretation of Hans-Walter Wolff,[26] Mic. 1–3 does not include any of the prophet's 'sermons'. In fact, the texts seem to have been integrated into a purposeful progression from the outset, reflecting the effects of the prophetic message (2.6-11; cf. 3.5-8) and showing evidence of harmonization with other prophetic books, especially Amos and Isaiah.

Given both its conceptual horizon (relationship to Samaria and the peoples; relations between the population already living in the land and those returning; renewed accusations due to the failure of the promised salvation to materialize as expected) as well as far-reaching literary references in the Old Testament, the texts in Mic. 4–5 and 6–7 point to editorial expansions (*Fortschreibung*) in stages from a later period.

The psalm-like final verses in Mic. 7.8-20 have a concluding character. They do not include any prophetic lamentations or accusations, but offer an assent to the preceding book text using 'we'.

## 12.30 Origins of the Book of Micah

The traditional notion that the core of the book is found in Mic. 1–3, which contains authentic material from the prophet Micah, still remains the most likely scenario. However, the noticeable use of the 1st person singular does not indicate anything about the collection's authenticity (see Ch. 12.29 above). Rather, it appears that these are also later texts in the 'I' style which were added to the authentic material.

25. E. Otto, 'Micha/Michabuch', *TRE* 22: 695–704.

26. H. W. Wolff, *Micah*.

The texts in Mic. 4–5 first stress that judgement is being realized with the triple use of 'now' (4.9, 11, 14 [NRSV 5.1]), mirroring the change to a prophecy of salvation in the early Persian period, while in Mic. 6–7 warnings and accusations (6.1–7.7) reappear combined with words of salvation (7.8-20), not unlike what is found in Isa. 56–66. This apparently reflects the need to account for the unfulfilled salvation prophecies in Mic. 5. Furthermore, various components of the text relate to the formation of the Book of Twelve as a whole (1.3-4/Amos 4.13; 1.7/Hos. 1-3; 7.18/Jonah 3.9; 4.2). 'Who is a God like you?' (7.18) is a play on the name 'Micah' ('Who is like Yah[weh]?'). Within the psalm-like conclusion to the book in Mic. 7.8-20, we find an addendum in Mic. 7.12-13 that evokes the notion of a universal world judgement, interrelated with similar corresponding texts in the prophetic books (Isa. 34.2-4; Jer. 25.27-31; Joel 4 [NRSV 3]).

## 12.31 Theology of the Book of Micah

At the heart of the book of Micah is its social critique, which denounces various grievances from diverse periods corresponding to the gradual development of the text over time. In keeping with the period in which it presumably originated, as with Amos this critique does not relate to morals, but the theology of history. The book of Micah does not primarily focus on bringing about repentance, but rather seeks to justify the proclamation of judgement. In this respect, the harsh announcement of disaster against Jerusalem (esp. 3.12) is striking: → *Zion* will be ploughed as a field, Jerusalem will become a heap of ruins and the Temple Mount will become a wooded height. This means that no less than the central place of God's presence in the world will be obliterated – a rather unthinkable idea for the book of Isaiah, for example, which was so strongly rooted in Jerusalemite theology.

While there are reasons for the rhythmic progression of the proclamation of disaster and salvation based on the text's origins, it also has theological value when read as a whole: it shows the transformation of God's will in the course of history, which ends in the long run with salvation for God's people.

## 12.32 Notes on the History of Reception

Micah appears to have been a formidable figure within the Old Testament itself, as is shown in the startling reference to him in Jer. 26, in the context of

Jeremiah's persecution on account of the judgement he announced against the temple of Yhwh.

> Jer. 26.17-19: 'And some of the elders of the land arose and said to all the assembled people, 'Micah of Moresheth, who prophesied during the days of King Hezekiah of Judah, said to all the people of Judah: 'Thus says Yhwh, Yhwh of hosts, Zion shall be ploughed as a field; Jerusalem shall become a heap of ruins, and the mountain of the house a wooded height.' Did King Hezekiah of Judah and all Judah actually put him to death? Did he not fear Yhwh and entreat his favor, and did not Yhwh change his mind about the disaster that he had pronounced against them? But we are about to bring great disaster on ourselves!"

In the New Testament Mic. 5.1 (NRSV 5.2) plays a notable role in the accounts of Jesus' birth in Matthew and Luke, in which the future prince of peace will come not from Jerusalem or from Nazareth – as was likely the case for the historical Jesus–but from Bethlehem, the birthplace of David.

In the late 20th century peace movement, the proclamation of Mic. 4.3 was often adopted because it promises the transformation of 'swords into ploughshares' (cf. also Isa. 2.4 as well as the inversion in Joel 4.10 [NRSV 3.10]).

# G The Book of Nahum

📖 Commentaries: L. Perlitt, *Die Propheten Nahum, Habakuk, Zephanja* (ATD 25/1. Göttingen: Vandenhoeck & Ruprecht, 2004); K. Spronk (Historical Commentary on the Old Testament. Kampen: Kok Pharos, 1997).

📖 K. Seybold, *Profane Prophetie: Studien zum Buch Nahum*. SBS 135. Stuttgart: Katholisches Bibelwerk, 1989.

## 12.33 Biblical Context

The book of Nahum can be easily divided into three sections: first, an → *acrostic* in Nah. 1.2-8 that runs through the first half of the Hebrew alphabet from Aleph to Kaf and is organized concentrically; then in 1.9–2.3 (NRSV 2.2) a disputation speech; and finally in 2.4–3.19 (NRSV 2.3–3.19) a conclusion with a three-part judgement against Nineveh. Precise dates are not given in the book, but repeated references to 'Nineveh' (the residence of the Assyrian king since the 8th cent. BCE) make the Neo-Assyrian background quite palpable.

| | | |
|---|---|---|
| 1.1 | | Superscription |
| 1.2-8 | | Acrostic theophany hymn |
| 1.9–2.3 (NRSV 2.2) | | Disputation speech against Judah and Nineveh |
| 2.4–3.19 (NRSV 2.3–3.19) | 2.4-14 (NRSV 2.3-13)<br>3.1-7<br>3.8-19 | Judgement against Nineveh |

# 12.34 Historical-Critical Analysis and Major Issues in the History of Critical Interpretation

Numerous vestiges of a process of literary growth are clear in the book of Nahum. Beginning with the duplicate superscription in 1.1, which may have been composed secondarily, the individual sections of the book as well as their component parts seem at first to have existed as independent sources before being brought together into one collection and further expanded. This is particularly noticeable in both the acrostic → *theophany* hymn in Nah. 1.2-8, and the poetry about Nineveh in 2.2, 4-11 (NRSV 2.1, 3-10); 3.1-3; 3.8-11, 12-15.

Also striking is the 'profane' design of the book in Nah. 2-3. The destruction of Nineveh dealt with here is merely described without little additional theological interpretation. In contrast, the 'Yhwh' passages in 2.14 (NRSV 2.13) and 3.4-7 stick out as additions. As evidenced by their intertextual relationships to the anti-Babylon texts in Isaiah (esp. Isa. 47), they see the downfall of Nineveh as the → *typological* model of the hoped-for destruction of Babylon. Occasionally, the argument has been made that Nahum as a whole is a redactional book within XII, but this opinion has lost its appeal in recent scholarship.

# 12.35 Origins of the Book of Nahum

The overwhelming consensus among scholars is that the previously independent texts in the third section constitute the core of the book, which was then expanded in stages by adding material to the beginning. The main support for this opinion is that the text includes statements whose contemporary context is transparent (3.8-11) such as references to the destruction of Thebes ('No-amon') in 664 BCE and the fall of Nineveh in 612 BCE, which fit with the anonymous first half of the book's superscription in 1.1a ('an oracle concerning Nineveh').

The oldest texts from Nah. 2.2, 4–3.19 (NRSV 2.1, 3–3.19) were likely written as a result of the fall of Nineveh, while the verses from Nah. 1.2–2.3 (NRSV 2.2) universalize the basic intention of the mocking poem in Nah. 3. In the process, the redactor at times incorporated existing material; in this way the acrostic theophany hymn in 1.2-8 was probably created separately before being inserted into the book (see the secondary inclusion in 1.*2-3).

Nahum and Habakkuk may have originally constituted a two-prophet scroll (see the similarities between Nah. 3 and Hab. 1) before the scroll was integrated into the Book of the Twelve. The sequence Nahum-Habakkuk reveals the following diptych structure:

| | | | |
|---|---|---|---|
| Nah. 1 | Nah. 2–3 | Hab. 1–2 | Hab. 3 |
| Theophany psalm | Judgement against Nineveh | Judgement against Babylon | Theophany psalm |

# 12.36 Theology of the Book of Nahum

We can only speak of explicit 'theology' in Nahum with regard to the book's overall composition, at which stage sections of text focused on reporting (esp. Nah. 2–3) and interpreting (esp. Nah. 1) have been combined. Nahum 1 interprets the 'profane' poetry about the fall of Nineveh as proof of the universal power of God in history which even determines the fate of great political powers and their capital cities – not just Nineveh but also Thebes and, by implication, Babylon.

# 12.37 Notes on the History of Reception

The book of Nahum acquires a special meaning in → *Qumran*. A pesher (commentary) on Nahum has been passed down[27] that relates the enemies of Israel named in the book to groups hostile to the Qumran-Essenes within Judaism.

27. Text in F. García Martínez and E. J. C. Tigchelaar, *The Dead Sea Scrolls* I, 334–41; G. Doudna, *4Q Pesher Nahum* (JSPSup 35, Sheffield: Sheffield Academic Press, 2001).

# H The Book of Habakkuk

Commentaries: F. I. Anderson (AB 25. New York: Doubleday, 2001); L. Perlitt, *Die Propheten Nahum, Habakuk, Zephanja* (ATD 25/1. Göttingen: Vandenhoeck & Ruprecht, 2004).

## 12.38 Biblical Context

The book of Habakkuk, which does not provide any specific details in 1.1 about its date, can be divided into two parts with two superscriptions. Habakkuk 1–2 comprises the prophet's complaint and corresponding oracles as well as a collection of oracles of woe, while Hab. 3, distinguished by its own superscription ('The Prayer of the Prophet Habakkuk'), offers a psalm containing depictions of a → *theophany* and judgement.

| | | |
|---|---|---|
| 1–2 | 1.1 | Superscription |
| | 1.2-4 | Complaint |
| | 1.5-11 | God's answer |
| | 1.12-17 | Complaint |
| | 2.1-5 | God's answer |
| | 2.6-19 | Words of woe |
| 3 | | |
| | 3.2-19 | Theophany hymn |

## 12.39 Historical-Critical Analysis and Major Issues in the History of Critical Interpretation

Although Habakkuk first appears to have a heterogeneous literary background, its orderly flow has caused some to interpret it as a prophetic liturgy, presuming a uniform composition, whether this is traced back to a historical cultic prophet Habakkuk or the book as a whole is viewed as → *pseudepigraphy* from the Hellenistic period.

Others consider a gradual development likely because of the problematic nature of the different conceptual horizons within Hab. 1–2 (social grievances in Jerusalem, proclamation of judgement against Babylon) and also in Hab. 3 (world judgement).

# 12.40 Origins of the Book of Habakkuk

The superscription in the book of Habakkuk does not indicate when the prophet was active; Hab. 1.6 clearly places the prophet in a Babylonian context: 'For I am rousing the Chaldeans [i.e., the Babylonians].'

Despite all the controversies, one can say with some certainty that in its theology of history the existing form of the book comes from the Hellenistic period.[28] One indication to support this is the view of world judgement in Hab. 3 as well as Israel's task as the people of salvation in favour of a division between righteous and sinners in Hab. 2. The idea that the current form of the book of Habakkuk is based on earlier preliminary literary stages of development, as some interpreters assume, is just as uncertain as the thesis of original literary unity. In the second case, Habakkuk could be read as a whole as scribal tradent prophecy. But the book of Habakkuk's compositional history might have been similar to the closely-related Nahum: the themes of Jerusalem and Babylon in Hab. 1–2, which may trace back to a historical prophet Habakkuk, would have been universalized subsequently by Hab. 3 in this case.

# 12.41 Theology of the Book of Habakkuk

Like the book of Nahum, Habakkuk highlights God's power to act in history, a power to which even Israel's enemies must bow. The complaint-answer pattern in Hab. 1–2 represents a feature unique to the book of Habakkuk that has often been interpreted as evidence of a cultic background, but in any case reveals a dialogical structure of prophecy.

Within the prophetic framework the content of these texts is also unique. They focus intensely on the problem of → *theodicy*, the question of the justice of God, otherwise at home in → *wisdom* literature:

28. In contrast, L. Perlitt (*Propheten*, 43) claims the book was 'complete' in the 4th century.

> 'O Lord, how long shall I cry for help, and you will not listen? Or cry to you "Violence!" and you will not save?' (Hab. 1.2).

## 12.42 Notes on the History of Reception

In → *Qumran* (1QpHab[29]), a pesher (interpretative commentary) on the book of Habakkuk has been preserved which interprets the book verse-by-verse. According to 1QpHab, Habakkuk recorded his prophecies himself but God did not announce 'the consummation of time' (7.1-5), meaning Habakkuk himself did not know precisely to what time his prophecies referred. The time of their fulfilment is only known by the author of the pesher: the prophecies are being fulfilled in that moment in the presence of the Qumran community.

In the additions to Daniel (*Bel and the Dragon*), the → *Septuagint* includes the legend that Habakkuk brought food to Daniel (Ch. 21B.3); this story often appeared in early Christian art. In → *apocalyptic literature* the statement in Hab. 2.3-4 played an important role:

> 'For there is still a vision for the appointed time; it speaks of the end, and does not lie. If it seems to tarry, wait for it; it will surely come, it will not delay. Look at the proud! Their spirit is not right in them, but the righteous live by their faith.'

This served as evidence for the belief that eschatological revelation was delayed. Meanwhile, Paul used Hab. 2.4 to argue for justification by faith (Rom. 1.17; Gal. 3.11). This scriptural evidence gains even more potency if we consider that Hab. 2.3-4 was considered the centre of the book in the Jewish interpretative tradition.

# I The Book of Zephaniah

📖 Commentaries: H. Irsigler (HTKAT. Freiburg: Herder, 2002); L. Perlitt, *Die Propheten Nahum, Habakuk, Zephanja* (ATD 25/1. Göttingen: Vandenhoeck & Ruprecht, 2004); M. A. Sweeney (Hermeneia. Minneapolis: Fortress, 2003); J. Vlaardingerbroek (Historical Commentary on the Old Testament. Leuven: Peeters, 1999).

📖 K. Seybold, *Satirische Prophetie: Studien zum Buch Zephaniah*. SBS 120. Stuttgart: Katholisches Bibelwerk, 1985.

29. Text in F. García Martínez and E. J. C. Tigchelaar, *The Dead Sea Scrolls* I, 10–21.

# 12.43 Biblical Context

The book of Zephaniah is generally divided according to the 'three-part → *eschatological* pattern', which envisages a course of events involving disaster for his own people, followed by disaster for foreign nations and finally salvation for his own people: after oracles against Jerusalem (1.4-16, framed by statements about world judgement in 1.2-3, 17-18) there are oracles against Philistines, Moab, Ammon, Cush, Assyria and Nineveh (2.4-15); 3.9-20 contains words of salvation.

Interspersed throughout this structure, however, are many elements that do not quite fit. In 2.1-3 there is an admonition and call to embrace righteousness, while 2.11 offers a utopic vision for all peoples, whereas 3.1-8 again presents oracles of judgment against Jerusalem. Alternate ways of organizing the book are thus possible[30] which do not fit exclusively into a 'three-part eschatological pattern'. Rather, as in many other writings, book structures overlap as the book develops through various redactions. The superscription in 1.1 places the book immediately before the destruction of Judah and Jerusalem.

| | | |
|---|---|---|
| 1.1 | | Superscription |
| | 1.2-3 World judgement | |
| 1.4-16 | | Judgement against Judah and Jerusalem |
| | 1.17-18 World judgement | |
| | 2.1-3 Word of warning | |
| 2.4-15 | | Judgement against foreign nations (Philistia, Moab, Ammon, Cush, Assyria, Nineveh) |
| | 3.1-8 Judgement against Jerusalem | |
| 3.9-20 | | Salvation for Judah and Jerusalem |

# 12.44 Historical-Critical Analysis and Major Issues in the History of Critical Interpretation

The elementary observations made about the book's structure point to a diachronic and gradual development in the book of Zephaniah. Individual texts also underwent a gradual process of literary development. So, for example, the

30. Cf. E. Zenger, *Einleitung*, 566–9.

Jerusalem texts from Zeph. 1 (judgement) can hardly have originated at the same time as those in Zeph. 3 (salvation). Meanwhile, verses 3.10, 12-13 assume the → *diaspora* situation of Israel, and the texts about world judgement in 1.2-3, 17-18 as well as 2.2-3, 11; 3.8 already reveal a proto-apocalyptic character (→ *apocalyptic*).

## 12.45 Origins of the Book of Zephaniah

The core of the book is formed by the accusations against Jerusalem in Zeph. 1. Correspondingly, verse 1.1 claims the prophet Zephaniah was active in the time of Josiah (639–609 BCE), although it is highly probable the written version of his words already assumes the destruction of Judah and Jerusalem. The conspicuous framing of the words against Jerusalem through 1.2-3, 17-18 interprets them as part of a comprehensive world judgement. It belongs to a group of prophetic texts which reflect on the collapse of the Persian Empire during the reign of Alexander III of Macedonia (*Alexander the Great*). The oracles against the nations in 2.4-15 are hard to situate in a particular context, but could easily have originated in the vicinity of Zeph. 1. Their geographical scope (Philistia, Moab, Ammon, Cush, Assyria) is entirely plausible for Judah in the 7th cent. BCE, as those named refer either to Judah's immediate neighbours or major powers which ceased to exist in the 7th cent. BCE (Cush [i.e., Ethiopia], Assyria).

The context for the theology of the 'poor' in 2.1-3 and 3.12-13 is postexilic piety and society; the book of Amos underwent a comparable revision within the Book of the Twelve.[31] The perspective on restoration in 3.9-20 developed in the postexilic period. At the same time, Zeph. 3.9-10, with its vision of the nations turning to Yhwh (cf. 2.11), should be seen in the context of the formation of the Book of the Twelve as a whole.

## 12.46 Theology of the Book of Zephaniah

As in Joel (Ch. 12B), the motif of the 'day of Yhwh' permeates the book of Zephaniah. Seen in the context of the book as a whole, the 'day of Yhwh' means

31. Cf. C. Levin, 'Das Amosbuch der Anawim', *ZTK* 94 (1997): 407–36, although the late dating of the related texts probably goes too far.

a terrible judgement against the whole world, yet the book also presents a view of the salvation in which those nations who turn to Yhwh will be integrated (2.11; 3.9). Furthermore, the book of Zephaniah is one of the more important representatives of a theology of the 'poor' in the Old Testament. While one dimension of this social critique is the option for the poor, another crucial aspect is how the image of God changes dramatically in this theology: God's will for salvation is no longer seen in the long-lasting prosperity of the king, people and state – the traditional view during the reigns of the kings – but it is newly qualified as rescuing the poor.

## 12.47 Notes on the History of Reception

Fragments from the two commentaries in → *Qumran* (1QpZef[32] and 4QpZef[33]) that relate to the book of Zephaniah understand the book as an announcement of the end of the world. Zeph. appears to have been similarly interpreted in the New Testament as well; Mt. 13.41 makes use of Zeph. 1.3, and Rev. 6.17 recalls Zeph. 1.14 (cf. Zeph. 3.8, 13 and Rev. 14.5; 16.1). With its equation of the 'day of Yhwh' with the 'day of wrath', Zeph. 1.14-15 is also the biblical model for the sequence *dies irae dies illa* in the requiem in the Roman missal used from 1570 to 1962. This could even be considered the most famous reception of Zephaniah.[34] In medieval → *iconography* Zephaniah is often depicted with a lantern because of Zeph. 1.12-13 ('I will search Jerusalem with lamps...'). Evidence for an → *apocryphal* → *apocalypse* of Zephaniah exists in a quote from Clement of Alexandria (StromV 5:11, 77), in which he provides information about the fate of the dead in heaven and hell.

# J The Book of Haggai

Commentaries: C. and E. Meyers, *Haggai, Zechariah 1–8* (AB 25B, New York: Doubleday, 1987); W. Rudolph, *Haggai, Sacharja 1–8, Sacharja 9–14, Maleachi* (KAT 12/4, Gütersloh: Gütersloher Verlagshaus, 1976); H. W. Wolff (Hermeneia. Transl. by M. Kohl. Minneapolis: Augsburg Fortress, 1988).

32. Text in F. García Martínez and E. J. C. Tigchelaar, *The Dead Sea Scrolls* I, 20–3.
33. Text in F. García Martínez and E. J. C. Tigchelaar, *The Dead Sea Scrolls* I, 340–1.
34. Cf. for more H. Irsigler, *Zephanja*, 32 with footnote 1.

J. Kessler, *The Book of Haggai: Prophecy and Society in Early Persian Yehud*. VTSup 91. Leiden: Brill, 2002.

## 12.48 Biblical Context

In its current form, the book of Haggai is embedded in a narrative framework,[35] so that, strictly speaking, it is a prophetic narrative, even though non-narrative material (e.g., sayings) predominates. The narrative framework has been harmonized with Zech. 1–8 (esp. Zech. 7–8), which has led to the consensus that Haggai + Zech. 1–8 once constituted a single coherent text, either because Haggai + Zech. 1–8 were edited at the same time or Zech. 1–8 was secondarily adapted to fit Haggai through Zech. 7–8. The latter is even more likely given the conspicuous cluster of references to Zech. 7–8 and Haggai's thematic originality. The apparent purpose of combining these texts is to facilitate understanding of Zech. 1–8 as a continuation of Haggai's prophecy: Haggai describes earthly changes such as the heavens and earth are shaken (2.6), while Zech. 1–8 provides a view of heaven: 'Zechariah sees the turning point announced in Hag. 2.21-23 in the seven night visions which constitute a single process set in motion as part of a heavenly strategy. The riders set out from heaven in order to inspect the situation on earth (Zech. 1.7-15). This is also the place from which the chariots are deployed in all four directions (6.1-8), in order to bring to fruition the events witnessed in the vision cycle.'[36]

The narrative passages divide the book into four sections: 1.1-15a; 1.15b–2.9; 2.10-19; 2.20-23. They also provide a unified form by including the precise dates when God spoke to Haggai (all dates occur in the second year of the Persian King Darius, i.e., 520 BCE).

The narrative starts with the people's resistance to rebuilding the temple: the Judeans who had stayed in the land resisted rebuilding the temple, as that would have meant independently bringing to an end the time of judgement that God had imposed (1.4). The exiles returning home, on the other hand, were focused on rebuilding their own homes first (1.9-11). Haggai conveys God's word in this situation, providing reassurance with a comprehensive view of salvation to be ushered in with the new Temple (1.15b–2.9). After

35. Hag. 1.1-3, 12-15; 2.1-2, 20-21.

36. R. Lux, 'Das Zweiprophetenbuch: Beobachtungen zu Aufbau und Struktur von Haggai und Sacharja 1–8', in *'Wort JHWH, das geschah...' (Hos 1:1): Studien zum Zwölfprophetenbuch* (Herders Biblische Studien 35; ed. E. Zenger; Freiburg: Herder, 2002), 191–217, 198.

that, the successful laying of the temple's foundation is interpreted as the dawn of a new era (2.10-19) accompanied by cosmic tremors (2.6-7). At the end, there is a → *messianic* promise to Zerubbabel (a descendant of King Jeconiah (Jehoiachin) according to 1 Chr. 3.17-19), the political official responsible for rebuilding the temple. This promise revokes Jeremiah's prophecy in Jer. 22.24-26 that the Davidic dynasty would be broken:

| | |
|---|---|
| Hag. 2.21-23: 'Speak to Zerubbabel, governor of Judah, saying, I am about to shake the heavens and the earth, and to overthrow the throne of kingdoms; I am about to destroy the strength of the kingdoms of the nations, and overthrow the chariots and their riders; and the horses and their riders shall fall, every one by the sword of a comrade. On that day, says Yhwh of hosts, I will take you, O Zerubbabel my servant, son of Shealtiel, says Yhwh, and make you like *a signet ring*; for I have chosen you, says Yhwh of hosts.' | Jer. 22.24-26: 'As I live, says Yhwh, even if King Coniah [Jehoiachin] son of Jehoiakim of Judah were *the signet ring* on my right hand, even from there I would tear you off and give you into the hands of those who seek your life, into the hands of those of whom you are afraid, even into the hands of King Nebuchadrezzar of Babylon and into the hands of the Chaldeans. I will hurl you and the mother who bore you into another country, where you were not born, and there you shall die.' |

## 12.49 Historical-Critical Analysis and Major Issues in the History of Critical Interpretation

The most important distinctive feature of the book's literary development is the distinction between the sayings and the narrative framework. Most scholars conclude that the narrative scaffolding cannot be traced back to the author of the sayings, as the narrative passages express a particular interest in the returning 'remnant' of Israel as well as the figure of Zerubbabel. In addition, the narrative framework can hardly be explained without considering the Zechariah tradition, which is comparable in this respect.

## 12.50 Origins of the Book of Haggai

The focus of the book of Haggai – initial resistance to rebuilding the temple, then laying the cornerstone of the temple – suggests the original text was created before the Second Temple was dedicated in 515 BCE. The figure of Haggai is also mentioned in Ezra 5.1 and 6.14, providing evidence of his historicity. Given the frequent and explicit naming of Haggai as a 'prophet' (1.1, 3, 12; 2.1, 10) and his vehement endorsement of the rebuilding of the temple, it has been assumed he was a cultic prophet, but this can neither be proved nor disproved. Some scholars have presumed the narrative framework was written by a 'Haggai chronicler' who would also have been active before 515 BCE, but this is unlikely.

The narrative, historicizing depiction of events that seeks to provide concrete dates, suggests instead that a certain interval of time has passed from the actual events. Another indication the narrative framework was added later is its tendency to give preferential treatment to the returning exiles over those living in the land. Prophetic legitimation in Haggai already presumes that the conflict between these groups is more advanced.

## 12.51 Theology of the Book of Haggai

Front and centre in the book of Haggai is the rebuilding of the temple destroyed by the Babylonians and the delayed beginning of construction in the early Persian period. The temple is not merely a place of worship, but above all the place where God is present in the world, so it is indispensable for the future well-being of Judah that the temple is rebuilt before any other private construction projects go forward. Conversely, as long as the temple lies in ruins the present will remain under the sign of judgement:

> Hag. 1.10: 'Therefore the heavens above you have withheld the dew, and the earth has withheld its produce.'

So Haggai reverses the arguments used by those opposing the temple's reconstruction: the economically difficult situation cannot be used as a justification for further postponing the rebuilding, but rather the completed temple will make economic prosperity possible. Once the temple has been rebuilt, then the peoples will acknowledge the sovereignty of Yhwh, and a Davidic ruler, Zerubbabel, will turn around the political situation. Haggai's prophecy gives voice to a view of restoration that was never realized in actuality, but remained alive in the unfolding of Israel's theological history.

## 12.52 Notes on the History of Reception

Ezra 5–6 documents the earliest *Wirkungsgeschichte* for the Haggai tradition: Haggai is specifically named along with Zechariah as promoting the rebuilding of the temple. Understandably, the major → *messianic* promise to Zerubbabel in 2.20-23 did not resonate with later generations because it was not fulfilled. This makes its long-term transmission within the book of Haggai even more noteworthy, as this shows that, even in antiquity, a prophecy's theological worth in the Old Testament did not rest entirely on its historical fulfilment.

# K The Book of Zechariah

📖 Commentaries: R. Hanhart (Zech. 1–8. BKAT 14/7.1. Neukirchen-Vluyn: Neukirchener, 1998); C. and E. Meyers, *Haggai, Zechariah 1–8* (AB 25B. New York: Doubleday, 1987); C. and E. Meyers (Zech. 9–14. AB 25C. New York: Doubleday, 1993); D. L. Petersen, *Zechariah 9-14 and Malachi: A Commentary* (OTL. London: SCM Press, 1995).

📖 H. Delkurt, *Sacharjas Nachtgesichte: Zur Aufnahme und Abwandlung prophetischer Traditionen*. BZAW 302. Berlin/New York: de Gruyter, 2000.

## 12.53 Biblical Context

As with the book of Haggai, Zechariah dates to the period when the temple was rebuilt under Darius (1.1, 7; 7.1). Three sections (1–8; 9–11; 12–14) are clearly separated from one another with partial book headings, among which 9.1 and 12.1 have the same form (*maśśā*ʾ 'declaration'), lending chapters 9–14 relative unity.

With its editorial heading system (1.1; 1.7; 7.1) and further correspondences, particularly in Zech. 7–8,[37] the first section (1–8) adheres closely to the book of Haggai. Scholars rightly assume that Haggai + Zech. 1–8 were edited to agree with one another. The references to Haggai in Zech. 7–8 as well as 1.1-6[38] speak for themselves in this respect.

Zechariah 1–8 essentially contains the so-called 'night visions of Zechariah', which sketch out a consistent vision for a Jerusalem with a

37. Cf. the configuration in C. and E. Meyers, *Haggai, Zechariah 1–8*, xlix.

38. ibid., liv.

reformed cult, existing within a community of nations that is once again peaceful. The current textual order presents eight visions, although the original cycle involved only seven (without Zech. 3) and had the following structure:

| I | II | III | IV(B) | V | VI | VII |
|---|---|---|---|---|---|---|
| 1.8-13, 14-15 | 2.1-4 (NRSV 1.18-21) | 2.5-9 (NRSV 2.1-5) | 4.1-6a, 10b-14 | 5.1-4 | 5.5-11 | 6.1-8 |
| Horses and Rider | Horns and Smiths | Man with the measuring line | Lampstand and olive trees | Flying Scroll | Woman in a basket (*Ephah*) | Chariot and horses |
| Patrolling the entire world | Disempowerment of the world | Jerusalem as a city without walls | Presence of Yhwh | Purge of the land | Elimination of idolatry | Sending out into the world |
| | | IV(A) 3.1-10 | | | | |
| | | Joshua before the heavenly court | | | | |

The seven original visions (I–VII) are arranged concentrically: Visions I and VII correspond in mentioning the horses, while II and VI are two-part visions (II: Horns, Smiths/VI: Woman, Deportation) and both involve the theme of foreigners; III and V correspond in terms of content in that III conceives of Jerusalem as a safe city without walls and V announces that the land will be purged of thieves and perjurors. Vision IV (B) describing the lampstand constitutes the middle, which was subsequently duplicated with IV(A).

## 12.54 Historical-Critical Analysis and Major Issues in the History of Critical Interpretation

The book of Zechariah with its three sections (1–8; 9–11; 12–14) clearly expanded through editorial activity over time. As early as the 18th century, observers recognized Zech. 9–14 could not have been written by the same author as Zech. 1–8. Chapters 9–11 are linguistically distinct from the poetic form of chs. 1–8, while 12–14 largely returns to prose. Above all, starting with Zech. 9, the text reflects a quite different situation from the rebuilding of the Second Temple in the first section: the temple has long since been rebuilt (11.13; 14.20-21); 9.1-8 apparently reflects the military campaign of Alexander III of Macedonia (*Alexander the Great*) from the fall of Tyre all the way to Gaza in the year 332 BCE, and 9.13 even explicitly names the sons of the 'Ionians' in Hebrew, meaning the Greeks. Within Zech. 9–14 there is evidence of multiple stages in the text's development, visible above all in shifting expectations about the end-time: thus Zech. 9–10 expects the restoration of all Israel, but this hope is apparently abandoned again in Zech. 11, while Zech. 12 and 14 present different views of the judgement of the nations. Zechariah 14 outlines an equally self-contained though far-reaching view of the end-times, extending all the way to a vision of the transformation of the cosmos itself.

Even the texts in Zech. 1–8 underwent a process of literary expansion: The visions in Zech 1–6, which make up the majority of that section, have been augmented in the current version of the book with the vision in 3.1-5, whose marked differences set it apart from the other visions (the interpreting angel is lacking, and the interpretative commentary is directed to Joshua and not the prophet). Furthermore, a number of commentaries and explanations (epexegesis) appear in 1.16-17; 2.10-17 (NRSV 2.6-13); 3.6-10; 4.6b-10a; 6.9-15, which interpret the visions. Chapters 7–8 likewise appear to be set apart from Zech. 1–6.

## 12.55 Origins of the Book of Zechariah

Similar to the traditional interpretation of Isaiah, scholars identified three prophetic individuals responsible for different sections of the book of Zechariah (1–8; 9–11; 12–14), of which only the first was named ('Zechariah'), while the authors of 9-11 and 12–14 were named 'Deutero-Zechariah' and 'Trito-Zechariah', respectively, as with the book of Isaiah. More recently, however, researchers have recognized that chapters 9–14 do not derive from an originally oral proclamation by an autonomous prophet but are examples of scribal tradent prophecy that has grown over time.

As with Haggai, the original version of the visions of Zechariah in Zech. *1–6 likely originated before the dedication of the temple in 515 BCE, although it remains difficult to determine exactly when the corresponding commentaries were added, as they essentially explicate the content of the visions. The passages 3.6-10 and 6.9-15, in which the high priest Joshua is accorded a central leadership function, clearly assume the historical disappearance of Zerubbabel from the political arena. While Zech. 4.6-10a still implies Zerubbabel is active, it appears to reflect on a crisis connected with Zerubbabel's mission.

Zechariah 7–8 provides a textual transition that binds the visions together with Haggai while at the same time connecting back to the → *Deuteronomistic* sermon calling for repentance in Zech. 1.1-6 (cf. 7.7, 8-15), which – as in Isa. 56–66 – was apparently a response to the delayed appearance of the promised salvation. The texts in Zech. 9–14, which know and use Zech. 1–8 and Malachi, can be dated to the later Hellenistic period based on contemporary allusions (see above Ch. 12.54), but they are not later than the conclusion of the prophetic → *canon* around the turn of the 3rd century BCE.

## 12.56 Theology of the Book of Zechariah

Although the central concern of the visions of Zechariah in their current form (as for the book of Haggai) is the reconstruction of the temple, they appear – as their thematic bias reveals – to have originally formulated a larger → *eschatological* view of salvation related to Jerusalem. Jerusalem is seen as the place where Yhwh is present in a world at peace once again. The focus on the rebuilding of the temple and its interpretation as an eschatological turning point towards salvation results especially from the secondary commentaries in Zech. 1–8 (esp. 7–8), in conjunction with the book of Haggai which has the same theological bent.

One noteworthy aspect of the visions is that, in contrast to the condemnations in Deut. 13 and in Jer. 23.25-40, they show that dreams could once again be considered a legitimate means of revelation (cf. also Gen. 37–50; Dan. 2). In keeping with developments in the theology of history, the visionary is neither looking at something he can understand directly nor is he gazing at God's own self (cf. Isa. 6; Jer. 1; Ezek. 1–3). Rather, the prophet requires an interpretative angel *(angelus interpres)* who must reveal and explain the meaning of what is seen.

Particularly interesting for the history of religion is the vision of the woman being carried away to Babylon in a basket (Ephah) (5.5-11), a transparent reference to the abolition of goddess worship in Judah.[39] Such veneration definitely had had a place in the cult of pre-exilic Israel and Judah. So Zech. 5 provides prophetic legitimation of cultic worship focused solely on the one God Yhwh from now on.

## 12.57 Notes on the History of Reception

Some scholars have occasionally placed the beginnings of → *apocalyptic literature*[40] in the book of Zechariah. Of course, one can identify and describe similar strands in how revelations are received in prophetic and apocalyptic traditions, yet Proto-Zechariah is still far removed thematically and theologically from the apocalyptic genre. Rather, illustrative material for the historical beginnings of apocalyptic literature exist in the Enoch discoveries from → *Qumran*, which demonstrate apocalyptic literature's background in priestly special knowledge.[41]

In the New Testament, the concept of a → *messiah* in the form of a servant was adopted, along with the idea that the saviour-king would ride on a donkey (Zech. 9.9) as seen in Mt. 21.4-5 and John 12.14-15. The artistic reception of Zechariah in particular adopted the images from the visions, the origins of which could often be linked with the motifs in religious art from the early Persian period.

# L The book of Malachi

📖 Commentaries: D. L. Petersen, *Zechariah 9-14 and Malachi: A Commentary* (OTL. London: SCM Press, 1995).

📖 O. H. Steck, *Der Abschluß der Prophetie im Alten Testament: Ein Versuch*

39. C. Uehlinger, 'Die Frau im Efa (Sach 5:5–11): Eine Programmvision von der Abschiebung der Göttin', *BK* 49 (1994): 93–103; a critical view is expressed by C. Körting, 'Sach 5:5–11 – Die Unrechtmäßigkeit wird an ihren Ort verwiesen', *Bib* 87 (2006): 477–92.
40. H. Gese, 'Anfang und Ende der Apokalyptik, dargestellt am Sacharjabuch', *ZTK* 70 (1973): 20–49. The same article can be found in idem, *Vom Sinai zum Zion: Alttestamentliche Beiträge zur biblischen Theologie* (BEvT 64; Munich: Kaiser, 1974), 202–30.
41. H. Stegemann, 'Die Bedeutung der Qumranfunde für die Erforschung der Apokalyptik', in *Apocalypticism in the Mediterranean World and the Near East* (2nd ed.; ed. D. Hellholm; Tübingen: Mohr Siebeck, 1983), 495–530.

*zur Frage der Vorgeschichte des Kanons*. Biblisch-theologische Studien 17. Neukirchen-Vluyn: Neukirchener 1991.

# 12.58 Biblical Context

According to the superscription in 1.1, the book of Malachi contains six disputations (1.2-5; 1.6–2.9; 2.10-16; 2.17 3.5; 3.6-12; 3.13-21 [NRSV 3.13–4.3]) which present accusations with reference to the addressee's objections. The book concludes with an epilogue (3.22-24 [NRSV 4.4-6]) which results in an inclusio reaching all the way back to the beginning of the canonical (→ *canon*) section of the 'prophets' (Josh. 1.7, 13).

Mal. 4.4: '*Remember the teaching of my servant Moses*, the statutes and ordinances that I *commanded* him at Horeb for all Israel.'

Josh. 1.7-8, 13: 'Only be strong and very courageous, being careful to act in accordance with all the law that my *servant Moses* commanded you; do not turn from it to the right hand or to the left, so that you may be successful wherever you go. This book of the *Torah* shall not depart out of your mouth; you shall meditate on it day and night, so that you may be careful to act in accordance with all that is written in it. For then you shall make your way prosperous, and then you shall be successful...'*Remember* the word that *Moses the servant of Yhwh commanded you*, saying, 'Yhwh your God is providing you a place of rest, and will give you this land."

# 12.59 Historical-Critical Analysis and Major Issues in the History of Critical Interpretation

Traditionally, the book of Malachi has been traced back to a prophet active in the 5th or 4th century BCE whose interest in sacrifice and the imparting of the Torah suggested a priestly background. More recent research in contrast has emphasized the text's close relationships to the book of Zechariah[42] as well as to other texts in the Old Testament. Scholars are now more likely to

42. See especially the headings in Zech. 9.1; 12.1 which have the same structure as Mal. 1.1, as well as the quote from Zech. 1.3 in Mal. 3.7.

believe Malachi as a whole represents late, scribal tradent prophecy. This is also suggested by the name Malachi ('my messenger', meaning a messenger of Yhwh, cf. → *LXX* on Mal. 1.1), likely a pen name as it is not otherwise attested in either the Bible or other inscriptions. In Palmyra the name 'Malachbel' ('Messenger of Bel'), which is the name of a god, is attested, suggesting from another perspective that Malachi is not a common name for a person.

## 12.60 Origins of the Book of Malachi

Although some still hold the view that there was a prophetic individual named Malachi, it seems far more likely that the book of Malachi as a whole is an example of scribal prophecy. The original text of the book (1.12–2.9; 3.6-12) appears to have been written as a continuation and development of Zech. 1–8 and may even have circulated under the name 'Zechariah'. With the gradual growth of the book of Zechariah around Zech. 9–14, the book of Malachi moved further away from Zech. 1–8. In the final phases of its development (2.17–3.5; 3.13-21 [NRSV 3.13–4.3], then 1.1; 2.10-12; 3.22-24 [NRSV 4.4-6]) it was separated from the Zechariah tradition and became its own book. What may also have played a role is the desire to have no fewer than twelve Minor Prophets – probably so that the number of prophets would match the number of patriarchs in Genesis: Abraham, Isaac and Jacob plus the twelve sons of Jacob correspond to the three Major Prophets (Isaiah, Jeremiah, Ezekiel) and the twelve Minor Prophets (Hosea–Malachi).

Particularly important is the concluding passage in 3.22-24 (NRSV 4.4-6), which establishes an inclusio with Josh. 1.7, 13, thus concluding the entire canonical section of the 'prophets' (see above Ch. 12.58). Scholars have long recognized that this reference is a literary technique, associated with the formation of this canonical section. So we are dealing with a text which provides a survey of no less than the entire 'big picture' of Joshua–Malachi.

## 12.61 Theology of the Book of Malachi

The theology of the book of Malachi is comparable to that of Trito-Isaianic texts (II Isa. 56-66;→ *Trito-Isaiah*), a text originating at approximately the same time: it belongs to those voices in the postexilic period which raised sharp accusations and saw social and cultic grievances as the crucial reason why the salvation of God could not fully break in. As with the 'Trito-Isaiah' texts in Isa. 56–66, the book of Malachi also abandons the unity of Israel as an entity with a salvific promise and sets up a distinction within Israel between sinners and righteous.

## 12.62 Notes on the History of Reception

The reception history of the book of Malachi is especially significant because of its promise that Elijah would return:

> Mal. 3.23-24 (NRSV 4.5-6): 'Lo, I will send you the prophet Elijah before the great and terrible day of Yhwh comes. He will turn the hearts of parents to their children and the hearts of children to their parents, so that I will not come and strike the land with a curse.'

In the New Testament the appearance of John the Baptist is associated with Elijah's return (Mt. 17.1-13; Lk. 1.17; Mk 9.11-13), while rabbinic Judaism anticipated the appearance of Elijah in the end-times as the one who would gather together the tribes of Israel and, as an intermediary, would be able to turn away the wrath of God.

# Part V
# The Literature of the Old Testament: Writings (*Ketuvim*)

In Jewish tradition, the books treated in Chs 13–23 constitute the third section of the Hebrew Bible following the 'Torah' and the 'Prophets'. They appear under the heading 'Writings' (Hebrew *kĕtûbîm*, Greek *[hagiai] graphai/Hagiographa/ [Holy] Scriptures*) at least since the Greek translation of the book of Ben Sirach (after 132 BCE; Ch. 27). The *order of the Writings* varies in the Jewish editions of the Bible (Ch. 1.2.1.3). Thus, for example, 1–2 Chronicles open the Ketuvim in the tradition of Palestinian Judaism and, therefore, precede Psalms. The concept of David as the founder of temple worship and liturgical prayer, with the Psalms understood as its material concretion, stands in the background of this placement of Chronicles. According to the tradition of Babylonian Judaism, 1–2 Chronicles follow Ezra-Nehemiah, thereby concluding the Ketuvim and the → *canon*. With the edict of the Persian King Cyrus (→ *Edict of Cyrus*), this placement culminates in a pilgrimage to the temple in Jerusalem. Other important variations in the arrangement of the text in the various Jewish editions of the Bible involve the position of the book of Job and the five festival scrolls (*Megilloth*).

In essence, two principles are involved in the *arrangement of the Megilloth*:[1]

(1) The *liturgical principle* involves the dates of the festivals (Ch. 3.3 excursus 'Festivals') to which the individual festival scrolls are assigned. In this regard, the beginning of the year occurs in the spring (Exod. 12.2) in accordance with the Babylonian calendar that was foundational in Israel since the exilic period (→ *exile*). This principle produced the arrangement Song of Songs, Ruth, Lamentations, Ruth, Ecclesiastes, and Esther.

(2) The *chronological principle* involves the fictive period of the action (= 'narrated time') or the period of composition (= 'time of the narrator')

1. P. Brandt, *Endgestalten des Kanons: Das Arrangement der Schriften Israels in der jüdischen und christlichen Bibel* (BBB 131; Berlin: Philo, 2001), 164–71.

indicated in the superscription to the book or proposed in medieval Jewish tradition. Accordingly, one finds the sequence Ruth, Song of Songs, Ecclesiastes, Lamentations and Esther:

(a) Ruth, because, according to 1.1, events transpired in the period of the judges (Ch. 7.6.3.3), according to 4.13-22, the heroine belonged in David's genealogy, and Samuel was considered the author;
(b) the Song of Songs because the young King Solomon appears as the author in 1.1;
(c) Ecclesiastes because, according to 1.1, the aged Solomon was considered the author;
(d) Lamentations, because it reflects the situation after the destruction of Jerusalem in 587/6 BCE and, according to Jewish tradition, Jeremiah was its author;
(e) Esther, because, according to 1.1, events transpired under the Persian King Xerxes (485–465 BCE).

In this textbook, the Writings will be presented in the sequence offered in the modern standard edition of the Hebrew Bible, the *Biblia Hebraica Stuttgartensia*:[2] Psalms, Job, Proverbs, Ruth, Song of Songs, Lamentations, Esther, Daniel, Ezra-Nehemiah and 1–2 Chronicles.

*Christian editions of the Bible*, which follow the ordering principle of the ancient Greek translation, the → *Septuagint* (LXX), disperse the Ketuvim across the three sections of the canon (historical, poetic and prophetic books). Thus, the books of Ruth, Chronicles, Ezra, Nehemiah and Esther appear among the historical books. Job, Psalms and the three books attributed to Solomon (Proverbs, Ecclesiastes and Song of Songs) constitute the complex of didactic books. Lamentations, as an appendix to the book of Jeremiah, and Daniel appear among the prophetic books.

In terms of *literary history*, the Ketuvim offer such a multiplicity of forms that they give the impression of a collection of exemplary ancient Israelite and Jewish literature. Thus, the books of Chronicles, Ezra and Nehemiah can be treated as a form of historiography, the book of Ruth as a short story, the

2. BHS, 5th ed., 1997. The position of 1–2 Chronicles at the end of the Ketuvim is only attributable to the modern editors of *BHS*, however, who here altered the sequence of Codex Leningradensis upon which the edition is based.

book of Esther as a novel, the book of Job, with some restrictions, as a kind of tragedy, the book of Ecclesiastes as a philosophical tractate, Song of Songs as an → *anthology* of love poems, Lamentations as a collection of elegies (songs of mourning), and Psalms as a collection of varied religious poems and prayers.

In terms of their *origins*, the majority of the Writings stem from the Persian-Hellenistic period. The Psalter (Ch. 13), which contains both a few prayers that belong, at least in their original state, as early as the monarchy, and compositions that originated or assumed their current form as late as the Hasmonean period, and parts of the book of Proverbs (Ch. 15) constitute exceptions.

A unifying *characteristic of the content* of the Writings is their establishment of religious identity and personal integrity that must be preserved through confidence in God's just administration in view of a world that often appears threatening. In this regard, both in their narrative portions and in their poetical sections, the Writings offer models for understanding and sustaining collective and individual lives.

# 13

# The Psalter

(Markus Witte – Translation by Mark Biddle)

## Chapter Outline




Commentaries: C. C. Broyles (NICOT. Peabody, Mass.: Hendrickson, 1999); W. Brueggemann, *The Message of the Psalms: A Theological Commentary*. Minneapolis: Augsburg, 1984; R. J. Clifford (2 vols. AOTC. Nashville, Tenn.: Abingdon, 2002, 2003); J. Day (OTG, Sheffield: JSOT, 1990); E. S. Gerstenberger (FOTL 14-15. Grand Rapids, Mich.: Eerdmans, 1988, 2001); F.-L. Hossfeld and E. Zenger (NEchtB 29 and 40. Würzburg: Echter, 1993, 2002); F.-L. Hossfeld and E. Zenger (Ps. 51–100. HTKAT. 2nd ed. Freiburg: Herder, 2000); F.-L. Hossfeld and E. Zenger (Ps. 100–150. HTKAT. 2nd ed. Freiburg: Herder, 2008).

Bibliography 10.1 Concepts of Old Testament Theology (B. Janowski, *Konfliktgespräche*). Further: O. Keel, *Die Welt der altorientalischen Bildsymbolik und das Alte Testament: Am Beispiel der Psalmen*. 5th ed. Neukirchen-Vluyn: Neukirchener, 1996; O. Loretz, *Psalmenstudien: Kolometrie, Strophik und Theologie ausgewählter Psalmen*. BZAW 309. Berlin/New York: de Gruyter, 2002; H. Spieckermann, *Heilsgegenwart: Eine Theologie der Psalmen*. FRLANT 148. Göttingen: Vandenhoeck & Ruprecht, 1989). German Classic: H. Gunkel and J. Begrich, *An Introduction to the Psalms: The Genres of the Religious Lyric of Israel*. Transl. by J. D. Nogalski. Macon, Ga.: Mercer University Press, 1998 (first German ed. Göttingen: Vandenhoeck & Ruprecht, 1933).

The designation *Psalms* traces back to the Greek term *psalmos* ('song accompanied by stringed instruments'), the Septuagint's rendering of the Hebrew psalm superscription *mizmôr* ('song'). The title *Psalter* is based on the Greek term *psalterion* ('stringed instrument' then 'song collection'). In Judaism, the term *sefer tĕhillîm* ('book of praises') and the abbreviation *tillîm* ('praises') are common. The Jewish philosopher *Philo of Alexandria* (b. circa 25 BCE) and the Jewish historiographer *Flavius Josephus* (approx. 37–100 CE) employed the Greek designation *hymnoi*. The term *biblos psalmōn* ('book of Psalms', Lk. 20.42; Acts 1.20) occurs in the NT (to designate an earlier form of the Psalter).

# 13.1 Biblical Context

## 13.1.1 Structure

A late redaction, perhaps following the 'Five Book of Moses', sub-divided the Psalter into five books (of various lengths). A concluding → *doxology* praising Yhwh, the God of Israel,[1] serves as a structuring characteristic. The hallelujah Psalm 150 constitutes the conclusion of the fifth book and of the whole Psalter. The secondary assignment of certain psalms to fictive characters or groups of authors or to liturgical occasions constitutes a second structural characteristic.

| **Book 1: Pss 1–41** | 1st Prologue: | The Torah | Ps. 1 | |
|---|---|---|---|---|
| | 2nd Prologue: | The Messiah | Ps. 2 | |
| | | Psalms of David | Pss 3–41 | |
| **Book 2: Pss 42–72** | | *Psalms of Korah* | *Pss 42–49* | |
| | | *Psalm of Asaph* | *Ps. 50* | |
| | | *Psalms of David* | *Pss 51–65* | |
| | | | *and 67–71* | *The So-Called Elohistic Psalter* |
| | | *Psalms of Solomon* | *Ps. 72* | |
| **Book 3: Pss 73–89** | | *Psalms of Asaph* | *Pss 73–83* | |
| | | Psalms of Korah | Pss 87–88 | |
| | | Psalm of Ethan | Ps. 89 | |

1. Cf. Pss 41.14 (NRSV 41.13); 72.18-19; 89.53 (NRSV 89.52); 106.48.

| | | | |
|---|---|---|---|
| **Book 4: Pss 90–106** | | Psalm of Moses | Ps. 90 |
| | | Sabbath Psalm | Ps. 92 |
| | | Todah Psalm | Ps. 100 |
| | | Psalms of David | Pss 101; 103 |
| **Book 5: Pss 107–150** | | Psalms of David | Pss 108–110 |
| | | Pilgrimage Psalms | Pss 120–134 |
| | | Psalms of David | Pss 138–145 |
| | 1st Epilogue: | The Messianic People | Ps. 149 |
| | 2nd Epilogue: | Praise of God | Ps. 150 |

| **Thematic Groups** | |
|---|---|
| Psalms of Complaint And Petition | Pss 3–6; 9–14; 22; 25–28 |
| Psalms of Thanksgiving and Praise | Pss 135–136; 138; 144–150 |
| 'Yhwh is King' Psalms | Pss 93–99 |

| **Topical Groups** | | |
|---|---|---|
| Early Church Penitential Psalms | | Pss 6; 32; 38; 51; 102; 130; 143 |
| Exilic Psalms | | Pss 44; 74; 79; 126; 137 |
| Historical Psalms | | Pss 77; 78; 105; 106; 114 |
| 'Yhwh is King' Psalms | | Pss 29; 47; 93–99 |
| Royal Psalms | | Pss 2; 18; 20; 21; 45; 68; 72; 89; 101; 110; 132; 144 |
| Vengeance Psalms | | Pss 69; 109; 137 |
| Creation Psalms | | Pss 8; 29; 104 |
| Torah Psalms | | Pss 1; 19; 119 |
| Wisdom Psalms | | Pss 37; 49; 73 |
| Zion Psalms | | Pss 46; 48; 76; 84; 87 |
| Hallel(ujah) Psalms: | | |
| | Egyptian Hallel | Pss 113–118 |
| | Great Hallel | Pss 135–136 |
| | Minor Hallel | Pss 146–150 |

## 13.1.2 The Enumeration of the 150 Psalms Differs in the Hebrew Bible and in the → *Septuagint*

The Septuagint combines Psalms 9–10 and 114–115 together into single psalms while it divides Psalms 116 and 147 into two. Moreover, the Septuagint, with (the → *deuterocanonical*) Psalm 151 (cf. Ch. 30 regarding Pr Man), has one more psalm than the Hebrew Bible.

| HB | LXX | HB | LXX | HB | LXX |
|---|---|---|---|---|---|
| 1–8 | 1–8 | 114/115 | 113 | 117–146 | 116–145 |
| 9/10 | 9 | 116.1–9 | 114 | 147.1–11 | 146 |
| 11–113 | 10–112 | 116.10–19 | 115 | 147.12–20 | 147 |
| | | | | 148–150 | 148–150 |
| | | | | | 151 |

## 13.1.3 Redactional Structures Extending Across the Psalter

In its final form, the Psalter manifests a *dual framework*. The external framework consists of Psalms 1 and 150: The study of the Torah (Ps. 1) flows into universal praise (Ps. 150). According to this framework, the Psalter serves as instruction in the praise of God (*doxology*). The internal framework consists of Psalms 2 and 149: The expectation of the → *messiah* (Ps. 2) corresponds to the world-wide recognition of the Messiah and the messianic people (Ps. 149). This dual framework conforms with the notion that the advent of the era of salvation is tied to Torah obedience.

The further structure of the Psalter becomes evident in the observation that there are *semantic, compositional and form-critical relationships* between neighbouring Psalms. Thus, two techniques, in particular, set individual psalms in the context of a more comprehensive relationship:[2] (1) *iuxtapositio*, i.e. intentional arrangement according to topical and thematic elements, and (2) *concatenatio*, i.e. linkage by keywords and motifs. The two techniques can also be employed in conjunction. Examples occur in the psalm groupings 3–14 or 22–26 and elsewhere.

2. Cf. already Fz. Delitzsch, *Biblical Commentary on the Psalms* (from the latest ed. specially rev. transl. by D. Eaton and J. E. Duguid; New York: Funk and Wagnalls, 1883) and, more recently, especially the work of F.-L. Hossfeld and E. Zenger.

| | | |
|---|---|---|
| **1) Pss 3–14: *'Alternation between Lament and Petition'*** | | |
| I | Lament and Petition | (Pss 3–7) |
| II | Praise of God (Hymn) | (Ps. 8) |
| III | Lament and Petition | (Pss 9–14) |

| | | | | |
|---|---|---|---|---|
| **2) Pss 3–7: *'Paradigmatic Situations of Suffering'*** | | | | |
| I | Enemies | (Ps. 3) | 'Morning' | (Ps. 3.6 [NRSV 3.5]) |
| II | Social Distress | (Ps. 4) | 'Evening' | (Ps. 4.9 [NRSV 4.8]) |
| III | Legal Distress | (Ps. 5) | 'Morning' | (Ps. 5.4 [NRSV 5.3]) |
| IV | Sickness | (Ps. 6) | 'Day' | (Ps. 6.7 [NRSV 6.6]) |
| V | Enemies | (Ps. 7) | 'Night' | (Ps. 7.12 [NRSV 7.11]) |

| | | | | | |
|---|---|---|---|---|---|
| **3) Pss 22–26: *'The Nearness of God'*** | | | | | |
| I | Lament | (Ps. 22) | Ps. 22.2 (NRSV 22.1) | → | Ps. 26.11 |
| II | Confidence | (Ps. 23) | Ps. 23.5 | par. | Ps. 22.27 (NRSV 22.26) |
| III | Temple | (Ps. 24) | Ps. 24.3-5 | par. | Ps. 23.6 |
| IV | Innocence | (Ps. 25) | Ps. 25.21 | par. | Ps. 24.4-5 |
| V | Vow of praise | (Ps. 26) | Ps. 26.12 | par. | Ps. 22.23 (NRSV 22.22) |

Occasionally, two psalms closely related in content and form are coupled and interpret one another.[3] Certain psalms fulfil a comprehensive function in the overall Psalter. The Royal Psalms 2; 72; 89 for example are located at interfaces of the Psalter. In their extrapolation related to God's eschatological saving activity and the Messiah, they lend the overall Psalter an → *eschatological* and messianic propensity.

Furthermore, the arrangement of the *superscriptions* of certain sub-collections manifests definite compositional arcs. With regard to Psalms 42–89, the Korah psalms constitute an *external framework* (Pss 42–49; 84–85 + 87–88) and the Asaph psalms (Pss 50; 73–83) an *internal framework* around the David psalms (Pss 51–72). In terms of content, this framework alternates between 'lament (L)' and 'God's response (R)'. At the centre of the framework stand 'didactic psalms (D)':

3. Cf. the 'twin Psalms' Pss 103/104, 105/106, 111/112, and 135/136.

| | |
|---|---|
| Korah psalms: | 42/43 (L); 45–48 (R); 49 (L) |
| Asaph psalms: | 50 (D) |
| David psalms: | 51–72 |
| Asaph psalms: | 73 (D); 74 (L); 75–76 (R); 77 (L); 78 (D); 79–80 (L); 81–82 (R); 83 (L) |
| Korah psalms: | 84–85 (L); 87 (R); 88 (L) |

# 13.2 Textual Issues and Major Issues in the History of Critical Interpretation

## 13.2.1 The Superscriptions of the Psalms

Many Psalms bear superscriptions, always in the first verse, all presumably tracing back to later additions. These superscriptions, not to be confused with the titles prefixed to some Psalms in modern translations of the Bible, divide into *four groups*: (1) some name exemplary *pious individuals in the Old Testament* as authors; (2) some indicate *guilds of temple singers* with the names of groups[4] (these guilds of singers were probably not the authors of the corresponding Psalms, but their tradents); (3) some identify *psalm genres*;[5] and (4) some mention *key liturgical and musical terms* concerning the worship function and instrumental accompaniment of the respective psalm.[6] The largely untranslatable term *Sela* (*selâ*; Septuagint: *diapsalma*, Ps. 3.3, 5, 9; 4.3 [NRSV 3.2, 4, 8; 4.2], etc.) may refer to an interlude; its precise meaning is unknown.

> *David* appears as the author of 73 Psalms (cf. e.g. Ps. 15), *Moses* as the author of Ps. 90 and *Solomon* as the author of Psalms 72 and 127. Outside the Hebrew Bible, some codices of the → *Septuagint* mention other authors. Thirteen Psalms in the Hebrew Bible and sixteen in the Septuagint offer additional *information concerning situations* in the life of David in which the respective Psalm is supposed to have originated.[7] The designation *lĕdawid* ('for/by/to David') was not originally

4. Cf. *Korahites* (Pss 42–49; 88.1), *Asaphites* (Pss 50; 73), *Heman* (Ps. 88.1) and *Ethan* (Ps. 89.1); see also 2 Chr. 20.19; 29.30; 1 Chr. 15.16-18.
5. Cf. the first verses of Pss 3; 16; 32; 48; 90; 120 and 145.
6. Cf. the first verses of Pss 4; 6; 54 and 100.
7. Cf. Ps. 3 to 2 Sam. 15–16 or Ps. 51 to 2 Sam. 11–12.

understood in terms of authorship ('by David'), but in terms of possession ('for David' or 'belonging to the Davidic [i.e. royal] psalm book'). The notion of David as a psalmist (cf. Amos 6.5) is based: (a) on his role as a lyre player at Saul's court (1 Sam. 16.16-23; 18.10; 19.9); (b) on his characterization as an author of funeral laments (2 Sam. 1.17-23; 3.31-34); and (c) on the → *deuteronomistic* depiction of him as a pious king (cf. the excursus to Ch. 7.6.3.4).

David is presented as a figure with whom the individual supplicant can identify. The books of Chronicles (Ch. 23) expand this presentation extensively (cf. 1 Chr. 16.7-36).

The attribution of Psalm 90 to the 'man of God, Moses' is based in the understanding of Moses as an exemplary intercessor for Israel (cf. Exod. 32.9-14).

The fictive attribution of Psalms 72 and 127 to Solomon is rooted in the tradition of the wise and just king and builder of the Jerusalem temple (1 Kgs 3; 6–8).

## 13.2.2 Phases of Psalm Research[8]

Modern interpretation of the Psalms, like all modern exegesis, is grounded in the interest, promoted by *Rationalism* and the *Enlightenment*, in understanding the biblical text in its 'original meaning'. The true fathers of the historical-critical interpretation of the Psalms were Johann Gottfried Eichhorn (1752–1827) and Johann Gottfried Herder (1744–1803). Both required that the Psalms, as very ancient prayers and songs, be understood in relation to their original intention, against the background of the situation in which they originated, and from the perspective of their original circle of addressees. *Four essential elements* of the historical-critical interpretation of the Psalms can be identified:

(1) While Luther divided the Psalms according to content into five groups ('prophecy', 'didactic poetry', 'prayers' [i.e. psalms of petition and lament], 'psalms of comfort', and 'psalms of praise/thanksgiving'),[9] since the eighteenth and nineteenth centuries, the Psalms have been categorized according to formal, i.e. linguistic and stylistic, criteria (→ *genres*/forms). Actual *form-critical interpretation* of the Psalms traces back to Wilhelm Martin Leberecht de Wette (1780–1849).

(2) After the origin of many psalms in the period *following* David had already been accepted in late medieval exegesis, historical-critical research concerned itself with

8. J. Becker, *Wege der Psalmenexegese* (SBS 78; Stuttgart: Katholisches Bibelwerk, 1975); M. Oeming, 'An der Quelle des Gebets: Neuere Untersuchungen zu den Psalmen', *TLZ* 127 (2002): 367–84.

9. Cf. M. Luther, 'Summarien über die Psalmen und Ursachen des Dolmetschens (1531–33)', in *D. Martin Luthers Werke: Kritische Gesamtausgabe* (vol. 38; Weimar: Böhlau, 1912 [= WA 38]), 1–69, here 17–18.

the discovery of the precise date of origin and the historical context of the Psalms. The major problems confronting dating the Psalms are the stereotypical nature of the language of prayer and the lack of clear references to historical events. The founder of modern *historicist interpretation* of the Psalms that assigns them *late dates* is *Ferdinand Hitzig* (1807–1875), who sought to derive from the psalms themselves an origin in the Maccabean/Hasmonean period (167–37 BCE) for most of the psalms. Julius Wellhausen (1844–1918) and Bernhard Duhm (1847–1928) continued this extreme late dating. After subsequent research had (rightly) given up such positions, they have most recently been given a modified revival by Manfred Oeming (2000).[10]

(3) Since the beginning of the twentieth century, the effort has been made to anchor Old Testament Psalms in specific cultic and ritual situations and to connect them to specific ancient Israelite festivals (Ch. 3.3 excursus 'Festivals') by means of *comparison from the perspective of the history of religion*[11] with prayers from Egypt, Mesopotamia and Asia Minor. The search for the 'worship occasion', the *Sitz im Leben*, or the socio-cultural location of individual psalms characterizes modern *form- and cult-critical interpretation*. It follows the work of Herder and de Wette, was established by Hermann Gunkel (1862–1932) and Sigmund Mowinckel (1884–1965), and was extended by Hans-Joachim Kraus (1918–2000) and Claus Westermann (1909–2000). The form-critical results obtained by Gunkel continue to be definitive.[12]

**Gunkel** established a ***typology*** in which he classified the Psalms according to three criteria:

(a) the formal diction employed,
(b) the motifs in evidence, and
(c) the origin of the psalm in worship (cult).

Gunkel's definitions of genres have prevailed in most cases. More recent research does not, however, draw direct inferences from the genres concerning

10. M. Oeming, *Das Buch der Psalmen: Psalm 1–41* (Neuer Stuttgarter Kommentar. Altes Testament 13/1; Stuttgart: Katholisches Bibelwerk, 2000).

11. J. Assmann, *Ägyptische Hymnen*; A. Falkenstein and W. v. Soden, *Sumerische und akkadische Hymnen und Gebete* (Zurich: Artemis Verlag, 1953); J. L. Foster, *Hymns, Prayers, and Songs: An Anthology of Ancient Egyptian Lyric Poetry* (Atlanta, Ga.: Scholars, 1995); M. Lichtheim, *Ancient Egyptian Literature* I-III; I. Singer, *Hittite Prayers* (Writings of the Ancient World 11; Atlanta, Ga.: SBL, 2002).

12. H. Gunkel, Die Psalmen (HK II/2; 4th ed., Göttingen: Vandenhoeck & Ruprecht, 1929 [repr. [6]1986]); idem and J. Begrich, Introduction.

experienced reality. Rather, the definition of genres serves to reveal linguistic and textual phenomena on the literary level (Ch. 2.1.1).

(4) Pre-critical scholarship assumed that the Psalms stemmed from *one* author and were of one piece. Since the eighteenth and nineteenth centuries, scholars have recognized traces of *redactional revisions* (expansions, abbreviations, reinterpretations) in some psalms. The commentaries by Erich Zenger and Frank-Lothar Hossfeld (1993; 2002, respectively) represent the current phase of *composition- and redaction-critical* interpretation, both of individual psalms and of the whole Psalter. They attempt to trace the literary development of each individual psalm. It becomes evident that Psalms, like all Old Testament literature, was subject up to the moment of its canonization (→ *canon*) to continuous literary revision that served theological actualization in the given period. At the same time, the works of Zenger and Hossfeld clarify the fact that Psalms has not been arranged capriciously. Rather, it becomes evident that (1) the sub-collections of psalms, like the overall Psalter, manifest redactional cross-references and theologically motivated interconnections and, (2) the Psalter can be read as *one* book in which the psalms appear as interrelated and reciprocally illuminating chapters.

**The fundamental rules of Old Testament poetry:** The psalms are poetical texts. As such, like poems from other linguistic and cultural realms, they have certain formal characteristics. In Hebrew, the smallest unit of poetry consists of a so-called stichos, also referred to in scholarship as a short verse, a semi-verse, a line of verse, an element of verse or a colon. As a rule, a (long) verse consists of two or three semi-verses (short verses, stichoi, cola). Accordingly, a (long) verse composed of two lines of verse (stichoi, cola) is also called a distich or bi-colon, a verse composed of three lines a tristich or tricolon.[13]

The *basic principle of Hebrew poetry*, which applies to the psalms as to the other poetic texts in the Old Testament, consists of *parallelismus membrorum*, i.e. the parallelism of the members (stichoi, cola) of a verse. Characteristically with regard to *parallelismus membrorum*, the essential elements of the parts of a verse correspond to one another formally and in terms of context. *Parallelismus membrorum* may be classified according to the nature of this formal and substantive correspondence. The English bishop Robert Lowth (1710–1787) first attempted such a typology of Hebrew poetry.

Current scholarship distinguishes five forms of parallelismus membrorum:

(1) *Synonymous parallelism*. Lines that belong together in terms of meaning render the same idea in different wordings:
'How long, Yhwh? Will you forget me forever?
How long will you hide your countenance from me?' (Ps. 13.2 [NRSV1]).

⇨

13. Regarding the varied terminology, see W. G. E. Watson, *Classical Hebrew Poetry: A Guide to its Techniques* (JSOTSup 26; Sheffield: JSOT, 1984 [repr. 2001]), 11–15.

(2) *Synthetic parallelism*. The second part of the verse or clause supplements the first without repeating it in altered form:
'Yhwh is my light and my salvation. Whom should I fear?
Yhwh guards my life. Who will frighten me?' (Ps. 27.1).

(3) *Antithetical parallelism*. The two members constitute a contrast:
'For my father and my mother have abandoned me,
but Yhwh will accept me' (Ps. 27.10).

(4) *Parabolic parallelism*. As in a comparison, one part of the verse conveys an image and the other its substance:
'Like a father has mercy on his children,
so Yhwh has mercy on those who fear him' (Ps. 103.13).

(5) *Climactic (repetitive or tautological) parallelism*. The individual parts of the verse (at most three) develop an idea in steps with a keyword repeated in each section:
'The floods have lifted up, O Yhwh,
the floods have lifted up their voice,
the floods have lifted up their roaring' (Ps. 93.3).

*Parallelismus membrorum* is not limited to Old Testament poetry, but already appears in Sumerian, Akkadian, Egyptian and Ugaritic poetry.

In addition to *parallelismus membrorum*, three other *peculiarities* distinguish poetic texts from prose texts in Hebrew. Thus, poetic diction is particularly concise. It avoids the use of the article and the relative pronoun and tends toward abbreviated (elliptic) constructions. Furthermore, there are a number of *stylistic devices*.[14] *Strophic construction* involves the combination of individual verses into topically (thematically) and formally cohesive units. Occasionally strophes are marked by a *chorus* (refrain).[15] *Alphabetic acrostics* constitute a peculiar strophic construction. In an acrostic, the beginning letters of the verses or strophes follow alphabetical order.[16] Finally, Hebrew poetry exhibits *metrical structure*. Since the pronunciation of Hebrew has changed in the course of the centuries and the text was initially transmitted unvocalized and unaccented, the question of the original metrical systems remains open. The *tradition of accentuation* in the synagogue's use of the Psalms traces back to the accent and intonation symbols of Jewish scholars in the early Middle Ages. Against this background, it is difficult to say how (individual) Old Testament psalms were originally performed musically.

J. L. Kugel, *The Idea of Biblical Poetry: Parallelism and Its History*. New Haven, Conn.: Yale University Press, 1981; K. Seybold, *Poetik der Psalmen*. Stuttgart: Kohlhammer, 2003; A. Wagner, ed., *Parallelismus Membrorum*. OBO 224. Fribourg: Academic Press/Göttingen: Vandenhoeck & Ruprecht, 2007.

14. Cf. L. Zogbo and E. R. Wendland, *Hebrew Poetry in the Bible: A Guide for Understanding and for Translation* (UBS Technical Helps; New York: United Bible Societies, 2000).

15. Cf. Ps. 42.6, 12/43.5; 42.10/43.2; 46.8, 12; 49.13, 21 (NRSV 42.5, 11/43.5; 42.9/43.2; 46.7, 11; 49.12, 20).

16. Cf. Pss 9/10; 25; 34; 37; 111–112; 119; 145; Prov. 31.10-31; Lam. 1–5.

# 13.3 Origins of the Psalms and of the Psalter

## 13.3.1 The Form of the Psalter and of the Individual Psalms

In its current form, the Psalter consists of a *book of prayers and meditations* assembled in several phases of redaction. It was composed from sub-collections, individual psalms and texts written specifically for this work ('redactional psalms', e.g. Ps. 1). At the beginning of the Psalter, as was also true of its sub-collections, stand *individual psalms* that belong to various → *genres*, stem from various times and socio-cultural contexts, and each have their own history of development and use. The discussion to follow will treat the *form, composition* and *redaction*, and function for individual psalms and for the Psalter separately. There are overlaps between the two presentations because some psalms were written as purely literary entities for a larger collection of texts and some psalms were revised for a more comprehensive context and in this sense received new functions.

## 13.3.2 The Basic Forms of Old Testament Psalms

The Individual and Communal Psalms of lament and petition and the Individual song of thanksgiving and the communal praise of God (hymn) constitute the most important *genres* of Old Testament psalms.

### *13.3.2.1 The Individual Psalm of Lament and Petition*

Individual psalms of lament or petition form the foundation of the Psalter. Approximately 35–40 psalms can be assigned to this genre.

Psalms of Individual lament and petition: Pss. 3–7; 10–14; 16–17; 22–23; 25–28; 35–36; 38–43; 51–59; 61–64; 69; 71; 86; 88; 102; 109; 130; 140; 141–143.

## Essential structural elements of the Individual lament are:

(1) the address to God;
(2) the description of existential distress (illness, guilt, persecution), the lament proper with up to three references
  (a) to the petitioners suffering, the *first person complaint*,
  (b) to Yhwh as the cause of the suffering, the *complaint to God*, that can develop further into an *accusation against God*,
  (c) to the surroundings the petitioner experienced as hostile, the *complaint about the enemy*, and questions about the duration ('how long' [*ʿad-matay, ʿad-ʾānâ*]) and the cause and purpose ('why'/'wherefore' [*lammâ*]) for the distress;
(3) the *request* for God's intervention to end the distress.

These three basic elements of the psalm of lament and petition can be supplemented with up to four additional components, all of which intend to provide additional motivation for God to intervene on behalf of the petitioner. The description of the distress can be expanded with elements of the *confession of innocence* (cf. Ps. 17.3) and of the *confession of confidence* (cf. Ps. 13.6; 22.10-11 [NRSV 13.5; 22.9-10]). The latter can develop into an independent *song of confidence* (cf. Ps. 23). The request for the end of suffering can be supplemented with the elements of a *vow of praise* (cf. Ps. 7.18; 13.6 [NRSV 7.17; 13.5]) and an expression of the *assurance of being heard* (cf. Ps. 6.9-10 [NRSV 6.8-9]; 28.6-8).

## Psalm 13 is a paradigmatic psalm of Individual lament and petition:

| | |
|---|---|
| 1 'To the leader. A Psalm of David. | → ***secondary superscription*** |
| 2(1) How long, O Yhwh? Will you forget me forever?<br>How long will you hide your face from me? | → ***address to God with lament to God and description of distress (first person complaint)*** |
| 3(2) How long must I bear pain in my soul,<br>And have sorrow in my heart all day long?<br>How long shall my enemy be exalted over me? | → ***complaint about the enemy*** |
| 4(3) Consider and answer me, Yhwh, my God!<br>Give light to my eyes, or I will sleep in death,<br>5(4) so that my enemy cannot say, 'I have prevailed';<br>and my foes cannot rejoice because I am shaken. | → ***petition*** |
| 6(5) But I trusted in your mercy; | → ***confession of confidence*** |

my heart shall rejoice in your help.
(6) I will sing to Yhwh, because he has treated me so well.' → ***vow of praise***

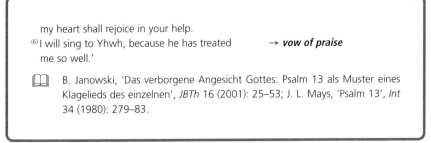

B. Janowski, 'Das verborgene Angesicht Gottes: Psalm 13 als Muster eines Klagelieds des einzelnen', *JBTh* 16 (2001): 25–53; J. L. Mays, 'Psalm 13', *Int* 34 (1980): 279–83.

The question of how to interpret the *petitioner's change of attitude* perceptible in the course of a psalm of lament and petition must be determined from case to case and cannot always be answered with a single possibility. Thus, the change of attitude may be interpreted in three ways: (1) *liturgically*, such that, after the lament recited before a priest, the petitioner received an oracle confirming that he had been heard, to which he responded with a confession of confidence (cf. Lam. 3.57); (2) *in terms of editorial technique*, such that formularies with laments, on the one hand, and prayers of confidence and petition, on the other, were preserved in the same place (e.g. the temple) and combined secondarily; and, (3) *psychologically*, such that the supplicant experienced initial relief from his suffering by expressing it and came to trust in God's deliverance in his prayer.[17]

### *13.3.2.2 The Communal Psalm of Lament and Petition or the Lament of the People*

This genre corresponds structurally to the psalm of individual lament and petition, but has a collective entity as the subject of the lament. This collective entity laments the destruction or the loss of state, city and/or temple.

Communal laments: Pss 44; 74; 79; 80; 83; 85; with Limilations, Pss 58; 60; 89; 106; 125; 137, and, outside the Psalter, Lam. 1; 2; 4; 5; Isa. 63.7–64.11 (NRSV 64.12); Jer. 14.2-9; *Pss. Sol.* 4; 7; 9; 1 Macc. 3.50-53; Sir. 36.1-22 (H)/33:1–13a + 16b–22 (G).
Like the Individual lament or petition, the ***communal lament*** has a fixed ***structure*** that combines certain invariable and interchangeable elements. The essential ⇨

17. See E. S. Gerstenberger, *Der bittende Mensch* (WMANT 51; Neukirchen-Vluyn: Neukirchener, 1980), 163–9.

components of the communal lament are: (1) the *address* to God, (2) the *lament*, and (3) the *petition*.

In a more developed form, the communal lament can include six elements:

(1) the address to God in the vocative and in the second person singular, which, in contrast to the psalm of individual lament and petition, can be joined by a hymnic predication of God's former saving activity (cf. Ps. 44.2–4 [NRSV 44.1–3]; 74.2);
(2) the supplicant (a choir or intercessor) speaking in the second person plural (cf. Ps. 74.1, 9) or, occasionally, in the collective first person singular (cf. Ps. 85.9 [NRSV 85.8]);
(3) the cry of despair and for assistance: the lament and the petition (cf. Ps. 79.9; 85.5 [NRSV 85.4]);
(4) the description of hardship with a view to political or natural crises which may contain the elements of the lament concerning the suffering of the people, God's activity, and the behaviour of the enemies. Usually, this description of the crisis includes the typical questions concerning the duration, cause and purpose of the crisis (cf. Ps. 74.3–11; 79.1-5, 10);
(5) the petition expressing the wish for the end of the catastrophe (cf. Ps. 74.2, 18–23);
(6) a (fictive) divine speech or divine pronouncement (cf. Ps. 60.8–10 [NRSV 60.6–8]).

*The objective of the communal psalm of lament and petition* is to motivate Yhwh to intervene on behalf of his people. Various arguments can be brought to bear: (1) a *retrospective* on the national history of salvation in contrast to the current crisis; (2) an *appeal* to God's name or honour, since Israel's fate is understood as reflecting God's power, as it were; (3) a *confession of sin* or a declaration of innocence; or (4) a declaration of *assurance of being heard* or a vow of praise.

Since the communal prayer of lament and petition addresses God in a *current* crisis, pointing to God's former saving activity and hoping for *future* intervention to deliver, it is a significant witness to a religiously oriented *historical awareness* such as is also found, in principle, elsewhere in the Ancient Near East. God's activity gives coherence to present, past and future, which appear pregnant with meaning against the background of his activity.

The relationship between the psalm of communal lament and petition and a prophetic oracle that may have been proclaimed following the communal lament (cf. Ps. 60.8-10; 85.9-14 [NRSV 60.6-8; 85.8-13]) is an open question in scholarship.

In any case, elaborate 'liturgies' consisting of a communal lament and an oracle appear in the prophetic tradition (e.g. Hos. 14.3-9 [NRSV 14.2-8]; Joel 1–2).

Texts comparable to Old Testament communal laments appear in *Israel's Ancient Near Eastern environment*, especially in Sumerian, Babylonian and Hittite psalms. Two characteristic examples are: (1) the Sumerian lament over the destruction of the southern Mesopotamian city of Ur ( = Erech) from ca. 1955 BCE (excerpts in W. Beyerlin, RTAT, 140-141 and in Context of Scripture I, 535-539.), and (2) the plague prayers of the Hittite king, Mursilis II (ca. 1325 BCE), laments concerning an epidemic understood as a divine visitation (excerpt in W. Beyerlin, RTAT, 191-196 and in Context of Scripture I, 156-160.).

### *13.3.2.3 The Psalm of Individual Thanksgiving*

The genre is represented in the Old Testament in about 20 psalms.

Individual thanksgivings: Pss. 9/10; 18; 30; 32; 34; 40.2-12 (NRSV 40.1-11); 41; 66; 92; 116; 118; 138, and, outside the Psalter, Isa. 38.10-20; Job 33.26-28; Jon. 2.3-10 (NRSV 2.2-9); Sir. 51.1-12 (17); *Pss. Sol.* 15; 16; etc.

The ***Individual song of thanksgiving*** involves two ***structural characteristics***:

(1) the *expression of thanks* in which the supplicant addresses God directly. The (introductory) formula is usually: 'I thank you' (cf. Ps. 118.21; Isa. 12.1; Sir. 51.1; see also Jon. 2.10 [NRSV 2.10]);

(2) the *testimony* in which the supplicant reports an act of God's deliverance that he has experienced personally. The report speaks of God in the third person singular (cf. Ps. 34.5 [NRSV 34.4]; 118.5).

The report of God's redemptive act itself can contain three additional motifs or elements:

(1) a retrospective on the supplicant's distress,
(2) a report of the appeal to God,
(3) an account of having been heeded.

The *function of the testimony*, given before the congregation or those invited to attend the sacrificial meal, is to report personal experience (cf. Ps. 22.23-26 [NRSV 22.22-25]; 66.16). With the report of deliverance, the supplicant invites his hearers to participate in (and identify with) his own fate. At the same time, he testifies that Yhwh is the God who intervenes in human suffering to deliver.

*Healing psalms*, which represent the prayer of someone recuperating from illness (cf. Pss 30; 32; 41; 69; 103), constitute a sub-group of the individual songs of thanksgiving.

#### *13.3.2.4 The Collective Psalm of Praise (Hymn): Formally, Two Types of Hymns may be Differentiated*

(1) the imperative hymn and (2) the participial hymn.

> Hymns: Pss 8; 19; 29; 33; 100; 103; 104; 105; 111; 113; 114; 135; 145; 146; 148; 149; 150.

A call, formulated in the imperative or cohortative, for the congregation to praise God introduces the *imperative hymn*, which continues with a performance (explication, corpus) of praise. In Hebrew, the particle *kî*, which can have affirmative ('indeed') and causative ('for') significance, introduces the praise. The development of the praise treats the theme of God's historical activity with Israel. The Song of Miriam in Exod. 15.21 constitutes the abbreviation of an imperative hymn.

The *participial hymn* praises God's creative power and righteousness in clauses constructed with participles in Hebrew which are usually rendered as relative clauses in English.[18] In later times, the two forms interfused.[19] In a few later hymns, one may distinguish between an imperatival conclusion in parallel to the imperatival opening (cf. Ps. 136).

#### *13.3.2.5 Additional 'Genres'*

In scholarship, one finds attempts to define additional genres beyond the four basic genres described here and to assign individual psalms to them. A common topic essentially unifies the psalms assembled in these groups, however. In most cases, the presumed cultic and institutional background is hypothetical. Consequently, it makes more sense to regard these psalms as thematically unified groups (see Ch. 13.1) and to assign them to a basic genre, in the event that they are not instances of *purely literary compositions* which are distinct from the cult ('*post-cultic psalms*').[20]

### 13.3.3 The Composition and Redaction of the Psalter

The Psalter took shape through the gradual combination of sub-collections. The process of tradition, revision and expansion began in the post-exilic period

18. Cf. Pss 104; 145; 146.
19. Cf. Pss 33; 113; 135; 136.
20. F. Stolz, *Psalmen im nachkultischen Raum* (ThSt 129; Zurich: Theologischer Verlag, 1983).

and concluded in the second century bce. Around 100 BCE, the qualitative, if not yet the quantitative 'canonicity' (→ canon) of the Psalter was established.

The literary growth of the Psalter presumably progressed from front to back. As a model (!) and hypothetically, *four large blocks* may be distinguished:

(1) **Pss 3–41** (*Davidic Psalter I*) constitute the foundation. For the most part, it involves *Individual psalms*. At points, the formation of small groups is evident (Pss 3–5; 18–21; 26–28; 38–41).

(2) The foundation was first linked to **Pss 42–89** (*Davidic Psalter III)* and introduced by the secondarily prefixed Ps. 2. *Individual psalms* also dominate in the second Davidic Psalter. Within the second Davidic Psalter, one finds a sub-collection (Pss 42–83), which underwent an *Elohistic redaction*, i.e. the exchange of the tetragrammaton (*Yhwh*) for the appellative *ʾĕlohîm* ('God'). Consequently, one also speaks of Pss 42–93 as the *Elohistic Psalter* (see Ch. 13.1). The framework of → *messianic* psalms (Pss 2; 89) characterizes the second Davidic Psalter.

(3) The collection consisting of Pss 2–89 was expanded with **Pss 90–119**. Ps. 1 was now prefixed as a prologue to the collection encompassing Pss 2–119. The → *wisdom* framework (Pss 1–119) characterizes the sub-collection Pss 1–119.

(4) The book of Psalms extending from Pss 1–119 was supplemented (in stages) by the block of **Pss 120–150**, which itself traces to various sections, including the *pilgrimage psalms* (Pss 120–134 with the 'great Hallel' in Pss 135–136).

The individual stimuli for the growth of the Psalter trace to certain theological intentions.

Two *redactional intentions* can be formally identified.

(1) The collection of the *Individual psalms* served to generate prayer formularies for individual supplicants. Their function is the inculcation of Yahwistic faith.

(2) The collection of the *communal psalms* served to generate examples of congregational prayer and singing and fulfils an essentially liturgical function.

## 13.3.4 The Composition and Redaction of the Individual Psalms

In view of the absence of direct evidence, dating the Psalms is always hypothetical (see Ch. 13.2.2) and depends on many factors. External criteria for outlining the history of development are the observation of dual traditions,[21]

21. Cf. Ps. 14 = Ps. 53; Ps. 40.14-18 (NRSV 40.13-17) = Ps. 70; Ps 57.8-12 + Ps. 60.7-14 (NRSV 57.7-11 + 60.5-12) = Ps. 108.2-14 (NRSV 108.1-13); 2 Sam. 22 par. Ps. 19.

the evidence of the reception of some psalms in other psalms,[22] and the genre categories. *Internal criteria* consist of the respective linguistic and motif repertoire and the complex of religio-historical and theological concepts perceptible in the respective psalm. One must always reckon with the fact that, in the course of transmission, psalms were revised, actualized theologically, and taken from the situation in which they were originally used and placed in another context.

The development of individual psalms may be divided *into five phases* as a hypothetical model (!): (1) *Cultic hymns* represent the oldest texts (cf. Pss 24*; 29*; 60*; 93*). Their setting in life was the pre-exilic royal temple cult. (2) The majority of communal *laments* stem from the exilic period (Pss 44; 74; 76; 79; 89; 137). (3) The majority of the *individual laments* originated in the exilic/post-exilic period. They could have been formulated either 'spontaneously' or as a component of ritual (Pss 42–43; 120 or Pss 6; 41, respectively). (4) In the early post-exilic period, the old hymnic heritage (esp. the 'Yhwh is King' Psalms) was received and revised (Pss 29*; 93), on the one hand, and *Festival Songs* were produced as literary model prayers for annual festivals, pilgrimages and 'special occasions', on the other. The primary gathering point was the celebration of the thanksgiving offering (Toda celebration, Pss 22; 30). (5) The origin of *post-cultic literary psalms* ('spiritual/religious songs', 'didactic psalms', Pss 1; 49; 73; 78; 104; 119; 136) occurred in the late post-exilic period (4th – 2nd centuries BCE).

The formation of the psalm collections and the revision of individual psalms ran parallel to these five phases. The former began in the exilic/post-exilic period and continued until the composition of the canonical Psalter and the latter also continued until canonization.

The continuous ***actualization*** (***relecture***) of the psalms can be divided into *four categories*:

(1) the interpretation of original votive/song offerings (liturgical formularies),
(2) the preparation of copies, recitations and citations,
(3) incidental expansions by readers,
(4) systematic theological revision: stylizations, abbreviations, classifications (addition of the situation in which the psalm was used, the genre of the psalm, an ideal situation, the musical accompaniment), the formation of series, the composition of junctures (Pss 1; 2; 72; 89; 119; 150).

22. Cf. Ps. 29 in Ps. 96; Ps. 115 in Ps. 135; Ps. 105 + 96 + 106 in 1 Chr. 16.7-36.

## 13.3.5 The Situation and Function of the Psalter

There are three theories regarding the original use of the Psalter in its final form:

(1) According to the *temple-liturgy thesis*, represented primarily in older scholarship,[23] the Psalter constituted the hymnal of the Second Temple. Thus, the Psalms were sung by a choir of Levites during the daily sacrifice and on special feast days (cf. 1 Chr. 16.4-18; Sir. 50.16). The congregation assembled in the temple responded with → *doxological* refrains (cf. Ps. 136). This thesis applies to individual psalm groups.[24] A general designation of the Psalter as the 'Hymnal of the Second Temple' is erroneous, however, from the perspectives of the history of religion and of literature.

(2) According to the *synagogue liturgy thesis*, the Psalter is the hymnal and prayerbook of the liturgy celebrated in the synagogue (Erhard S. Gerstenberger). The fact that there is no literary evidence for a use of the Psalter among the essential components (Torah reading, benedictions, the → *Šĕmaʿ yiśrāʾēl*) of the synagogue liturgy in the Second Temple period contradicts this theory.

(3) According to the *devotional thesis*, the Psalter contains readings for personal, meditative piety and the → *eschatological* hopes of certain circles in post-exilic Judaism (Erich Zenger). This thesis finds support in the overall flow of the Psalter and its structuring by → *wisdom* and eschatological texts.

## 13.3.6 The Situation and Function of Individual Psalms

Each psalm constitutes an independent work of art with its own history of development, its own degree of textual preservation, its own setting for its original use (*Sitz im Leben*), and its own history of secondary application (*relecture*). Thus, for each psalm, apart from its status in the Psalter, one must first inquire as to the original situation in which it was used and as to its original function. In this regard, one must take into account the fact that various situations and functions are to be attributed to a psalm in the course of the history of its redaction.

In general, the *Individual lament and petition psalm* originated in the specific distress of an individual. These prayers do not have a uniform setting in life,

23. Cf., for example, H. Schmidt, *Die Psalmen* (HAT I/15; Tübingen: Mohr Siebeck, 1934), iii.

24. Cf. the festival Pss 81 and 95, the collective lament and penitential liturgies and the weekly Psalms (in the sequence of the weekdays, beginning with the Sabbath: Pss 92; 24; 48; 82; 94; 81; 93).

however.[25] Hence, the decision must be made regarding each individual lament as to whether it was originally prayed in a penitential ceremony in the temple, where presumably lament formularies for appropriate situations were maintained, or in a private place. On the whole, it should be noted that the multi-dimensionality of the symbols employed in the psalms is open to several interpretations and that the individual laments are suitable as prayer formularies for a variety of situations in which a person may feel that his life is threatened.

The occasions for the *communal prayers of lament and petition* are mostly military or natural catastrophes that affect the whole people, catastrophes such as famine, droughts or epidemics.[26] The setting in life of the communal lament could have been a national fast (*ṣôm*).[27] Public lament ceremonies were held at the sanctuary in situations of war, imprisonment, plague or drought. Sacrifices were made, self-abasement rites[28] performed, and intercessory prayers made.[29] The communal laments preserved in the Old Testament probably contain pre-exilic elements, which are only preserved in a revised version from the post-exilic period, however. Most stem from the exilic period. It is possible to read in the exilic/post-exilic redaction how prayers originally anchored in a royal state-cult were actualized for the Second Temple period (Chs 4.3 and 4).

The setting in life for the *Individual song of thanksgiving* was originally the thanksgiving sacrifice or vow offered at the sanctuary with the family after one had experienced deliverance.[30] In addition, some thanksgiving songs lost their connection with the celebration of sacrifice, per se, and became independent.

The *communal praise of God* (hymn) has its original locus in the festival cult of the congregation assembled around the temple. Thus, like the communal lament, it originally belonged in the official cult. The category includes both hymns that actually originated in the Jerusalem temple and psalms originally at home in other Yhwh sanctuaries, such as Shiloh or Bethel, that were only adopted secondarily in the Jerusalem temple cult. In addition, 'post-cultic hymns' (Ps. 136), i.e. purely literary 'hymns', lost their connection with the

25. R. Achenbach, 'Zum Sitz im Leben mesopotamischer und altisraelitischer Klagegebete', *ZAW* 116 (2004): 364–78, 581–94.
26. Cf. Exod. 32.11-14; Deut. 9.25-29; Josh. 7.7-9; Judg. 20.3-26; 21.2-4; 1 Sam. 7.6; 1 Kgs 8; 21.9, 12; Joel 1–2; Hos. 7.14-15; Isa. 15.2; 58.3; Jer. 4.8; 6.2, 6; 14.1; 36.6, 9; Jon. 3.5-10; Mic. 1.8, 16; 4.14.
27. Cf. 1 Kgs 21.9, 12; Isa. 58.5; Jer. 36.9; Jon. 3.5.
28. These included fasting, crying, tearing the clothing, and smearing with dust and ashes.
29. Cf. Joel 2.17; 2 Chr. 20.6-13; Ps. 44; Jer. 3.25.
30. Cf. Ps. 50.14; 56.13 (NRSV 56.12); 66.13; 107.21-22; 116.17-19; 118.19.

cultic situation in the temple, but continued to utilize cultic diction. They spiritualized it, however, and praised God in the act of reading.

## 13.4 Theology of the Psalms and of the Psalter

In totality, Psalms document *the history of Yahwism*.[31] In this regard, the Psalter contains a condensed Old Testament theology and → *anthropology*. Thus, the Psalter constitutes a → *canon* within the canon, 'a little Bible' (M. Luther).[32] According to its framework in Psalms 1 and 150, the Psalter is *'Israel's' response* to the Torah given by Yhwh. At the same time, according to the guide for reading in Ps. 1.2, the Psalter itself appears as a Torah, i.e. as instruction for a life suitable for faith in Yhwh. The attribution of approximately half the psalms to David and their association with his life at points ('Davidization of the Psalter') intends to enable one to pray in the succession of David as *the seminal* → *messianic* figure.

Since the Psalms respond to God's activity and presence, they assume that *Yhwh is a personal and living counterpart* to human beings. All the psalms express the conviction that God's nature is primarily evident in his actions, specifically, in *creation* and *history*. In this regard, creation means that this will is not arbitrary but meaningful and purposeful (cf. Ps. 104). Creation points to the creator, but is not identical with him. God's activity is also evident in history. As with individuals, Yhwh stands behind the fate of individual nations (cf. Ps. 33). In liberation from Egypt, protection in the desert, and leadership into the cultivated land, the people of God sees the activity of its God (cf. Pss 113–114). Out of the experience that Yhwh once acted grows the hope in future protection (cf. Ps. 124). Out of the experience that Yhwh created the world and sends life anew daily arises the confidence that life will also be possible in the future and that Yhwh will deliver from death (cf. Pss 22; 49; 73).

31. R. G. Kratz, *Reste hebräischen Heidentums am Beispiel der Psalmen* (NAWG 1. Philologisch-Historische Klasse 2004/2; Göttingen: Vandenhoeck & Ruprecht, 2004).

32. M. Luther, 'Vorrede auf den Psalter', in *Die gantze Heilige Schrifft Deudsch, Wittenberg 1545* (ed. H. Volz *et al.*; Munich: Rogner und Bernhard, 1972), 964 (ET 'Preface to the Psalter (1545)', in *Luther's Works*, American Edition [55 vols.; ed. J. Pelikan and H. T. Lehmann; Philadelphia: Muhlenberg, 1955–86], 35:254).

To the extent that the main focus of the Psalter lies on the petitions and laments of individuals, the Psalter offers a *verbalization of fundamental human experience and an interpretation of human existence* before God. A person's existence moves between the poles of creaturely vulnerability and God-given majesty (Ps. 8). Both in his humility and in his grandeur, a human being stands in relation to God. His life can only succeed, as the Psalms understand it, if he leads it before and with the living God. A life without God and with no thought for God counts as a failed life (cf. Ps. 73).

*Prayer* belongs to a successful life. Both the individual and the communal cry of lament attest to the experience of powerlessness and anxiety (cf. Pss 6; 13 or Pss 80; 137, respectively). In contrast, the petitions and the expressions of hope are based on the experience of divine power (cf. Ps. 29). The goal of prayer is the incorporation of the human will into the divine will (cf. Ps. 73.23). The whole person of supplicants is always involved (Ps. 104.1). They place their trust entirely in God (cf. Ps. 23.4) and find their happiness only in communion with him (cf. Ps. 73.23). Central to the Psalter's view of humanity is the fact that human beings are just as aware of the radical difference between God and humanity, between divine righteousness and human sin (cf. Ps. 90 or Pss 51; 143, respectively) as of their dependence on a power greater than them. God's claim on people is balanced however, by the expectation that God will behave justly toward those who keep his commandments (cf. Pss 1; 146) and that his grace outweighs his wrath (cf. Ps. 103).

The psalms are first *prayers of the Old Testament people of God* (cf. Ps. 100). A universalist line also runs through the Psalter, however: Not just all peoples, but the whole cosmos is called upon to praise God (cf. Ps. 138.4; 150).

Therefore, the Psalter has great *kerygmatic power*: Every prayer offered before Yhwh (petition, praise, thanksgiving, lament) contains a confession to Yhwh and is directed at acknowledging him.

The particularist and the universalist lines in the Psalter meet in the tripartite concept of → *Zion* (cf. Ps. 46). Zion as the holy mountain on which Yhwh sits mysteriously enthroned is: (1) the site that survives the cosmic catastrophe of the eschaton, (2) the place to which all nations will one day come, and (3) the point from which Yhwh will establish universal peace. Until this moment, which simultaneously represents the end of history, Jews and Christians, but not they alone, are called upon to pray, 'Your kingdom come.'

# 13.5 Notes on the History of Reception

*Three trends* characterize the history of the reception and influence of Psalms. First, Psalms, in continuity with their cultic origins, have a central role in *worship* and in the personal piety of Judaism and Christianity to this day. Second, in extension of the inner-biblical *interpretation of scripture* that began already within the Psalter, the Psalms appear as the subject of extensive commentary. Finally, with their expression of basic human experiences, Psalms are the starting point for *paraphrases and original compositions*, musical and visual settings and dramatic presentation. This threefold form of the history of reception already begins – as, above all, the documents discovered in → *Qumran* demonstrate – in *ancient Judaism* with the collection of select psalms for liturgical and theological purposes,[33] with the commentaries on individual psalms (cf. 4QpPs37), and with the composition of post-biblical psalms (cf. 1QHodayot).[34] As in the Qumran documents, the Psalter belongs among the most cited texts in the New Testament. There are 110 literal citations from Psalms alone. Citations from the Individual prayers predominate.

With regard to the *musical setting* of psalms, reference will be made here only to Gregorian music, to the reformed Psalter tradition promoted by John Calvin, and to the composition of psalm-like songs undertaken by Martin Luther. *Illustrations* of psalms occur from Byzantine Bible manuscripts to Marc Chagall. The supposed authorship of David, who appears in medieval Christian and Jewish book illustrations, but also in sculpture, with a harp in his hand, was especially influential on → *iconography*.

33. Cf. the Psalm scrolls from caves 4 and 11 and the collection of biblical citations in 4QFlor(ilegium) (=4Q174, translation in F. García Martinez and E. J. C. Tigchelaar, *The Dead Sea Scrolls* I, 352–5.

34. Translation in ibid., 146–205.

# 14

# The Book of Job

## (Markus Witte – Translation by Mark Biddle)

## Chapter Outline




Commentaries: J. H. Eaton (OTG. Sheffield: JSOT, 1985); G. Fohrer (KAT. 2nd ed. Gütersloh: Gütersloher Verlagshaus, 1989); N. C. Habel (OTL. London: SCM, 1985); F. Hesse (ZBK 14. 2nd ed. Zurich: Theologischer Verlag, 1992); A. de Wilde (OTS 22. Leiden/Boston: Brill, 1981).

N. N. Glatzer, *The Dimensions of Job: A Study and Selected Readings*. New York: Leo Baeck Institute, 1969; T. Krüger *et al.*, eds, *Das Buch Hiob und seine Interpretationen*. ATANT 88. Zurich: Theologischer Verlag, 2007; H.-P. Müller, *Das Hiobproblem: Seine Stellung und Entstehung im Alten Orient und im Alten Testament*. EdF 84. 3rd ed. Darmstadt: Wissenschaftliche Buchgesellschaft, 1995; C. A. Newsom, *The Book of Job: A Contest of Moral Imaginations*. Oxford: Oxford University Press, 2003; D. S. Russell, *The Old Testament Pseudepigrapha: Patriarchs in Early Judaism*. London: SCM, 1987, 58–68.


Like the books of Jonah, Ruth, Esther and Daniel, the book bears the name, not of its author, but of its leading figure. In Hebrew, the name is *Ijob* (*ʾiyyôb*), while the → *Septuagint* renders it *Iob*.

The **name Job** means 'Where is the (divine) father?' and, in this form, presents a request for God's help. For Hebrew ears, the word *ʾôyēb* 'enemy' also echoes in the name *ʾîyyôb*, so that 'Job' can be understood as 'God's enemy' or 'the one hostile (to God)'.[1] The Koran associates the name (Arabic *ʾAyub*) with the word *ʾawab* ('repentant/penitent'), so that Job is the exemplary penitent (Sure 38:44). Neither the association with the Hebrew word *ʾôyēb* ('enemy') nor with the Arabic word *ʾawab* ('penitent') are authentic philological derivations, but they open associations for understanding the book which may have already been intended by the earliest tradents of the Job tradition.

# 14.1 Biblical Context

**1–2 Prologue: How the blessed Job came to great suffering**

| | |
|---|---|
| 1.1-5 | Presentation of the exemplarily pious and blessed Job |
| 1.6–2.10 | Job's dual trial |
| 2.11-13 | Arrival of the friends to comfort Job – Transition to the dialogue |

**3 Monologue: Job's complaint concerning his life marked by suffering**

**4–28 Dialogue: Job and his friends in search of the reason and objective of Job's suffering**

| | |
|---|---|
| 4–14 | First sequence of speeches: Just retribution |
| 15–21 | Second sequence of speeches: The fate of the evildoer |
| 22–28 | So-called 'third sequence of speeches': Job's accusation and turn against his friends |

**29–31 Monologue: Job challenges God to a legal contest**

**32–37 Monologue: Elihu's speeches to Job and his friends**

| | |
|---|---|
| 32.1-5 | Prologue: Introduction of Elihu |
| 32.6–33.33 | Elihu's first speech: On the pedagogical function of suffering and the interceding angel |
| 34–35 | Elihu's second and third speeches: On God's righteousness |
| 36–37 | Elihu's fourth speech: On the self-revealing, just creator God |

**38–42.6 Monologue: God outlines the cosmic world order**

| | |
|---|---|
| 38–39 | God's first speech: Creation and maintenance of creation |
| 40.1-5 | Interim response: Job's vow of silence |
| 40.6–41.26 (NRSV 41.34) | God's second speech: Right and might of the creator God |
| 42.1-6 | Concluding response: Job's confession of creaturehood |

**42.7-17 Epilogue: How the suffering Job was blessed anew**

The didactic poem of Job, who, like his friends, appears to be a paradigmatic figure, not an individual with a biography, consists of a *prologue* and *epilogue* writing in literary prose and a *poetic core*. The prologue and the epilogue

1. Cf. Job 13.24; 33.10 and the discussion in the Babylonian → *Talmud* (BB 16b; Nid 52a-b).

recount how Job stood the test of suffering. The poetic core offers extensive speeches, meditations and prayers. In its present form, the book manifests a pyramid-like *structure* in seven elements *(I-VII).*

The *prologue* (*I, chs. 1–2)* presents Job as an exemplarily devout and ethically responsible person and describes how, as the result of a dispute between God and the satan, he came to suffer. The prologue knows a dual setting: the land of Uz (*ʿûs*),[2] located in the east (*qedem*) or – as the pertinent Hebrew term may also be translated – in antiquity, whose name recalls a key word in the book of Job (the term 'to advise' [*yāʿaṣ*], 'counsel/plan' [*ʿeṣâ*]), and heaven, where Yhwh and his heavenly council meet.

**The heavenly council and the Satan:** From the perspective of the history of religions, the Old Testament concept of God's heavenly council[3] is based in Ancient Near Eastern myths, e.g., of El and Baal and the sons of god surrounding them in heaven and, in terms of its imagery, on scenes from the royal court of Ancient Near Eastern kings. In the Old Testament, the sons of God have been demoted to members of the heavenly world or to angels. The Satan, whose designation in Job 1–2 and in Zech. 3.1-2 is a title, not yet a proper name as in 1 Chr. 21.1 and the intertestamental texts (cf. Jub. 17.16), seems to belong to this heavenly council and to play there the role of a provocateur between God and humankind.

One of these meetings in heaven became the starting point for testing, with Job as the example, whether faith in God is the result of happiness, its cause, or is unrelated to it. The Satan's question, namely whether Job, blessed in every respect, fears God (in the dual sense of 'to worship' and 'to fear') without reason, i.e. without cause and objective ('for naught', Job 1.9), constitutes the engine of everything that follows: Job first loses his property and his family, then his health. He reacts to the 'messengers to Job' with a comprehensive rite of penitence, a confession of his creatureliness, and praise for God as the ground and objective of his life, thus refuting the Satan. For seven days, Job remains quiet in the face of his friends who have come to comfort him. Their

2. The geographical location of Uz points either to the realm of the southern trans-Jordan, to Edom (cf. Gen. 36.28; Jer. 25.20; Lam. 4.21; Jer. 49.7; Bar. 3.22-23), or to the northern trans-Jordan, to the region of Hauran or Safa (cf. Gen. 10.23, 29; 22.21; Josephus, Antiquities I:6:4; cf. Josephus, Flavius, Judean Antiquities (ed. S. Mason; Leiden/Boston: Brill, 2000ff., Vol. 3).
3. In addition to Job 1.6-12, cf. 1 Kgs 22.19; Ps. 82.1.

behaviour presents an exemplary narrative model of pastoral care: hearing of the suffering of their friend, they set out, get on the level of the sufferer, in solidarity, look and wait until the sufferer himself speaks (2.10-13).

*Job's* extensive *lament* (*II, ch. 3*) follows the prologue. The curse on the day of his birth (cf. Jer. 20.14-18; Sir. 40.1) with the questions about the cause and objective of his sorrow-shaped life develops into a dispute of God's creative power (cf. Job 3.4 with Gen. 1.3). Thus, Job 3 constitutes a poetic realization of Job's name ('Where is the father = the creator?') and of the question about the basis of piety, which is ultimately a question about God's nature (1.6-12). At the same time, Job 3 deals with the theological centre of the book of Job, which will reach its objective in the creator's self-presentation in the divine speeches.

In a meditative and circular fashion, the *dialogue* itself (*III, chs. 4–28*) discusses the relationship between justice, piety, fortune, and misfortune. The dispute is usually divided into three speech sequences (chs. 4–14, chs. 15–21, chs. 22–27/28). Yet, a subdivision into two speech sequences (chs. 4–14 and chs. 15–24) with an appendix (chs. 25–28) seems more appropriate. The basis of the argument is → *wisdom* informed by life experience and by confidence in a just world order. *Four ideas* are the focus: (1) there is a direct relationship between one's behaviour and one's fate ('*deed-consequence relationship*');[4] (2) God always requites justly; (3) suffering is a temporally limited punishment by God; and (4) in suffering, repentance is necessary and God's gracious attention is possible.

> In the *first speech sequence* (chs. 4–14), the friends develop these four points. In contrast, for Job, the notion of a God who loves the life of his creature and confidence in a just world order are shattered in view of the excess of suffering. Job's confession of his innocence, his questioning of God's righteousness, and his meditations on the frailty of life contrast with the wisdom counsel of his friends. *The main theme of the second sequence of speeches* (chs. 15–21) is the depiction of the horrid fate of the godless judged by God (chs. 15; 18; 20). Since this depiction has close affinities with the description of Job's suffering, Job learns indirectly that they equate him with a godless person. Thus, he turns,

4. This concept also appears in scholarship under the terms 'fate producing sphere of action' or 'connective justice'; see J. Assmann, *Ma'at: Gerechtigkeit und Unsterblichkeit im Alten Ägypten* (2nd ed., Munich: Beck, 1995), 66–7; G. Freuling, '*Wer eine Grube gräbt…': Der Tun-Ergehen-Zusammenhang und sein Wandel in der alttestamentlichen Weisheitsliteratur* (WMANT 102; Neukirchen-Vluyn: Neukirchener, 2004).

> disappointed, away from his friends. Because, as the author of suffering, God is the only one who can end it, it is not possible to flee God, and to do so would not end the suffering, Job hopes that God's grace is ultimately greater than his wrath (chs. 16–17; 19). Job produces statistical evidence that, contrary to the theory of just retribution in the world, the godless often prosper (ch. 21). Thus, he refutes the inference from a person's experience to a behaviour that justifies it. A direct accusation against Job that he had violated central commandments of humanity, further calls to repentance, and the repetition of the thesis, already formulated twice, concerning the unrighteousness of human beings contingent upon their creaturehood constitute the *last words of the friends* in the so-called third sequence of speeches (chs. 22; 25). Job closes the dialogue with a renewed confession of innocence, a reference to his failed search for God, a connection of his suffering with crises in the world, a hymn to the creative power of God that already alludes to the divine speeches, and a didactic speech. On the one hand, this speech repeats the descriptions of the fate of the godless offered by the friends but, on the other hand, sings of the cosmic wisdom accessible only to God (chs. 23–28). Although the book of Job, with its song to concealed wisdom (ch. 28), which recalls the song of the chorus in Greek tragedy in terms of dramaturgy and style, has attained an objective since people are offered the fear of God as the creation-conditioned replacement for the faulty capacity for absolute understanding of the world, the poet nonetheless begins a new speech sequence.

In a *tri-partite monologue (IV, chs. 29–31)*, the poet allows Job to look back on his blessed past (ch. 29), lament his current misfortune (ch. 30), and confess his innocence in a confession configured predominantly as an oath alluding to the commandments of the → *Decalogue* (ch. 31). Retrospective, lament, and confession culminate in an appeal to God finally to respond.

Before God himself speaks, retarding the pace *(V, chs. 32–37)*, a fourth friend appears: *Elihu* ('He, i.e. Yhwh, is my God'), the son of Barakel ('God blesses') from the tribe of Ram ('Exalted'). In *four distinct monologues*, Elihu concerns himself with a 'new' interpretation of suffering. Incensed at Job's contention that he is just and, equally, at the incapacity of the friends to refute Job, Elihu understands himself as an inspired advocate for the just creator God. The 'novelty' in Elihu's speeches consists in the interpretation of suffering as a pedagogical means of God, already indicated by Eliphaz (5.17), in the concept of an interceding angel (5.1) who can intercede with God for the sufferer who repents, and in the prospect of an imminent revelation of God (chs. 36–37).

Finally, *God speaks* (*VI, chs. 38–41)* – from the 'whirlwind' (38.1). With this single word, the poet indicates that he embeds the subsequent speech in an appearance of God ('theophany'; cf. Nah. 1.3). After a direct address to the *man* Job (Job 38.2-3), who feels surrounded by God himself (3.23), who hopes in God's adherence to justice (16.21), and who wants to approach God like a prince (31.37), Job is led in a long chain of rhetorical questions through the entire cosmos, through space and time. The creation of the animate and inanimate world and its maintenance by God, who knows the correct time for everything, refute Job's dispute of God's creative power in his initial lament. Job already becomes silent after the first divine speech (40.3-5): the rejection of an anthropocentric perspective – people are mentioned only once in the first divine speech – has shown Job that his fate is integrated into a larger plan of creation. The poet embarks immediately on a second divine speech (40.6–41.26 [NRSV 41.34]). An ironic challenge to Job's right and might and the extensive description of God's playful involvement with the Behemoth and the Leviathan, through which shine the mythical beings from the primordium and the eschaton, take the place of the brief depictions of animals in ch. 39. Once again, neither human beings nor Job's suffering are mentioned explicitly. Nonetheless, after this second divine speech, Job confesses God's omnipotence and his own creaturehood, and affirms that he has now seen God himself. Job 42.6 can be understood as an expression either of comfort or of Job's regret.

The book concludes with a *narrative assessment* of the dialogue and the description of Job's future good fortune (*VII, ch. 42.7-17)*. The epilogue, which begins as though God had been the last to speak, and not Job, characterizes Job's speeches as 'right' in contrast to those of his friends – apparently because he described reality, often enigmatic even if established by God, in harmony with his experience more truly (authentically) than the friends. Their speeches, which misconstrue Job's situation and person, are subject to the wrath of God which can only be overcome through the intercession of the righteous sufferer: in his suffering, he becomes the deliverer of his supposed comforters. Those who had actually come on a consolation visit to Job, smitten by God, become witnesses of the new blessing. Examples of this new blessing are Job's doubled property, the beauty of his daughters, explicitly named and provided with inheritances, and his advanced age, which he shares with Abraham, Isaac and Jacob.

# 14.2 Textual Issues and Major Issues in the History of Critical Interpretation

## 14.2.1 The Relationship between the Prose Framework and the Poetry

While Job appears in the prose prologue and epilogue as the example of a devout and patient sufferer, he appears in the poetic speeches with his friends as a rebel who vigorously complains about his suffering and accuses God. While the prologue knows the Satan as the initiator of Job's suffering, this figure appears in neither Job's speeches nor those of the friends or of God. While the prologue reports the death of Job's children, Job's lament in ch. 19 presupposes that they are still alive.

The ***designations for God*** are unusual. The proper name of the Old Testament God, Yhwh ('Lord'), surfaces only in parts of the prologue (1.6-12; 1.21; 2.1-7), in the epilogue (42.7-17), in the superscriptions to the divine speeches (38.1; 40.1, 3, 6, 42.1), and once in 12.9, while otherwise, the text speaks of *Elohim*, *El* or *Eloah* (each translated in English translations with 'God'), *Šadday* (usually rendered 'the Almighty') and once *Adonay* ('the Lord', 28.28). The use of *El*, *Eloah* and *Šadday* are limited to the poetry.

These (and other) differences in content and style between Job 1–2 and 42.7-17, on the one hand, and 3.1–42.6, on the other, already led in the 18th century to tracing the prose prologue and epilogue and the poetic speeches to different authors. *Four models* define the literary-historical relationship between the parts:[5]

(1) A framing narrative was secondarily written around the older poetry.
(2) The poetry was inserted secondarily into the older Job narrative.
(3) The author of the poetry adapted material from an older, already firmly fixed Job tradition to form the prologue and epilogue without completely harmonizing it with the poetry.
(4) The Job poetry and the Job narrative represent originally independent literary versions of the Job material, which were only combined with one another by a redactor.

5. Cf. the discussion in W.-D. Syring, *Hiob und sein Anwalt* (BZAW 336; Berlin/New York: de Gruyter, 2004), 47–9.

At the same time, attempts appear in more recent research to trace the book of Job to *one* author and to explain the differences mentioned in terms of content or composition.[6]

### 14.2.2 The Problem of the So-Called Third Sequence of Speeches (chs. 22–28)

In relation to chs. 4–21, chs. 22–28 exhibit a few peculiarities. The third friend, Zophar, no longer speaks; the speech of the second friend, Bildad, encompasses only five verses (25.2-6), and has close affinities in content with the first and second speeches of Eliphaz (cf. 4.17-10; 15.14-17), but does not have a framework comparable with other speeches by the friends. Job's speeches in 24.13-25 and 27.13-23 contradict his position in ch. 21 and resemble the speeches of the friends for lengthy sections. At points in 26.5-14 and 28.1-28 (cf. Prov. 8), Job anticipates the divine speeches (and Elihu's speeches). If these phenomena are not to be explained in terms of transmission technique by hypothesizing a secondarily corrupted text or in terms of dramaturgy by assuming a confusion of speakers at the end of the dialogue as intended by the poet, there remains only the (more likely) assumption of redactional revision of the poetry in Job.

### 14.2.3 The Problem of the Elihu Speeches (chs. 32–37)

The tri-partite speech of Job in chs. 29–31 leads toward a direct encounter with God. The block of Elihu's four monologues inserted between Job's final confession of innocence and the divine speech that reacts to it stand out from the rest of the book in terms of diction and content. The speeches of Elihu exhibit a strong Aramaic influence. In contrast to all preceding speeches by the friends, they address Job by name. They cite Job's speeches verbatim (33.9; 34.9; 35.2-3). The concept of an interceding and redeeming angel perceptible in chap. 33 differs from the → *angelology* perceptible elsewhere in the book. Finally, Elihu's speeches anticipate the content of chs. 38–39 although, from a compositional perspective, in ch. 37, they prepare for the divine speech as theophany. With a few exceptions, scholarship rightly regards the Elihu speeches as secondary, although there is some debate as to whether they are a literary unity or the redactor (or redactors) of chapters 32–37 is (or are) evident in other passages in the book of Job.[7]

6. See, e.g., N. Whybray, *Job* (Sheffield: Sheffield Academic Press, 1998).

7. T. Mende, *Durch Leiden zur Vollendung: Die Elihureden im Buch Ijob (Ijob 32–37)* (TThSt 49; Trier: Paulinus, 1990).

### 14.2.4 The Problem of the Divine Speeches (chs. 32.1–42.6)

Job's wish for a direct encounter with God (31.35-37) links to the direct address to Job in the opening of the first divine speech (38.2-3). The rhetorical questions to Job regarding the creation and maintenance of the world that follow in the first divine speech, however, nowhere explicitly treat Job's questions concerning the cause and objective of his suffering. It is not immediately clear how these explanations of cosmology offer Job a solution to the problem of the suffering of the righteous laid out in the poetry of Job. Consequently, scholarship repeatedly attempts to refute the originality of the divine speeches and to permit the poetry to end with an unheard cry by the righteous sufferer.[8] Considerations of content, form and dramaturgy speak against such a radical solution. Yet, questions arise as to (1) whether the two divine speeches are to be attributed to one author in view of their differences in language and motif, (2) how the brief divine speech in 40.1-12 and the two responses by Job in 40.3-5 and 42.1-6 relate to one another literarily, and (3) what constitutes the contribution of the divine speech(es) to the problem of Job.

## 14.3 Origins of the Book of Job

### 14.3.1 The Form and the Forms of the Book of Job

In its current form, the book offers a combination, unique in the Old Testament, of literary → *genres* and speech forms from various contexts. The prologue and the epilogue are written in literary prose, i.e. in a language that makes use of many poetic stylistic techniques but is not structured metrically. In all, the framework narrative can be characterized as a didactic novella or a → *wisdom* didactic narrative. In terms of narrative technique, it finds its nearest parallels in the books of Ruth and Jonah. With regard to the details, the Joban framework narrative employs elements of the fairy tale, the legend and the *myth*. In contrast, the essential genres of *Joban poetry* stem from the realms of wisdom, psalms, law and prophecy.

8. V. Maag, *Hiob: Wandlung und Verarbeitung des Problems in Novelle, Dialogdichtung und Spätfassungen* (FRLANT 128; Göttingen: Vandenhoeck & Ruprecht, 1982), 99–123, and to this J. v. Oorschot, *Gott als Grenze: Eine literar- und redaktionsgeschichtliche Studie zu den Gottesreden des Hiobbuches* (BZAW 170; Berlin/New York: de Gruyter, 1987).

*Wisdom speech forms* (Ch. 15) are:
(1) the aphorism/*māšāl* (cf. Ch. 4.11),
(2) the disputation, which constitutes the basic model for all the speeches of the friends (cf. Job 8),
(3) the didactic speech (cf. Job 27.11-23),
(4) meditations on the frailty of human existence (cf. Job 14.1-12), and
(5) the encyclopedic listing of the works of creation in the divine speeches (cf. Job 38.4–39.30), which are anchored in Ancient Near Eastern onomastic wisdom.

The following stem from the *psalmody* (Ch. 13):
(1) Job's laments and petitions addressed to God in the second person singular, which contain the central elements of the laments and petitions of the individual (cf. Job 7.7-21), and
(2) hymnic elements in individual speeches by Job (cf. Job 9.5-13; 10.8-12; 12.13-25; 23.8-9, 13-14; 26.5-14), the friends (cf. Job 11.7-9) and God (Job 38–41).

The following stem from the *realm of law* (Ch. 6):
(1) juridical vocabulary (cf. 'dispute' [*rîb*], 'law/statute' [*mišpāṭ*]),
(2) the challenge to God to engage in a legal dispute (Job 9.2-4.; 13.13-27; 23.3-7), and
(3) elements of the confession of innocence preserved in oath form in chapter 31.

Eliphaz' accusation of Job in Job 22.5-9 traces back to the *prophetic genre* of the critique of social misbehaviour ('prophetic social critique'; cf. Chs 4.2.1.3; 12.16.1; 12.31). The depiction of the reception of revelation in Job 4.12-16 also stems from prophetic literature (Ch. 12.55).

The transfer of individual genres from a specific *setting in life* into poetry has given them a *setting in the book*. In the meantime, individual genres in their new context in Joban poetry have acquired a function different than the one for which they were intended (Ch. 2.1.1). An intentional alienation of genres, a 'misuse', becomes evident when, for example, a motif from praise of the creator recurs in the accusation against God (cf. Job 7.17 with Ps. 8.5-6). In addition to the phenomena of genre-mixture and genre-appropriation, Joban poetry also manifests explicit or implicit references to other texts that precede the poetry of Job. Thus, the book of Job constitutes an exemplary intertextual work.[9]

9. M. Köhlmoos, *Das Auge Gottes: Textstrategie im Hiobbuch* (FAT 25; Tübingen: Mohr Siebeck, 1999).

## 14.3.2 The Composition and Redaction of the Book of Job

The book exhibits no indication of authorship. According to Jewish tradition, it was written by Moses (perhaps in the sense of an attribution of authority; cf. *b. B. Bat.* 14). The → *canon* of the Syriac Orthodox Bible (Peshitta), for example, which offers the book of Job following Deuteronomy, also reflects this tradition. Because of its wisdom character, with reservation, Luther attributed it, like Proverbs and Ecclesiastes, to Solomon. Considerations of literary and theological history speak for its origins in the course of the fifth to third centuries BCE. As the product of a long history of composition and redaction, it is not the unified literary word of one author. The *germ* of the book consists of a *Job legend*, which can no longer be reconstructed, that told of a man named Job who proved himself in suffering. The degree to which the aphorism transmitted in Ezek. 14.14, 20 concerning the three just men of the primordium, Daniel, Joab and Noah, actually traces back to an old tradition is controversial in contemporary scholarship in view of the unclarified circumstances of the redaction history of the book of Ezekiel (Ch. 11).

The *Joban material* was (1) literarily incorporated in the form of a grand *dialogical poem* that originally encompassed only chs. 3–27.6; 29–31; 38–39, on the one hand, and (2) treated in the form of a *novella* essentially preserved in 1.1-5, 13-21; 42.11-17, on the other. Both the Job novella and the presumably older Joban poetry were first revised and transmitted independently before (3) they were combined redactionally into one *book*. The novella was thereby given a new function as the framework narrative and the dialogical poetry were harmonized formally and in terms of content through the inclusion of: the heaven scenes (1.6-12; 2.1-6), the scene involving Job's illness (which depends on the second heaven scene), the subsequent discussion between Job and his wife (2.7-10), the visit by the three friends (2.11-13), and Job's intercession for his friends (42.7-10). The book that developed through the combination of novella and poetry underwent additional *redactional revisions* (4) until its inclusion among the 'Writings'. In the course of these revisions, the picture of Job and the interpretation of his suffering were repeatedly modified.

Viewed schematically, *four phases in the literary history* of the book result:

(1) the *Joban poetry* and its independent transmission and expansion,
(2) the *Job novella* and its independent transmission and expansion,

(3) the redactional *combination of the Job novella and the Joban poetry* into a *book of Job* consisting of a poetic core with a prose framework, and
(4) *redactional revisions* of the book of Job.

**The tradition of the righteous sufferer and the problematization of the concept of a just world order incorporated into the cosmos by the creator God**

The *Mesopotamian realm* offers poems analogous to theodicy (→ *theodicy*),[10] which share four essential structural assumptions with the Joban theme:

(1) the existence of a concept of guilt,
(2) the dignity of the individual,
(3) the relativization of → *polytheism* through belief in the personal god,
(4) the concept of retribution for good and evil in this world.

The 'Babylonian Theodicy' (translated in *COS* I, 492–5) represents the nearest parallel. In its redactional final form, this poem stems from the period around 800 BCE. The poem sometimes characterized as the 'Sumerian Job' (translated in *COS* I, 573–5) from the third millennium BCE involves an individual lament which offers its closest parallels to the book of Job in the meditations on suffering in chs. 7; 10; 14; 16; 19, and 29–30. The situation is similar with respect to the Babylonian poem *Ludlul bēl nēmeqi* ('I will praise the lord of wisdom', translated in *COS* I, 486–92).[11]

In addition to the Mesopotamian parallels, there are *Egyptian texts or groups* of texts:

(1) The 'Admonition of *Ipuwer*' (translated in Lichtheim, *AEL* I, 149–63) from the period around 2200 to 2040 BCE presents a lament over political and social grievance in the face of a comprehensive political crisis (cf. Job 21; 24).
(2) 'The Conversation of a Life-Weary Individual with his *Ba*' (translated in Lichtheim, *AEL* I, 163–9), also composed in the second millennium BCE, offers a poetical interchange between a sufferer and his *Ba* ('soul')[12] concerning just retribution, the future of the dead, and the structure of life.
(3) The 'Songs of the Harpist' (translated in Lichtheim, *AEL* I, 193–7; *AEL* II, 115–116), poetical reflections on life here and in the hereafter often placed in the mouth of a blind harpist, were sung at banquets and funeral ceremonies and called for the enjoyment of life in view of the inevitability of death (Ch. 18).
(4) 'The Laments of the Farmer/The Eloquent Peasant' (translated in *ANET*, 407–10)

10. A. Laato and J. C. de Moor, eds, *Theodicy in the World of the Bible* (Leiden/Boston: Brill, 2003).
11. Cf. Ps. 39.12-14 (NRSV 11-13); 35.13; 88.9 (NRSV 88.8); Jer. 12.6; 20.6; Lam. 3.4.
12. The term is difficult to translate; cf. H. Brunner, *Altägyptische Religion* (3rd ed., Darmstadt: Wissenschaftliche Buchgesellschaft, 1989), 138–44.

include an account with nine speeches, written entirely in poetry, by a farmer who demands justice in view of his experience of caprice.

(5) *Disputations between two persons from the papyrus Anastasi I* (translated in *ANET*, 475–9).

(6) *The 125th saying from the 'Book of the Dead'* from the 15th cent. BCE contains a 'negative confession of sins', comparable to Job's confession of innocence in ch. 31, i.e. a stereotypical list of misdeeds which, in the case of the 'Book of the Dead', the deceased had not committed in his life (translated in Lichtheim, *AEL* II, 124–32).

(7) Individual ethical and religious admonitions, which occur primarily in the friends' speeches in the poetry of Job and which, in terms of the history of forms and ideas, trace to Ancient Near Eastern proverbial wisdom, have older parallels in the *Instruction for Life* (translated in Lichtheim, *AEL* I, 58–80; II, 135–63; III, 159–217; cf. Chs 15 and 18).

(8) The list of natural phenomena in the *onomastica* ('lists of names') has affinities with Job 38f.

Two texts among the *literature transmitted in Aramaic* from the first millennium BCE are occasionally compared to the book of Job:

(1) the *Ahiqar Novella* (translated in *OTP* II, 479–507), which, apart from the literary parallel involving the redactional combination of a younger narrative with older poetic wisdom sayings and a few verbal parallels, is more reminiscent of the books of Esther and Daniel (Ch. 20; 21) and the → deuterocanonical book of Tobit, however;

(2) the 'Prayer of the Babylonion King Nabonidus' preserved only in fragments from cave 4 at → *Qumran*[13] from the first cent. BCE, which, apart from the parallel motif of suffering as a means of instruction, has tendencies which are more reminiscent of the biblical book of Daniel (21).

As early as the early church, the book of Job has been repeatedly compared with the classical *Greek tragedies*. There are parallels in structure and content with regard to the treatment of the question of the justice of the creator god, especially in the dramas of Aeschylus (525/4–456/5 BCE), especially with 'Prometheus Bound', and of Euripides (485/4–406 BCE), in the first instance with his 'Medea' and 'Bacchae'.[14]

With regard to all the texts mentioned from the environment of the Old Testament, one must first consider the particular cultural and religious context of each and its specific literary and formal character. In most cases, echoes of motifs are based on a common intellectual milieu in the eastern Mediterranean and the Near East and can be traced to a wisdom understanding of reality demonstrable throughout the Levant since the third millennium BCE.

⇨

13. 4QPrNab ar = 4Q242, translated in F. García Martínez and E. J. C. Tigchelaar, *The Dead Sea Scrolls* I, 486–89.

14. English translations are available in H. W. Smith, *Aeschylus: Suppliant maidens, Persian, Prometheus, Seven against Thebes* (LCL 145; Cambridge, Mass.: Harvard University Press, 1973, repr. 2001); D. Kovacs, ed., *Euripides: Cyclops, Alcestis, Medea* (LCL 12; Cambridge, Mass.: Harvard University Press, 1995); idem, *Bacchae* (LCL 495; Cambridge, Mass.: Harvard University Press, 2002).

F. Sedlmeier, 'Ijob und die Auseinandersetzungsliteratur im alten Mesopotamien'. Pages 85–136 in *Das Buch Ijob: Gesamtdeutung – Einzeltexte – Zentrale Themen*. ÖBS 31. Ed. by T. Seidl and S. Ernst. Frankfurt a. M.: Lang, 2007; C. Uehlinger, 'Das Hiob-Buch im Kontext der altorientalischen Literatur- und Religionsgeschichte'. Pages 97–163 in *Das Buch Hiob und seine Interpretationen*. ATANT 88. Ed. by T. Krüger *et al.* Zurich: Theologischer Verlag, 2007.

### 14.3.3 The Situation and Function of the Book of Job

The Babylonian → *Talmud* already expresses the justifiable suspicion that Job himself never lived, and that, therefore, the extant book does not represent a biographical survey of a historically verifiable occurrence, but a *didactic, parable-like fiction* (*māšāl*, cf. *b. B. Bat.* 15a). In more recent scholarship, one finds an entire palette of form-critical classifications (tragedy, comedy, epic, didactic poem, dramatized lament, concentrated legal dispute, and a work *sui generis*). Considering its redaction history, the question of the form of the book should be regarded with greater nuance and answered variously for each of its individual stages. The overall work lends itself to assignment to the category of *disputation literature* known especially from Egyptian wisdom. In terms of language and the history of tradition, the book of Job stems from learned wisdom circles in the Persian/Hellenistic period.

## 14.4 Theology of the Book of Job

The book of Job can be understood as a critically interpreted *kaleidoscope of Old Testament concepts and experiences of God*. The starting point for the discussion of God, both for the friends and for Job, is the *interpretation of the experiences of life* as experiences of God's activity. Three horizons of experience are evident: (1) *God's proximity*, which can be experienced as life-nurturing, but also as life-threatening, the latter in the case of Job who experiences God as so oppressively near that he desires time apart from God (Job 14.13); (2) *God's power*, which can be experienced as chaos-controlling and as life-destroying, the latter in the case of Job, who also suffers from his own impotence in relation to the God who withdraws from him (Job 16.12–17.7; 23.8-9); (3) *God's handling of justice*, which can be experienced as responsible, but also as capricious, the latter in the case of Job who understands his suffering as a breach of the law on God's part and a denunciation of the creator's solidarity with his creation (Job 9.15-35).

According to the book of Job, only a theology that (1) understands the ambivalence of experience of God, (2) also names the dark side of God and does not resolve the tensions in the image of God into dualism, and (3) views tradition, situation and person together is *upright speech about God.*

The question running throughout the whole book concerning God's nature ignites in the suffering of the righteous, which receives a multifaceted interpretation in the book itself. The number of theologies in the book confront a number of *interpretations of suffering*, from which a history of the interpretations of suffering in ancient Judaism can be inferred – a history that can be traced with variations down to today. While the oldest form of the Job novella understood suffering as a form of *testing* the righteous, the friends in the original poetry interpret it as *punishment* for concealed or public sins. Between the two interpretations stands the interpretation of sufferings as God's *pedagogical means*, an interpretation represented especially by Elihu. In contrast, the insertions in the speeches of the friends in 4.17-19; 15.14-17 and 25.1-6 treat the origin of suffering in the *sinfulness* of humankind which is a condition of its creaturehood. According to the divine speeches, suffering appears to be a *mystery*, which is incorporated into God's plan of creation, to be sure, but which ultimately escapes explanation. If all five of the interpretations of suffering mentioned possess partial truth, the decisive contribution of the book of Job does not lie in a general response to the question of the cause and goal of suffering, but in its guidance regarding proper *behaviour in suffering.*

Admittedly, in terms of → *genre*, the book of Job is not a handbook of pastoral care (M. Oeming), but a powerful literary engagement with the basic questions of human and divine existence. Nonetheless, it contains two central instructions for pastoral care, indeed, in the words of Job that open (3.1) and conclude (42.1-6) the book:[15] (1) Hearing precedes speaking for the pastoral caregiver; the first word should be the sufferer's. (2) A prescribed solution to the question of suffering will not succeed; only the sufferer himself can find such a solution in the encounter with God. Pastoral caregivers can accompany

15. G. Fischer, 'Heilendes Gespräch – Betrachtungen zur Kommunikation im Hiobbuch', in *Das Buch Ijob: Gesamtdeutungen – Einzeltexte – Zentrale Themen* (ÖBS 31; ed. T. Seidl and S. Ernst; Frankfurt a. M.: Lang, 2007), 103–200.

the sufferer on the way to this encounter. In the best case, they – like Job's friends – will be comforted and taught by the sufferer.

## 14.5 Notes on the History of Reception

The history of the literary reception and interpretation of the book of Job already begins in *ancient Judaism*. The *Targum of Job from → Qumran* (11QtgJob)[16] from the period around 100 BCE represents not only the oldest known preserved Aramaic translation of a biblical book, but offers in its reformulation of 42.9 ('and he, i.e. God, forgave their sins for [Job's] sake') a characteristic extrapolation of the image of Job and of the concept of sin. The version of Job$^{LXX}$ (→ *Septuagint*) that developed in the second/first century BCE, is approximately one-sixth shorter overall than the Hebrew book of Job. It offers in the prologue a long lament, not represented in the Hebrew text, by Job's wife concerning the loss of her children, makes Job's friends into kings, situates Job in Esau's family in another addition to the material in the epilogue of the Hebrew text, and lists Job among people who will one day rise from the dead. This concept of a resurrection, which goes beyond the this-wordly orientation of the Joban poetry, also occurs in the *Testament of Job*, a → *pseudepigraphic* document from the second cent. CE,[17] and in broad segments of the Christian reception of Job 19.25-27. The Hebrew basis of Job 19.25-27 refers to Job's hope to see God as his redeemer who will put him in the right in this life (cf. 42.5). The identification of the redeemer with Christ and the interpretation of Job's expectation as hope in a post-mortal bodily resurrection can be traced from the early church through pre-critical scholarship. It was recorded on many gravestones, especially in the Baroque period, and in individual church songs.

The *New Testament* mentions the book of Job or the hero of its title four times. The author of the Letter of James praises Job's patience, as does the Latin version of the book of Tobith (Ch. 26; cf. James 5.11; Tob. 2.15). In 1 Cor. 3.19, Paul appeals to Job 5.13, in Phil. 1.19 to Job 13.16 and in Rom. 11.35 to Job 41.3 (NRSV 41.11).

Since late antiquity, there have been many Jewish and Christian

16. Translated in F. García Martínez and E. J. C. Tigchelaar, *The Dead Sea Scrolls* II, 1184–1201.

17. Translation by R. P. Spittler, 'Testament of Job', in *OTP* I, 829–68.

commentaries on the book of Job. An intensive *literary engagement* with the book of Job as a work of art and with the problem of Job as the supposedly oldest treatment of the idea of → *theodicy* began with the Enlightenment. Immanuel Kant's essay 'Über das Misslingen aller philosophischen Versuche in der Theodizee' (1791), Johann Wolfgang Goethe's 'Faust' (1808/1832), Søren Kierkegaard's 'Gjentagelsen' (Repetition; 1843), and Josef Roth's *Hiob: Roman eines einfachen Mannes* (1930) can serve as representatives of the multitude.[18] In a particular manner, Job, who still functions as a symbol for the sufferer outright, has come to symbolize the unnumbered Job figures of the Shoah.[19]

In the graphic *arts*, depictions of Job already appear in the synagogue of Dura-Europos (ca. 250 CE) and in the Catacombs of Callixtus (4th cent. CE). Thenceforth, 'Job' appears throughout the history of Western art, beginning with illustrations in Christian and Jewish Bible manuscripts, continued in painting (Rembrandt, for example) to the lithographies (by Oskar Kokoschka, for example) and sculptures of modern art (Ernst Barlach, for example).[20] The focus is usually Job sitting in the dust, the sufferer conversing with his wife, or the man twisted in pain. Attempts to set the book of Job to music began in the eighteenth cent. (more recently, e.g., by Peter Eben, 'Eight Studies on the Book of Job').

18. Glatzer, *Dimensions of Job*.

19. K. Wolff, *Hiob 1943: Ein Requiem für das Warschauer Getto* (2nd ed., Berlin: Evangelische Verlagsanstalt, 1984).

20. C.-L. Seow, 'Job's Wife, with Due Respect', in *Das Buch Hiob und seine Interpretationen* (ATANT 88; ed. T. Krüger, *et al.*; Zurich, Theologischer Verlag, 2007), 351–73; S. Terrien, *The Iconography of Job: Through the Centuries: Artists as Biblical Interpreters* (University Park, Penn.: Pennsylvania State University Press, 1996).

# 15

# The Book of Proverbs (The Sayings of Solomon/Proverbs)

(Markus Witte – Translation by Mark Biddle)

## Chapter Outline



Commentaries: H. F. Fuhs (NEchtB 35. Würzburg: Echter, 2001); A. Meinhold (2 vols. ZBK 16. Zurich: Theologischer Verlag, 1991); R. E. Murphy (FOTL 13. Grand Rapids, Mich.: Eerdmans, 1981); idem (WBL 11. Nashville, Tenn.: T. Nelson, 1998).

I. Kottsieper, 'Alttestamentliche Weisheit'. *TRu* 67 (2002): 1–34. 201–22; J. v. Oorschot, 'Weisheit in Israel und im frühen Judentum'. *VF* 48 (2003): 59–89; L. G. Perdue, *Wisdom Literature: A Theological History*. Louisville, Ky.: Westminster John Knox, 2007, 37–76. 335–64; S. Weeks, *Instruction and Imagery in Proverbs 1–9*. Oxford: Oxford University Press, 2007; L. G. Perdue, ed., *Scribes, Sages and Seers: The Sage in the Eastern Mediterranean World*. FRLANT 219. Göttingen: Vandenhoeck & Ruprecht, 2008.

German Classic: G. von Rad, *Wisdom in Israel*. Transl. by J. D. Martin. London: SCM, 1972.

Jewish tradition refers to the book by its initial words, *mišlê (šělōmōh)* 'Proverbs (of Solomon)' (1.1). In keeping with the etymology of *māšāl* ('proverb'/'parable'/'aphorism'), the title refers to a linguistic expression that reveals reality by means of a comparative observation and that communicates life-nurturing knowledge. The translation 'Sayings (of Solomon)' chosen by the Luther and Zurich translations is fitting since the term 'saying' can, first, stand for the most widely varied forms of sayings,[1] and, second, encompasses the elements of demand, advice, appeal and objection. In contrast, the title 'Proverbs' (the standard translation) that traces back to the designations for the book in the → *Septuagint* (*paroimia*) and the → *Vulgate* (*proverbia*), limits the rich significance of the Hebrew title.

| | |
|---|---|
| 1.1–9.18 | **'Sayings of Solomon, the son of David, king of Israel'** |
| | 1.2-7 Proem |
| | 1.8–9.18 Ten didactic discourses and three wisdom poems (1.20-33; 8.1-36; 9.1-18) |
| **10.1–22.16** | **'Sayings of Solomon'** |
| **22.17–24.22** | **'*Words* of the Wise'** |
| **24.23-34** | **'These too are *Words* of the Wise'** |
| **25.1–29.27** | **'These too are Sayings of Solomon, collected by the men of Hezekiah, king of Judah'** |
| **30.1-33** | **'*Words* of Agur, the son of Yakem from Massa'** |
| **30.1-14** | Reflections and Prayer |
| **30.15-33** | Numerical sayings |
| **31.1-31** | **'*Words* of Lemuel, the king of Massa, which his mother taught him'** |
| **31.1-9** | Admonition for the king to live and judge rightly |
| **31.10-31** | Praise for the wise, God-fearing woman who acts independently |

# 15.1 Biblical Context

The book exhibits a *seven-part structure* marked by superscriptions.[2] The motif of the seven pillars of → *wisdom* (9.1) corresponds to this structural pattern. The superscription in 1.1 and the subsequent → *proem* (1.2-7), which cites the mediation of wisdom and the fear of God (i.e. piety) as the goal of the sayings, introduce both the first major section of the book (chs. 1–9) and the entire work. The motif of the fear of God fulfils a framing function (1.7; 31.30); it also appears in the middle of the book (15.33) and at other seams in the work.[3] Chapters 30–31, which offer a summation of the 'sayings, parables, words of the wise, and riddles' mentioned programmatically in 1.6

1. Biblical saying, motto, curse, mnemonic, blessing, aphorism, toast, spell, and many more.
2. Prov. 1.1; 10.1; 22.17; 24.23; 25.1; 30.1; 31.1.
3. Prov. 2.5; 3.7; 8.13; 9.10; 10.27; 14.2, 26; 15.16; 16.6; 19.23; 22.4; 23.17; 24.21.

and assembled in 1.8–29.27, constitute the conclusion to the frame. Thus, the educational programme of the sayings flows into: (1) a prayer (30.5-7), (2) an awed description of the world's riddles (30.15-33), (3) a call to justice and aid for the poor (31.8-9), and (4) praise for the exemplarily wise and pious woman (31.10-31). She appears as a counter-figure to the godless and as an ideal of lived belief in Yhwh. The extensive sequences of sayings attributed to Solomon in 10.1–22.16 and 25.1–29.27, each followed by two brief sequences of sayings without attribution or by non-Israelite wisdom teachers (22.17–24.22; 24.23-34 or 30; 31, respectively), manifest a *parallel structure*.

Following the *Introduction to instruction formulas* (→ *Lehreröffnungsformel*: 'Hear, my son...' / 'My son...'),[4] the most carefully crafted *first major section (1.8–9.18)* divides into ten didactic discourses. At their centre stands the call to fear God and the warnings against evildoing and adultery in the form of the admonitory description of the 'strange woman'. Poems to personified wisdom in 3.13-20; 8.1-36 and 9.1-8 and a series of numeral sayings in 6.1-19 (cf. 30.15-33) are inserted between the didactic discourses. Concentric correspondences between individual motifs and speech forms appear in the first major section.[5]

The sub-division of the second and fifth major sections (10.1-22:16 and 25.1–29.27, respectively) is based less on synchronic signals as on form- and tradition-critical observations. According to them, the *Solomonic collection* divides into the two sections, 10.1–15.33 and 16.1–22.16, and the *Hezekianic collection* into the two blocks, 25.1–27.27 and 28.1–29.27.

# 15.2 Textual Issues and Major Issues in the History of Critical Interpretation

## 15.2.1 The Book of Proverbs and Old Testament Wisdom Literature

Proverbs represents the book in the Old Testament most shaped by so-called wisdom (*ḥokmâ*). The term *ḥokmâ* designates, first, technical knowledge of

4. Prov. 1.8; 3.1, 21; 4.1, 10, 20; 5.1, 7 (variant); 6.20; 7.1.

5. Prov. 1.7 || 9.10; 1.20–33 || 8.1-36; 3.15 || 8.11.

a craft (cf. Exod. 31.1-11; 35.30-31). In an expanded meaning, it stands for a capacity for differentiation and orientation based on experience by means of which a person manages life. In this sense, wisdom aims at a successful life and is manifest as life skills. Its starting point is the observation of phenomena in nature and culture. Its horizons are all areas of human life in family and society. Its theoretical background is the notion that God incorporated a just order (*ṣĕdāqâ*, Egyptian → *Ma'at*) into this world. Adherence to it promises both individuals and communities the 'way of life' (Prov. 6.23), i.e. good fortune in every respect. Central is the conviction that a person's deeds and their consequences are contingent upon one another ('*deed-consequence relationship*', Ch. 14.1).[6] Those who observe themselves and their environment carefully, who heed the instruction of their predecessors, and who orient their lives according to the just world order are considered wise (*ḥākām*). Accordingly, those who do not pay careful attention to the world they live in and arrogantly disregard the tradition are considered idiots (*kĕsîl*) and fools (*'ĕwîl*). The righteous/pious (*ṣāddîq*) and the evildoer/godless (*rāšā'*) appear as (late) equivalents to the wise and the fool.

This wisdom for life and perspective based on experience and tradition and on the concept of an order that permeates the cosmos is *an international phenomenon* that appears in the Near East beginning in the third millennium BCE among the Sumerians, Akkadians and Egyptians and, since the second/first millennium BCE in the Syro-Palestinian realm.[7] In the realm of wisdom, the Old Testament is most evidently involved with Near Eastern cultures. The → *genres* that include the three → *canonical* (Proverbs, Job and Ecclesiastes) and two → *deuterocanonical* (Sirach and Wisdom of Solomon) wisdom books in the Old Testament and the sections shaped by wisdom patterns of language and thought in the historical, prophetic and psalm traditions have parallels in Mesopotamia, Syria, Egypt and Greece. In Mesopotamia, they occur primarily in the Sumerian *proverb collections* (1900–1800 BCE),[8] in Egypt in the *Instructions for Life*[9] attested from the Old Kingdom (2635-2155 BCE) to the period of → *Hellenism,* in the *onomastica*,

6. G. Freuling, *Wer eine Grube gräbt* (above, Ch. 14 n. 38).

7. D. J. A. Clines, A. Lichtenberger and H.-P. Müller, eds, *Weisheit in Israel* (Altes Testament und Moderne 12; Münster: Lit, 2003); R. J. Clifford, ed., *Wisdom Literature in Mesopotamia and Israel* (SBLSymS 36; Atlanta, Ga.: SBL, 2007).

8. Translated in *COS* I, 563–7.

9. Translated by M. Lichtheim, *AEL* III.

and among the Greeks, *proverbial wisdom* in the form of the proverb (*paroimia*), the aphorism (*gnōmē*), the contextualized motto (*apophthegma*) and the statement of advice (*hypothēkē*).[10] The Aramaic 'Sayings of Ahiqar' (Ch. 14.3) should be included.[11]

The aphorism/*māšāl* represents the simplest *genre* of Old Testament wisdom literature. The *didactic discourse*, the *didactic poem* attested primarily in wisdom Psalms,[12] the *reflections* (Ch. 18) that surface in Ecclesiastes, the *disputations* of the book of Job (Ch. 14), and the *didactic wisdom novella*[13] extant in the form of the Job novella (Ch. 14), the books of Jonah (Ch.12E), Ruth (Ch. 16), Esther (Ch. 20), Tobit, and in passages in the Joseph narrative (Gen. 37–50; Ch. 7.5) are more complex forms. The Old Testament manifests an internal *development* that led from an implicitly religious wisdom for everyday life to a considered theological wisdom.

The ***theologization of wisdom*** has four facets:

(1) an explicit grounding of wisdom rules for life in the activity and character of God. The goal of wisdom is life in the fear of God and oriented by the ethos required by Yhwh, namely by righteousness (*ṣĕdāqâ*) and mercy (*ḥesed*) in the sense of dependable behaviour appropriate for life in community;

(2) a *personification*, i.e. an interpretation of wisdom as the mediator of God's revelation, who, as 'Lady Wisdom', either invites people to successful life or, as a cosmic entity, must be sought (cf. Prov. 8.22-36; Job 28; Wis. 9);

(3) a connection of *wisdom* and *Torah*, i.e. an equation of cosmic wisdom with the Torah so that it appears as recorded wisdom and the true wise person is the one who orients life by the Torah (cf. Sir. 21.11; 24);

(4) an identification of the wise with the righteous and of the fool with the evildoer/godless.

10. R. Strömberg, *Griechische Sprichwörter* (Göteborg: Gumperts, 1961). Cf. C. Cavarnos, *The Seven Sages of Ancient Greece: the Lives and Teachings of the Earliest Greek Philosophers, Thales, Pittacos, Bias, Solon, Cleobulos, Myson, Chilon* (Belmont, Mass.: Institute for Byzantine and Modern Greek Studies, 1996).

11. Translated in *OTP* II, 479–93.

12. Cf. Pss 1; 19; 37; 49; 73; 78; 104; 105; 106; 119 (Ch. 13.1), each with a different focus.

13. H.-P. Müller, 'Die weisheitliche Lehrerzählung im Alten Testament und seiner Umwelt', in *Mensch – Umwelt – Eigenwelt: Gesammelte Aufsätze zur Weisheit Israels* (Stuttgart: Kohlhammer, 1992), 101–20; H. Strauss, 'Weisheitliche Lehrerzählungen im und um das Alten Testament', *ZAW* 116 (2004): 379–95.

## 15.2.2 Individual Sayings, Saying Collections and the Complete Composition

Self-contained individual sayings from various social contexts constitute the core of Proverbs. In addition to sayings from the realm of the family and the clan (‘*clan wisdom*’), there are sayings from the world of the royal court and scribal schools (‘*courtly wisdom*’) and sayings from wisdom teachers (‘*instructional wisdom*’). It may be that one should also take into account a wisdom stemming from the catechesis of the post-exilic (→ *exile*) community (‘*community wisdom*’).

The sayings in the book of Proverbs no longer appear as *individual sayings*, however, but in connection with thematically or stylistically related sayings in a *sequence of sayings*. Furthermore, as demonstrated by the superscriptions within the book, sequences of sayings are combined into *sayings collections*. Cross-references involving motifs and concepts link individual sayings collections, on the one hand,[14] whereas form, content and social history clearly distinguish them, on the other.[15] This observation raises the question of whether the book of Proverbs is the well-planned composition by an author, who may have employed sources of varied origins but combined them according to a unified design (Hans F. Fuhs), or whether it represents a multi-phased redactional fusion of originally independent *sub-collections* from various periods (the majority of interpreters). Another question involves the relationship between the *orality and literality* (Ch. 2.1.1) of the individual sayings, a question which cannot be given a categorical answer: Some sayings were probably transmitted orally at first and only secondarily recorded in writing, and others were genuine literary products (‘*literary sayings*’).

The following model of the ***development*** from isolated saying to a book of sayings is likely:

(1) the oral origination of proverbs and isolated sayings,
(2) recording at court and in school,
(3) collection of sayings series according to form and content criteria,
(4) the revision of extant sayings and the continued inclusion of others,

14. Cf., e.g., the correspondences in content and motif in the framing verses 1.8 || 10.1 || 31.2; 16.1 || 22.17; 9.18 || 24.22; 22.16 || 31.9; 24.34 || 27.7.

15. Cf., e.g., the dominance of two-lined sayings in 22.17–24.22 in contrast to the exclusively one-lined sayings in 10.1–22.16 and 28.1–29.33; or the doublets in 19.1 || 28.6 and 11.13 || 20.19.

(5) composition of sayings collections,
(6) composition of the book of Proverbs.
Thus, the process of oral origination and documentation could have overlapped and run in parallel.

### 15.2.3 The Hebrew and Greek Versions of the Book

The → *Septuagint* of Proverbs differs in three points from the Hebrew version that underlies English translations: (1) The Septuagint has modified the superscriptions (10.1; 22.17; 30.1; 31.1) so that the whole book appears as a collection of the sayings of Solomon; (2) the sequence of the text differs;[16] (3) some differences in the substance of the sayings are evident.

## 15.3 Origins of the Book of Proverbs and of Individual Sayings

### 15.3.1 The Form of the Book and of the Individual Sayings

In its final form, the book represents a *wisdom textbook* with its nearest parallels in the Egyptian *instructions for life*. Among these, its closest parallels in terms of form and history of development are the instructions of *Ankh-Sheshonq* and of the *Insinger Papyrus*.[17]

The basic formal model of all the poetic *individual sayings* is *parallelismus membrorum* (Ch. 13.2.2). Synonymous, synthetical and antithetical parallelism predominate. Since, in the Ancient Near Eastern understanding, wisdom depends primarily on cumulative experience, the survey of as many aspects of a phenomenon as possible, and the classification of people and

16. Thus, in the Septuagint, Prov. 30.1-14 stands between 24.22 and 23 and 30.15–31.9 between 24.34 and 25.1.
17. M. Lichtheim, *Late Egyptian Wisdom Literature in the International Context: A Study of Demotic Instructions* (OBO 52; Fribourg: Academic Press/Göttingen: Vandenhoeck & Ruprecht, 1983).

modes of behaviour (Ch. 15.2.1), *parallelismus membrorum* is particularly suited for concentrating insights into dense language.

15.3.1.1 *The Pronouncement or Assertion (declarative aphorism)* states the relationship between phenomena, modes of behaviour, and their consequences. It offers indirect instruction for behaviour:

> Whoever digs a pit will fall into it,
> and a stone will come back on the one who starts it rolling (Prov. 26.27).

The pronouncement or assertion developed historically from the usually one-line proverb (cf. Judg. 8.2, 21; 1 Kgs 20.11).

15.3.1.2 *The Comparison or Comparative ṭôb-('better than') saying* declares what is more beneficial. Here, too, the behavioural instruction is only implied:

> Better a piece of dry bread with quiet
> than a house full of feasting with strife (Prov. 17.1).

15.3.1.3 *The Numerical Saying Consists* of a *Title Line* followed by a catalogue/list. The first lines cite the common characteristic of the objects described and the number that have this characteristic. The list inventories the individual objects and describes specifically how they manifest the common characteristic:

> Four are the smallest things on earth / but they are (still) wiser than the wise:
> The ants, a people without strength/ but they provide their food in the summer;
> The badgers, a people without power / but they build their homes in the rocks;
> The locusts have no king / but they all march in rank;
> Lizards can be grasped with one's hands / but they can (still) be found in royal palaces'
> (Prov. 30.24-28).

The *Simple Numerical Saying* mentions only one number in the title line (cf. Prov. 30.24); the *layered numerical saying* contains two numbers, the second of which is one larger than the first:

> Three things are wondrous to me; / four I do not understand:
> the way of the eagle in the sky, / the way of the serpent on (the) rock,
> the way of a ship in the sea / and the way of a man with a maiden (Prov. 30.18-19).

Historically, the *riddle*[18] and *magical concepts* of the special significance and symbolism of certain numbers stand in the background of the numerical saying.

15.3.1.4 *The admonition (prompting aphorism)* is formulated in the imperative or vetative (= negated imperative) and, in contrast to declarative and comparative sayings, contains an explicit behavioural instruction. As a rule, it is associated with a justification that contains a motivation for the recommended behaviour and/or an indication of its consequences. Formulated positively, the admonition occurs as *advice* (cf. 22.17-19) and negatively as *warning* (cf. 22.22-23):

> Incline your ear and hear the words of the wise/
> and apply your mind to my teaching.
> For it will be pleasant if you keep them (i.e. the words) within you;/
> if all of them are ready on your lips.
> In order to put your trust in Yhwh,/
> I have made them known to you today, even to you (Prov. 22.17-19).

> Do not rob the poor because they are poor,/
> or crush the afflicted at the gate (= in court);
> for Yhwh pleads their cause
> and despoils of life those who despoil them (Prov. 22.22-23).

15.3.1.5 *The interjection ʾašrê* 'blessing/happy (is)' ('hail/well done') introduces the felicitation. It represents the most vivid form of advice. The behavioral instruction is applied to a certain behavior as blessed by Yhwh and, thus, in the recommendation to imitate it.

> Happy (is) the person who finds wisdom,/
> and the one who gains insight! (Prov. 3.13).

15.3.1.6 *The call to attention or the Introduction to instruction formula* (→ *Lehreröffnungsformel*) is a special form of the admonition. It addresses the student as son and calls for careful attention:

> And now, sons, listen to me/
> and attend to the words of my mouth! (Prov. 7.24).

18. H.-P. Müller, 'Der Begriff "Rätsel" im Alten Testament', in *Mensch – Umwelt – Eigenwelt: Gesammelte Aufsätze zur Weisheit Israels* (Stuttgart: Kohlhammer, 1992), 44–68.

The call for attention stems from education in the family and the school. In a secondary usage, it opens and structures a didactic or admonitory discourse.[19]

15.3.1.7 *The Didactic or Admonitory Discourse (instruction)* developed from the admonition. It depends on accumulating thematically related individual sayings into a sayings sequence and framing them with an *introduction* and a conclusion. It constitutes a lecture to addressees which, in its full form, opens with a call to attention (cf. 1.8) and concludes with a summary aphorism (*summary appraisal*; cf. 1.19). In its main expository, exhortatory or admonitory section (*actual instruction; corpus*), the didactic discourse can contain a *description* (cf. 5.3-6) or an *exemplary narrative* (cf. 7.6-23). Additional stylistic techniques of the didactic discourse include the rhetorical or didactic question, *question-answer play* (cf. 23.29-30) or the riddle (cf. 30.4-5).

15.3.1.8 *Individual Poems:* Prov. 1.20-33; 8.1-36; 9.1-18 offer poems on personified wisdom or folly. After an introduction that identifies the speaker, in a discourse formulated largely in the first person, 'Lady Wisdom' or 'Lady Folly' solicits adherents. A concluding section mentions the consequences of turning to wisdom or to folly (1.32-33; 8.32-36; 9.6, 18). In addition to wisdom poems, there are other poem-like sections[20] among which the warning against drunkenness (23.29-35) and the poem about the wife configured as an alphabetic → *acrostic* (31.10-31) stand out.

15.3.1.9 *Prayer:* Uniquely in Proverbs, language about God transforms into speech to God in the second person singular in 30.7-9 so that it constitutes a prayer. It may also include 30.1-3 and have its nearest parallel in one of Job's prayers of petition and lament (Job 13.18-21).

## 15.3.2 The Composition and the Redaction of the Book of Proverbs should be Considered Separately in Respect to the Book and its Sub-Collections.

15.3.2.1 *The Superscription to the Book* with the information that it involves sayings of Solomon, as is the case in the other → *canonical*, → *deuterocanonical*

19. Cf. Prov. 1.8; 2.1; 3.1, 11; 4.1, 10; 5.1, 20; 6.1, 20; 7.1.

20. Prov. 3.13; 6.1-9; 23.29-35; 24.30-34; 27.23-27.

and → *pseudepigraphic* Solomonic literature (Song of Songs, Ecclesiastes, Wisdom of Solomon, Psalms of Solomon, Odes of Solomon), should not be understood as information concerning authorship, but as an attribution of authority. In the background stands the notion of Solomon as the exemplarily wise and just king.[21] The Babylonian → *Talmud* already treated Solomonic authorship as a problem. According to *b B. Bat.* 15a, the book traces back to the Judean king Hezekiah (725/4–697/6 BCE) and his college (cf. the superscription in 25.1).

In terms of the history of literature and theology, the final form of the book probably dates to the fourth/third centuries BCE. One must take into account a process of composition and redaction encompassing several centuries. Traces of a late redaction are evident (1) in the sayings that give fear of God priority over or link it with wisdom,[22] (2) in allusions to the Torah,[23] the prophets (29.18) and parts of the Psalter,[24] and (3) in → *apocalyptically* oriented additions (2.21-22). In any case, the process of the redaction of Proverbs requires further clarification. Similarly, in view of the persistence of the conditions of ancient life and the general character of many sayings, the sayings collections can only be dated tentatively.

15.3.2.2 *The Collections:* Overall, the book traces back to three major collections and *five minor collections* that have independent histories of development and that were combined secondarily into a redactional unity. The book grew from the inside out. The *Solomonic collection* in 10.1–22.16 and the Hezekianic collection in 25.1–29.27 constitute the basis. To these were appended the *quasi-Egyptian instruction* in Prov. 22.17–24.22, the words of the wise in Prov. 23.24-34, the *words of Agur* in Prov. 30.1-14, the series of *numerical sayings* in Prov. 30.15-33, the *instructions for Lemuel* in 31.1-9 and the *praise of the wife* in Prov 31.10-31. The didactic discourse that opens the book in chapters 1–9 constitutes the youngest component.

15.3.2.2.1 *The Solomonic Collection* (10.1–22.16) contains 375 sayings of two lines each, a number that corresponds to the gematria of the name 'Solomon'.

21. Cf. 1 Kgs 3.28; 5.9-14 (NRSV 4.29-34); 10.1-9.

22. Cf. Prov. 1.7; 9.10; 15.33; 31.30.

23. Cf. Prov. 28.5; 29.18; 30.5-6.

24. Cf. Prov. 30.5 with Ps. 12.7 (NRSV 12.6); 18.31 (NRSV 18.30); 119.140.

**Gematria** is a technique for encryption and interpretation attested in the Ancient Near East and ancient Greece which plays with the numerical value of individual letters in the respective alphabets. Thus, the name Solomon (*šlmh*) corresponds to the number 375 since, in Hebrew, the letter *š* has the numerical value 300, the letter *l* the value 30, the letter *m* the value 40, and the letter *h* the value 5: therefore, *š* + *l* + *m* + *h* corresponds to 300 + 30 + 40 + 5 = 375. There is a whole series of instances of such number play in both the Old and the New Testament.

The collection consists of two sub-collections (10.1–15.33 and 16.1–22.16). The first sub-collection contains sayings formulated primarily as antitheses. In terms of content, it focuses on the contrast between the wise and the fool and the education of the wise 'son'. A rural milieu predominates (cf. 10.5; 12.4, 10-11). In the second sub-collection, synonymous or synthetical sayings appear in the foreground. Thematically, righteousness and mercy along with the contrast between poor and rich play important roles. The milieu of these sayings bears a more urban imprint. Aphorisms dealing with monarchy, commerce, and handcraft appear in concentrations here. In both sub-collections, the sayings are arranged largely by association. Still, on the level of language and style, certain patterns of arrangement are evident, e.g. the consonance (*paronomasia*) of words employed.

15.3.2.2.2 *The Quasi-Egyptian Instruction* (22.17–24.22) depends on the Egyptian *Instruction of Amenemope* from the twelfth century BCE.[25] The orientation of behaviour according to God's criterion of justice (22.19, 23; 23.11) give new accents to the Egyptian instruction, however. Like the 'Instruction of Amenemope', Prov. 22.17–24.22 consists of 30 sayings units. The possibility that Prov. 22.17–24.22 was composed during the monarchical period cannot be excluded, nor can a later origin since copies of and citations from the 'Instruction of Amenemope' can be identified as late as the second century CE.

The *sayings of the wise* in 24.23-24 assign two sayings each to three themes. Their origins and date are uncertain.

25. Translated in M. Lichtheim, *Ancient Egyptian Literature* II, 146–63; B. U. Schipper, 'Die Lehre des Amenemope und Prov 22,17–24,22: Eine Neubestimmung des literarischen Verhältnisses', *ZAW* 117 (2005): 53–72, 232–48.

15.3.2.2.3 *The Hezekianic Collection* (Prov. 25.1–29.27), which contains 137 sayings,[26] also consists of two sub-collections (chs. 25–27 and chs. 28–29): comparisons dominate in the first, antitheses in the second. Both sub-collections exhibit thematically oriented groupings of sayings and saying-sequences.

Both the Solomonic collection in 10.1–22.16 and the Hezekianic collection in chs. 25–29 can be located in the period of the monarchy based on the milieu assumed in the sayings. They are usually dated to the 8th century BCE.

15.3.2.2.4 *The Four Appendices to the Hezekianic Collection* (30.1–31.31) all belong to the post-exilic period. Notably, chs. 30 and 31 are attributed to Arabic wisdom teachers (cf. 1 Kgs 5.19 [NRSV 5.5]; Job. 2.11; Jer. 49.7). The *Words of Agur* (30.1-14) depend on Deuteronomy (cf. 30.5-6 and Deut. 4.2; 13.1 [NRSV 12.32]) and offer a summary of late wisdom thought oriented toward the word of God. The appended series of admonitions (30.10-14) constitutes a counterpart to the social commandments of the Torah (cf. Deut. 23.16 [NRSV 23.15]; Exod. 21.15, 17). The *series of numerical sayings* (30.15-33) serves as an illustration of the confession of the enigmatic character of the world God created (30.4-5; cf. Job 38.4–39.30). As evidenced by their superscription and their character as didactic discourse, the *Words of Lemuel* (31.1-9) correspond most closely to Egyptian royal instructions (cf. the *Instruction for Merikare* and the *Instruction of Amenemhet*).[27] Here, too, origins and precise date are uncertain. Since Lemuel's *mother* imparts this instruction (31.1), this text constitutes a bridge between the admonitions in 30.11 and the song of praise to the wise and god-fearing *wife* (31.10-31).

15.3.2.2.5 *The Didactic Discourses* in chs. 1–9 present a well-planned composition of ten discourses with two interludes and three wisdom poems. Although it contains older proverbial material, with its developed concept of wisdom (cf. Prov.

26. In gematria, the name Hezekiah as spelled in Prov. 25.1 (ḥzqyh) corresponds to the number 130: *ḥ* = 8, *z* = 7, *q* = 100, y = 10, *h* = 5, i.e. 8 + 7 + 100 + 10 + 5 = 130. The alternative orthography *ḥzqyhw* (cf. 2 Kgs 16.20, etc.) produces the number 136: *ḥ* = 8, *z* = 7, *q* = 100, *y* = 10, *h* = 5, *w* = 6, i.e. 8 + 7 + 100 + 10 + 5 + 6 = 136.

27. Both in M. Lichtheim, *Ancient Egyptian Literature* I, 97–109, 135–8; A. Wilke, *Kronerben der Weisheit: Gott, König und Frommer in der didaktischen Literatur Ägyptens und Israels* (FAT II/120; Tübingen: Mohr Siebeck, 2006).

8 with Job 38) and its parallels to Greek aretologies ('panegyrics') to the goddess Isis[28] (→ *Excursus* on Isis Ch. 25), it stems at the earliest from the Hellenistic period.

### 15.3.3 The Situation and Function of the Book of Proverbs

If the individual saying already aims at both the communication of knowledge and practical assistance for living, the same is especially true of the saying collection. Through the placement of the didactic discourses from the circle of wisdom teachers in chapters 1–9, the book appears as a grand collection of examples of behaviour. It is a textbook intended to transmit wisdom traditions and to inculcate the fear of God. Its most likely application was the instruction of young members of the Jerusalem upper class in the period of emergent → *Hellenism* (4th/3rd cent. BCE). Thus, in terms of its function and its → *genre*, the book stands alongside the somewhat younger Ecclesiastes (18) and proves to be a predecessor of the deuterocanonical wisdom books of Jesus Sirach (190/180 BCE; Ch. 27) and Wisdom of Solomon (1st cent. BCE/1st cent. CE Ch. 25).

## 15.4 Theology of the Book of Proverbs

Foundational for the theology of the book of Proverbs is the concept of a just order that *God as the Creator*[29] incorporated into the cosmos. In contrast to the foundation in creation theology, motifs from a theology of history as defined by the 'Torah' and the 'prophets' appear in the background. Via the designation of Solomon as 'son of David, king of Israel' mentioned in the superscription, the book is located historically, however, and the wisdom taught in it is imparted as *Israel's wisdom*.

*Justice* and *mercy* appear as central elements of God's nature and as criteria for human behaviour in community. The appropriate human attitude toward God is fear, i.e. an attitude that rejects that which is hostile to life and expresses itself in trust (16.20) and humility (22.4). At the same

28. Cf. the Isis aretalogy of Kyme, translated in R. S. Kraemer, ed., *Women's Religions in the Greco-Roman World: A Sourcebook* (Oxford: Oxford University Press, 2004), 456–7. (see also Ch. 25B).
29. Cf. Prov. 3.19-20; 8.22-31; 14.31; 17.5.

time, everyday human activity and behaviour should evidence the fear of God. Love of God and love for neighbour belong together[30] and should produce persons who are capable and responsible in their social, religious and political environment.

*Training and education* (*mûsar*, Prov. 1.3) are necessary for the proper configuration of social life. They find expression in the observance of the social commandments concerning the integrity of the life, dignity and property of the neighbour and concerning the preservation of marriage and justice, commandments also recorded in the → *Decalogue*. The ethos of Proverbs reaches its apex in the admonition to love one's enemy.[31]

The notion based on everyday *experience* that a certain deed brings about a certain consequence appears, on the one hand, as an engine of ethical behaviour, and on the other, as an expression of hope in dependability and justice. When the concept of the 'deed-consequence relationship' (Ch. 14A) has become an independent dogma, individual sayings themselves raise objections referring *theologically* to the transcendence of God (Prov. 16.1; 19.14) and → *anthropologically* to the limits of human knowledge and the capacity for learning.[32] When reality challenges the equation of good fortune for the righteous and destruction for the godless (cf. Prov. 11.31; 24.19), hope in the ultimate judgment of the godless arises. Thus, late sayings concerning eschatological salvation for the righteous and disaster for evildoers introduce an *eschatological* or → *apocalyptic* accent into the book (2.21-22). Thus, the book of Proverbs overall reflects the history of Old Testament wisdom and its theology, anthropology, and ethics.

## 15.5 Notes on the History of Reception

The inclusion of Proverbs in Holy Scriptures seems initially to have been controversial in *ancient Judaism*. Thus, the Babylonian → *Talmud* refers to internal contradictions.[33] In any case, Sir. 47.17 alludes to Prov. 1.6. Known also from →

30. Cf. Prov. 2.5-11; 3.1-12, 21-35; 14.21, 27, 31; 15.33; 18.2; 19.17; 22.9; 30.1-19.

31. Cf. Prov. 17.13; 20.22; 24.17; 25.21-22.

32. Cf. Prov. 16.2, 9; 19.21; 20.24; 21.30-31 and 12.1, 15; 17.24, respectively.

33. Cf. *b Šabb.* 30b with reference to Prov. 26.24f.

*Qumran*, the *Damascus Document*[34] (CD XI :20) cites Prov. 15.8 as scriptural evidence. In 4Q184, a → *wisdom* poem from the first century BCE.[35] one finds a text with close affinities to Prov. 7. In *b. B. Bat.* 14b, Proverbs appears among the Ketuvim. Finally, the 'Sayings of the Fathers' (*pirqê ʾābôt*),[36] a tractate of the → *Mishnah* in the Babylonian Talmud from the second century CE and the Greek-influenced sayings collection of Pseudo-Phocylides[37] demonstrate the endurance of wisdom sayings traditions in Judaism. In Rom. 12.20, Paul cites the maxim concerning love for one's enemy from Prov. 25.21-22. James 4.6 adduces Prov. 3.34 as scriptural evidence for God's grace toward the pious. Prov. 2.1-6 shines behind James 1.5-7. Hebr. 12.5-7 cites Prov. 3.11-12. The hymn of Christ in Col. 1.15-17 is a Christological interpretation of the wisdom poem from Prov. 8 (and Wis. Sol. 7.22ff.).

Despite the New Testament's depiction of Jesus as a wisdom teacher who utilized wisdom forms of discourse and speech, Proverbs has a very modest history of influence in Christianity in comparison to other Old Testament books. Above all, the assumption of Solomonic authorship and the personification of wisdom (Prov. 8.14; 9.1) have been influential on → *iconography* so that, since the Middle Ages, Solomon has often been portrayed as a teacher and wisdom as a richly clothed, crowned woman. Medieval → *allegory* personified wisdom as Mary, Christ or an angel; in the Baroque period, it was also associated with virtue.

The *Christian devaluation of Proverbs* that can sometimes be observed is based: (1) in the mistaken judgement evident in broad sections of the history of interpretation that Old Testament wisdom was a marginal phenomenon in Yahwism; (2) in the restriction of the worldview of Proverbs to a purely this-worldly orientation; (3) in the identification of the 'deed-consequence relationship' with the legal piety criticized in the New Testament; (4) in the negation of the enjoyment of life affirmed by Proverbs; and (5) in a non-historical transfer of certain ideals of education (13.24) and descriptions of gender relations (13.4; 31.10-31) into Christian social ethics.

Currently, Old Testament wisdom and Proverbs attract growing interest

34. F. García Martínez and E. J. C. Tigchelaar, *The Dead Sea Scrolls* I, 550–627.

35. Translated in ibid., 376–81.

36. Translated in R. T. Herford, ed., *The Ethics of the Talmud: The Sayings of the Fathers* (9th ed., New York: Schocken, 1978).

37. Translated by P. W. van der Horst, 'Pseudo-Phocylides', in *OTP* II, 565–82.

based on their intercultural character, their empirical epistemology, their understanding of education as a lifelong process, and their multi-dimensional, aspective approach to the world. The renaissance of Old Testament wisdom joins current interdisciplinary concerns with clarifying the concept of 'life',[38] which plays such a significant role in Proverbs.

38. E. Herms, ed., *Leben: Verständnis, Wissenschaft, Technik* (Veröffentlichungen der Wissenschaftlichen Gesellschaft für Theologie 24; Gütersloh: Gütersloher Verlagshaus, 2005).

# 16

# The Book of Ruth

(Markus Witte – Translation by Mark Biddle)

## Chapter Outline



Commentaries: I. Fischer (HTKAT. Freiburg: Herder, 2004); M. Köhlmoos (ATD 9,3. Göttingen: Vandenhoeck & Ruprecht, 2010); R. E. Murphy (FOTL 13. Grand Rapids, Mich.: Eerdmans, 1981), 83–94; K. Nielsen (OTL. London: SCM, 1997); E. Zenger (ZBK 8. 2nd ed. Zurich: Theologischer Verlag, 1992); Y. Zakovitch (SBS 177. Stuttgart: Katholisches Bibelwerk, 1999); J. Sasson (Sheffield: Sheffield Academic Press, 2nd ed., 1989); T. Frymer-Kensky and T. Cohn Eskenazi (JPS, Philadelphia: Jewish Publication Society, 2011).

## 16.1 Biblical Context

| | |
|---|---|
| **1.1-5** | **Prologue: The fate of the family of Elimelek** |
| **1.6-22** | **First act: Naomi's departure from Moab for Bethlehem** |
| **2.1-23** | **Second act: Ruth's encounter with Boaz in the fields of Bethlehem** |
| **3.1-18** | **Third act: Ruth's encounter with Boaz on the threshing-floor near Bethlehem** |
| **4.1-17** | **Fourth act: The answer for (redemption of) Elimelek's family in Bethlehem** |
| **4.18-22** | **Epilogue: Genealogy from Perez to David ('Perez toledot')** |

Corresponding to the settings of the action (Moab, fields of Bethlehem, threshing-floor near Bethlehem, Bethlehem), the book can be divided into *four sections* that coincide with the chapter divisions. The beginning of each section ('act') mentions the location of the main action.[1] A *narrative prologue*, which announces the themes of the book, and a *cataloguing epilogue*, which incorporates the narrative into David's background, serve as the framework. *Dialogues* between the protagonists, each of which offer interpretative retrospectives and prospectives at the end of an act,[2] constitute a second structural element. As a third compositional characteristic, the *chronological setting of the action* joins the spatial and dialogical structure. The narrative begins in the past, 'the period of the judges', i.e. Israel's pre- or non-state period (1.1). Afterward, the phases of the narrative periods become increasingly shorter. At the centre stands the encounter between Ruth and Boaz in *one* night (3.6-15). From this scene forward, the spans of narrated time broaden again until they reach an apex in the prospective on David's future. If David's genealogy is understood in a → *messianic* sense as an outlook on the ideal David,[3] then the book deals with the periods of 'Israel's beginning' and 'end'. The densest compositional structure consists of *keywords* that serve as guides for reading.

> Thus, the term 'to return' (*šûb*) appears twelve times in ch. 1, the word 'to harvest' (*lāqaṭ*) twelve times in ch. 2, the word 'to lie' (*šākab*) eight times in ch. 3, and the word 'to redeem' (*gāʾal*) fourteen times in ch. 4. The word 'child' (*yeled*) links the prologue and the epilogue (1.5; 4.16) and marks the acquisition of progeny as a central theme. Additional important keywords are the term 'fidelity' (*ḥesed*, 1.6; 2.20; 3.10), terms derived from the verb 'to bless' (*bārak*; 2.4, 20; 3.10; 4.14), and the significant names of the actors and settings.

The core motif of the book is the survival of a famine. By means of this motif, the major idea from the stories of Abraham and Joseph (cf. Gen. 12.10-20 and 37-50, respectively), namely God's guidance and protection in a strange land, become available as interpretative elements. The book offers the account of a crisis, an exodus, and God's mysterious guidance. *Elimelek* ('My God [Yhwh] is king') from Judean Bethlehem ('House of Bread') left his homeland along with his wife *Naomi* ('Delightful') and his sons *Machlon* ('Weak') and *Chilion* ('Sickly') to live

1. Cf. Ruth 1.6-7; 2.2; 3.2; 4.1.
2. Cf. Ruth 1.21; 2.22; 3.18; 4.17.
3. Cf. Isa. 9.1-6 (NRSV 9.2-7); 11.1-9; Zech. 9.9-10; Mic. 5.1-3 (NRSV 5.2-4) and E. Zenger (ZBK 8), 28.

as sojourners in neighbouring *Moab*. There, first the father, then both sons died. Naomi and her Moabite daughters-in-law *Ruth* ('Friend') and *Orpah* ('Stubborn'; 'She who turns around') survived as women without substantial rights (1.1-5).

***The sojourner (ger)***: In the Old Testament, the term *ger* describes the status of a person who, because of war, famine, epidemic, or some other catastrophe, must leave home and, alone or with closest family, go into asylum abroad. The basis for residence as a *ger* is the hospitality valued in ancient cultures (cf. Gen. 18; 19; Judg. 19). This hospitality made it possible for strangers to live for extended periods, even abroad, and to survive as guest workers. A sojourner had limited rights with regard to participation in legal affairs, to property ownership, and to involvement in the cult in his temporary home; but he was not completely without rights. Old Testament law regulates the status of a *ger* precisely. In the ideal case, he has legal, economic and social security. He may not be oppressed or enslaved (Exod. 22.20 [NRSV 22.21]; 23.9; Lev. 19.33-34). The *ger* enjoys the same protection as other people who have fallen from the bounds of solidarity of family (widows and orphans) and has a right to minimal economic assistance (Deut. 24.19-21). Late Old Testament legal texts motivate care for the *ger* ethically with a historical and theological reference to 'Israel's' past as a *ger* in Egypt (Lev. 19.34; Deut. 10.18-19; 23.8 [NRSV 23.7]; 26.5). The 'foreigner' (*nokrî*, Ruth 2.10) is legally and socially subordinate to the *ger* (Deut. 15.3; 23.21 [NRSV 23.20]).

📖 C. Bultmann, *Der Fremde im antiken Juda: Eine Untersuchung zum sozialen Typenbegriff 'ger' und seinem Bedeutungswandel in der alttestamentlichen Gesetzgebung*. FRLANT 153. Göttingen: Vandenhoeck & Ruprecht, 1992.

The gracious visitation of God (1.6)[4] effected the end of the famine in Judah and the return home (1.6-22). Out of solidarity (*ḥesed*) with their mother-in-law, the Moabitess Ruth converted to Yhwh (1.15-17) and accompanied Naomi to Bethlehem. There, she met *Boaz* ('in him is power'), a man who had all the rights of a free citizen in the local community, i.e. the right to speak in legal proceedings, to own property, and to self-defence (2.1-23). As close relatives of Naomi's deceased husband, the responsibilities of the *levirate* and of *redemption* (*ge᾽ullâ*) fell to him in the narrative (3.1-18).

***Levirate and Redemption*** (*ge᾽ullâ*): The *levirate* (in-law marriage, *Yibum*) means that the brother or a near male relative of a man who died without a son or a child is

⇨

4. Cf. Gen. 21.1; Exod. 3.16; 1 Sam. 2.1.

supposed to take his widow as wife (Deut. 25.5-10; Gen. 38). The firstborn of this union is considered the son and heir of the deceased. The levirate presupposes a polygamous and patriarchal society. It is meant: (1) to assure a male lineage, (2) to preserve the property situation within the family, and (3) to provide economic security for the widow. The levirate represents a social obligation required by the tribal ethos, but is not institutionally enforceable (cf. Gen. 38). The *ge'ullâ* refers to the duty of a wealthier family member to reacquire the property (*naḥălâ*) that a relative found necessary to sell in order to survive (cf. Lev. 25.23-28; Jer. 32.7-44). The relative who intercedes for his impoverished family member is designated *redeemer* (*go'ēl*). Also in the background here is the fact that property is supposed to remain within the family. The *ge'ullâ* is no more enforceable legally than the Levirate.

On Naomi's advice, Ruth, like a bride prepared for her wedding night,[5] went to the threshing-floor of Boaz and addressed him as the redeemer (*go'ēl*) of the family (3.1-18). Ruth's ideal character resounded once again when she acknowledged the duty of family solidarity (cf. 1.8). Boaz' praise for Ruth found expression in her designation as an *'ešet ḥayil* recognized in the 'city gate' (3.11), i.e. a woman who acts independently in the context of patriarchal society (cf. Prov. 31.10).

In the city gate, the central setting of the fourth act (4.1-17), the redeemer Boaz confirmed before witnesses that (1) the property (*naḥălâ*) would remain in the possession of the family, (2) whose name would not die out, and (3) Naomi and Ruth would have economic and legal security (vv. 9, 11). The narrative could have ended with the reference to Ruth's newborn in v. 17bα. Yet, just as it began primarily as an account about Naomi (cf. 1.6), it glances back on Naomi at the end (v. 14). The close relationship between Ruth and Naomi, indicated in 1.14 by the verb *dābaq* ('to remain', literally, 'to cling to someone', cf. 2.24), is underscored by the word 'to love' (*'āhab*). Ruth has proven to be a true friend (*rĕ'ût*). The blessing continues in praise over the newborn *Obed* ('servant'), Naomi's future caretaker (4.15-16).

The book concludes with a genealogy (*tôlĕdôt*) listing ten members from *Perez* to *David* (4.18-22). In analogy to the parallel of Ruth and Naomi with the matriarchs Leah and Rachel (4.1-17; Gen. 29–30), the genealogy of David can be read as an extension of the family trees in Genesis (Ch. 7.1). As with

5. Cf. Esth. 2.12; Cant. 1.3; 4.10; Jdt. 10.3-4.

them, the genealogy of David involves a literary construction as a 'summary history' of divine blessing. *Nachshon* stands in the accentuated fifth position. According to Num. 1.7, he was the exodus representative of the tribe of Judah. Thus, even the concluding genealogy characterizes the book of Ruth as an exodus story.

# 16.2 Textual Issues and Major Issues in the History of Critical Interpretation

Based on the conclusion of the book with a genealogy of David, Johann Wolfgang von Goethe already declared that the intention of the narrator was to provide the first king of Israel with 'reputable, interesting ancestors'.[6] The genealogy of David has a direct counterpart in 1 Chr. 2.5, 9-15, however, and stands out markedly from the narrative. Furthermore, the designation of Obed as Boaz' son contradicts the levirate concept assumed in 4.5, 10, according to which Obed must be Machlon's son. These circumstances suggest the thesis that the epilogue of the book in Ruth 4.18-22 is a later supplement. Reference could be made to structural parallels in the pentateuchal source P (→ *Pentateuch*; → *Priestly Document*; cf. Gen. 5; 11.10-32) and to the consonance of Ruth 1.1aα and 4.22 in favour of the original unity of narrative and genealogy: the setting of the account in the kingless period of the judges[7] (Ch. 7.6.3.3) contrasts with the prospective on Israel's first king. In any case, the originality of the first superscript (1.1aα), which gives the book a dual beginning, is by no means certain.

# 16.3 Origins of the Book of Ruth

## 16.3.1 The Form of the Book of Ruth

The book is an example of Old Testament *literary prose*. The timeless character of the events, the idealized milieu, and the pregnant personal names indicate that it

6. J. W. von Goethe, 'Noten und Abhandlungen zu besserem Verstehen des West-östlichen Divans', in *West-Östlicher Divan* (Manesse Bibliothek der Weltliteratur; Zurich: Manesse, 1952), 168–9.

7. Cf. Judg. 17.6; 18.1; 19.1; 21.25.

represents a *fictive account*. To be sure, it incorporates certain features and motifs of historically attested places, institutions and rites, but, overall, it constitutes a *parabolic narrative*. Based on the concentration on a few narrative elements, the focus on dialogues, and the description of a 'shocking event',[8] the book can be categorized as a → *wisdom novella*. Scholars in the Anglo-Saxon realm employ the terms *short story, folktale, comedy, saga and romance*. To the degree that the book engages legal questions concerning the institution of the 'redeemer', the handling of a disposable 'estate', and the levirate, associating these institutions with one another in a manner unique in the Old Testament, it constitutes a → *midrash-like* → *halakhah*, i.e. a narrative 'commentary on the law' or an interpretative legal narrative on the two legal texts, Lev. 25 (cf. Lev. 27.9-33) and Deut. 25.

## 16.3.2 The Composition and Redaction of the Book of Ruth

The book itself bears no indication of authorship. On grounds of literary and theological history, an origin in the Persian period is likely – in contrast to the date in the monarchical period sometimes proposed in older scholarship.

(1) The treatment of the question of the levirate depends on Deut. 25.5-10. The specific differences with Deut 25:5–10 can be explained as a conscious correction of the deuteronomic statute.

(2) The problematization of the redemption of the property is based on Lev. 25.

(3) The positive characterization of Moab engages critically with the deuteronomic prohibition against accepting Moabites into the congregation of Yhwh (Deut. 23.4-7 [NRSV 23.3-6]).

(4) The depiction of the foreigner, Ruth, as David's grandmother is directed critically against the prohibition against Judeans marrying foreign woman promulgated by Nehemiah (Neh. 13.3-13, 23-31; cf. Ch. 22).

(5) The pro-foreigner tendency corresponds to that of the book of Jonah, which stems from the Persian period, but also to late prophetic texts such as Isa. 19.24; 56.1-8.

(6) The inclusion in the Ketuvim, all of which stem from the Second Temple period, indicates composition in the Persian period.

The book of Ruth is not a literary unity; instead, *two layers* can be distinguished.[9]

8. J. W. von Goethe, 'Gespräch mit Eckermann vom 29.1.1827', in *Theorie der Novelle* (ed. H. Krämer; Stuttgart: Reclam, 1976), 29.

9. Cf. E. Zenger (ZBK 8), 10–14.

A *base narrative*, which essentially encompasses 1.1aβ–4.17bα, probably stems from the fifth/fourth century BCE. It presumably originated in educated circles in Jerusalem who were well-versed in the narrative and legal literature of Israel and Judah. A *redactional layer* from the third/second century BCE revised the book at points from an 'Israelocentric' perspective with appeal to 1 Chr. 2.5, 9-15. This layer (the '*Israel redaction*') included: (1) the incorporation into David's background (1.1aα; 4.17bβ, 18-22), (2) the parallels with the story of the patriarchs (4.11b-12; cf. Gen. 29–31; 38); (3) the explanation of the legal history of the institution of redeemer in 4.7b-8, and (4) a → *gloss* in 4.14b.

| | | |
|---|---|---|
| 1) | Base layer: | 1.1aβ–4.7a, 9–11a, 13-14a, 15-17bα |
| 2) | 'Israel redaction': | + 1.1aα; 4.7b-8, 11b-12, 14b, 17bβ, 18-22 |

### 16.3.3 The Situation and Function of the Book of Ruth

The book combines *theological historiography* with *actualizing legal interpretation*.[10] On the one hand, it seeks to entertain, on the other to instruct.

Meanwhile, several *narrative objectives* become evident: (1) the book offers an example of divine and human fidelity (*ḥesed*); (2) it supports solidarity in the family; (3) it advocates for the woman who acts independently (cf. Prov. 31.10-31; Esth.; Jdt.; see Ch. 20 and Ch. 24) and offers a contrast to the accounts of the active but mistreated women in Gen. 19; 34 and 38, but also to the negative picture of the Moabite women in Num. 25.1-4; and, (4) it concerns itself with the legitimization of David's Moabite ancestors.

In the form of an extensive parable set in 'Israel's' 'pre-state' period, the narrative from the 'post-state' period offers a model for interpreting and managing life and survival under foreign rule and in a foreign land.

## 16.4 Theology of the Book of Ruth

Two key theological ideas permeate the book. First, it adduces evidence that Yhwh, the God of individual and collective lives, is just and faithful. God's

10. For the Book of Ruth as reworking of pentateuchal law, see B. M. Levinson, *Legal Revision and Religious Renewal in Ancient Israel* (New York: Cambridge University Press, 2008). 33–45.

fidelity is manifest both toward his people and toward individuals since he always opens unexpected possibilities for life. Characteristically for the subtle 'missionary theology' of the book, Ruth's conversion does not take place on the basis of a special demonstration of God's power, as is the case of the heathen sailors surrounding Jonah (Jonah 1.9-16) or of the wondrously healed Aramaean Naaman (2 Kgs 5), but on the basis of her profound connection with Naomi (1.17). In the background stands the concept of Yhwh as a God who creates relationships, a concept evident throughout the Old Testament tradition. Even passages that speak of 'fate/chance' (*miqreh*; 2.3) do not abandon the notion of a personal God. Here, as in the other Old Testament books, Yhwh is a personal God, i.e. a God who can be addressed in prayer – both in praise and in lament, in petition and in thanksgiving – as 'thou' (cf. 1.8, 21; 2.4), who withdraws from a person and draws near again (cf. 1.6, 13), and who rewards and punishes a people according to their deeds (cf. 1.12).

The book of Ruth tells about this God using theological formulas. To this extent, it can be categorized as *narrative theology*. Significantly, it contains no divine speech set as a word of Yhwh. Ruth's rich gleanings, Boaz' acceptance of her, and Obed's birth do not appear as God's massive wonders, but as mysterious coincidences. The book stands for discreet discussion of Yhwh as Israel's God, to whom people of other religions come if they feel connections with his worshippers. Even if, ultimately, the wonder of divine protection for Naomi and Ruth stands at the centre of the book, it still invites one to see God at work behind every phenomenon.

The second central theological notion concerns *God's solidarity with the powerless*. Here, too, the book extends a basic line of Old Testament thought. Typical of God's involvement with power is (1) a relativization of human power and (2) concern for the powerless. With the account of God's concern for two powerless women, one of whom is a foreigner, the book of Ruth develops a concept recorded in the book of Exodus (cf. Exod. 1–15), in some psalms (cf. Ps. 8.2 [NRSV 8.1]), and in late prophetic texts (cf. Isa. 53), and which Paul also acknowledged (2 Cor. 12.9): God's power is mighty in the weak. Ruth stands for this insight and, not least for this reason, she appears in the genealogy of the one whom the Christian community acknowledges as God's suffering servant (cf. Mt. 1.1-17).

## 16.5 Notes on the History of Reception

The book of Ruth and its heroine have had an extraordinary history of reception and influence. In *Jewish liturgy* since the early Middle Ages, the book of Ruth has been assigned as the festival scroll for the → *Feast of Weeks*. *Illustrations* of the story of Ruth appear in Jewish and Christian manuscripts dating from the 12th and 14th centuries, respectively, and onward. The most popular portrayals are the threshing-floor scene and Ruth gathering grain between the harvesters in Boaz' field. This selection of images permeates the history of Western art from Hans Holbein the Elder and Rembrandt, via the Nazarenes to Marc Chagall. German classicism prized the literary character of the book highly (cf. Johann Gottfried Herder and Johann Wolfgang von Goethe). *Modern literature* includes poems on the theme and characters of the novella by Victor Hugo, Else Lasker-Schüler, or Nelly Sachs, for example. The French composer César Franck set the material of the book in an *oratorio* in 1846.

# 17

# The Song of Songs (Canticles)

(Markus Witte – Translation by Mark Biddle)

## Chapter Outline




Commentaries: A. Bloch and C. Bloch (New York: Random House, 1995); O. Keel (ZBK 18. 2nd ed. Zurich: Theologischer Verlag, 1992); H.-P. Müller, 'Das Hohelied'. Pages 1–90 in *Das Hohelied, Klagelieder, Das Buch Ester*. ATD 16/2. Ed. by H.-P. Müller, O. Kaiser and J. A. Loader. 4th ed. Göttingen: Vandenhoeck & Ruprecht, 1992; Y. Zakovith (HTKAT. Freiburg: Herder, 2004).

M. V. Fox, *The Song of Songs and the Ancient Egyptian Love Songs*. Madison, Wisc.: University of Wisconsin Press, 1985; A. C. Hagedorn, ed., *Perspectives on the Song of Songs/Perspektiven der Hoheliedauslegung*. BZAW 346. Berlin/New York: de Gruyter, 2005.


Jewish tradition refers to the book by its first words, *šîr haššîrîm* 'Song of Songs' (1.1). The phrase characterizes the book as the most beautiful song, as the definitive song. It appears in the → *Septuagint* under the title *asma (asmatōn)*, a literal translation that the → *Vulgate* renders accordingly with *canticum (canticorum)*. The German title 'Hoheslied', which paraphrases the term, can be traced back to Martin Luther.

# 17.1 Biblical Context

| | | | |
|---|---|---|---|
| **1.1** | **Superscription** | | |
| **1.2–2.7** | **Songs by the woman and the man alternate** | | **(A)** |
| | 1.2 | 'Love is sweeter than wine' | |
| | 2.5 | 'I am sick from love' | |
| | 2.7 | 'Do not stir up love' | |
| **2.8–3.11** | **Songs by the woman and a chorus alternate** | | **(B)** |
| | 2.16 | 'My friend is mine and I am his' | |
| | 3.1 | 'I sought him, but did not find him' | |
| | 3.5 | 'Do not stir up love' | |
| **4.1–5.1** | **Songs by the man** | | **(C)** |
| | 4.10 | 'Love is sweeter than wine' | |
| | 5.1 | 'Be drunk with love' | |
| **5.2–6.3** | **Songs by the woman and a chorus alternate** | | **(B)** |
| | 5.6 | 'I sought him, but did not find him' | |
| | 5.8 | 'I am sick from love' | |
| | 6.3 | 'My friend is mine and I am his' | |
| **6.4–7.10** | **Songs by the man and a chorus alternate** | | **(B')** |
| **7.11–8.7** | **Songs by the woman** | | **(C')** |
| | 8.4 | 'Do not stir up love' | |
| | 8.6 | 'Love is stronger than death' | |
| **8.8-10** | **Songs by the woman and a chorus alternate** | | **(B)** |
| **8.11-14** | **Songs by the man and the woman alternate** | | **(A)** |

The precise demarcation of the individual long songs, the identification of the persons who speak in them, and the question of overarching compositional structures are open questions in scholarship. To be sure, *refrain-like repetitions* of individual verses or parts of verses fulfil a structural function.[1] In addition, the blocks arranged according to *change of speaker* (woman, man, chorus) can be arranged (in accord with the structural outline above) chiastically or concentrically (A-B-C-B-B'-C'-B-A) with minor variations. So far, no structural scheme capable of winning majority assent has been proposed, even though more recent analyses agree in identifying 5.1b as the middle of the collection. The only theme of all the songs is love described with changing metaphors and varying lyrical forms.

1. Cf. Cant. 1.2b = 4.10b; 2.5b = 5.8c; 2.7 = 3.5 = 5.8* = 8.4*; 2.16 = 6.3a.

# 17.2 Textual Issues and Major Issues in the History of Critical Interpretation

## 17.2.1 Hermeneutics of the Song of Songs

Until the rise of historical criticism, the book was usually interpreted → *allegorically*; i.e. the relationship between the man and the woman in the Song of Songs was related, in connection with prophetic imagery, to the relationship between Yhwh and Israel or between Christ and the Church.[2] In the wake of the history of religions school and related comparative studies of Near Eastern literature, the book underwent a *culto-mythological interpretation*, according to which Canticles mirrors the concept of a union between a god and goddess drawn from Mesopotamian texts, a concept that was thought to have taken the form of the sacred marriage rite. Current research, following Johann G. Herder (1778), understands Canticles according to its 'natural meaning' as a *collection of profane love songs*. With regard to the elevation of the 'natural meaning', especially in the comparison of the lovers and their virtues with images from the plant and animal world, it should be noted that the point of comparison consists not in the figure, but in the Near Eastern symbolism of the chosen image and that multivalent terms are employed intentionally.

## 17.2.2 The Compositional Gaps in the Song of Songs

Canticles combines originally independent songs.[3] Sub-collections from various times and places of origin preceded the current composition. The debate concerns whether the final form of the book exhibits a continuous development of thought and whether overarching compositional structures are evident or whether it involves a collection arranged more by keywords and substantive commonalities. The absence of any plot progression contra-

2. Cf. Hos. 1–3; Jer. 2; Ezek. 16; 23; Isa. 5; L. Schwienhorst-Schönberger, 'Das Hohelied und die Kontextualität des Verstehens', in *Weisheit in Israel*, 81–91 (above, Ch. 15 n. 7).

3. Cant. 1.2-4, 5-6, 7-8, 9-11, 12, 13-14, 15-17; 2.1-3, 4-5, 6-7, 8-9, 10-13, 14, 15, 16-17; 3.1-5, 6-8, 9-10d, 10e-11; 4.1-7, 8, 9-11; 4.12–5.1, 2-8, 9-16; 6.1-3, 4-7, 8-10, 11; 6.12–7.1, 2-6, 7-10, 11, 12-13; 7.14–8.2, 3-4, 5ab, 5c-e, 6-7, 8-10, 11-12, 13-14 (O. Keel, *Hohelied*, 18).

dicts the interpretation of the book as *drama* popular in nineteenth century research. Individual songs are only occasionally arranged such that a kind of plot results.[4]

# 17.3 Origins of the Song of Songs

## 17.3.1 The Form and Forms of the Song of Songs

As a whole, the book can be described as a *collection of love songs. Parallels in the history of literature*, both to the individual songs and to the overall composition, consist of (1) early Egyptian love poetry[5] and (2) Greek *pastorals* (songs about an idealized farm and shepherding life, identified as a literary → *genre* since Theocritus [approx. 305 BCE]).[6] In the realm of ancient Jewish literature, one finds echoes in the description of Asenath in the Judeo-Hellenistic novel *Joseph and Asenath* (18.9–10)[7] and in a brief section of the Aramaic *Genesis Apocryphon*.[8]

## 17.3.2 The Composition and Redaction of the Song of Songs

The designation 'song' (*šîr*) employed in the superscription to the book is the general Hebrew designation for a song, usually with instrumental accompaniment, and, as a rule, with cheerful content. It can also be employed specifically for cultic songs (Ps. 120.1), drinking songs (Amos 6.5-6), and love songs (Isa. 5:1). The superscription's identification of Solomon as the author (Cant. 1.1) is due to redactional supplementation (cf. 1 Kgs 5.12 [NRSV 4.32]). It reflects the understanding of Solomon as a symbol for luxury and eroticism.[9] Linguistic, literary, and cultural observations suggest a significantly later origin. At least in its final form, the book may not have been completed prior to the third century BCE.

4. Cf. Cant. 5.2-8, 9-16; 6.1-3.
5. See J. L. Foster, *Love Songs of the New Kingdom* (Austin, Tex.: University of Texas Press, 1992), and the commentary by O. Keel (ZBK).
6. English translations are available in J. M. Edmonds, ed., *The Greek Bucolic Poets* (LCL 28; Cambridge, Mass.: Harvard University Press, 1960), 5–381.
7. Translated in *OTP* II, 177–247.
8. 1Qap Gen[ar] (20:1–8); translated in F. García Martínez and E. J. C. Tigchelaar, *The Dead Sea Scrolls* I, 27–49.
9. Cf. 1 Kgs 3.1; 10.1-10, 14-19; 11.1-3.

Based on the parallels with → *wisdom* literature, the bestowal of the authority of the exemplary wise king, Solomon (cf. Ecclesiastes, Proverbs, *Wisdom of Solomon*) and the elevated diction employed, wisdom circles seem the most likely authors. The reference to the 'daughters of Jerusalem' (1.5, etc.), the daughters of → *Zion* (3.11), and the fiction concerning Solomon (3.7, 9, 11; 8.11) support an origin in Jerusalem.

### 17.3.3 The Situation and Function of the Song of Songs

Earlier scholarship determined the setting in life to be a (week-long) marriage feast and was able to find support in a custom attested on into the nineteenth and twentieth century in Syria and Palestine in which the bride and bridegroom assumed the roles of queen and king. Indeed, more recent scholarship also locates individual songs in the context of banquets (cf. Cant. 2.4; 5.1b; 7.1b) and marriage celebrations, but, on the whole, leaves open the question of the setting of life of the book. In its extant form, it involves *literary verse* characterized by a contrived diction. Echoes of mythical diction do not point to a cultic pre-history for the songs, but are a conscious literary technique. In terms of social history, the collection may stem from prosperous but politically disenfranchised critics who compensated for their religious scepticism with a glorification of a nature-oriented joy in life.[10] In its extant form, the book would then be a Jewish reaction to the love poetry of the Alexandrian school of literature (Kallimachos, Apollonius of Rhodes, Theocritus),[11] offering its own contrasting contribution that grew out of Near Eastern tradition.

## 17.4 Theology of the Song of Songs

The Song of Songs, like the book of Esther (Ch. 20), contains no explicit designation for God.[12] In contrast to Esther, there is also no allusion to God or (apart

10. Cf. H.-P. Müller, *Hohelied*, 4.

11. Callimachus (LCL 129; ed. A. Mair; Cambridge, Mass.: Harvard University Press, 1955; and LCL 421; ed. C. A. Trypanis; Cambridge, Mass.: Harvard University Press, 1968); Greek Bucolic (LCL 28; ed. J. M. Edmonds; London: Heinemann, 1960); Philostratus I, *Life of Apollonius of Tyrana: Books I-IV* (LCL 1; ed. C. P. Jones; Cambridge, Mass.: Harvard University Press, 2010).

12. The expression *šalhebet-yâ* in Cant. 8.6, which HNAS (cf. NAU, NJB) translated 'flame of the Lord', contains the short form of the divine name *Yh(wh)* = *Yhwh* in the sense of an intensive suffix and designates a 'mighty flame'.

from the Solomon fiction) to the history of 'Israel'. At the same time, even without an → *allegorical* or → *typological* interpretation, it is possible to trace a religious profile by reading the Song of Songs in the overall context of Old Testament scriptures, especially its central → *anthropological* texts. An understanding against the background of the biblical Primeval History (Gen. 1–9), in particular, holds promise here. Like it, the Song of Songs understands a human being as a being created by God to cultivate *and* enjoy this world. The essential pleasures of life also include love between a man and a woman (Gen. 2.20-24). Like the Primeval History, the Song of Songs knows that human life is limited. At the same time, it knows that love is an ineffable gift. Even when described hyperbolically and sometimes personified mythically in the Song of Songs, love never appears as a goddess or as an entity separate from the lovers, but always as an experience between the lovers. As in Gen. 2.24, the beginnings of the phenomenon of personal love appear (Cant. 6.8-9; 8.11-12). In the framework of the Old Testament → *canon* and of the history of Jewish, and especially Christian, piety, the Song of Songs has the capacity to point out, contrary to a denigration of human sexuality, that it, too, is a gift of God. At the same time, it is ambivalent, like everything created.

## 17.5 Notes on the History of Reception

As was the case with the books of Proverbs (Ch. 15) and Ecclesiastes (Ch. 18), the inclusion of the Song of Song among the 'Holy Scriptures' was controversial in ancient Judaism. At the same time, the Song of Songs also enjoyed particularly high esteem, as indicated by a saying from Rabbi Aqiba transmitted in the Babylonian → *Talmud*:

> The whole world is not worth the day that the Song of Songs was given, for all the hagiographa are sacred, but the Song of Songs is most sacred (*Yad.* III:v).

Since the eighth century, the Song of Songs has been employed *in Jewish worship* as the scroll for the eighth day of the → *Passover/Mazzoth Festival*. This assignment is apparently based in its interpretation with regard to the love relationship between Yhwh, the God of the Exodus, and his people liberated from Egypt on Passover (cf. Hos. 11). The → *allegorical* interpretation led to the Song becoming one of the most beloved books in the Old Testament in Christianity on into the 17th century.

In the early church era and the Middle Ages, the allegorical interpretation appeared in three varieties:

(1) *Ecclesiologically*, the relationship between the man and woman in the Song of Songs was applied to the relationship between Christ as the bridegroom and the Church as the bride ('Ecclesia-Sponsa').
(2) *Mariologically*, the woman was identified with Mary as a type of the church ('Maria-Sponsa').
(3) *Mystically*, the relationship between the man and woman was interpreted in terms of the relationship of the soul of the believer with Christ ('Anima-Sponsa').

The Song of Songs exerted great influence overall on the language of piety, especially of mysticism, and on Western *literature*. Thus, Middle High German Minnesang fed on its language and imagery, as did the *West-Eastern Divan* by Johann Wolfgang von Goethe (1819). In the words placed in the mouth of his hero, Adson von Melk, the Song of Songs gained entrance into Umberto Eco's novel, *The Name of the Rose* (1980/82). In the *realm of the visual arts*, the allegorical interpretation, in particular, took root with greater intensity beginning in the twelfth century.

# 18

# Ecclesiastes (Solomon, the Preacher)

(Markus Witte – Translation by Mark Biddle)

## Chapter Outline




Commentaries: T. Krüger (Transl. by O. C. Dean, Jr. Minneapolis: Fortress, 2004); R. Murphy (WBC 23A. Dallas, Tex.: Word Books, 1992); L. Schwienhorst-Schönberger (HTKAT. Freiburg: Herder, 2004); R. N. Whybray (OTG. Sheffield: JSOT, 1989).

I. Kottsieper, 'Alttestamentliche Weisheit'. *TRu* (2002): 226–37; L. G. Perdue, *Wisdom Literature: A Theological History*. Louisville, Ky.: Westminster John Knox, 2007, 161–216; L. Schwienhorst-Schönberger, ed., *Das Buch Kohelet: Studien zur Struktur, Geschichte, Rezeption und Theologie*. BZAW 254. Berlin/New York: de Gruyter, 1997.


In the Hebrew tradition, the book is called *qohelet* in accord with the information in Eccl. 1.1 (cf. 1.2; 7.27 and 12.8-10). The word derives from the term *qāhāl* ('assembly') and signifies the 'leader of the assembly'. The term 'preacher' traces to the Greek translation of *qohelet* as *ecclēsiastēs*. The addition 'Solomon' is based on the equation of the son of David mentioned in Eccl. 1.1, 12 with his successor Solomon.[1]

1. Regarding the image of Solomon assumed in Eccl., cf. 1 Kgs 3.16-28; 5.9-14 (NRSV 4.29-34); 10.1-29.

# 18.1 Biblical Context

| | | |
|---|---|---|
| **1.1-3** | **Prologue with a statement of the theme of Qoheleth's learning** | |
| **1.4-11** | **Introduction: Reflection on the continual repetition of reality** | |
| **1.12–2.26** | **'Royal Travesty':[2] The royal Qoheleth in search of wisdom** | |
| **3.1-15** | **Reflections on time** | |
| **3.16–6.12** | **Reflections on the social and economic contexts of humanity** | |
| | 3.16-22 | Corrupt justice |
| | 4.1-16 | Corrupt society |
| | 4.17–5.6 (NRSV 5.7) | Religious practice |
| | 5.7 (NRSV 5.8)–6.9 | The handling of wealth |
| | 6.10-12 | God as the boundary condition of happiness |
| **7.1–8.15** | **Reflections on what is truly good for human beings** | |
| | 7:1–24 | Critique of traditional wisdom sayings |
| | 7:25–29 | Critique of wisdom's devaluation of woman |
| | 8:1–9 | Critique of the wisdom doctrine of the proper time |
| | 8:10–15 | Call to enjoy God-given joy |
| **8.16–10.20** | **Reflections on the utility of wisdom** | |
| | 8.16-17 | Limits of wisdom and knowledge |
| | 9.1-12 | Living in the face of death |
| | 9.13–10.20 | Observations on the strengths and weakness of wisdom |
| **11.1–12.7** | **Conclusion** | |
| | 11.1-8 | Call to presence of mind |
| | 11.9–12.7 | Instruction on the ability to enjoy oneself |
| **12.8-14** | **Epilogue with information about Qoheleth, the wisdom teacher** | |

In 1.1-3 and 12.8-14, the book contains a *prologue* and an *epilogue* that indicate the author and the motto of his document. This framework has a counterpart in 1.4-11 and 11.1–12.7 as an internal foreword and afterword indicating the question of humankind in the horizon of creation established by God as the theme of the book. One learns from the superscription (1.1) that it introduces a collection of *aphorisms* ('teachings') which, as is customary in Ancient Near Eastern literature, are composed *in poetic form* (Ch. 13.2.2). The attribution of the

2. A technical term for the literary guise of Qoheleth as king; Y. V. Koh, *Royal Autobiography in the Book of Qoheleth* (BZAW 369; Berlin/New York: de Gruyter, 2006).

teachings at hand to the *son of David* elicits the association with Solomon and with the tradition of the wise and just king tied to him. Ecclesiastes 1.2 concisely offers the *theme statement* of the document: 'Everything is extremely transitory (*hebel*),' says Qoheleth, 'everything is extremely transitory.' The term *hebel* designates the wind and, in a metaphorical sense, nothingness and transience.[3] Ecclesiastes 1.3 states the question that serves as the starting-point for all subsequent deliberation: 'What does one gain from all one's toil (*ʿāmāl*) that one has done under the sun?' The Preacher makes the question 'What is a human being?'[4] – known from Ps. 8.5 (NRSV 8.4) and stemming from the complaint about transience – the object of his pre-philosophical reflection. The description of human existence as *ʿāmāl* ('toil'/'adversity,' 2.24; 3.13; 5.18 [NRSV 5.19]) appears in place of the joyous confession of the world's design (Ps. 8). The person who has become the object of reflection is the person for whom the world is a riddle, existence is a crisis, and God is distant.

The well-planned composition concerning the constant order of the cosmos and the temporal structure of reality (1.4–3.15) already contains the *basic elements of the argument*. The series of topically coherent sayings that follow in 3.16–10.20 deepen 1.4–3.15 with reflections concerning social, economic, and religious contexts (3.16–6.12), what is truly good for human beings (7.1–8.15), and the utility of → *wisdom* (8.16–10.20).

Qoheleth's reflections consist mostly of *four steps*: (1) questions concerning human nature, (2) associations with a few observations on nature and culture, (3) a contrast with traditional wisdom sayings, and (4) thetic conclusions, often negatively formulated, in response to the question posed.

*Additional structural characteristics of the overall work* are *keywords* and *key formulas*, including the terms 'knowledge' (*daʿat*), 'transitory' (*hebel*), 'wisdom' (*ḥokmâ*), 'heart' (*lēb*), 'fate' (*miqrēh*), 'toil' (*ʿāmāl*), and 'joy' (*śimḥâ*). The most important *key formulas* include the expressions 'I said in my heart' (*ʿāmartî/dibbartî bĕlibbî*), 'everything is wholly transitory' (*hakkol hebel*), 'I recognized' (*yādaʿtî*), 'I saw' (*raʾitî*), 'snatching at the wind' (*rĕʿût rûăḥ*), and 'under the sun' (*taḥat haššemeš*).

3. The interpretation of the book changes depending on whether one translates the term hebel 'vanity,' 'futile,' 'breeze,' or 'absurd' (so D. Michel, *Qohelet* [EdF 258, Darmstadt: Wissenschaftliche Buchgesellschaft, 1988]); see D. B. Miller, *Symbol and Rhetoric in Ecclesiastes: The Place of Hebel in Qohelet's Work* (Academia Biblica 2; Leiden/Boston: Brill, 2002).
4. Cf. Ps. 144.3 and the perversion in Job 7.17.

# 18.2 Textual Issues and Major Issues in the History of Critical Interpretation

## 18.2.1 The Book of Ecclesiastes in the Context of the History of Old Testament Wisdom

The book engages critically with traditional → *wisdom* while relying on its linguistic forms. For Qoheleth, wisdom has only relative merit which must be newly proven in each situation. The notion that one can manage life with wisdom finds its limits in the times established by God. Realistic wisdom means embracing all of reality, i.e. the bright times of life as well as the dark, as given by God and acting within the limits of knowledge (3.14). The goal is to encourage following the 'golden mean'. The key lines of the argument in the *critique of wisdom* are the references to dependence on the inalterable present and the impossibility of planning the future (10.2-20). In view of this situation, Qoheleth emphasizes the significance of life positively[5] and calls for enjoying it ('carpe diem').[6]

***The carpe diem motif*** has many parallels in the Ancient Near East and antiquity. It has its oldest literary precursors demonstrable so far in a passage from the old Babylonian versions of the *Gilgamesh Epic* from the period around 1800 BCE (translated in *COS* I, 458–60) which is absent from the 'canonical version' of the Gilgamesh Epic, the Ninevite version from the 13th century BCE (the twelve-tablet epic). Other motif parallels occur in *Egyptian Songs of the Harpist* inscribed in the graves of the New Kingdom (16th–11th cent. BCE) that call for enjoyment of life in view of human mortality (translated in Lichtheim, *AEL* II, 115–116; I, 193–197). In addition, there are biographical grave inscriptions from Egypt (translated in *AEL* III, 51–52), Greek texts from the Hellenistic period, and Roman texts (cf. Horace, *Odes* I:11, who gave the motif its name).[7] No literary relationship between these texts can be demonstrated. Presumably, they constitute analogous developments in comparable social and intellectual circumstances.

5. Eccl. 9.4; cf. 1 Sam. 17.43; 24.15 (NRSV 25.14); Prov. 30.30; Homer, Odyssey XI:489 (English translation in G. E. Dimock, ed., *Homer: Odyssey: Books 1-12* [LCL 104; Cambridge, Mass.: Harvard University Press, 1998]).
6. Eccl. 9.7-10; further, Eccl. 2.24; 3.12, 22; 5.17-19; Wisd. Sol. 2.1-9.
7. English translation in N. Rudd, ed., *Horace: Odes and Epodes* (LCL 33; Cambridge, Mass.: Harvard University Press, 2004).

## 18.2.2 The Question of the Literary Character of the Book of Ecclesiastes

With regard to the question of its literary origins and overall interpretation, the work belongs to one of the most enigmatic books in the Old Testament. In essence, five factors are responsible for this situation: (1) the absence of analogies in the history of Old Testament literature; (2) the compositional differences between the carefully arranged tractate in 1.4–3.15 and the groups of sayings in 3.16–12.8, which are appended more on a principle of association and cohere around certain themes; (3) the critique of fundamental convictions of wisdom (Ch. 15.2); (4) the distance from the historical and prophetic traditions of the Old Testament; and (5) the proximity to Near Eastern and Greek wisdom texts.

The first three observations give rise to the *question of the literary unity of the book*, which is intensified with a view to apparent contradictions and the appendixes which are even configured as such (12.9-11; 12.12-14). The fourth and fifth observations provoke questions about the *status of the book in the context of the religious and cultural history* of the eastern Mediterranean in the second half of the first millennium BCE, especially its relationship to → *Hellenism*, and about its *status within Old Testament theology*. Most recent research posits the literary integrity of the book, apart from the two epilogues (12.9-11; 12.10-14) and glosses here and there, and explains the tensions in content between individual aphorisms by means of a theory of citation and argumentation.[8] Characterizations of the profile of the content of the work overall reach from a description of Qoheleth as a sceptic, representing an outsider in the Old Testament, to an assessment of him as a teacher of the Torah.[9]

8. Cf. D. Michel, *Qohelet*, 27–33 (above, n. 3).
9. See the overview in Kottsieper, *Weisheit*, 225–37.

# 18.3 Origins of the Book of Ecclesiastes

## 18.3.1 The Form of the Book of Ecclesiastes

In a manner unique in the Old Testament, the book combines → *genres* from → *wisdom* into extended reflections in the first person singular ('self-report') that take on the character of *tractates*.

*Wisdom genres* include: (a) proverbs (cf. 9.4b); (b) aphorisms (cf. 2.14; 7.11; 11.4); (c) comparative *ṭôb* ('better than') sayings (cf. 4.6; 7.1, 8; 9.18); (d) positive admonitions/advice (cf. 11.1-2); (e) negative admonitions/warnings (cf. 7.9, 16-17); (f) exhortations (cf. 4.17–5.6 [NRSV 5.7]; 9.7-10; 11.9–12.7); (g) benedictions (cf. 10.17); (h) rhetorical didactic questions (cf. 2.19). In addition, *forms of speech attested outside wisdom*, such as the woe (cf. 10.16-17), the comparison (cf. 2.13), the metaphor (cf. 9.14f.), or the → *allegory* (cf. 12.3-4a), also appear.

In terms of genre, the book constitutes an *instruction*, even though it lacks the typical *introduction to instruction formulas* (→ *Lehreröffnungsformel*) and the 'call to attention'. Ecclesiastes often cites aphorisms from the wisdom school to criticize them based on his own experience. *Parallels in the history of literature* occur in the Mesopotamian, Egyptian and Greek realms. According to the information given in Eccl. 1.1, the book is *instruction for living*. This genre has its closest parallels in ancient Egyptian instructions that often appear in the mouth of a king.[10] Greek literature offers parallels in *gnomic literature*.[11] The greatest similarities in form and context are with the *Egyptian Songs of the Harpist and complaints* (see above).[12]

10. Cf., for example, the 'Instruction of Merikare' or the 'Instruction of King Amenemhet', both translated in M. Lichtheim, *Ancient Egyptian Literature* I, 97–109; 135–9.
11. Cf., especially, the aphorisms collected under the name of Theognis of Megara (6th/5th cent. BCE); *Greek Elegiac Poetry from the Seventh to the Fifth Centuries B.C.* (LCL 258; ed. and transl. D. E. Gerber; Cambridge, Mass.: Harvard University Press, 2003).
12. Cf. the excursus on parallels to the book of Job (Ch. 14.3.2).

## 18.3.2 The Composition and Redaction of the Book of Ecclesiastes

As evidenced by its linguistic peculiarities, the influence of Aramaic and Persian, and its affinities with Greek thought, the book stems from the middle of the third century BCE, at the earliest. The book of Sirach, written around 190/180 BCE (Ch. 27), also engages critically with Ecclesiastes (cf. the '→ theodicy pericope' in Sir. 39.12-35 as an echo of Eccl. 3).

Whether the combination of the individual reflections stems from Qoheleth himself or from one of his students cannot be determined. The collection has received a *dual secondary framework*, however, which traces back to a first and second epilogist:

First Epilogist: + Eccl. 1.1*,2; 12.8-11
Second Epilogist: + Eccl. 12.12-14.

*Redactional revisions* are evident in four other passages: (1) Eccl. 3.17 and 11.9b interpret the call to fear God unilaterally in terms of Torah observance and link it with the idea of an eschatological judgement. (2) Eccl. 11.10b extends the restriction on the call to enjoyment in secondary phrase, 11.9b. (3) Eccl. 12.7 modifies the notion of the absolute death of human beings in terms of creation theology. Apart from the two epilogues and the four passages mentioned (3.17; 11.9b; 11.10b; 12.7), the book can be regarded a literary unity.[13]

## 18.3.3 The Situation and Function of the Book of Ecclesiastes

Under the influence of → *Hellenism*, the book mirrors the relationship between individual experience and a traditional, optimistic wisdom. Characteristic is the attempt to argue philosophically using the methods of Old Testament proverbial wisdom. According to the instruction in 11.9–12.7, Qoheleth may have been, like Ben Sirach after him, a scribe (*sôfer*) who taught young men from the Jerusalem upper class. The objective is instruction for a successful life in view of the ambivalence of life experience. The *starting point* was, not

13. In contrast, M. Rose (*Rien de nouveau: Nouvelles approches du livre de Qohéleth* [OBO 148; Fribourg: Academic Press/Göttingen: Vandenhoeck & Ruprecht, 1999]) proposes a multi-layered model of redaction.

least, the social and economic upheavals in Syria-Palestine caused by the expansion of Hellenism throughout the Near East (Ch. 4.4).

## 18.4 Theology of the Book of Ecclesiastes

Its *anthropological starting point* characterizes the theology of Ecclesiastes. Reflections about human beings lead to reflections about God. Qoheleth's own theology is a *theology of creation*.[14] The theme of salvation history established by God, which dominates Old Testament historical and prophetic traditions, plays no role. Human beings and the world surrounding them appear, ultimately, as an inscrutable, but meaningfully ordered work of God. The world and human experience in it are ambivalent. They have integrity in God, who withdraws from any human access, however. Consequently, Ecclesiastes consistently employs the general designations *ʾĕlôhîm* ('God') or *ha-ʾĕlôhîm* ('the God'/'the Deity') for God, and not, Yhwh, the proper name of the Old Testament God. God's activity is unpredictable by humans, but God does not act unjustly. Ecclesiastes avoids the question of *God's justice* with a reference to human injustice (7.20). The problem is not the justice of God, but the injustice of human beings. The question as to why human beings are unjust is not raised. Ecclesiastes describes the human tendency to miss the mark as an empirically demonstrable given, contingent on human creatureliness. Ecclesiastes would presumably respond to the resulting question as to why God apparently created a deficient humanity in a manner similar to Paul, later, in connection to Isa. 45.9 and Jer. 18.6 (cf. Rom. 3.20; 9.21-22). In view of the inscrutability of the world, the unpredictability of God, and the limitations of all created things and historical events, Qoheleth advises fear of God, on one hand, and *enjoyment of the moment*, on the other. The notion of the *fear of God*, which diminished to the notion of 'piety' in the history of Old Testament wisdom, has regained something of its original force: God, as unpredictable, is also the wholly other whose appearance evokes awe. In the fear of God, a human being acknowledges divine omnipotence and accepts the limits set by God and the *times of joy and sorrow* allocated by God.

14. L. G. Perdue, *Wisdom Literature*, 212–16.

Ecclesiastes 3.1-15 offers a reflection on *the nature of time*, which is unique in Ancient Near Eastern literature, even though there are corresponding motifs in Psalms 39 and 90 and the Egyptian Songs of the Harpist (see above). The term 'time' (*'et*) represents the time placed at the disposal of human beings, the moment that calls for action, the present moment, the *kairos*. In contrast, the term 'eternity' (*'ôlām*) denotes the time removed from humans and reserved for God. *'ôlām* is hidden time, *'et* is evident time. Both terms describe, not primarily duration, but a quality and a sphere: *'et* is human time, *'ôlām*, divine time; *'et* is the realm of humanity, *'ôlām* the realm of God. The two realms are interrelated, however. Time divides into qualified and mutually exclusive times. The task of humanity is to recognize what is appropriate to the time and to behave accordingly, thus acting 'in a timely fashion'. For the Preacher, everything that happens has the meaning God gives it in the moment it occurs (3.1-15). Time stands in direct relation to God. Human beings have a notion of the 'eternity' that surrounds the moment given them. The unity of time consists in its relationship to God. In any moment, a human being can discover something life-affirming *if* God allows him to perceive it. It is possible to engage with the given time *if* God permits it.[15]

For Qoheleth as for other biblical authors, this world is a dying world. Qoheleth only says this more clearly than they through his catchphrase 'everything is transitory'. Human and animal have the same mortal fate (*miqreh*, 3.10). With this assessment, Qoheleth stands in line with the traditional Old Testament *concept of death* as an absolute boundary.

***Old Testament concepts of life after death:*** Fundamentally, a strong this-worldly orientation permeates the Old Testament. Life, in the full sense of the word, exists only in this life. Yhwh is a God of the living (cf. Ps. 6.6 [NRSV 6.5]). After death, individuals continue to glimmer in *Sheol*, the underworld, as shades (cf. Isa. 14) only as long as people remember them. A few Old Testament texts that originated in close temporal proximity to Ecclesiastes hint at the notion that a person has a life after death which is more than shadowy vegetation in the underworld and which does not signify the absolute dissolution of relationship with God. Thus, at the latest since the middle of the third century BCE, one finds a series of different pictures of a post-mortal existence. One encounters essentially *four conceptual spheres*: (1) the hope for community with God that survives death (Ps. 73.23-24); (2) the expectation of a selective resurrection, i.e. the resurrection of the righteous to eternal

⇨

15. T. Gretler, *Zeit und Stunde: Theologische Zeitkonzepte zwischen Erfahrung und Ideologie in den Büchern Kohelet und Daniel* (Zurich: Theologischer Verlag, 2004).

life and the resurrection of the unrighteous to eternal shame (Dan. 12.1-3; 2 Macc. 7.9); (3) the conviction of the immortality of the soul of the pious (Ps. 49.16 [NRSV 49.15]; Wis 3.1). A common background in the history of ideas characterizes these three conceptual spheres. They all originate from the experience that there is no equalizing justice immanent in the world: if, on the one hand, even the just must suffer, and, on the other, faith in God's life-affirming justice is not to be abandoned, then there remains only the hope that the just will have a special fate. In addition to these three individually-oriented conceptual realms, there is also (4) the universal hope that God will one day deprive death of all its power (Isa. 25.6-8; 26.7-21). Its background in the history of tradition is the universalization (→ *universalism*) and monotheization (→ *monotheism*) of the Old Testament view of God: Because the God of Israel is simultaneously the creator of the whole world and because he is simultaneously the only God, he also has power over life-destroying death (Amos 9.2; Hos. 13.14; Job 26.5-6; Ps. 139.8). To be sure, God will only reveal his universal power at the end of time and in the context of the worldwide judgement of the nations. Thus, the Old Testament hope for overcoming the boundary of death has two immanent roots: (1) an extension of reflection on God's righteousness and (2) a development of the concept of God's universal kingship and creative activity. Egyptian and Persian notions of the judgement on the dead may have constituted external impulses. In 3.21, however, Qoheleth – like Jesus Sirach, who, two generations later, was also very conservative in this respect (cf. Sir. 14; 27) and then, in Jesus' time, the Sadducees (cf. Mk 12.18-27) – seems to reject decisively these → *eschatological* positions.

More insistently than other biblical witnesses, Ecclesiastes emphasizes the fact that human beings are absolutely dependent on the realms of life and times of life that God discloses. The significant element of this message is that Qoheleth recognizes the moments of happiness God sends in the conscious appreciation of everyday events. In the concentration on the moment sent by the Creator God and in the description of happiness as an encounter between Creator and creature manifest in the act of reception, Qoheleth proves to be a precursor to the words of Jesus in Mt. 6.25-34, in which the reference to Solomon is hardly accidental.

## 18.5 Notes on the History of Reception

The inclusion of Ecclesiastes in the 'Holy Scriptures' was still controversial in ancient Judaism as late as the first and second centuries CE. While the school of *Shammai* denied its holiness, the school of *Hillel* affirmed it.[16] *Philo of Alexandria* and the *New Testament* never cite the book.[17] *Josephus*, however, numbers it among the four → '*canonical*' books with hymnic and ethical content (Psalms; Proverbs; Canticles; Ecclesiastes).[18] Since the Middle Ages, Ecclesiastes has had a firm *place in Jewish worship* as the festival scroll for the → *Feast of Tabernacles.*

The book plays an important role in the *theology of the Reformers.* Luther interpreted it as a document in opposition to free will (1526). Finally, the book exercised major *influence on Western poetry* and was often *set to music.* As an example, attention may be drawn to the poems dealing with transience in German Baroque literature.[19]

16. Cf. b *Yad.* III:v; IV:vi; b *ʿEd.* V:iii; *b Meg.* 7a.
17. The reference to Eccl. 7.20 in Rom. 3.10 could be the sole exception. T. Krüger (*Qoheleth*, 32-33) lists possible New Testament allusions to Ecclesiastes.
18. Josephus, *Contra Apion* I, 8, translated in S. Mason, ed., *Flavius Josephus, Translation and Commentary*, Vol. 10.
19. Cf. e.g., A. Gryphius, 'Es ist alles eitell (*sic*)' (1643); idem, 'Die Herrlichkeit der Erden' (1650); M. Franck, 'Ach wie flüchtig, ach wie nichtig' (1652).

# 19

# The Book of Lamentations

(Markus Witte – Translation by Mark Biddle)

## Chapter Outline




📖 Commentaries: U. Berges (HTKAT. Freiburg: Herder, 2002); E. Gerstenberger (FOTL 15. Grand Rapids, Mich.: Eerdmans, 2001), 463–505; D. R. Hillers (AB 7a. 2nd ed. New York: Doubleday, 1992); O. Kaiser, 'Klagelieder'. Pages 91–198 in *Das Hohelied, Klagelieder, Das Buch Ester*. ATD 16/2. Ed. by H.-P. Müller, O. Kaiser and J. A. Loader. 4th ed. Göttingen: Vandenhoeck & Ruprecht, 1992; R. E. Murphy (FOTL 13. Grand Rapids, Mich.: Eerdmans, 1981); I. W. Provan (NCB Commentary. Grand Rapids, Mich.: Eerdmans, 1991).

📖 M. Emmendörfer, *Der ferne Gott*. FAT 21. Tübingen: Mohr Siebeck, 1997; C. Westermann, *Die Klagelieder: Forschungsgeschichte und Auslegung*. Neukirchen-Vluyn: Neukirchener, 1990.


Jewish tradition refers to the book by its first word, *ʾêkâ* ('Ah!/Woe!') or according to its designation in the Babylonian → *Talmud*, *qînôt* ('dirges', *B. Bat.* 15a). The → *Septuagint* and the → *Vulgate*, in which it occurs under the name *thrēnoi* or, Latinized, *threni*, or translated, *lamentations*, follow this designation. The designation 'Lamentations of *Jeremiah*' common in some traditions is based on three circumstances: (1) the expanded superscription in the Septuagint,[1] (2) a

1. And it came to pass that, after Israel was taken into captivity and Jerusalem was destroyed, Jeremiah sat crying and raised this lament over Jerusalem and said.

comment about Jeremiah as a singer of laments in 2 Chr. 35.25,[2] and (3) the location of Lamentations in the Septuagint and the Vulgate following the book of Jeremiah.

## 19.1 Biblical Context

| | | |
|---|---|---|
| 1 | **First Song: Jerusalem, the abandoned city** | |
| | 1.1-11 | Lament concerning the city's self-induced distress |
| | 1.12-22 | Call for retribution on the enemies who mock the city |
| 2 | **Second Song: The city stricken by God's wrath** | |
| | 2.1-12 | Report concerning Jerusalem's suffering |
| | 2.13-22 | Appeal for Yhwh to intervene with assistance |
| 3 | **Third Song: Meditation concerning God's wrath and grace** | |
| | 3.1-24 | Complaint of an individual sufferer |
| | 3.25-33 | Admonition concerning proper behaviour in suffering |
| | 3.34-39 | Reflection concerning God's righteousness |
| | 3.40-47 | Collective confession of sin |
| | 3.48-51 | Description of suffering |
| | 3.52-66 | Call for God's retribution |
| 4 | **Fourth Song: The city's sin and atonement** | |
| | 4.1-11 | Report concerning the suffering of Jerusalem's population |
| | 4.12-20 | Description of the misbehaviour of representatives of the city |
| | 4.21-22 | Confession of Jerusalem's sin with a wish for vengeance on Edom |
| 5 | **Fifth Song: God's memory** | |
| | 5.1-18 | Appeal to God's saving remembrance and collective lament |
| | 5.19-22 | Collective petition to Yhwh, praise of God, concluding question to God |

*Keywords* and *key motifs* interconnect the five songs. The following serve these functions: (1) God's wrath as the reason for the suffering,[3] (2) Jerusalem's sins as the cause for divine wrath,[4] (3) the confession of sins and the call to penitence as

2. And Jeremiah sang a lament over Josiah, and all the male and female singers lament in their songs of lament over Josiah until this day, and this became an established custom in Israel; and behold, they (i.e. the songs of lament) are recorded among the songs of lament.
3. Cf. Lam. 1.12; 2.1-4, 6, 21-22; 3.1; 4.11; 5.22.
4. Cf. Lam. 1.8, 14; 2.14; 3.42; 4.6, 13; 5.7.

means for appeasing God's wrath,[5] and (4) the call for confidence in God as the basis of hope in the face of God's continued absence.[6]

Additional *structural elements* include the variation of designations for God ('Yhwh', 'Lord', 'the Highest') and the modifications of the titles for the city repeatedly personified as a woman.[7] The chief characteristic of the overall composition is the *dramatic character* evident in the repeated change of speakers (individual reporter, the city) and audience (God, the city, the nations).

# 19.2 Textual Issues and Major Issues in the History of Critical Interpretation

Lamentations presumes the Babylonian conquest and destruction of Jerusalem in 587 BCE (Ch. 3.3). The songs exhibit such markedly stereotypical characteristics, however, that it is difficult to understand them as poetic eyewitness accounts. In addition, the songs record a progressive reflection on the loss of political independence and the destruction of the infrastructure of the official cult. Furthermore, the individual songs place different accents on the question of guilt. This variation indicates that the songs originated at a greater temporal distance to the events treated and stem from various authors.

# 19.3 Origins of the Book of Lamentations

## 19.3.1 The Form of the Book and of the Individual Songs

In the context of Old Testament literature, the book constitutes a unique → *genre*. In terms of the history of literature, it has its nearest relative in the Psalter (Ch. 13). Based on its scope and the interconnection of its individual

5. Cf. Lam. 1.14, 18; 2.18; 3.40; 5.16.
6. Cf. Lam. 1.20; 3.22, 25; 4.22; 5.21.
7. 'Daughter Zion', 'Jerusalem', 'Zion', 'Jacob', 'Judah', 'Israel', 'Daughter Jerusalem', 'widow', 'unclean woman', 'mother', and 'virgin.'

texts, however, Lamentations constitutes a much more dense composition. On the basis of its poetic form and its character as a continuous meditation, the generic designation → '*anthology of meditations*' seems suitable. The fact that exactly five laments were combined in a book may be associated with the structure of the → *Pentateuch* and the Psalter (Ch. 13).[8] Thus, the five books of Moses and the five books of David parallel the five lamentations of Jeremiah, all books which, according to Old Testament tradition, trace back to exemplary men of prayer.[9]

The five *songs* were originally *independent compositions* with their own theological profiles that were only secondarily combined into a collection. In terms of content and form, the first, second, fourth and fifth songs parallel closely while the third song constitutes an unusual unit. All the songs are alphabetic or quasi-alphabetic literary compositions (→ *acrostic*).

Furthermore, the basic form of the verse in all the songs consists of two cola (stichoi; → *colon*) that correspond to one another in content and form. The metre of the Hebrew funeral dirge dominates in the first four songs. In it, the first → *colon* of a bi-colon is longer than the second and a bi-colon always has 3 + 2 accented syllables. The songs themselves cannot be assigned to any specific *generic paradigm*, but constitute their own genre. They employ elements, primarily, from the *communal lament* and the *individual lament* (Ch. 13.3.2), from the *funeral dirge* (Qinah), and from the *wisdom admonition* ('*paranesis*'; Ch. 15).

***The funeral dirge*** can consist of six elements: (1) a cry of lamentation (*'êk* 'ah/how', cf. 2 Sam. 1.19, 25, 27), (2) an account of suffering utilizing the scheme contrasting the fortunate past ('once') and the unfortunate present ('now'), (3) a description of one's own crying and agony caused by suffering, (4) a list of those suffering or directly affected by the suffering, (5) the expression of waiting on the compassion of those passing by, and (6) a wish for vengeance.

Thus, Lamentations represents a *mixture of genres* and an *alteration of genres*. The sometimes verbal borrowings from Psalms and from the books of Isaiah, Jeremiah and Ezekiel characterize Lamentations as an *anthological (mosaic) composition*. Based on their alphabetic style, it can be assumed that,

8. Cf. also the division of the Ethiopian book of Enoch into five books (translated in *OTP* I, 5–89).

9. Cf. Exod. 32–34 (Moses); Pss 3–32 etc. (David); Jer. 15.15 (Jeremiah).

in essence, they are literary unities. Lamentations has a certain *form-critical analogy* in the Sumerian laments over the destruction of the city of Ur from the period around 1955 BCE.[10]

## 19.3.2 The Composition and Redaction of the Book of Lamentations

According to the expanded superscription in the → *Septuagint* and post-biblical Jewish tradition, Lamentations was written by Jeremiah (cf. *bB. Bat.* 15a). The fact that, from the perspective of the history of the → *canon*, Lamentations was transmitted as an independent entity in the context of the Ketuvim speaks against Jeremianic authorship. In addition, considerations of the history of literature and theology speak against both Jeremianic authorship and the assumption of an individual author. The songs all stand under the influence of the → *deuteronomistic* interpretation of the → *exile* and originated in the course of the sixth to fourth centuries BCE. The oldest song is probably the second, which may belong chronologically to the context of events surrounding the demise of Jerusalem in 587 BCE. The first song cites the second and goes beyond it to deal with the question of responsibility for Jerusalem's catastrophe. In turn, the fourth song appeals back to the first and second and exhibits a more extensive reflection on the question of guilt. The most recent song is the third.

From the perspective of the history of traditions, Lamentations 3 depends, on one side, on late prophecy, and on the other, on the late deuteronomistic theology of repentance (Ch. 7.2).[11] Moreoever, it assumes the complete book of Jeremiah (10). The many parallels to the book of Job (Ch. 14) are based on common roots in the diction of Psalms, especially in the language and motifs of the individual lament. With regard to its sceptical elements, Lamentations 3 has affinities with Psalm 14 (par. Ps. 53), Isa. 5.19 and parts of Job. Finally, Lamentations 3 reflects the beginnings of internal Jewish conflict between an → *eschatologically* oriented minority and an anti-eschatological majority. Thus, it belongs at least in the late Persian period (4th cent. BCE).

10. Transl. in COS I, 535–9; W. C. Gwaltney, 'The Biblical Book of Lamentations in the Context of Near Eastern Lament Literature', in *COS* II, 191–211.
11. Cf. v. 40 with Deut. 4.29-31; 30.1-10; 1 Kgs 8.46-51.

Thus, from the perspective of the history of literature, the following sequence results:

Lam. 2 → Lam. 1 → Lam. 4 → Lam. 5 → Lam. 3.

Scholarship debates the identity of the circle responsible for the composition of Lamentations. Based on the critique of priests and prophets, on the one hand, and the connection with the Jerusalem temple and the *scriptural scholarship* evident in the songs, on the other, it is most likely that levitical temple singers stood behind the composition. The secondary connection of Lamentations with the prophet Jeremiah is presumably based on formal and substantive parallels with the 'confessions of Jeremiah' (Jer. 11–20*), which, however, can no more be traced to the prophet himself than can Lamentations (Ch. 10.3).

### 19.3.3 The Situation and Function of the Book of Lamentations

The Lamentations are primarily *literary* texts by a pious individual suffering the consequences of the destruction of Jerusalem and its temple. They involve exegesis of scripture and *eschatological interpretation* of history. The latter is particularly evident in the juxtaposition of Jerusalem and the nations: Jerusalem's demise becomes the prelude to and the model for the final judgement. Yhwh, who did not spare his own city, will not spare the nations either. It is not possible to demonstrate a *liturgical use* in the environs of the destroyed temple or a connection with the exilic lamentation ceremonies mentioned in Zech. 7.3, 5; 8.15.

## 19.4 Theology of the Book of Lamentations

The theology of Lamentations centres on the acknowledgement of God's activity in history and of his righteousness. Lamentations joins seamlessly into the interpretation of historical events as God's acts, an interpretation that permeates the Old Testament. To the extent that Jerusalem's demise is attributed to the sins of its inhabitations ('guilt theology') and that change can only be attained through repentance and God's grace, the notion of a personal relationship with God stands behind the songs. The God of Lamentations appears as a God who freely turns toward people and can just as freely turn away from them. The absence of God is not a sign of divine impotence, but of divine punishment. The question of *God's righteousness*, sparked by the phenomenon of innocent suffering, finds an answer in the confession of the sins of the individual and the acknowledgement of a human community of guilt (Lam. 3.39). In view of individual and collective guilt as the obverse of human freedom, no human being can be sinless and escape God's wrath.[12] In this situation, the only option for a person is to trust that God's mercy is greater than his wrath and that his intention to preserve life is stronger than to destroy it (Lam. 3.22). As long as people live and suffer under the conditions of finality, especially in their own persons and existence, there remains hope in the ultimate turn to God brought about by God himself (Lam. 5.10). In this sense, the message of Lamentations lies in line with the petitions of the Lord's Prayer, 'your kingdom come' and 'deliver us from evil' (Mt. 6.10-13 *par.* Lk. 11.2-4). The transmission of Lamentations justified 'Israel's' enduring exile and demonstrated its significance: as long as tears are shed around and in Jerusalem, the cry of lamentation to God and penitence have their place. With this chain of thought, Lamentations has affinities with the eschatological hopes of later prophetic texts (Isa. 258; Rev. 21.4).

## 19.5 Notes on the History of Reception

Lamentations found a place in the liturgies of both post-biblical Judaism and early Christianity. Thus, *in Jewish worship* since the sixth century CE, Lamentations has been the festival scroll for the anniversary of the destruction of Jerusalem by the Babylonians in 587 BCE and by the Romans in 70 CE, both of which occurred on the ninth of the month of Av (July/August; 'Tisha be-Av').[13]

In connection with musical *arrangements* for Passion Week, Lamentations has often been set to music, by John Tuod (mid-15th cent.), Jan Disma Zelenka (1722), Rudolf Mauersberger in commemoration of the destruction of Dresden in WW II (1945), and Igor Stravinski (1958), for example.

12. Cf. Ps. 14 par. Ps. 53; 51; Eccl. 7.20; Job 25.4-6; W. Gross, 'Zorn Gottes – ein biblisches Theologumenon', in *Gott – ratlos vor dem Bösen?* (QD 177; ed. W. Beinert; Freiburg: Herder, 1997), 47–85.

13. The decree expelling the Jews from Spain was also promulgated on the ninth of Av in 1492.

# 20

# The Book of Esther

(Markus Witte – Translation by Mark Biddle)

## Chapter Outline



## A The Book of Esther (MT)

Commentaries J. D. Levenson (OTL. London: SCM, 1997); J. A. Loader, 'Das Buch Ester'. Pages 199–280 in *Das Hohelied, Klagelieder, Das Buch Ester*. ATD 16/2. Ed. by H.-P. Müller, O. Kaiser and J. A. Loader. 4th ed. Göttingen: Vandenhoeck & Ruprecht, 1992); A. Meinhold (ZBK 13. Zurich: Theologischer Verlag, 1983); C. A. Moore (AB 7B. 3rd ed. New York: Doubleday, 1979); R. E. Murphy (FOTL 13. Grand Rapids, Mich.: Eerdmans, 1988); H. M. Wahl (Berlin/New York: de Gruyter, 2009).

H. Koch, *Es kündet Dareios der König...: Vom Leben im persischen Großreich*. Kulturgeschichte der antiken Welt 55. 3rd ed. Mainz: Zabern, 2000; H. M. Wahl, 'Esther-Forschung'. *TRu* 66 (2001): 103–30; L. M. Wills, *The Jewish Novel in the Ancient World*. Ithaca, N.Y.: Cornell University Press, 1995, 93–131.

# 20.1 Biblical Context

| | | |
|---|---|---|
| **1.1–2.23** | **The Exposition** | |
| | 1.1–2.4 | The conflict between the Persian royal couple, Ahasuerus ( = Xerxes) and Vashti |
| | 2.5-20 | The appearance of Esther |
| | 2.21-23 | The appearance of Mordecai |
| **3.1–8.17** | **The Body** | |
| | 3.1-15 | The reason for and organization of the destruction of the Jews |
| | 4.1-17 | Mordecai's plan for deliverance |
| | 5.1-8 | Esther with King Xerxes |
| | 5.9–8.2 | The elevation of Mordecai and humiliation of Haman |
| | 8.3–8.8 | Esther with King Xerxes |
| | 8.9-14 | The Jew's plan for revenge |
| | 8.15-17 | The success and victory of the Jews |
| **9.1–10.3** | **The Conclusion** | |
| | 9.1-19 | Jewish counter-violence |
| | 9.20-32 | The establishment of the festival of Purim |
| | 10.1-3 | The importance of Mordecai |

The alternation between extensive descriptions of events and brief scenes characterizes the compositional structure of the book. These elements are first incorporated as narrative signals to be taken up again later.

The essential framework of the overall composition consists of:

(1) Indications of time,[1] (2) banquets arranged in pairs[2] and two fasts (4.3, 16), (3) the citation of written documents,[3] (4) individual *keywords* that shape the narrative (including especially the terms 'law' [*dāt*] and people [ *'am*]),[4] and, finally, (5) the constellation of actors:

1. Cf. Esth. 1.1, 5, 10; 2.16; 3.7, 12f.; 8.9; 9.1, 17, etc.
2. I: 1.3-4 || 1.5; II: 1.9 || 2.19; III: 5.4-6 || 5.8, 14; 6.14; 7.2, 7-8; IV: 8.17 || 9.17-18, 19.
3. Cf. Esth. 3.12-13; 8.9-12; 9.20-22, 29-32.
4. Cf. Esth. 1.8, 15; 2.8; 3.14-15; 4.3, 8, 16; 8.13-14, 17; 9.1, 14, etc. and 2.10; 3.8–14; 10.3, respectively.

| | | | |
|---|---|---|---|
| (a) | Xerxes and Vashti (1.1-2:4) | \|\| | Mordecai and Esther (2.5-7) |
| (b) | Xerxes and Esther (2.8-18; ch. 7) | \|\| | Mordecai and Haman (chs. 3; 6) |
| (c) | Xerxes and Haman (chs. 3; 6) | \|\| | Mordecai and Esther (ch. 4) |
| (d) | Xerxes, Esther and Haman (chs. 5; 7) | \|\| | Xerxes, Esther and Mordecai (ch. 9) |

The *starting point* of the programme for preserving Jewish identity abroad translated into narrative in the book is a feast given by King *Ahasuerus* (Xerxes; → *Septuagint*: Artaxerxes). The end of the *exposition* (Esth. 1.1–2.23) introduces three of the total of four central actors: the Persian king, who appears ironically as a marionette of his passions, court officials, and laws; the beautiful Jewess *Hadassah* ('Myrtle')/*Esther* ('Star'), who ascends to become queen without revealing her Jewish origins; and her foster-father *Mordecai*, one of the Jews deported by the Babylonians who is descended, programmatically, from Kish.[5]

The *body* (Esth. 3.1–8.17) begins by introducing the Persian *Haman/Aman* – according to his name (Hebrew *hāmam*, 'to destroy', Esth. 9.24) and his descent from *Agag* (1 Sam. 15.8-33) an archenemy of 'Israel' (Deut. 25.17-19). Haman's demand that all the servants working in the environs of the palace, including Mordecai, must perform proskynesis, i.e. render homage, forms the basis of the conflict that stands at the centre of the book: obedience to civil and divine power, the observation of the first commandment (Exod. 20.1-5) under the conditions of foreign rule that claims to be absolute. Mordecai's refusal to pay homage to Haman serves as the reason for destroying all the Jews in the realm of Ahasuerus (Xerxes). The notion that the alleged crime of an individual could result in collective punishment is based on the concept of a *corporate personality*, common in the Ancient Near East and antiquity. In order to determine the date when the extermination of the Jews should take place, lots were cast.[6] The royal edict of the thirteenth day of the first month,

5. This conceals an allusion to Saul, the son of Kish and the first king of Israel (1 Sam. 9.1-2; see Ch. 7.6.3.4).

6. The oracle by lot is also known, e.g., from 1 Sam. 14.42; Homer, *Iliad* III:314ff. (translated, e.g., in A. T. Murray and W. F. Wyatt, ed., *Homer: Iliad: Books 1-12* [LCL 170; Cambridge, Mass.: Harvard University Press, 1999]) and Herodotus, *Histories* III: 128 (translated in A. D. Godley, ed., *Herodotus: The Persian War: Books 3-4* [LCL 118; Cambridge, Mass.: Harvard University Press, 2006]).

Nisan (Esth. 3.13), which was the eve of the → *Passover* festival on the Jewish festal calendar and thus the memorial of the liberation from Egypt (Lev. 23.5), ordered the destruction of the Jews in writing. Now the Jewess who has ascended to become queen can become the deliverer of her people (Esth. 4–8). Her intervention with the king depicted dramatically, leads to Haman's loss of power, to Mordecai's installation in high office, and to the sparing of the Jews. Via Haman's fate, the narrator develops two *fundamental convictions of → wisdom*: (1) Pride goes before the fall (Prov. 16.18). (2) Whoever digs a grave for others will fall into it himself (Prov. 26.27). The Jewish resistance permitted in the end by the Persian court culminates in Jewish feasts of rejoicing and in worldwide conversions to Judaism (Esth. 8.17). With the comment that fear of the Jews fell on all the nations of the earth, the account reaches an emphatic conclusion (cf. Deut. 11.25).

A multi-part *appendix* (Esth. 9.1–10.3) arranges further events chronologically, reports in the fashion of → *annals* the number of their opponents the Jews killed, interprets the Esther story as the foundational legend of the → *Purim Festival*, and underscores Mordecai's importance.[7] Along with Esth. 8.15-16 and 2.5, Esth. 10.3 belongs among the verses to be spoken aloud by the congregation when the book of Esther is read in the synagogue.[8]

## 20.2 Textual Issues and Major Issues in the History of Critical Interpretation

The concentration in blocks on individual figures (Xerxes || Vashti; Mordecai || Haman; Xerxes || Esther || Mordecai), sometimes missing transitions between

7. Cf. Esth. 9.4 with Exod. 11.3 and Esth. 10.1-3 with Gen. 41.40ff., 42ff.; Dan. 2.48; 5.29; 6.29.

8. Esth. 2.5: 'Now there was a Jew in the citadel of Susa whose name was Mordecai son of Jair son of Shimei son of Kish, a Benjamite.'
Esth 8.15-16: 'And Mordecai went from (the audience with) the king in a royal robe of blue wool and white linen and with a large golden crown and a mantle of byssus and purple wool. And the city of Susa shouted and rejoiced. For the Jews there was light and gladness, joy and honour.'
Esth. 10.3: 'For Mordecai the Jew was next in rank to King Xerxes and powerful among the Jews and beloved by his many kindred. He (persistently) sought the good of his people and spoke peace (well-being) for all his descendants.'

blocks, and, in the body, the only loosely anchored foundation of the → *Purim Festival* (Esth. 3.7; 9.1-32) indicates that the book had *literary precursors*. Extensive additions found in the Greek (and Latin) tradition demonstrate that the book had a literary post-history (cf. Ch. 20B). It is the only book in the Hebrew → *canon* which is not attested (to date) among the texts from → *Qumran*.[9]

# 20.3 Origins of the Book of Esther

## 20.3.1 The Form of the Book of Esther

The book constitutes a *diaspora novella* (→ *diaspora*) with didactic character. Typical of this form are: (1) the concentration on an event, (2) the linkage to a situation, (3) the appearance of being a unique historical event, (4) the restriction to a few individuals, (5) the wondrous, symbolic, implausible turn to the good, and (6) the firm and unique conclusion.

Based on its comprehensive character, Esther resembles a *novel*. In the realm of biblical literature, as an overall work, it has its closest parallels in the → *deutero-canonical* books of Judith (Ch. 24) and Tobit (Ch. 26), both of which, however, exhibit a more pronounced religiosity. In individual sections, Esther has literary affinities with the Joseph story (Gen. 37–50) and the Daniel narratives (Dan. 1–6; 21). Indeed, in details, Esther seems to be the female counterpart of Joseph.

Esther endeavours to give the events portrayed the appearance of historicity.[10] The author demonstrates a certain familiarity with Persian affairs and vocabulary. Greek historians, especially Herodotus (484–425 BCE) and Xenophon (430–354 BCE), confirm individual locations, ceremonies at the Persian court, and administrative measures.

Nevertheless, the book exhibits **historical incongruencies**: it numbers Mordecai among the Judeans deported from Jerusalem in 598/7 BCE. (Esth. 2.5-6);[11] in contrast, Xerxes ruled from 486 to 465/4 BCE. The feast mentioned in Esth. 1.2-3 would then have taken place in 483 BCE and Esther's reception into the royal harem would have occurred, according to Esth. 2.17, in the seventh year of Xerxes' rule (479 BCE). Mordecai would have been at least 117 years old and

9. Although, the Aramaic manuscript 4Q550 (= 4QPrEsther$^{a-f}$) constitutes a text that offers Judeo-Persian court narratives with Esther material (translated in F. García Martínez and E. J. C. Tigchelaar, *The Dead Sea Scrolls* II, 1096–1103).

10. Cf. Esth. 1.1, 22; 3.12; 10.1-3.

11. Cf. 2 Kgs 24.14, 16; Jer. 52.28; *ANET*, 563–564.

> Esther would have been too old for the harem of Xerxes. This would be true even if Esth. 2.5-6 refers to Mordecai's grandfather and Mordecai's birth is placed around 547 BCE in → *exile*. Apart from these chronological considerations, neither the edicts in Esth. 1.20-22; 3.12-15; 8.9-14,[12] the juristic information in 8.8, the report concerning the mass conversions to Judaism (8.17), nor the massacre of the Persians (9.11-15) are historically plausible. According to Herodotus, at the time the Esther story was to have played out, Xerxes was married to Amestris.[13] At the time of the dramatic events surrounding Esther and Mordecai, Xerxes was at war with the Greeks (480/479 BCE). Finally, the Persian kings did not choose their wives from a harem, but from the noble women of the country.[14]

The idealized milieu, the fairytale motifs, and the skilful literary composition demonstrate that it is a *literary fiction*. Certain narrative elements may be based on historical motifs, as parallels in Herodotus, especially, indicate; overall, however, stereotypes predominate.

## 20.3.2 The Composition and Redaction of the Book of Esther

The book bears no indication of authorship. For reasons related to the history of literature and theology, an origin in the late Persian period or the early *Hellenistic period* is likely. A → *colophon* in the Greek version of the book from the time around 78 bce establishes the *terminus ad quem*.[15] The Hebrew of the book represents a late state of the language and exhibits Aramaic and Persian influence. In this regard, it has affinities with the books of Chronicles, Ecclesiastes, and Daniel. No Greek influences on the language are evident, a factor which can be adduced for locating the text, but not for dating it. If the

12. Regarding the practice of Persian kings of composing inscriptions in three languages, cf. the Behistun Inscription of Darius I (translated in R. G. Kent, *Old Persian. Grammar, Texts, Lexicon* [AOS 33; 2nd ed., New Haven, Conn.: American Oriental Society, 1989], 116–35).
13. Cf. Herodotus, Histories VII:61; VII:114; IX:108-112 (translated in A. D. Godley, ed., *Herodotus: The Persian War: Books 5-7* [LCL 119; Cambridge, Mass.: Harvard University Press, 2006] and idem, ed., *Herodotus: The Persian War: Books 8-9* [LCL 120; Cambridge, Mass.: Harvard University Press, 2001]).
14. Herodotus, *Histories*, III:84, 88 (translated in A. D. Godley, ed., *Herodotus: The Persian War: Books 3-4* [LCL 118; Cambridge, Mass.: Harvard University Press, 2006]).
15. 'In the fourth year of the reign of Ptolemy and Cleopatra, Dositheus, who claimed to be a priest and Levite, and his son Ptolemy delivered this Purim document. He said that it was (correct) and that Lysimachus, the son of Ptolemy from Jerusalem, had translated it.'

reference to the day of Mordecai in 2 Macc. 15.36-37 represents an allusion to Esther, then it must have originated prior to 124 BCE, the year 2 Maccabees was written (Ch. 29.2).

In terms of the history of its composition, three originally independent narratives have presumably been combined:

1) a *Vashti narrative* in which the Persian queen refuses a royal command,
2) a *Mordecai narrative* based on the fate of two royal officials,
3) an *Esther narrative* centred around the courageous behaviour of the beautiful foreign queen on behalf of her people.

Combined, these three narratives form the *foundation of the book* based on extant *traditions*, namely the tradition of an ascension story (cf. the accounts of Joseph and Daniel), the Exodus tradition, and the Saul tradition. This foundation underwent a threefold redaction (R1-R3) with a view to the → *Purim Festival.*

| | | |
|---|---|---|
| (1) | *Foundation:* | Esth. 1.1–8.17; 10.1-3 |
| (2) | *'Purim redactions':* | R1: + 9.1-19; R2: + 9.20-28; R3: + 9.29-32 |

Judging from the settings and theme of the book, its *provenance* was the eastern *diaspora*. The portrayal of the Persian palace at Susa and knowledge of Persian ceremonies point to origins in the Persian heartland.[16]

## 20.3.3 The Situation and Function of the Book of Esther

The book originated in the diaspora and deals with *Jewish life and survival abroad*. In contrast to treatments in the books of Ezra, Nehemiah and Daniel, Jewish identity is not assured by strict observance of purity regulations, but in militant and cunning intervention for the life of the Jewish people. Although in hyperbole, Esther seeks to demonstrate how Jews in the diaspora should behave, especially in situations of extreme existential danger: with loyalty to the state and in absolute confidence in God's protection. It cannot be determined, historically,

16. Cf. Esth. 5 or 1.15-16; 3.8-9; 5.11; 8.8, respectively.

whether a specific persecution of Jewish communities stands in the background of the book. So far, no systematic persecutions of the Jews have been attested for the Persian period. Since the book certainly originated before the Maccabean period, it cannot have been occasioned – as was the book of Daniel (Ch. 21) – by the anti-Jewish measures of the Syrian king Antiochus IV Epiphanes (167 BCE) either. The fact that it deals with the deliverance of Jews in a foreign land, not *from* a foreign land as, e.g., in the Exodus tradition, characterizes the book. Thereby, the book was open for reception in later Judaism, which was marked, at least since the period of → *Hellenism*, by diaspora existence. At the same time, however, it is open for reception in Christianity, which, in keeping with its Jewish roots, understood itself as the 'people of God', not in a national or geographical sense, but based on its personal relationship to God (cf. 1 Pet. 2.9; Heb. 4.9).

## 20.4 Theology of the Book of Esther

Besides the Song of Songs,[17] it is the only book in the Hebrew Bible that does not utilize either the name Yhwh or any other designation for God. It attests only indirectly that Yhwh is the God of Israel and the Lord of history. This conviction is evident in four passages:

(1) in Mordecai's remark that 'help may arise [for the Jews] from some other *place*' (4.14);

As was already the case in rabbinic Judaism and in Philo of Alexandria (b. ca. 25 BCE), the term '**place**' (Hebr. *māqōm*) is probably employed here as a substitute for 'God'.[18] The origin of this designation for God traces back to the tendency, identifiable generally in → *Hellenistic* Judaism, to exchange the names of God for substitutes. The background could be that the designation for the central cultic locus (*māqōm*), the Jerusalem temple, had become independent ('spiritualized').[19]

(2) in an → *acrostic* that exhibits the letters of the Tetragrammaton (*y-h-w-h* = *Yhwh*) and which occurs in the precise place where Esther first expresses *the* wish to Xerxes that brings about the change in the fate of Mordecai and the Jews (5.4): *yābô'* ('let come') *hammelek* ('the king') *wĕhāmān* ('and Haman') *hayyôm* ('today');

17. Regarding Cant. 8.6, see above, Ch. 17 n. 12.

18. See H. Köster, '*tópos*', *TDNT* 8:187–208, esp. 201; A. Marmorstein, *The Old Rabbinic Doctrine of God, I: The Names and Attributes of God*, (repr.; New York: Ktav, 1968), 92–3.

19. Cf. Deut. 12.5; 14.23; 1 Kgs 8.29-30; 2 Kgs 22.16; Jer. 7.3; 19.3.

(3) in the response of Haman's wife that the subjugation of Mordecai is impossible because he is 'from the Jewish race'.[20] Allegiance to Judaism, grounded in allegiance to Yhwh, determines the protection of individual Jews (10.3);
(4) in the concluding narrative comment that, after the wondrous repeal of the order to destroy the Jews, many gentiles converted to Judaism (8.17). The formulations in 9.1 ('and it was changed') and in 9.22 ('the month that had been turned for them from pain to joy and from mourning to a holiday') may also refer to God's activity (the so-called *passiva divina*). The notion of a divine determinism (cf. 4.14) can be derived from the motif of the oracular lot in 3.7: The day Haman established by lot as a day of destruction became the day of his own demise through mysterious coincidence.

Even though, as literature, it belongs among its masterworks, the book certainly does not stand at the theological centre of the Old Testament. In view of the innumerable pogroms that Jews had to suffer in the course of their history down to today repeatedly justified by the grounds modelled in Esth. 3.8-9, however, it should be read, as should Rom. 9–11 with which it is combined in *one* → *canon*, as testimony to the continued election of the people of God. The book can communicate to Christian readers, as well, that (1) there are limits to the complete adaptation to political and cultural systems, (2) there is a *status confessionis*, and (3) in certain situations, one's own identity and integrity can only be preserved by risking one's own life. Based on Lev. 19.18 and Mt. 22.31 (cf. also Mt. 5.43), if for no other reason, it goes without saying that the notion of revenge expressed, e.g., in Esth. 8.13, requires theological critique.

## 20.5 Notes on the History of Reception

In contrast to the book of Ruth and its heroine, the book of Esther and its major figures are not cited in the New Testament. In *ancient Judaism*, there were objections to its canonicity (→ *canon*; cf. *bMeg.* 7) on into the third century CE. Nevertheless, the Babylonian → *Talmud*, which devotes a tractate to it, can also rank the book above the prophets and Psalms or give priority to reading the book of Esther over studying the Torah (*bMeg.* 3b). Since the early Middle Ages, Judaism considered Esther the exemplary festival scroll (*mᶜgillâ*) and the text for the → *Purim Festival.*

20. Esth. 6.13; cf. Jer. 2.3; Zech. 2.12-13 (NRSV 2.8-9).

Even though the long Greek version (Ch. 20B) significantly theologized the book through the theology of history in its framework, the prayers it places in the mouths of Mordecai and Esther, and its inclusion of the Persian kings in the supreme God's plan for history, Christian theology paid it little attention. Luther's verdict that he found the book of Esther (and 2 Macc., too) 'so hostile' that he wished that it was not even available ('for they Judaize so much and have many pagan flaws,' *TR* no. 3391) is often cited. In any case, Luther could also treasure the book quite positively when, in the lectures on the letter to the Romans (1515/16), he viewed Esther and Mordecai in terms of medieval → *typology* as exemplary deliverers of their people and thus, as predecessors of Christ.

The oldest *graphic representation* of the Esther story known to date appears in the paintings in the synagogue of Dura-Europos (ca. 250 CE). Extensive illustrations also occur in the Hebrew Esther scrolls from the 16th and 17th centuries. In the Christian realm, depictions from Esther are attested beginning in the 11th century. Individual scenes received particular significance in the Christian Middle Ages through their *typological interpretation*. Thus, Esther could appear as an image for the church, for the bride of Christ, or as a type for Mary. Michelangelo placed Esther as a deliverer of Israel next to Judith in the Sistine Chapel. The Renaissance and the Baroque periods favoured scenes from the Esther story, not least because of their oriental milieu. Finally, one can refer to the *musical setting* of the Esther narrative in an oratorio by Georg Friedrich Handel (1732).

In connection with the book of Ruth and the → *deuterocanonical* book of Judith (Ch. 24), Esther belongs, lastly, to the central Old Testament components of a 'feminist theology' (Ch. 2.1.3).[21]

# B The 'Additions' to the Book of Esther

📖 K. H. Jobes, 'Esther'. Pages 424–40 in *A New English Translation of the Septuagint*. Ed. by A. Pietersma and B. G. Wright. Oxford: Oxford University Press, 2007 (NETS); G. G. Xeravits and J. Zsengellér, eds, *Deuterocanonical Additions of the Old Testament Books*. Deuterocanonical Literature Studies 4. Berlin/New York: de Gruyter, 2010.

📖 Commentaries: H. Bardtke (JSHRZ I/1. Gütersloh: Gütersloher Verlagshaus, 1973), 15–87; I. Kottsieper, 'Zusätze zu Ester' Pages 109–207 in *Das Buch Baruch, Der*

21. See A. Brenner, ed., *A Feminist Companion to Esther, Judith, and Susanna* (The Feminist Companion to the Bible 7; Sheffield: Sheffield Academic Press, 2005).

*Brief des Jeremia, Zusätze zu Ester und Daniel*. ATD.A 5. Ed. by O. H. Steck, R. G. Kratz and I. Kottsieper. Göttingen: Vandenhoeck & Ruprecht, 1998; C. A. Moore (AB 44. New York: Doubleday, 1977)

C. D. Harvey, *Finding Morality in the Diaspora? Moral Ambiguity and Transformed Morality in the Books of Esther*. BZAW 328. Berlin/New York: de Gruyter, 2003; U. Mittmann-Richert, *Einführung zu den historischen und legendarischen Erzählungen*. JSHRZ VI/1,1. Gütersloh: Gütersloher Verlagshaus, 2000, 97–113; K. De Troyer, *Rewriting the Sacred Text*. Leiden/Boston: Brill 2003.

# 20.6 Biblical Context

The expression 'Additions (*Additamenta*) to the book of Esther' refers to a surplus of roughly 100 verses in comparison to its Masoretic form (Ch. 20.2) evident in the book of Esther in the Septuagint (LXX) and, dependent on it, in the Vulgate (Vg). While these texts constitute integral components of the book of Esther in the LXX, Jerome placed them at the end of the (proto-)canonical book of Esther in his translation of the Hebrew Bible into Latin (Vg) as Esth. 10.4–16.21. The churches of the Reformation consider them apocryphal 'additions'. On grounds of the history of development, the treatment of this surplus should proceed from the LXX. While earlier scholarship cited the 'additions', in keeping with the LXX edition by A. Rahlfs (1935/1979/2006 = $LXX^{Ra}$) by indicating the respective chapter and verse with small letters, more recent scholarship cites according to the Göttingen edition of the LXX by R. Hanhart (2nd ed., 1983 = $LXX^{Gö}$) with the capital letters A–F.[22]

| | $LXX^{Ra}$ | $LXX^{Gö}$/NETS | Vg/NRSV.A |
|---|---|---|---|
| 1) Mardocai's dream[23] | 1.1a-l | A1-11 | 11.2-12 |
| Discovery of the plot | 1.1m-r | A12-17 | 12.1-6 |
| 2) Letter concerning the pogrom | 3.13a-g | B1-7 | 13.1-7 |
| 3) Mordecai's prayer | 4.17a-i | C1-11 | 13.8-18 |

⇨

22. For the sake of clarity, subsequent citations will be according to $LXX^{Gö}$, which also underlies newer translations (LXX.D, NETS, NRSV.A) and commentaries. The older enumeration will be given in parentheses only in explicit references to individual verses.

23. MT: Mordecai.

| | | | | |
|---|---|---|---|---|
| | Esther's prayer | 4.17-k-z | C12-30 | 14.1-19 |
| 4) | Esther before the king | 5.1a-f, 2a-b | D1-16 | 15.1/4-19 (16) |
| 5) | Letter delivering the Jews | 8.12a-x | E1-24 | 16.1-24 |
| 6) | Interpretation of the dream | 10.3a-g | F1-6 | 10.4-9 |
| | Appendix: Midrash on Purim | 10.3h-k | F7-10 | 10.10-13 |
| | Colophon | 10.3l | F11 | 11.1 |

**A 1–2.23 The exposition**

| | |
|---|---|
| *A1–11* | *Framework dealing with the theology of history: Mordecai's dream* |
| *A12–17* | *Mordecai's discovery of the plot (par. 2.21-23)* |
| 1.1–2.4 | The conflict between the Persian royal couple, Artaxerxes[24] and Astin[25] |
| 2.5-20 | The appearance of Esther |
| 2.21-23 | The appearance of Mardocai |

**3.1–8.17 The body**

| | |
|---|---|
| 3.1-13 | The reason for and organization of the destruction of the Jews |
| B1–17 | *Artaxerxes' edict calling for the destruction of the Jews* |
| 3.14-15 | The reason for and organization of the destruction of the Jews |
| 4.1-17 | Mardocai's plan for deliverance |
| *C1–11* | *Mardocai's prayer* |
| *C12–30* | *Esther's prayer* |
| *D1–16* | *Esther with King Artaxerxes (par. 5.1-2)* |
| 5:3–8 | Esther with King Artaxerxes |
| 5.9–8.2 | The elevation of Mordecai and humiliation of Haman |
| 8.3–8.8 | Esther with King Artaxerxes |
| *E1–24* | *Artaxerxes' edict legally recognizing the Jews* |
| 8.13-14 | The Jews' plan for revenge |
| 8.15-17 | The success and victory of the Jews |

**9.1–F11 The conclusion**

| | |
|---|---|
| 9.1-19 | Jewish counter-violence |
| 9.20-32 | The establishment of the festival of Purim |
| 10.1-3 | The importance of Mardocai |
| *F1–6* | *Framework dealing with the theology of history: the interpretation of Mordecai's dream* |
| *F7–10* | *Appendix: Midrash on Purim* |
| *F11* | *Colophon: The circumstances surrounding the translation of the book of Esther* |

24. MT: Ahasuerus.

25. MT: Vashti.

In its Greek form, the book of Esther has a framework dealing with the theology of history, a framework that incorporates the fate of the Jews in the Persian realm into a drama in world history with cosmic dimensions. Thus, Mardocai's dream that opens the book (A1–11) describes the battle between two dragons whose roar evokes the struggle of all nations against the 'people of the righteous' to whom help comes 'as though from a minor source' after they cry to God. The interpretation of the dream (F1–6) that concludes the book identifies the dragons as Mardocai and Haman, the 'people of the righteous' as Israel or the Jews under threat in the Persian Empire, and the 'minor source' as Esther. A brief account of Mardocai's discovery of the conspiracy between two Persian court officials against the king (A12–17), which prefigures and duplicates the account in 2.21-23, follows the description of the dream. Just as the cry for God's assistance in A8 already introduces the turning point, extensive prayers by Mardocai and Esther (C1–11; C12–30) stand at the centre of the Greek book of Esther. They are framed by the specific report of the content of the letter of the Persian king Artaxerxes, first concerning the planned destruction of the Jews as a 'misanthropic population perilous to the state' (B1–7: 4-5), then concerning the recognition of the Jews as citizens who live 'by the most just laws' and as 'sons of the highest, greatest, living God' (E1–24: 15-16).[26] The LXX expands the comment concerning Esther's appearance before the king, which encompasses only two verses in the Hebrew book of Esther (Esth. 5.1-2), into a dramatic appearance scene (D). An additional explanation of the name of the Purim Festival (F7–10), which plays with the motif of the lots (Hebrew *pûrîm*) that God created for individual nations, and a → *colophon*,[27] unique in this form in the context of biblical literature, which gives information concerning the time, author and tradents of the translation, end the Greek book of Esther.

In the context of the overall composition of the Greek book of Esther, the 'additions' have a certain concentric structure: thus, the 'dream' (A1–11) and the 'interpretation of the dream' (F1–6) correspond to the letters of Artaxerxes (B; E) and the prayers of Mardocai and Esther (C) at the centre of the composition.

26. Cf. Hos. 2.1 (NRSV 1.10).

27. Cf. also the prologue to the Greek book of Sirach (Ch. 27) and the pseudepigraphical Letter of Aristeas which reports the legend of the origins of the Septuagint (translated in *OTP* II, 7-34.).

# 20.7 Textual Issues and Major Issues in the History of Critical Interpretation

In contrast to the rare consideration still given the surpluses, especially in Protestant biblical studies,[28] they can only be understood appropriately, not only in terms of the history of development and composition but also hermeneutically and theologically, in the overall context of the Greek book of Esther. The discussion will continue to employ the term 'additions' only because of the history of scholarship.

Within the Greek tradition, two major streams can be distinguished in essence: (1) the text represented by the major LXX codices (the o' or B text) and (2) a shorter text represented so far by only four minuscules (the L' or A/Alpha text). The LXX edition by A. Rahlfs offers a critically reconstructed o' text, the LXX edition by R. Hanhart reproduces both forms of the text with pertinent critical apparati.[29] Both forms of the Greek text contain the surpluses mentioned. Both exhibit abbreviations and differences over against the MT at points, but also manifest characteristic differences from one another. There is some discussion as to whether these differences trace back to different Hebrew (or Aramaic) originals or to a conscious revision of the LXX by the author of the A Text.[30]

Since, in contrast to the 'additions' to the book of Daniel, the surpluses are only comprehensible in the context of the book of Esther, it is clear that they comprise supplements to the Hebrew book of Esther. Yet, it is an open question as to the phase in the history of the text and its development in which the 'additions' were inserted. Since they are only transmitted in Greek and, with respect to their explicit theology, they correspond to the overall tendency of the Greek book of Esther,[31] they could be genuine Greek expansions of the Greek text.[32] On the other hand, the 'additions' exhibit minor incongruencies in relation to the 'canonical' sections of the Greek book of Esther and do

28. U. Mittmann-Richert, *Einführung*, 97–113 constitutes an exception.

29. K. H. Jobes (in *NETS*) offers a translation of the Greek book of Esther (LXX and A).

30. Regarding the discussion, see Harvey, *Morality*, 4–12.

31. Cf. the explicit references to God in the Greek book of Esther (2.20; 4.8; 6.1, 13).

32. So, e.g., U. Mittmann-Richert, *Einführung*, 97–113.

not all lie on the same form-critical, linguistic, and tendential levels. Thus, Mordecai's dream and its interpretation (A1–11; F1–6), the two letters of Artaxerxes (B; E), the two doublets or embellishments (A12–17; D), the two prayers (C), and the bipartite appendix (F7–10, 11) have greater affinity with one another as pairs. This circumstance could indicate a development to be differentiated in terms of the history of language and composition.[33]

## 20.8 Origins of the 'Additions' to the Book of Esther

The original language and situation of origin can only be clearly determined in the case of the colophon (F11). It consists of an authentically Greek notice concerning the origins of the translation of the book of Esther, which it attributes to a certain Lysimachus in Jerusalem. If one relates the information in F11 to the complete Greek book of Esther and the fourth year of Ptolemy XII (=78/77 BCE), then the 'additions' originated between the second half of the second century and the beginning of the first century BCE. The designation of Haman as a 'Macedonian' (E 15), which differs from MT, also points to this period. It alludes retrospectively, on the one hand, to the destruction of the Achaeminid empire by the Macedonian, Alexander the Great, and contemporaneously, on the other, to the Seleucids (Ch. 4.4).

Based on their affinities with Hellenistic epistolary style, their specific vocabulary, and their parallels with 3 Macc. 3; 6; and 7 the two letters of Artaxerxes (B; E) may also be characterized with relative certainty as authentically Greek products. In terms of narrative technique and despite their fictive and stereotypical character, both letters profile the figure of Artaxerxes. Literarily, they serve to historicize the events depicted in the style of Hellenistic historiography. In terms of content, they emphasize the civic loyalty of Jews in the diaspora and thus fulfil an apologetic function (externally), on one side, and a parenetic function (internally), on the other.

The origins of 'additions' A, C, D and F1–10 are more difficult to determine. Here, one cannot exclude the possibility of Hebrew/Aramaic compositions and origins in Palestine. In this regard, 'Mordecai's dream' (A1–11) and its interpretation (F1–6) have parallels with → *apocalyptic* texts, especially with

33. So, e.g., I. Kottsieper, *Zusätze*, 109–36, who proposes a complex expansion hypothesis.

Daniel 7.[34] In terms of narrative technique, these two 'additions', as well as the duplication of the scene of the discovery of the plot (A12–17), emphasize the figure of Mardocai. The framework in A1–11 and F1–6 functions essentially to universalize and theologize events. The threat to the Jews in the Persian Empire appears to be a worldwide threat; history is understood explicitly as a God-directed process. The → *midrash* on the word *pûr* 'lot' in F7–10, which presents an alternative interpretation to explain the → *Purim Festival* in 9.26, is also indebted to this concept of the theology of history.

The prayers in C have their closest parallels in the communal prayers of petition and lament (Ps. 74; Ezr. 9.5-15.; Dan. 9; 13C2.2). Apparently C19–30 alludes to the restriction of the Jerusalem Yhwh cult under Antiochus IV Epiphanes (167/164 BCE).[35] From the perspective of narrative technique, the prayers serve to individualize Mardocai and Esther despite the formulaic character. These prayers, as with comparable insertions in Jewish narratives from the Hellenistic period,[36] basically function to portray the leading figures as model supplicants and, thus, to describe prayer as an essential option for human behaviour (C11).

The question of the original language and origin of the extended scene of Esther's encounter with the king in D can hardly be answered. Overall, the passage serves to emphasize Esther's beauty and the king's inconstant character, as well as to individualize the actors.

## 20.9 Theology of the 'Additions' to the Book of Esther

As with the whole Greek book of Esther, an explicit religiosity and theology and a focus on the fate of Israel as God's people characterize the 'additions'. While the Hebrew book of Esther does not employ a designation for God anywhere, but only indirectly recounts God's mysterious preservation of the Jews (Ch. 4.4.1), the Greek book of Esther refers explicitly to God's activity and to specifically Jewish rites. Thus, the saving intervention of God on behalf of his people, whom he chose as his

34. Cf. also Dan. 2.1, 19; 4.2, 16 (NRSV 4.5, 19) as well as Gen. 40.8; 41.1.
35. Cf. 1 Macc. 1.41-43; 2 Macc. 6; Dan. 9.27; 11.31; 12.11 (Ch. 4.4.1).
36. Cf. Dan.[LXX] 3.24-90; Jud. 9; Tob. 13.

heritage,[37] appears as a reaction to prayer.[38] Its essential characteristics are the praise of God's omnipotence, creative activity and omniscience (C2–5), and mercy and justice (C18), the confession of one's own sins (C17),[39] and the request for deliverance from distress (C8–10; C22–25). Israel's faith in the *one* God who intercedes for his people and demonstrates himself to be the lord of history (A11; D8; F1) stands in juxtaposition to the Gentiles' belief in many gods (C21). Mardocai, who refuses to do obeisance to Haman referring explicitly to the commandment concerning the exclusive worship of (C5–7), and Esther, who, like Daniel, refers to the observance of the purity commandments in the Gentile royal court (C26–29; Dan. 1.8-14), exemplify the preservation of Jewish identity under the conditions of non-Jewish dominion and non-Jewish culture. Consequently, the Greek text also explicitly mentions that the Gentiles who converted to Judaism 'underwent circumcision' (8.17).

## 20.10 Notes on the History of Reception

In essence, one can refer here to the presentation of the history of the reception of the Hebrew book of Esther (Ch. 20.5). One should note that the paraphrase of the Esther story in the Jewish historiographer, Flavius Josephus, presumes the 'additions' (with the exception of the passages A1–11; he probably omitted F1–10 intentionally).[40]

37. Cf. C8–10; C16; C20; F9; as well as Deut. 4.20-40; 9.26; 32.9; 1 Kgs 8.51; Ps. 33.12; 94.5; Jer. 3.19; 12.7ff.; 2 Macc. 1.26; Sir. 17.17 (NRSV 17.20).
38. Cf. A9; C2; C16.
39. Cf. Dan. 9.5-15; Tob. 3.4; Jud. 5.18.
40. Antiquities XI, 6, 1-13 ; cf. Josephus, Flavius, *Judean Antiquities* (ed. S. Mason; Leiden/Boston: Brill, 2000ff., Vol. 5).

# 21

# The Book of Daniel

(Markus Witte – Translation by Mark Biddle)

## Chapter Outline

# A The Book of Daniel (MT)

Commentaries: J. J. Collins (Hermeneia. Minneapolis: Fortress, 1993); ; J.-C. Lebram (ZBK 23. Zurich: Theologischer Verlag, 1984); C. L. Seow (Westminster Bible Companion. Louisville, Ky.: Westminster John Knox, 2003).

J. J. Collins and P. W. Flint, eds, *The Book of Daniel: Composition and Reception*. VTSup 83. 2 vols. Leiden/Boston: Brill, 2001; L. M. Wills, *The Jewish Novel in the Ancient World*. Ithaca, N.Y.: University of Cornell Press, 1995, 40–67; K. Bracht and D. S. du Toit, eds, *Die Geschichte der Daniel-Auslegung in Judentum, Christentum und Islam: Studien zur Kommentierung des Danielbuches in Literatur und Kunst*. BZAW 371. Berlin/New York: de Gruyter, 2007; K. Koch, T. Niewitsch and J. Tubach (EdF 144. Darmstadt: Wissenschaftliche Buchgesellschaft, 1980).

The book gets its title from the name of the hero, *Daniel*. This name can be translated either 'God (*ʾel*) judges (*dîn*)' or 'God is mighty (*dûn*)'. It indicates the programmatic theme of the book.

**1.1–21** **Exposition** (Hebrew)
**Daniel and his friends among the wise men at the Babylonian court**
*1.1* — *In the time of the Babylonian king, Nebuchadnezzar*

**2.1–7.28** **First major section** (*Aramaic*)
**Stories about the dream interpreter, Daniel, and his God**
2.1-49 — Nebuchadnezzar's dream about the statue with clay feet
*2.1* — *In the second year of the reign of the Babylonian king, Nebuchadnezzar*
3.1-30 — The preservation of the three young men in the oven

| | | | |
|---|---|---|---|
| | | *3.1* | *During the reign of the Babylonian king, Nebuchadnezzar* |
| | 3.31–4.34 (NRSV 4.37) | Nebuchadnezzar's dream about the arrogant tree | |
| | | *3.31* | *During the reign of the Babylonian king, Nebuchadnezzar* |
| | | 5.1-30 | The banquet of the arrogant Belshazzar |
| | | *5.1, 30* | *The last year of the reign of the Babylonian king, Belshazzar* |
| | 6.1-29 (NRSV 5.31–6.28) | The preservation of Daniel in the lion's den | |
| | | *6.1 (5.31)* | *During the reign of the 'Median' king, Darius* |
| | 7.1-28 | Daniel's dream about the animals and the vision of the Son of Man | |
| | | *7.1* | *In the first year of the reign of the Babylonian king, Belshazzar* |
| **8.1–12.13** | **Second major section** (Hebrew) | | |
| | **Daniel's visions of the Last Judgement** | | |
| | 8.1-27 | Daniel's vision of the ram and the goat | |
| | | *8.1* | *In the third year of the reign of the Babylonian king, Belshazzar* |
| | 9.1-19 | Daniel's study of the scriptures and his penitential prayer | |
| | | *9.1* | *In the first year of the reign of the 'Median' king, Darius* |
| | 9.20-27 | Daniel's instruction by the angel Gabriel | |
| | | *9.20-21* | *At the time of prayer during the evening sacrifice* |
| | 10.1–12.13 | Final vision and instruction concerning the future of his people | |
| | | *10.1* | *In the third year of the reign of the Persian king, Cyrus* |

# 21.1 Biblical Context

On one hand, based on the *change in style* from narratives to vision reports, the book divides into two parts (chs. 1–6; 7–12). On the other, close thematic interrelationships exist between the block composed in Aramaic (chs. 2–7) and the block extant in Hebrew (chs. 8–12). Chapter 1, written in Hebrew, precedes both blocks. Thus, a division into *three parts* seems appropriate. *Datings* of events seen and reported permeate the whole book as introductory elements.[1]

In a *first major section* (chs. 2–7), narratives about Daniel/Belshazzar and his three friends Hananiah/Shadrach, Mishael/Meshach and Azariah/Abednego at the Babylonian and Persian royal courts follow the *exposition* (ch. 12). At the centre of the first section stands *the narrative disclosure of God's kingship in the present*. The typical characteristics of the narratives in the first section appear with particular clarity in the depiction of Nebuchadnezzar's dream of the statue made of four or five different materials, with each material representing a certain empire replaced by a successor (ch. 2). An experience of or decision by the Gentile king sets in motion an encounter with the wise and pious Daniel or his friends that results in a confession by the Gentile of the power of Israel's God and the ascent of the Jewish hero at court. The concept, developed in the narrative of Nebuchadnezzar's dream, of four eras/empires, which has parallels in the Greek, Roman and Persian realms, returns in ch. 7 in the form of a vision report and is modified in chs. 8–12.

The narratives in the first section mirror one another: The report of Daniel's dream corresponds to the report of Nebuchadnezzar's dream (ch. 2 || 7). The account of the wondrous preservation of the three men in the oven has a counterpart in the account of the deliverance of Daniel in the lion's den (ch. 3 || 6). The report of Nebuchadnezzar's dream of the arrogant tree, which culminates in the Babylonian king's confession of the God of Israel, has its negative counterpart in the report of Belshazzar's banquet, which ends with the death of the arrogant king (ch. 4 || 5). The Gentile king's glorifying confession of Yhwh[2] and summaries of the special status of Daniel and his friends at court[3] conclude these narratives.

| ***Empire*** | ***Dan. 2*** | ***Dan. 7*** | ***Dan. 8*** |
|---|---|---|---|
| Babylonian (629–539 BCE) | gold | lion | |
| Medes (626–550 BCE) | silver | bear | ram |
| Persian (550/539–333 BCE) | bronze | panther | ram |
| Alexander the Great (333–323 BCE | iron | monster with iron teeth | goat |
| Seleucids/Ptolemies (323–62/30 BCE) | | ten horns | four horns |
| Antiochus IV (175–164 BCE) | | one horn | one horn |

1. Dan. 1.1; 2.1; 3.1; 5.30/6.1 (NRSV 5.31); 7.1; 8.1; 9.1(, 20-21); 10.1(; 11.1).
2. Dan. 2.46-47; 3.28-29; 4.34 (NRSV 4.37); 6.27-28 (6.26-27).
3. Dan. 1.19-21; 2.48-49; 3.30; 5.29; 6.29 (6.28).

Chapter 7 stands at the juncture with the *second major section*. Like chs. 8–12, it represents a vision report composed in the first person singular, yet, like chs. 2–6, is still written in Aramaic and, in terms of content, corresponds to ch. 2. The centre of the second section is *the visionary description of God's kingdom in the future*. Combined with the vision in ch. 7, is the view of a heavenly judgement scene in which the white-haired Ancient One ('Ancient of Days') sitting on a throne and surrounded by fire empowers the 'one like a son of man' (7.13) for eternal rule. If the 'Ancient of Days' can be identified, with relative certainty, as God in his function as the lord of time and eternity – which may have backgrounds, from the perspective of the history of religions, in an → *epithet* for the Syrian-Levantine god, El – the identity of the *son of man* is controversial, even today.

***The son of man:*** According to Dan. 7.13, the son of man (Aramaic *bar ʾĕnāš*, which initially meant simply 'human being') is an individual heavenly figure, an angel. In 7.18, 21-22, then, the 'holy ones of the highest' assume the functions of the son of man (cf. 9.14), who thereby becomes a collective entity, or at least the representative of such an entity. It is not clear whether the 'holy ones of the highest' is a designation for angels and/or for a group of people who are particularly faithful to Yhwh. In view of this textual ambiguity and of the appearance of the 'son of man' in extra-canonical (→ *canon*) Jewish texts from the Hellenistic period and in the New Testament, many efforts to explain the concept in terms of the history of religions and the option between an individual or a collective identification compete in scholarship. The term 'son of man', the Hebrew form of which (*ben ʾādām*) is a title for the prophet 93 times in the book of Ezekiel, in reference to a heavenly figure may, in fact, have originated with the author of Daniel 7. If this suspicion is correct, then the various types of a son of man and their association with concepts of a → *messiah* may have only been the product of the history of the reception of Daniel 7.

📖 K. Koch, 'Der "Menschensohn" in Daniel.' *ZAW* 119 (2007): 369–87.

The visions in the second major section group around a penitential prayer (9.4-19) that develops into a comprehensive communal confession of sin and of God's sole righteousness.[4] The two visions that follow focus on the fate of the Jerusalem temple (8.10-14; 9.26-27). In both cases, the angel Gabriel appears as interpreter (Latin *angelus interpres*). The grand concluding vision (10.1–12.13), in contrast, culminates in the description of the eschatological

4. Cf. Pss 44 and 80, on the one hand, and Jer. 14; Ezr. 9 and Neh. 9, on the other.

suffering of God's people and the future of the dead. Here, Daniel openly gives information concerning the imminent wars between the *Persians* and the *Greeks*, the struggles between the 'king of the South' (*Ptolemies*) and the 'king of the North' (*Seleucids*, Dan. 11.2-28) that will follow the disintegration of the *Empire of Alexander*, and the intervention of the 'ships from Kittim' (*Romans*). The visionary saw this period, when the province of Yehud/Judea (Ch. 4.4.1) was overrun by foreign and native troops, marked by the martyrdom of circles faithful to Yhwh, and torn apart by domestic Jewish disputes concerning the office of the high priest and the Yhwh cult, as the end time when the judgement between the pious and the evildoers would occur (12.1-11). The book ends with a beatitude on those who will experience this time and with the promise of the resurrection given to Daniel (12.12-13).

## 21.2 Textual Issues and Major Issues in the History of Critical Interpretation

The book has *formal and substantive peculiarities* in addition to the *change of languages* between ch. 1 (Hebrew), chs. 2–7 (Aramaic) and chs. 8–12 (Hebrew) and the *change in the narrative perspective* from third person account (chs. 1–6) to first person account (chs. 7–12) that indicate a long process of growth:

1. There are *contradictions in the chronology*. According to 1.5, Daniel was educated for three years at the court of Nebuchadnezzar without meeting the king; according to 2.5, he had already appeared before the king in the second year of Nebuchadnezzar's reign. According to 1.19-20 the king knew Daniel and his friends; according to 2.25, Daniel had yet to be presented to the king. Chapter 5 ends with the report of Belshazzar's death and the ascension of Darius (cf. 6.29 [NRSV 6.28]); in contrast, the events of ch. 7 still take place under Belshazzar. In addition to these tensions within the book, there is a contradiction between the dating of Nebuchadnezzar's siege of Jerusalem and the first deportation to Babylonia in Dan. 1.1-2, on one hand, and Jer. 25.1; 46.2; 2 Kgs 24.1-2, 6, 15, on the other (Ch. 4.3).
2. The *names of the heroes* differ in chs. 1–6. Thus, Daniel does not appear in ch. 3; it centres, instead, around the three pious Jews, Shadrach, Meshach and Abednego, who are identified in 1.7 (cf. Dan.$^{LXX}$ 3.64) with Daniel's three friends, Hananiah, Mishael and Azariah.
3. The *characterization of Daniel* varies. In chs. 1–6, Daniel appears as the ideal → *diaspora* Jew and wise dream interpreter who ascends to high office at the

foreign royal court under God's guidance. In chs. 7–12, Daniel appears as a lone recipient of revelations which are enigmatic even to him, frighten him, and must be interpreted by an angel.

4. Chs. 1–6 draw a different *picture of the foreign ruler* than do chs. 7–12. While the kings are capable of conversion and recognition in the narratives, they only appear as power hostile to God in the visions.
5. Varying *conceptions of the angels* appear. In the narratives, the angels appear on earth as deliverers (cf. 3; 6), in the visions as heavenly interpreters (cf. 7.16; 8.15), mediators of revelation (10.9), and representatives of the peoples (cf. 10.13; 12.1).
6. The *historical information* in chs. 1–6 manifests significant inaccuracies, while it becomes increasingly accurate beginning in ch. 7. According to Dan. 5.2, Belshazzar appears as Nebuchadnezzar's son, while, according to Babylonian and Greek sources, he was the son of Nabonidus and, contrary to Dan. 7.1 and 8.1, was never the independent king of Babylon. The Median Empire did not succeed the Babylonian, as 6.1 (NRSV 5.31) assumes, but was its contemporary; Darius I was not the Median king, but the Persian. According to 6.29 (NRSV 6.28) and 10.1 Cyrus II succeeded Darius I. Historically, Darius I followed Xerxes and Artaxerxes followed Darius II, while Cyrus II ruled before Cambyses and Darius I (Ch. 4.3). In contrast, the allusions in chs. 7–12 manifest in their non-predictive sections precise knowledge of contemporary events as attested in the → *deuterocanonical* books of Maccabees (cf. 1–2 Macc.; 29) and in extra-biblical Greek and Roman sources.
7. In the → *Septuagint* (LXX), the book differs substantially in form (1.2.1.2). Thus, between 3.23 and 3.24, the LXX offers a prayer of Azariah (Dan.$^{LXX}$ 3.24-50), a hymn of praise by the three men in the oven (Dan.$^{LXX}$ 3.51-90), and three additional narratives concerning Daniel not found in the Hebrew text. In English translations, these surpluses are produced either as chs. 13 and 14, following the Vulgate, or among the → *apocrypha* as 'Additions to the book of Daniel' (Ch. 21B). Finally, chs. 4–6 differ significantly in their LXX and Hebrew forms. Based on the major differences between the → *Masoretic* and the LXX versions, the early church adopted the younger Greek translation, which stands much closer to the Hebrew-Aramaic text and was falsely attributed to *Theodotion* (Th, Ch. 1.2.1.2). Accordingly, 'Theodotion's' version of Daniel found its way into the major Greek codices, while the older LXX version is completely attested today in only three manuscripts.[5] Critical editions of the LXX currently in use offer both Greek versions of the book of Daniel. Translations of the Greek additions (e.g. NRSV.A) reflect, as did Jerome's translation in the Vulgate, the 'Theodotion' text.

5. The Code Chicianus (= HS 88) from the 10th cent., the Syriac translation of Origen's Hexapla (Syrohexapla) and, in fragments, by Chester Beatty Papyrus 967 from the 3rd cent. CE. (J. Ziegler, *Susanna, Daniel, Bel et Draco* [Septuaginta: Vetus Testamentum Graecum auctoritate societatis litterarum Gottingensis editum XVI/2; 2nd ed., Göttingen: Vandenhoeck & Ruprecht, 1999]).

# 21.3 Origins of the Book of Daniel

## 21.3.1 The Form of the Book of Daniel

The book offers a mixture of *diaspora legends* (→ *diaspora*; chs. 1–6) and *vision reports* (chs. 7–12). The diaspora legends correspond to the genre of court and ascent narratives such as occur also in the Joseph story (Gen. 37–50, Ch. 7.5) or in the book of Esther (Ch. 20).[6] They centre around a figure who, because of adherence to Jewish identity abroad, comes into conflict with the Gentile power's claim to dominion encompassing all areas of life, is delivered by God from direct threat to his life, through this deliverance renders a living example of the strength of the God of Israel, and, consequently, has a career at the court of the foreign ruler. The court and ascent narratives have a historical certain complexion in that they date the events narrated[7] and contextualize them by means of references to (supposed) local customs.[8] On the other hand, the basic model for these narratives is based on popular fairytale and wonder motifs.

The *vision reports* have inner-biblical parallels and prototypes in the depictions of prophetic revelations. The depictions of visions in the book of Daniel consistently involve a *literary* depiction of history. Daniel's visions interpret specific historical occurrences as events predetermined by God ('meta-history'). The predictions cast as visions of the future are so-called *vaticinia ex eventu*, i.e. predictions which already look back on the event announced for the future and interpret it for the present. In this regard, the present is understood as the end time. The announcements beginning in Dan. 11.40, in which the author looks beyond his own time, constitute an exception.

The essential *characteristics of the vision reports* in the book of Daniel, which take the form of *symbolic dream visions* (Dan. 2; 4; 7; 8), on one hand, and of visions with the *appearance of a heavenly being* (Dan. 9–12), on the other, are: (1) the communication of special divine secrets; (2) the interpretation of these secrets by an angel; (3) the reference to contemporary events which

6. H. M. Wahl, 'Das Motiv des "Aufstiegs" in der Hofgeschichte: Am Beispiel von Joseph, Esther und Daniel', *ZAW* 112 (2000): 59–74.

7. Cf. Dan. 1.1; 2.1; 3.1; 6.1 (NRSV 5.31).

8. Cf. Dan. 6.2 (NRSV 6.1) with Esth. 1.1; 8.9 and Dan. 6.9, 13, 16 (NRSV 6.8, 12, 15) with Esth. 1.19.

are incorporated into the scheme of world eras; and (4) dualistic tendencies ('salvation' || 'judgement'; 'God-fearing' || 'godless'; 'deliverance' || 'annihilation').

These characteristics point to apocalyptic texts and mark the book of Daniel in its final form as an → *apocalypse*.

**Early Jewish apocalypticism:** The term ***apocalypticism*** (from the Greek, *apokalyptein* 'to reveal, disclose') refers to a specific eschatologically (i.e. end time) oriented complex of ideas characterized by:

1) a chronological scheme of history
2) the theory of a negative development of history and
3) reflections on the future of the dead.

Typically, apocalypticism adapts historical, geographical and astronomic-astrological traditions and develops them into a universal cosmological drama. Central to apocalyptic thought is the notion of a renewal of the world after its demise. Jewish apocalypticism drew nourishment, on one hand, from Old Testament → *wisdom* and prophecy, and was, on the other hand, a phenomenon of comprehensive political, religious and economic crises (as demonstrated by corresponding tendencies in the → *Hellenistic* environment of ancient Judaism).

The literary → *genre* which embodies apocalypticism is the ***apocalypse***. It displayed quite specific formal and substantive characteristics. *Formally*, the apocalypse involved *fictive depictions of visions* presented as the discussion of a problem by the visionary and God or an angel. The visionary is either instructed concerning the end time within the realm of history, like Daniel, or taken on a supramundane journey to heaven, like Enoch, for example (cf. 1 En. 14; 71). *In terms of content*, the apocalypse deals with the relationship between world history or human history and the kingdom of God. *Linguistically*, the apocalypse works with mythical allusions, symbols and (numerical) riddles. Their primary *addressees* are pious circles admonished and comforted in the face of political and religious crises. In the first instance, an apocalypse deals with the interpretation of the present, understood as the end time, not with predictions of the future. In order to lend their texts special authority, authors clothe apocalypses in the garb of a particular figure from salvation history or the primordium. Therefore, apocalypse involves → *pseudepigraphy*. The apex of Jewish apocalypses lies in the period from the second century BCE into the second century CE. Although the majority of these texts were not included in the Hebrew and Greek → *canon*,[9] they have attained enormous influence, not only in the New Testament, but also in the history of Christian and Jewish piety and art.

J. J. Collins, *The Apocalyptic Imagination: An Introduction to Jewish Apocalyptic Literature*. 2nd ed. Grand Rapids, Mich.: Eerdmans, 1998.

9. Cf. *As. Mos.*; *En.*; *4 Ezra*; *2 Bar.*; *3 Bar.*; *Apoc. El.*; *Apoc. Ab.*; *Apoc. Zeph.*; and *Sib. Or.*, all of which are available in the *OTP*, along with some of the Qumran documents, which can be found in English translation in F. García Martínez and E. J. C. Tigchelaar, *The Dead Sea Scrolls*.

## 21.3.2 The Composition and Redaction of the Book of Daniel

The literary historical peculiarities mentioned in section B can best be explained by means of a layer or supplementation hypothesis.[10] The Aramaic Daniel stories in chs. 2–6* constitute the foundation of the book. An Aramaic introduction comparable to ch. 1 presumably preceded them. The addition of the vision in ch. 7 (Aramaic) represented a first expansion. In a second phase of redaction, the Hebrew chs. 8 and 10–12 were attached. Each interprets ch. 7 and has, in turn, undergone actualizing expansions. Chapter 1 may have also been translated into Hebrew in conjunction with the addition of chs. 8 and 10–12. This Hebraicization presumably related to the fact that, after the rise of Aramaic as the vernacular in Palestine (Ch. 1.2.3 'Languages and Writing Materials'), Hebrew was regarded as the 'holy language' and, therefore, the Hebrew framework enabled inclusion among the 'Holy Scriptures'. The youngest component of the book is Daniel's penitential prayer in ch. 9. The fact the Greek book of Daniel evidences its own history of development notwithstanding, the successive expansion of the prayers in ch. 3 and the narratives of Susannah at the bath, of Daniel and the Bel/Marduk figure, and of Daniel and the dragon can be termed the fifth phase (see Ch. 21.2.3).

Viewed schematically, the 'book of Daniel' underwent four or five phases of configuration:

| | | |
|---|---|---|
| 1) | Aramaic | chs. 1*, 2–6 |
| 2) | Aramaic | chs. 1*, 2–6 +7 |
| 3) | Aramaic-Hebrew | chs. 1, 2-7 + 8, 10–12 |
| 4) | Aramaic-Hebrew | chs. 1–8, 10–12 + 9 |
| | | → the book of Daniel in the Hebrew Bible |
| 5) | Greek | chs. 1.1–3.23 + *vv. 24-90*; 3.24–12.13 + *'13.1–14.42'* |
| | | → the book of Daniel in the Latin Bible |

The appearance of a wise and just king named *Dan'ilu* in the Ugaritic Aqhat Epic (12th cent. BCE),[11] the reference to Daniel along with Noah and Job as

10. R. G. Kratz, 'Die Visionen des Daniel', in *Schriftauslegung in der Schrift: FS O. H. Steck* (BZAW 300; ed. R. G. Kratz, T. Krüger and K. Schmid; Berlin/New York: de Gruyter, 2000).

11. Translated in *COS* I, 343–58.

examples of righteousness and survivors of catastrophes in Ezek. 14.14, 20, the characterization of Daniel as a paradigm of wisdom in Ezek. 28.3, the additional Daniel narratives in the → *Septuagint* (Dan. 13–14), and the texts containing Daniel material known from Qumran (4Q243-245)[12] demonstrate that the Aramaic-Hebrew book of Daniel traces back to a selection from a broad stream of *Daniel traditions*.

In the configuration of the Daniel traditions, the authors have resorted to *Old Testament traditions* from prophecy and wisdom. The prophetic 'sources' of the book of Daniel include, above all, proto-apocalyptic texts.[13] Behind ch. 9, which especially evidences the *phenomenon of inner-biblical interpretation of scripture*, stand: (1) a scriptural citation from Jer. 25.11-12 and 29.10 in combination with Lev. 25-26, (2) the genre of a communal lament (Ch. 13.3.2.2) developed further into a confession of sin and repentance, and (3) the late deuteronomistic (Ch. 7.2.2, excursus on 'Deuteronomism') and chronistic (cf. 2 Chr. 26.21; Ch. 23.4) theology of history.

Scholars debate the degree to which Babylonian, Persian and Greek ideas have infused the book. In view of the Aramaic text *4QPrNab ar*[14] found at → *Qumran*, it is very likely that a tradition originally tied to the Babylonian king Nabonidus stands behind Daniel 4.

## 21.3.3 The Situation and Function of the Book of Daniel

The historicizing information in 1.1 and 10.1 indicate the period of the Babylonian → *exile* as the *narrated time* (= 'the fictive time of the action') which began with the first deportations of Judeans to Babylon in 598/7 BCE[15] and extended at least into the reign of the Persian king Cyrus II (559/8–530 BCE; Ch. 4.3). The *milieu* in which Daniel's narratives and visions are located is the Babylonian-Persian diaspora. In analogy to the book of Esther, the origins of the Aramaic narratives in Daniel (1) 2–6* are to be sought in this milieu. Additionally, as the differences between the Hebrew Bible and the Septuagint

12. Translated in F. García Martínez and E. J. C. Tigchelaar, *The Dead Sea Scrolls* I, 486–93.
13. Isa. 24–27; 65.17 and 66.22 and the books of Ezekiel and Zechariah (chs. 1–6), etc.
14. = 4Q242, translated in F. García Martínez and E. J. C. Tigchelaar, *The Dead Sea Scrolls* I, 486–7.
15. Cf. 2 Kgs 24.11-16; Jer. 52.27-28.

in Daniel 4–6 and the additions in Daniel 13–14 indicate, one must take into account Greek Daniel legends from the fourth century BCE.

The *events revealed* in Nebuchadnezzar's dreams and Daniel's visions extend, then, from the reign of Nebuchadnezzar II (605–562 BCE) to the threat to Jerusalem under Antiochus IV Epiphanes (175–164 BCE). Thus, the events described in Dan. 8.21-25 and 11.2-45 can be related unequivocally to Alexander the Great (336–323 BCE), to the conflicts surrounding his empire among the Diadochoi, and to the religio-political measures of Antiochus IV (167–165).

Since the events described in the visions involve → *Vaticinia ex eventu*, in its final form, the book traces back to the time of Antiochus IV. Dan. 11.40-42, 45 knows nothing of his death in 164 BCE. The 'abomination of desolation' (11.31), a disguised reference to an installation dedicated to Zeus erected in 167 BCE by Antiochus on the altar in the temple of Yhwh in Jerusalem (cf. 1 Macc. 1.54), has not yet been removed (cf. 1 Macc. 4.36-61). Thus, the final redaction falls in the time between 167 and 165 BCE. Consequently, Daniel is the youngest document in the Old Testament.

> Its late origins explain why it was not included in the prophetic section of the Hebrew → *canon*, which was probably closed around 200 BCE, but among the Writings (1.2.1.3). In the Septuagint, on grounds of content, the book appears among the prophetic books, indeed, after the book of Ezekiel which is related to it in many respects.

Those responsible for the *final redaction* were most likely educated, → *eschatologically* oriented circles in Jerusalem, who were probably included among those called 'insightful and wise' in 11.33 and 12.3.[16] The book originated in an *era* in which Syria-Palestine was the stage of six wars (the so-called Syrian Wars between 274 and 145 BCE), in which social conflicts based on the economic system of Ptolemaic then Seleucid dominion intensified. The progressive Hellenization of all areas of life also altered the traditional cult (Ch. 4.4).[17] The essential *function* of the book is the management of the crises that these changes had brought upon Palestinian Judaism and in which parties in Jerusalem open to → *Hellenism* participated significantly. The account of the preservation of Jewish identity in Babylonia and the visions concerning the final judgement on all the empires of the world were meant to encourage

16. Cf. 1 Macc. 2.42; 7.12-13; 2 Macc. 14.6 and 1QS II:13; IX:12.

17. Cf. Dan. 7.8-9, 25; 8.9-14 with 1 Macc. 1.41-64.

the pious in the land, admonish them to keep the Torah even under conditions of foreign rule, and comfort them with the prospect of the end of all human dominion and a just judgement at the end of time. Thus, Daniel is neither a book about history nor about the future from which the end of time can be calculated, but a *book of comfort*. In a specific historical situation, it keeps alive hope in God's justice and dominion with the assistance of the literary genre of the apocalypse and certain theological motifs.

## 21.4 Theology of the Book of Daniel

The theology of Daniel centres around the concept of Yhwh as the *director of time*.[18] In order to develop this notion, the book resorts to a hero from antiquity, portrays his fate in the paradigmatic period of judgement of the Babylonian Exile, has foreign rulers confess Yhwh as a power who changes history and culminates in a prospective on the end time. History appears as a process guided by Yhwh, which is simultaneously mysterious, that moves toward the worldwide recognition of God and culminates in the establishment of the universal and eternal kingdom of God. At the same time, this kingdom relativizes any human might and power.

As an expression of the universality of God (→ *universalism*), Daniel only rarely employs the proper name of the Old Testament God, speaking instead, of the 'God of heaven' (2.18), the 'Highest' (4.14 [NRSV 4.17]), the 'supreme God' (5.18), the 'King/Lord of heaven' (4.34 [NRSV 4.37]/5.23), or only of 'Heaven' (4.23 [NRSV 4.26]).

As the obverse of the concept of God's universality and transcendence, Daniel suggests a *doctrine of angels* (→ *angelology*).[19] The angels appear not just as deliverers and members of the heavenly court, but also as heavenly guards (4.10 [NRSV 4.13]), messengers (6.23 [NRSV 6.22]), revelators (10.5), interpreters (9.16; 10.21), holy ones (7.18) and representatives of the nations provided with proper names (9.16; 10.21; 12.1). Among them, the *son of man*, who will assume the kingdom of God at the end of time (7.14), stands out. This kingdom will dissolve all human dominion, mark the end of history, and be characterized by eternal life for the righteous.

18. T. Gretler, *Zeit und Stunde* (above, Ch. 18 n. 15).

19. F. V. Reiterer, T. Niklas and K. Schöpflin, eds, *Angels: The Concept of Celestial Beings – Origins, Development and Reception* (Deuterocanonical Literature Yearbook; Berlin/New York: de Gruyter, 2007).

In view of their negative experiences in this world, until the advent of the kingdom of God, the question repeatedly arises anew for *the pious* as to God's presence and righteousness. This question is accompanied by the necessity of trusting in God alone in a world which absolutizes itself and its images. *The commandments concerning exclusive worship and the prohibition against images* (cf. Exod. 20.2-6 || Deut. 5.6-9; Ch. 6.3.2) constitute guides for a life marked by → *wisdom* and piety. As the goal of this life, the *expectation of a final judgement* and of the *resurrection of the dead*, which surfaces in this form for the first and only time in the Old Testament,[20] grows for the pious out of the conviction that God is faithful. This expectation articulates the hope for an otherworldly retribution and fellowship with God that survives death (Ch. 18.4).

## 21.5 Notes on the History of Reception

Despite its marginal status in the Hebrew → *canon*, a status that traces back to the anti-apocalyptic propensities of rabbinic Judaism after the failed anti-Roman rebellions of 70 and 135 CE, the book of Daniel had an outstanding history of reception and influence *in ancient Judaism and in early and medieval Christianity*. 1 Maccabees 1.5 and 2.59-60 already cite Daniel. Daniel appears as a prophetic book in 4QFlor(ilegium) 2:3, a collection of scripture passages known from → *Qumran*,[21] in Flavius Josephus,[22] and in the New Testament (cf. Mt. 24.15). The concepts of angels, the sequence of empires, the son of man and the final judgement were adopted and extrapolated primarily in → *eschatologically* and apocalyptically oriented circles.[23]

In the New Testament, which offers over 200 allusions or verbatim citations from Daniel, the concept of the *Son of Man*, in particular, took root as a title

20. Cf. Dan. 12.1-3 and then 2 Macc. 7.9; 12.43-45. B. Schmitz, 'Auferstehung und Epiphanie', in *The Human Body in Death and Resurrection* (Deuterocanonical Literature Yearbook; ed. T. Nicklas, F. V. Reiterer and J. Verheyden; Berlin/New York: de Gruyter, 2009), 105–42.

21. = 1Q174, translated by F. García Martínez and E. J. C. Tigchelaar, *The Dead Sea Scrolls* I, 352–55.

22. *Contra Apion*, I, 8 (translated in S. Mason, ed., *Flavius Josephus: Translation and Commentary*, Vol. 10).

23. Cf. the 'Sectarian Rule' and the 'War Scroll' from Qumran (1QS and 1QM, respectively), Ethiopic Enoch (1 Enoch) or 4 Ezra.

for Jesus who acts with full authority in the present (cf. Mk 2.10) and who suffers (cf. Mk 8.31) or for the returning Christ (Mt. 24.27). Moreover, the gospel of John employs the term as a Christological title (John 9.35). The New Testament *Revelation of John*, the only canonical apocalypse other than Daniel,[24] is indebted to Daniel for essential elements of its constellation of ideas and worldview (cf. Rev. 5; 12.7; 13). Following the indications of the time for the destruction of Antiochus IV, understood as the final judgement,[25] one finds from late antiquity until the present historical speculation and attempts to identify the symbols of Daniel's visions with contemporary crises and powers and to develop a precise schedule for the end time – often involving the misperception of the original situation and function of Daniel as a book of comfort for people threatened in their existence and identity.[26]

In the *arts*, visualizations of Daniel's resurrection (together with Noah and Job, cf. Ezek. 14.14, 20) already occur in catacomb art. In Western painting, the scenes of Daniel in the lion's den and of the three men in the oven dominate; the motif of Daniel, the visionary, has also inspired painters and sculptors from the Middle Ages to the modern era. In addition to the *literary paraphrases* in Heinrich Heine's ballad 'Belsazer' (1822) or Carl Zuckmeyer's 'Gesang im Feuerofen' (1943) there are *musical settings* such as the oratorios of Georg Friedrich Handel (1745/1749), Karlheinz Stockhausen's 'Gesang der drei Jünglinge' (1956), and the rock oratorio 'Daniel' by Thomas Gabriel and Eugen Eckert (2002).

## B The 'Additions' to the Book of Daniel

R. T. McLay, 'Susanna/Daniel/Bel and the Dragon'. In *A New Translation of the Septuagint*. Ed. by A. Pietersma and G. G. Wright. Oxford: Oxford University Press, 2007 (NETS); G. G. Xeravits and J. Zsengellér, eds., *Deuterocanonical Additions of the Old Testament Books*. Deuterocanonical Literature Studies 4. Berlin/New York: de Gruyter, 2010.

24. Regarding extra-canonical apocalypses, see J. Charlesworth, 'Apocalyptic Literature and Testaments', *OTP* I, 1983.
25. Cf. Dan. 8.14; 9.27; 12.7.
26. Important in the history of reception was the equation of the fourth (iron) empire from Daniel 2 with the Roman Empire or its medieval legal successors in post-biblical Jewish and Christian historical speculation, which can be identified form late antiquity on into the 18th century.

Commentaries: K. Koch, *Deuterokanonische Zusätze zum Danielbuch*. AOAT 38. Kevelaer: Butzon und Bercker/Neukirchen-Vluyn: Neukirchener, 1987; I. Kottsieper, 'Zusätze zu Daniel'. Pages 209–328 in *Das Buch Baruch, Der Brief des Jeremia, Zusätze zu Ester und Daniel*. ATD.A 5. Ed. by O. H. Steck, R. G. Kratz and I. Kottsieper. Göttingen: Vandenhoeck & Ruprecht, 1998; C. A. Moore (AB 44. NewYork: Doubleday, 1977); O. Plöger (JSHRZ I/1. Gütersloh: Gütersloher Verlagshaus, 1973), 63–87.

D. S. Russell, *The Old Testament Pseudepigrapha: Patriarchs and Prophets in Early Judaism*. Philadelphia: Fortress, 1987, 44–57.

The expression 'Additions (*Additamenta*) to the book of Daniel' refers to the surpluses evidenced by the book of Daniel in the Septuagint (LXX), in the Greek translation of Theodotion (Th) and, following it, the Vulgate (Vg) in comparison to its Masoretic form (Ch. 21.2). The surpluses will be treated here in accordance with their arrangement in the LXX and the Vg: that is, the two prayers positioned between Dan. 3.23 and 24 (= Dan.$^{LXX}$ 3.24-50, 51-90) will be discussed first, then the stories of Susanna (DanSus, Dan. 13) and Bel and the Dragon (DanBel, Dan. 14).[27]

While the Greek versions (LXX, Th) exhibit minor, although somewhat significant, differences in the prayers in Dan. 3,[28] characteristic differences exist between the two versions with respect to the additional narratives.[29] Furthermore, there are differences in positioning: Thus, the original LXX version offers Sus. following Daniel 12 and before the account of Bel and the Dragon. In Th, the account of Bel and the Dragon also stands at the end of the book, but Sus. occurs before Dan. 1 – apparently because Daniel appears as a child (v. 45) in Th. Meanwhile, Sus. was also transmitted as an independent document. The critical editions of the LXX place Sus. before the actual book of Daniel. In comparison to the LXX, Th offers the smoother literary presentation in both cases.

The differences within the surpluses and the varied positions of the narratives in the textual tradition indicate that they lie on different levels in terms of the history of their development, even though the motif of the justice of Israel's God, who is the sole true God and universal ruler connects them thematically. The loose contextual connections in all cases suggest that the surpluses of the Greek

27. Subsequently, individual verses of the 'Additions' will be cited according to the NETS; divergent enumerations in NRSV.A will be given in parentheses.

28. For example, Th places greater emphasis on the roll of Azariah as the sole supplicant, while the LXX version accentuates the fact that all three friends, Hananiah, Azariah and Mishael, prayed.

29. R. T. McLay offers a synopsis of Th and LXX in *NETS*, 987–1027.

version are *supplementations* in relation to the Hebrew-Aramaic book of Daniel. Together with other non-canonical Daniel texts discovered at Qumran,[30] they attest to the popularity of the Daniel figure in Persian and Hellenistic Judaism.

Hermeneutically, it should be noted when reading the 'Additions' that they should be taken, from one perspective, as independent entities in terms of tradition and literary history, and, from another, as components that shape, structurally and theologically, the Greek (and Latin) book of Daniel in its various forms.[31]

# B.1 The Prayers of Azariah and of the Three Men in the Oven

## 21.6 Biblical Context

The Prayer of Azariah has a prose framework that connects it to its narrative context (vv. 24-25 [1] and 46-50 [23-27]). The major poetic section consists of a benediction (v. 26 [3]) and praise of God's justice (vv. 27-45 [4-22]) which includes a communal confession of sin, a request for deliverance, and the confession that the God of Israel is the sole God.

The Prayer of the Three Men in the Oven consists of a prose introduction (v. 51 [28]) and a bi-partite corpus (vv. 52-90 [29-68]). Part I (vv. 52-56 [29-34]) transmits benedictions (cf. Ps. 144.1) to the universal ruler of the world enthroned in his heavenly temple. Part II (vv. 57-85 + 90 [35-63 + 68]) contains a litany-like call to praise the creator. The reference to the 'just' and the designation of Azariah, Hananiah, and Mishael by name (vv. 86-89 [64–67]) link the prayer to the account in Daniel 3. The two prayers lend the account in Daniel 3 dramatic and liturgical character.

30. 4Q243-245 (= 4QpsDan), translated in F. García Martínez and E. J. C. Tigchelaar, *The Dead Sea Scrolls* I, 486–93.

31. See U. Mittmann-Richert, *Einleitung*, 118ff., 130ff., who, in contrast to a broad scholarly consensus, regards the 'Additions' as genuine extensions of the 'canonical' book of Daniel with no lengthy pre-history. R. T. McLay offers a translation of the Greek book of Daniel (LXX and Th) in NETS.

## 21.7 Textual Issues and Major Issues in the History of Critical Interpretation

The loose connections with the context and the collective orientation of the prayers suggest that they were originally independent and were not written as genuine 'literary texts' for their current textual context. Scholarship debates whether the prayers trace back to a Hebrew/Aramaic original or whether they were written in Greek.

## 21.8 Origins of the Prayers of Azariah and the Three Men in the Oven

The Prayer of Azariah is closest in terms of genre to the communal prayers of lament and petition (cf. Ps. 74; 79; 80; Ch. 13.2.2.2). Through its accent on the theology of history and its comprehensive understanding of sin, it has points of contact with Dan. 9.4-14; Neh. 9.5-15 and Bar. 1.15–3.8.[32] Based on the allusions to the restrictions of the Jerusalem cult under Antiochus IV Epiphanes (167/8–165/4 BCE; 4.4) in vv. 31–33 (9-10), 38-39 (15-16) and on grounds of the history of theology, it may have originated in the second century BCE.

In its second section, the Prayer of the Three Men in the Oven corresponds to the genre of the imperatival hymns (Ch. 13.2.2.4) and has its closest parallels in Ps. 103; 136 and 148. Like the Prayer of Azariah, it may have originally been independent and may stem from the Hellenistic period.

Like corresponding prayers in the Greek book of Esther (Ch. 20.6) and in the books of Judith (Ch. 24) and Tobit (Ch. 26), but also in Exod. 15, 2 Sam. 22, and 1 Kgs 8, both prayers function to portray the heroes of the account as model petitioners.

32. Cf. also the prayers contained in 4Q504-506 (translated in F. García Martínez and E. J. C. Tigchelaar, *The Dead Sea Scrolls* II, 1008–19).

# 21.9 Theology of the Prayers of Azariah and of the Three Men in the Oven

In the Prayer of Azariah, theological emphasis should be placed on the motif of the representation of the patriarchs (vv. 35-36 [12-13]) and on the atoning sacrifice of one's own life (v. 40 [17]). Characteristics of the theology of the Prayer of the Three Men are: (1) the concept of the heavenly temple, (2) the involvement of the whole living earthly and heavenly worlds in the praise of God, and (3) the confession of God's power over life and death, which represents a doxological contrast to → *eschatology* in Dan. 12.

# 21.10 Remarks on the History of Reception and Influence

By means of their inclusion in the so-called *odes* (*cantica*),[33] a collection of canonical and apocryphal poems,[34] the Prayers of Azariah and of the Three Men in the Oven found a place in (early) Christian liturgy. Iconographically, the youth praying in the oven already appear in the catacomb paintings and on early Christian sarcophaguses as an image for deliverance from mortal distress and for the resurrection.

# B.2 The Susannah Story

# 21.11 Biblical Context

Daniel 13 (DanSus) centres around the endangerment and deliverance of the beautiful and pious Jewess, Susannah (Hebrew *šûšan* 'lotus blossom').[35] Falsely

33. They are not to be confused with the Odes of Solomon, a collection of 42 anonymous poems, probably originally composed in Greek, from the 2nd cent. CE. (translated in *OTP* II, 725–69).
34. Ode 1: Exod. 15.1-19; Ode 2: Deut. 32.1-43; Ode 3: 1 Sam. 2.1-10; Ode 4: Hab. 3.2-19; Ode 5: Isa. 26.9-20; Ode 6: Jonah 2.3-10 (NRSV 2.2-9); Ode 7: Dan.$^{LXX}$ 3.26-45; Ode 8: Dan.$^{LXX}$ 3.52-88; Ode 9: Lk. 1.46-55, 68-79; Ode 10: Isa. 5.1-9; Ode 11: Isa. 38.10-20; Ode 12: OrMan; Ode 13: Lk. 2.29-32; Ode 14: a morning hymn.
35. Regarding the name and the associated symbolism, see Cant. 2.1-2, 16; 6.2-3; 7.3 (NRSV 7.2).

accused of adultery by two elders of the Jewish community who futilely sought to rape her, Susannah is saved from execution by Daniel who, based on his unusual wisdom, exposes the two elders in their lie.

| | | |
|---|---|---|
| **1-6** | **Prologue:** | **Introduction of Susannah, Joiachim's wife** |
| | | *1 (Th) In Babylon in Joiachim's house* |
| **7-62** | **Body:** | **Endangerment and Deliverance of Susannh** |
| | 7-27 | The two elders' attempt to rape Susannah |
| | | *7 In Joaichim's garden* |
| | 28-43 | Accusation against Susannah and the demand that she be punished with death |
| | | *28 In the synagogue (LXX)/ In Joaichim's house (Th)* |
| | 44-62 | Daniel's conviction of the elders and their execution |
| | | *45 On the way to the execution site* |
| | | *49 In Joiachim's house (Th)/ 51a In the synagogue (LXX)* |
| **63-64** | **Epilogue:** | **Praise of God and Daniel** |

Change of place and dialogue are the structural elements of the tri-partite account set in the Babylonian diaspora. The prayer of Susannah (vv. 42-43) and God's answer, made concrete in the inspiration of Daniel (vv. 44-45),[36] mark the turning point.

## 21.12 Textual Issues and Major Issues in the History of Critical Interpretation

The account, based on a Hebrew or Aramaic original, manifests only a loose connection with the canonical Daniel narratives. This circumstance and the special role of Daniel, who appears here in keeping with this name ('God judges') as a wise judge, speak for the assumption of an originally independent account that was only adopted as special content in the Greek translation of the proto-canonical book of Daniel. From a history of traditions perspective, the Daniel of Susannah is closer to the Daniel figure in Ezek. 14.14, 20; 28.3

36. Cf. Dan. 4.5, 6, 15 (NRSV 4.8, 9, 18).

and in the Ugaritic epic of Aqat than to the Daniel of the canonical accounts. Contrary to the hypothesis of a phased process of literary growth,[37] one can maintain with the majority of interpreters the essential literary unity of the foundation of the account represented by LXX and Th.[38]

## 21.13 Origins of the Susannah Narrative

Susannah has elements of the erotic novella and of the wisdom didactic narrative. The guiding motif, the persecution of the innocent righteous person (cf. Dan. 3.6), is also recorded in Genesis 34, the book of Esther (Ch. 20), the Ahiqar novel and in Sirach 2–5. Susannah appears extraordinarily to be the reverse of the failed seduction of Joseph (Gen. 39).[39] To the degree that legal texts from the Pentateuch play an important role in Susannah,[40] the text can also be understood, like the book of Ruth (Ch. 16), as the account of a legal case. There are also allusions to prophetic texts and to individual psalms, so that Susannah also has elements of a → *midrash.*

Based on references to canonical texts from the Pentateuch and the prophets,[41] the high esteem for the 'law of Moses' (v. 3; v. 62) and the social and historical milieu, the account stems from the Hellenistic period. In this regard, the LXX version exhibits a much more pronounced contemporary colour than the paradigmatic version of Theodotion.

## 21.14 Theology of the Susannah Narrative

Central to the theology of Susannah are: (1) the high value placed on prayer as a starting point for deliverance from distress,[42] (2) the notion that God gifts

37. See I. Kottsieper, *Zusätze*, 287–94.
38. Regarding the differences in content between Th and LXX, see K. Koenen, *Susanna*, and I. Kottsieper, *Zusätze*, 286–328.
39. Cf. Dan. 13.26 with Gen. 39.14-15 and Dan. 13.39 with Gen. 39.18. There are also parallels with 2 Sam. 11 (cf. esp. Dan. 13.15).
40. Cf. Dan. 13.8-20 with Exod. 20.17 par. Deut. 5.21; Dan. 13.21 with Lev. 20.10 and Deut. 22.22; Dan. 13.34 with Lev. 24.14 and Num. 5.18; Dan. 13.61-62 with Deut. 19.16-21.
41. See the sentence pronounced against Israel's false prophets in Jer. 29.21-23 (cf. Jer. 23.15).
42. V. 44; cf. Dan.$^{LXX}$ 3.24-50; Esth.$^{LXX}$ 4.17; 1 Macc. 4.20-34; 2 Macc. 3.15-24; 3 Macc. 2.

individuals for the benefit of others (v. 45), and (3) the conviction that the omnipotent God of Israel exercises just retribution.[43]

## 21.15 Remarks on the History of Reception and Influence

Susannah appears in the account as an individual, but, as the designation for Israel as a 'lotus blossom' in Hos. 14.6 (NRSV 14.5) indicates, is simultaneously a symbol for the true Israel (cf. v. 57) threatened by its own leaders and delivered by God through God-fearing charismatics. In the typological interpretation of the early and medieval church, Susannah appears as an exemplary petitioner, as the forerunner of Jesus in Gethsemane or before Pilate, and as a representative of the church. Since the Renaissance, the motif of the bathing Susannah, in particular, has enjoyed great popularity in Western art.

# B.3 The Stories of Bel and the Dragon

## 21.16 Biblical Context

Daniel 14 (DanBel) offers a dual account of Daniel in conflict with the Babylonian (so LXX) or Persian king (so Th), in which the Old Testament polemic against idol images and the confession of Yhwh as sole deity are translated into narrative using the example of the destruction of the cultic image of the god Bel (vv. 1-22) and of his cultic animal (vv. 23-42). The second account incorporates a report concerning the prophet Habakkuk (12.8), who was wondrously brought to Babylon.

| | | |
|---|---|---|
| **1-2** | **Prologue:** | **Daniel at the royal court** |
| **3-22** | **First account:** | **Daniel and the statue of Bel** |
| | 3-7 | Conflict over Bel's deity |
| | 8-21 | Daniel exposes the priests of Bel |

43. Vv. 42-43; 60-62 (63); cf. Dan. 2.22, 28-29, 47; 6.28.

| | | |
|---|---|---|
| | 22 | Execution of the priests of Bel and destruction of the cultic image |
| **23-42** | **Second account:** | **Daniel and the Dragon** |
| | 23-26 | Conflict over the deity of the Dragon |
| | 27-32 | Daniel destroys the Dragon |
| | ***33-39*** | ***Habakkuk provides for Daniel in the lion's den*** |
| | 40-42 | The king confesses the deity of Daniel's God |

The accounts exhibit a similar structure: After the Babylonian or Persian king confesses the power of his god, Daniel disputes it. Daniel's actions culminate in a demonstration of the impotence of the foreign god and in the pagan king's recognition of Daniel's God. The scenes of the feeding of the Bel statue, exposed as a fraud (vv. 8-21), stand juxtaposed with the wondrous provision for Daniel (vv. 33-39), as do the comments concerning the execution of the priests of Bel (vv. 22; 42) and of the Dragon (v. 27), on the one hand, and concerning the protection of Daniel (v. 40), on the other.

## 21.17 Textual Issues and Major Issues in the History of Critical Interpretation

Despite a few cross-references, the self-contained character of the stories of Bel, the Dragon and Habakkuk's journey to Babylon, the loose connection of v. 23 to v. 22, and the seamless continuation of v. 32 in v. 40 indicate that Daniel was formed from three originally independent accounts, each with its own tradition history. A Hebrew/Aramaic foundation seems to underlie each of the three. The relationship between the tradition and redaction history of the lion's den scenes in Daniel 6 and 14 is an open question. A superscription found only in the LXX traces the account of Bel and the Dragon back to a document by the prophet Habakkuk. The document *Vitae Prophetarum* (*VitProph*), a collection of legends about Old Testament prophets stemming from the first century CE, also attests to the extensive Habakkuk tradition in ancient Judaism.[44]

44. Translated in *OTP* II, 379–99; see U. Mittmann-Richert, *Einführung*, 156–71.

# 21.18 Origins of the Accounts of Bel and the Dragon

The two ironic accounts are satirical wisdom accounts with parenetic objectives. They employ stereotypical motifs such as the cleverness of the faithful Jew at the foreign royal court,[45] the destruction of thc foreign cultic image (and temple [so in Th]),[46] the threat to the piouis Jew posed by his pagan environment,[47] and the conversion of the pagan ruler to faith in Yhwh.[48] Likewise, the scene in which Habakkuk flees to Babylon with the aid of an angel incorporates biblical motifs.[49]

### Bel/Marduk

The common Semitic word 'bel' (Akkad. *belum*, Hebr. and Aram. *ba'al*) means 'lord' and appears in the Babylonian realm as a designation for various gods, above all the god Marduk (OT, Merodach, Jer. 50.2; 51.44; Isa. 46.1; Bar. 6.40). Originally, the patron god of the city of Babylon, beginning in the 2nd millennium BCE, Marduk rose to become the most important god in all Babylonia. The Babylonian epic *Enuma Elish* (*COS* I, 390–402) praises him as the one who created and ordered the world. Under Nebuchadnezzar II (604–562 BCE), the most famous Babylonian sanctuary, the stepped temple (*Ziggurat*) of Marduk in Babylon (*Etemenanki*, 'Tower of Babel', Gen. 11.1-9), was completed. In the neo-Babylonian period, Marduk, whose cultic statue was accompanied by the king to the festival hall during the New Year's processional, assumed elements of a universal god worshipped as creator, director of the cosmos, supreme judge and god of wisdom and could be equated with Zeus by the Greek historian Herodotus (ca. 484–430 BCE, *Histories* I:183).

T. Abusch, 'Marduk'. Pages 543–9 in *DDD*. 2nd ed. Leiden/Boston: Brill, 1999.

45. Cf. Dan. 1.19-20; Gen. 41.38-39.
46. Cf. Judg. 6.25-32; T. Job 4-5 (translated in *OTP* I, 840-41).
47. Cf. Esth. 3.6; Tob. 1.18-20.
48. Cf. 2 Kgs 5.17; Jdt. 14.6.
49. Cf. 1 Kgs 18.12; 2 Kgs 2.16-18 and, esp., Ezek. 3.12-14; 8.3.

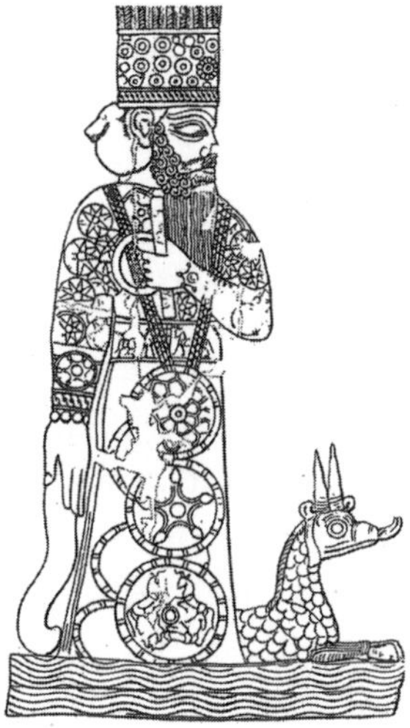

**Fig. 17:** Marduk and his dragon, detail from a stone seal cylinder of Marduk-zakir-šumi I. (854–819 BCE).

The period of origin for the three building blocks[50] and for the entire composition can only be estimated. The Jewish derision of the practice of feeding gods and of the veneration of idols,[51] and the concept of a single God to be worshipped aniconically that stands behind it (→ *monotheism*, the prohibition against images) presume texts in Deut. 4 and Isa. 44.6; 45.5; 46.9 that correspond from the perspective of the history of religion, but can also be understood against the backgrounds of both the Persian and the Hellenistic periods (cf. Wis. 13–15).

# 21.19 Theology of the Stories of Bel and the Dragon

As represented by the true monotheist, Daniel (vv. 5, 25), who appears as a priest in the LXX version (cf. Ezra. 8.2; Neh. 10.7 [NRSV 10.6]), in contrast

50. Vv. 3-22; 23-32 + 40-42; 33-39.

51. Cf. Isa. 40.18-20; 41.6-7; 42.17; 44.9-20; 46.5-7; Ps. 135.15-18; Wis. 13-15; Bar. 6 and see A. Berlejung, *Die Theologie der Bilder: Herstellung und Einweihung von Kultbildern in Mesopotamien und die alttestamentliche Bilderpolemik* (OBO 162; Fribourg: Academic Press/Göttingen: Vandenhoeck & Ruprecht, 1998).

to Dan. 1.6, the theology of Daniel 14 centres around the promotion of belief in a sole, living God who 'does not abandon those who love him' (v. 38, cf. 13.60Th).[52]

## 21.20 Notes on the History of Reception

Based on its interpretation as a symbol for the devil, death, or some other evil power, the dragon, which may already be understood 'meta-historically' in Daniel 14 as the embodiment of the chaos dragon,[53] gained widespread entry into Christian art. Thus, the motif of Daniel's poisoning of the dragon occurs often on early Christian sarcophaguses as a visualization of the destruction of death and of the hope in the resurrection (cf. 1 Cor. 15.26-55).

52. Cf. 1 Macc. 2.60-61; Neh. 1.5; Sir. 2.10; Hab. 2.4.

53. E. Haag, *Daniel* (NEchtB 30; Würzburg: Echter, 1993), 94.

# 22

# The Book of Ezra-Nehemiah

(Markus Witte – Translation by Mark Biddle)

## Chapter Outline




Commentaries: J. Blenkinsopp (OTL. London: SCM, 1988); A. H. J. Gunneweg (KAT XIX. 2 vols. Gütersloh: Gütersloher Verlagshaus, 1985, 1987); H. G. M. Williamson (OTG. Sheffield: JSOT, 1987).

P. R. Davies, ed., *Second Temple Studies 1. Persian Period*. JSOTSup 117. Sheffield: JSOT, 1991; H. Koch, *Es kündet Dareios der König...: Vom Leben im persischen Großreich*. Kulturgeschichte der antiken Welt 55. 3rd ed. Mainz: Zabern, 2000; R. G. Kratz, *The Composition of the Narrative Books of the Old Testament*. Transl. by J. Bowden. London: T&T Clark, 2005, 49–86; idem, *Das Judentum im Zeitalter des Zweiten Tempels*. FAT 42. Tübingen: Mohr Siebeck, 2004; O. Lipschits and M. Oeming, eds, *Judah and the Judeans in the Persian Period*. Winona Lake, Ind.: Eisenbrauns, 2006; J. Wiesehöfer, *Das frühe Persien: Geschichte eines antiken Weltreichs*. 2nd ed. München: Beck, 2002; T. Willi, *Juda – Jehud – Israel. Studien zum Selbstverständnis des Judentums in persischer Zeit*. FAT 12. Tübingen: Mohr Siebeck, 1995.


Jewish tradition transmits the books of Ezra and Nehemiah as one book. This circumstance can be inferred from (1) the fact that the → *Masoretic* → *colophon* of Ezra only appears after Neh. 13.31 and (2) the fact that the Masoretes indicate the centre of the unit Ezra-Nehemiah between Neh. 3.31 and 32. The oldest Greek biblical manuscripts, the lists of the → *canonical* books of the Old Testament by Melito of Sardis (d. before 190 CE), information concerning the history of the canon in the Babylonian → *Talmud* (cf. *BBat.* 15a; *San.* 93b), and the medieval rabbinic commentaries also treat Ezra-Nehemiah as one book. The division suggested by the superscription in Neh. 1.1 is first attested in Origen (d. circa 254 CE). In addition to Greek biblical manuscripts, it found its way into the Latin tradition, thence, beginning in 1448, into Hebrew biblical manuscripts and, finally, into modern translations of the Bible. The names of the books derive from the two key figures *Ezra* ('[God is] help') and *Nehemiah* ('Yhwh comforts'), who may also be the authors, at least of certain passages.

In addition to the canonical book of Ezra-Nehemiah, there are books of Ezra transmitted in Greek and Latin but which are enumerated differently in the Greek and Latin traditions. Thus, the → *Septuagint* contains a → *compilation* of 2 Chr. 35–36; Ezra 1–10; and Neh. 7.73 (NRSV 7.72) –8.13a that was written in Greek and originated in the 2nd or 1st century BCE, which is counted as Esdras α in the Septuagint but as 3 Ezra in the Latin tradition and as 1Esdras in NRSV.A. 3 Ezra contains a unique account of a competition between three pages at the Persian court, one of whom is identified with the Judean Zerubbabel (3 Ezr. 3.1–5.6), an account whose nearest parallel in the history of literature is the Daniel narratives (cf. Dan. 1–6).[54] Furthermore, an → *apocalypse* attributed to Ezra is known from the Latin tradition. It consists of the actual 4 Ezra along with 5 and 6 Ezra.

| **Hebrew Bible** | **Septuagint** | **Vulgate** | **Modern translations** | **NETS/NRSV.A** |
|---|---|---|---|---|
| | Esdras α | III Ezrae | 3 Esr | |
| Ezra | Esdras β | I Ezrae | Ezra } | 1 Esdras |
| Nehemiah | Esdras γ (formerly β) | II Ezrae | Nehemiah } | 2 Esdras |
| | | IV Ezrae | 4 Ezra (= *'4Ezr 3–14'*) | |
| | | | 5Ezra (= *'4Ezr 1–2'*) | |
| | | | 6Ezra (= *'4Ezr 15–16'*) | |

54. Other special material ('Sondergut' *S*) in 3 Ezra consists of an assessment of Josiah (3 Ezra 1.21-22), inserted between the portrayal of the Josianic period taken from 2 Chr. 35.1-19 and 2 Chr. 35.20–36.23 and the reordering of Ezra 4.7-24 after Ezra 1.11, giving the text of 3 Ezra the following order according to the numeration in NETS and LXX.D [NRSV.A]: 1.1-20 [1,1-22] (= 2 Chr. 35.1-19); *1.21-22 (S) [1,23-24]*; 1.23-55 [1,25-58] (= 2 Chr. 35.20–36.21); 2.1-14 [2.1-15] (= Ezra 1.1-11); 2.15-26 [2.16-30] (= Ezra 4.7-24); *3.1–5.6 (S)*; 5.7-70 [5.7-73] (= Ezra 2.1–4.5); 6.1–9.36 (= Ezra 5.1–10.44 MT); 9.37-55 (= Neh 7.72 [NRSV 73]–8.13a).

# 22.1 Biblical Context

| | | | |
|---|---|---|---|
| **Ezra 1–6** | **Reconstruction of the Jerusalem temple under Zerubbabel and Joshua** | | |
| | 1.1–2.70 | Edict of Cyrus and return of the Jews exiled in Babylon | |
| | 3.1–6.22 | Construction of the temple in the face of internal and external resistance | |
| | | 3.1-6 | *First burnt offering and Sukkoth Festival* for the returnees |
| | | 6.19-22 | *Feast of Passover* for the returnees |
| **Ezra 7–10** | **Implementation of the law for Judah under Ezra** | | |
| | 7.1–8.36 | Edict of *Artaxerxes* and the sending of Ezra from *Babylon* | |
| | 9.1–10.44 | Dissolution of the mixed marriages and the people's commitment ('covenant') | |
| | | 9.5-15 | Ezra's *penitential prayer* |
| **Neh 1–7** | **Reconstruction of Jerusalem's city walls under Nehemiah** | | |
| | 1.1–2.9 | Edict of Artaxerxes and the sending of Nehemiah from *Persia* | |
| | | 1.4-11 | Nehemiah's *penitential prayer* |
| | 2.10–7.72 | Construction of the wall in the face of internal and external resistance, (NRSV 7.73) social reforms | |
| **Neh 8–12** | **Submission to the law under Ezra and Nehemiah** | | |
| | 8–10 | Ezra's public reading of the law and the people's renewed commitment ('agreement') | |
| | | 8.13-18 | *Sukkoth Festival* |
| | | 9.5-37 | *Penitential prayer* of the people |
| | 11 | The settlement of Jerusalem and its environs ('synoikism') | |
| | 12 | The cultic personnel of the Jerusalem cult and its maintenance | |
| **Neh 13.1-31** | | **Enforcement of the obligation under Nehemiah** | |
| | 13.1-3 | Expulsion of the non-Israelites | |
| | 13.4-31 | Measures for the purity of the religious community | |
| | | 13.22 | *Sanctification of the Sabbath* |

A central *theme of the book* is the constitution of the pure community of Yhwh gathered under conditions that preserve the fundamental characteristics of Jewish identity in the sacred city of Jerusalem around the Yhwh temple as the centre of cosmic order and prosperous life. This theme unfolds in the following three measures: (1) in the reconstruction of the Jerusalem temple (Ezra 1–6), (2) in the protection, internally and externally, of the community gathered around the temple by means of the construction of the wall and by social equality (Ezra 7–10 + Neh. 1–7), and (3) in the establishment of the cultically pure community by means of commitment to the Torah of Moses (Neh. 8–12).

A kind of appendix repeats these steps once more in detail with the examples of the separation of the Jerusalem cultic community from its non-Jewish neighbours (13.1-3, 23-31), the purity of the temple (13.4-14), and the strict observance of the Sabbath (13.15-22). Here, too, the criterion is the written Torah, i.e., the 'book of Moses' (Neh. 13.1).[55]

The *span of narrated time* extends from the beginning of the reign of the Persians over the Near East under Cyrus II (539 BCE) to the conclusion of Nehemiah's reforms in Jerusalem after the 32nd year of the reign of Artaxerxes I (i.e., after 433 BCE; cf. Neh. 13.6). The *geographical setting* of the account reaches from the Near Eastern metropolises *Babylon* and *Susa* to the provinces of Samaria and Yehud ('Judah', Ch. 4.4) and is centred in *Jerusalem*, 'the holy city' (cf. Neh. 11.1, 18).

The individual sections of the book are structured similarly and are interconnected via *common motifs and key terms*. At the beginning of each new narrative stands an edict or a commission concerning Jerusalem.[56] In this manner, the Jewish actors who lead the various phases of the restoration of Jerusalem and the return of the Judeans deported to Babylonia are incorporated into the chronology of world politics determined by the Persian kings. Thus, the following appear in sequence: (1) *Sheshbazzar, Zerubbabel, and Joshua* who were responsible under the reigns of Cyrus II and Darius for reconstructing the temple and who were accompanied by the activity of the prophets *Haggai* and *Zechariah*; (2) the 'scribe and priest' *Ezra*, who was responsible under Artaxerxes (on the question as to whether Artaxerxes I or II was involved, see below) for implementing the Torah of Moses; and (3) the 'governor' *Nehemiah* responsible under Artaxerxes (I or II? see above) for reconstructing the Jerusalem city walls and for consolidating Judah's domestic and socio-political affairs.

The recurrence of the figure of Ezra in the context of the reading of the law (Neh. 8.1-12), the occasional references to Nehemiah in Ezra 2.2 and to Ezra in Neh. 12.36, and the two references to Ezra and Nehemiah together in Neh. 8.9 and 12.26 give the impression that the two protagonists were active simultaneously in Jerusalem.

***The date of Ezra-Nehemiah:*** Based on the references to the sons of Sanballat/Sîn-uballiṭ (cf. Neh. 2.10, 19; 3.33 [NRSV 4.1]) in the request by the Jewish community on Elephantine, an island in the Nile, written in 407 BCE to Bagohi

55. Cf. Ezra 3.2; 7.6, 10.

56. Cf. Ezra 1.1-4; 7.1-28; Neh. 2.1-9.

(Bagoas), the governor of the province of Yehud (translated in *COS* III, 125–30), the emperor under whom Nehemiah appears is clearly Artaxerxes I (465/4–425 BCE; 4.3). According to Neh. 1.1, then, Nehemiah's commission came in 445 BCE. The date of Ezra's mission is unclear. According to Ezra 7.8, Ezra was sent to Jerusalem in the seventh year of King Artahsasta (*Artaxerxes*). This statement refers either to Artaxerxes I or Artaxerxes II (404/359/8 BCE). In the first case, Ezra's mission is to be dated to 458 BCE, in the second, to 397 BCE. The biblical sequence of actors and the parallel activity of Ezra and Nehemiah assumed in Neh. 8.9 and 12.26 supports the assumption that Ezra's mission took place under Artaxerxes I, *before* Nehemiah. On the other hand, neither Nehemiah's reforms nor the request of the Jews from Elephantine mentioned above seem to presuppose Ezra's activity. Consequently, it is also possible that Ezra was active only *after* Nehemiah, under Artaxerxes II. A compromise suggestion places Ezra in the time between Nehemiah's first and second stays in Jerusalem (cf. Neh. 13.6), which, however, presupposes an alteration of the text in Ezra 7.8 from the seventh year of Artaxerxes I (458 BCE) to the twenty-seventh (438 BCE). However the historical question is to be answered,[57] the current order of the actors corresponds to the theological tendency of Ezra-Nehemiah with its high esteem for the law of Moses, which, on the level of the final form of the book, introduces and completes the political and social reforms in Jerusalem (Ezra 7; Neh. 8). The notion that Ezra, the 'scribe and priest' should be a purely fictional character is unlikely (despite the absence of extra-biblical evidence, a circumstance which pertains, however, to many Old Testament figures).

In each case, a *performance report* and a *list* of the Judeans who participated in the respective measures follows the royal edicts.[58] In each case, before the controversial reconstruction of the temple and the city walls and the regulation of the economic, social and religious integrity of Jerusalem's population could be successfully completed, it was necessary to overcome *opposition* posed sometimes by Jerusalem's neighbours, sometimes by Jewish opponents to the reforms of Ezra and Nehemiah. This circumstance includes: (1) the exchange of letters between the Persian emperor and the provincial governors in the → *satrapy* of Trans-Euphrates ('[region] beyond the Euphrates'), which included the territories of Samaria and Yehud, recorded in Ezra 4–6; (2) the dissolution of marriages between adherents of the Jerusalem upper-crust and non-Jewish

57. For other attempts to clarify the historical progression by means of the sequence of the high priests officiating at the time (cf. Ezra 10.6; Neh. 3.1; 12.10-11, 22) or of the references to Nehemiah's construction of the wall (cf. Ezra 9.9); Neh. 6.15), see H. Donner, *Geschichte*, 451–3.

58. Lists: Ezra 2.1-67 = Neh. 7.6-68 (NRSV 7.69); Ezra 8.1-14; Neh. 3.1-32; 10.1-18 (NRSV 9.38–10.17); 11.1-36; 12.1-26.

women recounted in Ezra 10 and Neh. 13.23-31; (3) the interventions against the reconstruction of the city walls organized by Nehemiah reported in Nehemiah 3–4; and (4) the internal political difficulties mentioned in Nehemiah 5–6.

Other *structuring elements* of the overall composition include: (1) the *description of feasts and the communication of prayers,*[59] which always appear in the context of overcoming opposition to the reforms of Ezra and Nehemiah; (2) the *contrast between the actors* (Cyrus || Nebuchadnezzar; Zerubbabel and Joshua || 'adversaries of Judah and Benjamin'; Nehemiah || Sanballat, Tobiah, and Geshem); (3) references to *the law of Moses;*[60] (4) references to the hand or the eye of God in relation to a *theology of history;*[61] (5) the *dating* of certain events;[62] and (6), in Nehemiah, the *reminder formula*, 'may God graciously remember the measures undertaken.'[63]

# 22.2 Textual Issues and Major Issues in the History of Critical Interpretation

Despite its formal coherence on the level of the final text, the book of Ezra-Nehemiah manifests a series of peculiarities that suggests a *complex history of development.*

## 22.2.1 The Alternation of Forms and Languages

Ezra 1.1–4.7; 6.19–7.11; 7.27–10.44 and Nehemiah have been transmitted in Hebrew, Ezra 4.8–6.18 and 7.12-26, in contrast, in Aramaic. Lists[64] and quotations of royal edicts[65] and letters[66] repeatedly interrupt the narrative thread. The list of returnees in Ezra 2.1-67 is identical with the population list in Neh. 7.6-68 (NRSV 7.69). Since the Aramaic sections contain not only documents

59. Sacrifices and feasts: Ezra 3.3-5; 6.17-18, 19-22; 8.35; Neh. 8.13-18.

60. Ezra 3.2; 7.6, 10; Neh. 8.1; 13.1.

61. Ezra 7.6, 9, 28; 8.18, 22, 31; Neh. 2.8, 19 and Ezra 5.5, respectively.

62. Ezra 1.1; 3.1; 6.19; 7.8; 8.31; Neh. 2.1; 7.72 (NRSV 7.73); 9.1.

63. Neh 5.19; 6.14; 13.4, 22, 31; cf. also Neh. 3.36-37.

64. Ezra 1.9-11; 8.1-14; 10.18-43; Neh. 3.1-32; 10.2-29 (NRSV 10.1-28); 11.3-26; 12.1-26.

65. Ezra 1.2-4; 6.3-12; 7.11-26.

66. Ezra 4.7-16, 17-22; 5.6-17.

or texts configured as such, but also narratives, the change of languages cannot be explained fundamentally as a literary technique meant to underscore the authenticity of the letters and edicts. Instead, the change of languages indicates different authors. The fact that the documents cited in Ezra 1.2-4; Neh. 2.6-8 and 6.6-7 appear in Hebrew also points in this direction.

### 22.2.2 Changes in Style

The narrative perspective varies frequently. Some passages speak about the major figures in the third person singular,[67] others in the first person.[68] The harsh transitions and new beginnings between the third person and first person accounts indicate that, here, too, one has to reckon, not with an author's literary technique, but with the combination of sources and redactional expansions.[69]

### 22.2.3 Changes of Actor

While Zerubbabel and Joshua are the central actors in Ezra 1–6 and the account is set in the time of Cyrus II (559/8–530 bce) or Darius I (522–486 BCE), *Ezra*, who appears in the time of Artaxerxes I/II (see above), stands at the centre of Ezra 7–10 and Neh. 8. In Neh. 1.1–7.5; 12.31–13.31, *Nehemiah*, the emissary of Artaxerxes I, determines events. An incidental reference to Ezra and Nehemiah together follows in Neh. 8.9 and 12.26. The abrupt appearance of Ezra in Nehemiah 8 after the broad description of Nehemiah's activity in Nehemiah 1–7 indicates that the joint appearance of Ezra and Nehemiah is secondary literarily and that, at an earlier level of tradition, the core of Ezra and the core of Nehemiah had independent histories of development.

### 22.2.4 The Law of Ezra and the Historicity of the Documents Cited

According to Ezra 7.6, 10, Ezra is a scribe, i.e. a scholar of scripture, who was an expert in the law (the Torah) that Yhwh had given Israel. As such, the Persian emperor commissioned him to introduce the 'law (*dātāʾ*) of the God

67. Ezra 1.1–7.26; 10.1-44 and Neh. (7.6-72 [NRSV 7.73];) 8.1–12.26.

68. Ezra 7.27-28; 8.15–9.5 (6-15) and Neh 1.1–7.5; 12.(27-30,) 31–13.31.

69. Cf. Ezra 7.26/27; 9.5(6-15)/10.1; Ezra 10.44/Neh. 1.1-2; Neh. 7.27/8.1 (cf. Neh. 8.9) and 12.26/27 (cf. v. 31).

of heaven' in Jerusalem (7.12, 21, 26). Accordingly, Ezra seems to have been legitimated by the Persians to promulgate, i.e. to make publicly known (→ '*Imperial authorization*'), the Torah as the law valid in the Persian province of Yehud ('Judah'). Indeed, on the level of the final text, the law of the God of heaven and the Torah, or the → *Pentateuch*, are identical. In the oldest layers of Ezra 7, however, a shorter law for regulating cultic and legal affairs in the province of Yehud ('Judah'), which is either no longer extant or was later integrated into the Pentateuch, lurks behind the law of Ezra. Furthermore, recent studies of philology and the history of motifs of both the edict of Artaxerxes in Ezra 7.12-26 and of the Aramaic documents in Ezra 4.8-22 demonstrate that they stand under the influence of → *Hellenistic* concepts and can only be adduced to a very limited degree in the reconstruction of Persian religious policy.[70]

# 22.3 Origins of the Book of Ezra-Nehemiah

## 22.3.1 The Form of the Book of Ezra-Nehemiah

The book belongs to the category of *theological historiography* (Ch. 3.2.2). The reproduction of royal *edicts, briefs* and *dialogues*, exact dates, and *lists of names* underscores its historiographical character. Interspersed *prayers*, references to the activity of God sometimes mediated by prophets (cf. Ezra 1.1; 5.1-2), and the scene between the cupbearer Nehemiah and the Persian king set in the style of the *court narrative* demonstrate[71] that, overall, it represents a literary composition with a very specific theological objective. It is not entirely fictional, however, although, as the historical incongruities in the sequence of Persian kings in Ezra 4 and trends in the history of religions imply that it was composed at some distance in time from the events recounted and with a clear interest in the present. The authors have employed a variety of source materials.

70. S. Grätz, *Das Edikt des Artaxerxes: Eine Untersuchung zum religionspolitischen und historischen Umfeld von Esra 7:12–26* (BZAW 337; Berlin/New York: de Gruyter. 2004).

71. Neh. 1.1b–2.8 cf. Dan. 1–6; Esth.; Jdt. 12.

## 22.3.2 The Composition and Redaction of the Book of Ezra-Nehemiah

The three narrative blocks of the book of Ezra-Nehemiah (Ezra 1–6: the Zerubbabel story; Ezra 7–10 + Neh. 8 [9–10]: the Ezra story; Neh. 1–7 + 11–13: the Nehemiah story) are based on several sources that have been redactionally linked. The precise demarcation of the source materials is controversial. A *block hypothesis* that reckons with the successive addition of narrative blocks, and a *layer hypothesis* that assumes a thorough redactional stratification alongside the blocks compete with the redaction-historical explanation.[72]

The most extensive, originally independent block consists of the *Nehemian story* cast as autobiography in Neh. *1.1–7.5; 12.31-43*; 13.4-31.* The social, cultic, and economic themes of this so-called *Nehemiah Memorandum* and the refrain-like remembrance formula lend it the character of an account given in relation to God and fellow humans. The addressees may have been Nehemiah's Jewish opponents. Certain sections of the memorandum have analogies in Ancient Near Eastern official and royal inscriptions. The inscription of the Egyptian head physician Udja-Hor-resent (519/518 BCE, translated in *AEL* III, 36–41) offers the most dense literary and contemporary parallels. At the same time, the stereotypical narrative clothing of the memorandum in Neh. 1–2 points to a conscious literary configuration and mixture of forms. Based on analogous practices in the Near East, and conjectured in the Greco-Roman realms, the notion that the Nehemiah memorandum, or an older core of it, was preserved in the Jerusalem temple archives, can be suspected,[73] but cannot be demonstrated.

Because of its framework with the → *Edict of Cyrus* concerning the reconstruction of the Jerusalem temple, the order of Darius based on this edict, and the account of the → *Passover* celebrated on the occasion of the completion of temple construction, the *Zerubbabel account* in Ezra 1–6 offers the most cohesive narrative block in Ezra-Nehemiah. The Aramaic *chronicle of the temple construction* in Ezra 4.8–6.19, secondarily expanded with the Hebrew portions in Ezra 1.1-11; 3.1–4.7

72. J. Pakkala, *Ezra the Scribe: The Development of Ezra 7–10 and Neh 8* (BZAW 347; Berlin/New York: de Gruyter, 2004; J. L. Wright, *Rebuilding Identity: The Nehemia-Memoir and its Earliest Readers* (BZAW 348; Berlin/New York: de Gruyter, 2004).

73. Cf., e.g., the documentation of the deeds of Augustus on the temple wall in Ancyra/Ankara (translated in *Res Gestae Divi Augusti* [ed. J. M. Moore and P. A. Brunt; Oxford: Oxford University Press, 1967]).

and 6.19-22, constitutes its earliest core. The Hebrew framing pieces, which incorporate additional source material in the temple inventory in 1.9-11 and the list of returnees in Ezra 2.1-67 (*par.* Neh. 7.6-68 [NRSV 7.69]), exhibit close stylistic and substantive relationships to the Hebrew *Ezra narrative* (Ezra 7.1-11; 8–10; Neh. 8; 12.31-43*) and to the *books of Chronicles* (Ch. 23.2.3 and 23.3.2).

While scholarship largely agrees with respect to the assumption of an originally independent Nehemiah memorandum, the existence of an analogous *Ezra Memoir* is controversial. Ezra 7–10 and Neh. 8 are the principle candidates for the basic elements of such an Ezra account. The displacement of Neh. 8 would then be attributable to a redactor who linked the original Ezra account (Ezra 7–10; Neh. 8) with the original Nehemiah account (Neh. 1–7*; 12–13*). In view of the multiple literary layers and the change of language in Ezra 7, the shift between first person and third person narrative in Ezra 7–10, the parallelism between the prayers in Ezra 9 and Neh. 9, and the appended legal measures on the question of mixed marriages in Ezra 10 and Neh. 10, it is more likely that Nehemiah 8 represents a redactional construct meant for its present place in the Ezra-Nehemiah composition and was not part of an originally independent Ezra source. This source must have been reduced in scope, maximally to Ezra 7–10* and minimally to the Edict of Artaxerxes in Ezra 7.12-16, if not to Ezra 7.21-22.

Starting from the assumption that the Nehemiah Memorandum, the chronicle of the Temple construction, and the Ezra source originated as three initially separate sources, and considering the redactional cross-references between Ezra 1–3; 6.19-22; 7.1-10; 8–10* and Neh. 8–10, a combination of block and redaction models seems feasible. It should be taken into account that the redactors incorporated additional sources and strengthened relationships with the book of Chronicles (Ch. 23.2.3 and Ch. 23.3.2).

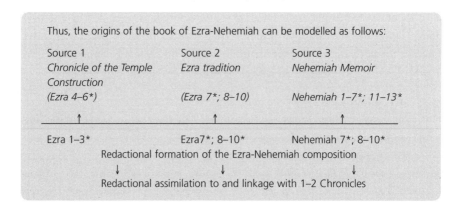

Thus, the origins of the book of Ezra-Nehemiah can be modelled as follows:

| Source 1 | Source 2 | Source 3 |
|---|---|---|
| *Chronicle of the Temple Construction* | *Ezra tradition* | *Nehemiah Memoir* |
| *(Ezra 4–6*)* | *(Ezra 7*; 8–10)* | *Nehemiah 1–7*; 11–13** |
| ↑ | ↑ | ↑ |
| Ezra 1–3* | Ezra7*; 8–10* | Nehemiah 7*; 8–10* |

Redactional formation of the Ezra-Nehemiah composition

↓ ↓ ↓

Redactional assimilation to and linkage with 1–2 Chronicles

## 22.3.3 The Situation and Function of the Book of Ezra-Nehemiah

The book of Ezra-Nehemiah represents the most important *source for the history of Yehud ('Judah')* from the beginning of Persian dominion over the Near East in 539 BCE until the middle of the fifth century BCE. In connection with (1) the → *Cyrus Cylinder*, a pro-Persian description of the acquisition of Babylon by Cyrus II,[74] (2) discoveries of coins and seals with the inscription *yhwd* (Yehud),[75] and (3) the Elephantine papyri,[76] it permits the following reconstruction of the period after the collapse of the kingdom of Judah in 587 BCE. Beginning in the late sixth century bce, for geo-political reasons, the Persians indulged, if they did not, in fact, promote (1) a return of Judeans deported to Babylon (Ch. 4.3.3), (2) the establishment of an independent province of Yehud as part of the large Persian → *satrapy* of the Trans-Euphrates, and (3) the resumption of the official cult in the Jerusalem temple. The precise date of these three steps is disputed. Data in Neh. 5.14-15, the designation of Yehud as a mědînâ ('province') in Ezra 5.8 and a Babylonian clay tablet from the 36th year of Darius I that mentions a Judean (?) governor,[77] indicate that Nehemiah was not the first governor of Yehud.

The missions of Ezra and Nehemiah belong in the *historical* context of the Persian interest in the political stabilization of the province of Yehud as a border post against Egypt, which repeatedly rebelled against Persian sovereignty. The description of Ezra and Nehemiah as reformers of Yehud's religion is the *literary* focus. To the extent that the inhabitants of Yehud ('Yehudeans' → Jews) gathered around the Jerusalem temple as the one cultic site chosen by Yhwh in faithful observance of the one Torah mediated by Moses and kept themselves free of all non-Jewish elements, they represented the 'true Israel'. The radical demand to disassociate from neighbours to the north ('Samaria'/'Samarians' → 'Samaritans'), to the south ('Arabs'/ 'Idumeans'), to the west ('Ashdod' as the epitome of Philistia and Phoenicia), and to the east ('Ammon' and 'Moab') and the concentration on

74. Translated in *COS* II, 314–16.

75. L. Mildenberg, 'Yĕhūd-Münzen', in *Palästina in vorhellenistischer Zeit* (Handbuch der Archäologie. Vorderasien II/1; ed. H. Weippert; Munich: Beck, 1988), 719–28 (+ tables 22–23).

76. Parts are translated *COS* III, 116–32.

77. See A. Meinhold, 'Serubbabel, der Tempel und die Provinz Jehud', in *Steine – Bilder – Texte: Historische Evidenz außerbiblischer und biblischer Quellen* (Arbeiten zur Geschichte der Bibel 5; ed. C. Hardmeier; Leipzig: Evangelische Verlagsanstalt, 2001), 193–212, here 197–8.

Jerusalem as the holy city where the 'true Israel' strictly observes the commandments of God, prove the Ezra-Nehemiah composition to be *Yehud's or Judaism's programmatic religious document.*

The earliest possible reference point for dating, at least of the sources incorporated in Ezra-Nehemiah, consists of the Edict of Cyrus in Ezra 6.3-5 from 538 BCE – if it is authentic. The reference to the king of Asshur in Ezra 6.33, which can only refer to the Seleucids who governed Syria-Palestine beginning in 200/198 BCE, the reception of Neh. 7.72 (NRSV 7.73)–8.13a in 3 Ezra (2nd/1st cent. BCE), and the close parallels between the prayers in Ezra 9, Neh. 9, and Dan. 9 (ca. 165 BCE) mark the latest possible moment for the redaction of the final form of the book. Origins in the time between the last third of the fifth century BCE (cf. the Nehemiah Memorandum) and the beginning of the third century BCE (cf. Ezra 6.22) are most likely.

The essential *function* of the book is to encourage the preservation of one's religious, cultural and genealogical identity, which can be summarized with the terms purity and unity. Their pillars are the observance of God's Torah given by Moses, dwelling in the city of Jerusalem once conquered by David, and praying, sacrificing and celebrating at the temple once erected by Solomon. The portrayal of Ezra's departure from Babylon as a second Exodus (Ezra 8) and the historical psalm, Neh. 9.6-37, which presupposes, in essence, the history encompassing Genesis 1 to 2 Kings 25 (Ch. 5), exemplify the strong roots of Ezra-Nehemiah in Israel's central traditions.

## 22.4 Theology of the Book of Ezra-Nehemiah

The dominant theological thread of the book can be deduced from the prologue in Ezra 1.1-3 and from the epilogue in Neh. 13.30-31. Behind the history of the 'true Israel' stands Yhwh himself, who used the Persian kings as tools to execute his plan for history (cf. Isa. 44.28). The reconstruction of Jerusalem and its temple, and the missions of Zerubbabel, Ezra and Nehemiah stand in the context of a history of divine guidance also found in narrative form, e.g., in the Joseph story (Ch. 7.5), in the books of Ruth (Ch. 16) and Esther (Ch. 20), and in poetic-reflective form in the prophetic books of the Old Testament. As in them, the motifs of God's eye, hand, wrath, grace or → *covenant* describe and define 'Israel's' experiences of and relationship with God. This 'Israel' understands itself to be a host of those delivered from the deportation and destruction (Ezra 9.13) and as a 'holy remnant' (Ezra 9.2, 8). With a strong orientation toward the present, the centre of 'Israel's' life is the Torah, the temple, and worship celebrated in accordance with the Torah under the leadership of the priests and Levites.

In terms of the history of religions, the particular emphasis on the 'awakening' of the Persian kings by Yhwh, the sole God (Neh. 9.6) and the God of heaven and earth (Ezra 5.11; cf. 1.2; 5.12; 7.12), may be a reaction to the self-concept of the Persian kings who regarded themselves rulers legitimated by the god Ahura Mazda, the creator of heaven and earth.

### The religion of the Achaemenids and Jewish religion in the Persian-Hellenistic period

The royal inscriptions of the Achaemenids suggest that they appealed to installation by *Ahuramazda*, the 'god of gods', 'the great god, who created heaven and earth'. As the → *Cyrus Cylinder* (translated in *COS* II, 314–16), the polyglot Darius statue from Susa,[78] inscriptions of Artaxerxes II, and the Persepolis tablets demonstrate, however, the Achaemenids were not monotheists (→ *monotheism*). The question of the Achaemenids' relationship to → *Zoroastrianism* is in dispute in light of the unclear chronology of the supposed 'founder of the religion', *Zoroaster* (the suggested dates range from the 12th to the early 6th centuries BCE) and the complicated state of the tradition of Zoroastrian writings (esp. the Avesta and the older Gathas contained in them, whose oldest manuscripts stem from no earlier than the 13th cent. BCE). The possibility cannot be excluded, however, that Old Testament monotheism, the Old Testament theology of creation and world order, as recorded especially in the → *Priestly Document* (cf. Gen. 1.1–2.3; 5*; 10*), and certain eschatological motifs in → *apocalyptic* literature (dualism, judgement of the world, life after death, Ch.18.4) formed in the encounter with Persian concepts.

P. Lecoq, *Les inscriptions de la Perse achéménide: Traduit du vieux perse, de élamite, du babylonien et de l'araméen, présenté et annoté*. Paris: Gallimard, 1997; R. G. Kent, *Old Persian: Grammar, Texts, Lexicon*. 2nd ed. New Haven, Conn.: American Oriental Society, 1953. Cf. also the excursus on Zarathustra and the Zoroastrian religion.

78. Cf. K. Mysliwiec, *The Twilight of Ancient Egypt* (Ithaca, N.Y.: Cornell University Press, 2000), 147–53.

## 22.5 Notes on the History of Reception

The → *deuterocanonical* books reflect the earliest literary reception of Ezra and Nehemiah. Thus, *Nehemiah* appears in the praise of the fathers in Jesus ben Sirach (Ch. 27), as in the biblical prototype, as the initiator of the post-exilic (→ *exile*) refortification of Jerusalem (Sir. 49.13). 2 Maccabees 2.13 may refer to the Nehemiah Memorandum. *Ezra*, who for some unknown reason is not mentioned in Sirach's praise of the fathers, rose in the Judaism of the Roman period to become the author of the → *apocalyptic* documents of 4–6 Ezra (origins in the 1st/2nd cent. CE). The Babylonian → *Talmud* declares Ezra to be the author of the books of Chronicles and large portions of Ezra (cf. *B. Bat.* 15a; *Sanh.* 93b). In later Jewish tradition, he appears as a paradigmatic scholar and as the second Moses attributed with the introduction of the Hebrew square script and the collection of the → *canonical* writings of the Hebrew Bible after the Exile. In connection with Ezra 7, this notion emanated as far as the historical-critical biblical scholarship of the early 19th century which, among other things, viewed Ezra as the redactor of the → *Pentateuch* (Ch. 5.2).

In particular, the notion of Ezra as a scribe influenced the *history of art*. Thus, since the frescoes in the synagogue of Dura-Europos (ca. 250 CE), one finds portrayals of Ezra with a scroll.

The particular esteem that the book of Ezra-Nehemiah continues to enjoy in Judaism because of its orientation toward identity formation often contrasts with a devaluation in the Christian realm because of the ethnic and religious particularism and rigour it proposes. The work demonstrates its continuing significance with regard to the historical situation in which the book originated as a form of cultural self-preservation in a world growing ever more differentiated in terms of religion, and in view of the conflicts surrounding Jerusalem recurrent throughout history. Finally, the concepts of human sin and God's absolute righteousness articulated in the penitential prayers in Ezra 9 and Neh. 9 point to central aspects of the New Testament. In this regard, but also with a view to the holy city,[79] the book of Ezra-Nehemiah, which concludes the canon of Hebrew scriptures according to the Palestinian tradition, constitutes an important linkage to the New Testament which also refers to Jerusalem, although transformed Christologically and → *eschatologically*, in its final book (cf. Rev. 21.9–22.5).

79. Cf. Isa. 60.1; 62.1-2; Ps. 48; 122; Lam.

# 23

# The Book of Chronicles

(Markus Witte – Translation by Mark Biddle)

## Chapter Outline




Commentaries: S. Japhet (OTL. London: SCM, 1993); idem (2 vols. HTKAT. Freiburg: Herder, 2002, 2003); G. H. Jones (OTG. Sheffield: JSOT, 1992); T. Willi (BKAT 24. Neukirchen-Vluyn: Neukirchener 1991ff.).

P. R. Davies, ed., *Second Temple Studies 1. Persian Period*. JSOTSup 117. Sheffield: JSOT, 1991; J. C. Endres, W. R. Millar and J. B. Burns, *Chronicles and Its Synoptic Parallels in Samuel, Kings, and Related Biblical Texts*. Collegeville, Minn.: Liturgical, 1998; I. Kalimi, *Zur Geschichtsschreibung des Chronisten: Literarisch-historiographische Abweichungen der Chronik von ihren Paralleltexten in den Samuel- und Königebüchern*. BZAW 226. Berlin/New York: de Gruyter, 1995; J. Kegler and M. Augustin, *Synopse zum Chronistischen Geschichtswerk*. BEATAJ 1. 2nd rev. ed. Frankfurt a.M. *et al*: Lang, 1991; R. G. Kratz, *The Composition of the Narrative Books of the Old Testament*. Transl. by J. Bowden. London: T&T Clark, 2005, 9–48; O. Lipschits and M. Oeming, eds, *Judah and the Judeans in the Persian Period*. Winona Lake, Ind.: Eisenbrauns, 2006; J. D. Newsome, Jr., *A Synoptic Harmony of Samuel, Kings, and Chronicles With Related Passages from Psalms, Isaiah, Jeremiah, and Ezra*. Grand Rapids, Mich.: Baker, 1986; J. Weinberg, *Der Chronist in seiner Mitwelt*. BZAW 239. Berlin/New York: de

Gruyter, 1996; T. Willi, *Juda – Jehud – Israel: Studien zum Selbstverständnis des Judentums in persischer Zeit*. FAT 12. Tübingen: Mohr Siebeck, 1995; idem, 'Zwei Jahrzehnte Forschung an Chronik und Esra-Nehemia'. *TRu* 67 (2002): 61–104.
German Classic: M. Noth, *The Chronicler's History.* JSOTSup 50. Transl. by H. G. M. Williamson. Sheffield: Sheffield University Press, 1987.

Jewish tradition refers to the two books of Chronicles as *dibrê hayyāmîm* ('Book of Days'/ → '*Annals*', cf. Esth. 2.23; 6.1; 10.2). The designation 'Chronicles' traces back to Hieronymus' (d. 420) Latin title for the work, *chronicon totius divinae historiae* ('Chronicle of the entire divine history'). The books appear in the → *Septuagint* under the names *prōton/deuteron tōn paraleipomenōn* ('First/Second [Book] of Things Omitted'). The background for this title could be either the observation concerning the literary history of Chronicles that, in comparison to the books of Samuel and Kings, with which it shares major sections of material including wording and order, it has extensive unique material, or the fact that, from the perspective of the history of the → *canon*, Chronicles was included in the Hebrew Bible quite late. There Chronicles originally appeared as *one* book, as the → *Masoretic* → *colophon* following 2 Chr. 36 demonstrates. The division made its way into Hebrew manuscripts of the Bible via the Septuagint.

# 23.1. Biblical Context

| | | |
|---|---|---|
| **I 1–10** | **The genealogical foyer or from Adam to the inhabitants of Jerusalem** | |
| | 1.1–2.2 | From Adam to the twelve sons of Israel/Jacob |
| | 2.3–9.1 | Israel as a people of twelve tribes |
| | 9.2-34 | The pre-exilic inhabitants of Jerusalem |
| | 9.35–10.14 | Saul's heritage (cf. 8.29-40) and story |
| **I 11–29** | **The history of David or of the establishment of the Jerusalem temple** | |
| | 16.7-36 | David's first song of thanksgiving on the occasion of the installation of the Ark (= Ps. 105.1-15; 96.1-13; 106.1, 47-48) |
| **II 1–9** | **The history of Solomon or of the construction of the Jerusalem temple** | |
| **II 10–36** | **The history of the kings of Judah or of the fate of the Jerusalem temple** | |
| | II 10–12 | The division of the kingdom under Rehoboam |
| | II 17–20 | Jehosaphat |
| | II 29–32 | Hezekiah |
| | II 34–35 | Josiah |

| | |
|---|---|
| II 36.1-21 | The last kings of Judah, the destruction of the temple and the deportation |
| II 36.22-23 | Edict of Cyrus concerning the reconstruction of the temple and the return of the deportees (= Ezra 1.1-3) |

Chronicles centres around the history of the Jerusalem temple and of the worship of God celebrated in its environs. The genealogical and geographical lists in 1 Chr. 1–10 lead up to its foundation by David.[1] They center around the lineage of Judah as the ancestor of David and the Judean kings (1 Chr. 2.3–4.23) and the lineage of Levi as the ancestor of Moses, Aaron, the priests, and the Levites (1 Chr. 5.27–6.66 [NRSV 6.1-81]).

***The Levites***, according to the (relatively late) founding legend, especially zealous worshippers of Yhwh (Gen. 34; cf. also Exod. 32), appear in the pre-exilic period (→ *exile*) as itinerant priests at local cultic sites distant from the central sanctuary (cf. Judg. 17.9-10). According to the Deuteronomic law governing priests (Deut. 18), all legitimate priests of Yhwh should be of Levite descent. In the post-exilic period, the theory was developed that all personnel in the Yhwh cult should be Levites. The performance of sacrifice was reserved to the Aaronides (secondarily inserted into the genealogy of the Levites). Cultic functions such as temple singers, doorkeepers, altar assistants, but also didactic activities such as teacher, preacher, judge, and scribe fell to the other Levitical clans – ordered hierarchically. Alongside the → *Priestly Document*, Chronicles and the books of Ezra and Nehemiah played a significant role in the rise of the Levites to functionaries responsible for all aspects of the cult of the Jerusalem temple.

With the edict of the Persian king Cyrus (→ *Edict of Cyrus*), who was commissioned by Yhwh, the God of heaven, concerning the reconstruction of the temple, Chronicles spans an arc from the creation (1 Chr. 1.1) to the pilgrimage to Jerusalem (2 Chr. 36.23). Between these two poles, it traces the history of the Judean monarchy in the form of *genealogies*, *lists*, *historical comments*, *paradigmatic narratives*, and *sermonic speeches* from its beginnings with Saul to its demise under Zedekiah. The weight-bearing framework of

1. 1 Chr. 15.1–17.14; 21.26-22:19; 28.10–29.22.

Chronicles is the chronology of the Jewish kings from David to Zedekiah. Formulaic elements of the royal history include (as in 1–2 Kgs) information concerning (a) the king's age when he began to rule, (b) the length of his reign, (c) his religious behaviour, and (d) his death, burial and successor.

> Uziah was sixteen years old when he began to reign, and he reigned fifty-two years in Jerusalem. His mother's name was Jecoliah of Jerusalem. He did what was right in the sight of Yhwh, just as his father Amaziah had done... Uzziah slept with his ancestors; they buried him near his ancestors in the burial field that belonged to the kings, for they said, 'He is leprous.'e His son Jotham succeeded him. (2 Chr. 26.3-4, 23)

This structure was not applied with strict uniformity; an element is occasionally omitted or other formulaic comments are added.

The central figure of the royal history is *David*, by whom all subsequent kings were measured. He is the ideal warrior, observer of the law, founder of the temple, and liturgist, a new Moses (1 Chr. 21.28-29), or, like him, truly a 'man of God'.[2] Only his son Solomon (2 Chr. 1–9) and the kings Jehosaphat (2 Chr. 17–20), Hezekiah (2 Chr. 29–32), and Josiah (2 Chr. 34–35) approach him. All other kings formulaically receive the predicate describing the degree to which they behaved in accordance with God's commandments. The piety of individual kings and of the people determines the fortune and misfortune of the community. Next to David, *Jehosaphat* (2 Chr. 17–20) figures as an exemplary king, whose military and economic successes were grounded in his impeccable religious policy, attention to the law, and fidelity to Yhwh.

Key theological *statements and motifs* permeate both books. They express the conviction that Yhwh requites justly and acts wondrously to guide history. These statements and motifs include, e.g., the motif of Israel's rest before its enemies,[3] and, in the area of the David-Solomon accounts, the conclusion of the individual segments of narrative with interpretative texts.[4] In addition, there are many internal cross-references to other passages in Chronicles.[5]

2. 2 Chr. 8.14; cf. 1 Chr. 23.14; 2 Chr. 30.16.
3. 1 Chr. 22.9, 18; 23.25; 2 Chr. 13.23 (NRSV 14.1); 14.4-6 (NRSV 14.5-7); 15.15; 20.30; 32.22; cf. also Neh. 9.28.
4. 1 Chr. 12.41 (NRSV 12.40); 17.27; 20.8; 29.29-30; 2 Chr. 1.18; 7.22; 9.29-31.
5. Cf. the list in J. Kegler and M. Augustin, *Synopse*, 26.

# 23.2 Textual Issues and Major Issues in the History of Critical Interpretation

## 23.2.1 The Relationship of Chronicles to the Books of Samuel and Kings

Beginning in 1 Chronicles 10, Chronicles largely follows 1 Sam. 31–2 Kgs 25 in terms of content and outline. At points, it exhibits a *different arrangement* of the material.[6] *Abridgements* of the narrative also occur. After reporting the so-called division of the kingdom,[7] it suppresses the subsequent history of the northern kingdom. For example, there are no counterparts to 1 Kgs 15.25–21.29 or 1 Kgs 22.52 (NRSV 22.51)–2 Kgs 8.16. It also omits accounts that could tarnish the image of the pious David, such as 2 Sam. 11.2–12.25 or 2 Sam. 13.1–21.17. It essentially reduces the broad treatment of Solomon's activity in 1 Kings 1–11 to his function as the builder of the Jerusalem temple (2 Chr. 1–9). In contrast, Chronicles has access to *special material* for the history of the monarchy in the form of narratives and lists that relate primarily to the construction, cultic and military projects of certain kings.

The extensive sections of verbatim agreement between Chronicles and 1 Sam. 31–2 Kgs 25 along with its simultaneous concentration on the history of Judah demonstrates that Chronicles employed the books of Samuel-Kings as a source. Indeed, the narratives that either have no counterpart at all in Samuel-Kings[8] or diverge in elements of their framework from the version in Samuel-Kings[9] demonstrate how Chronicles reshaped the extant tradition literarily and interpreted it theologically.[10]

6. Cf. 2 Sam. 5.1–6.23 with 1 Chr. 11.1-9 + 13.1–16.43.
7. Cf. 2 Chr. 10.1-19 with 1 Kgs 12.1-19.
8. Typical examples are the reports concerning Rehoboam's construction efforts (2 Chr. 11.5-10), Manasseh's repentance (2 Chr. 33.10-13), the Yhwh war under Jehosaphat (2 Chr. 20.1-30), or Hezekiah's regulation of the cult.
9. Cf. the reports concerning Solomon's construction of the temple (2 Chr. 3.1-5 in comparison to 1 Kgs 6.1-28) or concerning → *Josiah's reform* (2 Chr. 35.1-19 in comparison to 2 Kgs 23.21-23).
10. On the problem of the determination of the relationship between Chronicles and 1 Sam.–2 Kgs in terms of the history of tradition and literature, see also D. M. Carr, 'Empirische Perspektiven auf

## 23.2.2 The Changes of Style and Form in Chronicles

The genealogies (1 Chr. 1–9)[11] and lists (cf. 1 Chr. 23–27) that sometimes extend for several chapters, that often interrupt the narrative thread, and that are sometimes even repeated (1 Chr. 8.29-38 = 1 Chr. 9.35-40), indicate that Chronicles is not the product of a single literary effort. In the majority of cases, the lists can be explained more easily as supplementations than as pieces composed by the author of the foundation layer. If the insertions can be traced back to *a systematic redaction*, then one can distinguish between a first chronicler (*chronistic foundation layer*) and a second chronicler (*chronistic supplementary layer*). Otherwise, one can assume incidental expansions of the foundation layer.

## 23.2.3 The Relationship of Chronicles to the Book of Ezra and Nehemiah

Cyrus' call for the reconstruction of the temple that concludes Chronicles (2 Chr. 36.22-23) recurs as the opening of the book of Ezra-Nehemiah (Ezra 1.1-3). This book, with its accounts of the return of the deported Judeans to Jerusalem, of the restoration of the temple and city, and of the resumption of the cult, can be read as a seamless continuation of Chronicles. The compositional interchange between lists, genealogies and accounts, common to the books of Chronicles and Ezra-Nehemiah, the interest in the cult, in the priests and the Levites responsible for it, and in festivals[12] and prayers[13] articulated in both books, and the late variety of the language common to both books already gave rise in nineteenth-century scholarship to the theory of a *Chronistic History* encompassing 1-2 Chronicles, Ezra and Nehemiah.[14] According to its classical statement by Martin Noth (1943), this work traces back to a historian who undertook a thoroughly theological revision of the → *Deuteronomistic History* of the monarchy (Ch. 7.6.3.5) employing various source materials to develop the founding story of the post-exilic community surrounding the Jerusalem temple.

das Deuteronomistische Geschichtswerk', in *Die deuteronomistischen Geschichtswerke* (BZAW 365; ed. M. Witte *et al.*; Berlin/New York: de Gruyter, 2006), 1–17.

11. M. Oeming, *Das wahre Israel: Die 'genealogische Vorhalle' in 1 Chronik 1–9* (BWANT 128; Stuttgart: Kohlhammer, 1990).
12. Cf. 2 Chr. 30; 35; Ezra 3.1-6; 6.19-22; Neh. 8.13-18; 12.27-43.
13. Cf. 1 Chr. 29.10-19; Ezra 9.6-15; Neh. 1.4-11; 9.3-37.
14. L. Zunz, *Die gottesdienstlichen Vorträge der Juden, historisch entwickelt* (Berlin: Asher, 1832; 2nd ed., 1892, repr. Hildesheim: Olms, 1966).

Now, the likely sequence Chronicles – Ezra/Nehemiah has been scarcely attested in any Hebrew manuscript of the Bible.[15] It is apparently, rather, a product of the tradents of the → *Septuagint* through which this order made its way into the → *Vulgate* and finally into modern translations of the Bible. It should be noted that in the Septuagint, the book Ezra α (3 Ezra) still stands between Chronicles and Ezra-Nehemiah (Ch. 22). In addition, there are a series of substantive and theological differences between Chronicles on the one hand and Ezra-Nehemiah on the other, namely, with respect to: (1) the assessment of the Davidic dynasty and the prophets, (2) the attitude toward the inhabitants of the northern kingdom or Samaria, (3) the problem of mixed marriages, (4) the inclusion of miracle stories, (5) the emphasis on divine retribution as a factor that influences history, and (6) the 'autobiographical' sections in Ezra 7–9* and Neh. 1–7*; 12–13*.

While M. Noth attributed these differences to disparate source materials, narrative periods contingent on compositional factors, the Chronicler's tendencies, and post-Chronicler expansions, more recently, these differences have led to a general challenge to the thesis of a Chronistic History. At the moment, scholars propose versions of four basic models of the relationship between Chronicles and Ezra-Nehemiah:

(1) The ground form of Ezra-Nehemiah is regarded as a source for the author of a Chronistic History encompassing the books of Chronicles, Ezra and Nehemiah.
(2) Ezra-Nehemiah is identified as an older work that preceded Chronicles by the same circle of authors ('Chronistic School').
(3) Ezra-Nehemiah is regarded as a later continuation of Chronicles.
(4) The books of Chronicles, on one side, and of Ezra-Nehemiah, on the other, are regarded as primarily independent works, originally transmitted independently and transmitted with their own histories of composition and redaction (Ch. 22.3.2). The parallels between the two compositions, which proponents of this model also recognize, are attributed to a single redaction, or at least comparable redactions, which occurred quite late in either case.

None of these models satisfactorily answer the question as to why, almost without exception, the obvious sequence of the books, Chronicles, Ezra-Nehemiah, is not attested in the Jewish manuscript tradition.

15. Cf., for example, the 15th century manuscript, Sasson 499 (cited by R. Beckwith, *The Old Testament Canon of the New Testament Church and its Background in Early Judaism* [London: SPCK, 1985], 453).

# 23.3 Origins of the Book of Chronicles

## 23.3.1 The Form of Chronicles

These books, like the portrayal of the royal history in Samuel-Kings, belong to the category of *theological historiography* (Ch. 3.2.2). To the extent that Chronicles is based on the books Samuel-Kings, which utilize sources in turn (Chs 7.6.3.4 and Ch. 5), they can be viewed as *tertiary historiography*. At the same time, the rich list material and the references to sources cited heightens their historiographical character in comparison to Samuel-Kings.

> Now the acts of King David, from first to last, are written in the Chronicles of Samuel the seer, and in the Chronicles of Nathan the prophet, and in the Chronicles of Gad the seer (1 Chr. 29.29).[16]

At the same time, the extensive list sections retard the historically oriented course of the narrative. Sometimes the genealogies extend to the time of the author (cf. 1 Chr. 3.19-24). In contrast to the → *deuteronomistic* portrayal of history, the interest of Chronicles shifts to cultic-levitical considerations. By means of the interspersed prayers, the sermonic speeches by individual kings and prophets,[17] references to the direct relationship between piety and historical events, and the stories of royal examples of successful wars, the character of this historiography becomes especially clear: It involves *pragmatic and paradigmatic historiography*, i.e. a portrayal that reflects upon and interprets history with a view to cause and effect. It intends, with the help of examples, to instruct and to offer a model for future behaviour. Based on its inclusion, reconfiguration and interpretation of quasi-canonical material (→ *canon*), Chronicles, like the *deuterocanonical* book of Jubilees or certain paraphrases of the Pentateuch known from → *Qumran*,[18] can also be characterized as a *rewritten Bible*.[19]

16. Cf. similar comments in 2 Chr. 9.29; 16.11; 20.34; 24.27; 27.7; 32.32; 33.18-19, etc.
17. 1 Chr. 29.1-6, 10-19; 2 Chr. 13.4-12; 20.5-12; 29.5-11; 30.6-9.
18. Cf., e.g., 4Q364-367 or 4Q422 (both translated in F. García Martínez and E. J. C. Tigchelaar, *The Dead Sea Scrolls* II, 718–27 and 884–7).
19. Cf. 1 Chr. 21.1 with 2 Sam. 24.1 or Jub. 17.15-18 with Gen. 22.1.

## 23.3.2 The Composition and Redaction of Chronicles

The foundation of the work is an excerpt of the royal history from 1 Sam. 31–2 Kgs 25. Into it were inserted in phases, sometimes source-like, sometimes artificially constructed genealogies, lists concerning the construction, military and cultic measures undertaken by certain Judean kings, and purely chronistic exemplary accounts ('constructed reports').[20] The lists prefixed in 1 Chr. 1–10 are based on genealogical and geographical materials in the books of Genesis, Exodus, Numbers and Joshua and also offer special materials and creations of the Chronicler. This section, like the extensive complex concerning the Levites and the temple personnel in 1 Chr. 15–16 and 1 Chr. 23–27, may trace back, in essence, to later revisions.

Grossly simplified, then, the development may be depicted as follows (cf. Ch. 22.3.2):

| | | |
|---|---|---|
| *Source 1* | *Source 2* | *Source 3* |
| *Samuel-Kings* | *Lists from Gen.; Exod.; Num.; Josh.* | *Lists of unknown origin* |
| ↓ | ↓ | ↓ |

Composition of the Chronistic base layer (ChrBL: 1 Chr. 11–2 Chr. 36*)

| | | | |
|---|---|---|---|
| *ChrBL* | *Source 4* | *Source 5 (2)* | *Source 6 (3)* |
| *1 Chr. 2 Chr.** | *Ezra-Neh.** | *Lists from Gen.; Exod.; Num.; Josh.* | *Lists of unknown origin* |
| ↓ | ↓ | ↓ | ↓ |

Composition of the Chronistic History (ChrH: 1 Chr. 1–Neh. 13)

↓ ↓ ↓

Separation of the books and rearrangement contingent on canonization:

| | | |
|---|---|---|
| ↓ | ↓ | ↓ |
| Palestinian tradition | Babylonian tradition | Alexandrian tradition |
| Chr. [Ps...Dan] Ezra-Neh. | [Ps...Dan] Ezra-Neh., Chr. | [Gen.-2Kgs] Chr., 3 Ezra, Ezra-Neh. |

Whether the → *annals* and prophetic books cited refer to actual extra-biblical sources, or whether they represent a historiographical stylistic technique cannot be determined with certainty. In any case, these citations offer no material information beyond Samuel-Kings.

20. See the presentation in J. Kegler and M. Augustin, *Synopse*, 28–30.

The central problem in the determination of the relationship between Ezra-Nehemiah and Chronicles concerns the determination of the redactional phase in which the sources of Ezra-Nehemiah (Ch. 22) and the foundation of Chronicles were linked with one another. The differences between Ezra-Nehemiah, on the one hand, and Chronicles, on the other, suggest the theory of a pre-chronistic Ezra-Nehemiah composition. The topical and stylistic parallels between Chronicles and Ezra 1–3; 7.1-10; 8–9; Nehemiah 8–9; 12.27-47, in particular, support the assumption of a chronistic redaction of Ezra-Nehemiah. The differences and agreements can be explained most simply with the theory of a pre-chronistic Ezra-Nehemiah composition that was secondarily revised by the Chronicler. Thus, the model of a Chronistic History becomes applicable at a late stage of redaction, after all.

## 23.3.3 The Situation and Function of Chronicles

As evidenced by its dependence on the major collection, Genesis–2 Kings 25 (Ch. 5) and its integration of Ezra-Nehemiah*, the composition and redaction of Chronicles involving its base layer and expansions belong in the middle and the late Persian period (5th/4th cent. BCE). Individual sections point to the Maccabean period (2nd cent. BCE). It is unlikely, however, that Chronicles as a whole stems from as late as the Maccabean period.[21]

Earlier scholarship sometimes saw the separation of the Samaritans from the Jerusalem cultic community and an anti-Samaritan policy as the external motivation for the origins of Chronicles. The separation of the Samaritan Jews from the Jerusalemites was a long process, however, that came to a halt only in the second or first centuries BCE (Ch. 3.2.1). Only Ezra 4–6* and Nehemiah 3–6* deal with the supposed anti-Samaritan conflict based on religious grounds.

The actual motive that led to the composition of Chronicles involved theological engagement with native tradition and the theological interpretation of the current situation. This is especially clear in the appropriation and revision of the deuteronomistic royal history, in the citations from the Torah and the prophets,[22] in the focus on the Jerusalem temple, and in the high value

21. So G. Steins, *Die Chronik als kanonisches Abschlußphänomen: Studien zur Entstehung und Theologie von 1/2 Chronik* (BBB 93; Weinheim: Beltz, Athenäum, 1995).

22. Cf. 1 Chr. 29.18 with Gen. 6.5; 8.21; 2 Chr. 15.2 with Jer. 29.14; 2 Chr. 15.7 with Jer. 31.16; 2 Chr. 16.9 with Zech. 4.10; 2 Chr. 19.6-7 with Deut. 10.17; 2 Chr. 20.17 with Exod. 14.13; 2 Chr. 20.20

placed on prayers, feasts and sacrifices. In view of the deserved loss of their kingdom because of the sins of the kings and the people, it is appropriate to behave according to the Torah of Moses under the protection of the Persian kings and to celebrate properly the worship of God founded by David. The Levites appear as the essential personnel who guarantee the continuity from the Mosaic period through the Davidic era and into the present. They are responsible for both the correct interpretation of the Torah and the correct practice of the cult. Presumably, the composition and redaction of Chronicles also traces back to them or to a circle of scribes closely related to them.

## 23.4 Theology of the Book of Chronicles

The theology of Chronicles has both universalist and particularist orientations (with various nuances in its various literary layers). Alongside the 'primeval' beginning with the genealogy of Adam (1 Chr. 1.1) stands the confession of Yhwh as the creator of heaven and earth (2 Chr. 2.11 [NRSV 2.12]). In contrast to the portrayal in the → *Pentateuch*, the actual period of the foundation of 'Israel' is the era of David and Solomon. The reforms of kings Hezekiah and Josiah represent a second period of foundation.[23] The concentration on the history of the Judean kings corresponds to the concluding call for return to Jerusalem (2 Chr. 36.22-23). Yhwh is both the director of world history, who employs the kings of the Ancient Near East as tools of his action,[24] and the God of the patriarchs of 'Israel' (1 Chr. 29.18) whom he allows to live in blessing by means of his devout kings and whom he admonishes by means of his prophets (2 Chr. 36.15). The latter appear not only as repentance preachers (2 Chr. 12.5-8),[25] but also as inspired writers and interpreters of the Torah.[26]

Israel's history is part of the world history guided by Yhwh and centred in

with Exod. 14.31; Isa. 7.9; 2 Chr. 29.8 with Jer. 29.18; 2 Chr. 32.7 with Josh. 10.25; 2 Chr. 32.8 with Jer. 17.5; 2 Chr. 36.21 with Jer. 25.11-13.

23. H.-S. Bae, *Vereinte Suche nach JHWH: Die Hiskianische und Josianische Reform in der Chronik* (BZAW 355; Berlin/New York: de Gruyter, 2005).

24. Cf. 1 Chr. 5.26; 2 Chr. 36.17, 22.

25. Cf. 2 Chr. 15.1-7; 16.7-10; 19.2-3; 20.37; 21.12-15; 28.9-11.

26. Cf. 1 Chr. 29.29; 2 Chr. 9.29 and 2 Chr. 29.25, resp.

the temple in Jerusalem. The festivals celebrated there (2 Chr. 7.8-10; 30; 35) and the psalms prayed there (1 Chr. 16.7-36) reflect the religious ideal and represent the possibility of direct encounter with God. Chronicles has an → *eschatological* perspective only to the degree that the → *Edict of Cyrus* (2 Chr. 36.23) is open to the future. Chronicles never suggests (not even in 2 Chr. 6.40-42) that in this future a new Davidide will ascend the 'throne of God',[27] as the Chronicler, departing from his exemplar, describes the throne of the Judean kings. Indeed, in view of its profession of the eternal kingdom of God, such does not seem necessary (any longer; 1 Chr. 29.1-20).

## 23.5 Notes on the History of Reception

The earliest forms of the reception of Chronicles may consist of the portrait of David in the Praise of the Fathers by Ben Sira (cf. Sir. 47.8-10), in a fragment from → *Qumran* (4Q118), and in an allusion to 2 Chr. 24.20-21 in Mt. 23.35 (*par.* Lk. 11.51): This comment witnesses indirectly to the placement of Chronicles at the end of the Hebrew Bible, since it reports the first and last murders in the Hebrew Bible (Abel, Zechariah). Together with the picture of David as a psalmist generated in 2 Sam. 1.17-26; 3.31 and Amos 6.5 and extended in the great Psalm scroll from Qumran (11QPs$^a$),[28] the Chronicles' emphasis on David as the founder of temple worship and music influenced depictions of him as a musician in art from late antiquity to the modern era.

As a documentation of Jewish existence, which secured its own origins under the conditions of foreign domination and was oriented toward the essential forms of religious life (prayer, worship, feasts), Chronicles has extreme significance in the overall history of Judaism. With its concluding call for everyone who belongs to God's people to come up (*'ālâ*) to Jerusalem (2 Chr. 36.23), it established the programme for the *Aliyah*, the systematic immigration of Jews to Palestine founded in Zionism at the end of the nineteenth century.[29]

27. Cf. 1 Chr. 17.14; 28.5; 29.23; 2 Chr. 9.8; 13.8.
28. Col. XXVII:2-11: 'And David, Jesse's son, was wise and shone like the sunlight, a writer… and he wrote psalms: three thousand and six hundred… Thus total came to four thousand and fifty. And he spoke all of these through prophecy given him by the Highest' (cf. F. García Martínez and E. J. C. Tigchelaar, *The Dead Sea Scrolls* II, 1178–9.).
29. M. Krupp, *Die Geschichte des Zionismus*, Gütersloh: Gütersloher Verlagshaus, 2001).

# Part VI
# The Apocrypha or Deuterocanonical Books of the Old Testament

(Angelika Berlejung; Jan Christian Gertz; Konrad Schmid; Markus Witte)

Bibliography 1.6 Pseudepigrapha/Apocrypha. Further: O. Kaiser, *The Old Testament Apocrypha: An Introduction*. Peabody, Mass.: Hendrickson, 2004; D. J. Harrington 'Apocrypha, Apocryphal Writings I. Old Testament'. Pages 375–83 in vol. 2 of *The Encyclopedia of the Bible and its Reception*. Berlin/New York: de Gruyter, 2009.

The writings designated as Apocrypha or 'deuterocanonical' books are those which – although for the most part composed in Hebrew or Aramaic – have been included in the → *Septuagint* but not in the Hebrew → *canon* (Ch. 1.2.1). The specific books are Judith, the Wisdom of Solomon (*Sapientia Salomonis*), Tobit, Jesus Sirach (*Ben Sira*) and Baruch, together with the Letter of Jeremiah, 1 and 2 Maccabees, as well as the prayer of Manasseh. Finally there are the so-called additions to the books of Esther and Daniel. The books and 'additions' all originate from the Hellenistic-Roman period (→ *Hellenism*) and assume throughout that the Torah and Prophets are 'canonical'. Even though they were not accepted into the Hebrew Bible, several Apocryphal or → *deuterocanonical* books have had a significant history of reception within Judaism. The Christian traditions have differing approaches to these books. Within the Roman Catholic and Orthodox traditions they form part of the canon and are referred to as 'deuterocanonical' books. In contrast, Protestant traditions were oriented towards the Hebrew Bible resulting in the exclusion of these books from their canon. Luther included them in his Bible editions from 1534 and 1545 as an appendix under the title 'Apocrypha: These are books which are not on the same level as Holy Scripture, but are still useful and good to read.' Accordingly, these books have been termed 'Apocrypha' in the Protestant traditions.[1]

The following sections are devoted to the independent apocryphal books. Discussions of the apocryphal 'additions' are found in the treatments of the canonical books under the headings 'Additions to Esther' (Ch. 20B) and 'Additions to Daniel' (Ch. 21B).

1. In the Roman Catholic tradition the term 'apocrypha' is used for writings which appear in the Septuagint but did not become part of the canon.

# 24

# The Book of Judith

(Jan Christian Gertz – Translation by Peter Altmann)

## Chapter Outline




Commentaries: C. A. Moor (AB 40. Garden City, NY: Doubleday, 1985); E. Zenger (JSHRZ I/6. Gütersloh: Gütersloher Verlagshaus, 1981).

H. Engel, 'Das Buch Judit'. Pages 289–301 in *Einleitung in das Alte Testament*. Studienbücher Theologie 1,1. 7th ed. Ed. E. Zenger *et al*. Stuttgart: Kohlhammer, 2008: Bibliography; C. Rakel, *Judit – über Schönheit, Macht und Widerstand im Krieg: Eine feministisch-intertextuelle Lektüre*. BZAW 334. Berlin/New York: de Gruyter, 2003.


According to the → *Septuagint* the book of Judith belongs to the historical books and is found between the books of Esther and Tobit. There are two quite different forms of the text – the Greek text of the Septuagint and the subsequent ancient translations (Latin, Syriac, Ethiopian and Armenian) which depend upon it on the one hand and the → *Vulgate* of Jerome on the other. Though it includes expansions the Latin version of the Vulgate is about 20 per cent shorter, so that only about half of it agrees with the text found in the Septuagint. An Aramaic version like that mentioned by Jerome in his preface is no longer extant. The Medieval Hebrew copies most likely represent translations of the Vulgate back into Hebrew. The following discussion will be oriented towards the Septuagint, which is usually the basis for modern translations. Some translations, like the German 'Luther Bible', follow the Vulgate, however.

# 24.1 Biblical Context

| | | |
|---|---|---|
| I. 1–3 | **Nebuchadnezzar's Claim to World Dominion and Worship** | |
| | Nebuchadnezzar Defeats Media; Refusal to Give Allegiance to Nebuchadnezzar in the West (1.1-16) | |
| | Plan to Take Vengeance on All Who Deny Nebuchadnezzar's Authority (2.1-13) | |
| | Holofernes Attacks Judah (2.14–3.10) | |
| 4–7 | **Who Is God? Nebuchadnezzar or Yhwh** (LXX: *kyrios*; the Lord) | |
| | Israel's Fear, Cry for Help to Yhwh and Repentance (4.1-15) | |
| | The Speech of the Ammonite Achior before Holofernes about Israel and the Anger of Holofernes (5.1–6.21) | |
| | The Siege of Bethulia; the Distress of Those under Siege and Their Prayers to Yhwh (7.1-32) | |
| II. 8–16 | **Yhwh Alone Is the Ruler of the World and God.** | |
| | Introduction of the God-Fearing, Rich, and Beautiful Widow Judith (8.1–9.14) | |
| | Judith and Holofernes (10.1–13.10) | |
| | Yhwh's Power Made Manifest to the Assyrian Army (13.11–15.14) | |
| | Judith's Song Confessing and Praising Yhwh (16.1-17) | |
| | Epilogue: | Celebration in the Jerusalem Temple (16.18-20) |
| | | Judith Lives Many Years and Israel Lives in Peace During this Time (16.21-25) |

Against the backdrop of a fictive world history, the book of Judith depicts the highly dramatic conflict between the king of Assyria, Nabuchodonosor (Nebuchadnezzar) and Yhwh, the God of both Israel and the world. Nebuchadnezzar attempts to assert his claim that he is the sole ruler of the world and himself the only deity. The book is structured into two main parts: Jdt. 1–7 and 8–16. At the lowest point of the narrative, when Israel stands ready to capitulate and thereby acknowledge Nebuchadnezzar's claims, Judith is introduced through a rhetorical and syntactical resumption of Jdt. 4.1 (Jdt. 8.1, 8).

The first main section may be differentiated into two large parts: first there is a report of Nebuchadnezzar's military success in which his troops reach the Mediterranean coast (Jdt. 1–3). The point of the military expansion is clear – that Nebuchadnezzar's rule of the whole world be acknowledged and that he be worshipped as God (3.8). Whoever only views him as 'a man' (1.11), must expect to experience the wrath of the king and his cumulative military strength. This sets in motion the basic conflict of the book. Israel must remain true to its God Yhwh in this conflict until the end. Thus in the second part (Jdt. 4–7) Nebuchadnezzar's supreme commander, Holofernes, turns his attention to Israel. Israel manages to resist so that Holofernes asks in astonishment, 'Who is this people?' (Jdt. 5.3). The answer is provided by the Ammonite Achior through a retrospective of the history of Israel with its God Yhwh (Jdt. 5.5-21). Achior ends with the recommendation to not attack Israel because Israel can only be conquered when it falls away from its God and willingly bows before Nebuchadnezzar's claim. If instead a military confrontation ensues while Israel holds fast to its God, then Israel can be sure of the help of its God and the attacker can only expect the derision of the world. Holofernes does not listen, and instead praises 'Nebuchadnezzar, the Lord of the whole Earth' (Jdt. 6.4) and gives the command to attack.

The answer to Holofernes' irrationality and the exorbitant claims of his master is given in the second main section in the form of the beautiful, rich, and God-fearing widow Judith. She calls upon the despairing residents of the city Bethulia to stand strong. She offers a profession of faith looking back on Yhwh's actions in Israel's history: 'We know no other God but him, and so we hope that he will not disdain us or any of our nation' (Jdt. 8.20). After praying, she sets out for Holofernes' camp. Once there she masquerades as a defector, though she keeps the food and purity laws. On her fourth night in the camp she cuts off Holofernes' head, which is clouded by drink and lust. With the cry 'God, our God, is with us, still showing his power in Israel and his strength against our enemies, as he has done today!' (Jdt. 13.11), she returns to Bethulia. Overwhelmed by Judith's deed the Ammonite Achior becomes circumcised and is received by the Jewish community as a → *proselyte* (cf. Deut. 23.4). Then the enemy flees and a procession to Jerusalem takes place. The book ends with a notice about Judith's long life and that the Israelites lived in peace from their enemies.

## 24.2 Textual Issues and Major Issues in the History of Critical Interpretation

The original language of the book of Judith is debated. While no ancient Hebrew or Aramaic witnesses to the text exist, the Greek text exhibits stylistic idiosyncrasies that point to the conclusion that it is a translation from a Semitic original. Jerome also makes reference to an Aramaic version that he used as the basis for his version in the Vulgate, which represents not a literal translation but a rather free rendition. Also under discussion are the book's genre and the assessment of its obviously fictional character.

## 24.3 Origins of the Book of Judith

The search for the *original language* of the book cannot be answered decisively since on the one hand idiosyncrasies in the syntax and word choice in the narrative sections, as well as passages incomprehensible likely as a result of translation error speak for a Hebrew or Aramaic original.[2] On the other hand the Greek in the prayers and speeches does not come across like a translation and the citations of and allusions to older books of the Old Testament stem from the → *Septuagint* version rather than the Hebrew text.[3] Most likely the present form of the text can be explained as a revised Greek version of a no-longer-preserved Hebrew book of Judith. Either way the Greek text provides the foundation for work with this book.

The *dating* of the book is complicated by the quite divergent references found in the book (see below, Ch. 24.4). The description of the Israelites' hardship in Jdt. 4.1-15 likely reflects the experiences of 169/8 BCE and the subsequent period when Antiochus IV took Jerusalem and desecrated the temple and then Judas Maccabaeus retook and cleansed the temple (Ch. 4.4.1). Since the coastal road does not belong to Judean territory according to Jdt. 2.28, the capture of this region by Alexander Jannaeus (103–76 BCE) has not yet taken place.[4] The assumption of political authority by the high priests (cf. Jdt. 4.6-8) also points to the Maccabean period. The mention of Judith in 1 Clement (1 Clem. 55:4–5, ca. 96 CE) provides a definite → *terminus ad quem.*

In terms of → *genre*, the book is best described as a Jewish version of the → *Hellenistic* novel, which accounts for both poles of the book's literary form. On the one hand the book is animated by its inner-biblical references and allusions, while on the other hand the depiction of the interactions between Judith and

2. Cf. E. Zenger, Judit, 430–1.
3. Evidence can be found in H. Engel, '"Der HERR ist ein Gott, der Kriege zerschlägt:" Zur Frage der griechischen Originalsprache und der Struktur des Buches Judit', in *Goldene Äpfel in silbernen Schalen* (BEATAJ 20; ed. K. D. Schunk and M. Augustin; Frankfurt: Lang, 1992), 155–68. Citations from the Septuagint appear in Judith's prayer in Jdt. 9.1-9, 14 from Exod. 15.1, 21 (LXX)/ 15.3 (LXX), cf. Jdt. 9.7, 8 and E. Zenger, *Judit*, 494.
4. The Vulgate and German Luther translation have another geographic conception in this verse.

Holofernes corresponds somewhat to the flavour of the Greek-'Oriental' novelistic literature. The impressive artistry of the story appears particularly well in the ambiguity of Judith's speech before Holofernes, in which Judith allows him to believe that she accepts Nebuchadnezzar's claims and is ready to defect, while at the same time announcing Holofernes' gruesome end and professing that only Yhwh is God (Jdt. 10.5-19). The didactic intent, especially visible in the numerous speeches, prayers and historical retrospections, is unmistakable.

## 24.4 Theology of the Book of Judith

The book of Judith draws from the large pool of biblical traditions, especially the historical stories of military events. There are echoes of Abraham's victory over the kings of Mesopotamia (Gen. 14), the Kenite Jael's killing of Sisera (Judg. 4–5), David's victory over Goliath (1 Sam. 17), the portrayal in Chronicles of the deliverance of Jerusalem from Sennacherib in the year 701 BCE (2 Chr. 32.1-23), and the salvation of Jerusalem from Nicanor (1 Macc. 7; 2 Macc. 15). These echoes and a host of 'historical data' weave the portrayal of the book of Judith into a historical framework that is recognizable through and through as fiction. Nebuchadnezzar (605–562 BCE), in actuality the ruler of the Neo-Babylonian Empire and the enemy *par excellence* as a result of the destruction of Jerusalem and the temple, is introduced in the book of Judith as the king of the Assyrian Empire living in Nineveh. His attack on Israel follows the return from → *exile* made possible under the Persians (Jdt. 4.3; 5.18-19). The name 'Holofernes' calls up associations with the Persians, who are mentioned along with the Medes in the final chapter. At the same time, the assaults on the Jerusalem Temple under Antiochus IV beginning in 169/8 BCE (Ch. 4.4.1) are recognizable behind the destruction of the sanctuaries attributed to Nebuchadnezzar. The geographic information is a similar matter. Bethulia ('house of God') probably represents Jerusalem, which is explicitly mentioned elsewhere in the book. All of this must have been apparent to the book's original audience – assuming that they knew their Bible, their own time, and their land. The historical (and geographical) fiction therefore has little to do with the ignorance of an author that did not properly research his topic, but instead displays the theological intentions of the author who 'intends to portray the totality of [Israel's] historical experience within a single event'.[5] In this way

5. E. Zenger, *Judit*, 436.

the narrative concerning Nebuchadnezzar and Yhwh, Holofernes and Judith becomes universalized so that its assertions take on timeless significance. Thus it proclaims the one God Yhwh who in the course of history has proven to act for the good of the land and its residents even in the face of overpowering enemies – as long as Israel fulfils its obligations and unreservedly trusts God who hates iniquity (Jdt. 5.17). It is easy to overlook that the book, despite its warlike character and its depiction of violence, draws an explicitly unwarlike picture of God: 'For Yhwh is a God who crushes wars' (Jdt. 16.2).

## 24.5 Notes on the History of Reception

Even though the book of Judith was not received in the → *canon* of the Hebrew Bible, it still gave birth to a long tradition in the Jewish → *haggadah.* As a result of its proximity to the books of Maccabees it is closely associated with the tradition of the → *Hanukkah* celebration that commemorates the rededication of the Temple under Judas Maccabaeus (164 BCE; cf. Jdt. 16.31 in the Vulgate [missing in the LXX]). Other receptions of the book are quite ambivalent. Feminist interpretation notes both the comparable dislocation of typical gender roles in the book and the androcentric perspectives.[6] These divergent perceptions mirror the fact that interest in the book of Judith is obviously mainly due to its mix of themes covering the divine, power, sex, and death – a mix that has fascinated people at all times. A 'dash' of 'Orientalism' apparent in the contrast between Judith and Holofernes adds to this fascination: The pretty, rich, God-fearing Jewess Judith lives in seclusion wearing widow's clothes. She only beautifies herself and changes the black garb for elegant clothes and expensive accessories (Jdt. 10.3-4) as part of her plan to kill Holofernes. Holofernes, the Oriental leader of a murdering and land destroying army is depicted in contrast as the embodiment of spoilt luxury. He receives Judith while being served by a eunuch and resting on a bed under 'a canopy that was woven with purple and gold, emeralds and other precious stones,' (Jdt. 10.21). This motif has been accordingly taken up by art, literature, and film history. Gustav Klimt's 'Judith and Holofernes' (1901) belongs to the most famous portrayals of Judith as a femme fatale who beheads Holofernes.

6. Cf. C. Rakel, *Judit*; M. Stocker, *Judith: Sexual Warrior: Women and Power in Western Culture* (New Haven: Yale University Press, 1998).

# 25

# Wisdom of Solomon (Sapientia Salomonis)

(Markus Witte – Translation by Mark Biddle)

## Chapter Outline



Commentaries: D. Georgi (JSHRZ III/4. Gütersloh: Gütersloher Verlagshaus, 1980); H. Hübner (ATD.A 4. Göttingen: Vandenhoeck & Ruprecht, 1999); C. Larcher (3 vols. EBib.NS 1. Paris: J. Gabalda, 1982–1985); D. Winston (AB 43. New York: Doubleday, 1979); H. Engel (NSK.AT 16, Stuttgart: Katholisches Bibelwerk: 1998).

M. V. Blischke, *Die Eschatologie in der Sapientia Salomonis*. FAT II/26. Tübingen: Mohr Siebeck, 2007; J. J. Collins, *Jewish Wisdom in the Hellenistic Age*. OTL. Louisville, Ky.: Westminster John Knox, 1997, 178–221; M. Kepper, *Hellenistische Bildung im Buch der Weisheit: Studien zur Sprachgestalt und Theologie der Sapientia Salomonis*. BZAW 280. Berlin/New York: de Gruyter, 1999; M. Neher, *Wesen und Wirken der Weisheit in der Sapientia Salomonis*. BZAW 333. Berlin/New York: de Gruyter, 2004; A. Passaro and G. Bellia, eds, *The Book of Wisdom in Modern Research*. Deuterocanonical Literature Yearbook. Berlin/New York: de Gruyter, 2005; L. G. Perdue, *Wisdom Literature: A Theological History*. Louisville, Ky.: Westminster John Knox, 2007, 267–324.

The book takes its name from the super- or subscription, *sofia salōmōnos*, found in many Greek Bible manuscripts; the expanded title *panaretos sofia salōmōnos* ('The All-Virtuous Wisdom of Solomon') appears occasionally. The attribution to Solomon results from the identification of the speaker in

6.24-25;[1] 7.1; 9.7-8. The tradition of the wise Solomon (cf. 1 Kgs 3–10 and its derivative Sir. 47.12-17) stands in the background. The book itself contains neither the name Solomon nor any personal name whatsoever. In the Latin tradition, it appears under the simple designation *liber sapientiae* ('Book of Wisdom').

In the → *Septuagint, Sapientia (Wis)* appears after the book of Job (Ch. 14) and before the book of Sirach (Ch. 27). In the → *Vulgate*, which contains the Wisdom of Solomon in the form of the old Latin translation (→ *Vetus Latina*) from the second century CE since Hieronymus did not translate the book, it occurs as the last book of the Solomonic writings after the Song of Songs (Ch. 17) and before the book of Sirach.

# 25.1 Biblical Context

| | | |
|---|---|---|
| **1.1–6.21** | **Admonition** (*logos protreptikos*) **to righteous living** | |
| | *1.1 Introductory admonition* | |
| **6.22–11.1** | **In praise** (*enkōmion*) **of wisdom as the guide for living** | |
| **11.2–19.22** | **Seven analogies** (*synkriseis*) **to God's justice in the Exodus and the wilderness wandering** | |
| | 11.2-14 | First analogy |
| | 11.15–15.19 | Theological excursus |
| | 16.1–19.9 | Second through seventh analogies |
| | 19.10-22 | Epilogue |
| | 19.22 | *Concluding doxology* |

Part I (1.1–6.21) calls for the love of righteousness. Part II (6.22–11.1) offers a hymn of praise to wisdom. Part III (11.2–19.22) describes the activity of God in Israel's history. Part I and part II can be subsumed under the heading of divine righteousness. Part I looks forward to the last judgement thereby dealing with the transcendental aspect of divine righteousness, while part II describes God's retribution in Israel's history thereby emphasizing its immanence.

1. The various editions and translations of Wisdom of Solomon differ from one another in the enumeration of the verses. Citations here will follow the critical edition of the Septuagint by J. Ziegler (2nd ed.; Göttingen: Vandenhoeck & Ruprecht, 1980).

Internally, parts I and II exhibit a concentric structure (part I: 1.1-15 || 6.1-21; 1.16–2.24 || 5.1-23 centred around 3.1–4.20; part II: 6.22-25 || 9.1-18; 7.1-22a || 8.2-21 centred around 7.22b–8.1 and with an appendix in 10.1–11.1). Two theological excurses (11.15–12.27; 13.1-15, 19) have been inserted into the series of seven analogies (11.2–19.9) on the punitive and protective behaviour of God in history. The first and last verses of the book can be understood as the framework and the hermeneutical key to the overall work. The first calls the 'rulers of the world' and, with them, all humanity to love God (1.1); the latter confesses God's help for his people, help that spans time and space (19.22).

*The admonition to live a righteous life (Wis. 1.1–6.21):* Part I is held together formally by the address to rulers (1.1 *par.* 6.1) and topically by the theme of righteousness (1.1, 8, 15; 2.11; 5.6; 8.7). Wisdom appears as a counterpart to righteousness (1.1 *par.* 6.21). Both come from God and lead to him, who gives immortality to the just and, therewith, participation in his deity (3.4; 4.1; 5.15). This section centres around the contrast between the fates of the godless and of the just that climaxes in the portrayal of the eschatological judgement by the righteous, who are protected by God, of the godless (3.1–4.20). The just can also be called 'sons of God' (2.18; cf. Ps. 2.7; Mt. 27.43). The central theological motif of this first section is the concept of God as creator, who loves the life of his creatures (cf. 11.26), and as judge, who expects of his creatures a life of righteousness (cf. 12.12). The concentration on life leads to the climactic statement that God did not create death (11.13-15), but that it came into the world through the 'jealousy of the devil' (2.24; cf. *Vita Ad Ev* 10–17). Human beings, *per se*, were created for imperishability (Wis 2.23), which is evidence of the *imago dei* (Gen. 1.26-27). In the background of the description of the godless (1.16–5.23) stands a *carpe diem song* (2.1-20), such as is known from Qoheleth (Ch. 18.2). Here, the Wisdom of Solomon may explicitly dispute the preacher Solomon who calls for the enjoyment of life. It may also be a more general critique of a vulgar Epicureanism.

**Epicureanism** refers to the philosophical stream in the Hellenistic-Roman period (→ *Hellenism*) that traces back to the Greek philosopher Epicurus of Samos (341–270 BCE). The philosophy of Epicurus centres on an ethic that aims at the good fortune (*eudaimonía*) of the individual ('individual Hedonism'). By rational consideration of pleasures and self-control, the wise should be able to attain imperturbable ⇨

serenity (*ataraxia*). Death ultimately does not concern the wise because that which dissolves has no perception, and whatever has no perception does not concern people (Epicurus, *Principle Doctrine* 2). According to Epicurus, the gods also live in untroubled self-enjoyment – they are eternal and immortal, but care about nothing; i.e., there is neither the providence (*pronoia*) of the gods for the world and humanity proposed by the Stoa nor fate (*heimarmenē*). Epicurus denied transcendent powers as explanations for the world and the assumption that human souls are immortal. With a view to the question of → *theodicy* (Ch. 14.3.2), Lactantius (*De Ira Dei*, 13:19) reports: 'Epicurus says: "Either God wants to remove evil from the world but cannot, in which case he is weak; or he can but does not want to, in which case he is evil; or he cannot and does not want to, in which case he is weak and evil and is not God at all; or he can and wants to; where does evil come from then and why does he not remove it?"'

G. S. Kirk, J. E. Raven and M. Schofield, eds, *The Presocratic Philosophers: A Critical History with a Selection of Texts*. 2nd ed. Cambridge: Cambridge University Press, 1983; A. A. Long and D. N. Sedley, eds, *The Hellenistic Philosophers*. 2 vols. repr. Cambridge: Cambridge University Press, 1997–98.

*The praise of wisdom as the guide to life (Wis. 6.22–11.1):* The programmatic question 'What is wisdom?' (6.22) introduces part II and the profession of the activity of wisdom in history (11.1) concludes it. Sections of report (7.1-22a || 8.2-21) alternate with hymnic passages (7.22b–8.1|| 9.1-19; 10.1–11.1) within the second part. In terms of the history of literature and tradition, the second section of the book demonstrates most clearly the continued development of Jewish wisdom concepts. Thus, for one, it extrapolates the poems on personified wisdom in Prov. 8, Job 28 and Sir. 24 (Ch. 15.2). In Wis. 9.4, wisdom is even God's throne companion (*paredros*). For another, the book describes wisdom with terms from Platonic and Stoic philosophy. Like the Stoic pneuma, wisdom appears as the spirit that permeates everything (7.22b; 8.1).[2] In Platonic terminology, the book characterizes wisdom as 'the image of divine goodness' (7.26).[3] At the same time, wisdom continues to be related to the God of Israel (9.1). She is a gift of this God to 'his friends' (7.27) and finally reveals herself to those who recognized Israel's God as the God of the whole world. At the same time, wisdom appears as a principle active in history to guide the just and

2. Cf. J. v. Arnim, ed., *Stoicorum Veterum Fragmenta* II (Stuttgart: Teubner, 1902 [1964]), Nr. 1009.
3. Cf. Plato, *Politeia* 508b-c; *Timaios*, 92c.

to punish the unjust. The series of examples concerning the theology of history in 10.1–11.1 clarifies this role of wisdom. Without mentioning the individual names of the figures (the technique of *antonomasia*), this series summarizes the stories of Adam, Cain, Noah, Abraham, Lot, Jacob, Joseph and Moses under the theme of the deliverance of the just. By means of omitting the names of individual figures, the series takes the form of a → *typology* or *paradigm*, i.e.: Wisdom acts anew at all times and in all places to preserve the just in ongoing distress. At the same times, the series in 10.1–11.1 fulfils a → *parenetic* and *paracletic function.*

*The analogies concerning God's righteousness (Wis. 11.2–19.22):* The third part of the book offers an interpretation of the Egyptian plagues, of the Exodus from Egypt, and of Israel's wandering in the wilderness (cf. Ps. 78.5-55; Jub. 48.5-19). The section is based on Exod. 7–Num. 21. This form of interpretation has parallels in → *midrash*, a method preferred in post-biblical Jewish exegesis for interpreting texts as illuminated retellings. The author does not adhere to biblical chronology, however, but mixes individual accounts based on perspectives of motif and theme. Employing the stylistic technique of *synkrisis* (*distinctio*), i.e. a juxtaposition of opposites, known from Greek rhetoric,[4] he describes the just activity of God by way of contrasts. The comparisons all move toward clarifying God's just activity in the world.

Two theological excurses are embedded between the first and second *synkrisis* (11.2-14 and 16.1-4). They contain, first, a reflection on the nature and justice of God (11.15–12.27), and, second, encouragement to worship Yhwh as the sole God without idols (13.1–15.19). The polemic against idol worship (*idolatry*) is based on a corresponding critique of idols in → *Deutero-Isaiah* (cf. Isa. 44.9-20) and on the 'prohibition against images' (Exod. 20.4-5 *par.* Deut. 5.8-9; 4.16-19). The call for the exclusive worship of Yhwh corresponds to → *deuteronomistic* and deutero-Isaianic → *monotheism*,[5] but competes with the emphasis on the creative power and uniqueness of Zeus in → *Hellenistic* philosophy, especially in the Stoa, or of Isis in Hellenistic Isis theology.

4. Cf. H. Lausberg, *Handbook of Literary Rhetoric: A Foundation for Literary Study* (ed. D. E. Orton, R. D. Anderson and G. A. Kennedy; transl. M. T. Bliss and A. Jansen; Leiden/Boston: Brill, 1998).
5. Wis. 12.13; cf. Deut. 4.35; 6.4-5; Isa. 44.6.

The mother-goddess, **Isis**, who was already venerated in ancient Egypt, ascended together with Sarapis in Hellenistic times, starting from Ptolemaic Egypt, to become a universal goddess beloved throughout the Mediterranean region and praised in many hymns and aretalogies as creator, ruler of the world, source of justice, founder of culture, and saviour (*sōteira*).

J. Alvar, *Myth, Salvation and Ethics in the Cults of Cybele, Isis and Mithras*. Religion in the Graeco-Roman World 165. Leiden/Boston: Brill, 2008.

In the context of the second theological excursus (13.1–15.19), one finds a section on the recognition of God as the 'one who is' (*ho ōn*, 13.1; cf. Exod.$^{LXX}$ 3.14) from the works of creation, which, with a view to a 'natural theology', has close affinities with Pauline theology (cf. Rom. 1.20-32, but also Acts 17.22-31).

## 25.2 Textual Issues and Major Issues in the History of Critical Interpretation

The Wisdom of Solomon exists only in its Greek form and in translations based on it. Dependence on the historical and prophetic traditions of the Old Testament, parallels to the wisdom books (Prov., Eccl., Sir.), and affinities with Platonic and Stoic concepts point to a significant historical and intellectual distance from the era of Solomon (965–926 BCE). Formal and topical differences between the three parts (1.1–6.21; 6.22–11.1; 11.2–19.22) point to the book's long history of development. At the same time, cross-references support the assumption of a well-planned composition. Contemporary scholarship debates whether it traces back to one author who worked on his book for a long period,[6] to a group of authors,[7] or redactors working in succession.[8]

6. C. Larcher, *Sagesse* I, 119; H. Engel, *Das Buch der Weisheit* (Neuer Stuttgarter Kommentar. Altes Testament 16; Stuttgart: Katholisches Bibelwerk, 1998), 30–5.

7. D. Georgi, *Weisheit*, 394-395; S. Schroer, 'Das Buch der Weisheit', in *Einleitung in das Alte Testament* (ed. E. Zenger), 400–1.

8. M. V. Blischke, *Eschatologie*, 41–4.

'I am Isis . . .
I gave laws to the people and determined by law what none may alter. . .
I separated the earth from heaven.
I showed the stars their way.
I ordered the path of the sun and the moon. . .
I showed people the sacred things (*myēseis*).
I taught veneration of the images of the gods.
I built the temple of the gods.
I am the Lady of war. . .
I am the Lady of lightning. . .
I am called the lawgiver. . .
Everything is subject to me.
I free the captives. . .
I conquer fate. . .'

(From the Isis aretology of Kyme. For a translation in full see R. S. Kraemer, ed., *Women's Religions in the Greco-Roman world: A Sourcebook*. Oxford: Oxford University Press, 2004, 456–7. )

# 25.3 Origins of the Wisdom of Solomon

## 25.3.1 The Form of the Book

The thoroughly poetic book, i.e. it is written in *Parallelismus membrorum*, exhibits many of the primary wisdom forms (Ch. 15.3). Specifically, one finds sayings (*aphorisms*), admonitions, poems to wisdom, hymnic elements, prayers, discourses, legal descriptions, discussions, midrash-like considerations of history, parables, definitions, and lists. The differences in form between the three major sections may indicate that the author worked with extant school texts. In the context of biblical books, Wisdom of Solomon most closely parallels *Proverbs* (Ch. 15). With a view to the history of Greek literature, the Wisdom of Solomon can be characterized as a *logos protreptikos*, i.e. a 'prospectus', namely for wisdom. The forms of the panegyric (*enkōmion*) in 6.22–11.1 and the comparative juxtaposition (*synkrisis*) in 11.2–19.9* also stem from the sphere of Greek literature. As was already the case with Proverbs (Ch. 15) and Ecclesiastes (Ch. 18), the *instructions for life* known primarily from Egypt offer formal parallels in Near Eastern literature.

Wisdom of Solomon is grounded, on one side, in biblical tradition and, on the other, is influenced by → *Hellenistic* education (*paideia*). Biblical tradition is the source of: (1) the monotheistic orientation which is not even abandoned in the personification of wisdom, (2) the creation theology tendency, (3) the allusions to the Solomon tradition, (4) the depiction of the role of wisdom in history from Adam to Moses, which adheres to the outline of history found in the → *Pentateuch* and which has formal and traditional affinities with Old Testament historical psalms,[9] and (5) the *midrash-like* exegesis of the Exodus tradition. The following represent extensions or reinterpretations of biblical, especially wisdom, traditions: (1) the interpretation of the suffering of the innocent as a test,[10] (2) the portrayal of wisdom as an entity emanating from God,[11] and (3) the attempt to solve the problem of theodicy → *eschatologically*.[12] All three of these reinterpretations are also based on the combination of biblical and pagan ideas.

Examples of the Hellenistic education of the author of the Wisdom of Solomon include:

(1) the use of the terms *stoicheion* ('element', 7.17; 19.18), *pronoia* ('divine providence/provision,' 6.7; 13.16; 14.3; 17.2),[13] and *syneidēsis* ('conscience,' 17.11);
(2) the concept of the *pneuma noeron* ('spirit of reason,' 7.22);
(3) the interpretation of wisdom as the teacher of the four cardinal virtues of justice, prudence, insight, and courage (8.7; cf. Plato, *Nomoi*, 631c);
(4) the characterization of the body as an 'earthly tent' (9.15; cf. Plato, *Phaidon*, 81c);
(5) the idea of the creation of the world from 'formless material' (11.17; cf. Plato, *Timaios*, 51a);
(6) the notion of the pre-existence of the soul (8.19-20; cf. esp. Plato, *Phaidon*); and
(7) the explanation of belief in God in 13.2-9 and 14.15-21.

Presumably, commonalities in terminology and motif between the Wisdom of Solomon and Stoic and Platonic vocabulary are based on a common philosophical anguage. The familiarity with the vocabulary of Homer and the Greek tragedies (Aeschylus, Sophocles, Euripides) stems from a Hellenistic education.[14]

9. Cf. Ps. 78; 105–106; 135–136; Neh. 9; 1 Macc. 2.52-61; Sir. 44–49, 50.
10. Cf. Wis. 2.12-20 with Job 5.17.
11. Cf. Wis. 7.25; 9.4 with Prov. 8.22; Job 28; Sir. 24.
12. Cf. Wis. 2.23; 3.1 with Dan. 12.1-3; Ps. 49.16 (NRSV 49.15); *1 En.* 22; see also D. Winston, 'Theodicy in the Wisdom of Solomon', in *Theodicy in the World of the Bible* (ed. A. Laato and J. C. deMoor; Leiden: Brill, 2003), 525–45.
13. Cf. Dan.[LXX] 6.19; 2 Macc. 4.6; 3 Macc. 4.21; 5.30; 4 Macc. 9.24; 13.19; 17.22.
14. M. Kepper, *Bildung*, 95.

## 25.3.2 The Composition and Redaction of the Book

As in the case of the books of Proverbs (Ch. 15) or Ecclesiastes (Ch. 18), the Wisdom of Solomon represents a → *pseudepigraphic* work that was only attributed to Solomon in the course of later tradition. In any case, Solomonic authorship was already disputed in the early Church. In his prologue to the Solomonic literature, Hieronymus refers to the opinion that the Jewish philosopher *Philo of Alexandria* (b. ca. 25 BCE)[15] may have written the book. The fact that the speculation on the logos and the allegory typical of Philo's work does not appear in the book of Wisdom contradicts Philonic authorship. The Wisdom of Solomon shares with the work of Philo presumed origins in Alexandria and the openness of Judaism to Greco-Hellenistic ideas.

Wisdom of Solomon is an authentically Greek work. Theories that it may trace back to a Hebrew prototype, at least at points, have not prevailed in scholarship.

Linguistic, historical and intellectual grounds suggest a *date* for the Wisdom of Solomon in the period between the last quarter of the first century BCE and the second half of the first century CE.

Although the book consists of three quite different sections in terms of form and tradition and the three parts treat wisdom differently, the uniform diction and the continuous arc of the composition – apart from the excurses in 11.15–15.19 – argue for single authorship.

## 25.3.3 The Situation and Function of the Book

The Wisdom of Solomon represents the most important document from Hellenistic Judaism to have found its way into the Old Testament. The Hellenistic municipal culture of Alexandria shaped its *historical milieu*. Since the beginning of Ptolemaic rule in 301 BCE (Ch. 4.4), continuously growing number of Jews in Alexandria had, as was customary in Hellenistic cities, the status of a *politeuma*, i.e. a self-governed colony of foreigners. In Caesar's time (100–44 BCE), an ethnarch and later a council of elders (*gerusia*) led the Jewish *politeuma*.[16]

15. *The Works of Philo: Complete and Unabridged. New Updated Version* (transl. C. D. Younger, foreword by D. M. Scholer; 8th ed.; Peabody, Mass.: Hendrickson, 2006).

16. According to Philo (*In Flaccum* 43), one million Jews lived in Egypt in the first century CE.

Wisdom's familiarity with the concepts of the philosophical schools of the Stoa (Ch. 27.3.2), Platonism and Epicureanism (see above), with Hellenistic dedicatory inscriptions and hymns, epics, consolations, burial inscriptions and mystery religions[17] can be explained against the background of Alexandrian culture. The polemic against the animal cult (11.15-16) and the broad portrayal of the Egyptian plagues (11.2-14; 16.1–19.17) also support origins in Alexandria. Wis. 19.13-17 describes the phenomenon of xenophobia. Scholarship debates whether it reflects the specific experience of the Jewish population in Alexandria or whether it involves a literary topos.

The Wisdom of Solomon first addresses Jewish readers in the → *diaspora*. The address to the 'rulers of the earth' (1.1) and 'kings' (6.21) is a literary device explained in relation to the configuration of the book as a fictive discourse by King Solomon. The Wisdom of Solomon assumes significant knowledge of the Bible on the part of its readers. It presents its Jewish addressees with their own religion as the true wisdom. At the same time, it intends to encourage those who are disadvantaged in Alexandria because of their Jewish ancestry. Thus, the Wisdom of Solomon is an apology for the Jewish faith and theology, on one hand, and a paraclesis for the righteous, whose suffering is interpreted as a divine test, and who are supposed to be comforted eschatologically with the prospect of judgement for the dead and immortality.

## 25.4 Theology of the Wisdom of Solomon

At the centre of discourse about God in the Wisdom of Solomon stands the notion of *God as creator* and *God as director of history*. This God, who can also be addressed as 'Father',[18] is – as the Wisdom of Solomon extrapolates deuteronomistic and deutero-Isaianic → *monotheism* – the sole, all-powerful and all-effective God (6.7). In the context of Old Testament wisdom literature, the Wisdom of Solomon shares its orientation toward creation theology with Proverbs (Ch. 15.4), the book of Job (Ch. 14.4), and Ecclesiastes (Ch. 18.4). The integration of the theme of Israel's history into wisdom thought links

17. Cf. Wis. 14.22-25 and the term mystēria in 2.22; 6.22.

18. Wis. 2.16; 14.3; cf. Sir. 23.1; Isa. 63.16; 64.7 (NRSV 64.8); 1QH 17.35; 4Q372 Fragm. 1.16.

the Wisdom of Solomon with Ben Sirach (Ch. 27) and certain psalms (cf. Ps. 78; 105-106; 135-136). While for Ben Sirach, the divine glory represents the connection between creation and history, in the Wisdom of Solomon, it is the divine wisdom and justice. Both values, wisdom and justice, appear in the Wisdom of Solomon as God's modes of action, on one hand, and as the way to human immortality, on the other. The → *eschatology*, which transcends that implicit in canonical wisdom literature (→ *canon*), indicates the kinship of Wisdom of Solomon with the books of Daniel (Ch. 21) and *1 Enoch*, but also with wisdom texts found at → *Qumran* that contain a mixture of wisdom and eschatological elements.[19]

More clearly than all the other biblical books, the Wisdom of Solomon proposes the concept of the immortality of the soul of the righteous (3.1; cf. Ps. 49.16 [NRSV 49.15]) and of its rapture (4.10-11). It thereby extends the biblical concept of communion with God that survives death, on the one hand (cf. Ps. 73.24 taken together with Gen. 5.24; Sir. 44.16), and adapts ideas from the Greek environment, on the other (Ch. 18.4). At the same time, with its concept of the immortality of the soul and judgement for the dead, the Wisdom of Solomon approaches the New Testament interpretation. The statements concerning the *Holy Spirit* (1.5-7; 9.17; cf. Ps. 51.13 [NRSV 51.11]; Isa. 63.11f.), which, like wisdom, appears as a mode of God's activity, also approaches a New Testament motif.

The contextuality of the theology of the Wisdom of Solomon is particularly evident in its engagement with Hellenistic religions, especially in Egypt. Thus, the notion of the personified wisdom of Israel's God also responds to Hellenistic *Isis theology* (cf. Sir. 24). The polemic against *idolatry* (13.10-19) is also a Jewish reaction to the (→ *theriomorphic*) god figures encountered in Egyptian religion. The appeal to the rulers of the world to love justice (1.1) and to recognize their sovereignty as God-granted (6.3), and the critique of the divine veneration of images of rulers (14.16-21) are also a Jewish response to the ruler cult established in the Hellenistic monarchies and expanded by the Roman emperors (Ch. 4.4.2).

19. Cf. 1Q26; 4Q185; 4Q299–301; 4Q415–418 + 4Q423; see J. J. Collins, 'The Mysteries of God: Creation and Eschatology in 4QInstruction and *The Wisdom of Solomon*', in *Jewish Cult and Hellenistic Culture* (JSJSup 100; Leiden/Boston: Brill, 2005), 159–80.

# 25.5 Notes on the History of Reception

In rabbinic Judaism, the Wisdom of Solomon did not attain canonical significance because of its late origins (and its composition in Greek?). In contrast, the book gained entry into the canons of the Roman Catholic and Orthodox churches via the → *Septuagint*. The Wisdom of Solomon is one of the Old Testament books that exhibit the clearest relationship to the New Testament. The most prominent citations include Wis. 7.26 in Hebr. 1.3 (cf. 2 Cor. 4.4 and Wis. 7.22-24 in Hebr. 4.12-13). The expansion of the fourth Servant Song (Isa. 52.13–53.12) undertaken by the Wisdom of Solomon in 2.10-15 underwent further extension in the New Testament in the application of the motif of the just sufferer to Jesus.[20] Common origins in the history of tradition may explain parallels between the Wisdom of Solomon and Paul (cf. Rom. 1.18-32 with Wis. 13.1-18). The decisive difference between the Wisdom of Solomon and Paul consists in the fact that Paul does Jewish theology under the impression of the Christ event. In reference to the reinterpretation of the discourse about God's wisdom and righteousness in the Wisdom of Solomon, this means that God's wisdom and righteousness took form in Jesus Christ and that whoever trusts in Christ participates in God's wisdom and righteousness (1 Cor. 1). The Christological hymn in Col. 1.15-20 is a Christological reinterpretation of Wis. 7.22-23 and Prov. 8.

Even though Protestantism counts the Wisdom of Solomon among the → *apocrypha*, Luther devoted an extensive foreword to the book in his preface to the German Bible (1534/1545) in which he judged it to be a successful interpretation of the first commandment.

In *Christian art*, the notion of personified divine wisdom has been particularly influential (Ch. 15.5).

Finally, the Wisdom of Solomon plays an important role in modern proposals for feminist theology since Wisdom is understood as the feminine side of the biblical God. In the face of all justified objections to a patriarchal image of God and to a patriarchal theology, one must assert

20. Of the many references, cf. only Isa. 53.4 with Mt. 8.17; Isa. 53.5-6 with 1 Pet. 2.24-25; Isa. 53.7-8 with Acts 8.32-33 and Isa. 53.11-12 with Rom. 5.19.

with the Wisdom of Solomon that God is always more than the human intellect is able to comprehend and that any unilateral definition of God in *one* mode of discourse contradicts the transcendent nature of God, itself.

# 26

# The Book of Tobit (Tobias)

(Jan Christian Gertz – Translation by Peter Altmann)

## Chapter Outline



Commentaries: B. Ego (Pages 875–1007 in JSHRZ II.6. Gütersloh: Gütersloher Verlagshaus, 1999); J. A. Fitzmyer (Commentaries on Early Jewish Literature. Berlin/New York: de Gruyter, 2003); H. Schüngel-Straumann (HTKAT. Freiburg: Herder, 2000).

B. Ego, '"Heimat in der Fremde": Zur Konstituierung einer jüdischen Identität im Buch Tobit.' Pages 270–83 in *Jüdische Schriften in ihrem antik-jüdischen und urchristlichen Kontext*. JSHRZ. Studien 1. Ed. H. Lichtenberger and G. S. Oegema. Gütersloh: Gütersloher Verlagshaus, 2002; H. Engel, 'Das Buch Tobit'. Pages 278–88 in *Einleitung in das Alte Testament*. Studienbücher Theologie 1,1. 7th ed. Ed. E. Zenger *et al*. Stuttgart: Kohlhammer, 2008; M. Hallermayer, *Text und Überlieferung des Buches Tobit*. Deuterocanonical and Cognate Literature Studies 3. Berlin/New York: de Gruyter, 2008; G. Veravits and J. Zsengellér, eds. *The Book of Tobit: Text, Traditions, Theology*. JSJ Supplement Series 98. Leiden: Brill, 2005.

According to the → *Septuagint* the book of Tobit belongs to the historical books, generally placed between Judith and the books of Maccabees. The book has been passed on in various versions whose inner relationship is quite complicated (see below, Ch. 26.2). The Greek text appears in three different recensions: a short version ($G^{I}$), a long version ($G^{II}$), and a 'mixed version' ($G^{III}$). The → *Vulgate* (Tobias) offers a unique text complex. The following comments focus on the longer Greek version, which is the version the NRSV is based on.[1]

## 26.1 Biblical Context

| | |
|---|---|
| **1.1–2** | **Book Superscription** |
| **1.3–3.17** | **Exposition** |
| | A Self-Presentation and Prayer of Tobit in Nineveh (1.3–3.6) |
| | B Report about Sarah in Ecbatana and Sarah's Prayer (3.7-15) |
| | C The Granting of Both Prayers. The Sending of the Angel Raphael (3.16-17) |
| **4.1–14.1** | **Main Body: Tobias' Trip** |
| | A Tobit's Testament and Instructions for His Departing Son (4.1-21) |
| | B Preparation for the Trip and Hiring of Azariah/Raphael as Travel Companion (5.1–6.1) |
| | C Trip from Nineveh to Ecbatana (6.2–7.9a) |
| | D Marriage Celebration in Ecbatana (7.9a–10.13) |
| | C′ Trip from Ecbatana to Nineveh (11.1-18) |
| | B′ Raphael Reveals His Identity and Bids Farewell (12.1-22) |
| | A′ Tobit's Song of Praise (13.1–14.1) |
| **14.2–15** | **Epilogue** |
| | A Tobit's Testament, Death, and Burial (14.2-11) |
| | B Tobias' Later Life and Death (14.12-15) |

Through the example of Tobit from the tribe of Naphtali, his wife Anna, their son Tobias, and his wife Sarah, the artistically arranged book narrates a story of godly assistance in the midst of a life determined by both piety and suffering. The special attraction of this book is its juxtaposition and interweaving of scribal teaching, → *wisdom* instruction, and fable-like features. They together make the book into both a serious and entertaining narrative from the Hellenized East. After the book's superscription (1.1-2) the three-part exposition begins with the self-presentation of Tobit (1.3–2.14). Tobit reports on his youth, his journey from Israel into exile, and his alternating exilic fortunes between wealth and poverty, ascent and persecution. Having

1. For the book of Tobit NRSV follows the form of the Greek text found in codex Sinaiticus. Only where this text is defective, it is supplemented and corrected by other Greek manuscripts.

shown himself to be one of the few who kept the commandments of the God of Israel already in the time of his youth (1.3-9), he exhibits extraordinary piety also in → *exile* (1.11-18). He does not even abandon his piety after going blind (2.10). When his wife, however, berates him for both his fate and his attitude (2.14), he prays for death (3.1-6). After this prayer the story leaves Tobit in Nineveh to report on a situation in Ecbatana where a certain young Jewess 'Sarah' is praying 'at the same time'. At this point the narrative elegantly changes from the 'I'-form to the third person. Sarah is threatened by a jealous demon responsible for the loss of her previous seven husbands on their wedding nights. She is accused of murder by her maidservant (3.7-15). God hears both prayers and sends Raphael, one of the seven angels that stand before God's glory (12.15), to banish the demon and heal Tobit (3.16-17). The main body of the book, which is in the form of a ring composition, tells of the trip that Tobias' impoverished father sends him on to bring back money that he had once lent in far-off Media (4.1–14.1).[2] Tobias leaves after receiving a farewell warning, offering a prayer, and promising both to bury his parents (who seem on the verge of death) when he returns and to live a life pleasing to God. He sets out on his trip with his dog at his side (6.2; 11.4) and with the hired guide Azariah, in whose person the angel Raphael has hidden himself. On the way a large fish attacks Tobias by the river Tigris, but Azariah ('Yhwh helps')/Raphael ('God heals') saves him and advises him to take the heart, liver and gall bladder and keep them as remedies for casting out demons and healing blindness (in fact what is described here is identical with eye cataract). In Ecbatana he spends the night at Sarah's parents, and her father recognizes Tobias as the son of his brother ($G^{II}$), or rather of his cousin ($G^{I}$). Through Azariah/Raphael's intercession, Tobias successfully asks for Sarah's hand in marriage, defeats the demon, and returns after a 14-day wedding celebration with opulent gifts to his home (Azariah/Raphael had in the meantime collected the money). Once near Nineveh Tobias and his dog go on ahead and heal his father. When they try to compensate Azariah/Raphael with half of the new fortune, the angel makes his true identity known and disappears, while father and son extol and praise God. The main body ends with Tobit's song of praise, which serves as a counterpoint to his words of warning at the farewell to his son at the beginning. The song of praise extols the wonderful acts of God, prompting thanks and repentance, and flowing into an → *eschatological* song of praise for Jerusalem. The epilogue tells of Tobit's later years,

2. Cf. Engel, 'Tobit', 280–1.

his testament, as well as both his and his son's deaths at the respective ages of 112 and 117 ($G^{I}$: 127; 14.2-15).

# 26.2 Textual Issues and Major Issues in the History of Critical Interpretation

The book of Tobit has been passed on in a number of versions that in places diverge considerably. Placing these different versions in an order that explains how one version derived from another proves only partially successful. The oldest text manuscripts come from → *Qumran:* the single Hebrew (4Q200) and four Aramaic (4Q196–199) witnesses are all quite fragmentary. They come from the period between 100 BCE and 50 CE and include less than 25 per cent of the total content of the book. Even if the Hebrew version is generally considered a translation from Aramaic, this does not provide any certainty about the original language of the book. The oldest complete text comes from the Septuagint and exists in three different versions. The bulk of the manuscripts bear witness to a short form ($G^{I}$). R. Hanhart views this form as a secondary smoothing out of the long version ($G^{II}$), which, however, is almost only attested in Codex Siniaticus.[3] There are points of similarity between $G^{II}$ and the Old Latin version as well as the Qumran manuscripts – however, this does not necessarily make $G^{II}$ a translation of the 'original text'. A further version of the Septuagint offers something of a revised mixed form ($G^{III}$).

With respect to the textual history it hardly appears possible to reconstruct either a Hebrew or Aramaic 'original version' of the book of Tobit. In addition, at least the Greek tradition displays a tendency towards smoothing out and shortening the text. As a result statements about the compositional history of the book can only be offered with great reservation, since source- or redaction-critical arguments assume knowledge of the (non-extant) original text. It is therefore problematic to evaluate findings such as a change of perspective, an excess of motifs, scribal citations, or narrative elements that do not develop the plot or appear 'dispensable' as signs of textual growth. Something of a different case may be made for passages displaying a strong orientation towards Jerusalem (1.4-8; 13.1–14.1). Thus in $G^{II}$ the one praying in 13.1–14.1 is not yet identified, which could support the argument that it is

3. R. Hanhart, *Text und Textgeschichte des Buches Tobit* (MSU 17; Göttingen: Vandenhoek & Ruprecht, 1984).

a later → *Zion* Theology insertion or an earlier formed text taken up by the author of the book of Tobit.

## 26.3 Origins of the Book of Tobit

Besides the assumption of a redaction oriented towards Jerusalem, it is nearly impossible to make statements about the composition-historical growth of a supposed original form of the book. It is instead important to investigate the origins and usage of the received motifs, the → *genre*, as well as the provenance and dating of the book.

*Traditions and Motifs:* The book of Tobit makes liberal use of the richness of motifs found in earlier biblical books.[4] The portrayal of history is oriented to the nature of the portrayal in Kings; the speeches are laced with Deuteronomistic expressions and conceptions (→ *Deuteronomism*). There are direct allusions to prophetic tradition (2.6: Amos 8.10; 14.4-5: Nah. 3.7; Zeph. 2.13; Mic. 5.5; Isa. 10.5, 12; 14.25). The story of Tobit's suffering and the reaction of his wife that questions Tobit's righteousness is modelled after the frame story from Job (2.11-14: Job 2.7-10). Tobias' wedding with Sarah resembles that of Gen. 24 even in the details. The 'Law of Moses' plays a special role (1.8): under the conditions of the → *diaspora* the marriage from one's relatives (1.9; 4.12-13, etc.), the food laws (1.10–11), honouring one's parents (3.10; 5.1), the burial of the dead, especially of one's parents (1.17-20; 4.3-4; 14.10-13) are reckoned essential regulations. In addition the book of Tobit also calls on extra-biblical fables and fairytale motifs. In the version of the fairytale 'bride of the demon' closest to the book of Tobit the ghost of the dead subdues a demon that attempts to kill the hero on the wedding night as a way of giving thanks for his burial. In the book of Tobit the ghost of the dead is replaced by an angel of Yhwh sent by Yhwh in response to the hearing of a prayer. Another fairytale motif is that of the 'big fish' that provides the ingredients for a magic potion against demons as well as for medicine (6.2-9; 8.1-3; 11.4-13).

*Genre:* As a whole the book of Tobit can be described as a didactic → *wisdom* narrative. It takes up a number of contemporary literary forms with didactic purposes such as the testament (4; 14) and the instructions by an angel (12.6-11). In addition there are prayers and hymns of thanksgiving that characterize the piety and attitude of the protagonists. The 'I-form' of Tobit's

4. Cf. S. Weitzman, 'Allusion, Artifice, and Exile in the Hymn of Tobit', *JBL* 115 (1996): 49–61.

self-presentation has its closest contemporary analogies in the 'biographical' tomb inscriptions, the Ahiqar novella, and the Nehemiah memoir.

*Date and Social Background:* The numerous historical and geographic inaccuracies – Nineveh is located on the east side of the Tigris like Ecbatana (different in 6.2b), 'Naphtali' was deported under Tiglath-Pileser III (1.1-2: Shalmaneser V), Sargon II was successor to Shalmaneser V (1.15: Sennacherib), in spite of his old age, it is impossible that Tobit was born before the fall of Samaria (1.9-10) and then lived to see the fall of Nineveh in 612 BCE (14.15) – show clearly that the writing of the text did not take place in the same era as the narrated story. Instead the destructions of Samaria (722/1 BCE) and Jerusalem (587/6 BCE) lay far in the past. The world of the author is shaped by the → *diaspora,* which spread throughout the eastern Mediterranean to Persia. While there is an expectation that a return to Jerusalem will occur in the end times (13.3-18 [NRSV 13.3-17]), this is not a conceivable option – neither for the author nor for the protagonists of the book (14.12-15). The motif of the persecution of the Jews and the prohibition of burying executed Jews (1.18-20; 2.8) likely mirrors the experiences of conflicts in the Maccabean period. This and the Qumran finds suggest the development of the book occurred in the 2nd cent. BCE, while possible earlier stages of the text may come from the end of the Persian period or the early → *Hellenistic* decades. Possible locations are Palestine or the eastern diaspora. Since the defeated demon flees to Egypt (8.3) it is unlikely that the book originated in the Alexandrian diaspora. If the thoroughgoing references to Jerusalem are all seen as secondary, then it is possible to entertain the idea that Tobit originally represented a resident of Tebez in the region of Samaria. He was then only later made into a resident of a region loyal to the Jerusalem Temple. If this is the case then one could imagine earlier Samaritan stages of the text from the circle of the Tobiad dynasty that were later oriented towards Jerusalem.[5]

## 26.4 Theology of the Book of Tobit

In a superscription-like summation of his self-presentation Tobit names the central values of a pious life: truth, righteousness and charity (1.3). Each of these terms is attributed to God himself (3.2, 11) and serves at the same time

5. Cf. J. T. Milik, 'La Patrie de Tobie', *RB* 73 (1966): 522–30; M. Rabenau, *Studien zum Buch Tobit* (BZAW 220; Berlin/New York: de Gruyter, 1994), 149, 189.

as a guide for human action. Taking up these terms and corresponding themes repeatedly the book of Tobit unfolds them in the speeches and actions of the protagonists. In this manner the book develops a rich ethic of imitation, in which human action and divine direction correspond to each other according to the benchmarks of truth, righteousness and mercy. With the reception of the motif of the righteous sufferer, Tobit also shows that this correspondence is not always evident. Thus Tobit, who suffers as much as he is righteous, instructs his son to live piously and promises him a successful life (4.6-7), even though his own fortune seems to contradict this advice (4.7b according to $G^{II}$; 4.19 according to $G^{I}$; different in the Vulgate). The end of the book confirms Tobit's faith in the righteousness of God, a righteousness that can be believed in confidently in spite of the circumstances of the moment. The pious will be rescued from all hardship in the end. On the way one should preserve oneself by observing the Torah, reading the prophetic books, and following the wise instruction of the fathers, which includes sticking to the Golden Rule: 'And what you hate, do not do to anyone!' (4.15 according to $G^{I}$). The prayers for good leading to the praise of God have special significance in all this. The one praying can be sure that God – more precisely: his seven angels that then bring them to God – hear and respond to the prayers.

## 26.5 Notes on the History of Reception

The reasons why the book was not received into the Hebrew → *canon* can hardly be illuminated, though one possibility could be its differences from the rabbinic → *halakhah*. The text history suggests that the book was well loved even in the pre-Christian era and had already been produced in various translations. The New Testament has no explicit citations from the book of Tobit, but there are points of contact, such as the Golden Rule (cf. Mt. 7.12, cf. Lk. 6.31) and the call to joyful almsgiving (cf. Mt. 6.1-4; Lk. 6.30; 2 Cor. 9.7). In early Christianity the book of Tobit became canonical in the face of opposition. The motif of the guardian angel led to the book's entrance in the visual arts, literature, and many forms of everyday piety.

# 27

# Jesus Sirach (Ben Sira)

(Markus Witte – Translation by Mark Biddle)

## Chapter Outline




Commentaries: G. Sauer (ATD.A 1. Göttingen: Vandenhoeck & Ruprecht, 2000); J. Schreiner (Sir 1–24. NEchtB 38. Würzburg: Echter, 2002); P. W. Skehan and A. A. Di Lella (AB 39. New York: Doubleday 1987); B. M. Zapf (Sir 25–51. NEchtB 39. Würzburg: Echter, 2010.

P. C. Beentjes, *'Happy the One who Meditates on Wisdom' (Sir. 14,20): Collected Essays on the Book of Ben Sira*. CBET 43. Leuven: Peeters, 2006; J. J. Collins, *Jewish Wisdom in the Hellenistic Age*. OTL. Louisville, Ky.: Westminster John Knox, 1997, 23–111; R. Egger-Wenzel (ed.), *Ben Sira's God*. BZAW 321. Berlin/New York: de Gruyter, 2002; J. Marböck, *Weisheit und Frömmigkeit: Studien zur alttestamentlichen Literatur der Spätzeit*. ÖBS 29. Frankfurt a. M.: Lang, 2006; idem, *Gottes Weisheit unter uns. Zur Theologie des Buches Sirach*. Herders Biblische Studien 6. Freiburg: Herder, 1996; F. V. Reiterer, *'Alle Weisheit stammt vom Herrn...': Gesammelte Studien zu Ben Sira*. BZAW 375. Berlin/New York: de Gruyter, 2007; idem *et al.*, *Zählsynopse zum Buch Ben Sira*, Fontes et Subsidia ad Bibliam Pertinentes 1. Berlin/New York: de Gruyter, 2003; G. G. Xeravits/J. Zsengellér, eds, *Studies in the Book of Ben Sira*. JSJ Supplements 127. Leiden/Boston: Brill, 2008; A. Passaro/G. Bellia, eds, *The Wisdom of Ben Sira: Studies on Tradition, Redaction, and Theology*. Deuterocanonical Literature Studies 1. Berlin/New York: de Gruyter, 2008.

The Hebrew manuscript B ($H^B$) cites the author's name in 50.27 and 51.30-31 as 'Shimon (Simon), the son of Yeshua (Jesus), the son of Eleazar, the son of Sira' but in 51.30e as 'Shimon, the son of Yeshua, the son of Sirach'. The prologue to the Greek translation refers to the author simply as 'Jesus'. The Greek translation of 50.27 speaks of 'Jesus, the son of Sirach Eleazar, the Jerusalemite'. In the rabbinic tradition, the book appears under the designation 'Ben Sira', in the Greek tradition under '(Wisdom of) Jesus (the son of) Sirach', and in the Latin tradition under the name 'Ecclesiasticus' ('teacher of the church').[1]

In the → *Septuagint* and in the → *Vulgate*, which includes Sirach in the form of the old Latin translation (→ *Vetus Latina*) from the second century CE since Jerome did not translate the book, Sirach stands in final position among the wisdom literature, after the *Sapientia Salomonis* (Ch. 25).

# 27.1 Biblical Context

The book exhibits a very complicated textual history (see Ch. 27.2), which also impacts the portrayal of its structure, content and theology. The discussion of the biblical context deals with the Greek version (G), since it offers the oldest complete version of the book. One must take into account the fact that in the *Greek tradition* a *rearrangement of pages* has already happened in the area of chs. 30–36 so that the enumeration of the chapters differs between the Hebrew (H), Latin (La), Syriac (Syr) versions, on the one hand, and the Greek versions, on the other. Meanwhile, the versification differs significantly.[2] The 'correct' sequence of the content of chapters in G is: 1.1–30.24; 33.13b–36.16a; 30.25a–33.13a; 36.16b–51.30.

H 30.24 = G 30.25
H 30.25 = G 33.13b; H 31 = G 34; H 32 = G 35; H 33.1-16a = G 36.1-16a;
H 33.16b-33b = G 30.25a-40b; H 34 = G 31; H 35 = G 32; H 36.1-13a = G 33.1-13a[3]
H 36.16b = G 36.16b

1. In contrast to the Greek designation for the book of Qoheleth (Ch. 18), *ecclēsiastēs*.
2. In this discussion, the citations will largely follow the enumeration in the critical edition of the Septuagint by J. Ziegler (2nd ed.; 1980). F. V. Reiterer (*Zählsynopse*) provides a careful comparison of the different enumerations in the versions and translations.
3. Regarding the leap from 36.13a to 36.16b, see F. V. Reiterer, *Zählsynopse*, 194.

| | | |
|---|---|---|
| **[0** | **Prologue to the Greek translation]** | |
| **1.1–2.18** | **Introduction: Origin and Character of Wisdom** | |
| | *1.1–2.18* | *Appeal to* ***fear God*** *and trust God* |
| **3.1–6.17** | **Ethical admonitions** | |
| | *4.11-19* | *The doctrine of* ***wisdom*** |
| **6.18–14.19** | **Ethical admonitions** | |
| | *6.18-37* | *The search for* ***wisdom*** |
| | *10.19-24* | *Admonition to* ***fear God*** |
| **14.20–23.27** | **Ethical admonitions** | |
| | *14.20–15.10* | |
| | *21.6, 11* | *The gifts of* ***wisdom*** |
| **24.1–33.18** | **Reflections on the work of Wisdom in the World** | |
| | *24.1-29* | *Praise of* ***wisdom*** *and her Identification with the* ***Torah*** |
| **33.19–39.11** | **Reflections on the truly wise** | |
| | *36.1-22* | *Prayer for Zion's deliverance* |
| **39.12–43.33** | **Reflections on the order of creation and God's justice** | |
| | *40.18-27* | *Admonition to* ***fear God*** |
| | *42.15–43.22* | *Praise of God's glory* |
| **44.1–50.24** | **The praise of the fathers** | |
| **50.25–51.30** | **Conclusion** | |

The book does not evidence a well-planned literary structure. Instead, it is a collection of wisdom aphorisms, lectures, prayers, and poems that are sometimes arranged thematically, and sometimes stand in sequence with no points of connection. More extensive and more carefully structured units appear in the second half of the book.[4] Essential structural characteristics include: (1) poems to wisdom, (2) the hymn to God as creator (42.15–43.33), and (3) the self-contained section in the praise of the fathers (44.1–50.24). A song to wisdom (ch. 1) and a call to fidelity to God in difficult times (ch. 2), on one end, and a multi-part conclusion in 50.25–51.30, on the other, serve as a framework. If one follows internal structural elements such as the *introduction of instruction formula* (3.1; 33.19; 39.13; → *Lehreröffnungsformel*) or the direct address to the student (3.17; 6.18), the book divides into nine large blocks. At the centre stands the passage in which wisdom praises herself in ch. 24. Individual sayings and admonitions to fear God constitute a kind of refrain.[5]

4. Sir. 24.1-29; 38.24–39.11; 42.15–43.33; 44.1–49.16; 50; 51.13-30.

5. Sir. 1.11–2.18; 10.19-24; 19.20; 21.6, 11; 40.18-27.

*The prologue of the Greek translation:* The prologue written by the grandson of Ben Sira, which is also provided by the La, but not the Syr, contains important information concerning history (see Ch. 27.3.3), the history of the canon, and the text. First, the prologue refers to an existing collection of the sacred texts of Judaism (→ *canon*) consisting of the Torah, the Nevi᾿im and 'other writings'. Second, it incorporates the wisdom that flows from the Torah into the → *Hellenistic* ideal of education.[6] Third, it mentions the difficulties pertinent to the translation of a Hebrew work (→ *Septuagint*).[7]

*Poems to wisdom (Sir 1.1-10; 4.11-19; 6.18-37; 14.20–15.10; 24.1-29):* Small poetic compositions in which Ben Sira describes the origin, nature and function of wisdom occur at key junctures in the book. Parallels to Job 28, Prov. 8, and Bar. 3 characterize wisdom as a personified, cosmic entity, created by God (1.9). On one hand, like the Egyptian → *Ma᾿at*, she represents the order of creation, on the other, she is a gift for those who fear/love God (1.10), i.e. for those who keep God's commandments as formulated in Deuteronomy (Ch. 7.2). At the same time, Ben Sira takes pains to connect wisdom with the fear of God as proposed in the book of Proverbs (Ch. 15). Thus, Ben Sira also agrees that the fear of God is the beginning of wisdom (1.14; cf. Prov. 1.7; 9.10). Wisdom and the fear of God stand in a dialectic relationship: whoever fears God obtains wisdom; whoever is wise, fears God. In this way, wisdom enables one to find meaning in life (4.11-19). Consequently, the admonitions in Ben Sira call for the lifelong pursuit of wisdom.[8] This pursuit of wisdom corresponds to the study of the Torah (14.20; cf. Ps. 1). In other words, Ben Sira equates wisdom, the fear of God, and the Torah.

This equation is particularly clear in Sir. 24. The hymn in praise of personified wisdom characterizes the encounter between pagan Hellenistic and Jewish traditions present in Sirach. Thus, Ben Sira appropriates the → *genre* of the *Isis aretalogy* (Ch. 25.1) popular especially in Hellenized Egypt, on the one hand, and the → *deuteronomistic* Torah theology (cf. Deut. 4; 30), on the other. Sirach 24 applies to wisdom features attributed in Hellenistic

6. Sir. 24.30-34; 38.24-39:11; 51.13-30.

7. Instead of this (original) prologue by the grandson, the Greek → *Minuscule* 248 (13th cent.) contains a foreword that depicts the process of the transmission of the work entitled 'Wisdom of Jesus son of Sirach'. N. Peters (*Das Buch Jesus Sirach oder Ecclesiasticus* [EHAT 25; Münster: Aschendorff, 1913], 4-5.) offers a translation of this second prologue.

8. Sir. 6.18-37; 51.13-30.

veneration of Isis to the goddess. Yet, while Isis appears as an independent goddess, the wisdom Ben Sira discusses is a creation of God incarnate in the Torah (24.23-27).

*Reflections on human behaviour in family and society (Sir. 3.1–23.27; 25.1–39.11*):* Wisdom and the fear of God take form in the lives of individuals when they behave in family and society in keeping with Jewish tradition. Thus, broad sections of the book involve the admonition of individuals and the inculcation of Jewish social ethics. In this regard, Ben Sira stands in line with Old Testament wisdom that was articulated from its beginnings as knowledge concerning proper orientation in society and as training in proper behaviour (Ch. 15.2). At the same time, the specific admonitions and the array of themes addressed in Ben Sira indicate that he wrote in a period of cultural upheaval. In keeping with the → *Decalogue* (Exod. 20.12; Deut. 5.16), Ben Sira calls for social and intellectual *respect for parents* (Sir. 3.1-18; 7; 27-28). Ben Sira contrasts the individualism blossoming in the Hellenistic period, which introduced a dissolution of traditional social bonds, with the ideal of *friendship*.[9] The warnings against careless *involvement with women* that Ben Sira addresses to the young man (9.1-9) should also be seen against the background of Hellenism. Here, too, as in the comparable warnings against the strange woman in Prov. 7, concern for the loss of one's Jewish identity ultimately stands in the background. The aphorisms concerning shameful behaviour (41.1–42.14) also result from the same intention. Finally, Ben Sira admonishes a just harmony between *poor and rich* (13.1–14.19). Other examples of Ben Sira's 'modern' thought influenced by Hellenism are the references to behaviour at a banquet (*symposion*, 31.12–32.13), the value he places on educational travel (34.12-13; 39.4), and his assessment of physicians (38.1-15).

*A prayer for the deliverance of → Zion (Sir. 36.1-22):* In the style of a communal psalm of lament and petition (Ch. 13.3.2.2), Ben Sira prays for the deliverance of Israel.

In comparison with traditional communal laments in the Old Testament, this prayer exhibits four peculiarities: (1) the consistent address to God as the universal and sole God (vv. 1, 5, 22);[10] (2) the omission of a complaint

9. Sir. 6:5-17; 9.10; 12.8-9; 19.8-17; 22.19-26; 27.16-21; 37.1-6; see F. V. Reiterer, ed., *Freundschaft bei Ben Sira* (BZAW 244; Berlin/New York: de Gruyter, 1996).

10. Isa. 45.5, 7, 22-24; 43.10-11; 44.6.

> concerning the current distress with characteristic questions concerning the reason, the goal, and the endurance of suffering. In contrast, the prayer concentrates exclusively on the petition; (3) the use of → *eschatological* terms (v 10)[11] which bring the prayer into proximity with → *apocalyptic* texts (cf. Mk 13.31-32); and (4) a focus on the 'holy city/Jerusalem' and Zion, which appear as the centre of Israel and ultimately of the whole world (vv. 18-19).[12]

*The hymn of praise to God the creator (Sir. 42.15–43.33):* The hymnic description of God's works has its nearest parallels in Pss 8; 19; 31; 104; Job 37; 38–39; and Gen. 1. The attribution of all the works of creation to the word of God[13] is based on the tradition of creation by the word as encountered in the Bible in Gen. 1; Ps. 33.6; 147.15 (cf. also 4Q381, frg. 1.3)[14] and in the Egyptian realm, for example, in the 'memorial of Memphite theology' (9th/8th cent. BCE), where the god Ptah acts in creation through his 'word'.[15] The theological accent of the hymn praising the creator in the statement that the sole God is one and the same throughout the ages (42.21) and that God 'is all' (43.27) extrapolates deuteronomistic and deutero-Isaianic → *monotheism* (Deut. 4.35; Isa. 44.6) and represents the biblical counterpart to the Zeus hymn by the Stoic *Cleanthes* (304–233 BCE).[16]

*The praise of the fathers (Sir. 44–50):* Through the examples of select individuals, Ben Sira offers an overview of the history of Israel from antiquity to his time. A prologue in which Ben Sira describes the importance of historical memory (44.1-15) introduces the sequence of individual portraits unique in the area of biblical literature.[17] A section praising Enoch (44.16; 49.15), whom ancient Judaism considered an ancient, just and wise figure who experienced the unusual fate of being raptured to God (cf. Gen. 5.24 and the Jewish Enoch literature, esp. *1 En.*), frames the main section (44.16–49.16). The text then treats, in sequence, Noah, Abraham, Isaac, Jacob/Israel, Moses, Aaron, Phineas, Joshua, Caleb, the judges,

11. Cf. Dan. 8.19; 11.35; 12.9-13; Hab. 2.3; Ps. 102.14 (NRSV 102.13).
12. Cf. Sir. 24.11; 49.6; Isa. 61–62; Tob. 13.10-17; 11QPsa XXII:1–15 (translated in F. García Martinez andE. J. C. Tigchelaar, *The Dead Sea Scrolls* II, 1176–7).
13. Sir. 42.15; 43.5,10[11],26[28]; cf. Sir. 39.17.
14. Translated in F. García Martínez and E. J. C. Tigchelaar, *The Dead Sea Scrolls* II, 754–5.
15. Translated in *COS* I, 21–3.
16. J. C. Thom, *Cleanthes' Hymn to Zeus: Text, Translation and Comments* (Studien und Texte zu Antike und Christentum 33; Tübingen: Mohr Siebeck, 2005).
17. Cf. Neh. 9; 1 Macc. 2.51-60; 3 Macc 6.4-8; 4 Macc. 16.15-23; 18.9-19; Wis. 10.1–11.1.

Samuel, Nathan, David, Solomon, Rehoboam, Jeroboam, Elijah, Elisha, Hezekiah, Isaiah, Josiah, Jeremiah, Ezekiel, Job (only in H, Syr), the twelve prophets, Zerubbabel, Joshua ben Jehozadak, Nehemiah, Joseph, Shem, Seth, Enosh (only in H, Syr) and Adam. The focus is on the priestly figures Aaron and Phineas as the predecessors of the high priest, Simon, with whom the composition concludes (50.1-24). Structural elements of this biographically arranged portrayal of history are, first, the motif of the → '*covenant*' (*bĕrît*, *diathēkē*) and, second, the motif of divine glory (*kābôd*, *doxa*) with which some fathers were equipped.[18] The praise of the fathers is based on the → *Pentateuch* and the prophets and already presupposed the Dodekapropheton (cf. 49.10). In all, the praise of the fathers has an exemplary and → *doxological* character.

*The conclusion (Sir. 50.25–51.30):* The book ends with six (in H) or four (in G) disparate pieces:

1. a statement of disapproval of the neighbours of ancient Judah (50.25-26);
2. a first → *colophon* (50.27-29) contains information about the nature and function of the book and about its author;
3. an individual song of thanksgiving (51.1-12, Ch. 13.3.2.3);
4. a hymn attested only in $H^B$ (51.12a-o, Ch. 13.3.2.4);
5. a wisdom song (51.13-30) permits Ben Sira to tell in the first person singular of his pursuit of wisdom and his activity as a 'scholar' in a 'house of learning' (*byt mdrš*, v. 23);
6. a second → *colophon* (51.30e-g, only in $H^B$) offers yet a second indication of the author and a concluding doxology.[19]

Furthermore, 'Solomon's prayer' known from 1 Kgs 8.22-30 (*par.* 2 Chr. 6.14-21) occurs in the La/Vg as 52.1-13.

18. Sir. 44.17; 44.20-22; 45.15; 45.24-25; 50.24 (only in H).

19. Sir. 44.2; 44.19; 45.20; 45.23; furthermore, in G 46.2; 48.4; 49.16; 50.5.

# 27.2 Textual Issues and Major Issues in the History of Critical Interpretation

## 27.2.1 The Problem of the Transmission of the Text

Sirach was originally written in Hebrew, but, for centuries, was available only in Greek, Latin and Syriac, and the dependent Arabic and Persian translations. The authenticity of the Hebrew fragments that have been discovered in the Cairo Genizah since 1896 have been confirmed by discoveries at → *Qumran* and Massada.

### The Cairo Genizah

A genizah (from the Hebrew *gānaz* 'to enclose') involves a space for storing Jewish documents and ritual objects no longer employed for liturgical use because of some damage. A genizah was often adjoined to a synagogue. The Cairo Genizah, which belonged to the Ezra Synagogue of the Jewish Kairite sect ('readers of scripture'), is one of the most famous genizahs. Approximately 200,000 fragments of Jewish documents have been found here. In addition to the fragments of Sirach mentioned, discoveries there include: (1) a *Wisdom Document* (WCG) that has affinities at points with the book of Qoheleth (Ch. 18) and Sirach, but stems from no earlier than the Middle Ages;[20] (2) fragments of *Aquila's Greek translation of the Bible* (2nd cent. CE); (3) the *Damascus Document* (CD = Covenant of Damascus), an Essene document from the 1st cent. BCE, also attested through discoveries from Qumran, which speaks of a 'community of the new covenant' (cf. Jer. 31);[21] and (4) *Piyyutim*, i.e. religious poems. The majority of the finds from the Cairo Genizah are located today in the libraries of the universities of Cambridge (www.lib.cam.ac.uk/Taylor-Schechter/) and Princeton (www.princeton.edu/~geniza/).

S. C. Reif, 'The Discovery of the Cambridge Genizah Fragments of Ben Sira: Scholars and Texts'. Pages 1–22 in *The Book of Ben Sira in Modern Research*. BZAW 255. Ed. by P. C. Beentjes. Berlin/New York: de Gruyter, 1997.

Currently, approximately 68 per cent (as compared to the scope of the Greek text) of the Hebrew text, distributed among nine different manuscripts,

20. H. P. Rüger, *Die Weisheitsschrift aus der Kairoer Geniza: Text, Übersetzung und philologischer Kommentar* (WUNT 53; Tübingen: Mohr Siebeck, 1991).

21. F. García Martínez and E. J. C. Tigchelaar, *The Dead Sea Scrolls* I, 550–627.

has been identified. The texts from the Cairo Genizah ($H^{A-F}$) stem from the eleventh to twelfth centuries CE, the discoveries from Qumran[22] and Massada ($H^{Mas}$) from the period between the first century BCE and the first century CE.[23] None of the Hebrew fragments reflects the original text. It can only be obtained hypothetically by a comparison of the Hebrew, Greek, Latin and Syriac manuscripts. *The Greek translation* (G-I) represents the oldest complete version of the book. It was already expanded in antiquity, however (G-II). The expansions made their way into the versions represented by the major codices of the → *Septuagint*.[24] The *Latin translation* (La) derives from an expanded Greek text (G-II). The *Syriac translation* (Syr), which found its way into the *Peshitta*, was produced on the basis of a Hebrew prototype.

The most extensive fragment of the Hebrew text is $H^B$. Sections not yet attested in Hebrew include chapters 1–2; 17–18*; 21–24 and 28–29. As in the case of the Greek tradition, a distinction can be made for the Hebrew tradition between an older *Hebrew short text (H-I)* and a later *Hebrew long text (H-II)*. In view of the state of the tradition outlined and the fact that there is no Masoretic text (→ *Masoretes*) of Sirach, Sirach represents one of the most difficult books in the Old Testament not only from the standpoint of text-criticism, but also of hermeneutics.[25] The following text-critical rules of thumb apply:

1 The starting point is the Greek text of the → *Septuagint* since it contains the oldest complete version of Sirach available so far.
2 H-I most closely approximates the 'original text' and the prototype of the oldest Greek translation (G-I).
3 H-II is the closest relative of Syr and G-II.

Modern translations of and commentaries on Sirach reflect the complicated state of the tradition. All of the translations before 1896 are based on the

22. 2Q18; 11QPsa XXI,11–17; XXII,1 (F. García Martínez and E. J. C. Tigchelaar, *The Dead Sea Scrolls* II, 1174–7).
23. The standard edition of the Hebrew text of Sirach by P. C. Beentjes (*The Book of Ben Sira in Hebrew* [VTSup 68; Leiden: Brill, 1997/2006]) provides a detailed overview of the passages preserved in the Hebrew fragments. Regarding a new fragment of manuscript C from the Cairo Genizah, see R. Egger-Wenzel, 'Ein neues Fragment des MS C', *BN* 138 (2008): 107–14.
24. The standard critical edition of the text by J. Ziegler (2nd ed.; 1980) provides the text of G-II within the body of the text in small print (cf. NETS, 719–62). The older critical edition by A. Rahlfs (1935/1979 [2006]) reproduces the G-II text in a text-critical apparatus beneath the main text.
25. See F. Böhmisch, 'Die Textformen des Sirachbuches und ihre Zielgruppen', *PzB* 6 (1997): 87–122.

Greek or the Latin text. Translations prepared since the discovery of the Hebrew fragments offer a mixed text, i.e. when a Hebrew text is available, it is translated, otherwise the Greek short (or long) text is translated (cf. NRSV Apocrypha). Commentaries on the book display a similar picture.

## 27.2.2 The Problem of Composition

Sirach is the first biblical book to name its author by name. At the same time, it also contains the following indications that it was not written in one effort:

1. the formal unevenness between the minor compositions and the collections of aphorisms in chapters 1–23; 25–41, on the one hand, and the well-structured major compositions in chapters 24; 42–51, on the other;
2. the significant textual differences between the ancient Hebrew, Greek, Syriac and Latin versions;
3. several interspersed biographical sections[26] and the dual conclusion in 50.27-29 and 51.30 (H); and
4. sometimes abrupt thematic transitions, such as in 15.20/16.1; 36.22/23; 38.23/38.24.

In any case, scholarship concerning the literary and redaction history of the book of Sirach is just beginning. Usually, scholarship attributes the foundation of the Hebrew short version (H-I), to the degree that it is supported by the Greek short version (G-I), in essence to Ben Sira and explains the disparity of the text in terms of composition history. That is, an author may have combined pre-existent wisdom and hymnic texts and some minor compositions and edited in several phases. Three texts are especially controversial regarding their originality:

1. the prayer for the deliverance of → *Zion* (36.1-22) based on → *eschatological* components that are largely imperceptible elsewhere in the book;
2. the liturgical song of thanksgiving in 51.12a-o, which is preserved only in $H^B$;
3. the acrostic in 51.13-29.

Whether other eschatologically oriented → *glosses* should be taken into account depends on the interpretation of the corresponding passages and on the determination of the fundamental tendencies of Sirach. In late wisdom,

26. Sir. 16.24-25; 24.30-34; 33.16-18; 39.12-13.

at any rate, wisdom and eschatology do not constitute opposites, as can be demonstrated by the Wisdom of Solomon (Ch. 25).[27]

# 27.3 Origins of the Wisdom of Jesus Sirach

## 27.3.1 The Form of the Book

In its final form, the book constitutes a wisdom textbook that employs the *wisdom* → *genres* of the individual saying (*aphorism*), the sayings series, and the discourse known primarily from the book of Proverbs (Ch. 15). Like the book of Proverbs, Sirach is formulated in poetry, i.e., it is governed by the laws of *parallelismus membrorum*. In addition, it utilizes the genres of the *communal prayer of lament and petition* (36.1-22), the *creation hymn* (42.15–43.33), and the *song of thanksgiving* (51.1-12) known from Psalms (Ch. 13). Wisdom's hymn of self-praise in Sir. 24 has affinities with the → *Hellenistic* poems of praise (*Aretalogies*) to the goddess Isis. The praise of the fathers (44–50) depends on the historical psalms (cf. Pss 78; 105–106; 135–136). Moreover, the illustration of the history of Israel on the example of individual figures and the objective of the praise of the fathers in the extensive praise of Simon recall the Hellenistic genre of the Encomium.

## 27.3.2 The Composition and Redaction of the Book

The book stands in the tradition of Old Testament proverbial wisdom, but extends it in a quite unique fashion into a larger composition. Two phenomena characterize the innovation of Sirach:

1 An intensive *engagement with Jewish tradition*, as recorded in the books of the Torah and the prophets, which already have quasi-canonical status for Ben Sira. Sirach interacts with Deuteronomy (Ch. 7.2) in particular. The association of wisdom with the history of Israel depends on the tradition in the → *Pentateuch* and the former prophets. The high estimation of the cult of the Jerusalem temple is indebted to priestly and theocratic notions such as those present in the Priestly

27. B. G. Wright III and L. M. Wills, eds, *Conflicted Boundaries in Wisdom and Apocalypticism* (SBLSymS 35; Atlanta, Ga.: SBL Press, 2005).

source of the Pentatuch (P; Ch. 7.1) and in the Chronistic conception (Ch. 23).[28] In turn, Sirach submits the problematization of traditional wisdom, such as is articulated in the books of Job and Ecclesiastes (Ch. 14; Ch. 18), to critical revision.

2 An intensive *engagement with Hellenistic literature and culture*. Even more than Ecclesiastes, Sirach reflects the advance of Greek philosophical and pedagogical ideas. Sirach is familiar with the cosmological speculations of the Stoa, in particular.[29]

The **Stoa**, so called after the gathering place of its adherents in the *stoa poikilē* ('colourfully painted hall') in Athens, was a Greco-Roman school of philosophy that was concerned with logic, physics (natural philosophy), and ethics. The concentration on ethics and the notion of a logos that permeates the cosmos characterizes the Stoa throughout all the differences it exhibited in the course of its history, from Zenon (332–264 BCE), via Chrysippus (281/77–209/4 BCE) and Poseidonios (135–51 BCE), to Seneca (4 BCE–65 CE) and Marcus Aurelius (121–180 CE). The ideal wise person lives 'according to nature', is free of emotions, and finds happiness (*eudaimonia*) in virtue. This virtue is realized in an active configuration of the world in which, ultimately, everything is arranged beautifully and purposefully by divine providence (*pronoia*).

K. Ierodiakonou, ed., *Topics in Stoic Philosophy*. Oxford: Clarendon Press, 1999; W. Weinkauf, *Die Philosophie der Stoa: Ausgewählte Texte*. Reclam Universal-Bibliothek 18123. Stuttgart: Reclam, 2001.

The literary dependency of Ben Sira on Stoic texts cannot be demonstrated. There are, however, systematic affinities with a view to the concept of divine providence and the idea of the rational arrangement of the world (39.12-35).[30] In contrast to the Stoic model of a divine principle immanent in the world, Ben Sira maintains the biblical doctrine of a creator. Furthermore, echoes of the *Iliad*, the *Odyssey*, and the gnomic poetry of Theognis of Megara (6th cent. BCE) appear in Ben Sira. Finally, as is true of the books of Proverbs (Ch. 15) and Ecclesiastes (Ch. 18), there are parallels with Egyptian instructions for life.[31]

28. Cf. 1 Chr. 16; 2 Chr. 3.1–5.1; 7.8-10; 30; 31.2-19; 35.1-19.

29. U. Wicke-Reuter, *Göttliche Providenz und menschliche Verantwortung bei Ben Sira und in der Frühen Stoa* (BZAW 298; Berlin/New York: de Gruyter, 2000).

30. Cf. the description of the Stoic doctrine of God in Diogenes Laertius (*Lives of Eminent Philosophers* VII:147 [LCL 184-185; Cambridge, Mass.: Harvard University Press, 2006, 2005]).

31. Translated in M. Lichtheim, *Ancient Egyptian Literature* I-III; idem, *Late Egyptian Wisdom Literature in the International Context: A Study of Demotic Instructions* (OBO 52; Fribourg:

### 27.3.3 The Situation and Function of the Book

The information in the Greek prologue that the translator came to Alexandria in the thirty-eighth year of Euergetes (II = Ptolemaios VIII Physkon, 170–117 BCE) and there translated his grandfather's book implies that Ben Sirach lived in the first quarter of the second century BCE. The information in 50.27 (G, La) that he was a Jerusalemite comports with knowledge of topography and political situation in Jerusalem in the early second century BCE evident in his work. Ben Sira describes himself as a wisdom teacher who may have taught young men in a 'house of learning' (51.23). His time, after the rule of Alexander the Great (d. 323 BCE), was marked by an expansion of Hellenization throughout the entire Near East in all areas of life (Ch. 4.4). Ben Sira's petitions for the Zadokite priesthood (45.26; 50.23-24 [H]) and his prayer for the deliverance of Zion (36.1-22) may reflect conflicts between the high priest Onias III and the Seleucid ruler Seleucus IV (189–175 BCE; cf. 2 Macc. 3–4; Dan. 11.20). Ben Sira seems not yet aware of the deposition of the Zadokite high priest Onias III, compulsory Hellenization, and the prohibition of the exercise of Jewish religion under Antiochus IV Epiphanes (175–164 BCE) that ultimately led to the Maccabean rebellion in 165 BCE. His work will have originated, then, before 175 bce. The book's praise for the high priest Simon II, who held office from approximately 218 to 192 BCE (cf. 3 Macc. 2.1; Josephus, *Ant.* XII:4:1), also points to this time. An anti-Samaritan tendency (Ch. 3.2.1) is evident in Ben Sira in the execration in 50.25-26 and in the denigration of the history of the northern kingdom in the praise of the fathers (47.23-25).

## 27.4 Theology of the Wisdom of Jesus Sirach

Ben Sira presupposes the incipient consistent → *monotheism* in the late layers of Deuteronomy (Ch. 7.2) and the book of Isaiah (Ch. 9). He contrasts the confession of the God of Israel as the one and only God with the many gods in Hellenism and also with the designation of some Hellenistic gods as universal

Academic Press/Göttingen: Vandenhoeck & Ruprecht, 1983). Cf. esp. the Instructions of Cheti, of Ani, of the Chester Beatty Papyrus IV, of Amenemope, of Ankh-Sheshon and of the Insinger Papyrus.

deities. The God of Ben Sira – like the God of the whole Bible – is the creator of the world and, as such, is other than the world. To be sure, God and the world stand in relationship, but are essentially distinct from one another: 'for God is greater than all his works' (43.28). Continuing the biblical creation texts, Ben Sira advocated a theology that simultaneously defended the justice of the creator God (→ *theodicy*). In this respect, Ben Sira has affinities with the Elihu speeches in the book of Job (Job 32–37). The new element is that, in the context of his theodicy section,[32] Ben Sira points to polar structures in creation (33.14-15).

Ben Sira's picture of humanity corresponds to the → *anthropology* that can be derived from Gen. 1–3. Humans are mortal beings, who, with regard to their administrative role, are, however, god-like and capable of knowing (Sir. 17). The principal human capacity for knowledge and the ability to distinguish between good and evil allow human beings to make free moral decisions and to be occupied with the Torah as the source of wisdom (15.11-17; 17.11). The fundamental posture of human life is the fear of God (1.11–2.18). It should characterize human behaviour in all life situations. Prayer expresses the fear of God.[33] Ben Sira does not engage in the speculation concerning life after death that can be found in Judaism at least since the third century BCE (see the excursus in Ch. 18.4).[34]

At the juncture of Sira's theology and anthropology stand statements concerning wisdom and the cult. Thus, the cosmic wisdom identified with the Torah or incarnate in the Torah appears as a bridge between God and humanity (ch. 24). The authorized interpreter of the Torah is the high priest from the Zadokite family (45.17). The cult administered by the high priest in the Jerusalem temple is the definitive mediator of divine blessing (50.20-21).

## 27.5 Notes on the History of Reception

Admittedly, Sirach did not find acceptance into the → '*canon*' of the Hebrew Bible, but, as citations in the → *Talmud* demonstrate,[35] it was sometimes

32. Sir. 15.11–18.14; 33.7-15; 40.1-11; 41.1-13; see P. C. Beentjes, 'Theodicy in the Wisdom of Ben Sira', in Essays, 265–79.
33. Sir. 15.9-10; 17.6-10; 39.5-15; 43.27-33.
34. Sir. 14.12-19; 18.8-10; 41.3-4.
35. Cf. b. BQ 92b: Sir. 27.9; 13.15.

treated as a 'canonical book'. In the early church, the book was very popular and found entry into the canon of the Roman Catholic and Orthodox churches via the → *Septuagint*. In Protestantism, despite its inclusion among the apocrypha, Sirach exerted great influence on the catechisms and hymn-writing of the sixteenth and seventeenth centuries.[36]

No direct citations from Sirach appear in the New Testament, although there are over one hundred allusions or motif parallels. Two especially impressive examples are (1) the prologue to the Gospel of John (John 1), in which the notion of the indwelling of wisdom on → *Zion* and the incarnation of wisdom in the Torah (Sir. 24) was modified into the notion of the incarnation of the divine Logos in Jesus Christ and (2) the savior's call in Mt. 11.28-29, through which shines wisdom's invitation from Sir. 24.19 (cf. 51.26).

36. Cf. the hymns 'Nun danket alle Gott' by Martin Rinckart (ca. 1630) or 'Nun danket all und bringet Ehr' by Paul Gerhardt (1647).

# 28

# 1 Baruch and the Epistle of Jeremiah

(Konrad Schmid – Translation by Jennifer Adams-Maßmann)

## Chapter Outline



C. A. Moore, '1 Baruch'. Pages 255–316 in *Daniel, Esther, and Jeremiah: The Additions*. AB 44. Garden City, N.Y.: Doubleday, 1977; idem., 'Epistle of Jeremiah'. Pages 317–58 in *Daniel, Esther, and Jeremiah: The Additions*. AB 44. Garden City, N.Y.: Doubleday, 1977; O. H. Steck, R. G. Kratz and I. Kottsieper, *Das Buch Baruch, Der Brief Jeremias, Zusätze zu Ester und Daniel*. ATD.A 5. Göttingen: Vandenhoeck & Ruprecht, 1998; O. H. Steck, *Das apokryphe Baruchbuch: Studien zur Rezeption und Konzentration 'kanonischer' Überlieferung*. FRLANT 160. Göttingen: Vandenhoeck & Ruprecht, 1993.

In the Latin version of the Bible, Baruch and the Epistle of Jeremiah are united into one, six-chapter-long Book of Baruch in which the Epistle of Jeremiah counts as Bar. 6. These were originally two independent texts, however, although they appear closely related thematically in terms of the shared fictional situation drawn from the realm of Jeremiah-related literature (cf. Jer and the partial text sections Jer. 29 or Jer. 30–33 as well as Lamentations).

## 28.1 Biblical Context

1 Baruch is clearly divided into four sections: Bar. 1.1-15aα provides a narrative introduction to the text that follows, presenting it as a text written by Baruch, Jeremiah's scribe who is well known from the Book of Jeremiah (see Jer. 32, 36). The introduction also instructs that the text should be read in the Babylonian → *exile* as well as in Jerusalem. The actual text of the book begins with 1.15aβ with a prayer of penitence (1.15aβ–3.8) that Israel is supposed to use as a confession of sins. The next section, 3.9–4.4, is a speech admonishing Israel to turn back to the Torah. As in Sir. 24, Bar. 4.1 identifies the Torah with wisdom. The book concludes with words of encouragement and promise in 4.5–5.9, announcing to Israel and the inhabitants of Jerusalem that they will return to the land.

The Epistle of Jeremiah purports to be a copy of a letter by the prophet Jeremiah to the Babylonian exiles following the biblical example in Jer. 29, although it draws primarily from themes in Jer. 10. Its six sections demonstrate in a variety of ways that idols are not gods, arguing that, given their material nature and their ineffectiveness, they do not need to be feared.

## 28.2 Historical-Critical Analysis and Major Issues in the History of Scholarship

Because of the formal, linguistic and theological disparities between its four sections, scholars used to consider 1 Baruch a conglomerate of formerly independent texts. But closer observation has shown that the texts belong together conceptually and in terms of their genesis – that is, the process of reception and concentration of the biblical tradition (for more, see the reference works listed above, especially O. H. Steck). The three-step process of turning from sin, turning towards the Torah, and then returning to Israel constitutes the book's coherent message.

The Epistle of Jeremiah can be identified as a self-contained treatise based on its singular focus and the work's composition with strophic endings.

## 28.3 Origins of 1 Baruch and the Epistle of Jeremiah

We can be fairly confident that 1 Baruch, which is preserved in Greek but was probably originally written in Hebrew, goes back to a single author (for more on 3.38, see Ch. 28.5). It was certainly written several hundred years later than the exilic context in which it is set. This can be ascertained above all from the author's knowledge and use of texts from the 2nd cent. BCE such as Dan. 9, the inspiration for the composition of the penitential prayer in 1.15aβ–3.8, or Sir. 24, which was taken into consideration in the Torah passage 3.37–4.1. It does not assume the destruction of the Temple in Jerusalem by the Romans in 70 CE, however. So the most likely scenario is that the Book of Baruch was written immediately after the success of the Maccabean revolt in 163/162 BCE which was motivated by national-religious concerns. Such a historical context would certainly be plausible given the book's Torah orientation and perspectives on salvation.

The 7Q2 fragment of the Epistle of Jeremiah in → *Qumran* makes it clear that the epistle cannot be dated later than 100 BCE, and may originally have been in Aramaic. It is likely several decades older than Baruch: for the author of the Epistle, it appears the Maccabean crisis is not yet over. In addition, the text has been integrated into Jubilees 11–12 and 2 Macc. 2.2. Evidence that this text originated much later than the time of Jeremiah in which it purports to take place can also be found above all in the numerous scriptural references.

## 28.4 Theology of 1 Baruch and the Epistle of Jeremiah

The theology of Baruch belongs to the wider circle of → *deuteronomistic* thought, a long-lived tradition which influenced biblical and postbiblical texts through the 1st cent. CE. For the writer of Baruch, Israel has been under the judgement of God since the Babylonian exile but can attain salvation again through penitence and turning back to the Torah. By contrast, the speech of admonition in 3.9–4.4 with its → *wisdom* argumentation reflects the position of the Book of Sirach, although Baruch emphasizes much more strongly that wisdom is accessible only to Israel. In terms of the theology of the Epistle of Jeremiah, it focuses solely on the polemics against idols. The message is summarized in the refrain repeated in various forms multiple times: 'From this it is evident that they are not gods; so do not fear them!' (vv. 16, 23, 29b, 64-65, 69).

## 28.5 Reception History

The earliest evidence of 1 Baruch's reception history is the addition in 3.37, probably of Christian origin ('Afterwards (s)he appeared on earth and lived with humankind'), which relates to wisdom and apparently seeks to identify it with the incarnate Christ. In its reinterpreted form, 1 Baruch was an oft-read tract in Christianity. The Epistle of Jeremiah has its own only reception history before the Latin version and in areas where Latin was not prevalent. Thus it was absorbed into the *Jubilees*, in the prophetic Targum on Jer. 10.11 as well as in Christian apologetic works. In the Latin tradition it was read and understood within the framework of 1 Baruch.

# 29

# The Books of Maccabees

(Angelika Berlejung – Translation by Thomas Riplinger)

## Chapter Outline



The books 1 and 2 Maccabees (together with 3 and 4 Maccabees) are counted in the → *Septuagint* among the historical books. However, the → *Vulgate* accepted only 1 and 2 Maccabees as canonical. Both books enjoyed considerable esteem in the ancient church, and, at the Council of Trent in 1547, they were officially included in the Catholic Church's → *canon* of biblical books (Ch. 1.2.1). The names currently in use, 1 and 2 Maccabees, are attested since the 2nd cent. BCE. The name derives from the fact that the books deal with the revolt of the priest Mattathias, the son of Hasmon (hence the name 'Hasmoneans' given to the family) and his sons, Judas called 'Maccabaeus' (Hebr. 'Hammer') with his brothers

Jonathan and Simon. Although Judas was the first and only person to be given the sobriquet 'Maccabaeus' (1 Macc. 2.4), the whole family of Judas, his father and his four brothers, which according to 1 Macc. 2.1 came from Modein, is collectively known as the 'Maccabees'.

# A First Maccabees

J. R. Bartlett, *The First and Second Books of the Maccabees*. CBC. Cambridge University Press, 1973; idem, *1 Maccabees*. Guides to the Apocrypha and Pseudepigrapha. Sheffield: Sheffield Academic Press, 1998; J. J. Collins, *Daniel, First Maccabees, Second Maccabees, with an Excursus on the Apocalyptic Genre*, Wilmington, Del.: Glazier, 1981; J. A. Goldstein, *Maccabees* 1. AB 41. New York: Doubleday, 1976 (reprint 1977); K.-D. Schunck, *Historische und legendarische Erzählungen: 1. Makkabäerbuch*. JSHRZ I/4. Gütersloh: Mohn, 1980; D. S. Williams, 'Recent Research in 1 Maccabees'. *CurBS* 9 (2001): 169–84 (research report); idem, *The Structure of 1 Maccabees*. CBQMS 31. Washington: Catholic Biblical Association of America, 1999; G. G. Xeravits and J. Zsengellér, eds, *The Books of the Maccabees: History, Theology, Ideology: Papers of the Second International Conference on the Deuterocanonical Books, Pápa, Hungary, 9–11 June 2005*. JSJSup 118. Leiden: Brill, 2007; L. L. Grabbe, *Judaic Religion in the Second Temple Period: Belief and Practice from the Exile to Yavneh*. London: Routledge, 2000; O. Keel, *Die Geschichte Jerusalems und die Entstehung des Monotheismus*. Orte und Landschaften der Bibel IV,1. Göttingen: Vandenhoeck & Ruprecht, 2007, 1182–6; J. R. Bartlett, *Jews in the Hellenistic and Roman Cities*. New York: Routledge, 2002; J. J. Collins, *Between Athens and Jerusalem: Jewish Identity in Hellenistic Diaspora*. 2nd edition. Grand Rapids, Mich.: Eerdmans, 2000.

Numerous semiticisms and translation errors (1.1, 5, 16, 28-29, 36, 61; 2.29; 3.15; 4.19; 16.3; *et al.*) as well as a note from St. Jerome to this effect indicate that it was very early recognized that 1 Maccabees was originally written in Hebrew (or Aramaic), though the original is lost. In addition to the well-attested Greek tradition, there are also further ancient translations (Latin, Syrian, Arabic and Armenian). Of these, the → *Vetus Latina* is of special importance, because it arose on the basis of a Greek *Vorlage* which is older and qualitatively better than the surviving Greek manuscripts.

## 29.1 Biblical Context

The introduction to 1 Maccabees sketches the historical framework of the story which follows, beginning with the rise of Alexander the Great and his death, then relating the subsequent struggles of the Diadochi, and the victory of the Seleucids over the Ptolemies (→ Ch. 4.4.1). From 1 Macc. 1.10 on, the account concentrates on the Seleucid ruler Antiochus IV Epiphanes (175–164 BCE), whose policies are described as being anti-Jewish. Thus the ensuing struggle is foretold, so to speak, and the person responsible for it is identified. In ch. 2, the revolt of Mattathias, the son of Hasmon, is summarized, from its beginning to his death, so that, taken together, chapters 1 and 2 introduce the two opposing parties, which will continue to confront each other in the course of the events leading up to the death of Simon, the last son of Mattathias, which is related in ch. 16. Thus the book spans the years from 333 to 135/4 BCE.

*I. The Historical Background*

**1. 1–10** The **Prologue:** From Alexander the Great to Antiochus IV Epiphanes.

**1. 11–2.70 Introduction:** The crisis and the beginning of the revolt.

1.11-15 The apostasy of the Jews.

1.16-64 The catastrophe resulting from the apostasy (vv. 16-24); the plundering of the Temple; vv. 29-35 the construction of the citadel; vv. 41-64 measures against Jewish religious practice (including 1.54: the 'abomination of desolation' cf. Dan. 9.27; 11.31; 12.11).

2 The beginning of resistance under Mattathias, his testament and his death.

*II. The Main Part*

**1. 3.1–9.22: Judas.**

3.1-9 A hymn of praise for Judas.

3.10–9.22 The activities of Judas.

3.10–4.61 Battles; the purification of the Temple; and the renewal of the cult.

5.1-68 Battles against neighbouring peoples; liberation of the Jews; and the return to Jerusalem.

6.1-63 The death of Antiochus IV Epiphanes, and the attacks of Antiochus V; Judas besieges the citadel.

7.1–9.22 Conflicts under Demetrius I, the victory over Nicanor, the death of Judas on the battlefield.

**2. 9.23–12.53: Jonathan.**

9.23-73 The victory of Jonathan over Bacchides.

10.1-66 The rise of Alexander Balas and of Jonathan as high priest.

10.67–11.37 The rise of Demetrius II and the confirmation of Jonathan.

11.38–12.53 The break with Demetrius II and the murder of Jonathan.

**3. 13.1–16.22: Simon.**

13.1-14.3 The murder of Antiochus VI by Tryphon; the rise of Simon and his achievements.

14.4-15 A hymn of praise for Simon.

⇨

14.16–16.10 Confirmation of Simon by Demetrius II and Antiochus VII; the break between Antiochus VII and Simon.
16.11–22 The murder of Simon.
**Conclusion 16.23–24: Johannes Hyrcanus I.**

## 29.2 Textual Issues and Major Issues in the History of Critical Interpretation

First Maccabees is an example of a pro-Hasmonean royal interpretation of history in the guise of straightforward historical writing.[1] The generally narrative presentation of the actions of the various protagonists is enhanced with poems of lamentation (1.25-28, 36-40; 2.7-13; 3.45, 50b-53; 4.38; 7.17; 9.21, 41), which, echoing Lamentations and the lamentation psalms, recall various crises in the history of 'Israel'. For the persons of Judas Maccabaeus (3.1-9; 4.30–33) and Simon (14.4-15), there are only hymns of praise. The founder of the dynasty, Mattathias, together with his sons are compared in 1 Macc. 2.49-61 to Abraham, Joseph, Pinchas, Joshua, Caleb, David, Elijah, the three youths in the furnace, and Daniel, thus counting them among the most prominent figures of the history of 'Israel'. Intertextual references in 1 Maccabees are meant to draw parallels between Mattathias and Pinchas (compare 2.26, 54 with Num. 25.6-13); Judas Maccabaeus and Joshua (compare 5.5 with Josh. 6.17; 11.11) as well as David (compare 4.30 with 1 Sam. 14 and 17); Jonathan and the judges (compare 9.73 with Judg. 3.10; 10.2-3; 1 Sam. 7.15-16. *et al.*); and finally Simon and Samuel (compare 16.14 with 1 Sam. 7.16) as well as Solomon (compare 14.12-15 with 1 Kgs 5.5 [NRSV 5.19]; 6). From ch. 1 on, an opposition is constructed between the pagan peoples, who worship idols, and the Jews, who do not do so (1.43, 47; 3.48; 10.83-84; 13.47). Besides the references to the OT texts of the → *Pentateuch*, the Major and Minor Prophets, and the Psalter, the author also

1. See H. Lichtenberger, 'Geschichtsschreibung und Geschichtserzählung im 1. und 2. Makkabäerbuch', in *Die antike Historiographie und die Anfänge der christlichen Geschichtsschreibung* (BZNW 129; ed. E.-M. Becker; Berlin: de Gruyter, 2005), 197–212.

appears to have had access to the → *annals* of the Hasmonean Dynasty (see 16.23-24) in Jerusalem. He has integrated letters (5.10b-13; 10.18-20, 25b-45; 11.30-37; 12.6-18, 20-23; 13.36-40; 14.20b-23; 15.2-9, 16-21) and other documents (8.23-32; 14.27b-45) into his book, sometimes even in the form of verbatim citations, in order to create the impression of historical accuracy and objectivity. Nevertheless, in the individual case, it is necessary to inquire and to decide whether these texts might not in fact be literary fictions created for the sake of the narrative context.

Within the book, two different calendar system are used: the west-Seleucid numbering system to date Seleucid events [beginning in autumn 312], e.g. in 1.10, 20; 10.1, 57, 67; 14.1; but the east-Seleucid and Jewish numbering system [beginning in spring 312 or 311] e.g. 1.54; 4.52; 10.21, to date Jewish events. This leads to chronological problems with regard to 2 Maccabees and Flavius Josephus[2]. The different styles of dating led K.-D. Schunck[3] to propose a distinction of sources within 1 Maccabees, according to which the author of 1 Maccabees used a Seleucid chronicle and a Jewish biography of Judas, a Mattathias legend, and high-priestly annals for Jonathan and Simon. Against this theory, it is generally assumed with G. O. Neuhaus[4] that *only one author* wrote 1 Maccabees and that he used various literary genres and written sources such as letters and decrees. However, the conclusion of 1 Maccabees remains an object of discussion. According to D. S. Williams, there were two versions of 1 Maccabees, the first version comprised 1.1–14.15 (dated around 130 BCE); the second version included in addition ch. 14.16–16.24 (dated around 100 BCE). His principal argument is based on the polemic against the nations which is contained in 1.1–14.15 but which he claims is absent after 14.16. This claim, however, cannot be taken so strictly (see 14.33-34, 36; 15.33; 16.2). William's proposal revives the 'Addendum-Thesis' already proposed in the 19th cent., which treated 14.16–16.24 as a secondary addition, arguing that Flavius Josephus in his *Antiquitates* strictly follows 1 Maccabees only up to ch. 13, but thereafter goes his own way. However, because this is an argument from silence, contemporary research continues in the majority to regard 14.16–16.24 as having been part of 1 Maccabees from the beginning.

2. See J. Sievers, *Synopsis of the Greek Sources for the Hasmonean Period: 1 – 2 Maccabees and Josephus, War 1 and Antiquities 12-14* (SubBi 20; Rome: Pontificio Istituto Biblico, 2001).
3. K.-D. Schunck, *Die Quellen des I. und II. Makkabäerbuches* (Halle: Niemeyer, 1954).
4. G. O. Neuhaus, 'Quellen im 1. Makkabäerbuch? Eine Entgegnung auf die Analyse von K.-D. Schunck', *JSJ* 5 (1974): 162–75.

# 29.3 Origins of First Maccabees

For the origin of 1 Maccabees, the → *terminus post quem* (in view of 16.22-23) is generally taken to be the beginning of the reign of Johannes Hyrcanus in 135/4 (for the historical and religio-historical background, see Ch. 4.4). However, the Greek version of 1 Maccabees cannot have originated much earlier than 100 BCE.[5] This means that the Hebrew or Aramaic original of 1 Maccabees must have been written between 135/4 and 100 BCE. The anachronism in 1 Macc. 15.6, which attributes the minting of coins to Simon, whereas in fact it was Johannes Hyrcanus I (135/4–104 BCE) who issued the first coins, indicates the tendency of the author to back-date this sign of Jerusalem's autonomy to Simon. Furthermore, one should take into consideration that this anachronism implies a certain temporal distance to the real beginning of coinage under Johannes Hyrcanus I, so that the time of the origin of 1 Maccabees in both the original and the translation languages can be narrowed down to the reign of Alexander Jannaeus (103–76 BCE). The → *terminus ante quem* is in any case, 63 BCE, since the Romans are (still) viewed very positively.

The author of 1 Maccabees can be identified as a member of the Hasmonean court, who had access to various sources. It is debated, whether he belonged to the Pharisee or the Sadducee parties, but the historically attested connections of the Sadducees with the Hasmoneans at the time of Johannes Hyrcanus and Alexander Jannaeus speak more for the second view. As sources for 1 Maccabees, an already existing Judas vita (9.22), a Mattathias legend, and annals of the high priests Jonathan and Simon (16.24) have been discussed. The letters and decrees reproduced in the book could be citations of authentic documents from the Jerusalem archives, but they can also be viewed as literary compositions made up to illustrate the text (this is often proposed for 12.20-23), so that in the second view the question of their authenticity and provenience would be irrelevant. It is also conceivable that the author had a Seleucid chronicle at his disposal, on the basis of which he could synchronize the events of Seleucid history with those of Jerusalem. In its general style and in its closing formulae (see 9.22; 12.52b; 16.23-24), the narrative follows OT models (1 Kgs 11.41; 1 Chr. 29.29 *et al.*). The author himself has structured the text with the aid of various insertions (e.g. 2.49-68, the programmatic testament of Mattathias; cf. the various 'farewell discourses' of the OT),

5. So with R. Steiner, 'On the Dating of Hebrew Sound Changes (*Ḫ > Ḥ and * Ġ> ʿ) and Greek Translations (2 Esdras and Judith)', *JBL* 124/2 (2005): 229–67, here 256.

including the deliberate use of poetic pieces (1.25-28, 36-40; 2.7-13, 49b-68; 3.3-9a, 45, 50b-53; 4.30b-33, 38; 7.17; 9.21, 41; 14.4-15). 1 Maccabees is a book which makes clear, already at this early date, the high esteem accorded to the Torah, the Major and Minor Prophets, and the Psalter (cf. 7.17 and Ps. 79.2-3), but also to the book of Daniel (2.59-60; note, however, the critical attitude to the revolt in Dan. 11.34). These writings were taken up by the author of 1 Maccabees, and in a classical example of inner-biblical exegesis they are re-interpreted and actualized in the interests of the Maccabean Dynasty.

# 29.4 Theology of First Maccabees

## 29.4.1 Theology of History

Although Yhwh never intervenes directly in the events related (and is not even named explicitly), it is he that guides the story as a whole and the protagonists of the story in particular (4.30). When 'heaven' is mentioned in 3.18-19, 50, 60; 4.10, 24, 40, 55; 9.46; 12.15; 16.3, this term is a transparent reference to Yhwh, who saves 'Israel' through the hands of the Maccabees (3.6; 4.33-34; 5.62). Prayers (3.50-53; 4.24, 30-33, 55; 5.33; 7.40-42; 11.71), which are inserted in central positions within the narrative, show that Yhwh is the one who shapes events. The historiography of 1 Maccabees shows numerous echoes and parallels to the books of the Bible from Judges to 2 Kings as well as to the two books of Chronicles (see the closing formulae mentioned above). The wars of the Maccabees and their efforts to establish an independent Jerusalem are often set in relation to the → *conquest* by Joshua, to the events of the time of the judges (compare the Dtr judges pattern ['Richterschema'] [Ch. 7.6.3.3] with 1 Macc. 9.27, 73; 13.2), to Samuel's deeds as a judge, to David's rise to power (compare 2 Sam. 5.1-5 and 1 Macc. 14.25-26.), or to Solomon's peaceful reign. The author is concerned with the struggle for religious freedom, but also for the restoration of the 'national' grandeur of the Jewish state centred in Jerusalem on Mt. → *Zion* in analogy to the Davidic state. It is the history of salvation that provides the framework for the events narrated: the notion of a storm of the pagans against Zion (compare Ezek. 38.1-16; Mic. 4.11; Isa. 17.12 with 1 Macc. 3.27, 39; 12.53 *et al.*), the return of the dispersed Jews to Zion (compare Ezek. 39.28; Jer. 31.12 with 1 Macc. 5.23, 45, 53-54), or the epoch of peace for the land (compare 1 Kgs 5.5 [NRSV 5.19]; Zech. 3.10; 8.4 with 14.9-15), all of which is now achieved by the Maccabees in the present. This theological interpretation of history, however, cuts the ground away from the notion of a → *messiah*[6] or → *eschatological* expectations. The promises of the restoration of 'Israel' and the completion of salvation history are fulfilled not in the eschaton and not through a Davidide, but now through a Maccabee.

## 29.4.2 Royal Ideology

The Maccabees were the first royal house on Judean soil without a Davidic ancestry. First Maccabees compensates for this deficit by presenting the Maccabee/Hasmonean kings as chosen ones (5.62); they are instruments of God, in whom the saviour and conqueror figures of the past history of 'Israel' are reflected. God does not intervene actively in the events; instead he lets his chosen ones act. The Maccabees thus become God's warriors. Their wars are interpreted as wars of liberation, in which they do battle against and put to death the godless enemies, not only the heathen Seleucids but also the hellenized Jews, who sought to combine Jewish religion with → *Hellenistic* life-style. A further problem was raised by the fact that the Maccabees had assumed the office of the high priest without being Zadokites. In 1 Maccabees, their priesthood was legitimized above all by parallelizing Mattathias with Pinchas (compare Num. 25.6-13 with 1 Macc. 2.26, 50, 54, 64, 68), who, already before the Zadokite priests, had received the promise of an eternal priesthood and a covenant promise (Num. 25.12-13 → *covenant*). The author of 1 Maccabees emphasizes the Jerusalem Temple and the Torah as the pillars of 'Israel', and he underlines their restoration through the Maccabees with the aim of convincing the reader of the correctness and the necessity of the Maccabean rule. Without this dynasty, neither the one nor the other would exist (2.48). The reign of Simon is idealized as a time of salvation: with its inception, the restoration of 'Israel' based on the Temple and the Torah is ensured. Simon is a ruler who fulfils the demands of the Deuteronomic law of the king (compare Deut. 17.18-19 with 14.14), and in him diverse OT promises are fulfilled (Zech. 3; 8).

6. J. J. Collins, 'Messianism in the Maccabean Period', in *Judaisms and their Messiahs at the Turn of the Christian Era* (ed. J. Neusner; Cambridge: Cambridge University Press, 1987), 97–109.

### 29.4.3 Zeal and → 'Holy War'

Zeal for the Torah connects Mattathias with Pinchas and motivates his sons as well, who continue in his tradition. At the same time, it was Pinchas, who as chief priest began the 'holy war' (Num. 31.6), so that through him there is a connection between 'zeal for the Torah' (Num. 25.6-13) and 'holy war'. In analogy, 1 Maccabees gives the impression that the Maccabees, through their zeal for the law and with God's help in their guerilla tactics against the mighty armies of the Seleucids were fighting for the free practice of the Jewish religion and for the re-consecration of the Jerusalem Temple and thus were following in essence the rules for the 'holy war' (3.55-56; compare Deut. 20.5-9; Num. 31.6, 48-52). In doing so, they were repeating, in the eyes of the author of 1 Maccabees, the → *conquest* and were simply taking back what had always belonged to them (15.33-34!).

## 29.5 Notes on the History of Reception

The militant zeal for the law and the concept of 'holy war' with the help of God and to the honour of God, as well as the clear division of roles between the combatants (the warriors of God versus the enemies of God) are notions that have not only inspired the Zealots of New Testament times but also continue to find supporters to this day. In this way, the conflict between Jews and Greeks/pagans, as described in 1 Maccabees has become a paradigm of 'holy war' and of all wars of liberation from foreign domination. In particular, the figure of Judas Maccabaeus has inspired diverse artists. George F. Händel, for instance, composed an oratorio with this name, and Ludwig van Beethoven extracted from this work the choral piece 'See the conquering hero comes!' and composed (around 1796) 12 variations (for harpsichord/piano and cello). In → *iconography*, Judas has frequently been depicted as the warlike contender for God. In the Benedictine monastery of Brauweiler in the Cologne area, various scenes from the OT and the legends of the saints are depicted in paintings (from around 1149) on the walls, in the vaults, and on the ceiling; among them is a picture of Judas Maccabaeus. In the Protestant city parish church of Our Lady in Memmingen, Judas Maccabaeus is portrayed in knight's armour within the fresco cycle by Thomas Bocksberger (around 1470), which depicts the 12 Apostles and the 12 clauses of the Creed. Peter Paul Rubens painted the warlike-heroic Judas around 1618/20 as a military leader praying for the fallen warriors (Nantes, Musée des Beaux-Arts). In 2007, in the Cologne Cathedral, a 'Judas-Maccabaeus-Window' was dedicated; its place is in the east wall of the north transept.

# B Second Maccabees

J. A. Goldstein, *Maccabees 2*. AB 41A. New York: 1983 (reprint 1984); C. Habicht, *Historische und legendarische Erzählungen: 2. Makkabäerbuch*. JSHRZ I/3. 2nd edition. Gütersloh: Mohn, 1979; D. S. Williams, 'Recent Research in 2 Maccabees'. *CurBS* 2/1 (2003): 69–83 (research report); R. Zwick, 'Unterhaltung und Nutzen: Zum literarischen Profil des 2. Buches der Makkabäer'. Pages 125–49 in *Steht nicht geschrieben? FS Georg Schmuttermayr*. Ed. by J. Frühwald-König *et al*. Regensburg: Pustet, 2001; Keel, *Jerusalem*, 1177–82; S. Zeitlin, *The Second Book of Maccabees*. New York: Harper, 1954.

In the words of H. Cancik, 'in terms of its sources, its language, its rhetorical style, its motifs, its structure, and its psychagogical intentions, 2 Maccabees is an outstanding representative' of → *Hellenistic* historiography.[7] The book covers a shorter period of time than 1 Maccabees, since it deals essentially only with the activities of Judas Maccabaeus. In other respects as well, 2 Maccabees differs from 1 Maccabees. At times, it narrates other historical or historicized episodes (e.g. Heliodorus in 2 Macc. 3), and it gives details about names (e.g. 12.2: Hieronymus and Demophon; 12.36 Esdris). It emphasizes more strongly the inner-Jewish conflict regarding the binding character of the Torah and the Hellenization of Jerusalem (2 Macc. 4–5). It presents Judas Maccabaeus as the leader of the Hasideans/Hasidim (14.6 and 8.25-27; cf. 1 Macc. 2.39-43; 9.43-49). It also sets very different theological accents: God and his messengers intervene directly in the events (3.23-30; 10.29-30; 11.8); heavenly scenes with elevated historical figures from 'Israel's' past (Onias, Jeremiah [15.12-16]) accompany the narrated events. Detailed descriptions of horrible torture and correspondingly cruel punishment (compare 2 Macc. 7 with 9) are designed to entertain (2 Macc. 2.25; 15.38-39), to awaken emotions, and to impress what has been read in the memory of the reader. A strong apologetic intention is also evident: the Jews themselves do not start any wars, but instead are loyal citizens who only defend themselves when they are attacked or impeded in the practise of their religion. Finally, with the exception of the two opening letters 1.1-2, 18) and ch. 7, (which were

7. H. Cancik, 'Geschichtsschreibung', *Neues Bibellexion* I:813–22, here 820 (transl.).

originally written in Hebrew or Aramaic), 2 Maccabees was, from the start, written in Greek.

## 29.6 Biblical Context

Second Maccabees divides into two principal parts, part I consists of two letters of the Jews of Jerusalem to the Jews in the Egyptian → *diaspora* with the directive to celebrate the feast of the dedication of the Temple in the month of Kislev. Part II, the so-called epitome represents, according to the testimony of the author (2.23), an excerpt (Greek: *epitomé*) of a five-volume historical work of Jason of Cyrene. The book offers a classic example for the way in which the unity of the Jews and their fidelity to the law is supported by Yhwh's mercy and help, so that they are protected against danger. Only their disunity and infidelity to the law gives the Seleucids the opportunity to move successfully against them, against Jerusalem, and against the temple. Thus the suffering of the Jews in Jerusalem represents God's punishment of his people whom he has given into the hands of the pagans. The martyrs, therefore, whose story is recounted in 2 Macc. 6.18–7.42 take on central importance within the structure of the book, since their unmerited vicarious suffering for the Jews who have been untrue to the law and their prayers persuade Yhwh to relent, enabling Judas Maccabaeus in 2 Macc. 8 to move successfully against the Seleucids.

| | |
|---|---|
| *I. The two Festival Letters* | |
| **1.1-10a** | **First Letter** dated 124 BCE. |
| **1.10b–2.18** | **Second Letter** to Aristobulus (the tutor of Ptolemy VI), mentioning Nehemiah, Jeremiah, Solomon, Moses and offering to send copies of the documents contained in the Jerusalem library. |
| *II. The Epitome* | |
| **1. 2.19–3.40** | Foreword of the epitomist and the Heliodorus episode as an example of the power of Jewish unity:<br>2.19-32 *Preface* of the epitomist.<br>3.1-40 Account of the 'ideal situation' showing the effect of observance of the law and of prayer: prayers of petition turn back Heliodorus' attempt to seize the treasures of the Jerusalem Temple. |
| **2. 4.1–7.42** | The crisis in Jerusalem under Antiochus IV as a consequence of the disunity of the Jews and the punishment of God: |

⇨

| | |
|---|---|
| | 4.1–6.17 Infidelity to the law among the Hellenistic Jews, persecution of the Jews, and the desecration of the temple.<br>6.18–7.42 Vicarious fidelity to the law by Jews: the martyrdom of Eleasar and of the seven brothers with their mother, including their prayers. The *end* of the story of misfortune. |
| **3. 8.1–10.9** | Judas Maccabaeus as God's instrument against Antiochus IV and the feast of Hanukkah:<br>8.1–8.36 The *turning point*: from the story of calamity to the story of salvation, because God now shows mercy (8.5) and comes to the aid of those faithful to the law (8.23-24); Judas Maccabaeus is victorious over Nicanor for the first time.<br>9.1-29 The end of Antiochus IV.<br>10.1-9 The purification of the temple and the ceremonial re-consecration, the Hanukkah festival. |
| **4. 10.10–13.26** | Judas Maccabaeus as God's instrument against Antiochus V Eupator and Lysias:<br>10.10–11.38 Warlike threats to Jerusalem and Judea and the victory of Judas.<br>Contained therein: 11.16-38 four letters from the years 165/4–163:<br>1. Letter of Lysias (summer or autumn 164)<br>2. Letter of Antiochus V (shortly after 163)<br>3. Letter of Antiochus IV (March 164)<br>4. Letter of a Roman delegation (March, summer or autumn 164)<br>12.1-45 Warlike threats on the outskirts of Judea and in the Hellenistic cities; the victories of Judas.<br>13.1-26 Threats by Antiochus V and his retreat. |
| **5. 14.1–15.39** | Judas Maccabaeus as God's instrument against Demetrius I and Nicanor. The epilogue:<br>14.1-36 Intrigues of Alcimus and the threat to the Jerusalem Temple by Nicanor.<br>14.37-46 The suicide of Rasi.<br>15.1-36 Judas Maccabaeus defeats Nicanor for the second time. The end of Nicanor and the establishment of the day commemorating the end of Nicanor.<br>15.37-39 *Epilogue* of the epitomist. |

## 29.7 Textual Issues and Major Issues in the History of Critical Interpretation

Alongside the question of the origins of the two letters to the diaspora communities and their relationship to the epitome (question 1), the principal topic of discussion among scholars (question 2) is how 2 Macc. 2.19–15.39 is related to the no-longer-extant five-volume historical work of Jason of Cyrene, which is claimed as a source in 2.23.

To the 1st question: In all the manuscripts and translations since the 5th cent. CE, the letters in 1.1–2.18 have been transmitted together with the epitome. This by no means proves, however, that the epitomist himself had already placed them at the beginning of his work. Time and again various combinations have been suggested, for example a combination of only the first introductory letter with the epitome or of only the second letter with the epitome, in each case with a later insertion of the other letter. Since the letters and the epitome are otherwise unrelated – the epitome does not contain a single word about the letters; the letters appear to know nothing of the Nicanor Day; and the account of the end of Antiochus IV in 1.11-17 conflicts with the account in 9.1-17 – one can assume that the letters, which first had to be translated from a Semitic language, were unknown to both Jason of Cyrene and the epitomist, and that they were placed at the beginning of the work only by a later author or editor. The first letter from the year 124 BCE is generally regarded as an authentic document, whereas the second letter, which claims to be a message from the year 164 BCE, is generally regarded as a fiction. In view of the two traditions regarding the death of Antiochus IV, the epitomist can be excluded as the author of the second letter. It must derive, therefore, from a final editor of 2 Maccabees, who either himself composed the second letter or took it over from an existing source and placed it (together with the first letter) in front of the epitome.

To the 2nd question: The author himself calls his work an excerpt from the longer historical work of Jason of Cyrene. In the epitome, one can find traces of the divisions of the five-volume original, since it is possible to divide the epitome into five major sections on the basis of the stereotyped sentences in 2 Macc. 3.40; 7.42; 10.9; 13.26b; and 15.37a, which could represent the conclusions of the original five books. Jason was evidently a contemporary of Judas Maccabaeus and composed his work soon after Judas's death (160 BCE). To what extent this also holds for the epitomist, however, is debated.

Within the framework of a diachronistically oriented model, scholars have postulated a number of tradition levels for 2 Macc. 2.19–15.39. In this view, the basis of the epitome was the five-volume history of Jason of Cyrene, but he himself had various sources at his disposal, for example the letters from the years 165/4–163 cited in ch. 11, though their order is debated. Many scholars assume that the epitomist in the course of his summarizing work has re-arranged the authentic documents, which Jason himself had cited, and have thus proposed alternative historical arrangements of the documents, e.g. 11.27-33; 11.16-21; 11.34-38; 11.22-26, or a reverse sequence for the first two texts, namely, 11.16-21 and 11.27-33. Furthermore, there is a general consensus among the scholars that the following passages were not included in Jason's work but rather were added either by the epitomist or by a later, final redactor:

1 The passages consisting of the preface (2.19-32), the reflections and transitional commentaries (4.17; 5.17-20; 6.12-17; 9.28-29; 10.10) and the epilogue (15.37-39) stem from the epitomist and were inserted by him into Jason's account. Many scholars likewise treat the letter of the dying Antiochus IV Epiphanes cited in ch 9.18-27 as a work of the epitomist.
2 Ch. 7.1-42 has been translated from a Semitic language. This is a sign that this passage does not come from Jason but rather has been inserted in a prominent place by the epitomist. Since ch. 7 plays a central role in the overall structure of 2 Macc., it is certainly a part of the epitome and not a secondary addition of the final redactor.

Alongside these graded (re-)constructions of 2 Macc. 2.19–15.39, one also finds scholars (e.g. R. Zwick) who hold it to be conceivable that the literary figure of the epitome was not in fact based on any real original, but rather was made up by the 'epitomist' himself. Then he would be a mere 'author' (in the sense of a stand-alone narrator). For this proposal, it is argued that the linguistic, stylistic and syntactic mannerisms and rhetorical instruments (fondness for word-play and → *hapaxlegomena*) pervade the whole book in such a consistent way that 2.19–15.39 must be considered a unified work by a single author. In this view, the work of Jason is reduced at best to a quarry-like collection of historical notes used selectively by the author (so S. Zeitlin) or at worst to a fictitious source invented by the author to enhance the reliability of his 'epitome' and to praise its easy readability, by calling attention to its shortness (so R. Zwick). Fundamentally, the textual observations of this synchronic interpretation model rightly give greater weight to the contribution of the author/epitomist; however, in my opinion, they do not necessarily exclude the use of a pre-existing source, i.e. the work of Jason. One can understand the role of the epitomist not simply as compiling a shortened version of the original but also as creating an independent work with its own style based on the original. In that case, the observations about the textual consistency of the work can easily be reconciled with the epitomist's own description of his work in 2 Macc. 2.23.

## 29.8 Origins of Second Maccabees

The efforts to identify possible sources for Jason of Cyrene have proven quite hypothetical. Under discussion is a Judas vita that also might have served as a source for 1 Maccabees. According to the diachronic model favoured by the majority of scholars, the basic text of 2 Maccabees derives from the work of Jason of Cyrene, which the epitomist has summarized; in doing so, however, he used this text selectively and interpreted it in such a way as to create a work with its own character and intentions. In this connection, one should view the efforts to re-arrange the four letters cited in ch. 11, which are generally regarded as authentic: they presumably go back to the original work of Jason of Cyrene. The epitomist himself added the whole preface, the reflections and the epilogue, as well as ch. 7 and the fictive letter of Antiochus IV (9.18-27). The overall structure of the book as well as the linguistic-stylistic characteristics, the rhetorical devices, and the combination of various textual types from the most disparate literary and social contexts, i.e. letters, decrees, war stories, miracle accounts, martyr legends, apparition accounts, prayers, etc., show that the epitomist has composed his work as an authorial narrator with enormous linguistic-stylistic, rhetorical, narrative, and theological competence. The result is a multi-functional text answering to a variety of fundamental intentions. One can read 2 Maccabees: (1) as the festival legend for the → *Hanukkah* feast and the Nicanor Day; (2) as a deliberate counter-view to the pro-Hasmonean interpretation of history in 1 Maccabees; (3) as a theological project to put Yhwh's pedagogical dealings with his people into the foreground and to thematize the problem of → *theodicy*; (4) as a piece of propaganda for the Jerusalem Temple and the unity of God's people (especially aimed at the diaspora); and (5) as an apologetic insisting that the Jews conduct no wars of aggression but only wars of defense and that they even pray for their enemies (3.31-34).

As to the two opening letters, they are undoubtedly later additions by a final redactor designed to support the tendency of 2 Maccabees to bind the Egyptian diaspora on Jerusalem and to establish the new feast days.

The dating of the work is a matter of debate. Various dates have been proposed, ranging from as early as the middle of the 2nd cent. BCE (i.e. before

1 Maccabees) to as late as the year 70 CE. When one takes into account: (1) that the work of Jason of Cyrene must have been completed before the composition of 2 Maccabees; (2) that 2 Maccabees shares the same friendliness to the Romans as 1 Maccabees and therefore must have been written before 63 BCE; (3) that the first introductory letter dates to 124 BCE; and (4) that the expansionist politics of the Maccabees is nowhere mentioned, respectively that a critical attitude toward the policies of Johannes Hyrcanus is remarkable; then a variety of arguments speak for a composition of 2 Maccabees during the reign of Johannes Hyrcanus, i.e. 135/4–104. Both the overall structure of 2 Maccabees and the self-identification of the sender of the letters speak for an origin in Jerusalem. The authors of the individual parts as well as the final redactors were presumably members of the Jerusalem upper classes, who enjoyed a Greek education and had contacts with Alexandria: they were concerned about the temple and the Torah and wanted to bring about a closer connection of the → *diaspora* Jews of Egypt with the Jerusalem Temple.

## 29.9 Theology of Second Maccabees

By contrast to 1 Maccabees, the legitimation of the Hasmonean Dynasty is not a concern of 2 Maccabees. Judas is indeed positively regarded as a warrior and instrument of God, but his brother Simon Maccabaeus is criticized (10.19-20; 14.17). Much more important than the family of the Maccabees are the following theological themes:

### 29.9.1 Theology of the Temple

At the centre of the theology of 2 Maccabees is the temple in Jerusalem, as the centre of Jewish religiosity and the place of meeting between Yhwh and the pious Jews loyal to the law (wherever they may live). However, the temple and its cult are in danger when Jews fall away from their observance of the Torah (3.1; 4.16-17; 5.17-20; 6.12-17; 7.18, 32; 10.4). When that happens, God himself abandons his sanctuary (5.17) and allows the pagans to defile it. Thus the behaviour of 'Israel' is closely interwoven with the fate of the temple and of God's people. The rescue and restoration of the place of worship in 2 Macc. 10.2-3 are only possible because the guilt has been atoned for, 'Israel' has been reconciled with its God, and the divine wrath has been transformed into mercy. The story of 'Israel's' suffering thus appears as an expression of the divine will to educate his people, while leading them (6.12-16; 7.33; 10.4

cf. Wis. 3.5; 11.9, 15–12.27). In contrast to 1 Maccabees, where God himself does not actively intervene in the events, in 2 Maccabees Yhwh repeatedly acts directly to protect his sanctuary (3.24-34; 9.5; 14.34-35; 15.23-24, 34). The exclusive significance of the Jerusalem Temple, which is brought to expression in these passages, is meant especially as a message to the → *diaspora* Jews.

## 29.9.2 Theology of the Festivals

2 Maccabees provides the festival legends underlying the Hanukkah festival and the Nicanor Day. Both feasts are relatively new and are closely connected with the history of the Jerusalem Temple. The two introductory letters underscore the idea (only implicit in the epitome), that these feasts unite the Jews in the land and the Jews in the → diaspora in their praise of Yhwh.

## 29.9.3 Theology of the Martyrs

A single Jew who violates his fidelity to the law damages Yhwh's relationship to his people just as much as a single Jew who suffers martyrdom for the sake of his fidelity to the law can restore the relationship between Yhwh and his people (6.28; 7.37-38; 14.37-46). The vicarious suffering and intercessions of the righteous martyrs are the presuppositions for the reconciliation of the 'people' with its God.

## 29.9.4 Resurrection after Death

2 Maccabees 7 is – alongside Dan. 12, 1 En., and the LXX[8] – one of the oldest texts which have been handed down to us, that bring up the belief in the resurrection of the dead. The text takes up the terminology already known from Dan. 12. It is marked, on the one hand, by the theological interest in the active role of God in the resurrection and on the other by the emphasis on the bodily element of the risen person. The earthly martyrdom with its brutal destruction of the body will be counteracted by the bodily resurrection and the complete

8. On 'resurrection' in the LXX see A. van der Kooij, 'Ideas about the Afterlife in the Septuagint', in *Lebendige Hoffnung – ewiger Tod?! Jenseitsvorstellungen im Hellenismus, Judentum und Christentum* (Arbeiten zur Bibel und ihrer Geschichte 24; ed. M. Labahn and M. Lang; Leipzig: Evangelische Verlagsanstalt, 2007), 87–102; for a different view, see J. Schnocks, 'The Hope of Resurrection in the Book of Job', in *The Septuagint and Messianism* (BETL 195; ed. M. A. Knibb; Leuven: Peeters, 2006), 291–9.

bodily restitution in the eternal mode of resurrected existence (2 Macc. 7.11, 14). Individual hope in the resurrection and the theology of martyrdom are combined. The premature death of the just person puts to test the traditional 'Action-Consequence-Construct', according to which blessing automatically follows good action; disaster automatically follows sin (Ch. 14.1). By introducing the idea of a post-mortal resurrection and reward of the just person, the validity of this principle is maintained, but its ultimate fulfilment is put off to a time after death. In this connection, 2 Macc. 7.22-23 connects the resurrection of the martyrs with the theological notion of creation (*creatio ex nihilo* in 7.28). Sinners can expect *in this life* punishment mirroring their deeds (for Jason: 4.26; 5.9-10; for Menelaus: 13.8; for Antiochus IV: 9.6, 28; for Andronicus: 4.38; for Lysimachus: 4.42; for Nicanor 15.32-33); *in the next life*, they can expect not the resurrection to new life (see Antiochus IV. Epiphanes 7.14), but rather God's judgement, from which they will receive the punishment they deserve. In addition, 2 Macc. 12.43-45 indicates that one can posthumously redeem God's deceased warriors who have sinned by offering prayers of intercession and sacrifices of → *atonement*. Scenes in heaven (15.12-19) point to the idea that the just live together in heaven after their death and that, from heaven, they can act for the aid of the living.

## 29.10 Notes on the History of Reception

Second Maccabees is above all concerned with the theological aspects of the Maccabean revolt. It addresses and further develops numerous theological themes, which already had been prepared within the Hebrew OT. The remarks of 2 Maccabees on intercessory prayer, → *atonement*, vicarious suffering, and resurrection of the dead build a bridge to the NT, so that this book must be reckoned among the most important witnesses to the time between the testaments. To the history of reception belong the books of 3 and 4 Maccabees, which made use of 2 Maccabees as a source. A special reception history developed around the story in 2 Macc. 7, of the martyrdom of the seven brothers and their mother (who traditionally was given the name 'Salome' or 'Salomone'). As to the brothers themselves, although their names are not given in the biblical text and although they hardly were connected with the Maccabee family, they have traditionally been called the 'Holy Maccabees'. The extensive reception history of this tale is reflected in numerous rabbinical and patristic texts, as well as in the fact that these Jewish martyrs have been raised to Christian sainthood (whereas there is no mention of Jewish veneration or even of a 'Maccabee Synagogue'). Toward the end of the 4th cent. CE, there was already a Christian feast in their honor, and Augustine relates that in Antioch, the reputed place of their martyrdom, there was a Christian memorial basilica. According to St. Jerome (ca. 380 CE), their relics were also displayed in Antioch. Relics were also later brought to Constantinople and Rome, where to this day they are venerated in the church of San Pietro in Vincoli. According to a medieval legend, Reinald von Dassel received the 'Maccabee relics' together with the relics of the Three Kings from the Emperor Friedrich Barbarossa in Milan and brought them to Cologne in 1164. The same legend is quoted in the Latin inscription on the Maccabees Shrine in Cologne: 'Archbishop Reinald brought to this Ursuline Field in 1164 the holy bodies of the seven Maccabees, who illustrate the suffering of our Savior, as well as the body of their holy mother Salomone, who presaged the suffering of Holy Mary.' Ever since 1808, this shrine, which originally stood on a shelf of the high altar of the church of the Maccabees monastery in Cologne, can be viewed in the Dominican convent of St. Andreas in Cologne. The wooden casket in the form of a house with a gabled roof is covered with gilded copper plates and stems from the beginning of the 16th century. The side walls and also the roof surfaces of the shrine are decorated with a total of 40 scenes in relief, which depict the history of the martyrdom of the seven brothers and their mother (2 Macc. 7) and parallel to them – within the framework of a → *typological* interpretation of the OT and NT – scenes of the suffering of Christ and his mother, e.g. the scourging of the brothers is set alongside the scourging of Christ; the ascension of the brothers corresponds to the ascension of Christ. The Maccabees Altar in the church of St. Mary in Cologne (1756), which originally stood in the Maccabee Church, is a masterpiece of Baroque woodcarving. It too thematizes 2 Macc. 7 and exalts the mother of the seven martyrs and her sons. In addition to the Christian reception of the 2 Macc. 7 legend, the expulsion of Heliodorus from the temple (2 Macc. 3) has inspired the paintings of various artists, e.g. E. Delacroix's 'Studies on the expulsion of Heliodorus'; Raphael's frescos in the Heliodorus Stanza of the Vatican (1512–1514).

**Fig. 18a:** Perutah of Jehochanan/Hyrkan I. Obverse: Phoenician inscription in a wreath: יהוחנן הכהן הגדל וחבר היהודים A – "A Jehochanan, the high priest and the cooperative of the Jews". Reverse: double cornucopias with ribbons, hanging grapes, fruits and cereal ears.

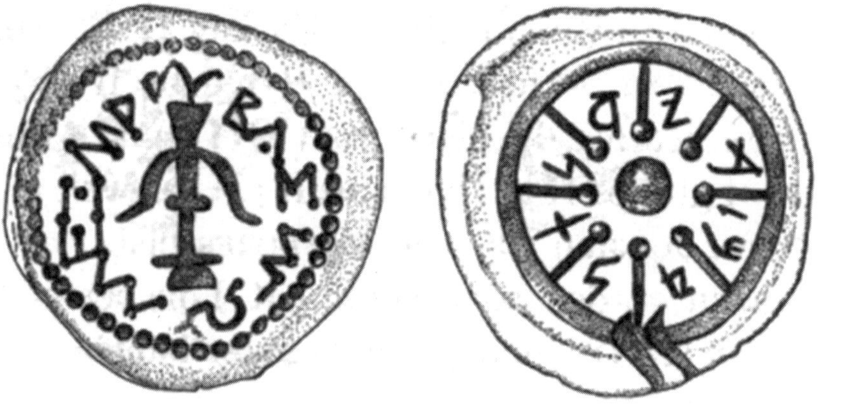

**Fig. 18b:** Perutah of Jehonatan/Alexander Jannaios. Obverse: Anchor encircled with a Greek inscription: *ΑΛΕΞΑΝΔΡΟΨ ΒΑΣΙΛΕΩ[Σ]* – "of King Alexander", in point circle. Reverse: Star with eight rays in a diadem, between the rays a phoenician inscription: ה·מל·ך·י·הו·נ·ת·ן – "the King Jehonatan".

# 30

# The Prayer of Manasseh (Oratio Manassae)

## (Markus Witte – Translation by Mark Biddle)

J. H. Charlesworth (Pages 625–37 in OTP 2. Garden City, N. Y.: Doubleday, 1985); E. Oswald (Pages 15–27 in JSHRZ IV.1. 2nd ed. Gütersloh: Gütersloher Verlagshaus, 1977; A.-M. Denis, *Introduction à la littérature religieuse judéo-hellénistique* I. Turnhout: Brepols, 2000, 659–79; G. S. Oegema, 'Poetische Schriften'. Pages 1–10 in JSHRZ VI.1,4. Gütersloh: Gütersloher Verlagshaus, 2002.

The prayer, transmitted in Greek and Latin, as well as in Syriac, Arabic, Armenian, Ethiopic, Coptic and Old Slavonic, represents a confession of sin placed in the mouth of King Manasseh (696–642 BCE) composed on the basis of the diction of Old Testament psalms (cf. esp. Ps. 51 [Ps. $50^{LXX}$]). Its → *anthological* style (*mosaic style)*, its fiction as a prayer of Manasseh, its prominent conversion theology, and its universal concept of God as the just ruler of all (*pantokratōr*) mark it as Judeo-Hellenistic role poetry with parallels in Dan. 9 and Jdt. 9.[1] The link for the content of the 15 verses of the poem composed originally in Greek[2] is the repentance of Manasseh recounted only in Chronicles (Ch. 23; 2 Chr. 33.11-19) and the summary of his prayer (2 Chr. 33.12-12, 18-19).

The Prayer of Manasseh (*Pr Man*) is transmitted in the *Codex Alexandrinus* in the so-called *Odes (Cantica)*, a collection of canonical and apocryphal poems appended to the Psalter (Ch. 13). Accordingly, the study edition of the Septuagint by Alfred Rahlfs (1935/1979) places it among the odes. In a few manuscripts of the Vulgate, it appears either as a supplement to 2 Chr.

1. See J. van Oorschot, 'Nachkultische Psalmen und spätbiblische Rollendichtung', *ZAW* 106 (1994): 69–86.
2. The Hebrew 'Prayer of Manasseh' found in cave 4 at Qumran (4Q381 33.8-11, translated in F. García Martínez and E. J. C. Tigchelaar, *The Dead Sea Scrolls* II, 758–9) has nothing to do with the text under discussion. It may stem from the pre-chronistic period and is an early witness to the intensive engagement with the figure of King Manasseh in later Judaism. The Hebrew version of the *Prayer of Manasseh* found in the Cairo Geniza (see the box in Ch. 27.2) is a late back-translation.

33.13, 19 or an appendix to 2 Chronicles. In the study edition of the Vulgate by Robert Weber (1969/4th ed., 1994), it begins the appendix. Martin Luther included it among the → *apocrypha* in the complete German Bible of 1534. Here, it assumes final position and, thus, stands directly before the New Testament. In view of its key theme, the confession of the creator God's justice and willingness to forgive, and its function, to call by example for repentance (*metanoia*), for trust in God's mercy, and for the praise of God (cf. vv. 7-8), this position is appropriate to its content.

Together with the five Syriac psalms transmitted in the *Peshitta*, the first of which is also known from the Septuagint tradition as Ps. 151 and the first through third in their Hebrew form from the great Psalm scroll from Qumran (11QPs[a]),[3] with the songs of praise from Qumran (1QH[a]),[4] with individual prayers interspersed in the → *apocrypha*,[5] or with the Psalms of Solomon,[6] the Prayer of Manasseh attests to the vitality of Jewish psalmody in the Hellenistic-Roman period.[7]

3. A. S. van der Woude, *Die fünf syrischen Psalmen (einschließlich Psalm 151)* (JSHRZ IV/1; Gütersloh: Gütersloher Verlagshaus, 1974), 29–47; F. García Martínez and E. J. C. Tigchelaar, *The Dead Sea Scrolls* II, 1172–9; G. S. Oegema, Poetische Schriften, 11–21.
4. F. García Martínez and E. J. C. Tigchelaar, *The Dead Sea Scrolls* I, 146–205.
5. Cf. Jdt. 9, Tob. 13, Dan.[LXX] 3.25-90 (Ch. 21B, Ch. 24 and Ch. 26) or Est.[LXX] 4.17a-z (Ch. 20B).
6. S. Holm-Nielsen, *Die Psalmen Salomos* (JSHRZ IV/2; Gütersloh: Gütersloher Verlagshaus, 1977), 51–112; G. S. Oegema, *Poetische Schriften*, 22–33; R. B. Wright, 'Psalms of Solomon', in *OTP* II (Garden City, N.Y.: Doubleday, 1985), 639–70.
7. See D. Flusser, 'Psalms, Hymns and Prayers', in *Jewish Writings of the Second Temple Period* (CRINT 2/2; ed. M. E. Stone; Assen: Van Gorcum, 1984), 551–77; R. Egger-Wenzel and J. Corley, eds, *Prayer from Tobit to Qumran* (Deuterocanonical Literature Yearbook; Berlin/New York: de Gruyter, 2004).

# Part VII
# Basic Outline of a Theology of the Old Testament

(Jan Christian Gertz – Translation by Peter Altmann)

Bibliography 10.1 Concepts of Old Testament Theology (B .S. Childs, *Theology*; W. Eichrodt, *Theology*; J. Jeremias, *Entwürfe;* R. Rendtorff, *Canonical Hebrew Bible;* W. H. Schmidt, *Faith;* W. Zimmerli, *Theology*); 10.2 The Question of Biblical Theology (C. Dohmen/T. Söding, *Bibel*). Further: A. de Pury and E. A. Knauf, 'La théologie de l'Ancien Testament: Kérygmatique ou descriptive?' *ETR* 70 (1995): 323–34; R. Smend, 'Theologie im Alten Testament'. Pages 104–17 in *Die Mitte des Alten Testaments: Gesammelte Studien 1*. BEvT 99. Munich: Kaiser, 1986.

*Preliminary Remarks*: The preceding discussions of the literature of the Old Testament/Hebrew Bible have also in and of themselves begun to develop a theology of the corresponding part of the → *canon* and texts. This approach is based on the presupposition that theology of the Old Testament should be understood as a descriptive task, attempting to describe the theological ideas of the authors and redactors of the biblical literature in their historical contexts. One can speak of 'theology' in the Old Testament wherever an overarching understanding of reality is expressed, which gives meaning to a contingent individual experience. Within the Old Testament literature such a concept of reality takes on different forms – although there are several points of contact between individual literary works and their fundamental theological ideas. The separate origins and profiles of the various conceptions should therefore be investigated. Correspondingly, in this textbook the description of the basic theological ideas has been included in the discussion of the individual textual complexes. Since this approach to a 'Theology of the Old Testament' is not the only possible nor sensible one, the following discussion will focus on the history and problems of the discipline as well as elucidate competing conceptions of the subject.

# 31

# Concepts in the History of Scholarship

## Chapter Outline



Bibliography 10.2 The Question of Biblical Theology (M. Oeming, *Theologien*). Further: J. H. Hayes and F. C. Prussner, *Old Testament Theology: Its History and Development*. Atlanta, Ga.: Westminster John Knox, 1985; J. Høgenhaven, *Problems and Prospects of Old Testament Theology*. Sheffield: JSOT Press, 1988; H.-J. Kraus, *Die Biblische Theologie: Ihre Geschichte und Problematik*. Neukirchen-Vluyn: Neukirchener, 1970, 15–125; W. Zimmerli, 'Biblische Theologie I'. Pages 426–55 in vol. 6 of *TRE*. Berlin/New York: de Gruyter: 1980.

## 31.1 From the Dicta Probantia of the Dogmatic Loci to the History of Religion of Israel

'Theology of the Old Testament' is a comparably new discipline that resulted from an ongoing process of differentiation in the recent history of theological studies. The foundational moment is commonly accepted to have been the inaugural lecture by Johann Philipp Gabler (1753–1826) held at the university of Altdorf on March 30, 1787. Its title was '*De justo discrimine theologiae biblicae et dogmaticae regundisque recte utriusque finibus*.'[1] The first step of differentiation therefore lay in the programmatic distinction (*discrimen*) between biblical studies and dogmatic theology. This distinction attempts to take seriously the intention of the biblical texts and their idiosyncrasies in opposition to the ruling dogmatics of the time.

A short overview of the state of theological and biblical studies at the time proves helpful when trying to understand Gabler's distinction. The churches of the Reformation had declared the 'Holy Scriptures' the exclusive source of Christian proclamation (*sola scriptura*). The consolidation of the Protestant church and its theology, however, inevitably led to the point in Protestant orthodoxy when the necessary development of a Protestant teaching mostly took the form of systematic description. The 'Holy Scripture' was pushed almost unavoidably into the subordinate role as a collection of individual biblical words or statements providing evidence (*dicta probantia*) for the doctrinal statements of the domains (*loci*) of dogmatic theology. Biblical studies in this regard became something of an auxiliary discipline to dogmatics, even if in individual cases it became its competitor as well. This occurred when a particular theology was detected *in* the Bible that was far closer to one's own theological conceptions than to the church's orthodoxy. This was the case especially for the two unequal children of the Enlightenment, Pietism which took recourse to personal faith experience and Neology which sought to develop rationally sufficient dogmatics. Both invoked the Bible against the positions of orthodoxy. The competition between biblical studies and dogmatics became more pointed through the introduction of historical-critical exegesis. Here, especially Johann Salomo Semler (1725) and his *Abhandlung von freier Untersuchung des Canon* ([ET: 'Treatise on a Free Investigation of the Canon'; 1771–75) should be named. The title speaks volumes: The → *canon* should be open for investigation unfettered by dogmatic guidelines just like all other literature. The result and presupposition of such an investigation is the insight that the biblical books and the canon

1. 'An Oration on the Proper Distinction between Biblical and Dogmatic Theology and the Specific Objectives of Each.' An English translation of the lecture can be found in *Old Testament Theology: Flowering and Future* (Sources for Biblical and Theological Study 1; ed. B. C. Ollenburger; 2nd ed; Winona Lake, Ind.: Eisenbrauns, 2004), 497–506. On Gabler see also R. Smend, 'Johann Philipp Gablers Begründung der Biblischen Theologie', in *Epochen der Bibelkritik: Gesammelte Studien 3* (BEvT 109; Munich: Kaiser, 1991 [original 1962]), 104–16.

are products of their time. Semler correspondingly differentiated between the 'Word of God', the lasting, always valid basic truths in the biblical writings, and the 'Holy Scriptures', the historically conditioned and transient statements of the biblical writers. At the same time this perspective on the historicality of biblical assertions fundamentally questioned the normative character of the text for present-day religion. How could biblical studies remain both historically precise and at the same time theologically productive?

Gabler's answer to this question was the already mentioned differentiation between biblical and dogmatic theology. Biblical theology works historically: its duty is to investigate and pass on what the biblical authors thought about divine matters. As a historical discipline it is concerned with invariable facts. This is different for dogmatic theology, which has an instructional character and teaches what a certain theologian thinks under the conditions of his time about divine matters. Because dogmatic theology is time-dependent it is subject to multiple changes. If dogmatics is to be biblically based, then there needs to be mediation between biblical and dogmatic theology. Gabler introduced a further distinction here within biblical theology itself. 'True biblical theology' is strictly historical: it explains the biblical writings historically and philologically and compares their theological conceptualizations. In addition there is a biblical theology that describes what remains valid in the biblical writings for the Christians of today. These basic ideas then become the foundation for dogmatic reflections oriented towards the present. This second type of biblical theology, more on the side of dogmatic theology, Gabler described as 'pure biblical theology'; 'pure' because it derives solely from the foundational ideals found in the Bible that are blended with the various temporal ideas and must first be separated from these time-bound statements.

The next distinction on the road to a discipline called 'Theology of the Old Testament' took place in the history-of-religion-differentiation between the Old and the New Testament, which can be traced back to Georg Lorenz Bauer (1755–1806). Decisive for this step was the historical insight into the self-understanding of the Old Testament writings as pre-Christian and non-Christian documents that reflect the faith of 'Israel' in its God in very different ways. For Bauer (and many others) the formulation of this insight was accompanied by a clear devaluation of the Old Testament. However, this does not change the objective correctness of treating the Old Testament as a self-contained unit separate from the New Testament. Namely as the 'Hebrew Bible' it is always also to be taken seriously as the document of another religion, even if the Christians of the early communities understood themselves as Jews. This is the case not only from the perspective of history, but also in view of the present in that the first and oldest part of the Christian Bible retains its pre-Christian character and remains simultaneously in relation to Judaism. The insight into the historicality of the biblical traditions problematized their use as theological statements with normative value and timeless claims. The insight into the history-of-religions and the unavoidable difference between the Old and New Testaments further presents the problem of the unity of biblical theology.

This problem grew even more acute in the subsequent period. The historical investigation necessarily led to differentiations in the understanding of the religious history within the two Testaments. In this regard Wilhelm Martin Leberecht de Wette (1780–1849) offered a groundbreaking work in his *Biblische Dogmatik Alten und Neuen Testaments* ('Biblical Dogmatics of the Old and New Testaments') published in 1813 whose subtitle named the most important inner differences: *kritische Darstellung der Religionslehre des Hebraismus, des Judenthums und des Urchristenthums* ('critical portrayal of the religious doctrine of "Hebraism", Judaism, and early Christianity'), in which the religion of the New Testament was further differentiated into the 'Teaching of Jesus' and the 'Teaching of the Apostles'. With regard to the Old Testament, the subsequent and most influential religious-historical differentiations stem from Bernhard Duhm (1847–1928)[2] and especially from Julius Wellhausen (1844–1918).[3] Following de Wette, but with a new source-critical foundation (Ch. 5.2) they differentiated the ancient Israelite religion of the pre-exilic period (→ *exile*), the Judaism of the post-exilic period, as well as a transitional phase between these two periods in which Deuteronomy was located. In addition they viewed the religion of pre-exilic prophecy as an independent phenomenon. The 'future', that is the end of the 19th century and the beginning of the 20th century, belonged to the description of the various religious phenomena and their placement in a historical chronology. Questions oriented towards an understanding of the whole of the Old Testament and its religion receded into the background. The terminological consequences of this change were drawn out by Rudolf

2. B. Duhm, *Theologie der Propheten als Grundlage für die innere Entwicklungsgeschichte der israelitischen Religion* (Bonn: Marcus, 1875).

3. J. Wellhausen, *Prolegomena to the History of Israel* (transl. and preface by W. R. Smith; Atlanta, Ga.: Scholars Press, 1994; transl. of *Prolegomena zur Geschichte Israels* [6th ed., Berlin/New York: de Gruyter, 1927; Student edition, 2001; 1st ed. 1878 under the title *Geschichte Israels I*]).

Smend, sr. (1851–1913), who titled his 1893 presentation *Alttestamentliche Religionsgeschichte* ('Old Testament History of Religion') and supported this choice with the argument that the name 'biblical theology' had been correct for a certain period of scholarly discussion but did not correspond with the essence of scholarship in the present moment.[4]

## 31.2 The History of Israelite Religion and the Theology of the Old Testament

The strong emphasis on the lack of continuity and on fractures within the Old Testament history of religion did not remain without a counter movement. The results of the religious-historical work itself led to a crisis in historicism and the search for something timeless in the stream of historical change. Also, by neglecting a comprehensive view on the Old Testament and instead focusing on the diverse historical phenomena the importance of the Old Testament for Christian theology was placed in question. The discipline was in danger of being transferred from theological studies into the realm of ancient Near Eastern religious history. The undeniable recognition of religious change within the texts of the Old Testament hindered a return to the approach to biblical theology as it was known before Gabler. For this reason a two-part presentation format, first the presentation of the historical development of Old Testament religion and then in a second part the religious content of the Old Testament, was introduced. The history of Israelite-Jewish religion and the theology of the Old Testament were seen as two different entities that did not exclude but rather complemented one another. This is naturally reminiscent of Gabler's distinction between 'true biblical theology' and 'pure biblical theology' and their interaction.

So theology of the Old Testament addressed the two connected problem areas to which Gabler had drawn attention and that became increasingly pressing: the normative validity of Old Testament statements about faith for Christian theology as well as the nature and unity of Old Testament religion. Addressing the question of the normative validity in fact led to a

4. R. Smend, sr., *Lehrbuch der alttestamentlichen Religionsgeschichte* (Freiburg: J. C. B. Mohr, 1893; rev. ed.; Tübingen: Mohr Siebeck, 1899).

particular approach. Walther Eichrodt (1890–1978), in his widely received *Theology of the Old Testament*,[5] was not concerned with the question of whether Old Testament religion was right or wrong to claim validity, but rather what the Old Testament actually meant and what was essential for its story. According to Eichrodt the intrinsic nature of the Old Testament reveals itself when viewed in the light of the Christ event – which is also what secures its relevance for present Christianity. Eichrodt viewed the Old Testament as moving beyond itself towards the New Testament. In this perspective, taken for itself the Old Testament is incomplete and first finds its completion in the appearance of Christ. This is proven by the negative example of post-biblical Judaism, which to Eichrodt features a 'torso-like appearance'.[6] It is obvious that the relevance of the Old Testament for the present here is bought at the price of an unhistorical as well as improper description of the Old Testament and Judaism. The inclusion of Old Testament statements about faith into a system of Christian theology Eichrodt assigned to dogmatics, for instance to the doctrine of Scripture. More attention was given to the question of the unity of Old Testament religion. It is inseparably connected with the search for an appropriate structure for a theology of the Old Testament. However, a dilemma loomed: in contrast to the history of religion, Old Testament Theology should offer a systematic presentation and provide fruitful connections for dogmatics. On the other hand it should not take its approach to the material from dogmatics but from the Old Testament itself. Yet this was made nearly impossible by the religious-historical differences within the Old Testament. Eichrodt argued that the unity of the Old Testament appears in a persistent tendency and its consistent foundational form. As a fundamental tendency he identified the previously mentioned movement towards the New Testament. The consistent foundational form he saw expressed in the term → *covenant* (Heb. *bĕrît*), which is developed in light of the relationships between God and the people, God and the world, as well as God and the individual. However, the attempt to establish the covenantal idea as the unity-forming organizational principle is problematic. In the Old Testament the term *covenant* serves neither as the exclusive nor the first conceptualization of the relationship to God. It instead concerns a relatively late theological concept that does not have the systematically central role

5. W. Eichrodt, *Theology*.

6. Cf. Ibid., Vol. 1.26-7.

that Eichrodt attributes to it. The term does indisputably offer a central category for determining the relationship between God and the people since the rise of → *Deuteronomism*. However, covenant already recedes to the background when turning to the description of the relationship between God and the world. It has almost no meaning for the relationship between God and the individual. Therefore, one cannot say that the unity and essence of the various Old Testament witnesses to God lie in the notion of covenant. As a result, a systematic presentation oriented towards the notion of covenant can only in a very limited manner assert that it arises from the Old Testament itself. A similar conclusion can be drawn for the attempt by Ludwig Köhler (1880–1956), who characterized the unity of the Old Testament with the concept 'The presence of the awe-inspiring Lord'. In any case, Köhler modelled the presentation of his theology clearly on the classical dogmatic outline with the sections theology, → *anthropology*, and → *soteriology*.

The results can be generalized: throughout this period no concept succeeded in doing justice to all the different aspects of Old Testament literature by applying one basic notion. The systematic presentation conceals the historical diversity. The statements of the Old Testament can hardly be systematized as a result of their historical nature and their close relationship to individual circumstances. Yet this is not a result of the notion of covenant not being historically central or the colouring with dogmatic categories. It is instead a product of the fundamental difficulty in providing historical arguments for any hermeneutic key. Every time an individual motif is raised up as the theological centre of the Old Testament this is a hermeneutical-dogmatic procedure rather than a historical undertaking.

## 31.3 Theology of the Old Testament as Retelling

Gerhard von Rad (1901–1971) also took part in the return from the 'history of religion' to 'theology', but he explicitly rejected a systematic mode of presentation since it is too much governed by dogmatics. Such presentations also tend to construe the Old Testament texts as thought complexes, e.g. with the theme 'God the creator', which the Old Testament itself never conceptualized. The Old Testament never makes its statements about God in the timeless fixed forms of doctrine about God, but rather in the form of narrative about God experienced in history. Therefore, a theology of the Old Testament should not be concerned with timeless teachings about God and humanity, but rather with the development of Old Testament witnesses to God's historical actions. As a result in his theology the contrary thesis is as follows: 'Thus, re-telling remains the most legitimate form of theological discourse on the Old Testament.'[7]

Von Rad dismissed the search for a concept unifying the various theologies of the Old Testament as the wrong question. He pointed to the fundamental meaning of the historically conditioned nature of Old Testament formulations of faith. The individual historical witnesses form neither an intellectual unity nor invoke the same revelatory experience. Since they are each referring to a different historical situation they necessarily differ. But this does not put the search for theological unity forever to rest. In place of a 'centre of the Old Testament' (however expressed), von Rad argued for a foundation built on the notion of a theology of history in Old Testament faith: the Old Testament works of literature 'confine themselves to representing Yahweh's relationship to Israel and the world in one aspect only, namely as a continuing divine activity in history'.[8] This thesis became the decisive criterion by which individual theological concepts within the Old Testament must be measured. Qoheleth, the → *apocalyptic* literature, and the postexilic understanding of law were criticized, while the → *Deuteronomistic History (DtrH)* received hermeneutical canonicity. No doubt this is also why the Psalms – the part of the Old Testament canon that has had the greatest influence in Christianity – and the → *wisdom* literature played minor roles in von Rad's theology. The search for the unity of Old Testament faith was then answered by noting what is typical of Yhwh faith, and according to von Rad this is its relation to history. However, the one-sidedness of the approach is certainly just as problematic as the formulation of a 'center of the Old Testament'. In addition, in his historically reflected retelling of the Old Testament witnesses of faith, von Rad drew the boundaries of historical examination only vaguely. He explicitly wanted to offer more than a history of Yhwh faith. Since Israel in its historical witnesses pointed not to its faith but to Yhwh, then the essential matter of a theology of the Old Testament is not faith, but only the revelation of God itself. In fact von Rad's presentation does not conform to this principle. Instead, it consistently develops the 'theology of the historical and the prophetic traditions of

7. G. von Rad, *Theology*, 1.121.

8. Ibid., 106.

Israel', which is the subtitle of both volumes. There is, however, nothing else possible since a theology 'presents not the object of faith, but faith itself in its own self-interpretation'.[9]

This brings up the ever-virulent problem of the normative value of Old Testament theological statements for present-day theology, which in the Christian context is inseparable from one's understanding of the relationship between the two Testaments. Far more than others von Rad investigated the relationship of the Old and New Testament and at least partially attempted to abrogate the separation that had been accepted since Bauer. The starting point was the tradition history of the Old Testament, which von Rad rightly described as a continual process of reinterpreting the extant tradition which thus forms new tradition. The New Testament contains the final hermeneutical repackaging and the definitive interpretation of salvation history according to von Rad. Against this tradition-historical classification of the two Testaments massive objections can be raised. As a historical discipline tradition-history is not bound to the (Christian) canon, meaning that it cannot be limited to the synchronic reception of the Old Testament in the New nor end diachronically with the New Testament. The special emphasis on the New Testament and the determination of its relationship to the Old Testament implies a theological judgement. This is not problematic in and of itself, but it simply cannot be derived by tradition-historical means. Instead, it results from the decision for one of numerous possibilities in the reception history of the Old Testament.

## 31.4 (New) Biblical Theology and Canonical Exegesis

Without question, von Rad's theology of the Old Testament constitutes the most important contribution to this discussion in the 20th century. Subsequent concepts have always referred positively and negatively to his work. Particular influence has been exercised by von Rad's call for 'a look at the Scriptures as a whole'[10] in the development of a (new) 'biblical theology' and specifically in its connection to a canonical approach. It implies a partial revision of the

9. R. Bultmann, *Theology of the New Testament* (2 vols. 2nd rev. ed. Waco, Tex.: Baylor University Press, 2007), 2.239.
10. G. von Rad, 'Grundprobleme einer biblischen Theologie des Alten Testaments', *TLZ* 68 (1943): 225–34, here 230.

differentiations held in biblical studies since Gabler. Thus, Brevard S. Childs' influential project claimed that because of its ecclesial usage, only the final canonical form of the Bible should be the mandatory entity for theology. This form alone has normative authority and should as such be interpreted.[11] The theological task of biblical theology according to Childs is 'to understand the various voices within the whole Christian Bible, New and Old Testament alike, as a witness to the one Lord Jesus Christ, the selfsame divine reality'.[12] In its character as 'witness of the faith of the one Lord Jesus Christ' Childs also grounded the relationship with the present and the normativity of the biblical writings as well as their unity. The Bible is therefore not to be read as a source for understanding the history of religion, but rather as an ongoing witness of faith. It is here that Childs' conception also crosses the border to dogmatics.

Numerous objections can be raised against this programme. Firstly, one should remember Semler's observation that canonization itself was also a historical process that stretched over an extended period of time and came to a certain conclusion also for the Old Testament scriptures first in post New Testament times. It is well known that the extent of the canon differs between the Christian denominations (Ch. 1.2.1.3).[13] The unity and normativity of the Old Testament statements of faith are therefore solely due to the retrospective view of a particular reception of the Old Testament just as in the earlier mentioned programmes for a theology of the Old Testament. It is presumably not by chance that Childs' biblical-theological and dogmatic reflections both in selection and order draw their inspiration from the *loci* of hidden but always present dogmatics.[14] And yet, more important is the theological objection. Viewed theologically as well as reception-historically one can say

11. B. S. Childs, *Theology*.
12. Ibid., 85.
13. Childs follows the canonical limits of the → *Masoretic* canon, which omits the → *apocrypha* found in the Catholic canon. He arranges the Old Testament books according to the order found in the → *Septuagint*. Differently, see R. Rendtorff, *Canonical Hebrew Bible*, whose canon follows the limits and order of the Masoretic canon and intentionally excludes the New Testament.
14. B. S. Childs, *Theology*, 349–716 (ch. 6): 1. The Identity of God; 2. God the Creator; 3. Covenant, Election, People of God; 4. Christ the Lord; 5. Reconciliation with God; 6. Law and Gospel; 7. Humanity: Old and New; 8. Biblical Faith; 9. God's Kingdom and Rule; and 10. The Shape of the Obedient Life: Ethics. Insofar as God's salvific presence in Israel is treated under the catchwords kingship, priesthood and prophecy, Childs orients himself on the teaching of the three offices of Christ (*munus triplex*).

that the texts of the canon as a collection of holy writings of Christianity and its denominations have an extraordinary position that essentially determines their identity – even though the various writings of the canon have always been weighted quite differently. However, Christianity is not a religion of the book in the sense that an eternal nature is attributed the biblical canon (like the Qur᾿an in Moslem orthodoxy). This means that questions asked about what preceded the final form are germane, especially since in terms of textual history this final form is rather elusive. In light of the formation of biblical traditions the notion holds true that every generation stands directly before God. In line with the Protestant understanding of scripture, God remains the free subject of the growth of traditions, and God is free to take the human witness as an instrument in the service of his self-realization 'when and where he desires' (Augsburg Confession Article V). Therefore also the older, only partially historically reconstructable stages of Old Testament faith statements as such are theologically relevant. Finally, a focus on the canon almost invariably leads exegesis to overplay the undeniable dissonance within the biblical writings at the price of rather vague generalizations.

## 31.5 Conclusion

The discipline 'Old Testament Theology' owes its existence to a process of progressive differentiation in the recent period of the history of theology. The basic steps have been the separation of biblical theology from dogmatics, the separation of the disciplines of the Old and New Testaments, as well as the religious-historical distinctions within Old Testament texts.

a The separation of biblical theology from dogmatics came about various reasons. In essence, it is based on the insight into the historical nature of the Bible. This led to the emancipation of the Bible from dogmatic presuppositions. From this perspective the separation from the authoritative ecclesial or theological doctrine belongs with the many cases in church history when the biblical texts developed their critic-producing potential. By taking the historicality seriously a problem arose that has so far only been solved in part: it concerns the question to what degree historical witnesses, which are necessarily particular and contingent, can provide a general and normative meaning also for the present.

b The second step of the differentiation process was the methodical separation of the Old and New Testaments that happened within biblical studies itself. It is also liberating insofar as the Old Testament is then able to receive its own historical significance. The above-named theological problems of the use of the

Old Testament in the context of Christian theology grow larger, however. To the historicality of the biblical traditions is now added the insight that the centuries-old Christian handling of the Old Testament does not correspond to its original intention – not least because from a historical perspective the scriptures collected in the Old Testament represent both a pre- and a non-Christian entity.

c All other differentiations took place within Old Testament scholarship. A growing historical understanding increasingly allows the diversity of the Old Testament witnesses to come to light. Acknowledging the multiplicity of the Old Testament discourse about God facilitates the recognition of the texts as entities with individual profiles and makes possible a deeper understanding of the texts. However, it also heightens the theological difficulty that comes with the historicality of the Bible: it no longer seems possible to even provide an answer to the question regarding what *the Old Testament as a whole* says about the nature and acts of God. This then directly influences the question of the normative significance of Old Testament statements of faith. In addition there is the insight that the salvation events reported in the Old Testament present a 'believed history' that witnesses to interpretative handling of historical experiences while the reported events themselves cannot be verified historically. At first glance this insight does not exactly promote the claim of Old Testament texts to normative validity. The question, i.e., what Moses and the Israelites' exodus through the Sea of Reeds means for the Christian faith, now turns into the question: what does it mean for Christian faith that the experiences of Israel of the early exilic period were processed by considering the believed exodus through the Sea of Reeds?

Taking a look back, it is especially the diversity of the Old Testament declarations of faith, the relationship between the religious-historical and the theological perspectives, and methods of presentation, as well as the level of importance given to Old Testament declarations of faith within Christian theology that mark the discussion about a theology of the Old Testament. Also, it is in the appraisal of these three factors that the concepts of a theology of the Old Testament differ.

# 32

# Unity and Diversity in the Theological Statements in the Old Testament

S. Gesundheit, 'Gibt es eine jüdische Theologie der hebräischen Bibel?' Pages 73–86 in *Theologie und Exegese des Alten Testaments/der Hebräischen Bibel: Zwischenbilanz und Zukunftsperspektiven*. SBS 200. Ed. by B. Janowski. Stuttgart: Katholisches Bibelwerk, 2005; J. D. Levenson, 'Warum Juden sich nicht für biblische Theologie interessieren'. *EvT* 51 (1991): 402–30; R. Murphy, 'Questions Concerning Biblical Theology'. *BTB* 30 (2000): 81–9; idem, 'Once again – the "Center" of the Old Testament'. *BTB* 31 (2001): 85–9; G. von Rad, 'Offene Fragen im Umkreis einer Theologie des Alten Testaments'. Pages 289–312 in *Gesammelte Studien zum AT II*. TB 48. Munich: Kaiser, 1973 (1963); H.-C. Schmitt, 'Die Einheit der Schrift und die Mitte des Alten Testaments'. Pages 326–45 in *Theologie in Prophetie und Pentateuch: Gesammelte Schriften*. BZAW 310. Berlin: de Gruyter, 2001; R. Smend, jr., 'Die Mitte des Alten Testaments'. Pages 40–84 in *Die Mitte des Alten Testaments: Gesammelte Studien 1*. BEvT 99. Munich: Kaiser, 1986.

The problem posed in the title of this section remains ever at hand in debates concerning the theology of the Old Testament. The history of religion approach at best identified a unity in the historical development of Old Testament religion. In intentional contrast, others attempted to construct a systematic picture of the whole expressing the unity of Old Testament religion, or determined the content of 'the centre of the Old Testament' (Ch. 31). In each case the basic intention is rather similar. It is concerned with the attempt to bring together opposing positions: the insight into the diversity of the Old Testament faith statements and the search for the unity of the Old Testament for the sake of its relevance for current theology. If the Old Testament is understood as a theological unity, then this makes a systematic presentation of its declarations of faith possible. A systematic presentation has the indisputable practical advantage that it can present the Old Testament notions of God, humanity, and the world in such a way that the Old Testament as a whole can be set in relationship with the theology of the New Testament and at the same time with a modern understanding. Though what might serve the application of the Old Testament to present-day faith (*applicatio*) cannot be provided from a historical perspective. To date, all attempts to determine the 'centre of the Old Testament', its 'unvarying principles', its 'basic idea', or 'overall unity' have shown themselves to be a proverbial '"Procrustean bed" in which essential sections of the book find no place, or more specifically, that cannot take into account how large the sections of the book are for which it has no place.'[1] The promises or the notion of → *covenant,* to cite two widely circulating determinations of the 'centre of the Old Testament', are appropriate for large swaths of the → *Pentateuch*, but they are absent from Proverbs, Qoheleth and the Song of Songs. A similar objection can be raised against von Rad's description of the Yhwh faith being based on a theology of history – which itself was formulated as an antithesis to the attempts to name a 'centre of the Old Testament'. The books named above also make no attempt, nor does the majority of the Psalms, to position themselves in relation to Israel's history of origins or to thematize this history. They are simply uninterested in 'salvation history', but they nevertheless are part of the Old Testament → *canon.*

In addition, most formulations of the 'centre of the Old Testament' or a compilation of its 'basic convictions' are clearly formed from the perspective of a particular reception of the Old Testament. This is especially apparent when two concepts describe the 'centre of the Old Testament' with a similar term yet mean two different things – such as 'Torah' in the Jewish perspective and 'law' in the sense of an abrupt antithesis between the Old and New Testaments – not to mention the variable meanings this specific term can take on within the Old Testament itself. Strictly speaking, the attempts at describing the theological unity of the Old Testament do not operate purely descriptively. Therefore the context for understanding the assumed unity as well as the individual theological statements must be defined in a twofold way: on the one hand, within the Old Testament itself and on the other, with respect to the reception history of a specific text and of the Old Testament as a whole. Should the respective statement be understood solely in its direct literary-historical context or should the interpretation cover a larger literary- and composition-historical context? If one decides here from the many conceivable possibilities in favour of a canonical approach that explains the text using the whole Old Testament as a frame for understanding, then the justified question may come from the reception-historical perspective whether this approach is any more justified than one that uses the entire

1. J. D. Levenson, 'Juden', 405.

Christian Bible or else a certain exegetical tradition (be it Christian or rabbinical) as a context for understanding.[2]

Despite the critique of attempts to transform the diversity of theological statements within the Old Testament into a theological unity, the concern is in and of itself justified. But the unity only arises from the perspective of the later reception of the Old Testament (Ch. 31). Besides, once the attempt at describing a theological unity is abandoned as the task of a theology of the Old Testament, the alternative is not necessarily to describe the theology of each individual Old Testament book and the innumerable phases of its compositional history. There are by all means recognizable conceptions within the Old Testament that transcend the books and their composition-historical phases. Therefore, following a suggestion by Hermann Spieckermann (who draws on von Rad) and leaning on the history of Old Testament literature one can differentiate between the theology of its historical traditions, the theology of its prophetic traditions, the theology of its cultic traditions, the theology of its → *wisdom* traditions, and finally the theology of its legal traditions.[3] These blocks of tradition are located by their literary-historical and social-historical locations as well as in regard to their basic theological principles in various degrees of proximity to one another. They each bring together quite different and sometimes opposing theological notions. For this reason in a theology of the Old Testament, they are to be acknowledged as discrete entities with their own conceptual contents and their own history. This is especially the case for the application of the Old (and New) Testament for present faith. The most noble task here is perhaps to bring the plurality of biblical theological notions into conversation with the plurality of present-day experiences of faith and their religious interpretation.[4]

2. Ibid., 426.
3. Cf. H. Spieckermann, 'Theologie II/1.1. Altes Testament', *TRE* 33 (2002): 268–68, and also G. von Rad, 'Offene Fragen', 294: 'Das Alte Testament [enthält] nicht nur eine, sondern eine Anzahl Theologien […], die sowohl in ihrer Struktur wie in der Art ihrer Argumentation weit voneinander divergieren.'
4. It should be noted that this final statement is formulated only with the *application* of biblical notions of faith in mind. Even if the Old Testament by all means knows of a 'discourse' between individual conceptions or – said more carefully – opinions, one should not make this discourse itself into the basic trajectory of the Old Testament. It is very uncertain whether in reality all Old Testament conceptions took part in such a discourse with one another or even wanted to take part.

# 33

# History of Religion and Theology of the Old Testament

I. Baldermann *et al*, eds, *Religionsgeschichte Israels oder Theologie des Alten Testaments?* Jahrbuch für Biblische Theologie 10. 2nd ed. Neukirchen-Vluyn: Neukirchener, 2001; O. Eissfeldt, 'Israelitisch-jüdische Religionsgeschichte und alttestamentliche Theologie', *ZAW* 44 (1926): 1–12; H.-C. Schmitt, 'Religionsgeschichte Israels oder Theologie des Alten Testaments?' Pages 346–66 in *Theologie in Prophetie und Pentateuch: Gesammelte Schriften*. BZAW 310. Berlin/New York: de Gruyter, 2001.

If the theology of the Old Testament is understood as a descriptive task that inquires about the theological principles of the authors and redactors of the biblical works of literature in their historical contexts and deliberately abstains from the formulation of a theological unity of the Old Testament, then one could be tempted to transform the task of theology of the Old Testament into a history of Israelite religion in the Old Testament period. Behind this suggestion that is repeatedly brought into the debate is the much-discussed alternative of theology and history of religions, which served a certain purpose at the end of the 19th and beginning of the 20th century (Ch. 31.2). However, in view of present scholarship this alternative seems the wrong approach and does not do justice to the purpose of either discipline anymore – even though there still are certain interdependences between the two.

The call for the history of religion to replace traditional theology of the Old Testament was originally formulated in opposition to dogmatic conceptions of Old Testament theology and was meant to account for the insight that 'the Old Testament lacks a temporal and formal unity'.[1] In addition the scholarly context of the outgoing 19th and incoming 20th century provided a certain level of optimism that the history of the religion(s) of ancient Israel could really be reconstructed on the basis of the Old Testament. The fact that the theological unity cannot substantiate on the basis of the Old Testament itself and the fact that the Old Testament contains numerable theologies is undisputed (here). This view corresponds with the descriptive approach that inquires about the theological conceptions within the Old Testament.

1. B. Duhm, *Theologie*, 25 (above, Ch. 31 n. 2).

Obviously, the search for the unity of the Old Testament and its relevance for current theology is not thereby solved, yet this search only arises from the reception of the Old Testament and therefore will only be satisfied from a commensurate standpoint. Within the 'concert' of theological studies as a whole this means that this task falls to the doctrine of Scripture within the prolegomena of dogmatics.

Turning to the possibilities of reconstructing a history of religion from the Old Testament sources, note should be made of the goals and methods of history of religion in the changed scholarly situation. The task of every history of religion is to trace the historical development of a religion and in doing so to take an interest in all aspects of religious life: praxis, customs, organizational forms, doctrine, and the formation of traditions in the respective religion, as well as the relation to other religions throughout its development from the beginnings until its transformation into new religious constellations. In order to reach this goal, a history of religion uses all available literary sources and other material legacies from the religion and its adherents. The stock of → *canonical* texts of the respective religion certainly is one of the sources for the history of religions – yet neither the only nor the primary one. Thus for history of religions the Old Testament represents one source among others. In addition, it is becoming increasingly clear that the Old Testament, even where it appears to simply narrate religious customs, is much more interpretative and an act of construal with regard to its own history than it seems at first glance.[2] Formulated differently, the Old Testament (also) reflects religious customs, but it only depicts these with a certain interpretation. One may say for both the history of Israel in general and the history of Israelite religion in particular that the picture of 'Israel' painted in the Old Testament is not identical with the course of history, although it is not completely fictional. The depiction of religious practice in the Old Testament portrayal(s) is also formed in service to the interpretation of the moment in which the texts were written. For this reason the history of religion has a different purpose from the description of Old Testament theology and its history. Therefore the repeatedly chosen title 'History of Israelite Religion in the Old Testament

2. This has been clearly recognized for P (→ *Priestly Document*) and the portrait of history in Chronicles during the 19th century, which made possible a historical depiction of the Old Testament and its religion(s) for the first time. For the older texts of the tradition this was less emphasized and was increasingly overlooked as a result of the influence of the tradition-historical inquiry into the preceding (oral) traditions.

Period' is anachronistic with regard to the history of scholarship, or else self-contradictory because the history of religion is tied to a canonical conception of history. Even the foundational term 'Old Testament' that suggests a certain unity owes its existence to a particular reception of the writings collected in the Old Testament, and the entity 'Israel' in these texts is much more a theological than a historical entity (Ch. 3.2.1).

On the other hand, in view of the Old Testament texts themselves, one must question whether a reading from a purely history-of-religions perspective is proper to the intentions of these texts and their present audience. It is indisputable that the culture of religious interpretation of life condensed in the writings of the Old Testament is a subject for the history of religion. However, in light of this purpose the texts are first to be interrogated for their theological concepts. After all the object of study is these textual concepts rather than the religious life of ancient Israel and Judah. The fact that the description of theological ideas itself is a discrete affair is brought to light easily by glancing at the extensive history of religion in this volume and the theological explanations included for each literary work of the Old Testament in their respective sections.

As a result, the task of a descriptively based theology, together with the compostion-history of the Old Testament and its parts, could be organized as a sub-discipline of the religious history of Palestine in the 1st millennium BCE (and would thereby be marginalized). However, one should always keep in mind here that the Old Testament is also the holy writing of present-day religious communities. These communities are no doubt interested more in understanding the content of 'their' texts than in an overall view of the historical development of a former religious age. This also goes without saying for theology whose subject matter is the reflection on the faith of these religious communities, its foundation (namely also its holy writings), and its objective statements. Observations concerning which theological principles lie at the foundation of the literary works of the Old Testament should therefore present more than simply an important sub-discipline of the history of the literature and religion of ancient Israel and Judah. It is, not least, present-day religious and theological interest in the writings of the Old Testament that compels Old Testament studies to work out the theological conceptions of the Old Testament so that they can be brought as simultaneous and at the same time as non-simultaneous voices into the present-day religious and theological conversations.

# 34

# The Old Testament as Part of the Christian Bible

J. Barr, *The Concept of Biblical Theology: An Old Testament Perspective*. London: SCM Press, 1999; E. Herms, 'Was haben wir an der Bibel? Versuch einer Theologie der christlichen Kanons'. Pages 99–192 in *Biblische Hermeneutik*. Jahrbuch für Biblische Theologie 12. Ed. by I. Baldermann. Neukirchen-Vluyn: Neukirchener, 1997; U. Luz, 'Was heißt "Sola Scriptura" heute? Ein Hilferuf für das protestantische Schriftprinzip', *EvT* 57 (1997): 28–35; B. Janowski, 'The One God of the Two Testaments: Basic Questions of a Biblical Theology', *ThTo* 57 (2000): 297–324; N. Slenczka, 'Das Verhältnis des Alten und Neuen Testaments'. Pages 90–109 in *Der Tod Gottes und das Leben des Menschen*. Göttingen: Vandenhoeck & Ruprecht, 2003; H. Spieckermann, 'God's Steadfast Love: Towards a New Conception of Old Testament Theology'. *Bib* 81 (2000): 305–27; idem, 'Die Verbindlichkeit des Alten Testaments: Unzeitgemäße Überlegungen zu einem ungeliebten Thema'. Pages 173–96 in *Gottes Liebe zu Israel: Studien zur Theologie des Alten Testaments*. FAT 33. Tübingen: Mohr Siebeck, 2001 (1997); K. Stock, *Die Theorie der christlichen Gewissheit: Eine enzyklopädische Orientierung*. Tübingen: Mohr Siebeck, 2005, 125–72; M. Welker, 'Sozio-metaphysische Theologie und Biblische Theologie: Zu Eilert Herms: "Was haben wir an der Bibel?"' Pages 309–22 in *Die Macht der Bilder*. Jahrbuch für Biblische Theologie 13. Ed. by I. Baldermann. Neukirchen-Vluyn: Neukirchener, 1999.

For all communities of faith for whom a clearly defined set of texts emerged as a foundation and norm during the communities' formative periods and then remained constant as it was passed on, this → *canon* helps to maintain identity over time and to serve as a defence against positions that threaten this identity. The relevance of the texts that have been collected into the canon for the present is therefore a given – simply due to the existence of the communities themselves. The literature collected in the Old Testament or TaNaK (Ch. 1.2.1.3) functions in varying extent and order as holy writings for the different religions and denominations. In Christianity it is as the Old Testament the oldest and first part of the Holy Scriptures. From this it derives its significance as orientation for life in a Christian context. The Old Testament is relevant for present-day Christian faith because it belongs to the canon of its Bible. From the perspective of religious self-definition the function of the canon will naturally be perceived in a different way. Namely, the canon is interpreted as a collection of texts that, because of their inspirational quality, earn the status of a record of revelation. Thus, all insights referring to life before God derive from the canon.

Irrespective of the diverse historical circumstances that led to the emergence of a fixed set of authoritative writings (Ch. 1.2.1.3), the establishment of the concrete text inventory as canon – be it only due to habit – belongs already in the reception history of these texts. The genesis of a collection of particular writings and their identity-building and preserving reception as canon within a particular community of faith should therefore be separated from one another. Canonization refers to the process of the delimitation and preservation of writings under retrospective canon-building points of view according to which a group of texts demonstrates itself as canonical while other competing texts are excluded. A similar matter is the (formal) unity of the collected writings brought about by their canonicity. Canonicity, and therefore relevance for the present time, is grounded in the reception of the writings, which can be seen already in the fact that these writings as TaNaK and Old Testament are equally holy scriptures to Judaism and Christianity. The viewpoint of canonization is in the one case that of the Pharisaic Judaism of the first century and in the other that of Christian Easter faith. In this respect from a historical perspective the following must be noted: 1. The above points of view only present one part of the historical possibilities. They represent the viewpoints of those early Jewish groups that after the destruction of the Second Temple in 70 CE could assert themselves, while other groups with their viewpoints – such as → *apocalyptic* circles or the Sadducees – sooner or later lost their influence on reception history. 2. Even if Christianity's determination of the inventory of the canon generally followed the guidelines of Pharisaic Judaism, the texts of the Old Testament nevertheless offer points of contact for both a specifically Jewish and a specifically Christian history of reception. Clarifying in this regard is the notion of the Hebrew Bible and its subsequent twofold history of reception.[1] 3. Finally, part of the specifically Christian reception history is the fact that since at least the 4th century the Old Testament has existed in combination with the New Testament writings as the Holy Scriptures known as the Old and New Testaments.

Against the conclusion that the unity of the Old Testament and its relevance as a guideline for present-day life in the context of Christian

1. Cf. K. Koch, 'Der doppelte Ausgang des Alten Testaments in Judentum und Christentum', in *Altes Testament und christlicher Glaube* (Jahrbuch für Biblische Theologie 6; ed. I. Baldermann; Neukirchen-Vluyn: Neukirchener, 1991), 315–42.

religion cannot be grounded in the texts of the Old Testament themselves one could point to the claim to authority that the texts of the Old Testament themselves raise as a canonical collection.[2] However, from a historical perspective one should always consider that the formulations making claims to authority hardly meant to apply to all times, including – viewed from the Hebrew Bible – post-canonical Christianity and its churches or post-biblical Judaism until the present.[3] Besides, the formulation of such a claim does not guarantee the acceptance of that claim by the individual or community. The Old Testament as a canonical collection has been able to assert its claim to validity to this day, which is solely due to the fact that Christianity in its religious behaviour has remained in continuity with the faith and exegesis of former generations. Formulated differently, the validity of the claim cannot be determined from the text, but lies in a particular form of reception – even if the religious community or the believing individual always understand their faith as being based on a claim manifest in the texts themselves.

The positive answer for the relevance of the Old Testament for present-day Christian belief is therefore represented in a '*reader*-oriented reception, which – to the degree that it is successful – makes possible an orientation to life and is accounted for theologically and ethically'.[4] The task of descriptively operating Old Testament theology is not to justify the relevance of the Old Testament or the like. Its task is much more a defence against a fundamental danger of reader-oriented receptions: the pure mirroring of preconceived opinions and ideas of the interpreters within the biblical text. In order to avoid this danger the text of the Old Testament must be allowed to speak with its idiosyncrasy and its foreignness. Only in this way is it possible for the believing individual to properly judge to what degree his or her existence is adequately explained by the biblical statements about the nature and work of God. Such a judgement surely does not occur outside of discourse and tradition, but under particular historically and socially mediated presuppositions. The fact that through historical inquiry the 'intention of the Old

2. H. Spieckermann, 'Verbindlichkeit'.
3. For this objection see E. Blum, 'Notwendigkeit und Grenzen historischer Exegese: Plädoyer für eine alttestamentliche "Exegetik"', in *Theologie und Exegese des Alten Testaments/der Hebräischen Bibel: Zwischenbilanz und Zukunftsperspektiven* (SBS 200; ed. B. Janowski; Stuttgart: Katholisches Bibelwerk, 2005), 11–40.
4. Cf. ibid., 36. See also for the following.

Testament' has proven manifold and polyphonic one may consider a loss or a chance – especially in view of the plurality of present life styles within the context of Christian religion. In any case, this finding cannot be altered – and is as such unambiguous.

# Appendix

## Chronological Tables[1]

### 1 Time Periods

| | |
|---|---|
| ca. 1 million years – 20,000 | Palaeolithic |
| 20,000 – 12,500 | Epipalaeolithic |
| 12,500 – 9,400 | Natufian |
| 9,400 – 6,400 | Pre-Pottery Neolithic A–C |
| 6,400 – 5,800 | Pottery Neolithic |
| 5,800 – 3,300 | Chalcolithic |
| 3,300 – 3,000 | Early Bronze Age I (EB Age) |
| 3,000 – 2,700 | Early Bronze Age II |
| 2,700 – 2,200 | Early Bronze Age III |
| 2,200 – 2,000 | Early Bronze Age IV = Middle Bronze Age I (MB Age) |
| 2,000 – 1,750 | Middle Bronze Age IIA |
| 1,750 – 1,550 | Middle Bronze Age IIB |
| 1,550 – 1,400 | Late Bronze Age I (LB Age) |
| 1,400 – 1,300 | Late Bronze Age IIA |
| 1,300 – 1,200/1,150 | Late Bronze Age IIB |
| 1,200/1,150 – 1,000 | Iron Age I |
| 1,000 – 926/900 | Iron Age IIA or 950/900 – 800/785/748 |
| 926/900 – 722/700 | Iron Age IIB or 800/785/748 – 722/700 |
| 722/700 – 587/6 | Iron Age IIC |
| 587/6 – 539/8 | Babylonian Period |
| 539/8 – 450/400 | Persian Period I |
| 450/400 – 333/2 | Persian Period II |
| 333/2 – 63 | Hellenistic Period |

1. Unless otherwise noted, all years should be understood as BCE.

## 2 Chronology of Important Dates in the History of 'Israel'

| | |
|---|---|
| 1,208 | First epigraphic mention of 'Israel' on the stele of Pharaoh Merneptah (*COS* II, 40–1). |
| 926/920/917 | Campaign of Pharaoh Shishak I from Gaza via Gezer to Megiddo with excursions into the interior. Activities in the Negev to secure the trade routes (1 Kgs 14.25-28; Stele fragment from Megiddo; Jerusalem is not mentioned in the Egyptian texts). |
| 853 | Ahab of Israel fights in the battle of Qarqar together with Hadadezer of Damascus against the Assyrian king Shalmaneser III (*COS* II, 261–4), whose advance is stopped. Further clashes of the coalition with the Assyrians follow. |
| 2nd half of the 9th century | Warfare between an unnamed king of Israel (probably Joram, 2 Kgs 1.1, 3. 4-27) and Mesha of Moab (*COS* II, 137–8). |
| 843/2 | Hazael becomes King of Damascus, war against Israel and Judah. Murder of the kings Joram of Israel and Ahaziah of Judah probably by Hazael of Damascus (*COS* II, 161–2) or, according to the OT account, by Jehu of Israel (2 Kgs 9.14-29; 2 Chr. 22.5-9).<br>Following the break between Hazael and Jehu, Israelite territorial losses in the north (Dan, Jezreel, Megiddo). |
| 841 | Shalmaneser III moves against Hazael of Damascus and others and receives tribute from Jehu of Israel (*COS* II, 264–71). |
| 796 | Adad-nirari III receives tribute from Joash of Israel (*COS* II, 276–7). |
| 738 | Menahem of Israel (like Rezin of Damascus) pays tribute to the Assyrian king Tiglath-Pileser III (*COS* II, 284–7; 2 Kgs 15.19-20). |
| 734 | Ahaz of Judah, the kings of Ammon, Moab and Edom pay tribute to Tiglath-Pileser III (*COS* II, 289–90; see also 2 Kgs 16.7). |
| 733/2 | Anti-Assyrian coalition of Rezin of Damascus, Hiram II of Tyre and Pekahiah of Israel. Ahaz of Judah becomes a vassal to the Assyrians (or already was one) and requests military aid against Israel (2 Kgs 16; Isa. 7.1); 'Syrian-Ephraimite War'. |

| | |
|---|---|
| 732 | Fall of Damascus, transformation of Aram-Damascus into an Assyrian province by Tiglath-Pileser III. Galilee and Transjordan are annexed. Defeat of the northern kingdom, deportation, overthrow of Pekah of Israel and appointment of Hoshea as king of Israel by the Assyrians. Tribute payment by the vassal Hoshea (*COS* II, 287–8; 2 Kgs 15.29–30; 16.9). |
| 724/3 | Siege of Samaria by Shalmaneser V. Capture of Hoshea (2 Kgs 17.4). |
| 722/1 | Overthrow of Samaria by Shalmaneser V, who dies shortly thereafter. Deportation, transformation of the northern kingdom into an Assyrian province (2 Kgs 17.5-6) only under Sargon II, who likewise claims a (second) conquest (around 720?) (*COS* II, 293–9). He settles Arabs in Samaria (*COS* II, 293–4). Hezekiah of Judah (ca. 723–695) constructs the Siloam-Tunnel in Jerusalem (*COS* II, 145–6; 2 Kgs 20.20). |
| 705 | Death of Sargon II leads to revolts in the west, which are put down in a punitive expedition by Sennacherib during his 3rd campaign. |
| 701 | Fall of Lachish and other Judean cities, deportation of Judean population elements. Partition of Judean territories among the kings of Ashdod, Ekron and Gaza. Unsuccessful siege of Jerusalem by Sennacherib and tribute payment by Hezekiah of Judah to the king (*COS* II, 302–4; 2 Kgs 18.13–19.36). |
| ca. 630 | Death of Ashurbanipal leads to the weakening of Assyrian influence in Palestine and to the strengthening of Egyptian influence. |
| 612 | End of the Assyrian kingdom by the coalition of the Medes and the Babylonians. |
| 609/8 | Pharaoh Neco II comes to the aid of the Assyrian king Ashur-uballit II in his rump state of Haran; Josiah's death at Megiddo (2 Kgs 23.29). |
| 605 | Battle of Carchemish between the Egyptians and the Babylonians leads to Egypt's loss to Nebuchadnezzar II of the Syro-Palestinian land-bridge (2 Kgs 24.7). |
| 598/7 | First conquest of Jerusalem by the Babylonian king Nebuchadnezzar II and the first wave of deportation; appointment of king Zedekiah by the Babylonians (*ANET*, 563–4; 2 Kgs 24.10-17). The Negev falls to Edom. |

| | |
|---|---|
| 587/6 | Second conquest of Jerusalem by the Babylonian king Nebuchadnezzar II and the second wave of deportation (2 Kgs 25). The southern Shephelah and southern portions of the Judean highlands fall to Edom. |
| 582 | Murder of the governor/vassal king Gedaliah in Mizpah; third deportation (Jer. 52.30) and flight of refugees to Egypt (Jer. 41–43; 2 Kgs 25.26). |
| 539 | End of the Neo-Babylonian Empire through Cyrus' II Conquest of Babylon (*ANET*, 306–7; *COS* II, 314–16). |
| 538 | Edict of Cyrus (Ezra 6.3-5; 1.2-4). |
| 525 | Egypt falls to the Persian Cambyses. |
| 520–515 | Administrative reform of Darius I Hystaspes. Construction of the Second Temple in Jerusalem (Hag. 1–2; Zech. 4.8-10; 8.9; Ezra 3–6). Laying of the first stone by the Davidide governor/vassal king Zerubbabel. |
| 480/50 | Construction of a Yhwh-temple on Mount Gerizim. |
| 445/444 | Reconstruction of the city wall of Jerusalem by the governor Nehemiah (Neh. 1–7). |
| 404 | Egypt secedes from the Persian Empire. |
| 333/2 | End of the Persian Empire and takeover of Palestine by Alexander the Great. |
| 312/301–200/198 | Palestine becomes part of the kingdom of the Ptolemies. |
| 200/198–63 | Palestine becomes part of the Seleucid Kingdom after the Battle of Paneas. |
| 188 | Peace of Apamea. |
| 167 | Antiochus IV Epiphanes forbids the observance of the Jewish law; desecration of the altar of sacrifice in the Jerusalem temple (1 Macc. 1; Dan. 9.27; 11.31). |
| 167–143/2 | Revolt of the Maccabees (1 Macc. 2–2 Macc.). |
| 164 | Re-consecration of the Jerusalem temple (Hanukkah celebration). |
| 161 | Victory of Judas Maccabaeus over Nicanor ('Day of Nicanor'). |
| 143/2–37 | The kingdom of the Hasmoneans. |
| 63 BCE | Roman conquest of the Jerusalem temple-complex by Pompey. |
| 37–4 BCE | Herod I (the Great). |
| 66–70 CE | 1st Jewish War. |
| 70 CE | Destruction of Jerusalem and of the Yhwh-temple by Titus |

| | |
|---|---|
| | (Titus Arch), likewise the fall of the Herodium, of Machaerus and of Masada. |
| 75 CE | Palestine becomes an imperial province with Roman governors. |
| 132–135 CE | 2nd Jewish War; Bar Kokhba revolt. |
| 135 CE | Judea is reorganized as the *provincia syria-palaestina* and Jerusalem is rebuilt as *aelia capitolina*. |

## 3 The Rulers of Israel and Judah[2]

| ***Judah*** | | ***Israel*** | |
|---|---|---|---|
| (?) 10th cent. | David | (?) 10th cent. | Saul |
| (?) 10th cent. | Solomon | | |
| (?)–910 | Rehoboam | (?)–907 | Jeroboam |
| (?) 910–908 | Abijam | (?) 907–906 | Nadab |
| (?) 908–868 | Asa | (?) 906–883 | Baasha |
| | | (?) 883–882 | Elah |
| | | 882/878 | Zimri |
| | | 882/878–871/0 | Omri |
| 868–852/47 | Jehoshaphat | 871/0–852/1 | Ahab |
| 852/47–842/2 | Jehoram | 852/1–851/0 | Ahaziah |
| 843/2 | Ahaziah | 851-70–843/2 | Jehoram/Joram |
| 843/2–838/7 | Athaliah | 843/2–816 | Jehu |
| 838/7–799 | Jehoash | 816–800 | Johoahaz |
| 799–771 | Amaziah | 800–785 | Jehoash |
| 785/771–734 | Uzziah | 785–745 | Jeroboam II |
| 757–742 | Jotham | 745 | Zachariah |
| 742/734–723 | Ahaz | 745–738/7 | Menahem |
| | | 738/7–736 | Pekahiah |
| | | 736–732 | Pekah |
| | | 731–724/3 | Hoshea |

2. The dating of the rulers of Israel and Judah in the 10th cent. BCE are highly uncertain. By comparison, the chronology from the time of King Omri of Samaria/Israel is relatively certain.

| *Judah* | | *Israel* |
|---|---|---|
| | | 722/0 *Fall of Israel* |
| 723–695 | Hezekiah | |
| 694–640 | Manasseh | |
| 640/39–638 | Amon | |
| 638–609/8 | Josiah | |
| 609/8 | Jehoahaz | |
| 609/8–598/7 | Eliakim/Jehoiakim | |
| 598/7 | Jehoiachin/Jeconiah | |
| 598/7–587/6 | Mattaniah/Zedekiah | |
| 587/6(?)–582 | Gedaliah (?) | |
| | *Fall of Judah* | |

# 4 Babylonian, Persian and 'Greek' Kings

| *The Babylonian Kings* | *The Persian Kings* | *The 'Greek' Kings* |
|---|---|---|
| Nabopolassar (626–605) | | |
| Nebuchadnezzar II (605–562) | | |
| Amel-Marduk/Ewil-Merodach (562–560) | | |
| Neriglissar (560–556) | Cyrus II (559/8–530) | |
| Nabonidus (556–539) with Belshazzar as crown prince and coregent | | |
| | Cambyses (530–522) | |
| | Darius I Hystaspes (522–486) | |
| | Xerxes (Ahasuerus; 486–465/4) | |
| | Artaxerxes I Longimanus (465/4–425) | |
| | Darius II (424–404) | |

| *The Babylonian Kings* | *The Persian Kings* | *The 'Greek' Kings* |
|---|---|---|
| | Artaxerxes II Mnemon (404–359/8) | |
| | Artaxerxes III Ochus (359/8–338) | Philipp II of Macedonia (359–336) |
| | Artaxerxes IV Arses (338–336) | |
| | Darius III Codomannus (336–331) | Alexander III of Macedonia (= the Great) (336–323) |
| | | Kings of the North: Seleucids (312–64)<br>Antiochus IV Epiphanes (175–164) |
| | | Kings of the South: Ptolemies (323–30) |

# 5 The 'Greek' Kings und the Jerusalem High Priests

| *Ptolemies* | *Seleucids (selected)* | *Jerusalem High Priests* |
|---|---|---|
| Ptolemy I Soter (satrap 323–306; king 305–283/2) | Seleucus I Nicator (312–281) (satrap 320/312–306; king 305–281) | Onias I (ca. 323–300) |
| Ptolemy II Philadelphus (283/2–246) | Antiochus I Soter (281–261)<br>Antiochus II Theos (261–246) | Simon I, son of Onias I<br>Eleasar, brother of Simon I |
| Ptolemy III Euergetes (246–221) | Seleucus II Callinicus (246–226)<br>Seleucus III Soter (226–223) | Manasseh, brother of Onias I |
| Ptolemy IV Philopator (221–205) | Antiochus III Megas (223–187) | Onias II, son of Simon I (until ca.196) |
| Ptolemy V Epiphanes (205–180) | | Simon II, son of Onias II |
| Ptolemy VI Philometor (180–145) | Seleucus IV Philopator (187–175) | 174 Onias III, son of Simon II, deposed |
| | Antiochus IV Epiphanes (175–164) | 174 Jason, brother of Onias III, appointed |
| | Antiochus V Eupator (164–162) | 173 Menelaus appointed<br>Ca. 169 Onias III/IV flees to Egypt |

| *Ptolemies* | *Seleucids (selected)* | *Jerusalem High Priests* |
|---|---|---|
| | Demetrius I (162–150) | 162 Alcimus appointed by Demetrius I. His successor was perhaps Judas Maccabaeus or possibly a seven-year vacancy followed. |
| | Alexander I Balas (150–145) | Jonathan, brother of Judas Maccabaeus (from 150) |
| Ptolemy VIII Euergetes II (145–116) | Demetrius II Nicator (145–139/8 and 129–125) | Simon, brother of Judas Maccabaeus (from 141–135/4) |
| | Antiochus VII Euergetes (139/8–129) | John Hyrcanus I, son of Simon Maccabaeus (135/4–104); first Hasmonean coinage |
| Ptolemy IX Soter II (116–107 and 88–80) | Antiochus VIII Epiphanes (125–96) | Aristobulus I (104–103)<br>Alexander Jannaeus (103–76) high priest and king |
| Ptolemy X Alexander I (107–88) | Demetrius III (95–88) | |
| Ptolemy XI Alexander II (80) | | |
| Ptolemy XII Neos Dionysos (80–51) | Antiochus XIII Asiaticus (69–64) | Alexandra Salome (76–67) appointed Hyrcanus II in 76 as high priest.<br>Aristobulus II interrupts this term of office (67–63). |
| | Philipp II (65–64) | Hyrcanus II (63–40) |

# 6 Literary-Historical Chronology of Biblical and Extra-biblical Sources for the History of Israel and Judah[3]

| | |
|---|---|
| ca. 1,360 | *Tell el-'Amārna-Correspondence* (*COS* III, 237–42) |
| ca. 1,221 | *Papyrus Anastasi III* ('Journal of an Egyptian frontier official'; *ANET*, 258–9) |
| 1,208 | *'Israel Stela' of Pharaoh Merneptah* (see p. 65; *COS* II, 40–1) |
| ca. 1,192 | *Papyrus Anastasi VI* ('Report of an Egyptian frontier official'; see p. 442; *COS* III, 16–17) |
| from the10th cent. | Narrative cycles about the beginnings of Israel and about events concerning its charismatic leaders and rulers, collections of sagas |

3. Unless otherwise indicated, all dates are BCE.

| | |
|---|---|
| 10th/9th cent. | *'The Gezer Calendar'* (see p. 87; *HAE* I, 30–7; *ANET*, 320) |
| from the 9th cent. | Excerpts from court annals (see p. 69) |
| 9th–7th cent. | *Assyrian Royal Inscriptions* (*COS* II, 261–306) |
| after 850 | Inscription of King Mesha of Moab (p. 107; *COS* II, 137–8) |
| ca. 843/2 | *Aramaic Inscription of Tell Dan* (see p. 134; *COS* II, 161–2) |
| 9th/8th cent. | *Hebrew and Phoenician inscriptions from Kuntillet ʿAjrûd* (pp. 38, 127–128; *HAE* I, 47–64; *COS* II, 171–3). |
| 1st half 8th cent. | *Hebrew → ostraca from Samaria* (p. 37–38; *HAE* I, 79–110; F.W. Dobbs-Allsopp *et al.*, *Hebrew Inscriptions*, 423–97). |
| 785 | *Aramaic Inscription of Zakkur* (*COS* II, 155). |
| mid 8th cent. | 'Grundschriften'[4] of the books of Amos and Hosea, the first law collections ('Covenant Code: Exod. 21–23*) |
| end 8th cent. | 'Grundschriften' of the books of (Proto-)Isaiah (Isa. 1–39*) and Micah |
| end 8th cent. | *Hebrew ostraca from Arad* (*HAE* I, 145–65; *COS* III, 85) |
| | *Hebrew inscription in the Siloam Tunnel* (p. 114; *COS* II, 145–6; 2 Kgs 20.20) |
| | *Hebrew sepulchral inscriptions in Jerusalem and in Khirbet el-Qom* (pp. 38, 127–128; *HAE* I, 199–211; *COS* II, 179) |
| end 8th cent. | 1) Redactional compilation of the narrative cycles about Samuel, Saul and David into the first comprehensive 'Royal History of Israel' (Sam.-Kgs*) |
| | 2) Composition of a first exodus-eisodus[5]-narrative (Exod.*; Num.*; Josh.*) |
| | 3) Composition of a first patriarchal history (Gen. 11–50*) |
| begin 7th cent. | *Hebrew sepulchral inscription in Jerusalem* (*HAE* I, 261–6; *COS* II, 180) |
| mid 7th cent. | *Hebrew ostracon from Meṣad Ḥashavyahu* (p. 119; *HAE* I, 315–29; *COS* III, 77–8) |
| end 7th cent. | First version of Deuteronomy – 'Urdeuteronomium' |
| | 'Grundschriften' of the books of Zephaniah, Nahum, Habakkuk |
| 607–598 | *Babylonian royal chronicles* (*ANET*, 563–4) |
| early 6th cent. | 'Grundschriften' of the books of Ezekiel and Jeremiah |
| | *Hebrew ostraca from Arad* (p. 120; HAE I, 347–403; *COS* III, 81–5) |
| ca. 588 | *Hebrew ostraca from Lachish* (p. 121; HAE I, 405–38; *COS* III, 78–81) |

4. Scholarly term (German: 'Basistext') for earlier documents used by later authors or redactors in compiling a new text.
5. Scholarly term for the immigration/penetration of the Israelites into Palestine, corresponding to 'exodus' as the term for their emigration/departure from Egypt → conquest.

| | |
|---|---|
| from the mid 6th cent. on | 1) Deuteronomistic redaction of the historical (and, in part, of the prophetic traditions): successive redactions of the Deuteronomistic History (1–2 Sam.*,1–2 Kgs*) and the Hexateuch-tradition (Exod.–Josh.*)<br>2) Redaction of the Deutero- and Trito-Isaiah collections (Isa. 40–55 and 56–66)<br>3) 'Grundschrift' of P (the Priestly Document) |
| 6th/5th cent. | *Achaemenid (Persian) royal inscriptions* (*ANET*, 306–7; *COS* II, 314–16) |
| 520 | 'Grundschriften' of the books of Haggai and (Proto-)Zechariah (Zech. 1–9) |
| 5th cent. | *Aramaic Elephantine-Papyri* (*TADAE*; *COS* III, 116–32) |
| end 5th/4th cent. | *Ketef Hinnom amulets from Jerusalem* (pp. 38, 127; *HAE* I, 447–56; *COS* II, 314) |
| Ca. 300 | 'Final redaction' of the Pentateuch (Torah) |
| 5th–3rd cent. | Ezra, Nehemiah, Chronicles |
| 3rd/2nd cent. | Tobit, Esther, final redaction of the Proverbs |
| 3rd–1st cent. | Completion of the → *Septuagint* |
| ca. 240 | 'Final redaction' of the Book of Twelve |
| ca. 190/180 | Jesus Sirach |
| ca. 150 | 'Final redaction' of the book of Daniel |
| 150/100 | Book of Judith |
| 130/100 | *Letter of Aristeas* |
| 135/100 | 2nd book of Maccabees |
| 100/70 | 1st book of Maccabees |
| 1st cent. BCE – 1st cent. CE | *most of the texts found at → Qumran* |
| 26 BCE/41 CE | Wisdom of Solomon |
| 1st half 1st cent. CE | *Greek writings of the Jewish philosopher Philo of Alexandria* |
| 70–100 CE | *Greek writings of the Jewish historian Flavius Josephus* |
| Ca. 100 CE | 'Canonization' (→ *canon*) of the TaNaK |

# Basic Literature for Old Testament Studies

**Preliminary Remark:** The following bibliography is limited to the most important literature for Old Testament studies. References to individual biblical books, respectively certain topics and questions are listed in the beginning of each paragraph. The footnotes refer to the following references by naming short titles. Bibliographical abbreviations follow (if not stated differently): P. H. Alexander *et al.*, eds, *The SBL Handbook of Style: For Ancient Near Eastern, Biblical, and Early Christian Studies*. Peabody, Mass.: Hendrickson, 1999. Furthermore the theological encyclopedias TRE, PPP and ABD are to be mentioned, which usually contain articles to all biblical books and the most important keywords and persons. The reference lists of this book do not refer to these articles, but they are occasionally quoted in footnotes.

## 1 Text Editions

### 1.1 Masoretic Text

*Biblia Hebraica Stuttgartensia*. Ed. by K. Elliger, W. Rudolph *et al.* Stuttgart 1967/1977 (BHS). Editio quinta emendata opera A. Schenker. Stuttgart: Deutsche Bibelgesellschaft, 1997.

A completely revised edition is planned: *Biblia Hebraica Quinta*. Editione cum apparatu critico novis curis elaborato. Ed. by A. Schenker *et al.* Stuttgart: Deutsche Bibelgesellschaft, 2004ff. (BHQ) (published so far: Biblia Hebraica Quinta Vol. 5: *Deuteronomy*. Stuttgart: Deutsche Bibelgesellschaft, 2007; Vol. 13: *The Twelve Minor Prophets*. Stuttgart: Deutsche Bibelgesellschaft, 2010; Vol. 17: *Proverbs*. Stuttgart: Deutsche Bibelgesellschaft, 2008; Vol. 18: *General Introduction and Megilloth*. Stuttgart: Deutsche Bibelgesellschaft, 2004; Vol. 20: *Ezra and Nehemiah*. Stuttgart: Deutsche Bibelgesellschaft, 2006).

*The Aleppo Codex*. Ed. by M. H. Goshen-Gottstein. Jerusalem: Magnes, 1976ff.

*Biblia Hebraica*. Ed. by R. Kittel *et al.* Stuttgart: Privilegierte Württembergische Bibelanstalt, 1937/1951 (BHK).

P. H. Kelley, D. S. Mynatt, T. G. Crawford, *The Masorah of Biblia Hebraica Stuttgartensia: Introduction and Annotated Glossary*. Grand Rapids, Mich.: Eerdmans, 1998.

## 1.2 Targums

*The Bible in Aramaic: Based on Old Manuscripts and Printed Texts*. Ed. by A. Sperber. Leiden/Boston: Brill, 1992ff.

*The Aramaic Bible: The Targums*. Ed. by M. McNamara. Wilmington, Del.: M. Glazier, 1987ff.

*Targum Neophyti I–VI*. Ed. by A. Diez Macho. Madrid: Consejo Superior de Investigaciones Científicas, 1968ff.

*Biblia Polyglotta Matritensia: Series IV Targum Palaestinense in Pentateuchum additur Targum Pseudojonathan ejusque hispanica versio*. Ed. by A. Díez Macho, Madrid: Consejo Superior de Investigaciones Científicas, 1977.

## 1.3 Septuagint

*Septuaginta: Id est Vetus Testamentum graece iuxta LXX interpretes*. Ed. by A. Rahlfs. Editio altera quam recognovit, et emendavit. Ed. by R. Hanhart. Stuttgart: Deutsche Bibelgesellschaft, 2006. (largely based on Codex Vaticanus).

*Septuaginta: Vetus Testamentum graecum auctoritate academiae scientiarum* [formerly: societatis scientiarum/societatis litterarum] *Gottingensis editum*. Göttingen: Vandenhoeck & Ruprecht, 1931ff.

*A New English Translation of the Septuagint*. Ed. by A. Pietersma and B. G. Wright. Oxford: Oxford University Press, 2007 (NETS).

*Septuaginta Deutsch. Das griechische Alte Testament in Übersetzung*. Ed. by W. Kraus and M. Karrer. Stuttgart: Deutsche Bibelgesellschaft, 2nd Ed. 2010 (LXXD).

Erlantengen und hommentare, Vol. I–II, Stuttgart: Dutsche Bibilgesllschult, 2011.

## 1.4 Vulgate

*Biblia Sacra iuxta Vulgatam versionem*. Ed. by R. Weber. 5th ed. Stuttgart: Deutsche Bibelgesellschaft, 2007.

## 1.5 Biblical Manuscripts from Qumran

*Discoveries in the Judaean Desert*. Oxford: Clarendon, 1955ff. (DJD).

The Qumran-Texts are also available on CD-ROM: *Dead Sea Scrolls Electronic Reference Library*. Vol. 1. Ed. by T. H. Lim. Leiden/Boston: Brill, 1997; Vol. 2. Ed. by E. Tov. Leiden/Boston: Brill, 1999; Vol. 3. Ed. by E. Tov. Leiden/Boston: Brill, 2006.

M. Abegg, P. Flint and E. Ulrich, *The Dead Sea Scrolls Bible*. San Francisco: Harper, 1999.

E. Ulrich, *The Biblical Qumran Scrolls: Transcriptions and Textual Variants*. VTSup 134. Leiden/Boston: Brill, 2010.

## 1.6 Pseudepigrapha/Apocrypha

*The Old Testament Pseudepigrapha* I–II. Ed. by J. H. Charlesworth. Garden City, N.Y.: Doubleday, 1983–1985 (OTP I-II).

*Jüdische Schriften aus hellenistisch-römischer Zeit*. Ed. by W. G. Kümmel and H. Lichtenberger. Gütersloh: Gütersloher Verlagshaus, 1973ff. (JSHRZ).

*Jüdische Schriften aus hellenistisch-römischer Zeit: Neue Folge*. Ed. by W. G. Kümmel and H. Lichtenberger, Gütersloh: Gütersloher Verlagshaus, 2005ff. (JSHRZ NF).

*Arbeitshilfen für das Studium der Pseudepigraphen*. Ed. by T. Knittel, C. Böttrich and J. Herzer, 2002. Online: http://www.uni-leipzig.de/~nt/asp/pseudep.htm.

*Jewish Writings of the Second Temple Period*. CRINT II/2. Ed. by M. E. Stone. Assen: Van Gorcum/ Philadelphia: Fortress, 1984.

G. W. E. Nickelsburg, Jewish Literature between the Bible and the Mishna. Second Edition with CD-ROM, Minneapolis: Fortress Press 2005.

# 2 Exegetical Resources

## 2.1 Concordances

A. Even-Shoshan, ed., *A New Concordance of the Bible: Thesaurus of the Language of the Bible, Hebrew and Aramaic Roots, Words, Proper Names, Phrases and Synonyms*. Jerusalem: Kiryat Sepher, 1993 (repr. of the renewed ed. of 1990).

E. Hatch and H. A. Redpath, *A Concordance to the Septuagint and the Other Greek Versions of the Old Testament* 1–3. Oxford: Clarendon, 1897–1906, 2nd rev. ed. Grand Rapids, Mich.: Baker, 1998.

G. Lisowsky and L. Rost, *Konkordanz zum Hebräischen Alten Testament*. Rev. ed. by H. P. Rüger. 3rd ed. Stuttgart: Deutsche Bibelgesellschaft, 1993.

S. Mandelkern, *Veteris Testamenti Concordantiae Hebraicae atque Chaldaicae*. 9th ed. Jerusalem/Tel Aviv: Schocken, 1971.

T. Muraoka, *Hebrew/Aramaic Index to the Septuagint: Keyed to the Hatch-Redpath Concordance*. Grand Rapids, Mich.: Baker, 1998.

## 2.2 Concordances on CD-ROM

*Accordance Scholar's Collection Core Bundle* (Mac). Version 9.4.3 on CD-ROM for Mac OS X. Oak-Tree Software, 2011.

*Bible Windows 7.0 on CD-ROM* (Windows). Silver Mountain Software, 2006.

*Bible Works 8 on CD-ROM* (Windows). Bible Works, LLC, 2008.

## 2.3 Dictionaries

F. I. Anderson and A. Dean Forbes, *The Vocabulary of the Old Testament*. Rome: Pontificio Istituto biblico, 1992.

F. Brown, S. Driver and C. Briggs, *Hebrew and English Lexicon*. 11th ed. Boston: Hendrickson, 1906, 2007.

D. J. A. Clines *et al.*, eds, *The Dictionary of Classical Hebrew*. Sheffield: Sheffield Academic Press, 1993ff. (published so far: Vol. I–VII [ר–א]) (DCH).

W. Gesenius and F. Buhl, *Hebräisches und Aramäisches Handwörterbuch über das Alte Testament*. 17th ed. (repr. of the ed. of 1915). Berlin: Springer, 1962.

W. Gesenius, *Hebräisches und Aramäisches Handwörterbuch über das Alte Testament*. 18th rev. ed. by R. Meyer and H. Donner. Berlin *et al.*: Springer, 1987ff. (published so far: Vol. I–VI [א (Hebr.) – ת (Aram.)]).

J. Hoftijzer and K. Jongeling, *Dictionary of the North-West Semitic Inscriptions*. HO 1. Abt., Der Nahe und Mittlere Osten 21. 2 vols. Leiden/Boston: Brill, 1995.

L. Köhler and W. Baumgartner, eds, *The Hebrew and Aramaic Lexicon of the Old Testament*. Subsequently Revised by W. Baumgartner and J. J. Stamm. Transl. and ed. under supervision of M. E. J. Richardson. Leiden/Boston: Brill, 2001.

J. Lust, E. Eynikel and K. Hauspie, *Greek-English Lexicon of the Septuagint*. Rev. ed. Stuttgart: Deutsche Bibelgesellschaft, 2003.

## 2.4 Atlases and Books on Applied Geography

Y. Aharoni, *The Land of the Bible: A Historical Geography*. Louisville, Ky.: Westminster John Knox, 2000.

Idem and M. Avi-Yonah, eds., *The Macmillan Bible Atlas*. New York: Macmillan, 1968.

O. Keel *et al.*, *Orte und Landschaften der Bibel: Ein Handbuch und Studienreiseführer zum Heiligen Land*. Vol. 1ff. Göttingen: Vandenhoeck & Ruprecht, 1982ff. (OLB).

S. Mittmann and G. Schmitt, eds, *Tübinger Bibelatlas: Auf der Grundlage des Tübinger Atlas des Vorderen Orients (TAVO)*. Stuttgart: Deutsche Bibelgesellschaft, 2001.

J. Murphy-O'Connor, *The Holy Land: An Oxford Archaeological Guide from Earliest Times to 1700*. 5th ed., rev. and expanded. Oxford: Oxford University Press, 2008.

A. F. Rainey and R. S. Notley, eds, *The Sacred Bridge: Carta's Atlas of the Biblical World*. Jerusalem: Carta, 2006.

W. Zwickel, *Einführung in die biblische Landes- und Altertumskunde*. Darmstadt: Wissenschaftliche Buchgesellschaft, 2002.

# 3 Exegetical Methods

A. A. Fischer, *Der Text des Alten Testaments: Neubearb. der Einführung in die Biblia Hebraica von Ernst Würthwein*. Stuttgart: Deutsche Bibelgesellschaft, 2009 (cf. E. Würthwein, *The Text of the Old Testament: An Introduction to the Biblia Hebraica*. Transl. by E. F. Rhodes. Grand Rapids, Mich.: Eerdmans, 1995).

J. Barton, *Reading the Old Testament: Method in Biblical Study*. London: Darton, Longman & Todd, 1984.

U. Becker, *Exegese des Alten Testaments: Ein Methoden- und Arbeitsbuch*. UTB 2664. 3rd ed. Tübingen: Mohr Siebeck, 2011.

M. J. Gorman, *Elements of Biblical Exegesis: A Basic Guide for Ministers and Students*. Peabody, Mass.: Hendrickson, 2010.

J. H. Hayes and C. R. Holladay, *Biblical Exegesis: A Beginner's Handbook*. 3rd ed. Louisville, Ky.: Westminster John Knox, 2007.

S. Kreuzer, D. Vieweger *et al.*, *Proseminar I: Altes Testament: Ein Arbeitsbuch*. 2nd ed. Stuttgart *et al.*: Kohlhammer, 2005.

K. McCarter Jr., *Textual Criticism: Recovering the Text of the Hebrew Bible*. Philadelphia: Fortress, 1986.

O. H. Steck, *Old Testament Exegesis: A Guide to the Methodology*. Transl. by J. D. Nogalski. Atlanta, Ga.: Scholars, 1998.

D. Stuart, *Old Testament Exegesis: A Handbook for Students and Pastors*. 4th ed. Louisville, Ky.: Westminster John Knox, 2009.

E. Tov, *Textual Criticism of the Hebrew Bible*. Minneapolis: Fortress /Assen: Van Gorcum, 2001.

G. M. Tucker, *Form Criticism of the Old Testament*. Philadelphia: Fortress, 1971.

## 3.1 Discussion of Methods and Alternative Approaches

### 3.1.1 General

J. Barr, *History and Ideology in the Old Testament: Biblical Studies at the End of a Millennium*. Oxford: Oxford University Press, 2000.

E. Blum, 'Von Sinn und Nutzen der Kategorie "Synchronie" in der Exegese'. Pages 16–30 in *David und Saul im Widerstreit - Diachronie und Synchronie im Wettstreit: Beiträge zur Auslegung des ersten Samuelbuches*. OBO 206. Ed. by W. Dietrich. Fribourg: Academic Press/Göttingen: Vandenhoeck & Ruprecht, 2004.

D. Clines, 'Beyond Synchronic/Diachronic', Pages 68–87 in *On the Way to the Postmodern: Old Testament Essays 1: 1967–1998*. JSOTSup 292. Sheffield: Sheffield Academic Press, 1998.

J. J. Collins, *The Bible after Babel: Historical Criticism in a Postmodern Age*. Grand Rapids, Mich.: Eerdmans, 2005.

G. Ebeling, 'Die Bedeutung der historisch-kritischen Methode für die protestantische Theologie und Kirche'. *ZTK* 46 (1950): 1–46. Repr. in *Wort und Glaube*. Vol. I. 3rd ed. Tübingen: Mohr Siebeck, 1967, 1–49 (ET 'The Significance of the Critical Historical Method for Church and Theology in Protestantism'. Pages 17–61 in *Word and Faith*. Philadelphia: Fortress, 1963).

Idem, 'Dogmatik und Exegese'. *ZTK* 77 (1980): 269–86. Repr. in *Wort und Glaube*. Vol. IV. Tübingen: Mohr Siebeck, 1995, 492–509.

J. C. Gertz, 'Auf dem Weg zum Text: Neuere methodische Entwicklungen in der alttestamentlichen Wissenschaft'. *Lernort Gemeinde* 20/4 (2002): 9–13.

S. L. McKenzie and S. R. Haynes, eds, *To Each its Own Meaning: An Introduction to Biblical Criticisms and their Application*. 2nd ed. Louisville, Ky.: Westminster John Knox, 1999.

E. Troeltsch, 'Über historische und dogmatische Methode in der Theologie'. Pages 729–53 in *Gesammelte Schriften*. Vol. II. Tübingen: Mohr Siebeck, 1913 (ET 'Historical and Dogmatic Method in Theology'. Pages 11–32 in *Religion in History*. Transl. by J. L. Adams and W. F. Bense. 2nd ed. Minneapolis: Fortress, 2007).

H. Weder, 'Exegese und Dogmatik: Überlegungen zur Bedeutung der Dogmatik für die Arbeit des Exegeten'. *ZTK* 84 (1987): 137–61. Repr. in *Einblick ins Evangelium: Exegetische Beiträge zur neutestamentlichen Hermeneutik: Gesammelte Aufsätze aus den Jahren 1980–1991*. Göttingen: Vandenhoeck & Ruprecht, 1992, 109–36.

### 3.1.2 Synchronic Methods: Canonical Approach, Structural Analysis, 'New Literary Criticism'

R. Alter, *The Art of Biblical Narrative*. 40th ed. New York: Basic Books, 2006.

Idem and F. Kermode, *The Literary Guide to the Bible*. 9th ed. Cambridge, Mass.: Harvard University Press, 1999.

S. Bar-Efrat, *Narrative Art in the Bible*. New York: T&T Clark, 2004.

J. Barr, *The Semantics of Biblical Language*. Oxford: Oxford University Press, 1961 (repr. 1991).

A. Berlin, *Poetics and Interpretation of Biblical Narrative*. Bible and Literature Series 9. Sheffield: Almond, 1983 (repr. 1999).

D. M. Gunn and D. N. Fewell, *Narrative in the Hebrew Bible*. Oxford: Oxford University Press, 1993.

C. Hardmeier, *Textwelten der Bibel entdecken: Grundlagen und Verfahren einer textpragmatischen Literaturwissenschaft der Bibel: Textpragmatische Studien zur Literatur- und Kulturgeschichte der Hebräischen Bibel*. 2 vols. Gütersloh: Gütersloher Verlagshaus, 2003, 2004.

M. Sternberg, *The Poetics of Biblical Narrative: Ideological Literature and the Drama of Reading*. 5th ed. Bloomington, Ind.: Indiana University Press, 1996.

J. Vette, 'Narrative Poetics and Hebrew Narrative: A Survey'. Pages 19–62 in *Literary Construction of Identity in the Ancient World: Proceedings of the Conference Literary Fiction and the Construction of Identity in Ancient Literatures*. Ed. by H. Liss and M. Oeming. Winona Lake, Ind.: Eisenbrauns, 2010 (research report).

### 3.1.3 Application-oriented Methods: Feminism, Social History and Liberation Theology

A. O. Bellis, *Helpmates, Harlots, Heroes: Women's Stories in the Hebrew Bible*. Louisville, Ky.: Westminster John Knox, 1994.

A. Brenner, ed., *A Feminist Companion to the Bible*. Sheffield: Sheffield Academic Press, 1993ff.

W. Dietrich and U. Luz, eds, *The Bible in a World Context: An Experiment in Contextual Hermeneutics*. Grand Rapids, Mich.: Eerdmans, 2002.

E. Drewermann, *Tiefenpsychologie und Exegese*. 2 vols. 5th ed. Olten: Walter, 1992.

J. H. Ellens and W. G. Rollins, eds, *Psychology and the Bible: A New Way to Read the Scriptures*. Westport, Conn.: Praeger, 2004.

I. Fischer, *Women who Wrestled with God: Biblical Stories of Israel's Beginnings*. Transl. by L. M. Maloney. Collegeville, Minn.: Liturgical Press, 2005.

T. S. Frymer-Kensky, *Studies in Bible and Feminist Criticism*. Philadelphia: Jewish Publication Society, 2006.

N. K. Gottwald, ed., *The Bible and Liberation: Political and Social Hermeneutics*. Maryknoll, N.Y.: Orbis, 1983.

Idem, *The Hebrew Bible in its Social World and in Ours*. Atlanta, Ga.: Scholars, 1993.

L. Schottroff, S. Schroer and M.-T. Wacker, *Feminist Interpretation: The Bible in Women's Perspective*. Transl. by B. Rumscheidt. Minneapolis: Fortress, 1998.

L. Schottroff and M.-T. Wacker, *Kompendium feministische Bibelauslegung*. 3rd ed. Gütersloh: Gütersloher Verlagshaus, 2007.

W. Schottroff and W. Stegemann, eds, *God of the Lowly: Socio-Historical Interpretations of the Bible*. Transl. by M. J. O'Connell. Maryknoll, N.Y.: Orbis, 1984.

R. R. Wilson, *Sociological Approaches to the Old Testament*. Philadelphia: Fortress, 1984.

## 4 Bible Dictionaries and Exegetical Reference Books for Old Testament Studies

*The Anchor Bible Dictionary*. 6 vols. Ed. by D. N. Freedman. New York: Doubleday, 1992 (ABD); also available on CD-ROM.

*Biblisch-Historisches Handwörterbuch: Landeskunde, Geschichte, Religion, Kultur, Literatur*. Ed. by B. Reicke and L. Rost. Göttingen: Vandenhoeck & Ruprecht, 1962–1979 [Paperback 1994] (BHH); also available on CD-ROM.

*Biblisches Reallexikon*. HAT 1.1. Ed. by K. Galling. 2nd ed. Tübingen: Mohr Siebeck, 1977 ($BRL^2$).

*Dictionary of Deities and Demons in the Bible*. Ed. by K. van der Toorn, B. Becking *et al.* 2nd ed. Leiden/Boston: Brill, 1999 ($DDD^2$).

*Handbuch theologischer Grundbegriffe zum Alten und Neuen Testament*. Ed. by A. Berlejung and C. Frevel. Darmstadt: Wissenschaftliche Buchgesellschaft, 2006 (HGANT).

*Neues Bibel-Lexikon*. 3 vols. Ed. by M. Görg and B. Lang. Zürich: Benziger, 1991–2001 (NBL).

*The New Interpreter's Dictionary of the Bible*. 5 vols. Ed. by. K. D. Sakenfeld. Nashville, Tenn.: Abingdon, 2006–2009.

*Theological Dictionary of the Old Testament*. Ed. by G. J. Botterweck and H. Ringgren. Transl. by J. T. Willis. Grand Rapids, Mich.: Eerdmans, 1977ff.

*Theological Lexicon of the Old Testament*. Ed. by E. Jenni and C. Westermann. Transl. by M. E. Biddle. Peabody, Mass.: Hendrickson, 1997.

## 5 Introductions and Histories of Literature

G. W. Anderson, *A Critical Introduction to the Old Testament*. 7th ed. London: G. Duckworth, 1959, 1972.

B. S. Childs, *Introduction to the Old Testament as Scripture*. London: SCM, 1979.

J. J. Collins, *Introduction to the Hebrew Bible*. Minneapolis: Fortress, 2004.

M. D. Coogan, *A Brief Introduction to the Old Testament: The Hebrew Bible in its Context*. Oxford: Oxford University Press, 2009.

P. R. Davies and J. Rogerson, *The Old Testament World*. 2nd completely rev. and expanded ed. Louisville, Ky.: Westminster John Knox, 2005.

O. Eißfeldt, *Einleitung in das Alte Testament*. 3rd rev. ed. Tübingen: Mohr Siebeck, 1964 (ET *The Old Testament: An Introduction, Including the Apocrypha and Pseudepigrapha, and also the Works of Similar Type from Qumran: The History of the Formation of the Old Testament*. Transl. by P. R. Ackroyd. New York: Harper and Row, 1965).

G. Fohrer, *Einleitung in das Alte Testament.* 12th rev. and extended ed. Heidelberg: Quelle & Meyer, 1979 (ET *Introduction to the Old Testament.* Transl. by D. Green. Nashville, Tenn.: Abingdon, 1968).

O. Kaiser, *Einleitung in das Alte Testament.* 5th rev. ed. Gütersloh: Gütersloher Verlagshaus, 1984.

Idem, *Grundriß der Einleitung in die kanonischen und deuterokanonischen Schriften des Alten Testaments.* 3 vols. Gütersloh: Gütersloher Verlagshaus, 1992–1994.

C. Levin, *The Old Testament: A Brief Introduction.* Transl. by M. Kohl. Princeton, N.J.: Princeton University Press, 2005.

S. L. McKenzie and J. Kaltner, *The Old Testament: Its Background, Growth & Content.* Nashville, Tenn.: Abingdon, 2007.

R. Rendtorff, *Das Alte Testament: Eine Einführung.* 7th ed. Neukirchen-Vluyn: Neukirchener, 2001 (ET *The Old Testament: An Introduction.* Transl. by J. Bowden. Philadelphia: Fortress, 1991).

K. Schmid, *Literaturgeschichte des Alten Testaments: Eine Einführung.* Darmstadt: Wissenschaftliche Buchgesellschaft, 2008.

W. H. Schmidt, *Einführung in das Alte Testament.* 5th ed. Berlin/New York: de Gruyter, 1995 (ET *Old Testament Introduction.* Transl. by M. J. O'Connell with D. J. Reimer. Berlin/New York: de Gruyter, 1999).

R. Smend, *Die Entstehung des Alten Testaments.* Theologische Wissenschaft 1. 5th rev. and extended ed. Stuttgart: Kohlhammer, 1995.

T. C. Vriezen and A. S. van der Woude, *Ancient Israelite and Early Jewish Literature.* Leiden/Boston: Brill, 2005.

E. Zenger *et al.*, *Einleitung in das Alte Testament.* Kohlhammer-Studienbücher Theologie 1.1. 7th rev. and extended ed. Stuttgart: Kohlhammer, 2008.

# 6 Extra-Biblical Sources

## 6.1 General and Methods

D. V. Edelman, ed., *The Fabric of History: Text, Artifact and Israel's Past.* JSOTSup 127. Sheffield: Continuum, 1991.

C. Hardmeier, ed., *Steine – Bilder – Texte: Historische Evidenz außerbiblischer und biblischer Quellen.* Arbeiten zur Bibel und ihrer Geschichte 5. Leipzig: Evangelische Verlagsanstalt, 2001.

T. E. Levy and T. Higham, ed., *The Bible and Radiocarbon Dating: Archaeology, Text and Science.* London/Oakville, Conn.: Equinox, 2005.

K. Meister, *Einführung in die Interpretation historischer Quellen: Schwerpunkt Antike: Vol. 1 Griechenland.* UTB.W 1923, Paderborn: Schöningh, 1997.

K. L. Sparks, *Ancient Texts for the Study of the Hebrew Bible: A Guide to the Background Literature.* 2nd ed. Peabody, Mass.: Hendrickson, 2006.

## 6.2 Sources in Writing

J. Assmann, *Ägyptische Hymnen und Gebete, übersetzt, kommentiert und eingeleitet.* OBO Sonderband. 2nd rev. and extended ed. Fribourg: Academic Press/Göttingen: Vandenhoeck & Ruprecht, 1999.

K. Beyer, *Die aramäischen Texte vom Toten Meer samt den Inschriften aus Palästina, dem Testament*

*Levis aus der Kairoer Genisa, der Fastenrolle und den alten talmudischen Zitaten.* Göttingen: Vandenhoeck & Ruprecht, 1984 (ATTM).

Idem, *Die aramäischen Texte vom Toten Meer samt den Inschriften aus Palästina, dem Testament Levis aus der Kairoer Genisa, der Fastenrolle und den alten talmudischen Zitaten, Ergänzungsband.* Göttingen: Vandenhoeck & Ruprecht, 1994 (ATTME).

Idem, *Die aramäischen Texte vom Toten Meer samt den Inschriften aus Palästina, dem Testament Levis aus der Kairoer Genisa, der Fastenrolle und den alten talmudischen Zitaten,* Vol. 2. Göttingen: Vandenhoeck & Ruprecht, 2004 (ATTM 2).

G. I. Davies, *Ancient Hebrew Inscriptions: Corpus and Concordance.* Cambridge: Cambridge University Press, 1991.

F. W. Dobbs-Allsopp *et al.*, *Hebrew Inscriptions: Texts from the Biblical Period of the Monarchy with Concordance.* London/New Haven, Conn.: Yale University Press, 2005,

H. Donner and W. Röllig, *Kanaanäische und aramäische Inschriften* 1–3. Vol. 1: 5th ed. Vol. 2: 3rd ed. Vol. 3: 3rd ed. Wiesbaden: Harrassowitz, 2002, 1973, 1976.

B. R. Foster, *Before the Muses: An Anthology of Akkadian Literature.* 3rd ed. Bethesda, Md.: CDL, 2005.

F. García Martínez and E. J. C. Tigchelaar, *The Dead Sea Scrolls: Study Edition* I-II. Leiden/Boston: Brill, 1997–1998.

J. C. L. Gibson, *Textbook of Syrian Semitic Inscriptions.* Oxford: Clarendon, 1971ff.

W. W. Hallo, ed., *The Context of Scripture: Canonical Compositions, Monumental Inscriptions and Archival Documents from the Biblical World.* 3 vols. Leiden/Boston: Brill, 1997–2002 (repr. 2003) (COS I-III).

B. Janowski and G. Wilhelm, eds, *Texte aus der Umwelt des Alten Testaments: Neue Folge.* Gütersloh: Gütersloher Verlagshaus, 2004ff. (TUAT NF). (published so far: Vol. 1, 2004; Vol. 2, 2005; Vol. 3, 2006; Vol. 4, 2008; Vol. 5, 2010).

*Flavius Josephus.* Transl. by H. S. J. Thackeray *et al.* 10 vols. LCL. London: Heinemann, 1950–1961.

*Flavius Josephus: Translation and Commentary.* Ed. by S. Mason, Leiden/Boston: Brill, 2000ff.

O. Kaiser *et al.*, eds, *Texte aus der Umwelt des Alten Testaments.* Gütersloh: Gütersloher Verlagshaus, 1982ff. (TUAT).

M. Lichtheim, *Ancient Egyptian Literature: A Book of Readings.* 3 vols. Berkeley, Calif.: University of California Press, 1973ff. (repr. 2006).

W. L. Moran, *The Amarna Letters.* Baltimore/London: Johns Hopkins University Press, 1992.

*Philo (of Alexandria), The Works of Philo.* Complete and Unabridged New Updated Version. Ed. by C. D. Yonge. Peabody, Mass.: Hendrickson, 2006.

B. Porten and A. Yardeni, eds, *Textbook of Aramaic Documents from Ancient Egypt.* 4 vols. Winona Lake, Ind.: Eisenbrauns, 1986–1999 (TADAE).

J. Renz and W. Röllig, eds, *Handbuch der althebräischen Epigraphik.* 3 vols. Darmstadt: Wissenschaftliche Buchgesellschaft, 1995–2003 (HAE).

D. Schwiderski, ed., *Die alt- und reichsaramäischen Inschriften/The Old and Imperial Aramaic Inscriptions.* Using the Database ARAM (by M. Sarther). Fontes et Subsidia ad Bibliam Pertinentes 2. Berlin/New York: de Gruyter, 2004.

*State Archives of Assyria*. Ed. by Neo-Assyrian Text Corpus Project of the Academy of Finland. Helsinki: Helsinki University Press, 1987ff. (SAA).

M. Weippert *et al.*, *Historisches Textbuch zum Alten Testament*. GAT 10. Göttingen/Oaksville, Conn.: Vandenhoeck & Ruprecht, 2010.

## 6.3 Archaeology and Iconography

J. Black and A. Green, *Gods, Demons and Symbols of Ancient Mesopotamia: An Illustrated Dictionary*. London: British Museum Press, 1992.

D. Collon, *First Impressions: Cylinder Seals in the Ancient Near East*. Chicago: University of Chicago Press/London: British Museum Publications, 1988.

I. Finkelstein, *The Archaeology of the Israelite Settlement*. Jerusalem: Israel Exploration Society, 1988.

V. Fritz, *An Introduction to Biblical Archaeology*. Transl. by B. Mänz-Davies. Sheffield: JSOT, 1994.

Z. Herzog, *Archaeology of the City: Urban Planning in Ancient Israel and Its Social Implications*. Tel Aviv: Yass Archaeology, 1997.

O. Keel, *Corpus der Stempelsiegel-Amulette aus Palästina/Israel: Einleitung; Katalog*. Vol. I–III: OBO Series Archaeologica 10; 13; 29; 31. Fribourg: Academic Press/Göttingen: Vandenhoeck & Ruprecht, 1995–2010.

Idem *et al.*, *Studien zu den Stempelsiegeln aus Palästina/Israel*. Vol. I–IV: OBO 67; 88; 100; 135. Fribourg: Academic Press/Göttingen: Vandenhoeck & Ruprecht, 1985–1994.

Idem and S. Schroer, *Die Ikonographie Palästinas/Israels und der Alte Orient: Eine Religionsgeschichte in Bildern*. Vol. 1. Fribourg: Academic Press, 2005 (IPIAO).

P. J. King and L. E. Stager, *Life in Biblical Israel: Library of Ancient Israel*, Louisville, Ky.: Westminster John Knox, 2001.

H.-P. Kuhnen, *Palästina in griechisch-römischer Zeit*. Handbuch der Archäologie, Vorderasien 2.2. München: Beck, 1990.

A. Mazar, *Archaeology of the Land of the Bible: 10,000-586 B.C.E.* New York: Doubleday, 1992.

E. M. Meyers, ed., *The Oxford Encyclopedia of Archaeology in the Near East*. Oxford: Oxford University Press, 1997 (OEANE).

J. B. Pritchard, *The Ancient Near East in Pictures: Relating to the Old Testament*. 2nd ed. Princeton, N.J.: Princeton University Press, 1969 (repr. 1994) (ANEP).

C. Renfrew and P. Bahn, *Archaeology: Theories, Methods and Practice*. 5th ed. London: Thames and Hudson, 2008.

E. Stern, *Archaeology of the Land of the Bible: Vol. 2 The Assyrian, Babylonian and Persian Periods, 732-332 BCE*. New York: Doubleday, 2001.

Idem *et al.*, eds, *The New Encyclopedia of Archaeological Excavations in the Holy Land*. Vol. I–V. Jerusalem: Israel Exploration Society, 1993ff; Supplement 2008 (NEAEHL).

H. Weippert, *Palästina in vorhellenistischer Zeit*. Handbuch der Archäologie, Vorderasien 2.1. München: Beck, 1988.

A. Weissenrieder and F. Wendt, 'Images as Communication: The Methods of Iconography'. Pages 3–49 in *Picturing the New Testament: Studies in Ancient Visual Images*. WUNT II/193. Ed. by A. Weissenrieder, F. Wendt and P. von Gemünden. Tübingen: Mohr Siebeck, 2005.

# 7 The History of the Ancient Near East and its Religions

J. Assmann, *The Mind of Egypt: History and Meaning in the Time of the Pharaohs*. Transl. by A. Jenkins. New York: Holt, 2002.

J. Botteró, *Religion in Ancient Mesopotamia*. Transl. by T. L. Fagaul. Chicago: University of Chicago Press, 2001.

P. Briant, *From Cyrus to Alexander: A History of the Persian Empire*. Transl. by P. T. Daniels. Winona Lake, Ind.: Eisenbrauns, 2002.

*Brill's New Pauly [Der Neue Pauly]: Encyclopaedia of the Ancient World*. Ed. by M. Landfester in collaboration with H. Cancik and H. Schneider, English ed. F. G. Gentry. 15 Vols. Leiden/Boston: Brill, 2006–2009.

I. E. S. Edwards *et al.*, eds, *The Cambridge Ancient History*. Cambridge: Cambridge University Press, 1977–1994.

H. Frankfort, *Ancient Egyptian Religion: An Interpretation*. New York: Harper & Row, 1961.

E. Hornung, *History of Ancient Egypt: An Introduction*. Transl. by D. Lorton. Ithaca, N.Y.: Cornell University Press, 1999.

H. Klengel, *Syria: 3000 to 300 B.C.* Berlin: Akademie, 1992.

A. Kuhrt. *The Ancient Near East: C. 3000-330 BC*. Routledge History of the Ancient World. 2 Vols. London: Routledge, 1995.

E. Lipiński, *The Aramaeans: Their Ancient History, Culture, Religion*. OLA 100. Leuven: Peeters, 2000.

G. E. Markoe, *Phoenicians: Peoples of the Past*. London: British Museum Press, 2002.

H. Niehr, *Religionen in Israels Umwelt: Einführung in die nordwestsemitischen Religionen Syrien-Palästinas*. NEchtB Supplements 5. Würzburg: Echter, 1998.

D. Pardee, *Ritual and Cult at Ugarit*. Atlanta, Ga.: SBL, 2002.

J. Sasson, ed., *Civilizations of the Ancient Near East*. Peabody, Mass.: Hendrickson, 2001.

B. E. Shafer, H. Baines and L. H. Lesko, *Religion in Ancient Egypt: Gods, Myths, and Personal Practice*. Ithaca, N.Y.: Cornell University Press, 1991.

I. Shaw, *The Oxford History of Ancient Egypt*. Oxford: Oxford University Press, 2003.

D. C. Snell, *Religions of the Ancient Near East*. Cambridge: Cambridge University Press, 2010.

M. Van de Mieroop, *A History of the Ancient Near East: Ca. 3000-323 B.C.* Malden, Mass.: Blackwell, 2007.

D. J. Wiseman, ed., *Peoples of Old Testament Times*. Oxford: Clarendon, 1973.

M. Witte and J. F. Diehl, eds, *Israeliten und Phönizier: Ihre Beziehungen im Spiegel der Archäologie und der Literatur des Alten Testaments und seiner Umwelt*. OBO 235. Fribourg: Academic Press/ Göttingen: Vandenhoeck & Ruprecht, 2008.

## 8 The History of Ancient Israel and Judah

G. W. Ahlström, *The History of Ancient Palestine from the Palaeolithic Period to Alexander's Conquest*. JSOTSup 146. Sheffield: Continuum, 1993.

R. Albertz, *Israel in Exile: The History and Literature of the Sixth Century B.C.E.* Transl. by D. Green. Atlanta, Ga.: SBL, 2003.

M. Avi-Yonah, *The Holy Land from the Persian to the Arab Conquest (536 BC-AD 640): A Historical Geography*. Jerusalem: Carta, 2002.

R. B. Coote and K. W. Whitelam, *The Emergence of Early Israel in Historical Perspective*. Sheffield: Almond, 1987.

P. R. Davies, *Memories of Ancient Israel: An Introduction to Biblical History – Ancient and Modern*. Louisville, Ky.: Westminster John Knox, 2008.

W. Dietrich, *The Early Monarchy in Israel: The Tenth Century B.C.E.* Transl. by J. Vette. Leiden/Boston: Brill, 2007.

H. Donner, *Geschichte des Volkes Israel und seiner Nachbarn in Grundzügen*. GAT 4/1 + 2. 4th ed. Göttingen: Vandenhoeck & Ruprecht, 2007; see also the review by M. Weippert, 'Geschichte Israels am Scheideweg'. *TRu* 58 (1993): 71–103.

D. Edelman, *The Origins of the 'Second' Temple: Persian Imperial Policy and the Rebuilding of Jerusalem*. London: Equinox, 2005.

P. F. Esler, *Ancient Israel: The Old Testament in Its Social Context*. London: SCM, 2005.

L. L. Grabbe, *Introduction to Second Temple Judaism: History and Religion of the Jews in the Time of Nehemiah, the Maccabees, Hillel, and Jesus*. London: Continuum, 2010.

Idem, *History of the Jews and Judaism in the Second Temple Period: Vol. 2 The Coming of the Greeks: The Early Hellenistic Period (335-175 BCE)*. Library of Second Temple Studies. London: Continuum, 2008.

J. Hayes and S. R. Mandell, *The Jewish People in Classical Antiquity: From Alexander to Bar Kochba*. Louisville, Ky.: Westminster John Knox, 1998.

M. Hengel, *Judaism and Hellenism: Studies in Their Encounter in Palestine during the Early Hellenistic Period*. Transl. by J. Bowden. Minneapolis: Fortress, 1991.

R. Kessler, *The Social History of Ancient Israel: An Introduction*. Transl. by L. M. Maloney. Minneapolis: Fortress, 2008.

T. Krüger, 'Theoretische und methodische Probleme der Geschichte des alten Israels in der neueren Diskussion'. *VF* 53 (2008): 4–22.

N. P. Lemche, *The Canaanites and Their Land*. JSOTSup 110. Sheffield: JSOT, 1991.

Idem, *Early Israel: Anthropological and Historical Studies on the Israelite Society Before the Monarchy*. VTSup 37. Leiden/Boston: Brill, 1985.

O. Lipschits, *The Fall and Rise of Jerusalem: Judah under Babylonian Rule*. Winona Lake, Ind.: Eisenbrauns, 2005.

Idem and J. Blenkinsopp, eds, *Judah and the Judeans in the Neo-Babylonian Period*. Winona Lake, Ind.: Eisenbrauns, 2003.

Idem, G. Knoppers and R. Albertz, eds, *Judah and the Judeans in the Fourth Century B.C.E.* Winona Lake, Ind.: Eisenbrauns, 2007.

Idem and M. Oeming, eds, *Judah and the Judeans in the Persian Period*. Winona Lake, Ind.: Eisenbrauns, 2006.

J. M. Miller and J. H. Hayes, *A History of Ancient Israel and Judah*, London: SCM, 2006.

E. Pfoh, *The Emergence of Israel in Ancient Palestine: Historical and Anthropological Perspectives*. Copenhagen International Seminar. London: Equinox, 2010.

D. B. Redford, *Egypt and Canaan in the New Kingdom*. Beer-Sheva: Ben-Gurion University of the Negev Press, 1990.

P. Sacchi, *The History of the Second Temple Period*. JSOTSup 285. Sheffield: Sheffield Academic Press, 2000.

E. Schürer, *The History of the Jewish People in the Age of Jesus Christ (175 B.C.–A.D. 135)*. A New English Version rev. and ed. by G. Vermes *et al.* 3 vols. Edinburgh: T&T Clark, 1973–1987 (rev. ed. 1995–2000).

T. L. Thompson, *Early History of the Israelite People: From the Written and Archaeological Sources*. SHANE 4. Leiden/Boston: Brill, 1992.

## 9 History of Religion of Ancient Israel

R. Albertz, *A History of Israelite Religion in the Old Testament Period*. Transl. by J. Bowden. Louisville, Ky.: Westminster John Knox, 1994.

G. Beckman and T. J. Lewis, eds, *Text, Artifact, and Image: Revealing Ancient Israelite Religion*. Providence, R.I.: Brown Judaic Studies, 2006.

L. L. Grabbe, *Judaic Religion in the Second Temple Period: Belief and Practice from the Exile to Yavneh*. London/New York: Routledge, 2000.

O. Keel, *Die Geschichte Jerusalems und die Entstehung des Monotheismus*. Orte und Landschaften der Bibel IV,1. Göttingen: Vandenhoeck & Ruprecht, 2007.

Idem and C. Uehlinger, *Gods, Goddesses, and Images of God in Ancient Israel*. Transl. by T. H. Trapp. Minneapolis: Fortress, 1998 (GGG).

P. D. Miller, *The Religion of Ancient Israel*. Library of Ancient Israel. Louisville, Ky.: Westminster John Knox, 2000.

B. A. Nakhai, *Archaeology and the Religions of Canaan and Israel*. ASOR 7. Boston: American Schools of Oriental Research, 2001.

S. Niditch, *Ancient Israelite Religion*. Oxford: Oxford University Press, 1997.

M. S. Smith, *The Origins of Biblical Monotheism: Israel's Polytheistic Background and the Ugarit Texts*. Oxford: Oxford University Press, 2000.

Idem, *The Memoirs of God: History, Memory, and the Experience of the Divine in Ancient Israel*. Minneapolis: Fortress, 2004.

F. Stavrakopoulou and J. Barton, eds, *Religious Diversity in Ancient Israel and Judah*. London: T&T Clark, 2010.

K. Van der Toorn, *Family Religion in Babylonia, Syria and Israel*. SHANE 7. Leiden/Boston: Brill, 1996.

Z. Zevit, *The Religions of Ancient Israel: A Synthesis of Parallactic Approaches*. London: Continuum, 2001.

# 10 Old Testament Theology and the History of Theology of Ancient Israel

## 10.1 Concepts of Old Testament Theology

W. Brueggemann, *Theology of the Old Testament*. Philadelphia: Fortress, 2005.

B. S. Childs, *Biblical Theology of the Old and New Testament: Theological Reflection on the Christian Bible*. London: SCM, 1992.

W. Eichrodt, *Theologie des Alten Testaments*. 3 vols. Vol. 1: Leipzig: Hinrichs, 1933. 8th ed. Stuttgart: Klotz, 1968; Vol. 2/3: Leipzig: Hinrichs 1935/1939. 6th ed. Göttingen: Vandenhoeck & Ruprecht, 1974 (ET *Theology of the Old Testament*. OTL. Transl. by J. A. Baker. London: SCM, 1961–1977).

J. H. Hayes and F. C. Prussner, *Old Testament Theology: Its History and Development*. Atlanta, Ga.: John Knox, 1985.

B. Janowski, *Konfliktgespräche mit Gott: Eine Anthropologie der Psalmen*. 3rd ed. Neukirchen-Vluyn: Neukirchener, 2009.

J. Jeremias, 'Neue Entwürfe zu einer "Theologie des Alten Testaments"'. Pages 125–58 in *Theologie und Exegese des Alten Testaments/der Hebräischen Bibel: Zwischenbilanz und Zukunftsperspektiven*. SBS 200. Ed. by B. Janowski. Stuttgart: Katholisches Bibelwerk, 2005.

O. Kaiser, *Der Gott des Alten Testaments: Wesen und Wirken: Theologie des Alten Testaments*. 3 vols. Göttingen: Vandenhoeck & Ruprecht, 1993–2003.

L. Köhler, *Theologie des Alten Testaments*. Tübingen: Mohr Siebeck, 1936. 4th ed. 1966 (ET *Old Testament Theology*. Library of Theological Translations. Transl. by A. S. Todd. Cambridge: James Clarke, 2002 [originally published, London: Lutterworth, 1957]).

J. L. McKenzie, *A Theology of the Old Testament*. Lanham, Md.: University Press of America, 1986.

L. G. Perdue, *Reconstructing Old Testament Theology: After the Collapse of History*. Philadelphia: Fortress, 2005.

G. von Rad, *Theologie des Alten Testaments*. 2 vols. München: Kaiser, Vol. 1: 1957. 10th ed. 1992; Vol. 2: 1960. 10th ed. 1993 (ET *Old Testament Theology*. 2 vols. Transl. by D. M. G. Stalker introduced by W. Brueggemann. Louisville, Ky.: Westminster John Knox, 2001).

R. Rendtorff, *Theologie des Alten Testaments: Ein kanonischer Entwurf*. 2 vols. Neukirchen-Vluyn: Neukirchener, 1999/2001 (ET *The Canonical Hebrew Bible: A Theology of the Old Testament*. Tools for Biblical Study 7. Transl. by D. E. Orton, Leiden: Deo, 2005).

W. H. Schmidt, *Alttestamentlicher Glaube in seiner Geschichte*. 10th rev. and expanded ed. Neukirchen-Vluyn: Neukirchener, 2007 (ET *The Faith of the Old Testament: A History*. Transl. by J. Sturdy. Philadelphia: Westminster, 1983).

W. Zimmerli, *Grundriß der alttestamentlichen Theologie*. 7th ed. Stuttgart: Kohlhammer, 1972, 1999 (ET *Old Testament Theology in Outline*. Transl. by D. E. Green. Edinburgh: Clark, 1978).

## 10.2 The Question of Biblical Theology

*Jahrbuch für Biblische Theologie*. Neukirchen-Vluyn: Neukirchener, 1986ff. (JBTh).

C. Dohmen and T. Söding, eds, *Eine Bibel – zwei Testamente: Positionen biblischer Theologie*. UTB.W 1893. Paderborn: Schöningh, 1995.

G. Ebeling, 'Was heißt "Biblische Theologie?"' Pages 69–89 in *Wort und Glaube* I. 3rd ed. with index. Tübingen: Mohr Siebeck, 1967 (ET: 'The Meaning of "Biblical Theology"'. Pages 79–97 in *Word and Faith*. Philadelphia: Fortress, 1963)

G. F. Hasel, *Old Testament Theology: Basic Issues in the Current Debate*. Grand Rapids, Mich.: Eerdmans, 1972.

M. Oeming, *Gesamtbiblische Theologien der Gegenwart: Das Verhältnis von AT und NT in der hermeneutischen Diskussion seit Gerhard von Rad*. 2nd ed. Stuttgart: Kohlhammer, 1987.

B. C. Ollenburger, E. A. Martens and G. F. Hasel, eds, *The Flowering of Old Testament Theology: A Reader in Twentieth-Century Old Testament Theology, 1930-1990*. Winona Lake, Ind.: Eisenbrauns, 1991.

## 10.3 Hermeneutics of the Old Testament

E. Blum, 'Notwendigkeit und Grenzen historischer Exegese: Plädoyer für eine alttestamentliche Exegetik'. Pages 11–40 in *Theologie und Exegese des Alten Testaments/der Hebräischen Bibel*. SBS 200. Ed. by B. Janowski. Stuttgart: Katholisches Bibelwerk, 2005.

C. Dohmen, *Vom Umgang mit dem Alten Testament*. Neuer Stuttgarter Kommentar Altes Testament 27. Stuttgart: Katholisches Bibelwerk, 1995.

Idem and G. Stemberger, *Hermeneutik der Jüdischen Bibel und des Alten Testaments*. Kohlhammer-Studienbücher Theologie 1.2. Stuttgart: Kohlhammer, 1996.

A. H. J. Gunneweg, *Vom Verstehen des Alten Testaments: Eine Hermeneutik*. GAT 5. 2nd rev. and extended ed. Göttingen: Vandenhoeck & Ruprecht, 1988 (ET *Understanding the Old Testament*. OTL. Transl. by J. Bowden. London: SCM, 1978).

O. Kaiser, 'Die Bedeutung des Alten Testaments für den christlichen Glauben'. *ZTK* 86 (1989): 1–17.

M. Oeming, *Biblische Hermeneutik: Eine Einführung*. 3rd ed. Darmstadt: Wissenschaftliche Buchgesellschaft, 2010 (ET *Contemporary Biblical Hermeneutics: An Introduction*. Transl. by J. F. Vette. Burlington, Vt.: Ashgate, 2006).

C. Westermann, *Essays on Old Testament Hermeneutics*. Transl. by J. L. Mays. Richmond, Va.: John Knox, 1963.

# 11 Commentary Series

*Das Alte Testament Deutsch* (ATD). Göttingen: Vandenhoeck & Ruprecht – generally understandable, historical-critical orientation (in German).

*Das Alte Testament Deutsch – Apokryphen* (ATD.A). Göttingen: Vandenhoeck & Ruprecht – supplement series to ATD with commentaries on the apocrypha or deuterocanonical books.

*The Anchor Bible* (AB). Garden City, N.Y.: Doubleday – historical-critical standard commentary in Northern America.

*Biblischer Kommentar – Altes Testament* (BKAT). Neukirchen-Vluyn: Neukirchener – detailed, scholarly commentary (in German).

*The Forms of the Old Testament Literature* (FOTL). Grand Rapids, Mich.: Eerdmans – short commentary with detailed description of the structure of the texts.

*Handbuch zum Alten Testament* (HAT). Tübingen: Mohr Siebeck – focused, accurate on philological questions, historical-critical orientation (in German).

*Herders Theologischer Kommentar zum Alten Testament* (HThK.AT). Freiburg: Herder – detailed, scholarly commentary, partly German translation of important international commentaries (in German).

*Hermeneia: A Critical and Historical Commentary on the Bible.* Philadelphia: Fortress – detailed, historical-critical orientation, partly translation of Continental-European commentaries; deals also with deuterocanonical/apocryphal and pseudepigraphic works.

*International Critical Commentary* (ICC). Edinburgh: T & T Clark – classic commentary, philological and historical-critical orientation.

*Old Testament Guides* (OTG). Sheffield: JSOT – short introduction and survey of the scholarly views.

*Old Testament Library* (OTL). London: SCM/Louisville, Ky.: Westminster John Knox – generally understandable, historical-critical orientation.

*Word Biblical Commentary* (WBC). Waco, Tx. *et al.*: Word Books/Thomas Nelson – detailed, rather conservative, accurate on philological questions.

*Zürcher Bibelkommentar – Altes Testament* (ZBK.AT). Zürich: Theologischer Verlag – generally understandable, historical-critical orientation (in German).

# 12 History of Exegesis and Reception of the Bible

## 12.1 General

P. Ackroyd, G. W. Lampe and S. L. Greenslade, eds., *The Cambridge History of the Bible* I–III. Cambridge: Cambridge University Press, 1963–1970.

M. Bocian, *Lexikon der biblischen Personen: Mit ihrem Fortleben in Judentum, Christentum, Islam, Dichtung, Musik und Kunst.* 2nd extended ed. Stuttgart: Kröner, 2004.

L. Diestel, *Geschichte des Alten Testaments in der christlichen Kirche.* Jena: Mauke, 1869 = Leipzig: Zentralantiquariat der DDR, 1981 (with an epilogue by S. Wagner).

*Encyclopedia of the Bible and its Reception* (EBR). Ed. by H.-J. Klauck *et al.* Berlin/New York: de Gruyter, 2009ff. (published so far: Vols 1–2: Aaron–Atheism); also available online.

H. Graf Reventlow, *History of Biblical Interpretation.* Atlanta, Ga.: SBL, 2009.

M. Sæbø, ed., *Hebrew Bible/Old Testament: The History of Its Interpretation.* 3 vols. Göttingen: Vandenhoeck & Ruprecht, 1996, 2000, 2008.

J. F. A. Sawyer, ed., *The Blackwell Companion to the Bible and Culture.* Oxford: Blackwell, 2006.

R. Smend, *From Astruc to Zimmerli: Old Testament Scholarship in Three Centuries.* Transl. by M. Kohl. Tübingen: Mohr Siebeck, 2007.

R. Smend, *Das Alte Testament im Protestantismus*. Grundtexte zur Kirchen- und Theologiegeschichte 3. Neukirchen-Vluyn: Neukirchener, 1995.

## 12.2 English Bible

B. Bobrick, *Wide as the Waters: The Story of the English Bible and the Revolution it Inspired.* New York: Penguin, 2002.

D. Daniell, *The Bible in English: Its History and Influence*. New Haven, Conn.: Yale University Press, 2005.

A. McGrath, *In the Beginning: The Story of the King James Bible and how it Changed a Nation, a Language, and a Culture*. New York: Harper Collins, 2002.

## 12.3 History of Literature

D. Jasper and S. Prickett, eds, *The Bible and Literature: A Reader*. Oxford: Blackwell, 1999.

D. L. Jeffrey, ed., *A Dictionary of Biblical Tradition in English Literature*. Grand Rapids, Mich.: Eerdmans, 1992.

W. A. Kort, *Take, Read: Scripture, Textuality and Cultural Practice*. University Park, Pa.: Pennsylvania State University Press, 1996.

R. Lemon *et al.*, eds, *The Blackwell Companion to the Bible in English Literature*. Chichester: Wiley-Blackwell, 2009.

## 12.3 Art History

*Die Bibel in der Kunst: The York Project*, DVD (PC + Mac). Online: www.zeno.org.

*Bildindex der Kunst und Architektur*. Ed. by Bildarchiv Foto Marburg, 2002. Online: http://www.bildindex.de.

J. Hall, *Dictionary of Subjects and Symbols in Art*. New York: Harper Collins, 1979.

E. Kirschbaum, ed., *Lexikon der christlichen Ikonographie*. Wien: Herder, 1968–76.

P. Murray and L. Murray, *The Oxford Companion to Christian Art and Architecture*. Oxford: Oxford University Press, 1996.

C. Wertle, *Die Bibel in der bildenden Kunst*. Reclam Universal-Bibliothek 18571. Stuttgart: Reclam, 2009.

## 12.4 Music History

R. C. von Ende, *Church Music: An International Bibliography*. Metuchen, N.J.: Scarecrow, 1980.

M. Gorali, *The Old Testament in Music*. Jerusalem: Maron, 1993.

M. McEntire and J. Emerson, *Raising Cain, Fleeing Egypt, and Fighting Philistines: The Old Testament in Popular Music*, Macon, Ga.: Smyth & Helwys, 2006.

## 12.5 Film History

J. S. Lang, *The Bible on the Big Screen: A Guide from Silent Films to Today's Movies*. Grand Rapids, Mich.: Baker, 2007.

L. J. Kreitzer, *The Old Testament in Fiction and Film: On Reversing the Hermeneutical Flow*. Sheffield: Sheffield Academic Press, 1994.

## 13 Web links

A useful collection of web links for research at the website of the Society of biblical Literature – Eductional Resources, http://www.sbl-site.org/educational/researchtools.aspx

*ABZU: A Guide to Information Related to the Study of the Ancient Near East on the Web*. Ed. by C .E. Jones, 1994–2004. Online: http://www.etana.org/abzu/.

*Bibelwissenschaftliche Literaturdokumentation Innsbruck* (BILDI). 2000ff. Online: http://www.uibk.ac.at/bildi/.

*Biblische Bibliographie Lausanne* (BIBIL). 2000ff. Online: https://wwwdbunil.unil.ch/bibil/bi/de/bibilhome.html.

*Das wissenschaftliche Bibel-Lexikon im Internet* (WiBiLex). Ed. by M. Bauks and K. Koenen. 2004ff. Online: http://www.wibilex.de.

*Informations-Stelle für Alttestamentliche Exegese* (ISATEX). Ed. by A. Wagner in cooperation with J. F. Diehl, 2003ff. Online: http://www.isatex.de.

*Society of Biblical Literature – Research Tools*. Online: http://www.sbl-site.org/educational/researchtools.aspx.

*WWW Virtual Library of Archaeology*. Ed. by Archaeological Research Institute at Arizona State University 2001ff. Online: http://archnet.asu.edu/.

# Glossary

This glossary explains various notions repeatedly mentioned in the text of this handbook without their being explained explicitly at the places where they occur or being otherwise evident in context. When an explicit explanation is offered at some particular place in the text of the book, this place is indicated here by a page number set in parentheses. Within the book text as well as here, those notions which are explained in this glossary are indicated by → and set *in italics*. Within a single paragraph or paragraph section, only the first occurrence of the term is marked in this way.

**acrostichon, acrostic:** a text so constructed that a successive reading of the initial letters of a sequence of words, sentences, lines, verses, stanzas, or chapters yields a new word or statement, or some otherwise significant sequence of letters, e.g. an alphabet (see p. 536).

**aetiology, aetiological:** legend recounted to explain the origins of particular practices, names, or other phenomena (see p. 336).

**allegory, allegorical:** a pictorial, visual way of speaking to illustrate an abstract notion, usually in the form of a story or anecdote.

**allochthonous:** immigrant, immigrated, used especially for population groups and their culture, language etc., which have moved into a territory already inhabited by a previous → *autochthonous* population.

**amphictyony:** a religious and political association of tribes around a common sanctuary (see p. 143).

**angelology:** beliefs and teachings about angels, i.e. supernatural beings, who as a rule serve as attendants and agents of God and as helpers of human beings.

**aniconism, aniconic:** renunciation or repudiation of pictorial or figurative images in a cultic context.

**annals:** chronologically ordered records of events, often in yearbook form (e.g. in royal archives).

**anthology, anthological:** (Greek: 'collection of flowers') collections of selected texts of an author or of an epoch or on a specific theme.

**anthropology, anthropological:** the study of and the teachings about human beings, their development, and their way of acting, from the point of view of the natural sciences and the humanities, but also of a particular religious group.

**anthropomorphic:** in a human form.

**apocalyptic, apocalyptical, apocalypse:** a manner of thinking related to the end times, the so called 'last things', and the literary genre in which such thinking is expressed (see p. 651).

**apocrypha, apocryphal:** writings not accepted into the biblical canon, but which are chronologically, stylistically, and thematically very near to canonical literature (see pp. 16; 695).

**apotropaic:** designed to avert or turn aside evil.

**ark of the covenant:** according to Exod. 25.10-22, a gold-plated chest of acacia wood equipped with golden rings at the four corners, into which gold-plated acacia shafts could be inserted to facilitate carrying. A 'mercy seat' with two enthroned cherubim rested atop of the chest. The cherubim faced each other and extended their wings upwards so as to overshadow the mercy seat.

In the course of Israel's cultic and literary history, **the ark, Hebr:** *ʿarôn*, was assigned various functions: originally, it evidently served as a military palladium, i.e. an object believed to afford effective protection or security; it was thought to represent the presence of Yahweh with his people and was carried before the advancing army (see Num. 10.35-36.). Later texts indicate that in the ark the tables of the law were preserved (see Deut. 10).

**atonement:** an event in which God does away with the sins of men and their consequences; it is often accomplished in the form of performing a sacrificial offering.

**autochthonous:** the long-established population or culture of a territory, especially in contrast to incoming 'foreign' → *allochthonous* population elements.

**Babylonian exile** → *exile*

**Babylonian Talmud** → *Talmud*

**baetylus:** a standing stone in upright position, having sacral meaning and functions, see also → *Mazzebah*.

**canon, canonical:** the authoritative collection of those writings which are considered to be normative for a community of believers. The authoritative character attributed to them is called **canonicity**. The process of collection and authorization is called **canonization** (see pp. 16–22).

**chthonic:** pertaining to the earth (or to the underworld).

**colon, pl. cola:** also called 'stichos', is the smallest poetic unit; two or three 'cola' constitute a 'bicolon' or a 'tricolon' (see p. 535).

**colophon:** a closing remark at the end of a text.

**compilation:** the creation of a larger text by combining already existing texts or pieces thereof, also used to designate the text thus produced.

**conoid:** a round body whose pointed or rounded top is notably smaller than its base, e.g. shaped like a cone, a bullet, or a bowling pin.

**conquest:** the forceful take-over and occupation of the promised land by the Israelites as described in the book of Joshua, also used to designate the Palestinian settlement of the Israelite tribes in general (see pp. 108–10; 356–60).

**covenant:** English translation of the Hebr. *bĕrît*. Like the so-called **Covenant Formula** 'You shall be my people, and I will be your God' (e.g. Jer. 30.22), this term describes God's relationship to Israel (see p. 377).

**Covenant Code:** a collection of legal prescriptions in Exod. 20.22–23.33 (see pp. 275–6).

**cult centralization:** the restriction of the worship of Yhwh to the Jerusalem temple as the only legitimate sanctuary, as this was commanded in Deut. 12 and enforced, according to 2 Kgs 22–23, by → *Josiah's reform* (see pp. 313–14).

**cult reform of Josiah** → *Josiah's reform*

**cursive → minuscule**

**Cyrus Cylinder:** a cuneiform text in which the Persian king Cyrus II (558–530 BCE) praises his benevolent decrees in favour of the Babylonians and the Marduk temple in Babylon (see. *COS* II, 314–316 and pp. 179; 426).

**Decalogue:** the so-called. 'ten words', i.e. the Ten Commandments in Exod. 20 and Deut. 5 (see p. 285).

**Deutero-Isaiah:** the scholarly name for Isa. 40–55 and the anonymous prophet-author(s) responsible for this section of the book of Isaiah (see II Isa; pp. 419–29).

**deuterocanonical literature, deuterocanonical:** texts contained in the Greek version (→ *Septuagint*) of the Bible, which are not contained in the Hebrew → *Masoretic* → *canon* (see pp. 16–22).

**Deuteronomism, deuteronomistic (Dtr):** texts and redactional layers of the Old Testament, which in terms of their theology and language are evidently oriented to the book of Deuteronomy (see pp. 310–11).

**Deuteronomistic history (DtrH):** according to M. Noth, a comprehensive historical work extending from Deut. to 2Kgs (see p. 260–3). In German publications this historical work is called DtrG ('Geschichtswerk'), while DtrH ('Historian') means the (first) author of this text.

**diaspora – communities:** regions in which the adherents of a religion or confession are in the minority; the term is used especially for Jewish communities outside of Palestine.

**doxology, doxological:** expression of praise of God's glory, often at the beginning or the end of a prayer or section of text. The **doxology of judgement** praises the justice exercised by God when acting as a judge.

**Edict of Cyrus:** according to Ezra 1.2-4; 6.3-5, a decree issued by the Persian king Cyrus in 539 BCE, allowing the Babylonian exiles to return to Judah and promising them political guarantees and material support for their reconstruction of the Jerusalem temple (see pp. 197–9).

**Elohist (E):** one of the sources of the Pentateuch according to the New Documentary Hypothesis; it is marked by the use of 'Elohim' as the name for God (see pp. 254; 256).

**Enneateuch:** a scholarly name for the entire narrative of the nine books Gen.–Deut., Josh., Judg., Sam., Kgs (see p. 242).

**epigraphy, epigraphic:** inscriptions as well as their collections and their study (see pp. 50–2).

**epithet:** a qualification or description added to a (divine) name based on some attribute deemed characteristic of the person or deity named.

**eschatology, eschatological:** teachings or beliefs about the last things with respect both to the individual person (*individual eschatology*) and/or to the world, or to the cosmos as a whole (*universal eschatology*).

**exile:** forced residence in a foreign land or place, in particular, the deportation of Israelites by the Assyrians in 722/1 BCE and the later deportations from Judah by the Babylonians in 587/6 BCE (i.e. the 'Babylonian exile') (see pp. 187–9).

**Feast of Tabernacles (Sukkoth):** an autumn religious feast in connection with the wine and olive harvest (see p. 84).

**Feast of Unleavened Bread (Mazzoth):** a spring religious festival corresponding to the beginning of the grain harvest (see p. 84).

**Feast of Weeks (Shavuoth):** originally a one-day religious festival in thanksgiving for the completion of the grain harvest (see p. 84).

**genre:** a generic literary category referring to a group of texts sharing the same formal characteristics (see p. 38).

**gloss:** explanation of an unclear expression; originally glosses were written either in the margin (marginal gloss) or between the lines (interlinear gloss); sometimes such glosses later came to be merged into the text itself.

**glyptic:** the art of carving or engraving gems, crystals and other rock forms, concretely, the technique of producing small figurines, reliefs or seals from stone, especially of gem quality, e.g. seals, cameos etc. and the objects thus produced. It is often used as a collective term to describe the whole class of such objects in a particular region or culture.

**golah (galut):** Hebr. 'exile', is used to refer to the deportation to Babylon in 597 BCE ('First Golah/Galut') and in 587 BCE ('Second Golah/Galut'); it is used also to refer to those thus deported, see also → *exile* and → *diaspora*.

**haggadah:** (Hebr.: 'telling') edifying and instructive tales to illustrate and explain biblical materials in the rabbinic tradition.

**halakhah:** (Hebr.: 'the way to go') individual Jewish religious prescriptions or the totality of such prescriptions, as they have been collected in the → *Mishnah* and further developed, through the interpretation and explanation of individual passages or themes of the Mishnah and the Bible, in the → *Talmud*.

**Hanukkah:** an early winter festival commemorating the (re-)consecration (Hebr. *ḥanukkâ*) of the temple in 164 BCE (see p. 761).

**hapaxlegomenon, pl. -a:** (Greek: 'said only once') a word which appears only once in a large textual corpus like the Bible.

**Hellenism, Hellenistic:** a term introduced in the 19th century by J. G. Droysen and J. Burckhardt to describe the historical cultural characteristics of the period from Alexander the Great (356–323 BCE) to the Roman conquest of the Egyptian kingdom of the Ptolemies (30 BCE) during which Greek culture became strongly intermingled with oriental elements and thus developed into a world-wide civilization.

**henotheism:** a special form of → *polytheism*; belief in a highest god without excluding in principle the worship of other inferior gods (see p. 74).

**holy war:** a notion found in the ancient oriental ideology of warfare, according to which wars of aggression or defence are fought in the name of and with the active assistance of the god of the city, the state, or the dynasty (for the OT see: Josh. 5.13–8.29; Judg. 7; 2 Chr. 20.1-30; 1 Macc. 3.33–4.25 etc.).

**iconography, iconographic:** the scholarly identification, description, classification and interpretation of the content of religious or artistic images (see pp. 52–6).

**Imperial authorization** → *Persian imperial authorization*

**Jehovist (JE):** an early combination of the → *Yahwist* and the → *Elohist* pentateuchal sources according to the New Documentary Hypothesis (see pp. 254–5).

**Josiah's reform:** a reform of the worship of Yahweh under King Josiah of Judah (638–609/8 BCE) connected, according to 2 Kgs 22–23, with the discovery of the book of Deuteronomy (see pp. 171–3).

**Lehreröffnungsformel:** the opening formula of a → *sapiential,* instructive discourse, typically 'Listen, my son, …' (see p. 571)

**LXX** → *Septuagint*

**Maʾat:** Egyptian term for the idea of and the divine symbol for the just order which rules in the world.

**majuscule:** a Greek or Latin manuscript written in capital letters.

**Masorah:** critical notes of the → *Masoretes* to the text of the Hebrew Bible. A distinction is made between the masora marginalis (marginal Masorah) written in the margins of the text and the masora finalis (closing or end Masorah) at the end of each book. The masora marginalis is subdivided into the masora parva written in the margins at each side of the text, which gives word statistics and calls attention to or explains special or remarkable usages, and the masora magna written in the upper and lower margins, which lists the biblical references for the notes of the masora parva. The masora finalis presents the masoretic material in alphabetical order.

**Masoretes:** groups of Jewish scribes and scholars working between the 7th and 11th centuries, who copied the Hebrew Bible, vocalizing the traditional consonantal spelling of words and introducing punctuation, cantilation symbols, and critical notes on the external form of the text – together these constitute the so called → *Masorah* – thus creating what has been handed down as the canonical text of the Hebrew Bible, the **Masoretic Text** (MT) (see pp. 12–13).

**Mazzebah (pl. mazzeboth):** a stone erected in an upright position, as a boundary mark or gravestone, but also for cultic purposes (see also → *baetylus*).

**Mazzoth (pl.)** → *Feast of Unleavened Bread*

**messiah, messianic (Hebr.:** 'anointed one'): a salvation-bringing king, whose coming is awaited in the end times.

**midrash, pl. midrashim:** rabbinic commentary on a book of the Bible (from Hebr. *dāraš* = 'to seek').

**minuscule:** a Greek or Latin manuscript written in small letters, for the most part in a running cursive hand **(cursive).**

**Mishnah (Hebr./Aram.:** 'repetition'): the first authoritative collection of Jewish religious laws and prescriptions, which was produced around 200 BCE. It was commented upon in the so-called Gemara and together with the latter forms the → *Talmud.*

**mono-yahwism, mono-yahwistic:** the notion that there is only one God Yahweh (opposite to → *poly-yahwism*).

**monolatry, monolatric:** worship of a single god despite the (theoretical) belief that other gods might exist (see p. 74).

**monotheism, monotheistic:** the conviction that there is only one single God, who alone can be the object of worship (see pp. 73–4).

**ostracon, pl. ostraca:** a fragment of pottery or limestone on which something has been written or inscribed.

**parenesis, parenetic:** advice, admonition, or exhortation, particularly of a moral or religious nature.

**Passover, Pesach:** a spring religious festival, originally a family celebration imbedded in the life of a pastoral population of cattle breeders and shepherds, later linked with the agrarian → *Feast of Unleavened Bread* (Mazzoth) (see pp. 86–8).

**Pentateuch:** the standard scholarly name for the first five books of the Bible, Gen. to Deut. (see pp. 237–42).

**Persian imperial authorization:** the practice of the Persians in recognizing local laws as laws of the Persian Empire (see p. 246).

**poly-yahwism, poly-yahwistic:** the notion, widespread in both the northern and the southern kingdoms during the era of the kings, that there existed numerous local manifestations of Yahweh (see p. 74).

**polytheism, polytheistic:** belief in the existence of many gods (see p. 74).

**Priestly Document (P):** one of the sources of the Pentateuch according to the New Documentary Hypothesis, so named because it reflects concerns typical of the Jewish priestly caste (see pp. 293–305).

**Privilegrecht:** juridical provisions governing duties owed to or otherwise related to Yhwh.

**proem:** preface, introduction to a text.

**proselyte:** a former 'heathen' without Jewish ancestors, who has converted to Judaism.

**Proto-Isaiah:** the standard scholarly designation for Isa. 1–39 (See I Isa.; pp. 410–19); see also → *Deutero-Isaiah* and → *Trito-Isaiah.*

**pseudepigraphy, pseudepigraphic:** the fictitious attribution of a text to a famous author in order to give it greater authority (see p. 16).

**Purim, Purim Festival:** according to the story in Esth. 9, the Purim festival commemorates the deliverance of the Jewish people within the Persian Empire from a plot to annihilate them thanks to the actions of Mordecai and his adopted daughter Esther (see p. 87).

**Qumran:** a locality in the vicinity of the Dead Sea, where since 1947, numerous, valuable manuscripts and manuscript fragments, some of them biblical, have been found, their origins going back to the 2nd cent. BCE (see pp. 12–13).

**Samaritan Pentateuch:** the Samaritan version of the Hebrew Pentateuch, which serves as the holy scripture of the Samaritans (see p. 13).

**sapiential** → *wisdom*

**satrapy:** the designation of a Persian province ruled by a royal governor called a **satrap**.

**scarab pl. scarabs:** a species of beetles regarded in Egypt as sacred and as symbolizing the sun-god.

***Šĕmaʿ yiśrāʾēl:*** the outstanding liturgical text of Judaism based on Deut. 6.4-5. (see pp. 307–8).

**Septuagint (LXX):** the ancient Greek translation of the Hebrew Bible (see pp. 15–16).

**Sin of Jeroboam:** according to 1Kgs 12, the installation of cult images at Bethel and Dan by King Jeroboam of the northern kingdom (see pp. 151; 373).

**soteriology:** teachings about divine deliverance or salvation.

**stichos** → *colon*

**subsistence economy:** a rural production system serving only to satisfy local, for the most part individual or familial needs, without producing a surplus for trading outside the local economic community.

**symbolic action:** an action performed by a prophet to signify or confirm a message (see p. 394).

**(the) tabernacle:** a (fictional) mobile sanctuary in the form of a tent, which, according to Exod. 25–40, Moses, at Yahweh's command, caused to be constructed at Sinai. The form ascribed to this tent sanctuary, in fact, corresponds on the whole to that of the Second Temple. In this way, the → *Priestly Document* attempted to link up the construction of the Second Temple with Moses.

**Talmud (Hebr./Aram.:** 'study/teaching'): the literature of the so-called halakhic tradition in Judaism; it consists of the → *Mishnah* and the Gemara commenting on the former. Alongside the larger Babylonian Talmud there is also the shorter Jerusalem Talmud.

**terminus a quo/post quem** (Lat. point in time *after which* something must be dated): *the earliest possible dating* for the composition of a text, whose exact dating is otherwise unknown, arguing on the basis of experiences and events which the text evidently presupposes or on the basis of its demonstrated awareness resp. use of other texts whose dates are known.

**terminus ad quem (Lat.:** point in time *up to which* something could be dated): the *latest possible dating* for the composition of a text, whose exact dating is otherwise unknown, arguing on the basis of events and experiences of which the text is evidently ignorant or on the basis of texts of known date, of which it shows no awareness.

**Tetrateuch:** scholarly term for the four books of Gen., Exod., Lev., and Num., but excluding Deut.

**theodicy:** the attempt to justify and explain God's existence, goodness and providential rule in the face of evident evil in the world appearing to contradict the notion of a good and just God or at least the notion of his having and exercising almighty power to rule the world.

**theophany:** an appearance or manifestation of a god at some particular place and time.

**theophoric element:** that part of the name of a person or place which is derived from the name of a god, e.g. 'Natania' (= the God Yhwh has given).

**theriomorphic:** in animal form.

**toledot (Hebr.:** 'genealogy'): the **toledot formula** ('. . .these are the descendents of. . .') is one of the structural characteristics of the → *Priestly Document* (see pp. 295–6).

**Trito-Isaiah:** within the framework of the three-book-hypothesis, this is the usual name for Isa. 56–66 (see pp. 404–5; 421–2); see also → *Proto-Isaiah* and → *Deutero-Isaiah.*

**typology, typological:** biblical figures and events are presented or interpreted as anticipations of future figures and events.

**uncials** → **majuscule**

**universalism:** the theological teaching that the formative and saving will of a deity extends to the whole (known) world.

**uraeus:** a species of cobra, which in ancient Egyptian art served as a symbol of a ruler.

***vaticinium ex eventu*** **(Lat.:** 'prophecy after the event'): prophetic or apocalyptic texts which claim to give exact, detailed predictions of future historical events. Because of their exact knowledge of the events they claim to predict, such prophecies are usually seen as ***vaticinia ex eventu*** and dated *after* the events they claim to predict.

**Vetus Latina:** (Lat.: 'the old Latin [translation]') a collective term for the various Latin Bible translations which circulated before or contemporary with the → *Vulgate*, i.e. up to and around 400 CE, and are sometimes reflected in even later texts which deviate from the Vulgate translation.

**Vulgate:** the Latin translation of the Bible produced by St. Jerome around 400 CE (see p. 16).

**wisdom, sapiential:** wisdom, Hebr. *ḥokmâ*, in the biblical usage, refers in general to the accumulation of technical knowledge and, in a more restricted sense, to the ability – based on experience – to make distinctions and to give directions. As such, it is the object of **wisdom** or **sapiential literature** (see pp. 571–3; 705–7; 730–1).

**Yahwist/Jahwist (J):** one of the sources of the Pentateuch according to the New Documentary Hypothesis; it is marked by the use of 'Yahweh' as the name for God (see pp. 253–4; 256).

**Zion/Zion Theology:** the traditional name for the (principal) hill of Jerusalem, which, in the Bible, also serves as the name of the whole city and of the temple within it. It is presented as the place of Yahweh's presence and, as such, the point of reference for a particular form of the theology of the Jerusalem temple (see p. 418).

**Zoroastrianism, Zoroastrian:** the name generally used today for contemporary (and older) forms of ancient Iranian religion which goes back to the figure of Zoroaster (see p. 215).

# Source of Figures

| | |
|---|---|
| Fig. 1 | D. Vieweger, *Archäologie der biblischen Welt*. Göttingen: Vandenhoeck & Ruprecht, 2003, 97. |
| Fig. 2 | D. Vieweger, *Archäologie der biblischen Welt*. Göttingen: Vandenhoeck & Ruprecht, 2003, 57. |
| Fig. 3 | A. Kuhrt, T*he Ancient Near East 3000–330 BC*. Vol. 1 London: Routledge, 1995 (reprint 1998), 1, 2. |
| Fig. 4 abd–f | *BRL*[2], 334, 335, 338, 339. |
| Fig. 4 c. | C. G. den Hertog (ed.), *Saxa loquentur: Studien zur Archäologie Palästinas/Israels. Festschrift für V. Fritz*. AOAT 302. Münster: Ugarit-Verlag, 2003, 117. |
| Fig. 5 a–f, k | O. Keel/C. Uehlinger, *GGG*, 52, 59, 98, 119, 379. |
| Fig. 5 g, h, j | C. Uehlinger, 'Anthropomorphic Cult Statuary in Iron Age Palestine and the Search for Yahweh's Cult Images'. Pages 91–155 in *The Image and the Book*: *Iconic Cults, Aniconism, and the Rise of Book Religion in Israel and the Ancient Near East,* CBET 21. Edited by K. van der Toorn. Leuven: Peeters, 1997, 113, 120. |
| Fig. 5 i | A. Berlejung private. |
| Fig. 5 l | T. Mettinger, *No Graven Image? Israelite Aniconism in Its Ancient Near Eastern Context*. ConBOT 42. Stockholm: Almquist & Wiksell 1995, 102. |
| Fig. 6 | J. M. Miller/J. H. Hayes, *A History of Ancient Israel and Judah*. Louisville: John Knox Press, 1986, 41. |
| Fig. 7 | J. M. Miller/J. H. Hayes, *A History of Ancient Israel and Judah*. Louisville: John Knox Press, 1986, 42. |
| Fig. 8 | A. Kuhrt, *The Ancient Near East 3000–330 BC*. Vol. 1. London: Routledge, 1995 (reprint 1998), 319. |
| Fig. 9 | S. Münger private. |
| Fig. 10 | H. Weippert, *Palästina*, 394. |
| Fig. 11 | J. Börker-Klähn, *Altvorderasiatische Bildstelen und vergleichbare Felsreliefs: Tafeln*. Baghdader Forschungen 4. Mainz: Zabern, 1982, Fig. 152a. |

| | |
|---|---|
| Fig. 12 | D. Vieweger, D. Vieweger, *Archäologie der biblischen Welt*. Göttingen: Vandenhoeck & Ruprecht, 2003, 324–5, Fig. 251.2 and 3. |
| Fig. 13 | O. Keel/C. Uehlinger, *GGG*, 308. |
| Fig. 14 a | A. Kurth ed., The Persian Empire. A Corpus of Sources from the Achaemenid Period. Vol. 1. Abingdon: Routledge, 2007, 190–191, Fig. 6.1. |
| Fig. 14 b | C. L. Meyers/E. M. Meyers, *Haggai, Zechariah 1–8: A New Translation with Introduction and Commentary*. AB 25 B. New York: Doubleday, 1987, xxxvi. |
| Fig. 15 | H. Keel-Leu/B. Teissier, *Die vorderasiatischen Rollsiegel der Sammlungen 'Bibel + Orient' der Universität Freiburg Schweiz*. OBO 200. Fribourg: Academic Press/Göttingen: Vandenhoeck & Ruprecht, 2004, 407, Nr. 236. |
| Fig. 16 | C. H. Kraeling (ed.), *The Synagogue: The Excavations at Dura-Europos: Final Report VIII.1*. New Haven: Yale University Press, 1956 (reprint 1979), Plate LXIX. Panel NC 1: Ezekiel, The Destruction and Restoration of National Life, Section A. |
| Fig. 17 | *ANEP*, 177, Nr. 523. |
| Fig. 18 a–b | S. Ostermann, *Die Münzen der Hasmonäer: Ein kritischer Bericht zur Systematik und Chronologie*. NTOA 55. Fribourg: Academic Press/Göttingen: Vandenhoeck & Ruprecht, 2005, 20, 27. |

# List of Contributors

Dr. Angelika Berlejung, Professor for Old Testament Studies at the Faculty of Theology of the University of Leipzig, Germany and Professor for Ancient Near Eastern Studies at the Faculty of Arts of the University of Stellenbosch, South-Africa.

Dr. Jan Christian Gertz, Professor for Old Testament Studies at the Faculty of Theology of the Ruprecht-Karls-University Heidelberg, Germany.

Dr. Konrad Schmid, Professor for Old Testament Studies at the Faculty of Theology of the University of Zurich, Switzerland.

Dr. Markus Witte, Professor for Old Testament Studies at the Faculty of Theology of the Humboldt-University Berlin, Germany.

# Index of People and Groups

# Index of Deities and Intermediate Beings

# Index of Places, Countries and Landscapes